WEBSTER'S
Concise
Pocket
Dictionary

FEDERAL
STREET
PRESS

A Division of Merriam-Webster, Incorporated.
Springfield, Massachusetts

This 2002 edition published by
Federal Street Press,
A division of Merriam-Webster, Incorporated.
P.O. Box 281
Springfield, MA 01102

Federal Street Press books are available for
bulk purchase for sales promotion and
premium use. For details write the manager
of special sales, Federal Street Press,
P.O. Box 281, Springfield, MA 01102

ISBN 1-892859-41-6

Printed in the United States of America

02   03   04   05   5   4   3   2   1

Preface

WEBSTER'S CONCISE POCKET DICTIONARY is an extremely concise reference to those words which form the very core of the English vocabulary.

Main entries follow one another in alphabetical order. Centered periods within the entries show points at which a hyphen may be put at the end of a line. Homographs of closely related origin are run into a single main entry, second and succeeding homographs being represented by a swung dash: ~. Homographs of distinctly different origin (as **¹fare** and **²fare**) are given separate entries with preceding raised numerals.

Variant spellings that are quite common appear at the main entry following a comma (as **judg•ment, judge•ment**).

Inflected forms of nouns, verbs, adjectives, and adverbs are shown when they are irregular, when adding the suffix makes a change, or when there might be doubt about their spelling. They are given either in full (as **bet•ter . . .; best** at **good**) or cut back to a convenient point of division (as **-ried; -ry•ing** at **hur•ry**).

Common variants of inflected forms are also shown even if they are regular (as **seed** or **seeds** at **seed**). When the inflected forms of a verb involve no irregularity except the doubling of a final consonant, the double consonant is shown instead of full or cutback inflected forms (as **lug . . . vb -gg-**).

Several other kinds of entries are also found in this dictionary. A variant or inflected form whose alphabetical place is distant from the main entry is entered at its own place with a cross-reference in small capital letters to the main entry (as **hung** past of HANG). A run-in entry is a term related to a main entry that appears within a definition (as **jet engine** at **jet-propelled**). It is set off by parentheses. An undefined run-on entry appears after all definitions of a main entry set off by a dash (as **—likeness** n at **²like**). Its meaning can be inferred from the meaning of the main entry where it appears and that of another main entry, often a suffix, elsewhere. A run-on phrase is a group of two or more words involving as a major element the main entry where it appears and having a special meaning of its own (as by **way** of **way** or **come** to at **come**). It always has a definition. Lists of undefined words whose meaning can be inferred from the meaning of a prefix and that of a word entered in the dictionary will be found at the following places: anti-, bi-, co-, counter-, extra-, hyper-, in-, inter-, mini-, multi-, non-, over-, post-, pre-, re-, self-, sub-, super-, un-, and vice-.

Information about the pronunciation of every entry in the dictionary is either given explicitly or implied. A full list of the symbols used is shown on the next page. Pronunciations are placed within slant lines (as \'dabəl\ at **dab•ble**).

Every main entry has an italic label (as *vb, n,* or *prefix*) indicating its grammatical function. All abbreviations used in these labels and all other abbreviations used in the dictionary are listed, along with a number of other common abbreviations, in a special section immediately following the dictionary proper. This section is followed in turn by a brief Handbook of Style discussing and illustrating the chief points of English punctutation, italicization, capitalization, and the formation of plurals.

Pronunciation Symbols

ə	banana, collide, abut; raised \ˈə\ in \ˈəl\, \ˈən\ as in battle, cotton, in \lˈə\, mˈə, rˈə\ as in French table, prisme, titre	ȯi	toy, sawing
		p	pepper, lip
		r	rarity
ˈə, ˌə	humbug, abut	s	source, less
ər	operation, further	sh	shy, mission
a	map, patch	t	tie, attack
ā	day, fate	th	thin, ether
ä	bother, cot, father	th	then, either
à	father as pronounced by those who do not rhyme it with *bother*	ü	boot, few \ˈfyü\
		u̇	put, pure \ˈpyu̇r\
		ue	German füllen
au̇	now, out	ue͞	French rue, German fühlen
b	baby, rib	v	vivid, give
ch	chin, catch	w	we, away
d	did, adder	y	yard, cue \ˈkyü\; raised \ʸ\ indicates that a preceding \l\, \n\, or \w\ is modified by the placing of the tongue tip against the lower front teeth, as in French digne \dēnʸ\
e	set, red		
ē	beat, nosebleed, easy		
f	fifty, cuff		
g	go, big		
h	hat, ahead		
hw	whale		
i	tip, banish	z	zone, raise
ī	site, buy	zh	vision, pleasure
j	job, edge	\	slant line used in pairs to mark the beginning and end of a transcription
k	kin, cook		
k̲	German ich, Buch	ˈ	mark at the beginning of a syllable that has primary (strongest) stress: \ˈpenmən,ship\
l	lily, cool		
m	murmur, dim		
n	nine, own; raised \ⁿ\ indicates that a preceding vowel or diphthong is pronounced through both nose and mouth, as in French bon \bōⁿ\	ˌ	mark at the beginning of a syllable that has secondary (next-strongest) stress: \ˈpenmən,ship\
		( )	indicate that what is symbolized between is present in some utterances but not in others: *factory* \ˈfakt(ə)rē\
ŋ	sing, singer, finger, ink		
ō	bone, hollow		
ȯ	saw, cork		
œ	French bœuf, German Hölle		
œ͞	French feu, German Höhle		

A

¹a \'ā\ *n, pl* **a's** *or* **as** \'āz\ : 1st letter of the alphabet

²a \ə, 'ā\ *indefinite article* : one or some—used to indicate an unspecified or unidentified individual

aard·vark \'ärd,värk\ *n* : ant-eating African mammal

aback \ə'bak\ *adv* : by surprise

aba·cus \'abəkəs\ *n, pl* **aba·ci** \-,sī, -,kē\ *or* **aba·cus·es** : calculating instrument using rows of beads

abaft \ə'baft\ *adv* : toward or at the stern

ab·a·lo·ne \,abə'lōnē\ *n* : large edible shellfish

¹aban·don \ə'bandən\ *vb* : give up without intent to reclaim —**aban·don·ment** *n*

²abandon *n* : thorough yielding to impulses

aban·doned \ə'bandənd\ *adj* : morally unrestrained

abase \ə'bās\ *vb* **abased; abas·ing** : lower in dignity —**abase·ment** *n*

abash \ə'bash\ *vb* : embarass —**abash·ment** *n*

abate \ə'bāt\ *vb* **abat·ed; abat·ing** : decrease or lessen

abate·ment \ə'bātmənt\ *n* : tax reduction

ab·at·toir \'abə,twär\ *n* : slaughterhouse

ab·bess \'abəs\ *n* : head of a convent

ab·bey \'abē\ *n, pl* **-beys** : monastery or convent

ab·bot \'abət\ *n* : head of a monastery

ab·bre·vi·ate \ə'brēvē,āt\ *vb* **-at·ed; -at·ing** : shorten —**ab·bre·vi·a·tion** \ə,brēvē'āshən\ *n*

ab·di·cate \'abdi,kāt\ *vb* **-cat·ed; -cat·ing** : renounce —**ab·di·ca·tion** \,abdi'kāshən\ *n*

ab·do·men \'abdəmən, ab'dōmən\ *n* **1** : body area between chest and pelvis **2** : hindmost part of an insect —**ab·dom·i·nal** \ab'dämən³l\ *adj* —**ab·dom·i·nal·ly** *adv*

ab·duct \ab'dəkt\ *vb* : kidnap —**ab·duc·tion** \-'dəkshən\ *n* —**ab·duc·tor** \-tər\ *n*

abed \ə'bed\ *adv or adj* : in bed

ab·er·ra·tion \,abə'rāshən\ *n* : deviation or distortion —**ab·er·rant** \a-'berənt\ *adj*

abet \ə'bet\ *vb* **-tt-** : incite or encourage —**abet·tor, abet·ter** \-ər\ *n*

abey·ance \ə'bāəns\ *n* : state of inactivity

ab·hor \ab'hȯr, ab-\ *vb* **-rr-** : hate —**ab·hor·rence** \-əns\ *n* —**ab·hor·rent** \-ənt\ *adj*

abide \ə'bīd\ *vb* **abode** \-'bōd\ *or* **abid·ed; abid·ing 1** : remain, last, or reside **2** : endure

ab·ject \'ab,jekt, ab'-\ *adj* : low in spirit or hope —**ab·jection** \ab-'jekshən\ *n* —**ab·ject·ly** *adv* —**ab·ject·ness** *n*

ab·jure \ab'jȯr\ *vb* **1** : renounce **2** : abstain from —**ab·ju·ra·tion** \,abjə'rāshən\ *n*

ablaze \ə'blāz\ *adj or adv* : on fire

able \'ābəl\ *adj* **abler** \-b(ə)lər\; **ablest** \-b(ə)ləst\ **1** : having sufficient power, skill, or resources **2** : skilled or efficient —**abil·i·ty** \ə'bilətē\ *n* —**ably** \'āblē\ *adv*

-able, -ible \əbəl\ *adj suffix* **1** : capable of, fit for, or worthy of **2** : tending, given, or liable to

ab·lu·tion \ə'blüshən, a'blü-\ *n* : washing of one's body

ab·ne·gate \'abni,gāt\ *vb* **-gat·ed; -gat·ing 1** : relinquish **2** : renounce —**ab·ne·ga·tion** \,abni'gāshən\ *n*

ab·nor·mal \ab'nȯrməl\ *adj* : deviating from the normal or average —**ab·nor·mal·i·ty** \,abnȯr'malətē, -(,)nȯr-\ *n* —**ab·nor·mal·ly** *adv*

aboard \ə'bȯrd\ *adv* : on, onto, or within a car, ship, or aircraft ~ *prep* : on or within

abode \ə'bōd\ *n* : residence

abol·ish \ə'bälish\ *vb* : do away with —**ab·o·li·tion** \,abə'lishən\ *n*

abom·i·na·ble \ə'bäm(ə)nəbəl\ *adj* : thoroughly unpleasant or revolting

abom·i·nate \ə'bämə,nāt\ *vb* **-nat·ed; -nat·ing** : hate —**abom·i·na·tion** \ə,bämə'nāshən\ *n*

ab·orig·i·nal \,abə'rij(ə)nəl\ *adj* **1** : original **2** : primitive

ab·orig·i·ne \-'rijənē\ *n* : original inhabitant

abort \ə'bȯrt\ *vb* : terminate prematurely —**abor·tive** \-'bȯrtiv\ *adj*

abor·tion \ə'bȯrshən\ *n* : removal or induced expulsion of a fetus

abound \ə'baȯnd\ *vb* : be plentiful

about \ə'baȯt\ *adv* : around ~ *prep* **1** : on every side of **2** : on the verge of **3** : having as a subject

above \ə'bəv\ *adv* : in or to a higher place ~ *prep* **1** : in or to a higher place than **2** : more than

above-board *adv or adj* : without deception

abrade \ə'brād\ *vb* **abrad·ed; abrad·ing** : wear away by rubbing —**abra·sion** \-'brāzhən\ *n*

abra·sive \ə'brāsiv\ *adj* **1** : tending to abrade **2** : causing irritation ~ *n* : substance for grinding, smoothing, or polishing —**abra·sive·ly** *adv* —**abra·sive·ness** *n*

abreast \ə'brest\ *adv or adj* **1** : side by side **2** : up to a standard or level

abridge \ə'brij\ *vb* **abridged; abridg·ing** : shorten or condense —**abridg·ment, abridge·ment** *n*

abroad \ə'brȯd\ *adv or adj* **1** : over a wide area **2** : outside one's country

ab·ro·gate \'abrəgāt\ *vb* **-gat·ed; -gat·ing** : annul or revoke —**ab·ro·ga·tion** \,abrə'gāshən\ *n*

abrupt \ə'brəpt\ *adj* **1** : sudden **2** : so quick as to seem rude —**abrupt·ly** *adv*

ab·scess \'ab,ses\ *n* : collection of pus surrounded by inflamed tissue —**ab·scessed** \-,sest\ *adj*

ab·scond \ab'skänd\ *vb* : run away and hide

ab·sent \'absənt\ *adj* : not present —**ab·sent** \ab'sent\ *vb* : keep oneself away —**ab·sence** \'absəns\ *n* —**ab·sen·tee** \,absən'tē\ *n*

ab·sent-mind·ed \,absənt'mīndəd\ *adj* : unaware of one's surroundings or action —**ab·sent-mind·ed·ly** *adv* —**ab·sent-mind·ed·ness** *n*

ab·so·lute \'absə,lüt, ,absə'-\ *adj* **1** : pure **2** : free from restricton **3** : definite —**ab·so·lute·ly** *adv*

ab·so·lu·tion \,absə'lüshən\ *n* : remission of sins

ab·solve \ab'zälv, -'sälv\ *vb* **-solved; -solv·ing** : set free of the consequences of guilt

ab·sorb \ab'sȯrb, -'zȯrb\ *vb* : suck up or take in as a sponge does **2** : engage (one's attention) —**ab·sor·ben·cy** \-'sȯrbənsē, -'zȯr-\ *n* —**ab·sor·bent** \-bənt\ *adj or n* —**ab·sorb·ing** *adj* —**ab·sorb·ing·ly** *adv*

ab·sorp·tion \ab'sȯrpshən, -'zȯrp-\ *n* : process of absorbing —**ab·sorp·tive** \-tiv\ *adj*

ab·stain \ab'stān\ *vb* : refrain from doing something —**ab·stain·er** *n* —**ab·sten·tion** \-'stenchən\ *n* —**ab·sti·nence** \'abstənəns\ *n*

ab·ste·mi·ous \ab'stēmēəs\ *adj* : sparing in use of food or drink —**ab·ste·mi·ous·ly** *adv*

ab·stract \ab'strakt, 'ab,-\ *adj* **1** : expressing a quality apart from an object **2** : not representing something specific ~ \'ab,-\ *n* : summary ~ \ab'-, 'ab,-\ *vb* **1** : remove or separate **2** : make an abstract of —**ab·stract·ly** *adv* —**ab·stract·ness** \-'strak(t)nəs, -,strak(t)-\ *n*

ab·strac·tion \ab'strakshən\ *n* **1** : act of abstracting **2** : abstract idea or work of art

ab·struse \ab'strüs, ab-\ *adj* : hard to understand —**ab·struse·ly** *adv* —**ab·struse·ness** *n*

ab·surd \ab'sərd, -'zərd\ *adj* : ridiculous or unreasonable —**ab·sur·di·ty** \-ətē\ *n* —**ab·surd·ly** *adv*

abun·dant \ə'bəndənt\ *adj* : more than enough —**abun·dance** \-dəns\ *n* —**abun·dant·ly** *adv*

abuse \ə'byüz\ *vb* **abused; abus·ing 1** : attack with words **2** : misuse **3** : mistreat ~ \-'byüs\ *n* **1** : corrupt practice **2** : improper use **3** : mistreatment **4** : coarse and insulting speech —**abus·er** *n* —**abu·sive** \-'byüsiv\ *adj* —**abu·sive·ly** *adv* —**abu·sive·ness** *n*

abut \ə'bət\ *vb* **-tt-** : touch along a border

abut·ment \ə'bətmənt\ *n* : structure that supports weight or withstands lateral pressure

abys·mal \ə'bizməl\ *adj* : immeasurably deep —**abys·mal·ly** *adv*

abyss \ə'bis\ *n* : bottomless pit

-ac \,ak\ *n suffix* : one affected with

aca·cia \ə'kāshə\ *n* : leguminous tree or shrub

ac·a·dem·ic \,akə'demik\ *adj* **1** : relating to schools or colleges **2** : theoretical —**ac·a·dem·i·cal·ly** \-ik(ə)lē\ *adv*

acad·e·my \ə'kadəmē\ *n, pl* **-mies 1** : private high school **2** : society of scholars or artists

acan·thus \ə'kanthəs\ *n* **1** : prickly Mediterranean herb **2** : ornament representing acanthus leaves

ac·cede \ak'sēd\ *vb* **-ced·ed; -ced·ing 1** : become a party to an agreement **2** : express approval **3** : enter upon an office

ac·cel·er·ate \ik'selə,rāt, ak-\ *vb* **-at·ed; -at·ing 1** : bring about earlier **2** : speed up **—ac·cel·er·a·tion** \-,selə'rāshən\ *n*

ac·cel·er·a·tor \ik'selə,rātər, ak-\ *n* : foot-operated pedal for controlling the speed of a motor vehicle

ac·cent \ak,sent\ *n* **1** : distinctive manner of pronunciation **2** : prominence given to one syllable of a word **3** : mark (as `, ´, ^`) over a vowel in writing or printing to indicate pronunciation ~ \'ak,-, ak'-\ *vb* : emphasize **—ac·cen·tu·al** \ak-'sench(ə)wəl\ *adj*

ac·cen·tu·ate \ak'senchə,wāt\ *vb* **-at·ed; -at·ing** : stress or show off by a contrast **—ac·cen·tu·a·tion** \-,senchə'wāshən\ *n*

ac·cept \ik'sept, ak-\ *vb* **1** : receive willingly **2** : agree to **—ac·cept·abil·i·ty** \ik,septə'bilətē, ak-\ *n* **—ac·cept·able** \-'septəbəl\ *adj* **—ac·cep·tance** \-'septəns\ *n*

ac·cess \'ak,ses\ *n* : capability or way of approaching **—ac·ces·si·bil·i·ty** \ik,sesə'bilətē, ak-\ *n* **—ac·ces·si·ble** \-'sesəbəl\ *adj*

ac·ces·sion \ik'seshən, ak-\ *n* **1** : something added **2** : act of taking office

ac·ces·so·ry \ik'ses(ə)rē, ak-\ *n, pl* **-ries 1** : nonessential addition **2** : one guilty of aiding a criminal **—acces·sory** *adj*

ac·ci·dent \'aksədənt\ *n* **1** : event occurring by chance or unintentionally **2** : chance **—ac·ci·den·tal** \,aksə-'dentᵊl\ *adj* **—ac·ci·den·tal·ly** \-'dentlē, -ᵊlē\ *adv*

ac·claim \ə'klām\ *vb or n* : praise

ac·cla·ma·tion \,aklə'māshən\ *n* **1** : eager applause **2** : unanimous vote

ac·com·mo·date \ə'kämə,dāt\ *vb* **-dat·ed; -dat·ing 1** : adapt **2** : provide with something needed **3** : hold without crowding

ac·com·mo·da·tion \ə,kämə'dāshən\ *n* **1** : quarters —usu. pl. **2** : act of accommodating

ac·com·pa·ny \ə'kəmp(ə)nē\ *vb* **-nied;**

-ny·ing 1 : go or occur with **2** : play supporting music **—ac·com·pa·ni·ment** \-mənt\ *n* **—ac·com·pa·nist** \-(ə)nəst\ *n*

ac·com·plice \ə'kämpləs, -'kəm-\ *n* : associate in crime

ac·com·plish \ə'kämplish, -'kəm-\ *vb* : do, fulfill, or bring about **—ac·com·plished** *adj* **—ac·com·plish·er** *n* **—ac·com·plish·ment** *n*

ac·cord \ə'kórd\ *vb* **1** : grant **2** : agree ~ *n* : agreement **—ac·cor·dance** \-'kórdᵊns\ *n* **—ac·cor·dant** \-ᵊnt\ *adj*

ac·cord·ing·ly \ə'kórdiŋlē\ *adv* : consequently

according to *prep* **1** : in conformity with **2** : as stated by

ac·cor·di·on \ə'kórdēən\ *n* : keyboard instrument with a bellows and reeds ~ *adj* : folding like an accordion bellows

ac·cost \ə'kóst\ *vb* : approach and speak to

ac·count \ə'kaunt\ *n* **1** : statement of business transactions **2** : credit arrangement with a vendor **3** : report **4** : worth **5** : sum deposited in a bank ~ *vb* : give an explanation

ac·count·able \ə'kauntəbəl\ *adj* : responsible **—ac·count·abil·i·ty** \-,kauntə'bilətē\ *n*

ac·coun·tant \ə'kauntᵊnt\ *n* : one skilled in accounting **—ac·coun·tan·cy** \-ᵊnsē\ *n*

ac·count·ing \ə'kauntiŋ\ *n* : financial record keeping

ac·cou·tre, ac·cou·ter \ə'kütər\ *vb* **-tred** *or* **-tered; -tring** *or* **-ter·ing** \-'kütəriŋ, -'kütriŋ\ : equip

ac·cred·it \ə'kredət\ *vb* **1** : approve officially **2** : attribute **—ac·cred·ita·tion** \-,kredə'tāshən\ *n*

ac·crue \ə'krü\ *vb* **-crued; -cru·ing** : be added by periodic growth **—ac·cru·al** \-əl\ *n*

ac·cu·mu·late \ə'kyümyə,lāt\ *vb* **-lat·ed; -lat·ing** : collect or pile up **—ac·cu·mu·la·tion** \-,kyümyə'lāshən\ *n* **—ac·cu·mu·la·tor** \-'kyümyə,lātər\ *n*

ac·cu·rate \'akyərət\ *adj* : free from error **—ac·cu·ra·cy** \-rəsē\ *n* **—ac·cu·rate·ly** *adv* **—ac·cu·rate·ness** *n*

ac·curs·ed \ə'kərst, -'kərsəd\, **ac·curst** \ə'kərst\ *adj* **1** : being under a curse **2** : damnable

ac·cuse \ə'kyüz\ *vb* **-cused; -cus·ing** : charge with an offense **—ac·cu·sa·tion** \,akyə'zāshən\ *n*

ac·cused \ə'kyüzd\ *n, pl* **-cused** : defendant in a criminal case

4

ac·cus·tom \ə'kəstəm\ *vb* : cause to treat something as usual or acceptable esp. through repeated experience

ace \'ās\ *n* : one that excels

acer·bic \a-,sər'bik, a-\ *adj* : sour or biting in temper, mood, or tone

ac·e·tate \'asə,tāt\ *n* : fast-drying fabric or plastic derived from acetic acid

acetic acid \ə,sētik-\ *n* : acid found in vinegar

acet·y·lene \ə'set°lən, -,lēn\ *n* : colorless gas used as a fuel in welding

ache \'āk\ *vb* **ached; ach·ing** 1 : suffer a dull persistent pain 2 : yearn —**ache** *n*

achieve \ə'chēv\ *vb* **achieved; achiev·ing** : gain by work or effort —**achieve·ment** *n* —**achiev·er** *n*

ac·id \'asəd\ *adj* 1 : sour or biting to the taste 2 : of or relating to an acid ~ *n* : sour water-soluble chemical compound that reacts with a base to form a salt —**acid·ic** \ə'sidik\ *adj* —**acid·i·fy** \ə'sidə,fī\ *vb* —**acid·i·ty** \-ətē\ *n*

ac·knowl·edge \ik'nälij, ak-\ *vb* **-edged; -edg·ing** 1 : admit as true 2 : admit the authority of 3 : express thanks for —**ac·knowl·edg·ment** *n*

ac·me \'akmē\ *n* : highest point

ac·ne \'aknē\ *n* : skin disorder marked esp. by pimples

ac·o·lyte \'akə,līt\ *n* : one who assists the clergyman in a service

acorn \ā,kȯrn, -kərn\ *n* : nut of the oak

acous·tic \ə'küstik\ *adj* : relating to hearing or sound —**acous·ti·cal** \-stikəl\ *adj* —**acous·ti·cal·ly** \-k(ə)lē\ *adv*

acous·tics \ə'küstiks\ *n sing or pl* 1 : science of sound 2 : qualities in a room that affect how sound is heard

ac·quaint \ə'kwānt\ *vb* 1 : inform 2 : make familiar

ac·quain·tance \ə'kwānt°ns\ *n* 1 : personal knowledge 2 : person with whom one is acquainted —**ac·quain·tance·ship** *n*

ac·qui·esce \,akwē'es\ *vb* **-esced; -esc·ing** : consent —**ac·qui·es·cence** \-'es°ns\ *n* —**ac·qui·es·cent** \-°nt\ *adj* —**ac·qui·es·cent·ly** *adv*

ac·quire \ə'kwī(ə)r\ *vb* **-quired; -quir·ing** : gain

ac·qui·si·tion \,akwə'zishən\ *n* : a gaining or something gained —**ac·quis·i·tive** \ə'kwizətiv\ *adj*

ac·quit \ə'kwit\ *vb* **-tt-** 1 : pronounce not guilty 2 : conduct (oneself) usu. well —**ac·quit·tal** \-°l\ *n*

acre \'ākər\ *n* 1 *pl* : lands 2 : 4840 square yards

acre·age \'āk(ə)rij\ *n* : area in acres

ac·rid \'akrəd\ *adj* : sharp and biting —**acrid·i·ty** \a'kridətē, ə-\ *n* —**ac·rid·ness** *n*

ac·ri·mo·ny \'akrə,mōnē\ *n, pl* **-nies** : harshness of language or feeling —**ac·ri·mo·ni·ous** \,akrə'mōnēəs\ *adj*

ac·ro·bat \'akrə,bat\ *n* : performer of tumbling feats —**ac·ro·bat·ic** \,akrə'batik\ *adj*

across \ə'krȯs\ *adv* 1 : to or on the opposite side ~ *prep* 1 : to or on the opposite side of 2 : on so as to cross

acryl·ic \ə'krilik\ *n* : plastic used for molded parts or in paints

act \'akt\ *n* 1 : thing done 2 : law 3 : main division of a play ~ *vb* 1 : perform in a play 2 : conduct oneself 3 : operate 4 : produce an effect

ac·tion \'akshən\ *n* 1 : legal proceeding 2 : manner or method of performing 3 : activity 4 : thing done over a period of time or in stages 5 : combat 6 : events of a literary plot 7 : operating mechanism

ac·ti·vate \'aktə,vāt\ *vb* **-vat·ed; -vat·ing** : make active or reactive —**ac·ti·va·tion** \,aktə'vāshən\ *n*

ac·tive \'aktiv\ *adj* 1 : causing action or change 2 : lively, vigorous, or energetic 3 : now in operation —**active** *n* —**ac·tive·ly** *adv*

ac·tiv·i·ty \ak'tivətē\ *n, pl* **-ties** 1 : quality or state of being active 2 : what one is actively doing

ac·tor \'aktər\ *n* : one that acts —**ac·tress** \-trəs\ *n*

ac·tu·al \'akch(əw)əl\ *adj* : really existing —**ac·tu·al·i·ty** \,akchə'walətē\ *n* —**ac·tu·al·iza·tion** \,akch(əw)ələ-'zāshən\ *n* —**ac·tu·al·ize** \'akch(əw)ə,līz\ *vb* —**ac·tu·al·ly** *adv*

ac·tu·ary \'akchə,werē\ *n, pl* **-ar·ies** : one who calculates insurance risks and premiums —**ac·tu·ar·i·al** \,akchə'werēəl\ *adj*

ac·tu·ate \'akchə,wāt\ *vb* **-at·ed; -at·ing** : put into action —**ac·tu·a·tor** \-,wātər\ *n*

acu·men \ə'kyümən\ *n* : mental keenness

acu·punc·ture \'akyu,pəŋkchər\ *n* : treatment by puncturing the body with needles —**acu·punc·tur·ist** \,akyu'pəŋkchərəst\ *n*

acute \ə'kyüt\ *adj* **acut·er; acut·est** 1 : sharp 2 : containing less than 90 degrees 3 : mentally alert 4 : severe —**acute·ly** *adv* —**acute·ness** *n*

ad \'ad\ *n* : advertisement

ad·age \'adij\ *n* : old familiar saying

ad·a·mant \'adəmənt, -,mant\ *adj* : insistent —**ad·a·mant·ly** *adv*

adapt \ə'dapt\ *vb* : adjust to be suitable for a new use or condition —**adapt·abil·i·ty** \ə,daptə'bilətē\ *n* —**adapt·able** *adj* —**ad·ap·ta·tion** \,ad-,ap'tāshən, adp-\ *n* —**adapt·er** *n* —**adap·tive** \ə'daptiv\ *adj*

add \'ad\ *vb* 1 : join to something else so as to increase in amount 2 : find a sum —**ad·di·tion** \ə'dishən\ *n*

ad·der \'adər\ *n* 1 : poisonous European snake 2 : No. American snake

ad·dict \'ad,)ikt\ *n* : one who is psychologically or physiologically dependent (as on a drug) ~ \ə'dikt\ *vb* : cause to become an addict —**ad·dic·tion** \ə'dikshən\ *n* —**ad·dic·tive** \-'diktiv\ *adj*

ad·di·tion·al \ə'dish(ə)nəl\ *adj* : existing as a result of adding —**ad·di·tion·al·ly** *adv*

ad·di·tive \'adətiv\ *n* : substance added to another

ad·dle \'ad²l\ *vb* **-dled; -dling** : confuse

ad·dress \ə'dres\ *vb* 1 : direct one's remarks to or deal with 2 : mark an address on ~ \ə'dres, 'ad,res\ *n* 1 : formal speech 2 : place where a person may be reached or mail may be delivered

ad·duce \ə'd(y)üs\ *vb* **-duced; -duc·ing** : offer as proof

ad·e·noid \'ad,noid, -²nòid\ *n* : enlarged tissue near the opening of the nose into the throat —usu. pl. —**adenoid, ad·e·noi·dal** \-²l\ *adj*

adept \ə'dept\ *adj* : highly skilled —**adept·ly** *adv* —**adept·ness** *n*

ad·e·quate \'adikwət\ *adj* : good or plentiful enough —**ad·e·qua·cy** \-kwəsē\ *n* —**ad·e·quate·ly** *adv*

ad·here \ad'hiər, əd-\ *vb* **-hered; -her·ing** 1 : remain loyal 2 : stick fast —**ad·her·ence** \-'hirəns\ *n* —**ad·her·ent** \-ənt\ *adj or n*

ad·he·sion \ad'hēzhən, əd-\ *n* : act or state of adhering

ad·he·sive \-'hēsiv, -ziv\ *adj* : tending to adhere ~ *n* : adhesive substance

adieu \ə'd(y)ü\ *n, pl* **adieus** *or* **adieux** \ə'd(y)üz\ : farewell

ad·ja·cent \ə'jāsᵊnt\ *adj* : situated near or next

ad·jec·tive \'ajiktiv\ *n* : word that serves as a modifier of a noun —**ad·jec·ti·val** \,ajik'tivəl\ *adj* —**ad·jec·ti·val·ly** *adv*

ad·join \ə'jòin\ *vb* : be next to

ad·journ \ə'jərn\ *vb* : end a meeting —**ad·journ·ment** *n*

ad·judge \ə'jəj\ *vb* **-judged; -judg·ing** 1 : think or pronounce to be 2 : award by judicial decision

ad·ju·di·cate \ə'jüdi,kāt\ *vb* **-cat·ed; -cat·ing** : settle judicially —**ad·ju·di·ca·tion** \ə,jüdi'kāshən\ *n*

ad·junct \'aj,əŋkt\ *n* : something joined or added but not essential

ad·just \ə'jəst\ *vb* : fix, adapt, or set right —**ad·just·able** *adj* —**ad·jus·ter, ad·jus·tor** \ə'jəstər\ *n* —**ad·just·ment** \ə'jəs(t)mənt\ *n*

ad·ju·tant \'ajətənt\ *n* : aide esp. to a commanding officer

ad–lib \'ad'lib\ *vb* : speak without preparation —**ad–lib** *n or adj*

ad·min·is·ter \əd'minəstər\ *vb* 1 : manage 2 : give out esp. in doses —**ad·min·is·tra·ble** \-strəbəl\ *adj*

ad·min·is·trant \-strənt\ *adj*

ad·min·is·tra·tion \əd,minə'strāshən, (,)ad-\ *n* 1 : process of managing 2 : persons responsible for managing —**ad·min·is·tra·tive** \əd'minə-,strā-tiv\ *adj* —**ad·min·is·tra·tive·ly** *adv*

ad·min·is·tra·tor \əd'minə,strātər\ *n* : one that manages

ad·mi·ra·ble \'adm(ə)rəbəl\ *adj* : worthy of admiration —**ad·mi·ra·bly** \-blē\ *adv*

ad·mi·ral \'adm(ə)rəl\ *n* : commissioned officer in the navy ranking next below a fleet admiral

ad·mire \ad'mī(ə)r\ *vb* **-mired; -mir·ing** : have high regard for —**ad·mi·ra·tion** \,admə'rāshən\ *n* —**ad·mir·er** *n* —**ad·mir·ing·ly** *adv*

ad·mis·si·ble \əd'misəbəl\ *adj* : that can be permitted —**ad·mis·si·bil·i·ty** \-,misə'bilətē\ *n*

ad·mis·sion \əd'mishən\ *n* 1 : acknowledgment of a fact 2 : act of admitting 3 : admittance or a fee paid for this

ad·mit \əd'mit\ *vb* **-tt-** 1 : allow to enter 2 : permit 3 : recognize as genuine —**ad·mit·ted·ly** *adv*

ad·mit·tance \əd'mit²ns\ *n* : permission to enter

ad·mix·ture \ad'mikschər\ *n* 1 : mixture 2 : thing added in mixing

ad·mon·ish \əd'mänish\ *vb* : rebuke —**ad·mo·ni·tion** \,admə'nishən\ *n* —**ad·mon·i·to·ry** \əd'mänə,tōrē\ *adj*

ado \ə'dü\ *n* 1 : fuss 2 : trouble

ado·be \ə'dōbē\ *n* : sun-dried building brick —**adobe** *adj*

ad·o·les·cence \,ad²l'es²ns\ *n* : period of growth between childhood and maturity —**ad·o·les·cent** \-²nt\ *adj or n*

adopt \ə'däpt\ *vb* 1 : take (a child of other parents) as one's own child 2

: take up and practice as one's own —**adop·tion** \-'däpshən\ n

adore \ə'dōr\ vb **adored; ador·ing 1** : worship **2** : be extremely fond of —**ador·able** adj —**ador·ably** adv —**ad·o·ra·tion** \,adə'rāshən\ n

adorn \ə'dōrn\ vb : decorate with ornaments —**adorn·ment** n

adrift \ə'drift\ adv or adj **1** : afloat without motive power or moorings **2** : without guidance or purpose

adroit \ə'dróit\ adj : dexterous or shrewd —**adroit·ly** adv —**adroit·ness** n

adult \ə'dəlt, 'ad,əlt\ adj : fully developed and mature ∼ n : grown-up person —**adult·hood** n

adul·ter·ate \ə'dəltə,rāt\ vb **-at·ed; -at·ing** : make impure by mixture —**adul·ter·a·tion** \-,dəltə'rāshən\ n

adul·tery \ə'dəlt(ə)rē\ n, pl **-ter·ies** : sexual unfaithfulness of a married person —**adul·ter·er** \-tərər\ n —**adul·ter·ess** \-t(ə)rəs\ n —**adul·ter·ous** \-t(ə)rəs\ adj

ad·vance \əd'vans\ vb **-vanced; -vanc·ing 1** : bring or move forward **2** : promote **3** : lend ∼ n **1** : forward movement **2** : improvement **3** : loan ∼ adj : being ahead of time —**ad·vance·ment** n

ad·van·tage \əd'vantij\ n **1** : superiority of position **2** : benefit or gain —**ad·van·ta·geous** \,ad,van'tājəs, -van-\ adj —**ad·van·ta·geous·ly** adv

Ad·vent \'ad,vent\ n : period before Christmas

ad·ven·ti·tious \,advən'tishəs\ adj : accidental —**ad·ven·ti·tious·ly** adv

ad·ven·ture \əd'venchər\ n **1** : risky undertaking **2** : exciting experience —**ad·ven·tur·er** \-'vench(ə)rər\ n —**ad·ven·ture·some** \-'venchərsəm\ adj —**ad·ven·tur·ous** \-'vench(ə)rəs\ adj

ad·verb \'ad,vərb\ n : word that modifies a verb, an adjective, or another adverb —**ad·ver·bi·al** \əd'vərbēəl\ adj —**ad·ver·bi·al·ly** adv

ad·ver·sary \'advə(r),serē\ n, pl **-sar·ies** : enemy or rival —**adversary** adj

ad·verse \əd'vərs, 'ad-\ adj : opposing or unfavorable —**ad·verse·ly** adv

ad·ver·si·ty \əd'vərsətē\ n, pl **-ties** : hard times

ad·vert \əd'vərt\ vb : refer

ad·ver·tise \'advər,tīz\ vb **-tised; -tis·ing** : call public attention to —**ad·ver·tise·ment** \,advər'tīzmənt, əd-'vərtəzmənt\ n —**ad·ver·tis·er** n

ad·ver·tis·ing \'advər,tīziŋ\ n : business of preparing advertisements

ad·vice \əd'vīs\ n : recommendation with regard to a course of action

ad·vis·able \əd'vīzəbəl\ adj : wise or prudent —**ad·vis·abil·i·ty** \-,vīzə'bilətē\ n

ad·vise \əd'vīz\ vb **-vised; -vis·ing** : give advice to —**ad·vis·er, ad·vi·sor** \-'vīzər\ n

ad·vise·ment \əd'vīzmənt\ n : careful consideration

ad·vi·so·ry \əd'vīz(ə)rē\ adj : having power to advise

ad·vo·cate \'advəkət, -,kāt\ n : one who argues or pleads for a cause or proposal ∼ \-,kāt\ vb **-cat·ed; -cat·ing** : recommend —**ad·vo·ca·cy** \-və-kə-sē\ n

adz, adze \'adz\ n : tool for shaping wood

ae·gis \'ējəs\ n : protection or sponsorship

ae·on \'ēən, 'ē,än\ n : indefinitely long time

aer·ate \'a(ə)r,āt\ vb **-at·ed; -at·ing** : supply or impregnate with air —**aer·a·tion** \,a(ə)'rāshən\ n —**aer·a·tor** \'a(ə)r,ātər\ n

ae·ri·al \'arēəl, ā'irēəl\ adj : inhabiting, occurring in, or done in the air ∼ n : antenna

ae·rie \'a(ə)rē, 'i(ə)rē\ n : eagle's nest

aer·o·bic \,a(ə)r'rōbik\ adj : using or needing oxygen

aero·dy·nam·ics \,arōdī'namiks\ n : science of the motion of gases —**aero·dy·nam·ic** \-ik\, **aero·dy·nam·i·cal** \-ikəl\ adj —**aero·dy·nam·i·cal·ly** \-ik(ə)lē\ adv

aero·nau·tics \,arə'nótiks\ n : science dealing with aircraft —**aero·nau·ti·cal** \-ikəl\, **aero·nau·tic** \-ik\ adj —**aero·nau·ti·cal·ly** \-ik(ə)lē\ adv

aero·sol \'arə,säl, -,sōl\ n **1** : liquid or solid particles suspended in a gas **2** : substance sprayed as an aerosol

aero·space \'arō,spās\ n : earth's atmosphere and the space beyond —**aerospace** adj

aes·thet·ic \es'thetik\ adj : relating to beauty —**aes·thet·i·cal·ly** \-ik(ə)lē\ adv

aes·thet·ics \-'thetiks\ n : branch of philosophy dealing with beauty

afar \ə'fär\ adv : from, at, or to a great distance —**afar** n

af·fa·ble \'afəbəl\ adj : easy to talk to —**af·fa·bil·i·ty** \,afə'bilətē\ n —**af·fa·bly** \'afəblē\ adv

af·fair \ə'faər\ n : something that relates to or involves one

¹**af·fect** \ə'fekt, a-\ vb : assume for

effect   —af·fec·ta·tion \,af,ek-
'tāshən\ n

²affect vb : produce an effect on

af·fect·ed \ə'fektəd, a-\ adj 1 : pretending to some trait 2 : artificially
assumed to impress —af·fect·ed·ly
adv

af·fect·ing \ə'fektiŋ, a-\ adj : arousing
pity or sorrow —af·fect·ing·ly adv

af·fec·tion \ə'fekshən\ n : kind or lov-
ing feeling —af·fec·tion·ate
\-sh(ə)nət\ adj —af·fec·tion·ate·ly
adv

af·fi·da·vit \,afə'dāvət\ n : sworn statement

af·fil·i·ate \ə'filē,āt\ vb -at·ed; -at·ing
: become a member or branch —af-
fil·i·ate \-ēət\ n —af·fil·i·a·tion
\-,filē'āshən\ n

af·fin·i·ty \ə'finətē\ n, pl -ties : close
attraction or relationship

af·firm \ə'fərm\ vb : assert positively
—af·fir·ma·tion \,afər'māshən\ n

af·fir·ma·tive \ə'fərmətiv\ adj : assert-
ing the truth or existence of something ~ n : statement of affirmation
or agreement

af·fix \ə'fiks\ vb : attach

af·flict \ə'flikt\ vb : cause pain and distress to —af·flic·tion \-'flikshən\ n

af·flu·ence \'af,lüən(t)s; ə'flü-, ə-\ n
: wealth —af·flu·ent \-ənt\ adj

af·ford \ə'fōrd\ vb 1 : manage to bear
the cost of 2 : provide

af·fray \ə'frā\ n : fight

af·front \ə'frənt\ vb or n : insult

af·ghan \'af,gan, -gən\ n : crocheted
or knitted blanket

afire \ə'fī(ə)r\ adj or adv : being on
fire

aflame \ə'flām\ adj or adv : flaming

afloat \ə'flōt\ adj or adv : floating

afoot \ə'füt\ adv or adj 1 : on foot 2
: in progress

afore·said \ə'fōr,sed\ adj : said or
named before

afraid \ə'frād, South also ə'fre(ə)d\
adj : filled with fear

afresh \ə'fresh\ adv : anew

aft \'aft\ adv : to or toward the stern
or tail

af·ter \'aftər\ adv 1 : at a later time 2
: at the back ~ prep 1 : behind in
place or time 2 : intent on gaining ~
conj : following the time when ~ adj
1 : later 2 : located toward the back

af·ter·life \'aftər,līf\ n : existence after
death

af·ter·math \-,math\ n : results

af·ter·noon \,aftər'nün\ n : time between noon and evening

af·ter·thought n : later thought

af·ter·ward \'aftə(r)wərd\, af·ter-
wards \-wərdz\ adv : at a later time

again \ə'gen, -'gin\ adv 1 : once more
2 : on the other hand 3 : in addition

against \ə'genst\ prep 1 : directly opposite to 2 : in opposition to 3 : so
as to touch or strike

agape \ə'gāp, -'gap\ adj or adv : having the mouth open in astonishment

ag·ate \'agət\ n : quartz with bands or
masses of various colors

age \'āj\ n 1 : length of time of life or
existence 2 : particular time in life
(as majority or the latter part) 3
: quality of being old 4 : long time 5
: period in history ~ vb : become old
or mature

-age \ij\ n suffix 1 : aggregate 2 : action
or process 3 : result of 4 : rate of 5
: place of 6 : state or rank 7 : fee

aged adj 1 \'ājəd\ : old 2 \'ājd\ : al-
lowed to mature

age·less \'ājləs\ adj : eternal

agen·cy \'ājənsē\ n, pl -cies 1 : one
through which something is accomplished 2 : office or function of an
agent 3 : government administrative
division

agen·da \ə'jendə\ n : list of things to
be done

agent \'ājənt\ n 1 : means 2 : person
acting or doing business for another

ag·gran·dize \ə'gran,dīz, 'agrən-\ vb
-dized; -diz·ing : make great or
greater —ag·gran·dize·ment \ə'gran-
dəzmənt, -,dīz-; ,agrən'dīz-\ n

ag·gra·vate \'agrə,vāt\ vb -vat·ed; -vat-
ing 1 : make more severe 2 : irritate
—ag·gra·va·tion \,agrə'vāshən\ n

ag·gre·gate \'agrigət\ adj : formed into
a mass ~ \-,gāt\ vb -gat·ed; -gat·ing
: collect into a mass ~ \-gət\ n 1
: mass 2 : whole amount

ag·gres·sion \ə'greshən\ n 1 : unpro-
voked attack 2 : hostile behavior —
ag·gres·sor \-'gresər\ n

ag·gres·sive \ə'gresiv\ adj 1 : easily
provoked to fight 2 : hard working
and enterprising —ag·gres·sive·ly
adv —ag·gres·sive·ness n

ag·grieve \ə'grēv\ vb -grieved; -griev-
ing 1 : cause grief to 2 : inflict injury
on

aghast \ə'gast\ adj : struck with
amazement or horror

ag·ile \'ajəl\ adj : able to move quickly
and easily —agil·i·ty \ə'jilətē\ n

ag·i·tate \'ajə,tāt\ vb -tat·ed; -tat·ing 1
: shake or stir back and forth 2
: excite or trouble the mind of 3 : try
to arouse public feeling —ag·i·ta·tion

\ˌajə'tāshən\ *n* —**ag·i·ta·tor** \'ajəˌtātər\ *n*

ag·nos·tic \ag'nästik, əg-\ *n* : one who doubts the existence of God

ago \ə'gō\ *adj or adv* : earlier than the present

agog \ə'gäg\ *adj* : full of excitement

ag·o·nize \'agəˌnīz\ *vb* -**nized; -niz·ing** : suffer mental agony —**ag·o·niz·ing·ly** *adv*

ag·o·ny \'agənē\ *n, pl* -**nies** : extreme pain or mental distress

agrar·i·an \ə'grerēən\ *adj* : relating to land ownership or farming interests —**agrarian** *n* —**agrar·i·an·ism** *n*

agree \ə'grē\ *vb* **agreed; agree·ing 1** : be of the same opinion **2** : express willingness **3** : get along together **4** : be similar **5** : be appropriate, suitable, or healthful

agree·able \-əbəl\ *adj* **1** : pleasing **2** : willing to give approval —**agree·able·ness** *n* —**agree·ably** *adv*

agree·ment \-mənt\ *n* **1** : harmony of opinion or purpose **2** : mutual understanding or arrangement

ag·ri·cul·ture \'agriˌkəlchər\ *n* : farming —**ag·ri·cul·tur·al** \ˌagri'kəlch(ə)rəl\ *adj* —**ag·ri·cul·tur·al·ist** \-rəst\, **ag·ri·cul·tur·al·ist** \-(ə)rə-ləst\ *n*

aground \ə'graùnd\ *adv or adj* : on or onto the bottom or shore

ague \'āgyü\ *n* **1** : fever with recurrent chills and sweating **2** : malaria

ahead \ə'hed\ *adv or adj* **1** : in or toward the front **2** : into or for the future **3** : in a more advantageous position

ahead of *prep* **1** : in front or advance of **2** : in excess of

ahoy \ə'hòi\ *interj* —used in hailing

aid \'ād\ *vb* : provide help or support ~ *n* : help

aide \'ād\ *n* : helper

ail \'āl\ *vb* **1** : trouble **2** : be ill

ai·le·ron \'āləˌrän\ *n* : movable part of an airplane wing

ail·ment \'ālmənt\ *n* : bodily disorder

aim \'ām\ *vb* **1** : point or direct (as a weapon) **2** : direct one's efforts ~ *n* **1** : an aiming or the direction of aiming **2** : something meant to be achieved —**aim·less** *adj* —**aim·less·ly** *adv* —**aim·less·ness** *n*

air \'aər\ *n* **1** : mixture of gases surrounding the earth **2** : compressed air **3** : travel by or use of aircraft **4** : medium of transmission of radio waves **5** : outward appearance **6** : artificial manner **7** : melody ~ *vb* **1**

: expose to the air **2** : broadcast —**air·borne** \-ˌbôrn\ *adj*

air-condition *vb* : equip with an apparatus (**air conditioner**) for filtering and cooling the air

air·craft *n, pl* **aircraft** : craft that flies

Aire·dale terrier \ˌaərˌdāl-\ *n* : large terrier with a hard wiry coat

air·field *n* : airport or its landing field

air force *n* : military organization for conducting warfare by aircraft

air·lift *n* : a transporting of esp. emergency supplies by aircraft —**airlift** *vb*

air·line *n* : air transportation system —**air·lin·er** *n*

air·mail *n* : system of transporting mail by airplane —**airmail** *vb*

air·man \-mən\ *n* : enlisted man in the air force in one of the 3 ranks below sergeant **2** : enlisted man in the air force ranking below airman first class and above airman basic **3** : aviator

airman basic *n* : enlisted man of the lowest rank in the air force

airman first class *n* : enlisted man in the air force ranking below sergeant and above airman

air·plane *n* : fixed-wing aircraft heavier than air

air·port *n* : place for landing aircraft and receiving passengers

air·ship *n* : propelled lighter-than-air aircraft

air·strip *n* : airfield runway

air·tight *adj* : tightly sealed to prevent flow of air

air·waves \-ˌwāvz\ *n pl* : medium of transmission of radio waves

airy \'a(ə)rē\ *adj* **air·i·er; -est 1** : delicate **2** : breezy

aisle \'īl\ *n* : passage between sections of seats

ajar \ə'jär\ *adj or adv* : partly open

akim·bo \ə'kimbō\ *adj or adv* : having the hand on the hip and the elbow turned outward

akin \ə'kin\ *adj* **1** : related by blood **2** : similar in kind

-al \əl\ *adj suffix* : of, relating to, or characterized by

al·a·bas·ter \'aləˌbastər\ *n* : white or translucent mineral

alac·ri·ty \ə'lakrətē\ *n* : cheerful readiness

alarm \ə'lärm\ *n* **1** : warning signal **2** : fear at sudden danger ~ *vb* **1** : warn **2** : frighten

alas \ə'las\ *interj* —used to express unhappiness, pity, or concern

al·ba·tross \'albə,tròs, -,träs\ n, pl **-tross** or **-trosses** : large seabird

al·be·it \òl'bēət, al-\ conj : even though

al·bi·no \al'bīnō\ n, pl **-nos** : person or animal with abnormally white skin —**al·bi·nism** \'albə,nizəm\ n

al·bum \'albəm\ n 1 : book for displaying a collection (as of photographs) 2 : phonograph record

al·bu·men \al'byümən\ n 1 : white of an egg 2 : albumin

al·bu·min \-mən\ n : protein found in blood, milk, egg white, and tissues

al·che·my \'alkəmē\ n : medieval chemistry —**al·chem·ic** \al'kemik\, **al·chem·i·cal** \-ikəl\ adj —**al·che·mist** \'alkəməst\ n

al·co·hol \'alkə,hòl\ n 1 : intoxicating element in liquor 2 : liquor —**al·co·hol·ic** \,alkə'hòlik, -'häl-\ n : person affected with alcoholism

al·co·hol·ism \'alkə,hòl,izəm\ n : addiction to alcoholic beverages

al·cove \'al,kōv\ n : recess in a room or wall

al·der·man \'òldərmən\ n : city official

ale \'āl\ n : beerlike beverage —**ale·house** n

alert \ə'lərt\ adj 1 : watchful 2 : quick to perceive and act ~ n : warning signal ~ vb : warn —**alert·ly** adv —**alert·ness** n

ale·wife n : fish of the herring family

al·fal·fa \al'falfə\ n : cloverlike forage plant

al·ga \'algə\ n, pl **-gae** \'(,)jē\ : any of a group of lower plants that includes seaweed —**al·gal** \-gəl\ adj

al·ge·bra \'aljəbrə\ n : branch of mathematics using symbols —**al·ge·bra·ic** \,aljə'brāik\ adj —**al·ge·bra·ical·ly** \-'brāik(ə)lē\ adv

alias \'ālēəs, 'ālyəs\ adv : otherwise called ~ n : assumed name

al·i·bi \'alə,bī\ n 1 : defense of having been elsewhere when a crime was committed 2 : justification ~ vb **-bied; -bi·ing** : offer an excuse

alien \'ālēən, 'ālyən\ adj : foreign ~ n : foreign-born resident

alien·ate \'ālēə,nāt, 'ālyə-\ vb **-at·ed; -at·ing** : cause to be no longer friendly —**alien·ation** \,ālēə'nāshən, ,ālyə-\ n

alight \ə'līt\ vb : dismount

align \ə'līn\ vb : bring into line —**alignment** n

alike \ə'līk\ adj : identical or very similar ~ adv : equally

al·i·men·ta·ry \,alə'ment(ə)rē\ adj

: relating to or functioning in nutrition

al·i·mo·ny \'alə,mōnē\ n, pl **-nies** : money paid to a separated or divorced spouse

alive \ə'līv\ adj 1 : having life 2 : lively or animated

al·ka·li \'alkə,lī\ n, pl **-lies** or **-lis** : strong chemical base —**al·ka·line** \-kələn, -,līn\ adj —**al·ka·lin·i·ty** \,alkə'linətē\ n

all \'òl\ adj 1 : the whole of 2 : greatest possible 3 : every one of ~ adv 1 : wholly 2 : so much 3 : for each side ~ pron 1 : every one 2 : every bit 3 : everything

Al·lah \'alə, ä'lä\ n : supreme being of the Muslims

all-around adj : versatile

al·lay \ə'lā\ vb : relieve or dispel

al·lege \ə'lej\ vb **-leged; -leg·ing** : state as a fact without proof —**al·le·ga·tion** \,ali'gāshən\ n —**al·leg·ed·ly** \ə'lejədlē\ adv

al·le·giance \ə'lējəns\ n : loyalty

al·le·go·ry \'alə,gòrē\ n, pl **-ries** : story in which figures and actions are symbols of general truths —**al·le·gor·i·cal** \alə'gòrikəl\ adj

al·le·lu·ia \,alə'lüyə\ interj : hallelujah

al·ler·gen \'alərjən\ n : something that causes allergy —**al·ler·gen·ic** \,alər'jenik\ adj

al·ler·gy \'alərjē\ n, pl **-gies** : abnormal reaction to a substance —**al·ler·gic** \ə'lərjik\ adj —**al·ler·gist** \'alərjəst\ n

al·le·vi·ate \ə'lēvē,āt\ vb **-at·ed; -at·ing** : relieve or improve —**al·le·vi·a·tion** \ə,lēvē'āshən\ n

al·ley \'alē\ n, pl **-leys** 1 : narrow passage between buildings 2 : place for bowling

al·li·ance \ə'līəns\ n : association

al·lied \ə'līd, 'al,īd\ adj : joined

al·li·ga·tor \'alə,gātər\ n : large aquatic reptile related to the crocodiles

al·lit·er·a·tion \ə,litə'rāshən\ n : repetition of initial sounds of words —**al·lit·er·a·tive** \-'litə,rātiv\ adj

al·lo·cate \'alə,kāt\ vb **-cat·ed; -cat·ing** : assign —**al·lo·ca·tion** \,alə'kāshən\ n

al·lot \ə'lät\ vb **-tt-** : distribute as a share —**al·lot·ment** n

al·low \ə'laù\ vb 1 : permit 2 : agree to the truth of —**al·low·able** adj

al·low·ance \-əns\ n 1 : allotted share 2 : money given regularly for expenses

al·loy \'al,òi, ə'lòi\ n : metals fused together —**alloy** vb

all right *adv or adj* **1** : satisfactorily **2** : yes **3** : certainly

all·spice \'ȯl‚spīs\ *n* : berry of a West Indian tree made into a spice

al·lude \ə'lüd\ *vb* **-lud·ed; -lud·ing** : refer indirectly —**al·lu·sion** \-'lüzhən\ *n* —**al·lu·sive** \-'lüsiv\ *adj* —**al·lu·sive·ly** *adv* —**al·lu·sive·ness** *n*

al·lure \ə'lu̇r\ *vb* **-lured; -lur·ing** : attract —**allure** *n* —**al·lure·ment** *n*

al·ly \ə'lī, 'al‚ī\ *vb* **-lied; -ly·ing** : unite in alliance ~ \'al‚ī, ə'lī\ *n, pl* **-lies** : member of an alliance

-al·ly \(ə)lē\ *adv suffix* : -ly

al·ma·nac \'ȯlmə‚nak, 'al-\ *n* : annual information book

al·mighty \ȯl'mītē\ *adj* : having absolute power

al·mond \'ämənd, 'am-; 'almənd\ *n* : tree with nutlike fruit kernels

al·most \'ȯl‚mōst, ȯl-'\ *adv* : only a little less than

alms \'ämz, 'almz\ *n, pl* **alms** : charitable gift

aloft \ə'lȯft\ *adv* : high in the air

alo·ha \ə'lōə, ä'lōhä\ *interj* —used to express greeting or farewell

alone \ə'lōn\ *adj* **1** : separated from others **2** : not including anyone or anything else —**alone** *adv*

along \ə'lȯŋ\ *prep* **1** : on or near in a lengthwise direction **2** : at a point on or during ~ *adv* **1** : forward **2** : as a companion **3** : all the time

along·side *adv* : along or by the side ~ *prep* : side by side with

alongside of *prep* : alongside

aloof \ə'lüf\ *adj* : indifferent and reserved —**aloof·ness** *n*

aloud \ə'lau̇d\ *adv* : so that the voice can be heard

al·paca \al'pakə\ *n* **1** : So. American mammal related to the llama **2** : alpaca wool or cloth made of this

al·pha·bet \'alfə‚bet, -bət\ *n* : ordered set of letters of a language —**al·pha·bet·i·cal** \‚alfə'betikəl\, **al·pha·bet·ic** \-'betik\ *adj* —**al·pha·bet·i·cal·ly** \-k(ə)lē\ *adv*

al·pha·bet·ize \'alfəbə‚tīz\ *vb* **-ized; -iz·ing** : arrange in alphabetic order —**al·pha·bet·iz·er** *n*

al·ready \ȯl'redē\ *adv* : by a given time

al·so \'ȯlsō\ *adv* : in addition

al·tar \'ȯltər\ *n* : structure for rituals

al·ter \'ȯltər\ *vb* : make different —**al·ter·a·tion** \‚ȯltə'rāshən\ *n*

al·ter·ca·tion \‚ȯltər'kāshən\ *n* : dispute

al·ter·nate \'ȯltərnāt, 'al-\ *adj* **1** : arranged or succeeding by turns **2** : every other ~ \-‚nāt\ *vb* **-nat·ed;** **-nat·ing** : occur or cause to occur by turns ~ \-nət\ *n* : replacement —**al·ter·nate·ly** *adv* —**al·ter·na·tion** \‚ȯltər'nāshən, ‚al-\ *n*

alternating current *n* : electric current that regularly reverses direction

al·ter·na·tive \ȯl'tərnətiv, al-\ *adj* : offering a choice —**alternative** *n*

al·ter·na·tor \'ȯltər‚nātər, 'al-\ *n* : alternating-current generator

al·though \ȯl'thō\ *conj* : even though

al·tim·e·ter \al'timətər, 'altə‚mētər\ *n* : instrument for measuring altitude

al·ti·tude \'altə‚t(y)üd\ *n* **1** : distance up from the ground **2** : angular distance above the horizon

al·to \'altō\ *n, pl* **-tos** : contralto

al·to·geth·er \‚ȯltə'gethər\ *adv* **1** : wholly **2** : on the whole

al·tru·ism \'altrü‚izəm\ *n* : concern for others —**al·tru·ist** \-'əst\ *n* —**al·tru·is·tic** \‚altrü'istik\ *adj* —**al·tru·is·ti·cal·ly** \-tik(ə)lē\ *adv*

al·um \'aləm\ *n* : crystalline compound containing aluminum

alu·mi·num \ə'lümənəm\ *n* : silver-white malleable ductile light metallic element

alum·na \ə'ləmnə\ *n, pl* **-nae** \-(‚)nē\ : woman graduate

alum·nus \ə'ləmnəs\ *n, pl* **-ni** \-‚nī\ : graduate

al·ways \'ȯlwēz, -wəz, -(‚)wāz\ *adv* **1** : at all times **2** : forever **3** : without exception

am *pres 1st sing of* BE

amal·gam \ə'malgəm\ *n* **1** : mercury alloy **2** : mixture

amal·gam·ate \ə'malgə‚māt\ *vb* **-at·ed;** **-at·ing** : unite —**amal·gam·a·tion** \-‚malgə'māshən\ *n*

am·a·ryl·lis \‚amə'riləs\ *n* : bulbous herb with clusters of colored flowers like lilies

amass \ə'mas\ *vb* : gather

am·a·teur \'amə‚tər, -‚ətər, -ə‚t(y)ür, -ə‚chu̇r, -əchər\ *n* **1** : person who does something for pleasure rather than for pay **2** : person who is not expert —**amateur** *adj* —**am·a·teur·ish** \‚amə'tərish, -'t(y)ür-\ *adj* —**am·a·teur·ism** \'amə‚tər‚izəm, -‚ətə‚riz-, -ə‚t(y)ür‚iz-, -‚chür‚iz-, -chə‚riz-\ *n*

am·a·to·ry \'amə‚tōrē\ *adj* : of or expressing sexual love

amaze \ə'māz\ *vb* **amazed; amaz·ing** : overwhelm with wonder —**amaze·ment** *n* —**amaz·ing·ly** *adv*

am·a·zon \'amə‚zän, -əzən\ *n* : tall strong woman —**am·a·zo·ni·an** \‚amə'zōnēən\ *adj*

am·bas·sa·dor \am'basədər\ *n* : country's representative in a foreign land —**am·bas·sa·do·ri·al** \ˌbasəˈdōrēəl\ adj —**am·bas·sa·dor·ship** n

am·ber \'ambər\ n : yellowish fossil resin or its color

am·ber·gris \'ambər.gris, -ˌgrēs\ n : waxy substance from certain whales used in making perfumes

am·bi·dex·trous \ˌambiˈdekstrəs\ adj : equally skilled with both hands — **am·bi·dex·trous·ly** adv

am·big·u·ous \amˈbigyəwəs\ adj : having more than one interpretation —**am·bi·gu·i·ty** \ˌambəˈgyüətē\ n

am·bi·tion \amˈbishən\ n : eager desire for success or power

am·bi·tious \-əs\ adj : characterized by ambition —**am·bi·tious·ly** adv

am·biv·a·lence \amˈbivələns\ n : simultaneous attraction and repulsion —**am·biv·a·lent** \-lənt\ adj

am·ble \'ambəl\ vb -**bled**; -**bling** : go at a leisurely gait —**amble** n

am·bu·lance \'ambyələns\ n : vehicle equipped for carrying injured or sick persons

am·bu·la·to·ry \'ambyələˌtōrē\ adj 1 : relating to or adapted to walking 2 : able to walk about

am·bush \'am.bush\ n : trap by which a surprise attack is made from a place of hiding —**ambush** vb

ame·lio·rate \əˈmēlyəˌrāt\ vb -**rat·ed**; -**rat·ing** : make or grow better —**ame·lio·ra·tion** \-ˌmēlyəˈrāshən\ n

amen \(ˈ)āˈmen, (ˈ)ä-\ interj —used esp. at the end of prayers

ame·na·ble \əˈmēnəbəl, -ˈmenə-\ adj : ready to yield or be influenced

amend \əˈmend\ vb 1 : improve 2 : alter in writing

amend·ment \əˈmen(d)mənt\ n : change made in a formal document (as a law)

amends \əˈmen(d)z\ n sing or pl : compensation for injury or loss

ame·ni·ty \əˈmenətē, -ˈmēnət-\ n, pl -**ties** 1 : agreeableness 2 : something serving to comfort or convenience 3 pl : social conventions

am·e·thyst \'aməthəst\ n : blue-purple gemstone

ami·a·ble \'āmēəbəl\ adj : easy to get along with —**ami·a·bil·i·ty** \ˌāmēəˈbilətē\ n —**ami·a·bly** \'āmēəblē\ adv

ami·ca·ble \'amikəbəl\ adj : friendly —**ami·ca·bly** \-blē\ adv

amid \əˈmid\, **amidst** \-ˈmidst\ prep : in or into the middle of

ami·no acid \əˌmēnō-\ n : nitrogen-containing acid

amiss \əˈmis\ adv : in the wrong way ~ adj : wrong

am·me·ter \'am,ētər\ n : instrument for measuring electric current

am·mo·nia \əˈmōnyə\ n 1 : colorless gaseous compound of nitrogen and hydrogen 2 : solution of ammonia in water

am·mu·ni·tion \ˌamyəˈnishən\ n 1 : projectiles fired from guns 2 : explosive items used in war

am·ne·sia \amˈnēzhə\ n 1 : sudden loss of memory —**am·ne·si·ac** \-z(h)ē-ˌak\, **am·ne·sic** \-zik, -sik\ n

am·nes·ty \'amnəstē\ n, pl -**ties** : a pardon for a group —**amnesty** vb

amoe·ba \əˈmēbə\ n, pl -**bas** or -**bae** \-(ˌ)bē\ : tiny one-celled animal that occurs esp. in water —**amoe·bic** \-bik\ adj

amok \əˈmək, -ˈmäk\ adv : in an uncontrolled often murderous way

among \əˈməŋ\ prep 1 : in or through 2 : in the number or class of 3 : in shares to each of

am·o·rous \'am(ə)rəs\ adj 1 : inclined to love 2 : being in love —**am·o·rous·ly** adv —**am·o·rous·ness** n

amor·phous \əˈmórfəs\ adj : shapeless

am·or·tize \'amər,tīz, əˈmór-\ vb -**tized**; -**tiz·ing** : get rid of (as a debt) gradually with periodic payments —**am·or·ti·za·tion** \ˌamortəˈzāshən, ə,mórt-\ n

amount \əˈmaunt\ vb 1 : reach as a total 2 : be equivalent ~ n : total number or quantity

amour \əˈmúr, ä-, a-\ n : love affair

am·pere \'am,piər\ n : unit of electric current

am·per·sand \'ampər,sand\ n : character & used for the word and

am·phib·i·ous \amˈfibēəs\ adj 1 : able to live both on land and in water 2 : adapted for both land and water —**am·phib·i·an** \-ən\ n

am·phi·the·ater \'amfə,thēətər\ n : oval or circular structure with rising tiers of seats around an arena

am·ple \'ampəl\ adj -**pler** \-plər\; -**plest** \-pləst\ 1 : large 2 : sufficient —**am·ply** \-plē\ adv

am·pli·fy \'amplə,fī\ vb -**fied**; -**fy·ing** : make louder, stronger, or more thorough —**am·pli·fi·ca·tion** \ˌampləfəˈkäshən\ n —**am·pli·fi·er** \'amplə,fī(ə)r\ n

am·pli·tude \-t(y)üd\ n 1 : fullness 2 : extent of a vibratory movement

am·pu·tate \'ampyə,tāt\ vb -**tat·ed**;

-tat·ing : cut off (a body part) —**am·pu·ta·tion** \,ampyə'tāshən\ n —**am·pu·tee** \,ampyə'tē\ n

amuck \ə'mək\ var of AMOK

am·u·let \'amyələt\ n : ornament worn as a charm against evil

amuse \ə'myüz\ vb **amused; amus·ing** 1 : engage the attention of in an interesting and pleasant way 2 : make laugh —**amuse·ment** n

an \ən, (')an\ indefinite article : a — used before words beginning with a vowel sound

-**an** \ən\, -**ian** \(ē)ən\, -**ean** \(ē)ən, 'ēən\ n suffix 1 : one that belongs to 2 : one skilled in ~ adj suffix 1 : of or belonging to 2 : characteristic of or resembling

anach·ro·nism \ə'nakrə,nizəm\ n : one that is chronologically out of place —**anach·ro·nis·tic** \ə,nakrə-'nistik\ adj

an·a·con·da \,anə'kändə\ n : large So. American snake

ana·gram \'anə,gram\ n : word or phrase made by transposing the letters of another word or phrase

anal \'ān°l\ adj : relating to the anus

an·al·ge·sic \,an°l'jēzik, -sik\ n : pain reliever

anal·o·gy \ə'nalajē\ n, pl -**gies** 1 : similarity between unlike things 2 : example of something similar —**an·a·log·i·cal** \,an°l'äjikəl\ adj —**an·a·log·i·cal·ly** \-ik(ə)lē\ adv —**anal·o·gous** \ə'naləgəs\ adj

anal·y·sis \ə'naləsəs\ n, pl -**y·ses** \-,sēz\ 1 : examination of a thing to determine its parts 2 : psychoanalysis —**an·a·lyst** \'an°ləst\ n —**an·a·lyt·ic** \,an°l'itik\, **an·a·lyt·i·cal** \-ikəl\ adj

an·a·lyze \'an°l,īz\ vb -**lyzed; -lyzing** : make an analysis of

an·ar·chism \'anər,kizəm\ n : theory that all government is undesirable —**an·ar·chist** \-kəst\ n —**an·ar·chis·tic** \,anər'kistik\ adj

an·ar·chy \'anərkē\ n : lack of government or order —**an·ar·chic** \a-'närkik\ adj

anath·e·ma \ə'nathəmə\ n 1 : solemn curse 2 : person or thing accursed or intensely disliked

anat·o·my \ə'natəmē\ n, pl -**mies** : science dealing with the structure of organisms —**an·a·tom·ic** \,anə-'tämik\, **an·a·tom·i·cal** \-ikəl\ adj —**an·a·tom·i·cal·ly** adv —**anat·o·mist** \ə'natəməst\ n

-**ance** \əns\ n suffix 1 : action or

process 2 : quality or state 3 : amount or degree

an·ces·tor \'an,sestər\ n : one from whom an individual is descended —**an·ces·tress** \-trəs\ n

an·ces·try \-trē\ n 1 : line of descent 2 : ancestors —**an·ces·tral** \an-'sestrəl\ adj

an·chor \'aŋkər\ n : heavy device that catches in the sea bottom to hold a ship in place ~ vb : hold or become held in place by or as if by an anchor —**an·chor·age** \-k(ə)rij\ n

an·chor·man \'aŋkər,man\ n : news broadcast coordinator

an·cho·vy \'an,chōvē, an'chō-\ n, pl -**vies** or -**vy** : small herringlike fish

an·cient \'ānshənt\ adj 1 : having existed for many years 2 : belonging to times long past —**ancient** n

-**an·cy** \ənsē\ n suffix : quality or state

and \ən(d), (')an(d)\ conj —used to indicate connection or addition

and·iron \'an,di(ə)rn\ n : one of 2 metal supports for wood in a fireplace

an·ec·dote \'anik,dōt\ n : brief story —**an·ec·dot·al** \,anik'dōt°l\ adj

ane·mia \ə'nēmēə\ n : blood deficiency —**ane·mic** \ə'nēmik\ adj

anem·o·ne \ə'nemənē\ n : small herb with showy usu. white flowers

an·es·the·sia \,anəs'thēzhə\ n : loss of bodily sensation

an·es·thet·ic \,anəs'thetik\ adj (agent or action) that produces anesthesia —**anes·the·tist** \ə'nesthətəst\ n —**anes·the·tize** \-thə,tīz\ vb

anew \ə'n(y)ü\ adv : over again

an·gel \'ānjəl\ n : spiritual being superior to humans —**an·gel·ic** \an-'jelik\, **an·gel·i·cal** \-ikəl\ adj —**an·gel·i·cal·ly** adv

an·ger \'aŋgər\ n : strong feeling of displeasure ~ vb : make angry

an·gi·na \an'jīnə\ n : painful disorder of heart muscles —**an·gi·nal** \an-'jīn°l\ adj

¹**an·gle** \'aŋgəl\ n 1 : figure formed by the meeting of 2 lines in a point 2 : sharp corner 3 : point of view ~ vb -**gled; -gling** : turn or direct at an angle

²**angle** vb **an·gled; an·gling** : fish with a hook and line —**an·gler** \-glər\ n —**an·gle·worm** n —**an·gling** n

an·go·ra \aŋ'gōrə, an-\ n : yarn or cloth made from the hair of an Angora goat or rabbit

an·gry \'aŋgrē\ adj -**gri·er; -est** : feeling or showing anger —an·gri·ly \-grəlē\ adv

an·guish \ˈaŋgwish\ n : extreme pain or distress of mind —an·guished \-gwisht\ adj

an·gu·lar \ˈaŋgyələr\ adj 1 : having many or sharp angles 2 : thin and bony —an·gu·lar·i·ty \ˌaŋgyə-ˈlarətē\ n

an·i·line \ˈanᵊlən\ n: oily poisonous liquid used esp. in making dyes

an·i·mal \ˈanəməl\ n 1 : living being capable of feeling and voluntary motion 2 : lower animal as distinguished from man

an·i·mate \ˈanəmət\ adj : having life \-ˌmāt\ vb -mat·ed; -mat·ing 1 : give life or vigor to 2 : make appear to move —an·i·mat·ed adj

an·i·ma·tion \ˌanəˈmāshən\ n 1 : liveliness 2 : animated cartoon

an·i·mos·i·ty \ˌanəˈmäsətē\ n, pl -ties : resentment

an·i·mus \ˈanəməs\ n : deep-seated hostility

an·ise \ˈanəs\ n : an herb related to the carrot with aromatic seeds (aniseed \-ə(s)ˌsēd\) used in flavoring

an·kle \ˈaŋkəl\ n : joint or region between the foot and the leg —an·kle-bone n

an·nals \ˈanᵊlz\ n pl : chronological record of history —an·nal·ist \-ᵊləst\ n

an·neal \əˈnēl\ vb : make less brittle by heating and then cooling

an·nex \əˈneks, ˈanˌeks\ vb : assume political control over (a territory) ~ \ˈanˌeks, -iks\ n : added building —an·nex·a·tion \ˌaˌnekˈsāshən\ n

an·ni·hi·late \əˈnīəˌlāt\ vb -lat·ed; -lat·ing : destroy —an·ni·hi·la·tion \-ˌnīəˈlāshən\ n

an·ni·ver·sa·ry \ˌanəˈvərs(ə)rē\ n, pl -ries : annual return of the date of a notable event or its celebration

an·no·tate \ˈanəˌtāt\ vb -tat·ed; -tat·ing : furnish with notes —an·no·ta·tion \ˌanəˈtāshən\ n —an·no·ta·tor \ˈanə-ˌtātər\ n

an·nounce \əˈnaúns\ vb -nounced; -nounc·ing : make known publicly —an·nounce·ment n —an·nounc·er n

an·noy \əˈnói\ vb : disturb or irritate —an·noy·ance \-ᵊns\ n —an·noy·ing·ly \-ˈnóiiŋlē\ adv

an·nu·al \ˈanyə(wə)l\ adj 1 : occurring once a year 2 : living only one year —annual n —an·nu·al·ly adv

an·nu·i·ty \əˈn(y)üətē\ n, pl -ities : amount payable annually or the right to such a payment

an·nul \əˈnəl\ vb -ll- : make legally void —an·nul·ment n

an·ode \ˈanˌōd\ n 1 : positive electrode 2 : negative battery terminal —an·od·ic \aˌnädik\, an·od·al \ˈnōdᵊl\ adj—an·od·i·cal·ly \-ik(ə)lē\, an·od·al·ly \-ᵊl(ē)\ adv

anoint \əˈnóint\ vb : apply oil to as a rite —anoint·ment n

anom·a·ly \əˈnäməlē\ n, pl -lies : something abnormal or unusual —anom·a·lous \əˈnämələs\ adj

anon·y·mous \əˈnänəməs\ adj : of unknown origin —an·o·nym·i·ty \ˌana-ˈnimətē\ n —anon·y·mous·ly adv

an·oth·er \əˈnəthər\ adj 1 : any or some other 2 : one more ~ pron 1 : one more 2 : one different

an·swer \ˈansər\ n 1 : something spoken or written in return to a question 2 : solution of a problem ~ vb 1 : reply to 2 : be responsible 3 : be adequate —an·swer·er n

an·swer·able \ˈans(ə)rəbəl\ adj : subject to taking blame or responsibility

ant \ˈant\ n : small social insect —ant·hill n

-ant \ənt\ n suffix 1 : one that performs or causes an action 2 : thing that is acted upon ~ adj suffix 1 : performing an action or being in a condition 2 : causing an action or process

an·tag·o·nism \anˈtagəˌnizəm\ n : active opposition or hostility —an·tag·o·nist \-ənəst\ n —an·tag·o·nis·tic \-ˌtagəˈnistik\ adj

ant·arc·tic \antˈärktik, -ˈärtik\ adj : relating to the region near the south pole

antarctic circle n : circle parallel to the equator approximately 23°27′ from the south pole

an·te·bel·lum \ˌantiˈbeləm\ adj : existing before the U.S. Civil War

an·te·ced·ent \ˌantəˈsēdᵊnt\ n : one that comes before —antecedent adj

an·te·lope \ˈantᵊlˌōp\ n, pl -lope or -lopes : deerlike mammal related to the ox

an·ten·na \anˈtenə\ n, pl -nae \-ˌnē\ or -nas 1 : one of the long slender paired sensory organs on the head of an arthropod 2 pl -nas : metallic device for sending or receiving radio waves

an·te·ri·or \anˈtirēər\ adj : located before in place or time

an·them \ˈanthəm\ n : song or hymn of praise or gladness

an·ther \'anthər\ n : part of a seed plant that contains pollen
an·thol·o·gy \an'thäləjē\ n, pl -gies : literary collection
an·thra·cite \'anthrə,sīt\ n : hard coal
an·thro·poid \'anthrə,poid\ adj : like humans ~ n : large ape
an·thro·pol·o·gy \,anthrə'päləjē\ n : science dealing with humans —an·thro·po·log·i·cal \-pə'läjikəl\ adj — an·thro·pol·o·gist \-'päləjəst\ n
anti- \,anti, -ē, ,an,tī\, ant-, anth- prefix 1 : opposite in kind, position, or action 2 : opposing or hostile toward 3 : defending against 4 : curing or treating

antiabortion
antiacademic
antiadministration
antiaggression
antiaggressive
antiaircraft
antialien
antianarchic
antianarchist
antiannexation
antiapartheid
antiaristocrat
antiaristocratic
antiart
antiatheism
antiatheist
antiauthoritarian
antiauthority
antibacterial
antibias
antibigotry
antiblack
antibourgeois
antiboxing
antiboycott
antibureaucratic
antiburglar
antiburglary
antibusiness
anticancer
anticapitalism
anticapitalist
anticapitalistic
anti-Catholic
anticensorship
anti-Christian
anti-Christianity
antichurch
anticigarette
anticlerical
anticollision
anticolonial
anticommunism

anticommunist
anticonservation
anticonservationist
anticonsumer
anticonventional
anticorrosion
anticorrosive
anticorruption
anticrime
anticruelty
anticult
anticultural
antidandruff
antidemocratic
antidiscrimination
antidrug
antidumping
antieavesdropping
antiestablishment
antievolution
antievolutionary
antifamily
antifanatic
antifascism
antifascist
antifatigue
antifemale
antifeminine
antifeminism
antifeminist
antifertility
antiforeign
antiforeigner
antifraud
antifungus
antigambling
antiglare
antigonorrheal
antigovernment
antigraft
antiguerrilla

antigun
antihijack
antihomosexual
antihuman
antihumanism
antihumanistic
antihumanity
antihunting
anti-imperialism
anti-imperialist
anti-inflation
anti-inflationary
anti-institutional
anti-integration
anti-intellectual
anti-intellectualism
antijamming
anti-Jewish
antilabor
antiliberal
antiliberalism
antilitter
antilittering
antiloitering
antilynching
antimale
antimanagement
antimaterialism
antimaterialist
antimaterialistic
antimicrobial
antimilitarism
antimilitarist
antimilitaristic
antimilitary
antimiscegenation
antimonopolist
antimonopoly
antimosquito
antinoise
antiobesity
antiobscenity
antipapal
antipersonnel
antipolice
antipollution
antipornographic
antipornography
antipoverty
antiprofiteering
antiprogressive
antiprostitution
antirabies
antiracing
antiracketeering
antiradical
antirape
antirealism
antirealistic

antirecession
antireform
antireligious
antirepublican
antirevolutionary
antiriot
antirobbery
antiromantic
antirust
antisegregation
antisex
antisexist
antisexual
antishoplifting
antislavery
antismoking
antismuggling
antismut
antispending
antistrike
antistudent
antisubmarine
antisubversion
antisubversive
antisuicide
antisyphilis
antitank
antitax
antitechnological
antitechnology
antiterrorism
antiterrorist
antitheft
antitobacco
antitotalitarian
antitoxin
antitraditional
antitrust
antituberculosis
antitumor
antityphoid
antiulcer
antiunemployment
antiunion
antiuniversity
antiurban
antivandalism
antiviolence
antiviral
antivivisection
antiwar
antiweed
anti-West
anti-Western
antiwhite
antiwiretapping
antiwoman

an·ti·bi·ot·ic \,antibī'ätik, -bē-\ *n* : substance that inhibits harmful microorganisms —**antibiotic** *adj*

an·ti·body \'anti,bädē\ *n* : bodily substance that counteracts the effects of a foreign substance or organism

an·tic \'antik\ *n* : playful act — *adj* : playful

an·tic·i·pate \an'tisə,pāt\ *vb* **-pat·ed; -pat·ing 1** : be prepared for **2** : look forward to —**an·tic·i·pa·tion** \-,tisə-'pāshən\ *n* —**an·tic·i·pa·to·ry** \-'tisəpə,tōrē\ *adj*

an·ti·cli·max \,anti'klī,maks\ *n* : something strikingly less important than what has preceded it —**an·ti·cli·mac·tic** \-klī'maktik\ *adj*

an·ti·dote \'anti,dōt\ *n* : remedy for poison

an·ti·freeze \'anti,frēz\ *n* : substance to prevent a liquid from freezing

an·ti·mo·ny \'antə,mōnē\ *n* : brittle white metallic chemical element

an·tip·a·thy \an'tipəthē\ *n, pl* **-thies** : strong dislike

an·ti·quar·i·an \,antə'kwerēən\ *adj* : relating to antiquities or old books —**antiquarian** *n* —**an·ti·quar·i·an·ism** *n*

an·ti·quary \'antə,kwerē\ *n, pl* **-quar·ies** : one who collects or studies antiquities

an·ti·quat·ed \'antə,kwātəd\ *adj* : out-of-date

an·tique \an'tēk\ *adj* : very old or out-of-date —**antique** *n*

an·tiq·ui·ty \an'tikwətē\ *n, pl* **-ties 1** : ancient times **2** *pl* : relics of ancient times

an·ti·sep·tic \,antə'septik\ *adj* : killing or checking the growth of germs —**antiseptic** *n* —**an·ti·sep·ti·cal·ly** \-tik(ə)lē\ *adv*

an·tith·e·sis \an'tithəsəs\ *n, pl* **-e·ses** \-,sēz\ : direct opposite

ant·ler \'antlər\ *n* : solid branched horn of a deer —**ant·lered** \-lərd\ *adj*

ant·onym \'antə,nim\ *n* : word of opposite meaning

anus \'ānəs\ *n* : the rear opening of the alimentary canal

an·vil \'anvəl\ *n* : heavy iron block on which metal is shaped

anx·i·ety \aŋ'zīətē\ *n, pl* **-eties** : uneasiness usu. over an expected misfortune

anx·ious \'aŋkshəs\ *adj* **1** : uneasy **2** : earnestly wishing —**anx·ious·ly** *adv*

any \'enē\ *adj* **1** : one chosen at random **2** : of whatever number or quantity ~ *pron* **1** : any one or ones **2**

: any amount ~ *adv* : to any extent or degree

any·body \-,bädē, -bəd-\ *pron* : anyone

any·how \-,haü\ *adv* **1** : in any way **2** : nevertheless

any·more \,enē'mōr\ *adv* : at the present time

any·one \-(,)wən\ *pron* : any person

any·place *adv* : anywhere

any·thing *pron* : any thing whatever

any·time *adv* : at any time whatever

any·way *adv* : anyhow

any·where *adv* : in or to any place

aor·ta \ā'ortə\ *n, pl* **-tas** *or* **-tae** \-ē\ : main artery from the heart —**aor·tic** \-'ortik\ *adj*

apart \ə'pärt\ *adv* **1** : separately in place or time **2** : aside **3** : to pieces

apart·heid \ə'pär,tāt, -,tīt\ *n* : racial segregation

apart·ment \ə'pärtmənt\ *n* : set of usu. rented rooms

ap·a·thy \'apəthē\ *n* : lack of emotion or interest —**ap·a·thet·ic** \,apə-'thetik\ *adj* —**ap·a·thet·i·cal·ly** \-ik(ə)lē\ *adv*

ape \'āp\ *n* : large tailless primate ~ *vb* **aped; ap·ing** : imitate

ap·er·ture \'apə(r),chúr, -chər\ *n* : opening

apex \'ā,peks\ *n, pl* **apex·es** *or* **api·ces** \'āpə,sēz, 'apə-\ : highest point

aphid \'āfəd, 'afəd\ *n* : small insect that sucks plant juices

aph·o·rism \'afə,rizəm\ *n* : short saying stating a general truth —**aph·o·ris·tic** \,afə'ristik\ *adj*

aph·ro·di·si·ac \,afrə'dizē,ak\ *n* : substance that excites sexual desire

api·a·rist \'āpēərəst\ *n* : beekeeper —**api·ary** \-pē,erē\ *n*

apiece \ə'pēs\ *adv* : for each one

aplomb \ə'pläm, -'plam\ *n* : complete calmness or self-assurance

apoc·a·lypse \ə'päkə,lips\ *n* : writing prophesying a cataclysm in which evil forces are destroyed —**apoc·a·lyp·tic** \-,päkə'liptik\ *adj*

apoc·ry·pha \ə'päkrəfə\ *n* : writings of dubious authenticity —**apoc·ry·phal** \-fəl\ *adj*

apol·o·get·ic \ə,pälə'jetik\ *adj* : expressing apology —**apol·o·get·i·cal·ly** \-ik(ə)lē\ *adv*

apol·o·gize \ə'pälə,jīz\ *vb* **-gized; -giz·ing** : make an apology —**apol·o·gist** \-jəst\ *n*

apol·o·gy \ə'päləjē\ *n, pl* **-gies 1** : formal justification for a wrong **2** : expression of regret for a wrong

ap·o·plexy \'apə,pleksē\ *n* : sudden

loss of consciousness caused by rupture or obstruction of an artery of the brain —**ap·o·plec·tic** \,apə-'plektik\ adj

apos·ta·sy \ə'pästəsē\ n, pl -sies : abandonment of a former loyalty —**apos·tate** \ə'päs,tāt, -'tət\ adj or n

apos·tle \ə'päsəl\ n : disciple or advocate —**apos·tle·ship** n —**ap·os·tol·ic** \,apə'stälik\ adj

apos·tro·phe \ə'pästrə,()fē\ n : punctuation mark ' to indicate the possessive case or the omission of a letter or figure

apoth·e·cary \ə'päthə,kerē\ n, pl -car·ies : druggist

ap·pall \ə'pȯl\ vb : fill with horror or dismay

ap·pa·ra·tus \,apə'ratəs, -'rāt-\ n, pl -tus·es or -tus 1 : equipment 2 : complex machine or device

ap·par·el \ə'parəl\ n : clothing

ap·par·ent \ə'parənt\ adj 1 : visible 2 : obvious 3 : seeming —**ap·par·ent·ly** adv

ap·pa·ri·tion \,apə'rishən\ n : ghost

ap·peal \ə'pēl\ vb 1 : try to have a court case reheard 2 : ask earnestly 3 : have an attraction —**appeal** n

ap·pear \ə'piər\ vb 1 : become visible or evident 2 : come into the presence of someone 3 : seem

ap·pear·ance \ə'pirəns\ n 1 : act of appearing 2 : outward aspect

ap·pease \ə'pēz\ vb -peased; -peas·ing : pacify with concessions —**ap·pease·ment** n

ap·pel·late \ə'pelət\ adj : having power to review decisions

ap·pend \ə'pend\ vb : attach

ap·pend·age \ə'pendij\ n : something attached

ap·pen·dec·to·my \,apən'dektəmē\ n, pl -mies : surgical removal of the appendix

ap·pen·di·ci·tis \ə,pendə'sītəs\ n : inflammation of the appendix

ap·pen·dix \ə'pendiks\ n, pl -dix·es or -di·ces \-də,sēz\ 1 : supplementary matter 2 : narrow closed tube extending from lower right intestine

ap·pe·tite \'apə,tīt\ n 1 : natural desire esp. for food 2 : preference

ap·pe·tiz·er \-,tīzər\ n : food or drink to stimulate the appetite

ap·pe·tiz·ing \-ziŋ\ adj : tempting to the appetite —**ap·pe·tiz·ing·ly** adv

ap·plaud \ə'plȯd\ vb : show approval esp. by clapping

ap·plause \ə'plȯz\ n : a clapping approval

ap·ple \'apəl\ n : rounded fruit with firm white flesh

ap·ple·jack \-,jak\ n : brandy made from cider

ap·pli·ance \ə'plīəns\ n : household machine or device

ap·pli·ca·ble \'aplikəbəl, ə'plikə-\ adj : capable of being applied —**ap·pli·ca·bil·i·ty** \,aplikə'bilətē, ə,plikə-\ n

ap·pli·cant \'aplikənt\ n : one who applies

ap·pli·ca·tion \,aplə'kāshən\ n 1 : act of applying or thing applied 2 : constant attention 3 : request

ap·pli·ca·tor \'aplə,kātər\ n : device for applying a substance

ap·pli·qué \,aplə'kā\ n : cut-out fabric decoration —**appliqué** vb

ap·ply \ə'plī\ vb -plied; -ply·ing 1 : place in contact 2 : put to practical use 3 : devote (one's) attention or efforts to something 4 : submit a request 5 : have reference or a connection

ap·point \ə'pȯint\ vb 1 : set or assign officially 2 : equip or furnish —**ap·poin·tee** \ə,pȯin'tē, ,a-\ n

ap·point·ment \ə'pȯintmənt\ n 1 : act of appointing 2 : nonelective political job 3 : arrangement for a meeting

ap·por·tion \ə'pȯrshən\ vb : distribute proportionately —**ap·por·tion·ment** n

ap·po·site \'apəzət\ adj : suitable —**ap·po·site·ly** adv —**ap·po·site·ness** n

ap·praise \ə'prāz\ vb -praised; -prais·ing : set value on —**ap·prais·al** \-'prāzəl\ n —**ap·prais·er** n

ap·pre·cia·ble \ə'prēshəbəl\ adj : considerable —**ap·pre·cia·bly** \-blē\ adv

ap·pre·ci·ate \ə'prēshē,āt\ vb -ated; -at·ing 1 : value justly 2 : be grateful for 3 : increase in value —**ap·pre·ci·a·tion** \-,prēshē'āshən\ n

ap·pre·cia·tive \ə'prēshətiv, -shē,āt-\ adj : showing appreciation

ap·pre·hend \,apri'hend\ vb 1 : arrest 2 : look forward to in dread 3 : understand —**ap·pre·hen·sion** \-'henchən\ n

ap·pre·hen·sive \-'hensiv\ adj : fearful —**ap·pre·hen·sive·ly** adv —**ap·pre·hen·sive·ness** n

ap·pren·tice \ə'prentəs\ n : person learning a craft ~ vb -ticed; -tic·ing : employ or work as an apprentice —**ap·pren·tice·ship** n

ap·prise \ə'prīz\ vb -prised; -pris·ing : inform

ap·proach \ə'prōch\ vb 1 : move nearer or be close to 2 : make initial advances or efforts toward —**ap-proach** *n* —**ap-proach-able** *adj*

ap-pro-ba-tion \ˌaprəˈbāshən\ *n* : approval

ap-pro-pri-ate \əˈprōprēˌāt\ *vb* -**at-ed; -at-ing 1** : take possession of **2** : set apart for a particular use ~ \-ˈprēət\ *adj* : suitable —**ap-pro-pri-ate-ly** *adv* —**ap-pro-pri-ate-ness** *n* —**ap-pro-pri-a-tion** \əˌprōprēˈāshən\ *n*

ap-prov-al \əˈprüvəl\ *n* : act of approving

ap-prove \əˈprüv\ *vb* -**proved; -prov-ing** : accept as satisfactory

ap-prox-i-mate \əˈpräksəmət\ *adj* : nearly correct or exact ~ \-ˌmāt\ *vb* -**mat-ed; -mat-ing** : come near —**ap-prox-i-mate-ly** *adv* —**ap-prox-i-ma-tion** \-ˌpräksəˈmāshən\ *n*

ap-pur-te-nance \əˈpərt(ə)nəns\ *n* : accessory —**ap-pur-te-nant** \-ˈpərt-nənt, -ᵊnənt\ *adj*

apri-cot \ˈaprəˌkät, ˈäprə-\ *n* : peach-like fruit

April \ˈāprəl\ *n* : 4th month of the year having 30 days

apron \ˈāprən, -pərn\ *n* : protective garment

ap-ro-pos \ˌaprəˈpō, ˈaprəˌpō\ *adv* : suitably ~ *adj* : being to the point

apropos of *prep* : with regard to

apt \ˈapt\ *adj* **1** : suitable **2** : likely **3** : quick to learn —**apt-ly** *adv* —**apt-ness** \ˈap(t)nəs\ *n*

ap-ti-tude \ˈaptəˌt(y)üd\ *n* **1** : capacity for learning **2** : natural ability

aqua \ˈakwə, ˈäk-\ *n, pl* **aquae** \ˈak(ˌ)wē, ˈäk̩wī\ *or* **aquas** \ˈ-\ : light greenish blue color

aquar-i-um \əˈkwēərēəm\ *n, pl* **-i-ums** *or* **-ia** \-ēə\ : container in which aquatic animals and plants are kept (as in the home)

aquat-ic \əˈkwätik, -ˈkwat-\ *adj* : of or relating to water —**aquatic** *n*

aq-ue-duct \ˈakwəˌdəkt\ *n* : conduit for carrying running water

aqui-line \ˈakwəˌlīn, -lən\ *adj* : hooked like an eagle's beak

-ar \ər\ *adj suffix* **1** : of, relating to, or being **2** : resembling

ar-a-besque \ˌarəˈbesk\ *n* : intricate design

ar-a-ble \ˈarəbəl\ *adj* : fit for crops

ar-bi-ter \ˈärbətər\ *n* : final authority

ar-bi-trary \ˈärbəˌtrerē\ *adj* **1** : selected at random **2** : autocratic —**ar-bi-trar-i-ly** \ˌärbəˈtrerəlē\ *adv* —**ar-bi-trar-i-ness** \ˈärbəˌtrerēnəs\ *n*

ar-bi-trate \ˈärbəˌtrāt\ *vb* -**trat-ed; -trat-ing** : settle a dispute as arbitrator —**ar-bi-tra-tion** \ˌärbəˈtrāshən\ *n*

ar-bi-tra-tor \ˈärbəˌtrātər\ *n* : one chosen to settle a dispute

ar-bor \ˈärbər\ *n* : shelter under branches or vines

ar-bo-re-al \ärˈbōrēəl\ *adj* : living in trees

arc \ˈärk\ *n* **1** : part of a circle **2** : bright streak of an electrical discharge ~ *vb* : form an arc

ar-cade \ärˈkād\ *n* : arched passageway between shops

ar-cane \ärˈkān\ *adj* : mysterious or secret

¹**arch** \ˈärch\ *n* : curved structure spanning an opening ~ *vb* : cover with or form into an arch

²**arch** *adj* **1** : chief —usu. in combination **2** : mischievous —**arch-ly** *adv* —**arch-ness** *n*

ar-chae-ol-o-gy, ar-che-ol-o-gy \ˌärkēˈäləjē\ *n* : study of past human life —**ar-chae-o-log-i-cal** \-kēəˈläjikəl\ *adj* —**ar-chae-ol-o-gist** \-kēˈäləjəst\ *n*

ar-cha-ic \ärˈkāik\ *adj* : belonging to an earlier time —**ar-cha-i-cal-ly** \-ik(ə)lē\ *adv*

arch-an-gel \ˈärkˌānjəl\ *n* : angel of high rank

arch-bish-op \ˈärchˈbishəp\ *n* : chief bishop —**arch-bish-op-ric** \-ˌə(ˌ)prik\ *n*

arch-di-o-cese \-ˈdī-əsəs, -ˌsēz, -ˌsēs\ *n* : diocese of an archbishop

ar-chery \ˈärch(ə)rē\ *n* : shooting with bow and arrows —**ar-cher** \ˈärchər\ *n*

ar-che-type \ˈärkiˌtīp\ *n* : original pattern or model

ar-chi-pel-a-go \ˌärkəˈpeləˌgō, ˌärchə-\ *n, pl* **-goes** *or* **-gos** : group of islands

ar-chi-tect \ˈärkəˌtekt\ *n* : building designer

ar-chi-tec-ture \ˈärkəˌtekchər\ *n* **1** : building design **2** : style of building —**ar-chi-tec-tur-al** \ˌärkəˈtekchərəl, -ˈtekshrəl\ *adj* —**ar-chi-tec-tur-al-ly** *adv*

ar-chives \ˈärˌkīvz\ *n pl* : public records or their storage place —**ar-chi-vist** \ˈärkəvəst, -ˌkī-\ *n*

arch-way *n* : passageway under an arch

arc lamp *n* : lamp that produces light when a current arcs between electrodes

arc-tic \ˈär(k)tik\ *adj* **1** : relating to the region near the north pole **2** : frigid

arctic circle *n* : circle parallel to the equator approximately 23°27′ from the north pole

-ard \ȯrd\ *n suffix* : one that is

ar·dent \'ärd³nt\ *adj* : characterized by warmth of feeling —**ar·dent·ly** *adv*

ar·dor \'ärdər\ *n* : warmth of feeling

ar·du·ous \'ärj(ə)wəs\ *adj* : difficult —**ar·du·ous·ly** *adv* —**ar·du·ous·ness** *n*

are *pres 2d sing or pres pl of* BE

ar·ea \'arēə\ *n* **1** : space for something **2** : amount of surface included **3** : region **4** : range covered by a thing or concept

area code *n* : 3-digit area-identifying telephone number

are·na \ə'rēnə\ *n* **1** : enclosed exhibition area **2** : sphere of activity

ar·gon \'är,gän\ *n* : colorless odorless gaseous chemical element

ar·got \'ärgət, -,gō\ *n* : special language (as of the underworld)

ar·gu·able \'ärgyəwəbəl\ *adj* : open to dispute

ar·gue \'ärgyü\ *vb* -**gued; -gu·ing** **1** : give reasons for or against something **2** : disagree in words

ar·gu·ment \'ärgyəmənt\ *n* **1** : reasons given to persuade **2** : dispute with words

ar·gu·men·ta·tive \,ärgyə'mentətiv\ *adj* : inclined to argue

ar·gyle \'är,gīl\ *n* : colorful diamond pattern in knitting

aria \'ärēə\ *n* : opera solo

ar·id \'arəd\ *adj* : dry and barren —**arid·i·ty** \ə'ridətē\ *n*

arise \ə'rīz\ *vb* **arose** \-'rōz\ **aris·en** \-'riz³n\; **aris·ing** \-'rīziŋ\ **1** : get up **2** : originate

ar·is·toc·ra·cy \,arə'stäkrəsē\ *n, pl* -**cies** : upper class —**aris·to·crat** \ə'ristə,krat\ *n* —**aris·to·crat·ic** \ə,ristə'kratik\ *adj*

arith·me·tic \ə'rithmə,tik\ *n* : mathematics that deals with numbers —**ar·ith·met·ic** \,arith'metik\, **ar·ith·met·i·cal** \-ikəl\ *adj*

ark \'ärk\ *n* : big boat

¹**arm** \'ärm\ *n* **1** : upper limb **2** : branch —**armed** \'ärmd\ *adj* —**arm·less** *adj*

²**arm** *vb* : furnish with weapons ∼ *n* **1** : weapon **2** : branch of the military forces **3** *pl* : family's heraldic designs

ar·ma·da \är'mädə, -'mäd-\ *n* : naval fleet

ar·ma·dil·lo \,ärmə'dilō\ *n, pl* -**los** : burrowing mammal covered with bony plates

ar·ma·ment \'ärməmənt\ *n* : military arms and equipment

ar·ma·ture \'ärmə,chür, -chər\ *n*

: part in an electric generator or motor in which the current is induced

armed forces *n pl* : military

ar·mi·stice \'ärməstəs\ *n* : truce

ar·mor \'ärmər\ *n* : protective covering —**ar·mored** \-mərd\ *adj*

ar·mory \'ärm(ə)rē\ *n, pl* -**mor·ies** : factory or storehouse for arms

arm·pit *n* : hollow under the junction of the arm and shoulder

ar·my \'ärmē\ *n, pl* -**mies** **1** : body of men organized for war esp. on land **2** : great number

aro·ma \ə'rōmə\ *n* : usu. pleasing odor —**ar·o·mat·ic** \,arə'matik\ *adj*

around \ə'raůnd\ *adv* **1** : in or along a circuit **2** : on all sides **3** : near **4** : in an opposite direction ∼ *prep* **1** : surrounding **2** : along the circuit of **3** : to or on the other side of **4** : near

arouse \ə'raůz\ *vb* **aroused; arous·ing** **1** : awaken from sleep **2** : stir up —**arous·al** \-'raůzəl\ *n*

ar·raign \ə'rān\ *vb* **1** : call before a court to answer to an indictment **2** : accuse —**ar·raign·ment** *n*

ar·range \ə'rānj\ *vb* -**ranged; -rang·ing** **1** : put in order **2** : settle or agree on **3** : adapt (a musical composition) for voices or instruments —**ar·range·ment** *n* —**ar·rang·er** *n*

ar·ray \ə'rā\ *vb* **1** : arrange in order **2** : dress esp. splendidly ∼ *n* **1** : arrangement **2** : rich clothing **3** : imposing group

ar·rears \ə'riərz\ *n pl* : state of being behind in paying debts

ar·rest \ə'rest\ *vb* **1** : stop **2** : take into legal custody —**arrest** *n*

ar·rive \ə'rīv\ *vb* -**rived; -riv·ing** **1** : reach a destination, point, or stage **2** : come near in time —**ar·riv·al** \-əl\ *n*

ar·ro·gant \'arəgənt\ *adj* : showing an offensive sense of superiority —**ar·ro·gance** \-gəns\ *n* —**ar·ro·gant·ly** *adv*

ar·ro·gate \-,gāt\ *vb* -**gat·ed; -gat·ing** : to claim without justification

ar·row \'arō\ *n* : slender missile shot from a bow —**ar·row·head** *n*

ar·royo \ə'roiō, -ō\ *n, pl* -**royos** **1** : watercourse **2** : gully

ar·se·nal \'ärsnəl, -³nəl\ *n* **1** : place where arms are made or stored **2** : store

ar·se·nic \'ärsnik, -³nik\ *n* : solid grayish poisonous chemical element

ar·son \'ärs³n\ *n* : malicious burning of property

art \'ärt\ *n* **1** : skill **2** : branch of learning 3 : creation of things of beauty or works so produced 4 : ingenuity

ar·te·rio·scle·ro·sis \ar,tirēōsklə'rō-səs\ n : hardening of the arteries —ar·te·rio·scle·rot·ic \-'rätik\ adj or n

ar·tery \'ärtərē\ n, pl -ter·ies 1 : tubular vessel carrying blood from the heart 2 : thoroughfare —ar·te·ri·al \är'tirēəl\ adj

art·ful \'ärtfəl\ adj 1 : ingenious 2 : crafty —art·ful·ly adv —art·ful·ness n

ar·thri·tis \är'thrītəs\ n, pl -ti·des \-'thritə,dēz\ : inflammation of the joints —ar·thrit·ic \-'thritik\ adj or n

ar·thro·pod \'ärthrə,päd\ n : invertebrate animal (as an insect or spider) with segmented body and jointed limbs —arthropod adj

ar·ti·choke \'ärtə,chōk\ n : tall thistlelike herb

ar·ti·cle \'ärtikəl\ n 1 : distinct part of a written document 2 : nonfictional published piece of writing 3 : word (as an, the) used to limit a noun 4 : item or piece

ar·tic·u·late \är'tikyələt\ adj : able to speak effectively \-,lāt\ vb -lat·ed: -lat·ing 1 : utter distinctly 2 : unite by joints —ar·tic·u·late·ly adv —ar·tic·u·late·ness n —ar·tic·u·la·tion \-,tikyə'lāshən\ n

ar·ti·fact \'ärtə,fakt\ n : object of human workmanship

ar·ti·fice \'ärtəfəs\ n 1 : trick or trickery 2 : ingenious device or ingenuity

ar·ti·fi·cial \,ärtə'fishəl\ adj 1 : man-made 2 : not genuine —ar·ti·fi·ci·al·i·ty \-,fishē'alətē\ n —ar·ti·fi·cial·ly adv —ar·ti·fi·cial·ness n

ar·til·lery \är'tilǝrē\ n, pl -ler·ies : large caliber firearms

ar·ti·san \'ärtəzan, -sən\ n : skilled craftsman

art·ist \'ärtəst\ n : one who creates art —ar·tis·tic \är'tistik\ adj —ar·tis·ti·cal·ly \-ik(ə)lē\ adv —ar·tis·try \'ärtəstrē\ n

art·less \'ärtləs\ adj : sincere or natural —art·less·ly adv —art·less·ness n

arty \'ärtē\ adj art·i·er: -est : pretentiously artistic —art·i·ly \'ärtlē\ adv —art·i·ness n

-ary \,erē\ adj suffix : of, relating to, or connected with

as \əz, (,)az\ adv 1 : to the same degree 2 : for example ~ conj 1 : in the same way or degree as 2 : while 3 : because 4 : though ~ pron —used after same or such ~ prep : in the capacity of

as·bes·tos \as'bestəs, az-\ n : fibrous incombustible mineral

as·cend \ə'send\ vb : move upward —as·cen·sion \-'senchən\ n

as·cen·dan·cy \ə'sendənsē\ n : domination

as·cen·dant \ə'sendənt\ n : dominant position ~ adj 1 : moving upward 2 : dominant

as·cent \ə'sent\ n 1 : act of moving upward 2 : degree of upward slope

as·cer·tain \,asər'tān\ vb : determine —as·cer·tain·able adj

as·cet·ic \ə'setik\ adj : self-denying ascetic n —as·cet·i·cism \-'setə,sizəm\ n

as·cribe \ə'skrīb\ vb -cribed: -crib·ing : attribute —as·crib·able adj —as·crip·tion \-'skripshən\ n

asep·tic \ā'septik\ adj : free of disease germs

¹ash \'ash\ n : tree related to the olives
²ash n : matter left when something is burned —ash·tray n

ashamed \ə'shāmd\ adj : feeling shame —asham·ed·ly \-'shāmədlē\ adv

ash·en \'ashən\ adj : deadly pale

ashore \ə'shōr\ adv : on or to the shore

aside \ə'sīd\ adv 1 : toward the side 2 : out of the way

aside from prep 1 : besides 2 : except for

as·i·nine \'asᵊn,īn\ adj : foolish —as·i·nin·i·ty \,asᵊn'inətē\ n

ask \'ask\ vb asked \'as(k)t\; ask·ing 1 : call on for an answer or help 2 : utter (a question or request) 3 : invite

askance \ə'skans\ adv 1 : with a side glance 2 : with mistrust

askew \ə'skyü\ adv or adj : out of line

asleep \ə'slēp\ adv or adj 1 : sleeping 2 : numbed 3 : inactive

as long as conj 1 : on condition that 2 : because

as of prep : from the time of

as·par·a·gus \ə'sparəgəs\ n : tall herb related to the lilies or its edible stalks

as·pect \'as,pekt\ n 1 : way something looks to the eye or mind 2 : phase

as·pen \'aspən\ n : poplar

as·per·i·ty \a'sperətē, ə-\ n, pl -ties 1 : roughness 2 : harshness

as·per·sion \ə'spərzhən\ n : remark that hurts someone's reputation

as·phalt \'as,fȯlt\, as·phal·tum \as'fȯltəm\ n : tarlike substance used in paving and in paints

as·phyx·ia \as'fiksēə\ n : lack of oxygen causing unconsciousness

as·phyx·i·ate \-se,āt\ vb -at·ed: -at·ing

: suffocate —**as·phyx·i·a·tion** \-,fiksē-
'āshən\ *n*

as·pi·ra·tion \,aspə'rāshən\ *n* : strong
desire to achieve a goal

as·pire \ə'spī(ə)r\ *vb* -**pired; -pir·ing**
: have an ambition —**as·pir·ant**
\'asp(ə)rənt, ə'spīrənt\ *n*

as·pi·rin \'asp(ə)rən\ *n, pl* **aspirin** or
aspirins : pain reliever

ass \'as\ *n* 1 : long-eared animal related to the horse 2 : stupid person

as·sail \ə'sāl\ *vb* : attack violently —
as·sail·able *adj* —**as·sail·ant** *n*

as·sas·si·nate \ə'sas⁰n,āt\ *vb* -**nat·ed;
-nat·ing** : murder esp. for political
reasons —**as·sas·sin** \-'sas⁰n\ *n* —
as·sas·si·na·tion \-,sas⁰n'āshən\ *n*

as·sault \ə'sólt\ *n or vb* : attack

as·say \'a,sā, a'sā\ *n* : analysis (as of
an ore) to determine quality or properties —**as·say** \a'sā, 'as,ā\ *vb*

as·sem·ble \ə'sembəl\ *vb* -**bled; -bling**
\-b(ə)liŋ\ 1 : collect into one place
2 : fit together the parts

as·sem·bly \-blē\ *n, pl* -**blies** 1 : meeting
2 *cap* : legislative body 3 : a fitting
together of parts

as·sem·bly·man \-mən\ *n* : member of
a legislative assembly —**as·sem·bly-
wom·an** *n*

as·sent \ə'sent\ *vb or n* : consent

as·sert \ə'sərt\ *vb* 1 : declare 2 : defend
—**as·ser·tion** \-'sərshən\ *n* —**assert-
ive** \-'sərtiv\ *adj* —**as·sert·ive-
ness** *n*

as·sess \ə'ses\ *vb* 1 : impose (as a tax)
2 : evaluate for taxation —**as·sess-
ment** *n* —**as·ses·sor** \-ər\ *n*

as·set \'as,et\ *n* 1 *pl* : individually
owned property 2 : advantage or resource

as·sid·u·ous \ə'sij(ə)wəs\ *adj* : diligent
—**as·si·du·i·ty** \,asə'd(y)üətē\ *n* —
as·sid·u·ous·ly *adv* —**as·sid·u·ous-
ness** *n*

as·sign \ə'sīn\ *vb* 1 : transfer to another 2 : appoint to a duty 3 : designate as a task 4 : attribute —**as-
sign·able** *adj* —**as·sign·ment** \-mənt\
n

as·sim·i·late \ə'simə,lāt\ *vb* -**lat·ed;
-lat·ing** 1 : absorb as nourishment 2
: understand —**as·sim·i·la·tion**
\-,simə-'lāshən\ *n*

as·sist \ə'sist\ *vb* : help —**assist** *n* —**as-
sis·tance** \-'sistəns\ *n* —**as·sis·tant**
\-tənt\ *n*

as·so·ci·ate \ə'sōs(h)ē,āt\ *vb* -**at·ed; -at-
ing** 1 : join in companionship or part-
nership 2 : connect in thought —**as-
so·ci·ate** \-s(h)ēət, -shət\ *n* —**asso-
ci·a·tion** \-,sōs(h)ē'āshən\ *n*

as soon as *conj* : when

as·sort·ed \ə'sórtəd\ *adj* : consisting of
various kinds

as·sort·ment \-mənt\ *n* : assorted collection

as·suage \ə'swāj\ *vb* -**suaged; -suag·ing**
: ease or satisfy

as·sume \ə'süm\ *vb* -**sumed; -sum·ing**
1 : take upon oneself 2 : pretend to
have 3 : take as granted

as·sump·tion \ə'səmpshən\ *n* : something assumed

as·sure \ə'shür\ *vb* -**sured; -sur·ing** 1
: give confidence or conviction to 2
: guarantee —**as·sur·ance** \-əns\ *n*

as·ter \'astər\ *n* : herb with daisylike
flowers

as·ter·isk \'astə,risk\ *n* : a character *
used as a reference mark or as an
indication of omission of words

astern \ə'stərn\ *adv or adj* 1 : behind
2 : at or toward the stern

as·ter·oid \'astə,róid\ *n* : small planet
between Mars and Jupiter —**aster-
oi·dal** \,astə'róid⁰l\ *adj*

asth·ma \'azmə\ *n* : disorder with a
cough and difficulty in breathing —
asth·mat·ic \az'matik\ *adj or n*

astig·ma·tism \ə'stigmə,tizəm\ *n*
: visual defect —**as·tig·mat·ic**
\,astig'matik\ *adj*

as to *prep* 1 : concerning 2 : according
to

as·ton·ish \ə'stänish\ *vb* : amaze —**as-
ton·ish·ing·ly** *adv* —**as·ton·ish·ment** *n*

as·tound \ə'staúnd\ *vb* : fill with confused wonder —**as·tound·ing·ly** *adv*

astrad·dle \ə'strad⁰l\ *adv or prep* : so
as to straddle

as·tral \'astrəl\ *adj* : relating to the
stars

astray \ə'strā\ *adv or adj* : off the right
way

astride \ə'strīd\ *adv* : with legs apart
or one on each side ~ *prep* : with
one leg on each side of

as·trin·gent \ə'strinjənt\ *adj* : causing
shrinking or puckering of tissues —
as·trin·gen·cy \-jənsē\ *n* —**astrin-
gent** *n*

as·trol·o·gy \ə'sträləjē\ *n* : prediction
of events by the stars —**as·trol·o·ger**
\-əjər\ *n* —**as·tro·log·i·cal** \,astrə-
'läjikəl\ *adj*

as·tro·naut \'astrə,nót\ *n* : space traveler

as·tro·nau·tics \,astrə'nótiks\ *n* : construction and operation of spacecraft —**as·tro·nau·tic** \-ik\, **as·tro-
nau·ti·cal** \-ikəl\ *adj*

as·tro·nom·i·cal \,astrə'nämikəl\ *adj* 1

: relating to astronomy 2 : extremely large

as·tron·o·my \ə'stränəmē\ *n, pl* **-mies** : study of the celestial bodies —**as·tron·o·mer** \-mər\ *n*

as·tute \ə'st(y)üt, a-\ *adj* : shrewd —**as·tute·ly** *adv* —**as·tute·ness** *n*

asun·der \ə'səndər\ *adv or adj* 1 : into separate pieces 2 : separated

asy·lum \ə'sīləm\ *n* 1 : refuge 2 : institution for care esp. of the insane

asym·met·ric \ˌāsə'metrik\, **asym·met·ri·cal** \-trikəl\ *adj* : not symmetrical —**asym·me·try** \(')ā'simətrē\ *n*

at \ət, (')at\ *prep* 1 —used to indicate a point in time or space 2 —used to indicate a goal 3 —used to indicate condition, means, cause, or manner

at all \ət'ȯl, ə'tȯl, at'ȯl\ *adv* : without restriction or under any circumstances

ate *past of* EAT

-ate \ət, ˌāt\ *n suffix* 1 : office or rank 2 : group of persons holding an office or rank ~ *adj suffix* 1 : brought into or being in a state 2 : marked by having

athe·ist \'āthēəst\ *n* : one who denies the existence of God —**athe·ism** \-ˌizəm\ *n* —**athe·is·tic** \ˌāthē'istik\ *adj*

ath·ero·scle·ro·sis \ˌathərōˌsklə'rōsəs\ *n* : arteriosclerosis with deposition of fatty substances in the arteries —**ath·ero·scle·rot·ic** \-'rätik\ *adj*

ath·lete \'ath.lēt\ *n* : one trained to compete in athletics

ath·let·ics \ath'letiks\ *n sing or pl* : exercises and games involving physical skill —**ath·let·ic** \-ik\ *adj*

-ation \'āshən\ *n suffix* : action or process

-ative \ˌātiv, ətiv\ *adj suffix* 1 : of, relating to, or connected with 2 : tending to

at·las \'atləs\ *n* : book of maps

at·mo·sphere \'atmə,sfiər\ *n* 1 : mass of air surrounding the earth 2 : surrounding influence —**at·mo·spher·ic** \ˌatmə'sfiərik, -'sfer-\ *adj* —**at·mo·spher·i·cal·ly** \-ik(ə)lē\ *adv*

at·oll \ə,tȯl, -ˌtäl, 'aˌ-\ *n* : ring-shaped coral island

at·om \'atəm\ *n* 1 : tiny bit 2 : smallest particle of a chemical element that can exist alone or in combination

atom bomb *n* : bomb utilizing the energy released by splitting the atom

atom·ic \ə'tämik\ *adj* : relating to atoms, atom bombs, or atomic energy

atomic energy *n* : energy liberated by changes in the nucleus of an atom

at·om·iz·er \'atə,mīzər\ *n* : device for reducing a liquid to a very fine spray

atone \ə'tōn\ *vb* **atoned; aton·ing** : make amends —**atone·ment** *n*

atop \ə'täp\ *prep* : on top of

atro·cious \ə'trōshəs\ *adj* : appalling or abominable —**atro·cious·ly** *adv* —**atro·cious·ness** *n*

atroc·i·ty \ə'träsətē\ *n, pl* **-ties** : savage act

at·ro·phy \'atrəfē\ *n, pl* **-phies** : wasting away of a bodily part or tissue —**at·ro·phy** *vb*

at·ro·pine \'atrə,pēn\ *n* : poisonous drug used esp. to relieve spasms

at·tach \ə'tach\ *vb* 1 : seize legally 2 : bind by personalities 3 : join —**at·tach·ment** *n*

at·ta·ché \ˌatə'shā, ˌa,ta-, ə,ta-\ *n* : technical expert on a diplomatic staff

at·tack \ə'tak\ *vb* 1 : try to hurt or destroy with violence or words 2 : set to work on ~ *n* 1 : act of attacking 2 : fit of sickness

at·tain \ə'tān\ *vb* 1 : achieve or accomplish 2 : reach —**at·tain·abil·i·ty** \ə,tānə'bilətē\ *n* —**at·tain·able** *adj* —**at·tain·ment** *n*

at·tempt \ə'tempt\ *vb* : make an effort toward —**attempt** *n*

at·tend \ə'tend\ *vb* 1 : handle or provide for the care of something 2 : accompany 3 : be present at 4 : pay attention —**at·ten·dance** \-'tendəns\ *n* —**at·ten·dant** \-dənt\ *adj or n*

at·ten·tion \ə'tenchən\ *n* 1 : concentration of the mind on something 2 : notice or awareness —**at·ten·tive** \-'tentiv\ *adj* —**at·ten·tive·ly** *adv* —**at·ten·tive·ness** *n*

at·ten·u·ate \ə'tenyə,wāt\ *vb* **-at·ed; -at·ing** 1 : make or become thin 2 : weaken —**at·ten·u·a·tion** \-,tenyə'wāshən\ *n*

at·test \ə'test\ *vb* : certify or bear witness —**at·tes·ta·tion** \ˌa,tes'tāshən\ *n*

at·tic \'atik\ *n* : space just below the roof

at·tire \ə'tī(ə)r\ *vb* **-tired; -tir·ing** : dress —**attire** *n*

at·ti·tude \'atə,t(y)üd\ *n* 1 : posture or relative position 2 : feeling, opinion, or mood

at·tor·ney \ə'tərnē\ *n, pl* **-neys** : legal agent

at·tract \ə'trakt\ *vb* 1 : draw to oneself 2 : have emotional or aesthetic appeal for —**at·trac·tion** \-'trakshən\

—at·trac·tive \-'traktiv\ *adj* —**at·trac·tive·ly** *adv* —**at·trac·tive·ness** *n*

at·tri·bute \'atrə,byüt\ *n* : inherent characteristic ~ \ə'tribyət\ *vb* -**trib·ut·ed; -ut·ing** 1 : regard as having a specific cause or origin 2 : regard as a characteristic —**at·trib·ut·able** *adj* —**at·tri·bu·tion** \,atrə'byüshən\ *n*

at·tune \ə't(y)ün\ *vb* : bring into harmony

au·burn \'ôbərn\ *adj* : reddish brown

auc·tion \'ôkshən\ *n* : public sale of property to the highest bidder —**auction** *vb* —**auc·tion·eer** \,ôkshə'niər\ *n*

au·dac·i·ty \ô'dasətē\ *n* : boldness or insolence —**au·da·cious** \ô'dāshəs\ *adj*

au·di·ble \'ôdəbəl\ *adj* : capable of being heard —**au·di·bly** \'ôdəblē\ *adv*

au·di·ence \'ôdēəns\ *n* 1 : formal interview 2 : group of listeners or spectators

au·dio \'ôdē,ō\ *adj* : relating to sound or its reproduction ~ *n* : television sound

au·dio·vi·su·al \,ôdēō'vizh(ə)wəl\ *adj* : relating to both hearing and sight

au·dit \'ôdət\ *vb* : examine financial accounts —**audit** *n* —**au·di·tor** \'ôdətər\ *n*

au·di·tion \ô'dishən\ *n* : tryout performance —**audition** *vb*

au·di·to·ri·um \,ôdə'tōrēəm\ *n* : room or building used for public gatherings

au·di·to·ry \'ôdə,tōrē\ *adj* : relating to hearing

au·ger \'ôgər\ *n* : boring tool

aug·ment \ôg'ment\ *vb* : enlarge or increase —**aug·men·ta·tion** \,ôgmən-'tāshən\ *n*

au·gur \'ôgər\ *n* : prophet ~ *vb* : predict —**au·gu·ry** \'ôg(y)ərē\ *n*

au·gust \ô'gəst\ *adj* : majestic

Au·gust \'ôgəst\ *n* : 8th month of the year having 31 days

auk \'ôk\ *n* : stocky diving seabird

aunt \'ant, 'änt\ *n* 1 : sister of one's father or mother 2 : wife of one's uncle

au·ra \'ôrə\ *n* 1 : distinctive atmosphere 2 : luminous radiation

au·ral \'ôrəl\ *adj* : relating to the ear or to hearing

au·ri·cle \'ôrikəl\ *n* 1 : external ear 2 : chamber of the heart that receives blood from the veins

au·ro·ra bo·re·al·is \ə,rōrə,bôrē'alis\ *n* : display of light in the night sky of northern latitudes

aus·pic·es \'ôspəsəz, -,sēz\ *n pl* : patronage and protection

aus·pi·cious \ô'spishəs\ *adj* : favorable

aus·tere \ô'stiər\ *adj* : severe —**aus·tere·ly** *adv* —**aus·ter·i·ty** \ô'sterətē\ *n*

au·then·tic \ə'thentik, ô-\ *adj* : genuine —**au·then·ti·cal·ly** \-ik(ə)lē\ *adv* —**au·then·tic·i·ty** \,ô,then'tisətē\ *n*

au·then·ti·cate \ə'thenti,kāt, ô-\ *vb* -**cat·ed; -cat·ing** : prove genuine —**au·then·ti·ca·tion** \-,thenti'kāshən\ *n*

au·thor \'ôthər\ *n* 1 : writer 2 : creator —**au·thor·ess** \-th(ə)rəs\ *n* —**au·thor·ship** *n*

au·thor·i·tar·i·an \ə,thärə'terēən, ə-, -,thôr-\ *adj* : marked by blind obedience to authority

au·thor·i·ta·tive \ə'thärə,tātiv, ô-, -'thôr-\ *adj* : being an authority —**au·thor·i·ta·tive·ly** *adv*

au·thor·i·ty \ə'thärətē, ô-, -'thôr-\ *n*, *pl* -**ties** 1 : expert 2 : right, responsibility, or power to influence 3 *pl* : persons in official positions

au·tho·rize \'ôthə,rīz\ *vb* -**rized; -riz·ing** : permit or give official approval for —**au·tho·ri·za·tion** \,ôth(ə)rə'zāshən\ *n*

au·to \'ôtō\ *n, pl* **autos** : automobile

au·to·bi·og·ra·phy \,ôtəbī'ägrəfē, -bē-\ *n* : writer's own life story —**au·to·bi·og·ra·pher** \-fər\ *n* —**au·to·bio·graph·i·cal** \-,bīə'grafikəl\ *adj*

au·toc·ra·cy \ô'täkrəsē\ *n, pl* -**cies** : government by one person having unlimited power —**au·to·crat** \'ôtə,krat\ *n* —**au·to·crat·ic** \,ôtə-'kratik\ *adj* —**au·to·crat·i·cal·ly** \-ik(ə)lē\ *adv*

au·to·graph \'ôtə,graf\ *n* : signature ~ *vb* : write one's name on

au·to·mate \'ôtə,māt\ *vb* -**mat·ed; -mat·ing** : make automatic —**au·to·ma·tion** \,ôtə'māshən\ *n*

au·to·mat·ic \,ôtə'matik\ *adj* 1 : involuntary 2 : designed to function without human intervention ~ *n* : automatic device (as a firearm) —**au·to·mat·i·cal·ly** \-ik(ə)lē\ *adv*

au·tom·a·ton \ô'tämətən, -ə,tän\ *n, pl* -**atons** *or* -**a·ta** \-ətə, -ə,tä\ : robot

au·to·mo·bile \,ôtəmō'bēl, -'mō,bēl\ *n* : 4-wheeled passenger vehicle with its own power source —**au·to·mo·bil·ist** \-'bēləst, -ēbi\ *n*

au·to·mo·tive \,ôtə'mōtiv\ *adj* : relating to automobiles

au·ton·o·mous \ô'tänəməs\ *adj* : self-governing —**au·ton·o·mous·ly** *adv* —**au·ton·o·my** \-mē\ *n*

au·top·sy \'ȯ,täpsē, 'ȯtəp-\ *n, pl* **-sies** : medical examination of a corpse

au·tumn \'ȯtəm\ *n* : season between summer and winter —**au·tum·nal** \ȯ'təmnəl\ *adj*

aux·il·ia·ry \ȯg'zilyərē, -'zil(ə)rē\ *adj* **1** : being a supplement or reserve **2** : accompanying a main verb form to express person, number, mood, or tense —**auxiliary** *n*

avail \ə'vāl\ *vb* : be of use or make use ~ *n* : use

avail·able \ə'vāləbəl\ *adj* **1** : usable **2** : accessible —**avail·abil·i·ty** \-,vālə'bilətē\ *n*

av·a·lanche \'avə,lanch\ *n* : mass of sliding or falling snow or rock

av·a·rice \'av(ə)rəs\ *n* : greed —**av·a·ri·cious** \,avə'rishəs\ *adj*

avenge \ə'venj\ *vb* **avenged; aveng·ing** : take vengeance for —**aveng·er** *n*

av·e·nue \'avə,n(y)ü\ *n* **1** : way of approach **2** : broad street

av·er·age \'av(ə)rij\ *adj* **1** : being about midway between extremes **2** : ordinary ~ *vb* **1** : be usually **2** : find the mean of ~ *n* : mean

averse \ə'vərs\ *adj* : feeling dislike or reluctance —**aver·sion** \-'vərzhən\ *n*

avert \ə'vərt\ *vb* : turn away

avi·ary \'āvē,erē\ *n, pl* **-ar·ies** : place where birds are kept

avi·a·tion \,āvē'āshən, ,avē-\ *n* : operation or manufacture of airplanes —**avi·a·tor** \'āvē,ātər, 'avē-\ *n*

av·id \'avəd\ *adj* **1** : greedy **2** : enthusiastic —**avid·i·ty** \a'vidətē, a-\ *n* —**av·id·ly** *adv*

av·o·ca·do \,avə'kädō, ,äv-\ *n, pl* **-dos** : tropical fruit

av·o·ca·tion \,avə'kāshən\ *n* : hobby

avoid \ə'vȯid\ *vb* **1** : keep away from **2** : prevent the occurrence of **3** : refrain from —**avoid·able** *adj* —**avoid·ance** \-³ns\ *n*

av·oir·du·pois \,avərdə'pȯiz\ *n* : system of weight based on the pound of 16 ounces

avow \ə'vaů\ *vb* : declare openly —**avow·al** \-'vaů(ə)l\ *n*

await \ə'wāt\ *vb* : wait for

awake \ə'wāk\ *vb* **awoke** \-'wōk\; **awaked** *or* **awok·en** \-'wōkən\; **awak·ing** : wake up —**awake** *adj*

awak·en \ə'wākən\ *vb* **-ened; -en·ing** : wake up

award \ə'wȯrd\ *vb* : give (something won or deserved) ~ *n* **1** : judgment **2** : prize

aware \ə'waər\ *adj* : having realization or consciousness —**aware·ness** *n*

awash \ə'wȯsh, -'wäsh\ *adv or adj* : flooded

away \ə'wā\ *adv* **1** : from this or that place or time **2** : out of the way **3** : in another direction **4** : from one's possession ~ *adj* **1** : absent **2** : distant

awe \'ȯ\ *n* : respectful fear or wonder ~ *vb* **awed; aw·ing** : fill with awe —**awe·some** \-səm\ *adj* —**awe·struck** *adj*

aw·ful \'ȯfəl\ *adj* **1** : inspiring awe **2** : extremely disagreeable **3** : very great —**aw·ful·ly** *adv*

awhile \ə'hwīl\ *adv* : for a while

awk·ward \'ȯkwərd\ *adj* **1** : clumsy **2** : embarrassing —**awk·ward·ly** *adv* —**awk·ward·ness** *n*

awl \'ȯl\ *n* : hole-making tool

aw·ning \'ȯniŋ\ *n* : window cover

awry \ə'rī\ *adv or adj* : wrong

ax, axe \'aks\ *n* : chopping tool

ax·i·om \'aksēəm\ *n* : generally accepted truth —**ax·i·om·at·ic** \,aksēə'matik\ *adj*

ax·is \'aksəs\ *n, pl* **ax·es** \-,sēz\ : center of rotation —**ax·i·al** \-sēəl\ *adj* —**ax·i·al·ly** *adv*

ax·le \'aksəl\ *n* : shaft on which a wheel revolves

aye \'ī\ *adv* : yes ~ *n* : a vote of yes

aza·lea \ə'zālyə\ *n* : rhododendron with funnel-shaped blossoms

az·i·muth \'az(ə)məth\ *n* **1** : arc measured along the horizon **2** : horizontal direction —**az·i·muth·al** \,azə'məthəl\ *adj*

azure \'azhər\ *n* : blue of the sky —**azure** *adj*

B

b \'bē\ *n, pl* **b's** *or* **bs** \'bēz\ : 2d letter of the alphabet

bab·ble \'babəl\ *vb* **-bled; -bling** **1** : utter meaningless sounds **2** : talk foolishly or too much —**babble** *n* —**bab·bler** *n*

babe \'bāb\ *n* : baby

ba·bel \'bābəl, 'bab-\ *n* : noisy confusion

ba·boon \ba'bün\ *n* : large Asian or African ape with a doglike muzzle

ba·by \'bābē\ *n, pl* **-bies** : very young

child ~ *vb* -**bied**; -**by·ing** : pamper — **baby** *adj* — **ba·by·hood** *n* — **ba·by·ish** *adj*

ba·by-sit *vb* -**sat**; -**sit·ting** : care for children while parents are away — **ba·by-sit·ter** *n*

bac·ca·lau·re·ate \,bakə'lòrēət\ *n* : bachelor's degree

bac·cha·na·lia \,bakə'nālyə\ *n, pl* -**lia** : drunken orgy — **bac·cha·na·lian** \-yən\ *adj or n*

bach·e·lor \'bach(ə)lər\ *n* 1 : holder of lowest 4-year college degree 2 : unmarried man — **bach·e·lor·hood** *n*

ba·cil·lus \bə'siləs\ *n, pl* -**li** \-,ī\ : rod-shaped bacterium — **bac·il·lary** \'basə,lerē\ *adj*

back \'bak\ *n* 1 : part of a human or animal body nearest the spine 2 : part opposite the front 3 : player farthest from the opponent's goal ~ *adv* 1 : to or at the back 2 : ago 3 : to or in a former place or state 4 : in reply — *adj* 1 : located at the back 2 : not paid on time 3 : moving or working backward 4 : not current ~ *vb* 1 : support 2 : go or cause to go back 3 : form the back of — **back·ache** *n* — **back·er** *n* — **back·ing** *n* — **back·less** *adj* — **back·rest** *n*

back·bite *vb* -**bit**; -**bit·ten**; -**bit·ing** : say spiteful things about someone absent — **back·bit·er** *n*

back·bone *n* 1 : bony column in the back that encloses the spinal cord 2 : firm character

back·drop *n* : painted cloth hung across the rear of a stage

back·fire *n* : explosion in the intake or exhaust passages of an internal-combustion engine — **back·fire** *vb*

back·gam·mon \'bak,gamən\ *n* : board game

back·ground *n* 1 : scenery behind something 2 : sum of a person's experience or training

back·hand *n* : stroke (as in tennis) made with the back of the hand turned forward — **backhand** *adj or vb* — **back·hand·ed** *adj*

back·lash *n* : adverse reaction — **back·lash·er** *n*

back·log *n* 1 : reserve of unfilled orders 2 : accumulation of things to be done — **backlog** *vb*

back·pack *n* : camping pack carried on the back ~ *vb* : hike with a backpack — **back·pack·er** *n*

back·slide *vb* -**slid**; -**slid** *or* -**slid·den** \-,slid°n\; -**slid·ing** : lapse in morals or religious practice — **back·slid·er** *n*

back·stage *adv or adj* : in or to an area behind a stage

back·up *n* : substitute

back·ward \'bakwərd\, **back·wards** *adv* 1 : toward the back 2 : with the back foremost 3 : in a reverse direction 4 : toward an earlier or worse state ~ *adj* 1 : directed, turned, or done backward 2 : retarded in development — **back·ward·ness** *n*

back·woods *n pl* : remote or isolated place

ba·con \'bākən\ *n* : salted and smoked meat from a pig

bac·te·ri·um \bak'tirēəm\ *n, pl* -**ria** \-ēə\ : microscopic plant — **bac·te·ri·al** \-ēəl\ *adj* — **bac·te·ri·o·log·ic** \-,tirēə'läjik\, **bac·te·ri·o·log·i·cal** \-əl\ *adj* — **bac·te·ri·ol·o·gist** \-ē-'äləjəst\ — **bac·te·ri·ol·o·gy** \-jē\ *n*

bad \'bad\ *adj* **worse** \'wərs\; **worst** \'wərst\ 1 : not good 2 : naughty 3 : faulty 4 : spoiled — **bad** *n or adv* — **bad·ly** *adv* — **bad·ness** *n*

bade *past of* BID

badge \'baj\ *n* : symbol of status

bad·ger \'bajər\ *n* : burrowing mammal with long claws on the forefeet ~ *vb* -**gered**; -**ger·ing** : harass

bad·min·ton \'bad,mint°n\ *n* : tennis-like game played with a shuttlecock

baf·fle \'bafəl\ *vb* -**fled**; -**fling** : perplex ~ *n* : device to alter flow (as of liquid or sound)

bag \'bag\ *n* : flexible usu. closable container ~ *vb* -**gg**- 1 : bulge out 2 : put in a bag 3 : catch in hunting

bag·a·telle \,bagə'tel\ *n* : trifle

ba·gel \'bāgəl\ *n* : hard doughnut-shaped roll

bag·gage \'bagij\ *n* : traveler's bags and belongings

bag·gy \'bagē\ *adj* -**gi·er**; -**est** : puffed out like a bag — **bag·gi·ly** *adv* — **bag·gi·ness** *n*

bag·pipe *n* : musical instrument with a bag, a tube with valves, and sounding pipes — often *pl*.

¹**bail** \'bāl\ *n* : container for scooping water out of a boat — **bail** *vb*

²**bail** *n* 1 : security given to guarantee a prisoner's appearance in court 2 : release secured by bail ~ *vb* : bring about the release of by giving bail — **bails·man** \'bālzmən\ *n*

bai·liff \'bāləf\ *n* 1 : British sheriff's aide 2 : minor officer of a U.S. court

bai·li·wick \'bālē,wik\ *n* : one's special field or domain

bait \'bāt\ *vb* 1 : harass with dogs usu. for sport 2 : furnish (a hook or trap) with bait ~ n : lure esp. for catching animals

bake \ˈbāk\ vb **baked; bak·ing** : cook in dry heat esp. in an oven ~ n : party featuring baked food —**bak·er** n —**bak·ery** \ˈbāk(ə)rē\ n —**bake·shop** n

bal·ance \ˈbaləns\ n 1 : weighing device 2 : counteracting weight, force, or influence 3 : equilibrium 4 : that which remains ~ vb **-anced; -anc·ing** 1 : compute the balance 2 : equalize 3 : bring into harmony or proportion —**bal·anced** adj

bal·co·ny \ˈbalkōnē\ n, pl **-nies** : platform projecting from a wall

bald \ˈbȯld\ adj 1 : lacking a natural or usual covering (as of hair) 2 : plain ~ vb : become bald —**bald·ly** adv

bal·der·dash \ˈbȯldər,dash\ n : nonsense

bale \ˈbāl\ n : large bundle ~ vb **baled; bal·ing** : pack in a bale —**bal·er** n

bale·ful \ˈbālfəl\ adj 1 : deadly 2 : ominous

balk \ˈbȯk\ n : hindrance ~ vb 1 : thwart 2 : stop short and refuse to go on —**balky** adj

¹**ball** \ˈbȯl\ n 1 : rounded mass 2 : game played with a ball ~ vb : form into a ball

²**ball** n : large formal dance —**ball·room** n

bal·lad \ˈbaləd\ n 1 : narrative poem 2 : slow romantic song —**bal·lad·eer** \,balə'di(ə)r\ n

bal·last \ˈbaləst\ n : heavy material to steady a ship or balloon ~ vb : provide with ballast

bal·le·ri·na \,balə'rēnə\ n : female ballet dancer

bal·let \ˈba,lā, ba'lā\ n : theatrical dancing

bal·lis·tics \bə'listiks\ n sing or pl : science of projectile motion —**ballistic** adj

bal·loon \bə'lün\ n : inflated bag ~ vb 1 : travel in a balloon 2 : swell out —**bal·loon·ist** n

bal·lot \ˈbalət\ n 1 : paper used to cast a vote 2 : system of voting ~ vb : vote

bal·ly·hoo \ˈbalē,hü\ n : publicity —**ballyhoo** vb

balm \ˈbä(l)m, ˈbȧlm\ n 1 : fragrant healing or soothing preparation 2 : spicy fragrant herb

balmy \ˈbä(l)mē, ˈbȧlmē\ adj **balm·i·er; -est** : gently soothing —**balm·i·ness** n

ba·lo·ney \bə'lōnē\ n : nonsense

bal·sa \ˈbȯlsə\ n : very light wood of a tropical tree

bal·sam \-səm\ n 1 : aromatic resinous plant substance 2 : balsam-yielding plant

bal·us·ter \ˈbaləstər\ n : upright support of a rail

bal·us·trade \-,strād\ n : row of balusters topped by a rail

bam·boo \bam'bü\ n : tall tropical grass with strong hollow stems

bam·boo·zle \bam'büzəl\ vb **-zled; -zling** : deceive

ban \ˈban\ vb **-nn-** : prohibit ~ n : legal prohibition

ba·nal \bə'näl, -'nal; 'bān²l\ adj : ordinary and uninteresting —**ba·nal·i·ty** \bə-'nal-ət-ē\ n

ba·nana \bə'nanə\ n : elongated fruit of a treelike tropical plant or the plant itself

¹**band** \ˈband\ n 1 : something that constrains or restrains 2 : strip that brings or holds together 3 : range of radio wavelengths ~ vb 1 : enclose with a band 2 : unite for a common end —**band·ed** adj —**band·er** n

²**band** n 1 : group 2 : musicians playing together

band·age \ˈbandij\ n : material used esp. in dressing wounds ~ vb : dress or cover with a bandage

ban·dan·na, ban·dana \ban'danə\ n : large colored figured handkerchief

ban·dit \ˈbandət\ n : outlaw or robber —**ban·dit·ry** \-,dətrē\ n

band·stand n : stage for band concerts

band·wag·on n : candidate, side, or movement gaining support

¹**ban·dy** \ˈbandē\ vb **-died; -dy·ing** : exchange in rapid succession

²**bandy** adj : curved outward

bane \ˈbān\ n 1 : poison 2 : cause of woe —**bane·ful** adj

¹**bang** \ˈbaŋ\ vb : strike, thrust, or move usu. with a loud noise ~ n 1 : blow 2 : sudden loud noise ~ adv : directly

²**bang** n : fringe of short hair over the forehead —usu. pl. ~ vb : cut in bangs

ban·gle \ˈbaŋgəl\ n : bracelet

ban·ish \ˈbanish\ vb 1 : force by authority to leave a country 2 : expel —**ban·ish·ment** n

ban·is·ter \-əstər\ n : upright support of a staircase handrail or the handrail itself

ban·jo \-,jō\ n, pl **-jos** : stringed instrument with a drumlike body —**ban·jo·ist** n

bank \ˈbaŋk\ n 1 : piled-up mass 2

: rising ground along a body of water **3** : sideways slope along a curve ~ *vb* **1** : form a bank **2** : cover (as a fire) to keep inactive **3** : incline (an airplane) laterally

²bank *n* : tier of objects

³bank *n* **1** : money institution **2** : reserve supply ~ *vb* : conduct business in a bank —**bank·book** *n* — **bank·er** *n* —**bank·ing** *n*

bank·rupt \'-(,)rəpt\ *n* : one required by law to forfeit assets to pay off debts ~ *adj* **1** : legally a bankrupt **2** : lacking something essential — **bankrupt** *vb* —**bank·rupt·cy** \-(,)rəp(t)sē\ *n*

ban·ner \'banər\ *n* : flag ~ *adj* : excellent

banns \'banz\ *n pl* : announcement in church of a proposed marriage

ban·quet \'baŋkwət\ *n* : ceremonial dinner —**banquet** *vb*

ban·shee \'banshē\ *n* : wailing female spirit that foretells death

ban·tam \'bantəm\ *n* : miniature domestic fowl

ban·ter \-ər\ *n* : good-natured joking —**banter** *vb*

ban·yan \'banyən\ *n* : large tree that grows new trunks from the limbs

bap·tism \'baptizəm\ *n* : Christian rite signifying spiritual cleansing —**bap·tis·mal** \bap'tizməl\ *adj*

bap·tize \bap'tīz, 'bap,tīz\ *vb* **-tized; -tiz·ing** : administer baptism to

bar \'bär\ *n* **1** : long narrow object used esp. as a lever, fastening, or support **2** : barrier **3** : body of practicing lawyers **4** : wide stripe **5** : food counter **6** : place where liquor is served **7** : vertical line across the musical staff ~ *vb* **-rr- 1** : obstruct with a bar **2** : shut out **3** : prohibit ~ *prep* : excluding —**barred** *adj* —**bar·room** *n* —**bar·tend·er** *n*

barb \'bärb\ *n* : sharp projection pointing backward —**barbed** *adj*

bar·bar·i·an \bär'berēən\ *adj* **1** : relating to people considered backward **2** : not refined —**barbarian** *n*

bar·bar·ic \-'barik\ *adj* : barbarian

bar·ba·rous \'bärb(ə)rəs\ *adj* **1** : lacking refinement **2** : mercilessly cruel —**bar·ba·rism** \-bə,rizəm\ *n* —**bar·bar·i·ty** \bär'barətē\ *n* —**bar·ba·rous·ly** *adv*

bar·be·cue \'bärbi,kyü\ *n* : gathering at which barbecued food is served ~ *vb* **-cued; -cu·ing** : cook over hot coals or on a spit often with a highly seasoned sauce

bar·ber \'bärbər\ *n* : one who cuts hair

bar·bi·tu·rate \bär'bichərət\ *n* : sedative or hypnotic drug

bard \'bärd\ *n* : poet

bare \'baər\ *adj* **bar·er; bar·est** *n* **1** : naked **2** : not concealed **3** : empty **4** : leaving nothing to spare **5** : plain ~ *vb* **bared; bar·ing** : make or lay bare —**bare·foot, bare·foot·ed** *adv or adj* —**bare·hand·ed** *adv or adj* —**bare·head·ed** *adv or adj* —**bare·ly** *adv* —**bare·ness** *n*

bare·back, bare·backed *adv or adj* : without a saddle

bare·faced *adj* : open and esp. brazen

bar·gain \'bärgən\ *n* **1** : agreement **2** : something bought for less than its value ~ *vb* **1** : negotiate **2** : barter

barge \'bärj\ *n* : broad flat-bottomed boat ~ *vb* **barged; barg·ing** : move rudely or clumsily —**barge·man** *n*

bari·tone \'barə,tōn\ *n* : male voice between bass and tenor

bar·i·um \'barēəm\ *n* : silver-white metallic chemical element

¹bark \'bärk\ *vb* **1** : make the sound of a dog **2** : speak in a loud curt tone ~ *n* : sound of a barking dog

²bark *n* : tough corky outer covering of a woody stem or root ~ *vb* : remove bark or skin from

³bark *n* : 3-masted ship

bark·er \'bärkər\ *n* : one who calls out to attract people to a sideshow

bar·ley \-lē\ *n* : cereal grass or its seeds

barn \'bärn\ *n* : building for keeping hay or livestock —**barn·yard** *n*

bar·na·cle \'bärnikəl\ *n* : marine crustacean

barn·storm \'-\ *vb* : tour through rural districts giving performances

ba·rom·e·ter \bə'rämətər\ *n* : instrument for measuring atmospheric pressure —**baro·met·ric** \,barə'metrik\, **baro·met·ri·cal** \-əl\ *adj*

bar·on \'barən\ *n* : British peer —**bar·on·age** \-ij\ *n* —**ba·ro·ni·al** \bə'rōnēəl\ *adj* —**bar·ony** \'barənē\ *n*

bar·on·ess \-ənəs\ *n* **1** : baron's wife **2** : woman holding a baronial title

bar·on·et \-ənət\ *n* : man holding a rank between a baron and a knight —**bar·on·et·cy** \-sē\ *n*

ba·roque \bə'rōk, -'räk\ *adj* : elaborately ornamented

bar·racks \'barəks\ *n sing or pl* : soldiers' housing

bar·ra·cu·da \,barə'küdə\ *n, pl* **-da** *or* **-das** : large predatory sea fish

bar·rage \bə'räzh, -'räj\ *n* : heavy artillery fire

bar·rel \'barəl\ *n* **1** : closed cylindrical container **2** : amount held by a barrel

3 : cylindrical part ~ *vb* **-reled** *or* **-relled; -rel·ing** *or* **-rel·ling** : pack in a barrel —**bar·reled** *adj*

bar·ren \'barən\ *adj* 1 : unproductive of life 2 : uninteresting —**bar·ren·ness** \-ənnəs\ *n*

bar·rette \bä'ret, bə-\ *n* : clasp for a woman's hair

bar·ri·cade \'barə,kād, ,barə'-\ *n* : barrier —**barricade** *vb*

bar·ri·er \'barēər\ *n* : something that separates or obstructs

bar·ring \'bäriŋ\ *prep* : omitting

bar·ris·ter \'barəstər\ *n* : British trial lawyer

bar·row \'barō\ *n* : wheelbarrow

bar·ter \'bärtər\ *vb* : trade by exchange of goods —**barter** *n*

ba·salt \bə'sȯlt, 'bā,-\ *n* : dark fine-grained igneous rock —**ba·sal·tic** \bə'sȯltik\ *adj*

¹**base** \'bās\ *n, pl* **bas·es** 1 : bottom 2 : fundamental part 3 : beginning point 4 : supply source of a force 5 : compound that reacts with an acid to form a salt ~ *vb* **based; bas·ing** : establish —**base·less** *adj*

²**base** *adj* **bas·er; -est** 1 : inferior 2 : contemptible —**base·ly** *adv* —**base·ness** *n*

base·ball *n* : game played with a bat and ball by 2 teams

base·ment \-mant\ *n* : part of a building below ground level

bash \'bash\ *vb* : strike violently ~ *n* : heavy blow

bash·ful \-fəl\ *adj* : self-conscious —**bash·ful·ness** *n*

ba·sic \'bāsik\ *adj* 1 : relating to or forming the base or essence 2 : relating to a chemical base —**ba·si·cal·ly** *adv* —**ba·sic·i·ty** \bā'sisətē\ *n*

ba·sil \'bazəl, 'bās-\ *n* : aromatic mint

ba·sil·i·ca \bə'silikə\ *n* : church or cathedral of high rank

ba·sin \'bās³n\ *n* 1 : large bowl or pan 2 : depression containing a pond or lake 3 : region drained by a river

ba·sis \'bāsəs\ *n, pl* **ba·ses** \-,sēz\ 1 : something that supports 2 : fundamental principle

bask \'bask\ *vb* : enjoy pleasant warmth

bas·ket \-ət\ *n* : woven container —**bas·ket·ful** *n*

bas·ket·ball *n* : game played with a ball on a court by 2 teams

bas-re·lief \,bäri'lēf\ *n* : flat sculpture with slightly raised design

¹**bass** \'bas\ *n, pl* **bass** *or* **bass·es** : spiny-finned sport and food fish

²**bass** \'bās\ *n* 1 : deep tone 2 : lowest male voice

bas·set hound \'basət-\ *n* : short-legged dog with long ears

bas·si·net \,basə'net\ *n* : baby's bed

bas·soon \bə'sün, ba-\ *n* : low-pitched wind instrument

bas·tard \'bastərd\ *n* 1 : illegitimate child 2 : offensive person ~ *adj* 1 : illegitimate 2 : inferior —**bas·tard·ize** *vb* —**bas·tardy** *n*

¹**baste** \'bāst\ *vb* **bast·ed; bast·ing** : sew temporarily with long stitches

²**baste** *vb* **bast·ed; bast·ing** : moisten with liquid at intervals while cooking

bas·tion \'baschən\ *n* : fortified position —**bas·tioned** *adj*

¹**bat** \'bat\ *n* 1 : stick or club 2 : sharp blow ~ *vb* **-tt-** : hit with a bat

²**bat** *n* : small flying mammal

³**bat** *vb* **-tt-** : wink or blink

batch \'bach\ *n* : quantity used or produced at one time

bate \'bāt\ *vb* **bat·ed; bat·ing** : moderate or reduce

bath \'bath, 'bàth\ *n, pl* **baths** \'bathz, 'baths, 'bàthz, 'bàths\ 1 : a washing of the body 2 : water for washing the body 3 : liquid in which something is immersed 4 : bathroom —**bath·tub** *n*

bathe \'bāth\ *vb* **bathed; bath·ing** 1 : wash in liquid 2 : flow against so as to wet 3 : shine light over 4 : take a bath or a swim —**bath·er** *n*

bath·robe *n* : robe worn around the house

bath·room *n* : room with a bathtub or shower and usu. a washbowl and toilet

ba·tiste \bə'tēst\ *n* : fine sheer fabric

ba·ton \bə'tän\ *n* : musical conductor's stick

bat·tal·ion \bə'talyən\ *n* : military unit composed of a headquarters and two or more companies

bat·ten \'bat³n\ *n* : strip of wood used to seal or reinforce ~ *vb* : furnish or fasten with battens

¹**bat·ter** \-ər\ *vb* : beat or damage with repeated blows

²**batter** *n* : mixture of flour and liquid

³**batter** *n* : player who bats

bat·tery \'bat(ə)rē\ *n, pl* **-ter·ies** 1 : illegal beating of a person 2 : group of artillery guns 3 : group of electric cells

bat·ting \-iŋ\ *n* : layers of cotton or wool for stuffing

bat·tle \'bat³l\ *n* : military fighting ~ *vb*

-tled; -tling : engage in battle —**bat-tle-field** n

bat-tle-ax n : long-handled ax formerly used as a weapon

bat-tle-ment \-mənt\ n : parapet on top of a wall

bat-tle-ship n : heavily armed warship

bat-ty \'bat-ē\ adj -ti-er; -est : crazy

bau-ble \'bȯbəl\ n : trinket

bawdy \'bȯdē\ adj bawd-i-er; -est : obscene or lewd —**bawd-i-ly** adv —**bawd-i-ness** n

bawl \'bȯl\ vb : cry loudly ~ n : long loud cry

1bay \'bā\ adj : reddish brown ~ n : bay-colored animal

2bay n : European laurel

3bay n 1 : compartment 2 : area projecting out from a building and containing a window (**bay window**)

4bay vb : bark with deep long tones ~ n 1 : position of one unable to escape danger 2 : baying of dogs

5bay n : body of water smaller than a gulf that is nearly surrounded by land

bay-ber-ry \-,berē\ n : shrub bearing small waxy berries

bay-o-net \'bāənət, ,bāə'net\ n : dagger that fits on the end of a rifle ~ vb -net-ed; -net-ing : stab with a bayonet

bay-ou \'bīō, -ü\ n : creek flowing through marshy land

ba-zaar \bə'zär\ n 1 : market 2 : fair for charity

ba-zoo-ka \-'zükə\ n : weapon that shoots armor-piercing rockets

BB n : small shot pellet

be \(')bē\ vb was \(')wəz, 'wäz\ were \(')wər\; been \(')bin\; be-ing \'bēiŋ\; am \əm, (')am\, is \(')iz, əz\, are \ər, (')är\ 1 : equal 2 : exist 3 : occupy a certain place 4 : occur ~ verbal auxiliary —used to show continuous action or to form the passive voice

beach \'bēch\ n : sandy shore of a sea, lake, or river ~ vb : drive ashore

beach-comb-er \-,kōmər\ n : one who searches the shore for useful objects

beach-head n : shore area held by an attacking force

bea-con \'bēkən\ n : guiding or warning light or signal —**beacon** vb

bead \'bēd\ n : small round body esp. strung on a thread ~ vb : form into a bead —**bead-ing** n —**beady** adj

bea-gle \'bēgəl\ n : small short-legged hound

beak \'bēk\ n : bill of a bird —**beaked** adj

bea-ker \'bēkər\ n 1 : large drinking cup 2 : laboratory vessel

beam \'bēm\ n 1 : large long piece of timber or metal 2 : ray of light 3 : directed radio signals for the guidance of pilots ~ vb 1 : send out light 2 : smile 3 : aim a radio broadcast

bean \'bēn\ n : edible plant seed borne in pods

1bear \'baər\ n, pl **bears** 1 or pl **bear** : large heavy mammal with shaggy hair 2 : gruff or sullen person —**bear-ish** adj

2bear vb **bore** \'bȯr\; **borne** \'bȯrn\; **bear-ing** 1 : carry 2 : give birth to or produce 3 : endure 4 : press —**bear-able** adj —**bear-er** n

beard \'biərd\ n 1 : facial hair on a man 2 : tuft like a beard ~ vb : confront boldly —**beard-ed** adj —**beard-less** adj

bear-ing n 1 : way of carrying oneself 2 : supporting object or purpose 3 : significance 4 : machine part in which another part turns 5 : direction with respect esp. to compass points

beast \'bēst\ n 1 : animal 2 : brutal person —**beast-li-ness** n —**beast-ly** adj

beat \'bēt\ vb **beat**; **beat-en** \'bētᵊn\ or **beat**; **beat-ing** 1 : strike repeatedly 2 : defeat 3 : act or arrive before 4 : throb ~ n 1 : single stroke or pulsation 2 : rhythmic stress in poetry or music ~ adj : exhausted —**beat-er** n

be-a-tif-ic \,bēə'tifik\ adj : blissful

be-at-i-fy \bē'atə,fī\ vb -**fied**; -**fy-ing** : make happy or blessed —**be-at-i-fi-ca-tion** \-,atəfə'kāshən\ n

be-at-i-tude \-'atə,t(y)üd\ n : saying in the Sermon on the Mount (Matthew 5:3-12) beginning "Blessed are"

beau \'bō\ n, pl **beaux** \'bōz\ or **beaus** : suitor

beau-ty \'byütē\ n, pl -**ties** : qualities that please the senses or mind —**beau-te-ous** \-ēəs\ adj —**beau-te-ous-ly** adv —**beau-ti-fi-ca-tion** \,byütəfə'kāshən\ n —**beau-ti-fi-er** \'byütə,fīər\ n —**beau-ti-ful** \-ifəl\ adj —**beau-ti-ful-ly** adv —**beau-ti-fy** \-ə,fī\ vb

bea-ver \'bēvər\ n : large fur-bearing rodent

be-cause \bi'kȯz, -'kəz\ conj : for the reason that

because of prep : by reason of

beck \'bek\ n : summons

beck-on \-ən\ vb : summon esp. by a nod or gesture

be·come \bi'kəm\ vb **-came** \-'kām\; **-come**; **-com·ing** : come to be 2 : be suitable **—be·com·ing** adj **—be·com·ing·ly** adv

bed \'bed\ n 1 : piece of furniture to sleep on 2 : flat or level surface ~ vb **-dd-** : put or go to bed **—bed·spread** n

bed·bug n : wingless bloodsucking insect

bed·clothes n pl : bedding

bed·ding n 1 : sheets and blankets for a bed 2 : soft material (as hay) for an animal's bed

be·deck \bi'dek\ vb : adorn

be·dev·il \-'devəl\ vb : harass

bed·lam \'bedləm\ n : uproar and confusion

be·drag·gled \bi'dragəld\ adj : dirty and disordered

bed·rid·den \'bed,ridʔn\ adj : kept in bed by illness

bed·rock n : solid subsurface rock **—bedrock** adj

bee \'bē\ n 1 : 4-winged honey-producing insect 2 : neighborly work session **—bee·hive** n **—bee·keep·er** n **—bees·wax** n

beech \'bēch\ n, pl **beech·es** or **beech** : tree with smooth gray bark and edible nuts (**beech·nuts**) **—beech·en** \-ən\ adj

beef \'bēf\ n, pl **beefs** \'bēfs\ or **beeves** \'bēvz\ : flesh of a steer, cow, or bull ~ vb : strengthen —used with up **—beef·steak** n

bee·line n : straight course

been past part of BE

beer \'biər\ n : alcoholic drink brewed from malt and hops **—beery** adj

beet \'bēt\ n : garden root vegetable

bee·tle \'bētəl\ n : 4-winged insect

be·fall \bi'fȯl\ vb **-fell**; **-fall·en** : happen to

be·fit \bi'fit\ vb : be suitable to

be·fore \bi'fōr\ adv 1 : in front 2 : earlier ~ prep 1 : in front of 2 : earlier than ~ conj : earlier than

be·fore·hand adv or adj : in advance

be·friend \bi'frend\ vb : act as friend to

be·fud·dle \-'fədʔl\ vb : confuse

beg \'beg\ vb **-gg-** : ask earnestly

be·get \bi'get\ vb **-got**; **-got·ten** or **-got**; **-get·ting** : produce (offspring) as a father

beg·gar \'begər\ n : one that begs ~ vb : make poor **—beg·gar·ly** adj **—beg·gar·y** n

be·gin \bi'gin\ vb **-gan** \-'gan\; **-gun** \-'gən\; **-gin·ning** 1 : start 2 : come into being **—be·gin·ner** n

be·gone \bi'gȯn\ vb : go away

be·go·nia \-'gōnyə\ n : tropical herb with waxy flowers

be·grudge \-'grəj\ vb 1 : concede reluctantly 2 : envy

be·guile \-'gīl\ vb **-guiled**; **-guil·ing** 1 : deceive 2 : amuse

be·half \-'haf, -'häf\ n : benefit

be·have \-'hāv\ vb **-haved**; **-hav·ing** : act in a certain way

be·hav·ior \-'hāvyər\ n : way of behaving **—be·hav·ior·al** \-əl\ adj

be·head \-'hed\ vb : cut off the head of

be·hest \-'hest\ n : command

be·hind \bi'hīnd\ adv : at the back ~ prep 1 : in back of 2 : less than 3 : supporting

be·hold \-'hōld\ vb **-held**; **-hold·ing** : see **—be·hold·er** n

be·hold·en \-'hōldən\ adj : indebted

be·hoove \-'hüv\, **be·hove** \-'hōv\ vb **-hooved** or **-hoved**; **-hoov·ing** or **-hov·ing** : be necessary for

beige \'bāzh\ n : yellowish brown **—beige** adj

be·ing \'bēiŋ\ n 1 : existence 2 : living thing

be·la·bor \bi'lābər\ vb 1 : beat 2 : carry on to absurd lengths

be·lat·ed \-'lātəd\ adj : delayed

belch \'belch\ vb 1 : expel stomach gas orally 2 : emit forcefully **—belch** n

be·lea·guer \bi'lēgər\ vb 1 : besiege 2 : harass

bel·fry \'belfrē\ n, pl **-fries** : bell tower

be·lie \bi'lī\ vb **-lied**; **-ly·ing** 1 : misrepresent 2 : prove false

be·lief \bə'lēf\ n 1 : trust 2 : something believed

be·lieve \-'lēv\ vb **-lieved**; **-liev·ing** 1 : trust in 2 : accept as true 3 : hold as an opinion **—be·liev·able** adj **—be·liev·ably** adv **—be·liev·er** n

be·lit·tle \bi'litʔl\ vb **-lit·tled**; **-lit·tling** : make seem unimportant or worthless

bell \'bel\ n : hollow metallic device that rings when struck ~ vb : provide with a bell

bel·la·don·na \,belə'dänə\ n : poisonous herb yielding a drug used esp. to relieve spasms or dilate the eye

belle \'bel\ n : beautiful woman

bel·li·cose \'beli,kōs\ adj : pugnacious **—bel·li·cos·i·ty** \,beli'käsətē\ n

bel·lig·er·ent \bə'lij(ə)rənt\ adj 1 : waging war 2 : truculent **—bel·lig·er·ence** \-rəns\ n **—bel·lig·er·en·cy** \-rənsē\ n **—belligerent** n

bel·low \'belō\ vb : make a loud deep roar or shout **—bellow** n

bel·lows \-ōz, -əz\ *n sing or pl* : device with sides that can be compressed to expel air

bell·weth·er \'-wethər, -,weth-\ *n* : leader

bel·ly \'belē\ *n, pl* **-lies** : abdomen ~ *vb* **-lied; -ly·ing** : bulge

be·long \bi'lȯŋ\ *vb* **1** : be suitable or proper **2** : be owned **3** : be a part of

be·long·ings \-iŋz\ *n pl* : possessions

be·loved \bi'ləv(ə)d\ *adj* : dearly loved —**beloved** *n*

be·low \-'lō\ *adv* : in or to a lower place ~ *prep* : lower than

belt \'belt\ *n* **1** : strip (as of leather) worn about the waist **2** : endless band passing around pulleys or cylinders and used to impart motion **3** : distinct region ~ *vb* **1** : put a belt around **2** : thrash

be·moan \bi'mōn\ *vb* : lament

be·muse \-'myüz\ *vb* : confuse

bench \'bench\ *n* **1** : long seat **2** : judge's seat **3** : court

bend \'bend\ *vb* **bent** \'bent\; **bend·ing 1** : curve or cause a change of shape in **2** : turn in a certain direction ~ *n* **1** : act of bending **2** : curve

be·neath \bi'nēth\ *adv or prep* : below

bene·dic·tion \,benə'dikshən\ *n* : closing blessing

bene·fac·tor \'benə,faktər\ *n* : one who gives esp. charitable aid —**bene·fac·tion** \,benə'fakshən\ *n* —**bene·fac·tress** \'benə,faktrəs\ *n*

ben·e·fi·cence \bə'nefəsəns\ *n* : quality of doing good —**ben·e·fi·cent** \-sənt\ *adj*

ben·e·fi·cial \,benə'fishəl\ *adj* : being of benefit —**ben·e·fi·cial·ly** *adv*

ben·e·fi·cia·ry \-'fishē,erē, -'fishərē\ *n, pl* **-ries** : one who receives benefits

ben·e·fit \'benə,fit\ *n* **1** : something that does good **2** : help **3** : fund-raising event —**benefit** *vb*

be·nev·o·lence \bə'nev(ə)ləns\ *n* **1** : charitable nature **2** : act of kindness —**be·nev·o·lent** \-lənt\ *adj*

be·night·ed \bi'nītəd\ *adj* : ignorant

be·nign \bi'nīn\ *adj* **1** : gentle or kindly **2** : not malignant —**be·nig·ni·ty** \-'nignətē\ *n*

be·nig·nant \-'nignənt\ *adj* : benign

bent \'bent\ *n* : aptitude or interest

be·numb \bi'nəm\ *vb* : make numb esp. by cold

ben·zene, ben·zine \'ben,zēn\ *n* : colorless flammable liquid

be·queath \bi'kwēth, -'kwēth\ *vb* **1** : give by will **2** : hand down

be·quest \bi'kwest\ *n* : something bequeathed

be·rate \-'rāt\ *vb* : scold harshly

be·reaved \-'rēvd\ *adj* : suffering the death of a loved one ~ *n, pl* **bereaved** : one who is bereaved —**be·reave·ment** *n*

be·reft \-'reft\ *adj* : deprived of or lacking something

be·ret \bə'rā\ *n* : round soft visorless cap

beri·beri \,berē'berē\ *n* : thiamine-deficiency disease

ber·ry \'berē\ *n, pl* **-ries** : small pulpy fruit

ber·serk \bə(r)'sərk, -'zərk\ *adj* : crazed —**berserk** *adv*

berth \'bərth\ *n* **1** : place where a ship lies at anchor **2** : place to sit or sleep esp. on a ship **3** : job ~ *vb* : to bring or come into a berth

ber·yl \'berəl\ *n* : light-colored silicate mineral

be·seech \bi'sēch\ *vb* **-sought** \-'sȯt\ *or* **-seeched; -seech·ing** : entreat

be·set \-'set\ *vb* **1** : harass **2** : hem in

be·side \-'sīd\ *prep* **1** : by the side of **2** : besides

be·sides \-'sīdz\ *adv* **1** : in addition **2** : moreover ~ *prep* **1** : other than **2** : in addition to

be·siege \-'sēj\ *vb* : lay siege to —**be·sieg·er** *n*

be·smirch \-'smərch\ *vb* : soil

be·sot \-'sät\ *vb* **-tt-** : become drunk

be·speak \bi-\ *vb* **-spoke; -spo·ken; -speak·ing** : indicate

best \'best\ *adj, superlative of* GOOD **1** : excelling all others **2** : most productive **3** : largest ~ *adv, superlative of* WELL **1** : in the best way **2** : most ~ *n* : one that is best ~ *vb* : outdo

bes·tial \'beschəl\ *adj* **1** : relating to beasts **2** : brutish —**bes·ti·al·i·ty** \,beschē'alətē\ *n*

be·stir \bi-\ *vb* : rouse to action

best man *n* : chief male attendant at a wedding

be·stow \bi'stō\ *vb* : give —**be·stow·al** \-əl\ *n*

bet \'bet\ *n* **1** : agreement that one whose guess about a result proves wrong will give something to one whose guess proves right **2** : money risked on a bet ~ *vb* **bet; bet·ting 1** : risk (as money) on an outcome **2** : make a bet with

be·tide \bi'tīd\ *vb* : happen to

be·to·ken \bi'tōkən\ *vb* : give an indication of

be·tray \bi'trā\ *vb* **1** : seduce **2** : deliver to an enemy by treachery **3** : prove unfaithful to **4** : reveal unintentionally —be·tray·al n —be·tray·er n

be·troth \-'träth, -'tròth, -'tróth, or with th \ vb : promise to marry —be·troth·al n —be·trothed n

bet·ter \'betǝr\ adj, comparative of GOOD 1 : more than half 2 : improved in health 3 : of higher quality ~ adv, comparative of WELL 1 : in a superior manner 2 : more ~ n 1 : one that is better 2 : advantage ~ vb 1 : improve 2 : surpass —bet·ter·ment \-mǝnt\ n

bet·tor, bet·ter \'betǝr\ n : one who bets

be·tween \bi'twēn\ prep 1 —used to show two things considered together 2 : in the space separating 3 —used to indicate a comparison or choice ~ adv : in an intervening space or interval

bev·el \'bevǝl\ n : slant on an edge ~ vb -eled or -elled; -el·ing or -el·ling 1 : cut or shape to a bevel 2 : incline

bev·er·age \'bev(ǝ)rij\ n : drink

bevy \'bevē\ n, pl bev·ies : large group

be·wail \bi'wāl\ vb : lament

be·ware \-'waǝr\ vb : be cautious

be·wil·der \-'wildǝr\ vb : confuse —be·wil·der·ment n

be·witch \-'wich\ vb 1 : affect by witchcraft 2 : charm —be·witch·ment n

be·yond \bē'änd\ adv 1 : farther 2 : besides ~ prep 1 : on or to the farther side of 2 : out of the reach of 3 : besides

bi- \(')bī, ,bi\ prefix 1 : two 2 : coming or occurring every two 3 : twice, doubly, or on both sides

bicolored	bimetal
biconcave	bimetallic
biconcavity	binational
biconvex	binationalism
biconvexity	biparental
bicultural	bipolar
bidirectional	biracial
biethnic	biracially
bifunctional	bitonal

bi·an·nu·al \(')bī-\ adj : occurring twice a year —bi·an·nu·al·ly adv

bi·as \'bīǝs\ n 1 : line diagonal to the grain of a fabric 2 : prejudice ~ vb -ased or -assed; -as·ing or -as·sing : prejudice

bib \'bib\ n : protective cover tied under a child's chin

Bi·ble \'bībǝl\ n 1 : sacred scriptures of Christians 2 : sacred scriptures of

Judaism or of some other religion —bib·li·cal \'biblikǝl\ adj

bib·li·og·ra·phy \,biblē'ägrǝfē\ n, pl -phies : list of writings on a subject or of an author —bib·li·og·ra·pher \-fǝr\ n —bib·lio·graph·ic \-lēǝ'grafik, bib·lio·graph·i·cal \-ǝl\ adj

bi·cam·er·al \bī'kam(ǝ)rǝl\ adj : having 2 legislative chambers

bi·car·bon·ate \-'kärbǝ,nāt, -nǝt\ n : acid carbonate

bi·cen·ten·ni·al \,bīsen'tenēǝl\ n : 200th anniversary —bicentennial adj

bi·ceps \'bī,seps\ n : large muscle of the upper arm

bick·er \'bikǝr\ vb or n : squabble

bi·cus·pid \bī'kǝspǝd\ n : double-pointed tooth

bi·cy·cle \'bī,sikǝl\ n : 2-wheeled vehicle moved by pedaling ~ vb -cled; -cling : ride a bicycle —bi·cy·cler \-(ǝ)lǝr\ n —bi·cy·clist \-list\ n

bid \'bid\ vb bade \'bad, 'bād\ or bid; bid·den \'bid²n\ or bid; bid·ding 1 : order 2 : invite 3 : express 4 : make a bid ~ n 1 : act of bidding 2 : buyer's proposed price —bid·da·ble \-ǝbǝl\ adj —bid·der n

bide \'bīd\ vb bode \'bōd\ or bid·ed; bided; bid·ing 1 : wait 2 : dwell

bi·en·ni·al \bī'enēǝl\ adj 1 : occurring once in 2 years 2 : lasting 2 years —biennial n —bi·en·ni·al·ly adv

bier \'biǝr\ n : stand for a coffin

bi·fo·cals \bī'fōkǝlz\ n pl : eyeglasses that correct for near and distant vision

big \'big\ adj -gg- : large in size, amount, or scope —big·ness n

big·a·my \'bigǝmē\ n : marrying one person while still married to another —big·a·mist \-mǝst\ n —big·a·mous \-mǝs\ adj

big·horn n, pl -horn or -horns : wild mountain sheep

bight \'bīt\ n 1 : loop of a rope 2 : bay

big·ot \'bigǝt\ n : one who is intolerant of others —big·ot·ed \-ǝtǝd\ adj —big·ot·ry \-ǝtrē\ n

big shot n : important person

big·wig n : big shot

bike \'bīk\ n : bicycle or motorcycle

bi·ki·ni \bǝ'kēnē\ n : woman's brief 2-piece bathing suit

bi·lat·er·al \bī-\ adj : involving 2 sides —bi·lat·er·al·ly adv

bile \'bīl\ n 1 : greenish liver secretion that aids digestion 2 : bad temper

bi·lin·gual \bī'lingwǝl\ adj : using 2 languages

bil·ious \'bilyəs\ *adj* : irritable —**bil·ious·ness** *n*

bilk \'bilk\ *vb* : cheat

¹**bill** \'bil\ *n* : jaws of a bird together with their horny covering ~ *vb* : caress fondly —**billed** *adj*

²**bill** *n* **1** : draft of a law **2** : list of things to be paid for **3** : printed advertisement **4** : piece of paper money ~ *vb* : submit a bill or account to

bill·board *n* : surface for displaying advertising bills

bil·let \'bilət\ *n* : soldiers' quarters ~ *vb* : lodge in a billet

bill·fold *n* : wallet

bil·liards \'bilyərdz\ *n* : game of driving balls into one another or into pockets on a table

bil·lion \-yən\ *n, pl* **billions** *or* **billion** : 1000 millions —**billion** *adj* —**bil·lionth** \-yənth\ *adj or n*

bil·low \'bilō\ *n* **1** : great wave **2** : rolling mass ~ *vb* : swell out —**bil·lowy** \'bilōwē\ *adj*

billy goat *n* : male goat

bin \'bin\ *n* : storage box

bi·na·ry \'bīnərē\ *adj* : consisting of 2 things —**binary** *n*

bind \'bīnd\ *vb* **bound** \'bàund\; **bind·ing 1** : tie **2** : obligate **3** : unite into a mass **4** : bandage —**bind·er** *n* —**bind·ing** *n*

binge \'binj\ *n* : spree

bin·go \'bingō\ *n, pl* **-gos** : game of covering numbers on a card

bin·oc·u·lar \bī'näkyələr, bə-\ *adj* : of or relating to both eyes ~ *n* : binocular optical instrument —usu. pl. **bin·oc·u·lar·ly** *adv*

bio·chem·is·try \,bīō-\ *n* : chemistry dealing with organisms —**bio·chem·i·cal** *adj or n* —**bio·chem·ist** *n*

bio·de·grad·able \,bīō-\ *adj* : able to be reduced to harmless products by organisms —**bio·de·grad·abil·i·ty** *n* —**bio·deg·ra·da·tion** *n* —**bio·de·grade** *vb*

bi·og·ra·phy \bī'ägrəfē, bē-\ *n, pl* **-phies** : written history of a person's life —**bi·og·ra·pher** \-fər\ *n* —**bio·graph·ic** \,bīə'grafik\, **bio·graph·i·cal** \-ikəl\ *adj*

bi·ol·o·gy \bī'äləjē\ *n* : science of living beings and life processes —**bio·log·i·cal** \,bīə'läjikəl\ *adj* —**bi·ol·o·gist** \bī'äləjəst\ *n*

bio·phys·ics \,bīō-\ *n* : application of physics to biological problems —**bio·phys·i·cal** *adj* —**bio·phys·i·cist** *n*

bi·op·sy \'bī,äpsē\ *n, pl* **-sies** : removal of live bodily tissue for examination

bi·par·ti·san \bī-\ *adj* : involving members of 2 parties

bi·ped \'bī,ped\ *n* : 2-footed animal

birch \'bərch\ *n* : deciduous tree with close-grained wood —**birch, birch·en** \-ən\ *adj*

bird \'bərd\ *n* : warm-blooded egg-laying vertebrate with wings and feathers —**bird·bath** *n* —**bird·house** *n* —**bird·seed** *n*

bird's-eye \'bərd,zī\ *adj* **1** : seen from above **2** : cursory

birth \'bərth\ *n* **1** : act or fact of being born or of producing young **2** : origin —**birth·day** *n* —**birth·place** *n* —**birth·rate** *n*

birth·mark *n* : unusual blemish on the skin at birth

birth·right *n* : something one is entitled to by birth

bis·cuit \'biskət\ *n* : a bread made with leavening other than yeast

bi·sect \'bī,sekt\ *vb* : divide into 2 parts —**bi·sec·tion** \'bī-\ *n* —**bi·sec·tor** \-tər\ *n*

bish·op \'bishəp\ *n* **1** : a clergyman higher than a priest or minister **2** : a chess piece

bish·op·ric \-rik\ *n* **1** : diocese **2** : office of bishop

bis·muth \'bizməth\ *n* : heavy brittle metallic chemical element

bi·son \'bīs²n, 'bīz-\ *n, pl* **-son** : large shaggy wild ox of central U.S.

bis·tro \'bēstrō, 'bis-\ *n, pl* **-tros** : small restaurant or bar

¹**bit** \'bit\ *n* **1** : part of a bridle that goes in a horse's mouth **2** : drilling tool —**bit·stock** *n*

²**bit** *n* **1** : small piece or quantity **2** : small degree

bitch \'bich\ *n* : female dog ~ *vb* : complain

bite \'bīt\ *vb* **bit** \'bit\; **bit·ten** \'bit²n\; **bit·ing** \'bītiŋ\ **1** : to grip or cut with teeth or jaws **2** : dig in or grab and hold **3** : sting **4** : take bait ~ *n* **1** : act of biting **2** : bit of food **3** : wound made by biting —**bit·ing** *adj*

bit·ter \'bitər\ *adj* **1** : having an acrid lingering taste **2** : intense or severe **3** : extremely harsh or resentful —**bit·ter·ly** *adv* —**bit·ter·ness** *n*

bit·tern \-ərn\ *n* : small heron

bi·tu·mi·nous coal \bə'tü(y)ümənəs-\ *n* : coal that yields volatile waste matter when heated

bi·valve \'bī-\ *n* : animal (as a clam) with a shell of 2 parts —**bivalve** *adj*

biv·ouac \'biv(ə),wak\ *n* : temporary camp ~ *vb* **-ouacked; -ouack·ing** : camp

33   **bizarre • blender**

bi·zarre \bə'zär\ *adj* : very strange — **bi·zarre·ly** *adv*

blab \'blab\ *vb* **-bb-** : talk too much

black \'blak\ *adj* 1 : of the color black 2 : Negro 3 : soiled 4 : lacking light 5 : wicked or evil 6 : gloomy ~ *n* 1 : black pigment or dye 2 : something black 3 : color of least lightness 4 : person of a dark-skinned race ~ *vb* : blacken —**black·ing** *n* —**black·ish** *adj* —**black·ly** *adv* —**black·ness** *n*

black-and-blue *adj* : darkly discolored from bruising

black·ball *n* : negative vote —**black·ball** *vb*

black·ber·ry \-‚berē\ *n* : black or purple fruit of a bramble

black·bird *n* : bird of which the male is largely or wholly black

black·board *n* : dark surface for writing on with chalk

black·en \-ən\ *vb* 1 : make or become black 2 : defame

black·guard \'blagərd, -‚ärd\ *n* : scoundrel

black·head *n* : small oily mass plugging the outlet of a skin gland

black·jack *n* 1 : flexible leather-covered club 2 : card game ~ *vb* : hit with a blackjack

black·list *n* : list of persons to be punished —**blacklist** *vb*

black·mail *n* 1 : extortion by threat of exposure 2 : something extorted by blackmail —**blackmail** *vb* —**black·mail·er** *n*

black·out *n* 1 : darkness due to electrical failure 2 : brief fainting spell — **black out** *vb*

black·smith *n* : one who forges iron

black·top *n* : dark material for surfacing roads —**blacktop** *vb*

blad·der \'bladər\ *n* : sac into which urine passes from the kidneys

blade \'blād\ *n* 1 : leaf esp. of grass 2 : something resembling the flat part of a leaf 3 : cutting part of an instrument or tool

blame \'blām\ *vb* **blamed; blam·ing** 1 : find fault with 2 : hold responsible or responsible for —**blam·able** *adj* —**blame** *n* —**blame·less** *adj* —**blame·less·ly** *adv* —**blame·wor·thi·ness** *n* —**blame·worthy** *adj*

blanch \'blanch\ *vb* : make or become white or pale

bland \'bland\ *adj* 1 : smooth in manner 2 : soothing 3 : tasteless —**bland·ly** *adv* —**bland·ness** *n*

blan·dish·ment \-ishmənt\ *n* : flattering or coaxing speech or act

blank \'blaŋk\ *adj* 1 : showing or causing a dazed look 2 : lacking expression 3 : empty 4 : free from writing 5 : downright ~ *n* 1 : an empty space 2 : form with spaces to write in 3 : unfinished form (as of a key) 4 : cartridge with no bullet ~ *vb* : cover or close up —**blank·ly** *adv* —**blank·ness** *n*

blan·ket \-ət\ *n* 1 : heavy covering for a bed 2 : covering layer ~ *vb* : cover ~ *adj* : applying to a group

blare \'blaər\ *vb* **blared; blar·ing** : make a loud harsh sound —**blare** *n*

blar·ney \'blärnē\ *n* : skillful flattery

bla·sé \blä'zā\ *adj* : indifferent to pleasure or excitement

blas·pheme \blas'fēm\ *vb* **-phemed; -phem·ing** : speak blasphemy

blas·phe·my \'blasfəmē\ *n, pl* **-mies** : irreverence toward God or anything sacred —**blas·phe·mous** *adj*

blast \'blast\ *n* 1 : violent gust of wind 2 : explosion ~ *vb* 1 : shrivel up 2 : shatter by or as if by explosive — **blast off** *vb* : take off esp. in a rocket

bla·tant \'blāt³nt\ *adj* : offensively showy —**bla·tan·cy** \-³nsē\ *n* —**bla·tant·ly** *adv*

¹blaze \'blāz\ *n* 1 : fire 2 : intense direct light 3 : strong display ~ *vb* **blazed; blaz·ing** : burn or shine brightly

²blaze *n* 1 : white mark on an animal's face 2 : mark made on a tree ~ *vb* **blazed; blaz·ing** : mark with blazes

blaz·er \-ər\ *n* : sports jacket

bleach \'blēch\ *vb* : whiten —**bleach** *n*

bleach·ers \-ərz\ *n sing or pl* : uncovered stand for spectators

bleak \'blēk\ *adj* 1 : desolately barren 2 : lacking cheering qualities — **bleak·ish** *adj* —**bleak·ly** *adv* —**bleak·ness** *n*

blear \'blir\ *adj* : dim with water or tears

bleary \'bli(ə)rē\ *adj* : dull or dimmed esp. from fatigue

bleat \'blēt\ *n* : cry of a sheep or goat or a sound like it —**bleat** *vb*

bleed \'blēd\ *vb* **bled \'bled\; bleed·ing** 1 : lose or shed blood 2 : feel distress 3 : flow from a wound 4 : draw fluid from 5 : extort money from —**bleed·er** *n*

blem·ish \'blemish\ *vb* : spoil by a flaw ~ *n* : noticeable flaw

¹blench \'blench\ *vb* : flinch

²blench *vb* : grow or make pale

blend \'blend\ *vb* 1 : mix thoroughly 2 : combine into an integrated whole ~ *n* : product of blending —**blend·er** *n*

bless \'bles\ vb **blessed** \'blest\; **bless-ing 1** : consecrate by religious rite **2** : invoke divine care for **3** : make happy —**bless-ed** \'blesəd\, **blest** \'blest\ adj —**bless-ed-ness** n —**bless-ing** n

blew past of BLOW

blight \'blīt\ n **1** : plant disorder marked by withering or an organism causing it **2** : harmful influence ~ vb : affect with or suffer from blight

blimp \'blimp\ n : small airship holding form by pressure of contained gas

blind \'blīnd\ adj **1** : lacking or grossly deficient in ability to see **2** : not intelligently controlled **3** : having no way out ~ vb **1** : to make blind **2** : dazzle ~ n **1** : something to conceal or darken **2** : place of concealment —**blind-ly** adv —**blind-ness** n

blind-fold vb : cover the eyes of —**blindfold** n

blink \'blink\ vb **1** : wink **2** : shine intermittently ~ n : wink

blink-er n : a blinking light

bliss \'blis\ n **1** : complete happiness **2** : heaven or paradise —**bliss-ful** adj —**bliss-ful-ly** adv

blis-ter \'blistər\ n **1** : raised area of skin containing watery fluid **2** : raised or swollen spot ~ vb : develop or cause blisters

blithe \'blīth, 'blīth\ adj **blith-er**; **blith-est** : cheerful —**blithe-ly** adv —**blithe-some** \-səm\ adj

blitz \'blits\ n **1** : series of air raids **2** : fast intensive campaign —**blitz** vb

bliz-zard \'blizərd\ n : severe windy snowstorm

bloat \'blōt\ vb : swell

blob \'bläb\ n : small lump or drop

bloc \'bläk\ n : group working together

block \'bläk\ n **1** : solid piece **2** : frame enclosing a pulley **3** : quantity considered together **4** : large building divided into separate units **5** : a city square or the distance along one of its sides **6** : obstruction **7** : interruption of a bodily or mental function ~ vb : obstruct or hinder

block-ade \blä'kād\ n : the shutting off of a place usu. by troops or ships ~ vb **-ad-ed; -ad-ing** : impose a blockade upon

block-head n : stupid person

blond, blonde \'bländ\ adj **1** : fair in complexion **2** : of a light color — **blond, blonde** n

blood \'bləd\ n **1** : red liquid that circulates in the heart, arteries, and veins of animals **2** : lifeblood **3** : lineage —**blood-ed** adj —**blood-less** adj

—**blood-stain** n —**blood-stained** adj
—**blood-suck-er** n —**blood-suck-ing** n
—**bloody** adj

blood-cur-dling adj : terrifying

blood-hound n : large hound with a keen sense of smell

blood-mo-bile \-mō‚bēl\ n : truck for collecting blood from donors

blood-shed n : slaughter

blood-shot adj : inflamed to redness

blood-stream n : blood in a circulatory system

blood-thirsty adj : eager to shed blood —**blood-thirst-i-ly** adv —**blood-thirst-i-ness** n

bloom \'blüm\ n **1** : flower **2** : period of flowering **3** : fresh or healthy look ~ vb : yield flowers —**bloomy** adj

bloo-mers \'blümərz\ n pl : woman's underwear of short loose trousers

bloop-er \'blüpər\ n : public blunder

blos-som \'bläsəm\ n or vb : flower

blot \'blät\ n **1** : stain **2** : blemish ~ vb **-tt- 1** : spot **2** : dry with absorbent paper —**blot-ter** n

blotch \'bläch\ n : large spot —**blotch** vb —**blotchy** adj

blouse \'blaús, 'blaúz\ n : loose garment reaching from the neck to the waist

¹**blow** \'blō\ vb **blew** \'blü\; **blown** \'blōn\; **blow-ing 1** : move forcibly **2** : send forth a current of air **3** : sound **4** : shape by blowing **5** : explode ~ n **1** : gale **2** : a blowing from the mouth —**blow-er** n —**blowy** adj

²**blow** n **1** : forcible stroke **2** pl : fighting **3** : calamity

³**blow** vb **blew; blown; blow-ing** : flower

blow-out n : bursting of a tire

blow-torch n : small torch that uses a blast of air

¹**blub-ber** \'bləbər\ n : fat of whales

²**blubber** vb : cry noisily

blud-geon \'bləjən\ n : short club ~ vb : hit with a bludgeon

blue \'blü\ adj **blu-er; blu-est 1** : of the color blue **2** : melancholy ~ n : color of the clear sky —**blu-ish** \-ish\ adj

blue-bell n : plant with blue bell-shaped flowers

blue-ber-ry \-‚berē, -b(ə)rē\ n : edible blue or blackish berry

blue-bird n : small bluish songbird

blue-fish n : bluish marine food fish

blue jay n : American crested jay

blue-print n **1** : photographic print in white on blue of a mechanical drawing **2** : plan of action —**blueprint** vb

blues \'blüz\ n pl **1** : depression **2**

: music in a usu. melancholy style of American Negro origin

¹bluff \'bləf\ *adj* 1 : rising steeply with a broad flat front 2 : frank ~ *n* : cliff

²bluff *vb* : deceive by pretense ~ *n* : act of bluffing —**bluff·er** \-ər\ *n*

blu·ing, blue·ing \'blüiŋ\ *n* : dye used in laundering to keep fabrics white

blun·der \'bləndər\ *vb* 1 : move clumsily 2 : make a stupid mistake ~ *n* : bad mistake

blun·der·buss \-,bəs\ *n* : obsolete short-barreled firearm

blunt \'blənt\ *adj* 1 : not sharp 2 : tactless ~ *vb* : make dull —**blunt·ly** *adv* —**blunt·ness** *n*

blur \'blər\ *n* 1 : smear 2 : something vaguely seen ~ *vb* -**rr**- : make or become indistinct —**blur·ry** \-ē\ *adj*

blurb \'blərb\ *n* : short publicity notice

blurt \'blərt\ *vb* : utter suddenly

blush \'bləsh\ *n* : reddening of the face —**blush** *vb* —**blush·ful** *adj*

blus·ter \'bləstər\ *vb* 1 : blow violently 2 : talk or act with boasts or threats —**bluster** *n* —**blus·tery** *adj*

boa \'bō·ə\ *n* 1 : a large snake (as the **boa con·stric·tor** \,bōəkən'striktər\) that crushes its prey 2 : fluffy scarf

boar \'bōr\ *n* : male swine

board \'bōrd\ *n* 1 : long thin piece of sawed lumber 2 : flat thin sheet esp. for games 3 : daily meals furnished for pay 4 : official body ~ *vb* 1 : go aboard 2 : cover with boards 3 : supply meals to —**board·er** *n*

board·walk *n* : wooden walk along a beach

boast \'bōst\ *vb* : praise oneself or one's possessions —**boast** *n* —**boast·er** *n* —**boast·ful** *adj* —**boast·ful·ly** *adv*

boat \'bōt\ *n* : vessel for traveling on water —**boat** *vb* —**boat·man** \-mən\ *n*

boat·swain \'bōsᵊn\ *n* : ship's officer in charge of the hull

¹bob \'bäb\ *vb* -**bb**- 1 : move up and down 2 : appear suddenly

²bob *n* 1 : float 2 : woman's short haircut ~ *vb* : cut hair in a bob

bob·bin \'bäbən\ *n* : spindle for holding thread

bob·ble \'bäbəl\ *vb* -**bled; -bling** : fumble —**bobble** *n*

bob·cat *n* : small American lynx

bob·o·link \'bäbə,liŋk\ *n* : American songbird

bob·sled \-,sled\ *n* : racing sled —**bobsled** *vb*

bob·white \(')bäb'hwīt\ *n* : quail

bock \'bäk\ *n* : dark beer

¹bode \'bōd\ *vb* **bod·ed; bod·ing** : indicate by signs

²bode *past of* BIDE

bod·ice \'bädəs\ *n* : close-fitting top of dress

bodi·ly \'bädᵊlē\ *adj* : relating to the body ~ *adv* 1 : in the flesh 2 : as a whole

body \'bädē\ *n, pl* **bod·ies** 1 : the physical whole of an organism 2 : human being 3 : main part 4 : mass of matter 5 : group —**bod·ied** *adj* —**bodi·less** \-iləs, -ᵊdləs\ *adj* —**body·guard** *n*

bog \'bäg, 'bȯg\ *n* : swamp ~ *vb* -**gg**- : sink in or as if in a bog —**bog·gy** *adj*

bo·gey \'bu̇gē, 'bō-\ *n, pl* -**geys** : someone or something frightening

bog·gle \'bägəl\ *vb* -**gled; -gling** : overwhelm with amazement

bo·gus \'bōgəs\ *adj* : fake

bo·he·mi·an \bō'hēmēən\ *n* : one living unconventionally —**bohemian** *adj*

¹boil \'bȯil\ *n* : inflamed swelling

²boil *vb* 1 : heat to a temperature (**boiling point**) at which vapor forms 2 : cook in boiling liquid 3 : be agitated —**boil** *n*

boil·er \'bȯilər\ *n* : tank holding hot water or steam

bois·ter·ous \'bȯist(ə)rəs\ *adj* : noisily turbulent —**bois·ter·ous·ly** *adv*

bold \'bōld\ *adj* 1 : courageous 2 : insolent 3 : daring —**bold·ly** *adv* —**bold·ness** \'bōl(d)nəs\ *n*

bo·le·ro \bə'le(ə)rō\ *n, pl* -**ros** 1 : Spanish dance 2 : short open jacket

boll \'bōl\ *n* : seed pod

boll weevil *n* : a small grayish weevil that infests the cotton plant

bo·lo·gna \bə'lōnē\ *n* : large smoked sausage

bol·ster \'bōlstər\ *n* : long pillow ~ *vb* -**stered; -ster·ing** : support

¹bolt \'bōlt\ *n* 1 : flash of lightning 2 : sliding bar used to fasten a door 3 : roll of cloth 4 : threaded pin used with a nut ~ *vb* 1 : move suddenly 2 : fasten with a bolt 3 : swallow hastily

²bolt *vb* : sift

bomb \'bäm\ *n* : explosive device ~ *vb* : attack with bombs —**bomb·proof** *adj*

bom·bard \bäm'bärd, bəm-\ *vb* : attack with or as if with artillery —**bom·bard·ment** *n*

bom·bar·dier \,bämbə(r)'diər\ *n* : one who releases the bombs from a bomber

bom·bast \'bäm,bast\ *n* : pretentious

language —**bom·bas·tic** \bäm-'bastik\ adj

bomb·er n 1 : one that bombs 2 : airplane for dropping bombs

bomb·shell n 1 : bomb 2 : great surprise

bo·na fide \'bōnə,fīd, 'bän-; ,bōnə'fīdē\ adj 1 : made in good faith 2 : genuine

bo·nan·za \bə'nanzə\ n : something yielding a rich return

bon·bon \'bän,bän\ n : piece of candy

bond \'bänd\ n 1 pl : fetters 2 : uniting force 3 : obligation made binding by money 4 : interest-bearing certificate ~ vb 1 : insure 2 : cause to adhere —**bond·hold·er** n

bond·age \'bändij\ n : slavery —**bond·man** \-mən\ n —**bond·wom·an** n

¹**bonds·man** \'bän(d)zmən\ n : slave

²**bondsman** n : surety

bone \'bōn\ n : skeletal material ~ vb **boned; bon·ing** : to free from bones —**bone·less** adj —**bony** \'bōnē\ adj

bon·er \'bōnər\ n : blunder

bon·fire \'bän,fī(ə)r\ n : outdoor fire

bo·ni·to \bə'nētō\ n, pl **-tos** or **-to** : medium-sized tuna

bon·net \'bänət\ n : hat for a woman or infant

bo·nus \'bōnəs\ n : extra payment

boo \'bü\ n, pl **boos** : shout of disapproval —**boo** vb

boo·by \'bübē\ n, pl **-bies** : dunce

book \'bük\ n 1 : paper sheets bound into a volume 2 : long literary work or a subdivision of one ~ vb : reserve —**book·case** n —**book·let** \-lət\ n —**book·mark** n —**book·sell·er** n —**book·shelf** n

book·end n : support to hold up a row of books

book·ie \-ē\ n : bookmaker

book·ish \-ish\ adj : fond of books and reading

book·keep·er n : one who keeps business accounts —**book·keep·ing** n

book·mak·er n : one who takes bets —**book·mak·ing** n

book·worm n : one devoted to reading

¹**boom** \'büm\ n 1 : long spar to extend the bottom of a sail 2 : beam projecting from the pole of a derrick

²**boom** vb 1 : make a deep hollow sound 2 : grow rapidly esp. in value ~ n 1 : booming sound 2 : rapid growth

boo·mer·ang \'bümə,raŋ\ n : angular club that returns to the thrower

¹**boon** \'bün\ n : benefit

²**boon** adj : congenial

boon·docks \'bün,däks\ n pl : rural area

boor \'bür\ n : rude person —**boor·ish** adj

boost \'büst\ vb 1 : raise 2 : promote —**boost** n —**boost·er** n

boot \'büt\ n 1 : covering for the foot and leg 2 : kick ~ vb : kick

boo·tee, boo·tie \'bütē\ n : infant's knitted sock

booth \'büth\ n, pl **booths** \'büthz, 'büths\ : small enclosed stall or seating area

boot·leg \'büt,leg\ vb : make or sell liquor illegally —**bootleg** adj or n —**boot·leg·ger** n

boo·ty \'bütē\ n, pl **-ties** : plunder

booze \'büz\ vb **boozed; booz·ing** : drink liquor to excess ~ n : liquor —**booz·er** n —**boozy** adj

bo·rax \'bōr,aks\ n : crystalline compound of boron

bor·der \'bȯrdər\ n 1 : edge 2 : boundary ~ vb 1 : put a border on 2 : be close

¹**bore** \'bōr\ vb **bored; bor·ing** 1 : pierce 2 : make by piercing ~ n : cylindrical hole or its diameter —**bor·er** n

²**bore** past of BEAR

³**bore** n : one that is dull ~ vb **bored; bor·ing** : tire with dullness —**bore·dom** \'bȯrdəm\ n

born \'bȯrn\ adj 1 : brought into life 2 : being such by birth

borne past part of BEAR

bo·ron \'bȯr,än\ n : dark-colored chemical element

bor·ough \'bərō\ n : incorporated town or village

bor·row \'bärō\ vb 1 : take as a loan 2 : take into use

bo·som \'büzəm, 'bü-\ n : breast ~ adj : intimate —**bo·somed** adj

boss \'bȯs\ n : employer or supervisor ~ vb : supervise —**bossy** adj

bot·a·ny \'bät(ə)nē\ n : plant biology —**bo·tan·i·cal** \bə'tanikəl\ adj —**bot·a·nist** \'bät(ə)nəst\ n —**bot·a·nize** \-ə,nīz\ vb

botch \'bäch\ vb : do clumsily —**botch** n

both \'bōth\ adj or pron : the one and the other ~ conj —used to show each of two is included

both·er \'bäthər\ vb 1 : annoy or worry 2 : take the trouble —**bother** n —**both·er·some** \-səm\ adj

bot·tle \'bät²l\ n : container with a narrow neck and no handles ~ vb **bottled; bot·tling** : put into a bottle

bot·tle·neck n : place or cause of congestion

bot·tom \'bätəm\ n 1 : supporting surface 2 : lowest part or place —**bottom** *adj* —**bot·tomed** *adj* —**bot·tom·less** *adj*

bot·u·lism \'bächə,lizəm\ *n* : acute food poisoning

bou·doir \'büd,wär, 'büd-\ *n* : woman's private room

bough \'baú\ *n* : large tree branch

bought *past of* BUY

bouil·lon \'bu,yän; 'bul,yän, -yən\ *n* : clear soup

boul·der \'bōldər\ *n* : large rounded rock —**boul·dered** *adj*

bou·le·vard \'bulə,värd, 'bü-\ *n* : broad thoroughfare

bounce \'baúns\ *vb* **bounced; bounc·ing 1** : spring back **2** : make bounce —**bounce** *n*

¹bound \'baúnd\ *adj* : intending to go

²bound *n* : limit or boundary ~ *vb* : be a boundary of —**bound·less** *adj* —**bound·less·ness** *n*

³bound *adj* **1** : obliged **2** : having a binding **3** : determined **4** : incapable of failing

⁴bound *n* : leap ~ *vb* : move by springing

bound·ary \'baúnd(ə)rē\ *n, pl* **-aries** : line marking extent or separation

boun·ty \'baúntē\ *n, pl* **-ties 1** : generosity **2** : reward —**boun·te·ous** \-ēəs\ *adj* —**boun·te·ous·ly** *adv* —**boun·ti·ful** \-ifəl\ *adj* —**boun·ti·ful·ly** *adv*

bou·quet \bō'kā, bü-\ *n* **1** : bunch of flowers **2** : fragrance

bour·bon \'bərbən\ *n* : corn whiskey

bour·geoi·sie \,bûrzh,wä'zē\ *n* : middle class of society —**bour·geois** \'bûrzh,wä, bûrzh'wä\ *n or adj*

bout \'baút\ *n* **1** : contest **2** : outbreak

bou·tique \bü'tēk\ *n* : specialty shop

bo·vine \'bō,vīn, -,vēn\ *adj* : relating to cattle —**bovine** *n*

¹bow \'baú\ *vb* **1** : submit **2** : bend the head or body ~ *n* : act of bowing

²bow \'bō\ *n* **1** : bend or arch **2** : weapon for shooting arrows **3** : knot with loops **4** : rod with stretched horsehairs for playing a stringed instrument ~ *vb* : curve or bend —**bow·man** \-mən\ *n* —**bow·string** *n*

³bow \'baú\ *n* : forward part of a ship —**bow** *adj*

bow·els \'baú(ə)ls\ *n pl* **1** : intestines **2** : inmost parts

bow·er \'baú(ə)r\ *n* : arbor

¹bowl \'bōl\ *n* : concave vessel or part —**bowl·ful** \-,fúl\ *n*

²bowl *n* : round ball for bowling ~ *vb* : roll a ball in bowling —**bowl·er** *n*

bowl·ing *n* : game in which balls are rolled to knock down pins

¹box \'bäks\ *n, pl* **box** *or* **box·es** : evergreen shrub —**box·wood** \-,wúd\ *n*

²box *n* **1** : container usu. with 4 sides and a cover **2** : small compartment ~ *vb* : put in a box

³box *n* : slap **1** : slap **2** : fight with the fists —**box·er** *n* —**box·ing** *n*

box·car *n* : roofed freight car

box office *n* : theater ticket office

boy \'bói\ *n* : male child —**boy·hood** *n* —**boy·ish** *adj* —**boy·ish·ly** *adv* —**boy·ish·ness** *n*

boy·cott \-,kät\ *vb* : refrain from dealing with —**boycott** *n*

brace \'brās\ *n* **1** : crank for turning a bit **2** : something that resists weight or supports ~ *vb* **braced; brac·ing 1** : make taut or steady **2** : invigorate **3** : strengthen

brace·let \'brāslət\ *n* : ornamental band for the wrist or arm

brack·et \'brakət\ *n* **1** : projecting support **2** : punctuation mark [or] **3** : class ~ *vb* **1** : furnish or fasten with brackets **2** : place within brackets **3** : group

brack·ish \-ish\ *adj* : salty

brad \'brad\ *n* : nail with a small head

brag \'brag\ *vb* **-gg-** : boast —**brag** *n*

brag·gart \'bragərt\ *n* : boaster

braid \'brād\ *vb* : interweave ~ *n* : something braided

braille \'brāl\ *n* : system of writing for the blind using raised dots

brain \'brān\ *n* **1** : organ of thought and nervous coordination enclosed in the skull **2** : intelligence ~ *vb* : smash the skull of —**brained** *adj* —**brain·less** *adj* —**brainy** *adj*

braise \'brāz\ *vb* **braised; brais·ing** : cook (meat) slowly in a covered dish

brake \'brāk\ *n* : device for slowing up ~ *vb* **braked; brak·ing** : slow or stop by a brake

bram·ble \'brambəl\ *n* : prickly shrub

bran \'bran\ *n* : broken grain husks

branch \'branch\ *n* **1** : division of a plant stem **2** : part ~ *vb* **1** : develop branches **2** : diverge —**branched** *adj*

brand \'brand\ *n* **1** : identifying mark made by burning **2** : stigma **3** : distinctive kind (as of goods from one firm) ~ *vb* : mark with a brand

bran·dish \'brandish\ *vb* : wave

brand-new *adj* : unused

bran·dy \'brandē\ *n, pl* **-dies** : liquor distilled from wine

brash \'brash\ *adj* **1** : impulsive **2** : aggressively self-assertive

brass \'bras\ *n* 1 : alloy of copper and zinc 2 : brazen self-assurance — **brassy** *adj*

bras·siere \brə'ziər\ *n* : woman's undergarment to support the breasts

brat \'brat\ *n* : ill-behaved child — **brat·ty** *adj*

bra·va·do \brə'vädō\ *n, pl* **-does** *or* **-dos** : false bravery

¹brave \'brāv\ *adj* **brav·er; brav·est** : showing courage ~ *vb* **braved; brav·ing** : face with courage — **brave·ly** *adv* — **brav·ery** \-(ə)rē\ *n*

²brave *n* : Indian warrior

bra·vo \'brävō\ *n, pl* **-vos** : shout of approval

brawl \'brȯl\ *n* : noisy quarrel or violent fight — **brawl** *vb* — **brawl·er** *n*

brawn \'brȯn\ *n* : muscular strength — **brawny** *adj*

bray \'brā\ *n* : harsh cry of a donkey — **bray** *vb*

bra·zen \'brāz²n\ *adj* 1 : made of brass 2 : bold — **bra·zen·ly** *adv* — **bra·zen·ness** \-(n)əs\ *n*

bra·zier \'brāzhər\ *n* : charcoal grill

breach \'brēch\ *n* 1 : breaking of a law, obligation, or standard 2 : gap ~ *vb* : make a breach in

bread \'bred\ *n* : baked food made of flour ~ *vb* : cover with bread crumbs

breadth \'bredth\ *n* : width

bread·win·ner *n* : wage earner

break \'brāk\ *vb* **broke** \'brōk\; **bro·ken** \'brōkən\; **break·ing** 1 : knock into pieces 2 : transgress 3 : force a way into or out of 4 : exceed 5 : interrupt 6 : fail ~ *n* 1 : act or result of breaking 2 : stroke of good luck — **break·able** *adj or n* — **break·age** \'brākij\ *n* — **break·er** *n* — **break in** *vb* 1 : enter by force 2 : interrupt 3 : train — **break out** *vb* 1 : erupt with force 2 : develop a rash

break·down *n* : physical or mental failure — **break down** *vb*

break·fast \'brekfəst\ *n* : first meal of the day — **breakfast** *vb*

breast \'brest\ *n* 1 : milk-producing gland esp. of a woman 2 : front part of the chest

breast·bone *n* : sternum

breath \'breth\ *n* 1 : slight breeze 2 : air breathed in or out — **breath·less** *adj* — **breath·less·ly** *adv*

breathe \'brēth\ *vb* **breathed; breath·ing** 1 : draw air into the lungs and expel it 2 : live 3 : utter

breath·tak·ing *adj* : exciting

breech·es \'brichəz\ *n pl* : trousers ending near the knee

breed \'brēd\ *vb* **bred** \'bred\; **breed·**

ing 1 : give birth to 2 : propagate 3 : raise ~ *n* 1 : kind of plant or animal usu. developed by man 2 : class — **breed·er** *n*

breeze \'brēz\ *n* : light wind ~ *vb* **breezed; breez·ing** : move fast — **breezy** *adj*

breth·ren \'breth(ə)rən, -ərn\ *pl of* BROTHER

bre·via·ry \'brēv(ə)ərē, -vē,erē\ *n, pl* **-ries** : prayer book used by Roman Catholic priests

brev·i·ty \'brevətē\ *n, pl* **-ties** : shortness or conciseness

brew \'brü\ *vb* : make by fermenting or infusing — **brew** *n* — **brew·er** *n* — **brew·ery** \'brüərē, 'brü(ə)rē\ *n*

bribe \'brīb\ *vb* **bribed; brib·ing** : corrupt or influence by gifts ~ *n* : something offered or given in bribing — **brib·ery** \-(ə)rē\ *n*

bric-a-brac \'brikə,brak\ *n pl* : small ornamental articles

brick \'brik\ *n* : building block of baked clay — **brick** *vb* — **brick·layer** *n* — **brick·lay·ing** *n*

bride \'brīd\ *n* : woman just married or about to be married — **brid·al** \-²l\ *adj*

bride·groom *n* : man just married or about to be married

brides·maid *n* : woman who attends a bride at her wedding

¹bridge \'brij\ *n* 1 : structure built for passage over a depression or obstacle 2 : upper part of the nose 3 : platform over the deck of a ship 4 : artificial replacement for missing teeth ~ *vb* : build a bridge over — **bridge·able** *adj*

²bridge *n* : card game for 4 players

bri·dle \'brīd²l\ *n* : headgear to control a horse ~ *vb* **-dled; -dling** 1 : put a bridle on 2 : restrain 3 : show hostility or scorn

brief \'brēf\ *adj* : short or concise ~ *n* : concise summary (as of a legal case) ~ *vb* : give final instructions or essential information to — **brief·ly** *adv* — **brief·ness** *n*

brief·case *n* : case for papers

¹bri·er, bri·ar \'brī(ə)r\ *n* : thorny plant

²brier, briar *n* : heath of southern Europe

¹brig \'brig\ *n* : 2-masted ship

²brig *n* : jail on a naval ship

bri·gade \brig'ād\ *n* 1 : a large military unit 2 : a group organized for a special activity

brig·a·dier general \,brigə,diər-\ *n*

: officer ranking next below a major general

brig·and \'brigənd\ n : bandit —**brig·and·age** \-ij\ n

bright \'brīt\ adj 1 : radiating or reflecting light 2 : cheerful 3 : intelligent —**bright·en** \-ᵊn\ vb —**bright·en·er** \'brītnər, -ᵊnər\ n —**bright·ly** adv —**bright·ness** n

bril·liant \'brilyənt\ adj 1 : very bright 2 : splendid 3 : very intelligent —**bril·liance** \-yəns\, **bril·lian·cy** \-yənsē\ n —**bril·liant·ly** adv

brim \'brim\ n : edge or rim —**brim·less** adj —**brimmed** adj

brim·ful \-'fül\ adj : full to the brim

brim·stone \'brim-\ n : sulfur

brin·dled \'brind²ld\ adj : gray or tawny with dark streaks or flecks

brine \'brīn\ n 1 : salt water 2 : ocean —**brin·i·ness** n —**briny** adj

bring \'briŋ\ vb **brought** \'brȯt\; **bring·ing** 1 : cause to come with one 2 : persuade 3 : produce 4 : sell for —**bring·er** n —**bring about** vb : make happen —**bring up** vb 1 : care for and educate 2 : cause to be noticed 3 : vomit

brink \'briŋk\ n : edge

bri·quette, bri·quet \brik'et\ n : pressed mass (as of charcoal)

brisk \'brisk\ adj 1 : lively 2 : invigorating —**brisk·ly** adv —**brisk·ness** n

bris·ket \'briskət\ n : breast or lower chest of a quadruped

bris·tle \'brisəl\ n : short stiff hair ~ vb -**tled; -tling** 1 : stand erect 2 : show angry defiance 3 : appear as if covered with bristles —**bris·tly** adj

brit·tle \'brit²l\ adj -**tler; -tlest** : easily broken or snapped

broach \'brōch\ n : pointed tool (as for opening casks) ~ vb 1 : pierce (as a cask) to open 2 : introduce for discussion

broad \'brȯd\ adj 1 : wide 2 : spacious 3 : clear or open 4 : obvious 5 : liberal in outlook 6 : widely applicable 7 : dealing with essential points —**broad·en** \-ᵊn\ vb —**broad·ly** adv —**broad·ness** n

broad·cast n 1 : transmission by radio waves 2 : radio or television program ~ vb -**cast; -cast·ing** 1 : scatter or sow in all directions 2 : make widely known 3 : send out on a broadcast —**broad·cast·er** n

broad·cloth n : fine cloth

broad·loom adj : woven on a wide loom esp. in solid color

broad–mind·ed adj : free from prejudice —**broad–mind·ed·ly** adv —**broad–mind·ed·ness** n

broad·side n 1 : simultaneous firing of all guns on one side of a ship 2 : verbal attack

bro·cade \brō'kād\ n : usu. silk fabric with a raised design

broc·co·li \'bräk(ə)lē\ n : green vegetable akin to cauliflower

bro·chure \brō'shùr\ n : pamphlet

brogue \'brōg\ n : Irish accent

broil \'brȯil\ vb : cook by radiant heat —**broil** n

broil·er n 1 : utensil for broiling 2 : chicken fit for broiling

¹**broke** \'brōk\ past of BREAK

²**broke** adj : out of money

bro·ken \'brōkən\ adj : imperfectly spoken —**bro·ken·ly** adv

bro·ken–heart·ed \-'härtəd\ adj : woeful

bro·ker \'brōkər\ n : agent who buys and sells for a fee —**bro·ker·age** \-k(ə)rij\ n

bro·mide \-,mīd\ n 1 : compound of bromine 2 : trite remark or notion —**bro·mid·ic** \brō'midik\ adj

bro·mine \-,mēn\ n : deep red liquid corrosive chemical element

bron·chi·tis \brän'kītəs, bräŋ-\ n : inflammation of the bronchi

bron·chus \'bräŋkəs\ n, pl **-chi** \-,kī, -,kē\ : division of the windpipe leading to a lung —**bron·chi·al** \-kēəl\ adj

bron·co \'bräŋkō\ n, pl **-cos** : small half-wild horse

bronze \'bränz\ vb **bronzed; bronz·ing** : make bronze in color ~ n 1 : alloy of copper and tin 2 : yellowish brown —**bronzy** \-ē\ adj

brooch \'brōch, 'brüch\ n : ornamental clasp or pin

brood \'brüd\ n : family of young ~ vb 1 : sit on eggs to hatch them 2 : ponder ~ adj : kept for breeding —**brood·er** n

¹**brook** \'brùk\ vb : tolerate

²**brook** n : small stream

broom \'brüm, 'brùm\ n 1 : flowering shrub 2 : implement for sweeping —**broom·stick** n

broth \'brȯth\ n, pl **broths** \'brȯths, 'brȯthz\ : liquid in which meat has been cooked

broth·el \'bräthəl, 'brȯth-\ n : house of prostitutes

broth·er \'brəthər\ n, pl **brothers** also **breth·ren** \'breth(ə)rən, 'brethərn\ 1 : male sharing one or both parents with another person 2 : kindred hu-

man being —**broth·er·hood** n —
broth·er·li·ness n —**broth·er·ly** adj

broth·er-in-law n, pl **brothers-in-law**
: brother of one's spouse or husband
of one's sister or of one's spouse's
sister

brought past of BRING

brow \'braù\ n 1 : eyebrow 2 : forehead 3 : edge of a steep place

brow·beat vb -beat; -beat·en or -beat;
-beat·ing : intimidate

brown \'braùn\ adj 1 : of the color
brown 2 : of dark or tanned complexion ~ n : a color like that of
coffee ~ vb : make or become brown

browse \'braùz\ vb browsed; brows-
ing 1 : graze 2 : look over casually
—**brows·er** n

bru·in \'brüən\ n : bear

bruise \'brüz\ vb bruised; bruis·ing 1
: make a bruise on 2 : become
bruised ~ n : surface injury to flesh

brunch \'brənch\ n : late breakfast,
early lunch, or combination of both

bru·net, bru·nette \brü'net\ adj : having dark skin, hair, and eyes —**bru-
net, brunette** n

brunt \'brənt\ n : main impact

¹brush \'brəsh\ n 1 : small cut
branches 2 : coarse shrubby vegetation

²brush n 1 : bristles set in a handle
used esp. for cleaning or painting 2
: light touch ~ vb 1 : apply a brush
to 2 : remove with or as if with a
brush 3 : dispose of in an offhand
way 4 : touch lightly —**brush up** vb
: renew one's skill

³brush n : skirmish

brush-off n : abrupt dismissal

brusque \'brəsk\ adj : curt or blunt in
manner —**brusque·ly** adv

bru·tal \'brüt³l\ adj : like a brute and
esp. cruel —**bru·tal·i·ty** \brü'talətē\
n —**bru·tal·ize** \'brüt³l,īz\ vb —**bru-
tal·ly** \-³lē\ adv

brute \'brüt\ adj 1 : of or typical of
beasts 2 : unreasoning 3 : purely
physical ~ n 1 : beast 2 : brutal person —**brut·ish** \-ish\ adj

bub·ble \'bəbəl\ vb -bled; -bling 1
: form, rise in, or give off bubbles ~
n : globule of gas in or covered with
a liquid —**bub·bly** \-(ə)lē\ adj

bu·bo \'b(y)übō\ n, pl **buboes** : inflammatory swelling of a lymph gland —
bu·bon·ic \b(y)ü'bänik\ adj

buc·ca·neer \,bəkə'niər\ n : pirate

buck \'bək\ n, pl **buck** or **bucks** 1
: male animal (as a deer) 2 : dollar ~
vb 1 : jerk forward 2 : oppose

buck·et \'bəkət\ n : pail —**buck·et·ful** n

buck·le \-əl\ n 1 : clasp (as on a belt)
for two loose ends 2 : bend or fold
~ vb -led; -ling 1 : fasten with a buckle 2 : apply oneself 3 : bend or crum-
ple

buck·ler \-lər\ n : shield

buck·shot n : coarse lead shot

buck·skin n : soft leather (as from the
skin of a buck) —**buckskin** adj

buck·tooth n : large projecting front
tooth —**buck-toothed** adj

buck·wheat n : herb whose seeds are
used as a cereal grain or the seeds
themselves

bu·col·ic \byü'kälik\ adj : rural

bud \'bəd\ n 1 : undeveloped plant
shoot 2 : partly opened flower ~ vb
-dd- 1 : form or put forth buds 2 : be
or develop like a bud

Bud·dhism \'bü,dizəm, 'büd,iz-\ n
: religion of eastern and central Asia
—**Bud·dhist** \'büdəst, 'büd-\ n or
adj

bud·dy \'bədē\ n, pl -dies : friend

budge \'bəj\ vb budged; budg·ing
: move from a place

bud·get \'bəjət\ n 1 : estimate of income and expenses 2 : plan for coordinating income and expenses —
budget vb or adj —**bud·get·ary**
\-ə,terē\ adj

buff \'bəf\ n 1 : dull yellow-orange
color 2 : enthusiast ~ adj : of the
color buff ~ vb : polish

buf·fa·lo \'bəfə,lō\ n, pl -**lo** or -**loes**
: wild ox (as a bison)

¹buff·er \'bəfər\ n : one that buffs

²buffer n : something that lessens
shock

¹buf·fet \-ət\ n : blow or slap ~ vb
: hit esp. repeatedly

²buf·fet \(,)bə'fā, bü-\ n 1 : sideboard
2 : meal at which people serve themselves

buf·foon \(,)bə'fün\ n : clown —**buf-
foon·ery** \-(ə)rē\ n

bug \'bəg\ n 1 : small usu. obnoxious
crawling creature 2 : 4-winged sucking insect 3 : unexpected imperfection 4 : disease-producing germ 5
: hidden microphone ~ vb -gg- 1
: pester 2 : conceal a microphone in

bug·a·boo \'bəgə,bü\ n, pl -boos : bogey

bug·bear n : source of dread

bug·gy \'bəgē\ n, pl -gies : light carriage

bu·gle \'byügəl\ n : trumpetlike brass
instrument —**bu·gler** \-glər\ n

build \'bild\ vb **built** \'bilt\; **build·ing**

1 : put together 2 : establish 3 : increase ~ n : physique —**build·er** n

build·ing \'bildiŋ\ n 1 : roofed and walled structure 2 : art or business of constructing buildings

bulb \'bəlb\ n 1 : large underground plant bud 2 : rounded or pear-shaped object —**bul·bous** \-əs\ adj

bulge \'bəlj\ n : swelling projecting part ~ vb bulged; bulg·ing : swell out

bulk \'bəlk\ n 1 : magnitude 2 : indigestible fibrous food residues 3 : large mass 4 : major portion ~ vb : have bulk —**bulky** \-ē\ adj

bulk·head n : ship's partition

[1]**bull** \'bul\ n 1 : adult male of a bovine or other large animal ~ adj : male

[2]**bull** n : papal letter

bull·dog n : compact short-haired dog

bull·doze \-,dōz\ vb 1 : move or level with a tractor (**bull·doz·er**) having a broad blade 2 : force

bul·let \'bulət\ n : missile to be shot from a gun —**bul·let-proof** adj

bul·le·tin \-ᵊn\ n 1 : brief public report 2 : periodical

bull·fight n : sport of taunting and killing bulls —**bull·fight·er** n

bull·frog n : large deep-voiced frog

bull·head·ed adj : stupidly stubborn

bul·lion \'bulyən\ n : gold or silver esp. in bars

bull·ock \-ək\ n 1 : young bull 2 : steer

bull's-eye n, pl bull's-eyes : center of a target

bul·ly \'bulē\ n, pl -lies : one who hurts or intimidates others ~ vb -lied; -ly·ing : act like a bully toward

bul·rush \'bul,rəsh\ n : tall coarse rush or sedge

bul·wark \-(,)wərk, -,wórk; 'bəl-(,)wərk\ n 1 : wall-like defense 2 : strong support or protection

bum \'bəm\ vb -mm- 1 : wander as a tramp 2 : seek by begging ~ n : idle worthless person ~ adj : worthless

bum·ble·bee \'bəmbəl,bē\ n : large hairy bee

bump \'bəmp\ vb : strike or knock forcibly ~ n 1 : sudden blow 2 : small bulge or swelling —**bumpy** adj

[1]**bum·per** \'bəmpər\ adj : unusually large

[2]**bump·er** \'bəmpər\ n : shock-absorbing bar at either end of a car

bump·kin \'bəmpkən\ n : awkward country person

bun \'bən\ n : sweet biscuit or roll

bunch \'bənch\ n : group ~ vb : form into a group —**bunchy** adj

bun·dle \'bəndᵊl\ n 1 : several items

bunched together 2 : something wrapped for carrying 3 : large amount ~ vb -dled; -dling : gather into a bundle

bun·ga·low \'bəngə,lō\ n : one-story house

bun·gle \'bəngəl\ vb -gled; -gling : do badly —**bungle** n —**bun·gler** n

bun·ion \'bənyən\ n : inflamed swelling of the first joint of the big toe

[1]**bunk** \'bəŋk\ n : built-in bed that is often one of a tier ~ vb : sleep

[2]**bunk** n : nonsense

bun·ker \-ər\ n 1 : storage compartment 2 : protective embankment

bun·kum, bun·combe \'bəŋkəm\ n : nonsense

bun·ny \'bənē\ n, pl -nies : rabbit

[1]**bun·ting** \'bəntiŋ\ n : small finch

[2]**bunting** n : flag material

buoy \'būē, 'bói\ n : floating marker anchored in water ~ vb 1 : keep afloat 2 : raise the spirits of —**buoy·an·cy** \'bóiənsē, 'būyən-\ n —**buoy·ant** \-ənt, -yənt\ adj

bur, burr \'bər\ n : rough or prickly covering of a fruit —**bur·ry** adj

bur·den \'bərdᵊn\ n 1 : something carried 2 : something oppressive 3 : cargo ~ vb : load or oppress —**bur·den·some** \-səm\ adj

bur·dock \'bər,däk\ n : tall coarse herb with prickly flower heads

bu·reau \'byúrō\ n 1 : chest of drawers 2 : administrative unit 3 : business office

bu·reau·cra·cy \byú'räkrəsē\ n, pl -cies 1 : body of government officials 2 : unwieldy administrative system —**bu·reau·crat** \'byúrə,krat\ n —**bu·reau·crat·ic** \,byúrə'kratik\ adj

bur·geon \'bərjən\ vb : grow

bur·glary \'bərglərē\ n, pl -glar·ies : forcible entry into a building to steal —**bur·glar** \-glər\ n —**bur·glar·ize** \'bərglə,rīz\ vb

bur·gle \'bərgəl\ vb -gled; -gling : commit burglary on or in

Bur·gun·dy \'bəndē\ n, pl -dies : kind of table wine

bur·i·al \'berēəl\ n : act of burying

bur·lap \'bər,lap\ n : coarse fabric usu. of jute or hemp

bur·lesque \(,)bər'lesk\ n 1 : witty or derisive imitation 2 : broadly humorous variety show ~ vb -lesqued; -lesqu·ing : mock

bur·ly \'bərlē\ adj -li·er; -est : strongly and heavily built

burn \'bərn\ vb burned \'bərnd, 'bərnt\ or burnt \'bərnt\; burn·ing 1 : be on fire 2 : feel or look as if on fire 3 : alter or become altered by or as if by fire or heat 4 : cause or make by fire ~ *n* : injury or effect produced by burning —**burn·er** *n*

burp \'bərp\ *n or vb* : belch

bur·ro \'bərō, 'bür-\ *n, pl -os* : small donkey

bur·row \'bərō\ *n* : hole in the ground made by an animal ~ *vb* : make a burrow —**bur·row·er** *n*

bur·sar \'bərsər\ *n* : treasurer esp. of a college

bur·si·tis \(,)bər'sītəs\ *n* : inflammation of a sac (**bur·sa** \'bərsə\) in a joint

burst \'bərst\ *vb* **burst** *or* **burst·ed; burst·ing** 1 : fly apart or into pieces 2 : enter or emerge suddenly ~ *n* : sudden outbreak or effort

bury \'berē\ *vb* **bur·ied; bury·ing** 1 : deposit in the earth 2 : hide

bus \'bəs\ *n, pl* **bus·es** *or* **bus·ses** : large motor-driven passenger vehicle ~ *vb* **bused** *or* **bussed; bus·ing** *or* **bus·sing** : travel or transport by bus

bus·boy *n* : waiter's helper

bush \'bush\ *n* 1 : shrub 2 : rough uncleared country 3 : a thick tuft or mat —**bushy** *adj*

bush·el \'bushəl\ *n* : 4 pecks

bush·ing \'bushiŋ\ *n* : metal lining used as a guide or bearing

busi·ness \'biznəs, -nəz\ *n* 1 : vocation 2 : commercial or industrial enterprise 3 : personal concerns —**busi·ness·man** \-,man\ *n* —**busi·ness·wom·an** \-,wümən\ *n*

¹**bust** \'bəst\ *n* 1 : sculpture of the head and upper torso 2 : breasts of a woman

²**bust** *vb* 1 : burst or break 2 : tame ~ *n* : punch 2 : failure

¹**bus·tle** \'bəsəl\ *vb* **-tled; -tling** : move or work briskly ~ *n* : energetic activity

²**bustle** *n* : pad or frame formerly worn under a woman's skirt

busy \'bizē\ *adj* **busi·er; -est** 1 : engaged in action 2 : being in use 3 : full of activity ~ *vb* **bus·ied; busy·ing** : make or keep busy —**busi·ly** *adv*

busy·body *n* : meddler

but \(')bət\ *conj* 1 : if not for the fact 2 : that 3 : without the accompanying condition 4 : rather 5 : yet nevertheless ~ *prep* : other than

butch·er \'buchər\ *n* 1 : one who slaughters animals or dresses their flesh 2 : brutal killer —**butcher** *vb* —**butch·ery** \-(ə)rē\ *n*

but·ler \'bətlər\ *n* : chief male household servant

¹**butt** \'bət\ *vb* : strike with a butt ~ *n* : blow with the head or horns

²**butt** *n* 1 : target 2 : victim

³**butt** *vb* : join edge to edge

⁴**butt** *n* : large end or bottom

⁵**butt** *n* : large cask

butte \'byüt\ *n* : isolated steep hill

but·ter \'bətər\ *n* : solid edible fat churned from cream ~ *vb* : spread with butter —**but·tery** *adj*

but·ter·cup *n* : yellow-flowered herb

but·ter·fat *n* : natural fat of milk and of butter

but·ter·fly *n* : insect with 4 broad wings

but·ter·milk *n* : liquid remaining after butter is churned

but·ter·nut *n* : edible nut of a tree related to the walnut or this tree

but·ter·scotch \-,skäch\ *n* : candy made from sugar, corn syrup, and water

but·tocks \'bətəks\ *n pl* : rear part of the hips

but·ton \'bətⁿn\ *n* 1 : small knob for fastening clothing 2 : buttonlike object ~ *vb* : fasten with buttons

but·ton·hole *n* : hole or slit for a button ~ *vb* : hold in talk

but·tress \'bətrəs\ *n* 1 : projecting structure to support a wall 2 : support —**buttress** *vb*

bux·om \'bəksəm\ *adj* : full-bosomed

buy \'bī\ *vb* **bought** \'bȯt\; **buy·ing** : purchase ~ *n* : bargain —**buy·er** *n*

buzz \'bəz\ *vb* : make a low humming sound ~ *n* : act or sound of buzzing

buz·zard \-ərd\ *n* : large bird of prey

buzz·er *n* : signaling device that buzzes

by \(')bī, bə\ *prep* 1 : near 2 : through 3 : beyond 4 : throughout 5 : no later than ~ \'bī\ *adv* 1 : near 2 : farther on

by·gone \'bī,gȯn\ *adj* : past —**bygone** *n*

by·law, bye·law *n* : organization's rule

by·line *n* : writer's name on an article

by·pass *n* : alternate route ~ *vb* : go around

by·prod·uct *n* : product in addition to the main product

by·stand·er *n* : spectator

by·way \'bī,wā\ *n* : side road

by·word *n* : proverb

C

c \'sē\ *n, pl* c's *or* cs \'sēz\ : 3d letter of the alphabet

cab \'kab\ *n* 1 : light closed horse-drawn carriage 2 : taxicab 3 : compartment for a driver —cab·bie, cabby *n* —cab·stand *n*

ca·bal \kə'bal\ *n* : group of conspirators —vb -ll- : plot

ca·bana \kə'ban(ə)ə\ *n* : shelter at a beach or pool

cab·a·ret \,kabə'rā\ *n* : nightclub

cab·bage \'kabij\ *n* : vegetable with a dense head of leaves

cab·in \-ish\ *n* 1 : private room on a ship 2 : small house 3 : airplane compartment

cab·i·net \-(ə)nət\ *n* 1 : display case or cupboard 2 : advisory council of a head of state —cab·i·net·mak·er *n* —cab·i·net·mak·ing *n* —cab·i·net·work *n*

ca·ble \'kābəl\ *n* 1 : strong rope, wire, or chain 2 : cablegram 3 : bundle of electrical wires ~ *vb* -bled; -bling : send a cablegram to

ca·ble·gram \-,gram\ *n* : message sent by a submarine telegraph cable

ca·boose \kə'büs\ *n* : crew car on a train

ca·cao \kə'kaù, -'kāō\ *n, pl* cacaos : So. American tree whose seeds (ca·cao beans) yield cocoa and chocolate

cache \'kash\ *n* 1 : hiding place 2 : something hidden ~ *vb* cached; cach·ing : place in a cache

cack·le \'kakəl\ *vb* -led; -ling : make a cry or laugh like the sound of a hen —cackle *n* —cack·ler *n*

ca·coph·o·ny \ka'käfənē\ *n, pl* -nies : harsh noise —ca·coph·o·nous \-nəs\ *adj*

cac·tus \'kaktəs\ *n, pl* cac·ti \-,tī\ *or* -tus·es : drought-resistant flowering plant with scales or prickles

cad \'kad\ *n* : ungentlemanly person —cad·dish \-ish\ *adj* —cad·dish·ly *adv* —cad·dish·ness *n*

ca·dav·er \kə'davər\ *n* : dead body —ca·dav·er·ous \-(ə)rəs\ *adj*

cad·die, cad·dy \'kadē\ *n, pl* -dies : golfer's helper —caddie, caddy *vb*

cad·dy \'kadē\ *n, pl* -dies : small tea chest

ca·dence \'kād²ⁿs\ *n* : measure of a rhythmical flow —ca·denced \-²ⁿst\ *adj*

ca·det \kə'det\ *n* : student in a military academy

cadge \'kaj\ *vb* cadged; cadg·ing : beg —cadg·er *n*

cad·mi·um \'kadmēəm\ *n* : grayish metallic chemical element

ca·dre \-rē\ *n* : nucleus of highly trained people

ca·fé \ka'fā, kə-\ *n* : restaurant

cafe·e·te·ria \,kafə'tirēə\ *n* : self-service restaurant

caf·fein \ka'fēn, 'ka,fēn\ *n* : stimulating alkaloid in coffee and tea

cage \'kāj\ *n* : box of wire or bars for confining an animal ~ *vb* caged; cag·ing : put or keep in a cage

ca·gey \-ē\ *adj* -gi·er; -est : shrewd —ca·gi·ly *adv* —ca·gi·ness *n*

cais·son \'kā,sän, 'käs²n\ *n* 1 : ammunition carriage 2 : watertight chamber for underwater construction

ca·jole \kə'jōl\ *vb* -joled; -jol·ing : persuade or coax —ca·jol·ery \-(ə)rē\ *n*

cake \'kāk\ *n* 1 : food of baked or fried usu. sweet batter 2 : solid mass ~ *vb* caked; cak·ing 1 : form into a cake 2 : encrust

cal·a·bash \'kalə,bash\ *n* : gourd

cal·a·mine \'kalə,mīn\ *n* : lotion of oxides of zinc and iron

ca·lam·i·ty \kə'lamətē\ *n, pl* -ties : disaster —ca·lam·i·tous \-ətəs\ *adj* —ca·lam·i·tous·ly *adv* —ca·lam·i·tous·ness *n*

cal·ci·fy \'kalsə,fī\ *vb* -fied; -fy·ing : harden —cal·ci·fi·ca·tion \,kalsəfə-'kāshən\ *n*

cal·ci·um \'kalsēəm\ *n* : silver-white soft metallic chemical element

cal·cu·late \'kalkyə,lāt\ *vb* -lat·ed; -lat·ing 1 : determine by mathematical processes 2 : judge —cal·cu·la·ble \-ləbəl\ *adj* —cal·cu·la·tion \,kalkyə'lāshən\ *n* —cal·cu·la·tor \'kalkyə,lātər\ *n*

cal·cu·lat·ing *adj* : shrewd

cal·cu·lus \'kalkyələs\ *n, pl* -li \-,lī\ : higher mathematics dealing with rates of change

cal·dron \'kóldrən\ *n* : large kettle

cal·en·dar \'kaləndər\ *n* : list of days, weeks, and months

¹calf \'kaf, 'kàf\ *n, pl* calves \'kavz, 'kàvz\ : young cow or related mammal —calf·skin *n*

²calf *n, pl* calves : back part of the leg below the knee

cal·i·ber, cal·i·bre \'kaləbər\ *n* 1 : diameter of a bullet or shell or of a gun bore **2** : degree of mental or moral excellence

cal·i·brate \-,brāt\ *vb* **-brat·ed; -brat·ing** : determine, correct, or put measuring marks on —**cal·i·bra·tion** \,kalə'brāshən\ *n*

cal·i·co \'kali,kō\ *n, pl* **-coes** *or* **-cos** : printed cotton fabric —**calico** *adj*

cal·i·pers, cal·li·pers \'kaləpərz\ *n* : measuring instrument with two adjustable legs

ca·liph, ca·lif \'kāləf, 'kal-\ *n* : title of head of Islam —**ca·liph·ate** \-,āt, -ət\ *n*

cal·is·then·ics \,kaləs'theniks\ *n sing or pl* : bending, stretching, and jumping exercises —**cal·is·then·ic** *adj*

calk \'kók\ *var of* CAULK

call \'kól\ *vb* **1** : shout **2** : summon **3** : demand **4** : telephone **5** : make a visit **6** : name —**call** *n* —**call·er** *n* — **call down** *vb* : reprimand —**call off** *vb* : cancel

call·ing *n* : vocation

cal·li·ope \kə'līə(,)pē, 'kalē,ōp\ *n* : musical instrument of steam whistles

cal·lous \'kaləs\ *adj* **1** : thickened and hardened **2** : unfeeling ~ *vb* : make callous —**cal·los·i·ty** \ka'läsətē\ *n* —**cal·lous·ly** *adv* —**cal·lous·ness** *n*

cal·low \'kalō\ *adj* : inexperienced or innocent —**cal·low·ness** *n*

cal·lus \'kaləs\ *n* : callous area on skin or bark ~ *vb* : form a callus

calm \'käm, 'kälm\ *n* **1** : period or condition of peacefulness or stillness ~ *adj* : still or tranquil ~ *vb* : make calm —**calm·ly** *adv* —**calm·ness** *n*

ca·lor·ic \kə'lórik\ *adj* : relating to heat or calories

cal·o·rie \'kal(ə)rē\ *n* : unit for measuring heat and energy value of food

ca·lum·ni·ate \kə'ləmnē,āt\ *vb* **-at·ed; -at·ing** : slander —**ca·lum·ni·a·tion** \-,ləmnē'āshən\ *n*

cal·um·ny \'kaləmnē\ *n, pl* **-nies** : false and malicious charge —**ca·lum·ni·ous** \kə'ləmnēəs\ *adj*

calve \'kav, 'käv\ *vb* **calved; calv·ing** : give birth to a calf

calves *pl of* CALF

ca·lyp·so \kə'lipsō\ *n, pl* **-sos** : West Indian style of music

ca·lyx \'kāliks, 'kal-\ *n, pl* **-lyx·es** *or* **-ly·ces** \-lə,sēz\ : sepals of a flower

cam \'kam\ *n* : bump (as on a shaft) for pushing another part

ca·ma·ra·de·rie \,käm(ə)'rädərē, ,kam-, -'rad-\ *n* : fellowship

cam·bric \'kāmbrik\ *n* : fine thin linen or cotton fabric

came *past of* COME

cam·el \'kaməl\ *n* : large hoofed mammal of desert areas

ca·mel·lia \kə'mēlyə\ *n* : shrub or tree grown for its showy roselike flowers or the flower itself

cam·eo \'kamē,ō\ *n, pl* **-eos** : gem carved in relief

cam·era \'kam(ə)rə\ *n* : box with a lens for taking pictures —**cam·era·man** \-,man, -mən\ *n*

cam·ou·flage \'kamə,fläzh, -,fläj\ *vb* : hide by disguising —**camouflage** *n*

camp \'kamp\ *n* **1** : place to stay temporarily esp. in a tent **2** : group living in a camp ~ *vb* : make or live in a camp —**camp·er** *n* —**camp·ground** *n* —**camp·site** *n*

cam·paign \kam'pān\ *n* : series of military operations or of activities meant to gain a result —**campaign** *vb* —**cam·paign·er** *n*

cam·pa·ni·le \,kampə'nēlē, -'nē(ə)l\ *n, pl* **-ni·les** *or* **-ni·li** \-'nēlē\ : bell tower

cam·phor \'kam(p)fər\ *n* : gummy volatile fragrant compound from an evergreen tree (**cam·phor tree**)

cam·pus \'kampəs\ *n* : grounds and buildings of a college or school

¹**can** \kən, (')kan\ *vb, past* **could** \kəd, (')kùd\; *pres sing & pl* **can 1** : be able to **2** : be permitted to by conscience or feeling **3** : have permission or liberty to

²**can** \'kan\ *n* : metal container ~ *vb* **-nn-** : preserve by sealing in airtight cans or jars —**can·ner** *n* —**can·nery** \-(ə)rē\ *n*

ca·nal \kə'nal\ *n* **1** : tubular passage in the body **2** : channel filled with water

can·a·pé \'kanəpē, -,pā\ *n* : appetizer

ca·nard \kə'närd\ *n* : false report

ca·nary \-'nerē\ *n, pl* **-nar·ies** : yellow or greenish finch

can·cel \'kansəl\ *vb* **-celed** *or* **-celled; -cel·ing** *or* **-cel·ling 1** : cross out **2** : destroy, neutralize, or match the force or effect of —**cancel** *n* —**can·cel·la·tion** \,kansə'lāshən\ *n* —**can·cel·er, can·cel·ler** *n*

can·cer \'kansər\ *n* **1** : malignant tumor that tends to spread **2** : slowly destructive evil —**can·cer·ous** \-(ə)rəs\ *adj* —**can·cer·ous·ly** *adv*

can·de·la·bra \,kandə'läbrə, -'lab-\ *n* : candelabrum

can·de·la·brum \-rəm\ *n, pl* **-bra** \-rə\ : ornamental branched candlestick

can·did \'kandəd\ *adj* **1** : frank **2** : unposed **—can·did·ly** adv **—can·did·ness** n

can·di·date \'kan(d)ə̩dāt, -(d)ədət\ n : one who seeks an office or membership **—can·di·da·cy** \-(d)ədəsē\ n

can·dle \'kand⁰l\ n : tallow or wax molded around a wick and burned to give light **—can·dle·light** n **—can·dle·stick** n

can·dor \'kandər\ n : frankness

can·dy \-dē\ n, pl **-dies** : food made from sugar ~ vb **-died; -dy·ing** : encrust in sugar

cane \'kān\ n 1 : slender plant stem 2 : a tall woody grass or reed 3 : stick for walking or beating ~ vb **caned; can·ing** 1 : beat with a cane 2 : weave or make with cane **—can·er** n

ca·nine \'kā̩nīn\ adj 1 : relating to dogs 2 : being the pointed tooth next to the incisors ~ n 1 : canine tooth 2 : dog

can·is·ter \'kanəstər\ n : small storage box

can·ker \'kaŋkər\ n : mouth ulcer **—can·ker·ous** \-k(ə)rəs\ adj

can·na·bis \'kanəbəs\ n : preparation derived from hemp

can·ni·bal \'kanəbəl\ n : human or animal that eats its own kind **—can·ni·bal·ism** \-bə̩lizəm\ n **—can·ni·bal·is·tic** \̩kanəbə'listik\ adj

can·ni·bal·ize \'kanəbə̩līz\ vb **-ized; -iz·ing** 1 : take usable parts from 2 : practice cannibalism

can·non \-ən\ n, pl **-nons** or **-non** : artillery piece **—can·non·ball** n **—can·non·eer** \̩kanə'niər\ n

can·non·ade \̩kanə'nād\ n : heavy artillery fire ~ vb **-ad·ed; -ad·ing** : bombard

can·not \'kan̩ät; kə'nät\ : can not **—cannot but** : be bound to

can·ny \'kanē\ adj **-ni·er; -est** : shrewd **—can·ni·ly** adv **—can·ni·ness** n

ca·noe \kə'nü\ n : narrow sharp-ended boat propelled by paddles **—canoe** vb **—ca·noe·ist** n

¹**can·on** \'kanən\ n 1 : regulation governing a church 2 : authoritative list 3 : an accepted principle

²**canon** n : clergyman in a cathedral

ca·non·i·cal \kə'nänikəl\ adj 1 : relating to or conforming to a canon 2 : orthodox **—ca·non·i·cal·ly** adv

can·on·ize \'kanə̩nīz\ vb **-ized** \-̩nīzd\; **-iz·ing** : recognize as a saint **—can·on·iza·tion** \̩kanənə'zāshən\ n

can·o·py \'kanəpē\ n, pl **-pies** : overhanging cover **—canopy** vb

¹**cant** \'kant\ n 1 : slanting surface 2 : slant ~ vb 1 : tip up 2 : lean to one side

²**cant** vb : talk hypocritically ~ n 1 : jargon 2 : insincere talk

can't \'kant, 'känt, 'känt\ : can not

can·ta·loupe \'kant⁰l̩ōp\ n : muskmelon with orange flesh

can·tan·ker·ous \kan'taŋk(ə)rəs\ adj : hard to deal with **—can·tan·ker·ous·ly** adv **—can·tan·ker·ous·ness** n

can·ta·ta \kən'tätə\ n : choral work

can·teen \kan'tēn\ n 1 : place of recreation for servicemen 2 : water container

can·ter \'kantər\ n : slow gallop **—canter** vb

can·ti·cle \'kantikəl\ n : liturgical song

can·ti·le·ver \'kant⁰l̩ēvər, -̩ev-\ n : beam or structure supported only at one end

can·to \'kan̩tō\ n, pl **-tos** : major division of a long poem

can·tor \'kantər\ n : synagogue official who sings liturgical music

can·vas \'kanvəs\ n 1 : strong cloth orig. used for making tents and sails 2 : set of sails 3 : oil painting

can·vass \-vəs\ vb : solicit votes, orders, or opinions from ~ n : act of canvassing **—can·vass·er** n

can·yon \-yən\ n : deep valley with steep sides

cap \'kap\ n 1 : covering for the head 2 : top or cover like a cap 3 : upper limit ~ vb **-pp-** 1 : provide or protect with a cap 2 : climax **—cap·ful** \-̩ful\ n

ca·pa·ble \'kāpəbəl\ adj : able to do something **—ca·pa·bil·i·ty** \̩kāpə'bilətē\ n **—ca·pa·bly** \'kāpəblē\ adv

ca·pa·cious \kə'pāshəs\ adj : able to contain much

ca·pac·i·tance \-'pasətəns\ n : ability to store electrical energy

ca·pac·i·tor \-ətər\ n : device for storing electrical energy

ca·pac·i·ty \-̩atē\ n, pl **-ties** 1 : ability to contain 2 : volume 3 : ability 4 : role or job ~ adj : equaling maximum capacity

¹**cape** \'kāp\ n : point of land jutting out into water

²**cape** n : garment that drapes over the shoulders

¹**ca·per** \'kāpər\ n : flower bud of a shrub pickled for use as a relish

²**caper** vb : leap or prance about ~ n 1 : frolicsome leap 2 : illegal escapade

cap·il·lary \'kapə̩lerē\ adj 1 : resembling a hair 2 : having a very small bore ~ n, pl **-lar·ies** : tiny thin-walled blood vessel

¹cap·i·tal \-ət³l\ adj **1** : punishable by death **2** : being in the series A, B, C rather than a, b, c **3** : relating to capital **4** : excellent ~ n **1** : capital letter **2** : seat of government **3** : wealth **4** : total face value of a company's stock **5** : capitalists as a group

²capital n : top part of a column

cap·i·tal·ism \-,izəm\ n : economic system of private ownership of capital

cap·i·tal·ist \-əst\ n **1** : person with capital invested in business **2** : believer in capitalism — adj **1** : owning capital **2** : practicing, advocating, or marked by capitalism — **cap·i·tal·is·tic** \,kapət³l'istik\ adj — **cap·i·tal·is·ti·cal·ly** \-k(ə)lē\ adv

cap·i·tal·ize \-,īz\ vb **-ized; -iz·ing 1** : write or print with a capital letter **2** : use as capital **3** : supply capital for **4** : turn something to advantage — **cap·i·tal·iza·tion** \,kapət³lə-'zāshən\ n

cap·i·tol \kapət³l\ n : building in which a legislature sits

ca·pit·u·late \kə'pichə,lāt\ vb **-lat·ed; -lat·ing** : surrender — **ca·pit·u·la·tion** \-,pichə'lāshən\ n

ca·pon \'kā,pän, -pən\ n : castrated male chicken

ca·price \kə'prēs\ n : whim — **ca·pri·cious** \-'prishəs\ adj

cap·size \'kap,sīz, kap'sīz\ vb **-sized; -siz·ing** : overturn

cap·stan \'kapstən, -,stan\ n : upright winch

cap·sule \'kapsəl, -,sül\ n **1** : enveloping cover (as for medicine) **2** : small pressurized compartment for astronauts ~ vb **-suled; -sul·ing** : put in compact form ~ adj : very brief or compact — **cap·su·lar** \-sələr\ adj — **cap·su·lat·ed** \-sə,lātəd\ adj

cap·tain \'kaptən\ n **1** : commander of a body of troops **2** : officer in charge of a ship **3** : commissioned officer in the navy ranking next below a rear admiral or a commodore **4** : commissioned officer (as in the army) ranking next below a major **5** : leader ~ vb : be captain of — **cap·tain·cy** n

cap·tion \-shən\ n **1** : title **2** : explanation with an illustration — **caption** vb

cap·tious \-shəs\ adj : tending to find fault — **cap·tious·ly** adv

cap·ti·vate \-tə,vāt\ vb **-vat·ed; -vat·ing** : attract and charm — **cap·ti·va·tion**

\,kaptə'vāshən\ n — **cap·ti·va·tor** \'kaptə,vātər\ n

cap·tive \-tiv\ adj **1** : made prisoner **2** : confined or under restraint — **captive** n — **cap·tiv·i·ty** \kap'tivətē\ n

cap·tor \'kaptər\ n : one that captures

cap·ture \-chər\ n : seizure by force or trickery ~ vb **-tured; -tur·ing** : take captive

car \'kär\ n **1** : vehicle moved on wheels **2** : cage of an elevator

ca·rafe \kə'raf, -'räf\ n : decanter

car·a·mel \'karəməl, 'kärməl\ n **1** : burnt sugar used for flavoring and coloring **2** : firm chewy candy

¹carat var of KARAT

²car·at \'karət\ n : unit of weight for precious stones

car·a·van \'karə,van\ n : travelers journeying together (as in a line)

car·a·way \'karə,wā\ n : aromatic herb with seeds used in seasoning

car·bine \'kär,bēn, -,bīn\ n : short-barreled rifle

car·bo·hy·drate \,kärbō'hī,drāt, -drət\ n : compound of carbon, hydrogen, and oxygen

car·bon \'kärbən\ n **1** : chemical element occurring in nature as diamond and graphite **2** : piece of carbon paper or a copy made with it

¹car·bon·ate \'kärbə,nāt, -nət\ n : salt or ester of a carbon-containing acid

²car·bon·ate \-,nāt\ vb **-at·ed; -at·ing** : impregnate with carbon dioxide — **car·bon·ation** \,kärbə'nāshən\ n

carbon paper n : thin paper coated with a pigment for making copies

car·bun·cle \'kär,bəŋkəl\ n : painful inflammation of the skin and underlying tissue

car·bu·re·tor \'kärb(y)ə,rātər\ n : device for mixing fuel and air

car·cass \-kəs\ n : dead body

car·cin·o·gen \kär'sinəjən\ n : agent causing cancer — **car·ci·no·gen·ic** \,kärs³nō'jenik\ adj

car·ci·no·ma \,kärs³n'ōmə\ n, pl **-mas** or **-ma·ta** \-mətə\ : malignant tumor — **car·ci·no·ma·tous** \-mətəs\ adj

¹card \'kärd\ vb : comb (fibers) before spinning ~ n : device for carding fibers — **card·er** n

²card n **1** : playing card **2** pl : game played with playing cards **3** : small flat piece of paper

card·board n : stiff material like paper

car·di·ac \'kärdē,ak\ adj : relating to the heart

car·di·gan \-igən\ n : sweater with an opening in the front

¹car·di·nal \'kärdnəl, -³nəl\ n **1** : offi-

cial of the Roman Catholic Church
2 : bright red songbird

²**cardinal** *adj* : of basic importance

cardinal number *n* : number (as 1, 82, 357) used in counting

car·di·ol·o·gy \,kärdē'äləjē\ *n* : study of the heart —**car·di·ol·o·gist** \-jəst\ *n*

car·dio·vas·cu·lar \-ō'vaskyələr\ *adj* : relating to the heart and blood vessels

care \'keər\ *n* 1 : anxiety 2 : watchful attention 3 : supervision ~ *vb* **cared; car·ing** 1 : feel anxiety or concern 2 : like 3 : provide care —**care·free** *adj* —**care·ful** \-fəl\ *adj* —**care·ful·ly** *adv* —**care·ful·ness** *n* —**care·less** *adj* —**care·less·ly** *adv* —**care·less·ness** *n*

ca·reen \kə'rēn\ *vb* 1 : lean over 2 : sway from side to side

ca·reer \kə'riər\ *n* : vocation ~ *vb* : go at top speed

ca·ress \kə'res\ *n* : tender touch ~ *vb* : touch lovingly or tenderly

car·et \'karət\ *n* : mark ∧ showing where something is to be inserted

care·tak·er *n* : one in charge for another or temporarily

car·go \'kärgō\ *n, pl* **-goes** *or* **-gos** : transported goods

car·i·bou \'karə,bü\ *n, pl* **-bou** *or* **-bous** : large No. American deer

car·i·ca·ture \'karika,chúr\ *n* : distorted representation for humor or ridicule —**caricature** *vb* —**car·i·ca·tur·ist** \-əst\ *n*

car·ies \'karēz\ *n, pl* **caries** : tooth decay

car·il·lon \'karə,län\ *n* : set of tuned bells

car·mine \'kärmən, -,mīn\ *n* : vivid red

car·nage \'kärnij\ *n* : slaughter

car·nal \'kärn³l\ *adj* : sensual —**car·nal·i·ty** \kär'nalətē\ *n* —**car·nal·ly** *adv*

car·na·tion \kär'nāshən\ *n* : showy flower

car·ni·val \'kärnəvəl\ *n* 1 : festival 2 : traveling enterprise offering amusements

car·ni·vore \-,vōr\ *n* : flesh-eating animal —**car·niv·o·rous** \kär'niv(ə)rəs\ *adj* —**car·niv·o·rous·ly** *adv* —**car·niv·o·rous·ness** *n*

car·ol \'karəl\ *n* : song of joy —**carol** *vb* —**car·ol·er, car·ol·ler** \-ələr\ *n*

car·om \-əm\ *n or vb* : rebound

ca·rouse \kə'rauz\ *vb* **-roused; -rous·ing** : drink and be boisterous —**carouse** *n* —**ca·rous·er** *n*

car·ou·sel, car·rou·sel \,karə'sel, 'karə,-\ *n* : merry-go-round

¹**carp** \'kärp\ *vb* : find fault

²**carp** *n, pl* **carp** *or* **carps** : freshwater fish

car·pel \'kärpəl\ *n* : modified leaf forming part of the ovary of a flower

car·pen·ter \'kärpəntər\ *n* : one who builds with wood —**carpenter** *vb* —**car·pen·try** \-trē\ *n*

car·pet \-pət\ *n* : fabric floor covering ~ *vb* : cover with a carpet —**car·pet·ing** \-iŋ\ *n*

car·port *n* : open-sided automobile shelter

car·riage \'karij\ *n* 1 : conveyance 2 : manner of holding oneself 3 : wheeled vehicle

car·ri·on \-ēən\ *n* : dead and decaying flesh

car·rot \-ət\ *n* : root vegetable

car·ry \'karē\ *vb* **-ried; -ry·ing** 1 : move while supporting 2 : hold (oneself) in a specified way 3 : support 4 : keep in stock 5 : reach to a distance 6 : win —**car·ri·er** \-ēər\ *n* —**carry on** *vb* 1 : conduct 2 : behave excitedly —**carry out** *vb* : put into effect

cart \'kärt\ *n* : wheeled vehicle ~ *vb* : carry in a cart —**cart·age** \-ij\ *n* —**cart·er** *n*

car·tel \kär'tel\ *n* : business combination designed to limit competition

car·ti·lage \'kärt³lij\ *n* : elastic skeletal tissue —**car·ti·lag·i·nous** \,kärt'lajənəs\ *adj*

car·tog·ra·phy \kär'tägrəfē\ *n* : making of maps —**car·tog·ra·pher** \-fər\ *n*

car·ton \'kärt³n\ *n* : cardboard box

car·toon \kär'tün\ *n* 1 : humorous drawing 2 : comic strip —**cartoon** *vb* —**car·toon·ist** *n*

car·tridge \'kärtrij\ *n* 1 : tube containing powder and a bullet or shot for a firearm 2 : container of material for insertion into an apparatus

carve \'kärv\ *vb* **carved; carv·ing** 1 : cut with care 2 : cut into pieces or slices —**carv·er** *n*

cas·cade \kas'kād\ *n* : small steep waterfall ~ *vb* **-cad·ed; -cad·ing** : fall in a cascade

¹**case** \'kās\ *n* 1 : particular instance 2 : convincing argument 3 : inflectional form esp. of a noun or pronoun 4 : fact 5 : lawsuit 6 : instance of disease —**in case** : if —**in case of** : in the event of

²**case** *n* 1 : box 2 : outer covering ~ *vb* **cased; cas·ing** 1 : enclose 2 : inspect

case·ment \-mənt\ *n* : window opening on hinges

cash \'kash\ *n* 1 : ready money 2

: money paid at the time of purchase ~ *vb* : give or get cash for

ca·shew \'kashü, ka'shü\ *n* : tropical American tree or its nut

¹ca·shier \ka'shiər\ *vb* : dismiss in disgrace

²cash·ier *n* : person who handles money

cash·mere \'kazh,miər, 'kash-\ *n* : fine goat's wool or a fabric of this

ca·si·no \kə'sēnō\ *n, pl* **-nos** : place for gambling

cask \'kask\ *n* : barrel-shaped container for liquids

cas·ket \'kaskət\ *n* : coffin

cas·se·role \'kasə,rōl, 'kaz-\ *n* : baking dish or the food cooked in this

cas·sette \kə'set, ka-\ *n* : case containing two reels of magnetic tape

cas·sock \'kasək\ *n* : long clerical garment

cast \'kast\ *vb* **cast; cast·ing** 1 : throw 2 : deposit (a ballot) 3 : assign parts in a play 4 : mold ~ *n* 1 : throw 2 : appearance 3 : rigid surgical dressing 4 : actors in a play

cas·ta·nets \,kastə'nets\ *n pl* : shells clicked together in the hand

cast·away \'kastə,wā\ *n* : survivor of a shipwreck —**castaway** *adj*

caste \'kast\ *n* : social class or rank

cast·er \'kastər\ *n* : small wheel on furniture

cas·ti·gate \'kastə,gāt\ *vb* **-gat·ed; -gat·ing** : chastise severely —**cas·ti·ga·tion** \,kastə'gāshən\ *n* —**cas·ti·ga·tor** \'kastə,gātər\ *n*

cast iron *n* : hard brittle alloy of iron

cas·tle \'kasəl\ *n* : fortified building

cast-off *adj* : thrown away —**cast·off** *n*

cas·trate \'kas,trāt\ *vb* **-trat·ed; -trat·ing** : remove the testes of —**cas·tra·tion** \ka'strāshən\ *n*

ca·su·al \'kazh(əw)əl\ *adj* 1 : happening by chance 2 : showing little concern 3 : informal —**ca·su·al·ly** \-ē\ *adv* —**ca·su·al·ness** *n*

ca·su·al·ty \-tē\ *n, pl* **-ties** 1 : serious or fatal accident 2 : one injured, lost, or destroyed

ca·su·ist·ry \'kazhəwəstrē\ *n, pl* **-ries** : adroit and esp. false reasoning —**ca·su·ist** \-wəst\ *n*

cat \'kat\ *n* 1 : small domestic mammal 2 : related animal (as a lion) —**cat·like** *adj*

cat·a·clysm \'katə,klizəm\ *n* : violent change —**cat·a·clys·mal** \,katə'klizmäl\, **cat·a·clys·mic** \-'klizmik\ *adj*

cat·a·comb \'katə,kōm\ *n* : underground burial place

cat·a·log, cat·a·logue \'kat³l,ȯg\ *n* 1 : list 2 : book containing a description of items ~ *vb* **-loged** *or* **-logued; -log·ing** *or* **-logu·ing** 1 : make a catalog of 2 : enter in a catalog —**cat·a·log·er, cat·a·logu·er** *n*

ca·tal·pa \kə'talpə\ *n* : tree with broad leaves and long pods

ca·tal·y·sis \-əsəs\ *n, pl* **-y·ses** \-,sēz\ : increase in the rate of chemical reaction caused by a substance (**cat·a·lyst** \'kat³ləst\) that is itself unchanged —**cat·a·lyt·ic** \,kat³l'itik\ *adj*

cat·a·ma·ran \,katəmə'ran\ *n* : boat with twin hulls

cat·a·mount \'katə,maùnt\ *n* : cougar

cat·a·pult \-,pəlt, -,pùlt\ *n* : device for hurling or launching —**catapult** *vb*

cat·a·ract \-,rakt\ *n* 1 : large waterfall 2 : cloudiness of the lens of the eye

ca·tarrh \kə'tär\ *n* : inflammation of the nose and throat

ca·tas·tro·phe \kə'tastrə(,)fē\ *n* 1 : great disaster or misfortune 2 : utter failure —**cat·a·stroph·ic** \,katə'sträfik\ *adj* —**cat·a·stroph·i·cal·ly** \-ik(ə)lē\ *adv*

cat·bird *n* : American songbird

cat·call *n* : noise of disapproval

catch \'kach, 'kech\ *vb* **caught** \'kȯt\; **catch·ing** 1 : capture esp. after pursuit 2 : trap 3 : detect esp. by surprise 4 : grasp 5 : get entangled 6 : become affected with or by 7 : seize and hold firmly ~ *n* 1 : act of catching 2 : something caught 3 : something that fastens 4 : hidden difficulty —**catch·er** *n*

catch·ing \-iŋ\ *adj* : infectious

catch·up \'kechəp, 'kach-; 'katsəp\ *var of* CATSUP

catch·word *n* : slogan

catchy \-ē\ *adj* **catch·i·er; -est** 1 : likely to catch interest 2 : easily remembered

cat·e·chism \'katə,kizəm\ *n* : set of questions and answers esp. to teach religious doctrine —**cat·e·chist** \-,kist\ *n* —**cat·e·chize** \-,kīz\ *vb*

cat·e·gor·i·cal \,katə'gȯrikəl\ *adj* : absolute —**cat·e·gor·i·cal·ly** \-k(ə)lē\ *adv*

cat·e·go·ry \'katə,gȯrē\ *n, pl* **-ries** : group or class —**cat·e·go·ri·za·tion** \,katigərə'zāshən\ *n* —**cat·e·go·rize** \'katigə,rīz\ *vb*

ca·ter \'kātər\ *vb* 1 : provide food for 2 : supply what is wanted —**ca·ter·er** *n*

cater-cor·ner \,katē'kȯrnər, ,katə-,**

,kitē-\, **cat·er·cor·nered** *adv or adj* : in a diagonal position

cat·er·pil·lar \'kata(r),pilər\ *n* : butterfly or moth larva

cat·er·waul \'katər,wȯl\ *vb* : make the harsh cry of a cat —**caterwaul** *n*

cat·fish *n* : big-headed fish with feelers about the mouth

cat·gut *n* : tough cord made usu. from sheep intestines

ca·thar·sis \kə'thärsəs\ *n, pl* **ca·thar·ses** \-,sēz\ : a purging —**ca·thar·tic** \kə'thärtik\ *adj or n*

ca·the·dral \-'thēdrəl\ *n* : principal church of a diocese

cath·e·ter \'kathətər\ *n* : tube for insertion into a body cavity

cath·ode \-,ōd\ *n* 1 : negative electrode 2 : positive battery terminal —**ca·thod·ic** \ka'thädik\ *adj*

cath·o·lic \'kath(ə)lik\ *adj* 1 : universal 2 *cap* : relating to Roman Catholics

Cath·o·lic *n* : member of the Roman Catholic Church —**Ca·thol·i·cism** \kə'thälə,sizəm\ *n*

cat·kin \'katkən\ *n* : long dense flower cluster

cat·nap *n* : short light nap —**catnap** *vb*

cat·nip \-,nip\ *n* : aromatic mint relished by cats

cat's-paw \'sē\ *n, pl* **cat's-paws** : person used as a tool

cat·sup \'kechəp, 'kach-; 'katsəp\ *n* : spicy tomato sauce

cat·tail *n* : marsh herb with furry brown spikes

cat·tle \'katᵊl\ *n pl* : domestic bovines —**cat·tle·man** \-mən, -,man\ *n*

cat·ty \'katē\ *adj* -**ti·er**; -**est** : mean or spiteful —**cat·ti·ly** *adv* —**cat·ti·ness** *n*

cat·walk *n* : high narrow walk

Cau·ca·sian \kȯ'kāzhən, -'kazh-\ *adj* : relating to the white race —**Caucasian** *n* —**Cau·ca·soid** \'kȯkə,sȯid\ *adj or n*

cau·cus \'kȯkəs\ *n* : political meeting —**caucus** *vb*

caught *past of* CATCH

cauldron *var of* CALDRON

cau·li·flow·er \'kȯli,flaú(ə)r, 'käl-\ *n* : vegetable having a compact head of undeveloped flowers

caulk \'kȯk\ *vb* : make seams watertight —**caulk·er** *n* —**caulk·ing** *n*

caus·al \'kȯzəl\ *adj* : relating to or being a cause —**cau·sal·i·ty** \kȯ'zalətē\ *n* —**caus·al·ly** \'kȯzəlē\ *adv*

cause \'kȯz\ *n* 1 : something that brings about a result 2 : reason 3 : lawsuit 4 : principle or movement to support ~ *vb* **caused**; **caus·ing** : be the cause of —**cau·sa·tion** \kȯ-

'zāshən,\ *n* —**caus·a·tive** \'kȯzətiv\ *adj* —**cause·less** *adj* —**caus·er** *n*

cause·way *n* : raised road esp. over water

caus·tic \'kȯstik\ *adj* 1 : corrosive 2 : sharp or biting —**caustic** *n*

cau·ter·ize \'kȯtə,rīz\ *vb* -**ized**; -**iz·ing** : burn to prevent infection or bleeding —**cau·ter·iza·tion** \,kȯtərə-'zāshən\ *n*

cau·tion \'kȯshən\ *n* 1 : warning 2 : care or prudence ~ *vb* : warn —**cau·tion·ary** \-shə,nerē\ *adj*

cau·tious \'kȯshəs\ *adj* : taking caution —**cau·tious·ly** *adv* —**cau·tious·ness** *n*

cav·al·cade \,kavəl'kād\ *n* 1 : procession on horseback 2 : series

cav·a·lier \,kavə'liər\ *n* : mounted soldier ~ *adj* : disdainful or arrogant —**cav·a·lier·ly** *adv*

cav·al·ry \'kavəlrē\ *n, pl* -**ries** : troops on horseback or in vehicles —**cav·al·ry·man** \-mən, -,man\ *n*

cave \'kāv\ *n* : natural underground chamber —**cave in** *vb* : collapse

cav·ern \'kavərn\ *n* : large cave —**cav·ern·ous** *adj* —**cav·ern·ous·ly** *adv*

cav·i·ar, cav·i·are \'kavē,är, 'käv-\ *n* : salted fish roe

cav·il \'kavəl\ *vb* -**iled** *or* -**illed**; -**il·ing** *or* -**il·ling** : find fault without good reason —**cavil** *n* —**cav·il·er, cav·il·ler** *n*

cav·i·ty \-ətē\ *n, pl* -**ties** 1 : unfilled place within a mass 2 : decay in a tooth

ca·vort \kə'vȯrt\ *vb* : prance or caper

caw \'kȯ\ *vb* : utter the harsh call of the crow —**caw** *n*

cay·enne pepper \,kī,en-, ,kā-\ *n* : ground dried fruits of a hot pepper

cay·man *var of* CAIMAN

cease \'sēs\ *vb* **ceased**; **ceas·ing** : stop

cease·less \-ləs\ *adj* : continuous

ce·dar \'sēdər\ *n* : cone-bearing tree with fragrant durable wood

cede \'sēd\ *vb* **ced·ed**; **ced·ing** : surrender —**ced·er** *n*

ceil·ing \'sēliŋ\ *n* 1 : overhead surface of a room 2 : upper limit

cel·e·brate \'selə,brāt\ *vb* -**brat·ed**; -**brat·ing** 1 : perform with appropriate rites 2 : honor with ceremonies 3 : extol —**cel·e·brant** \-brənt\ *n* —**cel·e·bra·tion** \,selə'brāshən\ *n* —**cel·e·bra·tor** \'selə,brātər\ *n*

cel·e·brat·ed \-əd\ *adj* : renowned

ce·leb·ri·ty \sə'lebrətē\ *n, pl* -**ties** 1 : renown 2 : well-known person

ce·ler·i·ty \sə'lerətē\ *n* : speed

cel·er·y \'sel(ə)rē\ *n, pl* **-er·ies** : herb grown for crisp edible stalks

ce·les·ta \sə'lestə\, **ce·leste** \sə'lest\ *n* : keyboard musical instrument

ce·les·tial \sə'leschəl\ *adj* **1** : relating to the sky **2** : heavenly

cel·i·ba·cy \'seləbəsē\ *n* **1** : state of being unmarried **2** : abstention from sexual intercourse —**cel·i·bate** \'seləbət\ *n or adj*

cell \'sel\ *n* **1** : small room **2** : tiny mass of protoplasm that forms the fundamental unit of living matter **3** : container holding an electrolyte for generating electricity —**celled** *adj*

cel·lar \'selər\ *n* : room or area below ground

cel·lo \'chelō\ *n, pl* **-los** : bass member of the violin family —**cel·list** \-əst\ *n*

cel·lo·phane \'selə,fān\ *n* : thin transparent cellulose wrapping

cel·lu·lar \-yələr\ *adj* : relating to or consisting of cells

cel·lu·lose \-yə,lōs\ *n* : complex plant carbohydrate

Cel·sius \'selsēəs\ *adj* : relating to a thermometer scale on which the freezing point of water is 0° and the boiling point is 100°

ce·ment \si'ment\ *n* **1** : powdery mixture of clay and limestone that hardens when wetted **2** : binding agent ~ *vb* : unite or cover with cement —**ce·ment·er** *n*

cem·e·tery \'semə,terē\ *n, pl* **-ter·ies** : burial ground

cen·ser \'sensər\ *n* : vessel for burning incense

cen·sor \-sər\ *n* : one with power to suppress anything objectionable (as in printed matter) ~ *vb* : be a censor of —**cen·so·ri·al** \sen'sōrēəl\ *adj* —**cen·sor·ship** \-,ship\ *n*

cen·so·ri·ous \sen'sōrēəs\ *adj* : critical —**cen·so·ri·ous·ly** *adv* —**cen·so·ri·ous·ness** *n*

cen·sure \'senchər\ *n* : official reprimand ~ *vb* **-sured; -sur·ing** : find blameworthy

cen·sus \-səs\ *n* : periodic population count

cent \'sent\ *n* : monetary unit equal to 1/100 of a basic unit of value

cen·taur \'sen,tȯr\ *n* : mythological creature that is half man and half horse

cen·ten·ni·al \sen'tenēəl\ *n* : 100th anniversary —**centennial** *adj*

cen·ter \'sentər\ *n* **1** : middle point **2** : point of origin or greatest concentration **3** : region of concentrated population **4** : player near the middle of his team ~ *vb* **1** : place, fix, or concentrate at or around a center **2** : have a center —**cen·tered** *adj* —**cen·ter·piece** *n*

cen·ti·grade \'sentə,grād, 'sänt-\ *adj* : Celsius

cen·ti·me·ter \'sentə,mētər, 'sänt-\ *n* : 1/100 meter

cen·ti·pede \'sentə,pēd\ *n* : long flat many-legged arthropod

cen·tral \'sentrəl\ *adj* **1** : constituting or being near a center **2** : essential or principal —**cen·tral·ly** *adv*

cen·tral·ize \-trə,līz\ *vb* **-ized; -iz·ing** : bring to a central point or under central control —**cen·tral·iza·tion** \,sentrələ'zāshən\ *n* —**cen·tral·iz·er** *n*

cen·tre *chiefly Brit var of* CENTER

cen·trif·u·gal \sen'trifyəgəl, -'trifigəl\ *adj* : acting in a direction away from a center or axis

cen·tri·fuge \'sentrə,fyüj\ *n* : machine that separates substances by spinning

cen·trip·e·tal \sen'tripət³l\ *adj* : acting in a direction toward a center or axis

cen·tu·ri·on \sen't(y)ürēən\ *n* : Roman military officer

cen·tu·ry \'sench(ə)rē\ *n, pl* **-ries** : 100 years

ce·ram·ic \sə'ramik\ *n* **1** *pl* : art or process of shaping and hardening articles from clay **2** : product of ceramics —**ceramic** *adj*

ce·re·al \'sirēəl\ *adj* : made of or relating to grain or to the plants that produce it ~ *n* **1** : grass yielding edible grain **2** : cereal grain used as food

cer·e·bel·lum \,serə'beləm\ *n, pl* **-bellums** *or* **-bel·la** \-'belə\ : part of the brain controlling muscular coordination —**cer·e·bel·lar** \-ər\ *adj*

cerebral palsy *n* : disorder caused by brain damage and marked esp. by defective muscle control

cer·e·brate \'serə,brāt\ *vb* **-brat·ed; -brat·ing** : think —**cer·e·bra·tion** \,serə'brāshən\ *n*

ce·re·brum \sə'rēbrəm, 'serə-\ *n, pl* **-brums** *or* **-bra** \-brə\ : part of the brain that contains the higher nervous centers —**ce·re·bral** \sə'rē-brəl, 'serə-\ —**ce·re·bral·ly** *adv*

cer·e·mo·ny \'serə,mōnē\ *n, pl* **-nies** **1** : formal act prescribed by law, ritual, or convention **2** : prescribed procedures —**cer·e·mo·ni·al** \,serə'mōnēəl\ *adj or n* —**cer·e·mo·ni·ous** \-nēəs\ *adj*

ce·rise \sə'rēs\ *n* : moderate red

cer·tain \'sərtⁿ\ *adj* 1 : settled 2 : true 3 : specific but not named 4 : bound 5 : assured ~ *pron* : certain ones —**cer·tain·ly** *adv* —**cer·tain·ty** \-tē\ *n*

cer·tif·i·cate \sər'tifikət\ *n* : document establishing truth or fulfillment

cer·ti·fy \'sərtə,fī\ *vb* **-fied; -fy·ing** 1 : verify 2 : endorse —**cer·ti·fi·able** \-,fīabəl\ *adj* —**cer·ti·fi·ably** \-blē\ *adv* —**cer·ti·fi·ca·tion** \,sərtəfə'kāshən\ *n* —**cer·ti·fi·er** *n*

cer·ti·tude \'sərtə,t(y)üd\ *n* : state of being certain

cer·vix \'sərviks\ *n, pl* **-vi·ces** \-və-,sēz\ *or* **-vixes** 1 : neck 2 : narrow end of the uterus —**cer·vi·cal** \-vikəl\ *adj*

ce·sar·e·an \si'zarēən\ *n* : surgical operation to deliver a baby —**cesarean** *adj*

ce·si·um \'sēzēəm\ *n* : silver-white soft ductile chemical element

ces·sa·tion \se'sāshən\ *n* : a halting

ces·sion \'seshən\ *n* : a yielding

cess·pool \'ses,pül\ *n* : underground sewage pit

Cha·blis \'shab,lē; sha'blē\ *n, pl* **Cha·blis** \-,lēz, -'blēz\ : dry white wine

chafe \'chāf\ *vb* **chafed; chaf·ing** 1 : fret 2 : make sore by rubbing

chaff \'chaf\ *n* 1 : debris separated from grain 2 : something worthless 3 : banter ~ *vb* : tease —**chaffy** *adj*

chaf·ing dish \'chāfiŋ-\ *n* : utensil for cooking at the table

cha·grin \shə'grin\ *n* : embarrassment or humiliation ~ *vb* : cause to feel chagrin

chain \'chān\ *n* 1 : flexible series of connected links 2 *pl* : fetters 3 : linked series ~ *vb* : bind or connect with a chain

chair \'cheər\ *n* 1 : seat with a back 2 : position of authority or dignity 3 : chairman ~ *vb* : act as chairman of

chair·man \-mən\ *n* : presiding officer —**chair·man·ship** *n* —**chair·wom·an** *n*

chaise longue \shāz'lôŋ\ *n, pl* **chaise longues** \-'lôŋ(z)\ : long couchlike chair

cha·let \sha'lā\ *n* : Swiss mountain cottage with overhanging roof

chal·ice \'chaləs\ *n* : eucharistic cup

chalk \'chók\ *n* 1 : soft limestone 2 : chalky material used as a crayon ~ *vb* : mark with chalk —**chalky** *adj* —**chalk up** *vb* 1 : credit 2 : achieve

chalk·board *n* : blackboard

chal·lenge \'chalənj\ *vb* **-lenged; -leng·ing** 1 : dispute 2 : invite or dare to

act or compete —**challenge** *n* —**chal·leng·er** *n*

cham·ber \'chāmbər\ *n* 1 : room 2 : enclosed space 3 : legislative meeting place or body 4 *pl* : judge's consultation room —**cham·bered** *adj*

cham·ber·maid *n* : bedroom maid

chamber music *n* : music by small group for a small audience

cha·me·leon \kə'mēlyən\ *n* : small lizard whose skin changes color

cham·ois \'shamē\ *n, pl* **cham·ois** \-ē(z)\ 1 : goatlike antelope 2 : soft leather

¹**champ** \'champ, 'chāmp\ *vb* : chew noisily

²**champ** \'champ\ *n* : champion

cham·pagne \sham'pān\ *n* : sparkling white wine

cham·pi·on \'champēən\ *n* 1 : advocate or defender 2 : winning contestant ~ *vb* : protect or fight for

cham·pi·on·ship \-,ship\ *n* : title of a champion 2 : contest to pick a champion

chance \'chans\ *n* 1 : unpredictable element of existence 2 : opportunity 3 : probability 4 : risk 5 : raffle ticket ~ *vb* **chanced; chanc·ing** 1 : happen 2 : encounter unexpectedly 3 : risk —**chance** *adj*

chan·cel \'chansəl\ *n* : part of a church around the altar

chan·cel·lery, chan·cel·lory \'chans(ə)lərē\ *n, pl* **-ler·ies** *or* **-lor·ies** 1 : position of a chancellor 2 : chancellor's office

chan·cel·lor \-s(ə)lər\ *n* 1 : chief or high state official 2 : head of a university —**chan·cel·lor·ship** *n*

chan·cre \'shaŋkər\ *n* : skin ulcer esp. from syphilis

chancy \'chansē\ *adj* **chanc·i·er; -est** : risky

chan·de·lier \shandə'liər\ *n* : hanging lighting fixture

chan·dler \'chandlər\ *n* : provisions dealer —**chan·dlery** *n*

change \'chānj\ *vb* **changed; chang·ing** 1 : make or become different 2 : exchange 3 : give or receive change for ~ *n* 1 : a changing 2 : excess from a payment 3 : money in smaller denominations 4 : coins —**change·able** *adj* —**change·less** *adj* —**chang·er** *n*

chan·nel \'chanⁿl\ *n* 1 : deeper part of a waterway 2 : means of passage or communication 3 : strait 4 : broadcast frequency ~ *vb* **-neled** *or* **-nelled; -nel·ing** *or* **-nel·ling** : make or direct through a channel chant \'chant\ *vb* : sing or speak in one tone —chant *n* —chant·er *n*

chan·tey, chan·ty \'shantē, 'chant-\ *n*, *pl* -teys *or* -ties : sailors' work song

Cha·nu·kah \'känəkə, 'hän-\ *var of* HANUKKAH

cha·os \'kā,äs\ *n* : complete disorder —cha·ot·ic \kā'ätik\ *adj* —cha·ot·i·cal·ly \-ik(ə)lē\ *adv*

¹chap \'chap\ *n* : fellow

²chap *vb* -pp- : dry and crack open usu. from wind and cold

cha·pel \'chapəl\ *n* : private or small place of worship

chap·er·on, chap·er·one \'shapə,rōn\ *n* : older person who accompanies young people at a social gathering ~ *vb* -oned; -on·ing : act as chaperon at or for —chap·er·on·age \-ij\ *n*

chap·lain \'chaplən\ *n* : clergyman in a military unit or a prison —chap·lain·cy \-sē\ *n*

chap·ter \'chaptər\ *n* 1 : main book division 2 : branch of a society

char \'chär\ *vb* -rr- 1 : burn to charcoal 2 : scorch

char·ac·ter \'kariktər\ *n* 1 : letter or graphic mark 2 : trait or distinctive combination of traits 3 : peculiar person 4 : fictional person —char·ac·ter·i·za·tion \,karikt(ə)rə'zäshən\ *n* —char·ac·ter·ize \'karikta,rīz\ *vb*

char·ac·ter·is·tic \,kariktə'ristik\ *adj* : typical ~ *n* : distinguishing quality —char·ac·ter·is·ti·cal·ly \-tik(ə)lē\ *adv*

cha·rades \shə'rādz\ *n sing or pl* : pantomime guessing game

char·coal \'chär,kōl\ *n* : porous carbon prepared by partial combustion

chard \'chärd\ *n* : leafy vegetable

charge \'chärj\ *vb* charged; charg·ing 1 : give an electric charge to 2 : impose a task or responsibility on 3 : command 4 : accuse 5 : rush forward in assault 6 : assume a debt for 7 : fix as a price ~ *n* 1 : excess or deficiency of electrons in a body 2 : tax 3 : responsibility 4 : accusation 5 : cost 6 : attack —charge·able *adj*

charg·er \-ər\ *n* : horse ridden in battle

char·i·ot \'chareət\ *n* : ancient 2-wheeled vehicle —char·i·o·teer \,chareə'tiər\ *n*

cha·ris·ma \kə'rizmə\ *n*, *pl* cha·ris·ma·ta \kə'rizmətə\ : special ability to lead —char·is·mat·ic \,karəz'matik\ *adj*

char·i·ty \'charətē\ *n*, *pl* -ties 1 : love for mankind 2 : generosity or leniency 3 : alms 4 : institution for relief of the needy —char·i·ta·ble

\-əbəl\ *adj* —char·i·ta·ble·ness *n* —char·i·ta·bly \-blē\ *adv*

char·la·tan \'shärlətan\ *n* : impostor

charm \'chärm\ *n* 1 : something with magic power 2 : appealing trait 3 : small ornament ~ *vb* : fascinate —charm·er *n* —charm·ing *adj* —charm·ing·ly *adv*

char·nel house \'chärn²l-\ *n* : place for dead bodies

chart \'chärt\ *n* 1 : map 2 : diagram ~ *vb* 1 : make a chart of 2 : plan

char·ter \-ər\ *n* 1 : document granting rights 2 : constitution ~ *vb* 1 : establish by charter 2 : rent —char·ter·er *n*

char·treuse \shär'trüz, -'trüs\ *n* : brilliant yellow green

char·wom·an \'chär,wümən\ *n* : cleaning woman

chary \'cha(ə)rē\ *adj* chari·er; -est : cautious —char·i·ly \'charəlē\ *adv*

¹chase \'chās\ *vb* chased; chas·ing 1 : follow trying to catch 2 : drive away —chase *n* —chas·er *n*

²chase *vb* chased; chas·ing : decorate (metal) by embossing or engraving

chasm \'kazəm\ *n* : gorge

chas·sis \'chasē, 'shas-\ *n*, *pl* chas·sis \-ēz\ : framework

chaste \'chāst\ *adj* chast·er; chast·est 1 : abstaining from all or unlawful sexual relations 2 : modest or decent 3 : severely simple —chaste·ly *adv* —chaste·ness *n* —chas·ti·ty \'chastətē\ *n*

chas·ten \'chās²n\ *vb* : discipline

chas·tise \chas'tīz\ *vb* -tised; -tis·ing 1 : punish 2 : censure —chas·tise·ment \-mənt, 'chastəz-\ *n*

chat \'chat\ *n* : informal talk —chat *vb* —chat·ty \-ē\ *adj*

châ·teau \sha'tō\ *n*, *pl* -teaus \-'tōz\ *or* -teaux \-'tō(z)\ 1 : large country house 2 : French vineyard estate

chat·tel \'chat²l\ *n* : item of tangible property other than real estate

chat·ter \'chatər\ *vb* 1 : utter rapidly succeeding sounds 2 : talk fast or too much —chatter *n* —chat·ter·er *n*

chat·ter·box *n* : incessant talker

chauf·feur \'shōfər, shō'fər\ *n* : hired car driver ~ *vb* : work as a chauffeur

chau·vin·ism \'shōvə,nizəm\ *n* 1 : excessive patriotism —chau·vin·ist \-vənəst\ *n* —chau·vin·is·tic \,shōvə'nistik\ *adj*

cheap \'chēp\ *adj* 1 : inexpensive 2 : shoddy —cheap *adv* —cheap·en \'chēpən\ *vb* —cheap·ly *adv* —cheap·ness *n*

cheap·skate *n* : stingy person

cheat \'chēt\ *n* **1** : act of deceiving **2** : one that cheats ~ *vb* **1** : deprive through fraud or deceit **2** : violate rules dishonestly —**cheat·er** *n*

check \'chek\ *n* **1** : sudden stoppage **2** : restraint **3** : test or standard for testing **4** : written order to a bank to pay money **5** : ticket showing ownership **6** : slip showing an amount due **7** : pattern in squares **8** : mark placed beside an item noted ~ *vb* **1** : slow down or stop **2** : restrain **3** : compare or correspond with a source or original **4** : inspect or test for condition **5** : mark with a check **6** : leave or accept for safekeeping or shipment **7** : checker —**check in** *vb* : report one's arrival —**check out** *vb* : settle one's account and leave

¹check·er \-ər\ *n* : piece in checkers ~ *vb* : mark with different colors or into squares

²checker *n* : one that checks

check·er·board \-ə(r)ˌbȯrd\ *n* : board of 64 squares of alternate colors

check·ers \-ərz\ *n* : game for 2 played on a checkerboard

check·mate *vb* : thwart completely —**checkmate** *n*

check·point *n* : place where traffic is checked

check·up *n* : physical examination

ched·dar \'chedər\ *n* : hard smooth cheese

cheek \'chēk\ *n* **1** : fleshy side part of the face **2** : impudence —**cheeked** \'chēkt\ *adj* —**cheeky** *adj*

cheep \'chēp\ *vb* : utter faint shrill sounds —**cheep** *n*

cheer \'chiər\ *n* **1** : good spirits **2** : food and drink for a feast **3** : shout of applause or encouragement ~ *vb* **1** : give hope or courage to **2** : make or become glad **3** : urge on or applaud with shouts —**cheer·er** *n* —**cheer·ful** \-fəl\ *adj* —**cheer·ful·ly** *adv* —**cheer·ful·ness** *n* —**cheer·lead·er** *n* —**cheer·less** *adj* —**cheer·less·ly** *adv* —**cheer·less·ness** *n*

cheery \'chi(ə)rē\ *adj* **cheer·i·er**; **-est** : cheerful —**cheer·i·ly** *adv* —**cheer·i·ness** *n*

cheese \'chēz\ *n* : curd of milk usu. pressed and cured —**cheesy** *adj*

cheese·cloth *n* : lightweight coarse cotton gauze

chee·tah \'chētə\ *n* : spotted swift-moving African cat

chef \'shef\ *n* : chief cook

chem·i·cal \'kemikəl\ *adj* **1** : relating to chemistry **2** : working or pro-

duced by chemicals ~ *n* : substance obtained by chemistry —**chem·i·cal·ly** \-k(ə)lē\ *adv*

che·mise \shə'mēz\ *n* **1** : woman's one-piece undergarment **2** : loose dress

chem·ist \'keməst\ *n* **1** : one trained in chemistry **2** *Brit* : pharmacist

chem·is·try \-əstrē\ *n, pl* **-tries** : science that deals with the composition and properties of substances

che·mo·ther·a·py \ˌkēmō-, ˌkemō-\ *n* : use of chemicals in the treatment of disease —**che·mo·ther·a·peu·tic** *adj*

che·nille \shə'nēl\ *n* : yarn with protruding pile or fabric of such yarn

cheque \'chek\ *chiefly Brit var of* CHECK 5

cher·ish \'cherish\ *vb* : hold dear

cher·ry \'cherē\ *n, pl* **-ries** : small fleshy fruit of a tree related to the roses or the tree or its wood

cher·ub \'cherəb\ *n* **1** *pl* **-u·bim** \-(y)ə-ˌbim\ : angel **2** *pl* **-ubs** : chubby child —**che·ru·bic** \chə'rübik\ *adj*

chess \'ches\ *n* : game for 2 played on a checkerboard —**chess·board** *n* —**chess·man** *n*

chest \'chest\ *n* **1** : boxlike container **2** : part of the body enclosed by the ribs and breastbone —**chest·ed** *adj*

chest·nut \'ches(ˌ)nət\ *n* : nut of a tree related to the beech or the tree

chev·i·ot \'shevēət\ *n* **1** : heavy rough wool fabric **2** : soft-finished cotton fabric

chev·ron \'shevrən\ *n* : V-shaped insignia

chew \'chü\ *vb* : crush or grind with the teeth ~ *n* : something to chew —**chew·able** *adj* —**chew·er** *n* —**chewy** *adj*

chic \'shēk\ *n* : smart elegance of dress or manner ~ *adj* **1** : stylish **2** : currently fashionable

chi·ca·nery \shik'ān(ə)rē\ *n, pl* **-ner·ies** : trickery

chick \'chik\ *n* : young chicken or bird

chick·a·dee \-ə(ˌ)dē\ *n* : small grayish American bird

chick·en \-ən\ *n* **1** : common domestic fowl or its flesh used as food **2** : coward

chicken pox *n* : acute contagious virus disease esp. of children

chi·cle \'chikəl\ *n* : gum from a tropical evergreen tree

chic·o·ry \'chik(ə)rē\ *n, pl* **-ries** : herb used in salad or its dried ground root used to adulterate coffee

chide \'chīd\ *vb* **chid** \'chid\ *or* **chid-**

ed \'chīdəd\; **chid** or **chid·den**
\'chidᵊn\ or **chided**; **chid·ing**
\'chīdiŋ\ : scold

chief \'chēf\ n : leader ~ adj 1 : highest
in rank 2 : most important —**chief·dom** n —**chief·ly** adv

chief·tain \'chēftən\ n : chief —**chief·tain·cy** \-sē\ n

chif·fon \shif'än, 'shif-\ n : sheer fabric

chig·ger \'chigər\ n : bloodsucking
mite

chi·gnon \'shēn,yän\ n : knot of hair

chil·blain \'chil,blān\ n : sore or inflamed swelling caused by cold

child \'chīld\ n, pl **chil·dren**
\'children\ 1 : unborn or recently
born person 2 : son or daughter —**child-bear·ing** n or adj —**child-birth**
n —**child·hood** n —**child·ish** adj —**child·ish·ly** adv —**child·ish·ness** n —**child·less** adj —**child·less·ness** n —**child·like** adj

chili, **chile**, **chil·li** \'chilē\ n, pl **chil·ies**
or **chil·es** or **chil·lies** 1 : hot pepper 2 : spicy stew of ground beef, chilies,
and beans

chill \'chil\ vb : make or become cold
or chilly ~ adj : moderately cold ~
n 1 : feeling of coldness with shivering 2 : moderate coldness

chilly \-ē\ adj **chill·i·er**; **-est** : noticeably cold —**chill·i·ness** n

chime \'chīm\ n : set of tuned bells or
their sound ~ vb : make bell-like
sounds —**chime in** vb : break into or
join in a conversation

chi·me·ra, **chi·mae·ra** \kī'mirə, kə-\ n : imaginary monster —**chi·me·ri·cal** \-'merikəl\ adj

chim·ney \'chimnē\ n, pl **-neys** 1 : passage for smoke 2 : glass tube around
a lamp flame

chimp \'chimp, 'shimp\ n : chimpanzee

chim·pan·zee \,chim,pan'zē, ,shim-;
chim'panzē, shim-\ n : manlike ape
smaller than a gorilla

chin \'chin\ n : part of the face below
the mouth —**chin·less** adj

chi·na \'chīnə\ n 1 : porcelain ware 2 : domestic pottery

chin·chil·la \chin'chilə\ n : small So.
American rodent with soft
pearl-gray fur

chink \'chiŋk\ n : small crack ~ vb : fill chinks of

chintz \'chints\ n : printed cotton cloth

chip \'chip\ n 1 : small thin flat piece
cut or broken off 2 : thin crisp morsel
of food 3 : counter used in games 4 : flaw where a chip came off 5

: small slice of semiconductor containing electronic circuits ~ vb **-pp-**
: cut or break chips from —**chip in**
vb : contribute

chip·munk \-,məŋk\ n : small striped
ground-dwelling squirrel

chip·per \-ər\ adj : lively and cheerful

chi·rop·o·dy \kə'räpədē, shə-\ n : podiatry —**chi·rop·o·dist** \-ədəst\ n

chi·ro·prac·tic \'kīrə,praktik\ n : system of healing based esp. on manipulation of body structures —**chi·ro·prac·tor** \-tər\ n

chirp \'chərp\ n : short sharp sound
like that of a bird or cricket —**chirp**
vb

chis·el \'chizəl\ n : sharp-edged metal
tool ~ vb **-eled** or **-elled**; **-el·ing** or **-el·ling** 1 : work with a chisel 2 : cheat —**chis·el·er** \-(ə)lər\ n

chit \'chit\ n : signed voucher for a
small debt

chit-chat \-,chat\ n : casual conversation

chiv·al·rous \'shivəlrəs\ adj 1 : relating
to chivalry 2 : honest, courteous, or
generous —**chiv·al·rous·ly** adv —**chiv·al·rous·ness** n

chiv·al·ry \-rē\ n, pl **-ries** 1 : system or
practices of knighthood 2 : spirit or
character of the ideal knight —**chi·val·ric** \shə'valrik\ adj

chive \'chīv\ n : herb related to the
onion

chlo·ride \'klōr,īd\ n : compound of
chlorine

chlo·ri·nate \-ə,nāt\ vb **-nat·ed**; **-nat·ing**
: treat or combine with chlorine —**chlo·ri·na·tion** \,klōrə'nāshən\ n —**chlo·ri·na·tor** \'klōrə,nātər\ n

chlo·rine \-,ēn\ n : chemical element
that is a heavy strong-smelling
greenish yellow irritating gas

chlo·ro·form \-ə,fòrm\ n : etherlike
colorless heavy fluid ~ vb : anesthetize or kill with chloroform

chlo·ro·phyll \-ə,fil\ n : green coloring
matter of plants

chock \'chäk\ n : wedge for blocking
the movement of a wheel —**chock** vb

chock-full \'chək'fùl, 'chäk-\ adj
: full to the limit

choc·o·late \'chäk(ə)lət, 'chòk-\ n 1
: ground roasted cacao beans or a
beverage made from them 2 : candy
made of or with chocolate 3 : dark
brown

choice \'chòis\ n 1 : act or power of
choosing 2 : one selected 3 : variety
offered for selection ~ adj **choic·er**;
choic·est 1 : worthy of being chosen

2 : selected with care 3 : of high quality

choir \'kwī(ə)r\ n : group of singers esp. in church —**choir·boy** n —**choir·mas·ter** n

choke \'chōk\ vb **choked; chok·ing** 1 : hinder breathing 2 : clog or obstruct ~ n 1 : a choking or sound of choking 2 : valve for controlling air intake in a gasoline engine

chok·er \-ər\ n : tight necklace

cho·ler \'kälər, 'kō-\ n : bad temper —**cho·ler·ic** \'kälərik, kə'ler-\ adj

chol·era \'kälərə\ n : disease marked by severe vomiting and dysentery

cho·les·ter·ol \kə'lestə,rōl, -,rōl\ n : waxy substance in animal tissues

choose \'chüz\ vb **chose** \'chōz\; **cho·sen** \'chōz³n\; **choos·ing** 1 : select after consideration 2 : see fit 3 : decide —**choos·er** n

choosy, choos·ey \'chüzē\ adj **choos·i·er; -est** : fussy in making choices

chop \'chäp\ vb **-pp-** 1 : cut by repeated blows 2 : cut into small pieces ~ n 1 : sharp downward blow 2 : small cut of meat often with part of a rib

chop·per \-ər\ n 1 : one that chops 2 : helicopter

chop·py \-ē\ adj **-pi·er; -est** 1 : rough with small waves 2 : jerky or disconnected —**chop·pi·ly** adv —**chop·pi·ness** n

chops \'chäps\ n pl : fleshy covering of the jaws

chop·sticks n pl : pair of sticks used in eating in oriental countries

cho·ral \'kōrəl\ adj : relating to or sung by a choir or chorus or in chorus —**cho·ral·ly** adv

cho·rale \kə'ral, -'räl\ n 1 : hymn tune or harmonization of a traditional melody 2 : chorus or choir

¹**chord** \'kord\ n : harmonious tones sounded together

²**chord** n 1 : cordlike anatomical structure 2 : straight line joining 2 points on a curve

chore \'chōr\ n 1 pl : daily household or farm work 2 : routine or disagreeable task

cho·re·og·ra·phy \,kōrē'ägrəfē\ n, pl **-phies** : art of dancing or of arranging dances —**cho·re·o·graph** \'kōrēə,graf\ vb —**cho·re·og·ra·pher** \,kōrē-'ägrəfər\ n —**cho·re·o·graph·ic** \-ēə'grafik\ adj

cho·ris·ter \'kōrəstər\ n : choir singer

chor·tle \'chort³l\ vb **-tled; -tling** : laugh or chuckle —**chor·tle** n

cho·rus \'kōrəs\ n 1 : group of singers

or dancers 2 : part of a song repeated at intervals 3 : composition for a chorus ~ vb : sing or utter together

chose past of CHOOSE

cho·sen \'chōz³n\ adj : favored

¹**chow** \'chaů\ n : food

²**chow** n : thick-coated muscular dog

chow·der \'chaůdər\ n : thick soup usu. of seafood and milk

chow mein \-'mān\ n : thick stew of shredded vegetables and meat

chris·ten \'kris³n\ vb 1 : baptize 2 : name —**chris·ten·ing** n

Chris·ten·dom \-dəm\ n : areas where Christianity prevails

Chris·tian \'krischən\ n : adherent of Christianity ~ adj : relating to or professing a belief in Christianity or Jesus Christ —**Chris·tian·ize** \'krischə,nīz\ vb

Chris·ti·an·i·ty \,krischē'anətē\ n : religion derived from the teachings of Jesus Christ

Christian name n : first name

Christ·mas \'krisməs\ n : December 25 celebrated as the birthday of Christ

chro·mat·ic \krō'matik\ adj 1 : relating to color 2 : proceeding by half steps of the musical scale

chrome \'krōm\ n : chromium or something plated with it

chro·mi·um \-ēəm\ n : a bluish white metallic element used esp. in alloys

chro·mo·some \-ə,sōm, -,zōm\ n : part of a cell nucleus that contains the genes —**chro·mo·som·al** \,krōmə-'sōməl, -'zō-\ adj

chron·ic \'kränik\ adj : frequent or persistent —**chron·i·cal·ly** \-(ə)lē\ adv

chron·i·cle \-əl\ n : history ~ vb **-cled; -cling** : record —**chron·i·cler** \-(ə)lər\ n

chro·no·log·i·cal \krə'näləjē\ n, pl **-gies** : list of events in order of their occurrence —**chron·o·log·i·cal** \,krän³l'äjikəl\ adj —**chron·o·log·i·cal·ly** \-ik(ə)lē\ adv

chro·nom·e·ter \krə'nämətər\ n : very accurate timepiece

chrys·a·lis \'krisələs\ n, pl **chrys·a·li·des** \kris'alə,dēz\ or **chrys·a·lis·es** : insect pupa enclosed in a shell

chrys·an·the·mum \kris'anthəməm\ n : plant with showy flowers

chub·by \'chəbē\ adj **-bi·er; -est** : fat —**chub·bi·ness** n

¹**chuck** \'chək\ vb 1 : tap 2 : toss ~ n 1 : light pat under the chin 2 : toss

²**chuck** n 1 : cut of beef 2 : machine part that holds work or another part

chuck·le \'chəkəl\ vb -led; -ling : laugh quietly —**chuckle** n

chug \'chəg\ n : sound of a laboring engine ~ vb -gg- : work or move with chugs

chum \'chəm\ n : close friend ~ vb -mm- : be chums —**chum·my** \-ē\ adj

chump \'chəmp\ n : fool

chunk \'chəŋk\ n 1 : short thick piece 2 : sizable amount

chunky \-ē\ adj **chunk·i·er; -est** 1 : stocky 2 : containing chunks

church \'chərch\ n 1 : building esp. for Christian public worship 2 : whole body of Christians 3 : denomination 4 : congregation —**church·go·er** n —**church·go·ing** adj or n

church·yard n : cemetery beside a church

churl \'chərl\ n : rude ill-bred person —**churl·ish** adj

churn \'chərn\ n : container in which butter is made ~ vb 1 : agitate in a churn 2 : shake violently

chute \'shüt\ n : trough or passage

chut·ney \'chətnē\ n, pl -neys : sweet and sour relish

chutz·pah, chutz·pa \'hútspə, 'kút-, -,)spä\ n : nerve or insolence

ci·ca·da \sə'kādə\ n : stout-bodied insect with transparent wings

ci·der \'sīdər\ n : apple juice

ci·gar \sig'är\ n : roll of leaf tobacco for smoking

cig·a·rette \,sigə'ret, 'sigə,ret\ n : cut tobacco rolled in paper for smoking

cinch \'sinch\ n 1 : strap holding a saddle or pack in place 2 : sure thing —**cinch** vb

cin·cho·na \siŋ'kōnə\ n : So. American tree that yields quinine

cinc·ture \'siŋkchər\ n : belt

cin·der \'sindər\ n 1 pl : ashes 2 : piece of partly burned wood or coal

cin·e·ma \'sinəmə\ n : movies or a movie theater —**cin·e·mat·ic** \,sinə 'matik\ adj

cin·na·mon \'sinəmən\ n : aromatic tree bark used as a spice

ci·pher \'sīfər\ n 1 : zero 2 : code

cir·ca \'sərkə\ prep : about

cir·cle \'sərkəl\ n 1 : closed symmetrical curve 2 : cycle 3 : group with a common tie ~ vb -cled; -cling 1 : enclose in a circle 2 : move or revolve around

cir·cuit \-kət\ n 1 : boundary 2 : regular tour of a territory 3 : complete path of an electric current

cir·cu·itous \,sər'kyüətəs\ adj : circular or winding

cir·cuit·ry \'sərkətrē\ n, pl -ries : arrangement of an electric circuit

cir·cu·lar \-kyələr\ adj 1 : round 2 : moving in a circle ~ n : advertising leaflet —**cir·cu·lar·i·ty** \,sərkyə 'larəntē\ n

cir·cu·late \'sərkyə,lāt\ vb -lat·ed; -lat·ing : move or cause to move in a circle or from place to place or person to person —**cir·cu·la·tion** \,sərkyə'lāshən\ n —**cir·cu·la·to·ry** \'sərkyələ,tōrē\ adj

cir·cum·cise \'sərkəm,sīz\ vb -cised; -cis·ing : cut off the foreskin of —**cir·cum·ci·sion** \,sərkəm'sizhən\ n

cir·cum·fer·ence \sər'kəmf(ə)rəns\ n : perimeter of a circle

cir·cum·flex \'sərkəm,fleks\ n : phonetic mark (as ⌃)

cir·cum·lo·cu·tion \,sərkəmlō'kyü-shən\ n : excessive use of words

cir·cum·nav·i·gate \,sərkəm-\ vb : sail completely around —**cir·cum·nav·i·ga·tion** n

cir·cum·scribe \'sərkəm,skrīb\ vb 1 : draw a line around 2 : limit

cir·cum·spect \'sərkəm,spekt\ adj : careful —**cir·cum·spec·tion** \,sərkəm'spekshən\ n

cir·cum·stance \'sərkəm,stans\ n 1 : fact or event 2 pl : surrounding conditions 3 pl : financial situation —**cir·cum·stan·tial** \,sərkəm-'stanchəl\ adj

cir·cum·vent \-'vent\ vb : get around esp. by trickery

cir·cus \'sərkəs\ n : show with feats of skill, animal acts, and clowns

cir·rho·sis \sə'rōsəs\ n, pl -rho·ses \-,sēz\ : fibrosis esp. of the liver —**cir·rhot·ic** \-'rätik\ adj or n

cir·rus \'sirəs\ n, pl -ri \-,ī\ : wispy white cloud

cis·tern \'sistərn\ n : underground water tank

cit·a·del \'sitəd³l, -ə,del\ n : fortress

cite \'sīt\ vb cit·ed; cit·ing 1 : summon before a court 2 : quote 3 : refer to esp. in commendation —**ci·ta·tion** \sī'tāshən\ n

cit·i·zen \'sitəzən\ n : member of a country —**cit·i·zen·ry** \-rē\ n —**cit·i·zen·ship** n

cit·ron \'sitrən\ n : lemonlike fruit

cit·rus \'sitrəs\ n, pl -rus or -rus·es : evergreen tree or shrub grown for its fruit (as the orange or lemon)

city \'sitē\ n, pl cit·ies : place larger or more important than a town

civ·ic \'sivik\ adj : relating to citizenship or civil affairs

civ·ics \-iks\ n : study of citizenship

civ·il \\'sivəl\\ *adj* 1 : relating to citizens 2 : polite 3 : relating to or being a lawsuit —**civ·il·ly** \\-(l)ē\\ *adv*

civ·il·ian \\sə'vilyən\\ *n* : person not in a military, police, or fire-fighting force

civ·il·i·ty \\sə'vilətē\\ *n, pl* -**ties** : courtesy

civ·i·li·za·tion \\,sivələ'zāshən\\ *n* 1 : high level of cultural development 2 : culture of a time or place

civ·i·lize \\'sivə,līz\\ *vb* -**lized**; -**liz·ing** : raise from a primitive stage of cultural development —**civ·i·lized** *adj*

civil liberty *n* : freedom from arbitrary governmental interference —usu. pl.

civil rights *n pl* : nonpolitical rights of a citizen

civil service *n* : government service

civil war *n* : war among citizens of one country

clack \\'klak\\ *vb* : make or cause a clatter —**clack** *n*

clad \\'klad\\ *adj* : covered

claim \\'klām\\ *vb* 1 : demand or take as the rightful owner 2 : maintain ~ *n* 1 : demand of right or ownership 2 : declaration 3 : something claimed —**claim·ant** \\-ənt\\ *n*

clair·voy·ant \\klaər'vóiənt\\ *adj* : able to perceive things beyond the senses —**clair·voy·ance** \\-əns\\ *n* —**clairvoyant** *n*

clam \\'klam\\ *n* : bivalve mollusk

clam·ber \\'klambər\\ *vb* : climb awkwardly

clam·my \\'klamē\\ *adj* -**mi·er**; -**est** : being damp, soft, and usu. cool —**clam·mi·ness** *n*

clam·or \\-ər\\ *n* 1 : uproar 2 : protest —**clamor** *vb* —**clam·or·ous** *adj*

clamp \\'klamp\\ *n* : device for holding things together —**clamp** *vb*

clan \\'klan\\ *n* : group of related families —**clan·nish** *adj* —**clan·nish·ness** *n*

clan·des·tine \\klan'destən\\ *adj* : secret

clang \\'klaŋ\\ *n* : loud metallic ringing —**clang** *vb*

clan·gor \\-ər\\ *n* : jumble of clangs

clank \\'klaŋk\\ *n* : brief sound of struck metal —**clank** *vb*

clap \\'klap\\ *vb* -**pp-** 1 : strike noisily 2 : applaud ~ *n* 1 : loud crash 2 : noise made by clapping the hands

clap·board \\'klabərd; 'kla(p),bōrd\\ *n* : narrow tapered board used for siding

clap·per \\'klapər\\ *n* : tongue of a bell

claque \\'klak\\ *n* : group hired to applaud at a performance

clar·et \\'klarət\\ *n* : dry red wine

clar·i·fy \\'klarə,fī\\ *vb* -**fied**; -**fy·ing** : make or become clear —**clar·i·fi·ca·tion** \\,klarəfə'kāshən\\ *n*

clar·i·net \\,klarə'net\\ *n* : woodwind instrument shaped like a tube —**clar·i·net·ist, clar·i·net·tist** \\-əst\\ *n*

clar·i·on \\'klarēən\\ *adj* : loud and clear

clar·i·ty \\'klarətē\\ *n* : clearness

clash \\'klash\\ *vb* 1 : make or cause a clash 2 : be in opposition or disharmony ~ *n* 1 : crashing sound 2 : hostile encounter

clasp \\'klasp\\ *n* 1 : device for holding things together 2 : embrace or grasp ~ *vb* 1 : fasten 2 : embrace or grasp

class \\'klas\\ *n* 1 : group of the same status or nature 2 : social rank 3 : course of instruction 4 : group of students ~ *vb* : classify —**class·less** *adj* —**class·mate** *n* —**class·room** *n*

clas·sic \\'klasik\\ *adj* 1 : serving as a standard of excellence 2 : classical ~ *n* : work of enduring excellence and esp. of ancient Greece or Rome —**clas·si·cal** \\-ikəl\\ *adj* —**clas·si·cal·ly** \\-k(ə)lē\\ *adv* —**clas·si·cism** \\'klasə,sizəm\\ *n* —**clas·si·cist** \\-səst\\ *n*

clas·si·fied \\'klasə,fīd\\ *adj* : restricted for security reasons

clas·si·fy \\-,fī\\ *vb* -**fied**; -**fy·ing** : arrange in or assign to classes —**clas·si·fi·ca·tion** \\,klasəfə'kāshən\\ *n*

clat·ter \\'klatər\\ *n* : rattling sound —**clatter** *vb*

clause \\'klöz\\ *n* 1 : separate part of a document 2 : part of a sentence with a subject and predicate

claus·tro·pho·bia \\,klöstrə'fōbēə\\ *n* : fear of closed or narrow spaces —**claus·tro·pho·bic** \\-bik\\ *adj*

clav·i·chord \\'klavə,kórd\\ *n* : early keyboard instrument

clav·i·cle \\-ikəl\\ *n* : collarbone

claw \\'klò\\ *n* : sharp curved nail or process (as on the toe of an animal) ~ *vb* : scratch or dig —**clawed** *adj*

clay \\'klā\\ *n* : plastic earthy material —**clay·ey** \\-ē\\ *adj*

clean \\'klēn\\ *adj* 1 : free from dirt or disease 2 : pure or honorable 3 : thorough ~ *adj* : make or become clean —**clean** *adv* —**clean·er** *n* —**clean·ly** \\-lē\\ *adv* —**clean·ness** *n*

clean·ly \\'klenlē\\ *adj* -**li·er**; -**est** : clean —**clean·li·ness** *n*

cleanse \\'klenz\\ *vb* **cleansed**; **cleans·ing** : make clean —**cleans·er** *n*

clear \\'kliər\\ *adj* 1 : bright 2 : free from clouds 3 : transparent 4 : easily heard, seen or understood 5 : free from doubt 6 : free from restriction or obstruction ~ *vb* **1** : make or become clear **2** : go away **3** : free from accusation or blame **4** : explain or settle **5** : net **6** : jump or pass without touching ~ *n* : clear space or part — **clear** *adv* — **clear·ance** \'klirəns\ *n* — **clear·ly** *adv* — **clear·ness** *n*

clear·ing \'kli(ə)riŋ\ *n* : land cleared of wood

cleat \'klēt\ *n* : projection that strengthens or prevents slipping

¹cleave \'klēv\ *vb* cleaved \'klēvd\ *or* **clove** \'klōv\; **cleav·ing** : adhere

²cleave *vb* cleaved \'klēvd\; **cleav·ing** : split apart — **cleav·age** \'klēvij\ *n*

cleav·er \'klēvər\ *n* : heavy chopping knife

clef \'klef\ *n* : sign on the staff in music to show pitch

cleft \'kleft\ *n* : crack

clem·ent \'klemənt\ *adj* **1** : merciful or temperate or mild — **clem·en·cy** \-ənsē\ *n*

clench \'klench\ *vb* **1** : hold fast **2** : close tightly

cler·gy \'klərjē\ *n* : body of religious officials — **clergy·man** \-jimən\ *n*

cler·ic \'klerik\ *n* : clergyman

cler·i·cal \-ikal\ *adj* **1** : relating to the clergy **2** : relating to a clerk or office worker

clerk \'klərk, *Brit* 'klärk\ *n* **1** : official responsible for record-keeping **2** : person doing general office work **3** : salesperson in a store — **clerk** *vb* — **clerk·ship** *n*

clev·er \'klevər\ *adj* **1** : resourceful **2** : marked by wit or ingenuity — **clev·er·ly** *adv* — **clev·er·ness** *n*

clew *var of* CLUE

cli·ché \kli'shā\ *n* : trite phrase — **cli·chéd** \-'shād\ *adj*

click \'klik\ *n* : slight sharp noise ~ *vb* : make or cause to make a click

cli·ent \'klīənt\ *n* **1** : person who engages professional services **2** : customer

cli·en·tele \,klīən'tel, ,klē-\ *n* : body of customers

cliff \'klif\ *n* : high steep face of rock

cli·mate \'klīmət\ *n* : average weather conditions over a period of years — **cli·mat·ic** \klī'matik\ *adj*

cli·max \'klī,maks\ *n* : the highest point ~ *vb* : come to a climax — **cli·mac·tic** \klī'maktik\ *adj*

climb \'klīm\ *vb* **1** : go up or down by use of hands and feet **2** : rise ~ *n* : a climbing — **climb·er** *n*

clinch \'klinch\ *vb* **1** : fasten securely **2** : settle **3** : hold fast or firmly — **clinch** *n* — **clinch·er** *n*

cling \'kliŋ\ *vb* clung \'kləŋ\; **cling·ing** **1** : adhere firmly **2** : hold on tightly

clin·ic \'klinik\ *n* : facility for diagnosis and treatment of outpatients — **clin·i·cal** \-əl\ *adj* — **clin·i·cal·ly** \-k(ə)lē\ *adv*

clink \'kliŋk\ *vb* : make a slight metallic sound — **clink** *n*

clin·ker \'kliŋkər\ *n* : fused stony matter esp. in a furnace

¹clip \'klip\ *vb* **-pp-** : fasten with a clip ~ *n* : device to hold things together

²clip *vb* **-pp- 1** : cut or cut off **2** : hit ~ *n* **1** : clippers **2** : sharp blow **3** : rapid pace

clip·per \'klipər\ *n* **1** *pl* : implement for clipping **2** : fast sailing ship

clique \'klēk, 'klik\ *n* : small exclusive group of people

cli·to·ris \'klitərəs, kli'tōrəs\ *n*, *pl* **cli·to·ri·des** \-'tōrə,dēz\ : small organ at the front of the vulva

cloak \'klōk\ *n* **1** : loose outer garment **2** : something that conceals ~ *vb* : cover or hide with a cloak

clob·ber \'kläbər\ *vb* : hit hard

clock \'kläk\ *n* : timepiece not carried on the person ~ *vb* : record the time of

clock·wise \-,wīz\ *adv or adj* : in the same direction as a clock's hands move

clod \'kläd\ *n* **1** : lump esp. of earth **2** : dull insensitive person

clog \'kläg\ *n* **1** : restraining weight **2** : thick-soled shoe ~ *vb* **-gg- 1** : impede with a clog **2** : obstruct passage through **3** : become plugged up

clois·ter \'klöistər\ *n* **1** : monastic establishment **2** : covered passage ~ *vb* : shut away from the world

clone \'klōn\ *n* **1** : offspring produced from a single organism **2** : copy

¹close \'klōz\ *vb* closed; **clos·ing** **1** : shut **2** : cease operation **3** : terminate **4** : bring or come together ~ *n* : conclusion or end

²close \'klōs\ *adj* clos·er; **clos·est** **1** : confining **2** : secretive **3** : strict **4** : stuffy **5** : having little space between items **6** : fitting tightly **7** : near **8** : intimate **9** : accurate **10** : nearly even — **close** *adv* — **close·ly** *adv* — **close·ness** *n*

clos·et \'kläzət, 'klöz-\ *n* : small compartment for household utensils or clothing ~ *vb* : take into a private room for a talk

clo·sure \'klōzhər\ *n* **1** : act of closing **2** : something that closes

clot \'klät\ *n* : dried mass of a liquid —**clot** *vb*

cloth \'klȯth\ *n, pl* **cloths** \'klȯthz, 'klȯths\ **1** : fabric **2** : tablecloth

clothe \'klȯth\ *vb* **clothed** *or* **clad** \'klad\; **cloth·ing** : dress

clothes \'klō(th)z\ *n pl* : clothing

cloth·ier \'klōthyər, -thēər\ *n* : maker or seller of clothing

cloth·ing \'klōthiŋ\ *n* : covering for the human body

cloud \'klau̇d\ *n* **1** : visible mass of particles in the air **2** : something that darkens, hides, or threatens ~ *vb* : darken or hide —**cloud·i·ness** *n* —**cloud·less** *adj* —**cloudy** *adj*

cloud·burst *n* : sudden heavy rain

clout \'klau̇t\ *n* **1** : blow **2** : influence ~ *vb* : hit forcefully

¹clove \'klōv\ *n* **1** : section of a bulb

²clove *past of* CLEAVE

³clove *n* : dried flower bud of an East Indian tree used as a spice

clo·ver \'klōvər\ *n* : leguminous herb with usu. 3-part leaves

clo·ver·leaf *n, pl* **-leafs** *or* **-leaves** : highway interchange without left-hand turns or direct crossings

clown \'klau̇n\ *n* : funny costumed entertainer esp. in a circus ~ *vb* : act like a clown —**clown·ish** *adj* —**clown·ish·ly** *adv* —**clown·ish·ness** *n*

cloy \'klȯi\ *vb* : disgust with excess —**cloy·ing·ly** \-iŋē\ *adv*

club \'kləb\ *n* **1** : heavy wooden stick **2** : playing card of a suit marked with a black figure like a clover leaf **3** : group associated for a common purpose ~ *vb* -**bb**- : hit with a club

club·foot *n* : misshapen foot twisted out of position from birth —**club·foot·ed** \-'fu̇təd\ *adj*

cluck \'klək\ *n* : sound made by a hen —**cluck** *vb*

clue, clew \'klü\ *n* : piece of evidence that helps solve a problem ~ *vb* **clued** *or* **clewed**; **clue·ing** *or* **clu·ing** *or* **clew·ing** : provide with a clue

clump \'kləmp\ *n* **1** : cluster **2** : heavy tramping sound ~ *vb* : tread heavily

clum·sy \'kləmzē\ *adj* **-si·er; -est 1** : lacking dexterity, nimbleness, or grace **2** : tactless —**clum·si·ly** *adv* —**clum·si·ness** *n*

clung *past of* CLING

clus·ter \'kləstər\ *n* : group ~ *vb* : grow or gather in a cluster

clutch \'kləch\ *vb* : grasp ~ *n* **1** : grasping hand or claws **2** : control or power **3** : coupling for connecting two working parts in machinery

clut·ter \'klətər\ *vb* : fill with things that get in the way —**clutter** *n*

co- *prefix* : with, together, joint, or jointly

coact	coinvent
coactor	coinventor
coauthor	coinvestigator
coauthorship	coleader
cocaptain	comanagement
cochairman	comanager
cochampion	co-officiate
cocomposer	co-organizer
coconspirator	co-own
cocreator	co-owner
codefendant	copartner
codesign	copartnership
codesigner	copresident
codevelop	coprincipal
codeveloper	coprisoner
codirect	coproduce
codirector	coproducer
codiscoverer	coproduction
codrive	copromote
codriver	copromoter
coedit	coproprietor
coeditor	coproprietorship
coexecutor	copublish
coexist	copublisher
coexistence	corecipient
coexistent	coresident
cofeature	cosignatory
cofinance	cosigner
cofound	cosponsor
cofounder	costar
coheir	cowinner
coheiress	coworker
cohost	cowrite
cohostess	

coach \'kōch\ *n* **1** : closed 2-door 4-wheeled carriage **2** : railroad passenger car **3** : bus **4** : 2d-class air travel **5** : one who instructs or trains performers ~ *vb* : instruct or direct as a coach

co·ag·u·late \kō'agyə,lāt\ *vb* **-lat·ed; -lat·ing** : clot —**co·ag·u·lant** \-lənt\ *n* —**co·ag·u·la·tion** \-,agyə'lāshən\ *n*

coal \'kōl\ *n* **1** : ember **2** : black solid mineral used as fuel —**coal·field** *n*

co·alesce \,kōə'les\ *vb* **-alesced; -alesc·ing** : grow together —**co·ales·cence** \-'les^ə ns\ *n*

co·ali·tion \-'lishən\ *n* : temporary alliance

coarse \'kȯrs\ *adj* **coars·er; coars·est 1** : composed of large particles **2** : rough or crude —**coarse·ly** *adv* —**coars·en** \-ə n\ *vb* —**coarse·ness** *n*

coast \'kōst\ *n* : seashore ~ *vb* : move without effort —**coast·al** \-ə l\ *adj* coast·er \-ər\ n 1 : one that coasts 2 : plate or mat to protect a surface

coast guard n : military force that guards or patrols a coast —coast·guards·man \'kōst,gärdzmən\ n

coast·line n : shape of a coast

coat \'kōt\ n 1 : outer garment for the upper body 2 : external growth of fur or feathers 3 : covering layer ~ vb : cover with a coat —coat·ed adj —coat·ing n

coax \'kōks\ vb : move to action or achieve by gentle urging or flattery

cob \'käb\ n : corncob

co·balt \'kō,bȯlt\ n : shiny silver-white magnetic metallic chemical element

cob·bler \'käblər\ n 1 : shoemaker 2 : deep-dish fruit pie —cob·ble \'käbəl\ vb

cob·ble·stone n : small round paving stone

co·bra \'kōbrə\ n : venomous snake

cob·web \'käb,web\ n : network spun by a spider or a similar filament

co·caine \kō'kān, 'kō,kān\ n : drug obtained from the leaves of a So. American shrub (co·ca \'kōkə\)

co·chlea \'kōklēə, 'käk-\ n, pl -chle·as or -chle·ae \-lē,ē, -,ī\ : the usu. spiral part of the inner ear —coch·le·ar \-lēər\ adj

cock \'käk\ n 1 : male fowl 2 : valve or faucet ~ vb 1 : draw back the hammer of a firearm 2 : tilt to one side —cock·fight n

cock·ade \kä'kād\ n : badge on a hat

cock·a·too \'käkə,tü\ n, pl -toos : large Australian parrot

cock·eyed \'käk'īd\ adj 1 : tilted to one side 2 : slightly crazy

cock·le \'käkəl\ n : edible shellfish

cock·pit \-,pit\ n : place for a pilot, driver, or helmsman

cock·roach \-,rōch\ n : nocturnal insect often infesting houses

cock·tail \'käk,tāl\ n 1 : iced drink of liquor and flavorings 2 : appetizer

cocky \-ē\ adj cock·i·er; -est : overconfident —cock·i·ness n

co·coa \'kōkō\ n 1 : cacao 2 : powdered chocolate or a drink made from this

co·co·nut \-kə(,)nət\ n : nutlike fruit of a tropical palm (coconut palm)

co·coon \kə'kün\ n : case protecting an insect pupa

cod \'käd\ n, pl cod : food fish of the No. Atlantic

cod·dle \'käd³l\ vb -dled; -dling : pamper

code \'kōd\ n 1 : system of laws or rules 2 : system of signals

co·deine \'kō,dēn, 'kōdēən\ n : narcotic drug used in cough remedies

cod·ger \'käjər\ n : odd fellow

cod·i·cil \'kädəsəl, -,sil\ n : postscript to a will

cod·i·fy \'kädə,fī, 'kōd-\ vb -fied; -fy·ing : arrange systematically —cod·i·fi·ca·tion \,kädəfə'kāshən, ,kōd-\ n

co·ed \'kō,ed\ n : female student in a coeducational institution —coed adj

co·ed·u·ca·tion \,kō-\ n : education of the sexes together —co·ed·u·ca·tion·al adj

co·ef·fi·cient \,kōə'fishənt\ n 1 : number that is a multiplier of another 2 : number that serves as a measure of some property

co·erce \kō'ərs\ vb -erced; -erc·ing : force —co·er·cion \-'ərzhən, -shən\ n —co·er·cive \-'ərsiv\ adj

cof·fee \'kȯfē\ n : drink made from the roasted and ground seeds (coffee beans) of a tropical shrub —cof·fee·house n —cof·fee·pot n

cof·fer \'kȯfər\ n : box for valuables

cof·fin \-fən\ n : box for burial

cog \'käg\ n : tooth on the rim of a gear —cogged \'kägd\ adj —cog·wheel n

co·gent \'kōjənt\ adj : compelling or convincing —co·gen·cy \-jənsē\ n

cog·i·tate \'käjə,tāt\ vb -tat·ed; -tat·ing : think over —cog·i·ta·tion \,käjə'tāshən\ n —cog·i·ta·tive \'käjə,tātiv\ adj

co·gnac \'kōn,yak\ n : French brandy

cog·nate \'käg,nāt\ adj : related —cognate n

cog·ni·tion \käg'nishən\ n : act or process of knowing —cog·ni·tive \'kägnətiv\ adj

cog·ni·zance \'kägnəzəns\ n : notice or awareness —cog·ni·zant \'kägnəzənt\ adj

co·hab·it \kō'habət\ vb : live together as husband and wife —co·hab·i·ta·tion \-,habə'tāshən\ n

co·here \kō'hiər\ vb -hered; -her·ing : stick together

co·her·ent \-'hirənt\ adj 1 : able to stick together 2 : logically consistent —co·her·ence \-əns\ n —co·her·ent·ly adv

co·he·sion \-'hēzhən\ n : a sticking together —co·he·sive \-siv\ adj —co·he·sive·ly adv —co·he·sive·ness n

co·hort \'kō,hȯrt\ n 1 : group of soldiers 2 : companion

coif·fure \kwä'fyur\ n : hair style

coil \'kȯil\ vb : wind in a spiral ~ n : series of loops (as of rope)

coin \'kȯin\ n : piece of metal used as

61

money ~ vb 1 : make (a coin) by stamping 2 : create —**coin·age** \-ij\ n —**coin·er** n

co·in·cide \ˌkōən'sīd, 'kōən,sīd\ vb **-cid·ed; -cid·ing** 1 : be in the same place 2 : happen at the same time 3 : be alike —**co·in·ci·dence** \kō-'insədəns\ n —**co·in·ci·dent** \-ənt\ adj —**co·in·ci·den·tal** \-,insə'dent²l\ adj

co·itus \'kōətəs\ n : sexual intercourse —**co·ital** \-ət²l\ adj

coke \'kōk\ n : fuel made by heating soft coal

co·la \'kōlə\ n : carbonated soft drink

col·an·der \'kələndər, 'käl-\ n : perforated utensil for draining food

cold \'kōld\ adj 1 : having a low or below normal temperature 2 : lacking warmth of feeling 3 : suffering from lack of warmth ~ n 1 : low temperature 2 : minor respiratory illness —**cold·ly** adv —**cold·ness** \'kōl(d)nəs\ n —**in cold blood** : with premeditation

cold–blood·ed adj 1 : cruel or merciless 2 : having a body temperature that varies with the temperature of the environment

cole·slaw \'kōl,slo\ n : cabbage salad

col·ic \'kälik\ n : sharp abdominal pain —**col·icky** adj

col·i·se·um \ˌkälə'sēəm\ n : arena

col·lab·o·rate \kə'labə,rāt\ vb **-rat·ed; -rat·ing** 1 : work jointly with others 2 : help the enemy —**col·lab·o·ra·tion** \-,labə'rāshən\ n —**col·lab·o·ra·tor** \-'labə,rātər\ n

col·lapse \kə'laps\ vb **-lapsed; -laps·ing** 1 : fall in 2 : break down physically or mentally 3 : fold down ~ n : breakdown —**col·laps·ible** adj

col·lar \'kälər\ n : part of a garment around the neck ~ vb 1 : seize by the collar 2 : grab —**col·lar·less** adj

col·lar·bone n : bone joining the breastbone and the shoulder blade

col·lards \'kälərdz\ n pl : kale

col·late \kə'lāt; 'käl,āt, 'kōl-\ vb **-lat·ed; -lat·ing** 1 : compare carefully 2 : assemble in order

col·lat·er·al \kə'lat(ə)rəl\ adj 1 : secondary 2 : descended from the same ancestors but not in the same line 3 : similar ~ n : property used as security for a loan

col·league \'käl,ēg\ n : associate

col·lect \kə'lekt\ vb 1 : bring, come, or gather together 2 : receive payment of ~ adv or adj : to be paid for by the receiver —**col·lect·ible, col·lect-**

able adj —**col·lec·tion** \-'lekshən\ n —**col·lec·tor** \-'lektər\ n

col·lec·tive \-tiv\ adj : denoting or shared by a group ~ n : a cooperative unit —**col·lec·tive·ly** adv

col·lege \'kälij\ n : institution of higher learning granting a bachelor's degree —**col·le·gian** \kə'lējən\ n —**col·le·giate** \kə'lējət\ adj

col·lide \kə'līd\ vb **-lid·ed; -lid·ing** : strike together —**col·li·sion** \-'lizhən\ n

col·lie \'kälē\ n : large long-haired dog

col·loid \'käl,oid\ n : tiny particles in suspension in a fluid —**col·loi·dal** \kə'loid²l\ adj

col·lo·qui·al \kə'lōkwēəl\ adj : used in informal conversation —**col·lo·qui·al·ism** \-ə,lizəm\ n

col·lo·quy \'käləkwē\ n, pl **-quies** : formal conversation or conference

col·lu·sion \kə'lüzhən\ n : secret cooperation for deceit —**col·lu·sive** \-'lüsiv\ adj

co·logne \kə'lōn\ n : perfumed liquid

¹co·lon \'kōlən\ n, pl **colons** or **co·la** \-lə\ : lower part of the large intestine —**co·lon·ic** \kō'länik\ adj

²colon n, pl **colons** : punctuation mark used esp. to direct attention to following matter

col·o·nel \'kərn²l\ n : commissioned officer (as in the army) ranking next below a brigadier general

col·on·nade \ˌkälə'nād\ n : row of supporting columns

col·o·ny \'kälənē\ n, pl **-nies** 1 : people who inhabit a new territory or the territory itself 2 : animals of one kind (as bees) living together —**co·lo·nial** \kə'lōnēəl\ adj or n —**colo·nist** \'kälənəst\ n

col·o·nize \'kälə,nīz\ vb **-nized; -niz·ing** 1 : establish a colony in 2 : settle in a colony —**col·o·ni·za·tion** \ˌkälənə-'zāshən\ n —**col·o·niz·er** n

col·or \'kələr\ n 1 : quality of visible things distinct from shape that results from light reflection 2 pl : flag 3 : liveliness ~ vb 1 : give color to 2 : blush —**col·or·fast** adj —**col·or·ful** adj —**col·or·less** adj

col·or–blind adj : unable to distinguish colors —**color blindness** n

col·ored \'kələrd\ adj 1 : having color 2 : of a race other than the white ~ n, pl **colored** or **coloreds** : colored person

co·los·sal \kə'läsəl\ adj : very large or great

co·los·sus \-əs\ n, pl **-sus·es** or **-si** \-'läs-,ī\ : something of great size or scope

colt \'kōlt\ *n* : young male horse — **colt·ish** *adj*

col·umn \'käləm\ *n* 1 : vertical section of a printed page 2 : special item (as in a newspaper) 3 : pillar 4 : row (as of soldiers) — **col·um·nar** \kə'ləmnər\ *adj* — **col·um·nist** \'käləm-(n)əst\ *n*

co·ma \'kōmə\ *n* : deep prolonged unconsciousness — **co·ma·tose** \-,tōs, 'kämə-\ *adj*

comb \'kōm\ *n* 1 : toothed instrument for arranging the hair 2 : crest on a fowl's head — **comb** *vb* — **combed** \'kōmd\ *adj*

com·bat \kəm'bat, 'käm,bat\ *vb* -**bat·ed** *or* -**bat·ted**; -**bat·ing** *or* -**bat·ting** : fight — **com·bat** \'käm,bat\ *n* — **com·bat·ant** \kəm'bat⁹nt\ *n* — **com·bat·ive** \kəm'bativ\ *adj*

com·bi·na·tion \,kämbə'nāshən\ *n* 1 : process or result of combining 2 : code for opening a lock

com·bine \kəm'bīn\ *vb* -**bined**; -**bin·ing** : join together — **com·bine** \'käm,bīn\ *n* 1 : association for business or political advantage 2 : harvesting machine

com·bus·ti·ble \kəm'bəstəbəl\ *adj* : apt to catch fire — **com·bus·ti·bil·i·ty** \-,bəstə'bilətē\ *n* — **combustible** *n*

com·bus·tion \-'bəschən\ *n* : process of burning

come \'kəm\ *vb* came \'kām\; come; com·ing 1 : move toward or arrive at something 2 : reach a state 3 : originate or exist 4 : amount — **come across** *vb* : meet or find by chance — **come off** *vb* : succeed — **come to** *vb* : regain consciousness — **come to pass** : happen — **come upon** : come across

come·back *n* 1 : retort 2 : return to a former position — **come back** *vb*

co·me·di·an \kə'mēdēən\ *n* 1 : comic actor 2 : funny person 3 : entertainer specializing in comedy — **co·me·di·enne** \-,mēdē'en\ *n*

com·e·dy \'kämədē\ *n, pl* -**dies** 1 : an amusing play 2 : humorous entertainment

come·ly \'kəmlē\ *adj* -**li·er**; -**est** : good-looking — **come·li·ness** *n*

com·et \'kämət\ *n* : small bright celestial body having a tail

com·fort \'kəmfərt\ *n* 1 : consolation 2 : well-being or something that gives it ~ *vb* : give hope to 2 : console — **com·fort·able** \'kəmftəbəl, 'kəmfərt-\ *adj* — **com·fort·ably** \-blē\ *adv* — **com·fort·less** *adj*

com·fort·er \'kəmfə(r)tər\ *n* 1 : one that comforts 2 : quilt

com·ic \'kämik\ *adj* 1 : relating to comedy 2 : funny ~ *n* 1 : comedian 2 : sequence of cartoons — **com·i·cal** *adj*

com·ing \'kəmiŋ\ *adj* : next

com·ma \'kämə\ *n* : punctuation mark used esp. to separate sentence parts

com·mand \kə'mand\ *vb* 1 : order 2 : control ~ *n* 1 : act of commanding 2 : an order given 3 : mastery 4 : troops under a commander — **com·man·dant** \'kämən,dant, -,dänt\ *n*

com·man·deer \,kämən'dir\ *vb* : seize by force

com·mand·er \kə'mandər\ *n* 1 : officer commanding an army or subdivision of an army 2 : commissioned officer in the navy ranking next below a captain

com·mand·ment \-'man(d)mənt\ *n* : order

command sergeant major *n* : noncommissioned officer in the army ranking above a first sergeant

com·mem·o·rate \kə'memə,rāt\ *vb* -**rat·ed**; -**rat·ing** : celebrate or honor — **com·mem·o·ra·tion** \-,memə'rāshən\ *n* — **com·mem·o·ra·tive** \-'mem(ə)rətiv, -'memə,rāt-\ *adj*

com·mence \kə'mens\ *vb* -**menced**; -**menc·ing** : start

com·mence·ment \-mənt\ *n* 1 : beginning 2 : graduation ceremony

com·mend \kə'mend\ *vb* 1 : entrust 2 : recommend 3 : praise — **com·mend·able** \-əbəl\ *adj* — **com·men·da·tion** \,kämən'dāshən, -,en-\ *n*

com·men·su·rate \kə'mens(ə)rət, -'mench(ə)-\ *adj* : equal in measure or extent

com·ment \'käm,ent\ *n* : statement of opinion or remark — **comment** *vb*

com·men·tary \-ən,terē\ *n, pl* -**tar·ies** : series of comments

com·men·ta·tor \-ən,tātər\ *n* : one who discusses news

com·merce \'käm(,)ərs\ *n* : business

com·mer·cial \kə'mərshəl\ *adj* : designed for profit or for mass appeal ~ *n* : broadcast advertisement — **com·mer·cial·ize** \-,īz\ *vb* — **com·mer·cial·ly** \-ē\ *adv*

com·min·gle \kə'miŋgəl\ *vb* : mix

com·mis·er·ate \kə'mizə,rāt\ *vb* -**at·ed**; -**at·ing** : sympathize — **com·mis·er·a·tion** \-,mizə'rāshən\ *n*

com·mis·sary \'kämə,serē\ *n, pl* -**sar·ies** : store esp. for military personnel

com·mis·sion \kə'mishən\ *n* 1 : order

granting power or rank **2** : panel to judge, approve, or act **3** : the doing of an act **4** : agent's fee ~ vb **1** : confer rank or authority to or for **2** : request something be done or made

com·mis·sion·er \-'mish(ə)nər\ n **1** : member of a commission **2** : head of a government department

com·mit \-'mit\ vb -tt- **1** : turn over to someone for safekeeping or confinement **2** : perform or do **3** : pledge —**com·mit·ment** n —**com·mit·tal** \-ºl\ n

com·mit·tee \-'mitē\ n : panel that examines or acts on something

com·mo·di·ous \kə-'mōdēəs\ adj : spacious

com·mod·i·ty \-'mädətē\ n, pl -ties : article for sale

com·mo·dore \'kämə,dōr\ n **1** : former commissioned officer in the navy ranking next below a rear admiral **2** : officer commanding a group of merchant ships

com·mon \'kämən\ adj **1** : public **2** : shared by several **3** : widely known, found, or observed **4** : ordinary ~ n : community land —**com·mon·ly** adv —**in common** : shared together

com·mon·place \'kämən,plās\ n : cliché ~ adj : ordinary

common sense n : good judgment

com·mon·weal \-,wēl\ n : general welfare

com·mon·wealth \-,welth\ n : state

com·mo·tion \kə-'mōshən\ n : disturbance

¹com·mune \kə-'myün\ vb -muned; -mun·ing : communicate intimately

²com·mune \'käm,yün; kə-'myün\ n : community that shares all ownership and duties —**com·mu·nal** \-ºl\ adj

com·mu·ni·cate \kə-'myünə,kāt\ vb -cat·ed; -cat·ing **1** : make known **2** : exchange information or opinions —**com·mu·ni·ca·ble** \-'myünikəbəl\ adj —**com·mu·ni·ca·tion** \-,myünə-'kāshən\ n —**com·mu·ni·ca·tive** \-'myüni,kātiv, -kət-\ adj

Com·mu·nion \-'myünyən\ n : Christian sacrament of partaking of bread and wine

com·mu·ni·qué \kə-'myünə,kā, -,myü-nə'kā\ n : official bulletin

com·mu·nism \'kämyə,nizəm\ n **1** : social organization in which goods are held in common **2** cap : political doctrine based on revolutionary Marxist socialism —**com·mu·nist**

\-nəst\ n or adj, often cap —**com·mu·nis·tic** \,kämyə'nistik\ adj, often cap

com·mu·ni·ty \kə-'myünətē\ n, pl -ties : body of people living in the same place under the same laws

com·mute \kə-'myüt\ vb -mut·ed; -mut·ing **1** : reduce (a punishment) **2** : travel back and forth regularly ~ n : trip made in commuting —**com·mu·ta·tion** \,kämyə'tāshən\ n —**com·mut·er** n

¹com·pact \kəm'pakt, (')käm-\ adj **1** : hard **2** : small or brief ~ vb : pack together ~ \'käm,pakt\ n **1** : cosmetics case **2** : small car —**com·pact·ly** adv —**com·pact·ness** n

²com·pact \'käm,pakt\ n : agreement

com·pan·ion \kəm'panyən\ n **1** : close friend **2** : one of a pair —**com·pan·ion·able** adj —**com·pan·ion·ship** n

com·pa·ny \'kəmp(ə)nē\ n, pl -nies **1** : business organization **2** : group of performers **3** : guests **4** : infantry unit

com·par·a·tive \kəm'parətiv\ adj **1** : relating to or being an adjective or adverb form that denotes increase **2** : relative —**comparative** n —**com·par·a·tive·ly** adv

com·pare \kəm'paər\ vb -pared; -par·ing **1** : represent as similar **2** : check for likenesses or differences ~ n : comparison —**com·pa·ra·ble** \'kämp(ə)rəbəl\ adj

com·par·i·son \kəm'parəsən\ n **1** : act of comparing **2** : change in the form and meaning of an adjective or adverb to show different levels of quality, quantity, or relation

com·part·ment \-'pärtmənt\ n : section or room

com·pass \'kəmpəs, 'käm-\ n **1** : scope **2** : device for drawing circles **3** : device for determining direction

com·pas·sion \kəm'pashən\ n : pity —**com·pas·sion·ate** \-(ə)nət\ adj

com·pat·i·ble \-'patəbəl\ adj : harmonious —**com·pat·i·bil·i·ty** \-,patə-'bilətē\ n

com·pa·tri·ot \kəm'pātrēət, -trē,ät\ n : fellow countryman

com·pel \kəm'pel\ vb -ll- : cause through necessity

com·pen·di·um \-'pendēəm\ n, pl -di·ums or -dia \-dēə\ : summary

com·pen·sate \'kämpən,sāt\ vb -sat·ed; -sat·ing **1** : offset or balance **2** : repay —**com·pen·sa·tion** \,kämpən'sā-shən\ n —**com·pen·sa·to·ry** \kəm'pensə,tōrē\ adj

com·pete \kəm'pēt\ vb -pet·ed; -pet·ing : strive to win —**com·pe·ti·tion**

\,kämpə'tishən\ n —com·pet·i·tive \kəm'petətiv\ adj —com·pet·i·tive·ness n —com·pet·i·tor \kəm'petətər\ n

com·pe·tent \'kämpətənt\ adj : capable —com·pe·tence \-əns\ n —com·pe·ten·cy \-ənsē\ n

com·pile \kəm'pīl\ vb -piled; -pil·ing : collect or compose from several sources —com·pi·la·tion \,kämpə-'lāshən\ n —com·pil·er \kəm'pīlər\ n

com·pla·cence \kəm'plāsᵊns\ n : self-satisfaction —com·pla·cen·cy \-ᵊnsē\ n —com·pla·cent \-ᵊnt\ adj

com·plain \kəm'plān\ vb 1 : express grief, pain, or discontent 2 : make an accusation —com·plain·ant n —com·plain·er n

com·plaint \-'plānt\ n 1 : expression of grief or discontent 2 : ailment 3 : formal accusation

com·ple·ment \'kämpləmənt\ n 1 : something that completes 2 : full number or amount ~ \-,ment\ vb : complete —com·ple·men·ta·ry \,kämplə'ment(ə)rē\ adj

com·plete \kəm'plēt\ adj -plet·er; -est 1 : having no part lacking 2 : finished 3 : total ~ vb -plet·ed; -plet·ing 1 : make whole 2 : finish —com·plete·ly adv —com·plete·ness n —com·ple·tion \-'plēshən\ n

com·plex \käm'pleks, kəm-; 'käm,pleks\ adj 1 : having many parts 2 : intricate ~ \'käm,pleks\ n : psychological problem —com·plex·i·ty \kəm'pleksətē, käm-\ n

com·plex·ion \kəm'plekshən\ n : hue or appearance of the skin esp. of the face —com·plex·ioned adj

com·pli·cate \'kämplə,kāt\ vb -cat·ed; -cat·ing : make complex or hard to understand —com·pli·cat·ed \-əd\ adj —com·pli·ca·tion \,kämplə-'kāshən\ n

com·plic·i·ty \kəm'plisətē\ n, pl -ties : participation in guilt

com·pli·ment \'kämpləmənt\ n 1 : flattering remark 2 pl : greeting ~ \-,ment\ vb : pay a compliment to —com·pli·men·ta·ry \,kämplə-'ment(ə)rē\ adj 1 : praising 2 : free

com·ply \kəm'plī\ vb -plied; -ply·ing : obey —com·pli·ance \-əns\ n —com·pli·ant \-ənt\ n

com·po·nent \kəm'pōnənt, 'käm,pō-\ n : part of something larger ~ adj : serving as a component

com·port \kəm'pōrt\ vb 1 : agree 2 : behave —com·port·ment \-mənt\ n

com·pose \kəm'pōz\ vb -posed; -pos-

ing 1 : create (as by writing) or put together 2 : calm 3 : set type —com·pos·er n —com·po·si·tion \,kämpə-'zishən\ n

com·pos·ite \käm'päzət, kəm-\ adj : made up of diverse parts —com·posite n

com·post \'käm,pōst\ n : decayed organic fertilizing material

com·po·sure \kəm'pōzhər\ n : calmness

com·pote \'käm,pōt\ n : fruits cooked in syrup

¹com·pound \(')käm'paùnd, kəm-\ vb 1 : combine or add 2 : pay (interest) on principal and accrued interest ~ \'käm,paùnd\ adj : made up of 2 or more parts ~ \'käm,paùnd\ n : something compounded

²com·pound \'käm,paùnd\ n : enclosure

com·pre·hend \,kämpri'hend\ vb 1 : understand 2 : include —com·pre·hen·si·ble \-'hensəbəl\ adj —com·pre·hen·sion \-'henchən\ n —com·pre·hen·sive \-siv\ adj

com·press \kəm'pres\ vb : squeeze together ~ \'käm,pres\ n : pad for pressing on a wound —com·pressed adj —com·pres·sion \-'preshən\ n —com·pres·sor \-'presər\ n

compressed air n : air under pressure greater than that of the atmosphere

com·prise \kəm'prīz\ vb -prised; -pris·ing 1 : contain or cover 2 : be made up of

com·pro·mise \'kämprə,mīz\ vb -mised; -mis·ing : settle differences by mutual concessions —compromise n

comp·trol·ler \kən'trōlər, 'kämp,trō-\ n : financial officer

com·pul·sion \kəm'pəlshən\ n 1 : coercion 2 : irresistible impulse —com·pul·sive \-siv\ adj —com·pul·so·ry \-'pəls(ə)rē\ adj

com·punc·tion \-'pəŋkshən\ n : remorse

com·pute \-'pyüt\ vb -put·ed; -put·ing : calculate —com·pu·ta·tion \,käm-pyü'tāshən\ n

com·put·er \-'pyütər\ n : electronic data processing machine —com·put·er·iza·tion \-,pyütərə'zāshən\ n —com·put·er·ize \-'pyütə,rīz\ vb

com·rade \'käm,rad, -rəd\ n : companion —com·rade·ship n

¹con \'kän\ adv : against ~ n : opposing side or person

²con vb -nn- : swindle

con·cave \(')kän'kāv\ adj : curved like

the inside of a sphere —**con·cav·i·ty** \kän'kavətē\ n

con·ceal \kən'sēl\ vb : hide —**con·ceal·ment** n

con·cede \-'sēd\ vb -**ced·ed; -ced·ing** : grant

con·ceit \-'sēt\ n : excessively high opinion of oneself —**con·ceit·ed** \-əd\ adj

con·ceive \-'sēv\ vb -**ceived; -ceiv·ing** 1 : become pregnant 2 : think of —**con·ceiv·able** \-'sēvəbəl\ adj —**con·ceiv·ably** \-blē\ adv

con·cen·trate \'känsən,trāt\ vb -**trat·ed; -trat·ing** 1 : gather together 2 : make stronger 3 : fix one's attention on one thing ~ n : something concentrated —**con·cen·tra·tion** \,känsən'trāshən\

con·cen·tric \kən'sentrik\ adj : having a common center

con·cept \'kän,sept\ n : thought or idea

con·cep·tion \kən'sepshən\ n 1 : act of conceiving 2 : idea

con·cern \kən'sərn\ vb 1 : relate to 2 : involve — n 1 : affair 2 : worry 3 : business —**con·cerned** \-'sərnd\ adj —**con·cern·ing** \-'sərniŋ\ prep

con·cert \-'sərt\ vb 1 : plan together ~ \'kän(,)sərt\ n 1 : agreement or joint action 2 : public performance of music

con·cer·ti·na \,känsər'tēnə\ n : accordionlike instrument

con·cer·to \kən'chertō\ n, pl -**ti** \-(,)ē\ or -**tos** : orchestral work with solo instruments

con·ces·sion \-'seshən\ n 1 : act of conceding 2 : something conceded 3 : right to do business on a property

conch \'käŋk, 'känch\ n, pl **conchs** \'käŋks\ or **conch·es** \'känchəz\ : large spiral-shelled marine mollusk

con·cil·i·ate \kən'silē,āt\ vb -**at·ed; -at·ing** : gain the goodwill of —**con·cil·i·a·tion** \-,silē'āshən\ n —**con·cil·ia·to·ry** \-'silyə,tōrē, -'silē-\ adj

con·cise \kən'sīs\ adj : said in few words —**con·cise·ly** adv —**con·cise·ness** n

con·clave \'kän,klāv\ n : private meeting

con·clude \kən'klüd\ vb -**clud·ed; -clud·ing** 1 : end 2 : decide —**con·clu·sion** \-'klüzhən\ n —**con·clu·sive** \-siv\ adj —**con·clu·sive·ly** adv

con·coct \kən'käkt, kän-\ vb : prepare or devise —**con·coc·tion** \-'käkshən\ n

con·com·i·tant \-'kämətənt\ adj : accompanying —**concomitant** n

con·cord \'kän,kord, 'käŋ-\ n : agreement

con·cor·dance \kən'kord³ns\ n 1 : agreement 2 : index of words —**con·cor·dant** \-³nt\ adj

con·course \'kän,kōrs\ n : open space where crowds gather

con·crete \kän'krēt, 'kän,krēt\ adj 1 : naming something real 2 : actual or substantial 3 : made of concrete ~ \'kän,krēt, kän'krēt\ n : hard building material made of cement, sand, gravel, and water

con·cre·tion \kän'krēshən\ n : hard mass

con·cu·bine \'käŋkyu,bīn\ n : mistress

con·cur \kən'kər\ vb -**rr-** : agree —**con·cur·rence** \-'kərəns\ n

con·cur·rent \-ənt\ adj : happening at the same time

con·cus·sion \kən'kəshən\ n 1 : shock 2 : brain injury from a blow

con·demn \-'dem\ vb 1 : declare to be wrong, guilty, or unfit for use 2 : sentence —**con·dem·na·tion** \,kän,dem'nāshən\ n

con·dense \kən'dens\ vb -**densed; -dens·ing** 1 : make or become more compact 2 : change from vapor to liquid —**con·den·sa·tion** \,kän,den'sāshən, -dən-\ n —**con·dens·er** n

con·de·scend \,kändi'send\ vb 1 : lower oneself 2 : act haughtily —**con·de·scen·sion** \-'senchən\ n

con·di·ment \'kändəmənt\ n : pungent seasoning

con·di·tion \kən'dishən\ n 1 : necessary situation or stipulation 2 pl : state of affairs 3 : state of being ~ vb 1 : limit by a condition 2 : put into proper condition —**con·di·tion·al** \kən'dish(ə)nəl\ adj —**con·di·tion·al·ly** \-ē\ adv

con·dole \kən'dōl\ vb -**doled; -dol·ing** : express sympathy —**con·do·lence** \kən'dōləns, 'kändə-\ n

con·do·min·i·um \,kändə'minēəm\ n, pl -**ums** : individually owned apartment

con·done \kən'dōn\ vb -**doned; -don·ing** : overlook or forgive

con·dor \'kändər, -,dór\ n : large western American vulture

con·du·cive \kən'd(y)üsiv\ adj : tending to help or promote

con·duct \'kän(,)dəkt\ n 1 : management 2 : behavior ~ \kən'dəkt\ vb 1 : guide 2 : manage or direct 3 : be a channel for 4 : behave —**con·duc·tion** \-'dəkshən\ n —**con·duc·tive** \-'dəktiv\ adj —**con·duc·tiv·i·ty**

\,kən,dək'tivātē\ n —con·duc·tor \-'dəktər\ n

con·duit \'kän,d(y)üət, -d(w)ət\ n : channel (as for conveying fluid)

cone \'kōn\ n 1 : scaly fruit of pine and related trees 2 : solid figure having a circular base and tapering sides

Con·es·to·ga \,känə'stōgə\ n : covered wagon

con·fec·tion \kən'fekshən\ n : sweet dish or candy —con·fec·tion·er \-sh(ə)nər\ n

con·fed·er·a·cy \kən'fed(ə)rəsē\ n, pl -cies 1 : league 2 cap : 11 southern states that seceded from the U.S. in 1860 and 1861

con·fed·er·ate \-rət\ adj 1 : united in a league 2 cap : relating to the Confederacy ~ n 1 : ally 2 cap : adherent of the Confederacy ~ \-,fedə,rāt\ vb -at·ed; -at·ing : unite —con·fed·er·a·tion \-,fedə'rāshən\ n

con·fer \kən'fər\ vb -rr- 1 : give 2 : meet to exchang views —con·fer·ee \,känfə'rē\ n —con·fer·ence \'känf(ə)rəns\ n

con·fess \kən'fes\ vb 1 : acknowledge or disclose one's misdeed, fault, or sin 2 : declare faith in —con·fes·sion \'feshən\ n —con·fes·sion·al \-'fesh(ə)nəl\ n or adj

con·fes·sor \kən'fesər, 2 also 'kän,fes-\ n 1 : one who confesses 2 : priest who hears confessions

con·fet·ti \kən'fetē\ n : bits of paper or ribbon thrown in celebration

con·fi·dant \'känfə,dant, -,dänt\ n : one to whom secrets are confided

con·fide \kən'fīd\ vb -fid·ed; -fid·ing 1 : share private thoughts 2 : reveal in confidence

con·fi·dence \'känfədəns\ n 1 : trust 2 : self-assurance 3 : something confided —con·fi·dent \-ənt\ adj —con·fi·den·tial \,känfə'denchəl\ adj —con·fi·den·tial·ly \-ē\ adv —con·fi·dent·ly adv

con·fig·u·ra·tion \kən,figyə'rāshən\ n : arrangement

con·fine \-'fīn\ vb -fined; -fin·ing 1 : restrain or restrict to a limited area 2 : put in prison —con·fine·ment n —con·fin·er n

confines \'kän,fīnz\ n pl : bounds

con·firm \kən'fərm\ vb 1 : ratify 2 : verify 3 : admit as a full member of a church or synagogue —con·fir·ma·tion \,känfər'māshən\ n —con·firmed adj

con·fis·cate \'känfə,skāt\ vb -cat·ed; -cat·ing : take by authority —con·fis·ca·tion \,känfə'skāshən\ n

con·fla·gra·tion \,känflə'grāshən\ n : great fire

con·flict \'kän,flikt\ n 1 : war 2 : clash of ideas ~ \kən'flikt\ vb : clash

con·form \kən'fōrm\ vb 1 : make or be like 2 : obey —con·for·mi·ty \kən'fōrmətē\ n

con·found \kən'faúnd, kän-\ vb : confuse

con·front \kən'frənt\ vb : oppose or face —con·fron·ta·tion \,känfrən'tāshən\ n

con·fuse \kən'fyüz\ vb -fused; -fus·ing 1 : make mentally uncertain 2 : jumble —con·fu·sion \-'fyüzhən\ n

con·fute \-'fyüt\ vb -fut·ed; -fut·ing : overwhelm by argument

con·geal \kən'jēl\ vb 1 : freeze 2 : become thick and solid

con·ge·nial \kən'jēnyəl\ adj : kindred or agreeable —con·ge·ni·al·i·ty n

con·gen·i·tal \kən'jenət°l\ adj : existing from birth

con·gest \kən'jest\ vb 1 : overcrowd or overfill —con·ges·tion \-'jeschən\ n —con·ges·tive \-'jestiv\ adj

con·glom·er·ate \kən'gläm(ə)rət\ adj : made up of diverse parts ~ \-ə,rāt\ vb -at·ed; -at·ing : form into a mass ~ \-(ə)rət\ n 1 : rock composed of fragments and a cementing material 2 : diversified corporation —con·glom·er·a·tion \-,gläm(ə)'rāshən\ n

con·grat·u·late \kən'grachə,lāt\ vb -lat·ed; -lat·ing : express pleasure to for good fortune —con·grat·u·la·tion \-,grachə'lāshən\ n —con·grat·u·la·to·ry \-'grachələ,tōrē\ adj

con·gre·gate \'kängri,gāt\ vb -gat·ed; -gat·ing : assemble

con·gre·ga·tion \,kängri'gāshən\ n 1 : assembly of people at worship 2 : religious group —con·gre·ga·tion·al \-sh(ə)nəl\ adj

con·gress \'kängrəs\ n : assembly of delegates or of senators and representatives —con·gres·sio·nal \kən'gresh(ə)nəl, kän-\ adj —con·gress·man \'kängrəsmən\ n —con·gress·wom·an n

con·gru·ence \kən'grüəns, 'kängrəwəns\ n : likeness —con·gru·ent \-ənt\ adj

con·gru·ity \kən'grüətē, kän-\ n : correspondence between things —con·gru·ous \'kängrəwəs\ adj

con·ic \'känik\ adj : relating to or like a cone —con·i·cal \-ikəl\ adj

co·ni·fer \'känəfər, 'kōn-\ n : cone-bearing tree —co·nif·er·ous \kō'nif(ə)rəs\ adj

con·jec·ture \kən'jekchər\ *n* or *vb*
: guess —**con·jec·tur·al** \-əl\ *adj*

con·join \kən-\ *vb* : join together

con·ju·gal \'känjigəl, kən'jü-\ *adj* : relating to marriage

con·ju·gate \'känjə,gāt\ *vb* **-gat·ed·**
-gat·ing : give the inflected forms of
(a verb) —**con·ju·ga·tion** \,känjə-
'gāshən\ *n*

con·junc·tion \kən'jəŋkshən\ *n* **1**
: combination **2** : occurrence at the
same time **3** : a word that joins other
words together —**con·junc·tive** \-'tiv\
adj

con·jure \'känjər, 'kən-\ *vb* **-jured·**
-jur·ing **1** : summon by sorcery **2**
: practice sleight of hand **3** : entreat
—**con·jur·er, con·ju·ror** \'känjərər,
'kən-\ *n*

con·nect \kə'nekt\ *vb* : join or associate —**con·nec·tion** \-'nekshən\ *n* —
con·nec·tive \-tiv\ *n* or *adj* —**con·nec·tor** *n*

con·nive \kə'nīv\ *vb* **-nived·**· **niv·ing** **1**
: pretend ignorance of wrongdoing **2**
: cooperate secretly —**con·niv·ance** *n*

con·nois·seur \,känə'sər\ *n* : expert
judge esp. of art

con·note \kə'nōt\ *vb* **-not·ed·** **-not·ing**
: suggest additional meaning —**con·no·ta·tion** \,känə'tāshən\ *n*

con·nu·bi·al \kə'n(y)übēəl\ *adj* : relating to marriage

con·quer \'käŋkər\ *vb* : defeat or overcome —**con·quer·or** \-kərər\ *n*

con·quest \'kän,kwest, 'käŋ-\ *n* **1** : act
of conquering **2** : something conquered

con·science \'känchəns\ *n* : awareness
of right and wrong

con·sci·en·tious \,känchē'enchəs\ *adj*
: honest and hard-working —**con·sci·en·tious·ly** *adv*

con·scious \'känchəs\ *adj* **1** : aware **2**
: mentally awake or alert **3** : intentional —**con·scious·ly** *adv* —**con·scious·ness** *n*

con·script \kən'skript\ *vb* : draft for
military service —**con·script** \'kän-
,skript\ *n* —**con·scrip·tion** \kən-
'skripshən\ *n*

con·se·crate \'känsə,krāt\ *vb* **-crat·ed·**
-crat·ing **1** : declare sacred **2** : devote
to a solemn purpose —**con·se·cra·tion** \,känsə'krāshən\ *n*

con·sec·u·tive \kən'sek(y)ətiv\ *adj*
: following in order —**con·sec·u·tive·ly** *adv*

con·sen·sus \-'sensəs\ *n* **1** : agreement
in opinion **2** : collective opinion

con·sent \-'sent\ *vb* : give permission
or approval —**consent** *n*

con·se·quence \'känsə,kwens\ *n* **1** : result or effect **2** : importance —**con·se·quent** \-kwənt, -,kwent\ *adj* —
con·se·quent·ly *adv*

con·se·quen·tial \,känsə'kwenchəl\
adj : important

con·ser·va·tion \,känsər'vāshən\ *n*
: planned management of natural
resources —**con·ser·va·tion·ist**
\-sh(ə)nəst\ *n*

con·ser·va·tive \kən'sərvətiv\ *adj* **1**
: disposed to maintain the status quo
2 : cautious —**con·ser·va·tism**
\-və,tizəm\ *n* —**conservative** *n*
—**con·ser·va·tive·ly** *adv*

con·ser·va·to·ry \kən'sərvə,tōrē\ *n*, *pl*
-ries : school for art or music

con·serve \-'sərv\ *vb* **-served·** **-serv·ing**
: keep from wasting ~ \'kän,sərv\
n : candied fruit or fruit preserves

con·sid·er \kən'sidər\ *vb* **1** : think
about **2** : give thoughtful attention to
3 : think that —**con·sid·er·ate**
\-'sid(ə)rət\ *adj* —**con·sid·er·ate·ly**
adv —**con·sid·er·ate·ness** *n* —**con·sid·er·ation** \-,sidə'rāshən\ *n*

con·sid·er·able   \-'sidər(ə)bəl,
-'sidrəbəl\ *adj* **1** : significant **2** : noticeably large —**con·sid·er·a·bly**
\-blē\ *adv*

con·sid·er·ing \-(ə)riŋ\ *prep* : taking
notice of

con·sign \kən'sīn\ *vb* **1** : transfer **2**
: send to an agent for sale —**con·sign·ee** \,känsə'nē, -,sī-; kən,sī-\ *n*
—**con·sign·ment** \kən'sīnmənt\ *n* —
con·sign·or \,känsə'nōr, -,sī-;
kən,sī-\ *n*

con·sist \kən'sist\ *vb* **1** : be inherent —
used with *in* **2** : be made up —used
with *of*

con·sis·ten·cy \-'sistənsē\ *n*, *pl* **-cies** **1**
: degree of thickness or firmness **2**
: quality of being consistent

con·sis·tent \-tənt\ *adj* : being steady
and regular —**con·sis·tent·ly** *adv*

[1]con·sole \kən'sōl\ *vb* **-soled·** **-sol·ing**
: soothe the grief of —**con·so·la·tion**
\,känsə'lāshən\ *n*

[2]con·sole \'kän,sōl\ *n* : cabinet or part
with controls

con·sol·i·date \kən'sälə,dāt\ *vb* **-dat·ed·** **-dat·ing** : unite or compact —**con·sol·i·da·tion** \-,sälə'dāshən\ *n*

con·som·mé \,känsə'mā\ *n* : clear soup

con·so·nance \'käns(ə)nəns\ *n* : agreement or harmony —**con·so·nant**
\-s(ə)nənt\ *adj*

con·so·nant \-s(ə)nənt\ *n* **1** : speech
sound marked by constriction or

closure in the breath channel 2 : letter other than *a, e, i, o,* and *u* —con·so·nan·tal \ˌkänsə'nant'l\ *adj*

con·sort \'kän,sȯrt\ *n* : spouse ~ \kən'sȯrt\ *vb* : keep company

con·spic·u·ous \kən'spikyəwəs\ *adj* : very noticeable —con·spic·u·ous·ly *adv*

con·spire \kən'spī(ə)r\ *vb* -spired; -spir·ing : secretly plan an unlawful act —con·spir·a·cy \-'spirəsē\ *n* —con·spir·a·tor \-'spirətər\ *n*

con·sta·ble \'känstəbəl, 'kän-\ *n* : police officer

con·stab·u·lary \kən'stabyə,lerē\ *n, pl* -lar·ies : police force

con·stant \'känstənt\ *adj* 1 : steadfast or faithful 2 : not varying 3 : continually recurring ~ *n* : something unchanging —con·stan·cy \-stənsē\ *n* —con·stant·ly *adv*

con·stel·la·tion \ˌkänstə'lāshən\ *n* : group of stars

con·ster·na·tion \ˌkänstər'nāshən\ *n* : amazed dismay

con·sti·pa·tion \ˌkänstə'pāshən\ *n* : difficulty of defecation —con·sti·pate \'känstə,pāt\ *vb*

con·stit·u·ent \kən'stichəwənt\ *adj* 1 : component 2 : having power to elect ~ *n* 1 : component part 2 : one who may vote for a representative —con·stit·u·en·cy \-wənsē\ *n*

con·sti·tute \'känstə,t(y)üt\ *vb* -tut·ed; -tut·ing 1 : establish 2 : be all or a basic part of

con·sti·tu·tion \ˌkänstə't(y)üshən\ *n* 1 : physical composition or structure 2 : the basic law of an organized body or the document containing it —con·sti·tu·tion·al \-əl\ *adj* —con·sti·tu·tion·al·i·ty \-ˌt(y)üshə'nalətē\ *n*

con·strain \kən'strān\ *vb* 1 : compel 2 : confine 3 : restrain —con·straint \-'strānt\ *n*

con·strict \-'strikt\ *vb* : draw or squeeze together —con·stric·tion \-'strikshən\ *n* —con·stric·tive \-'striktiv\ *adj*

con·struct \kən'strəkt\ *vb* : build or make —con·struc·tion \-'strəkshən\ *n* —con·struc·tive \-tiv\ *adj*

con·strue \kən'strü\ *vb* -strued; -stru·ing : explain or interpret

con·sul \'känsəl\ *n* 1 : Roman magistrate 2 : government commercial official in a foreign country —con·sul·ar \-sələr\ *adj* —con·sul·ate \-lət\ *n*

con·sult \kən'səlt\ *vb* 1 : ask the advice or opinion of 2 : confer —con-

sul·tant \-ənt\ *n* —con·sul·ta·tion \ˌkänsəl'tāshən\ *n*

con·sume \kən'süm\ *vb* -sumed; -sum·ing : eat or use up —con·sum·able *adj* —con·sum·er *n*

con·sum·mate \kən'səmət\ *adj* : complete or perfect ~ \'känsə,māt\ *vb* -mat·ed; -mat·ing : make complete —con·sum·ma·tion \ˌkänsə'māshən\ *n*

con·sump·tion \kən'səmpshən\ *n* 1 : act of consuming 2 : use of goods 3 : tuberculosis —con·sump·tive \-tiv\ *adj or n*

con·tact \'kän,takt\ *n* 1 : a touching 2 : association or relationship 3 : connection or communication ~ *vb* 1 : come or bring into contact 2 : communicate with

con·ta·gion \kən'tājən\ *n* 1 : spread of disease by contact 2 : disease spread by contact —con·ta·gious \-jəs\ *adj*

con·tain \-'tān\ *vb* 1 : enclose or include 2 : have or hold within 3 : restrain —con·tain·er *n* —con·tain·ment *n*

con·tam·i·nate \kən'tamə,nāt\ *vb* -nat·ed; -nat·ing : soil or infect by contact or association —con·tam·i·na·tion \-,tamə'nāshən\ *n*

con·tem·plate \'käntəm,plāt\ *vb* -plat·ed; -plat·ing : view or consider thoughtfully —con·tem·pla·tion \ˌkäntəm'plāshən\ *n* —con·tem·pla·tive \kən'templətiv; 'käntəm,plāt-\ *adj*

con·tem·po·ra·ne·ous \kən,tempə-'rānēəs\ *adj* : contemporary

con·tem·po·rary \-tempə,rerē\ *adj* 1 : occurring or existing at the same time 2 : of the same age —contemporary *n*

con·tempt \kən'tempt\ *n* 1 : feeling of scorn 2 : state of being despised 3 : disobedience to a court or legislature —con·tempt·ible \-'temptəbəl\ *adj*

con·temp·tu·ous \-'tempchə(wə)s\ *adj* : feeling or expressing contempt —con·temp·tu·ous·ly *adv*

con·tend \-'tend\ *vb* 1 : strive against rivals or difficulties 2 : argue 3 : maintain or claim —con·tend·er *n*

¹con·tent \kən'tent\ *adj* : satisfied ~ *vb* : satisfy ~ *n* : ease of mind —con·tent·ed *adj* —con·tent·ed·ly *adv* —con·tent·ed·ness *n* —con·tent·ment *n*

²con·tent \'kän,tent\ *n pl* : something contained 2 *pl* : subject matter (as of a book) 3 : essential meaning 4 : proportion contained

con·ten·tion \kən'tenchən\ *n* : state of

contending **—con·ten·tious** \-chəs\ *adj*

con·test \kən'test\ *vb* : dispute or challenge ~ \'kän,test\ *n* 1 : struggle 2 : game **—con·test·able** \kən-'testəbəl\ *adj* **—con·test·ably** \-blē\ *adv* **—con·tes·tant** \-'testənt\ *n*

con·text \'kän,tekst\ *n* : words surrounding a word or phrase

con·tig·u·ous \kən'tigyəwəs\ *adj* : connected to or adjoining **—con·ti·gu·i·ty** \,käntə'gyüətē\ *n*

con·ti·nence \'känt°nəns\ *n* : self-restraint **—con·ti·nent** \-ənt\ *adj*

con·ti·nent \'känt°nənt, 'käntnənt\ *n* : great division of land on the globe **—con·ti·nen·tal** \,känt°n'ent°l\ *adj*

con·tin·gen·cy \kən'tinjənsē\ *n, pl* **-cies** : possible event

con·tin·gent \-jənt\ *adj* : dependent on something else ~ *n* : a quota from an area or group

con·tin·u·al \kən'tinyə(wə)l\ *adj* 1 : continuous 2 : steadily recurring **—con·tin·u·al·ly** \-ē\ *adv*

con·tin·ue \kən'tinyü\ *vb* **-tin·ued; -tin·u·ing** 1 : remain in a place or condition 2 : endure 3 : resume after an intermission 4 : extend **—con·tin·u·ance** \-yəwəns\ *n* **—con·tin·u·a·tion** \-,tinyə'wāshən\ *n*

con·tin·u·ous \-'tinyəwəs\ *adj* : continuing without interruption **—con·ti·nu·ity** \,känt°n'(y)üətē\ *n* **—con·tin·u·ous·ly** *adv*

con·tort \kən'tórt\ *vb* : twist out of shape **—con·tor·tion** \-'tórshən\ *n*

con·tour \'kän,túr\ *n* 1 : outline 2 *pl* : shape

con·tra·band \'käntrə,band\ *n* : illegal goods

con·tra·cep·tion \,käntrə'sepshən\ *n* : prevention of conception **—con·tra·cep·tive** \-'septiv\ *adj or n*

con·tract \'kän,trakt\ *n* : binding agreement ~ \kən'trakt, *1 usu* 'kän,trakt\ *vb* 1 : establish or undertake by contract 2 : become ill with 3 : draw together so as to shorten 4 : shorten (a word) by omission **—con·trac·tion** \kən'trakshən\ *n* **—con·trac·tor** \'kän,traktər, kən'trak-\ *n* **—con·trac·tu·al** \kən'trak-chə(wə)l\ *adj*

con·tra·dict \,käntrə'dikt\ *vb* : state the contrary of **—con·tra·dic·tion** \-'dikshən\ *n* **—con·tra·dic·to·ry** \-'dikt(ə)rē\ *adj*

con·tral·to \kən'traltō\ *n, pl* **-tos** : lowest female voice

con·trap·tion \kən'trapshən\ *n* : device or contrivance

con·trary \'kän,trerē; *4 often* kən'tre(ə)rē\ *adj* 1 : opposite in character, nature, or position 2 : mutually opposed 3 : unfavorable 4 : uncooperative or stubborn **—con·trari·ly** \-,trerəlē, -'trer-\ *adv* **—con·trari·wise** \-,wiz\ *adv* **—con·trary** \'kän,trerē\ *n*

con·trast \'kän,trast\ *n* 1 : unlikeness shown by comparing 2 : unlike color or tone of adjacent parts ~ \kən'trast\ *vb* 1 : show differences 2 : compare so as to show differences

con·tra·vene \,käntrə'vēn\ *vb* **-vened; -ven·ing** : go or act contrary to

con·trib·ute \kən'tribyət\ *vb* **-ut·ed; -ut·ing** : give or help along with others **—con·tri·bu·tion** \,käntrə'byü-shən\ *n* **—con·trib·u·tor** \kən-'tribyətər\ *n* **—con·trib·u·to·ry** \-yə,tórē\ *adj*

con·trite \'kän,trīt, kən'trīt\ *adj* : repentant **—con·tri·tion** \kən'trishən\ *n*

con·trive \kən'trīv\ *vb* **-trived; -triv·ing** 1 : devise or make with ingenuity 2 : bring about **—con·triv·ance** \-'trīvəns\ *n* **—con·triv·er** *n*

con·trol \-'trōl\ *vb* **-ll-** 1 : exercise power over 2 : dominate or rule ~ *n* 1 : power to direct or regulate 2 : restraint 3 : regulating device **—con·trol·la·ble** *adj* **—con·trol·le** \-'trōlər, 'kän,-\ *n*

con·tro·ver·sy \'käntrə,vərsē\ *n, pl* **-sies** : clash of opposing views **—con·tro·ver·sial** \,käntrə'vərshəl, -sēəl\ *adj*

con·tro·vert \'käntrə,vərt, ,käntrə'-\ *vb* : contradict **—con·tro·vert·ibl** *adj*

con·tu·ma·cious \,känt(y)ə'māshəs\ *adj* : stubborn or insubordinate **—con·tu·ma·cy** \kən't(y)üməsē, 'känt(y)ə-\ *n*

con·tu·me·ly \kən't(y)üməlē, 'känt(y)ə,mēlē\ *n* : rudeness

con·tu·sion \kən't(y)üzhən\ *n* : bruise **—con·tuse** \-'t(y)üz\ *vb*

co·nun·drum \kə'nəndrəm\ *n* : riddle

con·va·lesce \,känvə'les\ *vb* **-lesced; -lesc·ing** : gradually recover health **—con·va·les·cence** \-°ns\ *n* **—con·va·les·cent** \-°nt\ *adj or n*

con·vec·tion \kən'vekshən\ *n* : circulation in fluids due to warmer portions rising and colder ones sinking **—con·vec·tion·al** \-'veksh(ə)nəl\ *adj* **—con·vec·tive** \-'vektiv\ *adj*

con·vene \kən'vēn\ *vb* **-vened; -ven·ing** : assemble or meet

con·ve·nience \-'vēnyəns\ n 1 : personal comfort or ease 2 : device that saves work

con·ve·nient \-nyənt\ adj 1 : suited to one's convenience 2 : near at hand —**con·ve·nient·ly** adv

con·vent \'känvənt, -,vent\ n : community of nuns

con·ven·tion \kən'venchən\ n 1 : agreement esp. between nations 2 : large meeting 3 : body of delegates 4 : accepted usage or way of behaving —**con·ven·tion·al** \-'vench(ə)nəl\ adj —**con·ven·tion·al·ly** adv

con·verge \kən'vərj\ vb -verged; -verg·ing : approach a single point —**con·ver·gence** \-'vərjəns\ n —**con·ver·gen·cy** \-jənsē\ n —**con·ver·gent** \-jənt\ adj

con·ver·sant \-'vərsənt\ adj : having knowledge and experience

con·ver·sa·tion \,känvər'sāshən\ n : an informal talking together —**con·ver·sa·tion·al** \-sh(ə)nəl\ adj

¹con·verse \kən'vərs\ vb -versed; -vers·ing : engage in conversation —**con·verse** \'kän,vərs\ n

²con·verse \kən'vərs, 'kän,vərs\ adj : opposite —**con·verse** \'kän,vərs\ n —**con·verse·ly** adv

con·ver·sion \kən'vərzhən\ n 1 : change 2 : adoption of religion

con·vert \kən'vərt\ vb 1 : turn from one belief or party to another 2 : change ~ \'kän,vərt\ n : one who has undergone religious conversion —**con·vert·er, con·ver·tor** \-ər\ n —**con·vert·ible** adj

con·vert·ible \kən'vərtəbəl\ n : automobile with a removable top

con·vex \kän'veks, 'kän,-, kän'-\ adj : curved or rounded like the outside of a sphere —**con·vex·i·ty** \kən-'veksətē, kän-\ n

con·vey \kən'vā\ vb -veyed; -vey·ing : transport or transmit —**con·vey·ance** \-'vāəns\ n —**con·vey·er, con·vey·or** \-ər\ n

con·vict \kən'vikt\ vb : find guilty ~ \'kän,vikt\ n : person in prison

con·vic·tion \kən'vikshən\ n 1 : act of convicting 2 : strong belief

con·vince \-'vins\ vb -vinced; -vinc·ing : cause to believe —**con·vinc·ing·ly** adv

con·viv·i·al \-'vivyəl, -'vivēəl\ adj : cheerful or festive —**con·viv·i·al·i·ty** \-,vivē'alətē\ n

con·voke \kən'vōk\ vb -voked; -vok·ing : call together to a meeting —**con·vo·ca·tion** \,känvə'kāshən\ n

con·vo·lut·ed \'känvə,lütəd\ adj 1 : intricately folded 2 : intricate

con·vo·lu·tion \,känvə'lüshən\ n : convoluted structure

con·voy \'kän,vȯi, kən'vȯi\ vb : accompany for protection ~ \'kän,-vȯi\ n : group of vehicles or ships moving together

con·vul·sion \kən'vəlshən\ n : violent involuntary muscle contraction —**con·vulse** \-'vəls\ vb —**con·vul·sive** \-'vəlsiv\ adj

coo \'kü\ n : sound of a pigeon —**coo** vb

cook \'kuk\ n : one who prepares food ~ vb : prepare food —**cook·book** n —**cook·er** n —**cook·ery** \-(ə)rē\ n —**cook·ware** n

cook·ie, cooky \'kukē\ n, pl -ies : small sweet flat cake

cool \'kül\ adj 1 : moderately cold 2 : not excited 3 : showing dislike ~ vb : make or become cool ~ n 1 : cool time or place 2 : composure —**cool·ant** \-ənt\ n —**cool·er** n —**cool·ly** \'kül(l)ē\ adv —**cool·ness** n

coo·lie \'külē\ n : unskilled Oriental laborer

coop \'küp, 'kup\ n : enclosure usu. for poultry ~ vb : confine in or as if in a coop

co-op \'kō,äp\ n : cooperative

coo·per \'kupər, 'kü-\ n : barrel maker —**cooper** vb

co·op·er·ate \kō'äpə,rāt\ vb : act jointly —**co·op·er·a·tion** \-,äpə'rā-shən\ n

co·op·er·a·tive \kō'äp(ə)rətiv, -'äpə-,rāt-\ adj : willing to work with others ~ n : enterprise owned and run by those using its services

co-opt \kō'äpt\ vb 1 : elect as a colleague 2 : take over

co·or·di·nate \-'ȯrd'nət, -'ȯrdnət\ adj : equal esp. in rank ~ n : any of a set of numbers used in specifying the location of a point on a surface or in space ~ \-'n,āt\ vb -nat·ed; -nat·ing 1 : make or become coordinate 2 : work or act together harmoniously —**co·or·di·na·tion** \-,ȯrd'n'āshən\ n —**co·or·di·na·tor** \-'n,ātər\ n

coot \'küt\ n : dark-colored ducklike bird

cop \'käp\ n : police officer

¹cope \'kōp\ n : cloaklike ecclesiastical vestment

²cope vb coped; cop·ing : deal with difficulties

co-pi·lot \'kō-\ n : assistant airplane pilot

cop·ing \'kōpiŋ\ n : top layer of a wall

co·pi·ous \'kōpēəs\ *adj* : very abundant —**co·pi·ous·ly** *adv* —**co·pi·ous·ness** *n*

cop·per \'käpər\ *n* 1 : malleable reddish metallic chemical element 2 : penny —**cop·pery** *adj*

cop·per·head *n* : largely coppery brown venomous snake

co·pra \'kōprə\ *n* : dried coconut meat

copse \'käps\ *n* : thicket

cop·u·la \'käpyələ\ *n* : verb linking subject and predicate —**cop·u·la·tive** \-,lätiv\ *adj*

cop·u·late \'käpyə,lät\ *vb* -**lat·ed**; -**lat·ing** : engage in sexual intercourse —**cop·u·la·tion** \,käpyə'lāshən\ *n*

copy \'käpē\ *n, pl* **cop·ies** 1 : imitation or reproduction of an original 2 : writing to be set for printing —*vb* **cop·ied**; **copy·ing** 1 : make a copy of 2 : imitate —**copi·er** \-ər\ *n* —**copy·ist** *n*

copy·right *n* : sole right to a literary or artistic work —*vb* : get a copyright on

co·quette \kō'ket\ *n* : flirt

cor·al \'kȯrəl\ *n* 1 : skeletal material of colonies of tiny sea polyps 2 : deep pink —**coral** *adj*

cord \'kȯrd\ *n* 1 : usu. heavy string 2 : long slender anatomical structure 3 : measure of firewood equal to 128 cu. ft. 4 : small electrical cable —*vb* 1 : tie or furnish with a cord 2 : pile in cords

cor·dial \'kȯrjəl\ *adj* : warmly welcoming —*n* : liqueur —**cor·di·al·i·ty** \,kȯrj(ē)'alātē, kȯrd'yal-\ *n* —**cor·dial·ly** \'kȯrjəlē\ *adv*

cor·don \'kȯrdᵊn\ *n* : encircling line of troops or police —**cordon** *vb*

cor·do·van \-əvən\ *n* : soft fine-grained leather

cor·du·roy \-ə,rȯi\ *n* 1 : heavy ribbed fabric 2 *pl* : trousers of corduroy

core \'kȯr\ *n* 1 : central part of some fruits 2 : inmost part —*vb* **cored**; **cor·ing** : take out the core of —**cor·er** *n*

cork \'kȯrk\ *n* 1 : tough elastic bark of a European oak (**cork oak**) 2 : stopper of cork —*vb* : stop up with a cork —**corky** *adj*

cork·screw *n* : device for drawing corks from bottles

cor·mo·rant \'kȯrm(ə)rənt, -ə,rant\ *n* : dark seabird

¹corn \'kȯrn\ *n* : cereal grass or its seeds —*vb* : cure or preserve in brine —**corn·meal** *n* —**corn·stalk** *n* —**corn·starch** *n*

²corn *n* : local hardening and thickening of skin

corn·cob *n* : axis on which the kernels of Indian corn are arranged

cor·nea \'kȯrnēə\ *n* : transparent part of the coat of the eyeball —**cor·ne·al** *adj*

cor·ner \'kȯrnər\ *n* 1 : point or angle formed by the meeting of lines or sides 2 : place where two streets meet 3 : inescapable position 4 : control of the supply of something ~ *vb* 1 : drive into a corner 2 : get a corner on 3 : turn a corner

cor·ner·stone *n* 1 : stone at a corner of a wall 2 : something basic

cor·net \kȯr'net\ *n* : trumpetlike instrument

cor·nice \'kȯrnəs\ *n* : horizontal wall projection

cor·nu·co·pia \,kȯrn(y)ə'kōpēə\ *n* : goat's horn filled with fruits and grain emblematic of abundance

co·rol·la \kə'rälə\ *n* : petals of a flower

cor·ol·lary \'kȯrə,lerē\ *n, pl* -**lar·ies** 1 : logical deduction 2 : consequence or result

co·ro·na \kə'rōnə\ *n* : shining ring around the sun seen during eclipses

cor·o·nary \'kȯrə,nerē\ *adj* : relating to the heart or its blood vessels ~ *n* : thrombosis of an artery supplying the heart

cor·o·na·tion \,kȯrə'nāshən\ *n* : crowning of a monarch

cor·o·ner \'kȯrənər\ *n* : public official who investigates causes of suspicious deaths

¹cor·po·ral \'kȯrp(ə)rəl\ *adj* : bodily

²corporal *n* : noncommissioned officer ranking next below a sergeant

cor·po·ra·tion \,kȯrpə'rāshən\ *n* : legal creation with the rights and liabilities of a person —**cor·po·rate** \'kȯrp(ə)rət\ *adj*

cor·po·re·al \kȯr'pōrēəl\ *adj* : physical or material —**cor·po·re·al·ly** *adv*

corps \'kȯr\ *n, pl* **corps** \'kȯrz\ 1 : subdivision of a military force 2 : working group

corpse \'kȯrps\ *n* : dead body

cor·pu·lence \'kȯrpyələns\ *or* **cor·pu·len·cy** \-lənsē\ *n* : excessive fatness —**cor·pu·lent** \-lənt\ *adj*

cor·pus \'kȯrpəs\ *n, pl* -**po·ra** \-pərə\ 1 : corpse 2 : body of writings

cor·pus·cle \'kȯr(,)pəsəl\ *n* : blood cell

cor·ral \kə'ral\ *n* : enclosure for animals —**corral** *vb*

cor·rect \kə'rekt\ *vb* 1 : make right 2 : chastise —*adj* 1 : true or factual 2 : conforming to a standard —**cor·rec·tion** \-'rekshən\ *n* —**cor·rec·tive** \-'rektiv\ *adj* —**cor·rect·ly**

\-'rek(t)lē\ *adv* —**cor·rect·ness** \-'rek(t)nəs\ *n*

cor·re·late \'kòrə,lāt\ *vb* -**lat·ed**; -**lat·ing** : show a connection between —**cor·re·late** \-lət, -,lāt\ *n* —**cor·re·la·tion** \,kòrə'lāshən\ *n*

cor·rel·a·tive \kə'relətiv\ *adj* : regularly used together —**correlative** *n*

cor·re·spond \,kòrə'spänd\ *vb* 1 : match 2 : communicate by letter —**cor·re·spon·dence** \-'spändəns\ *n* —**cor·re·spond·ing·ly** \-'spändiŋlē\ *adv*

cor·re·spon·dent \-'spändənt\ *n* 1 : person one writes to 2 : reporter

cor·ri·dor \'kòrədər, -ə,dòr\ *n* : passageway connecting rooms

cor·rob·o·rate \kə'räbə,rāt\ *vb* -**rat·ed**; -**rat·ing** : support with evidence —**cor·rob·o·ra·tion** \-,räbə'rāshən\ *n*

cor·rode \kə'rōd\ *vb* -**rod·ed**; -**rod·ing** : wear away by chemical action —**cor·ro·sion** \-'rōzhən\ *n*, —**cor·ro·sive** \-'rōsiv\ *adj* or *n*

cor·ru·gate \'kòrə,gāt\ *vb* -**gat·ed**; -**gat·ing** : form into ridges and grooves —**cor·ru·gat·ed** *adj* —**cor·ru·ga·tion** \,kòrə'gāshən\ *n*

cor·rupt \kə'rəpt\ *vb* 1 : change from good to bad 2 : bribe ~ *adj* : morally debased —**cor·rupt·ible** *adj* —**cor·rup·tion** \-'rəpshən\ *n*

cor·sage \kòr'säzh, -'säj\ *n* : bouquet worn by a woman

cor·set \'kòrsət\ *n* : woman's stiffened undergarment

cor·tege \kòr'tezh, 'kòr,-\ *n* : funeral procession

cor·tex \'kòr,teks\ *n*, *pl* -**ti·ces** \'kòrtə,sēz\ *or* -**tex·es** : outer or covering layer of an organism or part (as the brain) —**cor·ti·cal** \'kòrtikəl\ *adj*

cor·ti·sone \'kòrtə,sōn, -zōn\ *n* : adrenal hormone

cos·met·ic \käz'metik\ *n* : beautifying preparation ~ *adj* : relating to beautifying

cos·mic \'käzmik\ *adj* 1 : relating to the universe 2 : vast or grand

cos·mo·naut \'käzmə,nöt\ *n* : Soviet astronaut

cos·mo·pol·i·tan \,käzmə'pälət²n\ *adj* : belonging to all the world —**cosmopolitan** *n*

cos·mos \'käzməs *also* -,mōs, -,mäs\ *n* : universe

cos·sack \'käs,ak, -ək\ *n* : Russian czarist cavalryman

cost \'kòst\ *n* 1 : amount paid for something 2 : loss or penalty ~ *vb* cost; cost·ing 1 : require too much in

payment 2 : cause to pay, suffer, or lose —**cost·li·ness** \-lēnəs\ *n* —**cost·ly** \-lē\ *adj*

cos·tume \'käs,t(y)üm\ *n* : clothing

co·sy \'kōzē\ *var of* COZY

cot \'kät\ *n* : small bed

cote \'kōt, 'kät\ *n* : small shed or coop

co·te·rie \'kōtə,rē, ,kōtə'-\ *n* : exclusive group of persons

co·til·lion \kō'tilyən\ *n* : formal ball

cot·tage \'kätij\ *n* : small house

cot·ton \'kät²n\ *n* : soft fibrous plant substance or thread or cloth made of it —**cot·ton·seed** *n* —**cot·tony** *adj*

cot·ton·mouth \'kät²n\ *n* : poisonous snake

couch \'kauch\ *vb* 1 : lie or place on a couch 2 : phrase ~ *n* : bed or sofa

cou·gar \'kügər, -,gär\ *n* : large tawny wild American cat

cough \'kòf\ *vb* : force air from the lungs with short sharp noises —**cough** *n*

could \kəd, (')kúd\ *past of* CAN

coun·cil \'kaúnsəl\ *n* 1 : assembly or meeting 2 : body of lawmakers —**coun·cil·lor**, **coun·cil·or** \-s(ə)lər\ *n* —**coun·cil·man** \-mən\ *n* —**coun·cil·wom·an** *n*

coun·sel \'kaúnsəl\ *n* 1 : advice 2 : deliberation together 3 *pl* -**sel** : lawyer ~ *vb* -**seled** *or* -**selled**; -**sel·ing** *or* -**sel·ling** 1 : advise 2 : consult together —**coun·sel·or**, **coun·sel·lor** \-s(ə)lər\ *n*

¹**count** \'kaúnt\ *vb* 1 : name or indicate one by one to find the total number 2 : recite numbers in order 3 : rely 4 : be of value or account ~ *n* 1 : act of counting or the total obtained by counting 2 : charge in an indictment —**count·able** *adj*

²**count** *n* : European nobleman

coun·te·nance \'kaúnt²nəns, 'kaúntnəns\ *n* : face or facial expression ~ *vb* -**nanced**; -**nanc·ing** : allow or encourage

¹**count·er** \'kaúntər\ *n* 1 : piece for reckoning or games 2 : surface over which business is transacted

²**count·er** *n* : one that counts

³**count·er** *vb* : oppose ~ *adv* : in an opposite direction ~ *n* 1 : offsetting force or move ~ *adj* : contrary

counter- *prefix* 1 : contrary or opposite 2 : opposing 3 : retaliatory

counteraccusation	counterattack
	counterbid
counteraggression	counterblockade
	counterblow
counterargue	countercampaign
counterassault	

counterchallenge
countercharge
counterclaim
countercom-
plaint
countercoup
countercriticism
counterdemand
counterdemon-
stration
counterdemon-
strator
countereffect
countereffort
counterembargo
counterevidence
counterguerrilla
counterinfla-
tionary
counterinfluence
counterintrigue
countermeasure
countermove
countermove-
ment
counteroffer
counterpetition
counterploy
counterpower
counterpressure

counterpropa-
ganda
counterproposal
counterprotest
counterquestion
counterraid
counterrally
counterrebuttal
counterreform
counterresponse
counterretalia-
tion
counterrevolu-
tion
counterrevolu-
tionary
counterstrategy
counterstyle
countersue
countersugges-
tion
countersuit
countertendency
counterterror
counterterrorism
counterterrorist
counterthreat
counterthrust
countertrend

liant sudden action or plan 2 : sudden overthrow of a government

cou·pé, coupe \\kü'pā, 'küp\\ n : 2-door
automobile with an enclosed body

cou·ple \\kəpəl\\ vb **-pled; -pling** : link
together ~ n 1 : pair 2 : two persons
closely associated or married

cou·pling \\kəpliŋ\\ n : connecting device

cou·pon \\k(y)ü,pän\\ n : certificate redeemable for goods or a cash discount

cour·age \\kərij\\ n : ability to conquer
fear or despair —**cou·ra·geous**
\\kə'rājəs\\ adj

cou·ri·er \\kürēər, 'kərē-\\ n : messenger

course \\kōrs\\ n 1 : progress 2
: ground over which something
moves 3 : part of a meal served at
one time 4 : method of procedure 5
: subject taught in a series of classes
~ vb **coursed; cours·ing** 1 : hunt with
dogs 2 : run speedily —**of course** : as
might be expected

court \\kōrt\\ n 1 : residence of a sovereign 2 : sovereign and his officials
and advisers 3 : area enclosed by a
building 4 : space marked for playing
a game 5 : place where justice is
administered ~ vb : woo —**court-
house** n —**court·room** n —**court·ship**
\\-,ship\\ n

cour·te·ous \\kərtēəs\\ adj : showing
politeness and respect for others —
cour·te·ous·ly adv

cour·te·san \\kōrtəzən, 'kərt-\\ n
: prostitute

cour·te·sy \\kərtəsē\\ n, pl **-sies** : courteous behavior

cour·ti·er \\kōrtēər, 'kōrtyər\\ n : person in attendance at a royal court

court·ly \\kōrtlē\\ adj **-li·er; -est** : polite
or elegant —**court·li·ness** n

court–mar·tial n, pl **courts–martial**
: military trial court —**court–martial**
vb

court·yard n : enclosure open to the
sky that is attached to a house

cous·in \\kəz²n\\ n : child of one's uncle or aunt

cove \\kōv\\ n : sheltered inlet or bay

cov·e·nant \\kəv(ə)nənt\\ n : binding
agreement —**cov·e·nant** \\-(ə)nənt,
-ə,nant\\ vb

cov·er \\kəvər\\ vb 1 : place something
over or upon 2 : protect or hide 3
: include or deal with ~ n : something that covers —**cov·er·age**
\\-(ə)rij\\ n

cov·er·let \\-lət\\ n : bedspread

coun·ter·act vb : lessen the force of

coun·ter·bal·ance n : balancing influence or weight ~ vb : oppose or balance

coun·ter·clock·wise adv or adj : opposite to the way a clock's hands move

coun·ter·feit \\'kaúntər,fit\\ vb 1 : copy
in order to deceive 2 : pretend ~ adj
: spurious ~ n : fraudulent copy —
coun·ter·feit·er n

coun·ter·mand \\-,mand\\ vb : super-
sede with a contrary order

coun·ter·part n : one that is similar or
corresponds

coun·ter·point n : music with inter-
woven melodies

coun·ter·sign n : secret signal ~ vb
: add a confirming signature to

count·ess \\'kaúntəs\\ n : wife or widow
of a count or an earl or a woman
holding that rank in her own right

count·less \\-ləs\\ adj : too many to be
numbered

coun·try \\'kəntrē\\ n, pl **-tries** 1 : nation
2 : rural area ~ adj : rural —**coun·
try·man** \\-mən\\ n

coun·try·side n : rural area or its people

coun·ty \\'kaúntē\\ n, pl **-ties** : local government division esp. of a state

coup \\'kü\\ n, pl **coups** \\'küz\\ 1 : brilco·vert \'kō(ˌ)vərt, 'kōvərt, 'kəvərt\ adj : secret ~ \'kōvərt, 'kəvərt, 'kō-\ n : thicket that shelters animals

cov·et \'kəvət\ vb : desire enviously —cov·et·ous adj

cov·ey \'kəvē\ n, pl -eys 1 : bird with her young 2 : small flock (as of quail)

¹cow \'kaů\ n : adult female of a bovine animal —cow·hide n

²cow vb : intimidate

cow·ard \'kaů(ə)rd\ n : one who lacks courage —cow·ard·ice \-əs\ n —cow·ard·ly adv or adj

cow·boy n : a mounted ranch hand who tends cattle —cow·girl n

cow·er \'kaů(ə)r\ vb : shrink from fear or cold

cowl \'kaůl\ n : monk's hood

cow·lick \'kaů,lik\ n : turned-up tuft of hair that resists control

cow·slip \-ˌslip\ n : yellow flower

cox·swain \'käksən, -ˌswān\ n : person who steers a boat

coy \'kói\ adj : shy or pretending shyness

coy·ote \'kī,ōt, kī'ōt-ē\ n, pl coy·otes or coyote : small No. American wild dog

coz·en \'kəzⁿn\ vb : cheat

co·zy \'kōzē\ adj -zi·er; -est : snug

crab \'krab\ n : short broad shellfish with pincers

crab·by \'krabē\ adj -bi·er; -est : cross

¹crack \'krak\ vb 1 : break with a sharp sound 2 : fail in tone 3 : break without completely separating ~ n 1 : sudden sharp noise 2 : witty remark 3 : narrow break 4 : sharp blow 5 : try

²crack adj : extremely proficient

crack·down n : disciplinary action —crack down vb

crack·er \-ər\ n : thin crisp bakery product

crack·le \'krakəl\ vb -led; -ling 1 : make snapping noises 2 : develop fine cracks in a surface —crackle n

crack·pot \'krak,pät\ n : eccentric

crack-up n : crash

cra·dle \'krādⁿl\ n : baby's bed ~ vb -dled; -dling 1 : place in a cradle 2 : hold securely

craft \'kraft\ n 1 : occupation requiring special skill 2 : craftiness 3 pl usu craft : structure designed to provide transportation 4 pl usu craft : small boat —crafts·man \'kraftsmən\ n —crafts·man·ship \-ˌship\ n

crafty \'kraftē\ adj craft·i·er; -est : sly —craft·i·ness n

crag \'krag\ n : steep cliff —crag·gy \-ē\ adj

cram \'kram\ vb -mm- 1 : eat greedily

2 : pack in tight 3 : study intensely for a test

cramp \'kramp\ n 1 : sudden painful contraction of muscle 2 pl : sharp abdominal pains ~ vb 1 : affect with cramp 2 : restrain

cran·ber·ry \'kran,berē, -b(ə)rē\ n : red acid berry of a trailing plant

crane \'krān\ n 1 : tall wading bird 2 : machine for lifting heavy objects ~ vb craned; cran·ing : stretch one's neck to see

cra·ni·um \'krānēəm\ n, pl -ni·ums or -nia \-nēə\ : skull —cra·ni·al \-əl\ adj

crank \'krank\ n 1 : bent lever turned to operate a machine 2 : eccentric ~ vb : start or operate by turning a crank

cranky \'krankē\ adj crank·i·er; -est : irritable

cran·ny \'kranē\ n, pl -nies : crevice

craps \'kraps\ n : dice game

crash \'krash\ vb 1 : break noisily 2 : fall and hit something with noise and damage ~ n 1 : loud sound 2 : action of crashing 3 : failure

crass \'kras\ adj : crude or unfeeling

crate \'krāt\ n : wooden shipping container —crate vb

cra·ter \'krātər\ n : volcanic depression

cra·vat \'krə'vat\ n : necktie

crave \'krāv\ vb craved; crav·ing : long for —crav·ing n

cra·ven \'krāvən\ adj : cowardly —craven n

craw·fish \'kró,fish\ n : crayfish

crawl \'król\ vb 1 : move slowly (as by drawing the body along the ground) 2 : swarm with creeping things ~ n : very slow pace

cray·fish \'krā,fish\ n : lobsterlike freshwater crustacean

cray·on \'krā,än, -ən\ n : stick of chalk or wax used for drawing or coloring —crayon vb

craze \'krāz\ vb crazed; craz·ing : make or become insane ~ n : fad

cra·zy \'krāzē\ adj cra·zi·er; -est 1 : mentally disordered 2 : wildly impractical —cra·zi·ly adv —cra·zi·ness n

creak \'krēk\ vb or n : squeak —creaky adj

cream \'krēm\ n 1 : yellowish fat-rich part of milk 2 : thick smooth sauce, confection, or cosmetic 3 : choicest part ~ vb : beat into creamy consistency —creamy adj

cream·ery \-(ə)rē\ n, pl -er·ies : place where butter and cheese are made

crease \ˈkrēs\ n : line made by folding —**crease** vb

cre·ate \krēˈāt\ vb **-at·ed; -at·ing** : bring into being —**cre·a·tion** \krēˈāshən\ n —**cre·ative** \-iv\ adj —**cre·ativ·i·ty** \krē(,)āˈtivətē, ,krēə-\ n —**cre·ator** \krēˈātər\ n

crea·ture \ˈkrēchər\ n : lower animal or human being

cre·dence \ˈkrēdᵊns\ n : belief

cre·den·tials \kriˈdenchəlz\ n : evidence of qualifications or authority

cred·i·ble \ˈkredəbəl\ adj : believable —**cred·i·bil·i·ty** \,kredəˈbilətē\ n

cred·it \ˈkredət\ n 1 : balance in a person's favor 2 : time given to pay for goods 3 : belief 4 : esteem 5 : source of honor ~ vb 1 : believe 2 : give credit to

cred·it·able \-əbəl\ adj : worthy of esteem or praise —**cred·it·ably** \-əblē\ adv

cred·i·tor \-ər\ n : person to whom money is owed

cred·u·lous \ˈkrejələs\ adj : easily convinced —**cre·du·li·ty** \kriˈd(y)ülətē\ n

creed \ˈkrēd\ n : statement of essential beliefs

creek \ˈkrēk, ˈkrik\ n : small stream

creel \ˈkrēl\ n : basket for carrying fish

creep \ˈkrēp\ vb **crept** \ˈkrept\; **creep·ing** 1 : crawl 2 : grow over a surface like ivy —**creep** n —**creep·er** n

cre·mate \ˈkrē,māt\ vb **-mat·ed; -mat·ing** : burn up (a corpse) —**cre·ma·tion** \kriˈmāshən\ n —**cre·ma·to·ry** \ˈkrēmə,tōrē, ˈkrem-\ n

cre·o·sote \ˈkrēə,sōt\ n : oily wood preservative

crepe, crêpe \ˈkrāp\ n : light crinkled fabric

cres·cen·do \krəˈshendō\ adv or adj : growing louder —**crescendo** n

cres·cent \ˈkresᵊnt\ n : shape of the moon between new moon and first quarter

crest \ˈkrest\ n 1 : tuft on a bird's head 2 : top of a hill or wave 3 : part of a coat of arms ~ vb : rise to a crest

crest·fall·en \ˈkrest-\ adj : sad

cre·tin \ˈkrētᵊn\ n : person with marked mental deficiency —**cre·tin·ism** \-,izəm\ n

cre·vasse \kriˈvas\ n : deep fissure esp. in a glacier

crev·ice \ˈkrevəs\ n : narrow fissure

crew \ˈkrü\ n : body of workers (as on a ship) —**crew·man** \-mən\ n

crib \ˈkrib\ n 1 : manger 2 : grain storage bin 3 : baby's bed ~ vb **-bb-** : put in a crib

crib·bage \-ij\ n : card game scored by moving pegs on a board (**cribbage board**)

crick \ˈkrik\ n : muscle spasm

¹**crick·et** \ˈkrikət\ n : insect noted for the chirping of the male

²**cricket** n : bat and ball game played on a field with wickets

cri·er \ˈkrī(ə)r\ n : one who calls out announcements

crime \ˈkrīm\ n : serious violation of law

crim·i·nal \ˈkrimənᵊl\ adj : relating to or being a crime or its punishment ~ n : one who commits a crime

crimp \ˈkrimp\ vb : cause to become crinkled, wavy, or bent —**crimp** n

crim·son \ˈkrimzən\ n : deep red —**crimson** adj

cringe \ˈkrinj\ vb **cringed; cring·ing** : shrink in fear

crin·kle \ˈkriŋkəl\ vb **-kled; -kling** : wrinkle —**crinkle** n —**crin·kly** \-k(ə)lē\ adj

crin·o·line \ˈkrinᵊlən\ n 1 : stiff cloth 2 : full stiff skirt or petticoat

crip·ple \ˈkripəl\ n : disabled person ~ vb **-pled; -pling** : disable

cri·sis \ˈkrīsəs\ n, pl **cri·ses** \-,sēz\ : decisive or critical moment

crisp \ˈkrisp\ adj 1 : easily crumbled 2 : firm and fresh 3 : lively 4 : invigorating —**crisp** vb —**crisp·ly** adv —**crisp·ness** n —**crispy** adj

criss·cross \ˈkris,krós\ n : pattern of crossed lines ~ vb : mark with or follow a crisscross

cri·te·ri·on \krīˈtirēən\ n, pl **-ria** \-ēə\ : standard

crit·ic \ˈkritik\ n : judge of literary or artistic works

crit·i·cal \-ikəl\ adj 1 : inclined to criticize 2 : being a crisis 3 : relating to criticism or critics —**crit·i·cal·ly** \-ik(ə)lē\ adv

crit·i·cize \-ə,sīz\ vb **-cized; -cizing** 1 : judge as a critic 2 : find fault —**crit·i·cism** \-ə,sizəm\ n

cri·tique \krəˈtēk\ n : critical estimate

croak \ˈkrōk\ n : hoarse harsh cry (as of a frog) —**croak** vb

cro·chet \krōˈshā\ n : needlework done with a hooked needle —**crochet** vb

crock \ˈkräk\ n : thick earthenware pot or jar —**crock·ery** \-(ə)rē\ n

croc·o·dile \ˈkräkə,dīl\ n : reptile of tropical waters

cro·cus \ˈkrōkəs\ n, pl **-cus·es** : herb with spring flowers

crone \ˈkrōn\ n : ugly old woman

cro·ny \ˈkrōnē\ n, pl **-nies** : chum

crook \'krůk\ *n* 1 : bent or curved tool or part 2 : thief *~ vb* : curve sharply

crook·ed \'krůkəd\ *adj* 1 : bent 2 : dishonest —**crook·ed·ness** *n*

croon \'krün\ *vb* : sing softly —**croon·er** *n*

crop \'kräp\ *n* 1 : pouch in the throat of a bird or insect 2 : short riding whip 3 : something that can be harvested *~ vb* **-pp-** 1 : trim 2 : appear unexpectedly —used with *up*

cro·quet \krō'kā\ *n* : lawn game of driving balls through wickets

cro·quette \-'ket\ *n* : mass of minced food deep fried

cro·sier \'krōzhər\ *n* : bishop's staff

cross \'krós\ *n* 1 : figure or structure consisting of an upright and a cross piece 2 : interbreeding of unlike strains *~ vb* 1 : intersect 2 : cancel 3 : go or extend across 4 : interbreed *~ adj* 1 : going across 2 : contrary 3 : marked by bad temper —**cross·ing** *n* —**cross·ly** *adv*

cross·bow \-,bō\ *n* : short bow mounted on a rifle stock

cross·breed *vb* **-bred; -breed·ing** : hybridize

cross-ex·am·ine *vb* : question about earlier testimony —**cross-ex·am·i·na·tion** *n*

cross-eyed *adj* : having the eye turned toward the nose

cross-re·fer *vb* : refer to another place (as in a book) —**cross-ref·er·ence** *n*

cross·roads *n* : place where 2 roads cross

cross section *n* : representative portion

cross·walk *n* : path for pedestrians crossing a street

cross·ways *adv* : crosswise

cross·wise \-,wīz\ *adv* : so as to cross something —**crosswise** *adj*

crotch \'kräch\ *n* : angle formed by the parting of 2 legs or branches

crotch·et \'krächət\ *n* : odd notion —**crotch·ety** *adj*

crouch \'krauch\ *vb* : stoop over —**crouch** *n*

croup \'krüp\ *n* : laryngitis of infants

crou·ton \'krü,tän\ *n* : bit of toast

¹**crow** \'krō\ *n* : large glossy black bird

²**crow** *vb* 1 : make the loud sound of the cock 2 : gloat *~ n* 1 : cry of the cock

crow·bar *n* : metal bar used as a pry or lever

crowd \'kraůd\ *vb* : collect or cram together *~ n* : large number of people

crown \'kraůn\ *n* 1 : wreath of honor or victory 2 : royal headdress 3 : top

or highest part *~ vb* 1 : place a crown on 2 : honor —**crowned** \'kraůnd\ *adj*

cru·cial \'krüshəl\ *adj* : vitally important

cru·ci·ble \'krüsəbəl\ *n* : heat-resisting container

cru·ci·fix \-,fiks\ *n* : representation of Christ on the cross

cru·ci·fix·ion \,krüsə'fikshən\ *n* : act of crucifying

cru·ci·fy \-,fī\ *vb* **-fied; -fy·ing** 1 : put to death on a cross 2 : persecute

crude \'krüd\ *adj* **crud·er; -est** 1 : not refined 2 : lacking grace or elegance *~ n* : unrefined petroleum —**crude·ly** *adv* —**cru·di·ty** \-ətē\ *n*

cru·el \'krüəl\ *adj* **-el·er** *or* **-el·ler; -el·est** *or* **-el·lest** : causing suffering to others —**cru·el·ly** \-ē\ *adv* —**cru·el·ty** \-tē\ *n*

cru·et \'krüət\ *n* : bottle for salad dressings

cruise \'krüz\ *vb* **cruised; cruis·ing** 1 : sail to several ports 2 : travel at the most efficient speed —**cruise** *n*

cruis·er \'krüzər\ *n* 1 : warship 2 : police car

crumb \'krəm\ *n* : small fragment

crum·ble \'krəmbəl\ *vb* **-bled; -bling** : break into small pieces —**crum·bly** \-b(ə)lē\ *adj*

crum·ple \-pəl\ *vb* **-pled; -pling** 1 : crush together 2 : collapse

crunch \'krənch\ *vb* : chew or press with a crushing noise *~ n* : crunching sound —**crunchy** *adj*

cru·sade \krü'sād\ *n* 1 *cap* : medieval Christian expedition to the Holy Land 2 : reform movement —**crusade** *vb* —**cru·sad·er** *n*

crush \'krəsh\ *vb* 1 : squeeze out of shape 2 : grind or pound to bits 3 : suppress *~ n* 1 : severe crowding 2 : infatuation

crust \'krəst\ *n* 1 : hard outer part of bread or a pie 2 : hard surface layer —**crust·al** *adj* —**crusty** *adj*

crus·ta·cean \,krəs'tāshən\ *n* : aquatic arthropod having a firm shell

crutch \'krəch\ *n* : support for use by the disabled in walking

crux \'krəks, 'krůks\ *n, pl* **crux·es** : hard problem 2 : crucial point

cry \'krī\ *vb* **cried; cry·ing** 1 : call out 2 : weep *~ n, pl* **cries** 1 : shout 2 : fit of weeping 3 : characteristic sound of an animal

crypt \'kript\ *n* : underground chamber

cryp·tic \'kriptik\ *adj* : enigmatic

cryp·tog·ra·phy \krip'tägrəfē\ *n* : cod-

ing and decoding of messages —
cryp·tog·ra·pher \-fər\ n

crys·tal \'krist^əl\ n 1 : transparent
quartz 2 : something (as glass) like
crystal 3 : body formed by solidifi-
cation that has a regular repeating
atomic arrangement —**crys·tal·line**
\-tələn\ adj

crys·tal·lize \-tə,līz\ vb **-lized; -liz·ing**
: form crystals or a definite shape
—**crys·tal·li·za·tion**   \,kristəla-
'zāshən\ n

cub \'kəb\ n : young animal

cub·by·hole \'kəbē,hōl\ n : small confined space

cube \'kyüb\ n 1 : solid having 6 equal
square sides 2 : product obtained by
taking a number 3 times as a factor
~ vb **cubed; cub·ing** 1 : raise to the
3d power 2 : form into a cube 3 : cut
into cubes —**cu·bic** \'kyübik\ adj

cu·bi·cle \-bikəl\ n : small room

cu·bit \-bət\ n : unit of length equal to
about 18 inches

cuck·old \'kəkəld, 'kùk-\ n : man
whose wife is unfaithful

cuck·oo \'kükü, 'kùk-\ n, pl **-oos**
: brown European bird ~ adj : silly

cu·cum·ber \'kyü(,)kəmbər\ n : fleshy
fruit related to the gourds

cud \'kəd\ n : food chewed again by
ruminating animals

cud·dle \'kəd^əl\ vb **-dled; -dling** : lie
close

cud·gel \'kəjəl\ n or vb : club

¹**cue** \'kyü\ n : signal —**cue** vb

²**cue** n : stick used in pool

¹**cuff** \'kəf\ n 1 : part of a sleeve encircling the wrist 2 : folded trouser
hem

²**cuff** vb or n : slap

cui·sine \kwi'zēn\ n : manner of cooking

cu·li·nary \'kələ,nerē, 'kyülə-\ adj : of
or relating to cookery

cull \'kəl\ vb : select

cul·mi·nate \'kəlmə,nāt\ vb **-nat·ed;
-nat·ing** : rise to the highest point —
cul·mi·na·tion \,kəlmə'nāshən\ n

cul·pa·ble \'kəlpəbəl\ adj : deserving
blame

cul·prit \'kəlprət\ n : guilty person

cult \'kəlt\ n 1 : religious system 2
: faddish devotion —**cult·ist** n

cul·ti·vate \'kəltə,vāt\ vb **-vat·ed; -vat-
ing** 1 : prepare for crops 2 : foster
the growth of 3 : refine —**cul·ti·va-
tion** \,kəltə'vāshən\ n

cul·ture \'kəlchər\ n 1 : cultivation 2
: refinement of intellectual and artistic taste 3 : particular form or stage
of   civilization   —**cul·tur·al**

\'kəlch(ə)rəl\   adj   —**cul·tured**
\'kəlchərd\ adj

cul·vert \'kəlvərt\ n : drain crossing
under a road or railroad

cum·ber \'kəmbər\ vb : burden —**cum-
ber·some** \-bərsəm\ —**cum·brous** \-brəs\
adj

cu·mu·la·tive \'kyümyələtiv, -,lāt-\ adj
: increasing by additions

cu·mu·lus \-ləs\ n, pl **-li** \-,lī, -,lē\
: massive rounded cloud

cun·ning \'kəniŋ\ adj 1 : crafty 2
: clever 3 : appealing ~ n 1 : skill 2
: craftiness

cup \'kəp\ n 1 : small drinking vessel
2 : contents of a cup ~ vb **-pp-**
: shape like a cup —**cup·ful** n

cup·board \'kəbərd\ n : small storage
closet

cup·cake n : small cake

cu·pid·i·ty \kyü'pidətē\ n, pl **-ties** : excessive desire for money

cu·po·la \'kyüpələ, -,lō\ n : small rooftop structure

cur \'kər\ n : mongrel dog

cu·rate \'kyùrət\ n : clergyman —**cu·
ra·cy** \-əsē\ n

cu·ra·tor \kyù'rātər\ n : one in charge
of a museum or zoo

curb \'kərb\ n 1 : restraint 2 : raised
edging along a street ~ vb : hold
back

curd \'kərd\ n : coagulated milk

cur·dle \'kərd^əl\ vb **-dled; -dling** 1
: form curds 2 : sour

cure \'kyùr\ n 1 : recovery from disease 2 : remedy ~ vb **cured; cur·ing**
1 : restore to health 2 : process for
storage or use —**cur·able** adj

cur·few \'kər,fyü\ n : requirement to
be off the streets at a set hour

cu·rio \'kyùrē,ō\ n, pl **-ri·os** : rare or
unusual article

cu·ri·ous \'kyùrēəs\ adj 1 : eager to
learn 2 : strange —**cu·ri·os·i·ty**
\,kyùrē'äsətē\ n

curl \'kərl\ vb 1 : form into ringlets 2
: curve ~ n 1 : ringlet of hair 2
: something with a spiral form —
curl·er n —**curly** adj

cur·lew \-(y)ü\ n, pl **-lews** or **-lew**
: long-legged brownish bird

curl·i·cue \'kərli,kyü\ n : fanciful curve

cur·rant \'kərənt\ n 1 : small seedless
raisin 2 : berry of a shrub

cur·ren·cy \'kərənsē\ n, pl **-cies** 1
: general use or acceptance 2
: money

cur·rent \'kərənt\ adj : occurring in or
belonging to the present ~ n 1
: swiftest part of a stream 2 : flow of
electricity

cur·ric·u·lum \kə'rikyələm\ *n, pl* -la \-lə\ : course of study

¹cur·ry \'kərē\ *vb* -ried; -ry·ing : brush (a horse) with a wire brush (currycomb) —curry favor : seek favor by flattery

²curry *n, pl* -ries : blend of spices or a food seasoned with this

curse \'kərs\ *n* 1 : a calling down of evil or harm upon one 2 : affliction ~ *vb* cursed; curs·ing 1 : call down injury upon 2 : swear at 3 : afflict

cur·sor \'kərsər\ *n* : indicator on a computer screen

cur·so·ry \'kərs(ə)rē\ *adj* : hastily done

curt \'kərt\ *adj* : rudely abrupt —curt·ly *adv*

cur·tail \(,)kər'tāl\ *vb* : shorten —cur·tail·ment *n*

cur·tain \'kərtᵊn\ *n* : hanging screen that can be drawn back or raised — curtain *vb*

curt·sy, curt·sey \'kərtsē\ *n, pl* -sies or -seys : courteous bow made by bending the knees —curtsy, curtsey *vb*

cur·va·ture \'kərvə,chùr\ *n* : amount or state of curving

curve \'kərv\ *vb* curved; curv·ing : bend from a straight line or course ~ *n* 1 : a bending without angles 2 : something curved

cush·ion \'kùshən\ *n* 1 : soft pillow 2 : something that eases or protects ~ *vb* 1 : provide with a cushion 2 : soften the force of

cusp \'kəsp\ *n* : pointed end

cus·pid \'kəspəd\ *n* : a canine tooth

cus·pi·dor \'kəspə,dòr\ *n* : spittoon

cus·tard \'kəstərd\ *n* : sweetened cooked mixture of milk and eggs

cus·to·dy \'kəstədē\ *n, pl* -dies : immediate care or charge —cus·to·di·al \,kəs'tōdēəl\ *adj* —cus·to·di·an \-ēən\ *n*

cus·tom \'kəstəm\ *n* 1 : habitual course of action 2 *pl* : import taxes ~ *adj* : made to personal order —cus·tom·ar·i·ly \,kəstə'merəlē\ *adv* —cus·tom·ary \'kəstə,merē\ *adj* —cus·tom-built *adj* —cus·tom-made *adj*

cus·tom·er \'kəstəmər\ *n* : buyer

cut \'kət\ *vb* cut; cut·ting 1 : penetrate or divide with a sharp edge 2 : experience the growth of (a tooth)

through the gum 3 : shorten 4 : remove by severing 5 : intersect ~ *n* 1 : something separated by cutting 2 : reduction —cut *in vb* : thrust oneself between others

cu·ta·ne·ous \kyù'tānēəs\ *adj* : relating to the skin

cute \'kyüt\ *adj* cut·er; -est : pretty

cu·ti·cle \'kyütikəl\ *n* : outer layer (as of skin)

cut·lass \'kətləs\ *n* : short heavy curved sword

cut·lery \-lərē\ *n* : cutting utensils

cut·let \-lət\ *n* : slice of meat

cut·ter \'kətər\ *n* 1 : tool or machine for cutting 2 : small armed motorboat 3 : light sleigh

cut·throat *n* : murderer ~ *adj* : ruthless

-cy \sē\ *n suffix* 1 : action or practice 2 : rank or office 3 : body 4 : state or quality

cy·a·nide \'sīə,nīd, -nəd\ *n* : poisonous chemical salt

cy·cle \'sīkəl, 4 *also* 'sikəl\ *n* 1 : period of time for a series of repeated events 2 : recurring round of events 3 : long period of time 4 : bicycle or motorcycle ~ *vb* -cled; -cling : ride a cycle —cy·clic \'sīklik, 'sik-\, cy·cli·cal \-əl\ *adj* —cy·clist \'sīk(ə)ləst, 'sik-\ *n*

cy·clone \'sī,klōn\ *n* : tornado —cy·clon·ic \sī'klänik\ *adj*

cy·clo·pe·dia, cy·clo·pae·dia \,sīklə'pēdēə\ *n* : encyclopedia

cyl·in·der \'siləndər\ *n* 1 : long round body or figure 2 : rotating chamber in a revolver 2 : piston chamber in an engine —cy·lin·dri·cal \sə'lindrikəl\ *adj*

cym·bal \'simbəl\ *n* : one of a pair of concave brass plates clashed together

cyn·ic \'sinik\ *n* : one who attributes all actions to selfish motives —cyn·i·cal \-ikəl\ *adj* —cyn·i·cism \-ə,sizəm\ *n*

cy·no·sure \'sīnə,shùr, 'sinə-\ *n* : center of attraction

cy·press \'sīprəs\ *n* : evergreen tree related to the pines

cyst \'sist\ *n* : abnormal bodily sac —cys·tic \'sistik\ *adj*

czar \'zär\ *n* : ruler of Russia until 1917 —czar·ist *n or adj*

D

d \'dē\ *n, pl* **d's** *or* **ds** \'dēz\ : 4th letter of the alphabet

¹dab \'dab\ *n* : gentle touch or stroke ~ *vb* **-bb-** : touch or apply lightly

²dab *n* : small amount

dab·ble \'dabəl\ *vb* **-bled; -bling 1** : splash **2** : work without serious effort

dachs·hund \'däks,hunt\ *n* : small dog with a long body and short legs

dad \'dad\ *n* : father

dad·dy \'dadē\ *n, pl* **-dies** : father

daf·fo·dil \'dafə,dil\ *n* : narcissus with trumpetlike flowers

daft \'daft\ *adj* : foolish —**daft·ness** *n*

dag·ger \'dagər\ *n* : knife for stabbing

dahl·ia \'dalyə, 'dāl-\ *n* : tuberous herb with showy flowers

dai·ly \'dālē\ *adj* **1** : occurring, done, or used every day or every weekday **2** : computed in terms of one day ~ *n, pl* **-lies** : daily newspaper —**daily** *adv*

dain·ty \'dāntē\ *n, pl* **-ties** : something delicious ~ *adj* **-ti·er; -est** : delicately pretty —**dain·ti·ly** *adv* —**dain·ti·ness** *n*

dairy \'de(ə)rē\ *n, pl* **-ies** : farm that produces or company that processes milk —**dairy·ing** \'derēiŋ\ *n* —**dairy·maid** *n* —**dairy·man** \-mən, -,man\ *n*

da·is \'dāəs, 'dī-\ *n* : raised platform (as for a speaker)

dai·sy \'dāzē\ *n, pl* **-sies** : tall leafy-stemmed plant bearing showy flowers

dale \'dāl\ *n* : valley

dal·ly \'dalē\ *vb* **-lied; -ly·ing 1** : flirt **2** : dawdle —**dal·li·ance** \-əns\ *n*

dal·ma·tian \dal'māshən\ *n* : large dog having a spotted white coat

¹dam \'dam\ *n* : female parent of a domestic animal

²dam *n* : barrier to hold back water —**dam** *vb*

dam·age \'damij\ *n* **1** : loss or harm due to injury **2** *pl* : compensation for loss or injury ~ *vb* **-aged; -ag·ing 1** : do damage to

dam·ask \-əsk\ *n* : firm lustrous figured fabric

dame \'dām\ *n* : woman of rank or authority

damn \'dam\ *vb* **1** : condemn to hell **2** : curse —**dam·na·ble** \-nəbəl\ *adj*

dam·na·tion \dam'nāshən\ *n* —**damned** *adj*

damp \'damp\ *n* : moisture ~ *vb* **1** : reduce the draft in **2** : restrain **3** : moisten ~ *adj* : moist —**damp·ness** *n*

damp·en \'dampən\ *vb* **1** : diminish in activity or vigor **2** : make or become damp

damp·er \'dampər\ *n* : movable plate to regulate a flue draft

dam·sel \'damzəl\ *n* : young woman

dance \'dans\ *vb* **danced; danc·ing** : move rhythmically to music ~ *n* : act of dancing or a gathering for dancing —**danc·er** *n*

dan·de·li·on \'dandʰl,īən\ *n* : common yellow-flowered herb

dan·der \'dandər\ *n* : temper

dan·druff \'dandrəf\ *n* : whitish scurf on the scalp

dan·dy \'dandē\ *n, pl* **-dies 1** : man too concerned with clothes **2** : something excellent ~ *adj* **-di·er; -est** : very good

dan·ger \'dānjər\ *n* **1** : exposure to injury or evil **2** : something that may cause injury —**dan·ger·ous** \'dānj(ə)rəs\ *adj*

dan·gle \'daŋgəl\ *vb* **-gled; -gling 1** : hang and swing freely **2** : be left without support or connection **3** : allow or cause to hang

dank \'daŋk\ *adj* : unpleasantly damp

dap·per \'dapər\ *adj* : neat and stylishly dressed

dap·ple \-əl\ *vb* **-pled; -pling** : mark with colored spots

dare \'dar\ *vb* **dared; dar·ing 1** : have sufficient courage **2** : urge or provoke to contend —**dare** *n* —**dar·ing** \'da(ə)riŋ\ *n or adj*

dare·dev·il *n* : recklessly bold person

dark \'därk\ *adj* **1** : having little or no light **2** : not light in color **3** : gloomy ~ *n* : absence of light —**dark·en** \-ən\ *vb* —**dark·ly** *adv* —**dark·ness** *n*

dar·ling \'därliŋ\ *n* **1** : beloved **2** : favorite ~ *adj* **1** : dearly loved **2** : very pleasing

darn \'därn\ *vb* : mend with interlacing stitches —**darn·er** *n*

dart \'därt\ *n* **1** : small pointed missile **2** *pl* : game of throwing darts at a target **3** : tapering fold in a garment

4 : quick movement ~ *vb* : move suddenly or rapidly

dash \\'dash\\ *vb* 1 : knock or hurl violently or impetuously 2 : smash 3 : ruin 4 : perform or finish hastily 5 : move quickly ~ *n* 1 : sudden burst, splash, or stroke 2 : punctuation mark — 3 : tiny amount 4 : showiness or liveliness 5 : sudden rush 6 : short race

dash•board *n* : instrument panel

dash•ing \\'dashiŋ\\ *adj* : dapper and charming

das•tard \\'dastərd\\ *n* : one who sneakingly commits malicious acts

das•tard•ly \\-lē\\ *adj* : base or malicious

da•ta \\'dātə, 'dat-, 'dät-\\ *n sing or pl* : factual information

¹date \\'dāt\\ *n* : edible fruit of a palm

²date *n* 1 : day, month, or year when something is done or made 2 : historical time period 3 : social engagement or the person one goes out with ~ *vb* **dat•ed; dat•ing** 1 : determine or record the date of 2 : have a date with 3 : originate **—to date** : up to now

dat•ed \\-əd\\ *adj* : old-fashioned

da•tum \\'dātəm, 'dat-, 'dät-\\ *n, pl* **-ta** \\-ə\\ *or* **-tums** : piece of data

daub \\'dob\\ *vb* : smear ~ *n* : something daubed on **—daub•er** *n*

daugh•ter \\'dotər\\ *n* : human female offspring

daugh•ter-in-law *n, pl* **daughters-in-law** : wife of one's son

daunt \\'dont\\ *vb* : lessen the courage of

daunt•less \\-ləs\\ *adj* : fearless

dav•en•port \\'davən,pōrt\\ *n* : sofa

daw•dle \\'dodᵊl\\ *vb* **-dled; -dling** 1 : waste time 2 : loiter

dawn \\'don\\ *vb* 1 : grow light as the sun rises 2 : begin to appear, develop, or be understood ~ *n* : first appearance (as of daylight)

day \\'dā\\ *n* 1 : period of light between one night and the next 2 : 24 hours 3 : specified date 4 : particular time or age 5 : period of work for a day **—day•light** *n* **—day•time** *n*

day•break *n* : dawn

day•dream *n* : fantasy of wish fulfillment **—daydream** *vb*

daylight saving time *n* : time one hour ahead of standard time

daze \\'dāz\\ *vb* **dazed; daz•ing** 1 : stun by a blow 2 : dazzle **—daze** *n*

daz•zle \\'dazəl\\ *vb* **-zled; -zling** 1 : overpower with light 2 : impress greatly **—dazzle** *n*

DDT \\,dē(,)dē'tē\\ *n* : long-lasting insecticide

dea•con \\'dēkən\\ *n* : subordinate church officer **—dea•con•ess** *n*

dead \\'ded\\ *adj* 1 : lifeless 2 : unresponsive or inactive 3 : exhausted 4 : obsolete 5 : precise ~ *n, pl* **dead** 1 : one that is dead —usu. with *the* 2 : most lifeless time ~ *adv* 1 : completely 2 : directly **—dead•en** \\'ded°n\\ *vb*

dead•beat *n* : one who will not pay debts

dead end *n* : end of a street with no exit **—dead-end** *adj*

dead•line *n* : time by which something must be finished

dead•lock *n* : struggle that neither side can win **—deadlock** *vb*

dead•ly \\'dedlē\\ *adj* **-li•er; -est** 1 : capable of causing death 2 : very accurate 3 : fatal to spiritual progress 4 : suggestive of death 5 : very great ~ *adv* : extremely **—dead•li•ness** *n*

dead•pan *adj* : expressionless **—deadpan** *vb*

dead•wood *n* : something useless

deaf \\'def\\ *adj* : unable or unwilling to hear **—deaf•en** \\-ən\\ *vb* **—deaf•ness** *n*

deaf-mute *n* : deaf person unable to speak

deal \\'dēl\\ *n* 1 : indefinite quantity 2 : distribution of playing cards 3 : negotiation or agreement 4 : treatment received 5 : bargain ~ *vb* **dealt** \\'delt\\; **deal•ing** \\'dēliŋ\\ 1 : distribute playing cards 2 : be concerned with 3 : take action 4 : sell **—dealer** *n* **—deal•ing** *n*

dean \\'dēn\\ *n* 1 : head of a group of clergymen 2 : university or school administrator 3 : senior member

dear \\'dir\\ *adj* 1 : highly valued or loved 2 : expensive 3 : loved one **—dear•ly** *adv* **—dear•ness** *n*

dearth \\'dərth\\ *n* : scarcity

death \\'deth\\ *n* 1 : end of life 2 : cause of loss of life 3 : state of being dead 4 : destruction or extinction **—death•less** *adj* **—death•ly** *adj or adv*

de•ba•cle \\di'bäkəl, -'bakəl\\ *n* : disaster or fiasco

de•bar \\di'bär\\ *vb* : bar from something

de•bark \\-'bärk\\ *vb* : disembark **—de•bar•ka•tion** \\,dē,bär'kāshən\\ *n*

de•base \\di'bās\\ *vb* : disparage **—de•base•ment** *n*

de•bate \\-'bāt\\ *vb* **-bat•ed; -bat•ing** : discuss a question by argument

—de·bat·able adj **—debate** n **—de·bat·er** n

de·bauch \-'bȯch\ vb : seduce or corrupt **—de·bauch·ery** \-(ə)rē\ n

de·bil·i·tate \-'bilə,tāt\ vb **-tat·ed; -tat·ing** : make ill or weak

de·bil·i·ty \-'bilətē\ n, pl **-ties** : physical weakness

deb·it \'debət\ n : account entry of a payment or debt ~ vb : record as a debit

deb·o·nair \,debə'naər\ adj : gracefully charming

de·bris \də'brē, dā-; 'dā,brē\ n, pl **-bris** \-'brēz, -,brēz\ : remains of something destroyed

debt \'det\ n 1 : sin 2 : something owed 3 : state of owing money **—debt·or** \-ər\ n

de·bunk \dē'bəŋk\ vb : expose as false

de·but \'dā,byü, dā'byü\ n 1 : first public appearance 2 : formal entrance into society **—debut** vb **—deb·u·tante** \'debyü,tänt\ n

de·cade \'dek,ād, -əd; de'kād\ n : 10 years

dec·a·dence \'dekədəns; di'kād°ns\ n : deterioration **—dec·a·dent** \-ənt; -°nt\ adj or n

de·cal \'dē,kal, di'kal, 'dekəl\ n : picture or design for transfer from prepared paper

de·camp \di'kamp\ vb : depart suddenly

de·cant \-'kant\ vb : pour gently

de·cant·er \-ər\ n : ornamental bottle for decanting and serving

de·cap·i·tate \di'kapə,tāt\ vb **-tat·ed; -tat·ing** : behead **—de·cap·i·ta·tion** \-,kapə'tāshən\ n

de·cay \di'kā\ vb 1 : decline in condition 2 : decompose **—decay** n

de·cease \-'sēs\ n : death **—decease** vb

de·ceit \-'sēt\ n 1 : deception 2 : dishonesty **—de·ceit·ful** \-fəl\ adj **—de·ceit·ful·ly** adv **—de·ceit·ful·ness** n

de·ceive \-'sēv\ vb **-ceived; -ceiv·ing** : trick or mislead **—de·ceiv·er** n

de·cel·er·ate \dē'selə,rāt\ vb **-at·ed; -at·ing** : slow down

De·cem·ber \di'sembər\ n : 12th month of the year having 31 days

de·cent \'dēs°nt\ adj 1 : good, right, or just 2 : clothed 3 : not obscene 4 : fairly good **—de·cen·cy** \-°nsē\ n **—de·cent·ly** adv

de·cep·tion \di'sepshən\ n 1 : act or fact of deceiving 2 : fraud **—de·cep·tive** \-'septiv\ adj **—de·cep·tive·ly** adv

de·cide \di'sīd\ vb **-cid·ed; -cid·ing** 1 : make a choice or judgment 2

: bring to a conclusion 3 : cause to decide

de·cid·ed \di'sīdəd\ adj 1 : unmistakable 2 : resolute **—de·cid·ed·ly** adv

de·cid·u·ous \di'sijəwəs\ adj : having leaves that fall annually

dec·i·mal \'des(ə)məl\ n : fraction in which the denominator is a power of 10 expressed by a point (**decimal point**) placed at the left of the numerator **—decimal** adj

de·ci·pher \di'sīfər\ vb : make out the meaning of **—de·ci·pher·able** adj

de·ci·sion \-'sizhən\ n 1 : act or result of deciding 2 : determination

de·ci·sive \-'sīsiv\ adj 1 : having the power to decide 2 : conclusive 3 : showing determination **—de·ci·sive·ly** adv **—de·ci·sive·ness** n

deck \'dek\ n 1 : floor of a ship 2 : pack of playing cards ~ vb 1 : array or dress up 2 : knock down

de·claim \di'klām\ vb : speak loudly or impressively **—dec·la·ma·tion** \,deklə'māshən\ n

de·clare \di'klaər\ vb **-clared; -clar·ing** 1 : make known formally 2 : state emphatically **—dec·la·ra·tion** \,deklə'rāshən\ n **—de·clar·a·tive** \di'klarətiv\ adj **—de·clar·a·to·ry** \di'klarə,tȯrē\ adj **—de·clar·er** n

de·clen·sion \di'klenchən\ n : inflectional forms of a noun, pronoun, or adjective

de·cline \di'klīn\ vb **-clined; -clin·ing** 1 : turn or slope downward 2 : wane 3 : refuse to accept 4 : inflect ~ n 1 : gradual wasting away or change to a lower state or level 3 : a descending slope **—dec·li·na·tion** \,deklə'nāshən\ n

de·code \dē'kōd\ vb : decipher (a coded message) **—de·cod·er** n

de·com·pose \,dēkəm'pōz\ vb 1 : separate into parts 2 : decay **—de·com·po·si·tion** \dē,kämpə'zishən\ n

de·con·ges·tant \,dēkən'jestənt\ n : agent that relieves congestion

de·cor, dé·cor \dā'kȯr, 'dā,kȯr\ n : room design or decoration

dec·o·rate \'dekə,rāt\ vb **-rat·ed; -rat·ing** 1 : add something attractive to 2 : honor with a medal **—dec·o·ra·tion** \,dekə'rāshən\ n **—dec·o·ra·tive** \'dek(ə)rətiv\ adj **—dec·o·ra·tor** \'dekə,rātər\ n

de·co·rum \di'kōrəm\ n : proper behavior **—dec·o·rous** \'dekərəs, di-'kōrəs\ adj **—dec·o·rous·ly** adv **—dec·o·rous·ness** n

de·coy \'dē,kȯi, di'-\ n : something that tempts ~ vb : tempt de·crease \di'krēs\ vb -creased; -creas·ing : grow or cause to grow less — decrease \'dē,krēs\ n

de·cree \di'krē\ n : official order — decree vb

de·crep·it \di'krepət\ adj : impaired by age

de·cre·scen·do \,dākrə'shendō\ adv or adj : with a decrease in volume

de·cry \di'krī\ vb : condemn

ded·i·cate \'dedi,kāt\ vb -cat·ed; -cat·ing 1 : set apart for a purpose (as honor or worship) 2 : address to someone as a compliment —ded·i·ca·tion \,dedi'kāshən\ n —ded·i·ca·to·ry \'dedikə,tōrē\ adj

de·duce \di'd(y)üs\ vb -duced; -duc·ing : derive by reasoning —de·duc·ible adj

de·duct \di'-dəkt\ vb : subtract —de·duct·ible adj

de·duc·tion \-'dəkshən\ n 1 : subtraction 2 : reasoned conclusion —de·duc·tive \-'dəktiv\ adj

deed \'dēd\ n 1 : exploit 2 : document showing ownership ~ vb : convey by deed

deem \'dēm\ vb : think

deep \'dēp\ adj 1 : extending far in a specified direction down, back, within, or outward 2 : occupied 3 : dark and rich in color 4 : low in tone ~ adv 1 : deeply 2 : far along in time ~ n : deep place —deep·en \'dēpən\ vb —deep·ly adv

deep-seat·ed \-'sētəd\ adj : firmly established

deer \'diər\ n, pl deer : ruminant mammal with antlers in the male —deer·skin n

de·face \di'fās\ vb : mar the surface of —de·face·ment n

de·fame \di'fām\ vb -famed; -fam·ing : injure the reputation of —def·a·ma·tion \,defə'māshən\ n —de·fam·a·to·ry \di'famə,tōrē\ adj

de·fault \di'fölt\ n : failure in a duty —default vb —de·fault·er n

de·feat \di'fēt\ vb 1 : frustrate 2 : win victory over ~ n : loss of a battle or contest

def·e·cate \'defi,kāt\ vb -cat·ed; -cat·ing : discharge feces from the bowels —def·e·ca·tion \,defi'kāshən\ n

de·fect \'dē,fekt, di'fekt\ n : imperfection ~ \di'-\ vb : desert —de·fec·tion \-'fekshən\ n —de·fec·tor \-'fektər\ n

de·fec·tive \di'fektiv\ adj : faulty or deficient —defective n

de·fend \di'fend\ vb 1 : protect from

danger or harm 2 : take the side of —de·fend·er n

de·fen·dant \-'fendənt\ n : person charged or sued in a court

de·fense, de·fence \-'fens\ n 1 : act of defending 2 : something that defends 3 : party, group, or team that opposes another —de·fense·less adj —de·fen·si·ble adj —de·fen·sive adj or n

¹de·fer \di'fər\ vb -rr- : postpone —de·fer·ment \di'fərmənt\ n —de·fer·ra·ble \-əbəl\ adj

²defer vb -rr- : yield to the opinion or wishes of another —def·er·ence \'def(ə)rəns\ n —def·er·en·tial \,defə'renchəl\ adj

de·fi·ance \di'fīəns\ n : act or state of defying —de·fi·ant \-ənt\ adj

de·fi·cient \di'fishənt\ adj : lacking something necessary —de·fi·cien·cy \-'fishənsē\ n

def·i·cit \'defəsət\ n : shortage esp. in money

de·file \di'fīl\ vb -filed; -fil·ing 1 : make filthy or corrupt 2 : profane or dishonor —de·file·ment n

de·fine \di'fīn\ vb -fined; -fin·ing 1 : fix or mark the limits of 2 : clarify in outline 3 : set forth the meaning of —de·fin·able adj —de·fin·ably adv —de·fin·er n —def·i·ni·tion \,defə'nishən\ n

def·i·nite \'def(ə)nət\ adj 1 : having distinct limits 2 : clear in meaning, intent, or identity 3 : typically designating an identified or immediately identifiable person or thing —def·i·nite·ly adv

de·fin·i·tive \di'finətiv\ adj 1 : conclusive 2 : authoritative

de·flate \di'flāt\ vb -flat·ed; -flat·ing 1 : release air or gas from 2 : reduce —de·fla·tion \-'flāshən\ n

de·flect \di'flekt\ vb : turn aside —de·flec·tion \-'flekshən\ n

de·fo·li·ate \dē'fōlē,āt\ vb -at·ed; -at·ing : deprive of leaves esp. prematurely —de·fo·li·ant \-lēənt\ n —de·fo·li·a·tion \-,fōlē'āshən\ n

de·form \di'förm\ vb 1 : distort 2 : disfigure —de·for·ma·tion \,dē,för-'māshən, defər-\ n —de·for·mi·ty \di'förmətē\ n

de·fraud \di'fröd\ vb : cheat

de·fray \di'frā\ vb : pay

de·frost \di'fröst\ vb 1 : thaw out 2 : free from ice —de·frost·er n

deft \'deft\ adj : quick and skillful —deft·ly adv —deft·ness n

de·funct \di'fəŋkt\ adj : dead

de·fy \-'fī\ *vb* **-fied; -fy·ing** 1 : challenge 2 : boldly refuse to obey

de·gen·er·ate \di'jen(ə)rət\ *adj* : degraded or corrupt ~ *n* : degenerate person ~ \-ə,rāt\ *vb* : become degenerate **—de·gen·er·a·cy** \-'(ə)rəsē\ *n* **—de·gen·er·a·tion** \-,jenə'rāshən\ *n* **—de·gen·er·a·tive** \-'jenə,rātiv\ *adj*

de·grade \di'grād\ *vb* 1 : reduce from a higher to a lower rank or degree 2 : debase **—de·grad·able** \-əbəl\ *adj* **—deg·ra·da·tion** \,degrə'dāshən\ *n*

de·gree \di'grē\ *n* 1 : step in a series 2 : extent, intensity, or scope 3 : title given to a college graduate 4 : a 360th part of the circumference of a circle

de·hy·drate \dē'hī,drāt\ *vb* 1 : remove water from 2 : lose liquid **—de·hy·dra·tion** \,dēhī'drāshən\ *n*

de·i·fy \'dēə,fī\ *vb* **-fied; -fy·ing** : make a god of **—de·i·fi·ca·tion** \,dēəfə-'kāshən\ *n*

deign \'dān\ *vb* : condescend

de·i·ty \'dēətē\ *n, pl* **-ties** 1 *cap* : God 2 : a god or goddess

de·ject·ed \di'jektəd\ *adj* : sad **—de·jec·tion** \-shən\ *n*

de·lay \di'lā\ *n* : a putting off of something ~ *vb* 1 : postpone 2 : stop or hinder for a time

de·lec·ta·ble \di'lektəbəl\ *adj* : delicious

del·e·gate \'deligət, -,gāt\ *n* : representative ~ \-,gāt\ *vb* **-gat·ed; -gat·ing** 1 : entrust to another 2 : appoint as one's delegate **—del·e·ga·tion** \,deli'gāshən\ *n*

de·lete \di'lēt\ *vb* **-let·ed; -let·ing** : eliminate something written **—de·le·tion** \-'lēshən\ *n*

del·e·te·ri·ous \,delə'tirēəs\ *adj* : harmful

de·lib·er·ate \di'lib(ə)rət\ *adj* 1 : determined after careful thought 2 : intentional 3 : not hurried ~ \-ə,rāt\ *vb* **-at·ed; -at·ing** : consider carefully **—de·lib·er·ate·ly** *adv* **—de·lib·er·ate·ness** *n* **—de·lib·er·a·tion** \-,libə-'rāshən\ *n* **—de·lib·er·a·tive** \-'libə-,rātiv, -'lib(ə)rət-\ *adj*

del·i·ca·cy \'delikəsē\ *n, pl* **-cies** 1 : something special and pleasing to eat 2 : fineness 3 : frailty

del·i·cate \'delikət\ *adj* 1 : subtly pleasing to the senses 2 : dainty and charming 3 : sensitive or fragile 4 : requiring fine skill or tact **—del·i·cate·ly** *adv*

del·i·ca·tes·sen \,delikə'tes⁰n\ *n* : store that sells ready-to-eat food

de·li·cious \di'lishəs\ *adj* : very pleas-

ing esp. in taste or aroma **—de·li·cious·ly** *adv*

de·light \di'līt\ *n* 1 : great pleasure 2 : source of great pleasure ~ *vb* 1 : take great pleasure 2 : satisfy greatly **—de·light·ful** \-fəl\ *adj* **—de·light·ful·ly** *adv*

de·lin·e·ate \di'linē,āt\ *vb* **-eat·ed; -eat·ing** : sketch or portray **—de·lin·e·a·tion** \-,linē'āshən\ *n*

de·lin·quent \-'liŋkwənt\ *n* : delinquent person ~ *adj* 1 : violating duty or law 2 : overdue in payment **—de·lin·quen·cy** \-kwənsē\ *n*

de·lir·i·um \di'lirēəm\ *n* : mental disturbance **—de·lir·i·ous** \-ēəs\ *adj*

de·liv·er \di'livər\ *vb* 1 : set free 2 : hand over 3 : assist in birth 4 : say or speak 5 : send to an intended destination **—de·liv·er·ance** \-(ə)rəns\ *n* **—de·liv·er·er** *n* **—de·liv·ery** \-(ə)rē\ *n*

dell \'del\ *n* : small secluded valley

del·ta \'deltə\ *n* : triangle of land at the mouth of a river

de·lude \di'lüd\ *vb* **-lud·ed; -lud·ing** : mislead or deceive

del·uge \'delyüj\ *n* 1 : flood 2 : drenching rain ~ *vb* **-uged; -ug·ing** 1 : flood 2 : overwhelm

de·lu·sion \di'lüzhən\ *n* : false belief

de·luxe \di'lüks, -'ləks, -'lüks\ *adj* : very luxurious or elegant

delve \'delv\ *vb* **delved; delv·ing** 1 : dig 2 : seek information in records

dem·a·gogue, dem·a·gog \'demə,gäg\ *n* : politician who appeals to emotion and prejudice **—dem·a·gogu·ery** \-,gäg(ə)rē\ *n* **—dem·a·gogy** \-,gägē, -,gäjē\ *n*

de·mand \di'mand\ *n* 1 : act of asking esp. with authority 2 : something claimed as due 3 : ability and desire to buy 4 : urgent need ~ *vb* 1 : ask for with authority 2 : require

de·mar·cate \di'mär,kāt, 'dē,mär-\ *vb* **-cat·ed; -cat·ing** : mark the limits of **—de·mar·ca·tion** \,dē,mär'kāshən\ *n*

de·mean \di'mēn\ *vb* : degrade

de·mean·or \-'mēnər\ *n* : behavior

de·ment·ed \-'mentəd\ *adj* : crazy

de·mer·it \-'merət\ *n* : mark given an offender

demi·god \'demi,gäd\ *n* : mythological being less powerful than a god

de·mise \di'mīz\ *n* 1 : death 2 : loss of status

demi·tasse \'demi,tas\ *n* : small cup of coffee

de·mo·bi·lize \di-, dē-\ *vb* : disband

from military service —**de·mo·bi·li·za·tion** n

de·moc·ra·cy \di'mäkrəsē\ n, pl **-cies** 1 : government in which the supreme power is held by the people 2 : political unit with democratic government

dem·o·crat \'demə,krat\ n : adherent of democracy

dem·o·crat·ic \,demə'kratik\ adj : relating to or favoring democracy — **de·moc·ra·tize** \di'mäkrə,tīz\ vb

de·mol·ish \di'mälish\ vb 1 : tear down or smash 2 : put an end to — **de·mo·li·tion** \,demə'lishən, dē-\ n

de·mon \'dēmən\ n : evil spirit — **de·mon·ic** \di'mänik\ adj

dem·on·strate \'demən,strāt\ vb **-strat·ed**; **-strat·ing** 1 : show clearly or publicly 2 : prove 3 : explain — **de·mon·stra·ble** \di'mänstrəbəl\ adj — **dem·on·stra·tion** \,demən'strāshən\ n — **de·mon·stra·tive** \di'mänstrətiv\ adj or n — **dem·on·stra·tor** \'demən,strātər\ n

de·mor·al·ize \di'mórə,līz\ vb : destroy the enthusiasm of

de·mote \-'mōt\ vb **-mot·ed**; **-mot·ing** : reduce to a lower rank — **de·mo·tion** \-'mōshən\ n

de·mur \-'mər\ vb -rr- : object — **de·mur** n

de·mure \di'myúr\ adj : modest — **de·mure·ly** adv

den \'den\ n 1 : animal's shelter 2 : hiding place 3 : cozy private little room

de·na·ture \dē'nāchər\ vb **-tured**; **-tur·ing** : make (alcohol) unfit for drinking

de·ni·al \di'nī(ə)l\ n : rejection of a request or of the validity of a statement

den·i·grate \'deni,grāt\ vb **-grat·ed**; **-grat·ing** : speak ill of

den·im \'denəm\ n 1 : durable twilled cotton fabric 2 pl : pants of denim

den·i·zen \-əzən\ n : inhabitant

de·nom·i·na·tion \di,nämə'nāshən\ n 1 : religious body 2 : value or size in a series — **de·nom·i·na·tion·al** \-sh(ə)nəl\ adj

de·nom·i·na·tor \-'nämə,nātər\ n : part of a fraction below the line

de·note \di'nōt\ vb 1 : mark out plainly 2 : mean — **de·no·ta·tion** \,dēnō'tāshən\ n — **de·no·ta·tive** \'dēnō,tātiv, di'nōtətiv\ adj

de·noue·ment \,dā,nü'mäⁿ\ n : final outcome (as of a drama)

de·nounce \di'naúns\ vb **-nounced**; **-nounc·ing** 1 : criticize severely 2 : inform against

dense \'dens\ adj **dens·er**; **-est** 1 : thick, compact, or crowded 2 : stupid — **dense·ly** adv — **dense·ness** n — **den·si·ty** \'densətē\ n

dent \'dent\ n : small depression — **dent** vb

den·tal \-ᵊl\ adj : relating to teeth or dentistry

den·ti·frice \'dentəfrəs\ n : preparation for cleaning teeth

den·tin \'dentᵊn\, **den·tine** \'den,tēn, ,den'-\ n : bonelike component of teeth

den·tist \'dentəst\ n : one who cares for and replaces teeth — **den·tist·ry** n

den·ture \'denchər\ n : artificial teeth

de·nude \di'n(y)üd\ vb **-nud·ed**; **-nud·ing** : strip of covering

de·nun·ci·a·tion \di,nənsē'āshən\ n : act of denouncing

de·ny \-'nī\ vb **-nied**; **-ny·ing** 1 : declare untrue 2 : disavow 3 : refuse to grant

de·odor·ant \dē'ōdərənt\ n : preparation to prevent unpleasant odors — **de·odor·ize** \-,rīz\ vb

de·part \di'pärt\ vb 1 : go away or away from 2 : die — **de·par·ture** \-'pärchər\ n

de·part·ment \di'pärtmənt\ n 1 : area of responsibility or interest 2 : functional division — **de·part·men·tal** \di,pärt'mentᵊl, ,dē-\ adj

de·pend \di'pend\ vb 1 : rely for support 2 : be determined by or based on something else — **de·pend·abil·i·ty** \-,pendə'bilətē\ n — **de·pend·able** adj — **de·pen·dence** \di'pendəns\ n — **de·pen·den·cy** \-dənsē\ n — **de·pen·dent** \-ənt\ adj or n

de·pict \di'pikt\ vb : show by or as if by a picture — **de·pic·tion** \-'pikshən\ n

de·plete \di'plēt\ vb **-plet·ed**; **-plet·ing** : use up resources of — **de·ple·tion** \-'plēshən\ n

de·plore \di'plōr\ vb **-plored**; **-plor·ing** : regret strongly — **de·plor·able** \-əbəl\ adj

de·ploy \-'plói\ vb : spread out for battle — **de·ploy·ment** \-mənt\ n

de·port \di'pōrt\ vb 1 : behave 2 : send out of the country — **de·por·ta·tion** \,dē,pōr'tāshən, dē-\ n — **de·port·ment** \di'pōrtmənt\ n

de·pose \di'pōz\ vb **-posed**; **-pos·ing** 1 : remove (a ruler) from office 2 : testify — **de·po·si·tion** \,depə'zishən, ,dē-\ n

de·pos·it \di'päzət\ vb **-it·ed**; **-it·ing** 1 : put away for safekeeping 2 : give as a pledge 3 : lay or put down ~ *n* 1 : state of being deposited 2 : something deposited 3 : act of depositing —**de·pos·i·tor** \-'päzətər\ *n*

de·pos·i·to·ry \di'päzə,törē\ *n, pl* **-ries** : place for deposit

de·pot *l usu* 'depō, *2 usu* 'dēp-\ *n* 1 : place for storage 2 : bus or railroad station

de·prave \di'prāv\ *vb* **-praved; -praving** : corrupt morally —**de·praved** *adj* —**de·prav·i·ty** \-'pravətē\ *n*

dep·re·cate \'depri,kāt\ *vb* **-cat·ed; -cat·ing** 1 : express disapproval of 2 : belittle —**dep·re·ca·tion** \,depri-'kāshən\ *n* —**dep·re·ca·to·ry** \'depri-kə,törē\ *adj*

de·pre·ci·ate \di'prēshē,āt\ *vb* **-at·ed; -at·ing** 1 : lessen in value 2 : belittle —**de·pre·ci·a·tion** \-,prēshē'āshən\ *n*

dep·re·da·tion \,deprə'dāshən\ *n* : a laying waste or plundering —**dep·re·date** \'deprə,dāt\ *vb*

de·press \di'pres\ *vb* 1 : press down 2 : lessen the activity or force of 3 : discourage 4 : decrease the market value of —**de·pres·sant** \-ⁿnt\ *n or adj* —**de·pressed** *adj* —**de·pres·sive** \-iv\ *adj or n* —**de·pres·sor** \-ər\ *n*

de·pres·sion \di'preshən\ *n* 1 : act of depressing or state of being depressed 2 : period of low economic activity

de·prive \-'prīv\ *vb* **-prived; -priving** : take or keep something away from —**de·pri·va·tion** \,deprə'vāshən\ *n*

depth \'depth\ *n, pl* **depths** \'dep(th)s\ 1 : something that is deep 2 : distance down from a surface 3 : distance from front to back 4 : quality of being deep

dep·u·ta·tion \,depyə'tāshən\ *n* : delegation

dep·u·ty \'depyətē\ *n, pl* **-ties** : person appointed to act for another —**dep·u·tize** \-yə,tīz\ *vb*

de·rail \di'rāl\ *vb* : run off the rails —**de·rail·ment** *n*

de·range \-'rānj\ *vb* **-ranged; -rang·ing** 1 : disarrange or upset 2 : make insane —**de·range·ment** *n*

der·by \'dərbē, *Brit* 'där-\ *n, pl* **-bies** : horse race 2 : stiff felt hat with dome-shaped crown

der·e·lict \'derə,likt\ *adj* 1 : abandoned 2 : negligent ~ *n* 1 : something abandoned 2 : bum —**der·e·lic·tion** \,derə'likshən\ *n*

de·ride \di'rīd\ *vb* **-rid·ed; -rid·ing** : make fun of —**de·ri·sion** \-'rizhən\ *n* —**de·ri·sive** \-'rīsiv\ *adj*

de·rive \di'rīv\ *vb* **-rived; -riv·ing** 1 : obtain from a source or parent 2 : come from a certain source 3 : infer or deduce —**der·i·va·tion** \,derə-'vāshən\ *n* —**de·riv·a·tive** \di'rivə-tiv\ *adj or n*

der·ma·tol·o·gy \,dərmə'täləjē\ *n* : study of the skin and its disorders —**der·ma·tol·o·gist** \-jəst\ *n*

de·rog·a·to·ry \di'rägə,törē\ *adj* : intended to lower the reputation

der·rick \'derik\ *n* 1 : hoisting apparatus 2 : framework over an oil well

de·scend \di'send\ *vb* 1 : move or climb down 2 : come down from a stock or source 3 : extend downward 4 : make a sudden attack —**de·scen·dant, de·scen·dent** \-ənt\ *adj or n* —**de·scent** \di'sent\ *n*

de·scribe \-'skrīb\ *vb* **-scribed; -scrib·ing** : represent in words —**de·scrib·able** *adj* —**de·scrib·ably** *adv* —**de·scrip·tion** \-'skripshən\ *n* —**de·scrip·tive** \-'skriptiv\ *adj*

de·scry \di'skrī\ *vb* **-scried; -scry·ing** : catch sight of

des·e·crate \'desi,krāt\ *vb* **-crat·ed; -crat·ing** : treat (something sacred) with disrespect —**des·e·cra·tion** \,desi'krāshən\ *n*

de·seg·re·gate \dē-\ *vb* : eliminate esp. racial segregation in —**de·seg·re·ga·tion** *n*

¹**des·ert** \'dezərt\ *n* : dry barren region —**desert** *adj*

²**de·sert** \di'zərt\ *n* : what one deserves

³**de·sert** \di'zərt\ *vb* : abandon —**de·sert·er** *n* —**de·ser·tion** \-'zərshən\ *n*

de·serve \-'zərv\ *vb* **-served; -serv·ing** : be worthy of

des·ic·cate \'desi,kāt\ *vb* **-cat·ed; -cat·ing** : dehydrate —**des·ic·ca·tion** \,desi'kāshən\ *n*

de·sign \di'zīn\ *vb* 1 : create and work out the details of 2 : make a pattern or sketch of ~ *n* 1 : mental project or plan 2 : purpose 3 : preliminary sketch 4 : underlying arrangement of elements 5 : decorative pattern —**de·sign·er** *n*

des·ig·nate \'dezig,nāt\ *vb* **-nat·ed; -nat·ing** 1 : indicate, specify, or name 2 : appoint —**des·ig·na·tion** \,dezig'nāshən\ *n*

de·sire \di'zīr\ *vb* **-sired; -sir·ing** 1 : feel desire for 2 : request ~ *n* 1 : strong conscious impulse to have, be, or do something 2 : something desired —**de·sir·abil·i·ty** \-,zīrə-'bilətē\ *n* —**de·sir·able** \-'zīrəbəl\ *adj* —**de·sir·ous** \-'zīrəs\ *adj*

de·sist \di'zist, -'sist\ *vb* : stop

desk \'desk\ *n* : table esp. for writing and reading

des·o·late \'desələt, 'dez-\ *adj* 1 : lifeless 2 : disconsolate ~ \-,lāt\ *vb* **-lat·ed; -lat·ing** : lay waste —**des·o·la·tion** \,desə'lāshən, ,dez-\ *n*

de·spair \di'spaər\ *vb* : lose all hope ~ *n* : loss of hope

des·per·a·do \,despə'rädō, -'rād-\ *n, pl* **-does** *or* **-dos** : desperate criminal

des·per·ate \'despə)rət\ *adj* 1 : hopeless 2 : rash 3 : extremely intense —**des·per·ate·ly** *adv* —**des·per·a·tion** \,despə'rāshən\ *n*

de·spi·ca·ble \di'spikəbel, 'despik-\ *adj* : deserving scorn

de·spise \di'spīz\ *vb* **-spised; -spis·ing** : feel contempt for

de·spite \-'spīt\ *prep* : in spite of

de·spoil \-'spóil\ *vb* : strip of possessions or value

de·spon·den·cy \-'spändənsē\ *n* : dejection —**de·spon·dent** \-dənt\ *adj*

des·pot \'despət, -,pät\ *n* : tyrant —**des·pot·ic** \des'pätik\ *adj* —**des·po·tism** \'despə,tizəm\ *n*

des·sert \di'zərt\ *n* : sweet food, fruit, or cheese ending a meal

des·ti·na·tion \,destə'nāshən\ *n* : place where something or someone is going

des·tine \'destən\ *vb* **-tined; -tin·ing** 1 : designate, assign, or determine in advance 2 : direct

des·ti·ny \'destənē\ *n, pl* **-nies** : that which is to happen in the future

des·ti·tute \'destə,t(y)üt\ *adj* 1 : lacking something 2 : very poor —**des·ti·tu·tion** \,destə't(y)üshən\ *n*

de·stroy \di'strói\ *vb* : kill or put an end to

de·stroy·er \-'strói(ə)r\ *n* 1 : one that destroys 2 : small speedy warship

de·struc·tion \-'strəkshən\ *n* 1 : action of destroying 2 : ruin —**de·struc·ti·bil·i·ty** \-,strəktə'bilətē\ *n* —**de·struc·ti·ble** \-'strəktəbəl\ *adj* —**de·struc·tive** \-'strəktiv\ *adj*

des·ul·to·ry \'desəl,tōrē\ *adj* : aimless

de·tach \di'tach\ *vb* : separate

de·tached \-'tacht\ *adj* 1 : separate 2 : aloof or impartial

de·tach·ment \-'tachmənt\ *n* 1 : separation 2 : troops or ships on special service 3 : aloofness 4 : impartiality

de·tail \di'tāl, 'dē,tāl\ *n* : small item or part ~ *vb* : give details of

de·tain \di'tān\ *vb* 1 : hold in custody 2 : delay

de·tect \di'tekt\ *vb* : discover —**de-**

tect·able *adj* —**de·tec·tion** \-'tekshən\ *n* —**de·tec·tor** \-'tər\ *n*

de·tec·tive \-'tektiv\ *n* : one who investigates crime

dé·tente \dā'tä⁽ⁿ⁾t\ *n* : relaxation of tensions between nations

de·ten·tion \di'tenchən\ *n* : confinement

de·ter \-'tər\ *vb* **-rr-** : discourage or prevent —**de·ter·rence** \-əns\ *n* —**de·ter·rent** \-ənt\ *adj or n*

de·ter·gent \di'tərjənt\ *n* : cleansing agent

de·te·ri·o·rate \-'tirēə,rāt\ *vb* **-rat·ed; -rat·ing** : make or grow worse —**de·te·ri·o·ra·tion** \-,tirēə'rāshən\ *n*

de·ter·mi·na·tion \di,tərmə'nāshən\ *n* 1 : act of deciding or fixing 2 : firm purpose

de·ter·mine \-'tərmən\ *vb* **-mined; -min·ing** \-'tərm(ə)niŋ\ 1 : decide on, establish, or settle 2 : find out 3 : be the cause of

de·test \-'test\ *vb* : hate —**de·test·able** *adj* —**de·tes·ta·tion** \,dē,tes'tāshən\ *n*

det·o·nate \'det⁽ə⁾n,āt, 'detə,nāt\ *vb* **-nat·ed; -nat·ing** : explode —**det·o·na·tion** \,det⁽ə⁾n'āshən, ,detə'nā-\ *n* —**det·o·na·tor** \-ər\ *n*

de·tour \'dē,túr\ *n* : temporary indirect route —**detour** *vb*

de·tract \di'trakt\ *vb* : take away —**de·trac·tion** \-'trakshən\ *n* —**de·trac·tor** \-'traktər\ *n*

det·ri·ment \'detrəmənt\ *n* : damage —**det·ri·men·tal** \,detrə'ment⁽ᵊ⁾l\ *adj* —**det·ri·men·tal·ly** *adv*

deuce \'d(y)üs\ *n* 1 : 2 in cards or dice 2 : tie in tennis 3 : devil—used as an oath

deut·sche mark \,dóichə-\ *n* : monetary unit of West Germany

de·val·ue \dē-\ *vb* : reduce the value of —**de·val·u·a·tion** *n*

dev·as·tate \'devə,stāt\ *vb* **-tat·ed; -tat·ing** : ruin —**dev·as·ta·tion** \,devə'stāshən\ *n*

de·vel·op \di'veləp\ *vb* 1 : grow, increase, or evolve gradually 2 : cause to grow, increase, or reach full potential —**de·vel·op·er** *n* —**de·vel·op·ment** *n* —**de·vel·op·men·tal** \-,veləp'ment⁽ᵊ⁾l\ *adj*

de·vi·ate \'dēvē,āt\ *vb* **-at·ed; -at·ing** : change esp. from a course or standard —**de·vi·ant** \-vēənt\ *adj or n* —**de·vi·ate** \-vēət, -vē,āt\ *n* —**de·vi·a·tion** \,dēvē'āshən\ *n*

de·vice \di'vis\ *n* 1 : specialized piece of equipment or tool 2 : design

dev·il \'devəl\ *n* 1 : personified su-

preme spirit of evil **2** : demon **3**
: wicked person ~ *vb* **-iled** *or* **-illed:**
il·ing *or* **il·ling 1** : pester **2** : mash
or chop (food) and season highly —
dev·il·ish \'dev(ə)lish\ *adj* — **dev·il·**
ry \'devəlrē\, **dev·il·try** \-trē\ *n*

de·vi·ous \'dēvēəs\ *adj* : tricky

de·vise \di'vīz\ *vb* **-vised; -vis·ing**
1 : invent **2** : plot **3** : give by will

de·void \-'void\ *adj* : entirely lacking

de·vote \di'vōt\ *vb* **-vot·ed; -vot·ing**
: set apart for a special purpose

de·vot·ed \-əd\ *adj* : ardent

dev·o·tee \,devə'tē, -'tā\ *n* : zealous
follower

de·vo·tion \di'vōshən\ *n* **1** : prayer —
usu. pl. **2** : strong affection — **devo·**
tion·al \-sh(ə)nəl\ *adj*

de·vour \di'vaů(ə)r\ *vb* : consume rav-
enously — **de·vour·er** *n*

de·vout \-'vaůt\ *adj* **1** : devoted to religion **2** : sincere — **de·vout·ly** *adv*
— **de·vout·ness** *n*

dew \'d(y)ü\ *n* : moisture condensed
at night — **dew·drop** *n* — **dewy** *adj*

dex·ter·ous, **dex·trous** \'dekst(ə)rəs\
adj : skillful with the hands — **dex·**
ter·i·ty \dek'sterətē\ *n* — **dex·ter·**
ous·ly *adv*

dex·trose \'dek,strōs\ *n* : plant or
blood sugar

di·a·be·tes \,dīə'bētēz, -'bētəs\ *n* : disorder in which the body has too little
insulin and too much sugar — **dia·**
bet·ic \-'betik\ *adj or n*

di·a·bol·ic \-'bälik\, **di·a·bol·i·cal**
\-ikəl\ *adj* : fiendish

di·a·crit·ic \-'kritik\ *n* : mark accompanying a letter and indicating a specific sound value — **di·a·crit·i·cal**
\-'kritikəl\ *adj*

di·a·dem \'dīə,dem\ *n* : crown

di·ag·no·sis \,dīig'nōsəs, -əg-\ *n, pl*
-no·ses \-,sēz\ : identifying of a disease from its symptoms — **di·ag·nose**
\'dīig,nōs, -əg-\ *vb* — **di·ag·nos·tic**
\,dīig'nästik, -əg-\ *adj*

di·ag·o·nal \dī'ag(ə)nəl\ *adj* : extending from one corner to the opposite
corner ~ *n* : diagonal line, direction,
or arrangement — **di·ag·o·nal·ly** \-ē-\
adv

di·a·gram \'dīə,gram\ *n* : explanatory
drawing or plan ~ *vb* **-gramed** *or*
-grammed; -gram·ing *or* **gram·ming**
: represent by a diagram — **di·a·**
gram·mat·ic \,dīəgrə'matik\ *adj*

di·al \'dī(ə)l\ *n* **1** : face of a clock,
meter, or gauge **2** : control knob or
wheel ~ *vb* **-aled** *or* **alled; -al·ing**
or **-al·ling** : turn a dial to call, operate,
or select

di·a·lect \'dīə,lekt\ *n* : variety of language confined to a region or group

di·a·logue, di·a·log \-,lòg\ *n* : conversation

di·am·e·ter \dī'amətər\ *n* **1** : straight
line through the center of a circle **2**
: thickness

di·a·met·ric \,dīə'metrik\, **di·a·met·ri·**
cal \-trikəl\ *adj* : completely opposite — **di·a·met·ri·cal·ly** \-(ə)lē\ *adv*

di·a·mond \'dī(ə)mənd\ *n* **1** : hard brilliant mineral that consists of crystalline carbon **2** : flat figure having 4
equal sides, 2 acute angles, and 2
obtuse angles **3** : playing card of a
suit marked with a red diamond **4**
: baseball field

di·a·per \'dī(ə)pər\ *n* : folded material
drawn up between a baby's legs and
fastened at the waist ~ *vb* : put a
diaper on

di·a·phragm \'dīə,fram\ *n* **1** : sheet of
muscle between the chest and ab-
dominal cavity **2** : contraceptive device

di·ar·rhea, di·ar·rhoea \,dīə'rēə\ *n*
: abnormal discharge of loose matter
from the bowels

di·a·ry \'dī(ə)rē\ *n, pl* **-ries** : daily record of personal experiences — **di·a·**
rist \'dīərəst\ *n*

di·a·tribe \'dīə,trīb\ *n* : denunciation

dice \'dīs\ *n, pl* **dice** : die or a game
played with dice ~ *vb* **diced; dic·ing**
: cut into small cubes

dick·er \'dikər\ *vb* : bargain

dic·tate \'dik,tāt\ *vb* **-tat·ed; -tat·ing**
1 : speak for a person or a machine
to record **2** : command ~ *n* : order
— **dic·ta·tion** \dik'tāshən\ *n*

dic·ta·tor \'dik,tātər\ *n* : person ruling
absolutely and often brutally — **dic·**
ta·to·ri·al \,diktətō'rēəl\ *adj* — **dicta·**
tor·ship \dik'tātər,ship, 'dik,-\ *n*

dic·tion \'dikshən\ *n* **1** : choice of the
best word **2** : precise pronunciation

dic·tio·nary \-shə,nerē\ *n, pl* **-nar·ies**
: reference book of words with information about their meanings

dic·tum \'diktəm\ *n, pl* **-ta** \-tə\ : authoritative or formal statement

did *past of* DO

di·dac·tic \dī'daktik\ *adj* : intended to
teach a moral lesson

¹die \'dī\ *vb* **died; dy·ing** \'dīiŋ\ **1**
: stop living **2** : pass out of existence
3 : stop or subside **4** : long

²die \'dī\ *n, pl* **dice** \'dīs\ : small
marked cube used in gambling **2** *pl*
dies \'dīz\ : form for stamping or
cutting

die·sel \'dēzəl, -səl\ *n* : engine in which

high compression causes ignition of the fuel

di·et \'dīət\ n : food and drink regularly consumed (as by a person) ~ vb : eat less or according to certain rules —**di·e·tary** \,dīə,terē\ adj or n —**di·et·er** n

di·e·tet·ics \,dīə'tetiks\ n sing or pl : science of nutrition —**di·e·tet·ic** adj —**di·e·ti·cian** \-'tishən\ n

dif·fer \'difər\ vb 1 : be unlike 2 : disagree —**dif·fer·ence** \'difərns, 'dif(ə)rəns\ n

dif·fer·ent \-ərnt, -(ə)rənt\ adj : not the same —**dif·fer·ent·ly** adv

dif·fer·en·ti·ate \,difə'renchē,āt\ vb -at·ed; -at·ing 1 : make or become different 2 : distinguish —**dif·fer·en·ti·a·tion** \-,renchē'āshən\ n

dif·fi·cult \'difi(,)kəlt\ adj : hard to do, understand, or deal with

dif·fi·cul·ty \-(,)kəltē\ n, pl -ties 1 : difficult nature 2 : great effort 3 : something hard to do, understand, or deal with

dif·fi·dent \'difədənt\ adj : reserved —**dif·fi·dence** \-əns\ n

dif·fuse \dif'yüs\ adj 1 : wordy 2 : scattered ~ \-'yüz\ vb -fused; -fus·ing : pour out or spread widely —**dif·fu·sion** \-'yüzhən\ n

dig \'dig\ vb dug \'dəg\; dig·ging 1 : turn up soil 2 : hollow out or form by removing earth 3 : uncover by turning up earth 4 : discover 5 : poke ~ n : thrust 2 : cutting remark

¹di·gest \'dī,jest\ n : body of information in shortened form

²di·gest \dī'jest, də-\ vb 1 : think over 2 : convert (food) into a form that can be absorbed 3 : summarize —**di·gest·ible** adj —**di·ges·tion** \-'jeschən\ n —**di·ges·tive** \-'jestiv\ adj

dig·it \'dijət\ n 1 : any of the figures 1 to 9 inclusive and usu. the symbol 0 2 : finger or toe

dig·i·tal \-ᵊl\ adj : providing information in numerical digits —**dig·i·tal·ly** adv

dig·ni·fy \'dignə,fī\ vb -fied; -fy·ing : give dignity to

dig·ni·tary \-,terē\ n, pl -taries : person of high position

dig·ni·ty \'dignətē\ n, pl -ties 1 : quality or state of being worthy or honored 2 : formal reserve (as of manner)

di·gress \dī'gres, də-\ vb : wander from the main subject —**di·gres·sion** \-'greshən\ n

dike \'dīk\ n : earth bank or dam

di·lap·i·dat·ed \də'lapə,dātəd\ adj : fallen into partial ruin —**di·lap·i·da·tion** \-,lapə'dāshən\ n

di·late \dī'lāt, 'dī,lāt\ vb -lat·ed; -lat·ing : swell or expand —**dil·a·ta·tion** \,dilə'tāshən\ n —**di·la·tion** \dī-'lāshən\ n

dil·a·to·ry \'dilə,tōrē\ adj 1 : delaying 2 : not prompt

di·lem·ma \də'lemə\ n : choice between equally undesirable alternatives

dil·et·tante \'dilə,tänt, -,tant; ,dilə'tänt(ē), -'tant(ē)\ n, pl -tantes or -tan·ti \-'tänt(ē), -'tantē\ : one who dabbles in a field of interest

dil·i·gent \'dilə jənt\ adj : attentive and busy —**dil·i·gence** \-jəns\ n —**dil·i·gent·ly** adv

dill \'dil\ n : herb with aromatic leaves and seeds

dil·ly-dal·ly \'dilē,dalē\ vb : waste time by delay

di·lute \dī'lüt, də-\ vb -lut·ed; -lut·ing : lessen the consistency or strength of by mixing with something else ~ adj : weak —**di·lu·tion** \-'lüshən\ n

dim \'dim\ adj -mm- 1 : not bright or distinct 2 : having no luster 3 : not seeing or understanding clearly —**dim** vb —**dim·ly** adv —**dim·mer** n —**dim·ness** n

dime \'dīm\ n : U.S. coin worth 1/10 dollar

di·men·sion \də'menchən, dī-\ n 1 : measurement of extension (as in length, height, or breadth) 2 : extent —**di·men·sion·al** \-'mench(ə)nəl\ adj

di·min·ish \də'minish\ vb 1 : make less or cause to appear less 2 : dwindle

di·min·u·tive \də'minyətiv\ adj : extremely small

dim·ple \'dimpəl\ n : small depression esp. in the cheek or chin

din \'din\ n : loud noise

dine \'dīn\ vb dined; din·ing : eat dinner

din·er \'dīnər\ n 1 : person eating dinner 2 : railroad dining car or restaurant in the shape of one

din·ghy \'diŋ(k)ē, -gē\ n, pl -ghies : light rowboat

din·gy \'dinjē\ adj -gi·er; -est : not fresh, bright, or light —**din·gi·ness** n

din·ner \'dinər\ n : main daily meal

di·no·saur \'dīnə,sȯr\ n : extinct often huge reptile

dint \'dint\ n : force—in the phrase by dint of

di·o·cese \'dīəsəs, -,sēz, -,sēs\ n, pl -ces·es \-əz, 'dīə,sēz\ : territorial jurisdiction of a bishop —**di·oc·e·san** \di'äsəsən, ˌdiə'sēz°n\ *adj or n*

dip \'dip\ *vb* -**pp**- **1** : plunge into a liquid **2** : take out with a ladle **3** : lower and quickly raise again **4** : sink or slope downward suddenly ~ *n* **1** : plunge into water for sport **2** : sudden downward movement or incline —**dip·per** *n*

diph·the·ria \dif'thirēə, dip-\ *n* : acute contagious disease

diph·thong \'dif,thòŋ, 'dip-\ *n* : two vowel sounds joined to form one speech sound (as *ou* in *out*)

di·plo·ma \də'plōmə\ *n, pl* -**mas** : record of graduation from a school

di·plo·ma·cy \-məsē\ *n* **1** : business of conducting negotiations between nations **2** : tact —**dip·lo·mat** \'dipləˌmat\ *n* —**dip·lo·mat·ic** \ˌdiplə'matik\ *adj*

dire \'dī(ə)r\ *adj* **dir·er**; -**est 1** : very horrible **2** : extreme

di·rect \də'rekt, dī-\ *vb* **1** : address **2** : cause to move or to follow a certain course **3** : show (someone) the way **4** : regulate the activities or course of **5** : request with authority — *adj* **1** : leading to or coming from a point without deviation or interruption **2** : frank —**direct** *adv* —**di·rect·ly** \-'rek(t)lē\ *adv* —**di·rect·ness** \-'rek(t)nəs\ *n* —**di·rec·tor** \-tər\ *n*

direct current *n* : electric current flowing in one direction only

di·rec·tion \də'rekshən, dī-\ *n* **1** : supervision **2** : order **3** : course along which something moves —**di·rec·tion·al** \-sh(ə)nəl\ *adj*

di·rec·tive \-tiv\ *n* : order

di·rec·to·ry \-t(ə)rē\ *n, pl* -**ries** : alphabetical list of names and addresses

dirge \'dərj\ *n* : funeral hymn

di·ri·gi·ble \'dirəjəbəl, də'rijə-\ *n* : airship

dirt \'dərt\ *n* **1** : mud, dust, or grime that makes something unclean **2** : soil

dirty \-ē\ *adj* **dirt·i·er**; -**est 1** : not clean **2** : unfair **3** : indecent ~ *vb* **dirt·ied**; **dirty·ing** : make or become dirty —**dirt·i·ness** *n*

dis·able \dis'ābəl, -'ā-\ *vb* -**abled**; -**abling** \-b(ə)liŋ\ : make unable to function —**dis·abil·i·ty** \ˌdisə'bilətē\ *n*

dis·abuse \ˌdisə'byüz\ *vb* : free from error

dis·ad·van·tage \ˌdis-\ *n* : something that hinders success —**dis·ad·van·ta·geous** *adj*

dis·af·fect \ˌdis-\ *vb* : cause discontent in —**dis·af·fec·tion** *n*

dis·agree \ˌdis-\ *vb* **1** : fail to agree **2** : differ in opinion —**dis·agree·ment** *n*

dis·agree·able \ˌdis-\ *adj* : unpleasant

dis·al·low \ˌdis-\ *vb* : refuse to admit or recognize

dis·ap·pear \ˌdis-\ *vb* **1** : pass out of sight **2** : cease to be —**dis·ap·pear·ance** *n*

dis·ap·point \ˌdisə'pòint\ *vb* : fail to fulfill the expectation or hope of —**dis·ap·point·ment** *n*

dis·ap·prove \ˌdis-\ *vb* **1** : condemn or reject **2** : feel or express dislike or rejection —**dis·ap·prov·al** *n*

dis·arm \dis'ärm\ *vb* **1** : take weapons from **2** : reduce armed forces **3** : make harmless or friendly —**dis·ar·ma·ment** \-'ärmamənt\ *n*

dis·ar·range \ˌdis-\ *vb* : throw into disorder —**dis·ar·range·ment** *n*

dis·ar·ray \ˌdis-\ *n* : disorder

dis·as·ter \diz'astər, dis-\ *n* : sudden great misfortune —**di·sas·trous** \-'astrəs\ *adj*

dis·avow \ˌdisə'vaù\ *vb* : deny responsibility for —**dis·avow·al** \-'vaù(ə)l\ *n*

dis·band \dis-\ *vb* : break up the organization of

dis·bar \dis-\ *vb* : expel from the legal profession —**dis·bar·ment** *n*

dis·be·lieve \ˌdis-\ *vb* : hold not to be true or real —**dis·be·lief** *n*

dis·burse \dis'bərs\ *vb* -**bursed**; -**bursing** : pay out —**dis·burse·ment** *n*

disc *var of* DISK

dis·card \dis'kärd, 'dis,kärd\ *vb* : get rid of as unwanted —**dis·card** \'dis,kärd\ *n*

dis·cern \dis'ərn, diz-\ *vb* : discover with the eyes or the mind —**dis·cern·ible** *adj* —**dis·cern·ment** *n*

dis·charge \dis'chärj, 'dis,chärj\ *vb* **1** : unload **2** : shoot **3** : set free **4** : dismiss from service **5** : let go or let off **6** : give forth fluid ~ \'dis,-, dis'-\ *n* **1** : act of discharging **2** : a flowing out (as of blood) **3** : dismissal

dis·ci·ple \dis'ipəl\ *n* : one who helps spread his master's teachings

dis·ci·pli·nar·i·an \ˌdisəplə'nerēən\ *n* : one who enforces order

dis·ci·pline \'disəplən\ *n* **1** : field of study **2** : training that corrects, molds, or perfects **3** : punishment **4** : control gained by obedience or training ~ *vb* -**plined**; -**plin·ing 1** : punish **2** : train in self-control —**dis·ci·plin·ary** \'disəplə,nerē\ *adj*

dis·claim \dis'klām\ *vb* : disavow

dis·close \-'klōz\ *vb* : reveal —**dis·clo·sure** \-'klōzhər\ *n*

dis·col·or \dis'kələr\ *vb* 1 : change the color of 2 : stain —**dis·col·or·ation** \dis,kələ'rāshən\ *n*

dis·com·fit \dis'kəmfət\ *vb* : upset —**dis·com·fi·ture** \dis'kəmfə,chùr\ *n*

dis·com·fort \dis'kəmfərt\ *n* : lack of comfort

dis·con·cert \,diskən'sərt\ *vb* : upset

dis·con·nect \,diskə'nekt\ *vb* : undo the connection of

dis·con·so·late \dis'känsələt\ *adj* : hopelessly sad

dis·con·tent \,diskən'tent\ *n* : uneasiness of mind —**dis·con·tent·ed** *adj*

dis·con·tin·ue \,diskən'tinyü\ *vb* : end —**dis·con·tin·u·ance** *n*

dis·cord \'dis,kórd\ *n* : lack of harmony —**dis·cor·dant** \dis'kórd°nt\ *adj* —**dis·cor·dant·ly** *adv*

dis·count \'dis,kaúnt\ *n* : reduction from a regular price ~ \'dis,-, dis'-\ *vb* 1 : reduce the amount of 2 : disregard

dis·cour·age \dis'kərij\ *vb* -**aged**; -**ag·ing** 1 : deprive of courage, confidence, or enthusiasm 2 : dissuade —**dis·cour·age·ment** *n*

dis·course \'dis,kórs\ *n* 1 : conversation 2 : formal treatment of a subject ~ \dis'-\ *vb* -**coursed**; -**cours·ing** : talk at length

dis·cour·te·ous \dis'kərtēəs\ *adj* : lacking courtesy —**dis·cour·te·ous·ly** *adv* —**dis·cour·te·sy** *n*

dis·cov·er \dis'kəvər\ *vb* 1 : make known 2 : obtain the first sight or knowledge of —**dis·cov·er·er** *n* —**dis·cov·ery** \-(ə)rē\ *n*

dis·cred·it \dis'kredət\ *vb* 1 : disbelieve 2 : destroy confidence in ~ *n* 1 : loss of reputation 2 : disbelief —**dis·cred·it·able** *adj*

dis·creet \dis'krēt\ *adj* : capable of keeping a secret —**dis·creet·ly** *adv*

dis·crep·an·cy \dis'krepənsē\ *n*, *pl* -**cies** : difference or disagreement

dis·crete \dis'krēt, 'dis,-\ *adj* : individually distinct

dis·cre·tion \dis'kreshən\ *n* 1 : discreet quality 2 : power of decision or choice —**dis·cre·tion·ary** *adj*

dis·crim·i·nate \dis'krimə,nāt\ *vb* -**nat·ed**; -**nat·ing** 1 : distinguish 2 : show favor or disfavor unjustly —**dis·crim·i·na·tion** \-,krimə'nāshən\ *n* —**dis·crim·i·na·to·ry** \-'krimənə,tōrē\ *adj*

dis·cur·sive \dis'kərsiv\ *adj* : passing from one topic to another —**dis·cur·sive·ly** *adv* —**dis·cur·sive·ness** *n*

dis·cus \'diskəs\ *n*, *pl* -**cus·es** : disk hurled for distance in a contest

dis·cuss \dis'kəs\ *vb* : talk about or present —**dis·cus·sion** \-'kəshən\ *n*

dis·dain \dis'dān\ *n* : feeling of contempt ~ *vb* : look upon or reject with disdain —**dis·dain·ful** \-fəl\ *adj* —**dis·dain·ful·ly** *adv*

dis·ease \diz'ēz\ *n* : condition of a body that impairs its functioning —**dis·eased** \-'ēzd\ *adj*

dis·em·bark \,disəm'bärk\ *vb* : get off a ship —**dis·em·bar·ka·tion** \dis-,em,bär'kāshən\ *n*

dis·em·bod·ied \,disəm'bädēd\ *adj* : having no substance or reality

dis·en·chant \,dis°n'chant\ *vb* : to free from illusion —**dis·en·chant·ment** *n*

dis·en·gage \-°n'gāj\ *vb* : release —**dis·en·gage·ment** *n*

dis·en·tan·gle \-°n'taŋgəl\ *vb* : free from entanglement

dis·fa·vor \dis-\ *n* : disapproval

dis·fig·ure \dis-\ *vb* : spoil the appearance of —**dis·fig·ure·ment** *n*

dis·fran·chise \dis-\ *vb* : deprive of the right to vote —**dis·fran·chise·ment** *n*

dis·gorge \dis'górj\ *vb* : spew forth

dis·grace \dis'grās\ *vb* : bring disgrace to ~ *n* 1 : shame 2 : cause of shame —**dis·grace·ful** \-fəl\ *adj* —**dis·grace·ful·ly** *adv*

dis·grun·tle \dis'grənt°l\ *vb* -**tled**; -**tling** : put in bad humor

dis·guise \dis'gīz\ *vb* -**guised**; -**guis·ing** : hide the true identity or nature of ~ *n* : something that conceals

dis·gust \-'gəst\ *n* : strong aversion ~ *vb* : provoke disgust in —**dis·gust·ed·ly** *adv* —**dis·gust·ing·ly** *adv*

dish \'dish\ *n* 1 : vessel for serving food or the food it holds 2 : food prepared in a particular way ~ *vb* : put in a dish —**dish·cloth** *n* —**dish·rag** *n* —**dish·wash·er** *n* —**dish·wa·ter** *n*

dis·har·mo·ny \dis'härmənē\ *n* : lack of harmony —**dis·har·mo·ni·ous** \,dis(,)här'mōnēəs\ *adj*

dis·heart·en \dis'härt°n\ *vb* : discourage

di·shev·el \dish'evəl\ *vb* -**eled** or -**elled**; -**el·ing** or -**el·ling** : throw into disorder —**di·shev·eled, di·shev·elled** *adj*

dis·hon·est \dis-\ *adj* : not honest —**dis·hon·est·ly** *adv* —**dis·hon·es·ty** *n*

dis·hon·or \dis-\ *n* or *vb* : disgrace —**dis·hon·or·able** *adj* —**dis·hon·or·ably** *adv*

dis·il·lu·sion \,disə'lüzhən\ *vb* : to free from illusion —**dis·il·lu·sion·ment** *n*

dis·in·cli·na·tion \dis-\ *n* : unwillingness —**dis·in·cline** \,dis*n*'klīn\ *vb*

dis·in·fect \,dis*n*'fekt\ *vb* : destroy disease germs in or on —**dis·in·fec·tant** \-'fektant\ *adj or n* —**dis·in·fec·tion** \-'fekshən\ *n*

dis·in·her·it \,dis-\ *vb* : prevent from inheriting property

dis·in·te·grate \dis'intə,grāt\ *vb* : break into parts or small bits —**dis·in·te·gra·tion** \dis,intə'grāshən\ *n*

dis·in·ter·est·ed \dis-\ *adj* 1 : not interested 2 : not prejudiced —**dis·in·ter·est·ed·ness** *n*

dis·joint·ed \dis'jóintəd\ *adj* 1 : separated at the joint 2 : incoherent

disk \'disk\ *n* : something round and flat

dis·like \dis'līk\ *vb* : regard with dislike ~ *n* : feeling that something is unpleasant and to be avoided

dis·lo·cate \'dislō,kāt, dis-\ *vb* : move out of the usual or proper place —**dis·lo·ca·tion** \,dis(,)lō'kāshən\ *n*

dis·lodge \dis-\ *vb* : force out of a place

dis·loy·al \dis-\ *adj* : not loyal —**dis·loy·al·ty** *n*

dis·mal \'dizməl\ *adj* : showing or causing gloom —**dis·mal·ly** *adv*

dis·man·tle \dis'mant⁹l\ *vb* -**tled**; -**tling** : take apart

dis·may \dis'mā\ *vb* -**mayed**; -**may·ing** : discourage —**dismay** *n*

dis·mem·ber \dis'membər\ *vb* : cut into pieces —**dis·mem·ber·ment** *n*

dis·miss \dis'mis\ *vb* 1 : send away 2 : remove from service 3 : put aside or out of mind —**dis·miss·al** *n*

dis·mount \dis-\ *vb* 1 : get down from something 2 : take apart

dis·obey \,disə'bā\ *vb* : refuse to obey —**dis·obe·di·ence** \-'bēdēəns\ *n* —**dis·obe·di·ent** \-ənt\ *adj*

dis·or·der \dis'órdər\ *vb* : cause disorder of ~ *n* 1 : lack of order 2 : breach of public order 3 : abnormal state of body or mind —**dis·or·der·li·ness** *n* —**dis·or·der·ly** *adj*

dis·or·ga·nize \dis-\ *vb* : throw into disorder —**dis·or·ga·ni·za·tion** *n*

dis·own \dis'ōn\ *vb* : repudiate

dis·par·age \-'parij\ *vb* -**aged**; -**ag·ing** : say bad things about —**dis·par·age·ment** *n*

dis·pa·rate \dis'parət, 'disp(ə)rət\ *adj* : different in quality or character —**dis·par·i·ty** \dis'parətē\ *n*

dis·pas·sion·ate \dis'pash(ə)nət\ *adj* : not influenced by strong feeling —**dis·pas·sion** \-ən\ *n*

dis·patch \dis'pach\ *vb* 1 : send 2 : kill 3 : attend to rapidly ~ *n* 1 : message 2 : news item from a correspondent 3 : promptness and efficiency —**dis·patch·er** *n*

dis·pel \dis'pel\ *vb* -**ll**- : clear away

dis·pen·sa·ry \-'pens(ə)rē\ *n, pl* -**ries** : place where medical or dental aid is provided

dis·pen·sa·tion \,dispən'sāshən\ *n* 1 : system of principles or rules 2 : exemption from a rule 3 : act of ispensing

dis·pense \dis'pens\ *vb* -**pensed**; -**pens·ing** 1 : portion out 2 : make up and give out (remedies) —**dis·pens·able** *adj* —**dis·pens·er** *n* —**dispense with** : do without

dis·perse \dis'pərs\ *vb* -**persed**; -**pers·ing** : scatter —**dis·per·sal** \-'pərsəl\ *n* —**dis·per·sion** \-'pərzhən\ *n*

dis·place \dis-\ *vb* 1 : expel or force to flee from home or native land 2 : take the place of —**dis·place·ment** \-mənt\ *n*

dis·play \dis'plā\ *vb* : present to view —**display** *n*

dis·please \dis-\ *vb* : arouse the dislike of —**dis·plea·sure** \-'plezhər\ *n*

dis·port \dis'pōrt\ *vb* 1 : amuse 2 : frolic

dis·pose \dis'pōz\ *vb* -**posed**; -**pos·ing** 1 : give a tendency to 2 : settle —**dis·pos·able** \-'pōzəbəl\ *adj* —**dis·pos·al** \-'pōzəl\ *n* —**dis·pos·er** *n* —**dispose of** 1 : determine the fate, condition, or use of 2 : get rid of

dis·po·si·tion \,dispə'zishən\ *n* 1 : act or power of disposing of 2 : arrangement 3 : natural attitude

dis·pos·sess \,dispə'zes\ *vb* : deprive of possession or occupancy —**dis·pos·ses·sion** \-'zeshən\ *n*

dis·pro·por·tion \,disprə'pōrshən\ *n* : lack of proportion —**dis·pro·por·tion·ate** \-sh(ə)nət\ *adj*

dis·prove \dis-\ *vb* : prove false —**dis·proof** *n*

dis·pute \dis'pyüt\ *vb* -**put·ed**; -**put·ing** 1 : argue 2 : deny the truth or rightness of 3 : struggle against or over ~ *n* : debate or quarrel —**dis·put·able** \-əbəl, 'dispyət-\ *adj* —**dis·put·ably** \-blē\ *adv* —**dis·pu·ta·tion** \,dispyə'tāshən\ *n*

dis·qual·i·fy \dis-\ *vb* : make ineligible —**dis·qual·i·fi·ca·tion** *n*

dis·qui·et \dis-\ *vb* : make uneasy or restless ~ *n* : anxiety

dis·re·gard \,dis-\ *vb* : pay no attention to ~ *n* : neglect

dis·re·pair \,dis-\ *n* : need of repair

dis·rep·u·ta·ble \dis-\ *adj* : having a bad reputation

dis·re·pute \,dis-\ *n* : low regard

dis·re·spect \,dis-\ *n* : lack of respect —**dis·re·spect·ful** *adj*

dis·robe \dis-\ *vb* : undress

dis·rupt \dis'rəpt\ *vb* : throw into disorder —**dis·rup·tion** \-'rəpshən\ *n* —**dis·rup·tive** \-'rəptiv\ *adj*

dis·sat·is·fac·tion \dis,atəs'fakshən\ *n* : dissatisfied feeling

dis·sat·is·fy \dis'atəs,fī\ *vb* : fail to satisfy —**dis·sat·is·fied** *adj*

dis·sect \dis'ekt\ *vb* : cut into parts esp. to examine —**dis·sec·tion** \-'ekshən\ *n*

dis·sem·ble \dis'embəl\ *vb* **-bled; -bling** : disguise feelings or intention —**dis·sem·bler** *n*

dis·sem·i·nate \dis'emə,nāt\ *vb* **-nat·ed; -nat·ing** : spread around —**dis·sem·i·na·tion** \-,emə'nāshən\ *n*

dis·sen·sion \dis'enchən\ *n* : discord

dis·sent \dis'ent\ *vb* : object or disagree ~ *n* : difference of opinion —**dis·sent·er** *n* —**dis·sen·tient** \-'enchənt\ *adj* *n*

dis·ser·ta·tion \,disər'tāshən\ *n* : long written study of a subject

dis·ser·vice \dis'ərvəs\ *n* : injury

dis·si·dent \'disədənt\ *n* : one who differs openly —**dis·si·dence** \-əns\ *n* —**dissident** *adj*

dis·sim·i·lar \dis'imələr\ *adj* : different —**dis·sim·i·lar·i·ty** \dis,imə'larətē\ *n*

dis·si·pate \'disə,pāt\ *vb* **-pat·ed; -pat·ing** 1 : break up and drive off 2 : squander 3 : drink to excess —**dis·si·pa·tion** \,disə'pāshən\ *n*

dis·so·ci·ate \dis'ōs(h)ē,āt\ *vb* **-at·ed; -at·ing** : separate from association —**dis·so·ci·a·tion** \dis,ōs(h)ē'āshən\ *n*

dis·so·lute \'disə,lüt\ *adj* : loose in morals or conduct

dis·so·lu·tion \,disə'lüshən\ *n* : act or process of dissolving

dis·solve \diz'älv\ *vb* 1 : break up or bring to an end 2 : pass or cause to pass into solution

dis·so·nance \'disənəns\ *n* : discord —**dis·so·nant** \-nənt\ *adj*

dis·suade \dis'wād\ *vb* **-suad·ed; -suad·ing** : persuade not to do something —**dis·sua·sion** \-'wāzhən\ *n*

dis·tance \'distəns\ *n* 1 : measure of separation in space or time 2 : reserve

dis·tant \-tənt\ *adj* 1 : separate in space 2 : remote in time, space, or relationship 3 : reserved

dis·taste \dis'tāst\ *n* : dislike —**dis·taste·ful** *adj*

dis·tem·per \dis'tempər\ *n* : virus disease of dogs

dis·tend \dis'tend\ *vb* : swell out —**dis·ten·sion, dis·ten·tion** \-'tenchən\ *n*

dis·till \dis'til\ *vb* : obtain by distillation —**dis·til·late** \'distə,lāt, -lət\ *n* —**dis·till·er** *n* —**dis·till·ery** \dis-'til(ə)rē\ *n*

dis·til·la·tion \,distə'lāshən\ *n* : purification of liquid by evaporating then condensing

dis·tinct \dis'tiŋkt\ *adj* 1 : distinguished from others 2 : clearly seen or heard —**dis·tinct·ly** *adv* —**dis·tinct·ness** *n*

dis·tinc·tion \-'tiŋkshən\ *n* 1 : act of distinguishing 2 : difference 3 : special recognition

dis·tinc·tive \-'tiŋktiv\ *adj* 1 : setting one apart 2 : characteristic —**dis·tinc·tive·ly** *adv* —**dis·tinc·tive·ness** *n*

dis·tin·guish \dis'tiŋgwish\ *vb* 1 : perceive as different 2 : set apart 3 : discern 4 : make outstanding —**dis·tin·guish·able** *adj* —**dis·tin·guished** \-gwisht\ *adj*

dis·tort \dis'tórt\ *vb* : twist out of shape, condition, or true meaning —**dis·tor·tion** \-'tórshən\ *n*

dis·tract \dis'trakt\ *vb* : divert the mind or attention of —**dis·trac·tion** \-'trakshən\ *n*

dis·traught \dis'tröt\ *adj* : agitated with mental conflict

dis·tress \-'tres\ *n* 1 : suffering 2 : misfortune 3 : state of danger or great need ~ *vb* : subject to strain or distress —**dis·tress·ful** *adj*

dis·trib·ute \-'tribyət\ *vb* **-ut·ed; -ut·ing** 1 : divide among many 2 : spread or hand out —**dis·tri·bu·tion** \,distrə-'byüshən\ *n* —**dis·trib·u·tive** \-'tribyətiv\ *adj* —**dis·trib·u·tor** \-ər\ *n*

dis·trict \'dis(,)trikt\ *n* : territorial division

dis·trust \dis'trəst\ *vb or n* : mistrust —**dis·trust·ful** \-fəl\ *adj*

dis·turb \dis'tərb\ *vb* 1 : interfere with 2 : destroy the peace, composure, or order of —**dis·tur·bance** \-'tərbəns\ *n* —**dis·turb·er** *n*

dis·use \-'yüs\ *n* : lack of use

ditch \dich\ *n* : trench ~ *vb* 1 : dig a ditch in 2 : get rid of

dith·er \'dithər\ *n* : highly nervous or excited state

dit·to \'ditō\ *n, pl* **-tos** : more of the same

dit·ty \'ditē\ *n, pl* **-ties** : short simple song

di·uret·ic \,dī(y)ə'retik\ *adj* : tending to increase urine flow —**diuretic** *n*

di·ur·nal \dī'ərn^əl\ adj : daily 2 : of or occurring in the daytime

di·van \'dī,van, dī-\ n : couch

dive \'dīv\ vb **dived** \'dīvd\ or **dove** \'dōv\; **dived; div·ing** 1 : plunge into water headfirst 2 : submerge 3 : descend quickly ~ n 1 : act of diving 2 : sharp decline —**div·er** n

di·verge \də'vərj, dī-\ vb **-verged; -verg·ing** 1 : move in different directions 2 : differ —**di·ver·gence** \-'vərjəns\ n —**di·ver·gent** \-jənt\ adj

di·vers \'dīvərz\ adj : various

di·verse \dī'vərs, də-, 'dī,vərs\ adj : involving different forms —**di·ver·si·fi·ca·tion** \də,vərsəfə'kāshən, dī-\ n —**di·ver·si·fy** \-'vərsə,fī\ vb —**di·ver·si·ty** \-sətē\ n

di·vert \də'vərt, dī-\ vb 1 : turn from a course or purpose 2 : distract 3 : amuse —**di·ver·sion** \-'vərzhən\ n

di·vest \dī'vest, də-\ vb : strip of clothing, possessions, or rights

di·vide \də'vīd\ vb **-vid·ed; -vid·ing** 1 : separate 2 : distribute 3 : share 4 : subject to mathematical division ~ n : watershed —**di·vid·er** n

div·i·dend \'divə,dend\ n 1 : individual share 2 : bonus 3 : number to be divided by another

div·i·na·tion \,divə'nāshən\ n : practice of trying to foretell future events

di·vine \də'vīn\ adj **-vin·er; -est** 1 : relating to or being God or a god 2 : supremely good ~ n : clergyman ~ vb **-vined; -vin·ing** 1 : infer 2 : prophesy —**di·vine·ly** adv —**di·vin·er** n —**di·vin·i·ty** \-'vinətē\ n

di·vis·i·ble \-'vizəbəl\ adj : capable of being divided —**di·vis·i·bil·i·ty** \-,vizə'bilətē\ n

di·vi·sion \-'vizhən\ n 1 : distribution 2 : part of a whole 3 : disagreement 4 : process of finding out how many times one number is contained in another —**di·vi·sion·al** \-'vizh(ə)nəl\ adj

di·vi·sive \də'vīsiv, -'viziv\ adj : creating dissension

di·vi·sor \-'vīzər\ n : number by which a dividend is divided

di·vorce \də'vōrs\ n : legal breaking up of a marriage —**di·vorce** vb

di·vor·cée \-,vōr'sā, -'sē\ n : divorced woman

di·vulge \də'vəlj, dī-\ vb **-vulged; -vulg·ing** : reveal

diz·zy \'dizē\ adj **-zi·er; -est** 1 : having a sensation of whirling 2 : causing or caused by giddiness —**diz·zi·ly** adv —**diz·zi·ness** n

do \('')dü\ vb **did** \('')did\; **done** \'dən\; **do·ing** \'düiŋ\; **does** \('')dəz\ 1 : work to accomplish (an action or task) 2 : behave 3 : prepare or fix up 4 : fare 5 : finish 6 : serve the needs or purpose of 7 —used as an auxiliary verb —**do away with** 1 : get rid of 2 : destroy —**do by** : act toward in a specified way —**do in** vb 1 : ruin 2 : kill

doc·ile \'däsəl\ adj : easily managed —**do·cil·i·ty** \dä'silətē\ n

¹**dock** \'däk\ vb 1 : shorten 2 : reduce

²**dock** n 1 : berth between 2 piers to receive ships 2 : loading wharf or platform ~ vb : bring or come into dock —**dock·hand** n —**dock·work·er** n

³**dock** n : place in a court for a prisoner

dock·et \'däkət\ n 1 : record of the proceedings in a legal action 2 : list of legal causes to be tried —**docket** vb

doc·tor \'däktər\ n 1 : person holding one of the highest academic degrees 2 : one (as a surgeon) skilled in healing arts ~ vb 1 : give medical treatment to 2 : repair or alter —**doc·tor·al** \-t(ə)rəl\ adj

doc·trine \'däktrən\ n : something taught —**doc·tri·nal** \-trən^əl\ adj

doc·u·ment \'däkyəmənt\ n : paper that furnishes information or legal proof —**doc·u·ment** \-,ment\ vb —**doc·u·men·ta·tion** \,däkyəmən'tāshən\ n

doc·u·men·ta·ry \,däkyə'ment(ə)rē\ adj 1 : of or relating to documents 2 : giving a factual presentation —**documentary** n

dod·der \'dädər\ vb : become feeble usu. from age

dodge \'däj\ vb **dodged; dodg·ing** 1 : move quickly aside or out of the way of 2 : evade —**dodge** n

do·do \'dōdō\ n, pl **-does** or **-dos** 1 : heavy flightless extinct bird 2 : stupid person

doe \'dō\ n, pl **does** or **doe** : adult female deer —**doe·skin** \-,skin\ n

do·er \'düər\ n : one that does

does pres 3d sing of DO

doff \'däf\ vb : remove

dog \'dȯg\ n : flesh-eating domestic mammal ~ vb 1 : hunt down or track like a hound 2 : worry as if by dogs —**dog·catch·er** n —**dog·gy** \-ē\ n or adj —**dog·house** n

dog-ear \'dȯg,iər\ n : turned-down corner of a page —**dog-eared** \-,iərd\ adj

dog·ged \'dȯgəd\ *adj* : stubbornly determined

dog·ma \'dȯgmə\ *n* : tenet or code of tenets

dog·ma·tism \-,tizəm\ *n* : unwarranted stubbornness of opinion —**dog·mat·ic** \dȯg'matik\ *adj*

dog·wood *n* : flowering tree

doi·ly \'dȯilē\ *n*, *pl* **-lies** : small decorative mat

do·ings \'düiŋz\ *n pl* : deeds

dol·drums \'dōldrəmz,'däl-\ *n pl* **1** : spell of listlessness or despondency **2** : windless ocean near the equator

dole \'dōl\ *n* : distribution esp. of money to the needy or unemployed ~ *vb* : give out in small portions

dole·ful \'dōlfəl\ *adj* : full of grief —**dole·ful·ly** *adv*

doll \'däl, 'dȯl\ *n* : small figure of a person used esp. as a child's toy

dol·lar \'dälər\ *n* : any of various basic monetary units (as in the U.S. and Canada)

dol·ly \'dälē\ *n*, *pl* **-lies** : wheeled frame for moving heavy objects

dol·phin \'dälfən\ *n* **1** : sea mammal related to the whales **2** : saltwater food fish

dolt \'dōlt\ *n* : stupid person —**dolt·ish** *adj*

-dom \dəm\ *n suffix* **1** : office or realm **2** : state or fact of being **3** : those belonging to a group

do·main \dō'mān, də-\ *n* **1** : territory over which someone reigns **2** : sphere of activity

dome \'dōm\ *n* : large hemispherical roof

do·mes·tic \də'mestik\ *adj* **1** : relating to the household or family **2** : relating and limited to one's own country **3** : tame ~ *n* : household servant —**do·mes·ti·cal·ly** \-tik(ə)lē\ *adv*

do·mes·ti·cate \-ti,kāt\ *vb* **-cat·ed; -cat·ing** : tame —**do·mes·ti·ca·tion** \-,mesti'kāshən\ *n*

dom·i·cile \'dämə,sīl, 'dō-; 'däməsəl\ *n* : home —**domicile** *vb*

dom·i·nance \'dämənəns\ *n* : control —**dom·i·nant** \-nənt\ *adj*

dom·i·nate \-,nāt\ *vb* **-nat·ed; -nat·ing** **1** : have control over **2** : rise high above —**dom·i·na·tion** \,dämə'nāshən\ *n*

dom·i·neer \,dämə'niər\ *vb* : exercise arbitrary control

do·min·ion \də'minyən\ *n* **1** : supreme authority **2** : governed territory

dom·i·no \'dämə,nō\ *n*, *pl* **-noes** *or* **-nos**

: flat rectangular block used as a piece in a game (**dominoes**)

don \'dän\ *vb* **-nn-** : put on (clothes)

do·nate \'dō,nāt\ *vb* **-nat·ed; -nat·ing** : make a gift of —**do·na·tion** \dō-'nāshən\ *n*

¹done \'dən\ *past part of* DO

²done *adj* **1** : finished or ended **2** : cooked sufficiently

don·key \'däŋkē, 'dəŋ-\ *n*, *pl* **-keys** : domestic ass

do·nor \'dōnər\ *n* : one that gives

doo·dle \'düd³l\ *vb* **-dled; -dling** : draw or scribble aimlessly —**doodle** *n*

doom \'düm\ *n* **1** : judgment **2** : fate **3** : ruin —**doom** *vb*

door \'dōr\ *n* : passage for entrance or a movable barrier that can open or close such a passage —**door·jamb** *n* —**door·knob** *n* —**door·mat** *n* —**door·step** *n* —**door·way** *n*

dope \'dōp\ *n* **1** : narcotic preparation **2** : stupid person **3** : information ~ *vb* doped; dop·ing : drug

dor·mant \'dȯrmənt\ *adj* : not actively growing or functioning —**dor·man·cy** \-mənsē\ *n*

dor·mer \'dȯrmər\ *n* : window built upright in a sloping roof

dor·mi·to·ry \'dȯrmə,tōrē\ *n*, *pl* **-ries** : residence hall (as at a college)

dor·mouse \'dȯr,maůs\ *n* : squirrellike rodent

dor·sal \'dȯrsəl\ *adj* : relating to or on the back —**dor·sal·ly** *adv*

do·ry \'dōrē\ *n*, *pl* **-ries** : flat-bottomed boat

dose \'dōs\ *n* : quantity (as of medicine) taken at one time ~ *vb* dosed; dos·ing : give medicine to —**dos·age** \'dōsij\ *n*

dot \'dät\ *n* **1** : small spot **2** : small round mark made with or as if with a pen ~ *vb* **-tt-** : mark with dots

dot·age \'dōtij\ *n* : senility

dote \'dōt\ *vb* doted; dot·ing **1** : act feebleminded **2** : be foolishly fond

dou·ble \'dəbəl\ *adj* **1** : consisting of 2 members or parts **2** : being twice as great or as many **3** : folded in two ~ *n* **1** : something twice another **2** : one that resembles another ~ *adv* : doubly ~ *vb* -bled; -bling **1** : make or become twice as great **2** : fold or clench

dou·ble-cross *vb* : deceive by trickery —**dou·ble-cross·er** *n*

dou·bly \'dəblē\ *adv* : to twice the degree

doubt \'daůt\ *vb* **1** : be uncertain about **2** : mistrust **3** : consider unlikely ~ *n* **1** : uncertainty **2** : mistrust **3** : inclination not to believe **—doubt·ful** \-fəl\ adj **—doubt·ful·ly** adv **— doubt·less** \-ləs\ adv

douche \'düsh\ n : jet of fluid for cleaning a body part

dough \'dō\ n : stiff mixture of flour and liquid **—doughy** \'dō-ē\ adj

dough·nut \-(ˌ)nət\ n : small fried ring-shaped cake

dough·ty \'daütē\ adj **-ti·er; -est** : able, strong, or valiant

dour \'du̇(ə)r, 'dau̇r\ adj 1 : severe 2 : gloomy or sullen

douse \'dau̇s, 'dau̇z\ vb **doused; dous·ing** 1 : plunge into or drench with water 2 : extinguish

¹dove \'dəv\ n : small wild pigeon

²dove \'dōv\ past of DIVE

dove·tail \'dəv,tāl\ n 1 : flaring tenon and its mortise ~ vb 1 : join by dovetails 2 : fit together neatly

dow·a·ger \'daüijər\ n 1 : widow with wealth or a title 2 : dignified elderly woman

dowdy \'daüdē\ adj **dowd·i·er; -est** : lacking neatness and charm

dow·el \'daü(ə)l\ n : peg used for fastening two pieces

dow·er \'daü(ə)r\ n : property given a widow for life ~ vb : supply with a dower

¹down \'daün\ adv 1 : toward or in a lower position or state 2 : to a lying or sitting position 3 : as a cash deposit 4 : on paper ~ adj 1 : lying on the ground 2 : directed or going downward 3 : being at a low level— prep : toward the bottom of ~ vb 1 : cause to go down 2 : defeat

²down n : fluffy feathers

down·cast adj 1 : sad 2 : directed down

down·fall n : ruin or cause of ruin **— down·fall·en** \-ˌfȯlən\ adj

down·grade n : downward slope ~ vb : lower in grade or position

down·heart·ed adj : sad

down·pour n : heavy rain

down·right adv : thoroughly ~ adj : absolute or thorough

downs \'daünz\ n pl : rolling treeless uplands

down·stairs adv : on or to a lower floor and esp. the main floor **—downstairs** adj or n

down-to-earth adj : practical

down·town adv : to, toward, or in the business center of a town **—downtown** n or adj

down·trod·den \-ˌträd²n\ adj : suffering oppression

down·ward \'daünwərd\, **down·wards** \-wərdz\ adv : to a lower place or condition **—downward** adj

down·wind adv or adj : in the direction the wind is blowing

downy \'daünē\ adj **-i·er; -est** : resembling or covered with down

dow·ry \'daü(ə)rē\ n, pl **-ries** : property a woman gives her husband in marriage

dox·ol·o·gy \däk'säləjē\ n, pl **-gies** : hymn of praise to God

doze \'dōz\ vb **dozed; doz·ing** : sleep lightly **—doze** n

doz·en \'dəz²n\ n, pl **-ens** or **-en** : group of 12 **—doz·enth** \-²nth\ adj

drab \'drab\ adj **-bb-** : dull **—drab·ness** n

dra·co·ni·an \drā'kōnēən, dra-\ adj, often cap : harsh, cruel

draft \'draft, 'draft\ n 1 : act of drawing or hauling 2 : act of drinking 3 : amount drunk at once 4 : preliminary outline or rough sketch 5 : selection from a pool or the selection process 6 : order for the payment of money 7 : air current ~ vb 1 : select usu. on a compulsory basis 2 : make a preliminary sketch, version, or plan of ~ adj : drawn from a container **—draft·ee** \draf'tē, dräf-\ n **—drafty** \'draftē\ adj

drafts·man \'draftsmən, 'draft-\ n : one who draws plans

drag \'drag\ n 1 : something dragged over a surface or through water 2 : something that hinders progress or is boring 3 : act or an instance of dragging ~ vb **-gg-** 1 : haul 2 : move or work with difficulty 3 : pass slowly 4 : search or fish with a drag **—drag·ger** n

drag·net \-ˌnet\ n 1 : trawl 2 : planned actions for finding a criminal

drag·on \'dragən\ n : fabled winged serpent

drag·on·fly n : large 4-winged insect

drain \'drān\ vb 1 : draw off or flow off gradually or completely 2 : exhaust ~ n : means or act of draining **—drain·age** \-ij\ n **—drain·er** n **—drain·pipe** n

drake \'drāk\ n : male duck

dra·ma \'drämə, 'dram-\ n 1 : composition for theatrical presentation esp. on a serious subject 2 : series of events involving conflicting forces **—dra·mat·ic** \drə'matik\ adj **—dra·mat·i·cal·ly** \-ik(ə)lē\ adv **— dram·a·tist** \'dramətəst, 'dräm-\ n **—dram·a·ti·za·tion** \ˌdramətə'zāshən, ˌdräm-\ n **—dram·a·tize** \'dramə,tīz, 'dräm-\ vb

drank past of DRINK

drape \\'drāp\\ vb **draped; drap·ing** 1 : cover or adorn with folds of cloth 2 : cause to hang in flowing lines or folds ~ n : curtain

drap·ery \\'drāp(ə)rē\\ n, pl **-er·ies** : decorative fabric hung esp. as a heavy curtain

dras·tic \\'drastik\\ adj : extreme or harsh —**dras·ti·cal·ly** \\-tik(ə)lē\\ adv

draught \\'draft\\, **draughty** \\'draftē\\ chiefly Brit var of DRAFT, DRAFTY

draw \\'drȯ\\ vb **drew** \\'drü\\ **drawn** \\'drȯn\\ **draw·ing** 1 : move or cause to move (as by pulling) 2 : attract or provoke 3 : extract 4 : take or receive (as money) 5 : bend a bow in preparation for shooting 6 : leave a contest undecided 7 : sketch 8 : write out 9 : deduce ~ n 1 : act, process, or result of drawing 2 : tie —**draw out** : cause to speak candidly —**draw up** 1 : write out 2 : pull oneself erect 3 : bring or come to a stop

draw·back n : disadvantage

draw·bridge n : bridge that can be raised

draw·er \\'drȯ(ə)r\\ n 1 : one that draws 2 : sliding boxlike compartment 3 pl : underpants

draw·ing \\'drȯiŋ\\ n 1 : occasion of choosing by lot 2 : act or art of making a figure, plan, or sketch with lines 3 : something drawn

drawl \\'drȯl\\ vb : speak slowly — **drawl** n

dread \\'dred\\ vb : feel extreme fear or reluctance ~ n : great fear ~ adj : causing dread —**dread·ful** \\-fəl\\ adj —**dread·ful·ly** adv

dream \\'drēm\\ n 1 : series of thoughts or visions during sleep 2 : dreamlike vision 3 : something notable 4 : ideal ~ vb **dreamed** \\'dremt, 'drēmd\\ or **dreamt** \\'dremt\\ **dream·ing** 1 : have a dream 2 : imagine —**dream·er** n —**dream·like** adj —**dreamy** adj

drea·ry \\'dri(ə)rē\\ adj **-ri·er; -est** : dismal —**drea·ri·ly** \\'drirəlē\\ adv

¹dredge \\'drej\\ n : machine for removing earth esp. from under water ~ vb **dredged; dredg·ing** : dig up or search with a dredge —**dredg·er** n

²dredge vb **dredged; dredg·ing** : coat (food) with flour

dregs \\'dregz\\ n pl 1 : sediment 2 : most worthless part

drench \\'drench\\ vb : wet thoroughly

dress \\'dres\\ vb 1 : put clothes on 2 : decorate 3 : prepare (as a carcass) for use 4 : apply dressings, remedies, or fertilizer to ~ n 1 : apparel 2 : single garment of bodice and skirt ~ adj : suitable for a formal event —**dress·mak·er** n —**dress·mak·ing** n

dress·er \\'dresər\\ n : bureau with a mirror

dress·ing n 1 : act or process of dressing 2 : sauce or a seasoned mixture 3 : material to cover an injury

dressy \\-ē\\ adj **dress·i·er; -est** 1 : showy in dress 2 : stylish

drew past of DRAW

drib·ble \\'dribəl\\ vb **-bled; -bling** 1 : fall or flow in drops : drool — **dribble** n

drier comparative of DRY

driest superlative of DRY

drift \\'drift\\ n 1 : motion or course of something drifting 2 : mass blown up by wind 3 : general intention or meaning ~ vb 1 : float or be driven along (as by a current) 2 : wander without purpose 3 : pile up under force —**drift·er** n —**drift·wood** n

¹drill \\'dril\\ vb 1 : bore with a drill 2 : instruct by repetition ~ n 1 : boring tool 2 : strict training and instruction —**drill·er** n

²drill n : seed-planting implement

³drill n : twill-weave cotton fabric

drily var of DRYLY

drink \\'driŋk\\ vb **drank** \\'draŋk\\ **drunk** \\'drəŋk\\ or **drank; drink·ing** 1 : swallow liquid 2 : absorb 3 : drink alcoholic beverages esp. to excess ~ n 1 : beverage 2 : alcoholic liquor —**drink·able** adj —**drink·er** n

drip \\'drip\\ vb **-pp-** : fall or let fall in drops ~ n 1 : a dripping 2 : sound of falling drops

drive \\'drīv\\ vb **drove** \\'drōv\\ **driv·en** \\'drivən\\ **driv·ing** 1 : urge or force onward 2 : direct the movement or course of 3 : compel 4 : cause to become 5 : propel forcefully ~ n 1 : trip in a vehicle 2 : driveway 3 : intensive campaign 4 : aggressive or dynamic quality 5 : basic need —**driv·er** n

drive-in adj : accommodating patrons in cars —**drive-in** n

driv·el \\'drivəl\\ vb **-eled** or **-elled; -el·ing** or **-el·ling** 1 : drool 2 : talk stupidly ~ n : nonsense

drive·way n : private road from the street to a house

driz·zle \\'drizəl\\ n : fine misty rain — **drizzle** vb

droll \\'drōl\\ adj : humorous or whimsical —**droll·ery** n —**drol·ly** \\'drȯ(l)lē\\ adv

drom·e·dary \\'drämə‚derē\\ n, pl **-dar·ies** : speedy one-humped camel

drone \\'drōn\ *n* **1** : male honeybee **2** : deep hum or buzz ~ *vb* **droned; dron·ing** : make a dull monotonous sound

drool \\'drül\ *vb* : let liquid run from the mouth

droop \\'drüp\ *vb* **1** : hang or incline downward **2** : lose strength or spirit —**droop** *n*

drop \\'dräp\ *n* **1** : quantity of fluid in one spherical mass **2** *pl* : medicine used by drops **3** : decline or fall **4** : distance something drops ~ *vb* **-pp- 1** : fall in drops **2** : let fall **3** : convey **4** : go lower or become less strong or less active —**drop·let** \-lət\ *n* —**drop back** *vb* : move toward the rear —**drop behind** : fail to keep up —**drop in** *vb* : pay an unexpected visit

drop·per *n* : device that dispenses liquid by drops

drop·sy \\'dräpsē\ *n* : abnormal accumulation of serous fluid in the body

dross \\'dräs\ *n* : waste matter

drought, drouth \\'draut(h)\ *n* : long dry spell

¹drove \\'drōv\ *n* : crowd of moving people or animals

²drove *past of* DRIVE

drown \\'draun\ *vb* **1** : suffocate in water **2** : overpower or become overpowered

drowse \\'drauz\ *vb* **drowsed; drows·ing** : doze —**drowse** *n*

drowsy \\'drauzē\ *adj* **drows·i·er; -est** : sleepy —**drows·i·ly** *adv* —**drows·i·ness** *n*

drub \\'drab\ *vb* **-bb-** : beat severely

drudge \\'draj\ *vb* **drudged; drudg·ing** : do hard or boring work —**drudge** *n* —**drudg·ery** \-(ə)rē\ *n*

drug \\'drag\ *n* **1** : substance used as or in medicine **2** : narcotic ~ *vb* **-gg-** : affect with drugs —**drug·gist** \-əst\ *n* —**drug·store** *n*

dru·id \\'drüəd\ *n* : ancient Celtic priest

drum \\'drəm\ *n* **1** : musical instrument that is a skin-covered cylinder beaten with sticks **2** : drum-shaped object (as a container) ~ *vb* **-mm- 1** : beat a drum **2** : drive, force, or bring about by steady effort —**drum·beat** *n* —**drum·mer** *n*

drum·stick *n* **1** : stick for beating a drum **2** : lower segment of a fowl's leg

drunk \\'drəŋk\ *adj* : having the faculties impaired by alcohol ~ *n* : one who is drunk —**drunk·ard** \\'drəŋkərd\ *n* —**drunk·en** \-kən\ *adj* —**drunk·en·ly** *adv* —**drunk·en·ness** *n*

dry \\'drī\ *adj* **dri·er** \\'drī(ə)r\; **dri·est** \\'drīəst\ **1** : lacking water or moisture **2** : thirsty **3** : marked by the absence of alcoholic beverages **4** : uninteresting **5** : not sweet ~ *vb* **dried; dry·ing** : make or become dry —**dry·ly** *adv* —**dry·ness** *n*

dry-clean *vb* : clean (fabrics) chiefly with solvents other than water —**dry cleaning** *n*

dry·er \\'drī(ə)r\ *n* : device for drying

dry goods *n pl* : textiles, clothing, and notions

dry ice *n* : solid carbon dioxide

du·al \\'d(y)üəl\ *adj* : twofold —**du·al·ism** \-ə,lizəm\ *n* —**du·al·i·ty** \d(y)ü'alətē\ *n*

dub \\'dəb\ *vb* **-bb-** : name

du·bi·ous \\'d(y)übēəs\ *adj* **1** : uncertain **2** : questionable —**du·bi·ous·ly** *adv* —**du·bi·ous·ness** *n*

du·cal \\'d(y)ükəl\ *adj* : relating to a duke or dukedom

duch·ess \\'dəchəs\ *n* **1** : wife of a duke **2** : woman holding a ducal title

duchy \-ē\ *n, pl* **-ies** : territory of a duke or duchess

¹duck \\'dək\ *n, pl* : swimming bird related to the goose and swan ~ *vb* **1** : thrust or plunge under water **2** : lower the head or body suddenly **3** : evade —**duck·ling** \-liŋ\ *n*

²duck *n* : cotton fabric

duct \\'dəkt\ *n* : canal for conveying a fluid —**duct·less** \-ləs\ *adj*

duc·tile \\'dəkt?l\ *adj* : able to be drawn out or shaped —**duc·til·i·ty** \,dək-'tilətē\ *n*

dude \\'d(y)üd\ *n* : dandy

dud·geon \\'dəjən\ *n* : ill humor

due \\'d(y)ü\ *adj* **1** : owed **2** : appropriate **3** : attributable **4** : expected ~ *n* **1** : something due **2** *pl* : fee ~ *adv* : directly

du·el \\'d(y)üəl\ *n* : combat between 2 persons —**duel** *vb* —**du·el·ist** *n*

du·et \d(y)ü'et\ *n* : musical composition for 2 performers

due to *prep* : because of

dug *past of* DIG

dug·out \\'dəg,aut\ *n* **1** : boat made by hollowing out a log **2** : shelter made by digging

duke \\'d(y)ük\ *n* : nobleman of the highest rank —**duke·dom** *n*

dull \\'dəl\ *adj* **1** : mentally slow **2** : blunt **3** : not brilliant or interesting ~ *n* : make or become dull —**dull·ard** \\'dələrd\ *n* —**dull·ness, dul·ness** *n* —**dul·ly** \\'dəl(l)ē\ *adv*

du·ly \'d(y)ülē\ *adv* : in a due manner, time, or degree

dumb \'dəm\ *adj* 1 : mute 2 : stupid — **dumb·ly** *adv*

dumb·bell \'dəm,bel\ *n* 1 : short bar with weights on the ends 2 : stupid person

dumb·found, dum·found \,dəm'faúnd\ *vb* : amaze

dum·my \'dəmē\ *n, pl* -**mies** 1 : dumb person 2 : imitation of something (as a human figure)

dump \'dəmp\ *vb* : unload or discard in a mass ~ *n* : place for dumping something (as refuse) —**in the dumps** : sad

dump·ling \'dəmpliŋ\ *n* : small mass of boiled or steamed dough

dumpy \'dəmpē\ *adj* **dump·i·er; -est** : short and thick in build

¹dun \'dən\ *adj* : brownish gray

²dun *vb* -**nn**- : hound for payment of a debt

dunce \'dəns\ *n* : stupid person

dune \'d(y)ün\ *n* : hill of sand

dung \'dəŋ\ *n* : manure

dun·ga·ree \,dəŋgə'rē\ *n* 1 : blue denim 2 *pl* : work clothes made of dungaree

dun·geon \'dənjən\ *n* : underground prison

dunk \'dəŋk\ *vb* : dip or submerge temporarily in liquid

duo \'d(y)ü(,)ō\ *n, pl* **du·os** : pair

du·o·de·num \,d(y)üə'dēnəm, d(y)ü-'äd³nəm\ *n, pl* -**na** \-'dēnə, -³nə\ *or* -**nums** : part of the small intestine nearest the stomach —**du·o·de·nal** \-'dēn³l, -³nəl\ *adj*

dupe \'d(y)üp\ *n* : one easily deceived or cheated —**dupe** *vb*

du·plex \'d(y)ü,pleks\ *adj* : double ~ *n* : 2-level apartment or 2-family house

du·pli·cate \'d(y)üplikət\ *adj* 1 : consisting of 2 identical items 2 : being just like another ~ *n* : exact copy ~ \-,kāt\ *vb* -**cat·ed; -cat·ing** 1 : make an exact copy of 2 : repeat or equal —**du·pli·ca·tion** \,d(y)üpli'kāshən\ *n* —**du·pli·ca·tor** \'d(y)üpli,kātər\ *n*

du·plic·i·ty \d(y)ü'plisətē\ *n, pl* -**ties** : deception

du·ra·ble \'d(y)ürəbəl\ *adj* : lasting

a long time —**du·ra·bil·i·ty** \,d(y)ürə'bilətē\ *n*

du·ra·tion \d(y)ü'rāshən\ *n* : length of time something lasts

du·ress \-'res\ *n* : coercion

dur·ing \,d(y)üriŋ\ *prep* 1 : throughout 2 : at some point in

dusk \'dəsk\ *n* : twilight —**dusky** *adj*

dust \'dəst\ *n* : powdered matter ~ *vb* 1 : remove dust from 2 : sprinkle with fine particles —**dust·er** *n* — **dust·pan** *n* —**dusty** *adj*

du·ty \'d(y)ütē\ *n, pl* -**ties** 1 : action required by one's occupation or position 2 : moral or legal obligation 3 : tax —**du·te·ous** \-əs\ *adj* —**du·ti·able** \-əbəl\ *adj* —**du·ti·ful** \'d(y)ütifəl\ *adj*

dwarf \'dwórf\ *n, pl* **dwarfs** \'dwó(ə)rfs\ *or* **dwarves** \'dwórvz\ : one that is much below normal size ~ *vb* 1 : stunt 2 : cause to seem smaller —**dwarf·ish** *adj*

dwell \'dwel\ *vb* **dwelt** \'dwelt\ *or* **dwelled** \'dweld, 'dwelt\; **dwell·ing** 1 : reside 2 : keep the attention directed —**dwell·er** *n* —**dwell·ing** *n*

dwin·dle \'dwind³l\ *vb* -**dled; -dling** : become steadily less

dye \'dī\ *n* : coloring material ~ *vb* **dyed; dye·ing** : give a new color to

dying *pres part of* DIE

dyke *var of* DIKE

dy·nam·ic \dī'namik\ *adj* 1 : relating to physical force producing motion 2 : energetic or forceful

dy·na·mite \'dīnə,mīt\ *n* : explosive made of nitroglycerin —**dynamite** *vb*

dy·na·mo \-,mō\ *n, pl* -**mos** : electrical generator

dy·nas·ty \'dīnastē, -,nas-\ *n, pl* -**ties** : succession of rulers of the same family —**dy·nas·tic** \dī'nastik\ *adj*

dys·en·tery \'dis³n,terē\ *n, pl* -**ter·ies** : disorder marked by diarrhea

dys·lex·ia \dis'leksēə\ *n* : disturbance of the ability to read —**dys·lex·ic** \-'sik\ *adj*

dys·pep·sia \-'pepshə, -sēə\ *n* : indigestion —**dys·pep·tic** \-'peptik\ *adj or n*

dys·tro·phy \'distrəfē\ *n, pl* -**phies** : disorder involving nervous and muscular tissue

E

ea·ger \'ēgər\ *adj* : enthusiastic or anxof the alphabet

each \'ēch\ *adj* : being one of the class

named ~ *pron* : every individual one ~ *adv* : apiece

ea·ger \'ēgər\ *adj* : enthusiastic or anx

ious **—ea·ger·ly** adv **—ea·ger·ness** n

ea·gle \'ēgəl\ n : large bird of prey

-ean —see **-AN**

¹ear \'iər\ n : organ of hearing or the outer part of this **—ear·ache** n **—eared** adj **—ear·lobe** \-ˌlōb\ n

²ear n : fruiting head of a cereal

ear·drum n : thin membrane that receives and transmits sound waves in the ear

earl \'ərl\ n : British nobleman **—earl·dom** \-dəm\ n

ear·ly \'ərlē\ adj **-li·er; -est 1** : relating to or occurring near the beginning or before the usual time **2** : ancient **—early** adv

ear·mark vb : designate for a specific purpose

earn \'ərn\ vb **1** : receive as a return for service **2** : deserve

ear·nest \'ərnəst\ n : serious state of mind **—earnest** adj **—ear·nest·ly** adv **—ear·nest·ness** n

earn·ings \'ərniŋz\ n pl : something earned

ear·phone n : device that reproduces sound and is worn over or in the ear

ear·ring n : earlobe ornament

ear·shot n : range of hearing

earth \'ərth\ n **1** : soil or land **2** : planet inhabited by man **—earth·li·ness** n **—earth·ly** adj **—earth·ward** \-wərd\, **earth·wards** adv

earth·en \'ərthən\ adj : made of earth or baked clay **—earth·en·ware** \-ˌwaər\ n

earth·quake n : shaking or trembling of the earth

earth·worm n : long segmented worm

earthy \'ərthē\ adj **earth·i·er; -est 1** : consisting of or resembling soil **2** : practical **3** : coarse **—earth·i·ness** n

ease \'ēz\ n **1** : comfort **2** : naturalness of manner **3** : freedom from difficulty ~ vb **eased; eas·ing 1** : relieve from distress **2** : lessen the tension of **3** : make easier

ea·sel \'ēzəl\ n : frame to hold a painter's canvas upright

east \'ēst\ adv : to or toward the east ~ adj : situated toward or at or coming from the east ~ n **1** : direction of sunrise **2** cap : regions to the east **—east·er·ly** \'ēstərlē\ adv or adj **—east·ward** adv or adj **—east·wards** adv

Eas·ter \'ēstər\ n : church feast celebrating Christ's resurrection

east·ern \'ēstərn\ adj **1** cap : relating to a region designated East **2** : lying

toward or coming from the east **—East·ern·er** n

easy \'ēzē\ adj **eas·i·er; -est 1** : marked by ease **2** : lenient **—eas·i·ly** \'ēz(ə)lē\ adv **—eas·i·ness** \-ēnəs\ n

easy-go·ing adj : taking life easily

eat \'ēt\ vb **ate** \'āt\; **eat·en** \'ēt³n\; **eat·ing 1** : take in as food **2** : use up or corrode **—eat·able** adj or n **—eat·er** n

eaves \'ēvz\ n pl : overhanging edge of a roof

eaves·drop vb : listen secretly **—eaves·drop·per** n

ebb \'eb\ n **1** : outward flow of the tide **2** : decline ~ vb **1** : recede from the flood state **2** : wane

eb·o·ny \'ebənē\ n, pl **-nies** : hard heavy wood of tropical trees (**ebony trees**) ~ adj **1** : made of ebony **2** : black

ebul·lient \i'bu̇lyənt, -'bəl-\ adj : exuberant **—ebul·lience** \-yəns\ n

ec·cen·tric \ik'sentrik\ adj **1** : odd in behavior **2** : being off center **—eccentric** n **—ec·cen·tri·cal·ly** \-trik(ə)lē\ adv **—ec·cen·tric·i·ty** \ˌek-ˌsen'trisətē\ n

ec·cle·si·as·tic \ik-ˌlēzē'astik\ n : clergyman

ec·cle·si·as·ti·cal \-tikəl\, **ecclesiastic** adj : relating to a church **—ec·cle·si·as·ti·cal·ly** \-tik(ə)lē\ adv

ech·e·lon \'eshəˌlän\ n **1** : steplike arrangement **2** : level of authority

echo \'ekō\ n, pl **ech·oes** : repetition of a sound caused by a reflection of the sound waves **—echo** vb

éclair \ā'klaər\ n : custard-filled pastry

eclec·tic \e'klektik, i-\ adj : drawing or drawn from varied sources **—eclec·tic** n

eclipse \i'klips\ n : total or partial obscuring of one celestial body by another **—eclipse** vb

ecol·o·gy \i'käləjē, e-\ n, pl **-gies** : science concerned with the interaction of organisms and their environment **—eco·log·i·cal** \ˌēkə'läjikəl, ˌek-\ adj **—eco·log·i·cal·ly** adv **—ecol·o·gist** \i'kälə̇jəst, e-\ n

eco·nom·ic \ˌekə'nämik, ˌēkə-\ adj : relating to the satisfaction of man's material needs

eco·nom·ics \-'nämiks\ n : branch of knowledge dealing with goods and services **—econ·o·mist** \i'känəməst\ n

econ·o·mize \i'känəˌmīz\ vb **-mized; -miz·ing** : be thrifty

econ·o·my \-mē\ n, pl **-mies 1** : thrifty management of resources **2** : economic system **—eco·nom·i·cal** \ˌekəˈnämikəl, ˌēkə-\ adj **—eco·nom·i·cal·ly** adv **—economy** adj

ecru \ˈekrü, ˈäkrü\ n : beige

ec·sta·sy \ˈekstəsē\ n, pl **-sies** : extreme emotional excitement **—ec·stat·ic** \ek-ˈstatik, ik-\ adj **—ec·stat·i·cal·ly** \-ik(ə)lē\ adv

ec·u·men·i·cal \ˌekyəˈmenikəl\ adj : promoting worldwide Christian unity

ec·ze·ma \igˈzēmə, ˈegzəmə, ˈeksə-\ n : itching skin inflammation

¹-ed \d after a vowel or b, g, j, l, m, n, ŋ, r, t͟h, v, z, zh; əd, id after d, t; t after other sounds\ vb suffix or adj suffix **1** —used to form the past participle of regular verbs **2** : having or having the characteristics of

²-ed vb suffix —used to form the past tense of regular verbs

ed·dy \ˈedē\ n, pl **-dies** : whirlpool **—eddy** vb

ede·ma \iˈdēmə\ n : dropsy **—edem·a·tous**\-ˈdemətəs\ adj

Eden \ˈēd⁹n\ n : paradise

¹edge \ˈej\ n **1** : cutting something of a blade **2** : line where something begins or ends ~ vb **edged; edg·ing 1** : give or form an edge **2** : move gradually **—edg·er** n

edgy \ˈejē\ adj **edg·i·er; -est** : nervous **—edg·i·ness** n

ed·i·ble \ˈedəbəl\ adj : fit or safe to be eaten **—ed·i·bil·i·ty** \ˌedəˈbilətē\ n **—edible** n

edict \ˈēˌdikt\ n : decree

ed·i·fi·ca·tion \ˌedəfəˈkāshən\ n : instruction or information **—ed·i·fy** \ˈedəˌfī\ vb

ed·i·fice \ˈedəfəs\ n : large building

ed·it \ˈedət\ vb : revise and prepare for publication **—ed·i·tor** \-ər\ n **—ed·i·tor·ship** n

edi·tion \iˈdishən\ n **1** : form in which a text is published **2** : total number published at one time

ed·i·to·ri·al \ˌedəˈtōrēəl\ adj **1** : relating to an editor **2** : expressing opinion ~ n : article (as in a newspaper) expressing the views of an editor **—ed·i·to·ri·al·ize** \-ēə,līz\ vb **—ed·i·to·ri·al·ly** adv

ed·u·cate \ˈejə,kāt\ vb **-cat·ed; -cat·ing 1** : give instruction to **2** : develop mentally and morally **—ed·u·ca·ble** \ˈejəkəbəl\ adj **—ed·u·ca·tion** \ˌejəˈkāshən\ n **—ed·u·ca·tion·al** \-sh(ə)nəl\ adj **—ed·u·ca·tor** \-ər\ n

-ee n suffix **1** : recipient or beneficiary of **2** : person who performs

eel \ˈēl\ n : snakelike fish

-eer n suffix : one that is concerned with, conducts, or produces

ee·rie \ˈi(ə)rē\ adj **-ri·er; -est** : weird **—ee·ri·ly** \ˈirəlē\ adv

ef·face \iˈfās, e-\ vb **-faced; -fac·ing** : obliterate by rubbing out **—ef·face·ment** n

ef·fect \iˈfekt\ n **1** : result **2** : meaning **3** : influence **4** pl : goods or possessions ~ vb : accomplish or produce **—in effect** : in substance

ef·fec·tive \iˈfektiv\ adj **1** : producing a strong or desired effect **2** : being in operation **—ef·fec·tive·ly** adv **—ef·fec·tive·ness** n

ef·fec·tu·al \iˈfekchə(wə)l\ adj : producing an intended effect **—ef·fec·tu·al·ly** adv **—ef·fec·tu·al·ness** n

ef·fem·i·nate \əˈfemənət\ adj : unsuitably womanish **—ef·fem·i·na·cy** \-nəsē\ n

ef·fer·vesce \ˌefərˈves\ vb **-vesced; -vesc·ing 1** : bubble and hiss as gas escapes **2** : show exhilaration **—ef·fer·ves·cence** \-ˈves⁹ns\ n **—ef·fer·ves·cent** \-⁹nt\ adj **—ef·fer·ves·cent·ly** adv

ef·fete \eˈfēt\ adj : decadent or worn out

ef·fi·ca·cious \ˌefəˈkāshəs\ adj : effective **—ef·fi·ca·cy** \ˈefikəsē\ n

ef·fi·cient \iˈfishənt\ adj : working well with little waste **—ef·fi·cien·cy** \-ənsē\ n **—ef·fi·cient·ly** adv

ef·fi·gy \ˈefəjē\ n, pl **-gies** : image of a person

ef·fort \ˈefərt\ n **1** : a putting forth of strength **2** : use of resources toward a goal **3** : product of effort **—ef·fort·less** adj **—ef·fort·less·ly** adv

ef·fron·tery \iˈfrəntərē\ n, pl **-ter·ies** : insolence

ef·fu·sion \iˈfyüzhən, e-\ n : a gushing forth **—ef·fu·sive** \-ˈfyüsiv\ adj **—ef·fu·sive·ly** adv

¹egg \ˈeg, ˈāg\ vb : urge to action

²egg n **1** : rounded usu. hard-shelled reproductive body esp. of birds and reptiles from which the young hatches **2** : ovum **—egg·shell** n

egg·nog \-ˌnäg\ n : drink of eggs and cream

egg·plant n : edible purplish fruit of a plant related to the potato

ego \ˈēgō\ n, pl **egos** : self-esteem

ego·cen·tric \ˌēgōˈsentrik\ adj : self-centered

ego·tism \ˈēgəˌtizəm\ n : exaggerated sense of self-importance **—ego·tist** \-təst\ n **—ego·tis·tic** \ˌēgəˈtistik\, **ego·tis·ti·cal** \-tikəl\ adj **—ego·tis·ti·cal·ly** adv

egre·gious \i'grējəs\ *adj* : notably bad —**egre·gious·ly** *adv*

egress \'ē,gres\ *n* : a way out

egret \'ēgrət, i'gret, 'egrət\ *n* : long-plumed heron

ei·der \'īdər\ *n* : northern sea duck that yields a soft down (**eiderdown**)

eight \'āt\ *n* 1 : one more than 7 2 : 8th in a set or series 3 : something having 8 units —**eight** *adj or pron* —**eighth** \'āt̲th\ *adj or adv or n*

eigh·teen \'ā,(')tēn\ *n* : one more than 17 —**eigh·teen** *adj or pron* —**eigh·teenth** \-'tēnth\ *adj or n*

eighty \'ātē\ *n, pl* **eight·ies** : 8 times 10 —**eight·i·eth** \'ātēəth\ *adj or n* —**eighty** *adj or pron*

ei·ther \'ēt̲hər, 'ī-\ *adj* 1 : both 2 : being the one or the other of two ~ *pron* : one of two or more ~ *conj* : one or the other

ejac·u·late \i'jakyə,lāt\ *vb* **-lat·ed; -lat·ing** 1 : say suddenly 2 : eject a fluid (as semen) —**ejac·u·la·tion** \-,jak-yə'lāshən\ *n*

eject \i'jekt\ *vb* : drive or throw out —**ejec·tion** \-'jekshən\ *n*

eke \'ēk\ *vb* **eked; ek·ing** : barely gain with effort —usu. with *out*

elab·o·rate \i'lab(ə)rət\ *adj* : planned in detail & complex and ornate ~ \-ə,rāt\ *vb* **-rat·ed; -rat·ing** : work out in detail —**elab·o·rate·ly** *adv* —**elab·o·rate·ness** *n* —**elab·o·ra·tion** \-,labə'rāshən\ *n*

elapse \i'laps\ *vb* **elapsed; elaps·ing** : slip by

elas·tic \i'lastik\ *adj* 1 : springy 2 : flexible ~ *n* 1 : elastic material 2 : rubber band —**elas·tic·i·ty** \-,las-'tisətē, ,ē,las-\ *n*

elate \i'lāt\ *vb* **elat·ed; elat·ing** : fill with joy —**ela·tion** \-'lāshən\ *n*

el·bow \'el,bō\ *n* 1 : joint of the arm 2 : elbow-shaped bend or joint ~ *vb* : push aside with the elbow

el·der \'eldər\ *adj* : older ~ *n* 1 : one who is older 2 : church officer

el·der·ber·ry \'eldə(r),berē\ *n* : edible black or red fruit of a tree or shrub bearing these

el·der·ly \'eldərlē\ *adj* : past middle age

el·dest \'eldəst\ *adj* : oldest

elect \i'lekt\ *adj* : elected but not yet in office ~ *n* **elect** *pl* : exclusive group ~ *vb* : choose esp. by vote —**elec·tion** \i'lekshən\ *n* —**elec·tive** \i'lektiv\ *n or adj* —**elec·tor** \i'lektər\ *n* —**elec·tor·al** \-t(ə)rəl\ *adj*

elec·tor·ate \i'lekt(ə)rət\ *n* : body of persons entitled to vote

elec·tric \i'lektrik\ *adj* 1 : relating to or run by electricity 2 : thrilling —**elec·tri·cal** \-trikəl\ *adj* —**elec·tri·cal·ly** *adv*

elec·tri·cian \i,lek'trishən\ *n* : one who installs or repairs electrical equipment

elec·tric·i·ty \-'tris(ə)tē\ *n, pl* **-ties** 1 : fundamental form of energy occurring naturally (as in lightning) or produced artificially 2 : electric current

elec·tri·fy \i'lektrə,fī\ *vb* **-fied; -fy·ing** 1 : charge with electricity 2 : equip for use of electric power 3 : thrill —**elec·tri·fi·ca·tion** \-,lektrəfə'kāshən\ *n*

elec·tro·car·dio·gram \i,lektrō'kärdēə,gram\ *n* : tracing made by an electrocardiograph

elec·tro·car·dio·graph \-,graf\ *n* : instrument for recording the changes of electrical potential occurring during the heartbeat

elec·tro·cute \i'lektrə,kyüt\ *vb* **-cut·ed; -cut·ing** : kill by an electric shock —**elec·tro·cu·tion** \-,lektrə'kyüshən\ *n*

elec·trode \i'lek,trōd\ *n* : conductor at a nonmetallic part of a circuit

elec·trol·y·sis \i,lek'träləsəs\ *n* 1 : production of chemical changes by passage of an electric current through a substance 2 : destruction of hair roots with an electric current —**elec·tro·lyt·ic** \-,trə'litik\ *adj*

elec·tro·lyte \i'lektrə,līt\ *n* : nonmetallic electric conductor

elec·tro·mag·net \i,lektrō'magnət\ *n* : magnet created with electric current —**elec·tro·mag·net·ic** \-,mag-'netik\ *adj* —**elec·tro·mag·net·i·cal·ly** \-ik(ə)lē\ *adv*

elec·tron \i'lek,trän\ *n* : negatively charged particle within the atom

elec·tron·ic \i,lek'tränik\ *adj* : relating to electrons or electronics —**elec·tron·i·cal·ly** \-ik(ə)lē\ *adv*

elec·tron·ics \-iks\ *n* : physics of electrons and their use

elec·tro·plate \i'lektrə,plāt\ *vb* : coat (as with metal) by electrolysis

el·e·gance \'eligəns\ *n* : refined gracefulness —**el·e·gant** \-gənt\ *adj* —**el·e·gant·ly** *adv*

el·e·gy \'eləjē\ *n, pl* **-gies** : poem expressing grief for one who is dead —**ele·gi·ac** \,elə'jīək, -,ak\ *adj*

el·e·ment \'eləmənt\ *n* 1 *pl* : weather conditions 2 : natural environment 3 : constituent part 4 *pl* : simplest principles 5 : substance not separable by ordinary chemical means —**el·e·men·tal** \,elə'ment²l\ *adj*

el·e·men·ta·ry \ˌeləˈment(ə)rē\ *adj* 1 : simple 2 : relating to the basic subjects of education

el·e·phant \ˈeləfənt\ *n* : huge mammal with a trunk and 2 ivory tusks

el·e·vate \ˈeləˌvāt\ *vb* **-vat·ed; -vat·ing** 1 : lift up 2 : exalt

el·e·va·tion \ˌeləˈvāshən\ *n* 1 : height or a high place

el·e·va·tor \ˈeləˌvātər\ *n* 1 : cage or platform for raising or lowering something 2 : grain storehouse

elev·en \iˈlevən\ *n* 1 : one more than 10 2 : 11th in a set or series 3 : something having 11 units — **eleven** *adj or pron* — **elev·enth** \-ənth\ *adj or n*

elf \ˈelf\ *n, pl* **elves** \ˈelvz\ : mischievous fairy — **elf·in** \ˈelfən\ *adj* — **elf·ish** \ˈelfish\ *adj*

elic·it \iˈlisət\ *vb* : draw forth

el·i·gi·ble \ˈeləjəbəl\ *adj* : qualified to participate or to be chosen — **el·i·gi·bil·i·ty** \ˌeləjəˈbilətē\ *n* — **eligible** *n*

elim·i·nate \iˈliməˌnāt\ *vb* **-nat·ed; -nat·ing** : get rid of — **elim·i·na·tion** \iˌliməˈnāshən\ *n*

elite \āˈlēt\ *n* : choice or select group

elix·ir \iˈliksər\ *n* : medicinal solution

elk \ˈelk\ *n* : large deer

el·lipse \iˈlips, e-\ *n* : oval — **el·lip·tic** \-ˈliptik\, **el·lip·ti·cal** \-tikəl\ *adj*

el·lip·sis \iˈlipsəs\ *n, pl* **-lip·ses** \-ˌsēz\ 1 : omission of a word 2 : marks (as . . .) to show omission — **el·lip·ti·cal** \-tikəl\, **el·lip·tic** \-ˈliptik\ *adj*

elm \ˈelm\ *n* : tall shade tree

el·o·cu·tion \ˌeləˈkyüshən\ *n* : art of public speaking

elon·gate \iˈlôŋˌgāt\ *vb* **-gat·ed; -gat·ing** : make or grow longer — **elon·ga·tion** \(ˌ)ēˌlôŋˈgāshən\ *n*

elope \iˈlōp\ *vb* **eloped; elop·ing** : run away esp. to be married — **elope·ment** *n*

el·o·quent \ˈeləkwənt\ *adj* : forceful and persuasive in speech — **el·o·quence** \-kwəns\ *n* — **el·o·quent·ly** *adv*

else \ˈels\ *adv* 1 : in a different way, time, or place 2 : otherwise ~ *adj* 1 : other 2 : more

else·where *adv* : in or to another place

elu·ci·date \iˈlüsəˌdāt\ *vb* **-dat·ed; -dat·ing** : explain — **elu·ci·da·tion** \iˌlüsəˈdāshən\ *n*

elude \ēˈlüd\ *vb* **elud·ed; elud·ing** : evade — **elu·sive** \ēˈlüsiv\ *adj* — **elu·sive·ly** *adv* — **elu·sive·ness** *n*

elves *pl of* ELF

ema·ci·ate \iˈmāshēˌāt\ *vb* **-at·ed; -at·ing** : become or make very thin — **ema·ci·a·tion** \iˌmā(sh)ēˈāshən\ *n*

em·a·nate \ˈeməˌnāt\ *vb* **-nat·ed; -nat·ing** : come forth — **em·a·na·tion** \ˌeməˈnāshən\ *n*

eman·ci·pate \iˈmansəˌpāt\ *vb* **-pat·ed; -pat·ing** : set free — **eman·ci·pa·tion** \iˌmansəˈpāshən\ *n* — **eman·ci·pa·tor** \iˈmansəˌpātər\ *n*

emas·cu·late \iˈmaskyəˌlāt\ *vb* **-lat·ed; -lat·ing** 1 : castrate 2 : weaken — **emas·cu·la·tion** \iˌmaskyəˈlāshən\ *n*

em·balm \imˈbäm, -ˈbälm\ *vb* : preserve (a corpse) — **em·balm·er** *n*

em·bank·ment \imˈbaŋkmənt\ *n* : protective barrier of earth

em·bar·go \imˈbärgō\ *n, pl* **-goes** : ban on trade — **embargo** *vb*

em·bark \-ˈbärk\ *vb* 1 : go on board a ship or airplane 2 : make a start — **em·bar·ka·tion** \ˌemˌbärˈkāshən\ *n*

em·bar·rass \imˈbarəs\ *vb* : cause distress and self-consciousness — **em·bar·rass·ment** *n*

em·bas·sy \ˈembəsē\ *n, pl* **-sies** : residence and offices of an ambassador

em·bed \imˈbed\ *vb* **-dd-** : fix firmly

em·bel·lish \-ˈbelish\ *vb* : decorate — **em·bel·lish·ment** *n*

em·ber \ˈembər\ *n* : smoldering fragment from a fire

em·bez·zle \imˈbezəl\ *vb* **-zled; -zling** : steal (money) by falsifying records — **em·bez·zle·ment** *n* — **em·bez·zler** \-(ə)lər\ *n*

em·bit·ter \imˈbitər\ *vb* : make bitter

em·bla·zon \-ˈblāzᵊn\ *vb* : display conspicuously

em·blem \ˈembləm\ *n* : symbol — **em·blem·at·ic** \ˌembləˈmatik\ *adj*

em·body \imˈbädē\ *vb* **-bod·ied; -body·ing** : give definite form or expression to — **em·bodi·ment** \-ˈbädimənt\ *n*

em·boss \-ˈbäs, -ˈbòs\ *vb* : ornament with raised work

em·brace \-ˈbrās\ *vb* **-braced; -brac·ing** 1 : clasp in the arms 2 : welcome 3 : include — **embrace** *n*

em·broi·der \-ˈbròidər\ *vb* : ornament with or do needlework — **em·broi·dery** \-(ə)rē\ *n*

em·broil \imˈbròil\ *vb* : involve in conflict or difficulties

em·bryo \ˈembrēˌō\ *n* : living being in its earliest stages of development — **em·bry·on·ic** \ˌembrēˈänik\ *adj*

emend \ēˈmend\ *vb* : correct — **emen·da·tion** \ˌēˌmenˈdāshən\ *n*

em·er·ald \ˈem(ə)rəld\ *n* : green gem ~ *adj* : bright green

emerge \iˈmərj\ *vb* **emerged; emerg·ing** : rise, come forth, or appear — **emer·gence** \-ˈmərjəns\ *n* — **emer·gent** \-jənt\ *adj*

emer·gen·cy \i'mərjənsē\ *n, pl* **-cies** : condition requiring prompt action

em·ery \'em(ə)rē\ *n, pl* **-er·ies** : dark granular mineral used for grinding

emet·ic \i'metik\ *n* : agent that induces vomiting —**emetic** *adj*

em·i·grate \'emə,grāt\ *vb* **-grat·ed; -grat·ing** : leave a country to settle elsewhere —**em·i·grant** \-igrant\ *n* —**em·i·gra·tion** \,emə'grāshən\ *n*

em·i·nence \'emənəns\ *n* **1** : prominence or superiority **2** : person of high rank

em·i·nent \-nənt\ *adj* : prominent —**em·i·nent·ly** *adv*

em·is·sary \'emə,serē\ *n, pl* **-sar·ies** : agent

emit \ē'mit\ *vb* **-tt-** : give off or out —**emis·sion** \-'mishən\ *n*

emol·u·ment \i'mälyəmənt\ *n* : salary or fee

emote \i'mōt\ *vb* **emot·ed; emot·ing** : express emotion

emo·tion \i'mōshən\ *n* : intense feeling —**emo·tion·al** \-sh(ə)nəl\ *adj* —**emo·tion·al·ly** *adv*

em·per·or \'empərər\ *n* : ruler of an empire

em·pha·sis \'emfəsəs\ *n, pl* **-pha·ses** \-,sēz\ : stress

em·pha·size \-,sīz\ *vb* **-sized; -siz·ing** : stress

em·phat·ic \im'fatik, em-\ *adj* : uttered with emphasis —**em·phat·i·cal·ly** \-'fatik(ə)lē\ *adv*

em·pire \'em,pī(ə)r\ *n* : large state or a group of states

em·pir·i·cal \im'pirikəl\ *adj* : based on observation —**em·pir·i·cal·ly** \-ik(ə)lē\ *adv*

em·ploy \im'plói\ *vb* **1** : use **2** : occupy ~ *n* : paid occupation —**em·ploy·ee, em·ploye** \im,ploi'ē, -'plói(ē),ē\ *n* —**em·ploy·er** *n* —**em·ploy·ment** \-mənt\ *n*

em·pow·er \im'pau(ə)r\ *vb* : authorize

em·press \'emprəs\ *n* **1** : wife of an emperor **2** : woman holding an imperial title

emp·ty \'emptē\ *adj* **1** : containing nothing **2** : not occupied **3** : lacking value, sense, or purpose ~ *vb* **-tied; -ty·ing** : make or become empty —**emp·ti·ness** \-tēnəs\ *n*

emu \'ēmyü\ *n* : Australian bird related to the ostrich

em·u·late \'emyə,lāt\ *vb* **-lat·ed; -lat·ing** : try to equal or excel —**em·u·la·tion** \,emyə'lāshən\ *n*

emul·si·fy \i'məlsə,fī\ *vb* **-fied; -fy·ing** : convert into an emulsion —**emul-**

si·fi·ca·tion \i,məlsəfə'kāshən\ *n* —**emul·si·fi·er** \-'fī(ə)r\ *n*

emul·sion \i'məlshən\ *n* : mixture of mutually insoluble liquids —**emul·sive** \-'məlsiv\ *adj*

-en \ən, ³n\ *vb suffix* **1** : become or cause to be **2** : cause or come to have

en·able \in'ābəl\ *vb* **-abled; -abling** : give power, capacity, or ability to

en·act \in'akt\ *vb* **1** : make into law **2** : act out —**en·act·ment** *n*

enam·el \in'aməl\ *n* **1** : glasslike substance used for coating metal or pottery **2** : hard outer layer of a tooth **3** : glossy paint —**enamel** *vb*

en·am·or \in'amər\ *vb* : inflame with love

en·camp \in'kamp\ *vb* : make camp —**en·camp·ment** *n*

en·case \in'kās\ *vb* : enclose in or as if in a case

-ence \əns, ³ns\ *n suffix* **1** : action or process **2** : quality or state

en·ceph·a·li·tis \in,sefə'lītəs\ *n, pl* **-lit·i·des** \-'litə,dēz\ : inflammation of the brain

en·chant \in'chant\ *vb* **1** : bewitch **2** : fascinate —**en·chant·er** *n* —**en·chant·ment** *n* —**en·chant·ress** \-'chantrəs\ *n*

en·cir·cle \in'sərkəl\ *vb* : surround

en·close \in'klōz\ *vb* **1** : shut up or surround **2** : include —**en·clo·sure** \in-'klōzhər\ *n*

en·co·mi·um \en'kōmēəm\ *n, pl* **-mi·ums** *or* **-mia** \-mēə\ : high praise

en·com·pass \in'kəmpəs, -'käm-\ *vb* : surround or include

en·core \'än,kōr\ *n* : further performance

en·coun·ter \in'kauntər\ *vb* **1** : fight **2** : meet unexpectedly —**encounter** *n*

en·cour·age \in'kərij\ *vb* **-aged; -ag·ing** **1** : inspire with courage and hope **2** : foster —**en·cour·age·ment** *n*

en·croach \in'krōch\ *vb* : enter upon another's property or rights —**en·croach·ment** *n*

en·crust \in'krəst\ *vb* : form a crust on

en·cum·ber \in'kəmbər\ *vb* : burden —**en·cum·brance** \-brəns\ *n*

-en·cy \ənsē, ³n-\ *n suffix* : -ence

en·cyc·li·cal \in'siklikəl, en-\ *n* : papal letter to bishops

en·cy·clo·pe·dia \in,sīklə'pēdēə\ *n* : reference work on many subjects —**en·cy·clo·pe·dic** \-'pēdik\ *adj*

end \'end\ *n* **1** : point at which something stops or no longer exists **2** : cessation **3** : purpose ~ *vb* **1** : stop or finish **2** : be at the end of —**end-**

ed *adj* —**end·less** *adj* —**end·less·ly** *adv*

en·dan·ger \in'dānjər\ *vb* : bring into danger

en·dear \in'diər\ *vb* : make dear —**en·dear·ment** \-mənt\ *n*

en·deav·or \in'devər\ *vb or n* : attempt

end·ing \'endiŋ\ *n* : end

en·dive \'en,dīv\ *n* : salad plant

en·do·crine \'endəkrən, -,krīn, -,krēn\ *adj* : producing secretions distributed by the bloodstream —**endocrine** *n*

en·dorse \in'dórs\ *vb* -**dorsed**; -**dorsing** 1 : sign one's name to 2 : approve —**en·dorse·ment** *n*

en·dow \in'daú\ *vb* 1 : furnish with funds 2 : furnish naturally —**en·dow·ment** *n*

en·dure \in'd(y)úr\ *vb* -**dured**; -**during** 1 : last 2 : suffer patiently 3 : tolerate —**en·dur·able** *adj* —**en·dur·ance** \-əns\ *n*

en·e·ma \'enəmə\ *n* : injection of liquid into the rectum

en·e·my \-mē\ *n, pl* -**mies** : one that attacks or tries to harm another

en·er·get·ic \,enər'jetik\ *adj* : full of energy or activity —**en·er·get·i·cal·ly** \-ik(ə)lē\ *adv*

en·er·gize \'enər,jīz\ *vb* -**gized**; -**giz·ing** : give energy to

en·er·gy \'enərjē\ *n, pl* -**gies** 1 : capacity for action 2 : vigorous action 3 : capacity for doing work

en·er·vate \'enər,vāt\ *vb* -**vat·ed**; -**vat·ing** : make weak or listless —**en·er·va·tion** \,enər'vāshən\ *n*

en·fold \in'fōld\ *vb* : surround or embrace

en·force \-'fōrs\ *vb* 1 : compel 2 : carry out —**en·force·able** \-əbəl\ *adj* —**en·force·ment** *n*

en·fran·chise \-'fran,chīz\ *vb* -**chised**; -**chis·ing** : grant voting rights to —**en·fran·chise·ment** \-,chīzmənt, -chəz-\ *n*

en·gage \in'gāj\ *vb* -**gaged**; -**gag·ing** 1 : participate or cause to participate 2 : bring or come into working contact 3 : bind by a pledge to marry 4 : hire 5 : bring or enter into conflict —**en·gage·ment** \-mənt\ *n*

en·gag·ing *adj* : attractive

en·gen·der \in'jendər\ *vb* -**dered**; -**der·ing** : create

en·gine \'enjən\ *n* 1 : machine that converts energy into mechanical motion 2 : locomotive

en·gi·neer \,enjə'niər\ *n* 1 : one trained in engineering 2 : engine operator ~ *vb* : lay out or manage as an engineer

en·gi·neer·ing \-iŋ\ *n* : practical application of science and mathematics

en·grave \in'grāv\ *vb* -**graved**; -**grav·ing** : cut into a surface —**en·grav·er** *n* —**en·grav·ing** *n*

en·gross \-'grōs\ *vb* : occupy fully

en·gulf \-'gəlf\ *vb* : swallow up

en·hance \-'hans\ *vb* -**hanced**; -**hanc·ing** : improve in value —**en·hance·ment** *n*

enig·ma \i'nigmə\ *n* : puzzle or mystery —**enig·mat·ic** \,enig'matik, ,ē-\ *adj*

en·join \in'jóin\ *vb* 1 : command 2 : forbid

en·joy \-'jói\ *vb* : take pleasure in —**en·joy·able** *adj* —**en·joy·ment** *n*

en·large \-'lärj\ *vb* -**larged**; -**larg·ing** : make or grow larger —**en·large·ment** *n* —**en·larg·er** *n*

en·light·en \-'līt᷃n\ *vb* : give knowledge or spiritual insight to —**en·light·en·ment** *n*

en·list \-'list\ *vb* 1 : join the armed forces 2 : get the aid of —**en·list·ee** \-,lis'tē\ *n* —**en·list·ment** \-'lis(t)mənt\ *n*

en·liv·en \in'līvən\ *vb* : give life or spirit to

en·mi·ty \'enmətē\ *n, pl* -**ties** : mutual hatred

en·no·ble \in'ōbəl\ *vb* -**bled**; -**bling** : make noble

en·nui \'än'wē\ *n* : boredom

enor·mi·ty \i'nórmətē\ *n, pl* -**ties** 1 : great wickedness 2 : huge size

enor·mous \i'nórməs\ *adj* : great in size, number, or degree —**enor·mous·ly** *adv* —**enor·mous·ness** *n*

enough \i'nəf, ᵊn'əf\ *adj* : adequate ~ *adv* 1 : in an adequate manner 2 : in a tolerable degree ~ *pron* : adequate number, quantity, or amount

en·quire \in'kwī(ə)r\, **en·qui·ry** \'in-,kwī(ə)rē, in'-; 'inkwərē, 'iŋ-\ *var of* **inquire, inquiry**

en·rage \in'rāj\ *vb* : fill with rage

en·rich \-'rich\ *vb* : make rich —**en·rich·ment** *n*

en·roll, en·rol \-'rōl\ *vb* -**rolled**; -**roll·ing** 1 : enter on a list 2 : become enrolled —**en·roll·ment** *n*

en route \ä᷃'rüt, en-, in-\ *adv or adj* : on or along the way

en·sconce \in'skäns\ *vb* -**sconced**; -**sconc·ing** : settle snugly

en·sem·ble \ä᷃'sämbəl\ *n* 1 : small group 2 : costume

en·shrine \in'shrīn\ *vb* 1 : put in a shrine 2 : cherish

en·sign \'ensən, *l also* 'en,sīn\ *n* 1 : flag 2 : commissioned officer in the navy ranking next below a lieutenant junior grade

en·slave \in'slāv\ vb : make a slave of **—en·slave·ment** n

en·snare \-'snaor\ vb : snare

en·sue \-'sü\ vb -sued; -su·ing : follow as a consequence

en·sure \-'shúr\ vb -sured; -sur·ing : guarantee

en·tail \-'tāl\ vb : involve as a necessary result

en·tan·gle \-'tangəl\ vb : tangle **—en·tan·gle·ment** n

en·ter \'entər\ vb 1 : go or come in or into 2 : start 3 : set down (as in a list)

en·ter·prise \'entər,prīz\ n 1 : an undertaking 2 : business organization 3 : initiative

en·ter·pris·ing \-,prīziŋ\ adj : showing initiative

en·ter·tain \,entər'tān\ vb 1 : treat or receive as a guest 2 : hold in mind 3 : amuse **—en·ter·tain·er** n **—en·ter·tain·ment** n

en·thrall, en·thral \in'thról\ vb -thralled; -thrall·ing : hold spellbound

en·thu·si·asm \-'th(y)üzē,azəm\ n : strong excitement of feeling or its cause **—en·thu·si·ast** \-,ast, -əst\ n **—en·thu·si·as·tic** \-,th(y)üzē'astik\ adj **—en·thu·si·as·ti·cal·ly** \-,tik(ə)lē\ adv

en·tice \in'tīs\ vb -ticed; -tic·ing : tempt **—en·tice·ment** n

en·tire \in'tī(ə)r\ adj : complete or whole **—en·tire·ly** adv **—en·tire·ty** \-'tīrətē, -'tī(ə)rtē\ n

en·ti·tle \-'tīt⁹l\ vb -tled; -tling 1 : name 2 : give a right to

en·ti·ty \'entətē\ n, pl -ties : something with separate existence

en·to·mol·o·gy \,entə'mäləjē\ n : study of insects **—en·to·mo·log·i·cal** \-mə'läjikəl\ adj **—en·to·mol·o·gist** \-'mäləjəst\ n

en·tou·rage \,äntú'räzh\ n : retinue

en·trails \'entrəlz, -,trālz\ n pl : intestines

¹en·trance \'entrəns\ n 1 : act of entering 2 : means or place of entering **—en·trant** \'entrənt\ n

²en·trance \in'trans\ vb -tranced; -tranc·ing : fascinate or delight

en·trap \in'trap\ vb : trap **—en·trap·ment** n

en·treat \-'trēt\ vb : ask earnestly **—en·treaty** \-'trētē\ n

en·trée, en·tree \'än,trā\ n : principal dish of the meal

en·trench \in'trench\ vb : establish in a strong position **—en·trench·ment** n

en·tre·pre·neur \,äntrəprə'nər\ n : organizer or promoter of an enterprise

en·trust \in'trəst\ vb : commit to another with confidence

en·try \'entrē\ n, pl -tries 1 : entrance 2 : an entering in a record or an item so entered

en·twine \in'twīn\ vb : twine together or around

enu·mer·ate \i'n(y)ümə,rāt\ vb -at·ed; -at·ing 1 : count 2 : list **—enu·mer·a·tion** \i,n(y)ümə'rāshən\ n

enun·ci·ate \ē'nənsē,āt\ vb -at·ed; -at·ing 1 : announce 2 : pronounce **—enun·ci·a·tion** \-,nənsē'āshən\ n

en·vel·op \in'veləp\ vb : surround **—en·vel·op·ment** n

en·ve·lope \'envə,lōp, 'än-\ n : paper container for a letter

en·vi·ron·ment \in'vīrənmənt\ n : surroundings **—en·vi·ron·men·tal** \-,vīrən'ment⁹l\ adj

en·vi·ron·men·tal·ist \-⁹ləst\ n : one concerned about the human environment

en·vi·rons \in'vīrənz\ n pl : vicinity

en·vis·age \in'vizij\ vb -aged; -ag·ing : have a mental picture of

en·voy \'en,vói, 'än-\ n : diplomat

en·vy \'envē\ n 1 : resentful awareness of another's advantage 2 : object of envy ~ vb -vied; -vy·ing : feel envy toward or on account of **—en·vi·able** \-vēəbəl\ adj **—en·vi·ous** \-vēəs\ adj

en·zyme \'en,zīm\ n : complex mostly protein product of living cells

eon \'ēən, ē,än\ n var of AEON

ep·au·let \,epə'let\ n : shoulder ornament on a uniform

ephem·er·al \i'fem(ə)rəl\ adj : short-lived

ep·ic \'epik\ n : long poem about a hero **—epic** adj

ep·i·cure \'epi,kyúr\ n : person with fastidious taste esp. in food and wine **—ep·i·cu·re·an** \,epikyú'rēən, -'kyúrē-\ n or adj

ep·i·dem·ic \,epə'demik\ adj : affecting many persons at one time **—epidemic** n

ep·i·der·mis \,epə'dərməs\ n : outer layer of skin

ep·i·gram \'epə,gram\ n : short witty poem or saying **—ep·i·gram·mat·ic** \,epəgrə'matik\ adj

ep·i·lep·sy \'epə,lepsē\ n, pl -sies : nervous disorder marked by convulsive attacks **—ep·i·lep·tic** \,epə'leptik\ adj or n

epis·co·pal \i'piskəpəl\ adj : governed by bishops

ep·i·sode \'epə‚sōd, -‚zōd\ n : occurrence —**ep·i·sod·ic** \‚epə'sädik, -'zäd-\ adj

epis·tle \i'pisəl\ n : letter

ep·i·taph \'epə‚taf\ n : inscription in memory of a dead person

ep·i·thet \'epə‚thet, -thət-\ n : characterizing often abusive word or phrase

epit·o·me \i'pitəmē\ n 1 : summary 2 : ideal example —**epit·o·mize** \-‚mīz\ vb

ep·och \'epək, 'ep‚äk\ n : extended period —**ep·och·al** \'epəkəl, 'ep‚äkəl\ adj

ep·oxy \'ep‚äksē, ep'äksē\ n : synthetic resin used esp. in adhesives ~ vb -**ox·ied** or -**oxyed**; -**oxy·ing** : glue with epoxy

equa·ble \'ekwəbəl, 'ēkwə-\ adj : free from unpleasant extremes —**equa·bil·i·ty** \‚ekwə'bilətē, ‚ē-\ n —**equa·bly** \-blē\ adv

equal \'ēkwəl\ adj : of the same quantity, value, quality, number, or status as another ~ n : one that is equal ~ vb equaled or equalled; equal·ing or equal·ling : be or become equal to —**equal·i·ty** \i'kwälətē\ n —**equal·ize** \'ēkwə‚līz\ vb —**equal·ly** \'ēkwəlē\ adv

equa·nim·i·ty \‚ēkwə'nimətē, ‚ek-\ n, pl -ties : calmness

equate \i'kwāt\ vb equat·ed; equat·ing : treat or regard as equal

equa·tion \i'kwāzhən, -shən\ n : mathematical statement that two things are equal

equa·tor \i'kwātər\ n : imaginary circle that separates the northern and southern hemispheres —**equa·to·ri·al** \‚ēkwə'tōrēəl, ‚ek-\ adj

eques·tri·an \i'kwestrēən\ adj : relating to horses or horsemanship ~ n : horseback rider

equi·lat·er·al \‚ēkwə'lat(ə)rəl\ adj : having equal sides

equi·lib·ri·um \‚ēkwə'librēəm\ n, pl -ri·ums or -ria \-rēə\ : state of balance

equine \'ē‚kwīn, 'ek‚wīn\ adj : relating to the horse —**equine** n

equi·nox \'ēkwə‚näks, 'ek-\ n : time when day and night are everywhere of equal length

equip \i'kwip\ vb -pp- : furnish with needed resources —**equip·ment** \-mənt\ n

eq·ui·ta·ble \'ekwətəbəl\ adj : fair

eq·ui·ty \'ekwətē\ n, pl -ties 1 : justice 2 : value of a property less debt

equiv·a·lent \i'kwiv(ə)lənt\ adj : equal

—equiv·a·lence \-ləns\ n —**equiva·lent** n

equiv·o·cal \i'kwivəkəl\ adj : ambiguous or uncertain

equiv·o·cate \i'kwivə‚kāt\ vb -cat·ed; -cat·ing : use misleading language —**equiv·o·ca·tion** \-‚kwivə'kāshən\ n

¹-er \ər\ adj suffix or adv suffix —used to form the comparative degree of adjectives and adverbs of esp. those of one or two syllables

²-er \ər\, -ier \ēər, yər\, -yer \yər\ n suffix 1 : one that is associated with 2 : one that performs or is the object of an action 3 : one that is

era \'irə, 'erə, 'ērə\ n : period of time associated with something

erad·i·cate \i'radə‚kāt\ vb -cat·ed; -cat·ing : do away with —**erad·i·ca·ble** \-əkəbəl\ adj

erase \i'rās\ vb erased; eras·ing : rub or scratch out —**eras·er** n —**era·sure** \i'rāshər\ n

ere \(‚)eər\ prep or conj : before

erect \i'rekt\ adj : not leaning or lying down ~ vb 1 : build 2 : bring to an upright position —**erec·tion** \i'rek-shən\ n

er·mine \'ərmən\ n : weasel with white winter fur or its fur

erode \i'rōd\ vb erod·ed; erod·ing : wear away gradually

ero·sion \i'rōzhən\ n : process of eroding

erot·ic \i'rätik\ adj : sexually arousing —**erot·i·cal·ly** \-ik(ə)lē\ adv —**erot·i·cism** \i'rätə‚sizəm\ n

err \'eər, 'ər\ vb : be or do wrong

er·rand \'erənd\ n : short trip taken to do something often for another

er·rant \-ənt\ adj 1 : traveling about 2 : going astray

er·rat·ic \ir'atik\ adj : irregular or eccentric —**er·rat·i·cal·ly** \-ik(ə)lē\ adv

er·ro·ne·ous \ir'ōnēəs, e'rō-\ adj : wrong —**er·ro·ne·ous·ly** adv

er·ror \'erər\ n 1 : something that is not accurate 2 : state of being wrong

er·satz \'er‚säts\ adj : synthetic or phony

erst·while \'ərst‚hwīl\ adv : in the past ~ adj : former

er·u·di·tion \‚er(y)ə'dishən\ n : great learning —**er·u·dite** \'er(y)ə‚dīt\ adj

erupt \i'rəpt\ vb : burst forth esp. suddenly and violently —**erup·tion** \i'rəpshən\ n —**erup·tive** \-tiv\ adj

-ery \(ə)rē\ n suffix 1 : character or condition 2 : practice 3 : place of doing

¹-es \əz, iz after s, z, sh, ch; z after v

or a vowel\ *n pl suffix* —used to form the plural of some nouns

²-es *vb suffix* —used to form the 3d person singular present of some verbs

es·ca·late \'eskə,lāt\ *vb* -lat·ed; -lat·ing : become quickly larger or greater —es·ca·la·tion \,eskə'lāshən\ *n*

es·ca·la·tor \'eskə,lātər\ *n* : moving stairs

es·ca·pade \'eskə,pād\ *n* : mischievous adventure

es·cape \is'kāp\ *vb* -caped; -cap·ing : get away or away from ~ *n* 1 : flight from or avoidance of something unpleasant 2 : leakage 3 : means of escape ~ *adj* : providing means of escape —es·cap·ee \is-,kā'pē, ,es(,)kā-\ *n*

es·ca·role \'eskə,rōl\ *n* : salad green

es·carp·ment \is'kärpmənt\ *n* : cliff

es·chew \is'chü\ *vb* : shun

es·cort \'es,kort\ *n* : one accompanying another —es·cort \is'kort, es-\ *vb*

es·crow \'es,krō\ *n* : deposit to be delivered upon fulfillment of a condition

esoph·a·gus \i'säfəgəs\ *n, pl* -gi \-,gī, -,jī\ : muscular tube connecting the mouth and stomach

es·o·ter·ic \,esə'terik\ *adj* : mysterious or secret

es·pe·cial·ly \is'pesh(ə)lē\ *adv* : particularly or notably

es·pi·o·nage \'espēə,näzh, -nij\ *n* : practice of spying

es·pou·sal \is'pauzəl\ *n* 1 : betrothal 2 : wedding 3 : a taking up as a supporter —es·pouse \-'pauz\ *vb*

es·pres·so \e'spresō\ *n, pl* -sos : strong steam-brewed coffee

es·py \is'pī\ *vb* -pied; -py·ing : catch sight of

es·quire \'es,kwī(ə)r\ *n* —used as a title of courtesy

-ess \əs, ,es\ *n suffix* : female

es·say \'es,ā\ *n* : literary composition ~ *vb* \e'sā, 'es,ā\ : attempt —es·say·ist \'es,āəst\ *n*

es·sence \'es²ns\ *n* 1 : fundamental nature or quality 2 : extract 3 : perfume

es·sen·tial \i'senchəl\ *adj* : basic or necessary —essential *n* —es·sen·tial·ly *adv*

-est \əst, ist\ *adj suffix or adv suffix* —used to form the superlative degree of adjectives and adverbs and esp. those of 1 or 2 syllables

es·tab·lish \is'tablish\ *vb* 1 : bring into existence 2 : put on a firm basis 3 : cause to be recognized

es·tab·lish·ment \-'mənt\ *n* 1 : business or a place of business 2 : an establishing or being established 3 : controlling group

es·tate \is'tāt\ *n* 1 : one's possessions 2 : large piece of land with a house

es·teem \-'tēm\ *n or vb* : regard

es·ter \'estər\ *n* : organic chemical compound

esthetic *var of* AESTHETIC

es·ti·ma·ble \'estəməbəl\ *adj* : worthy of esteem

es·ti·mate \'estə,māt\ *vb* -mat·ed; -mat·ing : judge the approximate value, size, or cost ~ \-mət\ *n* 1 : rough or approximate calculation 2 : statement of the cost of a job —es·ti·ma·tion \,estə'māshən\ *n* —es·ti·ma·tor \'estə,mātər\ *n*

es·trange \is'trānj\ *vb* -tranged; -trang·ing : make hostile —es·trange·ment *n*

es·tro·gen \'estrəjən\ *n* : hormone that produces female characteristics

es·tu·ary \'eschə,werē\ *n, pl* -ar·ies : arm of the sea at a river's mouth

et cet·era \et'setərə, -'setrə\ : and others esp. of the same kind

etch \'ech\ *vb* 1 : make lines on with acid 2 : produce by etching —etch·er *n* —etch·ing *n*

eter·nal \i'tərn²l\ *adj* : lasting forever —eter·nal·ly *adv*

eter·ni·ty \-nətē\ *n, pl* -ties : infinite duration

eth·ane \'eth,ān\ *n* : gaseous hydrocarbon

eth·a·nol \'ethə,nol, -,nōl\ *n* : alcohol

ether \'ēthər\ *n* : light flammable liquid used as an anesthetic

ethe·re·al \i'thirēəl\ *adj* 1 : celestial 2 : exceptionally delicate

eth·i·cal \'ethikəl\ *adj* 1 : relating to ethics 2 : honorable —eth·i·cal·ly *adv*

eth·ics \-iks\ *n sing or pl* 1 : study of good and evil and moral duty 2 : moral principles or practice

eth·nic \'nik\ *adj* : relating to races or groups of people with common customs ~ *n* : member of a minority ethnic group

eth·nol·o·gy \eth'näləjē\ *n* : study of the races of mankind —eth·no·log·i·cal \,ethnə'läjikəl\ *adj* —eth·nol·o·gist \eth'näləjəst\ *n*

eth·yl \'ethəl\ *n* : hydrocarbon radical

et·i·quette \'etikət, -,ket\ *n* : good manners

et·y·mol·o·gy \,etə'mäləjē\ *n, pl* -gies 1 : history of a word 2 : study of etymologies —et·y·mo·log·i·cal

\-mə'läjikəl\ adj —et·y·mol·o·gist \-'mäləjəst\ n

eu·ca·lyp·tus \,yükə'liptəs\ n, pl -ti \-,tī\ or -tus·es : Australian evergreen tree

Eu·cha·rist \'yük(ə)rəst\ n : Communion —eu·cha·ris·tic \,yükə'ristik\ adj

eu·lo·gy \'yüləjē\ n, pl -gies : speech in praise —eu·lo·gis·tic \,yülə'jistik\ adj —eu·lo·gize \'yülə,jīz\ vb

eu·nuch \'yünək\ n : castrated man

eu·phe·mism \'yüfə,mizəm\ n : substitution of a pleasant expression for an unpleasant or offensive one —eu·phe·mis·tic \,yüfə'mistik\ adj

eu·pho·ni·ous \yü'fōnēəs\ adj : pleasing to the ear —eu·pho·ny \'yüfənē\ n

eu·pho·ria \yü'fōrēə\ n : elation —eu·phor·ic \-'förik\ adj

eu·tha·na·sia \,yüthə'näzh(ē)ə\ n : mercy killing

evac·u·ate \i'vakyə,wāt\ vb -at·ed; -at·ing 1 : discharge wastes from the body 2 : remove or withdraw from —evac·u·a·tion \i,vakyə'wāshən\ n

evade \i'vād\ vb evad·ed; evad·ing : manage to avoid

eval·u·ate \i'valyə,wāt\ vb -at·ed; -at·ing : appraise —eval·u·a·tion \i,valyə'wāshən\ n

evan·gel·i·cal \,ē,van'jelikəl, ,evən-\ adj : relating to the Christian gospel

evan·ge·lism \i'vanjə,lizəm\ n : the winning or revival of personal commitments to Christ —evan·ge·lis·tic \i,vanjə'listik\ adj

evap·o·rate \i'vapə,rāt\ vb -rat·ed; -rat·ing 1 : pass off in or convert into vapor 2 : disappear quickly —evap·o·ra·tion \i,vapə'rāshən\ n —evap·o·ra·tive \i'vapə,rātiv\ adj —evap·o·ra·tor \-,rātər\ n

eva·sion \i'vāzhən\ n : act or instance of evading —eva·sive \i'vāsiv\ adj —eva·sive·ness n

eve \'ēv\ n : evening

even \'ēvən\ adj 1 : smooth 2 : equal or fair 3 : fully revenged 4 : divisible by 2 ~ adv 1 : already 2 —used for emphasis ~ vb : make or become even —even·ly adv —even·ness n

eve·ning \'ēvniŋ\ n : early part of the night

event \i'vent\ n 1 : occurrence 2 : noteworthy happening 3 : eventuality —event·ful adj

even·tu·al \i'vench(əw)əl\ adj : later —even·tu·al·ly adv

even·tu·al·i·ty \i,venchə'walətē\ n, pl

-ties : possible occurrence or outcome

ev·er \'evər\ adv 1 : always 2 : at any time 3 : in any case

ev·er·green adj : having foliage that remains green —evergreen n

ev·er·last·ing \,evər'lastiŋ\ adj : lasting forever

ev·ery \'evrē\ adj 1 : being each one of a group 2 : all possible

ev·ery·body \'evri,bädē, -bəd-\ pron : every person

ev·ery·day \'evri,dā\ adj : ordinary

ev·ery·one \-(,)wən\ pron : every person

ev·ery·thing pron : all that exists

ev·ery·where adv : in every place or part

evict \i'vikt\ vb : force (a person) to move from a property —evic·tion \i-'vikshən\ n

ev·i·dence \'evədəns\ n 1 : outward sign 2 : proof or testimony

ev·i·dent \-dənt\ adj : clear or obvious —ev·i·dent·ly \-ədəntlē, -ə,dent-\ adv

evil \'ēvəl\ adj evil·er or evil·ler; evil·est or evil·lest : wicked ~ n 1 : sin 2 : source of sorrow or distress —evil·do·er \,ēvəl'düər\ n —evil·ly adv

evince \i'vins\ vb evinced; evinc·ing : show

evis·cer·ate \i'visə,rāt\ vb -at·ed; -at·ing : remove the viscera of —evis·cer·a·tion \i,visə'rāshən\ n

evoke \i'vōk\ vb evoked; evok·ing : call forth or up —evo·ca·tion \,ēvō-'kāshən, ,evə-\ n —evoc·a·tive \i'väkətiv\ adj

evo·lu·tion \,evə'lüshən\ n : process of change by degrees —evo·lu·tion·ary \-shə,nerē\ adj

evolve \i'välv\ vb evolved; evolv·ing : develop or change by degrees

ewe \'yü\ n : female sheep

ew·er \'yüər\ n : vase-shaped jug

ex·act \ig'zakt\ vb : compel to furnish ~ adj : precisely correct —ex·act·ing adj —ex·ac·tion \-'zakshən\ n —ex·ac·ti·tude \-'zakta,t(y)üd\ n —ex·act·ly adv —ex·act·ness n

ex·ag·ger·ate \ig'zajə,rāt\ vb -at·ed; -at·ing : say more than is true —ex·ag·ger·at·ed·ly adv —ex·ag·ger·a·tion \-,zajə'rāshən\ n —ex·ag·ger·a·tor \-'zajə,rātər\ n

ex·alt \ig'zólt\ vb : glorify —ex·al·ta·tion \,eg,zól'tāshən, ,ek,sól-\ n

ex·am \ig'zam\ n : examination

ex·am·ine \ig'zam,ən\ vb -ined; -in·ing 1 : inspect closely 2 : test by questioning —ex·am·i·na·tion \-,zamə'nāshən\ n

ex·am·ple \-'zampəl\ *n* 1 : representative sample 2 : model 3 : problem to be solved for teaching purposes

ex·as·per·ate \-'zaspə,rāt\ *vb* **-at·ed; -at·ing** : thoroughly annoy —**ex·as·per·a·tion** \-,zaspə'rāshən\ *n*

ex·ca·vate \'ekskə,vāt\ *vb* **-vat·ed; -vat·ing** : dig or hollow out —**ex·ca·va·tion** \,ekskə'vāshən\ *n* —**ex·ca·va·tor** \'ekskə,vātər\ *n*

ex·ceed \ik'sēd\ *vb* 1 : go or be beyond the limit of 2 : do better than

ex·ceed·ing·ly, ex·ceed·ing *adv* : extremely

ex·cel \ik'sel\ *vb* **-ll-** : do extremely well or far better than

ex·cel·lence \'eks(ə)ləns\ *n* : quality of being excellent

ex·cel·len·cy \-(ə)lənsē\ *n, pl* **-cies** — used as a title of honor

ex·cel·lent \-(ə)lənt\ *adj* : very good —**ex·cel·lent·ly** *adv*

ex·cept \ik'sept\ *vb* : omit ~ *prep* 1 : excluding 2 : but ~ *conj* : but —**ex·cep·tion** \-'sepshən\ *n*

ex·cep·tion·al \-'sepsh(ə)nəl\ *adj* : superior —**ex·cep·tion·al·ly** *adv*

ex·cerpt \'ek,sərpt, 'eg,zərpt\ *n* : brief passage ~ \ek'-, eg'-, 'ek,-, 'eg,-\ *vb* : select an excerpt

ex·cess \ik'ses, 'ek,ses\ *n* : amount left over —**excess** *adj* —**ex·ces·sive** \ik'sesiv\ *adj* —**ex·ces·sive·ly** *adv*

ex·change \iks'chānj, 'eks,chānj\ *n* 1 : the giving or taking of one thing in return for another 2 : marketplace esp. for securities ~ *vb* **-changed; -chang·ing** : transfer in return for some equivalent —**ex·change·able** \iks'chānjəbəl\ *adj*

¹**ex·cise** \'ek,sīz, -,sīs\ *n* : tax

²**ex·cise** \ik'sīz\ *vb* **-cised; -cis·ing** : cut out —**ex·ci·sion** \-'sizhən\ *n*

ex·cite \ik'sīt\ *vb* **-cit·ed; -cit·ing** 1 : stir up 2 : kindle the emotions of —**ex·cit·abil·i·ty** \-,sītə'bilətē\ *n* —**ex·cit·able** \-'sītəbəl\ *adj* —**ex·ci·ta·tion** \,ek,sī'tāshən, -sə-\ *n* —**ex·cit·ed·ly** *adv* —**ex·cite·ment** \ik'sītmənt\ *n*

ex·claim \iks'klām\ *vb* : cry out esp. in delight —**ex·cla·ma·tion** \,eksklə'māshən\ *n* —**ex·clam·a·to·ry** \iks'klamə,tōrē\ *adj*

exclamation point *n* : punctuation mark ! used esp. after an interjection or exclamation

ex·clude \iks'klüd\ *vb* **-clud·ed; -clud·ing** : leave out —**ex·clu·sion** \-'klüzhən\ *n*

ex·clu·sive \-'klüsiv\ *adj* 1 : reserved for particular persons 2 : stylish 3 : sole —**ex·clu·sive·ly** *adv* —**ex·clu·sive·ness** *n*

ex·com·mu·ni·cate \,ekskə'myünə,kāt\ *vb* : expel from a church —**ex·com·mu·ni·ca·tion** \-,myünə'kāshən\ *n*

ex·cre·ment \'ekskrəmənt\ *n* : bodily waste —**ex·cre·men·tal** \,ekskrə'mentᵊl\ *adj*

ex·crete \ik'skrēt\ *vb* **-cret·ed; -cret·ing** : eliminate wastes from the body —**ex·cre·tion** \-'skrēshən\ *n* —**ex·cre·to·ry** \'ekskrə,tōrē\ *adj*

ex·cru·ci·at·ing \ik'skrüshē,ātiŋ\ *adj* : intensely painful —**ex·cru·ci·at·ing·ly** *adv*

ex·cul·pate \'ek(,)skəl,pāt\ *vb* **-pat·ed; -pat·ing** : clear from alleged fault

ex·cur·sion \ik'skərzhən\ *n* : pleasure trip

ex·cuse \ik'skyüz\ *vb* **-cused; -cus·ing** 1 : pardon 2 : release from an obligation 3 : justify ~ \-'skyüs\ *n* 1 : justification 2 : apology

ex·e·cute \'eksi,kyüt\ *vb* **-cut·ed; -cut·ing** 1 : carry to completion 2 : enforce 3 : put to death —**ex·e·cu·tion** \,eksi'kyüshən\ *n* —**ex·e·cu·tion·er** \-sh(ə)nər\ *n*

ex·ec·u·tive \ig'zek(y)ətiv\ *adj* : relating to the carrying out of decisions, plans, or laws ~ *n* 1 : branch of government with executive duties 2 : administrator

ex·ec·u·tor \-(y)ətər\ *n* : one who settles an estate —**ex·ec·u·trix** \-(y)ə,triks\ *n*

ex·em·pla·ry \ig'zemplərē\ *adj* : so commendable as to serve as a model

ex·em·pli·fy \-plə,fī\ *vb* **-fied; -fy·ing** : serve as an example of —**ex·em·pli·fi·ca·tion** \-,zemplə·fə'kāshən\ *n*

ex·empt \ig'zempt\ *adj* : being free from some liability ~ *vb* : make exempt —**ex·emp·tion** \-'zempshən\ *n*

ex·er·cise \'eksər,sīz\ *n* 1 : a putting into action 2 : exertion to develop endurance or a skill 3 *pl* : public ceremony ~ *vb* **-cised; -cis·ing** 1 : exert 2 : engage in exercise —**ex·er·cis·er** *n*

ex·ert \ig'zərt\ *vb* : put into action —**ex·er·tion** \-'zərshən\ *n*

ex·hale \eks'hāl\ *vb* **-haled; -hal·ing** : breathe out —**ex·ha·la·tion** \eks(h)ə'lāshən\ *n*

ex·haust \ig'zòst\ *vb* 1 : draw out or develop completely 2 : use up 3 : tire or wear out ~ *n* : waste steam or gas from an engine or a system for removing it —**ex·haus·tion**

ex·haus·tive \-'zóschən\ n —**ex·haus·tive** \-'zóstiv\ adj

ex·hib·it \ig'zibət\ vb : display esp. publicly ~ n 1 : act of exhibiting 2 : something exhibited —**ex·hi·bi·tion** \,eksə'bishən\ n —**ex·hib·i·tor** \ig'zibətər\ n

ex·hil·a·rate \ig'zilə,rāt\ vb -rat·ed; -rat·ing : thrill —**ex·hil·a·ra·tion** \-,zilə'rāshən\ n

ex·hort \-'zórt\ vb : urge earnestly —**ex·hor·ta·tion** \,eks,ór'tāshən, ,egz-, -ər-\ n

ex·hume \igz'(y)üm, iks'(h)yüm\ vb -humed; -hum·ing : dig up (a buried corpse) —**ex·hu·ma·tion** \,eks(h)yü-'māshən, ,egz(z)yü-\ n

ex·i·gen·cy \'eksajənsē, ig'zijən-\ n, pl -cies 1 : urgent need 2 pl : requirements of the situation —**ex·i·gent** \'eksajənt\ adj

ex·ile \'eg,zīl, 'ek,sīl\ n 1 : banishment 2 : person banished from his country —exile vb

ex·ist \ig'zist\ vb 1 : have real or actual being 2 : live —**ex·is·tence** \-əns\ n —**ex·is·tent** \-ənt\ adj

ex·it \'egzət, 'eksət\ n 1 : departure 2 : way out of an enclosed space —exit vb

ex·o·dus \'eksədəs\ n : mass departure

ex·on·er·ate \ig'zänə,rāt\ vb -at·ed; -at·ing : free from blame —**ex·on·er·a·tion** \-,zänə'rāshən\ n

ex·or·bi·tant \ig'zórbətənt\ adj : exceeding what is usual or proper

ex·or·cise \'ek,sór,sīz, -sər-\ vb -cised; -cis·ing : drive out (as an evil spirit) —**ex·or·cism** \-,sizəm\ n —**ex·or·cist** \-,sist\ n

ex·ot·ic \ig'zätik\ adj 1 : foreign 2 : strange and exciting —exotic n —**ex·ot·i·cal·ly** \-ik(ə)lē\ adv —**ex·ot·i·cism** \-,zätə,sizəm\ n

ex·pand \ik'spand\ vb : enlarge

ex·panse \-'spans\ n : very large area

ex·pan·sion \-'spanchən\ n 1 : act or process of expanding 2 : expanded part

ex·pan·sive \-'spansiv\ adj 1 : tending to expand 2 : warmly benevolent 3 : of large extent —**ex·pan·sive·ly** adv —**ex·pan·sive·ness** n

ex·pa·tri·ate \ek'spātrē,āt, -ət\ n : exile —expatriate \-,āt\ adj or vb

ex·pect \ik'spekt\ vb 1 : look forward to 2 : consider probable or one's due —**ex·pec·tan·cy** \-ənsē\ n —**ex·pec·tant** \-ənt\ adj —**ex·pec·tant·ly** adv —**ex·pec·ta·tion** \,ek,spek'tāshən\ n

ex·pe·di·ent \ik'spēdēənt\ adj : convenient or advantageous rather than right or just ~ n : convenient often makeshift means to an end

ex·pe·dite \'ekspə,dīt\ vb -dit·ed; -dit·ing : carry out or handle promptly —**ex·pe·dit·er** n

ex·pe·di·tion \,ekspə'dishən\ n : long journey for work or research or the people making this

ex·pe·di·tious \-əs\ adj : prompt and efficient

ex·pel \ik'spel\ vb -ll- : force out

ex·pend \-'spend\ vb 1 : pay out 2 : use up —**ex·pend·able** adj

ex·pen·di·ture \-'spendichər, -də-,chür\ n : act of using or spending

ex·pense \ik'spens\ n : cost —**ex·pen·sive** \-'spensiv\ adj —**ex·pen·sive·ly** adv

ex·pe·ri·ence \ik'spirēəns\ n 1 : a participating in or living through an event 2 : an event that affects one 3 : knowledge from doing ~ vb -enced; -enc·ing : undergo

ex·per·i·ment \ik'sperəmənt\ n : test to discover something ~ vb : make experiments —**ex·per·i·men·tal** \-,sperə'ment°l\ adj —**ex·per·i·men·ta·tion** \-mən'tāshən\ n —**ex·per·i·men·ter** \-'sperə,mentər\ n

ex·pert \'ek,spərt\ adj : thoroughly skilled ~ n : person with special skill —**ex·pert·ly** adv —**ex·pert·ness** n

ex·per·tise \,ek,spər'tēz\ n : skill

ex·pi·ate \'ekspē,āt\ vb : make amends for —**ex·pi·a·tion** \,ekspē'āshən\ n

ex·pire \ik'spī(ə)r, ek-\ vb -pired; -pir·ing 1 : breathe out 2 : die 3 : end —**ex·pi·ra·tion** \,ekspə'rāshən\ n

ex·plain \ik'splān\ vb 1 : make clear 2 : give the reason for —**ex·plain·able** \-əbəl\ adj —**ex·pla·na·tion** \,eksplə'nāshən\ n —**ex·plan·a·to·ry** \ik'splana,tōrē\ adj

ex·ple·tive \'eksplətiv\ n : usu. profane exclamation

ex·pli·ca·ble \'ek'splikəbəl, 'ek-(,)splik-\ adj : capable of being explained —**ex·pli·ca·bly** \-blē\ adv

ex·plic·it \ik'splisət\ adj : absolutely clear or precise —**ex·plic·it·ly** adv —**ex·plic·it·ness** n

ex·plode \ik'splōd\ vb -plod·ed; -plod·ing 1 : discredit 2 : burst or cause to burst violently

ex·ploit \'ek,splóit\ n : heroic act ~ \ik'splóit\ vb 1 : utilize 2 : use unfairly —**ex·ploi·ta·tion** \,ek,splói'tāshən\ n

ex·plore \ik'splór\ vb -plored; -plor·ing : examine or range over thoroughly —**ex·plo·ra·tion** \,eksplə'rāshən\ n

—ex·plor·a·to·ry \ik'splōrə,tōrē\ *adj*
—ex·plor·er *n*

ex·plo·sion \ik'splōzhən\ *n* : process
or instance of exploding

ex·plo·sive \-siv\ *adj* 1 : able to cause
explosion 2 : likely to explode —
explosive *n* —ex·plo·sive·ly *adv*

ex·po·nent \ik'spōnənt, 'ek,spō-\ *n* 1
: mathematical symbol showing how
many times a number is to be repeated as a factor 2 : advocate —ex-
po·nen·tial \,ekspə'nenchəl\ *adj* —
ex·po·nen·tial·ly *adv*

ex·port \ek'spōrt, 'ek,spōrt\ *vb* : send
to foreign countries —export \'ek,-\
n —ex·por·ta·tion \,ek,spōr'tāshən\
n —ex·port·er \ek'spōrtər, 'ek,-
spōrt-\ *n*

ex·pose \ik'spōz\ *vb* -posed; -pos·ing 1
: deprive of shelter or protection 2
: subject (film) to light 3 : make
known —ex·po·sure \-'spōzhər\ *n*

ex·po·sé, ex·pose \,ekspō'zā\ *n* : exposure of something discreditable

ex·po·si·tion \,ekspə'zishən\ *n* : public
exhibition

ex·pound \ik'spaúnd\ *vb* : set forth or
explain in detail

¹ex·press \-'spres\ *adj* 1 : clear 2 : specific 3 : traveling at high speed with
few stops —express *adv or n* —ex-
press·ly *adv*

²express *vb* 1 : make known in words
or appearance 2 : press out (as juice)
—ex·press·ible \-əbəl\ *adj* —ex-
press·ibly \-əblē\ *adv*

ex·pres·sion \-'spreshən\ *n* 1 : utterance 2 : mathematical symbol 3
: significant word or phrase 4 : look
on one's face —ex·pres·sion·less *adj*
—ex·pres·sive \-'spresiv\ *adj* —ex-
pres·sive·ness *n*

ex·press·way \ik'spres,wā\ *n* : high-
speed divided highway

ex·pul·sion \-'spəlshən\ *n* : an expel-
ling or being expelled

ex·pur·gate \'ekspər,gāt\ *vb* -gat·ed;
-gat·ing : censor —ex·pur·ga·tion
\,ekspər'gāshən\ *n*

ex·qui·site \'ek'skwizət, 'ek,(,)skwiz-\
adj 1 : flawlessly beautiful and delicate 2 : keenly sensitive

ex·tant \'ekstənt; ek'stant\ *adj* : existing

ex·tem·po·ra·ne·ous \ek,stempə'rā-
nēəs\ *adj* : impromptu —ex·tem-
po·ra·ne·ous·ly *adv*

ex·tend \ik'stend\ *vb* 1 : stretch forth
or out 2 : prolong 3 : enlarge —ex-
tend·able, ex·tend·ible \-'stendəbəl\
adj

ex·ten·sion \-'stenchən\ *n* 1 : an extending or being extended 2 : additional part

ex·ten·sive \ik'stensiv\ *adj* : of considerable extent —ex·ten·sive·ly *adv*

ex·tent \'stent\ *n* : size, length, or degree of something

ex·ten·u·ate \ik'stenyə,wāt\ *vb* -at·ed;
-at·ing : lessen the seriousness of —
ex·ten·u·a·tion \-,stenyə'wāshən\ *n*

ex·te·ri·or \ek'stirēər\ *adj* : external ~
n : external part or surface

ex·ter·mi·nate \ik'stərmə,nāt\ *vb* -nat-
ed; -nat·ing : destroy utterly —ex-
ter·mi·na·tion \-,stərmə'nāshən\ *n*
—ex·ter·mi·na·tor \-'stərmə,nātər\
n

ex·ter·nal \ek'stərn³l\ *adj* : relating to
or on the outside —ex·ter·nal·ly *adv*

ex·tinct \ik'stiŋkt\ *adj* : no longer existing —ex·tinc·tion \-'stiŋkshən\ *n*

ex·tin·guish \-'stiŋgwish\ *vb* : put out
(as a fire) —ex·tin·guish·able *adj* —
ex·tin·guish·er *n*

ex·tir·pate \'ekstər,pāt\ *vb* -pat·ed;
-pat·ing : destroy

ex·tol \ik'stōl\ *vb* -ll- : praise highly

ex·tort \-'stort\ *vb* : obtain by force or
improper pressure —ex·tor·tion
\-'stórshən\ *n* —ex·tor·tion·er *n* —
ex·tor·tion·ist *n*

ex·tra \'ekstrə\ *adj* 1 : additional 2
: superior —extra *n or adv*

extra- *prefix* : outside or beyond

extra-atmo-spheric	extragalactic
extracampus	extragovern-mental
extraclassroom	extrahuman
extracommunity	extralegal
extraconstitu-tional	extramarital
extracontinental	extranational
extradepart-mental	extraplanetary
extradiocesan	extrascholastic
extrafamilial	extrasensory
	extraterrestrial
	extravehicular

ex·tract \ik'strakt\ *vb* 1 : pull out forcibly 2 : withdraw (as a juice) —
\'ek,-\ *n* 1 : excerpt 2 : product (as
a juice) obtained by extracting —ex-
tract·able *adj* —ex·trac·tion \ik-
'strakshən\ *n* —ex·trac·tor \-tər\ *n*

ex·tra·cur·ric·u·lar \,ekstrəkə-
'rikyələr\ *adj* : lying outside the
regular curriculum

ex·tra·dite \'ekstrə,dīt\ *vb* -dit·ed; -dit-
ing : bring or deliver a suspect to a
different jurisdiction for trial —ex-
tra·di·tion \,ekstrə'dishən\ *n*

ex·tra·ne·ous \ek'strānēəs\ *adj* : not

essential or relevant —**ex·tra·ne·ous·ly** adv

ex·traor·di·nary \ik'strȯrd³n,erē, ,ekstrə'ȯrd-\ adj : notably unusual or exceptional —**ex·traor·di·nar·i·ly** \ik,strȯrd³n'erəlē, ,ekstrə,ȯrd-\ adv

ex·trav·a·gant \ik'stravigənt\ adj : wildly excessive, lavish, or costly —**ex·trav·a·gance** \-gəns\ n —**ex·trav·a·gant·ly** adv

ex·trav·a·gan·za \-,stravə'ganzə\ n : spectacular event

ex·treme \ik'strēm\ adj 1 : very great or intense 2 : very severe or drastic 3 : not moderate 4 : most remote ~ n 1 : extreme state 2 : something located at one end or the other of a range —**ex·treme·ly** adv

ex·trem·i·ty \-'stremətē\ n, pl -ties 1 : most remote part 2 : human hand or foot 3 : extreme degree or state (as of need)

ex·tri·cate \'ekstrə,kāt\ vb -cat·ed; -cat·ing : set or get free from an entanglement or difficulty —**ex·tri·ca·ble** \ik'strikəbəl, ek-; 'ek,(,)strik-\ adj **ex·tri·ca·tion** \,ekstrə'kāshən\ n

ex·tro·vert, ex·tra·vert \'ekstrə,vərt\ n : person more interested in the world than in the inner self —**ex·tro·ver·sion** \,ekstrə'vərzhən\ n —**ex·tro·vert·ed** \'ekstrə,vərtəd\ adj

ex·u·ber·ant \ig'züb(ə)rənt\ adj : joy- ously unrestrained —**ex·u·ber·ance** \-b(ə)rəns\ n —**ex·u·ber·ant·ly** adv

ex·ude \ig'züd\ vb -ud·ed; -ud·ing 1 : discharge slowly through pores 2 : give off —**ex·u·date** \'eks(y)ü,dāt\ n —**ex·u·da·tion** \,eks(y)ü'dāshən\ n

ex·ult \ig'zəlt\ vb : rejoice in triumph —**ex·ul·tant** \-'zəlt³nt\ adj —**ex·ul·tant·ly** adv —**ex·ul·ta·tion** \,ek(,)səl'tāshən, ,eg(,)zəl-\ n

-ey —see -Y

eye \'ī\ n 1 : organ of sight consisting of a globular structure (**eye·ball**) in a socket of the skull with thin movable covers (**eye·lids**) bordered with hairs (**eye·lash·es**) 2 : vision 3 : judgment 4 : something suggesting an eye ~ vb **eyed**; **eye·ing** or **ey·ing** : look at — **eye·brow** \-,braü\ n —**eyed** \'īd\ adj —**eye·strain** n

eye·drop·per n : dropper

eye·glass·es n pl : glasses

eye·let \'īlət\ n : small hole (as in cloth) for a lacing or rope

eye-open·er n : something startling — **eye-open·ing** adj

eye·piece n : lens at the eye end of an optical instrument

eye·sight n : sight

eye·sore n : unpleasant sight

eye·tooth n : upper canine tooth

eye·wit·ness n : person who actually sees something happen

ey·rie \'ī(ə)rē, or like AERIE\ var of AERIE

F

f \'ef\ n, pl **f's** or **fs** \'efs\ : 6th letter of the alphabet

fa·ble \'fābəl\ n 1 : legendary story 2 : story that teaches a lesson —**fa·bled** \-bəld\ adj

fab·ric \'fabrik\ n 1 : structure 2 : material made usu. by weaving or knitting fibers

fab·ri·cate \-ri,kāt\ vb -cat·ed; -cat·ing 1 : construct 2 : invent —**fab·ri·ca·tion** \,fabri'kāshən\ n

fab·u·lous \'fabyələs\ adj 1 : like, told in, or based on fable 2 : incredible or marvelous —**fab·u·lous·ly** adv

fa·cade \fə'säd\ n 1 : principal face of a building 2 : false or superficial appearance

face \'fās\ n 1 : front or principal surface (as of the head) 2 : presence 3 : facial expression 4 : grimace 5 : outward appearance ~ vb **faced**; **fac·ing** 1 : challenge or resist firmly or brazenly 2 : cover with different material 3 : sit or stand with the face toward 4 : front on —**faced** \'fāst\ adj —**face·less** adj —**face·less·ness** n —**fa·cial** \'fāshəl\ adj or n

face·down adv : with the face downward

fac·et \'fasət\ n 1 : surface of a cut gem 2 : phase —**fac·et·ed** adj

fa·ce·tious \fə'sēshəs\ adj : jocular —**fa·ce·tious·ly** adv —**fa·ce·tious·ness** n

fac·ile \'fasəl\ adj 1 : easy 2 : fluent

fa·cil·i·tate \fə'silə,tāt\ vb -tat·ed; -tat·ing : make easier

fa·cil·i·ty \-'silətē\ n, pl -ties 1 : ease in doing or using 2 : something built or installed to serve a purpose or facilitate an activity

fac·ing \'fāsiŋ\ n : lining or covering or material for this

fac·sim·i·le \fak'siməlē\ n : exact copy

fact \'fakt\ n 1 : act or action 2 : something that exists or is real —**fac·tu·al** \'fakchə(wə)l\ *adj* —**fac·tu·al·ly** *adv*

fac·tion \'fakshən\ *n* : part of a larger group —**fac·tion·al** *adj* —**fac·tion·al·ism** \-shə)nə,lizəm\ *n*

fac·tious \'fakshəs\ *adj* : causing discord

fac·ti·tious \fak'tishəs\ *adj* : artificial

fac·tor \'faktər\ *n* 1 : something that has an effect 2 : gene 3 : number used in multiplying

fac·to·ry \'fakt(ə)rē\ *n, pl* -ries : place for manufacturing

fac·to·tum \fak'tōtəm\ *n* : employee with varied duties

fac·ul·ty \'fakəltē\ *n, pl* -ties 1 : ability to act 2 : power of the mind or body 3 : body of teachers or department of instruction

fad \'fad\ *n* : briefly popular practice or interest —**fad·dish** *adj* —**fad·dist** *n*

fade \'fād\ *vb* **fad·ed; fad·ing** 1 : wither 2 : lose or cause to lose freshness or brilliance 3 : grow dim 4 : vanish

fag \'fag\ *vb* **-gg-** 1 : drudge 2 : tire or exhaust

fag·ot, fag·got \'fagət\ *n* : bundle of twigs

Fahr·en·heit \'farən,hīt\ *adj* : relating to a thermometer scale with the boiling point at 212 degrees and the freezing point at 32 degrees

fail \'fāl\ *vb* 1 : decline in health 2 : die away 3 : stop functioning 4 : be unsuccessful 5 : become bankrupt 6 : disappoint or abandon 7 : neglect ~ *n* : act of failing

fail·ing *n* : slight defect in character or conduct ~ *prep* : in the absence or lack of

faille \'fīl\ *n* : closely woven ribbed fabric

fail·ure \'fālyər\ *n* 1 : absence of expected action or performance 2 : bankruptcy 3 : deficiency 4 : one that has failed

faint \'fānt\ *adj* 1 : cowardly or spiritless 2 : weak and dizzy 3 : lacking vigor 4 : indistinct ~ *vb* : lose consciousness ~ *n* : act or condition of fainting —**faint·heart·ed** —**faint·ly** *adv* —**faint·ness** *n*

¹**fair** \'faər\ *adj* 1 : attractive in appearance 2 : not stormy or cloudy 3 : just or honest 4 : conforming with the rules 5 : open to legitimate pursuit or attack 6 : light in color 7 : adequate —**fair·ness** *n*

²**fair** *adv* : FAIRLY

³**fair** *n* : exhibition for judging or selling —**fair·ground** *n*

fair·ly \'fa(ə)rlē\ *adv* 1 : quite 2 : in a fair manner 3 : moderately

fairy \'fa(ə)rē\ *n, pl* **fair·ies** : usu. small imaginary being —**fairy tale**

fairy·land \-,land\ *n* 1 : land of fairies 2 : beautiful or charming place

faith \'fāth\ *n, pl* **faiths** \'fāths, 'fāthz\ 1 : allegiance 2 : belief and trust in God 3 : confidence 4 : system of religious beliefs —**faith·ful** \-fəl\ *adj* —**faith·ful·ly** *adv* —**faith·ful·ness** *n* —**faith·less** *adj* —**faith·less·ly** *adv* —**faith·less·ness** *n*

fake \'fāk\ *vb* **faked; fak·ing** 1 : falsify 2 : counterfeit 3 : pretend ~ *n* : copy, counterfeit, or trick ~ *adj* : not genuine —**fak·er** *n*

fa·kir \fə'kiər\ *n* : wandering beggar of India

fal·con \'falkən, 'fô(l)-\ *n* : long-winged hawk esp. used for hunting —**fal·con·ry** \-rē\ *n*

fall \'fòl\ *vb* **fell** \'fel\; **fall·en** \'fòlən\; **fall·ing** 1 : go down by gravity 2 : hang freely 3 : go lower 4 : be defeated or ruined 5 : commit a sin 6 : happen at a certain time 7 : become gradually ~ *n* 1 : act of falling 2 : autumn 3 : downfall 4 *pl* : waterfall 5 : distance something falls

fal·la·cy \'faləsē\ *n, pl* -cies 1 : false idea 2 : false reasoning —**fal·la·cious** \fə'lāshəs\ *adj*

fal·li·ble \'faləbəl\ *adj* : capable of making a mistake

fall·out *n* : radioactive particles from a nuclear explosion

fal·low \'falō\ *n* : land plowed but not planted —**fallow** *vb* or *adj*

false \'fòls\ *adj* **fals·er; fals·est** 1 : not genuine, true, faithful, or permanent 2 : misleading —**false·ly** *adv* —**false·ness** *n* —**fal·si·fi·ca·tion** \,fòlsəfə-'kāshən\ *n* —**fal·si·fy** \'fòlsə,fī\ *vb* —**fal·si·ty** \'fòlsətē\ *n*

false·hood \'fòls,hüd\ *n* : lie

fal·set·to \fòl'setō\ *n, pl* **-tos** : artificially high singing voice

fal·ter \'fòltər\ *vb* **-tered; -ter·ing** 1 : move unsteadily 2 : hesitate —**fal·ter·ing·ly** *adv*

fame \'fām\ *n* : public reputation —**famed** \'fāmd\ *adj*

fa·mil·ial \fə'milyəl\ *adj* : relating to a family

¹**fa·mil·iar** \fə'milyər\ *n* 1 : companion 2 : guardian spirit

²**familiar** *adj* 1 : closely acquainted 2 : forward 3 : frequently seen or experienced —**fa·mil·iar·i·ty** \fə,mil-'yaratē, -,milē'(y)ar-\ *n* —**fa·mil·iar·**

ize \fə'milyə‚rīz\ vb —**fa‧mil‧iar‧ly** adv

fam‧i‧ly \'fam(ə)lē\ n, pl **-lies 1** : persons of common ancestry **2** : group living together **3** : parents and children **4** : group of related individuals

fam‧ine \'famən\ n : extreme scarcity of food

fam‧ish \-ish\ vb : starve

fa‧mous \'fāməs\ adj : widely known or celebrated

fa‧mous‧ly adv : very well

¹fan \'fan\ n : device for producing a current of air ~ vb -nn- **1** : move air with a fan **2** : direct a current of air upon **3** : stir to activity

²fan n : enthusiastic follower or admirer

fa‧nat‧ic \fə'natik\, **fa‧nat‧i‧cal** \-ikəl\ adj : excessively enthusiastic or devoted —**fanatic** n —**fa‧nat‧i‧cism** \-'natə‚sizəm\ n

fan‧ci‧er \'fansēər\ n : one devoted to raising a particular plant or animal

fan‧cy \'fansē\ n, pl **-cies 1** : liking **2** : whim **3** : imagination ~ vb **-cied; -cy‧ing 1** : like **2** : imagine ~ adj **-ci‧er; -est 1** : not plain **2** : of superior quality —**fan‧ci‧ful** \-sifəl\ —**fan‧ci‧ful‧ly** \-f(ə)lē\ adv —**fan‧ci‧ly** adv

fan‧dan‧go \fan'dango\ n, pl **-gos** : lively Spanish dance

fan‧fare \'fan‚faər\ n : a sounding of trumpets **2** : showy display

fang \'faŋ\ n : long tooth of a venomous snake

fan‧light n : semicircular window

fan‧ta‧sia \fan'tāzhə, -z(h)ēə; ‚fanta‧'zēə\ n : music written to fancy rather than to form

fan‧tas‧tic \fan'tastik\ adj **1** : imaginary or unrealistic **2** : exceedingly or unbelievably great —**fan‧tas‧ti‧cal‧ly** \-tik(ə)lē\ adv

fan‧ta‧sy \'fantəsē\ n **1** : imagination **2** : product (as a daydream) of the imagination **3** : fantasia —**fan‧ta‧size** \'fantə‚sīz\ vb

far \'fär\ adv **farther** \-thər\ or **further** \'fər-\; **farthest** or **furthest** \-thəst\ **1** : at or to a distance **2** : much **3** : to a degree **4** : to an advanced point or extent ~ adj **farther** or **further**; **farthest** or **furthest 1** : remote **2** : long **3** : being more distant

far‧away adj : distant

farce \'färs\ n **1** : satirical comedy with an improbable plot **2** : ridiculous action —**far‧ci‧cal** \-sikəl\ adj

¹fare \'faər\ vb **fared; far‧ing** : get along

²fare n **1** : price of transportation **2** : range of food

fare‧well \faar'wel\ n **1** : wish of welfare at parting **2** : departure —**farewell** \‚faar‚wəl\ adj

far-fetched adj : not probable or reasonable

fa‧ri‧na \fə'rēnə\ n : fine meal made from cereal grains

farm \'färm\ n : place where something is raised ~ vb **1** : use (land) as a farm **2** : raise something —**farm‧er** n —**farm‧hand** \-‚hand\ n —**farm‧house** n —**farm‧ing** n —**farm‧land** \-‚land\ n —**farm‧yard** n

far-off adj : remote in time or space

far‧ri‧er \'farēər\ n : blacksmith who shoes horses

far‧row \'farō\ vb : give birth to a litter of pigs —**farrow** n

far‧sight‧ed adj **1** : better able to see distant things than near **2** : judicious or shrewd —**far‧sight‧ed‧ness** n

far‧ther \'färthər\ adv **1** : at or to a greater distance or more advanced point **2** : more completely ~ adj : more distant

far‧ther‧most adj : most distant

far‧thest \'färthəst\ adj : most distant ~ adv **1** : to or at the greatest distance **2** : to the most advanced point **3** : by the greatest extent

fas‧ci‧cle \'fasikəl\ n **1** : small bundle **2** : division of a book published in parts —**fas‧ci‧cled** \-kəld\ adj

fas‧ci‧nate \'fas⁹n‚āt\ vb **-nat‧ed; -nat‧ing** : transfix and hold spellbound —**fas‧ci‧na‧tion** \‚fas⁹n'āshən\ n

fas‧cism \'fash‚izəm\ n : dictatorship that exalts nation and race —**fas‧cist** \-əst\ n or adj —**fas‧cis‧tic** \fa‧'shistik\ adj

fash‧ion \'fashən\ n **1** : manner **2** : prevailing custom or style ~ vb : form or construct —**fash‧ion‧able** \-(ə)nəbəl\ —**fash‧ion‧ably** \-blē\ adv

¹fast \'fast\ adj **1** : firmly fixed, bound, or shut **2** : faithful **3** : moving or acting quickly **4** : indicating ahead of the correct time **5** : deep and undisturbed **6** : permanently dyed **7** : wild or promiscuous ~ adv **1** : so as to be secure or bound **2** : soundly or deeply **3** : swiftly

²fast vb : abstain from food or eat sparingly ~ n : act or time of fasting

fas‧ten \'fas⁹n\ vb : attach esp. by pinning or tying —**fas‧ten‧er** n —**fas‧ten‧ing** n

fas·tid·i·ous \fas'tidēəs\ *adj* : hard to please —**fas·tid·i·ous·ly** *adv* —**fas·tid·i·ous·ness** *n*

fat \'fat\ *adj* **-tt-** 1 : having much fat 2 : thick ～ *n* : animal tissue rich in greasy or oily matter —**fat·ness** *n* —**fat·ten** \'fatᵊn\ *vb* —**fat·ty** *adj or n*

fa·tal \'fātᵊl\ *adj* : causing death or ruin —**fa·tal·i·ty** \fā'talətē, fə-\ *n* —**fa·tal·ly** *adv*

fa·tal·ism \'fātᵊl,izəm\ *n* : belief that fate determines events —**fa·tal·ist** \-əst\ *n* —**fa·tal·is·tic** \,fātᵊl'istik\ *adj*

fate \'fāt\ *n* 1 : cause beyond human control held to determine events 2 : end or outcome —**fat·ed** *adj* —**fate·ful** \-fəl\ *adj* —**fate·ful·ly** *adv*

fa·ther \'fäthər, 'fath-\ *n* 1 : male parent 2 *cap* : God 3 : originator —**father** *vb* —**fa·ther·hood** \-,hũd\ *n* —**fa·ther·land** \-,land\ *n* —**fa·ther·less** *adj* —**fa·ther·ly** *adj*

father-in-law *n, pl* **fa·thers-in-law** : father of one's spouse

fath·om \'fathəm\ *n* : nautical unit of length equal to 6 feet ～ *vb* 1 : measure by sounding 2 : understand —**fath·om·able** *adj* —**fath·om·less** *adj*

fa·tigue \fə'tēg\ *n* 1 : weariness from labor or use 2 : tendency to break under repeated stress ～ *vb* **-tigued; -tigu·ing** : tire out

fat·u·ous \'fach(ə)wəs\ *adj* : foolish or stupid —**fat·u·ous·ly** *adv* —**fat·u·ous·ness** *n*

fau·cet \'fȯsət, 'fäs-\ *n* : fixture for drawing off a liquid

fault \'fȯlt\ *n* 1 : weakness in character 2 : something wrong or imperfect 3 : responsibility for something wrong 4 : fracture in the earth's crust ～ *vb* : find fault in or with —**fault·find·er** *n* —**fault·find·ing** *n* —**fault·i·ly** \'fȯltəlē\ *adv* —**fault·less** *adj* —**fault·less·ly** *adv* —**faulty** *adj*

fau·na \'fȯnə\ *n* : animals or animal life esp. of a region —**fau·nal** \-ᵊl\ *adj*

faux pas \'fō'pä\ *n, pl* **faux pas** \-'pä(z)\ : social blunder

fa·vor \'fāvər\ *n* 1 : approval 2 : partiality 3 : act of kindness ～ *vb* : regard or treat with favor —**fa·vor·able** \'fāv(ə)rəbəl\ *adj* —**fa·vor·ably** \-blē\ *adv*

fa·vor·ite \'fāv(ə)rət\ *n* : one favored —**favorite** *adj* —**fa·vor·it·ism** \-,izəm\ *n*

¹**fawn** \'fȯn\ *vb* : seek favor by groveling

²**fawn** *n* : young deer

faze \'fāz\ *vb* **fazed; faz·ing** : disturb the composure of

fear \'fiər\ *n* : unpleasant emotion caused by expectation or awareness of danger ～ *vb* : be afraid of —**fear·ful** \-fəl\ *adj* —**fear·ful·ly** *adv* —**fear·less** *adj* —**fear·less·ly** *adv* —**fear·less·ness** *n* —**fear·some** \-səm\ *adj*

fea·si·ble \'fēzəbəl\ *adj* : capable of being done —**fea·si·bil·i·ty** \,fēzə'bilətē\ *n* —**fea·si·bly** \'fēzəblē\ *adv*

feast \'fēst\ *n* 1 : large or fancy meal 2 : religious festival ～ *vb* : eat plentifully

feat \'fēt\ *n* : notable deed

feath·er \'fethər\ *n* : one of the light horny outgrowths that form the external covering of a bird's body —**feather** *vb* —**feath·ered** \-ərd\ *adj* —**feath·er·less** *adj* —**feath·ery** *adj*

fea·ture \'fēchər\ *n* 1 : shape or appearance of the face 2 : part of the face 3 : prominent characteristic 4 : special attraction ～ *vb* : give prominence to —**fea·ture·less** *adj*

Feb·ru·ary \'feb(y)ə,werē, 'febrə-\ *n* : 2d month of the year having 28 and in leap years 29 days

fe·ces \'fē,sēz\ *n pl* : intestinal body waste —**fe·cal** \-kəl\ *adj*

feck·less \'fekləs\ *adj* : irresponsible

fe·cund \'fekənd, 'fē-\ *adj* : prolific —**fe·cun·di·ty** \fi'kəndətē, fe-\ *n*

fed·er·al \'fed(ə)rəl\ *adj* : of or constituting a government with power distributed between a central authority and constituent units —**fed·er·al·ism** \-rə,lizəm\ *n* —**fed·er·al·ist** \-ləst\ *n or adj* —**fed·er·al·ly** *adv*

fed·er·ate \'fedə,rāt\ *vb* **-at·ed; -at·ing** : join in a federation

fed·er·a·tion \,fedə'rāshən\ *n* : union of organizations

fe·do·ra \fi'dōrə\ *n* : soft felt hat

fed up *adj* : out of patience

fee \'fē\ *n* : fixed charge

fee·ble \'fēbəl\ *adj* **-bler; -blest** : weak or ineffective —**fee·ble·mind·ed** \,fēbəl'mīndəd\ *adj* —**fee·ble·mind·ed·ness** *n* —**fee·ble·ness** *n* —**fee·bly** \-blē\ *adv*

feed \'fēd\ *vb* **fed** \'fed\; **feed·ing** 1 : give food to 2 : eat 3 : furnish ～ *n* : food for livestock —**feed·er** *n*

feel \'fēl\ *vb* **felt** \'felt\; **feel·ing** 1 : perceive or examine through physical contact 2 : think or believe 3 : be conscious of 4 : seem esp. to the touch 5 : have sympathy ～ *n* 1 : sense of touch 2 : quality of a thing imparted through touch —**feel·er** *n*

feel·ing \\'fēliŋ\ n 1 : sense of touch 2 : state of mind 3 pl : sensibilities 4 : opinion

feet pl of FOOT

feign \\'fān\ vb : pretend

feint \\'fānt\ n : mock attack intended to distract attention —**feint** vb

fe·lic·i·tate \fi'lisə,tāt\ vb **-tat·ed; -tat·ing** : congratulate —**fe·lic·i·ta·tion** \-,lisə'tāshən\ n

fe·lic·i·tous \fi'lisətəs\ adj : aptly expressed —**fe·lic·i·tous·ly** adv

fe·lic·i·ty \-'lisətē\ n, pl **-ties** 1 : great happiness 2 : pleasing faculty esp. in art or language

fe·line \\'fē,līn\ adj : relating to cats —**feline** n

¹fell \\'fel\ vb : cut or knock down

²fell past of FALL

fel·low \\'felō\ n 1 : companion or associate 2 : man or boy —**fel·low·ship** \-,ship\ n

fel·low·man \,felō'man\ n : kindred human being

fel·on \\'felən\ n : one who has committed a felony

fel·o·ny \\'felənē\ n, pl **-nies** : serious crime —**fe·lo·ni·ous** \fə'lōnēəs\ adj

¹felt \\'felt\ n : cloth made of pressed wool and fur

²felt past of FEEL

fe·male \\'fē,māl\ adj : relating to or being the sex that bears young —**female** n

fem·i·nine \\'femənən\ adj : relating to the female sex —**fem·i·nin·i·ty** \,femə'ninətē\ n

fem·i·nism \\'femə,nizəm\ n : organized activity on behalf of women's rights —**fem·i·nist** \-nəst\ n or adj

fe·mur \\'fēmər\ n, pl **fe·murs** or **fem·o·ra** \\'fem(ə)rə\ : long bone of the thigh —**fem·o·ral** \\'fem(ə)rəl\ adj

fence \\'fens\ n : enclosing barrier esp. of wood or wire ~ vb **fenced; fenc·ing** 1 : enclose with a fence 2 : practice fencing —**fenc·er** n

fenc·ing \\'fensiŋ\ n 1 : combat with swords for sport 2 : material for building fences

fend \\'fend\ vb : ward off

fend·er \\'fendər\ n : guard over an automobile wheel

fen·nel \\'fen²l\ n : herb related to the carrot

fer·ment \fər'ment\ vb : cause or undergo fermentation ~ \\'fər,ment\ n : agitation

fer·men·ta·tion \,fərmən'tāshən, -,men-\ n : chemical decomposition of an organic substance in the absence of oxygen

fern \\'fərn\ n : flowerless seedless green plant

fe·ro·cious \fə'rōshəs\ adj : fierce or savage —**fe·ro·cious·ly** adv —**fe·ro·cious·ness** n —**fe·roc·i·ty** \-'räsətē\ n

fer·ret \\'ferət\ n : white European polecat ~ vb : find out by searching

fer·ric \\'ferik\, **fer·rous** \\'ferəs\ adj : relating to or containing iron

fer·rule \\'ferəl\ n : metal band or ring

fer·ry \\'ferē\ vb **-ried; -ry·ing** : carry by boat over water ~ n, pl **-ries** : boat used in ferrying —**fer·ry·boat** n

fer·tile \\'fərt²l\ adj 1 : producing plentifully 2 : capable of developing or reproducing —**fer·til·i·ty** \(,)fər'tilətē\ n

fer·til·ize \\'fərt²l,īz\ vb **-ized; -iz·ing** : make fertile —**fer·til·iza·tion** \,fərt²lə'zāshən\ n —**fer·til·iz·er** n

fer·vid \\'fərvəd\ adj : ardent or zealous —**fer·vid·ly** adv

fer·vor \\'fərvər\ n : passion —**fer·ven·cy** \-vənsē\ n —**fer·vent** \-vənt\ adj —**fer·vent·ly** adv

fes·ter \\'festər\ n : pus-filled sore ~ vb 1 : form pus 2 : become more bitter or malignant

fes·ti·val \\'festəvəl\ n : time of celebration

fes·tive \-tiv\ adj : joyous or happy —**fes·tive·ly** adv —**fes·tiv·i·ty** \fes-'tivətē\ n

fes·toon \fes'tün\ n : decorative chain or strip hanging in a curve —**festoon** vb

fe·tal \\'fēt²l\ adj : of, relating to, or being a fetus

fetch \\'fech\ vb 1 : go or come after and bring or take back 2 : sell for

fetch·ing \\'fechiŋ\ adj : attractive —**fetch·ing·ly** adv

fête \\'fāt, 'fet\ n : lavish party ~ vb **fêt·ed; fêt·ing** : honor or commemorate with a fête

fet·id \\'fetəd\ adj : having an offensive smell

fe·tish \\'fetish, 'fēt-\ n 1 : object believed to have magical powers 2 : object of unreasoning devotion or concern

fet·lock \\'fet,läk\ n : projection on the back of a horse's leg above the hoof

fet·ter \\'fetər\ n : chain or shackle for the feet —**fetter** vb

fet·tle \\'fet²l\ n : state of fitness

fe·tus \\'fētəs\ n : vertebrate not yet born or hatched

feud \\'fyüd\ n : lasting conflict between families or clans —**feud** vb

feu·dal \'fyüd³l\ *adj* : of or relating to feudalism

feu·dal·ism \-,izəm\ *n* : medieval political order in which land is granted in return for service —**feu·dal·is·tic** \,fyüd³l'istik\ *adj*

fe·ver \'fēvər\ *n* 1 : abnormal rise in body temperature 2 : state of heightened emotion —**fe·ver·ish** *adj* —**fe·ver·ish·ly** *adv*

few \'fyü\ *pron* : not many ~ *adj* : some but not many —often with *a* ~ *n* : small number —often with *a*

few·er \-ər\ *pron* : smaller number of things

fez \'fez\ *n, pl* **fez·zes** : round flat-crowned hat

fi·an·cé \,fē,än'sā\ *n* : man one is engaged to

fi·an·cée \,fē,än'sā\ *n* : woman one is engaged to

fi·as·co \fē'askō\ *n, pl* **-coes** : ridiculous failure

fi·at \'fēat, -,at, -,ät; 'fīət, -,at\ *n* : decree

fib \'fib\ *n* : trivial lie —**fib** *vb* —**fib·ber** *n*

fi·ber, fi·bre \'fībər\ *n* 1 : threadlike substance or structure (as a muscle cell or fine root) 2 : element that gives texture or substance —**fi·brous** \-brəs\ *adj*

fi·ber·board *n* : construction material made of compressed fibers

fi·ber·glass *n* : glass in fibrous form in various products (as insulation)

fi·bril·la·tion \,fibrə'lāshən, ,fīb-\ *n* : rapid irregular contractions of muscle fibers (as of the heart) —**fib·ril·late** \'fibrə,lāt, 'fīb-\ *vb*

fib·u·la \'fibyələ\ *n, pl* **-lae** \-lē, -,lī\ *or* **-las** : outer of the two leg bones below the knee —**fib·u·lar** \-lər\ *adj*

fick·le \'fikəl\ *adj* : unpredictably changeable —**fick·le·ness** *n*

fic·tion \'fikshən\ *n* : a made-up story or literature consisting of these —**fic·tion·al** \-sh(ə)nəl\ *adj*

fic·ti·tious \fik'tishəs\ *adj* : made up or pretended

fid·dle \'fid³l\ *n* : violin ~ *vb* **-dled; -dling** 1 : play on the fiddle 2 : move the hands restlessly —**fid·dler** \'fidlər, -³lər\ *n*

fid·dle·sticks *n* : nonsense —used as an interjection

fi·del·i·ty \fə'delətē, fī-\ *n, pl* **-ties** 1 : quality or state of being faithful 2 : quality of reproduction

fidg·et \'fijət\ *n* 1 *pl* : restlessness 2 : one that fidgets ~ *vb* : move restlessly —**fidg·ety** *adj*

fi·du·cia·ry \fə'd(y)üshē,erē, -shərē\ *adj* : held or holding in trust —**fiduciary** *n*

field \'fēld\ *n* 1 : open country 2 : cleared land 3 : land yielding some special product 4 : sphere of activity 5 : area for sports 6 : region or space in which a given effect (as magnetism) exists ~ *vb* : put into the field —**field** *adj* —**field·er** *n*

fiend \'fēnd\ *n* 1 : devil 2 : extremely wicked person —**fiend·ish** *adj* —**fiend·ish·ly** *adv*

fierce \'fiərs\ *adj* **fierc·er; -est** 1 : violently hostile or aggressive 2 : intense 3 : menacing looking —**fierce·ly** *adv* —**fierce·ness** *n*

fiery \'fī(ə)rē\ *adj* **fi·er·i·er; -est** 1 : burning 2 : hot or passionate —**fi·eri·ness** \'fī(ə)rēnəs\ *n*

fi·es·ta \fē'estə\ *n* : festival

fife \'fīf\ *n* : small flute

fif·teen \fif'tēn\ *n* : one more than 14 —**fifteen** *adj or pron* —**fif·teenth** \-'tēnth\ *adj or n*

fifth \'fifth\ *n* 1 : one that is number 5 in a countable series 2 : one of 5 equal parts of something —**fifth** *adj or adv*

fif·ty \'fiftē\ *n, pl* **-ties** : 5 times 10 —**fif·ti·eth** \-tēəth\ *adj or n* —**fifty** *adj or pron*

fif·ty-fif·ty *adv or adj* : shared equally

fig \'fig\ *n* : pear-shaped edible fruit

fight \'fīt\ *vb* **fought** \'fȯt\; **fight·ing** 1 : contend against another in battle 2 : box 3 : struggle ~ *n* 1 : hostile encounter 2 : boxing match 3 : verbal disagreement —**fight·er** *n*

fig·ment \'figmənt\ *n* : something imagined or made up

fig·u·ra·tive \'fig(y)ərətiv\ *adj* : metaphorical —**fig·u·ra·tive·ly** *adv*

fig·ure \'figyər\ *n* 1 : symbol representing a number 2 *pl* : arithmetical calculations 3 : price 4 : shape or outline 5 : illustration 6 : pattern or design 7 : prominent person ~ *vb* **-ured; -ur·ing** 1 : be important 2 : calculate —**fig·ured** *adj*

fig·u·rine \,fig(y)ə'rēn\ *n* : small statue

fil·a·ment \'filəmənt\ *n* : fine thread or threadlike part —**fil·a·men·tous** \,filə'mentəs\ *adj*

fil·bert \'filbərt\ *n* : edible nut of a European hazel

filch \'filch\ *vb* : steal furtively

¹file \'fīl\ *n* : tool for smoothing or sharpening ~ *vb* **filed; fil·ing** : rub or smooth with a file

²file *vb* **filed; fil·ing** 1 : arrange in order

2 : enter or record officially ~ *n* : device for keeping papers in order

³**file** *n* : row of persons or things one behind the other ~ *vb* **filed; fil·ing** : march in file

fil·ial \'filēəl, 'filyəl\ *adj* : relating to a son or daughter

fil·i·bus·ter \'filə₁bəstər\ *n* : long speeches to delay a legislative vote —**filibuster** *vb* —**fil·i·bus·ter·er** *n*

fil·i·gree \-₁grē\ *n* : ornamental designs of fine wire —**fil·i·greed** \-₁grēd\ *adj*

fill \'fil\ *vb* **1** : make or become full **2** : stop up **3** : feed **4** : satisfy **5** : occupy fully **6** : spread through ~ *n* **1** : full supply **2** : material for filling —**fill·er** *n* —**fill in** *vb* **1** : provide information to or for **2** : substitute

fil·let \'filat, fi'lā, 'fil₍₎ā\ *n* : piece of boneless meat or fish ~ *vb* : cut into fillets

fill·ing *n* : material used to fill something

fil·ly \'filē\ *n, pl* **-lies** : young female horse

film \'film\ *n* **1** : thin skin or membrane **2** : thin coating or layer **3** : strip of material used in taking pictures **4** : movie ~ *vb* : make a movie of —**filmy** *adj*

film·strip *n* : strip of film with photographs for still projection

fil·ter \'filtər\ *n* **1** : device for separating matter from a fluid **2** : device (as on a camera lens) that absorbs light ~ *vb* **1** : pass through a filter **2** : remove by means of a filter —**fil·ter·able** *adj* —**fil·tra·tion** \fil'trāshən\ *n*

filth \'filth\ *n* : repulsive dirt or refuse —**filth·i·ness** *n* —**filthy** \'filthē\ *adj*

fin \'fin\ *n* **1** : thin external process controlling movement in an aquatic animal **2** : fin-shaped part (as on an airplane) **3** : flipper —**finned** \'find\ *adj*

fi·na·gle \fə'nāgəl\ *vb* **-gled; -gling** : get by clever or tricky means —**fi·na·gler** *n*

fi·nal \'fin³l\ *adj* **1** : not to be changed **2** : ultimate **3** : coming at the end —**final** *n* —**fi·nal·ist** \'fin³last\ *n* —**fi·nal·i·ty** \fi'nalətē, fə-\ *n* —**fi·nal·ize** \-,īz\ *vb* —**fi·nal·ly** *adv*

fi·na·le \fə'nalē, fi'näl-\ *n* : last or climactic part

fi·nance \fə'nans, 'fī,nans\ *n* **1** *pl* : money resources **2** : management of money affairs ~ *vb* **-nanced; -nanc·ing 1** : raise funds for **2** : give necessary funds to **3** : sell on credit

fi·nan·cial \fə'nanchəl, fī-\ *adj* : relating to finance —**fi·nan·cial·ly** *adv*

fi·nan·cier \,finən'siər, ,fī,nan-\ *n* : person who invests large sums of money

finch \'finch\ *n* : songbird (as a sparrow or linnet)

find \'find\ *vb* **found** \'faund\; **find·ing 1** : discover or encounter **2** : obtain by effort **3** : experience or perceive **4** : gain or regain the use of **5** : decide on (a verdict) ~ *n* **1** : act or instance of finding **2** : something found —**find·er** *n* —**find·ing** *n* —**find out** *vb* : learn, discover, or verify something

fine \'fin\ *n* : money paid as a penalty ~ *vb* **fined; fin·ing** : impose a fine on ~ *adj* **fin·er; -est 1** : free from impurity **2** : small or thin **3** : not coarse **4** : superior in quality or appearance ~ *adv* : finely —**fine·ly** *adv* —**fine·ness** *n*

fin·ery \'fin(ə)rē\ *n, pl* **-er·ies** : showy clothing and jewels

fi·nesse \fə'nes\ *n* **1** : delicate skill **2** : craftiness —**finesse** *vb*

fin·ger \'fingar\ *n* **1** : one of the 5 divisions at the end of the hand and esp. one other than the thumb **2** : something like a finger **3** : part of a glove for a finger ~ *vb* **1** : touch with the fingers **2** : identify as if by pointing —**fingered** *adj* —**fin·ger·nail** *n* —**fin·ger·tip** *n*

fin·ger·ling \-garlin\ *n* : small fish

fin·ger·print *n* : impression of the pattern of marks on the tip of a finger —**fingerprint** *vb*

fin·icky \'finikē\ *adj* : excessively particular in taste or standards

fin·ish \'finish\ *vb* **1** : come or bring to an end **2** : use or dispose of entirely **3** : put a final coat or surface on ~ *n* **1** : end **2** : final treatment given a surface —**fin·ish·er** *n*

fi·nite \'fī,nīt\ *adj* : having definite limits

fink \'fiŋk\ *n* : contemptible person

fiord *var of* FJORD

fir \'fər\ *n* : erect evergreen tree or its wood

fire \'fī(ə)r\ *n* **1** : light or heat and esp. the flame of something burning **2** : destructive burning of something (as a house) **3** : enthusiasm **4** : discharge of firearms ~ *vb* **fired; fir·ing 1** : kindle **2** : stir up or enliven **3** : dismiss from employment **4** : shoot **5** : bake —**fire·bomb** *n or vb* —**fire·less** *adj* —**fire·proof** *adj or vb* —**fire·wood** *n*

fire·arm *n* : weapon (as a rifle) that works by an explosion of gunpowder

fire•ball n 1 : ball of fire 2 : brilliant meteor

fire-boat n : ship equipped for fighting fire

fire-box n 1 : chamber (as of a furnace) that contains a fire 2 : fire-alarm box

fire•break n : cleared land for checking a forest fire

fire•bug n : person who deliberately sets destructive fires

fire-crack•er n : small firework that makes noise

fire•fly n : night-flying beetle that produces a soft light

fire•man \-mən\ n 1 : member of a company organized to put out fires 2 : stoker

fire•place n : opening made in a chimney to hold an open fire

fire-plug n : hydrant

fire•side n 1 : place near the fire or hearth 2 : home ~ adj : having an informal quality

fire•trap n : place apt to catch on fire

fire•work n : device that explodes to produce noise or a display of light

¹firm \'fərm\ adj 1 : securely fixed in place 2 : strong or vigorous 3 : not subject to change 4 : resolute ~ vb : make or become firm —**firm•ly** adv —**firm•ness** n

²firm n : business enterprise

fir•ma•ment \'fərməmənt\ n : sky

first \'fərst\ adj 1 : being number one 2 : foremost ~ adv 1 : before any other 2 : for the first time ~ n 1 : number one 2 : one that is first —**first class** n —**first–class** adj or adv —**first•ly** adv —**first–rate** adj or adv

first aid n : emergency care

first lieutenant n : commissioned officer ranking next below a captain

first sergeant n 1 : noncommissioned officer serving as the chief assistant to the commander of a military unit (as a company) 2 : rank in the army below a command sergeant major and in the marine corps below a sergeant major

firth \'fərth\ n : estuary

fis•cal \'fiskəl\ adj : relating to money

¹fish \'fish\ n, pl fish or fish•es : water animal with fins, gills, and usu. scales ~ vb 1 : try to catch fish 2 : grope —**fisher** n —**fish•hook** n —**fish•ing** n

fish•er•man \-mən\ n : one who fishes

fish•ery \'fish(ə)rē\ n, pl -er•ies : fishing business or a place for this

fishy \'fishē\ adj fish•i•er; -est 1 : relating to or like fish 2 : questionable

fis•sion \'fishən, 'fizh-\ n : splitting of

an atomic nucleus —**fis•sion•able** \-(ə)nəbəl\ adj

fis•sure \'fishər\ n : crack

fist \'fist\ n : hand doubled up —**fist•ed** \'fistəd\ adj —**fist•ful** \-,fu̇l\ n

fist•i•cuffs \'fisti,kəfs\ n pl : fist fight

¹fit \'fit\ n : sudden attack of illness or emotion

²fit adj -tt- 1 : suitable 2 : qualified 3 : sound in body ~ vb -tt- 1 : be suitable to 2 : insert or adjust correctly 3 : make room for 4 : supply or equip 5 : belong ~ n 1 : state of fitting or being fitted —**fit•ly** adv —**fit•ness** n —**fit•ter** n

fit•ful adj : restless —**fit•ful•ly** adv

fit•ting adj : suitable ~ n : a small part

five \'fīv\ n 1 : one more than 4 2 : 5th in a set or series 3 : something having 5 units —**five** adj or pron

fix \'fiks\ vb 1 : attach 2 : establish 3 : make right 4 : prepare 5 : improperly influence ~ n 1 : predicament 2 : determination of location —**fix•er** n

fix•a•tion \fik'sāshən\ n : obsessive attachment —**fix•ate** \'fik,sāt\ vb

fixed \'fikst\ adj 1 : stationary 2 : settled —**fixed•ly** \'fiksədlē\ adv —**fixed•ness** \-nəs\ n

fix•ture \'fikschər\ n : permanent part of something

fizz \'fiz\ vb : make a hissing sound ~ n : effervescence

fiz•zle \'fizəl\ vb -zled; -zling 1 : fizz 2 : fail ~ n : failure

fjord \fē'ȯrd\ n : inlet of the sea between cliffs

flab \'flab\ n : flabby flesh

flab•ber•gast \'flabər,gast\ vb : astound

flab•by \'flabē\ adj -bi•er; -est : not firm —**flab•bi•ness** n

flac•cid \'flaksəd, 'flasəd\ adj : not firm

¹flag \'flag\ n : flat stone

²flag n 1 : fabric that is a symbol (as of a country) 2 : something used to signal ~ vb -gg- : signal with a flag —**flag•pole** n —**flag•staff** n

³flag vb -gg- : lose strength or spirit

flag•el•late \'flajə,lāt\ vb -lat•ed; -lat•ing : whip —**flag•el•la•tion** \,flajəh'lā-shən\ n

flag•on \'flagən\ n : container for liquids

fla•grant \'flāgrənt\ adj : conspicuously bad —**fla•grant•ly** adv

flag•ship n : ship carrying a commander

flag•stone n : flag

flail \'flāl\ n : tool for threshing grain ~ vb : beat with or as if with a flail

flair \'flaər\ n : natural aptitude

flak \'flak\ n, pl flak : antiaircraft fire

flake \'flāk\ n : small flat piece ~ vb flaked; flak·ing : separate or form into flakes

flam·boy·ant \flam-'bóiənt\ adj : showy —flam·boy·ance \-əns\ n —flam·boy·ant·ly adv

flame \'flām\ n 1 : glowing part of a fire 2 : state of combustion 3 : burning passion —flame vb —flam·ing adj

fla·min·go \flə'miŋgō\ n, pl -gos : long-legged long-necked tropical water bird

flam·ma·ble \'flaməbəl\ adj : easily ignited

flange \'flanj\ n : rim

flank \'flaŋk\ n : side of something ~ vb 1 : attack or go around the side of 2 : be at the side of

flan·nel \'flan²l\ n : soft napped fabric

flap \'flap\ n 1 : slap 2 : something flat that hangs loose ~ vb -pp- 1 : move (wings) up and down 2 : swing back and forth noisily

flap·jack \-.jak\ n : pancake

flare \'flaər\ vb flared; flar·ing : become suddenly bright or excited ~ n : blaze of light

flash \'flash\ vb 1 : give off a sudden flame or burst of light 2 : appear or pass suddenly ~ n 1 : sudden burst of light or inspiration 2 : instant ~ adj : coming suddenly

flash·light n : small battery-operated light

flashy \'flashē\ adj flash·i·er; -est : showy —flash·i·ly adv —flash·i·ness n

flask \'flask\ n : flattened bottle

¹flat \'flat\ adj -tt- 1 : smooth 2 : broad and thin 3 : definite 4 : uninteresting 5 : deflated 6 : below the true pitch ~ n 1 : level surface of land 2 : flat note in music 3 : deflated tire ~ adv -tt- 1 : exactly 2 : below the true pitch ~ vb -tt- : make flat —flat·ly adv —flat·ness n —flat·ten \-²n\ vb

²flat n 1 : story in a building 2 : apartment

flat·car n : railroad car without sides

flat·fish n : flattened fish with both eyes on the upper side

flat·foot n, pl flat·feet : foot condition in which the arch is flattened —flat·foot·ed adj

flat·ter \'flatər\ vb 1 : praise insincerely 2 : judge or represent too favorably —flat·ter·er n —flat·tery \'flatərē\ n

flat·u·lent \'flachələnt\ adj : full of gas —flat·u·lence \-ləns\ n

flat·ware n : eating utensils

flaunt \'flónt\ vb : display ostentatiously —flaunt n

fla·vor \'flāvər\ n 1 : quality that affects the sense of taste 2 : something that adds flavor ~ vb : give flavor to —fla·vor·ful adj —fla·vor·ing \'flāv(ə)riŋ\ n —fla·vor·some adj

flaw \'fló\ n : fault —flaw·less adj —flaw·less·ly adv

flax \'flaks\ n : plant from which linen is made

flax·en \'flaksən\ adj : made of or like flax

flay \'flā\ vb 1 : strip off the skin of 2 : criticize harshly

flea \'flē\ n : leaping bloodsucking insect

fleck \'flek\ vb or n : streak or spot

fledg·ling \'flejliŋ\ n : young bird

flee \'flē\ vb fled \'fled\; flee·ing : run away

fleece \'flēs\ n : sheep's wool ~ vb fleeced; fleec·ing 1 : shear 2 : get money from dishonestly —fleecy adj

¹fleet \'flēt\ vb : pass rapidly ~ adj : swift —fleet·ing adj —fleet·ness n

²fleet n : group of ships

fleet admiral n : commissioned officer of the highest rank in the navy

flesh \'flesh\ n 1 : soft parts of an animal's body 2 : soft plant tissue (as fruit pulp) —fleshed \'flesht\ adj —fleshy adj

flesh·ly \'fleshlē\ adj : sensual

flew past of FLY

flex \'fleks\ vb : bend

flex·i·ble \'fleksəbəl\ adj 1 : capable of being flexed 2 : adaptable —flex·i·bil·i·ty \,fleksə'bilətē\ n —flex·i·bly \-əblē\ adv

flick \'flik\ n : light jerky stroke ~ vb 1 : strike lightly 2 : flutter

flick·er \'flikər\ vb 1 : waver 2 : burn unsteadily ~ n 1 : sudden movement 2 : wavering light

fli·er \'flī(ə)r\ n 1 : aviator 2 : advertising circular

¹flight \'flīt\ n 1 : act or instance of flying 2 : ability to fly 3 : a passing through air or space 4 : series of stairs —flight·less adj

²flight n : act or instance of running away

flighty \-ē\ adj flight·i·er; -est 1 : capricious 2 : silly

flim·flam \'flim,flam\ n : trickery

flim·sy \-zē\ adj -si·er; -est 1 : not strong or well made 2 : not believable —flim·si·ly adv —flim·si·ness n

flinch \'flinch\ vb : shrink from pain

fling \'fliŋ\ vb flung \'fləŋ\; fling·ing 1 : move brusquely 2 : throw ~ n 1

: act or instance of flinging **2** : attempt **3** : period of self-indulgence

flint \'flint\ n : hard quartz that gives off sparks when struck with steel —**flinty** adj

flip \'flip\ vb -pp- **1** : cause to turn over quickly or many times **2** : move with a quick push ~ adj : insolent —**flip** n

flip-pant \'flipənt\ adj : not serious enough —**flip-pan-cy** \-ənsē\ n

flip-per \-ər\ n : paddlelike limb (as of a seal) for swimming

flirt \'flərt\ vb **1** : be playfully romantic **2** : trifle ~ n : one who flirts —**flir-ta-tion** \ˌflər'tāshən\ n —**flir-ta-tious** \-shəs\ adj

flit \'flit\ vb -tt- : dart

float \'flōt\ n **1** : something that floats **2** : vehicle carrying an exhibit ~ vb **1** : rest on or in a fluid without sinking **2** : finance by issuing stock or bonds —**float-er** n

flock \'fläk\ n : group of animals (as birds) or people ~ vb : gather or move as a group

floe \'flō\ n : mass of floating ice

flog \'fläg\ vb -gg- : beat with a rod or whip —**flog-ger** n

flood \'fləd\ n **1** : great flow of water over the land **2** : overwhelming volume ~ vb : cover or fill esp. with water —**flood-wa-ter** n

floor \'flōr\ n **1** : bottom of a room on which one stands **2** : story of a building **3** : lower limit ~ vb **1** : furnish with a floor **2** : knock down or overwhelm —**floor-board** n —**floor-ing** \-iŋ\ n

floo-zy, floo-zie \'flüzē\ n, pl -zies : tawdry woman

flop \'fläp\ vb -pp- **1** : flap **2** : slump heavily **3** : fail —**flop** n

flop-py \'fläpē\ adj -pier; -est : soft and flexible

flo-ra \'flōrə\ n : plants or plant life of a region

flo-ral \'flōrəl\ adj : relating to flowers

flor-id \'flörəd\ adj **1** : excessively flowery in style **2** : reddish

flor-ist \'flörəst\ n : flower dealer

flo-ta-tion \flō'tāshən\ n : process or instance of floating

flo-til-la \flō'tilə\ n : small fleet

flot-sam \'flätsəm\ n : floating wreckage

¹**flounce** \'flaůns\ vb **flounced; flounc-ing** : move with exaggerated jerky motions —**flounce** n

²**flounce** n : fabric border

¹**floun-der** \'flaůndər\ n, pl flounder or flounders : flatfish

²**flounder** vb **1** : struggle for footing **2** : proceed clumsily

flour \'flaů(ə)r\ n : finely ground meal ~ vb : coat with flour —**floury** adj

flour-ish \'flərish\ vb **1** : thrive **2** : wave threateningly ~ n **1** : embellishment **2** : ostentatious action

flout \'flaůt\ vb : scorn

flow \'flō\ vb **1** : move in a stream **2** : proceed smoothly and readily ~ n : uninterrupted stream

flow-er \'flaů(ə)r\ n **1** : showy plant shoot that bears seeds **2** : state of flourishing ~ vb **1** : produce flowers **2** : flourish —**flow-ered** adj —**flow-er-i-ness** n —**flow-er-less** adj —**flow-er-pot** n —**flow-ery** -ē\ adj

flown past part of FLY

flu \'flü\ n **1** : influenza **2** : minor virus ailment

flub \'fləb\ vb -bb- : bungle —**flub** n

fluc-tu-ate \'fləkchəˌwāt\ vb -at-ed; -at-ing : change rapidly esp. up and down —**fluc-tu-a-tion** \ˌfləkchə-'wā-shən\ n

flue \'flü\ n : smoke duct

flu-ent \'flüənt\ adj : speaking with ease —**flu-en-cy** \-ənsē\ n —**flu-ent-ly** adv

fluff \'fləf\ n **1** : something soft and light **2** : blunder ~ vb **1** : make fluffy **2** : make a mistake —**fluffy** -ē\ adj

fluid \'flüəd\ adj : flowing ~ n : substance that can flow —**flu-id-i-ty** \flü-'idətē\ n

fluid-ounce n : unit of liquid measure equal to ¹⁄₁₆ pint

fluke \'flük\ n : stroke of luck

flume \'flüm\ n : channel for water

flung past of FLING

flunk \'fləŋk\ vb : fail in school work

flun-ky, flun-key \'fləŋkē\ n, pl -kies or keys : obsequious or insignificant person

flu-o-res-cence \ˌflu̇(ə)r'es°ns\ n : emission of light after initial absorption —**flu-o-resce** \-'es\ vb —**flu-o-res-cent** \-'es°nt\ adj

flu-o-ri-date \'flu̇(ə)rə,dāt\ vb -dat-ed; -dat-ing : add fluoride to —**flu-o-ri-da-tion** \ˌflu̇(ə)r'dāshən\ n

flu-o-ride \'flu̇(ə)r,īd\ n : compound of fluorine

flu-o-rine \'flu̇(ə)r,ēn, -ən\ n : toxic gaseous chemical element

flu-o-ro-car-bon \ˌflu̇(ə)rō'kärbən\ n : compound containing fluorine and carbon

flu-o-ro-scope \'flu̇rə,skōp\ n : instrument for internal examination —**flu-o-ro-scop-ic** \ˌflu̇rə'skäpik\ adj —**flu-o-ros-co-py** \ˌflu̇(ə)r'äskəpē\ n

flur·ry \'flərē\ n, pl **-ries** 1 : light snowfall 2 : bustle 3 : brief burst of activity — **flurry** vb

¹**flush** \'fləsh\ vb : cause (a bird) to fly from cover

²**flush** n 1 : sudden flow (as of water) 2 : surge of emotion 3 : blush ~ vb 1 : blush 2 : wash out with a rush of liquid ~ adj 1 : filled to overflowing 2 : of a reddish healthy color 3 : smooth or level 4 : abutting — **flush** adv

³**flush** n : cards of the same suit

flus·ter \'fləstər\ vb : upset — **fluster** n

flute \'flüt\ n 1 : pipelike musical instrument 2 : groove — **flut·ed** adj — **flut·ing** n — **flut·ist** \-əst\ n

flut·ter \'flətər\ vb 1 : flap the wings rapidly 2 : move with quick wavering or flapping motions 3 : behave in an agitated manner ~ n 1 : a fluttering 2 : state of confusion — **flut·tery** \-ərē\ adj

flux \'fləks\ n : state of continuous change

¹**fly** \'flī\ vb **flew** \'flü\; **flown** \'flōn\; **fly·ing** 1 : move through the air with wings 2 : float or soar 3 : flee 4 : move or pass swiftly 5 : operate an airplane

²**fly** n, pl **flies** : garment closure

³**fly** n, pl **flies** : winged insect

fly-by-night adj : transitory

fly·er var of FLIER

fly·pa·per n : sticky paper for catching flies

fly·speck n 1 : speck of fly dung 2 : something tiny

fly·wheel n : rotating wheel that regulates the speed of machinery

f-number n : number expressing the effectiveness of a camera lens

foal \'fōl\ n : young horse — **foal** vb

foam \'fōm\ n 1 : mass of bubbles on top of a liquid 2 : material of cellular form ~ vb : form foam — **foamy** adj

fob \'fäb\ n : short chain for a pocket watch

fo'·c'sle var of FORECASTLE

fo·cus \'fōkəs\ n, pl **-cus·es** or **-ci** \-,sī\ 1 : point at which reflected or refracted rays meet 2 : adjustment (as of eyeglasses) for clear vision 3 : central point ~ vb : bring to a focus — **fo·cal** \-kəl\ adj — **fo·cal·ly** adv

fod·der \'fädər\ n : food for livestock

foe \'fō\ n : enemy

fog \'fòg, 'fäg\ n 1 : fine particles of water suspended near the ground 2 : mental confusion ~ vb -gg- : obscure or be obscured with fog — **fog·gy** adj

fog·horn n : warning horn sounded in a fog

fo·gy \'fōgē\ n, pl **-gies** : person with old-fashioned ideas

foi·ble \'fòibəl\ n : minor character fault

¹**foil** \'fòil\ vb : defeat ~ n : fencing sword

²**foil** n 1 : thin sheet of metal 2 : one that sets off another by contrast

foist \'fòist\ vb : force another to accept

¹**fold** \'fōld\ n 1 : enclosure for sheep 2 : group with a common interest

²**fold** vb 1 : lay one part over another 2 : embrace ~ n : part folded

fold·er \'fōldər\ n 1 : one that folds 2 : circular 3 : folded cover or envelope for papers

fol·de·rol \'fäldə,räl\ n : nonsense

fo·liage \'fōl(ē)ij\ n : plant leaves

fo·lio \'fōlē,ō\ n, pl **-lios** : sheet of paper folded once

folk \'fōk\ n, pl **folk** or **folks** 1 : people in general **folks** pl : one's family ~ adj : relating to the common people

folk·lore n : customs and traditions of a people — **folk·lor·ist** n

folksy \'fōksē\ adj **folks·i·er**; **-est** : friendly and informal

fol·li·cle \'fälikəl\ n : small anatomical cavity or gland

fol·low \'fälō\ vb 1 : go or come after 2 : pursue 3 : obey 4 : proceed along 5 : keep one's attention fixed on 6 : result from — **fol·low·er** n

fol·low·ing \'fäləwiŋ\ adj : next ~ n : group of followers ~ prep : after

fol·ly \'fälē\ n, pl **-lies** : foolishness

fo·ment \'fō'ment\ vb : incite — **fo·men·ta·tion** \,fōmən'tāshən, -,men-\ n

fond \'fänd\ adj 1 : strongly attracted 2 : affectionate 3 : dear — **fond·ly** \'fän(d)lē\ adv — **fond·ness** \-nəs\ n

fon·dle \'fändᵊl\ vb **-dled**; **-dling** : touch lovingly

fon·due \fän'd(y)ü\ n : preparation of melted cheese

font \'fänt\ n 1 : baptismal basin 2 : fountain

food \'füd\ n : material eaten to sustain life

fool \'fül\ n 1 : stupid person 2 : jester ~ vb 1 : waste time 2 : meddle 3 : deceive — **fool·ery** \'fül(ə)rē\ n — **fool·ish** \'fülish\ adj — **fool·ish·ly** adv — **fool·ish·ness** n — **fool·proof** adj

fool·har·dy \'fül,härdē\ adj : rash — **fool·har·di·ness** n

foot \'fůt\ n, pl **feet** \'fēt\ 1 : terminal part of a leg 2 : unit of length equal to ⅓ yard **3** : unit of verse meter **4** : bottom —**foot·age** \-ij\ *n* —**foot·path** *n* —**foot·print** *n* —**foot·race** *n* —**foot·rest** *n* —**foot·wear** *n*

foot·ball *n* : ball game played by 2 teams on a rectangular field

foot·bridge *n* : bridge for pedestrians

foot·ed \'fŭtəd\ *adj* : having feet or such or so many feet

foot·hill *n* : hill at the foot of higher hills

foot·hold *n* : support for the feet

foot·ing *n* **1** : foothold **2** : basis

foot·lights *n pl* : stage lights along the floor

foot·lock·er *n* : small trunk

foot·loose *adj* : having no ties

foot·man \-mən\ *n* : male servant

foot·note *n* : note at the bottom of a page

foot·step *n* **1** : step **2** : distance covered by a step **3** : footprint

foot·stool *n* : stool to support the feet

foot·work *n* : skillful movement of the feet (as in boxing)

fop \'fäp\ *n* : dandy —**fop·pery** \-(ə)rē\ *n* —**fop·pish** *adj*

for \fər, (')fȯr\ *prep* **1** —used to show preparation or purpose **2** : because of **3** —used to show a recipient **4** : in support of **5** : so as to support or help cure **6** : so as to be equal to **7** : concerning **8** : through the period of ~ *conj* : because

for·age \'fȯrij\ *n* **1** : food for animals **2** : search for provisions ~ *vb* -**aged**; -**ag·ing 1** : hunt food **2** : make a search

for·ay \'fȯr,ā\ *vb* : raid for plunder —**foray** *n*

¹**for·bear** \fȯr'baər\ *vb* -**bore** \-'bȯr\; -**borne** \-'bȯrn\; -**bear·ing 1** : refrain from **2** : be patient —**for·bear·ance** \-'barəns\ *n*

²**forbear** *var of* FOREBEAR

for·bid \fər'bid\ *vb* -**bade** \-'bad, -'bād\ *or* -**bad** \-'bad\; -**bid·den** \-'bidᵊn\; -**bid·ding 1** : prohibit **2** : order not to do something

for·bid·ding *adj* : tending to discourage

force \'fȯrs\ *n* **1** : exceptional strength or energy **2** : military strength : body (as of persons) available for a purpose **4** : violence **5** : influence (as a push or pull) that causes motion ~ *vb* **forc·ing 1** : compel **2** : gain against resistance **3** : break open —**force·ful** \-fəl\ *adj* —**force·ful·ly** *adv* —**in force 1** : in great numbers **2** : valid

for·ceps \'fȯrsəps\ *n, pl* **forceps** : surgical instrument for grasping objects

forc·ible \'fȯrsəbəl\ *adj* **1** : done by force **2** : showing force —**forc·i·bly** \-blē\ *adv*

ford \'fȯrd\ *n* : place to wade across a stream ~ *vb* : wade across

fore \'fȯr\ *adv* : in or toward the front ~ *adj* : being or coming before in time, place, or order ~ *n* : front

fore-and-aft *adj* : lengthwise

fore·arm \'fȯr-\ *n* : part of the arm between the elbow and the wrist

fore·bear, for·bear \'fȯr,baər, 'fȯr-\ *n* : ancestor

fore·bode \fȯr'bōd, fȯr-\ *vb* : predict —**fore·bod·ing** *n*

fore·cast \'fȯr,kast\ *vb* -**cast** *or* -**cast·ed**; -**cast·ing** : predict —**forecast** *n* —**fore·cast·er** *n*

fore·cas·tle \'fōksəl\ *n* : forward part of a ship

fore·close \fȯr'klōz\ *vb* : take legal measures to terminate a mortgage —**fore·clo·sure** \-'klōzhər\ *n*

fore·fa·ther \'fȯr-\ *n* : ancestor

fore·fin·ger \'fȯr-\ *n* : finger next to the thumb

fore·foot \'fȯr-\ *n* : front foot of a quadruped

fore·front \'fȯr-\ *n* : foremost position or place

fore·gath·er *var of* FORGATHER

¹**fore·go** \fȯr'gō\ *vb* -**went**; -**gone**; -**go·ing** : precede

²**forego** *var of* FORGO

fore·go·ing *adj* : preceding

fore·gone *adj* : determined in advance

fore·ground \'fȯr-\ *n* : part of a scene nearest the viewer

fore·hand \'fȯr-\ *n* : a stroke with the palm of the hand turned in the direction of movement —**forehand** *adj*

fore·head \'fȯrəd, 'fȯr,hed\ *n* : part of the face above the eyes

for·eign \'fȯrən\ *adj* **1** : situated outside a place or country and esp. one's own country **2** : belonging to a different place or country **3** : not pertinent **4** : related to or dealing with other nations —**for·eign·er** \-ər\ *n*

fore·know \fȯr'nō\ *vb* -**knew**; -**known**; -**know·ing** : know beforehand —**fore·knowl·edge** *n*

fore·leg \'fȯr-\ *n* : front leg

fore·lock \'fȯr-\ *n* : front lock of hair

fore·man \'fȯrmən\ *n* **1** : spokesman of a jury **2** : workman in charge

fore·most \'fȯr-\ *adj* : first in time, place, or order —**foremost** *adv*

fore·noon \'fȯr-\ *n* : morning

fo·ren·sic \fə'rensik\ *adj* : relating to courts or public speaking or debate

fo·ren·sics \-siks\ *n pl* : art or study of speaking or debating

fore·or·dain \ˌfȯr-\ *vb* : decree beforehand

fore·quar·ter \ˈfȯr-\ *n* : front half on one side of the body of a quadruped

fore·run·ner \ˈfȯr-\ *n* : one that goes before

fore·see \fȯrˈsē\ *vb* -saw; -seen; -see·ing : see or realize beforehand — **fore·see·able** *adj*

fore·shad·ow \ˈfȯr-\ *vb* : hint or suggest beforehand

fore·sight \ˈfȯr-\ *n* : care or provision for the future — **fore·sight·ed** *adj* — **fore·sight·ed·ness** *n*

for·est \ˈfȯrəst\ *n* : large thick growth of trees and underbrush — **for·est·ed** \ˈfȯrəstəd\ *adj* — **for·est·er** \-əstər\ *n* — **for·est·land** \-ˌland\ *n* — **for·est·ry** \-əstrē\ *n*

fore·stall \fȯrˈstȯl, fȯr-\ *vb* : prevent by acting in advance

fore·swear *var of* FORESWEAR

fore·taste \ˈfȯr-\ *n* : advance indication or notion ~ *vb* : anticipate

fore·tell \fȯrˈtel\ *vb* -told; -tell·ing : predict

fore·thought \ˈfȯr-\ *n* : foresight

for·ev·er \fȯrˈevər\ *adv* 1 : for a limitless time 2 : always

for·ev·er·more \-ˌevərˈmȯr\ *adv* : forever

fore·warn \ˈfȯr-\ *vb* : warn beforehand

fore·word \ˈfȯr-\ *n* : preface

¹**forge** \ˈfȯrj\ *n* : smithy ~ *vb* **forged; forg·ing** 1 : form (metal) by heating and hammering 2 : imitate falsely esp. to defraud — **forg·er** *n* — **forg·ery** \-(ə)rē\ *n*

²**forge** *vb* **forged; forg·ing** : move ahead steadily

for·get \fərˈget, fȯr-\ *vb* -got \-ˈgät\; -got·ten \-ˈgätᵊn\ *or* -got; -get·ting 1 : be unable to think of or recall 2 : fail to think of at the proper time — **for·get·ful** \-fəl\ *adj* — **for·get·ful·ly** *adv*

for·get-me-not *n* : small herb with blue or white flowers

for·give \fərˈgiv\ *vb* -gave \-ˈgāv\; -giv·en \-ˈgivən\; -giv·ing : pardon — **for·giv·able** *adj* — **for·give·ness** *n*

for·go, fore·go \fȯrˈgō, fȯr-\ *vb* -went; -gone; -go·ing : give up

fork \ˈfȯrk\ *n* 1 : implement with prongs for lifting, holding, or digging

2 : forked part 3 : a dividing into branches or a place where something branches ~ *vb* 1 : divide into branches 2 : move with a fork — **forked** \ˈfȯrkt, ˈfȯrkəd\ *adj*

fork·lift *n* : hoisting machine with a fork-shaped lever

for·lorn \fərˈlȯrn\ *adj* 1 : deserted 2 : wretched — **for·lorn·ly** *adv*

form \ˈfȯrm\ *n* 1 : shape 2 : set way of doing or saying something 3 : document with blanks to be filled in 4 : behavior or performance with respect to what is expected 5 : mold 6 : variety 7 : one of the ways in which a word is changed to show difference in use ~ *vb* 1 : give form or shape to 2 : train 3 : develop 4 : constitute — **for·ma·tive** \ˈfȯrmətiv\ *adj* — **form·less** \-ləs\ *adj*

for·mal \ˈfȯrməl\ *adj* : following established custom ~ *n* : formal social event — **for·mal·i·ty** \fȯrˈmalətē\ *n* — **for·mal·ize** \ˈfȯrməˌlīz\ *vb* — **for·mal·ly** *adv*

form·al·de·hyde \fȯrˈmaldəˌhīd\ *n* : colorless pungent gas used as a preservative and disinfectant

for·mat \ˈfȯrˌmat\ *n* : general style or arrangement of something — **format** *vb*

for·ma·tion \fȯrˈmāshən\ *n* 1 : a giving form to something 2 : something formed 3 : arrangement

for·mer \ˈfȯrmər\ *adj* : coming before in time — **for·mer·ly** *adv*

for·mi·da·ble \ˈfȯrmədəbəl, fȯrˈmid-\ *adj* 1 : causing fear or dread 2 : very difficult — **for·mi·da·bly** \-blē\ *adv*

for·mu·la \ˈfȯrmyələ\ *n, pl* -las *or* -lae \-ˌlē, -ˌlī\ 1 : set form of words for ceremonial use 2 : recipe 3 : milk mixture for a baby 4 : group of symbols or figures expressing a single rule or idea 5 : set form or method

for·mu·late \-ˌlāt\ *vb* -lat·ed; -lat·ing : state definitely and clearly — **for·mu·la·tion** \ˌfȯrmyəˈlāshən\ *n*

for·ni·ca·tion \ˌfȯrnəˈkāshən\ *n* : illicit sexual intercourse — **for·ni·cate** \ˈfȯrnəˌkāt\ *vb* — **for·ni·ca·tor** \-ˌkātər\ *n*

for·sake \fərˈsāk\ *vb* -sook \-ˈsuk\; -sak·en \-ˈsākən\; -sak·ing : abandon

for·swear, fore·swear \fȯrˈswaer, fȯr-, -ˈswear\ *vb* -swore; -sworn; -swear·ing 1 : renounce under oath 2 : perjure

for·syth·ia \fərˈsithēə\ *n* : shrub grown for its yellow flowers

fort \\'fōrt\\ *n* 1 : fortified place 2 : permanent army post

forte \\'fōrt, 'fōr,tā\\ *n* : something in which a person excels

forth \\'fōrth\\ *adv* : forward

forth·com·ing *adj* : coming or available soon

forth·right *adj* : direct —**forth·right·ly** *adv* —**forth·right·ness** *n*

forth·with *adv* : immediately

for·ti·fy \\'fōrt·ə,fī\\ *vb* **-fied; -fy·ing** : make strong —**for·ti·fi·ca·tion** \\,fōrtəfə'kāshən\\ *n*

for·ti·tude \\'fōrta,t(y)ūd\\ *n* : ability to endure

fort·night \\'fōrt,nīt\\ *n* : 2 weeks —**fort·night·ly** *adj or adv*

for·tress \\'fōrtras\\ *n* : strong fort

for·tu·itous \\fōr'tü(y)ütas\\ *adj* : accidental

for·tu·nate \\'fōrch(ə)nat\\ *adj* 1 : coming by good luck 2 : lucky —**for·tu·nate·ly** *adv*

for·tune \\'fōrchən\\ *n* 1 : apparent cause of something that happens to one unexpectedly 2 : good or bad luck 3 : destiny 4 : wealth

for·tune-tell·er \\-,telər\\ *n* : one who foretells a person's future —**for·tune-tell·ing** \\-iŋ\\ *n or adj*

for·ty \\'fōrtē\\ *n, pl* **forties** : 4 times 10 —**for·ti·eth** \\-ēəth\\ *adj or n* —**forty** *adj or pron*

for·ty-nin·er \\-'nīnər\\ *n* : person in the gold rush to California in 1849

fo·rum \\'fōrəm\\ *n, pl* **-rums** 1 : Roman marketplace 2 : medium for open discussion

for·ward \\'fōrwərd\\ *adj* 1 : being near or at or belonging to the front 2 : brash ~ *adv* : toward what is in front ~ *n* : player near the front of his team ~ *vb* 1 : help onward 2 : send on —**for·ward·er** \\-wərdər\\ *n* —**for·ward·ness** *n*

for·wards \\'fōrwərdz\\ *adv* : forward

fos·sil \\'fäsəl\\ *n* : preserved trace of an ancient plant or animal ~ *adj* : being or originating from a fossil —**fos·sil·ize** *vb*

fos·ter \\'fōstər\\ *adj* : being, having, or relating to substitute parents ~ *vb* : help to grow or develop

fought *past of* FIGHT

foul \\'faül\\ *adj* 1 : offensive 2 : clogged with dirt 3 : abusive 4 : wet and stormy 5 : unfair ~ *n* 1 : a breaking of the rules in a game ~ *adv* : foully ~ *vb* 1 : make or become foul or filthy 2 : tangle —**foul·ly** *adv* —**foul-mouthed** \\-'maüthd, -'maütht\\ *adj* —**foul·ness** *n*

fou·lard \\fü'lärd\\ *n* : lightweight silk

foul-up *n* : error or state of confusion —**foul up** *vb* : bungle

¹found \\'faünd\\ *past of* FIND

²found *vb* 1 : establish —**found·er** *n*

³found *vb* : melt (metal) and pour into a mold —**found·er** *n* —**found·ry** \\'faündrē\\ *n*

foun·da·tion \\faün'dāshən\\ *n* 1 : act of founding 2 : basis for something 3 : endowed institution 4 : supporting structure —**foun·da·tion·al** \\-sh(ə)nəl\\ *adj*

foun·der \\'faündər\\ *vb* : sink

found·ling \\'faün(d)liŋ\\ *n* : abandoned infant that is found

fount \\'faünt\\ *n* : fountain

foun·tain \\'faünt²n\\ *n* 1 : spring of water 2 : source 3 : artificial jet of water

four \\'fōr\\ *n* 1 : one more than 3 2 : 4th in a set or series 3 : something having 4 units —**four** *adj or pron*

four·fold *adj* : quadruple —**four·fold** *adv*

four·score *adj* : 80

four·some \\'fōrsəm\\ *n* : group of 4

four·teen \\fōr'tēn\\ *n* : one more than 13 —**fourteen** *adj or pron* —**four·teenth** \\-'tēnth\\ *adj or n*

fourth \\'fōrth\\ *n* 1 : one that is 4th 2 : one of 4 equal parts of something —**fourth** *adj or adv*

fowl \\'faül\\ *n, pl* **fowl** *or* **fowls** 1 : bird 2 : chicken

fox \\'fäks\\ *n, pl* **fox·es** *or* **fox** 1 : small mammal related to wolves 2 : clever person ~ *vb* : trick —**foxy** \\'fäksē\\ *adj*

fox·glove *n* : flowering plant that provides digitalis

fox·hole \\'fäks,hōl\\ *n* : pit for protection against enemy fire

foy·er \\'fȯiər, 'fȯi,(y)ā\\ *n* : entrance hallway

fra·cas \\'frākəs, 'frak-\\ *n, pl* **-cas·es** \\-əsəz\\ : brawl

frac·tion \\'frakshən\\ *n* 1 : number indicating one or more equal parts of a whole 2 : portion —**frac·tion·al** \\-sh(ə)nəl\\ *adj* —**frac·tion·al·ly** *adv*

frac·tious \\-shəs\\ *adj* : hard to control

frac·ture \\-chər\\ *n* : a breaking of something —**fracture** *vb*

frag·ile \\'frajəl, -,jīl\\ *adj* : easily broken —**fra·gil·i·ty** \\frə'jilətē\\ *n*

frag·ment \\'fragmənt\\ *n* : part broken off ~ \\-,ment\\ *vb* : break into parts —**frag·men·tary** \\'fragmən,terē\\ *adj* —**frag·men·ta·tion** \\,fragmən'tāshən, -,men-\\ *n*

fra·grant \\'frāgrənt\\ *adj* : sweet-

smelling —**fra·grance** \-grəns\ n —
fra·grant·ly adv

frail \'frāl\ adj : weak or delicate —
frail·ty \'frā(ə)ltē\ n

frame \'frām\ vb **framed; fram·ing** 1
: plan 2 : formulate 3 : construct or
arrange 4 : enclose in a frame 5
: make appear guilty ~ n 1 : makeup
of the body 2 : supporting or enclosing structure 3 : state or disposition
(as of mind) —**frame·work** n

franc \'fraŋk\ n : monetary unit (as of
France)

fran·chise \'fran,chīz\ n 1 : special
privilege 2 : the right to vote —**fran-
chi·see** \,fran,chī'zē, -chə-\ n

fran·gi·ble \'franjəbəl\ adj : breakable
—**fran·gi·bil·i·ty** \,franjə'bilətē\ n

¹**frank** \'fraŋk\ adj : direct and sincere
—**frank·ly** adv —**frank·ness** n

²**frank** vb : mark (mail) with a sign
showing it can be mailed free ~ n
: sign on franked mail

frank·furt·er, frank·fort·er \'fraŋk-
fə(r)tər, -,fort-\, **frank·furt, frank·
fort** \-fərt\ n : cooked sausage

frank·in·cense \'fraŋkən,sens\ n : incense resin

fran·tic \'frantik\ adj : wildly excited
—**fran·ti·cal·ly** \-ik(ə)lē\ adv —**fran-
tic·ly** \-iklē\ adv

fra·ter·nal \frə'tərnᵊl\ adj 1 : brotherly
2 : of a fraternity —**fra·ter·nal·
ly** adv

fra·ter·ni·ty \frə'tərnətē\ n, pl **-ties**
: social club of males

frat·er·nize \'fratər,nīz\ vb **-nized;
-niz·ing** 1 : mingle as friends 2 : associate with citizens or troops of a
hostile nation —**frat·er·ni·za·tion**
\,fratərnə-'zāshən\ n

frat·ri·cide \'fratrə,sīd\ n : killing of a
brother or sister —**frat·ri·cid·al**
\,fratrə'sīdᵊl\ adj

fraud \'frod\ n : trickery —**fraud·u-
lent** \'frojələnt\ adj —**fraud·u·lent-
ly** adv

fraught \'frot\ adj : bearing promise
or menace

¹**fray** \'frā\ n : fight

²**fray** vb : wear by rubbing 2 : separate the threads of 3 : irritate

frazzle \'frazəl\ vb **-zled; -zling** : wear
out ~ n : exhaustion

freak \'frēk\ n 1 : something abnormal
or unusual 2 : enthusiast —**freak·ish**
adj —**freak out** vb : experience
nightmarish hallucinations from
drugs

freck·le \'frekəl\ n : brown spot on the
skin —**freckle** vb

free \'frē\ adj **fre·er; fre·est** 1 : having
liberty or independence 2 : not taxed
3 : given without charge 4
: voluntary 5 : not in use 6 : not
fastened ~ adv : without charge —
vb **freed; free·ing** : set free —**free** adv
—**free·born** adj —**free·dom**
\'frēdəm\ n —**free·ly** adv

free·boo·ter \-,bütər\ n : pirate

free-for-all n : fight with no rules

free·load vb : live off another's generosity —**free·load·er** n

free·stand·ing adj : standing without
support

free·way \'frē,wā\ n : expressway

free will n : independent power to
choose —**free·will** adj

freeze \'frēz\ vb **froze** \'frōz\; **fro·zen**
\'frōzᵊn\; **freez·ing** 1 : harden into
ice 2 : become chilled 3 : damage by
frost 4 : stick fast 5 : become motionless 6 : fix at one stage or level
~ n 1 : very cold weather 2 : state
of being frozen —**freez·er** n

freeze-dry vb : preserve by freezing
then drying —**freeze-dried** adj

freight \'frāt\ n 1 : carrying of goods
or payment for this 2 : shipped goods
~ vb : load or ship goods —**freight-
er** n

french fry vb : fry in deep fat —**french
fry** n

fre·net·ic \fri'netik\ adj : frenzied
—**fre·net·i·cal·ly** \-ik(ə)lē\ adv

fren·zy \'frenzē\ n, pl **-zies** : violent
agitation —**fren·zied** \-zēd\ adj

fre·quen·cy \'frēkwənsē\ n, pl **-cies** 1
: frequent or regular occurrence 2
: number of cycles or sound waves
per second

fre·quent \'frēkwənt\ adj : happening
often ~ \'frē'kwent, 'frēkwənt\ vb
: go to habitually —**fre·quent·er** n
—**fre·quent·ly** adv

fres·co \'freskō\ n, pl **-coes** or **-cos**
: painting on fresh plaster

fresh \'fresh\ adj 1 : not salt 2 : invigorating 3 : not preserved 4 : not
stale 5 : like new 6 : insolent —**fresh-
en** \-ən\ vb —**fresh·ly** adv —**fresh·
ness** n

fresh·et \-ət\ n : overflowing stream

fresh·man \-mən\ n : first-year student

fresh·wa·ter n : water that is not
salt

fret \'fret\ vb **-tt-** 1 : worry or become
irritated 2 : fray 3 : agitate ~ n 1
: worn spot 2 : irritation —**fret·ful**
\'fretfəl\ adj —**fret·ful·ly** adv —**fret·
ful·ness** n

fri·a·ble \'frīəbəl\ adj : easily pulverized

fri·ar \ˈfrī(ə)r\ n : member of a religious order

fri·ary \-ē-\ n, pl **-ar·ies** : monastery of friars

fric·as·see \ˈfrikə,sē, ˌfrikəˈ-\ n : meat stewed in a gravy ~ vb **-seed; -see·ing** : stew in gravy

fric·tion \ˈfrikshən\ n 1 : a rubbing between 2 surfaces 2 : clash of opinions —**fric·tion·al** adj

Fri·day \ˈfrīdē\ n : 6th day of the week

friend \ˈfrend\ n : person one likes —**friend·less** \ˈfren(d)ləs\ adj —**friend·li·ness** \ˈfren(d)lēnəs\ n —**friend·ly** adj —**friend·ship** \ˈfren(d)ˌship\ n

frieze \ˈfrēz\ n : ornamental band around a room

frig·ate \ˈfrigət\ n : warship smaller than a destroyer

fright \ˈfrīt\ n : sudden fear —**fright·en** \-ᵊn\ vb —**fright·ful** \-fəl\ adj —**fright·ful·ly** adv —**fright·ful·ness** n

frig·id \ˈfrijəd\ adj : intensely cold —**fri·gid·i·ty** \frijˈidətē\ n

frill \ˈfril\ n 1 : ruffle 2 : pleasing but nonessential addition —**frilly** adj

fringe \ˈfrinj\ n 1 : ornamental border of short hanging threads or strips 2 : border ~ vb : furnish with or serve as a fringe

frisk \ˈfrisk\ vb 1 : leap about 2 : search (a person) esp. for weapons

frisky \ˈfriskē\ adj **frisk·i·er; -est** : frolicsome —**frisk·i·ly** adv —**frisk·i·ness** n

¹frit·ter \ˈfritər\ n : fried batter containing fruit or meat

²fritter vb : waste little by little

friv·o·lous \ˈfriv(ə)ləs\ adj : not important or serious —**fri·vol·i·ty** \frivˈälətē\ n —**friv·o·lous·ly** adv

frizz \ˈfriz\ vb : curl tightly —**frizz** n —**frizzy** adj

fro \ˈfrō\ adv : away

frock \ˈfräk\ n 1 : loose outer garment 2 : dress

frog \ˈfrȯg, ˈfräg\ n 1 : leaping amphibian 2 : hoarseness 3 : ornamental braid fastener 4 : small holder for flowers

frog·man \-ˌman, -mən\ n : underwater swimmer

frol·ic \ˈfrälik\ vb **-icked; -ick·ing** : romp ~ n : fun —**frol·ic·some** \-səm\ adj

from \(ˈ)frəm, ˈfräm\ prep —used to show a starting point

frond \ˈfränd\ n : fern leaf

front \ˈfrənt\ n 1 : face 2 : behavior 3 : main side of a building 4 : forward part 5 : boundary between air

masses ~ vb 1 : face 2 : serve as a front —**fron·tal** \-ᵊl\ adj

front·age \ˈfrəntij\ n : length of boundary line on a street

fron·tier \ˌfrənˈtiər\ n : outer edge of settled territory —**fron·tiers·man** \-ˈtiarzmən\ n

fron·tis·piece \ˈfrəntə,spēs\ n : illustration facing a title page

frost \ˈfrȯst\ n 1 : freezing temperature 2 : ice crystals on a surface ~ vb 1 : cover with frost 2 : put icing on (a cake) —**frosty** adj

frost·bite \ˈfrȯs(t),bīt\ n : partial freezing of part of the body —**frost·bit·ten** \-,bitᵊn\ adj

frost·ing n : icing

froth \ˈfrȯth\ n, pl **froths** \ˈfrȯths, ˈfrȯthz\ : bubbles on a liquid —**frothy** adj

fro·ward \ˈfrō(w)ərd\ adj : willful

frown \ˈfraün\ vb or n : scowl

frow·sy, frow·zy \ˈfraüzē\ adj **-si·er or -zier; -est** : untidy

froze past of FREEZE

frozen past part of FREEZE

fru·gal \ˈfrügəl\ adj : thrifty —**fru·gal·i·ty** \früˈgalətē\ n —**fru·gal·ly** adv

fruit \ˈfrüt\ n 1 : usu. edible and sweet part of a seed plant 2 : result ~ vb : bear fruit —**fruit·cake** n —**fruit·ed** \-əd\ adj —**fruit·ful** adj —**fruit·ful·ness** n —**fruit·less** adj —**fruity** adj

fru·ition \früˈishən\ n : completion

frumpy \ˈfrəmpē\ adj **frump·i·er; -est** : dowdy

frus·trate \ˈfrəs,trāt\ vb **-trat·ed; -trat·ing** 1 : block 2 : cause to fail —**frus·trat·ing·ly** adv —**frus·tra·tion** \ˌfrəsˈtrāshən\ n

¹fry \ˈfrī\ vb **fried; fry·ing** 1 : cook esp. with fat or oil 2 : be cooked by frying ~ n, pl **fries** 1 : something fried 2 : social gathering with fried food

²fry n, pl **fry** : recently hatched fish

fud·dle \ˈfədᵊl\ vb **-dled; -dling** : muddle

fud·dy-dud·dy \ˈfədē,dədē\ n, pl **-dies** : one who is old-fashioned or unimaginative

fudge \ˈfəj\ vb **fudged; fudg·ing** : cheat or exaggerate ~ n : creamy candy

fu·el \ˈfyüəl\ n : substance burned to produce heat or power ~ vb **-eled or -elled; -el·ing or -el·ling** : provide with or take in fuel

fu·gi·tive \ˈfyüjətiv\ adj 1 : running away or trying to escape 2 : not lasting —**fugitive** n

-ful \fəl\ adj suffix 1 : full of 2 : having the qualities of 3 : -able ~ n suffix : quantity that fills

ful·crum \'fu̇lkrəm, 'fəl-\ *n, pl* **-crums** *or* **-cra** \-krə\ : support on which a lever turns

ful·fill, ful·fil \fu̇l'fil\ *vb* **-filled; -fill·ing** 1 : perform 2 : satisfy —**ful·fill·ment** *n*

¹full \'fu̇l\ *adj* 1 : filled 2 : complete 3 : rounded 4 : having an abundance of something ~ *adv* : entirely ~ *n* : utmost degree —**full·ness** \'fu̇lnəs\ *n* —**ful·ly** \-(l)ē\ *adv*

²full *vb* : shrink and thicken woolen cloth —**full·er** *n*

full–fledged \'fu̇l'flejd\ *adj* : fully developed

ful·some \'fu̇lsəm\ *adj* : offensive

fum·ble \'fəmbəl\ *vb* **-bled; -bling** : fail to hold something properly —**fum·ble** *n*

fume \'fyüm\ *n* : irritating gas ~ *vb* **fumed; fum·ing** 1 : give off fumes 2 : show annoyance

fu·mi·gate \-mə,gāt\ *vb* **-gat·ed; -gat·ing** : treat with pest-killing fumes —**fu·mi·gant** \'fyümigənt\ *n* —**fu·mi·ga·tion** \,fyümə'gāshən\ *n*

fun \'fən\ *n* 1 : something providing amusement or enjoyment 2 : enjoyment

func·tion \'fəŋkshən\ *n* 1 : special purpose 2 : formal ceremony or social affair ~ *vb* 1 : serve 2 : operate —**func·tion·al** \-sh(ə)nəl\ *adj* —**func·tion·al·ly** *adv* —**func·tion·less** *adj*

func·tion·ary \-shə,nerē\ *n, pl* **-ar·ies** : official

fund \'fənd\ *n* 1 : store 2 : sum of money intended for a special purpose 3 *pl* : available money ~ *vb* : provide funds for

fun·da·men·tal \,fəndə'mentªl\ *adj* 1 : basic 2 : of central importance or necessity —**fundamental** *n* —**fun·da·men·tal·ly** *adv*

fu·ner·al \'fyün(ə)rəl\ *n* : ceremony for a dead person —**funeral** *adj* —**fu·ne·re·al** \fyü'nirēəl\ *adj*

fun·gi·cide \'fənjə,sīd, 'fəngə-\ *n* : agent that kills fungi —**fun·gi·cid·al** \,fənjə'sīdªl, ,fəngə-\ *adj*

fun·gus \'fəŋgəs\ *n, pl* **fun·gi** \'fən,jī, 'fəŋ,gī\ : lower plant that lacks chlorophyll —**fun·gal** \'fəŋgəl\ *adj* —**fun·gous** \-gəs\ *adj*

funk \'fəŋk\ *n* : state of paralyzed fear

funky \'fəŋkē\ *adj* **funk·i·er; -est** : unconventional and unsophisticated

fun·nel \'fənªl\ *n* 1 : cone-shaped utensil with a tube 2 : ship's smokestack ~ *vb* **-neled; -nel·ing** : move to a central point or into a central channel

fun·nies \'fənēz\ *n pl* : section of comic strips

fun·ny \'fənē\ *adj* **-ni·er; -est** 1 : amusing 2 : strange

fur \'fər\ *n* 1 : hairy coat of a mammal 2 : article of clothing made with fur —**fur** *adj* —**furred** \'fərd\ *adj* —**fur·ry** \-ē\ *adj*

fur·bish \'fərbish\ *vb* : make lustrous or new looking

fu·ri·ous \'fyu̇rēəs\ *adj* : fierce or angry —**fu·ri·ous·ly** *adv*

fur·long \'fər,lȯŋ\ *n* : a unit of length equal to 220 yards

fur·lough \'fərlō\ *n* : authorized absence from duty —**furlough** *vb*

fur·nace \-nəs\ *n* : enclosed structure in which heat is produced

fur·nish \-nish\ *vb* 1 : provide with what is needed 2 : make available for use

fur·nish·ings \-iŋs\ *n pl* 1 : articles or accessories of dress 2 : furniture

fur·ni·ture \'fərnichər\ *n* : movable equipment necessary for a room

fu·ror \'fyu̇r,ȯr\ *n* 1 : anger 2 : sensational craze

fur·ri·er \'fərēər\ *n* : dealer in furs

fur·row \'fərō\ *n* 1 : trench made by a plow 2 : wrinkle or groove —**furrow** *vb*

fur·ther \'fərthər\ *adv* 1 : at or to a more advanced point 2 : more ~ *adj* : additional ~ *vb* : promote —**fur·ther·ance** \-(ə)rəns\ *n*

fur·ther·more \'fərthə(r),mōr\ *adv* : in addition

fur·ther·most \-thər,mōst\ *adj* : most distant

fur·thest \'fərthəst\ *adv or adj* : farthest

fur·tive \'fərtiv\ *adj* : slyly or secretly done —**fur·tive·ly** *adv* —**fur·tive·ness** *n*

fu·ry \'fyu̇rē\ *n, pl* **-ries** 1 : violent anger 2 : violence

¹fuse \'fyüz\ *n* 1 : tube lighted to transmit fire to an explosive 2 *usu* **fuze** : device for exploding a charge ~, **fuze** *vb* **fused** *or* **fuzed; fus·ing** *or* **fuz·ing** : equip with a fuse

²fuse *vb* **fused; fus·ing** 1 : melt and run together 2 : unite ~ *n* : electrical safety device —**fus·i·ble** *adj*

fu·se·lage \'fyüsə,läzh, -zə-\ *n* : main body of an airplane

fu·sil·lade \'fyüsə,läd, -,läd, ,fyüsə'-, -zə-\ *n* : volley of fire

fu·sion \'fyüzhən\ *n* 1 : process of merging by melting 2 : union of atomic nuclei

fuss \'fəs\ *n* 1 : needless bustle or excitement 2 : unusual amount of attention or interest 3 : objection or protest ~ vb 1 : shower flattering attention 2 : pay undue attention to details

fuss·bud·get \-,bəjət\ n : one who fusses about trifles

fussy \'fəsē\ adj **fuss·i·er; -est** 1 : irritable 2 : fastidious —**fuss·i·ly** adv —**fuss·i·ness** n

fu·tile \'fyüt²l, 'fyü,tīl\ adj : useless or vain —**fu·til·i·ty** \fyü'tilətē\ n

fu·ture \'fyüchər\ adj : coming after the present ~ n 1 : time yet to come 2 : what will happen —**fu·tur·is·tic** \,fyüchə'ristik\ adj

fuze var of FUSE

fuzz \'fəz\ n : fine particles or fluff

fuzzy \-ē\ adj **fuzz·i·er; -est** 1 : covered with or like fuzz 2 : indistinct —**fuzz·i·ness** n

-fy \,fī\ vb suffix : make —**-fi·er** \,fī(ə)r\ n suffix

G

g \'jē\ n, pl **g's** or **gs** \'jēz\ 1 : 7th letter of the alphabet 2 : unit of gravitational force

gab \'gab\ vb **-bb-** : chatter —**gab** n —**gab·by** \'gabē\ adj

gab·ar·dine \'gabər,dēn\ n : durable twilled fabric

ga·ble \'gābəl\ n : triangular part of the end of a building —**ga·bled** \-bəld\ adj

gad \'gad\ vb **-dd-** : roam about —**gad·der** n

gad·fly n : persistently critical person

gad·get \'gajət\ n : device —**gad·get·ry** \'gajətrē\ n

gaff \'gaf\ n : metal hook for lifting fish —**gaff** vb

gaffe \'gaf\ n : social blunder

gag \'gag\ vb **-gg-** 1 : prevent from speaking or crying out by stopping up the mouth 2 : retch or cause to retch ~ n 1 : something that stops up the mouth 2 : laugh-provoking remark or act

gage var of GAUGE

gag·gle \'gagəl\ n : flock of geese

gai·ety \'gāətē\ n, pl **-eties** : gay spirits

gai·ly \'gālē\ adv : in a gay manner

gain \'gān\ n 1 : profit 2 : obtaining of profit or possessions 3 : increase ~ vb 1 : get possession of 2 : win 3 : arrive at 4 : increase or increase in 5 : profit —**gain·er** n —**gain·ful** adj —**gain·ful·ly** adv

gain·say \gān'sā\ vb **-said** \-'sād, -'sed\; **-say·ing; -says** \-'sāz, -'sez\ : deny or dispute —**gain·say·er** n

gait \'gāt\ n : manner of walking or running —**gait·ed** adj

gal \'gal\ n : girl

ga·la \'gālə, 'galə, 'gälə\ n : festive celebration —**gala** adj

gal·axy \'galəksē\ n, pl **-ax·ies** : system of stars, nebulas, and dust —**ga·lac·tic** \gə'laktik\ adj

gale \'gāl\ n 1 : strong wind 2 : outburst

¹**gall** \'gȯl\ n 1 : bile 2 : insolence

²**gall** n 1 : sore on the skin caused by chafing 2 : swelling of plant tissue caused by parasites ~ vb 1 : chafe 2 : irritate or vex

gal·lant \gə'lant, -'länt; 'galənt\ n : man very attentive to women ~ \galənt; gə'lant, -'länt\ adj 1 : splendid 2 : brave 3 : polite and attentive to women —**gal·lant·ly** adv —**gal·lant·ry** \'galəntrē\ n

gall·blad·der n : pouch attached to the liver in which bile is stored

gal·le·on \'galēən\ n : large sailing ship formerly used for war and commerce esp. by the Spanish

gal·lery \'gal(ə)rē\ n, pl **-ler·ies** 1 : outdoor balcony 2 : long narrow room or passage 3 : room or building for exhibiting art 4 : spectators —**gal·ler·ied** \-rēd\ adj

gal·ley \'galē\ n, pl **-leys** 1 : old ship propelled by oars and sails 2 : kitchen of a ship or airplane

gal·li·um \'galēəm\ n : bluish white metallic chemical element

gal·li·vant \'galə,vant\ vb 1 : be socially active esp. with members of the opposite sex 2 : travel about for pleasure

gal·lon \'galən\ n : unit of liquid measure equal to 4 quarts

gal·lop \-əp\ n : fast 3-beat gait of a horse —**gallop** vb —**gal·lop·er** n

gal·lows \-ōz\ n, pl **-lows** or **-lows·es** : upright frame for hanging criminals

gall·stone n : abnormal concretion in the gallbladder or bile passages

ga·lore \gə'lȯr\ adj : in abundance

ga·losh \-'läsh\ n : overshoe —usu. pl.

gal·va·nize \'galvə,nīz\ vb **-nized; -niz·ing** 1 : shock into action 2 : coat (iron or steel) with zinc —**gal·va·ni·**

za·tion \,galvənə'zāshən\ n —gal·va·niz·er n

gam·bit \'gambət\ n 1 : opening tactic in chess 2 : risky stratagem

gam·ble \'bəl\ vb -bled; -bling 1 : play a game for stakes 2 : bet 3 : take a chance ~ n : risky undertaking —gam·bler \-blər\ n

gam·bol \-bəl\ vb -boled or -bolled; -bol·ing or -bol·ling : skip about in play —gambol n

game \'gām\ n 1 : playing activity 2 : competition according to rules 3 : animals hunted for sport or food ~ vb gamed; gam·ing : gamble ~ adj 1 : plucky 2 : lame —game·ly adv —game·ness n

game·cock n : male fighting cock

game·keep·er n : person in charge of game animals or birds

gam·ete \gə'mēt, 'gam,ēt\ n : matured germ cell —ga·met·ic \gə'metik\ adj

ga·mine \ga'mēn\ n : charming tomboy

gam·ut \'gamət\ n : entire range or series

gamy or gam·ey \'gāmē\ adj gam·i·er; -est : having the flavor of game esp. when slightly tainted —gam·i·ness n

¹gan·der \'gandər\ n : male goose

²gander n : glance

gang \'gaŋ\ n 1 : group of persons working together 2 : group of criminals ~ vb : attack in a gang —with up

gan·gling \'gaŋgliŋ\ adj : lanky

gan·gli·on \'gaŋglēən\ n, pl -glia \-glēə\ : mass of nerve cells —gan·gli·on·ic \,gaŋglē'änik\ adj

gang·plank n : platform used in boarding or leaving a ship

gan·grene \'gaŋ,grēn, gaŋ'-; 'gan,gan-\ n : local death of body tissue —gangrene vb —gan·gre·nous \'gaŋgrənəs\ adj

gang·ster \'gaŋstər\ n : member of criminal gang

gang·way \-,wā\ n : passage in or out

gan·net \'ganət\ n : large fish-eating marine bird

gan·try \'gantrē\ n, pl -tries : frame structure supported over or around something

gap \'gap\ n 1 : break in a barrier 2 : mountain pass 3 : empty space

gape \'gāp, 'gap\ vb gaped; gap·ing 1 : open widely 2 : stare with mouth open —gape n

ga·rage \gə'räzh, -'räj\ n : building for housing or repairing automobiles ~ vb -raged; -rag·ing : put or keep in a garage

garb \'gärb\ n : clothing ~ vb : dress

gar·bage \'gärbij\ n 1 : food waste 2 : trash

gar·ble \'gärbəl\ vb -bled; -bling : distort the sense or sound of

gar·den \'gärdᵊn\ n 1 : plot for growing fruits, flowers, or vegetables 2 : public recreation area ~ vb : work in a garden —gar·den·er \'gärdnər, -ᵊnər\ n

gar·de·nia \gär'dēnyə\ n : tree or shrub with fragrant white or yellow flowers or the flower

gar·gan·tuan \gär'ganch(ə)wən\ adj : having tremendous size or volume

gar·gle \'gärgəl\ vb -gled; -gling : rinse the throat with liquid —gargle n

gar·goyle \'gär,goil\ n : waterspout in the form of a grotesque human or animal

gar·ish \'ga(ə)rish\ adj : offensively bright or gaudy

gar·land \'gärlənd\ n : wreath of leaves or flowers ~ vb : form into or deck with a garland

gar·lic \'gärlik\ n : herb with pungent bulbs used in cooking —gar·licky \-likē\ adj

gar·ment \-mənt\ n : article of clothing

gar·ner \-nər\ vb : acquire by effort

gar·net \-nət\ n : deep red mineral

gar·nish \-nish\ vb : add decoration to (as food) —garnish n

gar·nish·ee \,gärnə'shē\ vb -eed; -ee·ing : take (as a debtor's wages) by legal authority

gar·nish·ment \'gärnishmənt\ n : attachment of property to satisfy a creditor

gar·ret \'garət\ n : attic

gar·ri·son \-əsən\ n : military post or the troops stationed there —garrison vb

gar·ru·lous \'garələs\ adj : talkative —gar·ru·li·ty \gə'rülətē\ n —gar·ru·lous·ly adv —gar·ru·lous·ness n

gar·ter \'gärtər\ n : band to hold up a stocking or sock

gas \'gas\ n, pl gas·es 1 : fluid (as hydrogen or air) that tends to expand indefinitely 2 : gasoline ~ vb gassed; gas·sing 1 : treat with gas 2 : fill with gasoline —gas·eous \-ēəs, 'gashəs\ adj

gash \'gash\ n : deep long cut —gash vb

gas·ket \'gaskət\ n : material to seal a joint against leakage

gas·light n : light of burning illuminating gas

gas·o·line \'gasə,lēn, ,gasə'-\ n : flammable liquid from petroleum

gasp \'gasp\ vb 1 : catch the breath with emotion 2 : breathe laboriously —**gasp** n

gas·tric \'gastrik\ adj : relating to or located near the stomach

gas·tron·o·my \gas'tränəmē\ n : art of good eating —**gas·tro·nom·ic** \,gastrə'nämik\, **gas·tro·nom·i·cal** \-ikəl\ adj

gate \'gāt\ n : an opening for passage in a wall or fence —**gate·keep·er** n —**gate·post** n

gate·way n : way in or out

gath·er \'gaṯhər\ vb 1 : bring or come together 2 : harvest 3 : pick up little by little 4 : deduce —**gath·er·er** n —**gath·er·ing** n

gauche \'gōsh\ adj : crude or tactless

gaudy \'gȯdē\ adj **gaud·i·er; -est** : tastelessly showy —**gaud·i·ly** \'gȯdᵊlē\ adv —**gaud·i·ness** n

gauge \'gāj\ n : instrument for measuring ~ vb **gauged; gaug·ing** : measure

gaunt \'gȯnt\ adj : thin or emaciated —**gaunt·ness** n

¹**gaunt·let** \-lət\ n 1 : protective glove 2 : challenge to combat

²**gauntlet** n : ordeal

gauze \'gȯz\ n : thin often transparent fabric —**gauzy** adj

gave past of GIVE

gav·el \'gavəl\ n : mallet of a presiding officer or auctioneer

gawk \'gȯk\ vb : stare stupidly

gawky \-ē\ adj **gawk·i·er; -est** : clumsy

gay \'gā\ adj 1 : merry 2 : bright and lively 3 : homosexual —**gay** n

gaze \'gāz\ vb **gazed; gaz·ing** : fix the eyes in a steady intent look —**gaze** n —**gaz·er** n

ga·zelle \gə'zel\ n : small swift antelope

ga·zette \-'zet\ n : newspaper

gaz·et·teer \,gazə'tiər\ n : geographical dictionary

gear \'gir\ n 1 : clothing 2 : equipment 3 : toothed wheel that interlocks with another for transmitting motion ~ vb 1 : provide with gears 2 : make ready or adjust —**gear·ing** n

gear·shift n : mechanism by which automobile gears are shifted

geese pl of GOOSE

gei·sha \'gāshə, 'gē-\ n, pl **-sha** or **-shas** : Japanese girl trained to entertain men

gel·a·tin \'jelətᵊn\ n : sticky substance obtained from animal tissues by boiling —**ge·lat·i·nous** \jə'latnəs, -ᵊnəs\ adj

geld \'geld\ vb : castrate

geld·ing \-iŋ\ n : castrated horse

gem \'jem\ n : cut and polished valuable stone —**gem·stone** n

gen·der \'jendər\ n 1 : sex 2 : division of a class of words (as nouns) that determines agreement of other words

gene \'jēn\ n : complex chemical unit of a chromosome that carries heredity —**gen·ic** \'jēnik, 'je-\, **jen-**\ adj

genera pl of GENUS

n, pl -gies : study of family pedigrees —**ge·ne·a·log·i·cal** \-ē·ə'läjikəl\ adj —**ge·ne·a·log·i·cal·ly** adv —**ge·ne·al·o·gist** \-ē'äləjəst, -'al-\ n

genera pl of GENUS

gen·er·al \'jen(ə)rəl\ adj 1 : relating to the whole 2 : applicable to all of a group 3 : common or widespread ~ n 1 : something that involves or is applicable to the whole 2 : commissioned officer ranking next below a general of the army or a general of the air force 3 : commissioned officer of the highest rank in the marine corps —**gen·er·al·ly** adv —**in general** : for the most part

gen·er·al·i·ty \,jenə'ralətē\ n, pl **-ties** : general statement

general of the air force : commissioned officer of the highest rank in the air force

general of the army : commissioned officer of the highest rank in the army

gen·er·al·ize \'jenə,rīz\ vb **-ated; -at·ing** : reach a general conclusion esp. on the basis of particular instances —**gen·er·al·iza·tion** \-(ə)rələ'zāshən\ n

general of the air force : commissioned officer of the highest rank in the air force

general of the army : commissioned officer of the highest rank in the army

gen·er·ate \'jenə,rāt\ vb **-at·ed; -at·ing** : create or produce

gen·er·a·tion \,jenə'rāshən\ n 1 : living beings constituting a single step in a line of descent 2 : production —**gen·er·a·tive** \'jenə,rātiv, -rət-\ adj

gen·er·a·tor \'jenə,rātər\ n 1 : one that generates 2 : machine that turns mechanical into electrical energy

ge·ner·ic \jə'nerik\ adj 1 : general 2 : not protected by a trademark 3 : relating to a genus —**generic** n

gen·er·ous \'jen(ə)rəs\ adj : freely giving or sharing —**gen·er·os·i·ty** \,jenə'räsətē\ n —**gen·er·ous·ly** adv —**gen·er·ous·ness** n

ge·net·ics \jə'netiks\ n : biology dealing with heredity and variation —**ge·net·ic** \-ik\ adj —**ge·net·i·cal·ly** adv —**ge·net·i·cist** \-'netəsəst\ n

ge·nial \'jēnyəl\ adj : cheerful —**ge·nial·i·ty** \jēnē'alətē, jēn'yal-\ n —**ge·nial·ly** \'jēnyəlē\ adv

ge·nie \'jēnē\ n : supernatural spirit that often takes human form

gen·i·tal \'jenətᵊl\ adj : concerned with reproduction **—gen·i·tal·ly** \-tālē\ adv

gen·i·ta·lia \ˌjenə'tālyə\ n pl : external genital organs

gen·i·tals \'jenətᵊlz\ n pl : genitalia

ge·nius \'jēnyəs\ n 1 : single strongly marked capacity 2 : extraordinary intellectual power of a person having such power

geno·cide \'jenəˌsīd\ n : systematic destruction of a racial or cultural group

genre \'zhänrə, 'zhäⁿrə, 'zhäⁿ(ə)r\ n : category esp. of literary composition

gen·teel \jen'tēl\ adj : polite or refined

gen·tile \'jenˌtīl\ n : person who is not Jewish **—gentile** adj

gen·til·i·ty \jen'tilətē\ n, pl **-ties** 1 : good birth and family 2 : good manners

gen·tle \'jentᵊl\ adj **-tler; -tlest** 1 : of a family of high social station 2 : not harsh, stern, or violent 3 : soft or delicate ~ vb **-tled; -tling** : make gentle **—gen·tle·ness** n **—gent·ly** adv

gen·tle·man \-mən\ n : man of good family or manners **—gen·tle·man·ly** adv

gen·tle·wom·an \-ˌwu̇mən\ n : woman of good family or breeding

gen·try \'jentrē\ n, pl **-tries** : people of good birth or breeding

gen·u·flect \'jenyəˌflekt\ vb : bend the knee in worship **—gen·u·flec·tion** \ˌjenyə'flekshən\ n

gen·u·ine \'jenyəwən\ adj : being the same in fact as in appearance **—gen·u·ine·ly** adv **—gen·u·ine·ness** n

ge·nus \'jēnəs\ n, pl **gen·er·a** \'jenərə\ : category of biological classification

ge·ode \'jēˌōd\ n : stone having a mineral-lined cavity

geo·des·ic \ˌjēə'desik, -'dēs-\ adj : made of a framework of light straight-sided polygons in tension

ge·og·ra·phy \jē'ägrəfē\ n : study of the earth and its climate, products, and inhabitants **—ge·og·ra·pher** \-fər\ n **—geo·graph·ic** \ˌjēə'grafik\, geo·graph·i·cal \-ikəl\ adj **—geo·graph·i·cal·ly** adv

ge·ol·o·gy \jē'äləjē\ n : study of the history of the earth and its life esp. as recorded in rocks **—geo·log·ic** \ˌjēə'läjik\, geo·log·i·cal \-ikəl\ adj **—geo·log·i·cal·ly** adv **—ge·ol·o·gist** \jē'äləjəst\ n

ge·om·e·try \jē'ämətrē\ n, pl **-tries**

: mathematics of the relations, properties, and measurements of solids, surfaces, lines, and angles **—ge·om·e·ter** \-ətər\ n **—geo·met·ric** \ˌjēə'metrik\, geo·met·ri·cal \-rikəl\ adj **—geo·met·ri·cal·ly** \-'fizəsəst\ n

geo·phys·ics \ˌjēə'fiziks\ n : physics of the earth **—geo·phys·i·cal** \-ikəl\ adj **—geo·phys·i·cist** \-'fizəsəst\ n

geo·ther·mal \ˌjēə'thərməl\ adj : relating to the heat of the earth's interior

ge·ra·ni·um \jə'rānēəm\ n : garden plant with clusters of white, pink, or scarlet flowers

ger·bil \'jərbəl\ n : burrowing desert rodent

ge·ri·at·ric \ˌjerē'atrik\ adj : relating to aging or the aged

ge·ri·at·rics \-triks\ n : medicine dealing with the aged and aging

germ \'jərm\ n 1 : microorganism 2 : source or rudiment

ger·mane \(ˌ)jər'mān\ adj : relevant

ger·ma·ni·um \-'mānēəm\ n : grayish white hard chemical element

ger·mi·cide \'jərməˌsīd\ n : agent that destroys germs **—ger·mi·cid·al** \ˌjərmə'sīdᵊl\ adj

ger·mi·nate \'jərməˌnāt\ vb **-nat·ed; -nat·ing** : begin to develop **—ger·mi·na·tion** \ˌjərmə'nāshən\ n

ger·ry·man·der \ˌjerē'mandər, 'jerē,-, ˌgerē'-, 'gerē,-\ vb : divide into election districts so as to give one political party an advantage **—gerrymander** n

ger·und \'jərənd\ n : word having the characteristics of both verb and noun

ge·sta·po \gə'stäpō\ n, pl **-pos** : secret police

ges·ta·tion \je'stāshən\ n : pregnancy or incubation **—ges·tate** \'jes,tāt\ vb

ges·ture \'jeschər\ n 1 : movement of the body or limbs that expresses something 2 : something said or done for its effect on the attitudes of others **—ges·tur·al** \-chərəl\ adj **—gesture** vb

ge·sund·heit \gə'zu̇ntˌhīt\ interj : used to wish good health to one who has just sneezed

get \'get\ vb **got** \'gät\; **got** or **got·ten** \'gätᵊn\; **get·ting** 1 : gain or be in possession of 2 : succeed in coming or going 3 : cause to come or go or to be in a certain condition or position 4 : become 5 : be subjected to 6 : understand 7 : be obliged **—get along** vb 1 : get by 2 : be on friendly terms **—get by** : meet one's needs

get·away \'getəˌwā\ n 1 : escape 2 : a starting or getting under way

gey·ser \'gīzər\ *n* : spring that intermittently shoots up hot water and steam

ghast·ly \'gastlē\ *adj* **-li·er; -est** : horrible or shocking

gher·kin \'gərkən\ *n* : small pickle

ghet·to \'getō\ *n, pl* **-tos** *or* **-toes** : part of a city in which members of a minority group live

ghost \'gōst\ *n* : disembodied soul —**ghost·ly** *adv*

ghost·write *vb* **-wrote; -writ·ten** : write for and in the name of another —**ghost·writ·er** *n*

ghoul \'gül\ *n* : legendary evil being that feeds on corpses —**ghoul·ish** *adj*

GI \(')jē'ī\ *n, pl* **GI's** *or* **GIs** : member of the U.S. armed forces

gi·ant \'jīənt\ *n* **1** : huge legendary being **2** : something very large or very powerful —**giant** *adj*

gib·ber \'jibər\ *vb* **-bered; -ber·ing** : speak rapidly and foolishly

gib·ber·ish \'jib(ə)rish\ *n* : unintelligible speech or language

gib·bon \'gibən\ *n* : manlike ape

gibe \'jīb\ *vb* **gibed; gib·ing** : jeer at —**gibe** *n*

gib·lets \'jibləts\ *n pl* : edible fowl viscera

gid·dy \'gidē\ *adj* **-di·er; -est 1** : silly **2** : dizzy —**gid·di·ness** *n*

gift \'gift\ *n* **1** : something given **2** : talent —**gift·ed** *adj*

gi·gan·tic \jī'gantik\ *adj* : very big

gig·gle \'gigəl\ *vb* **-gled; -gling** : laugh in a silly manner —**giggle** *n* —**gig·gly** \-(ə)lē\ *adj*

gig·o·lo \'jigə,lō\ *n, pl* **-los** : man living on the earnings of a woman

Gi·la monster \'hēlə-\ *n* : large venomous lizard

gild \'gild\ *vb* **gild·ed** \'gildəd\ *or* **gilt** \'gilt\; **gild·ing** : cover with or as if with gold —**gild·ing** *n*

gill \'gil\ *n* : organ of a fish for obtaining oxygen from water

gilt \'gilt\ *adj* : gold-colored ~ *n* : gold or goldlike substance on the surface of an object

gim·bal \'gimbəl, 'jim-\ *n* : device that allows something to incline freely

gim·let \'gimlət\ *n* : small boring tool

gim·mick \'gimik\ *n* : new and ingenious scheme, feature, or device —**gim·mick·ry** *n* —**gim·micky** \-ikē\ *adj*

gimpy \'gimpē\ *adj* : lame

¹gin \'jin\ *n* : machine to separate seeds from cotton —**gin** *vb*

²gin *n* : clear liquor flavored with juniper berries

gin·ger \'jinjər\ *n* : pungent aromatic spice from a tropical plant —**gin·ger·bread** *n*

gin·ger·ly *adj* : very cautious or careful —**gingerly** *adv*

ging·ham \'giŋəm\ *n* : cotton clothing fabric

gin·gi·vi·tis \,jinjə'vītəs\ *n* : inflammation of the gums

gink·go \'giŋ(,)kō\ *n, pl* **-goes** *or* **-gos** : tree of eastern China

girt \'gərt\; **gird·ing 1** : encircle or **gird** \'gərd\ *vb* **gird·ed** *or* : aromatic root of a Chinese herb

gi·raffe \jə'raf\ *n* : African mammal with a very long neck

gird \'gərd\ *vb* **gird·ed** \'gərdəd\ *or* **girt** \'gərt\; **gird·ing 1** : encircle or fasten with or as if with a belt **2** : prepare

gird·er \'gərdər\ *n* : horizontal supporting beam

gir·dle \-ᵊl\ *n* : woman's supporting undergarment ~ *vb* : surround

girl \'gərl\ *n* **1** : female child **2** : sweetheart —**girl·hood** \-,hùd\ *n* —**girl·ish** *adj*

girlfriend *n* : frequent or regular female companion of a boy or man

girth \'gərth\ *n* : measure around something

gist \'jist\ *n* : main point of a matter

give \'giv\ *vb* **gave** \'gāv\; **giv·en** \'givən\; **giv·ing 1** : put into the possession or keeping of another **2** : pay **3** : perform **4** : contribute or donate **5** : produce **6** : utter **7** : yield to force, strain, or pressure ~ *n* : capacity or tendency to yield to force or strain —**give in** *vb* : surrender —**give out** *vb* : become used up or exhausted —**give up** *vb* **1** : let out of one's control **2** : cease from trying, doing, or hoping

give·away *n* **1** : unintentional betrayal **2** : something given free

giv·en \'givən\ *adj* **1** : prone or disposed **2** : having been specified

giz·zard \'gizərd\ *n* : muscular usu. horny-lined enlargement following the crop of a bird

gla·cial \'glāshəl\ *adj* : of or relating to glaciers —**gla·cial·ly** *adv*

gla·cier \'glāshər\ *n* : large body of ice moving slowly

glad \'glad\ *adj* **-dd- 1** : experiencing or causing pleasure, joy, or delight **2** : very willing —**glad·den** \-ᵊn\ *vb* —**glad·ly** *adv* —**glad·ness** *n*

glade \'glād\ *n* : grassy open space in a forest

glad·i·a·tor \'gladē,ātər\ *n* : one who fought to the death for the entertainment of ancient Romans —**glad·i·a·to·ri·al** \,gladē'tôrēəl\ adj

glad·i·o·lus \,gladē'ōləs\ n, pl **-li** \-,)lē, -,lī\ : plant related to the irises

glam·our, glam·or \'glamər\ n : romantic or exciting attractiveness —**glam·or·ize** \-ə,rīz\ vb —**glam·or·ous** \-(ə)rəs\ adj

glance \'glans\ vb **glanced; glanc·ing 1** : strike and fly off to one side **2** : give a quick look ~ n : quick look

gland \'gland\ n : group of cells that secretes a substance —**glan·du·lar** \'glanjələr\ adj

glans \'glanz\ n, pl **glan·des** \-,dēz\ : conical vascular body forming the extremity of the penis or clitoris

glare \'glaər\ vb **glared; glar·ing 1** : shine with a harsh dazzling light **2** : gaze angrily ~ n **1** : harsh dazzling light **2** : angry stare —**glar·ing** \'gla(ə)riŋ\ adj —**glar·ing·ly** adv

glass \'glas\ n **1** : usu. transparent substance made by melting sand and other materials **2** : something made of glass **3** pl : lenses used to correct defects of vision —**glass** adj —**glass·ful** \-,fûl\ n —**glass·ware** \-,waər\ n —**glassy** adj

glass-blow·ing n : art of shaping a mass of molten glass by blowing air into it —**glass·blow·er** n

glau·co·ma \glaú'kōmə, glò-\ n : state of increased pressure within the eyeball

glaze \'glāz\ vb **glazed; glaz·ing 1** : furnish with glass **2** : apply glaze to ~ n : glassy surface or coating

gla·zier \'glāzhər\ n : one who sets glass in window frames

gleam \'glēm\ n **1** : transient or partly obscured light **2** : faint trace ~ vb : send out gleams

glean \'glēn\ vb : collect little by little —**glean·able** n —**glean·er** n

glee \'glē\ n : joy —**glee·ful** adj

glen \'glen\ n : valley

glib \'glib\ adj **-bb-** : speaking or spoken with ease —**glib·ly** adv

glide \'glīd\ vb **glid·ed; glid·ing** : move or descend smoothly and effortlessly ~ n : smooth motion or descent

glid·er \'glīdər\ n : winged aircraft having no engine

glim·mer \'glimər\ vb : shine faintly or unsteadily ~ n **1** : faint light **2** : small amount

glimpse \'glimps\ vb **glimpsed; glimps·ing** : take a brief look at —**glimpse** n

glint \'glint\ vb : gleam or sparkle —**glint** n

glis·ten \'glis²n\ vb : shine or sparkle by reflection —**glisten** n

glit·ter \'glitər\ vb : shine with brilliant or metallic luster ~ n : small glittering ornaments —**glit·tery** adj

gloat \'glōt\ vb : think of something with pride or self-satisfaction

glob \'gläb\ n : large rounded lump

glob·al \'glōbəl\ adj : worldwide —**glob·al·ly** adv

globe \'glōb\ n **1** : sphere **2** : the earth or a model of it

glob·u·lar \'gläbyələr\ adj **1** : round **2** : made up of globules

glob·ule \'gläbyül\ n : tiny ball

glock·en·spiel \'gläkən,s(h)pēl\ n : portable musical instrument consisting of tuned metal bars

gloom \'glüm\ n **1** : darkness **2** : sadness —**gloom·i·ly** adv —**gloom·i·ness** n —**gloomy** adj

glop \'gläp\ n : messy mass or mixture

glo·ri·fy \'glōrə,fī\ vb **-fied; -fy·ing 1** : make to seem glorious **2** : worship —**glo·ri·fi·ca·tion** \,glōrəfə'kāshən\ n

glo·ry \'glōrē\ n, pl **-ries 1** : praise or honor offered in worship **2** : cause for praise or renown **3** : magnificence **4** : heavenly bliss ~ vb **-ried; -ry·ing** : rejoice proudly —**glo·ri·ous** \'glōrēəs\ adj —**glo·ri·ous·ly** adv

¹**gloss** \'gläs, 'glòs\ n : luster ~ vb : treat rapidly or superficially —**gloss·i·ly** \-ə'lē\ adv —**gloss·i·ness** \-ēnəs\ n —**glossy** \-ē\ adj

²**gloss** n : brief explanation or translation ~ vb : translate or explain

glos·sa·ry \'gläs(ə)rē, 'glòs-\ n, pl **-ries** : dictionary —**glos·sar·i·al** \glä-'sarēəl, glò-\ adj

glove \'gləv\ n : hand covering with sections for each finger

glow \'glō\ vb **1** : shine with or as if with intense heat **2** : show exuberance ~ n : brightness or warmth of color or feeling

glow·er \'glaú(ə)r\ vb : stare angrily —**glower** n

glow·worm n : insect or insect larva that emits light

glu·cose \'glü,kōs\ n : sugar found esp. in blood, plant sap, and fruits

glue \'glü\ n : substance used for sticking things together —**glue** vb —**glu·ey** \'glüē\ adj

glum \'gləm\ adj **-mm- 1** : sullen **2** : dismal

glut \'glət\ vb **-tt-** : fill to excess —**glut** n

glu·ten \'glüt⁹n\ n : gluey protein substance in flour

glu·ti·nous \'glüt⁹nəs\ adj : sticky

glut·ton \'glət⁹n\ n : one who eats to excess —**glut·ton·ous** \'glət⁹nəs\ adj —**glut·tony** \'glät⁹nē\ n

glyc·er·in, glyc·er·ine \'glis(ə)rən\ n : syrupy liquid used as a solvent and moistener

gnarled \'närld\ adj 1 : knotty 2 : gloomy or sullen

gnash \'nash\ vb : grind (as teeth) together

gnat \'nat\ n : small biting fly

gnaw \'nȯ\ vb : bite or chew on —**gnaw·er** \'nȯ(ə)r\ n

gnome \'nōm\ n : dwarf of folklore —**gnom·ish** adj

gnu \'n(y)ü\ n, pl **gnu** or **gnus** : large African antelope

go \'gō\ vb **went** \'went\; **gone** \'gȯn, 'gän\; **go·ing** \'gȯiŋ\; **goes** \'gōz\ 1 : move, proceed, run, or pass 2 : leave 3 : extend or lead 4 : sell or amount —with *for* 5 : happen 6 —used in present participle to show intent or imminent action 7 : become 8 : fit or harmonize 9 : belong ~ n, pl **goes** 1 : act or manner of going 2 : vigor 3 : attempt —**go back on** : betray —**go by the board** : be discarded —**go for** : favor —**go off** : explode —**go one better** : outdo —**go over** 1 : examine 2 : study —**go to town** : be very successful —**on the go** : constantly active

goad \'gōd\ n : something that urges —**goad** vb

goal \'gōl\ n 1 : mark to reach in a race 2 : purpose 3 : object in a game through which a ball is propelled

goal·ie \'gōlē\ n : player who defends the goal

goal·keep·er n : goalie

goat \'gōt\ n : horned ruminant mammal related to the sheep —**goat·skin** n

goa·tee \gō'tē\ n : small pointed beard

gob \'gäb\ n : lump

¹**gob·ble** \'gäbəl\ vb **-bled; -bling** : eat greedily

²**gobble** vb **-bled; -bling** : make the noise of a turkey (**gobbler**)

gob·ble·dy·gook, gob·ble·de·gook \'gäbəldē'gük, -'gük\ n : nonsense

gob·let \'gäblət\ n : large stemmed drinking glass

gob·lin \-lən\ n : ugly mischievous sprite

god \'gäd, 'gȯd\ n 1 cap : supreme being 2 : being with supernatural powers —**god·dess** \-əs\ n —**god·like** adj —**god·ly** adj

god·child n : person one sponsors at baptism —**god·daugh·ter** n —**god·son** n

god·less \-ləs\ adj : not believing in God —**god·less·ness** n

god·par·ent n : sponsor at baptism —**god·fa·ther** n —**god·moth·er** n

god·send \-,send\ n : something needed that comes unexpectedly

goes pres 3d sing of GO

go·get·ter \'gō,getər\ n : enterprising person —**go·get·ting** \-iŋ\ adj or n

gog·gle \'gägəl\ vb **-gled; -gling** : stare wide-eyed

gog·gles \-əlz\ n pl : protective glasses

go·ings-on \,gȯiŋz'ȯn, -'än\ n pl : events

goi·ter \'gȯitər\ n : abnormally enlarged thyroid gland —**goi·trous** adj

gold \'gōld\ n : malleable yellow metallic chemical element —**gold·smith** \-,smith\ n

gold·brick \-,brik\ n : person who shirks duty —**goldbrick** vb

gold digger n : woman interested only in a man's money

gold·en \'gōldən\ adj 1 : made of, containing, or relating to gold 2 : having the color of gold 3 : precious or favorable

gold·en·rod \'gōldən,räd\ n : herb having tall stalks with tiny yellow flowers

gold·finch \'gōl(d),finch\ n : yellow American finch

gold·fish \-,fish\ n : small usu. orange or golden carp

golf \'gälf, 'gȯlf\ n : game played by hitting a small ball (**golf ball**) with clubs (**golf clubs**) into holes placed in a field (**golf course**) —**golf** vb —**golf·er** n

go·nad \'gō,nad\ n : sex gland

gon·do·la \'gändələ (usual for 1), gän-'dō-\ n 1 : long narrow boat used on the canals of Venice 2 : car suspended from a cable

gon·do·lier \,gändə'liər\ n : gondola boatman

gone \'gȯn\ adj 1 : past 2 : involved

gon·er \'gȯnər\ n : hopeless case

gong \'gäŋ, 'gȯŋ\ n : metallic disk that sounds when struck

gon·or·rhea \,gänə'rēə\ n : bacterial inflammatory venereal disease of the genital tract —**gon·or·rhe·al** \-'rēəl\ adj

goo \'gü\ n : thick or sticky substance —**goo·ey** \-ē\ adj

good \'gúd\ adj **bet·ter** \'betər\; **best**

\\'best\\ 1 : satisfactory 2 : salutary 3 : considerable 4 : desirable 5 : well-behaved, kind, or virtuous ~ *n* 1 : something good 2 : benefit 3 *pl* : personal property 4 *pl* : wares — **good—heart·ed** \\-'härtəd\\ *adj* — **good·ish** *adj* — **good-look·ing** *adj* — **good-na·tured** *adj* — **good·ness** *n* — **good-tem·pered** \\-'tempərd\\ *adj*

good-bye, good·by \\gud'bī, gə(d)-\\ *n* : parting remark

good-for-noth·ing *n* : idle worthless person

Good Friday *n* : Friday before Easter observed as the anniversary of the crucifixion of Christ

good·ly *adj* **-li·er; -est** : considerable

good·will *n* 1 : good intention 2 : kindly feeling

goody \\-ē\\ *n, pl* **good·ies** : something that is good esp. to eat

goody-goody *adj* : affectedly or annoyingly sweet or self-righteous — **goody-goody** *n*

goof \\'güf\\ *vb* 1 : blunder 2 : waste time —usu. with *off* or *around* — **goof** *n* —**goof-off** *n*

goofy \\'güfē\\ *adj* **goof·i·er; -est** : crazy — **goof·i·ness** *n*

goose \\'güs\\ *n, pl* **geese** \\'gēs\\ : large bird with webbed feet

goose·ber·ry \\'güs,berē, 'güz-, -b(ə)rē\\ *n* : berry of a shrub related to the currant

goose·flesh *n* : roughening of the skin caused usu. by cold or fear

goose pimples *n pl* : gooseflesh

go·pher \\'gōfər\\ *n* : burrowing rodent

¹**gore** \\'gōr\\ *n* : blood

²**gore** *vb* **gored; gor·ing** : pierce or wound with a horn or tusk

¹**gorge** \\'gōrj\\ *n* : narrow ravine

²**gorge** *vb* **gorged; gorg·ing** : eat greedily

gor·geous \\'gōrjəs\\ *adj* : supremely beautiful

go·ril·la \\gə'rilə\\ *n* : African manlike ape

gory \\'gōrē\\ *adj* **gor·i·er; -est** : bloody

gos·hawk \\'gäs,hók\\ *n* : long-tailed hawk with short rounded wings

gos·ling \\'gäzliŋ, 'góz-\\ *n* : young goose

gos·pel \\'gäspəl\\ *n* 1 : teachings of Christ and the apostles 2 : something accepted as infallible truth — **gospel** *adj*

gos·sa·mer \\'gäsəmər, gäz(ə)mər\\ *n* 1 : film of cobweb 2 : light filmy substance

gos·sip \\'gäsəp\\ *n* 1 : person who re- veals personal information 2 : rumor or report of an intimate nature ~ *vb* : spread gossip — **gos·sipy** *adj*

got *past of* GET

Goth·ic \\'gäthik\\ *adj* : relating to a medieval style of architecture

gotten *past part of* GET

gouge \\'gaúj\\ *n* 1 : rounded chisel 2 : cavity or groove scooped out ~ *vb* **gouged; goug·ing** 1 : cut or scratch a groove in 2 : overcharge — **goug·er** *n*

gou·lash \\'gü,läsh, -,lash\\ *n* : beef stew with vegetables and paprika

gourd \\'gōrd, 'gùrd\\ *n* 1 : any of a group of vines including the cucumber, squash, and melon 2 : inedible hard-shelled fruit of a gourd

gour·mand \\'gùr,mänd\\ *n* : person who loves good food and drink

gour·met \\'gùr,mā, gùr'mā\\ *n* : connoisseur of food and drink

gout \\'gaút\\ *n* : disease marked by painful inflammation and swelling of the joints — **gouty** *adj*

gov·ern \\'gəvərn\\ *vb* 1 : control and direct policy in 2 : guide or influence strongly 3 : restrain — **gov·ern·ment** \\-ər(n)mənt\\ *n* — **gov·ern·men·tal** \\,gəvər(n)'ment⁹l\\ *adj*

gov·ern·ess \\'gəvərnəs\\ *n* : female teacher in a private home

gov·er·nor \\'gəv(ə)nər, 'gəvərnər\\ *n* 1 : head of a political unit 2 : automatic speed-control device — **gov·er·nor·ship** *n*

gown \\'gaún\\ *n* 1 : loose flowing outer garment 2 : woman's formal evening dress — **gown** *vb*

grab \\'grab\\ *vb* **-bb-** : take by sudden grasp — **grab** *n*

grace \\'grās\\ *n* 1 : unmerited divine assistance 2 : short prayer before or after a meal 3 : respite 4 : ease of movement or bearing ~ *vb* **graced; grac·ing** 1 : honor 2 : adorn — **grace·ful** \\-fəl\\ *adj* — **grace·ful·ly** *adv* — **grace·ful·ness** *n* — **grace·less** *adj*

gra·cious \\'grāshəs\\ *adj* : marked by kindness and courtesy or charm and taste — **gra·cious·ly** *adv* — **gra·cious·ness** *n*

grack·le \\'grakəl\\ *n* : American blackbird

gra·da·tion \\grā'dāshən, grə-\\ *n* : step, degree, or stage in a series

grade \\'grād\\ *n* 1 : stage in a series, order, or ranking 2 : division of school representing one year's work 3 : mark of accomplishment in school 4 : degree of slope ~ *vb* **grad·ed; grad·ing** 1 : arrange in grades 2

137

grader • gratuitous

: make level or evenly sloping **3** : give a grade to —**grad·er** n

grade school n : school including the first 6 or 8 grades

gra·di·ent \'grādēənt\ n : slope

grad·u·al \'graj(əw)əl\ adj : going by steps or degrees —**grad·u·al·ly** adv

grad·u·ate \'grajə,wət, -ə,wāt\ n : holder of a diploma ~ adj : of or relating to studies beyond the bachelor's degree ~ \-ə,wāt\ vb -**at·ed; -at·ing 1** : grant or receive a diploma **2** : mark with degrees of measurement —**grad·u·a·tion** \,grajə-'wāshən\ n

graf·fi·to \gra'fētō, grə-\ n, pl -**ti** \-,(,)ē\ : inscription on a wall

graft \'graft\ vb : join one thing to another so that they grow together ~ n **1** : grafted plant **2** : the getting of money dishonestly or the money so gained —**graft·er** n

grain \'grān\ n **1** : seeds or fruits of cereal grasses **2** : small hard particle **3** : arrangement of fibers in wood —**grained** \'grānd\ adj —**grain·field** n —**grainy** adj

gram, gramme \'gram\ n : metric unit of weight nearly equal to one cubic centimeter of water at its maximum density

gram·mar \'gramər\ n : study of words and their functions and relations in the sentence —**gram·mar·i·an** \grə'mereən, -'mar-\ n —**gram·mat·i·cal** \-'matikəl\ adj —**gram·mat·i·cal·ly** adv

grammar school n : grade school

gra·na·ry \'grān(ə)rē, 'gran-\ n, pl -**ries** : storehouse for grain

grand \'grand\ adj **1** : large or striking in size or scope **2** : fine and imposing **3** : very good —**grand·ly** \'gran(d)lē\ adv —**grand·ness** \-nəs\ n

grand·child \'gran(d),chīld\ n : child of one's son or daughter —**grand·daugh·ter** \-,dotər\ n —**grand·son** n

gran·deur \'granjər\ n : quality or state of being grand

gran·dil·o·quence \gran'diləkwəns\ n : pompous speaking —**gran·dil·o·quent** \-kwənt\ adj

gran·di·ose \'grandē,ōs, ,grandē-'\ adj **1** : impressive **2** : affectedly splendid —**gran·di·ose·ly** adv

grand·par·ent \-,parənt\ n : parent of one's father or mother —**grand·fa·ther** \-,fäthər, -,fath-\ n —**grand·moth·er** \-,məthər\ n

grand·stand \-,stand\ n : usu. roofed stand for spectators

grange \'grānj\ n : farmers association

gran·ite \'granət\ n : hard igneous rock —**gra·nit·ic** \gra'nitik\ adj

grant \'grant\ vb **1** : consent to **2** : give **3** : admit as true ~ n **1** : act of granting **2** : something granted —**grant·ee** \grant'ē\ n —**grant·er** \'grantər\ n —**grant·or** \-ər-, -,ȯr\ n

gran·u·late \'granyə,lāt\ vb -**lat·ed; -lat·ing** : form into grains or crystals —**gran·u·la·tion** \,granyə'lāshən\ n

gran·ule \'granyül\ n : small particle —**gran·u·lar** \-yələr\ adj —**gran·u·lar·i·ty** \,granyə'larətē\ n

grape \'grāp\ n : smooth juicy edible berry of a woody vine (**grape-vine**)

grape·fruit n : large edible yellow-skinned citrus fruit

graph \'graf\ n : diagram that shows relationships between things —**graph** vb

graph·ic \'grafik\ adj **1** : vividly described **2** : relating to the arts (**graphic arts**) of representation and printing on flat surfaces —**graph·i·cal·ly** \-ik(ə)lē\ adv —**graph·ics** \-iks\ n

graph·ite \'graf,īt\ n : soft carbon used for lead pencils and lubricants

grap·nel \'grapnəl\ n : small anchor with several claws

grap·ple \'grapəl\ vb -**pled; -pling 1** : seize or hold with or as if with a hooked implement **2** : wrestle

grasp \'grasp\ vb **1** : take or seize firmly **2** : understand ~ n **1** : one's hold or control **2** : one's reach **3** : comprehension

grass \'gras\ n : plant with jointed stem and narrow leaves —**grassy** adj

grass·hop·per \-,häpər\ n : leaping plant-eating insect

grass·land n : land covered with grasses

¹**grate** \'grāt\ n **1** : framework with bars across it **2** : frame of iron bars to hold burning fuel

²**grate** vb **grat·ed; -ing 1** : pulverize by rubbing against something rough **2** : irritate —**grat·er** n —**grat·ing·ly** adv

grate·ful \'grātfəl\ adj : thankful or appreciative —**grate·ful·ly** adv —**grate·ful·ness** n

grat·i·fy \'grata,fī\ vb -**fied; -fy·ing** : give pleasure to —**grat·i·fi·ca·tion** \,gratəfə'kāshən\ n

grat·ing \'grātiŋ\ n : grate

gra·tis \'gratəs, 'grāt-\ adv or adj : free

grat·i·tude \'gratə,t(y)üd\ n : state of being grateful

gra·tu·itous \grə't(y)üətəs\ adj **1** : free **2** : uncalled-for

gra·tu·i·ty \-ətē\ *n, pl* **-ities** : tip

¹**grave** \'grāv\ *n* : place of burial —**grave·stone** *n* —**grave·yard** *n*

²**grave** *adj* **grav·er; grav·est 1** : threatening great harm or danger **2** : solemn —**grave·ly** *adv* —**grave·ness** *n*

grav·el \'gravəl\ *n* : loose rounded fragments of rock —**grav·el·ly** *adj*

grav·i·tate \'gravə,tāt\ *vb* **-tat·ed; -tat·ing** : move toward something

grav·i·ta·tion \,gravə'tāshən\ *n* : natural force of attraction that tends to draw bodies together —**grav·i·ta·tion·al** \-sh(ə)nəl\ *adj* —**grav·i·ta·tion·al·ly** *adv* —**grav·i·ta·tive** \'gravə,tātiv\ *adj*

grav·i·ty \'gravətē\ *n, pl* **-ties 1** : serious importance **2** : attraction of bodies toward the center of the earth —**gravity** *adj*

gra·vy \'grāvē\ *n, pl* **-vies** : sauce made from thickened juices of cooked meat

gray \'grā\ *adj* **1** : of the color gray **2** : having gray hair ~ *n* : neutral color between black and white ~ *vb* : make or become gray —**gray·ish** \-ish\ *adj* —**gray·ness** *n*

¹**graze** \'grāz\ *vb* **grazed; graz·ing** : feed on herbage or pasture —**graz·er** *n*

²**graze** *vb* **grazed; graz·ing** : touch lightly in passing

grease \'grēs\ *n* : thick oily material or fat ~ \'grēs, 'grēz\ *vb* **greased; greas·ing** : smear or lubricate with grease —**greasy** \'grēsē, -zē\ *adj*

great \'grāt, *South also* 'gre(ə)t\ *adj* **1** : large in size or number **2** : larger than usual —**great·ly** *adv* —**great·ness** *n*

grebe \'grēb\ *n* : diving bird related to the loon

greed \'grēd\ *n* : selfish desire beyond reason —**greed·i·ly** \-ᵊlē\ *adv* —**greed·i·ness** \-ēnəs\ *n* —**greedy** \'grēdē\ *adj*

green \'grēn\ *adj* **1** : of the color green **2** : unripe **3** : inexperienced ~ *vb* : become green ~ *n* **1** : color between blue and yellow **2** *pl* : leafy parts of plants —**green·ish** *adj* —**green·ness** \'grēnnəs\ *n*

green·ery \'grēn(ə)rē\ *n, pl* **-er·ies** : green foliage or plants

green·horn *n* : inexperienced person

green·house *n* : glass structure for the growing of plants

greet \'grēt\ *vb* **1** : address with expressions of kind wishes **2** : react to —**greet·er** *n*

greet·ing *n* **1** : friendly address on meeting **2** *pl* : best wishes

gre·gar·i·ous \gri'garēəs, -'ger-\ *adj* : social or companionable —**gre·gar·i·ous·ly** *adv* —**gre·gar·i·ous·ness** *n*

grem·lin \'gremlən\ *n* : small mischievous gnome

gre·nade \grə'nād\ *n* : small missile filled with explosive or chemicals

grew *past of* GROW

grey *var of* GRAY

grey·hound \'grā,haûnd\ *n* : tall slender dog noted for speed

grid \'grid\ *n* **1** : grate **2** : metal plate for conducting current in a storage battery

grid·dle \'gridᵊl\ *n* : flat metal surface for cooking

grid·iron \'grid,ī(ə)rn\ *n* **1** : grate for broiling **2** : football field

grief \'grēf\ *n* **1** : emotional suffering caused by or as if by bereavement **2** : disaster

griev·ance \'grēvəns\ *n* : complaint

grieve \'grēv\ *vb* **grieved; griev·ing** : feel or cause to feel grief or sorrow

griev·ous \'grēvəs\ *adj* **1** : oppressive **2** : causing grief or sorrow —**griev·ous·ly** *adv*

grill \'gril\ *vb* **1** : cook on a grill **2** : question intensely ~ *n* **1** : griddle **2** : informal restaurant

grille, grill \'gril\ *n* : grate forming a barrier or screen —**grill·work** *n*

grim \'grim\ *adj* **-mm- 1** : harsh and forbidding in appearance **2** : relentless —**grim·ly** *adv* —**grim·ness** *n*

gri·mace \'griməs, grim'ās\ *n* : facial expression of disgust —**grimace** *vb*

grime \'grīm\ *n* : embedded or accumulated dirt —**grimy** *adj*

grin \'grin\ *vb* **-nn-** : smile so as to show the teeth —**grin** *n*

grind \'grīnd\ *vb* **ground** \'graûnd\; **grind·ing 1** : reduce to powder **2** : wear down or sharpen by friction **3** : operate or produce by turning a crank ~ *n* : monotonous labor or routine —**grind·er** *n* —**grind·stone** \'grīn,stōn\ *n*

grip \'grip\ *vb* **-pp-** : seize or hold firmly ~ *n* **1** : grasp **2** : control **3** : device for holding

gripe \'grīp\ *vb* **griped; grip·ing 1** : cause pains in the bowels **2** : complain —**gripe** *n*

grippe \'grip\ *n* : influenza

gris·ly \'grizlē\ *adj* **-li·er; -est** : horrible or gruesome

grist \'grist\ *n* : grain to be ground or already ground —**grist·mill** *n* gris•tle \'grisəl\ n : cartilage —gris•tly \-(ə)lē\ adj

grit \'grit\ n 1 : hard sharp granule 2 : material composed of granules 3 : unyielding courage — vb -tt- : press with a grating noise —grit•ty adj

grits \'grits\ n pl : coarsely ground hulled grain

griz•zled \'grizəld\ adj : streaked with gray

groan \'grōn\ vb 1 : moan 2 : creak under a strain —groan n

gro•cer \'grōsər\ n : food dealer —gro•cery \'grōs(ə)rē\ n

grog \'gräg\ n : rum diluted with water

grog•gy \-ē\ adj -gier; -est : dazed and unsteady on the feet —grog•gi•ly adv —grog•gi•ness n

groin \'grȯin\ n : juncture of abdomen and thigh

grom•met \'grämət, 'grəm-\ n : eyelet

groom \'grüm, 'grum\ n 1 : one who cleans and brushes horses 2 : bridegroom — vb 1 : clean and care for (as a horse) 2 : make neat, attractive, or acceptable

groove \'grüv\ n 1 : long narrow channel 2 : fixed routine —groove vb

grope \'grōp\ vb groped; grop•ing : search for by feeling

gros•beak \'grōs,bēk\ n : finch with large conical bill

¹gross \'grōs\ adj 1 : glaringly noticeable 2 : bulky 3 : consisting of an overall total exclusive of deductions 4 : vulgar ~ n : the whole before any deductions ~ vb : earn as a total —gross•ly adv —gross•ness n

²gross n, pl gross : 12 dozen

gro•tesque \grō'tesk\ adj 1 : absurdly distorted or repulsive 2 : ridiculous —gro•tesque•ly adv

grot•to \'grätō\ n, pl -toes : cave

grouch \'grauch\ n : complaining person —grouch vb —grouchy adj

¹ground \'graund\ n 1 : bottom of a body of water 2 pl : sediment 3 : basis for something 4 : surface of the earth 5 : conductor that makes electrical connection with the earth or a framework ~ vb 1 : force or bring down to the ground 2 : instruct in fundamental principles 3 : connect with an electrical ground —ground•less adj

²ground past of GRIND

ground•hog n : woodchuck

ground•wa•ter n : underground water

ground•work n : foundation

group \'grüp\ n : number of associated individuals ~ vb : gather or collect into groups

grou•per \'grüpər\ n : large fish of warm seas

grouse \'graus\ n, pl grouse or grouses : game bird

grout \'graut\ n : mortar for filling cracks —grout vb

grove \'grōv\ n : small group of trees

grov•el \'grävəl, 'grəv-\ vb -eled or -elled; -el•ing or -el•ling : abase oneself

grow \'grō\ vb grew \'grü\; grown \'grōn\; grow•ing 1 : come into existence and develop to maturity 2 : be able to grow 3 : advance or increase 4 : become 5 : cultivate —grow•er \'grō(ə)r\ n

growl \'graul\ vb : utter a deep threatening sound —growl n

grown-up \'grōn,əp\ n : adult —grown-up adj

growth \'grōth\ n 1 : stage in growing 2 : process of growing 3 : result of something growing

grub \'grəb\ vb -bb- : root out by digging ~ n 1 : thick wormlike larva 2 : food

grub•by \'grəbē\ adj -bi•er; -est : dirty —grub•bi•ness n

grub•stake n : supplies for a prospector

grudge \'grəj\ vb grudged; grudg•ing : be reluctant to give ~ n : feeling of ill will

gru•el \'grüəl\ n : thin porridge

gru•el•ing, gru•el•ling \-əliŋ\ adj : requiring extreme effort

grue•some \'grüsəm\ adj : horribly repulsive

gruff \'grəf\ adj : rough in speech or manner —gruff•ly adv

grum•ble \'grəmbəl\ vb -bled; -bling : mutter in discontent —grum•bler \-b(ə)lər\ n

grumpy \-pē\ adj grump•i•er; -est : cross —grump•i•ly adv —grump•i•ness n

grun•ion \'grənyən\ n : fish of the California coast

grunt \'grənt\ n : deep guttural sound —grunt vb

gua•no \'gwänō\ n : excrement of seabirds used as fertilizer

guar•an•tee \,garən'tē\ n 1 : assurance of the fulfillment of a condition 2 : something given or held as a security ~ vb -teed; -tee•ing 1 : promise to be responsible for 2 : state with certainty —guar•an•tor \,garən'tor\ n

guar•an•ty \'garəntē\ n, pl -ties 1 : promise to answer for another's failure to pay a debt **2** : guarantee **3** : pledge ~ *vb* **-tied; -ty·ing** : guarantee

guard \\'gärd\\ *n* **1** : defensive position **2** : act of protecting **3** : an individual or group that guards against danger **4** : protective or safety device ~ *vb* **1** : protect or watch over **2** : take precautions —**guard·house** *n* — **guard·room** *n*

guard·ian \\'gärdēən\\ *n* : one who has responsibility for the care of a person or property —**guard·ian·ship** *n*

gua·va \\'gwävə\\ *n* : shrubby tree or its mildly acid fruit

gu·ber·na·to·ri·al \\ˌg(y)übə(r)nə-'tōrēəl\\ *adj* : relating to a governor

guer·ril·la, guer·ril·la \\gə'rilə\\ *n* : soldier engaged in small-scale harassing tactics

guess \\'ges\\ *vb* **1** : form an opinion from little evidence **2** : state correctly solely by chance **3** : think or believe —**guess** *n*

guest \\'gest\\ *n* **1** : person to whom hospitality (as of a house) is extended **2** : patron of a commercial establishment (as a hotel) **3** : person not a regular cast member who appears on a program

guf·faw \\(ˌ)gə'fȯ, 'gəˌfȯ\\ *n* : loud burst of laughter —**guf·faw** \\(ˌ)gə'fȯ\\ *vb*

guide \\'gīd\\ *n* **1** : one that leads or gives direction to another **2** : device on a machine to direct motion ~ *vb* **guid·ed; guid·ing 1** : show the way to **2** : direct —**guid·able** *adj* —**guid·ance** \\'gīd°ns\\ *n* —**guide·book** *n*

guild \\'gild\\ *n* : association

guile \\'gīl\\ *n* : craftiness —**guile·ful** *adj* —**guile·less** *adj* —**guile·less·ness** *n*

guil·lo·tine \\'gilə,tēn; ˌgē(y)ə'tēn, 'gē(y)ə,-\\ *n* : machine for beheading persons —**guillotine** *vb*

guilt \\'gilt\\ *n* **1** : fact of having committed an offense **2** : feeling of responsibility for offenses —**guilt·i·ly** *adv* —**guilt·i·ness** *n* —**guilty** \\'giltē\\ *adj*

guinea \\'ginē\\ *n* **1** : old gold coin of United Kingdom **2** : 21 shillings

guinea pig *n* : small So. American rodent

guise \\'gīz\\ *n* : external appearance

gui·tar \\gə'tär, gi-\\ *n* : 6-stringed musical instrument played by plucking

gulch \\'gəlch\\ *n* : ravine

gulf \\'gəlf\\ *n* **1** : extension of an ocean or a sea into the land **2** : abyss

¹gull \\'gəl\\ *n* : seabird with webbed feet

²gull *vb* : make a dupe of ~ *n* : dupe —**gull·ible** *adj*

gul·let \\'gələt\\ *n* : throat

gul·ly \\-ē\\ *n, pl* **-lies** : trench worn by running water

gulp \\'gəlp\\ *vb* : swallow hurriedly or greedily —**gulp** *n*

¹gum \\'gəm\\ *n* : tissue along the jaw at the base of the teeth

²gum *n* **1** : sticky plant substance **2** : gum usu. of sweetened chicle prepared for chewing —**gum·my** *adj*

gum·bo \\'gəmbō\\ *n* : thick soup

gum·drop *n* : gumlike candy

gump·tion \\'gəmpshən\\ *n* : initiative

gun \\'gən\\ *n* **1** : cannon **2** : portable firearm **3** : discharge of a gun **4** : something like a gun ~ *vb* **-nn-** : hunt with a gun —**gun·fight** *n* —**gun·fight·er** *n* —**gun·fire** *n* —**gun·man** \\-man\\ *n* —**gun·pow·der** *n* —**gun·shot** *n* —**gun·smith** *n*

gun·boat *n* : small armed ship

gun·ner \\'gənər\\ *n* : person who uses a gun

gun·nery sergeant \\'gən(ə)rē-\\ *n* : non-commissioned officer in the marine corps ranking next below a first sergeant

gun·ny \\'gənē\\ *n* : coarse jute material for making sacks (gunnysacks)

gun·sling·er \\-ˌsliŋər\\ *n* : gunman in the old West

gun·wale \\'gən°l\\ *n* : upper edge of a boat's side

gup·py \\'gəpē\\ *n, pl* **-pies** : tiny tropical fish

gur·gle \\'gərgəl\\ *vb* **-gled; -gling** : make a sound like that of a flowing and gently splashing liquid —**gurgle** *n*

gu·ru \\gə'rü, 'gü(ə)r(ˌ)ü\\ *n, pl* **-rus** : personal religious teacher in Hinduism

gush \\'gəsh\\ *vb* : pour forth violently or enthusiastically —**gush·er** \\'gəshər\\ *n*

gushy \\-ē\\ *adj* **gush·i·er; -est** : effusively sentimental

gust \\'gəst\\ *n* **1** : sudden brief rush of wind **2** : sudden outburst —**gust** *vb* —**gusty** *adj*

gus·ta·to·ry \\'gəstəˌtōrē\\ *adj* : relating to the sense of taste

gus·to \\'gəstō\\ *n* : zest

gut \\'gət\\ *n* **1** : intestines **2** : digestive canal **3** *pl* : courage ~ *vb* **-tt-** : eviscerate

gut·ter \\'gətər\\ *n* : channel for carrying off rainwater

gut·tur·al \\'gətərəl\\ *adj* : sounded in the throat —**guttural** *n*

¹guy \'gī\ *n* : rope, chain, or rod attached to something to steady it — **guy** *vb*

²guy *n* : person

guz·zle \'gəzəl\ *vb* **-zled; -zling** : drink greedily

gym \'jim\ *n* : gymnasium

gym·na·si·um \jim'nāzēəm, -zhəm\ *n*, *pl* **-si·ums** *or* **-sia** \-zēə, -zhə\ : place for indoor sports

gym·nas·tics \jim'nastiks\ *n* : physical exercises performed in a gymnasium —**gym·nast** \'jim,nast\ *n*—**gym·nas·tic** *adj*

gy·ne·col·o·gy \,gīnə'käləjē, ,jin-\ *n* : branch of medicine dealing with the diseases of women —**gy·ne·co·log·ic** \-ikə'läjik\, **gy·ne·co·log·i·cal**

\-ikəl\ *adj* —**gy·ne·col·o·gist** \-ə'käləjəst\ *n*

gyp \'jip\ *n* 1 : cheat 2 : trickery —**gyp** *vb*

gyp·sum \'jipsəm\ *n* : calcium-containing mineral

gy·rate \'jī,rāt\ *vb* **-rat·ed; -rat·ing** : revolve around a center —**gy·ra·tion** \jī'rāshən\ *n*

gy·ro·com·pass \'jīrō,kəmpəs, -,käm-\ *n* : compass in which the axis of a spinning gyroscope points to the north

gy·ro·scope \-,skōp\ *n* : wheel mounted to spin rapidly about an axis that is free to turn in various directions

H

h \'āch\ *n*, *pl* **h's** *or* **hs** \'āchəz\ : 8th letter of the alphabet

hab·er·dash·er \'habə(r),dashər\ *n* : men's clothier —**hab·er·dash·ery** \-(ə)rē\ *n*

hab·it \'habət\ *n* 1 : monk's or nun's clothing 2 : usual behavior —**hab·it-form·ing** *adj*

hab·it·able \-əbəl\ *adj* : capable of being lived in

hab·i·tat \'habə,tat\ *n* : place where a plant or animal naturally occurs

hab·i·ta·tion \,habə'tāshən\ *n* 1 : occupancy 2 : dwelling place

ha·bit·u·al \hə,bich(əw)əl\ *adj* 1 : commonly practiced or observed 2 : doing, practicing, or acting by habit —**ha·bit·u·al·ly** *adv* —**ha·bit·u·al·ness** *n*

ha·bit·u·ate \hə'bicha,wāt\ *vb* **-at·ed; -at·ing** : accustom

ha·ci·en·da \,(h)äsē'endə\ *n* : ranch house

¹hack \'hak\ *vb* 1 : cut with repeated irregular blows 2 : cough in a short dry manner 3 : manage successfully —**hack** *n* —**hack·er** *n*

²hack *n* 1 : horse or vehicle for hire 2 : saddle horse 3 : writer for hire — **hack** *adj* —**hack·man** \-mən\ *n*

hack·le \'hakəl\ *n* 1 : long feather on the neck or lower back of a bird 2 *pl* : hairs that can be erected 3 *pl* : temper

hack·ney \-nē\ *n*, *pl* **-neys** 1 : horse for riding or driving 2 : carriage for hire

hack·neyed \-nēd\ *adj* : trite

hack·saw *n* : saw for metal

had *past of* HAVE

had·dock \'hadək\ *n*, *pl* **haddock** : Atlantic food fish

Ha·des \'hād(,)ēz\ *n* 1 : mythological abode of the dead 2 *often not cap* : hell

haft \'haft\ *n* : handle of a weapon or tool

hag \'hag\ *n* 1 : witch 2 : ugly old woman

hag·gard \'hagərd\ *adj* : worn or emaciated —**hag·gard·ly** *adv*

hag·gle \'hagəl\ *vb* **-gled; -gling** : argue in bargaining —**hag·gler** *n*

¹hail \'hāl\ *n* 1 : precipitation in small lumps of ice 2 : something like a rain of hail ~ *vb* : rain hail —**hail·stone** *n* —**hail·storm** *n*

²hail *vb* 1 : greet or salute 2 : summon ~ *n* : expression of greeting or praise —often used as an interjection

hair \'haər\ *n* : threadlike growth from the skin —**hair·brush** *n* —**hair·cut** *n* —**hair·dress·er** *n* —**haired** *adj* —**hair·i·ness** *n* —**hair·less** *adj* —**hair·pin** *n* —**hair·style** *n* —**hair·styl·ing** *n* —**hair·styl·ist** *n* —**hairy** *adj*

hair·breadth \-,bredth\, **hairs·breadth** \'haərz-\ *n* : tiny distance or margin

hair·do \-,dü\ *n*, *pl* **-dos** : style of wearing hair

hair·line *n* 1 : thin line 2 : outline of the hair on the head

hair·piece *n* : toupee

hair·rais·ing *adj* : causing terror or astonishment

hake \'hāk\ *n* : marine food fish

hal·cy·on \'halsēən\ *adj* : prosperous or most pleasant

¹hale \'hāl\ *adj* : healthy or robust

²**hale** \vb **haled; hal·ing** 1 : haul 2 : compel to go

half \'haf, 'häf\ n, pl **halves** \'havz, 'hävz\ : one of 2 equal parts — adj 1 : being a half or nearly a half 2 : partial —**half** adv

half-breed n : offspring of parents of different races —**half-breed** adj

half brother n : brother by one parent only

half-heart·ed \-'härtəd\ adj : without enthusiasm —**half-heart·ed·ly** adv — **half-heart·ed·ness** n

half-life n : time for half of something to undergo a process

half sister n : sister by one parent only

half·way adj : midway between 2 points —**half·way** adv

half-wit \-,wit\ n : foolish person — **half-wit·ted** \-'witəd\ adj

hal·i·but \'haləbət\ n, pl **halibut** : large edible marine flatfish

hal·i·to·sis \,halə'tōsəs\ n : bad breath

hall \'hol\ n 1 : large public or college or university building 2 : lobby 3 : auditorium

hal·le·lu·jah \,halə'lüyə\ interj —used to express praise, joy, or thanks

hall·mark \'hol,märk\ n : distinguishing characteristic

hal·low \'halō\ vb : consecrate —**hallowed** \-ōd, -əwad\ adj

Hal·low·een \,halə'wēn, ,häl-\ n : evening of October 31 observed esp. by children in merrymaking and masquerading

hal·lu·ci·na·tion \hə,lüs'n'āshən\ n : perception of objects or events that are not real —**hal·lu·ci·nate** \hə-'lüs'n,āt\ vb —**hal·lu·ci·na·to·ry** \-'lüs'nə,tōrē\ adj

hal·lu·ci·no·gen \hə'lüs'nəjən\ n : substance that induces hallucinations — **hal·lu·ci·no·gen·ic** \-,lüs'nə'jenik\ adj

hall·way n : entrance hall

ha·lo \'hālō\ n, pl **-los** or **-loes** : circle of light appearing to surround a shining body

¹**halt** \'holt\ adj : lame

²**halt** vb : stop or cause to stop —**halt** n

hal·ter \'holtər\ n 1 : rope or strap for leading or tying an animal 2 : brief blouse held up by straps ~ vb : catch (an animal) with a halter

halt·ing \'holtiŋ\ adj : uncertain — **halt·ing·ly** adv

halve \'hav, 'häv\ vb **halved; halv·ing** 1 : divide into halves 2 : reduce to half

halves pl of HALF

ham \'ham\ n 1 : thigh 2 : cut esp. of pork from the thigh 3 : showy actor 4 : amateur radio operator ~ vb -**mm**- : overlay a part —**ham** vb

ham·burg·er \'ham,bərgər\, **ham·burg** \-,bərg\ n : ground beef or a sandwich made with this

ham·let \'hamlət\ n : small village

ham·mer \-ər\ n 1 : hand tool for pounding 2 : gun part whose striking explodes the charge ~ vb 1 : beat, drive, or shape with a hammer 2 : produce by repeated blows

ham·mer·head n 1 : striking part of a hammer 2 : shark with a hammerlike head

ham·mock \'hamək\ n : swinging bed hung by cords at each end

¹**ham·per** \-pər\ vb : impede

²**hamper** n : large covered basket

ham·ster \-stər\ n : stocky short-tailed rodent

ham·string \-,striŋ\ vb -**strung** \-,strəŋ\; -**string·ing** \-,striŋiŋ\ 1 : cripple by cutting the leg tendons 2 : make ineffective or powerless

hand \'hand\ n 1 : end of a front limb adapted for grasping 2 : side 3 : promise of marriage 4 : handwriting 5 : assistance or participation 6 : applause 7 : cards held by a player 8 : worker ~ vb : lead, assist, give, or pass with the hand —**hand·clasp** n —**hand·craft** vb —**hand·ful** n — **hand·gun** n —**hand·less** adj —**handmade** adj —**hand·rail** n —**hand·saw** n —**hand·wo·ven** adj —**hand·writ·ing** n —**hand·writ·ten** adj

hand·bag n : woman's purse

hand·ball n : game played by striking a ball with the hand

hand·bill n : printed advertisement or notice distributed by hand

hand·book n : concise reference book

hand·cuffs n pl : locking bracelets that bind the wrists together —**handcuff** vb

hand·i·cap \'handi,kap\ n 1 : advantage given or disadvantage imposed to equalize a competition 2 : disadvantage —**handicap** vb —**hand·i·capped** adj —**hand·i·cap·per** n

hand·i·craft \'handi,kraft\ n 1 : manual skill 2 : article made by hand — **hand·i·craft·er** n —**hand·i·crafts·man** \-,kraftsmən\ n

hand·i·work \-,wərk\ n : work done personally

hand·ker·chief \'haŋkərchəf, -,chēf\ n, pl **-chiefs** \-chəfs, -,chēfs\ : small piece of cloth carried for personal use

han·dle \'hand^əl\ n : part to be grasped ~ vb -dled; -dling 1 : touch, hold, or manage with the hands 2 : deal with 3 : deal or trade in —**han·dle·bar** n —**han·dled** \-d^əld\ adj — **han·dler** \'han(d)lər\ n

hand·maid·en, **hand·maid** n : female attendant

hand·out n : something given out

hand·pick vb : select personally

hand·shake n : clasping of hands (as in greeting)

hand·some \'hansəm\ adj 1 : sizable 2 : generous 3 : nice-looking —**hand·some·ly** adv —**hand·some·ness** n

hand·spring n : somersault on the hands

hand·stand n : a balancing upside down on the hands

handy \'handē\ adj **hand·i·er; -est** 1 : conveniently near 2 : easily used 3 : dexterous —**hand·i·ly** adv —**hand·i·ness** n

handy·man \-,man\ n : one who does odd jobs

hang \'haŋ\ vb **hung** \'həŋ\ or **hanged** \'haŋd\; **hang·ing** 1 : fasten or remain fastened to an elevated point without support from below 2 : put or come to death by suspending with a rope around the neck 3 : droop ~ n 1 : way a thing hangs 2 : knack — **hang·er** n —**hang·ing** n or adj

han·gar \'haŋər\ n : airplane shelter

hang·dog \'haŋ,dòg\ adj : ashamed or guilty

hang·man \-mən\ n : public executioner

hang·nail n : loose skin near a fingernail

hang·out n : place where one likes to spend time

hang·over n : sick feeling following heavy drinking

hank \'haŋk\ n : coil or loop

han·ker \'haŋkər\ vb : desire strongly —**han·ker·ing** n

han·ky-pan·ky \,haŋkē'paŋkē\ n : underhand activity

han·som \'hansəm\ n : 2-wheeled covered carriage

Ha·nuk·kah \'känəkə, 'hän-\ n : 8-day Jewish holiday commemorating the rededication of the Temple of Jerusalem after its defilement by Antiochus of Syria

hap·haz·ard \hap'hazərd\ adj : having no plan or order —**hap·haz·ard·ly** adv

hap·less \'hapləs\ adj : unfortunate —**hap·less·ly** adv —**hap·less·ness** n

hap·pen \'hapən\ vb 1 : take place 2 : be fortunate to encounter something unexpectedly —often used with infinitive

hap·pen·ing \-(ə)niŋ\ n : occurrence

hap·py \'hapē\ adj -**pi·er; -est** 1 : fortunate 2 : content, pleased, or joyous —**hap·pi·ly** \'ha,pəlē\ adv — **hap·pi·ness** n

ha·rangue \hə'raŋ\ n : ranting or scolding speech —**harangue** vb — **ha·rangu·er** \-'raŋər\ n

ha·rass \hə'ras, 'harəs\ vb 1 : worry and impede (an enemy) by repeated raids 2 : annoy continually —**ha·rass·ment** n

har·bin·ger \'härbənjər\ n : one that announces or foreshadows what is coming

har·bor \-bər\ n : protected body of water suitable for anchorage ~ vb 1 : give refuge to 2 : hold as a thought or feeling

hard \'härd\ adj 1 : not easily penetrated 2 : firm or definite 3 : close or searching 4 : severe or unfeeling 5 : strenuous or difficult 6 : physically strong or intense —**hard** adv —**hard·ness** n

hard·en \'härd^ən\ vb : make or become hard or harder —**hard·en·er** n

hard·head·ed \-'hedəd\ adj 1 : stubborn 2 : realistic —**hard·head·ed·ly** adv —**hard·head·ed·ness** n

hard·heart·ed \-'härtəd\ adj : lacking sympathy —**hard·heart·ed·ly** adv — **hard·heart·ed·ness** n

hard·ly \-lē\ adv 1 : only just 2 : certainly not

hard·ship \-,ship\ n : suffering or privation

hard·tack \-,tak\ n : hard biscuit

hard·ware n : cutlery or tools made of metal

hard·wood n : wood of a broad-leaved usu. deciduous tree —**hardwood** adj

har·dy \'härdē\ adj -**di·er; -est** : able to withstand adverse conditions — **har·di·ly** adv —**har·di·ness** n

hare \'haər\ n, pl **hare** or **hares** : longeared mammal related to the rabbit

hare·lip n : deformity in which the upper lip is vertically split —**hare·lipped** \-'lipt\ adj

ha·rem \'harəm\ n : house or part of a house allotted to women in a Muslim household or the women and servants occupying it

hark \'härk\ vb : listen

har·le·quin \'härlik(w)ən\ n : clown

har·lot \'härlət\ n : prostitute

harm \'härm\ n 1 : physical or mental damage 2 : mischief ~ vb : cause harm —**harm·ful** \-fəl\ adj —**harm-**

ful·ly adv —harm·ful·ness n —harm·less adj —harm·less·ly adv —harm·less·ness n

har·mon·ic \här'mänik\ adj 1 : of or relating to musical harmony 2 : pleasing to hear —har·mon·i·cal·ly \-ik(ə)lē\ adv

har·mon·i·ca \här'mänikə\ n : small wind instrument with metallic reeds

har·mo·ny \'härmənē\ n, pl -nies 1 : musical combination of sounds 2 : pleasing arrangement of parts 3 : lack of conflict 4 : internal calm —har·mo·ni·ous \här'mōnēəs\ adj —har·mo·ni·ous·ly adv —har·mo·ni·ous·ness n —har·mo·ni·za·tion \,härmənə'zāshən\ n —har·mo·nize \'härmə,nīz\ vb

har·ness \'härnəs\ n : gear of a draft animal ~ vb 1 : put a harness on 2 : put to use

harp \'härp\ n : musical instrument with many strings plucked by the fingers ~ vb 1 : play on a harp 2 : dwell on a subject tiresomely —harp·er n —harp·ist n

har·poon \här'pün\ n : barbed spear used in hunting whales —harpoon vb —har·poon·er n

harp·si·chord \'härpsi,kòrd\ n : keyboard instrument with strings that are plucked

har·py \'härpē\ n, pl -pies : shrewish woman

har·row \'harō\ n : implement used to break up soil —vb 1 : cultivate with a harrow 2 : distress

har·ry \'harē\ vb -ried; -ry·ing : torment by or as if by constant attack

harsh \'härsh\ adj 1 : disagreeably rough 2 : severe —harsh·ly adv —harsh·ness n

hart \'härt\ n : stag

har·um-scar·um \,harəm'skarəm\ adv : recklessly

har·vest \'härvəst\ n 1 : act or time of gathering in a crop 2 : mature crop —harvest vb —har·vest·er n

has pres 3d sing of HAVE

hash \'hash\ vb : chop into small pieces ~ n : chopped meat mixed with potatoes and browned

hash·ish \'hash,ēsh, -,(,)ish\ n : unadulterated intoxicating resin from female hemp plants

hasp \'hasp\ n : hinged strap fastener esp. for a door

has·sle \'hasəl\ n 1 : quarrel 2 : struggle —hassle vb

has·sock \'hasək\ n : cushion used as a seat or leg rest

haste \'hāst\ n 1 : rapidity of motion 2

: rash action 3 : excessive eagerness —hast·i·ly \'hāstəlē\ adv —hast·i·ness \-stēnəs\ n —hasty \-stē\ adj

has·ten \'hās³n\ vb : hurry

hat \'hat\ n : covering for the head

¹hatch \'hach\ n : small door or opening —hatch·way n

²hatch vb : emerge from an egg —hatch·ery \-(ə)rē\ n

hatch·et \'hachət\ n : short-handled ax

hate \'hāt\ n : intense hostility and aversion ~ vb hat·ed; hat·ing 1 : express or feel hate 2 : dislike —hate·ful \-fəl\ adj —hate·ful·ly adv —hate·ful·ness n —hat·er n

ha·tred \'hātrəd\ n : hate

hat·ter \'hatər\ n : one that makes or sells hats

haugh·ty \'hòtē\ adj -ti·er; -est : disdainfully proud —haugh·ti·ly adv —haugh·ti·ness n

haul \'hòl\ vb 1 : draw or pull 2 : transport or carry ~ n 1 : amount collected 2 : load or the distance it is transported —haul·age \-ij\ n —haul·er n

haunch \'hònch\ n : hip or hindquarter —usu. pl.

haunt \'hònt\ vb 1 : visit often 2 : visit or inhabit as a ghost ~ n : place habitually frequented —haunt·er n —haunt·ing·ly adv

have \(')hav, (h)əv, v; in sense 2 before "to" usu 'haf\ vb had \(')had, (h)əd\; hav·ing \'haviŋ\; has \(')haz, (h)əz, in sense 2 before "to" usu 'has\ 1 : hold in possession, service, or affection 2 : be compelled or forced to 3 —used as an auxiliary with the past participle to form the present perfect, past perfect, or future perfect 4 : obtain or receive 5 : undergo 6 : cause to 7 : bear —have to do with : have in the way of connection or relation with or effect on

ha·ven \'hāvən\ n : place of safety

hav·oc \'havək\ n 1 : wide destruction 2 : great confusion

¹hawk \'hòk\ n : small or medium-sized day-flying bird of prey —hawk·ish adj

²hawk vb : offer for sale by calling out in the street —hawk·er n

haw·ser \'hòzər\ n : large rope

haw·thorn \'hò,thòrn\ n : spiny shrub or tree with pink or white fragrant flowers

hay \'hā\ n : herbage mowed and cured for fodder —hay n —hay·fork n —hay·loft n —hay·mow \-,maù\ n —hay·stack n

hay·cock \'hā,käk\ n : small pile of hay

hay·rick \-,rik\ n : large outdoor stack of hay

hay·seed \'hā,sēd\ n : bumpkin

hay·wire adj : being out of order

haz·ard \'hazərd\ n 1 : source of danger 2 : chance ~ vb : venture or risk —**haz·ard·ous** adj

¹**haze** \'hāz\ n : fine dust, smoke, or light vapor in the air that reduces visibility

²**haze** vb **hazed; haz·ing** : harass by abusive and humiliating tricks

ha·zel \'hāzəl\ n : shrub or small tree bearing edible nuts (**ha·zel·nuts**)

hazy \'hāzē\ adj **haz·i·er; -est** 1 : obscured by haze 2 : vague or indefinite —**haz·i·ly** adv —**haz·i·ness** n

he \('hē, ē\ pron 1 : that male one 2 : a or the person

head \'hed\ n 1 : front or upper part of the body 2 : mind 3 : upper or higher end 4 : director or leader 5 : place of leadership or honor ~ vb 1 : provide with or form a head 2 : put, stand, or be at the head 3 : point or proceed in a certain direction —**head·ache** n —**head·band** n —**head·dress** n —**head·ed** adj —**head·first** adv or adj —**head·gear** n —**head·less** adj —**head·man** \-'man, -,man\ n —**head·rest** n —**head·ship** n —**head·waiter** n

head·ing \-iŋ\ n 1 : direction in which a plane or ship heads 2 : something (as a title) standing at the top or beginning

head·land \'hedlənd, -,land\ n : promontory

head·light n : light on the front of an automobile

head·line n : introductory line of a newspaper story printed in large type

head·long \-'lòŋ\ adv 1 : head foremost 2 : in a rash or reckless manner —**head·long** \-,lòŋ\ adj

head·mas·ter n : male head of a private school

head·mis·tress n : female head of a private school

head-on adj : having the front facing in the direction of initial contact —**head-on** adv

head·phone n : an earphone held on by a band over the head

head·quar·ters n sing or pl : command or administrative center

head·stone n : stone at the head of a grave

head·strong adj : stubborn or willful

head·wa·ters n pl : source of a stream

head·way n : forward motion

heady \'hedē\ adj **head·i·er; -est** 1 : intoxicating 2 : shrewd

heal \'hēl\ vb : make or become sound or whole —**heal·er** n

health \'helth\ n : sound physical or mental condition

health·ful \-fəl\ adj : beneficial to health —**health·ful·ly** adv —**health·ful·ness** n

healthy \'helthē\ adj **health·i·er; -est** : enjoying or typical of good health —**health·i·ly** adv —**health·i·ness** n

heap \'hēp\ n : pile ~ vb : throw or lay in a heap

hear \'hir\ vb **heard** \'hərd\, **hear·ing** \'hi(ə)riŋ\ 1 : perceive by the ear 2 : heed 3 : learn —**hear·er** \'hirər\ n

hear·ing n 1 : process or power of perceiving sound 2 : earshot 3 : session in which witnesses are heard

hear·ken \'härkən\ vb : give attention

hear·say n : rumor

hearse \'hərs\ n : vehicle for carrying the dead to the grave

heart \'härt\ n 1 : hollow muscular organ that keeps up the circulation of the blood 2 : playing card of a suit marked with a red heart 3 : whole personality or the emotional or moral part of it 4 : courage 5 : essential part —**heart·beat** n —**heart·ed** adj

heart·ache n : anguish of mind

heart·break n : crushing grief —**heart·break·er** n —**heart·break·ing** adj —**heart·bro·ken** adj

heart·burn n : burning distress behind the lower sternum

heart·en \'härtᵊn\ vb : encourage

hearth \'härth\ n 1 : area in front of a fireplace 2 : home —**hearth·stone** n

heart·less \-ləs\ adj : cruel

heart-rend·ing \-,rendiŋ\ adj : causing intense grief or anguish

heart·sick adj : very despondent —**heart·sick·ness** n

heart·strings n pl : deepest emotions

heart·throb n : sweetheart

heart·warm·ing adj : inspiring sympathetic feeling

heart·wood n : central portion of wood

hearty \'härtē\ adj **heart·i·er; -est** 1 : vigorously healthy 2 : nourishing —**heart·i·ly** adv —**heart·i·ness** n

heat \'hēt\ vb : make or become warm or hot ~ n 1 : condition of being hot 2 : form of energy that causes a body to rise in temperature 3 : intensity of feeling —**heat·ed·ly** adv —**heat·er** n —**heat·less** adj

heath \'hēth\ n 1 : often evergreen shrubby plant of wet acid soils 2 : tract of wasteland —**heathy** adj

hea·then \'hēthən\ n, pl **-thens** or **-then** : uncivilized or godless person —**heathen** adj

heath·er \'hethər\ n : evergreen heath with lavender flowers —**heath·ery** adj

heat·stroke n : disorder that follows prolonged exposure to excessive heat

heave \'hēv\ vb **heaved** or **hove** \'hōv\; **heav·ing** 1 : rise or lift upward 2 : throw 3 : rise and fall ~ n 1 : an effort to lift or raise 2 : throw

heav·en \'hevən\ n 1 pl : sky 2 : abode of the Deity and of the blessed dead 3 : place of supreme happiness **heav·en·ly** —**heav·en·ward** adv or adj

heavy \'hevē\ adj **heavi·er**; **-est** 1 : having great weight 2 : hard to bear 3 : greater than the average —**heavi·ly** adv —**heavi·ness** n —**heavy·weight** n

heavy–du·ty adj : able to withstand unusual strain

heavy·set adj : stocky and compact in build

heck·le \'hekəl\ vb **-led**; **-ling** : harass with gibes —**heck·ler** \-(ə)lər\ n

hec·tic \'hektik\ adj : filled with excitement or confusion —**hec·ti·cal·ly** \-tik(ə)lē\ adv

hedge \'hej\ n 1 : fence or boundary of shrubs or small trees 2 : means of protection ~ vb **hedged**; **hedg·ing** 1 : protect oneself against loss 2 : evade the risk of commitment —**hedg·er** n

hedge·hog n : spiny mammal (as a porcupine)

he·do·nism \'hēd³n,izəm\ n : way of life devoted to pleasure —**he·do·nist** \-³nəst\ n —**he·do·nis·tic** \,hēd-³n'istik\ adj

heed \'hēd\ vb : pay attention ~ n : attention —**heed·ful** \-fəl\ adj —**heed·ful·ly** adv —**heed·ful·ness** n —**heed·less** adj —**heed·less·ly** adv —**heed·less·ness** n

¹**heel** \'hēl\ n 1 : back of the foot 2 : crusty end of a loaf of bread 3 : solid piece forming the back of the sole of a shoe —**heel·less** \'hēlləs\ adj

²**heel** vb : tilt to one side

heft \'heft\ n : weight ~ vb : judge the weight of by lifting

hefty \'heftē\ adj **heft·i·er**; **-est** : big and bulky

he·ge·mo·ny \hi'jemənē\ n : preponderant influence esp. of one nation over others

heif·er \'hefər\ n : young cow

height \'hīt, 'hītth\ n 1 : highest part or point 2 : distance from bottom to top 3 : altitude

height·en \'hīt³n\ vb : increase in amount or degree

hei·nous \'hānəs\ adj : shockingly evil —**hei·nous·ly** adv —**hei·nous·ness** n

heir \'aər\ n : one who inherits or is entitled to inherit property —**heir·ship** n

heir·ess \'arəs\ n : female heir esp. to great wealth

heir·loom \'aər,lüm\ n : something handed on from one generation to another

held past of HOLD

he·li·cal \'helikəl, 'hē-\ adj : spiral

he·li·cop·ter \'helə,käptər, 'hē-\ n : aircraft supported in the air by rotors

he·lio·trope \'hēlyə,trōp\ n : garden herb with small fragrant white or purple flowers

he·li·um \'hēlēəm\ n : very light nonflammable gaseous chemical element

he·lix \'hēliks\ n, pl **-li·ces** \'helə,sēz, 'hē-\ : something spiral

hell \'hel\ n 1 : nether world in which the dead continue to exist 2 : realm of the devil 3 : place or state of torment or destruction —**hell·ish** adj

hell·gram·mite \'helgrə,mīt\ n : aquatic insect larva

hel·lion \'helyən\ n : troublesome person

hel·lo \hə'lō, he-\ n, pl **-los** : expression of greeting

helm \'helm\ n : lever or wheel for steering a ship —**helms·man** \'helmzmən\ n

hel·met \'helmət\ n : protective covering for the head

help \'help\ vb 1 : supply what is needed 2 : be of use 3 : refrain from or prevent ~ n 1 : something that helps or a source of help 2 : one who helps another —**help·er** n —**help·ful** \-fəl\ adj —**help·ful·ly** adv —**help·ful·ness** n —**help·less** adj —**help·less·ly** adv —**help·less·ness** n

help·ing \'helpiŋ\ n : portion of food

help·mate n 1 : helper 2 : wife

help·meet \-,mēt\ n : helpmate

hel·ter–skel·ter \,heltər'skeltər\ adv : in total disorder

hem \'hem\ n : border of an article of cloth doubled back and stitched down ~ *vb* **-mm-** 1 : sew a hem 2 : surround restrictively —**hem·line** *n*

he·ma·tol·o·gy \,hēma'tälǝjē\ *n* : study of the blood and blood-forming organs —**hema·to·log·ic** \-mǝt'əl'äjik\ *adj* —**he·ma·tol·o·gist** \-'tälǝjǝst\ *n*

hemi·sphere \'hema,sfiǝr\ *n* : one of the halves of the earth divided by the equator into northern and southern parts (**northern hemisphere, southern hemisphere**) or by a meridian into eastern and western parts (**eastern hemisphere, western hemisphere**) —**hemi·spher·ic** \,hemǝ-'sfiǝrik, -'sfer-\, **hemi·spher·i·cal** \-'sfirikǝl, -'sfer-\ *adj*

hem·lock \'hem,läk\ *n* 1 : poisonous herb related to the carrot 2 : evergreen tree related to the pines

he·mo·phil·ia \,hēmǝ'fēlēǝ\ *n* : tendency to severe prolonged bleeding —**he·mo·phil·i·ac** \-ē,ak\ *adj or n*

hem·or·rhage \'hem(ǝ)rij\ *n* : large discharge of blood —**hemorrhage** *vb* —**hem·or·rhag·ic** \,hemǝ'rajik\ *adj*

hem·or·rhoids \'hem(ǝ),roidz\ *n pl* : swollen mass of dilated veins at or just within the anus

hemp \'hemp\ *n* 1 : tall Asian herb grown for its tough fiber —**hemp·en** \'hempǝn\ *adj*

hen \'hen\ *n* : female domestic fowl

hence \'hens\ *adv* 1 : away 2 : therefore 3 : from this source or origin

hence·forth *adv* : from this point on

hence·for·ward *adv* : henceforth

hench·man \'henchmǝn\ *n* : trusted follower

hen·na \'henǝ\ *n* : reddish brown dye obtained from the leaves of a tropical shrub

hen·peck \'hen,pek\ *vb* : subject (one's husband) to persistent nagging

he·pat·ic \hi'patik\ *adj* : relating to or resembling the liver

hep·a·ti·tis \,hepǝ'tītǝs\ *n, pl* **-tit·i·des** \-'titǝ,dēz\ : inflammation of the liver or a disease of which this is a feature

her \(h)ǝr, ,hǝr\ *adj* : of or relating to her or herself ~ \ǝr, (')hǝr\ *pron, objective case of* SHE

her·ald \'herǝld\ *n* 1 : official crier or messenger 2 : harbinger ~ *vb* : give notice

her·al·dry \'herǝldrē\ *n, pl* **-ries** : practice of devising and granting arms —**he·ral·dic** \he'raldik, hǝ-\ *adj*

herb \'(h)ǝrb\ *n* 1 : seed plant that lacks woody tissue 2 : plant or plant part valued for medicinal or savory qualities —**herb·a·ceous** \,(h)ǝr-'bāshǝs\ *adj* —**herb·age** \'(h)ǝr-bij\ *n* —**herb·al** \-bal\ *n or adj* —**herb·al·ist** \-balǝst\ *n*

her·bi·cide \'(h)ǝrbǝ,sīd\ *n* : agent that destroys plants —**her·bi·cid·al** \,(h)ǝrbǝ'sīd'l\ *adj*

her·biv·o·rous \,(h)ǝr'bivǝrǝs\ *adj* : feeding on plants —**her·bi·vore** \'(h)ǝrbǝ,vŏr\ *n*

her·cu·le·an \,hǝrkyǝ'lēǝn, ,hǝr'kyü-lēǝn\ *adj* : of extraordinary power, size, or difficulty

herd \'hǝrd\ *n* : group of animals of one kind ~ *vb* : assemble or move in a herd —**herd·er** *n* —**herds·man** \'hǝrdzmǝn\ *n*

here \'hiǝr\ *adv* 1 : in or at this place 2 : now 3 : at or in this point or particular 4 : in the present life or state ~ *n* : this place —**here·abouts** \'hirǝ,baůts\, **here·about** \-,baůt\ *adv*

here·af·ter *adv* : in some future time or state ~ *n* : existence beyond earthly life

here·by *adv* : by means of this

he·red·i·tary \hǝ'redǝ,terē\ *adj* 1 : genetically passed or passable from parent to offspring 2 : passing by inheritance

he·red·i·ty \-ǝtē\ *n* : the passing of characteristics from parent to offspring

here·in *adv* : in this

here·of *adv* : of this

here·on *adv* : on this

her·e·sy \'herǝsē\ *n, pl* **-sies** : opinion or doctrine contrary to church dogma —**her·e·tic** \-,tik\ *n* —**he·ret·i·cal** \hǝ'retikǝl\ *adj*

here·to·fore \'hirtǝ,fŏr\ *adv* : up to this time

here·un·der *adv* : under this

here·un·to *adv* : to this

here·upon *adv* : on this

here·with *adv* 1 : with this 2 : hereby

her·i·tage \'heritij\ *n* 1 : inheritance 2 : birthright

her·maph·ro·dite \(,)hǝr'mafrǝ,dīt\ *n* : animal or plant having both male and female reproductive organs —**hermaphrodite** *adj* —**her·maph·ro·dit·ic** \-,mafrǝ'ditik\ *adj*

her·met·ic \hǝr'metik\ *adj* : sealed airtight —**her·met·i·cal·ly** \-ik(ǝ)lē\ *adv*

her·mit \'hǝrmǝt\ *n* : one who lives in solitude

her·nia \'hərnēə\ *n, pl* **-ni·as** *or* **-ni·ae** \-nē,ē, -nē,ī\ : a protruding of a bodily part through the weakened wall of its enclosure —**her·ni·ate** \-nē,āt\ *vb* —**her·ni·a·tion** \,hərnē'āshən\ *n*

he·ro \'hērō\ *n, pl* **-roes** : one that is much admired or shows great courage —**he·ro·ic** \hi'rōik\ *adj* —**he·ro·i·cal·ly** \-ik(ə)lē\ *adv* —**he·ro·ics** \-iks\ *n pl* —**her·o·ism** \'herə,wizəm\ *n*

her·o·in \'herəwən\ *n* : strongly addictive narcotic

her·o·ine \'herəwən\ *n* : woman of heroic achievements or qualities

her·on \'herən\ *n* : long-legged longbilled wading bird

her·pes \'hərpēz\ *n* : virus disease characterized by the formation of blisters

her·pe·tol·o·gy \,hərpə'täləjē\ *n* : study of reptiles and amphibians —**her·pe·tol·o·gist** \-pə'täləjəst\ *n*

her·ring \'heriŋ\ *n, pl* **-ring** *or* **-rings** : narrow-bodied Atlantic food fish

hers \'hərz\ *pron* : one or the ones belonging to her

her·self \(h)ər'self\ *pron* : she, her —used reflexively or for emphasis

hertz \'herts, 'hərts\ *n, pl* **hertz** : unit of frequency equal to one cycle per second

hes·i·tant \'hezətənt\ *adj* : tending to hesitate —**hes·i·tance** \-ten(t)s\ *n* —**hes·i·tan·cy** \-tənsē\ *n* —**hes·i·tant·ly** *adv*

hes·i·tate \'hezə,tāt\ *vb* **-tat·ed; -tat·ing** 1 : hold back esp. in doubt 2 : pause —**hes·i·ta·tion** \,hezə'tāshən\ *n*

het·er·o·ge·neous \,het(ə)rə'jēnēəs, -nyəs\ *adj* : consisting of dissimilar ingredients or constituents —**het·er·o·ge·ne·i·ty** \-jə'nēətē\ *n* —**het·er·o·ge·neous·ly** *adv* —**het·er·o·ge·neous·ness** *n*

het·er·o·sex·u·al \,hetərō'seksh(əw)əl\ *adj* : oriented toward the opposite sex —**heterosexual** *n*

hew \'hyü\ *vb* **hewed; hewed** *or* **hewn** \'hyün\; **hew·ing** 1 : cut or shape with or as if with an ax 2 : conform strictly —**hew·er** *n*

hex \'heks\ *vb* : put an evil spell on —**hex** *n*

hexa·gon \'heksə,gän\ *n* : 6-sided polygon —**hex·ag·o·nal** \hek'sagən⁹l\ *adj*

hey·day \'hā,dā\ *n* : time of flourishing

hi·a·tus \hī'ātəs\ *n* : lapse in continuity

hi·ba·chi \hi'bächē\ *n* : brazier

hi·ber·nate \'hībər,nāt\ *vb* **-nat·ed; -nat·ing** : pass the winter in a torpid or resting state —**hi·ber·na·tion** \,hībər'nāshən\ *n* —**hi·ber·na·tor** \'hībər,nātər\ *n*

hic·cup \'hik(,)əp\ *n* : spasmodic inhalation with sudden closing of the glottis accompanied by a peculiar sound —**hiccup** *vb*

hick \'hik\ *n* : awkward provincial person —**hick** *adj*

hick·o·ry \'hik(ə)rē\ *n, pl* **-ries** : No. American hardwood tree —**hickory** *adj*

¹**hide** \'hīd\ *vb* **hid** \'hid\; **hid·den** \'hid⁹n\ *or* **hid; hid·ing** : put or remain out of sight

²**hide** *n* : animal skin

hid·eous \'hidēəs\ *adj* : very ugly —**hid·eous·ly** *adv* —**hid·eous·ness** *n*

hie \'hī\ *vb* **hied; hy·ing** *or* **hie·ing** : hurry

hi·er·ar·chy \'hī(ə),rärkē\ *n, pl* **-chies** : persons or things arranged in a graded series —**hi·er·ar·chi·cal** \,hī(ə)'rärkikəl\ *adj*

hi·er·o·glyph·ic \,hī(ə)rə'glifik\ *n* : character in the picture writing of the ancient Egyptians

high \'hī\ *adj* 1 : having large extension upward 2 : elevated in pitch 3 : exalted in character 4 : of greater degree or amount than average 5 : expensive 6 : excited or stupefied by alcohol or a drug ~ *adv* : at or to a high place or degree ~ *n* 1 : elevated point or level 2 : automobile gear giving the highest speed —**high·ly** *adv*

high·boy *n* : high chest of drawers on legs

high·brow \-,braů\ *n* : person of superior learning or culture —**high·brow** *adj*

high-flown *adj* : pretentious

high-hand·ed *adj* : willful and arrogant —**high-hand·ed·ly** *adv* —**high-hand·ed·ness** *n*

high·land \'hīlənd\ *n* : hilly country —**high·land·er** \-ləndər\ *n*

high·light *n* : event or detail of major importance ~ *vb* 1 : emphasize 2 : be a highlight of

high·ness \-nəs\ *n* 1 : quality or degree of being high 2 —used as a title (as for kings)

high-rise *adj* : having several stories

high school *n* : school usu. comprising the 9th to 12th or 10th to 12th grades

high-spir·it·ed *adj* : lively

high-strung \-'strəŋ\ *adj* : very nervous or sensitive

high·way *n* : public road

high·way·man \-mən\ *n* : one who robs travelers on a road

hi·jack, high-jack \'hī,jak\ *vb* : steal esp. by commandeering a vehicle — **hijack** *n* — **hi·jack·er** *n*

hike \'hīk\ *vb* **hiked; hik·ing** 1 : raise quickly 2 : take a long walk ~ *n* 1 : long walk 2 : increase — **hik·er** *n*

hi·lar·i·ous \hil'arēəs, hī'lar-\ *adj* : extremely funny — **hi·lar·i·ous·ly** *adv* — **hi·lar·i·ty** \-ətē\ *n*

hill \'hil\ *n* : place where the land rises — **hill·side** *n* — **hill·top** *n* — **hilly** *adj*

hill·bil·ly \'hil,bilē\ *n, pl* **-lies** : person from a backwoods area

hill·ock \'hilək\ *n* : small hill

hilt \'hilt\ *n* : handle of a sword

him \im, 'him\ *pron, objective case of* HE

him·self \(h)im'self\ *pron* : he, him — used reflexively or for emphasis

¹hind \'hīnd\ *n* : female deer

²hind *adj* : back

hin·der \'hindər\ *vb* : obstruct or hold back

hind·most *adj* : farthest to the rear

hind·quar·ter *n* : back half of a complete side of a carcass

hin·drance \'hindrəns\ *n* : something that hinders

hind·sight *n* : understanding of an event after it has happened

Hin·du·ism \'hindü,izəm\ *n* : body of religious beliefs and practices native to India — **Hin·du** *n or adj*

hinge \'hinj\ *n* : jointed piece on which one piece (as a door) turns or swings ~ *vb* **hinged; hing·ing** 1 : attach by or furnish with hinges 2 : depend

hint \'hint\ *n* 1 : indirect suggestion 2 : clue 3 : very small amount — **hint** *vb*

hin·ter·land \'hintər,land\ *n* : remote region

hip \'hip\ *n* : part of the body on either side just below the waist — **hip·bone** *n*

hip·pie, hip·py \'hipē\ *n, pl* **-pies** : usu. young person who rejects conventional society

hip·po·pot·a·mus \,hipə'pätəməs\ *n, pl* **-mus·es** *or* **-mi** \-,mī\ : large thick-skinned African river animal

hire \'hī(ə)r\ *n* 1 : payment for labor 2 : employment ~ *vb* **hired; hir·ing** : employ for pay

hire·ling \'hī(ə)rlin\ *n* : one who serves another only for gain

hir·sute \'hər,süt, 'hiər-\ *adj* : hairy

his \(h)iz, ,hiz\ *adj* : of or belonging to him ~ \'hiz\ *pron* : ones belonging to him

hiss \'his\ *vb* 1 : make a sharp sibilant sound 2 : show dislike by hissing — **hiss** *n*

his·to·ri·an \his'tōrēən\ *n* : writer of history

his·to·ry \'hist(ə)rē\ *n, pl* **-ries** 1 : chronological record of significant events 2 : study of past events — **his·tor·ic** \his'tòrik\, **his·tor·i·cal** \-ikəl\ *adj* — **his·tor·i·cal·ly** \-k(ə)lē\ *adv*

hit \'hit\ *vb* **hit; hit·ting** 1 : reach with a blow 2 : come or cause to come in contact 3 : affect detrimentally ~ *n* 1 : blow 2 : something very successful — **hit·ter** *n*

hitch \'hich\ *vb* 1 : move by jerks 2 : catch by a hook 3 : hitchhike ~ *n* 1 : jerk 2 : sudden halt

hitch·hike \'hich,hīk\ *vb* : travel by securing free rides from passing vehicles — **hitch·hik·er** *n*

hith·er \'hithər\ *adv* : to this place

hith·er·to \-,tü\ *adv* : up to this time

hive \'hīv\ *n* 1 : container housing honeybees 2 : colony of bees — **hive** *vb*

hives \'hīvz\ *n sing or pl* : allergic disorder

hoard \'hòrd\ *n* : hidden accumulation — **hoard** *vb* — **hoard·er** *n*

hoar·frost \'hòr,fròst\ *n* : frost

hoarse \'hòrs\ *adj* **hoars·er; -est** 1 : harsh in sound 2 : speaking in a harsh strained voice — **hoarse·ly** *adv* — **hoarse·ness** *n*

hoary \'hòrē\ *adj* **hoar·i·er; -est** : gray or white with age — **hoar·i·ness** *n*

hoax \'hōks\ *n* : act intended to trick or dupe — **hoax** *vb* — **hoax·er** *n*

hob·ble \'häbəl\ *vb* **-bled; -bling** : limp along ~ *n* : hobbling movement

hob·by \-ē\ *n, pl* **-bies** : interest engaged in for relaxation — **hob·by·ist** \-ēəst\ *n*

hob·gob·lin \-,gäblən\ *n* 1 : mischievous goblin 2 : bogey

hob·nail \-,nāl\ *n* : short nail for studding shoe soles — **hob·nailed** \-,nāld\ *adj*

hob·nob \-,näb\ *vb* **-bb-** : associate socially

¹hobo \'hōbō\ *n, pl* **-boes** : tramp

¹hock \'häk\ *n* : joint or region in the hind limb of a quadruped corresponding to the human ankle

²hock *n or vb* : pawn

hock·ey \'häkē\ *n* : game played on ice or a field by 2 teams

hod \'häd\ *n* 1 : carrier for bricks or mortar 2 : scuttle

hodge·podge \'häj,päj\ *n* : heterogeneous mixture

hoe \'hō\ *n* : long-handled tool for cultivating or weeding —**hoe** *vb*

hog \'hóg, 'hág\ *n* 1 : domestic adult swine 2 : glutton ~ *vb* : take selfishly —**hog·gish** *adj*

hogs·head \'hógz,hed, 'hágz-\ *n* : large cask or barrel

hog·wash *n* : nonsense

hoist \'hóist\ *vb* : lift ~ *n* 1 : lift 2 : apparatus for hoisting

¹hold \'hōld\ *vb* **held** \'held\; **hold·ing** 1 : possess 2 : restrain 3 : have a grasp on 4 : remain or keep in a particular situation or position 5 : contain 6 : regard 7 : cause to occur 8 : occupy esp. by appointment or election ~ *n* 1 : act or manner of holding 2 : restraining or controlling influence —**hold·er** *n* —**hold forth** : speak at length —**hold to** : adhere to —**hold with** : agree with

²hold *n* : cargo area of a ship

hold·ing \'hōldiŋ\ *n* : property owned —usu. pl.

hold·up *n* 1 : robbery at the point of a gun 2 : delay

hole \'hōl\ *n* 1 : opening into or through something 2 : hollow place (as a pit) 3 : den —**hole** *vb*

hol·i·day \'hälə,dā\ *n* 1 : day of freedom from work 2 : vacation —**holi·day** *vb*

ho·li·ness \'hōlēnəs\ *n* : quality or state of being holy

hol·ler \'hälər\ *vb* : cry out —**holler** *n*

hol·low \'häl-ō\ *adj* -**low·er** \-əwər\; -**est** 1 : sunken 2 : having a cavity within 3 : sounding like a noise made in an empty place 4 : empty of value or meaning ~ *vb* : make or become hollow ~ *n* 1 : surface depression 2 : cavity —**hol·low·ness** *n*

hol·ly \-ē\ *n, pl* -**lies** : evergreen tree or shrub

hol·ly·hock \-,häk, -,hök\ *n* : tall perennial herb grown for its showy flowers

ho·lo·caust \'hälə,kóst, 'hō-, 'hó-\ *n* : thorough destruction esp. by fire

hol·stein \'hōl,stēn, -,stīn\ *n* : large black-and-white dairy cow

hol·ster \'hōlstər\ *n* : case for a pistol

ho·ly \'hōlē\ *adj* -**li·er**; -**est** 1 : sacred 2 : spiritually pure

hom·age \'(h)ämij\ *n* : reverent regard

home \'hōm\ *n* 1 : residence 2 : congenial environment 3 : place of origin or refuge ~ *vb* **homed**; **hom·ing** : go or return home —**home·bred** *adj* —**home·com·ing** *n* —**home·grown** *adj* —**home·land** \-,land\ *n* —**home·less** *adj* —**home·made** \-,(m)ād\ *adj*

home·ly \-lē\ *adj* -**li·er**; -**est** : plain or unattractive —**home·li·ness** *n*

home·mak·er *n* : one who manages a household —**home·mak·ing** *n*

home·sick *adj* : longing for home —**home·sick·ness** *n*

home·spun \-,spən\ *adj* : simple

home·stead \-,sted\ *n* : home and land (as a tract acquired from U.S. public lands) occupied and worked by a family —**home·stead·er** \-ər\ *n*

home·stretch *n* 1 : last part of a race-track 2 : final stage

¹home·ward \-wərd\, **home·wards** \-wərdz\ *adv* : toward home

²homeward *adj* : in the direction of home

home·work *n* : school lessons to be done outside the classroom

hom·ey \'hōmē\ *adj* hom·i·er; -est : intimate in nature

ho·mi·cide \'hämə,sīd, 'hō-\ *n* : the killing of one human being by another —**hom·i·cid·al** \,hämə'sīd⁹l\ *adj*

hom·i·ly \'häməlē\ *n, pl* -**lies** : sermon —**hom·i·let·ic** \,hämə'letik\ *adj*

hom·i·ny \'hämənē\ *n* : type of processed hulled corn

ho·mo·ge·neous \,hōmə'jēnēəs, -nyəs\ *adj* : of the same or a similar kind —**ho·mo·ge·ne·i·ty** \-jə'nēətē\ *n* —**ho·mo·ge·neous·ly** *adv* —**ho·mo·ge·neous·ness** *n*

ho·mog·e·nize \hō'mäjə,nīz, hə-\ *vb* -**nized**; -**niz·ing** : make the particles (as in milk or paint) of uniform size and even distribution —**ho·mog·e·ni·za·tion** \-,mäjənə'zāshən\ *n* —**ho·mog·e·niz·er** *n*

ho·mo·graph \'hämə,graf, 'hōmə-\ *n* : one of 2 or more words (as the noun *conduct* and the verb *conduct*) spelled alike but different in origin or meaning or pronunciation

hom·onym \'hämə,nim, 'hōmə-\ *n* 1 : homophone 2 : homograph 3 : one of 2 or more words (as *pool* of water and *pool* the game) spelled and pronounced alike but different in meaning

ho·mo·phone \'hämə,fōn, 'hōmə-\ *n* : one of 2 or more words (as *to, too,* and *two*) pronounced alike but different in origin or meaning or spelling

Ho·mo sa·pi·ens \,hōmō'sapēənz, -'sä-\ *n* : man or mankind

ho·mo·sex·u·al \,hōmə'seksh(ə)wəl\ *adj* : oriented toward one's own sex —**homosexual** *n*

hone \'hōn\ *n* : sharpening stone — **hone** *vb* —**hon·er** *n*

hon·est \'änəst\ *adj* **1** : free from deception **2** : trustworthy **3** : frank — **hon·est·ly** *adv* —**hon·es·ty** \-əstē\ *n*

hon·ey \'hənē\ *n, pl* -**eys** : sweet sticky substance made by bees (**hon·ey·bees**) from the nectar of flowers

hon·ey·comb *n* : mass of 6-sided wax cells built by honeybees or something like it ~ *vb* : make or become full of holes like a honeycomb

hon·ey·moon *n* : holiday taken by a newly married couple —**honeymoon** *vb*

hon·ey·suck·le \-ˌsəkəl\ *n* : shrub or vine with flowers rich in nectar

honk \'häŋk, 'hȯŋk\ *n* : cry of a goose or a similar sound —**honk** *vb* —**honk·er** *n*

hon·or \'änər\ *n* **1** : good name **2** : outward respect or symbol of this **3** : privilege **4** : person of superior rank or position—used esp. as a title **5** : something or someone worthy of respect **6** : integrity ~ *vb* **1** : regard with honor **2** : confer honor on **3** : fulfill the terms of —**hon·or·able** \'än(ə)rəbəl\ *adj* —**hon·or·ably** \-blē\ *adv* —**hon·or·ari·ly** \ˌänəˈrerəlē\ *adv* —**hon·or·ary** \'änəˌrerē\ *adj*

hood \'hu̇d\ *n* **1** : part of a garment that covers the head **2** : covering over an automobile engine compartment —**hood·ed** *adj*

-hood \ˌhu̇d\ *n suffix* **1** : state, condition, or quality **2** : individuals sharing a state or character

hood·lum \'hu̇dləm, 'hu̇d-\ *n* : thug

hood·wink \'hu̇dˌwiŋk\ *vb* : deceive

hoof \'hu̇f, 'hüf\ *n, pl* **hooves** \'hu̇vz, 'hüvz\ *or* **hoofs** : horny covering of the toes of some mammals (as horses or cattle) —**hoofed** \'hu̇ft, 'hüft\ *adj*

hook \'hu̇k\ *n* : curved or bent device for catching, holding, or pulling ~ *vb* : seize or make fast with a hook —**hook·er** *n*

hoo·kah \'hu̇kə, 'hü-\ *n* : pipe for smoking so arranged that the smoke passes through water

hook·worm *n* : parasitic intestinal worm

hoo·li·gan \'hüligən\ *n* : thug

hoop \'hüp, 'hu̇p\ *n* : circular strip, figure, or object

hoot \'hüt\ *vb* **1** : shout in contempt **2** : make the cry of an owl —**hoot** *n* —**hoot·er** *n*

¹hop \'häp\ *vb* -**pp**- : move by quick springy leaps —**hop** *n*

²hop *n* : vine whose ripe dried flowers are used to flavor malt liquors

hope \'hōp\ *vb* **hoped; hop·ing** : desire with expectation of fulfillment ~ *n* **1** : act of hoping **2** : something hoped for —**hope·ful** \-fəl\ *adj* —**hope·ful·ly** *adv* —**hope·ful·ness** *n* —**hope·less** *adj* —**hope·less·ly** *adv* —**hope·less·ness** *n*

hop·per \'häpər\ *n* : container that releases its contents through the bottom

horde \'hȯrd\ *n* : throng or swarm

hore·hound \'hȯrˌhau̇nd\ *n* : aromatic bitter mint

ho·ri·zon \hə'rīz³n\ *n* : line marking the apparent junction of earth and sky

hor·i·zon·tal \ˌhȯrəˈzänt³l\ *adj* : parallel to the horizon —**hor·i·zon·tal·ly** *adv*

hor·mone \'hȯrˌmōn\ *n* : cell product in body fluids that has a specific effect on other cells —**hor·mon·al** \hȯr'mōn³l\ *adj*

horn \'hȯrn\ *n* **1** : one of the hard bony projections on the head of many hoofed animals **2** : brass wind instrument —**horned** *adj* —**horn·less** *adj* —**horny** *adj*

hor·net \'hȯrnət\ *n* : large social wasp

ho·rol·o·gy \hə'räləjē\ *n* : science of measuring time or making clocks —**hor·o·log·ic** \ˌhȯrəˈläjik\ *adj* —**ho·rol·o·gist** \hə'räləjəst\ *n*

horo·scope \'hȯrəˌskōp\ *n* : astrological forecast

hor·ren·dous \hȯ'rendəs\ *adj* : horrible

hor·ri·ble \'hȯrəbəl\ *adj* **1** : having or causing horror **2** : highly disagreeable —**hor·ri·ble·ness** *n* —**hor·ri·bly** \-blē\ *adv*

hor·rid \'hȯrəd\ *adj* : horrible —**hor·rid·ly** *adv*

hor·ri·fy \-ə,fī\ *vb* -**fied; -fy·ing** : cause to feel horror

hor·ror \-ər\ *n* **1** : intense fear, dread, or dismay **2** : intense repugnance **3** : something horrible

hors d'oeuvre \ȯr'dərv\ *n, pl* **hors d'oeuvres** \-'dərv(z)\ : appetizer

horse \'hȯrs\ *n* : large solid-hoofed domesticated mammal —**horse·back** *n or adv* —**horse·hair** *n* —**horse·hide** *n* —**horse·less** *adj* —**horse·man** *n* —**horse·man·ship** *n* —**horse·wom·an** *n* —**hors·ey, horsy** *adj*

horse·fly *n* : large fly with bloodsucking female

horse·play *n* : rough boisterous play

horse·pow·er *n* : unit of mechanical power

horse·rad·ish *n* : herb with a pungent root used as a condiment

horse·shoe \'hȯrs(,)shü\ *n* : protective metal plate fitted to the rim of a horse's hoof

hor·ta·to·ry \'hȯrtə,tōrē\ *adj* : giving exhortation

hor·ti·cul·ture \'hȯrtə,kəlchər\ *n* : science of growing fruits, vegetables, and flowers —**hor·ti·cul·tur·al** \,hȯrtə'kəlch(ə)rəl\ *adj* —**hor·ti·cul·tur·ist** \-rəst\ *n*

ho·san·na \hō'zanə, -'zän-\ *interj* — used as a cry of acclamation and adoration

hose \'hōz\ *n* **1** *pl* **hose** : stocking or sock **2** *pl* **hos·es** : flexible tube for conveying fluids ~ *vb* **hosed**; **hos·ing** : spray, water, or wash with a hose

ho·siery \'hōzh(ə)rē, 'hōz(ə)-\ *n* : stockings or socks

hos·pice \'häspəs\ *n* **1** : lodging (as for travelers) maintained by a religious order **2** : facility or program for those with fatal illnesses

hos·pi·ta·ble \hä'spitəbəl, 'häs,(,)pit-\ *adj* : given to generous and cordial reception of guests —**hos·pi·ta·bly** \-blē\ *adv*

hos·pi·tal \'häs,pit³l\ *n* : institution where the sick or injured receive medical care —**hos·pi·tal·iza·tion** \,häs,pit³lə'zāshən\ *n* —**hos·pi·tal·ize** \'häs,pit³l,īz\ *vb*

hos·pi·tal·i·ty \,häspə'talətē\ *n*, *pl* **-ties** : hospitable treatment, reception, or disposition

¹host \'hōst\ *n* **1** : army **2** : multitude

²host *n* : one who receives or entertains guests —**host** *vb*

³host *n* : eucharistic bread

hos·tage \'hästij\ *n* : person held to guarantee that promises will be kept or demands met

hos·tel \'häst³l\ *n* : lodging for youth —**hos·tel·er** *n*

hos·tel·ry \-rē\ *n*, *pl* **-ries** : hotel

host·ess \'hōstəs\ *n* : woman who is host

hos·tile \'häst³l, -,tīl\ *adj* : openly or actively unfriendly or opposed to someone or something —**hostile** *n* —**hos·tile·ly** *adv* —**hos·til·i·ty** \häs-'tilətē\ *n*

hot \'hät\ *adj* **-tt-** **1** : having a high temperature **2** : giving a sensation of heat or burning **3** : ardent **4** : pungent —**hot** *adv* —**hot·ly** *adv* —**hot·ness** *n*

hot·bed *n* : environment that favors rapid growth

hot dog *n* : frankfurter

ho·tel \hō'tel\ *n* : building where lodging and personal services are provided

hot·head·ed *adj* : impetuous —**hot·head** *n* —**hot·head·ed·ly** *adv* —**hot·head·ed·ness** *n*

hot·house *n* : glass-enclosed house for raising plants

hound \'haůnd\ *n* : long-eared hunting dog ~ *vb* : pursue relentlessly

hour \'aů(ə)r\ *n* **1** : 24th part of a day **2** : time of day —**hour·ly** *adv or adj*

hour·glass *n* : glass vessel for measuring time

house \'haůs, *n* **1** *pl* **hous·es** \'haůzəz\ **1** : building to live in **2** : household **3** : legislative body **4** : business firm ~ \'haůz\ *vb* **housed**; **hous·ing** : provide with or take shelter —**house·boat** \'haůs-\ *n* —**house·clean** \'haůs-\ *vb* —**house·clean** \'haůs-\ *vb* —**house·ful** \-,fůl\ *n* —**house·keep·er** *n* —**house·keep·ing** *n* —**house·maid** *n* —**house·wares** *n pl* —**house·work** *n*

house·break *vb* **·broke**; **·bro·ken**; **·break·ing** : train to excretory habits acceptable in indoor living

house·fly *n* : two-winged fly common about human habitations

house·hold \-,hōld\ *n* : those who dwell as a family under the same roof ~ *adj* **1** : domestic **2** : common or familiar —**house·hold·er** *n*

house·warm·ing *n* : party to celebrate moving into a house

house·wife \'haůs-,wīf\ *n* : married woman in charge of a household —**house·wife·ly** *adj* —**house·wif·ery** \-,wif(ə)rē\ *n*

hous·ing \'haůziŋ\ *n* **1** : dwellings for people **2** : protective covering

hove *past of* HEAVE

hov·el \'həvəl, 'häv-\ *n* : small wretched house

hov·er \'həvər, 'häv-\ *vb* **1** : remain suspended in the air **2** : move about in the vicinity

how \'haů\ *adv* **1** : in what way or condition **2** : for what reason **3** : to what extent ~ *conj* : in what manner or condition

how·ev·er \haů'evər\ *conj* : in whatever manner ~ *adv* **1** : to whatever degree or in whatever manner **2** : in spite of that

how·itz·er \'haůətsər\ *n* : short cannon

howl \'haůl\ *vb* : emit a loud long doleful sound like a dog —**howl** *n* —**howl·er** *n*

hoy·den \\'hȯid⁰n\\ n : girl or woman of saucy or carefree behavior

hub \\'həb\\ n : central part (as of a wheel) —**hub·cap** n

hub·bub \\'həb,əb\\ n : uproar

hu·bris \\'hyübrəs\\ n : excessive pride

huck·le·ber·ry \\'həkəl,berē\\ n 1 : shrub related to the blueberry or its berry 2 : blueberry

huck·ster \\'həkstər\\ n : peddler

hud·dle \\'həd³l\\ vb -dled; -dling 1 : crowd together 2 : confer —**huddle** n

hue \\'hyü\\ n : attribute of colors that permits them to be classed as red, yellow, green, blue, or an intermediate color —**hued** \\'hyüd\\ adj

huff \\'həf\\ n : fit of pique —**huffy** adj

hug \\'həg\\ vb -gg- 1 : press tightly in the arms 2 : stay close to —**hug** n

huge \\'hyüj\\ adj large or extensive —**huge·ly** adv —**huge·ness** n

hu·la \\'hülə\\ n : Polynesian dance

hulk \\'həlk\\ n 1 : bulky or unwieldy person or thing 2 : old ship unfit for service —**hulk·ing** adj

hull \\'həl\\ n 1 : outer covering of a fruit or seed 2 : frame or body of a ship ~ vb : remove the hulls of —**hull·er** n

hul·la·ba·loo \\'hələbə,lü\\ n, pl -loos : uproar

hum \\'həm\\ vb -mm- : make a prolonged sound like that of the speech sound \\m\\ —**hum** n —**hum·mer** n

hu·man \\'(h)yümən\\ adj 1 : of or relating to the species people belong to 2 : by, for, or like people —**human** n —**human·kind** n —**hu·man·ly** adv —**hu·man·ness** n

hu·mane \\(h)yü'mān\\ adj : showing compassion or consideration for others —**hu·mane·ly** adv —**hu·mane·ness** n

hu·man·ism \\'(h)yümə,nizəm\\ n : doctrine or way of life centered on human interests or values —**hu·man·ist** \\-nəst\\ n or adj —**hu·man·is·tic** \\,(h)yümə'nistik\\ adj

hu·man·i·tar·i·an \\(h)yü,manə'terēən\\ n : person promoting human welfare —**humanitarian** adj —**hu·man·i·tar·i·an·ism** n

hu·man·i·ty \\(h)yü'manətē\\ n, pl -ties 1 : human or humane quality or state 2 : mankind

hu·man·ize \\'(h)yümə,nīz\\ vb -ized; -iz·ing : make human or humane —**hu·man·iza·tion** \\,(h)yümənə'zāshən\\ n

hu·man·oid \\'(h)yümə,nȯid\\ adj : having human form —**humanoid** n

hum·ble \\'(h)əmbəl\\ adj -bler; -blest 1 : not proud or haughty 2 : not pretentious ~ vb -bled; -bling : make humble —**hum·ble·ness** n —**humbler** n —**hum·bly** \\-blē\\ adv

hum·bug \\'həm,bəg\\ n : nonsense

hum·drum \\-,drəm\\ adj : monotonous

hu·mid \\'(h)yüməd\\ adj : containing or characterized by moisture —**hu·mid·i·fi·ca·tion** \\hyü,midəfi'kāshən\\ n —**hu·mid·i·fi·er** \\-'midə,fī(ə)r\\ n —**hu·mid·i·fy** \\-,fī\\ vb —**hu·mid·ly** adv

hu·mid·i·ty \\(h)yü'midətē\\ n, pl -ties : atmospheric moisture

hu·mi·dor \\'(h)yümə,dȯr\\ n : humidified storage case

hu·mil·i·ate \\(h)yü'milē,āt\\ vb -at·ed; -at·ing : injure the self-respect of —**hu·mil·i·at·ing·ly** adv —**hu·mil·i·a·tion** \\-,milē'āshən\\ n

hu·mil·i·ty \\(h)yü'milətē\\ n : humble quality or state

hum·ming·bird \\'həmiŋ,bərd\\ n : tiny American bird

hum·mock \\'həmək\\ n : mound or knoll

hu·mor \\'(h)yümər\\ n 1 : mood 2 : quality of being laughably ludicrous or incongruous 3 : appreciation of what is ludicrous or incongruous 4 : something intended to be funny ~ vb : comply with the wishes or mood of —**hu·mor·ist** \\-(ə)rəst\\ n —**hu·mor·less** adj —**hu·mor·less·ly** adv —**hu·mor·less·ness** n —**hu·mor·ous** \\'(h)yümə(ə)rəs\\ adj —**hu·mor·ous·ly** adv —**hu·mor·ous·ness** n

hump \\'həmp\\ n : rounded protuberance —**humped** adj

hump·back n : hunchback —**hump·backed** adj

hu·mus \\'(h)yüməs\\ n : dark organic part of soil

hunch \\'hənch\\ vb : assume or cause to assume a bent or crooked posture ~ n : strong intuitive feeling

hunch·back n 1 : back with a hump 2 : person with a crooked back —**hunch·backed** adj

hun·dred \\'həndrəd\\ n, pl -dreds or -dred : 10 times 10 —**hundred** adj —**hun·dredth** \\-drədth\\ adj or n

hung past of HANG

hun·ger \\'həŋgər\\ n 1 : craving or urgent need for food 2 : strong desire —**hunger** vb —**hun·gri·ly** \\-grəlē\\ adv —**hun·gry** adj

hunk \\'həŋk\\ n : large piece

hun·ker \\'həŋkər\\ vb : squat down

hunt \\'hənt\\ vb 1 : pursue for food or

hur·dle \'hərd³l\ n 1 : barrier to leap over 2 : obstacle —**hurdle** vb —**hur·dler** n

hurl \'hərl\ vb : throw with violence —**hurl** n —**hurl·er** n

hur·rah \hu̇-'rȯ, -'rä\ interj —used to express joy or approval

hur·ri·cane \'hər-ə-ˌkān\ n : tropical storm with winds of 74 miles per hour or greater

hur·ry \'hər-ē\ vb -ried; -ry·ing : go or cause to go with haste ~ n : extreme haste —**hur·ried·ly** adv —**hur·ried·ness** n

hurt \'hərt\ vb hurt; hurt·ing 1 : feel or cause pain 2 : do harm to ~ n 1 : bodily injury 2 : harm —**hurt·ful** \-fəl\ adj

hur·tle \'hərt³l\ vb -tled; -tling : move with rapid force

hus·band \'həz-bənd\ n : married man ~ vb : manage prudently

hus·band·ry \-bən-drē\ n 1 : careful use 2 : agriculture

hush \'həsh\ vb : make or become quiet ~ n : silence

husk \'həsk\ n : outer covering of a seed or fruit ~ vb : strip the husk from —**husk·er** n

¹**husky** \'həs-kē\ adj -ki·er; -est : hoarse —**husk·i·ly** adv —**husk·i·ness** n

²**husky** adj -ki·er; -est : burly —**husk·i·ness** n

³**husky** n, pl -kies : working dog of the arctic

hussy \'həz-ē, 'həs-\ n, pl -sies 1 : brazen woman 2 : mischievous girl

hus·tle \'həs-əl\ vb -tled; -tling 1 : hurry 2 : work energetically —**hustle** n —**hus·tler** \'həs-lər\ n

hut \'hət\ n : small often temporary dwelling

hutch \'həch\ n 1 : cupboard with open shelves 2 : pen for an animal

hy·a·cinth \'hī-ə-ˌsinth\ n : bulbous herb grown for bell-shaped flowers

hy·brid \'hī-brəd\ n : offspring of genetically differing parents —**hybrid** adj —**hy·brid·iza·tion** \ˌhī-brə-də-'zāshən\ n —**hy·brid·ize** \'hī-brəd-ˌīz\ vb —**hy·brid·iz·er** n

hy·drant \'hī-drənt\ n : pipe from which water may be drawn to fight fires

hy·drau·lic \hī-'drȯ-lik\ adj : operated by liquid forced through a small hole —**hy·drau·lics** \-liks\ n

hy·dro·car·bon \ˌhī-drə-'kärbən\ n : organic compound of carbon and hydrogen

hy·dro·elec·tric \ˌhī-drō-i-'lek-trik\ adj : producing electricity by waterpower —**hy·dro·elec·tric·i·ty** \-ˌlek-'tris-ət-ē\ n

hy·dro·gen \'hī-drəjən\ n : gaseous colorless odorless flammable chemical element —**hy·drog·e·nous** \hī-'dräjənəs\ adj

hydrogen bomb n : powerful bomb that derives its energy from the union of atomic nuclei

hy·dro·pho·bia \ˌhī-drə-'fōbēə\ n : rabies

hy·dro·plane \'hī-drə-ˌplān\ n : speedboat that skims the water

hy·drous \'hī-drəs\ adj : containing water

hy·e·na \hī-'ē-nə\ n : nocturnal carnivorous mammal of Asia and Africa

hy·giene \'hī-ˌjēn\ n : conditions or practices conducive to health —**hy·gien·ic** \ˌhī-jē-'enik; hī-'jen-, -'jēn-\ adj —**hy·gien·i·cal·ly** \-ik(ə)lē\ adv —**hy·gien·ist** \hī-'jēnəst, -'jen-; 'hī-jēn-\ n

hy·grom·e·ter \hī-'grämət-ər\ n : instrument for measuring atmospheric humidity

hying pres part of HIE

hymn \'him\ n : song of praise esp. to God —**hymn** vb —**hym·nal** \'himnəl\ n

hyper- prefix 1 : above or beyond 2 : excessively or excessive

hyperacid	hypermasculine
hyperacidity	hypermilitant
hyperactive	hypermoralistic
hyperacute	hypernational-
hyperaggressive	istic
hyperanxious	hyperreactive
hypercautious	hyperrealistic
hyperclean	hyperromantic
hypercon-	hypersensitive
scientious	hypersensi-
hypercorrect	tiveness
hypercritical	hypersensitivity
hyperemotional	hypersexual
hyperenergetic	hypersusceptible
hyperexcitable	hypersuspicious
hyperfastidious	hypertense
hyperintense	hypervigilant

hy·per·bo·le \hī-'pərbə-(ˌ)lē\ n : extravagant exaggeration

hy·per·ten·sion \ˌhīpər-ˌtenchən\ n : high blood pressure —**hy·per·ten·sive** \ˌhīpər-'tensiv\ adj or n

hy·phen \'hī-fən\ n : punctuation mark

- used to divide or compound words —hyphen *vb*

hy·phen·ate \'hīfə,nāt\ *vb* -at·ed; -at·ing : connect or divide with a hyphen —hy·phen·a·tion \,hīfə'nāshən\ *n*

hyp·no·sis \hip'nōsəs\ *n, pl* -no·ses \-,sēz\ : induced state like sleep in which the subject is responsive to suggestions of the inducer (**hyp·no·tist** \'hipnətəst\) —**hyp·no·tism** \'hipnə,tizəm\ *n* —**hyp·no·tiz·able** \-,tīzəbəl\ *adj* —**hyp·no·tize** \-,tīz\ *vb*

hyp·not·ic \hip'nätik\ *adj* : relating to hypnosis —hypnotic *n* —hyp·not·i·cal·ly \-ik(ə)lē\ *adv*

hy·po·chon·dria \,hīpə'kändrēə\ *n* : morbid concern for one's health —hy·po·chon·dri·ac \-drē,ak\ *adj or n*

hy·poc·ri·sy \hip'äkrəsē\ *n, pl* -sies : a feigning to be what one is not —**hyp·o·crite** \'hipə,krit\ *n* —**hyp·o·crit·i·cal** \,hipə'kritikəl\ *adj* —**hyp·o·crit·i·cal·ly** *adv*

hy·po·der·mic \,hīpə'dərmik\ *adj* : used for or given by injection beneath the skin ~ *n* : hypodermic syringe

hy·pot·e·nuse \hī'pät²n,(y)üs, -,(y)üz\ *n* : side of a right-angled triangle opposite the right angle

hy·poth·e·sis \hī'päthəsəs\ *n, pl* -e·ses \-,sēz\ : assumption made in order to test its consequences —hy·poth·e·size \-,sīz\ *vb* —hy·po·thet·i·cal \,hīpə'thetikəl\ *adj* —hy·po·thet·i·cal·ly *adv*

hys·ter·ec·to·my \,histə'rektəmē\ *n, pl* -mies : surgical removal of the uterus —hys·ter·ec·to·mize \-,mīz\ *vb*

hys·te·ria \his'terēə, -tir-\ *n* : uncontrollable fear or emotion —hys·ter·i·cal \-'terikəl\ *adj* —hys·ter·i·cal·ly *adv*

hys·ter·ics \-'teriks\ *n pl* : uncontrollable laughter or crying

I

i \'ī\ *n, pl* i's *or* is \'īz\ : 9th letter of the alphabet

I \(')ī, ə\ *pron* : the speaker

-ial *adj suffix* : of, relating to, or characterized by

-ian —see -AN

ibis \'ībəs\ *n, pl* ibis *or* ibis·es : wading bird with a down-curved bill

-ible —see -ABLE

ice \'īs\ *n* 1 : frozen water 2 : frozen dessert ~ *vb* iced; ic·ing 1 : freeze 2 : chill 3 : cover with icing

ice·berg \'īs,bərg\ *n* : large floating mass of ice

ice·box *n* : refrigerator

ice·break·er *n* : ship equipped to cut through ice

ice cream *n* : sweet frozen food

ice-skate *vb* : skate on ice —ice skater

ich·thy·ol·o·gy \,ikthē'äləjē\ *n* : study of fishes —ich·thy·ol·o·gist \-jəst\ *n*

ici·cle \'ī,sikəl\ *n* : hanging mass of ice

ic·ing \'īsiŋ\ *n* : sweet usu. creamy coating for baked goods

icon \'ī,kän\ *n* : religious image

icon·o·clast \ī'känə,klast\ *n* : attacker

of cherished beliefs or institutions —icon·o·clasm \-,klazəm\ *n*

icy \'īsē\ *adj* ic·i·er; -est 1 : covered or consisting of ice 2 : very cold —ic·i·ly *adv* —ic·i·ness *n*

id \'id\ *n* : unconscious part of the mind

idea \ī'dēə\ *n* 1 : something imagined in the mind 2 : purpose or plan

ide·al \ī'dē(ə)l\ *adj* 1 : imaginary 2 : perfect ~ *n* 1 : standard of excellence 2 : model 3 : aim —ide·al·ly *adv*

ide·al·ism \ī'dē(ə),lizəm\ *n* : adherence to ideals 2 : tendency to see things as they should be —ide·al·ist \-ləst\ *n* —ide·al·is·tic \ī,dē(ə)'listik\ *adj* —ide·al·is·ti·cal·ly \-tik(ə)lē\ *adv*

ide·al·ize \ī'dē(ə),līz\ *vb* -ized; -iz·ing : think of or represent as ideal —ide·al·iza·tion \-,dē(ə)'zāshən\ *n*

iden·ti·cal \ī'dentikəl\ *adj* 1 : being the same 2 : exactly or essentially alike

iden·ti·fi·ca·tion \ī,dentəfə'kāshən\ *n* 1 : act of identifying 2 : evidence of identity

iden·ti·fy \ī'dentə,fī\ *vb* -fied; -fy·ing 1 : associate 2 : establish the identity of —iden·ti·fi·able \-,fīəbəl\ *adj* —iden·ti·fi·er \-,fī(-ə)r\ *n*

iden·ti·ty \ī'dentətē\ *n, pl* -ties 1

: sameness of essential character 2
: individuality 3 : fact of being what
is supposed

ide·ol·o·gy \ˌīdē'äləjē, ˌid-\ n, pl -gies
: body of beliefs —ide·o·log·i·cal
\ˌīdēə'läjikəl, ˌid-\ adj

id·i·om \'idēəm\ n 1 : language peculiar to a person or group 2 : expression with a special meaning —id·i-
om·at·ic \ˌidēə'matik\ adj —id·i·om-
at·i·cal·ly \-ik(ə)lē\ adv

id·i·o·syn·cra·sy \ˌidēə'sigkrəsē\ n, pl
-sies : personal peculiarity —id·i·o-
syn·crat·ic \-ōsin'kratik\ adj —id·i·o-
syn·crat·i·cal·ly \-'kratik(ə)lē\ adv

id·i·ot \'idēət\ n : feebleminded or
foolish person —id·i·o·cy \-əsē\ n —
id·i·ot·ic \ˌidē'ätik\ adj —id·i·ot·i-
cal·ly \-ik(ə)lē\ adv

idle \'id°l\ adj idler; idlest 1 : worthless 2 : inactive : lazy ~ vb idled;
idling : spend time doing nothing —
idle·ness n —idler n —idly \'idlē\
adv

idol \'id°l\ n 1 : image of a god 2
: object of devotion —idol·iza·tion
\ˌīd°lə'zāshən\ n —idol·ize
\'īd°līz\ vb

idol·a·ter \ī'dälətər\ n : worshiper of
idols —idol·a·trous \-trəs\ adj —
idol·a·try \-trē\ n

-ier —see -ER

if \(ˌ)if, əf\ conj 1 : in the event that 2
: whether 3 : even though

-ify \ə,fī\ vb suffix : -fy

ig·loo \'iglü\ n, pl -loos : hut made of
snow blocks

ig·nite \ig'nīt\ vb -nit·ed; -nit·ing : set
afire or catch fire —ig·nit·able
\-'nītəbəl\ adj

ig·ni·tion \ig'nishən\ n 1 : a setting on
fire 2 : process or means of igniting
fuel

ig·no·ble \ig'nōbəl\ adj : not honorable
—ig·no·bly \-blē\ adv

ig·no·min·i·ous \ˌignə'minēəs\ adj 1
: dishonorable 2 : humiliating —ig-
no·min·i·ous·ly adv —ig·no·mi·ny
\'ignə,minē, ig'nämənē\ n

ig·no·ra·mus \ˌignə'rāməs\ n : ignorant person

ig·no·rant \'ignərənt\ adj 1 : lacking
knowledge 2 : stupid 3 : unaware —
ig·no·rance \-rəns\ n —ig·no·rant·ly
adv

ig·nore \ig'nōr\ vb -nored; -nor·ing
: refuse to notice

igua·na \i'gwänə\ n : tropical American lizard

ilk \'ilk\ n : kind

ill \'il\ adj worse \'wərs\; worst
\'wərst\ 1 : sick 2 : bad 3 : inferior

4 : hostile ~ adv worse; worst 1
: with displeasure 2 : harshly 3
: scarcely 4 : badly ~ n 1 : evil 2
: misfortune 3 : sickness

il·le·gal \il'(l)ēgəl\ adj : not lawful —
il·le·gal·i·ty \ˌili'galətē\ n —il·le·gal-
ly \il'(l)ēgəlē\ adv

il·leg·i·ble \il'(l)ejəbəl\ adj : not legible
—il·leg·i·bil·i·ty \il,(l)ejə'bilətē\ n —
il·leg·i·bly \il'(l)ejəblē\ adv

il·le·git·i·mate \ˌili'jitəmət\ adj 1 : born
of unmarried parents 2 : illegal —il·le-
git·i·ma·cy \-əməsē\ n —il·le·git·i-
mate·ly adv

il·lic·it \il'(l)isət\ adj : not lawful —il-
lic·it·ly adv

il·lim·it·able \il'(l)imətəbəl\ adj
: boundless —il·lim·it·ably \-blē\
adv

il·lit·er·ate \il'(l)it(ə)rət\ adj : unable
to read or write —il·lit·er·a·cy
\-(ə)rəsē\ n —illiterate n

ill-na·tured \-'nāchərd\ adj : cross —
ill-na·tured·ly adv

ill·ness \'ilnəs\ n : sickness

il·log·i·cal \il'(l)äjikəl\ adj : contrary to
logic —il·log·i·cal·ly adv

ill-starred \'il'stärd\ adj : unlucky

il·lu·sive \il'üsiv\ adj : illusory

il·lu·so·ry \il'üs(ə)rē, -'üz-\ adj : based
on or producing illusion

il·lus·trate \'iləs,trāt\ vb -trat·ed; -trat-
ing 1 : explain by example 2 : provide
with pictures or figures —il·lus-
tra·tor \-ər\ n

il·lus·tra·tion \ˌiləs'trāshən\ n 1 : example that explains 2 : pictorial
explanation

il·lus·tra·tive \il'əstrativ\ adj : designed to illustrate —il·lus·tra·tive·ly
adv

il·lus·tri·ous \-'trēəs\ adj : notably or
brilliantly outstanding —il·lus·tri-
ous·ness n

ill will n : unfriendly feeling

im·age \'imij\ n 1 : likeness 2 : visual
counterpart of an object formed by
a lens or mirror 3 : mental picture ~
vb -aged; -ag·ing : create a representation of

im·ag·ery \'imij(ə)rē\ n 1 : images 2
: figurative language

imag·i·nary \im'ajə,nerē\ adj : existing only in the imagination

imag·i·na·tion \im,aj·ə'nāshən\ *n* 1 : act or power of forming a mental image 2 : creative ability —imag·i·na·tive \im'aj(ə)nətiv, -ə,nātiv\ *adj* —imag·i·na·tive·ly *adv*

imag·ine \im'ajən\ *vb* -ined; -in·ing : form a mental picture of something not present —imag·in·able \-'aj(ə)nəbəl\ *adj* —imag·in·ably \-blē\ *adv*

im·bal·ance \(')im'baləns\ *n* : lack of balance

im·be·cile \'imbəsəl, -,sil\ *n* : feeble-minded or foolish person —imbecile, im·be·cil·ic \,imbə'silik\ *adj* —im·be·cil·i·ty \-'silətē\ *n*

im·bibe \im'bīb\ *vb* -bibed; -bib·ing : drink —im·bib·er *n*

im·bro·glio \im'brōlyō\ *n, pl* -glios : complicated situation

im·brue \im'brü\ *vb* -brued; -bru·ing : steep

im·bue \-'byü\ *vb* -bued; -bu·ing : fill (as with color or a feeling)

im·i·tate \'imə,tāt\ *vb* -tat·ed; -tat·ing 1 : follow as a model 2 : mimic —im·i·ta·tive \-,tātiv\ *adj* —im·i·ta·tor \-ər\ *n*

im·i·ta·tion \,imə'tāshən\ *n* 1 : act of imitating 2 : copy —imitation *adj*

im·mac·u·late \im'akyələt\ *adj* : without stain or blemish —im·mac·u·late·ly *adv*

im·ma·te·ri·al \,imə'tirēəl\ *adj* 1 : spiritual 2 : not relevant —im·ma·te·ri·al·i·ty \-,tirē'alətē\ *n*

im·ma·ture \,imə't(y)ur\ *adj* : not yet mature —im·ma·tu·ri·ty \-ətē\ *n*

im·mea·sur·able \(')im'ezh(ə)rəbəl\ *adj* : indefinitely extensive —im·mea·sur·ably \-blē\ *adv*

im·me·di·a·cy \im'ēdēəsē\ *n, pl* -cies : urgency

im·me·di·ate \-ēət\ *adj* 1 : direct 2 : being next in line 3 : made or done at once 4 : not distant —im·me·di·ate·ly *adv*

im·me·mo·ri·al \,imə'mōrēəl\ *adj* : old beyond memory

im·mense \im'ens\ *adj* : vast —im·mense·ly *adv* —im·men·si·ty \-'ensətē\ *n*

im·merse \im'ərs\ *vb* -mersed; -mers·ing 1 : plunge or dip esp. into liquid 2 : engross —im·mer·sion \-'ərzhən\ *n*

im·mi·grant \'imigrənt\ *n* : one that immigrates

im·mi·grate \'imə,grāt\ *vb* -grat·ed; -grat·ing : come into a place and take up residence —im·mi·gra·tion \,imə'grāshən\ *n*

im·mi·nent \'imənənt\ *adj* : ready to take place —im·mi·nence \-nəns\ *n* —im·mi·nent·ly *adv*

im·mo·bile \(')im'ōbəl\ *adj* : incapable of being moved —im·mo·bil·i·ty \,imō'bilətē\ *n* —im·mo·bi·lize \im-'ōbəlīz\ *vb*

im·mod·er·ate \(')im'äd(ə)rət\ *adj* : not moderate —im·mod·er·a·cy \-(ə)rəsē\ *n* —im·mod·er·ate·ly *adv*

im·mod·est \(')im'ädəst\ *adj* : not modest —im·mod·est·ly *adv* —im·mod·es·ty \-əstē\ *n*

im·mo·late \'imə,lāt\ *vb* -lat·ed; -lat·ing : offer in sacrifice —im·mo·la·tion \,imə'lāshən\ *n*

im·mor·al \(')im'örəl\ *adj* : not moral —im·mo·ral·i·ty \,imō'ralətē, ,imə-\ *n* —im·mor·al·ly *adv*

im·mor·tal \(')im'ört?l\ *adj* 1 : not mortal 2 : having lasting fame ~ *n* : one exempt from death or oblivion —im·mor·tal·i·ty \,im,ör'talətē\ *n* —im·mor·tal·ize \im'ört?l,īz\ *vb*

im·mov·able \(')im'üvəbəl\ *adj* 1 : stationary 2 : unyielding —im·mov·abil·i·ty \(,)im,üvə'bilətē\ *n* —im·mov·ably *adv*

im·mune \im'yün\ *adj* : not liable esp. to disease —im·mu·ni·ty \im-'yünətē\ *n* —im·mu·ni·za·tion \,imyənə'zāshən\ *n* —im·mu·nize \'imyə,nīz\ *vb*

im·mu·nol·o·gy \,imyə'näləjē\ *n* : science of immunity —im·mu·no·log·ic \-yən?l'äjik\, im·mu·no·log·i·cal \-ikəl\ *adj* —im·mu·no·log·i·cal·ly \-ik(ə)lē\ *adv* —im·mu·nol·o·gist \,imyə'näləjəst\ *n*

im·mu·ta·ble \(')im'yütəbəl\ *adj* : unchangeable —im·mu·ta·bil·i·ty \(,)im,yütə'bilətē\ *n* —im·mu·ta·bly *adv*

imp \'imp\ *n* 1 : demon 2 : mischievous child

im·pact \im'pakt\ *vb* 1 : press close 2 : have an effect on ~ \'im,pakt\ *n* 1 : forceful contact 2 : influence

im·pact·ed \im'paktəd\ *adj* : wedged between the jawbone and another tooth

im·pair \im'paər\ *vb* : diminish in quantity or value —im·pair·ment *n*

im·pa·la \im'palə\ *n* : large antelope

im·pale \im'pāl\ *vb* -paled; -pal·ing : pierce with something pointed —im·pale·ment *n*

im·pal·pa·ble \(')im'palpəbəl\ *adj* : incapable of being felt —im·pal·pa·bly *adv*

im·pan·el \im'pan?l\ *vb* : enter in or on a panel

158

im·part \-'pärt\ *vb* : give from or as if from a store

im·par·tial \(')im'pärshəl\ *adj* : not partial —**im·par·tial·i·ty** \(,)im-,pärshē'alətē, -,pär'shal-\ *n* —**im·par·tial·ly** *adv*

im·pass·able \(')im'pasəbəl\ *adj* : not passable —**im·pass·ably** \-'pasəblē\ *adv*

im·passe \'im,pas\ *n* : inescapable predicament

im·pas·sioned \im'pashənd\ *adj* : filled with passion

im·pas·sive \im'pasiv\ *adj* : showing no feeling or interest —**im·pas·sive·ly** *adv* —**im·pas·siv·i·ty** \,im-,pas'ivətē\ *n*

im·pa·tiens \im'pāshənz, -shəns\ *n* : annual herb with showy irregular flowers

im·pa·tient \(')im'pāshənt\ *adj* : not patient —**im·pa·tience** \-shəns\ *n* —**im·pa·tient·ly** *adv*

im·peach \im'pēch\ *vb* 1 : charge an official with misconduct 2 : cast doubt on —**im·peach·ment** *n*

im·pec·ca·ble \(')im'pekəbəl\ *adj* : faultless —**im·pec·ca·bly** *adv*

im·pe·cu·nious \,impi'kyünyəs, -nēəs\ *adj* : broke —**im·pe·cu·nious·ness** *n*

im·pede \im'pēd\ *vb* **-ped·ed; -ped·ing** : interfere with

im·ped·i·ment \-'pedəmənt\ *n* 1 : hindrance 2 : speech defect

im·pel \-'pel\ *vb* **-pelled; -pel·ling** : urge forward

im·pend \-'pend\ *vb* : be about to occur

im·pen·e·tra·ble \(')im'penətrəbəl\ *adj* : incapable of being penetrated or understood —**im·pen·e·tra·bil·i·ty** \(,)im,penətrə'bilatē\ *n* —**im·pen·e·tra·bly** *adv*

im·pen·i·tent \(')im'penətənt\ *adj* : not penitent —**im·pen·i·tence** \-təns\ *n*

im·per·a·tive \im'perətiv\ *adj* 1 : expressing a command 2 : urgent ~ *n* 1 : imperative mood or verb form 2 : unavoidable fact, need, or obligation —**im·per·a·tive·ly** *adv*

im·per·cep·ti·ble \,impər'septəbəl\ *adj* : not perceptible —**im·per·cep·ti·bly** *adv*

im·per·fect \(')im'pərfikt\ *adj* : not perfect —**im·per·fec·tion** *n* —**im·per·fect·ly** *adv*

im·pe·ri·al \im'pirēəl\ *adj* 1 : relating to an empire or an emperor 2 : royal

im·pe·ri·al·ism \im'pirēə,lizəm\ *n* : policy of controlling other nations —**im·pe·ri·al·ist** \-ləst\ *n* or *adj* —**im·pe·ri·al·is·tic** \-,pirēə'listik\ *adj*

im·pe·ri·al·is·ti·cal·ly \-tik(ə)lē\ *adv*

im·per·il \im'perəl\ *vb* **-iled** or **-illed; -il·ing** or **-il·ling** : endanger

im·pe·ri·ous \im'pirēəs\ *adj* : arrogant or domineering —**im·pe·ri·ous·ly** *adv*

im·per·ish·able \(')im'perishəbəl\ *adj* : not perishable

im·per·ma·nent \-'pərmənənt\ *adj* : not permanent —**im·per·ma·nent·ly** *adv*

im·per·me·able \-'pərmēəbəl\ *adj* : not permeable

im·per·mis·si·ble \,impər'misəbəl\ *adj* : not permissible

im·per·son·al \(')im'pərsnəl, -°nəl\ *adj* : not involving human personality or emotion —**im·per·son·al·i·ty** \(,)im,pərs°n'alətē\ *n* —**im·per·son·al·ly** \-ē\ *adv*

im·per·son·ate \im'pərs°n,āt\ *vb* **-at·ed; -at·ing** : assume the character of —**im·per·son·a·tion** \-,pərs°n'āshən\ *n* —**im·per·son·a·tor** \-'pərs°n,ātər\ *n*

im·per·ti·nent \(')im'pərt°nənt\ *adj* 1 : irrelevant 2 : insolent —**im·per·ti·nence** \-°nəns\ *n* —**im·per·ti·nent·ly** *adv*

im·per·turb·able \,impər'tərbəbəl\ *adj* : calm and steady

im·per·vi·ous \(')im'pərvēəs\ *adj* : incapable of being penetrated or affected

im·pet·u·ous \im'pech(ə)wəs\ *adj* : impulsive —**im·pet·u·os·i·ty** \(,)im-,pechə'wäsətē\ *n* —**im·pet·u·ous·ly** *adv*

im·pe·tus \'impətəs\ *n* : driving force

im·pi·ety \(')im'pīətē\ *n* : quality or state of being impious

im·pinge \im'pinj\ *vb* **-pinged; -ping·ing** : encroach —**im·pinge·ment** \-'pinjmənt\ *n*

im·pi·ous \'impēəs, (')im'pī-\ *adj* : not pious

imp·ish \'impish\ *adj* : mischievous —**imp·ish·ly** *adv* —**imp·ish·ness** *n*

im·pla·ca·ble \(')im'plakəbəl, -'plā-\ *adj* : not capable of being appeased or changed —**im·pla·ca·bil·i·ty** \(,)im,plakə'bilətē, -,plā-\ *n* —**im·pla·ca·bly** \(')im'plakəblē\ *adv*

im·plant \im'plant\ *vb* 1 : set firmly or deeply 2 : fix in the mind or spirit

im·plau·si·ble \(')im'plòzəbəl\ *adj* : not plausible —**im·plau·si·bil·i·ty** \(,)im,plòzə'bilətē\ *n*

im·ple·ment \'impləmənt\ *n* : piece of equipment for performing a hand or mechanical operation ~ \-,ment\ *vb*

: put into practice —**im·ple·men·ta·tion** \,implǝmǝn'tāshǝn\ n

im·pli·cate \'implǝ,kāt\ vb -cat·ed; -cat·ing : involve

im·pli·ca·tion \,implǝ'kāshǝn\ n 1 : an implying 2 : something implied

im·plic·it \im'plisǝt\ adj 1 : understood though only implied 2 : complete and unquestioning —**im·plic·it·ly** adv

im·plode \im'plōd\ vb -plod·ed; -plod·ing : burst inward —**im·plo·sion** \-'plōzhǝn\ n —**im·plo·sive** \-'plō-siv\ adj

im·plore \im'plōr\ vb -plored; -plor·ing : entreat

im·ply \-'plī\ vb -plied; -ply·ing : express indirectly

im·po·lite \,impǝ'līt\ adj : not polite

im·pol·i·tic \(')im'pälǝ,tik\ adj : not politic

im·pon·der·a·ble \(')im'pänd(ǝ)rǝbǝl\ adj : incapable of being precisely evaluated —**imponderable** n

im·port \im'pōrt\ vb 1 : mean 2 : bring in from an external source ~ \'im,-pōrt\ n 1 : meaning 2 : importance 3 : something imported —**im·por·ta·tion** \,im,pōr'tāshǝn\ n —**im·port·er** n

im·por·tant \im'pōrt³nt\ adj : having great worth, significance, or influence —**im·por·tance** \-³ns\ n —**im·por·tant·ly** adv

im·por·tu·nate \im'pōrch(ǝ)nǝt\ adj : troublesomely persistent or urgent

im·por·tune \,impǝr't(y)ün, im-'pōrchǝn\ vb -tuned; -tun·ing : urge or beg persistently —**im·por·tu·ni·ty** \,impǝr't(y)ünǝtē\ n

im·pose \im'pōz\ vb -posed; -pos·ing 1 : establish as compulsory 2 : take unwarranted advantage of —**im·po·si·tion** \,impǝ'zishǝn\ n

im·pos·ing \im'pōziŋ\ adj : impressive

im·pos·si·ble \(')im'päsǝbǝl\ adj 1 : incapable of occurring 2 : hopeless —**im·pos·si·bil·i·ty** \(,)im,päsǝ'bilǝtē\ n —**im·pos·si·bly** \-'päsǝblē\ adv

im·post \im,pōst\ n : tax

im·pos·tor, im·pos·ter \im'pästǝr\ n : one who assumes an identity or title to deceive —**im·pos·ture** \-'päschǝr\ n

im·po·tent \'impǝtǝnt\ adj 1 : lacking power 2 : sterile —**im·po·tence** \-pǝtǝns\ n —**im·po·ten·cy** \-ǝnsē\ n —**im·po·tent·ly** adv

im·pound \im'paúnd\ vb : seize and hold in legal custody —**im·pound·ment** n

im·pov·er·ish \im'päv(ǝ)rish\ vb : make poor —**im·pov·er·ish·ment** n

im·prac·ti·ca·ble \(')im'praktikǝbǝl\ adj : not practicable

im·prac·ti·cal \-'praktikǝl\ adj : not practical

im·pre·cise \,impri'sīs\ adj : not precise —**im·pre·cise·ly** adv —**im·pre·cise·ness** n —**im·pre·ci·sion** \-'sizhǝn\ n

im·preg·na·ble \im'pregnǝbǝl\ adj : able to resist attack —**im·preg·na·bil·i·ty** \(,)im,pregnǝ'bilǝtē\ n

im·preg·nate \im'preg,nāt\ vb -nat·ed; -nat·ing 1 : make pregnant 2 : saturate with some other substance —**im·preg·na·tion** \,im,preg'nāshǝn\ n

im·pre·sa·rio \,imprǝ'särē,ō\ n, pl -ri·os : one who sponsors an entertainment

¹im·press \im'pres\ vb 1 : apply with or produce by pressure 2 : press, stamp, or print in or upon 3 : produce a vivid impression of 4 : affect (as the mind) forcibly ~ \'im,-\ n 1 : product of pressure or influence 2 : impression or effect —**im·press·ible** adj

²im·press \im'pres\ vb : force into naval service —**im·press·ment** n

im·pres·sion \im'preshǝn\ n 1 : mark made by impressing 2 : marked influence or effect 3 : printed copy 4 : vague notion or recollection —**im·pres·sion·able** \-'presh(ǝ)nǝbǝl\ adj

im·pres·sive \im'presiv\ adj : making a marked impression —**im·pres·sive·ly** adv —**im·pres·sive·ness** n

im·pri·ma·tur \,imprǝ'mä,tü(ǝ)r\ n : official approval (as of a publication by a censor)

im·print \im'print, 'im,-\ vb : stamp or mark by or as if by pressure ~ \'im,-\ n : something imprinted or printed

im·pris·on \im'priz³n\ vb : put in prison —**im·pris·on·ment** n \-'prizǝnmǝnt\

im·prob·a·ble \(')im'präbǝbǝl\ adj : unlikely to be true or to occur —**im·prob·a·bil·i·ty** \(,)im,präbǝ-'bilǝtē\ n —**im·prob·a·bly** adv

im·promp·tu \im'prämpt(y)ü\ adj : not planned beforehand —**impromptu** adv or n

im·prop·er \(')im'präpǝr\ adj : not proper —**im·prop·er·ly** adv

im·pro·pri·ety \,imprǝ'prīǝtē\ n, pl -eties : state or instance of being improper

im·prove \im'prüv\ vb -proved; -prov·ing 1 : grow or make better 2 : make

good use of **—im·prov·able**
\-'prüvəbəl\ *adj* **—im·prove·ment** *n*

im·prov·i·dent \(')im'prävədənt\ *adj*
: not providing for the future **—im-
prov·i·dence** \-əns\ *n*

im·pro·vise \'imprə,vīz, 'imprə,vīz\
vb **-vised; -vis·ing** : make, invent, or
arrange offhand **—im·pro·vi·sa·tion**
\im,prävə'zāshən, ,imprəvə-\ *n* —
im·pro·vis·er, im·pro·vi·sor \,imprə-
'vīzər, 'imprəvī-\ *n*

im·pru·dent \(')im'prüd°nt\ *adj* : not
prudent **—im·pru·dence** \-°ns\ *n*

im·pu·dent \'impyədənt\ *adj* : insolent
—im·pu·dence \-əns\ *n* **—im·pu·
dent·ly** *adv*

im·pugn \im'pyün\ *vb* : attack as false

im·pulse \'im,pəls\ *n* **1** : moving force
2 : sudden inclination

im·pul·sion \im'pəlshən\ *n* : act of im-
pelling

im·pul·sive \im'pəlsiv\ *adj* : acting on
impulse **—im·pul·sive·ly** *adv* **—im·
pul·sive·ness** *n*

im·pu·ni·ty \im'pyünətē\ *n* : exemption from punishment or harm

im·pure \(')im'pyür\ *adj* : not pure **—
im·pu·ri·ty** \-'pyürətē\ *n*

im·pute \im'pyüt\ *vb* **-put·ed; -put·ing**
: credit to or blame on a person or
cause **—im·pu·ta·tion** \,impyə-
'tāshən\ *n*

in \(')in, ən, °n\ *prep* **1** —used to in-
dicate location, inclusion, situation,
or manner **2** : into **3** : during ~ \'in\
adv : to or toward the inside ~ \'in\
adj : located inside

in- \(')in, ,in\ *prefix* **1** : not **2** : lack of

inability	inappropriately
inaccessibility	inappropriate-
inaccessible	ness
inaccuracy	inapt
inaccurate	inarguable
inaction	inartistic
inactive	inartistically
inactivity	inattentive
inadequacy	inattentively
inadequate	inattentiveness
inadequately	inaudible
inadmissibility	inaudibly
inadmissible	inauspicious
inadvisability	inauthentic
inadvisable	incapability
inapparent	incapable
inapplicable	incautious
inapposite	incoherence
inappositely	incoherent
inappositeness	incoherently
inappreciative	incohesive
inapproachable	incombustible
inappropriate	incommensurate

incommodious	indistinctly
incommunicable	indistinctness
incompatibility	indivisibility
incompatible	indivisible
incomplete	ineducable
incompletely	ineffective
incompleteness	ineffectively
incomprehen-	ineffectiveness
sible	ineffectual
inconceivable	ineffectually
inconceivably	ineffectualness
inconclusive	inefficiency
incongruent	inefficient
inconsecutive	inefficiently
inconsiderate	inelastic
inconsiderately	inelasticity
inconsiderate-	inelegance
ness	inelegant
inconsistency	ineligibility
inconsistent	ineligible
inconsistently	ineradicable
inconspicuous	inessential
inconspicuously	inexact
inconstancy	inexactly
inconstant	inexpedient
inconstantly	inexpensive
inconsumable	inexperience
incontestable	inexperienced
incontestably	inexpert
incorporeal	inexpertly
incorporeally	inexpertness
incorrect	inexplicable
incorrectly	inexplicably
incorrectness	inexplicit
incorruptible	inexpressible
inculpable	inexpressibly
incurable	inextinguishable
incurious	inextricable
indecency	infeasibility
indecent	infeasible
indecently	infelicitous
indecipherable	infelicity
indecisive	infertile
indecisively	infertility
indecisiveness	inflexibility
indecorous	inflexible
indecorously	inflexibly
indecorousness	infrequent
indefensible	infrequently
indefinable	inglorious
indefinably	ingloriously
indescribable	ingratitude
indescribably	inhumane
indestructibility	inhumanely
indestructible	injudicious
indigestible	injudiciously
indiscernible	injudiciousness
indiscreet	inoffensive
indiscretion	inoperable
indisputable	inoperative
indisputably	insalubrious
indistinct	insensitive

insensitivity	intolerable
inseparable	intolerably
insignificant	intolerance
insincere	intolerant
insincerely	intractable
insincerity	invariable
insolubility	invariably
insoluble	inviable
instability	invisibility
insubstantial	invisible
insufficiency	invisibly
insufficient	involuntarily
insufficiently	involuntary
insupportable	invulnerability
intangibility	invulnerable
intangible	invulnerably
intangibly	

in·ad·ver·tent \,inəd'vərtᵊnt\ *adj* : unintentional **—in·ad·ver·tence** \-ᵊns\ *n* **—in·ad·ver·ten·cy** \-ᵊnsē\ *n* **—in·ad·ver·tent·ly** *adv*

in·alien·able \(')in'ālyənəbəl, -'āleānə-\ *adj* : incapable of being transferred or given up **—in·alien·abil·i·ty** \(,)in,ālyənə'bilətē, -'āleānə-\ *n* **—in·alien·ably** *adv*

inane \in'ān\ *adj* **inan·er; -est** : silly or stupid **—inan·i·ty** \in'anətē\ *n*

in·an·i·mate \(')in'anəmət\ *adj* : not animate or animated **—in·an·i·mate·ly** *adv* **—in·an·i·mate·ness** *n*

in·a·ni·tion \,inə'nishən\ *n* : weakness from lack of food and water

in·ap·pre·cia·ble \,inə'prēshəbəl\ *adj* : too small to be perceived **—in·ap·pre·cia·bly** *adv*

in·ar·tic·u·late \,inär'tikyələt\ *adj* : without the power of speech or of effective expression **—in·ar·tic·u·late·ly** *adv*

in·as·much as \,inəz,məchəz\ *conj* : because

in·at·ten·tion \,inə'tenchən\ *n* : failure to pay attention

in·au·gu·ral \in'ógyərəl, -g(ə)rəl\ *adj* : relating to an inauguration ~ *n* 1 : inaugural speech 2 : inauguration

in·au·gu·rate \in'óg(y)ə,rāt\ *vb* **-rat·ed; -rat·ing** 1 : install in office 2 : start **—in·au·gu·ra·tion** \-,óg(y)ə'rāshən\ *n*

in·board \'in,bōrd\ *adv* : inside a craft **—inboard** *adj*

in·born \'in'bórn\ *adj* : present from birth

in·bred \'in'bred\ *adj* : inborn

in·breed·ing \'in,brēdiŋ\ *n* : interbreeding of closely related individuals **—in·breed** \-'brēd\ *vb*

in·cal·cu·la·ble \(')in'kalkyələbəl\ *adj*

: too large to be calculated **—in·cal·cu·la·bly** *adv*

in·can·des·cent \,inkən'desᵊnt\ *adj* 1 : glowing with heat 2 : brilliant **—in·can·des·cence** \-ᵊns\ *n*

in·can·ta·tion \,in,kan'tāshən\ *n* : use of spoken or sung charms or spells as a magic ritual

in·ca·pac·i·tate \,inkə'pasə,tāt\ *vb* **-tat·ed; -tat·ing** : disable

in·ca·pac·i·ty \,inkə'pasətē\ *n, pl* **-ties** : quality or state of being incapable

in·car·cer·ate \in'kärsə,rāt\ *vb* **-at·ed; -at·ing** : imprison **—in·car·cer·a·tion** \(,)in,kärsə'rāshən\ *n*

in·car·nate \in'kärnət, -,nāt\ *adj* : having bodily form and substance **—in·car·nate** \-,nāt\ *vb* **—in·car·na·tion** \-,kär'nāshən\ *n*

in·cen·di·ary \in'sendē,erē\ *adj* 1 : pertaining to or used to ignite fire 2 : tending to excite **—incendiary** *n*

in·cense \'in,sens\ *n* : material burned to produce a fragrant odor or its smoke ~ \in'sens\ *vb* **-censed; -cens·ing** : make very angry

in·cen·tive \in'sentiv\ *n* : inducement to do something

in·cep·tion \in'sepshən\ *n* : beginning

in·ces·sant \(')in'sesᵊnt\ *adj* : continuing without interruption **—in·ces·sant·ly** *adv*

in·cest \'in,sest\ *n* : sexual intercourse between close relatives **—in·ces·tu·ous** \in'seschəwəs\ *adj*

inch \'inch\ *n* : unit of length equal to 1/12 foot ~ *vb* : move by small degrees

in·cho·ate \in'kōət, 'inkə,wāt\ *adj* : new and not fully formed or ordered

in·ci·dent \'insədənt\ *n* : occurrence **—in·ci·dence** \-əns\ *n* **—incident** *adj*

in·ci·den·tal \,insə'dentᵊl\ *adj* 1 : subordinate, nonessential, or attendant 2 : met by chance ~ *n* 1 : something incidental 2 *pl* : minor expenses that are not itemized **—in·ci·den·tal·ly** *adv*

in·cin·er·ate \in'sinə,rāt\ *vb* **-at·ed; -at·ing** : burn to ashes **—in·cin·er·a·tor** \-,rātər\ *n*

in·cip·i·ent \in'sipēənt\ *adj* : beginning to be or appear

in·cise \in'sīz\ *vb* **-cised; -cis·ing** : carve into

in·ci·sion \in'sizhən\ *n* : surgical wound

in·ci·sive \in'sīsiv\ *adj* : keen and discerning **—in·ci·sive·ly** *adv*

in·ci·sor \in'sīzər\ *n* : tooth for cutting

in•cite \in'sīt\ vb -cit•ed; -cit•ing : arouse to action —in•cite•ment n

in•ci•vil•i•ty \,insə'vilətē\ n : rudeness

in•clem•ent \(')in'klemənt\ adj : stormy —in•clem•en•cy \-ənsē\ n

in•cline \in'klīn\ vb -clined; -clin•ing 1 : bow 2 : tend toward an opinion 3 : slope ~ n : slope —in•cli•na•tion \,inklə'nāshən\ n

inclose, inclosure var of ENCLOSE, ENCLOSURE

in•clude \in'klüd\ vb -clud•ed; -clud•ing : take in or comprise —in•clu•sion \in'klüzhən\ n —in•clu•sive \-'klüsiv\ adj

in•cog•ni•to \,in,käg'nētō, in'kägnə,tō\ adv or adj : with one's identity concealed

in•come \'in,kəm\ n : money gained (as from work or investment)

in•com•ing \'in,kəmiŋ\ adj : coming in

in•com•mu•ni•ca•do \,inkə,myünə'kädō\ adv or adj : without means of communication

in•com•pa•ra•ble \(')in'kämp(ə)rəbəl\ adj : eminent beyond comparison

in•com•pe•tent \(')in'kämpətənt\ adj : lacking sufficient knowledge or skill —in•com•pe•tence \-pətəns\ n —in•com•pe•ten•cy \-ənsē\ n —incompetent n

in•con•gru•ous \(')in'käŋgrəwəs\ adj : inappropriate or out of place —in•con•gru•i•ty \,inkən'grüətē, ,kän-\ n —in•con•gru•ous•ly adv

in•con•se•quen•tial \,in,känsə'kwenchəl\ adj : unimportant —in•con•se•quence \(')in'känsə,kwens\ n —in•con•se•quen•tial•ly adv

in•con•sid•er•able \,inkən'sidər(ə)bəl, -'sidrəbəl\ adj : trivial

in•con•sol•able \,inkən'sōləbəl\ adj : incapable of being consoled —in•con•sol•ably adv

in•con•ve•nience \,inkən'vēnyəns\ n 1 : discomfort 2 : something that causes trouble or annoyance ~ vb : cause inconvenience to —in•con•ve•nient \,inkən'vēnyənt\ adj —in•con•ve•nient•ly adv

in•cor•po•rate \in'kórpə,rāt\ vb -rat•ed; -rat•ing 1 : blend 2 : form into a legal body —in•cor•po•rat•ed adj —in•cor•po•ra•tion \-,kórpə'rāshən\ n

in•cor•ri•gi•ble \(')in'kórəjəbəl\ adj : incapable of being corrected or reformed —in•cor•ri•gi•bil•i•ty \(')in,kórəjə'bilətē\ n —in•cor•ri•gi•bly \(')in'kórəjəblē\ adv

in•crease \in'krēs, 'in,krēs\ vb -creased; -creas•ing : make or become greater ~ \'in,-, in'-\ n

: enlargement in size 2 : something added —in•creas•ing•ly \-'krēsiŋlē\ adv

in•cred•i•ble \(')in'kredəbəl\ adj : too extraordinary to be believed —in•cred•ibil•i•ty \(,)in,kredə'bilətē\ n —in•cred•i•bly \(')in'kredəblē\ adv

in•cred•u•lous \(')in'krejələs\ adj : skeptical —in•cre•du•li•ty \,inkri-'d(y)ülətē\ n —in•cred•u•lous•ly adv

in•cre•ment \'iŋkrəmənt, 'in-\ n : increase or amount of increase —in•cre•men•tal \,iŋkrə'ment³l, ,in-\ adj

in•crim•i•nate \in'krimə,nāt\ vb -nat•ed; -nat•ing : show to be guilty of a crime —in•crim•i•na•tion \-,krimə'nāshən\ n —in•crim•i•na•to•ry \-'krim(ə)nə,tōrē\ adj

in•cu•bate \'iŋkyə,bāt, 'in-\ vb -bat•ed; -bat•ing : keep (as eggs) under conditions favorable for development —in•cu•ba•tion \,iŋkyə'bāshən, ,in-\ n —in•cu•ba•tor \'iŋkyə,bātər, 'in-\ n

in•cul•cate \in'kəl,kāt, 'in(,)kəl-\ vb -cat•ed; -cat•ing : instill by repeated teaching —in•cul•ca•tion \,in(,)kəl-'kāshən\ n

in•cum•bent \in'kəmbənt\ n : holder of an office ~ adj : obligatory —in•cum•ben•cy \-bənsē\ n

in•cur \in'kər\ vb -rr- : become liable or subject to

in•cur•sion \in'kərzhən\ n : invasion

in•debt•ed \in'detəd\ adj : owing something —in•debt•ed•ness n

in•de•ci•sion \,indi'sizhən\ n : inability to decide

in•deed \in'dēd\ adv : without question

in•de•fat•i•ga•ble \,indi'fatigəbəl\ adj : not tiring —in•de•fat•i•ga•bly \-blē\ adv

in•def•i•nite \(')in'def(ə)nət\ adj 1 : not defining or identifying 2 : not precise 3 : having no fixed limit or amount —in•def•i•nite•ly adv

in•del•i•ble \in'deləbəl\ adj : not capable of being removed or erased —in•del•i•bly adv

in•del•i•cate \(')in'delikət\ adj : improper —in•del•i•ca•cy \in'deləkəsē\ n

in•dem•ni•fy \in'demnə,fī\ vb -fied; -fy•ing : repay for a loss —in•dem•ni•fi•ca•tion \-,demnəfə'kāshən\ n

in•dem•ni•ty \in'demnətē\ n, pl -ties : security against loss or damage

¹in•dent \in'dent\ vb : leave a space at the beginning of a paragraph —in•dent n

²in·dent *vb* : force inward so as to form a depression or dent

in·den·ta·tion \ˌin̩den̍tāshən\ *n* **1** : notch, recess, or dent **2** : action of indenting **3** : space at the beginning of a paragraph

in·den·ture \in̍denchər\ *n* : contract binding one person to work for another for a given period —usu. in pl. ~ *vb* **-tured**; **-tur·ing** : bind by indentures

Independence Day *n* : July 4 observed as a legal holiday in commemoration of the adoption of the Declaration of Independence in 1776

in·de·pen·dent \ˌində̍pendənt\ *adj* **1** : not governed by another **2** : not requiring or relying on something or somebody else **3** : not easily influenced —**in·de·pen·dence** \-dəns\ *n* —**independent** *n* —**in·de·pen·dent·ly** *adv*

in·de·ter·mi·nate \ˌindi̍tərm(ə)nət\ *adj* : not definitely determined —**in·de·ter·mi·na·cy** \-(ə)nəsē\ *n* —**in·de·ter·mi·nate·ly** *adv*

in·dex \ˈin̩deks\ *n, pl* **-dex·es** *or* **-di·ces** \-də̩sēz\ **1** : alphabetical list of items (as topics in a book) **2** : a number that serves as a measure or indicator of something ~ *vb* **1** : provide with an index **2** : serve as an index of

index finger *n* : forefinger

in·di·cate \ˈində̩kāt\ *vb* **-cat·ed**; **-cat·ing 1** : point out or to **2** : reveal or suggest **3** : state briefly —**in·di·ca·tion** \ˌində̍kāshən\ *n* —**in·di·ca·tor** \ˈində̩kātər\ *n*

in·dic·a·tive \in̍dikətiv\ *adj* : serving to indicate

in·dict \in̍dīt\ *vb* : charge with a crime —**in·dict·able** *adj* —**in·dict·ment** *n*

in·dif·fer·ent \in̍difərnt, -̍dif(ə)rənt\ *adj* **1** : having no preference **2** : showing neither interest nor dislike **3** : mediocre —**in·dif·fer·ence** \-̍difərns, -̍dif(ə)rəns\ *n* —**in·dif·fer·ent·ly** *adv*

in·dig·e·nous \in̍dijənəs\ *adj* : native to a particular region

in·di·gent \ˈindijənt\ *adj* : needy —**in·di·gence** \-jəns\ *n*

in·di·ges·tion \ˌindī̍jeschən, -də-\ *n* : discomfort from inability to digest food

in·dig·na·tion \ˌindig̍nāshən\ *n* : anger aroused by something unjust or unworthy —**in·dig·nant** \in̍dignənt\ *adj* —**in·dig·nant·ly** *adv*

in·dig·ni·ty \in̍dignətē\ *n, pl* **-ties 1** : offense against self-respect **2** : humiliating treatment

in·di·go \ˈindi̩gō\ *n, pl* **-gos** *or* **-goes 1** : blue dye **2** : dark blue or violet color

in·di·rect \ˌində̍rekt, -dī-\ *adj* : not straight or straightforward —**in·di·rec·tion** \-̍rekshən\ *n* —**in·di·rect·ly** *adv* —**in·di·rect·ness** *n*

in·dis·crim·i·nate \ˌindis̍krimənət\ *adj* **1** : not careful or discriminating **2** : haphazard —**in·dis·crim·i·nate·ly** *adv*

in·dis·pens·able \ˌindis̍pensəbəl\ *adj* : absolutely essential —**in·dis·pens·abil·i·ty** \-̩pensə̍bilətē\ *n* —**indispensable** *n* —**in·dis·pens·ably** \-̍pensəblē\ *adv*

in·dis·posed \-̍pōzd\ *adj* : slightly ill —**in·dis·po·si·tion** \(̩)in̩dispə̍zishən\ *n*

in·dis·sol·u·ble \ˌindis̍älyəbəl\ *adj* : not capable of being dissolved or broken

in·di·vid·u·al \ˌində̍vij(əw)əl\ *n* **1** : single member of a category **2** : person —**individual** *adj* —**in·di·vid·u·al·ly** *adv*

in·di·vid·u·al·i·ty \-̩vijə̍walətē\ *n* : special quality that distinguishes an individual

in·di·vid·u·al·ize \-̍vijə(wə)̩līz\ *vb* **-ized**; **-iz·ing 1** : make individual **2** : treat individually

in·doc·tri·nate \in̍däktrə̩nāt\ *vb* **-nat·ed**; **-nat·ing** : instruct in fundamentals (as of a doctrine) —**in·doc·tri·na·tion** \(̩)in̩däktrə̍nāshən\ *n*

in·do·lent \ˈindələnt\ *adj* : lazy —**in·do·lence** \-ləns\ *n*

in·dom·i·ta·ble \in̍dämətəbəl\ *adj* : invincible —**in·dom·i·ta·bly** \-blē\ *adv*

in·door \ˌin̩dòr\ *adj* : relating to the inside of a building

in·doors \in̍dòrz\ *adv* : in or into a building

in·du·bi·ta·ble \(̍)in̍d(y)übətəbəl\ *adj* : being beyond question —**in·du·bi·ta·bly** \-blē\ *adv*

in·duce \in̍d(y)üs\ *vb* **-duced**; **-duc·ing 1** : persuade **2** : bring about —**in·duce·ment** *n* —**in·duc·er** *n*

in·duct \in̍dəkt\ *vb* **1** : put in office **2** : admit as a member **3** : enroll (as for military service) —**in·duct·ee** \(̩)in̩dək̍tē\ *n*

in·duc·tion \in̍dəkshən\ *n* **1** : act or instance of inducting **2** : reasoning from particular instances to a general conclusion

in·duc·tive \in̍dəktiv\ *adj* : reasoning by induction

in·dulge \in̍dəlj\ *vb* **-dulged**; **-dulg·ing**

: yield to the desire of or for —**in-dul-gence** \-'dǝljǝns\ n —**in-dul-gent** \-jǝnt\ adj —**in-dul-gent-ly** adv

in-dus-tri-al \in'dǝstrēǝl\ adj : having to do with industry —**in-dus-tri-al-ist** \-ǝlǝst\ n —**in-dus-tri-al-iza-tion** \-,dǝstrēǝlǝ'zāshǝn\ n —**in-dus-tri-al-ize** \-'dǝstrēǝ,līz\ vb —**in-dus-tri-al-ly** \-ē\ adv

in-dus-tri-ous \in'dǝstrēǝs\ adj : diligent or busy —**in-dus-tri-ous-ly** adv —**in-dus-tri-ous-ness** n

in-dus-try \'in,dǝstrē\ n, pl -tries 1 : diligence 2 : manufacturing enterprises or activity

ine-bri-ate \in'ēbrē,āt\ vb -at-ed; -at-ing : make drunk ~ n : one who is drunk —**ine-bri-a-tion** \-,ēbrē-'āshǝn\ n

in-ef-fa-ble \in'efǝbǝl\ adj : incapable of being expressed in words —**in-ef-fa-bly** \-blē\ adv

in-ept \in'ept\ adj 1 : inappropriate or foolish 2 : generally incompetent —**in-ep-ti-tude** \in'eptǝ,t(y)üd\ n —**in-ept-ly** adv —**in-ept-ness** n

in-equal-i-ty \,ini'kwälǝtē\ n : quality of being unequal or uneven

in-ert \in'ǝrt\ adj 1 : powerless to move or act 2 : sluggish —**in-ert-ly** adv —**in-ert-ness** n

in-er-tia \in'ǝrsh(ē)ǝ\ n : tendency of matter to remain at rest or in motion —**in-er-tial** \-shǝl\ adj

in-es-cap-able \,inǝ'skāpǝbǝl\ adj : inevitable —**in-es-cap-ably** \-blē\ adv

in-es-ti-ma-ble \(')in'estǝmǝbǝl\ adj : incapable of being estimated —**in-es-ti-ma-bly** \-blē\ adv

in-ev-i-ta-ble \in'evǝtǝbǝl\ adj : incapable of being avoided or escaped —**in-ev-i-ta-bil-i-ty** \(,)in-,evǝtǝ'bilǝtē\ n —**in-ev-i-ta-bly** \in'evǝtǝblē\ adv

in-ex-cus-able \,inik'skyüzǝbǝl\ adj : being without excuse or justification —**in-ex-cus-ably** \-blē\ adv

in-ex-haust-ible \,inig'zȯstǝbǝl\ adj : incapable of being used up or tired out —**in-ex-haust-ibly** \-blē\ adv

in-ex-o-ra-ble \(')in'eks(ǝ)rǝbǝl\ adj : unyielding or relentless —**in-ex-o-ra-bly** adv

in-fal-li-ble \(')in'falǝbǝl\ adj : incapable of error —**in-fal-li-bil-i-ty** \(,)in-,falǝ'bilǝtē\ n —**in-fal-li-bly** adv

in-fa-mous \'infǝmǝs\ adj : having the worst kind of reputation —**in-fa-mous-ly** adv

in-fa-my \-mē\ n, pl -mies : evil reputation

in-fan-cy \'infǝnsē\ n, pl -cies 1 : early

childhood 2 : early period of existence

in-fant \'infǝnt\ n : baby

in-fan-tile \'infǝn,tīl, -tᵊl, -,tēl\ adj : relating to infants

in-fan-try \'infǝntrē\ n, pl -tries : soldiers that fight on foot

in-fat-u-ate \in'fachǝ,wāt\ vb -at-ed; -at-ing : inspire with foolish love or admiration —**in-fat-u-a-tion** \-,fachǝ'wāshǝn\ n

in-fect \in'fekt\ vb : contaminate with disease-producing matter —**in-fec-tion** \-'fekshǝn\ n —**in-fec-tious** \-shǝs\ adj —**in-fec-tive** \-'fektiv\ adj

in-fer \in'fǝr\ vb -rr- : deduce —**in-fer-ence** \'inf(ǝ)rǝns\ n —**in-fer-en-tial** \,infǝ'renchǝl\ adj

in-fe-ri-or \in'firēǝr\ adj : being lower in position, degree, rank, or merit —**inferior** n —**in-fe-ri-or-i-ty** \in-,firē'ȯrǝtē\ n

in-fer-nal \in'fǝrnᵊl\ adj : of or like hell—often used as a general expression of disapproval —**in-fer-nal-ly** adv

in-fer-no \in'fǝrnō\ n, pl -nos : place or condition suggesting hell

in-fest \in'fest\ vb : swarm or grow in or over —**in-fes-ta-tion** \,in,fes'tā-shǝn\ n

in-fi-del \'infǝdᵊl, -fǝ,del\ n : one who does not believe in a particular religion

in-fi-del-i-ty \,infǝ'delǝtē, -fī-\ n, pl -ties : lack of faithfulness

in-field \'in,fēld\ n : baseball field inside the base lines —**in-field-er** n

in-fil-trate \in'fil,trāt, 'in(,)fil-\ vb -trat-ed; -trat-ing : enter or become established in without being noticed —**in-fil-tra-tion** \,in(,)fil'trāshǝn\ n

in-fi-nite \'infǝnǝt\ adj 1 : having no limit or extending indefinitely 2 : vast —**infinite** n —**in-fi-nite-ly** adv —**in-fin-i-tude** \in'finǝ,t(y)üd\ n

in-fin-i-tes-i-mal \(,)in,finǝ'tesǝmǝl\ adj : very minute —**in-fin-i-tes-i-mal-ly** adv

in-fin-i-tive \in'finǝtiv\ n : verb form in English usu. used with to

in-fin-i-ty \in'finǝtē\ n, pl -ties 1 : quality or state of being infinite 2 : indefinitely great number or amount

in-firm \in'fǝrm\ adj : feeble from age —**in-fir-mi-ty** \-'fǝrmǝtē\ n

in-fir-ma-ry \in'fǝrm(ǝ)rē\ n, pl -ries : place for the care of the sick

in-flame \in'flām\ vb -flamed; -flam-ing 1 : excite to intense action or feeling 2 : affect or become affected with

inflammation —in·flam·ma·to·ry \-'flamə,tōrē\ *adj*

in·flam·ma·ble \in'flaməbəl\ : flammable

in·flam·ma·tion \,inflə'māshən\ *n* : response to injury in which an affected area becomes red and painful and congested with blood

in·flate \in'flāt\ *vb* **-flat·ed; -flat·ing 1** : swell or puff up (as with gas) **2** : expand or increase abnormally —**in·flat·able** *adj*

in·fla·tion \in'flāshən\ *n* **1** : act of inflating **2** : abnormal increase in the volume of money and credit with a continuing rise in prices —**in·fla·tion·ary** \-shə,nerē\ *adj*

in·flec·tion \in'flekshən\ *n* **1** : change in pitch or loudness of the voice **2** : change in form of a word —**in·flect** \-'flekt\ *vb* —**in·flec·tion·al** \-'flekshənəl\ *adj*

in·flict \in'flikt\ *vb* : give by or as if by hitting —**in·flic·tion** \-'flikshən\ *n*

in·flu·ence \'in,flüəns\ *n* **1** : power or capacity of causing an effect in indirect or intangible ways **2** : one that exerts influence ~ *vb* **-enced; -enc·ing** : affect or alter by influence —**in·flu·en·tial** \,inflü'enchəl\ *adj*

in·flu·en·za \,inflü'enzə\ *n* : acute very contagious virus disease

in·flux \'in,fləks\ *n* : a flowing in

in·form \in'fȯrm\ *vb* : give information or knowledge to —**in·for·mant** \-ənt\ *n* —**in·form·er** *n*

in·for·mal \in'fȯrməl\ *adj* **1** : without formality or ceremony **2** : for ordinary or familiar use —**in·for·mal·i·ty** \,infȯr'malətē, -fər-\ *n* —**in·for·mal·ly** *adv*

in·for·ma·tion \,infər'māshən\ *n* : knowledge obtained from investigation, study, or instruction —**in·for·ma·tion·al** \-sh(ə)nəl\ *adj*

in·for·ma·tive \in'fȯrmətiv\ *adj* : giving knowledge

in·frac·tion \in'frakshən\ *n* : violation

in·fra·red \(,)infrə'red\ *adj* : being, relating to, or using radiation of wavelengths longer than those of red light —**infrared** *n*

in·fringe \in'frinj\ *vb* **-fringed; -fring·ing** : violate another's right or privilege —**in·fringe·ment** *n*

in·fu·ri·ate \in'fyūrē,āt\ *vb* **-at·ed; -at·ing** : make furious —**in·fu·ri·at·ing·ly** \-,ātiŋlē\ *adv*

in·fuse \in'fyüz\ *vb* **-fused; -fus·ing 1** : instill a principle or quality in **2** : steep in liquid without boiling —**in·fu·sion** \-'fyüzhən\ *n*

¹-ing \iŋ\ *vb suffix or adj suffix* —used to form the present participle and sometimes an adjective resembling a present participle

²-ing *n suffix* **1** : action or process **2** : something connected with or resulting from an action or process

in·ge·nious \in'jēnyəs\ *adj* : very clever —**in·ge·nious·ly** *adv* —**in·ge·nious·ness** *n*

in·ge·nue or **in·gé·nue** \'anjə,nü, 'än-; 'aⁿzhə-, 'äⁿ-\ *n* : naive young woman

in·ge·nu·i·ty \,injə'n(y)üətē\ *n*, *pl* **-ities** : skill or cleverness in planning or inventing

in·gen·u·ous \in'jenyəwəs\ *adj* : innocent and candid —**in·gen·u·ous·ly** *adv* —**in·gen·u·ous·ness** *n*

in·gest \in'jest\ *vb* : eat —**in·ges·tion** \-'jeschən\ *n*

in·gle·nook \'iŋgəl,nuk\ *n* : corner by the fireplace

in·got \'iŋgət\ *n* : block of metal

in·grained \(')in'grānd\ *adj* : deepseated

in·grate \'in,grāt\ *n* : ungrateful person

in·gra·ti·ate \in'grāshē,āt\ *vb* **-at·ed; -at·ing** : gain favor for (oneself) —**in·gra·ti·at·ing** *adj*

in·gre·di·ent \in'grēdēənt\ *n* : one of the substances that make up a mixture

in·grown \'in,grōn\ *adj* : grown in and esp. into the flesh

in·hab·it \in'habət\ *vb* : live or dwell in —**in·hab·it·able** *adj* —**in·hab·it·ant** \-ətənt\ *n*

in·hale \in'hāl\ *vb* **-haled; -hal·ing** : breathe in —**in·ha·lant** \-ənt\ *n* —**in·ha·la·tion** \,in(h)ə'lāshən\ *n* —**in·hal·er** *n*

in·here \in'hiər\ *vb* **-hered; -her·ing** : be inherent

in·her·ent \in'hirənt, -'her-\ *adj* : being an essential part of something —**in·her·ent·ly** *adv*

in·her·it \in'herət\ *vb* : receive from one's ancestors —**in·her·it·able** \-əbəl\ *adj* —**in·her·i·tance** \-ətəns\ *n* —**in·her·i·tor** \-ətər\ *n*

in·hib·it \in'hibət\ *vb* : hold in check —**in·hi·bi·tion** \,in(h)ə'bishən\ *n*

in·hu·man \(')in'(h)yümən\ *adj* : cruel or impersonal —**in·hu·man·i·ty** \-(h)yü'manətē\ *n* —**in·hu·man·ly** *adv*

in·im·i·cal \in'imikəl\ *adj* : hostile or harmful —**in·im·i·cal·ly** *adv*

in·im·i·ta·ble \(')in'imətəbəl\ *adj* : not capable of being imitated

in·iq·ui·ty \in'ikwətē\ *n, pl* **-ties** : wickedness **—in·iq·ui·tous** \-wətəs\ *adj*

ini·tial \in'ishəl\ *adj* 1 : of or relating to the beginning 2 : first ~ *n* : 1st letter of a word or name ~ *vb* **-tialed** *or* **-tialled**: **-tial·ing** *or* **-tial·ling** : put initials on **—ini·tial·ly** *adv*

ini·ti·ate \in'ishē,āt\ *vb* **-at·ed**: **-at·ing** 1 : start 2 : induct into membership **—initiate** \-'ish(ē)ət\ *n* **—ini·ti·a·tion** \-,ishē'āshən\ *n* **—ini·tia·to·ry** \-'ishēə,tōrē\ *adj*

ini·tia·tive \in'ishətiv\ *n* 1 : first step 2 : readiness to undertake something on one's own

in·ject \in'jekt\ *vb* : force or introduce into something **—in·jec·tion** \-'jekshən\ *n*

in·junc·tion \in'jəŋkshən\ *n* : court writ requiring one to do or to refrain from doing a specified act

in·jure \'injər\ *vb* **-jured**; **-jur·ing** : do damage, hurt, or a wrong to

in·ju·ry \'inj(ə)rē\ *n, pl* **-ries** 1 : act that injures 2 : hurt, damage, or loss sustained **—in·ju·ri·ous** \in'jūrēəs\ *adj*

in·jus·tice \(')in'jəstəs\ *n* : unjust act

ink \'iŋk\ *n* : usu. liquid and colored material for writing and printing ~ *vb* : put ink on **—ink·well** \-,wel\ *n* **—inky** *adj*

in·kling \'iŋkliŋ\ *n* : hint or idea

in·land \'in,land, -lənd\ *n* : interior of a country **—inland** *adj or adv*

in·law \'in'lò\ *n* : relative by marriage

in·lay \(')in'lā, 'in,lā\ *vb* **-laid** \-'lād\; **-lay·ing** : set into a surface for decoration ~ \'in,lā\ *n* 1 : inlaid work 2 : shaped filling cemented into a tooth

in·let \'in,let, -lət\ *n* : bay or recess in a shore

in·mate \'in,māt\ *n* : person confined to an asylum or prison

in me·mo·ri·am \,inmə'mōrēəm\ *prep* : in memory of

in·most \'in,mōst\ *adj* : deepest within

inn \'in\ *n* : hotel

in·nards \'inərdz\ *n pl* : internal parts

in·nate \in'āt\ *adj* 1 : inborn 2 : inherent **—in·nate·ly** *adv*

in·ner \'inər\ *adj* : being on the inside

in·ner·most \'inər,mōst\ *adj* : farthest inward

in·ner·sole \,inər'sōl\ *n* : insole

in·ning \'iniŋ\ *n* : baseball team's turn at bat

inn·keep·er \'in,kēpər\ *n* : owner of an inn

in·no·cent \'inəsənt\ *adj* 1 : free from guilt 2 : harmless 3 : not sophisti-

cated **—in·no·cence** \-səns\ *n* **—innocent** *n* **—in·no·cent·ly** *adv*

in·noc·u·ous \in'äkyəwəs\ *adj* 1 : harmless 2 : inoffensive

in·no·va·tion \,inə'vāshən\ *n* : new idea or method **—in·no·vate** \'inə,vātiv\ *adj* **—in·no·va·tor** \-,vātər\ *n*

in·nu·en·do \,inyə'wendō\ *n, pl* **-dos** *or* **-does** : insinuation

in·nu·mer·a·ble \in'(y)üm(ə)rəbəl\ *adj* : countless

in·oc·u·late \in'äkyə,lāt\ *vb* **-lat·ed**: **-lat·ing** : treat with something esp. to establish immunity **—in·oc·u·la·tion** \-,äkyə'lāshən\ *n*

in·op·por·tune \(,)in,äpər't(y)ün\ *adj* : happening at the wrong time **—in·op·por·tune·ly** *adv*

in·or·di·nate \in'ordnət, -³nət\ *adj* : unusual or excessive **—in·or·di·nate·ly** *adv*

in·or·gan·ic \,in,òr'ganik\ *adj* : made of mineral matter

in·pa·tient \'in,pāshənt\ *n* : patient who stays in a hospital

in·put \'in,pût\ *n* : something put in **—input** *vb*

in·quest \'in,kwest\ *n* : inquiry esp. before a jury

in·quire \in'kwī(ə)r\ *vb* **-quired**; **-quir·ing** 1 : ask 2 : investigate **—in·quir·er** *n* **—in·quir·ing·ly** *adv* **—in·qui·ry** \'in,kwī(ə)rē, in'kwī(ə)rē; 'inkwərē, 'iŋ-\ *n*

in·qui·si·tion \,inkwə'zishən, ,iŋ-\ *n* 1 : official inquiry 2 : severe questioning **—in·quis·i·tor** \in'kwizətər\ *n* **—in·quis·i·to·ri·al** \-,kwizə'tōrēəl\ *adj*

in·quis·i·tive \in'kwizətiv\ *adj* : curious **—in·quis·i·tive·ly** *adv* **—in·quis·i·tive·ness** *n*

in·road \'in,rōd\ *n* : encroachment

in·rush \'in,rəsh\ *n* : influx

in·sane \(')in'sān\ *adj* 1 : not sane 2 : foolish **—in·sane·ly** *adv* **—in·san·i·ty** \in'sanətē\ *n*

in·sa·tia·ble \(')in'sāshəbəl\ *adj* : incapable of being satisfied

in·sa·ti·ate \(')in'sāsh(ē)ət\ *adj* : insatiable

in·scribe \in'skrīb\ *vb* 1 : write 2 : engrave 3 : dedicate (a book) to someone **—in·scrip·tion** \-'skripshən\ *n*

in·scru·ta·ble \in'skrütəbəl\ *adj* : mysterious **—in·scru·ta·bly** *adv*

in·seam \'in, sēm\ *n* : inner seam (of a garment)

in·sect \'in,sekt\ *n* : small usu. winged animal with 6 legs

in·sec·ti·cide \in'sektə,sīd\ *n* : insect

poison **—in·sec·ti·cid·al** \(,)in-
,sektə⁻'sīdᵊl\ *adj*

in·se·cure \,insi'kyúr\ *adj* 1 : uncertain
2 : unsafe 3 : fearful **—in·se·**
cure·ly *adv* **—in·se·cu·ri·ty**
\-'kyúrətē\ *n*

in·sem·i·nate \in'semə,nāt\ *vb* **-nat·ed;**
-nat·ing : introduce semen into **—in-**
sem·i·na·tion \-,semə'nāshən\ *n*

in·sen·si·ble \(')in'sensəbəl\ *adj* 1 : un-
conscious 2 : unable to feel 3 : unaware **—in·sen·si·bil·i·ty** \(,)in-
,sensə'bilətē\ *n* **—in·sen·si·bly** *adv*

in·sen·tient \(')in'sench(ē)ənt\ *adj*
: lacking feeling **—in·sen·tience**
\-ch(ē)əns\ *n*

in·sert \in'sərt\ *vb* : put in **—insert**
\'in,sərt\ *n* **—in·ser·tion** \in-
'sərshən\ *n*

in·set \'in,set\ *vb* **inset** *or* **in·set·ted; in-**
set·ting : set in **—inset** *n*

in·shore \in'shōr\ *adj* 1 : situated near
shore 2 : moving toward shore ~ *adv*
: toward shore

in·side \in'sīd, 'in,sīd\ *n* 1 : inner side
2 *pl* : innards ~ *prep* 1 : in or into
the inside of 2 : before the end of ~
adv 1 : on the inner side 2 : into the
interior **—inside** *adj* **—in·sid·er** \in-
'sīdər\ *n*

inside of *prep* : inside

in·sid·i·ous \in'sidēəs\ *adj* 1 : treacherous 2 : seductive **—in·sid·i·ous·ly**
adv **—in·sid·i·ous·ness** *n*

in·sight \'in,sīt\ *n* : understanding **—**
in·sight·ful \'in,sitfəl, in'sīt-\ *adj*

in·sig·nia \in'signēə\, **in·sig·ne** \-(,)nē\
n, pl **-nia** *or* **-ni·as** : badge of authority or office

in·sin·u·ate \in'sinyə,wāt\ *vb* **-at·ed;**
-at·ing 1 : imply 2 : bring in artfully
—in·sin·u·a·tion \(,)in,sinyə-
'wāshən\ *n*

in·sip·id \in'sipəd\ *adj* 1 : tasteless 2
: not stimulating **—in·si·pid·i·ty**
\,insə'pidətē\ *n*

in·sist \in'sist\ *vb* : be firmly demand-
ing **—in·sis·tence** \in'sistəns\ *n* **—in-**
sis·tent \-tənt\ *adj* **—in·sis·tent·ly**
adv

insofar as \,insə,färəz\ *conj* : to the
extent that

in·sole \'in,sōl\ *n* : inside sole of a shoe

in·so·lent \'insələnt\ *adj* : contemp-
tuously rude **—in·so·lence** \-ləns\ *n*

in·sol·vent \(')in'sälvənt\ *adj* : unable
or insufficient to pay debts **—in·sol-**
ven·cy \-vənsē\ *n*

in·som·nia \in'sämnēə\ *n* : inability to
sleep

in·so·much as \,insə,məchəz\ *conj*
: inasmuch as

insomuch that *conj* : to such a degree
that

in·sou·ci·ance \in'süsēəns, aⁿsüsyäⁿs\
n : lighthearted indifference **—in-**
sou·ci·ant \in'süsēənt, aⁿsüsyäⁿ\
adj

in·spect \in'spekt\ *vb* : view closely
and critically **—in·spec·tion**
\-'spekshən\ *n* **—in·spec·tor** \-tər\
n

in·spire \in'spī(ə)r\ *vb* **-spired; -spir-**
ing 1 : inhale 2 : influence by example 3 : bring about ~ stir to action
—in·spi·ra·tion \,inspə'rāshən\ *n*
—in·spi·ra·tion·al \-'rāsh(ə)nəl\ *adj* **—**
in·spir·er *n*

in·stall, in·stal \in'stòl\ *vb* **-stalled;**
-stall·ing 1 : induct into office 2 : set
up for use **—in·stal·la·tion** \,in-
stə'lāshən\ *n*

in·stall·ment \in'stòlmənt\ *n* : partial
payment

in·stance \'instəns\ *n* 1 : request or
instigation 2 : example

in·stant \'instənt\ *n* : moment ~ *adj*
1 : immediate 2 : ready to mix **—in-**
stan·ta·neous \,instən'tānēəs\ *adj* **—**
in·stan·ta·neous·ly *adv* **—in·stant·ly**
adv

in·stead \in'sted\ *adv* : as a substitute
or alternative

instead of \in,stedə(v), -,stid-\ *prep*
: as a substitute for alternative to

in·step \'in,step\ *n* : part of the foot in
front of the ankle

in·sti·gate \'instə,gāt\ *vb* **-gat·ed;**
-gat·ing : incite **—in·sti·ga·tion**
\,instə'gāshən\ *n* **—in·sti·ga·tor**
\'instə,gātər\ *n*

in·still \in'stil\ *vb* **-stilled; -still·ing**
: impart gradually

in·stinct \'in,stiŋkt\ *n* 1 : natural talent
2 : natural inherited or subcon-
sciously motivated behavior **—in-**
stinc·tive \in'stiŋktiv\ *adj* **—in·stinc-**
tive·ly *adv* **—in·stinc·tu·al**
\in'stiŋ(k)chə(wə-)l\ *adj*

in·sti·tute \'instə,t(y)üt\ *vb* **-tut·ed;**
-tut·ing 1 : establish 2 : start ~ *n* 1
: organization promoting a cause 2
: school

in·sti·tu·tion \,instə't(y)üshən\ *n* 1
: act of instituting 2 : custom 3
: corporation or society of a public
character **—in·sti·tu·tion·al**
\-'t(y)üsh(ə)nəl\ *adj* **—in·sti·tu·tion-**
al·ize \-,īz\ *vb* **—in·sti·tu·tion-**
al·ly *adv*

in·struct \in'strəkt\ *vb* : teach **—in-**
struc·tion \in'strəkshən\ *n* **—in-**
struc·tion·al \-sh(ə)nəl\ *adj* **—in-**
struc·tive \in'strəktiv\ *adj* **—in-**

struc·tor \in'strəktər\ n —**in·struc·tor·ship** n

in·stru·ment \'instrəmənt\ n 1 : means 2 : implement 3 : something that produces music 4 : legal document 5 : device for controlling or regulating something —**in·stru·men·tal** \,instrə'mentᵊl\ adj —**in·stru·men·tal·ist** \-əst\ n —**in·stru·men·tal·i·ty** \,instrəmən'talətē, ,men-\ n —**in·stru·men·ta·tion** \,instrəmən'tāshən, ,-men-\ n

in·sub·or·di·nate \,insə'bordnət, -ᵊnət\ adj : not obeying —**in·sub·or·di·na·tion** \-,bordᵊn'āshən\ n

in·suf·fer·able \(')in'səf(ə)rəbəl\ adj : unbearable —**in·suf·fer·ably** \-blē\ adv

in·su·lar \'ins(y)ələr, 'inshələr\ adj 1 : relating to an island 2 : isolated 3 : narrow-minded —**in·su·lar·i·ty** \,ins(y)ə'larətē, ,inshə'lar-\ n

in·su·late \'insə,lāt\ vb -**lat·ed**; -**lat·ing** : protect from heat loss or electricity —**in·su·la·tion** \,insə'lāshən\ n —**in·su·la·tor** \'insə,lātər\ n

in·su·lin \'ins(ə)lən\ n : hormone used by diabetics

in·sult \in'səlt\ vb : treat with contempt ~ \in,səlt\ n : insulting act or remark —**in·sult·ing·ly** \-iŋlē\ adv

in·su·per·a·ble \(')in'süp(ə)rəbəl\ adj : too difficult —**in·su·per·a·bly** \-blē\ adv

in·sure \in'shür\ vb -**sured**; -**sur·ing** 1 : guarantee against loss 2 : make certain —**in·sur·able** \-əbəl\ adj —**in·sur·ance** \-əns\ n —**in·sured** \in-'shürd\ n —**in·sur·er** n

in·sur·gent \in'sərjənt\ n : rebel —**in·sur·gence** \-jəns\ n —**in·sur·gen·cy** \-jənsē\ n —**in·sur·gent** adj

in·sur·mount·able \,insər'maüntəbəl\ adj : too great to be overcome —**in·sur·mount·ably** \-blē\ adv

in·sur·rec·tion \,insə'rekshən\ n : revolution —**in·sur·rec·tion·ist** n

in·tact \in'takt\ adj : undamaged

in·take \'in,tāk\ n 1 : opening through which something enters 2 : act of taking in 3 : amount taken in

in·te·ger \'intijər\ n : number that is not a fraction and does not include a fraction

in·te·gral \'intigrəl\ adj : essential

in·te·grate \'intə,grāt\ vb -**grat·ed**; -**grat·ing** 1 : unite 2 : end segregation of or at —**in·te·gra·tion** \,intə'grāshən\ n

in·teg·ri·ty \in'tegrətē\ n 1 : soundness 2 : adherence to a code of values 3 : completeness

in·tel·lect \'intᵊl,ekt\ n : power of knowing or thinking —**in·tel·lec·tu·al** \,intᵊl'ekch(əw)əl\ adj or n —**in·tel·lec·tu·al·ism** \-ch(ə)wə,lizəm\ n —**in·tel·lec·tu·al·ly** adv

in·tel·li·gence \in'teləjəns\ n 1 : ability to learn and understand 2 : information

in·tel·li·gent \in'teləjənt\ adj : having or showing intelligence —**in·tel·li·gent·ly** adv

in·tel·li·gi·ble \in'teləjəbəl\ adj : understandable —**in·tel·li·gi·bil·i·ty** \-,teləjə'bilətē\ n —**in·tel·li·gi·bly** adv

in·tem·per·ance \(')in'temp(ə)rəns\ n : lack of moderation —**in·tem·per·ate** \-p(ə)rət\ adj —**in·tem·per·ate·ness** n

in·tend \in'tend\ vb : have as a purpose

in·tend·ed \-'tendəd\ n : engaged person —**intended** adj

in·tense \in'tens\ adj 1 : extreme 2 : deeply felt —**in·tense·ly** adv —**in·ten·si·fi·ca·tion** \-,tensəfə'kāshən\ n —**in·ten·si·fy** \-'tensə,fī\ vb —**in·ten·si·ty** \in'tensətē\ n —**in·ten·sive** \in-'tensiv\ adj —**in·ten·sive·ly** adv

¹**in·tent** \in'tent\ n : purpose —**in·ten·tion** \-'tenchən\ n —**in·ten·tion·al** \-'tench(ə)nəl\ adj —**in·ten·tion·al·ly** adv

²**intent** adj : concentrated —**in·tent·ly** adv —**in·tent·ness** n

in·ter \in'tər\ vb -**rr-** : bury

inter- prefix : between or among

interagency	interethnic
interatomic	interfaculty
interbank	interfamily
interborough	interfiber
interbusiness	interfraternity
intercampus	intergalactic
interchurch	intergang
intercity	intergovern-
interclass	mental
intercoastal	intergroup
intercollegiate	interhemispheric
intercolonial	interindustry
intercommunal	interinstitutional
intercommunity	interisland
intercompany	interlibrary
intercontinental	intermolecular
intercounty	intermountain
intercultural	interoceanic
interdenomi-	interoffice
national	interparticle
interdepart-	interparty
mental	interpersonal
interdivisional	interplanetary
interelectronic	interpopulation

interprovincial
interpupil
interracial
interregional
interreligious
interscholastic
intersectional
interstate
interstellar
intersystem
interterm

interterminal
intertribal
intertroop
intertropical
interuniversity
interurban
intervalley
intervillage
interwar
interzonal
interzone

in·ter·ac·tion \ˌintərˈakshən\ *n* : mutual influence —**in·ter·act** \-ˈakt\ *vb* —**in·ter·ac·tive** *adj*

in·ter·breed \ˌintərˈbrēd\ *vb* -**bred** \-ˈbred\; -**breed·ing** : breed together

in·ter·ca·late \inˈtərkəˌlāt\ *vb* -**lat·ed**; -**lat·ing** : insert —**in·ter·ca·la·tion** \-ˌtərkəˈlāshən\ *n*

in·ter·cede \ˌintərˈsēd\ *vb* -**ced·ed**; -**ced·ing** : act to reconcile —**in·ter·ces·sion** \-ˈseshən\ *n* —**in·ter·ces·sor** \-ˈsesər\ *n* —**in·ter·ces·so·ry** \-ˈses(ə)rē\ *adj*

in·ter·cept \ˌintərˈsept\ *vb* : interrupt the progress of —**in·ter·cept** \ˈintərˌsept\ *n* —**in·ter·cep·tion** \ˌintərˈsepshən\ *n* —**in·ter·cep·tor** \-ˈseptər\ *n*

in·ter·change \ˌintərˈchānj\ *vb* 1 : exchange 2 : change places ~ \ˈintərˌchānj\ *n* 1 : exchange 2 : junction of highways —**in·ter·change·able** \ˌintərˈchānjəbəl\ *adj*

in·ter·course \ˈintərˌkōrs\ *n* 1 : relations between persons or nations 2 : copulation

in·ter·de·pen·dent \ˌintərdiˈpendənt\ *adj* : mutually dependent —**in·ter·de·pen·dence** \-dəns\ *n*

in·ter·dict \ˌintərˈdikt\ *vb* : prohibit —**in·ter·dic·tion** \-ˈdikshən\ *n*

in·ter·est \ˈint(ə)rəst, -tərest\ *n* 1 : right 2 : benefit 3 : charge for borrowed money 4 *pl* : group financially involved in something 5 : readiness to pay special attention 6 : quality that causes interest ~ *vb* 1 : concern 2 : get the attention of —**in·ter·est·ing** *adj* —**in·ter·est·ing·ly** *adv*

in·ter·face \ˈintərˌfās\ *n* : common boundary —**in·ter·fa·cial** \ˌintərˈfāshəl\ *adj*

in·ter·fere \ˌintə(r)ˈfiər\ *vb* -**fered**; -**fer·ing** 1 : collide or be in opposition 2 : try to collide with the affairs of others —**in·ter·fer·ence** \-ˈfirəns\ *n*

in·ter·im \ˈintərəm\ *n* : time between —**interim** *adj*

in·te·ri·or \inˈtirēər\ *adj* : being on the inside ~ *n* 1 : inside 2 : inland area

in·ter·ject \ˌintərˈjekt\ *vb* : stick in between

in·ter·jec·tion \-ˈjekshən\ *n* : an exclamatory word —**in·ter·jec·tion·al·ly** \-sh(ə)nəlē\ *adv*

in·ter·lace \ˌintərˈlās\ *vb* : cross or cause to cross one over another

in·ter·lard \ˌintərˈlärd\ *vb* : intersperse

in·ter·lin·ear \ˌintərˈlinēər\ *adj* : between written or printed lines

in·ter·lock \ˌintərˈläk\ *vb* 1 : interlace 2 : connect for mutual effect —**in·ter·lock** \ˈintərˌläk\ *n*

in·ter·lope \ˌintərˈlōp\ *vb* -**loped**; -**lop·ing** 1 : encroach 2 : interfere —**in·ter·lop·er** *n*

in·ter·lude \ˈintərˌlüd\ *n* : intervening period

in·ter·mar·ry \ˌintərˈmarē\ *vb* 1 : marry each other 2 : marry within a group —**in·ter·mar·riage** \-ˈmarij\ *n*

in·ter·me·di·ary \ˌintərˈmēdēˌerē\ *n*, *pl* -**ar·ies** : agent between individuals or groups —**intermediary** *adj*

in·ter·me·di·ate \ˌintərˈmēdēət\ *adj* : between extremes —**intermediate** *n*

in·ter·ment \inˈtərmənt\ *n* : burial

in·ter·mi·na·ble \(ˈ)inˈtərm(ə)nəbəl\ *adj* : endless —**in·ter·mi·na·bly** *adv*

in·ter·min·gle \ˌintərˈmiŋgəl\ *vb* : mingle

in·ter·mis·sion \ˌintərˈmishən\ *n* : break in a performance

in·ter·mit·tent \-ˈmitⁿnt\ *adj* : coming at intervals —**in·ter·mit·tent·ly** *adv*

in·ter·mix \ˌintərˈmiks\ *vb* : mix together —**in·ter·mix·ture** \-ˈmikschər\ *n*

¹**in·tern** \ˈinˌtərn, inˈtərn\ *vb* : confine —**in·tern·ee** \ˌinˌtərˈnē\ *n* —**in·tern·ment** *n*

²**in·tern, in·terne** \ˈinˌtərn\ *n* : advanced student (as in medicine) gaining supervised experience ~ *vb* : act as an intern —**in·tern·ship** *n*

in·ter·nal \inˈtərnᵊl\ *adj* 1 : inward 2 : inside of the body 3 : relating to or existing in the mind —**in·ter·nal·ly** *adv*

in·ter·na·tion·al \ˌintərˈnash(ə)nəl\ *adj* : affecting 2 or more nations ~ *n* : something having international scope —**in·ter·na·tion·al·ism** \-ˌizəm\ *n* —**in·ter·na·tion·al·ize** \-ˌīz\ *vb* —**in·ter·na·tion·al·ly** *adv*

in·ter·nist \ˈinˌtərnəst\ *n* : specialist in nonsurgical medicine

in·ter·play \ˈintərˌplā\ *n* : interaction

in·ter·po·late \inˈtərpəˌlāt\ *vb* -**lat·ed**;

-lat-ing : insert —in-ter-po-la-tion \-,tərpə'lāshən\ n

in-ter-pose \,intər'pōz\ vb -posed; -pos-ing 1 : place between 2 : intrude —in-ter-po-si-tion \-pə'zishən\ n

in-ter-pret \in'tərprət\ vb : explain the meaning of —in-ter-pre-ta-tion \in-,tərprə'tāshən\ n —in-ter-pre-ta-tive \-'tərprə,tātiv\ adj —in-ter-pret-er n —in-ter-pre-tive \-'tərprətiv\ adj

in-ter-re-late \,intə(r)ri'lāt\ vb : have a mutual relationship —in-ter-re-lat-ed-ness \-'lātədnəs\ n —in-ter-re-la-tion \-'lāshən\ n —in-ter-re-la-tion-ship n

in-ter-ro-gate \in'terə,gāt\ vb -gat-ed; -gat-ing : question —in-ter-ro-ga-tion \-,terə'gāshən\ n —in-ter-rog-a-tive \,intə'rägətiv\ adj or n —in-ter-ro-ga-tor \-'terə,gātər\ n —in-ter-rog-a-to-ry \,intə'rägə,tōrē\ adj

in-ter-rupt \,intə'rəpt\ vb : intrude so as to hinder or end continuity —in-ter-rupt-er n —in-ter-rup-tion \-'rəpshən\ n —in-ter-rup-tive \-'rəptiv\ adv

in-ter-sect \in,tər'sekt\ vb 1 : cut across or divide 2 : cross —in-ter-sec-tion \-'sekshən\ n

in-ter-sperse \,intər'spərs\ vb -spersed; -spers-ing : insert at intervals —in-ter-sper-sion \-'spərzhən\ n

in-ter-stice \in'tərstəs\ n, pl -stic-es \-stə,sēz, -stəsəz\ : space between —in-ter-sti-tial \,intər'stishəl\ adj

in-ter-twine \,intər'twīn\ vb : twist together

in-ter-val \'intərvəl\ n 1 : time between 2 : space between

in-ter-vene \,intər'vēn\ vb -vened; -ven-ing 1 : happen between events 2 : intercede —in-ter-ven-tion \-'venchən\ n

in-ter-view \'intər,vyü\ n : a meeting to get information —interview vb —in-ter-view-er n

in-ter-weave \,intər'wēv\ vb -wove \-'wōv\; -wo-ven \-'wōvən\; -weav-ing : weave together —in-ter-wo-ven \-'wōvən\ adj

in-tes-tate \in'tes,tāt, -tət\ adj : not leaving a will

in-tes-tine \in'testən\ n : tubular part of the digestive system after the stomach forming a long narrow upper part (**small intestine**) followed by a broader shorter lower part (**large intestine**) —in-tes-ti-nal \-tən[ə]l\ adj

in-ti-mate \'intə,māt\ vb -mat-ed; -mat-ing : hint ~ \'intəmət\ adj 1 : very friendly 2 : suggesting privacy 3

: very personal ~ n : close friend —in-ti-ma-cy \'intəməsē\ n —in-ti-mate-ly adv —in-ti-ma-tion \,intə'māshən\ n

in-tim-i-date \in'timə,dāt\ vb -dat-ed; -dat-ing : make fearful —in-tim-i-da-tion \-,timə'dāshən\ n

in-to \,intü, 'intü\ prep 1 : to the inside of 2 : to the condition of 3 : against

in-to-na-tion \,intə'nāshən\ n : way of singing or speaking

in-tone \in'tōn\ vb -toned; -ton-ing : chant

in-tox-i-cate \in'täksə,kāt\ vb -cat-ed; -cat-ing : make drunk —in-tox-i-cant \-sikənt\ n —in-tox-i-ca-tion \-,täksə'kāshən\ n

in-tra-mu-ral \,intrə'myürəl\ adj : within a school

in-tran-si-gent \in'transəjənt\ adj : uncompromising —in-tran-si-gence \-jəns\ n —intransigent n

in-tra-ve-nous \,intrə'vēnəs\ adj : by way of the veins —in-tra-ve-nous-ly adv

in-trep-id \in'trepəd\ adj : fearless —in-tre-pid-i-ty \,intrə'pidətē\ n

in-tri-cate \'intrikət\ adj : very complex and delicate —in-tri-ca-cy \-trikəsē\ n —in-tri-cate-ly adv

in-trigue \in'trēg\ vb -trigued; -trigu-ing 1 : scheme 2 : arouse curiosity of ~ n : secret scheme —in-trigu-ing-ly \-iglē\ adv

in-trin-sic \in'trinzik, -sik\ adj : essential —in-trin-si-cal-ly \-zik(ə)lē, -si-\ adv

in-tro-duce \,intrə'd(y)üs\ vb -duced; -duc-ing 1 : bring in esp. for the 1st time 2 : cause to be acquainted 3 : bring to notice 4 : put in —in-tro-duc-tion \-dəkshən\ n —in-tro-duc-to-ry \-'dəkt(ə)rē\ adj

in-troit \in'trōət, -,tróit\ n : part of the Mass or music for it

in-tro-spec-tion \,intrə'spekshən\ n : examination of one's own thoughts or feelings —in-tro-spect \-'spekt\ vb —in-tro-spec-tive \-'spektiv\ adj —in-tro-spec-tive-ly adv

in-tro-vert \'intrə,vərt\ n : shy or retiring person —in-tro-ver-sion \,intrə'vərzhən\ n —introvert adj —in-tro-vert-ed \'intrə,vərtəd\ adj

in-trude \in'trüd\ vb -trud-ed; -trud-ing 1 : thrust in 2 : encroach —in-trud-er n —in-tru-sion \-'trüzhən\ n —in-tru-sive \-'trüsiv\ adj —in-tru-sive-ness n

in-tu-ition \,int(y)ü'ishən\ n : quick and ready insight —in-tu-it \in-

't(y)üət\ *vb* —**in·tu·i·tive** \in-'t(y)üətiv\ *adj* —**in·tu·i·tive·ly** *adv*

in·un·date \'inən,dāt\ *vb* **-dat·ed; -dat·ing** : flood —**in·un·da·tion** \,inən-'dāshən\ *n*

in·ure \in'(y)ur\ *vb* **-ured; -ur·ing** : accustom to accept something undesirable

in·vade \in'vād\ *vb* **-vad·ed; -vad·ing** : enter for conquest —**in·vad·er** *n* —**in·va·sion** \-'vāzhən\ *n*

¹**in·val·id** \in'valəd\ *adj* : not true or legal —**in·va·lid·i·ty** \,invə'lidətē\ *n* —**in·val·id·ly** *adv*

²**in·val·id** \'invələd\ *adj* : sickly ~ *n* : one chronically ill —**in·va·lid·ism** \-,izəm\ *n*

in·val·i·date \(')in'valə,dāt\ *vb* : make invalid

in·valu·able \(')in'valyə(wə)bəl\ *adj* : extremely valuable

in·vec·tive \in'vektiv\ *n* : abusive language —**invective** *adj*

in·veigh \in'vā\ *vb* : protest or complain forcefully

in·vei·gle \in'vāgəl, -'vē-\ *vb* **-gled; -gling** : win over or get by flattery

in·vent \in'vent\ *vb* **1** : think up **2** : create for the 1st time —**in·ven·tion** \-'venchən\ *n* —**in·ven·tive** \-iv\ *adj* —**in·ven·tive·ness** *n* —**in·ven·tor** \-'ventər\ *n*

in·ven·to·ry \'invən,tōrē\ *n, pl* **-ries 1** : list of goods **2** : stock —**inventory** *vb*

in·verse \(')in'vərs, 'in,vərs\ *adj* : opposite —**in·verse·ly** *adv*

in·vert \in'vərt\ *vb* **1** : turn upside down or inside out **2** : reverse —**in·ver·sion** \-'vərzhən\ *n*

in·ver·te·brate \(')in'vərtəbrət, -,brāt\ *adj* : lacking a backbone ~ *n* : invertebrate animal

in·vest \in'vest\ *vb* **1** : give power or authority to **2** : endow with a quality **3** : commit money to someone else's use in hope of profit —**in·vest·ment** \-'vest(t)mənt\ *n* —**in·ves·tor** \-'vestər\ *n*

in·ves·ti·gate \in'vestə,gāt\ *vb* **-gat·ed; -gat·ing** : study closely and systematically —**in·ves·ti·ga·tion** \-,vestə-'gāshən\ *n* —**in·ves·ti·ga·tor** \-'vestə,gātər\ *n*

in·ves·ti·ture \in'vestə,chúr, -chər\ *n* : act of establishing in office

in·vet·er·ate \in'vet(ə)rət\ *adj* : acting out of habit —**in·vet·er·a·cy** \-(ə)rəsē\ *n*

in·vid·i·ous \in'vidēəs\ *adj* **1** : detestable **2** : injurious —**in·vid·i·ous·ly** *adv*

in·vig·o·rate \in'vigə,rāt\ *vb* **-rat·ed;**

-rat·ing : give life and energy to —**in·vig·o·ra·tion** \-,vigə'rāshən\ *n*

in·vin·ci·ble \(')in'vinsəbəl\ *adj* : incapable of being conquered —**in·vin·ci·bil·i·ty** \(,)in,vinsə'bilətē\ *n* —**in·vin·ci·bly** \(')in'vinsəblē\ *adv*

in·vi·o·la·ble \(')in'vīələbəl\ *adj* : safe from violation or desecration —**in·vi·o·la·bil·i·ty** \(,)in, vīələ'bilətē\ *n*

in·vi·o·late \(')in'vīələt\ *adj* : not violated or profaned

in·vite \in'vīt\ *vb* **-vit·ed; -vit·ing 1** : entice **2** : increase the likelihood of **3** : request the presence or participation of **4** : encourage —**in·vi·ta·tion** \,invə'tāshən\ *n* —**in·vit·ing** \in'vītiŋ\ *adj*

in·vo·ca·tion \,invə'kāshən\ *n* **1** : prayer **2** : incantation

in·voice \'in,vóis\ *n* **1** : itemized bill for goods shipped ~ *vb* **-voiced; -voic·ing** : bill

in·voke \in'vōk\ *vb* **-voked; -vok·ing 1** : call on for help **2** : cite as authority **3** : conjure **4** : carry out

in·volve \in'välv\ *vb* **-volved; -volv·ing 1** : draw in as a participant **2** : relate closely **3** : require as a necessary part **4** : occupy fully —**in·volve·ment** *n*

in·volved \-'välvd\ *adj* : intricate

¹**in·ward** \'inwərd\ *adj* : inside

²**inward, in·wards** \-wərdz\ *adv* : toward the inside, center, or inner being

in·ward·ly *adv* **1** : mentally or spiritually **2** : internally **3** : to oneself

io·dide \'īə,dīd\ *n* : compound of iodine

io·dine \'īə,dīn, -ədᵉn\ *n* : nonmetallic chemical element

io·dize \'īə,dīz\ *vb* **-dized; -diz·ing** : treat with iodine or an iodide

ion \'īən, 'ī,än\ *n* : electrically charged particle —**ion·ic** \ī'änik\ *adj* —**ion·iz·able** \'īə,nīzəbəl\ *adj* —**ion·iza·tion** \,īənə'zāshən\ *n* —**ion·ize** \'īə,nīz\ *vb* —**ion·iz·er** \'īə,nīzər\ *n*

-ion *n suffix* **1** : act or process **2** : state or condition

ion·o·sphere \ī'änə,sfiər\ *n* : layer of the upper atmosphere with charged particles —**ion·o·spher·ic** \ī,änə-'sfi(ə)rik, -'sfer-\ *adj*

io·ta \ī'ōtə\ *n* : small quantity

IOU \,ī(,)ō'yü\ *n* : acknowledgment of a debt

iras·ci·ble \ir'asəbəl, ī'ras-\ *adj* : marked by hot temper —**iras·ci·bil·i·ty** \-,asə'bilətē, -,ras-\ *n*

irate \ī'rāt\ *adj* : roused to intense anger —**irate·ly** *adv*

ire \ˈī(ə)r\ *n* : anger

ir·i·des·cence \ˌir·ə'des²ns\ *n* : rainbowlike play of colors —**ir·i·des·cent** \-²nt\ *adj*

iris \ˈīrəs\ *n, pl* **iris·es** *or* **iri·des** \ˈīrə,dēz, 'ir-\ **1** : colored part around the pupil of the eye **2** : plant with long leaves and large showy flowers

irk \ˈərk\ *vb* : make weary, irritated, or bored —**irk·some** \-səm\ *adj* —**irk·some·ly** *adv*

iron \ˈī(ə)rn\ *n* **1** : metallic chemical element **2** : something made of iron **3** : heated device for pressing clothes ~ *vb* : press or smooth out with an iron —**iron·er** *n* —**iron·ware** *n* —**iron·work** *n* —**iron·work·er** *n* —**iron·works** *n pl*

iron·clad \-'klad\ *adj* **1** : sheathed in iron armor **2** : strict or exacting

iron·ing \ˈī(ə)rniŋ\ *n* : clothes to be ironed

iron·wood \-,wu̇d\ *n* : tree or shrub with very hard wood

iro·ny \ˈīrənē\ *n, pl* **-nies 1** : use of words to express the opposite of the literal meaning **2** : incongruity between the actual and expected result of events —**iron·ic** \ī'ränik\, **iron·i·cal** \-ikəl\ *adj* —**iron·i·cal·ly** \-ik(ə)lē\ *adv*

ir·ra·di·ate \ir'ādē,āt\ *vb* **-at·ed; -at·ing** : treat with radiation —**ir·ra·di·a·tion** \-,ādē'āshən\ *n*

ir·ra·tio·nal \(')ir'ash(ə)nəl\ *adj* **1** : incapable of reasoning **2** : not based on reason —**ir·ra·tio·nal·i·ty** \(,)ir,-ashə'nalətē\ *n* —**ir·ra·tio·nal·ly** *adv*

ir·rec·on·cil·able \(,)ir,ekən'sīləbəl\ *adj* : impossible to reconcile —**ir·rec·on·cil·abil·i·ty** \-,sīlə'bilətē\ *n*

ir·re·cov·er·able \,iri'kəv(ə)rəbəl\ *adj* : not capable of being recovered —**ir·re·cov·er·ably** \-blē\ *adv*

ir·re·deem·able \,iri'dēməbəl\ *adj* : not redeemable

ir·re·duc·ible \,iri'd(y)üsəbəl\ *adj* : not reducible —**ir·re·duc·ibly** \-blē\ *adv*

ir·ref·u·ta·ble \,iri'fyütəbəl, (')ir-'r(ef)yət-\ *adj* : impossible to refute

ir·reg·u·lar \(')ir'egyələr\ *adj* : not regular or normal —**irregular** *n* —**ir·reg·u·lar·i·ty** \(,)ir,egyə'larətē\ *n* —**ir·reg·u·lar·ly** *adv*

ir·rel·e·vant \ir'eləvənt\ *adj* : not relevant —**ir·rel·e·vance** \-vəns\ *n*

ir·re·li·gious \,iri'lijəs\ *adj* : not following religious practices

ir·rep·a·ra·ble \(')ir'ep(ə)rəbəl\ *adj*

: impossible to make good, undo, or remedy

ir·re·place·able \,iri'plāsəbəl\ *adj* : not replaceable

ir·re·press·ible \-'presəbəl\ *adj* : impossible to repress or control

ir·re·proach·able \-'prōchəbəl\ *adj* : blameless

ir·re·sist·ible \-'zistəbəl\ *adj* : impossible to successfully resist —**ir·re·sist·ibly** \-blē\ *adv*

ir·res·o·lute \(')ir'ezəlüt\ *adj* : uncertain —**ir·res·o·lute·ly** *adv* —**ir·res·o·lu·tion** \-,ezə'lüshən\ *n*

ir·re·spec·tive of \,iri'spektiv-\ *prep* : without regard to

ir·re·spon·si·ble \,iri'spänsəbəl\ *adj* : not responsible —**ir·re·spon·si·bil·i·ty** \-,spänsə'bilətē\ *n* —**ir·re·spon·si·bly** *adv*

ir·re·triev·able \,iri'trēvəbəl\ *adj* : not retrievable

ir·rev·er·ence \(')ir'ev(ə)rəns\ *n* **1** : lack of reverence **2** : irreverent act or utterance —**ir·rev·er·ent** \-(ə)rənt\ *adj*

ir·re·vers·ible \,iri'vərsəbəl\ *adj* : incapable of being reversed

ir·re·vo·ca·ble \(')ir'evəkəbəl\ *adj* : incapable of being revoked —**ir·rev·o·ca·bly** \-blē\ *adv*

ir·ri·gate \'irə,gāt\ *vb* **-gat·ed; -gat·ing** : supply with water by artificial means —**ir·ri·ga·tion** \,irə'gāshən\ *n*

ir·ri·tate \'irə,tāt\ *vb* **-tat·ed; -tat·ing 1** : excite to anger **2** : make sore or inflamed —**ir·ri·ta·bil·i·ty** \,irətə'bilətē\ *n* —**ir·ri·ta·ble** \'irətəbəl\ *adj* —**ir·ri·ta·bly** *adv* —**ir·ri·tant** \'irətənt\ *adj or n* —**ir·ri·tat·ing·ly** *adv* —**ir·ri·ta·tion** \,irə-'tāshən\ *n*

is *pres 3d sing of* BE

-ish \ish\ *adj suffix* **1** : characteristic of **2** : somewhat

isin·glass \ˈīz²n,glas, 'iziŋ-\ *n* **1** : gelatin from the air bladders of fish **2** : mica

Is·lam \is'läm, iz-, -'läm\ *n* : religious faith of Muslims —**Is·lam·ic** \-ik\ *adj*

is·land \ˈīlənd\ *n* : body of land surrounded by water —**is·land·er** \'īləndər\ *n*

isle \ˈīl\ *n* : small island

is·let \ˈīlət\ *n* : small island

-ism \,izəm\ *n suffix* **1** : act or practice **2** : characteristic manner **3** : condition **4** : doctrine

iso·late \ˈīsə,lāt, 'isə-\ *vb* **-lat·ed; -lat·ing** : place or keep by itself —**iso·la·tion** \,īsə'lāshən, ,isə-\ *n*

iso·met·rics \,īsə'metriks\ *n sing or pl*

: exercise against unmoving resistance **—isometric** *adj*

isos·ce·les \ī'säsə,lēz\ *adj* : having 2 equal sides

iso·tope \'īsə,tōp\ *n* : species of atom of a chemical element **—iso·to·pic** \,īsə'täpik, -'tō-\ *adj* **—iso·to·pi·cal·ly** \-ik(ə)lē\ *adv*

is·sue \'ish(,)ü\ *vb* **-sued; -su·ing** 1 : go, come, or flow out 2 : descend from a specified ancestor 3 : emanate or result 4 : put forth or distribute officially ~ *n* 1 : action of issuing 2 : offspring 3 : result 4 : point of controversy 5 : act of giving out or printing 6 : quantity given out or printed **—is·su·ance** \'ishəwəns\ *n* **—is·su·er** *n*

-ist \əst\ *n suffix* 1 : one that does 2 : one that plays 3 : one that specializes in 4 : follower of a doctrine

isth·mus \'isməs\ *n* : narrow strip of land connecting 2 larger portions

it \('))it, ət\ *pron* 1 : that one —used of a lifeless thing or an abstract entity 2 —used as an anticipatory subject or object ~ *n* : player who tries to catch others (as in a game of tag)

ital·ic \ə'talik, ī-, ī-\ *n* : style of type with slanting letters **—italic** *adj* —

ital·i·ci·za·tion \ə,taləsə'zāshən, ī-, ī-\ *n* **—ital·i·cize** \ə'talə,sīz, ī-, ī-\ *vb*

itch \'ich\ *n* 1 : uneasy irritating skin sensation 2 : skin disorder 3 : persistent desire **—itch** *vb* **—itchy** *adj*

item \'ītəm\ *n* 1 : particular in a list, account, or series 2 : piece of news **—item·iza·tion** \,ītəmə'zāshən\ *n* **—item·ize** \'ītə,mīz\ *vb*

itin·er·ant \ī'tinərənt, ə-\ *adj* : traveling from place to place

itin·er·ary \ī'tinə,rerē, ə-\ *n, pl* **-ar·ies** : route or outline of a journey

its \(,)its, əts\ *adj* : relating to it

it·self \it'self, ət-\ *pron* : it—used reflexively or for emphasis

-ity \ətē\ *n suffix* : quality, state, or degree

-ive \iv\ *adj suffix* : that performs or tends toward an action

ivo·ry \'īv(ə)rē\ *n, pl* **-ries** 1 : hard creamy-white material of elephants' tusks 2 : pale yellow color

ivy \'īvē\ *n, pl* **ivies** : trailing woody vine with evergreen leaves

-ize \,īz\ *vb suffix* 1 : cause to be, become, or resemble 2 : subject to an action 3 : treat or combine with 4 : engage in an activity

J

j \'jā\ *n, pl* **j's** or **js** \'jāz\ : 10th letter of the alphabet

jab \'jab\ *vb* **-bb-** : thrust quickly or abruptly ~ *n* : short straight punch

jab·ber \'jabər\ *vb* : talk rapidly or unintelligibly **—jabber** *n*

jack \'jak\ *n* 1 : mechanical device to raise a heavy body 2 : small flag 3 : small 6-pointed metal object used in a game (**jacks**) 4 : electrical socket ~ *vb* 1 : raise with a jack 2 : increase

jack·al \'jakəl, -,ȯl\ *n* : wild dog smaller than a wolf

jack·ass *n* : male ass

jack·et \'jakət\ *n* : garment for the upper body **—jack·et·ed** *adj*

jack·ham·mer \'jak,hamər\ *n* : pneumatic tool for drilling

jack·knife \'jak,nīf\ *n* : pocketknife

jack-o'-lan·tern \'jakə,lantərn\ *n* : lantern made of a carved pumpkin

jack·pot \'jak,pät\ *n* : sum of money won

jack·rab·bit \-,rabət\ *n* : large hare of western No. America

jade \'jād\ *n* : usu. green gemstone

jad·ed \'jādəd\ *adj* : dulled or bored by having too much

jag·ged \'jagəd\ *adj* : sharply notched

jag·uar \'jag(yə),wär\ *n* : black-spotted tropical American cat

jai alai \'hī,lī, ,hī-\ *n* : game with a ball propelled by a basket on the hand

jail \'jāl\ *n* : prison ~ *vb* : put in jail **—jail·break** *n* **—jail·er, jail·or** *n*

ja·lopy \jə'läpē\ *n, pl* **-lopies** : dilapidated automobile

jal·ou·sie \'jaləsē\ *n* : door or window with louvers

jam \'jam\ *vb* **-mm-** 1 : press into a close or tight position 2 : cause to become wedged so as to be unworkable ~ *n* 1 : crowded mass that blocks or impedes 2 : difficult situation 3 : thick sweet food made of cooked fruit

jamb \'jam\ *n* : upright framing piece of a door

jam·bo·ree \,jambə'rē\ *n* : large festive gathering

jan·gle \'jaŋgəl\ *vb* **-gled; -gling** : make a harsh ringing sound **—jangle** *n*

jan·i·tor \'janətər\ *n* : person who has the care of a building —**jan·i·to·ri·al** \ˌjanəˈtōrēəl\ *adj*

Jan·u·ary \'janyəˌwerē\ *n* : 1st month of the year having 31 days

¹jar \'jär\ *vb* -**rr**- 1 : have a harsh or disagreeable effect 2 : vibrate or shake ~ *n* 1 : jolt 2 : painful effect

²jar *n* : broad-mouthed container

jar·gon \'järgən, -ˌgän\ *n* : special vocabulary of a group

jas·mine \'jazmən\ *n* : climbing shrub with fragrant flowers

jas·per \'jaspər\ *n* : red, yellow, or brown opaque quartz

jaun·dice \'jóndəs\ *n* : yellowish discoloration of skin, tissues, and body fluids

jaun·diced \-dəst\ *adj* : exhibiting envy or hostility

jaunt \'jónt\ *n* : short pleasure trip

jaun·ty \'jóntē\ *adj* -**ti·er**; -**est** : lively in manner or appearance —**jaun·ti·ly** \'jóntᵊlē\ *adv* —**jaun·ti·ness** *n*

jave·lin \'jav(ə)lən\ *n* : light spear

jaw \'jó\ *n* 1 : either of the bony or cartilaginous structures that support the mouth 2 : one of 2 movable parts for holding or crushing ~ *vb* : talk indignantly or at length —**jaw·bone** \-ˌbōn, -ˌbón\ *n* —**jawed** \'jód\ *adj*

jay \'jā\ *n* : noisy brightly colored bird

jay·bird *n* : jay

jay·walk *vb* : cross a street carelessly —**jay·walk·er** *n*

jazz \'jaz\ *vb* : enliven ~ *n* 1 : kind of American music involving improvisation 2 : empty talk —**jazzy** *adj*

jeal·ous \'jeləs\ *adj* : suspicious of a rival or of one believed to enjoy an advantage —**jeal·ous·ly** *adv* —**jeal·ou·sy** \-əsē\ *n*

jeans \'jēnz\ *n pl* : pants made of durable twilled cotton cloth

jeep \'jēp\ *n* : 4-wheel army vehicle

jeer \'jiər\ *vb* 1 : speak or cry out in derision 2 : ridicule ~ *n* : taunt

Je·ho·vah \ji'hōvə\ *n* : God

je·june \ji'jün\ *adj* : dull or childish

jell \'jel\ *vb* 1 : come to the consistency of jelly 2 : take shape

jel·ly \'jelē\ *n, pl* -**lies** : a substance (as food) with a somewhat elastic consistency —**jelly** *vb*

jel·ly·fish *n* : sea animal with a saucer-shaped jellylike body

jen·ny \'jenē\ *n, pl* -**nies** : female bird or donkey

jeop·ar·dy \'jepərdē\ *n* : exposure to death, loss, or injury —**jeop·ar·dize** \-ər,dīz\ *vb*

jerk \'jərk\ *vb* 1 : give a sharp quick push, pull, or twist 2 : move in short abrupt motions ~ *n* 1 : short quick pull or twist 2 : stupid or foolish person —**jerk·i·ly** *adv* —**jerky** *adj*

jer·kin \'jərkən\ *n* : close-fitting sleeveless jacket

jer·ry-built \'jerē,bilt\ *adj* : built cheaply and flimsily

jer·sey \'jərzē\ *n, pl* -**seys** 1 : plain knit fabric 2 : knitted shirt

jest \'jest\ *n* : witty remark —**jest** *vb*

jest·er \'jestər\ *n* : one employed to entertain a court

¹jet \'jet\ *n* : velvet-black coal used for jewelry

²jet *vb* -**tt**- 1 : spout or emit in a stream 2 : travel by jet ~ *n* 1 : forceful rush of fluid through a narrow opening 2 : jet-propelled airplane

jet-propelled *adj* : driven by an engine (**jet engine**) that produces propulsion (**jet propulsion**) by the rearward discharge of a jet of fluid

jet·sam \'jetsəm\ *n* : jettisoned goods

jet·ti·son \'jetəsən\ *vb* 1 : throw (goods) overboard 2 : discard —**jettison** *n*

jet·ty \'jetē\ *n, pl* -**ties** : pier or wharf

Jew \'jü\ *n* : one whose religion is Judaism —**Jew·ish** *adj*

jew·el \'jüəl\ *n* 1 : ornament of precious metal 2 : gem ~ *vb* -**eled** or -**elled**; -**el·ing** or -**el·ling** : adorn with jewels —**jew·el·er**, **jew·el·ler** \-ər\ *n* —**jew·el·ry** \-rē\ *n*

jib \'jib\ *n* : triangular sail

jibe \'jīb\ *vb* **jibed**; **jib·ing** : be in agreement

jif·fy \'jifē\ *n, pl* -**fies** : short time

jig \'jig\ *n* : lively dance ~ *vb* -**gg**- : dance a jig

jig·ger \'jigər\ *n* : measure used in mixing drinks

jig·gle \'jigəl\ *vb* -**gled**; -**gling** : move with quick little jerks —**jiggle** *n*

jig·saw *n* : machine saw with a narrow blade that moves up and down

jilt \'jilt\ *vb* : woman who jilts a man ~ *vb* : drop (one's lover) unfeelingly

jim·my \'jimē\ *n, pl* -**mies** : small crowbar ~ *vb* -**mied**; -**my·ing** : pry open

jim·son·weed \'jimsən,wēd\ *n* : coarse poisonous weed

jin·gle \'jiŋgəl\ *vb* -**gled**; -**gling** : make a light tinkling sound ~ *n* 1 : light tinkling sound 2 : short verse or song

jin·go·ism \'jiŋgō,izəm\ *n* : extreme chauvinism or nationalism —**jin·go·ist** \-əst\ *n* —**jin·go·is·tic** \ˌjiŋgō-'istik\ *adj*

jinx \'jiŋks\ *n* : one that brings bad luck —**jinx** *vb*

jit·ney \\'jitnē\\ *n, pl* **-neys** : small bus

jit·ters \\'jitərz\\ *n pl* : extreme nervousness —**jit·tery** \\-ərē\\ *adj*

job \\'jäb\\ *n* 1 : something that has to be done 2 : regular employment —**job·hold·er** *n* —**job·less** *adj*

job·ber \\'jäbər\\ *n* : middleman

jock·ey \\'jäkē\\ *n, pl* **-eys** : one who rides a horse in a race ~ *vb* **-eyed; -ey·ing** : manipulate or maneuver adroitly

jo·cose \\jō'kōs\\ *adj* : jocular

joc·u·lar \\'jäkyələr\\ *adj* : marked by jesting —**joc·u·lar·i·ty** \\,jäkyə-'larətē\\ *n*

jo·cund \\'jäkənd\\ *adj* : full of mirth or gaiety

jodh·purs \\'jädpərz\\ *n pl* : riding breeches

¹jog \\'jäg\\ *vb* **-gg-** 1 : give a slight shake or push to 2 : run or ride at a slow pace ~ *n* 1 : slight shake 2 : slow pace —**jog·ger** *n*

²jog *n* : brief abrupt change in direction or line

join \\'join\\ *vb* 1 : come or bring together 2 : become a member of —**join·er** *n*

joint \\'joint\\ *n* 1 : point of contact between bones 2 : place where 2 parts connect 3 : often disreputable place ~ *adj* : common to 2 or more —**joint·ed** *adj* —**joint·ly** *adv*

joist \\'joist\\ *n* : beam supporting a floor or ceiling

joke \\'jōk\\ *n* : something said or done to provoke laughter ~ *vb* **jok·ing** : make jokes —**jok·er** *n* —**jok·ing·ly** \\'jōkiŋlē\\ *adv*

jol·li·ty \\'jälətē\\ *n, pl* **-ties** : gaiety or merriment

jol·ly \\'jälē\\ *adj* **-li·er; -est** : full of high spirits

jolt \\'jolt\\ *vb* 1 : move with a sudden jerky motion 2 : give a jolt to ~ *n* 1 : abrupt jerky blow or movement 2 : sudden shock —**jolt·er** *n*

jon·quil \\'jänkwəl\\ *n* : narcissus with white or yellow flowers

josh \\'jäsh\\ *vb* : tease or joke

jos·tle \\'jäsəl\\ *vb* **-tled; -tling** : push or shove

jot \\'jät\\ *n* : least bit ~ *vb* **-tt-** : write briefly and hurriedly

jounce \\'jauns\\ *vb* **jounced; jounc·ing** : jolt —**jounce** *n*

jour·nal \\'jərn⁹l\\ *n* 1 : brief account of daily events 2 : periodical (as a newspaper)

jour·nal·ism \\'jərn⁹l,izəm\\ *n* : business of reporting or printing news —

jour·nal·ist \\-əst\\ *n* —**jour·nal·is·tic** \\,jərn⁹l'istik\\ *adj*

jour·ney \\'jərnē\\ *n, pl* **-neys** : a going from one place to another ~ *vb* **-neyed; -ney·ing** : make a journey

jour·ney·man \\-mən\\ *n* : worker who has learned a trade and works for another person

joust \\'jaust\\ *n* : combat on horseback between 2 knights with lances —**joust** *vb*

jo·vial \\'jōvēəl\\ *adj* : marked by good humor —**jo·vi·al·i·ty** \\,jōvē'alətē\\ *n* —**jo·vi·al·ly** \\'jōvēəlē\\ *adv*

¹jowl \\'jaul\\ *n* 1 : lower jaw 2 : cheek

²jowl *n* : loose flesh about the lower jaw or throat

joy \\'joi\\ *n* 1 : feeling of happiness 2 : source of happiness —**joy** *vb* —**joy·ful** *adj* —**joy·ful·ly** *adv* —**joy·less** *adj* —**joy·ous** \\'joiəs\\ *adj* —**joy·ous·ly** *adv* —**joy·ous·ness** *n*

joy·ride *n* : reckless ride for pleasure —**joy·rid·er** *n* —**joy·rid·ing** *n*

ju·bi·lant \\'jübələnt\\ *adj* : expressing great joy —**ju·bi·lant·ly** *adv* —**ju·bi·la·tion** \\,jübə'lāshən\\ *n*

ju·bi·lee \\'jübə,lē\\ *n* 1 : 50th anniversary 2 : season or occasion of celebration

Ju·da·ism \\'jüdə,izəm\\ *n* : religion developed among the ancient Hebrews —**Ju·da·ic** \\jü'däik\\ *adj*

judge \\'jəj\\ *vb* **judged; judg·ing** 1 : form an opinion 2 : decide as a judge ~ *n* 1 : public official authorized to decide questions brought before a court 2 : one who gives an authoritative opinion —**judge·ship** *n*

judg·ment, judge·ment \\'jəjmənt\\ *n* 1 : decision or opinion given after judging 2 : capacity for judging

ju·di·ca·ture \\'jüdikə,chùr\\ *n* : administration of justice

ju·di·cial \\jü'dishəl\\ *adj* : relating to judicature or the judiciary —**ju·di·cial·ly** *adv*

ju·di·cia·ry \\jü'dishē,erē. -'dishərē\\ *n* : system of courts of law or the judges of them —**judiciary** *adj*

ju·di·cious \\jü'dishəs\\ *adj* : having or characterized by sound judgment —**ju·di·cious·ly** *adv* —**ju·di·cious·ness** *n*

ju·do \\'jüdō\\ *n* : form of wrestling —**judo·ist** *n*

jug \\'jəg\\ *n* : large deep container with a narrow mouth and a handle

jug·ger·naut \\'jəgər,not\\ *n* : massive inexorable force or object

jug·gle \\'jagəl\\ *vb* **-gled; -gling** \\-(ə)liŋ\\ 1 : keep several objects in motion in the air at the same time 2 : manipulate for an often tricky purpose — **jug·gler** \\'jəglər\ *n*

jug·u·lar \\'jəgyələr\ *adj* : in or on the throat or neck

juice \\'jüs\ *n* **1** : extractable fluid contents of cells or tissues **2** : electricity —**juic·er** *n* —**juic·i·ly** \\'jüsəlē\ *adv* —**juic·i·ness** \-sēnəs\ *n* —**juicy** \\'jüsē\ *adj*

ju·jube \\'jü,jüb, 'jüjü,bē\ *n* : gummy candy

juke·box \\'jük,bäks\ *n* : coin-operated record player

ju·lep \\'jüləp\ *n* : mint-flavored bourbon drink

Ju·ly \\ju'lī\ *n* : 7th month of the year having 31 days

jum·ble \\'jəmbəl\ *vb* -**bled**; -**bling** : mix in a disorderly mass —**jumble** *n*

jum·bo \\'jəmbō\ *n, pl* -**bos** : very large version —**jumbo** *adj*

jump \\'jəmp\ *vb* **1** : rise into or through the air esp. by muscular effort **2** : pass over **3** : give a start **4** : rise or increase sharply ~ *n* **1** : a jumping **2** : sharp sudden increase **3** : initial advantage

¹jump·er \\'jəmpər\ *n* : one that jumps

²jumper *n* : sleeveless one-piece dress

jumpy \\'jəmpē\ *adj* **jump·i·er**; -**est** : nervous or jittery

junc·tion \\'jəŋkshən\ *n* **1** : a joining **2** : place or point of meeting

junc·ture \\'jəŋkchər\ *n* **1** : joint or connection **2** : critical time or state of affairs

June \\'jün\ *n* : 6th month of the year having 30 days

jun·gle \\'jəŋgəl\ *n* : thick tangled mass of tropical vegetation

ju·nior \\'jünyər\ *n* **1** : person who is younger or of lower rank than another **2** : student in the next-to-last year ~ *adj* : younger or lower in rank

ju·ni·per \\'jünəpər\ *n* : evergreen shrub or tree

¹junk \\'jəŋk\ *n* **1** : discarded articles **2** : shoddy product ~ *vb* : discard or scrap —**junky** *adj*

²junk *n* : flat-bottomed ship of Chinese waters

jun·ket \\'jəŋkət\ *n* : trip made by an official at public expense

jun·ta \\'hüntə, 'jəntə, 'həntə\ *n* : group of persons controlling a government

ju·ris·dic·tion \\jürəs'dikshən\ *n* **1** : right or authority to interpret and apply the law **2** : limits within which authority may be exercised —**ju·ris·dic·tion·al** \-sh(ə)nəl\ *adj*

ju·ris·pru·dence \-'prüd²ns\ *n* **1** : system of laws **2** : science or philosophy of law

ju·rist \\'jürəst\ *n* : lawyer or judge

ju·ror \\'jürər\ *n* : member of a jury

ju·ry \\'jürē\ *n, pl* -**ries** : body of persons sworn to give a verdict on a matter

just \\'jəst\ *adj* **1** : reasonable **2** : correct or proper **3** : morally or legally right **4** : deserved ~ \(,)jəst, (,)jist\ *adv* **1** : exactly **2** : very recently **3** : barely **4** : only —**just·ly** *adv* —**just·ness** *n*

jus·tice \\'jəstəs\ *n* **1** : administration of what is just **2** : judge **3** : administration of law **4** : fairness

jus·ti·fy \\'jəstə,fī\ *vb* -**fied**; -**fy·ing** : prove to be just, right, or reasonable —**jus·ti·fi·able** *adj* —**jus·ti·fi·ca·tion** \,jəstəfə'kāshən\ *n*

jut \\'jət\ *vb* -**tt**- : stick out

jute \\'jüt\ *n* : strong glossy fiber from a tropical herb

ju·ve·nile \\'jüvə,nīl, -vən²l\ *adj* : relating to children or young people ~ *n* : young person

jux·ta·pose \\'jəkstə,pōz\ *vb* -**posed**; -**pos·ing** : place side by side —**jux·ta·po·si·tion** \,jəkstəpə'zishən\ *n*

K

k \\'kā\ *n, pl* **k's** *or* **ks** \\'kāz\ : 11th letter of the alphabet

kai·ser \\'kīzər\ *n* : German ruler

kale \\'kāl\ *n* : curly cabbage

ka·lei·do·scope \kə'līdə,skōp\ *n* : device containing loose bits of colored glass reflecting in many patterns —**ka·lei·do·scop·ic** \-,līdə'skäpik\ *adj* —**ka·lei·do·scop·i·cal·ly** \-ik(ə)lē\ *adv*

kan·ga·roo \,kaŋgə'rü\ *n, pl* -**roos** : large leaping Australian mammal

ka·olin \\'kāələn\ *n* : fine white clay

kar·at \\'karət\ *n* : unit of gold content

ka·ra·te \kə'rätē\ *n* : art of self-defense by crippling kicks and punches

ka·ty·did \\'kātē,did\ *n* : large American grasshopper

kay·ak \\'kī,ak\ *n* : Eskimo canoe

ka·zoo \kə'zü\ n, pl -zoos : toy musical instrument

keel \'kēl\ n : central lengthwise strip on the bottom of a ship —**keeled** \'kēld\ adj

keen \'kēn\ adj 1 : sharp 2 : severe 3 : enthusiastic 4 : mentally alert —**keen·ly** adv —**keen·ness** \'kēnnəs\ n

keep \'kēp\ vb **kept** \'kept\; **keep·ing** 1 : perform 2 : guard 3 : maintain 4 : retain in one's possession 5 : detain 6 : continue in good condition 7 : refrain ~ n 1 : fortress 2 : means by which one is kept —**keep·er** n

keep·ing \'kēpiŋ\ n : conformity

keep·sake \'kēp,sāk\ n : souvenir

keg \'keg\ n : small cask or barrel

kelp \'kelp\ n : coarse brown seaweed

ken \'ken\ n : range of sight or understanding

ken·nel \'kenᵊl\ n : dog shelter —**kennel** vb

ker·chief \'kərchəf, -,chēf\ n : square of cloth worn as a head covering

ker·nel \'kərnᵊl\ n 1 : inner softer part of a seed or nut 2 : whole seed of a cereal 3 : central part

ker·o·sene, ker·o·sine \'kerə,sēn, ,kerə'-, 'kar-, ,kar-\ n : thin flammable oil from petroleum

ketch·up var of CATSUP

ket·tle \'ketᵊl\ n : vessel for boiling liquids

ket·tle·drum \-,drum\ n : brass or copper drum with a top of animal skin

¹key \'kē\ n 1 : metal piece to open a lock 2 : explanation 3 : lever pressed by a finger in playing an instrument or operating a machine 4 : leading individual or principle 5 : system of musical tones or pitch ~ vb 1 : attune 2 : make nervous ~ adj : basic —**key·hole** n

²key n : low island or reef

key·board n : arrangement of keys

key·note \-,nōt\ n 1 : 1st note of a scale 2 : central fact, idea, or mood ~ vb 1 : set the keynote of 2 : deliver the major speech

key·punch n : keyboard machine to punch cards —**keypunch** vb —**keypunch·er** n

key·stone n : wedge-shaped piece at the crown of an arch

kha·ki \'kakē, 'käk-\ n : light yellowish brown

khan \'kän, 'kan\ n : Mongol leader

kib·butz \kib'üts, -'üts\ n, pl -but·zim \-,üt'sēm, -,üt-\ : Israeli collective farm or settlement

ki·bitz·er \'kibətsər, kə'bit-\ n : one who offers unwanted advice —**kib·itz** \'kibəts\ vb

kick \'kik\ vb 1 : strike out or hit with the foot 2 : object strongly 3 : recoil ~ n 1 : thrust with the foot 2 : recoil of a gun 3 : stimulating effect —**kick·er** n

kid \'kid\ n 1 : young goat 2 : child ~ vb -dd- 1 : deceive as a joke 2 : tease —**kid·der** n —**kid·ding·ly** adv —**kid·dish** \'kidish\ adj

kid·nap \'kid,nap\ vb -napped or -naped \-,napt\; -nap·ping or -nap·ing : carry a person away by illegal force —**kid·nap·per, kid·nap·er** n

kid·ney \'kidnē\ n, pl -neys : either of a pair of organs that excrete urine

kill \'kil\ vb 1 : deprive of life 2 : finish 3 : use up (time) ~ n : act of killing —**kill·er** n

kiln \'kil(n)\ n : heated enclosure for burning, firing, or drying —**kiln** vb

ki·lo \'kēlō\ n, pl -los 1 : kilogram 2 : kilometer

kilo·cy·cle \'kilə,sīkəl\ n : kilohertz

ki·lo·gram \'kēlə,gram, 'kilə-\ n : 1000 grams

ki·lo·hertz \'kilə,hərts, 'kēlə-, -,herts\ n : 1000 hertz

ki·lo·me·ter \kil'ämətər, 'kilə,mēt-\ n : 1000 meters

ki·lo·volt \'kilə,vōlt\ n : 1000 volts

kilo·watt \'kilə,wät\ n : 1000 watts

kilt \'kilt\ n : knee-length pleated skirt

kil·ter \'kiltər\ n : proper condition

ki·mo·no \kə'mōnə\ n, pl -nos : loose robe

kin \'kin\ n 1 : one's relatives 2 : kinsman

kind \'kīnd\ n 1 : essential quality 2 : group with common traits 3 : variety ~ adj 1 : of a sympathetic nature 2 : arising from sympathy —**kind·heart·ed** adj —**kind·ness** n

kin·der·gar·ten \'kindər,gärtᵊn\ n : class for young children —**kin·der·gart·ner** \-,gärtnər\ n

kin·dle \'kindᵊl\ vb -dled; -dling 1 : set on fire or start burning 2 : stir up

kin·dling \'kin(d)liŋ, 'kinlən\ n : material for starting a fire

kind·ly \'kīndlē\ adj -lier; -est : of a sympathetic nature ~ adv 1 : sympathetically 2 : courteously —**kind·li·ness** n

kin·dred \'kindrəd\ n 1 : related individuals 2 : kin ~ adj : of a like nature

kin·folk \'kin,fōk\, **kinfolks** \n pl : kin

king \'kiŋ\ n : male sovereign —**king·dom** \-dəm\ n —**king·less** adj —**king·ly** adj —**king·ship** n

king·fish·er \-ˌfishər\ n : bright-colored crested bird

kink \ˈkiŋk\ n 1 : short tight twist or curl 2 : cramp —**kinky** adj

kin·ship n : relationship

kins·man \ˈkinzmən\ n : male relative

kins·wom·an \-ˌwümən\ n : female relative

kip·per \ˈkipər\ n : dried or smoked fish —**kipper** vb

kiss \ˈkis\ vb : touch with the lips as a mark of affection —**kiss** n

kit \ˈkit\ n : set of articles (as tools or parts)

kitch·en \ˈkichən\ n : room with cooking facilities

kite \ˈkīt\ n 1 : small hawk 2 : covered framework flown at the end of a string

kith \ˈkith\ n : familiar friends

kit·ten \ˈkitᵊn\ n : young cat —**kit·ten·ish** adj

¹**kit·ty** \ˈkitē\ n, pl -ties : kitten

²**kitty** n, pl -ties : fund or pool (as in a card game)

kit·ty-cor·ner, kit·ty-cor·nered var of CATERCORNER

ki·wi \ˈkēˌwē\ n : flightless New Zealand bird

klep·to·ma·nia \ˌkleptəˈmānēə\ n : neurotic impulse to steal —**klep·to·ma·ni·ac** \-nēˌak\ n

knack \ˈnak\ n 1 : clever way of doing something 2 : natural aptitude

knap·sack \ˈnapˌsak\ n : case for carrying supplies

knave \ˈnāv\ n : rogue —**knav·ery** \ˈnāv(ə)rē\ n —**knav·ish** \ˈnāvish\ adj

knead \ˈnēd\ vb 1 : work and press with the hands 2 : massage —**knead·er** n

knee \ˈnē\ n : joint in the middle part of the leg —**kneed** \ˈnēd\ adj

knee·cap \ˈnēˌkap\ n : bone forming the front of the knee

kneel \ˈnēl\ vb **knelt** \ˈnelt\ or **kneeled; kneel·ing** : fall or rest on the knees

knell \ˈnel\ n : stroke of a bell

knew past of KNOW

knick·ers \ˈnikərz\ n pl : pants gathered at the knee

knick·knack \ˈnikˌnak\ n : small decorative object

knife \ˈnīf\ n, pl **knives** \ˈnīvz\ : sharp blade with a handle ~ vb **knifed; knif·ing** : stab or cut with a knife

knight \ˈnīt\ n 1 : mounted warrior of feudal times 2 : man honored by a sovereign ~ vb : make a knight of —**knight·hood** n —**knight·ly** adv

knit \ˈnit\ vb **knit** or **knit·ted; knit·ting** 1 : link firmly or closely 2 : form a fabric by interlacing yarn or thread ~ n : knitted garment —**knit·ter** n

knob \ˈnäb\ n : rounded protuberance or handle —**knobbed** \ˈnäbd\ adj —**knob·by** \ˈnäbē\ adj

knock \ˈnäk\ vb 1 : strike with a sharp blow 2 : collide 3 : find fault with ~ n : sharp blow —**knock out** vb : make unconscious

knock·er n : device hinged to a door to knock with

knoll \ˈnōl\ n : small round hill

knot \ˈnät\ n 1 : interlacing (as of string) that forms a lump 2 : base of a woody branch in the stem 3 : group 4 : one nautical mile per hour ~ vb -tt- : tie in or with a knot —**knot·ty** adj

know \ˈnō\ vb **knew** \ˈn(y)ü\; **known** \ˈnōn\; **know·ing** 1 : perceive directly or understand 2 : be familiar with —**know·able** adj —**know·er** n

know·ing \ˈnōiŋ\ adj : shrewdly and keenly alert —**know·ing·ly** adv

knowl·edge \ˈnälij\ n 1 : understanding gained by experience 2 : range of information —**knowl·edge·able** adj

knuck·le \ˈnəkəl\ n : rounded knob at a finger joint —**knuck·le·bone** n

ko·ala \kōˈälə, kəˈwäl-\ n : furry Australian animal

kohl·ra·bi \kōlˈrabē, -ˈräb-\ n, pl -bies : cabbage that forms no head

Ko·ran \kəˈran, -ˈrän\ n : book of writings accepted by Muslims as revelations made to Muhammad by Allah

ko·sher \ˈkōshər\ adj : ritually fit for use according to Jewish law

kow·tow \kaüˈtaü, ˈkaüˌtaü\ vb : show excessive deference

kryp·ton \ˈkripˌtän\ n : gaseous chemical element

ku·dos \ˈk(y)üˌdäs, -ˌdōz\ n : fame and renown

kum·quat \ˈkəmˌkwät\ n : small citrus fruit

L

l \'el\ *n, pl* **l's** *or* **ls** \'elz\ : 12th letter of the alphabet

lab \'lab\ *n* : laboratory

la·bel \'lābǝl\ *n* 1 : identification slip 2 : identifying word or phrase ~ *vb* **-beled** *or* **-belled; -bel·ing** *or* **-bel·ling** : put a label on

la·bi·al \'lābēǝl\ *adj* : of or relating to the lips

la·bor \'lābǝr\ *n* 1 : physical or mental effort 2 : physical activities of childbirth 3 : task 4 : people who work for wages ~ *vb* : work esp. with great effort —**la·bor·er** *n*

lab·o·ra·to·ry \'lab(ǝ)rǝ,tōrē\ *n, pl* **-ries** : place for experimental testing and analysis

Labor Day *n* : 1st Monday in September observed as a legal holiday in recognition of the workingman

la·bo·ri·ous \lǝ'bōrēǝs\ *adj* : requiring great effort —**la·bo·ri·ous·ly** *adv*

lab·y·rinth \'labǝ,rinth\ *n* : maze —**lab·y·rin·thine** \,labǝ'rinthǝn\ *adj*

lace \'lās\ *n* 1 : cord or string for tying 2 : fine net usu. figured fabric ~ *vb* **laced; lac·ing** 1 : tie 2 : adorn with lace —**lacy** \'lāsē\ *adj*

lac·er·ate \'lasǝ,rāt\ *vb* **-at·ed; -at·ing** : tear roughly —**lac·er·a·tion** \,lasǝ'rāshǝn\ *n*

lach·ry·mose \'lakrǝ,mōs\ *adj* : tearful

lack \'lak\ *vb* : be missing or deficient in ~ *n* : deficiency

lack·a·dai·si·cal \,lakǝ'dāzikǝl\ *adj* : lacking spirit —**lack·a·dai·si·cal·ly** \-k(ǝ)lē\ *adv*

lack·ey \'lakē\ *n, pl* **-eys** 1 : liveried retainer 2 : toady

lack·lus·ter \'lak,lǝstǝr\ *adj* : dull

la·con·ic \lǝ'känik\ *adj* : sparing of words —**la·con·i·cal·ly** \-ik(ǝ)lē\ *adv*

lac·quer \'lakǝr\ *n* : glossy surface coating —**lacquer** *vb*

la·crosse \lǝ'krós\ *n* : ball game played with long-handled rackets

lac·tate \'lak,tāt\ *vb* **-tat·ed; -tat·ing** : secrete milk —**lac·ta·tion** \lak-'tāshǝn\ *n*

lac·tic \'laktik\ *adj* : relating to milk

la·cu·na \lǝ'k(y)ünǝ\ *n, pl* **-nae** \-(,)nē\ *or* **-nas** : blank space or missing part

lad \'lad\ *n* : boy

lad·der \'ladǝr\ *n* : device with steps or rungs for climbing

lad·en \'lādǝn\ *adj* : loaded

la·dle \'lādⁿl\ *n* : spoon with a deep bowl —**ladle** *vb*

la·dy \'lādē\ *n, pl* **-dies** 1 : woman of rank or authority 2 : woman

la·dy·bird \'lādē,bǝrd\ *n* : ladybug

la·dy·bug \-,bǝg\ *n* : brightly colored beetle

lag \'lag\ *vb* **-gg-** : fail to keep up ~ *n* 1 : a falling behind 2 : interval

la·ger \'lägǝr\ *n* : beer

lag·gard \'lagǝrd\ *adj* : slow ~ *n* : one that lags —**lag·gard·ly** *adv or adj* —**lag·gard·ness** *n*

la·gniappe \'lan,yap\ *n* : bonus

la·goon \lǝ'gün\ *n* : shallow sound, channel, or pond near or connecting with a larger body of water

laid *past of* LAY

lain *past part of* LIE

lair \'laǝr\ *n* : den

lais·sez–faire \,les,ā'faǝr\ *n* : doctrine opposing government interference in business

la·ity \'lāǝtē\ *n* : people who are not clergy

lake \'lāk\ *n* : inland body of water

la·ma \'lämǝ\ *n* : Buddhist monk

lamb \'lam\ *n* : young sheep or its flesh used as food

lam·baste, lam·bast \lam'bāst, -'bast\ *vb* 1 : beat 2 : censure

lam·bent \'lambǝnt\ *adj* : light or bright —**lam·ben·cy** \-bǝnsē\ *n* —**lam·bent·ly** *adv*

lame \'lām\ *adj* **lam·er; lam·est** : having a limb disabled 2 : weak ~ *vb* **lamed; lam·ing** : make lame —**lame·ly** *adv* —**lame·ness** *n*

lamé \lä'mā, la-\ *n* : cloth with tinsel threads

lame·brain \'lām,brān\ *n* : fool

la·ment \lǝ'ment\ *vb* 1 : mourn 2 : express sorrow for ~ *n* : mourning —**lam·en·ta·ble** \'lamǝntǝbǝl,lǝ-'mentǝ-\ *adj* —**lam·en·ta·bly** \-blē\ *adv* —**lam·en·ta·tion** \,lamǝn-'tāshǝn\ *n*

lam·i·nat·ed \'lamǝ,nātǝd\ *adj* : made of thin layers of material —**lam·i·nate** \-,nāt\ *vb* —**lam·i·nate** \-nǝt\ *n or adj* —**lam·i·na·tion** \,lamǝ-'nāshǝn\ *n*

lamp \'lamp\ *n* : device for producing light or heat

lam·poon \lam'pün\ *n* : satire —**lampoon** *vb*

lam·prey \'lamprē\ *n, pl* **-preys** : sucking eellike water animal

lance \'lans\ *n* : spear ~ *vb* **lanced;**

lanc·ing \ : pierce or open with a lancet

lance corporal n : enlisted man in the marine corps ranking above a private first class and below a corporal

lan·cet \'lansət\ n : pointed surgical instrument

land \'land\ n 1 : solid part of the surface of the earth 2 : country ~ vb 1 : go ashore 2 : catch or gain 3 : touch the ground or a surface —**land·less** adj

land·fill n : dump

land·hold·er n : owner of land —**land·hold·ing** adj or n

land·ing \'landiŋ\ n 1 : action of one that lands 2 : place for loading passengers and cargo 3 : level part of a staircase

land·locked adj : enclosed by land

land·lord n : owner of property —**land·la·dy** n

land·lub·ber \-,ləbər\ n : one with little sea experience

land·mark \'lan(d),märk\ n 1 : object that marks a boundary or serves as a guide 2 : event that marks a turning point

land·scape \-,skāp\ n : view of natural scenery ~ vb -scaped; -scap·ing : beautify a piece of land (as by decorative planting)

land·slide n 1 : slipping down of a mass of earth 2 : overwhelming victory

land·ward \'landwərd\ adj : toward the land —**landward** adv

lane \'lān\ n : narrow way

lan·guage \'laŋgwij\ n : words and the methods of combining them for communication

lan·guid \'laŋgwəd\ adj 1 : weak 2 : sluggish —**lan·guid·ly** adv —**lan·guid·ness** n

lan·guish \'laŋgwish\ vb : become languid or discouraged

lan·guor \'laŋ(g)ər\ n : listless indolence —**lan·guor·ous** adj —**lan·guor·ous·ly** adv

lank \'laŋk\ adj 1 : thin 2 : limp

lanky \'laŋkē\ adj lank·i·er; -est : tall and thin

lan·o·lin \'lan³lən\ n : fatty wax used in ointments

lan·tern \'lantərn\ n : enclosed portable light

¹lap \'lap\ n 1 : front part of the lower trunk and thighs of a seated person 2 : overlapping part 3 : one complete circuit ~ vb -pp- 1 : fold over or around

²lap vb -pp- 1 : scoop up with the tongue 2 : splash gently

lap·dog n : small dog

la·pel \lə'pel\ n : fold of the front of a coat

lap·i·dary \'lapə,derē\ n : one who cuts and polishes gems ~ adj : relating to gems

lapse \'laps\ n 1 : slight error 2 : termination of a right or privilege 3 : interval ~ vb **lapsed; laps·ing** 1 : slip 2 : subside 3 : cease

lar·board \'lärbərd\ n : port side

lar·ce·ny \'lärsnē, -²nē\ n, pl -nies : theft —**lar·ce·nous** \'lärsnəs, -²nəs\ adj

larch \'lärch\ n : conical evergreen

lard \'lärd\ n : pork fat

lar·der \'lärdər\ n : pantry

large \'lärj\ adj larg·er; larg·est : greater than average —**large·ly** adv —**large·ness** n

lar·gess, lar·gesse \lär'zhes, -'jes; 'lär-,jes\ n : liberal giving

lar·i·at \'lareət\ n : lasso

¹lark \'lärk\ n : small songbird

²lark vb or n : romp

lar·va \'lärvə\ n, pl -vae \-(,)vē\ : wormlike form of an insect —**lar·val** \-vəl\ adj

lar·yn·gi·tis \,lərən'jītəs\ n : inflammation of the larynx

lar·ynx \'lariŋks\ n, pl -ryn·ges \lə'rin,jēz\ or -ynx·es : upper part of the trachea —**la·ryn·ge·al** \,larən-'jēəl, lə'rinjēəl\ adj

las·civ·i·ous \lə'sivēəs\ adj : lewd —**las·civ·i·ous·ness** n

la·ser \'lāzər\ n : device that produces an intense light beam

¹lash \'lash\ vb : whip ~ n 1 : stroke esp. of a whip 2 : eyelash

²lash vb : bind with a rope or cord

lass \'las\ n : girl

lass·ie \'lasē\ n : girl

las·si·tude \'lasə,t(y)üd\ n 1 : fatigue 2 : listlessness

las·so \'lasō, la'sü\ n, pl -sos or -soes : rope with a noose for catching livestock —**lasso** vb

¹last \'last\ vb : continue in existence or operation

²last adj 1 : following all the rest 2 : previous ~ adv 1 : at the end 2 : most recently 3 : in conclusion ~ n : something that is last —**last·ly** adv —**at last** : finally

³last n : form on which a shoe is shaped

latch \'lach\ vb : catch or get hold ~ n : catch that holds a door closed

late \'lāt\ adj lat·er; lat·est 1 : coming or staying after the proper time 2 : advanced toward the end 3 : recently deceased 4 : recent —**late** adv

—late·com·er \-ˌkəmər\ n —late·ly \-lē\ adv —late·ness n

lat·er·al \ˈlat(ə)rəl\ adj : on or toward the side —lat·er·al·ly adv

la·tex \ˈlā,teks\ n, pl -ti·ces \ˈlātəˌsēz, ˈlat-\ or -tex·es : emulsion of synthetic rubber or plastic

lath \ˈlath, ˈlath\ n, pl laths or lath : building material (as a thin strip of wood) used as a base for plaster —lath·ing \-iŋ\ n

lathe \ˈlāth\ n : machine that rotates material for shaping

lath·er \ˈlathər\ n : foam ~ vb : form or spread lather

lat·i·tude \ˈlatəˌt(y)üd\ n 1 : distance north or south from the earth's equator 2 : freedom of action

la·trine \ləˈtrēn\ n : toilet

lat·ter \ˈlatər\ adj 1 : more recent 2 : being the second of 2 —lat·ter·ly adv

lat·tice \ˈlatəs\ n : framework of crossed strips

laud vb or n : praise —laud·able adj —laud·ably adv

laugh \ˈlaf, ˈläf\ vb : show mirth, joy, or scorn with a smile and explosive sound —laugh n —laugh·able adj —laugh·ing·ly \-iŋlē\ adv

laugh·ing·stock \ˈlafiŋˌstäk, ˈläf-\ n : object of ridicule

laugh·ter \ˈlaftər, ˈläf-\ n : action or sound of laughing

¹launch \ˈlȯnch\ vb 1 : hurl or send off 2 : set afloat 3 : start —launch n —launch·er n

²launch n : small open boat

laun·der \ˈlȯndər\ vb : wash or iron fabrics —laun·der·er n —laun·dress \-drəs\ n —laun·dry \-drē\ n

lau·re·ate \ˈlȯrēət\ n : recipient of honors —lau·re·ate·ship n

lau·rel \ˈlȯrəl\ n 1 : small evergreen tree 2 : honor

la·va \ˈlävə, ˈlav-\ n : volcanic molten rock

lav·a·to·ry \ˈlavəˌtōrē\ n, pl -ries : bathroom

lav·en·der \ˈlavəndər\ n 1 : aromatic plant used for perfume 2 : pale purple

lav·ish \ˈlavish\ adj : expending or expended profusely ~ vb : expend or give freely —lav·ish·ly adv

law \ˈlȯ\ n 1 : established rule of conduct 2 : body of such rules 3 : principle of construction or procedure 4 : rule stating uniform behavior under uniform conditions 5 : lawyer's

profession —law·break·er n —law·giv·er n —law·less adj —law·less·ly adv —law·less·ness n —law·mak·er n —law·man \-mən\ n —law·suit n

law·ful \ˈlȯfəl\ adj : permitted by law —law·ful·ly adv

lawn \ˈlȯn\ n : grass-covered yard

law·yer \ˈlȯyər\ n : legal practitioner

lax \ˈlaks\ adj : not strict or tense —lax·i·ty \ˈlaksətē\ n —lax·ly adv

lax·a·tive \ˈlaksətiv\ n : drug relieving constipation

¹lay \ˈlā\ vb laid \ˈlād\ lay·ing 1 : put on a surface 2 : produce eggs 3 : bet 4 : impose as a duty or burden 5 : place (as stress) on something 6 : put forward ~ n : way something lies or is laid

²lay past of LIE

³lay n : song

⁴lay adj : of the laity —lay·man \-mən\ n —lay·wom·an \-ˌwümən\ n

lay·er \ˈlāər\ n 1 : one that lays 2 : one thickness over or under another

lay·off \ˈlā,of\ n : temporary dismissal of a worker

lay·out \ˈlā,aut\ n 1 : arrangement 2 : outfit

la·zy \ˈlāzē\ adj -zi·er; -est : disliking activity or exertion —la·zi·ly \ˈlāzəlē\ adv —la·zi·ness n

lea \ˈlē, ˈlā\ n : meadow

leach \ˈlēch\ vb : remove (a soluble part) with a solvent

¹lead \ˈlēd\ vb led \ˈled\ lead·ing 1 : direct or run on a course 2 : direct the activity of 3 : go at the head of 4 : bring or tend to a definite result ~ n : position in front —lead·er n —lead·er·less adj —lead·er·ship n

²lead \ˈled\ n 1 : heavy bluish white chemical element 2 : marking substance in a pencil —lead·en \ˈledᵊn\ adj

leaf \ˈlēf\ n, pl leaves \ˈlēvz\ 1 : green outgrowth of a plant stem 2 : leaflike thing ~ vb 1 : produce leaves 2 : turn book pages —leaf·age \ˈlēfij\ n —leafed \ˈlēft\ adj —leaf·less adj —leafy adj —leaved \ˈlēfd\ adj

leaf·let \ˈlēflət\ n : pamphlet

¹league \ˈlēg\ n : unit of distance equal to about 3 miles

²league n : association for a common purpose —league vb —leagu·er n

leak \ˈlēk\ vb 1 : enter or escape through a leak 2 : become or make known ~ n : opening that accidentally admits or lets out a substance —leak·age \ˈlēkij\ n —leaky adj

¹lean \ˈlēn\ vb 1 : bend from a vertical

position **2** : rely on for support **3** : incline in opinion —**lean** n

²lean adj **1** : lacking in flesh **2** : lacking richness —**lean·ness** \'lēnnəs\ n

leap \'lēp\ vb **leapt** or **leaped** \'lēpt, 'lept\; **leap·ing** : jump —**leap** n

leap year n : 366-day year

learn \'lərn\ vb **1** : gain understanding or skill by study or experience **2** : memorize **3** : find out —**learn·er** n

learn·ed \-əd\ adj : having great learning

learn·ing \-iŋ\ n : knowledge gained by study

lease \'lēs\ n : contract transferring real estate for a term and usu. for rent ~ vb **leased; leas·ing** : grant by or hold under a lease

leash \'lēsh\ n : line to hold an animal —**leash** vb

least \'lēst\ adj **1** : lowest in importance or position **2** : smallest **3** : scantiest ~ n : one that is least ~ adv : in the smallest or lowest degree

leath·er \'letḥər\ n : dressed animal skin —**leath·ern** \-ərn\ adj —**leath·ery** adj

¹leave \'lēv\ vb **left** \'left\; **leav·ing** **1** : bequeath **2** : allow or cause to remain **3** : have as a remainder **4** : go away ~ n **1** : permission **2** : authorized absence **3** : departure

²leave vb **leaved; leav·ing** : leaf

leav·en \'levən\ n : substance for producing fermentation ~ vb : raise dough with a leaven

leaves pl of LEAF

lech·ery \'lechərē\ n : inordinate indulgence in sex —**lech·er** \'lechər\ n —**lech·er·ous** adj —**lech·er·ous·ness** n

lec·ture \'lekchər\ n : instructive talk —**lecture** vb —**lec·tur·er** n —**lec·ture·ship** n

led past of LEAD

ledge \'lej\ n : shelflike projection

led·ger \'lejər\ n : account book

lee \'lē\ n : side sheltered from the wind —**lee** adj

leech \'lēch\ n : segmented freshwater worm

leek \'lēk\ n : onionlike herb

leer \'liər\ n : suggestive look —**leer** vb

leery \'li(ə)rē\ adj : suspicious or wary

lees \'lēz\ n pl : dregs

lee·ward \'lēwərd, 'lüərd\ adj : situated away from the wind ~ n : the lee side

lee·way \'lē,wā\ n : allowable margin

¹left \'left\ adj : on the same side of the body as the heart ~ n : left hand —**left** adv

²left past of LEAVE

leg \'leg\ n **1** : limb of an animal that supports the body or something like it **2** : clothing to cover the leg ~ vb -**gg**- : walk or run —**legged** \'legəd\ adj —**leg·less** adj

leg·a·cy \'legəsē\ n, pl -**cies** : inheritance

legal \'lēgəl\ adj **1** : relating to law or lawyers **2** : lawful —**le·gal·is·tic** \,lēgə'listik\ adj —**le·gal·i·ty** \li'galətē\ n —**le·gal·ize** \'lēgə,līz\ vb —**le·gal·ly** \-gəlē\ adv

leg·ate \'legət\ n : official representative

le·ga·tion \li'gāshən\ n **1** : diplomatic mission **2** : official residence and office of a diplomat

leg·end \'lejənd\ n **1** : story handed down from the past **2** : inscription **3** : explanation of map symbols —**leg·end·ary** \-ən,derē\ adj

leg·er·de·main \,lejərdə'mān\ n : sleight of hand

leg·ging, leg·gin \'legən, -in\ n : leg covering

leg·i·ble \'lejəbəl\ adj : capable of being read —**leg·i·bil·i·ty** \,lejə'bilətē\ n —**leg·i·bly** \'lejəblē\ adv

le·gion \'lējən\ n **1** : large military force **2** : multitude **3** : association of former servicemen —**le·gion·ary** \-,erē\ n —**le·gion·naire** \,lējən'aər\ n

leg·is·late \'lejəs,lāt\ vb -**lat·ed; -lat·ing** : enact or bring about with laws —**leg·is·la·tion** \,lejə'slāshən\ n —**leg·is·la·tive** \'lejəs,lātiv\ adj —**leg·is·la·tor** \-ər\ n

leg·is·la·ture \'lejə,slāchər\ n : organization with authority to make laws

le·git·i·mate \li'jitəmət\ adj **1** : lawfully begotten **2** : genuine **3** : conforming with law or accepted standards —**le·git·i·ma·cy** \-məsē\ n —**le·git·i·mate·ly** adv

le·gume \'leg,yüm, li'gyüm\ n : plant bearing pods —**le·gu·mi·nous** \li'gyümənəs\ adj

lei \'lā,(ē)\ n : necklace of flowers

lei·sure \'lēzhər, 'lezh-, 'lāzh-\ n **1** : free time **2** : comfort **3** : convenience —**lei·sure·ly** adv

lem·ming \'lemiŋ\ n : short-tailed rodent

lem·on \'lemən\ n : yellow citrus fruit —**lem·ony** adj

lem·on·ade \,lemə'nād\ n : sweetened lemon beverage

lend \'lend\ vb **lent** \'lent\; **lend·ing** **1**

: give for temporary use **2** : furnish
—**lend·er** *n*

length \'length\ *n* **1** : longest dimension **2** : duration in time **3** : piece to be joined to others —**length·en** \'lengthən\ *vb* —**length·wise** *adv or adj* —**lengthy** *adj*

le·nient \'lēnēənt, -nyənt\ *adj* : of mild and tolerant disposition or effect — **le·ni·en·cy** \-nēənsē, -nyəns,\ *n* —**le·ni·ent·ly** *adv*

len·i·ty \'lenətē\ *n* : leniency

lens \'lenz\ *n* **1** : curved piece for forming an image in an optical instrument **2** : transparent body in the eye that focuses light rays

Lent \'lent\ *n* : 40-day period of penitence and fasting from Ash Wednesday to Easter —**Lent·en** \-ᵊn\ *adj*

len·til \'lent-ᵊl\ *n* : Old World legume

le·o·nine \'lēə,nīn\ *adj* : like a lion

leop·ard \'lepərd\ *n* : large tawny black-spotted cat

le·o·tard \'lēə,tärd\ *n* : close-fitting garment

lep·er \'lepər\ *n* : person with leprosy

lep·re·chaun \'leprə,kän\ *n* : mischievous Irish elf

lep·ro·sy \'leprəsē\ *n* : chronic bacterial disease —**lep·rous** \-rəs\ *adj*

les·bi·an \'lezbēən\ *n* : female homosexual —**lesbian** *adj* —**les·bi·an·ism** \-,izəm\ *n*

le·sion \'lēzhən\ *n* : abnormal area in the body due to injury or disease

less \'les\ *adj* **1** : fewer **2** : of lower rank, degree, or importance **3** : smaller ~ *adv* : to a lesser degree ~ *n, pl* **less** : smaller portion ~ *prep* : minus —**less·en** \-ᵊn\ *vb*

-less \ləs\ *adj suffix* **1** : not having **2** : unable to act or be acted on

les·see \le'sē\ *n* : tenant under a lease

less·er \'lesər\ *adj* **1** : smaller **2** : inferior

les·son \'lesᵊn\ *n* **1** : reading or exercise to be studied by a pupil **2** : something learned

les·sor \'les,or, le'sòr\ *n* : one who transfers property by a lease

lest \,lest\ *conj* : for fear that

¹let \'let\ *n* : hindrance or obstacle

²let *vb* **let; let·ting 1** : cause to **2** : rent **3** : permit

-let \lət\ *n suffix* : small one

le·thal \'lēthəl\ *adj* : deadly —**le·thal·ly** *adv*

leth·ar·gy \'lethərjē\ *n* : state of being lazy or indifferent —**le·thar·gic** \li'thärjik\ *adj*

let·ter \'letər\ *n* **1** : unit of an alphabet

2 : written or printed communication **3** *pl* : literature or learning **4** : literal meaning ~ *vb* : mark with letters —**let·ter·er** *n*

let·tuce \'letəs\ *n* : garden plant with crisp leaves

leu·ke·mia \lü'kēmēə\ *n* : cancerous blood disease —**leu·ke·mic** \-mik\ *adj or n*

lev·ee \'levē\ *n* : embankment to prevent flooding

lev·el \'levəl\ *n* **1** : device for establishing a flat surface **2** : horizontal surface **3** : position in a scale ~ *vb* **-eled** *or* **-elled; -el·ing** *or* **-el·ling 1** : make flat or level **2** : aim **3** : raze ~ *adj* **1** : having a smooth surface **2** : of the same height or rank —**lev·el·er** *n* —**lev·el·ly** *adv* —**lev·el·ness** *n*

le·ver \'levər, 'lē-\ *n* : bar for prying or dislodging something —**le·ver·age** \'lev(ə)rij, 'lēv-\ *n*

le·vi·a·than \li'vīəthən\ *n* **1** : large sea animal **2** : enormous thing

lev·i·ty \'levətē\ *n* : unseemly frivolity

levy \'levē\ *n, pl* **lev·ies** : imposition or collection of a tax ~ *vb* **lev·ied; levy·ing 1** : impose or collect legally **2** : enlist for military service **3** : wage

lewd \'lüd\ *adj* **1** : sexually unchaste **2** : salacious —**lewd·ly** *adv* —**lewd·ness** *n*

lex·i·cog·ra·phy \,leksə'kägrəfē\ *n* : dictionary making —**lex·i·cog·ra·pher** \-fər\ *n* —**lex·i·co·graph·i·cal** \-kō'grafikəl\ *or* **lex·i·co·graph·ic** \-ik\ *adj*

lex·i·con \'leksə,kän\ *n, pl* **-i·ca** \-sikə\ *or* **-icons** : dictionary

li·a·ble \'līəbəl\ *adj* **1** : legally obligated **2** : probable **3** : susceptible —**li·a·bil·i·ty** \,līə'bilətē\ *n*

li·ai·son \'lēə,zän, lē'ā-\ *n* **1** : close bond **2** : communication between groups

li·ar \'līər\ *n* : one who lies

li·bel \'lībəl\ *n* : action, crime, or an instance of injuring a person's reputation esp. by something written ~ *vb* **-beled** *or* **-belled; -bel·ing** *or* **-bel·ling** : make or publish a libel —**li·bel·er** *n* —**li·bel·ist** *n* —**li·bel·ous, li·bel·lous** \-bələs\ *adj*

lib·er·al \'lib(ə)rəl\ *adj* : not stingy, narrow, or conservative —**liberal** *n* —**lib·er·al·ism** \-,izəm\ *n* —**lib·er·al·i·ty** \,libə'ralətē\ *n* —**lib·er·al·ize** \'lib(ə)rə,līz\ *vb* —**lib·er·al·ly** \-rəlē\ *adv*

lib·er·ate \'libə,rāt\ *vb* **-at·ed; -at·ing** : set free —**lib·er·a·tion** \,libə'rā·shən\ *n* —**lib·er·a·tor** \'libə,rātər\ *n*

lib·er·tine \'libər,tēn\ n : one who leads a dissolute life

lib·er·ty \'libərtē\ n, pl **-ties 1** : quality or state of being free **2** : action going beyond normal limits

li·bi·do \lə'bēdō, -'bid-\ n, pl **-dos** : sexual drive —**li·bid·i·nal** \lə'bid-ᵊnal\ adj —**li·bid·i·nous** \-əs\ adj

li·brary \'lī,brerē\ n, pl **-brar·ies 1** : place where books are kept for use **2** : collection of books —**li·brar·i·an** \lī'brerēən\ n

li·bret·to \lə'bretō\ n, pl **-tos** or **-ti** \-ē\ : text of an opera —**li·bret·tist** \-əst\ n

lice pl of LOUSE

li·cense, li·cence \'līsᵊns\ n **1** : legal permission to engage in some activity **2** : document or tag evidencing a license granted **3** : irresponsible use of freedom —**license** vb —**li·cens·ee** \,līsᵊn'sē\ n

li·cen·tious \lī'senchəs\ adj : disregarding sexual restraints —**li·cen·tious·ly** adv —**li·cen·tious·ness** n

li·chen \'līkən\ n : complex lower plant made up of an alga and a fungus —**li·chen·ous** adj

lic·it \'lisət\ adj : lawful

lick \'lik\ vb **1** : draw the tongue over **2** : beat ~ n **1** : stroke of the tongue **2** : small amount

lic·o·rice \'lik(ə)rish, -rəs\ n : dried root of a European leguminous plant or candy flavored with an extract from it

lid \'lid\ n **1** : movable cover **2** : eyelid

¹**lie** \'lī\ vb **lay** \'lā\; **lain** \'lān\; **ly·ing** \'līiŋ\ **1** : be in, rest in, or assume a horizontal position **2** : occupy a certain relative position ~ n : position in which something lies

²**lie** vb **lied; ly·ing** \'līiŋ\ : tell a lie ~ n : untrue statement

liege \'lēj\ n : feudal superior or vassal

lien \'lēn, 'lēən\ n : legal claim on the property of another

lieu·ten·ant \lü'tenənt\ n **1** : representative **2** : first lieutenant or second lieutenant **3** : commissioned officer in the navy ranking next below a lieutenant commander —**lieu·ten·an·cy** \-ənsē\ n

lieutenant colonel n : commissioned officer (as in the army) ranking next below a colonel

lieutenant commander n : commissioned officer in the navy ranking next below a commander

lieutenant general n : commissioned officer (as in the army) ranking next below a general

lieutenant junior grade n, pl **lieutenants junior grade** : commissioned officer in the navy ranking next below a lieutenant

life \'līf\ n, pl **lives** \'līvz\ **1** : quality that distinguishes a vital and functional being from a dead body or inanimate matter **2** : physical and mental experiences of an individual **3** : biography **4** : period of existence **5** : way of living **6** : liveliness —**life·less** adj —**life·like** adj

life·blood n : basic source of strength and vitality

life·boat n : boat for use in saving lives at sea

life·guard n : one employed to safeguard bathers

life·long adj : continuing through life

life·sav·ing n : art or practice of saving lives —**life·sav·er** \-,sāvər\ n

life·time n : duration of an individual's existence

lift \'lift\ vb **1** : move upward or cause to move upward **2** : put an end to —**lift** n

lift–off \'lif,tȯf\ n : vertical takeoff by a rocket

lig·a·ment \'ligəmənt\ n : band of tough tissue that holds bones together

lig·a·ture \'ligə,chu̇r, -chər\ n : something that binds or ties

¹**light** \'līt\ n **1** : radiation that makes vision possible **2** : daylight **3** : source of light **4** : public knowledge **5** : aspect **6** : celebrity **7** : flame for lighting — adj **1** : bright **2** : weak in color ~ vb **light·ed** or **lit; light·ing 1** : make or become light **2** : cause to burn —**light·er** n —**light·ness** n —**light·proof** adj

²**light** adj : not heavy, serious, or abundant —**light** adv —**light·ly** adv —**light·ness** n —**light·weight** adj

³**light** adj **light·ed** or **lit** \'lit\; **light·ing** : settle or dismount

¹**light·en** \'lītᵊn\ vb **1** : make light or bright **2** : give out flashes of lightning

²**lighten** vb **1** : relieve of a burden **2** : become lighter

light·heart·ed \-'härtəd\ adj : GAY —**light·heart·ed·ly** adv —**light·heart·ed·ness** n

light·house n : structure with a powerful light for guiding sailors

light·ning \'lītniŋ\ n : flashing discharge of atmospheric electricity

light–year \'līt,yiər\ n : distance traveled by light in one year equal to about 5.878 trillion miles

lig·nite \'lig,nīt\ n : brownish black soft coal

¹like \'līk\ vb **liked; lik·ing 1** : enjoy **2** : desire ~ n : preference —**lik·able, like·able** \'līkəbəl\ adj

²like adj : similar ~ prep **1** : similar or similarly to **2** : typical of **3** : such as ~ n : counterpart ~ conj : as or as if —**like·ness** n —**like·wise** adv

-like \,līk\ adj comb form : resembling, suggesting, or characteristic of

like·li·hood \'līklē,hu̇d\ n : probability

like·ly \'līklē\ adj **-li·er; -est 1** : probable **2** : believable ~ adv : in all probability

lik·en \'līkən\ vb : compare

lik·ing \'līkiŋ\ n : favorable regard

li·lac \'līlək, -,lak, -,läk\ n : shrub with clusters of fragrant pink, purple, or white flowers

lilt \'lilt\ n : rhythmical swing or flow

lily \'lilē\ n, pl **lil·ies** : tall bulbous herb with funnel-shaped flowers

lima bean \,līmə-\ n : bushy or tall bean grown for its flat edible seed or the seed

limb \'lim\ n **1** : projecting appendage used in moving or grasping **2** : tree branch —**limb·less** adj

lim·ber \'limbər\ adj : supple or agile ~ vb : make or become limber

lim·bo \'limbō\ n, pl **-bos** : place or state of confinement or oblivion

¹lime \'līm\ n : caustic white oxide of calcium

²lime n : small green lemonlike citrus fruit —**lime·ade** \-,ād\ n

lime·light n : center of public attention

lim·er·ick \'lim(ə)rik\ n : light poem of 5 lines

lime·stone n : rock that yields lime when burned

lim·it \'limət\ n **1** : boundary **2** : something that restrains or confines ~ vb : set limits on —**lim·i·ta·tion** \,limə-'tāshən\ n —**lim·it·less** adj

lim·ou·sine \'limə,zēn, ,limə'-\ n : large luxurious sedan

limp \'limp\ vb : walk lamely ~ n : limping movement or gait ~ adj : lacking firmness and body —**limp·ly** adv —**limp·ness** n

lim·pid \'limpəd\ adj : clear or transparent

lin·den \'lindən\ n : tree with large heart-shaped leaves

¹line \'līn\ vb **lined; lin·ing** : cover the inner surface of —**lin·ing** n

²line n **1** : cord, rope, or wire **2** : row or something like a row **3** : note **4** : course of action or thought **5** : state of agreement **6** : occupation **7** : limit **8** : transportation system **9** : long narrow mark ~ vb **lined; lin·ing 1** : mark with a line **2** : place in a line **3** : form a line

lin·eage \'linēij\ n : descent from a common ancestor

lin·eal \'linēəl\ adj **1** : linear **2** : in a direct line of ancestry

lin·ea·ments \'linēəmənts\ n pl : features or contours esp. of a face

lin·ear \'linēər\ adj **1** : straight **2** : long and narrow

lin·en \'linən\ n **1** : cloth or thread made of flax **2** : household articles made of cloth

lin·er \'līnər\ n **1** : one that lines **2** : ship or airplane belonging to a line

line·up \'līn,əp\ n **1** : line of persons for inspection or identification **2** : list of players in a game

-ling \liŋ\ n suffix **1** : one connected with or having the quality of **2** : young, small, or inferior one

lin·ger \'liŋgər\ vb : be slow to leave or act

lin·ge·rie \,länjə'rā, ,laⁿzhə-, -'rē\ n : women's underwear

lin·go \'liŋgō\ n, pl **-goes** : usu. strange language

lin·guist \'liŋgwəst\ n **1** : person skilled in speech or languages **2** : student of language —**lin·guis·tic** \liŋ'gwistik\ adj —**lin·guis·tics** n pl

lin·i·ment \'linəmənt\ n : liquid medication rubbed on the skin

link \'liŋk\ n : connecting structure (as a ring of a chain) **2** : bond —**link** vb —**link·age** \-ij\ n —**link·er** n

li·no·leum \lə'nōlēəm\ n : floor covering with hard surface

lin·seed \'lin,sēd\ n : seeds of flax yielding an oil (**linseed oil**)

lint \'lint\ n : fine fluff or loose short fibers from fabric

lin·tel \'lintⁿl\ n : horizontal piece over a door or window

li·on \'līən\ n : large cat of Africa and Asia —**li·on·ess** \'līənəs\ n

li·on·ize \'līə,nīz\ vb **-ized; -iz·ing** : treat as very important —**li·on·iza·tion** \,līənə'zāshən\ n

lip \'lip\ n **1** : either of the 2 fleshy folds surrounding the mouth **2** : edge of something hollow —**lipped** \'lipt\ adj —**lip·read·ing** n

lip·stick \'lip,stik\ n : stick of cosmetic to color lips

liq·ue·fy \'likwə,fī\ vb **-fied; -fy·ing** : make or become liquid —**liq·ue·fac·tion** \,likwə'fakshən\ n —**liq·ue-**

fi·able \-'fīəbəl\ adj —**liq·ue·fi·er** \'likwə,fīər\ n

li·queur \li'kər\ n : sweet or aromatic alcoholic liquor

liq·uid \'likwəd\ adj 1 : flowing freely like water 2 : neither solid nor gaseous 3 : of or convertible to cash —**liquid** n —**li·quid·i·ty** \lik'widətē\ n

liq·ui·date \'likwə,dāt\ vb -**dat·ed; -dat·ing** 1 : pay off 2 : dispose of —**liq·ui·da·tion** \,likwə'dāshən\ n

li·quor \'likər\ n : liquid substance and esp. a distilled alcoholic beverage

lisp \'lisp\ vb : pronounce s and z imperfectly —**lisp** n

lis·some \'lisəm\ adj : supple or agile

¹list \'list\ n 1 : series of names or items ~ vb 1 : make a list of 2 : put on a list

²list vb : tilt or lean over ~ n : slant

lis·ten \'lis³n\ vb 1 : pay attention in order to hear 2 : heed —**lis·ten·er** \'lisnər, -³nər\ n

list·less \'listləs\ adj : having no desire to act —**list·less·ly** adv —**list·less·ness** n

lit \'lit\ past of LIGHT

lit·a·ny \'lit³nē\ n, pl -**nies** : prayer said as a series of responses to a leader

li·ter \'lētər\ n : unit of liquid measure equal to about 1.06 quarts

lit·er·al \'lit(ə)rəl\ adj : being exactly as stated —**lit·er·al·ly** adv

lit·er·ary \'litə,rerē\ adj : relating to literature

lit·er·ate \'lit(ə)rət\ adj : able to read and write —**lit·er·a·cy** \'lit(ə)rəsē\ n

lit·er·a·ture \'lit(ə)rə,chùr, -chər\ n : writings of enduring interest

lithe \'līth, 'līth\ adj 1 : supple 2 : graceful —**lithe·some** \-səm\ adj

lith·o·graph \'lithə,graf\ n : print from a drawing on stone —**li·thog·ra·pher** \lith'ägrəfər, 'lithə,grafər\ n —**lith·o·graph·ic** \,lithə'grafik\ adj —**li·thog·ra·phy** \lith'ägrəfē\ n

lit·i·gate \'litə,gāt\ vb -**gat·ed; -gat·ing** : carry on a lawsuit —**lit·i·gant** \'litigənt\ n —**lit·i·ga·tion** \,litə-'gāshən\ n —**li·ti·gious** \lə'tijəs, li-\ adj —**li·ti·gious·ness** n

lit·mus \'litməs\ n : coloring matter that turns red in acid solutions and blue in alkaline

lit·ter \'litər\ n 1 : animal offspring of one birth 2 : stretcher 3 : rubbish ~ vb 1 : give birth to young 2 : strew with litter

lit·tle \'lit³l\ adj **lit·tler** \'litlər, -³lər\ or **less** \'les\ or **less·er** \'lesər\; **lit·tlest** \'litləst, -³ləst\ or **least** \'lēst\ 1 : not big 2 : not much 3 : not im-

portant ~ adv **less** \'les\; **least** \'lēst\ 1 : slightly 2 : not often ~ n : small amount —**lit·tle·ness** n

lit·ur·gy \'litərjē\ n, pl -**gies** : rite of worship —**li·tur·gi·cal** \lə'tərjikəl\ adj —**li·tur·gi·cal·ly** \-k(ə)lē\ adv —**lit·ur·gist** \'litərjəst\ n

liv·able \'livəbəl\ adj : suitable for living in or with —**liv·a·bil·i·ty** \,livə'bilətē\ n

¹live \'liv\ vb **lived; liv·ing** 1 : be alive 2 : conduct one's life 3 : subsist 4 : reside

²live \'līv\ adj 1 : having life 2 : burning 3 : connected to electric power 4 : not exploded 5 : of continuing interest 6 : involving the actual presence of real people

live·li·hood \'līvlē,hùd\ n : means of subsistence

live·long \,liv'lòŋ\ adj : whole

live·ly \'līvlē\ adj -**li·er; -est** : full of life and vigor —**live·li·ness** n

liv·en \'līvən\ vb : enliven

liv·er \'livər\ n : organ that secretes bile —**liv·ered** \'livərd\ adj

liv·ery \'liv(ə)rē\ n, pl -**er·ies** 1 : uniform for household servants 2 : care of horses for pay —**liv·er·ied** \-rēd\ adj —**liv·ery·man** \-mən\ n

lives pl of LIFE

live·stock \'liv,stäk\ n : farm animals

liv·id \'livəd\ adj 1 : discolored by bruising 2 : pale 3 : enraged

liv·ing \'liviŋ\ adj : having life ~ n : livelihood

liz·ard \'lizərd\ n : scaly reptile

lla·ma \'lämə\ n : So. American mammal related to the camel

lo \'lō\ interj —used to call attention

load \'lōd\ n 1 : cargo 2 : supported weight 3 : burden ~ vb 1 : put a load on 2 : burden 3 : put ammunition in

¹loaf \'lōf\ n, pl **loaves** \'lōvz\ : mass of bread

²loaf vb : waste time —**loaf·er** n

loam \'lōm, 'lüm\ n : soil —**loamy** adj

loan \'lōn\ n 1 : money borrowed at interest 2 : something lent temporarily 3 : permission to use ~ vb : lend

loath \'lōth, 'lōth\ adj : very reluctant

loathe \'lōth\ vb **loathed; loath·ing** : hate

loath·ing \'lōthiŋ\ n : extreme disgust

loath·some \'lōthsəm, 'lōth-\ adj : repulsive

lob \'läb\ vb -**bb-** : throw or hit in a high arc —**lob** n

lob·by \'läbē\ n, pl -**bies** 1 : public waiting room at the entrance of a building 2 : persons lobbying ~ vb -**bied**:

-by·ing : try to influence legislators **—lob·by·ist** \-ist\ n

lobe \'lōb\ n : rounded part **—lo·bar** \'lōbər\ adj **—lobed** \'lōbd\ adj

lo·bot·o·my \lō'bätəmē\ n, pl **-mies** : severance of nerve fibers in the brain

lob·ster \'läbstər\ n : marine crustacean with 2 large pincerlike claws

lo·cal \'lōkəl\ adj : confined to or serving a limited area **—local** n **—lo·cal·ly** adv

lo·cale \lō'kal\ n : setting for an event

lo·cal·i·ty \lō'kalətē\ n, pl **-ties** : particular place

lo·cal·ize \'lōkə,līz\ vb **-ized; -iz·ing** : confine to a definite place **—lo·cal·iza·tion** \,lōkələ'zāshən\ n

lo·cate \'lō,kāt, lō'kāt\ vb **-cat·ed; -cat·ing 1** : settle **2** : find a site for **3** : discover the place of **—lo·ca·tion** \lō'kāshən\ n

¹lock \'läk\ n : tuft or strand of hair

²lock n **1** : fastener using a bolt **2** : enclosure in a canal to raise or lower boats **~** vb **1** : make fast with a lock **2** : confine **3** : interlock

lock·er \'läkər\ n : storage compartment

lock·et \'läkət\ n : small case worn on a necklace

lock·jaw n : tetanus

lock·out n : closing of a plant by an employer during a labor dispute

lock·smith \-,smith\ n : one who makes or repairs locks

lo·co·mo·tion \,lōkə'mōshən\ n : power of moving **—lo·co·mo·tive** \-'mōtiv\ adj

lo·co·mo·tive \-'mōtiv\ n : vehicle that moves railroad cars

lo·co·weed \'lōkō,wēd\ n : western plant poisonous to livestock

lo·cust \'lōkəst\ n **1** : migratory grasshopper **2** : cicada **3** : tree with hard wood

lo·cu·tion \lō'kyüshən\ n : way of saying something

lode \'lōd\ n : ore deposit

lode·stone n : magnetic rock

lodge \'läj\ vb **lodged; lodg·ing 1** : provide quarters for **2** : come to rest **3** : file **~** n **1** : special house (as for hunters) **2** : animal's den **3** : branch of a fraternal organization **—lodg·er** \'läjər\ n **—lodg·ing** n **—lodg·ment, lodge·ment** \-mənt\ n

loft \'loft\ n **1** : attic **2** : upper floor (as of a warehouse)

lofty \'loftē\ adj **loft·i·er; -est** : tall or high **—loft·i·ly** adv **—loft·i·ness** n

¹log \'log, 'läg\ n **1** : unshaped timber

2 : daily record of a ship's or plane's progress **~** vb **-gg- 1** : cut trees for lumber **2** : enter in a log

²log n : logarithm

log·a·rithm \'logə,rithəm, 'läg-\ n : exponent to which a base number is raised to produce a given number **—log·a·rith·mic** \,logə'rithmik, ,läg-\ adj

loge \'lōzh\ n : box in a theater

log·ger \-ər\ n : one engaged in logging

log·ger·head \'logər,hed, 'läg-\ n : large Atlantic sea turtle **—at log·gerheads** : in disagreement

log·ic \'läjik\ n **1** : science of reasoning **2** : sound reasoning **—log·i·cal** \-ikal\ adj **—log·i·cal·ly** adv **—lo·gi·cian** \lō'jishən\ n

lo·gis·tics \lō'jistiks\ n sing or pl : procurement and movement of people and supplies **—lo·gis·tic** adj

lo·go \'lōgō, 'lóg-, 'läg-\ n, pl **lo·gos** \-ōz\ : advertising symbol

loin \'lóin\ n **1** : part of the body on each side of the spine between the hip and lower ribs **2** pl : abdominal regions

loi·ter \'lóitər\ vb : remain around a place idly **—loi·ter·er** n

loll \'läl\ vb : lounge

lol·li·pop, lol·ly·pop \'läli,päp\ n : hard candy on a stick

lone \'lōn\ adj **1** : alone or isolated **2** : only **—lone·li·ness** n **—lone·ly** adj **—lon·er** \'lōnər\ n

lone·some \-səm\ adj : sad from lack of company **—lone·some·ly** adv **—lone·some·ness** n

long \'lóŋ\ adj **lon·ger** \'lóŋgər\; **lon·gest** \'lóŋgəst\ **1** : extending far or for a considerable time **2** : having a specified length **3** : tedious **4** : well supplied—used with on **~** adv : for a long time **~** n : long period **~** vb : feel a strong desire **—long·ing** \lóŋiŋ\ n **—long·ing·ly** adv

lon·gev·i·ty \län'jevətē\ n : long life

long·hand n : handwriting

long·horn n : cattle with long horns

lon·gi·tude \'länjə,t(y)üd\ n : angular distance east or west from a meridian

lon·gi·tu·di·nal \,länjə't(y)üdnəl, -ᵊnəl\ adj : lengthwise **—lon·gi·tu·di·nal·ly** adv

long·shore·man \'lóŋ'shōrmən\ n : one who loads and unloads ships

look \'lük\ vb **1** : see **2** : seem **3** : direct one's attention **4** : face **~** n **1** : movement of the eyes to see something **2** : appearance of the face **3**

: aspect —**look after** : take care of —
look for 1 : expect 2 : search for

look-out \n 1 : one who watches 2 : careful watch

¹loom \'lüm\ n : frame or machine for weaving

²loom vb : appear large and indistinct or impressive

loon \'lün\ n : black-and-white diving bird

loo-ny, loo-ney \'lünē\ adj -ni-er; -est : crazy

loop \'lüp\ n 1 : doubling of a line that leaves an opening 2 : something like a loop —**loop** vb

loop-hole \'lüp,hōl\ n : means of evading

loose \'lüs\ adj loos-er; -est 1 : not fixed tight 2 : not restrained 3 : not dense 4 : slack 5 : not exact ~ vb loosed; loos-ing 1 : release 2 : untie or relax —**loose** adv —**loose-ly** adv —**loos-en** \'lüsᵊn\ vb —**loose-ness** n

loot \'lüt\ n or vb : plunder —**loot-er** n

lop \'läp\ vb -pp- : cut off

lope \'lōp\ n : bounding gait —**lope** vb

lop-sid-ed \'läp'sīdəd\ adj 1 : leaning to one side 2 : not symmetrical —**lop-sid-ed-ly** adv —**lop-sid-ed-ness** n

lo-qua-cious \lō'kwāshəs\ adj : very talkative —**lo-quac-i-ty** \-'kwasətē\ n

lord \'lȯrd\ n 1 : one with authority over others 2 : British nobleman

lord-ly \-lē\ adj -li-er; -est : haughty

lord-ship \-,ship\ n : rank of a lord

Lord's Supper n : Communion

lore \'lōr\ n : traditional knowledge

lose \'lüz\ vb lost \'lȯst\; los-ing \'lüzin\ 1 : have pass from one's possession 2 : be deprived of 3 : waste 4 : be defeated in 5 : fail to keep to or hold —**los-er** n

loss \'lȯs\ n 1 : something lost 2 pl : killed, wounded, or captured soldiers 3 : failure to win

lost \'lȯst\ adj 1 : not used, won, or claimed 2 : unable to find the way

lot \'lät\ n 1 : object used in deciding something by chance 2 : share 3 : fate 4 : plot of land 5 : much

loth \'lōth, 'lōth\ var of LOATH

lo-tion \'lōshən\ n : liquid to rub on the skin

lot-tery \'lätərē\ n, pl -ter-ies : drawing of lots with prizes going to winners

lo-tus \'lōtəs\ n 1 : legendary fruit that causes forgetfulness 2 : water lily

loud \'laud\ adj 1 : high in volume of sound 2 : noisy 3 : obtrusive in color or pattern —**loud** adv —**loud-ly** adv —**loud-ness** n

loud-speak-er n : device that amplifies sound

lounge \'launj\ vb lounged; loung-ing : act or move lazily ~ n : room with comfortable furniture

lour \'lau(ə)r\ var of LOWER

louse \'laus\ n, pl lice \'līs\ : parasitic insect

lousy \'lauzē\ adj lous-i-er; -est 1 : infested with lice 2 : not good —**lous-i-ly** adv —**lous-i-ness** n

lout \'laut\ n : stupid awkward person —**lout-ish** adj —**lout-ish-ly** adv

lou-ver, lou-vre \'lüvər\ n : opening having parallel slanted slats for ventilation or such a slat

love \'ləv\ n 1 : strong affection 2 : warm attachment 3 : beloved person ~ vb loved; lov-ing 1 : feel affection for 2 : enjoy greatly —**lov-able** \-əbəl\ adj —**love-less** adj —**lov-er** n —**lov-ing-ly** adv

love-lorn \-,lȯrn\ adj : deprived of love or of a lover

love-ly \'ləvlē\ adj -li-er; -est : beautiful —**love-li-ness** n

¹low \'lō\ vb or n : moo

²low adj low-er; low-est 1 : not high or tall 2 : below the normal level 3 : not loud 4 : humble 5 : sad 6 : less than usual 7 : falling short of a standard 8 : unfavorable ~ n 1 : something low 2 : automobile gear giving the slowest speed —**low** adv —**low-ness** n

low-brow \'lō,braủ\ n : person without intellectual interests or culture

¹low-er \'laủ(ə)r\ vb 1 : scowl 2 : become dark and threatening

²low-er \'lō(ə)r\ adj : relatively low (as in rank)

³low-er \'lō(ə)r\ vb 1 : drop 2 : let descend 3 : reduce in value

low-land \'lōland, -,land\ n : low flat country

low-ly \'lōlē\ adj -li-er; -est : humble —**low-li-ness** n

loy-al \'lȯi(ə)l\ adj : faithful to a country, cause, or friend —**loy-al-ist** n —**loy-al-ly** adv —**loy-al-ty** \'lȯi(ə)ltē\ n

loz-enge \'läzᵊnj\ n : small medicated candy

LSD \,el,es'dē\ n : hallucinogenic drug

lu-bri-cant \'lübrikənt\ n : material to reduce friction

lu-bri-cate \-,kāt\ vb -cat-ed; -cat-ing : apply a lubricant to —**lu-bri-ca-tion** \,lübrə'kāshən\ n —**lu-bri-ca-tor** \'lübrə,kātər\ n

lu-cid \'lüsəd\ adj 1 : clear-minded 2 : easily understood —**lu-cid-i-ty** \lü-

'sidətē\ *n* —**lu·cid·ly** *adv* —**lu·cid·ness** *n*

luck \'lək\ *n* **1** : chance **2** : good fortune —**luck·i·ly** *adv* —**luck·i·ness** = *n* —**luck·less** *adj* —**lucky** *adj*

lu·cra·tive \'lükrətiv\ *adj* : profitable —**lu·cra·tive·ly** *adv* —**lu·cra·tive·ness** *n*

lu·di·crous \'lüdəkrəs\ *adj* : comically ridiculous —**lu·di·crous·ly** *adv* —**lu·di·crous·ness** *n*

lug \'ləg\ *vb* **-gg-** : drag or carry laboriously

lug·gage \'ləgij\ *n* : baggage

lu·gu·bri·ous \lü'gübrēəs\ *adj* : mournful —**lu·gu·bri·ous·ly** *adv* —**lu·gu·bri·ous·ness** *n*

luke·warm \'lük'wörm\ *adj* **1** : moderately warm **2** : not enthusiastic

lull \'ləl\ *vb* : make or become quiet or relaxed ∼ *n* : temporary calm

lul·la·by \'lələ,bī\ *n, pl* **-bies** : song to lull children to sleep

lum·ba·go \,ləm'bāgō\ *n* : rheumatic back pain

lum·ber \'ləmbər\ *n* : timber dressed for use ∼ *vb* : cut logs —**lum·ber·man** *n* —**lum·ber·yard** *n*

lum·ber·jack \-,jak\ *n* : logger

lu·mi·nary \'lümə,nerē\ *n, pl* **-nar·ies** : very famous person

lu·mi·nes·cence \,lümə'nes⁹ns\ *n* : low-temperature emission of light —**lu·mi·nes·cent** \-⁹nt\ *adj*

lu·mi·nous \'lümənəs\ *adj* : emitting light —**lu·mi·nance** \-nəns\ *n* —**lu·mi·nos·i·ty** \,lümə'näsətē\ *n* —**lu·mi·nous·ly** *adv*

lump \'ləmp\ *n* **1** : mass of irregular shape **2** : abnormal swelling ∼ *vb* : heap together —**lump·ish** *adj* —**lumpy** *adj*

lu·na·cy \'lünəsē\ *n, pl* **-cies** : insanity

lu·nar \'lünər\ *adj* : of the moon

lu·na·tic \'lünə,tik\ *adj* : insane —**lunatic** *n*

lunch \'lənch\ *n* : noon meal ∼ *vb* : eat lunch

lun·cheon \'lənchən\ *n* : usu. formal lunch

lung \'ləŋ\ *n* : breathing organ in the chest —**lunged** \'ləŋd\ *adj*

lunge \'lənj\ *n* **1** : sudden thrust **2** : sudden move forward —**lunge** *vb*

lurch \'lərch\ *n* : sudden swaying —**lurch** *vb*

lure \'lür\ *n* **1** : something that attracts

2 : artificial fish bait ∼ *vb* **lured; lur·ing** : attract

lu·rid \'lürəd\ *adj* **1** : gruesome **2** : sensational —**lu·rid·ly** *adv*

lurk \'lərk\ *vb* : lie in wait

lus·cious \'ləshəs\ *adj* **1** : pleasingly sweet in taste or smell **2** : sensually appealing —**lus·cious·ly** *adv* —**lus·cious·ness** *n*

lush \'ləsh\ *adj* : covered with abundant growth

lust \'ləst\ *n* **1** : intense sexual desire **2** : intense longing —**lust** *vb* —**lust·ful** *adj*

lus·ter, lus·tre \'ləstər\ *n* **1** : brightness from reflected light **2** : magnificence —**lus·ter·less** *adj* —**lus·trous** \-trəs\ *adj*

lusty \'ləstē\ *adj* **lust·i·er; -est** : full of vitality —**lust·i·ly** *adv* —**lust·i·ness** *n*

lute \'lüt\ *n* : pear-shaped stringed instrument —**lute·nist, lu·ta·nist** \'lüt⁹nəst\ *n*

lux·u·ri·ant \,ləg'zhürēənt, ,lək'shür-\ *adj* **1** : growing plentifully **2** : rich and varied —**lux·u·ri·ance** \-ēəns\ *n* —**lux·u·ri·ant·ly** *adv*

lux·u·ri·ate \-ē,āt\ *vb* **-at·ed; -at·ing** : revel

lux·u·ry \'ləksh(ə)rē, 'ləgzh-\ *n, pl* **-ries** **1** : great comfort **2** : something desirable but costly **3** : something adding to pleasure or comfort —**lux·u·ri·ous** \,ləg'zhürēəs, ,lək'shür-\ *adj* —**lux·u·ri·ous·ly** *adv*

-ly \lē\ *adv, after* 1 *usu* ē; (*corresponding adjectives may end in* əl, *as* "*double*"); *-ically is* ik(ə)lē\ *adv suffix* **1** : in a specified way **2** : from a specified point of view

ly·ce·um \lī'sēəm, 'līsē-\ *n* : hall for public lectures

lye \'lī\ *n* : caustic alkaline substance

lying *pres part of* LIE

lymph \'limf\ *n* : bodily liquid consisting chiefly of blood plasma and white blood cells —**lym·phat·ic** \lim'fatik\ *adj*

lynch \'linch\ *vb* : put to death by mob action —**lynch·er** *n*

lynx \'liŋks\ *n, pl* **lynx** *or* **lynx·es** : wildcat

lyre \'lī(ə)r\ *n* : ancient Greek stringed instrument

lyr·ic \'lirik\ *adj* **1** : suitable for singing **2** : expressing direct personal emotion ∼ *n* **1** : lyric poem **2** *pl* : words of a song —**lyr·i·cal** \-ikəl\ *adj*

M

m \'em\ *n, pl* **m's** *or* **ms** \'emz\ : 13th letter of the alphabet

ma'am \'mam, *after "yes" often* əm\ *n* : madam

ma·ca·bre \mə'käb(rə), -'käbər, -'käbrə\ *adj* : gruesome

mac·ad·am \mə'kadəm\ *n* : pavement of cemented broken stone —**mac·ad·am·ize** \-ˌīz\ *vb*

mac·a·ro·ni \ˌmakə'rōnē\ *n* : tubes of dried wheat paste used as food

mac·a·roon \ˌmakə'rün\ *n* : cookie of ground almonds or coconut

ma·caw \mə'kô\ *n* : large long-tailed parrot

¹mace \'mās\ *n* **1** : heavy spiked club **2** : ornamental staff as a symbol of authority

²mace *n* : spice from the fibrous coating of the nutmeg

ma·chete \mə'shetē\ *n* : large heavy knife

mach·i·na·tion \ˌmakə'nāshən, ˌmashə-\ *n* : plot or scheme —**mach·i·nate** \'makəˌnāt, 'mash-\ *vb*

ma·chine \mə'shēn\ *n* : combination of mechanical or electrical parts ~ *vb* **-chined; -chin·ing** : modify by machine-operated tools —**ma·chin·able** *adj* —**ma·chin·ery** \-(ə)rē\ *n* —**ma·chin·ist** *n*

mack·er·el \'mak(ə)rəl\ *n, pl* **-el** *or* **-els** : No. Atlantic food fish

mack·i·naw \'makəˌnô\ *n* : short heavy plaid coat

mac·ra·mé \ˌmakrə'mā\ *n* : coarse lace or fringe made by knotting

mac·ro \'mak(ˌ)rō\ *adj* : very large

mac·ro·cosm \'makrəˌkäzəm\ *n* : universe

mad \'mad\ *adj* **-dd- 1** : insane or rabid **2** : rash and foolish **3** : angry **4** : carried away by enthusiasm —**mad·den** \'madᵊn\ *vb* —**mad·den·ing·ly** \-ᵊniŋ-\ *adv* —**mad·ly** *adv* —**mad·ness** *n*

mad·am \'madəm\ *n, pl* **mes·dames** \mā'däm\ —used in polite address to a woman

ma·dame \mə'dam, *before a surname also* ˌmadəm\ *n, pl* **mes·dames** \mā'däm\ —used as a title for a woman not of English-speaking nationality

mad·cap \'madˌkap\ *adj* : wild or zany —**madcap** *n*

made *past of* MAKE

Ma·dei·ra \mə'dirə\ *n* : amber-colored dessert wine

ma·de·moi·selle \ˌmad(ə)m(w)ə'zel, ˌmam'zel\ *n, pl* **ma·de·moi·selles** \-'zelz\ *or* **mes·de·moi·selles** \ˌmād(ə)m(w)ə'zel\ : an unmarried girl or woman —used as a title for a woman esp. of French nationality

mad·house \-ˌ\ *n* **1** : insane asylum **2** : place of great uproar or confusion

mad·man \-ˌman, -mən\ *n* : lunatic —**mad·wom·an** *n*

mad·ri·gal \'madrigəl\ *n* : elaborate song for several voice parts

mael·strom \'mālstrəm\ *n* : whirlpool

ma·e·stro \'mīstrō\ *n, pl* **-stros** *or* **-stri** \-ˌstrē\ : eminent composer or conductor

Ma·fia \'mäfēə\ *n* : secret criminal organization

ma·fi·o·so \ˌmäfē'ō(ˌ)sō\ *n, pl* **-si** \-(ˌ)sē\ : member of the Mafia

mag·a·zine \ˌmagə'zēn\ *n* **1** : storehouse **2** : publication issued at regular intervals **3** : cartridge container in a gun

ma·gen·ta \mə'jentə\ *n* : deep purplish red

mag·got \'magət\ *n* : wormlike fly larva —**mag·goty** *adj*

mag·ic \'majik\ *n* **1** : art of using supernatural powers **2** : extraordinary power or influence **3** : sleight of hand —**magic, mag·i·cal** \-ikəl\ *adj* —**mag·i·cal·ly** \-ik(ə)lē\ *adv* —**ma·gi·cian** \mə'jishən\ *n*

mag·is·te·ri·al \ˌmajə'stirēəl\ *adj* **1** : authoritative **2** : relating to a magistrate

mag·is·trate \'majəˌstrāt\ *n* : judge —**mag·is·tra·cy** \-strəsē\ *n*

mag·ma \'magmə\ *n* : molten rock

mag·nan·i·mous \mag'nanəməs\ *adj* : noble or generous —**mag·na·nim·i·ty** \ˌmagnə'nimətē\ *n* —**mag·nan·i·mous·ly** *adv* —**mag·nan·i·mous·ness** *n*

mag·ne·sia \mag'nēshə, -zhə\ *n* : oxide of magnesium used as a laxative

mag·ne·sium \mag'nēzēəm, -zhəm\ *n* : silver-white metallic chemical element

mag·net \'magnət\ *n* **1** : body that attracts iron **2** : something that attracts —**mag·net·ic** \mag'netik\ *adj* —**mag·net·i·cal·ly** \-ik(ə)lē\ *adv* —**mag·ne·tism** \'magnəˌtizəm\ *n*

mag·ne·tite \'magnəˌtīt\ *n* : black iron ore

mag·ne·tize \'magnə,tīz\ *vb* **-tized; -tiz·ing 1** : attract like a magnet **2** : give magnetic properties to —**mag·ne·tiz·able** *adj* —**mag·ne·ti·za·tion** \,magnətə'zāshən\ *n* —**mag·ne·tiz·er** *n*

mag·nif·i·cent \mag'nifəsənt\ *adj* : splendid —**mag·nif·i·cence** \-səns\ *n* —**mag·nif·i·cent·ly** *adv*

mag·ni·fy \'magnə,fī\ *vb* **-fied; -fy·ing 1** : intensify **2** : enlarge —**mag·ni·fi·ca·tion** \,magnəfə'kāshən\ *n* —**mag·ni·fi·er** \'magnə,fī(ə)r\ *n*

mag·ni·tude \'magnə,t(y)üd\ *n* **1** : greatness of size or extent **2** : quantity

mag·no·lia \mag'nōlyə\ *n* : shrub with large fragrant flowers

mag·pie \'mag,pī\ *n* : long-tailed black-and-white bird

ma·hog·a·ny \mə'hägənē\ *n, pl* **-nies** : tropical evergreen tree or its reddish brown wood

maid \'mād\ *n* **1** : unmarried young woman **2** : female servant

maid·en \'mād³n\ *n* : unmarried young woman ~ *adj* **1** : unmarried **2** : first —**maid·en·hood** \-,hüd\ *n* —**maid·en·ly** *adj*

maid·en·hair \-,haar\ *n* : fern with delicate feathery fronds

¹mail \'māl\ *n* **1** : something sent or carried in the postal system **2** : postal system ~ *vb* : send by mail —**mail·box** \-,bäks\ *n* —**mail·man** \-,man, -mən\ *n*

²mail *n* : armor of metal links or plates

maim \'mām\ *vb* : seriously wound or disfigure

main \'mān\ *n* **1** : force **2** : ocean **3** : principal pipe, duct, or circuit of a utility system ~ *adj* : chief —**main·ly** *adv*

main·land \'man,land, -lənd\ *n* : part of a country on a continent

main·stay *n* : chief support

main·stream *n* : prevailing current or direction of activity or influence —**mainstream** *adj*

main·tain \mān'tān\ *vb* **1** : keep in an existing state (as of repair) **2** : sustain **3** : declare —**main·tain·abil·i·ty** \-,tānə'bilətē\ *n* —**main·tain·able** \-'tānəbəl\ *adj* —**main·te·nance** \'māntnəns, -ⁿəns\ *n*

mai·tre d'hôtel \,mātrədō'tel, ,me-\ *n* : head of a dining room staff

maize \'māz\ *n* : corn

maj·es·ty \'majəstē\ *n, pl* **-ties 1** : sovereign power or dignity —used as a title **2** : grandeur or splendor —**ma·jes·tic** \mə'jestik\ *adj* —**ma·jes·ti·cal·ly** \-tik(ə)lē\ *adv*

ma·jor \'mājər\ *adj* **1** : larger or greater **2** : noteworthy or conspicuous ~ *n* **1** : commissioned officer (as in the army) ranking next below a lieutenant colonel **2** : main field of study ~ *vb* **-jored; -jor·ing** : pursue an academic major

ma·jor-do·mo \,mājər'dōmō\ *n, pl* **-mos** : head steward

major general *n* : commissioned officer (as in the army) ranking next below a lieutenant general

ma·jor·i·ty \mə'jorətē\ *n, pl* **-ties 1** : age of full civil rights **2** : quantity more than half

make \'māk\ *vb* **made** \'mād\; **mak·ing 1** : cause to exist, occur, or appear **2** : fashion or manufacture **3** : formulate in the mind **4** : constitute **5** : prepare **6** : cause to be or become **7** : carry out or perform **8** : compel **9** : gain **10** : have an effect —used with *for* ~ *n* : brand —**mak·er** *n*

make do *vb* : get along with what is available —**make good** *vb* **1** : repay **2** : succeed —**make out** *vb* **1** : draw up or write **2** : discern or understand **3** : fare —**make up** *vb* **1** : invent **2** : become reconciled **3** : compensate for

make-be·lieve *n* : a pretending to believe ~ *adj* : imagined or pretended

make·shift *n* : temporary substitute —**makeshift** *adj*

make·up \-,əp\ *n* **1** : way in which something is constituted **2** : cosmetics

mal·ad·just·ed \,malə'jəstəd\ *adj* : poorly adjusted (as to one's environment) —**mal·ad·just·ment** \-'jəs(t)mənt\ *n*

mal·adroit \,malə'droit\ *adj* : clumsy or inept

mal·a·dy \'malədē\ *n, pl* **-dies** : disease or disorder

mal·aise \mə'lāz, ma-\ *n* : sense of being unwell

mal·a·mute \'malə,myüt\ *n* : powerful heavy-coated dog

mal·a·prop·ism \'malə,präp,izəm\ *n* : humorous misuse of a word

ma·lar·ia \mə'lerēə\ *n* : disease transmitted by a mosquito —**ma·lar·i·al** \-əl\ *adj*

mal·ar·key \mə'lärkē\ *n* : foolishness

mal·con·tent \,malkən'tent\ *adj* : dissatisfied with the state of affairs —**malcontent** *n*

male \'māl\ *adj* **1** : relating to the sex that performs a fertilizing function **2**

: masculine ~ n : male individual — **male·ness** n

male·dic·tion \,malə'dikshən\ n : curse

male·fac·tor \'malə,faktər\ n : one who commits an offense esp. against the law

ma·lef·i·cent \mə'lefəsənt\ adj : harmful

ma·lev·o·lent \mə'levələnt\ adj : malicious or spiteful —**ma·lev·o·lence** \-ləns\ n

mal·fea·sance \mal'fēz°ns\ n : misconduct by a public official

mal·for·ma·tion \,malfór'māshən\ n : distortion or faulty formation — **mal-formed** \mal'fórmd\ adj

mal·func·tion \mal'fəŋkshən\ vb : fail to operate properly —**malfunction** n

mal·ice \'maləs\ n : ill will —**ma·li·cious** \mə'lishəs\ adj —**ma·li·cious·ly** adv

ma·lign \mə'līn\ adj 1 : wicked 2 : malignant ~ vb : speak evil of

ma·lig·nant \mə'lignənt\ adj 1 : harmful 2 : likely to cause death —**ma·lig·nan·cy** \-nənsē\ n —**ma·lig·nant·ly** adv —**ma·lig·ni·ty** \-nətē\ n

ma·lin·ger \mə'liŋgər\ vb : pretend illness to avoid duty —**ma·lin·ger·er** n

mall \'mól\ n 1 : shaded promenade 2 : concourse providing access to rows of shops

mal·lard \'malərd\ n, pl -**lard** or -**lards** : common wild duck

mal·lea·ble \'malēəbəl\ adj : easily shaped —**mal·lea·bil·i·ty** \,malēə'bilətē\ n

mal·let \'malət\ n : hammerlike tool

mal·nour·ished \mal'nərisht\ adj : poorly nourished

mal·nu·tri·tion \,maln(y)ü'trishən\ n : inadequate nutrition

mal·odor·ous \mal'ōdərəs\ adj : foul-smelling —**mal·odor·ous·ly** adv — **mal·odor·ous·ness** n

mal·prac·tice \-'praktəs\ n : failure of professional duty

malt \'mólt\ n : sprouted grain used in brewing

mal·treat \mal'trēt\ vb : treat badly —**mal·treat·ment** n

ma·ma, mam·ma \'mämə\ n : mother

mam·mal \'maməl\ n : vertebrate animal that nourishes its young with milk —**mam·ma·li·an** \mə'mālēən, ma-\ adj or n

mam·ma·ry \'mamərē\ adj : relating to the milk-secreting glands

mam·moth \'maməth\ n : large hairy extinct elephant ~ adj : enormous

man \'man\ n, pl **men** \'men\ 1 : human being 2 : adult male 3 : mankind ~ vb -**nn**- 1 : station people to work on or at 2 : physically operate —

man·hood n —**man·hunt** n —**man-like** adj —**man·li·ness** n —**man·ly** adj or adv —**man·made** adj —**man·nish** adj —**man·nish·ly** adv —**man·nish·ness** n —**man-size, man-sized** adj

man·a·cle \'manikəl\ n : shackle for the hands —**manacle** vb

man·age \'manij\ vb -**aged; -ag·ing** 1 : control 2 : direct or carry on business or affairs 3 : cope —**man·age·abil·i·ty** \,manijə'bilətē\ n —**man·age·able** \'manijəbəl\ adj —**man·age·able·ness** n —**man·age·ably** \-blē\ adv —**man·age·ment** \'manijmənt\ n —**man·age·men·tal** \,manij'ment°l\ adj —**man·ag·er** \'manijər\ n —**man·a·ge·ri·al** \,manə'jirēəl\ adj

man·da·rin \'mandərən\ n : Chinese imperial official

man·date \'man,dāt\ n : authoritative command

man·da·to·ry \'mandə,tōrē\ adj : obligatory

man·di·ble \'mandəbəl\ n : lower jaw —**man·dib·u·lar** \man'dibyələr\ adj

man·do·lin \,mandə'lin, 'mand°lən\ n : stringed musical instrument

man·drake \'man,drāk\ n : herb with a large forked root

mane \'mān\ n : animal's neck hair —**maned** \mānd\ adj

ma·neu·ver \mə'n(y)üvər\ n 1 : planned movement of troops or ships 2 : military training exercise 3 : procedure involving expert physical movement 4 : skillful often evasive action or management —**maneuver** vb —**ma·neu·ver·abil·i·ty** \-,n(y)üvərə'bilətē\ n

man·ful \'manfəl\ adj : courageous —**man·ful·ly** adv

man·ga·nese \'maŋgə,nēz, -,nēs\ n : gray metallic chemical element

mange \'mānj\ n : skin disease of domestic animals —**mangy** \'mānjē\ adj

man·ger \'mānjər\ n : feeding trough for livestock

man·gle \'maŋgəl\ vb -**gled; -gling** 1 : mutilate 2 : bungle —**man·gler** \-g(ə)lər\ n

man·go \'maŋgō\ n, pl -**goes** : yellowish red tropical fruit

man·grove \'man,grōv, 'maŋ-\ n : tropical tree growing in salt water

man·han·dle \'-\ vb : handle roughly

man·hole n : entry to a sewer

ma·nia \'mānēə, -nyə\ n 1 : insanity 2

: excessive enthusiasm —**ma·ni·ac** \-nē,ak\ n —**ma·ni·a·cal** \mə'nīə-kəl\ adj —**man·ic** \'manik\ adj or n

man·i·cure \'manə,kyu̇r\ n : treatment for the fingernails ~ vb **-cured; -cur·ing 1** : do manicure work on **2** : trim precisely —**man·i·cur·ist** \-,kyu̇rəst\ n

¹man·i·fest \'manə,fest\ adj : clear to the senses or to the mind ~ vb : make evident —**man·i·fes·ta·tion** \,manəfə'stāshən\ n —**man·i·fest·ly** adv

²manifest n : invoice of cargo or list of passengers

man·i·fes·to \,manə'festō\ n, pl **-tos** or **-toes** : public declaration of policy or views

man·i·fold \'manə,fōld\ adj : marked by diversity or variety ~ n : pipe fitting with several outlets for connections

ma·nila paper \mə,nilə-\ n : durable brownish paper

ma·nip·u·late \mə'nipyə,lāt\ vb **-lated; -lat·ing 1** : treat or operate manually or mechanically **2** : influence esp. by cunning —**ma·nip·u·la·tion** \mə,nipyə'lāshən\ n —**ma·nip·u·la·tive** \-'nipyə,lātiv\ adj —**ma·nip·u·la·tor** \-,lātər\ n

man·kind \'man'kīnd\ n : human race

man·na \'manə\ n : something valuable that comes unexpectedly

manned \'mand\ adj : carrying or performed by a man

man·ne·quin \'manikən\ n : dummy used to display clothes

man·ner \'manər\ n **1** : kind **2** : usual way of acting **3** : artistic method **4** pl : social conduct

man·nered \-ərd\ adj **1** : having manners of a specified kind **2** : artificial

man·ner·ism \'manə,rizəm\ n : individual peculiarity of action

man·ner·ly \-lē\ adj : polite —**man·ner·li·ness** n

man-of-war \,manə(v)'wȯr\ n, pl **men-of-war** \,men-\ : warship

man·or \'manər\ n : country estate —**ma·no·ri·al** \mə'nȯrēəl\ adj —**ma·no·ri·al·ism** \-ə,lizəm\ n

man·pow·er n : supply of people available for service

man·sard \'man,särd\ n : roof with two slopes on all sides and the lower slope the steeper

manse \'mans\ n : parsonage

man·ser·vant n, pl **men·ser·vants** : a male servant

man·sion \'manchən\ n : very big house

man·slaugh·ter n : unintentional killing of a person

man·tel \'mant²l\ n : shelf above a fireplace

man·tis \'mantəs\ n, pl **-tis·es** or **-tes** \'man,tēz\ : large insect with stout foreleg

man·tle \'mant²l\ n **1** : sleeveless cloak **2** : something that covers, enfolds, or envelopes ~ vb **-tled; -tling** : cover

man·tra \'mantrə\ n : mystical chant

man·u·al \'manyə(wə)l\ adj : involving the hands or physical force ~ n : handbook —**man·u·al·ly** adv

man·u·fac·ture \,man(y)ə'fakchər\ n : process of making wares by hand or by machinery ~ vb **-tured; -tur·ing** : make from raw materials —**man·u·fac·tur·er** n

ma·nure \mə'n(y)u̇r\ n : animal excrement used as fertilizer —**ma·nu·ri·al** adj

manu·script \'manyə,skript\ n : something written or typed

many \'menē\ adj **more** \'mȯr\; **most** \'mōst\ : consisting of a large number —**many** n or pron

map \'map\ n : representation of a geographical area ~ vb **-pp- 1** : make a map of **2** : plan in detail —**map·pa·ble** \-əbəl\ adj —**map·per** n

ma·ple \'māpəl\ n : tree with hard light-colored wood

mar \'mär\ vb **-rr-** : damage

mar·a·schi·no \,marə'skēnō, -'shē-\ n, pl **-nos** : preserved cherry

mar·a·thon \'marə,thän\ n **1** : long-distance race **2** : test of endurance

ma·raud \mə'rȯd\ vb : plunder —**ma·raud·er** n

mar·ble \'märbəl\ n **1** : crystallized limestone **2** : small glass ball used in a children's game (**marbles**)

mar·bling \-b(ə)liŋ\ n : intermixture of fat and lean in meat

march \'märch\ vb : move with regular steps or in a purposeful manner ~ n **1** : distance covered in a march **2** : measured stride **3** : forward movement **4** : music for marching —**march·er** n

March \'märch\ n : 3d month of the year having 31 days

mar·chio·ness \'märshənəs\ n **1** : wife or widow of a marquess **2** : woman holding the rank of a marquess

Mar·di Gras \'märdē,grä\ n : Tuesday before the beginning of Lent often observed with parades and merrymaking mare \'maər\ n : female horse

mar·ga·rine \'märj(ə)rən, -ə,rēn\ n : butter substitute made usu. from vegetable oils

mar·gin \'märjən\ n 1 : edge 2 : spare amount, measure, or degree — mar·gin·al \-ə¹\ adj — mar·gin·al·ly adv

mari·gold \'marə,gōld, 'mer-\ n : garden plant with showy flower heads

mari·jua·na \,marə'(h)wänə\ n : intoxicating drug obtained from the hemp plant

ma·ri·na \mə'rēnə\ n : place for mooring boats

mar·i·nate \'marə,nāt\ vb -nat·ed; -nat·ing : soak in a savory sauce

ma·rine \mə'rēn\ adj 1 : relating to the sea 2 : relating to marines ~ n : infantry soldier associated with a navy

mar·i·ner \'marənər\ n : sailor

mar·i·o·nette \,marēə'net, ,mer-\ n : puppet

mar·i·tal \'marət°l\ adj : relating to marriage

mar·i·time \'marə,tīm\ adj : relating to the sea or commerce on the sea

mar·jo·ram \'märj(ə)rəm\ n : aromatic mint used as a seasoning

¹mark \'märk\ n 1 : something aimed at 2 : something (as a line) designed to record position 3 : visible sign 4 : written symbol 5 : grade 6 : lasting impression 7 : blemish ~ vb 1 : designate or set apart by a mark or make a mark on 2 : characterize 3 : remark — mark·er n

²mark n : monetary unit of East Germany

marked \'märkt\ adj : noticeable — mark·ed·ly \'märkədlē\ adv

mar·ket \'märkət\ n 1 : buying and selling of goods or the place this happens 2 : demand for commodities 3 : store ~ vb : sell — mar·ket·able adj

mar·ket·place \-,plās\ n 1 : market 2 : world of trade or economic activity

marks·man \'märksmən\ n : good shooter — marks·man·ship n

mar·lin \'märlən\ n : large oceanic fish

mar·ma·lade \'märmə,lād\ n : jam with pieces of fruit and rind

mar·mo·set \'märmə,set\ n : small bushy-tailed monkey

mar·mot \'märmət\ n : burrowing rodent

¹ma·roon \mə'rün\ vb : isolate without hope of escape

²maroon n : dark red

mar·quee \mär'kē\ n : canopy over an entrance

mar·quess \'märkwəs\, mar·quis \'märkwəs, mär'kē\ n, pl -quess·es

or -quis·es or -quis : British noble ranking next below a duke

mar·row \'marō\ n : soft tissue in the \-'kēz(əz)\ : marchioness

mar·riage \'marij\ n 1 : state of being married 2 : wedding ceremony — mar·riage·able adj

mar·row \'marō\ n : soft tissue in the cavity of bone

mar·ry \'marē\ vb -ried; -ry·ing 1 : join as husband and wife 2 : take or give in marriage — mar·ried adj or n

marsh \'märsh\ n : soft wet land — marshy adj

mar·shal \'märshəl\ n 1 : leader of ceremony 2 : usu. high military or administrative officer ~ -shaled or -shalled; -shal·ing or -shal·ling 1 : arrange in order, rank, or position 2 : lead with ceremony

marsh·mal·low \'märsh,melō, -,mal\ n : spongy candy

mar·su·pi·al \mär'süpēəl\ n : Australian mammal that nourishes young in an abdominal pouch — marsupial adj

mart \'märt\ n : market

mar·ten \'märt°n\ n, pl -ten or -tens : weaselike mammal

mar·tial \'märshəl\ adj 1 : relating to war or an army 2 : warlike

mar·tin \'märt°n\ n : small swallow

mar·ti·net \,märt°n'et\ n : strict disciplinarian

mar·tyr \'märtər\ n : one who dies or makes a great sacrifice for a cause ~ vb : make a martyr of — mar·tyr·dom \-dəm\ n

mar·vel \'märvəl\ vb -veled or -velled; -vel·ing or -vel·ling : feel surprise or wonder ~ n : something amazing — mar·vel·ous, mar·vel·lous \'märv-(ə)ləs\ adj — mar·vel·ous·ly adv — mar·vel·ous·ness n

Marx·ism \'märk,sizəm\ n : political and social principles of Karl Marx — Marx·ist \-səst\ n or adj

mas·cara \mas'karə\ n : eye cosmetic

mas·cot \'mas,kät, -kət\ n : one believed to bring good luck

mas·cu·line \'maskyələn\ adj : relating to the male sex — mas·cu·lin·i·ty \,maskyə'linətē\ n

mash \'mash\ n 1 : crushed steeped grain for fermenting 2 : soft pulpy mass ~ vb 1 : reduce to a pulpy mass 2 : smash — mash·er n

mask \'mask\ n : disguise for the face ~ vb 1 : disguise 2 : cover to protect

mas·och·ism \'masə,kizəm, 'maz-\ n : pleasure in being abused — mas·

och·ist \-kəst\ n —**mas·och·is·tic** \,masə'kistik, ,maz-\ adj

ma·son \'mās³n\ n : workman who builds with stone or brick —**ma·son·ry** \-rē\ n

mas·quer·ade \,maskə'rād\ n 1 : costume party 2 : disguise ~ vb -ad·ed; -ad·ing 1 : disguise oneself 2 : take part in a costume party —**mas·quer·ad·er** n

mass \'mas\ n 1 : large amount of matter or number of things 2 : expanse or magnitude 3 : great body of people —usu. pl. ~ vb : form into a mass —**mass·less** \-ləs\ adj —**massy** adj

Mass n : worship service of the Roman Catholic Church

mas·sa·cre \'masikər\ n : wholesale slaughter —**massacre** vb

mas·sage \mə'säzh, -'säj\ n : a rubbing of the body —**massage** vb

mas·seur \ma'sər\ n : man who massages

mas·seuse \-'sə(r)z, -'süz\ n : woman who massages

mas·sive \'masiv\ adj 1 : being a large mass 2 : large in scope —**mas·sive·ly** adv —**mas·sive·ness** n

mast \'mast\ n : tall pole supporting sails —**mast·ed** adj

mas·ter \'mastər\ n 1 : male teacher 2 : holder of an academic degree between a bachelor's and a doctor's 3 : one highly skilled 4 : one in authority ~ vb 1 : subdue 2 : become proficient in —**mas·ter·ful** \-fəl\ adj —**mas·ter·ful·ly** adv —**mas·ter·ly** adj —**mas·tery** \'mast(ə)rē\ n

master chief petty officer n : petty officer of the highest rank in the navy

master gunnery sergeant n : noncommissioned officer in the marine corps ranking above a master sergeant

mas·ter·piece \'mastər,pēs\ n : great piece of work

master sergeant n 1 : noncommissioned officer in the army ranking next below a sergeant major 2 : noncommissioned officer in the air force ranking next below a senior master sergeant 3 : noncommissioned officer in the marine corps ranking next below a master gunnery sergeant

mas·ter·work n : masterpiece

mas·tic \'mastik\ n : pasty glue

mas·ti·cate \'mastə,kāt\ vb -cat·ed; -cat·ing : chew —**mas·ti·ca·tion** \,mastə'kāshən\ n

mas·tiff \'mastəf\ n : large dog

mast·odon \'mastə,dän\ n : extinct elephantlike animal

mas·toid \'mas,tóid\ n : bone behind the ear —**mastoid** adj

mas·tur·ba·tion \,mastər'bāshən\ n : stimulation of sex organs by hand —**mas·tur·bate** \'mastər,bāt\ vb

¹**mat** \'mat\ n 1 : coarse woven or plaited fabric 2 : mass of tangled strands 3 : thick pad ~ vb -tt- : form into a mat

²**mat, matt, matte** \'mat\ adj : not shiny ~ n 1 : border around a picture 2 : dull finish

mat·a·dor \'matə,dór\ n : bullfighter

¹**match** \'mach\ n 1 : one equal to another 2 : 2 things that go well together 3 : game 4 : marriage ~ vb 1 : set in competition 2 : marry 3 : be or provide the equal of 4 : fit or go together —**match·less** adj —**match·mak·er** n

²**match** n : piece of wood or paper material with a combustible tip

mate \'māt\ n 1 : companion 2 : subordinate officer on a ship 3 : one of a pair ~ vb **mat·ed; mat·ing** 1 : fit together 2 : come together as a pair

ma·te·ri·al \mə'tirēəl\ adj 1 : natural 2 : relating to matter 3 : important 4 : of a physical or worldly nature ~ n : stuff something is made of —**ma·te·ri·al·ly** adv

ma·te·ri·al·ism \mə'tirēə,lizəm\ n 1 : theory that matter is the only reality 2 : preoccupation with material and not spiritual things —**ma·te·ri·al·ist** \-ləst\ n or adj —**ma·te·ri·al·is·tic** \-,tirēə'listik\ adj

ma·te·ri·al·ize \mə'tirēə,līz\ vb -ized; -iz·ing : take or cause to take bodily form —**ma·te·ri·al·iza·tion** \mə,tirēələ'zāshən\ n

ma·té·ri·el, ma·te·ri·el \mə,tirē'el\ n : military supplies

ma·ter·nal \mə'tərn³l\ adj : motherly —**ma·ter·nal·ly** adv

ma·ter·ni·ty \mə'tərnətē\ n, pl -ties 1 : state of being a mother 2 : hospital's childbirth facility —**maternity** adj

math \'math\ n : mathematics

math·e·mat·ics \,mathə'matiks\ n pl : science of numbers and of space configurations —**math·e·mat·i·cal** \-ikəl\ adj —**math·e·mat·i·cal·ly** adv —**math·e·ma·ti·cian** \,mathəmə'tishən\ n

mat·i·nee, mat·i·née \,mat³n'ā\ n : afternoon performance

mat·ins \'mat³nz\ n : morning prayers

ma·tri·arch \'mātrē,ärk\ n : woman who rules a family —**ma·tri·ar·chal**

\\,mātrē'ärkəl\\ adj —ma•tri•ar•chy \\'mātrē,ärkē\\ n

ma•tri•cide \\'matrə,sīd, 'mā-\\ n : murder of one's mother —ma•tri•cid•al \\,matrə'sīdᵊl, ,mā-\\ adj

ma•tric•u•late \\mə'trikyə,lāt\\ vb -lat•ed; -lat•ing : enroll in school —ma•tric•u•la•tion \\-,trikyə'lāshən\\ n

mat•ri•mo•ny \\'matrə,mōnē\\ n : marriage —mat•ri•mo•ni•al \\,matrə'mōnēəl\\ adj —mat•ri•mo•ni•al•ly adv

ma•trix \\'mātriks\\ n, pl -tri•ces \\'mātrə,sēz, 'ma-\\ or -trix•es \\'mātriksəz\\ 1 : something within which something else originates or develops 2 : mold

ma•tron \\'mātrən\\ n 1 : dignified mature woman 2 : woman supervisor —ma•tron•ly adj

matt, matte var of MAT

mat•ter \\'matər\\ n 1 : subject of interest 2 pl : circumstances 3 : trouble 4 : physical substance ~ vb : be important

mat•tock \\'matək\\ n : a digging tool

mat•tress \\'matrəs\\ n : pad to sleep on

ma•ture \\mə't(y)ùr\\ adj -tur•er; -est 1 : carefully considered 2 : fully grown or developed 3 : due for payment ~ vb -tured; -tur•ing : become mature —mat•u•ra•tion \\,machə'rāshən\\ n —mat•u•ra•tion•al \\-sh(ə)nəl\\ adj —ma•tu•ri•ty \\-ətē\\ n

maud•lin \\'mòdlən\\ adj : stupidly sentimental

maul \\'mòl\\ n : heavy wooden hammer ~ vb 1 : beat 2 : handle roughly

mau•so•le•um \\,mòsə'lēəm, ,mòzə-\\ n, pl -leums or -lea \\-'lēə\\ : large above-ground tomb

mauve \\'mōv, 'mòv\\ n : lilac color

ma•ven, ma•vin \\'māvən\\ n : expert

mav•er•ick \\'mav(ə)rik\\ n 1 : unbranded range animal 2 : nonconformist

maw \\'mò\\ n 1 : stomach 2 : throat, esophagus, or jaws

mawk•ish \\'mòkish\\ adj : sickly sentimental —mawk•ish•ly adv —mawk•ish•ness n

max•im \\'maksəm\\ n : proverb

max•i•mum \\'maks(ə)məm\\ n, pl -ma \\-səmə\\ or -mums \\-s(ə)məmz\\ 1 : greatest quantity 2 : upper limit 3 : largest number —maximum adj —max•i•mize \\-sə,mīz\\ vb

may \\(')mā\\ verbal auxiliary, past might \\(')mīt\\; pres sing & pl may 1 : have permission 2 : be likely to 3 —used to express desire, purpose, or contingency

May \\'mā\\ n : 5th month of the year having 31 days

may•ap•ple \\n : woodland herb having edible fruit

may•be \\'mābē, 'mebē\\ adv : perhaps

may•flow•er n : spring-blooming herb

may•fly n : fly with an aquatic larva

may•hem \\'mā,hem, 'māəm\\ n : crippling or mutilation of a person

may•on•naise \\'māə,nāz\\ n : thick salad dressing

may•or \\'māər\\ n : chief city official —may•or•al \\-əl\\ adj —may•or•al•ty \\-əltē\\ n

maze \\'māz\\ n : confusing network of passages —mazy adj

ma•zur•ka \\mə'zərkə\\ n : Polish dance

me \\(')mē\\ pron, objective case of I

mead \\'mēd\\ n : alcoholic beverage brewed from honey

mead•ow \\'medō\\ n : low-lying usu. level grassland —mead•ow•land \\-,land\\ n

mead•ow•lark n : songbird with a yellow breast

mea•ger, mea•gre \\'mēgər\\ adj 1 : thin 2 : scanty —mea•ger•ly adv —mea•ger•ness n

¹meal \\'mēl\\ n 1 : food to be eaten at one time 2 : act of eating —meal•time n

²meal n : ground grain —mealy adj

¹mean \\'mēn\\ adj 1 : humble 2 : worthy of or showing little regard 3 : stingy 4 : malicious —mean•ly adv —mean•ness n

²mean \\'mēn\\ vb meant \\'ment\\; mean•ing \\'mēniŋ\\ 1 : intend 2 : serve to convey, show, or indicate 3 : be important

³mean n 1 : middle point 2 pl : something that helps gain an end 3 pl : material resources 4 : sum of several quantities divided by the number of quantities ~ adj : being a mean

me•an•der \\mē'andər\\ vb -dered; -der•ing \\-d(ə)riŋ\\ 1 : follow a winding course 2 : wander aimlessly —mean•der n

mean•ing \\'mēniŋ\\ n : idea conveyed or intended to be conveyed —mean•ing•ful \\-fəl\\ adj —mean•ing•ful•ly adv —mean•ing•less adj

mean•time \\'mēn,tīm\\ n : intervening time —meantime adv

mean•while \\-,hwīl\\ n : meantime —meanwhile adv

mea•sles \\'mēzəlz\\ n pl : disease that is marked by red spots on the skin

mea•sly \\'mēz(ə)lē\\ adj -sli•er; -est : contemptibly small in amount

mea·sure \'mezhər, 'mäzh-\ n 1 : moderate amount 2 : dimensions or amount 3 : something to show amount 4 : unit or system of measurement 5 : act of measuring 6 : means to an end ~ vb -sured; -sur·ing 1 : regulate by a standard 2 : find out or mark off size or amount of 3 : have a specified measurement —**mea·sur·able** \'mezh(ə)rəbəl, 'mäzh-\ adj —**mea·sur·ably** \-blē\ adv —**mea·sure·less** adj —**mea·sure·ment** n —**mea·sur·er** n

meat \'mēt\ n 1 : food 2 : animal flesh used as food —**meat·ball** n —**meaty** adj

me·chan·ic \mi'kanik\ adj : manual ~ n : worker who repairs machines

me·chan·i·cal \mi'kanikəl\ adj 1 : relating to machines or mechanics 2 : involuntary —**me·chan·i·cal·ly** adv

me·chan·ics \-iks\ n sing or pl 1 : branch of physics dealing with energy and forces in relation to bodies 2 : mechanical details

mech·a·nism \'mekə,nizəm\ n 1 : piece of machinery 2 : technique for gaining a result 3 : basic processes producing a phenomenon —**mech·a·nis·tic** \,mekə'nistik\ adj —**mech·a·nis·ti·cal·ly** \-tik(ə)lē\ adv —**mech·a·ni·za·tion** \,mekənə'zāshən\ n —**mech·a·nize** \'mekə,nīz\ vb —**mech·a·niz·er** n

med·al \'med³l\ n 1 : religious pin or pendant 2 : coinlike commemorative metal piece

me·dal·lion \mə'dalyən\ n : large medal

med·dle \'med³l\ vb -dled; -dling : interfere —**med·dler** \'medlər, -³lər\ n —**med·dle·some** \'med³lsəm\ adj

me·dia \'mēdēə\ n pl : communications organizations

me·di·an \'mēdēən\ n : middle value in a range —**median** adj

me·di·ate \'mēdē,āt\ vb -at·ed; -at·ing : help settle a dispute —**me·di·a·tion** \,mēdē'āshən\ n —**me·di·a·tor** \'mēdē,ātər\ n

med·ic \'medik\ n : medical worker esp. in the military

med·i·ca·ble \'medikəbəl\ adj : curable

med·ic·aid \'medi,kād\ n : government program of medical aid for the poor

med·i·cal \'medikəl\ adj : relating to medicine —**med·i·cal·ly** \-k(ə)lē\ adv

medi·care \'medi,keər\ n : government program of medical care for the aged

med·i·cate \'medə,kāt\ vb -cat·ed; -cat-ing : treat with medicine —**med·i·ca·tion** \,medə'kāshən\ n

med·i·cine \'medəsən\ n 1 : preparation used to treat disease 2 : science dealing with the cure of disease —**me·dic·i·nal** \mə'disnəl, -³nəl\ adj —**me·dic·i·nal·ly** adv

me·di·eval, me·di·ae·val \,mēd(ē)'ēval, ,med-, ,mid-\ adj : of or relating to the Middle Ages —**me·di·eval·ism** \-,izəm\ n —**me·di·eval·ist** \-əst\ n

me·di·o·cre \,mēdē'ōkər\ adj : not very good —**me·di·oc·ri·ty** \-'äkrətē\ n

med·i·tate \'medə,tāt\ vb -tat·ed; -tat·ing : contemplate —**med·i·ta·tion** \,medə'tāshən\ n —**med·i·ta·tive** \'medə,tātiv\ adj —**med·i·ta·tive·ly** adv

me·di·um \'mēdēəm\ n, pl -di·ums or -dia \-ēə\ 1 : middle position or degree 2 : means of effecting or conveying something 3 : surrounding substance 4 : means of communication 5 : mode of artistic expression —**medium** adj

med·ley \'medlē\ n, pl -leys : series of songs performed as one

meek \'mēk\ adj 1 : mild-mannered 2 : weak —**meek·ly** adv —**meek·ness** n

meer·schaum \'miərshəm, -,shôm\ n : claylike tobacco pipe

¹**meet** \'mēt\ vb met \'met\; meet·ing 1 : run into 2 : join 3 : oppose 4 : assemble 5 : satisfy 6 : be introduced to ~ n : sports team competition

²**meet** adj : proper

meet·ing \'mētiŋ\ n : a getting together —**meet·ing·house** n

mega·cy·cle \'megə,sīkəl\ n : megahertz

mega·hertz \-,hərts, -,heərts\ n : one million hertz

mega·phone \'megə,fōn\ n : coneshaped device to intensify or direct the voice

mel·an·choly \'melən,kälē\ n : depression —**mel·an·chol·ic** \,melən'kälik\ adj —**melancholy** adj

mela·no·ma \,melə'nōmə\ n, pl -mas : usu. malignant tumor

me·lee \'mā,lā, mā'lā\ n : brawl

me·lio·rate \'mēlyə,rāt, 'mēlēə-\ vb -rat·ed; -rat·ing : improve —**me·lio·ra·tion** \,mēlyə'rāshən, ,mēlēə-\ n —**me·lio·ra·tive** \'mēlyə,rātiv, 'mēlēə-\ adj

mel·lif·lu·ous \me'lifləwəs, mə-\ adj : sweetly flowing —**mel·lif·lu·ous·ly** adv —**mel·lif·lu·ous·ness** n

mel·low \'melō\ adj 1 : grown gentle

or mild 2 : rich and full —**mellow** vb
—**mel·low·ness** n

melo·dra·ma \'melə,drämə, -,dram-\ n
: overly theatrical play —**melo·dra-mat·ic** \,melədrə'matik\ adj —**melo-dra·ma·tist** \,melə'dramətəst,
-'dräm-\ n

mel·o·dy \'melədē\ n, pl **-dies** 1 : agree-able sound 2 : succession of musical notes —**me·lod·ic** \mə'lädik\ adj —**me·lod·i·cal·ly** \-ik(ə)lē\ adv —**me·lo·di·ous** \mə'lōdēəs\ adj —**me·lo·di·ous·ly** adv —**me·lo·di·ous·ness** n

mel·on \'melən\ n : gourdlike fruit

melt \'melt\ vb 1 : change from solid to liquid usu. by heat 2 : dissolve or disappear gradually 3 : move or be moved emotionally

mem·ber \'membər\ n 1 : part of a person, animal, or plant 2 : one of a group 3 : part of a whole —**mem·ber-ship** \-,ship\ n

mem·brane \'mem,brān\ n : thin layer esp. of animal or plant tissue —**mem-bra·nous** \-brənəs\ adj

me·men·to \mi'mentō\ n, pl **-tos** or **-toes** : souvenir

memo \'memō\ n, pl **mem·os** : memo-randum

mem·oirs \'mem,wärz\ n pl : auto-biography

mem·o·ra·bil·ia \,memərə'bilēə, -'bilyə\ n pl 1 : memorable things 2 : mementos

mem·o·ra·ble \'mem(ə)rəbəl\ adj : worth remembering —**mem·o·ra-bil·i·ty** \,memərə'bilətē\ n —**mem·o-ra·ble·ness** \'mem(ə)rəbəlnəs\ n —**mem·o·ra·bly** \-blē\ adv

mem·o·ran·dum \,memə'randəm\ n, pl **-dums** or **-da** \-də\ : informal note

me·mo·ri·al \mə'mōrēəl\ n : some-thing (as a monument) meant to keep remembrance alive —**memorial** adj —**me·mo·ri·al·ize** vb

Memorial Day n : last Monday in May or formerly May 30 observed as a legal holiday in commemoration of dead servicemen

mem·o·ry \'mem(ə)rē\ n, pl **-ries** 1 : power of remembering 2 : some-thing remembered 3 : commemora-tion 4 : time within which past events are remembered —**mem·o·ri-za·tion** \,memərə'zāshən\ n —**mem·o·rize** \'memə,rīz\ vb —**mem·o·riz·er** n

men pl of MAN

men·ace \'menəs\ n : threat of danger ~ vb **-aced; -ac·ing** 1 : threaten 2 : endanger —**men·ac·ing·ly** adv

me·nag·er·ie \mə'naj(ə)rē\ n : collec-tion of wild animals

mend \'mend\ vb 1 : improve 2 : repair 3 : heal —**mend** n —**mend·er** n

men·da·cious \men'dāshəs\ adj : dis-honest —**men·da·cious·ly** adv —**men·dac·i·ty** \-'dasətē\ n

men·di·cant \'mendikənt\ n : beggar —**men·di·can·cy** \-kənsē\ n —**mendi-cant** adj

men·ha·den \men'hād°n, mən-\ n, pl **-den** : fish related to the herring

me·nial \'mēnēəl, -nyəl\ adj 1 : relat-ing to servants 2 : humble ~ n : do-mestic servant —**me·ni·al·ly** adv

men·in·gi·tis \,menən'jītəs\ n, pl **-git-i·des** \-'jitə,dēz\ : disease of the brain and spinal cord

meno·pause \'menə,pòz\ n : time when menstruation ends —**meno-paus·al** \,menə'pòzəl\ adj

men·stru·a·tion \,menstrə'wāshən, men'strā-\ n : monthly discharge of blood from the uterus —**men·stru·al** \'menstra(wə)l\ adj —**men·stru·ate** \'menstrə,wāt, -,strāt\ vb

-ment \mənt\ n suffix 1 : result or means of an action 2 : action or process 3 : place of an action 4 : state or condition

men·tal \'ment°l\ adj : relating to the mind or its disorders —**men·tal·i·ty** \men'talətē\ n —**men·tal·ly** adv

men·thol \'men,thòl, -,thōl\ n : sooth-ing substance from oil of peppermint —**men·tho·lat·ed** \-,thə,lātəd\ adj

men·tion \'menchən\ vb : refer to —**mention** n

men·tor \'men,tòr, 'mentər\ n : in-structor

menu \'menyü, 'mān-\ n : restaurant's list of food

me·ow \mē'aù\ n : characteristic cry of a cat —**meow** vb

mer·can·tile \'mərkən,tēl, -,tīl\ adj : relating to merchants or trade

mer·ce·nary \'mərs°n,erē\ n, pl **-nar-ies** : hired soldier ~ adj : serving only for money —**mer·ce·nar·i·ly** \,mərs°n'erəlē\ adv —**mer·ce·nari-ness** \'mərs°nerənəs\ n

mer·cer \'mərsər\ n : textile dealer

mer·chan·dise \'mərchən,dīz, -,dīs\ n : goods bought and sold ~ vb **-dised; -dis·ing** : buy and sell —**mer·chan-dis·er** n

mer·chant \'mərchənt\ n : one who buys and sells

merchant marine n : commercial ships

mer·cu·ri·al \,mər'kyúrēəl\ adj : un-predictable —**mer·cu·ri·al·ly** adv —**mer·cu·ri·al·ness** n

mer·cu·ry \'mərkyərē\ n : liquid metallic chemical element —**mer·cu·ric** \,mər'kyürik\ adj —**mer·cu·rous** \,mər'kyürəs, 'mərkyərəs\ adj

mer·cy \'mərsē\ n, pl -**cies 1** : show of pity or leniency **2** : divine blessing —**mer·ci·ful** \-sifəl\ adj—**mer·ci·ful·ly** adv —**mer·ci·less** \-siləs\ adj —**mer·ci·less·ly** adv —mercy adj

mere \'miər\ adj **mer·est** : simple —**mere·ly** adv

merge \'mərj\ vb **merged; merg·ing 1** : unite **2** : blend —**merg·er** \'mərjər\ n

me·rid·i·an \mə'ridēən\ n : imaginary circle on the earth's surface passing through the poles —meridian adj

me·ringue \mə'raŋ\ n : dessert topping of baked beaten egg whites

me·ri·no \mə'rēnō\ n, pl -**nos 1** : kind of sheep **2** : fine soft woolen yarn

mer·it \'merət\ n **1** : praiseworthy quality **2** pl : rights and wrongs of a legal case ~ vb : deserve —**mer·i·to·ri·ous** \,merə'tōrēəs\ adj —**mer·i·to·ri·ous·ly** adv —**mer·i·to·ri·ous·ness** n

mer·maid \'mər,mād\ n : legendary female sea creature

mer·ry \'merē\ adj -**ri·er; -est** : full of high spirits —**mer·ri·ly** adv —**mer·ri·ment** \'merimənt\ n —**mer·ry·mak·er** \'merē,mākər\ n —**mer·ry·mak·ing** \'merē,mākiŋ\ n

merry-go-round n : revolving amusement ride

me·sa \'māsə\ n : steep flat-topped hill

mesdames pl of MADAM or of MADAME or of MRS.

mesdemoiselles pl of MADEMOISELLE

mesh \'mesh\ n **1** : one of the openings in a net **2** : net fabric **3** : working contact ~ vb : fit together properly —**meshed** \'mesht\ adj

mes·mer·ize \'mezmə,rīz\ vb -**ized; -ing** : hypnotize —**mes·mer·ic** \mez'merik\ adj —**mes·mer·ism** \'mezmə,rizəm\ n

mess \'mes\ n **1** : meal eaten by a group **2** : confused, dirty, or offensive state **3** : state of disorder or distress ~ vb **1** : make dirty or untidy **2** : putter **3** : interfere —**messy** adj

mes·sage \'mesij\ n : news, information, or a command sent by one person to another

mes·sen·ger \'mesⁿjər\ n : one who carries a message or does an errand

Mes·si·ah \mə'sīə\ n **1** : expected deliverer of the Jews **2** : Jesus Christ **3** not cap : great leader

messieurs pl of MONSIEUR

Messrs. pl of MR.

mes·ti·zo \me'stēzō\ n, pl -**zos** : person of mixed blood

met past of MEET

me·tab·o·lism \mə'tabə,lizəm\ n : sum of the processes of life support and esp. the processes by which a substance is assimilated or eliminated by the body —**met·a·bol·ic** \,metə-'bälik\ adj —**me·tab·o·lize** \mə-'tabə,līz\ vb

met·al \'metⁿl\ n : lustrous, fusible, ductile substance —**me·tal·lic** \mə-'talik\ adj —**met·al·ware** n —**met·al·work** n —**met·al·work·er** n —**met·al·work·ing** n

met·al·lur·gy \'metⁿl,ərjē\ n : science of metals —**met·al·lur·gi·cal** \,metⁿl'ərjikəl\ adj —**met·al·lur·gist** \'metⁿl,ərjist\ n

meta·mor·pho·sis \,metə'mórfəsəs\, n, pl -**pho·ses** \-,sēz\ : sudden and drastic change (as of form) —**meta·morphose** \-,fōz, -,fōs\ vb

met·a·phor \'meta,fór, -fər\ n : use of a word denoting one kind of object or idea in place of another to suggest a likeness between them —**met·a·phor·i·cal** \,metə'fórikəl\ adj

meta·phys·ics \,metə'fiziks\ n : study of the causes and nature of things —**meta·phys·i·cal** \-'fizəkəl\ adj —**meta·phy·si·cian** \-fə'zishən\ n

mete \'mēt\ vb **met·ed; met·ing** : allot

me·te·or \'mētēər, -ē,ór\ n : small piece of matter in the solar system

me·te·or·ic \,mētē'órik\ adj **1** : relating to a meteor **2** : sudden and brilliant —**me·te·or·i·cal·ly** \-i-k(ə)lē\ adv

me·te·or·ite \'mētēə,rīt\ n : meteor that reaches the earth —**me·te·or·it·ic** \,mētēə'ritik\ adj

me·te·o·rol·o·gy \,mētēə'räləjē\ n : science of weather —**me·te·o·ro·log·ic** \-,rə'läjik\, **me·te·o·ro·log·i·cal** \-'läjikəl\ adj —**me·te·o·rol·o·gist** \-ēə'räləjəst\ n

¹**me·ter** \'mētər\ n : rhythm in verse or music

²**meter** n : unit of length equal to 39.37 inches

³**meter** n : measuring instrument

meth·a·done \'methə,dōn\ n : synthetic addictive narcotic

meth·ane \'meth,ān\ n : colorless odorless flammable gas

meth·a·nol \'methə,nól, -,nōl\ n : volatile flammable poisonous liquid

meth·od \'methəd\ n **1** : procedure for achieving an end **2** : orderly arrangement or plan —**me·thod·i·cal** \mə'thädikəl\ adj —**me·thod·i·cal·ly** \-k(ə)lē\ adv —**me·thod·i·cal·ness** n

me·tic·u·lous \mə'tikyələs\ *adj* : extremely careful in attending to details —**me·tic·u·lous·ly** *adv* —**me·tic·u·lous·ness** *n*

met·ric \'metrik\, **met·ri·cal** \-trikəl\ *adj* : relating to meter or the metric system —**met·ri·cal·ly** *adv*

met·ri·ca·tion \metri'kāshən\ *n* : conversion into or expression in the metric system

metric system *n* : system of weights and measures using the meter and kilogram

me·tro·nome \'metrə,nōm\ *n* : instrument that produces regular repeated ticks

me·trop·o·lis \mə'träp(ə)ləs\ *n* : major city —**met·ro·pol·i·tan** \,metrə'pälət\(^{\partial}\)n\ *adj*

met·tle \'met\(^{\partial}\)l\ *n* : spirit or courage —**met·tle·some** \-səm\ *adj*

mez·za·nine \'mez\(^{\partial}\)n,ēn, ,mez\(^{\partial}\)n'ēn\ *n* 1 : shopping level between 2 main floors 2 : lowest balcony

mez·zo-so·pra·no \,metsōsə'pranō, ,me(d)z-\ *n* : voice between soprano and contralto

mi·as·ma \mī'azmə\ *n* : noxious vapor —**mi·as·mic** \-mik\ *adj*

mi·ca \'mīkə\ *n* : mineral separable into thin transparent sheets

mice *pl of* MOUSE

mi·cro \'mīkrō\ *adj* : very small

mi·crobe \'mī,krōb\ *n* : disease-causing microorganism —**mi·cro·bi·al** \mī'krōbēəl\ *adj*

mi·cro·bi·ol·o·gy \,mīkrōbī'äləjē\ *n* : biology dealing with microscopic life —**mi·cro·bi·o·log·i·cal** \'mīkrō,bīə'läjikəl\ *adj* —**mi·cro·bi·ol·o·gist** \,mīkrōbī'äləjəst\ *n*

mi·cro·cosm \'mīkrə,käzəm\ *n* : one thought of as a miniature universe

mi·cro·film \-,film\ *n* : small film recording printed matter —**microfilm** *vb*

mi·crom·e·ter \mī'krämətər\ *n* : instrument for measuring minute distances

mi·cro·min·ia·ture \,mīkrō'minēə,chùr, -'mini,chùr, -chər\ *adj* : reduced to a very small size —**mi·cro·min·ia·tur·iza·tion** \-,minēə,chùrə-'zāshən, ,mini,chùr-, -chər-\ *n* —**mi·cro·min·ia·tur·ized** \-'minēəchə-,rīzd, -'minichə-\ *adj*

mi·cron \'mī,krän\ *n* : 1/1,000,000 meter

mi·cro·or·gan·ism \,mīkrō'ȯrgə,nizəm\ *n* : tiny being

mi·cro·phone \'mīkrə,fōn\ *n* : instrument for changing sound waves into variations of an electric current

mi·cro·scope \-,skōp\ *n* : optical device for magnifying tiny objects —**mi·cro·scop·ic** \,mīkrə'skäpik\, **mi·cro·scop·i·cal** \-ikəl\ *adj* —**mi·cro·scop·i·cal·ly** *adv* —**mi·cros·co·py** \mī-'kräskəpē\ *n*

mi·cro·wave \'mīkrə,wāv\ *n* : short radio wave

mid \'mid\ *adj* : middle —**mid·point** *n* —**mid·stream** *n* —**mid·sum·mer** *n* —**mid·town** *n or adj* —**mid·week** *n* —**mid·win·ter** *n* —**mid·year** *n*

mid·air *n* : a point well above the ground

mid·day *n* : noon

mid·dle \'mid\(^{\partial}\)l\ *adj* 1 : equally distant from the extremes 2 : being at neither extreme ~ *n* : middle part or point

Middle Ages *n pl* : period from about A.D. 500 to about 1500

mid·dle·man \-,man\ *n* : dealer or agent between the producer and consumer

mid·dling \'midliŋ, -lən\ *adj* 1 : of middle or medium size, degree, or quality 2 : mediocre

midge \'mij\ *n* : very tiny fly

midg·et \'mijət\ *n* : very small person or thing

mid·land \'midlənd, -,land\ *n* : interior of a country

mid·most *adj* : being nearest the middle —**midmost** *adv*

mid·night *n* : 12 o'clock at night

mid·riff \'mid,rif\ *n* : mid-region of the torso

mid·ship·man \'mid,shipmən, (')mid-'ship-\ *n* : student naval officer

midst \'midst\ *n* : position close to or surrounded by others —**midst** *prep*

mid·way \'mid,wā\ *n* : concessions and amusements at a carnival ~ *adv* : in the middle

mid·wife \'mid,wīf\ *n* : woman who aids at childbirth —**mid·wife·ry** \-,wīf(ə)rē\ *n*

mien \'mēn\ *n* : appearance

miff \'mif\ *vb* : upset or peeve

¹might \(')mīt\ *past of* MAY —used to express permission or possibility or as a polite alternative to *may*

²might \'mīt\ *n* : power or resources

mighty \'mītē\ *adj* **might·i·er; -est** 1 : very strong 2 : great —**might·i·ly** *adv* —**might·i·ness** *n* —**mighty** *adv*

mi·graine \'mī,grān\ *n* : severe headache and often nausea

mi·grant \'mīgrənt\ *n* : one who moves frequently to find work

mi·grate \ˈmī.grāt\ vb **-grat·ed; -grat·ing** 1 : move from one place to another 2 : pass periodically from one region or climate to another —**mi·gra·tion** \mīˈgrāshən\ n —**mi·gra·tion·al** \-sh(ə)nəl\ adj —**mi·gra·to·ry** \ˈmīgrə,tōrē\ adj

mild \ˈmīld\ adj 1 : gentle in nature or behavior 2 : moderate in action or effect —**mild·ly** adv —**mild·ness** n

mil·dew \ˈmil,d(y)ü\ n : whitish fungal growth —**mildew** vb

mile \ˈmīl\ n : unit of length equal to 5280 feet

mile·age \ˈmīlij\ n 1 : allowance per mile for traveling expenses 2 : amount or rate of use expressed in miles

mile·stone n : significant point in development

mi·lieu \mēlˈyə(r), -ˈyü\ n, pl **-lieus** or **-lieux** \-ˈyə(r)(z), -ˈyüz\ : surroundings or setting

mil·i·tant \ˈmilətənt\ adj : aggressively active or hostile —**mil·i·tan·cy** \-tənsē\ n —**militant** n —**mil·i·tant·ly** adv

mil·i·ta·rism \ˈmilətə,rizəm\ n : dominance of military ideals or of a policy of aggressive readiness for war —**mil·i·ta·rist** \-,rəst\ n —**mil·i·ta·ris·tic** \,milətəˈristik\ adj

mil·i·tary \ˈmilə,terē\ adj 1 : relating to soldiers, arms, or war 2 : relating to or performed by armed forces ~ n : armed forces or the people in them —**mil·i·tar·i·ly** \,miləˈterəlē\ adv

mil·i·tate \-,tāt\ vb **-tat·ed; -tat·ing** : have an effect

mi·li·tia \məˈlishə\ n : civilian soldiers —**mi·li·tia·man** \-mən\ n

milk \ˈmilk\ n : nutritive fluid secreted by female mammals for feeding their young ~ vb : draw off the milk of —**milk·er** n —**milk·i·ness** \-ēnəs\ n —**milky** adj

milk·man \-,man, -mən\ n : man who sells or delivers milk

milk·weed n : herb with milky juice

¹**mill** \ˈmil\ n 1 : building in which grain is ground into flour 2 : manufacturing plant 3 : machine used esp. for forming or processing ~ vb 1 : subject to a process in a mill 2 : move in a circle —**mill·er** n

²**mill** n : 1/10 cent

mil·len·ni·um \məˈlenēəm\ n, pl **-nia** \-ēə\ or **-niums** : a period of 1000 years

mil·let \ˈmilət\ n : cereal and forage grass with small seeds

mil·li·gram \ˈmilə,gram\ n : 1/1000 gram

mil·li·li·ter \-,lētər\ n : 1/1000 liter

mil·li·me·ter \-,mētər\ n : 1/1000 meter

mil·li·ner \ˈmilənər\ n : person who makes or sells women's hats —**mil·li·nery** \ˈmilə,nerē\ n

mil·lion \ˈmilyən\ n, pl **millions** or **million** : 1000 thousands —**million** adj —**mil·lionth** \-yənth\ adj or n

mil·lion·aire \,milyəˈnaər, ˈmilyə,naər\ n : person worth a million or more (as of dollars)

mil·li·pede \ˈmilə,pēd\ n : long-bodied arthropod with 2 pairs of legs on most segments

mill·stone n : either of 2 round flat stones used for grinding grain

mime \ˈmīm, ˈmēm\ n 1 : mimic 2 : art of telling a story by body movements —**mime** vb

mim·eo·graph \ˈmimēə,graf\ n : machine for making many stencil copies —**mimeograph** vb

mim·ic \ˈmimik\ n : one that mimics ~ vb **-icked; -ick·ing** 1 : imitate closely 2 : ridicule by imitation —**mim·ic·ry** \ˈmimikrē\ n

min·a·ret \,minəˈret\ n : tower attached to a mosque

mince \ˈmins\ vb **minced; minc·ing** 1 : cut into small pieces 2 : choose (one's words) carefully 3 : walk in a prim affected manner —**minc·ing** adj

mind \ˈmīnd\ n 1 : memory 2 : the part of an individual that feels, perceives, and esp. reasons 3 : intention 4 : normal mental condition 5 : opinion 6 : intellectual ability ~ vb 1 : attend to 2 : obey 3 : be concerned about 4 : be careful —**mind·ed** adj —**mind·less** \ˈmīndləs\ adj —**mind·less·ly** adv —**mind·less·ness** n

mind·ful \-fəl\ adj : aware or attentive —**mind·ful·ly** adv —**mind·ful·ness** n

¹**mine** \ˈmīn\ pron : one or the ones belonging to me

²**mine** \ˈmīn\ n 1 : excavation from which minerals are taken 2 : encased explosive for destroying enemy vehicles or vessels ~ vb mined; **min·ing** 1 : get ore from 2 : place military mines —**min·er** n

min·er·al \ˈmin(ə)rəl\ n 1 : crystalline substance not of animal or vegetable origin 2 : useful natural substance (as coal) obtained from the ground —**mineral** adj —**min·er·al·ize** \-,īz\ vb

min·er·al·o·gy \,minəˈrāləjē, -ˈral-\ n : science dealing with minerals —**min·er·al·og·i·cal** \,min(ə)rəˈläj-**

ik\əl\ *adj* —**min·er·al·o·gist** \,minə-'rälə\jəst. -'ral-\ *n*

min·gle \'miŋgəl\ *vb* -**gled; -gling** : bring together or mix

mini- *comb form* : miniature or of small dimensions

minibook	mini-opera
miniboom	minipanic
minibrain	minipark
minibudget	miniplan
minibus	minipool
minicab	miniprice
minicalculator	miniproblem
minicamera	minipump
minicar	minirebellion
minicoat	minirecession
miniclock	miniriot
minicomponent	minirobot
minicomputer	minirose
miniconvention	miniscandal
minicourse	minischool
minicrisis	minisearch
minidrama	minisedan
minidress	miniseries
minifair	miniski
minifarm	miniskirt
minifestival	minislump
minifeud	minisociety
miniflaw	ministate
minigarden	ministrike
minigrant	minisub
minigroup	minisubmarine
miniguide	minisurvey
minihospital	minisystem
minileague	miniterritory
minilecture	minitheater
minimarket	minitrain
minimiracle	minivacation
minimuseum	minivan
minination	miniversion
mininetwork	miniwar
mininovel	minizoo

min·ia·ture \'minēə,chùr, 'mini,chùr. -chər\ *n* : tiny copy or very small version —**miniature** *adj* —**min·ia·tur·ist** \-,chùrəst, -chər-\ *n* —**min·ia·tur·ize** \-ēəchə,riz, -icha-\ *vb*

min·i·mal \'minəməl\ *adj* : relating to or being a minimum —**min·i·mal·ly** *adv*

min·i·mize \'minə,miz\ *vb* -**mized; -mizing 1** : reduce to a minimum **2** : estimate at a minimum

min·i·mum \'minəməm\ *n, pl* -**ma** \-mə\ *or* -**mums** : lowest quantity or amount —**minimum** *adj*

min·ion \'minyən\ *n* **1** : servile dependent **2** : subordinate official

min·is·ter \'minəstər\ *n* **1** : Protestant clergyman **2** : high officer of state **3**

: diplomatic representative ~ *vb* : give aid or service —**min·is·te·ri·al** \,minə'stirēəl\ *adj* —**min·is·tra·tion** *n*

min·is·try \'minəstrē\ *n, pl* -**tries 1** : office or duties of a minister **2** : body of ministers **3** : government department headed by a minister

mink \'miŋk\ *n, pl* **mink** *or* **minks** : weasellike mammal or its soft brown fur

min·now \'minō\ *n, pl* -**nows** : small freshwater fish

mi·nor \'mīnər\ *adj* : less in size, importance, or value ~ *n* **1** : person not yet of legal age **2** : secondary field of academic specialization

mi·nor·i·ty \mə'nòrətē, mī-\ *n, pl* -**ties 1** : time or state of being a minor **2** : smaller number (as of votes) **3** : part of a population differing from others (as in race or religion)

min·strel \'minstrəl\ *n* **1** : medieval singer of verses **2** : performer in a program usu. of Negro songs and jokes —**min·strel·sy** \-sē\ *n*

¹mint \'mint\ *n* **1** : place where coins are made **2** : vast sum —**mint** *vb* —**mint·age** \-ij\ *n* —**mint·er** *n*

²mint *n* : herb with fragrant foliage —**minty** *adj*

min·u·et \,minyə'wet\ *n* : slow graceful dance

mi·nus \'mīnəs\ *prep* : diminished by **2** : lacking ~ *n* : negative quantity or quality

mi·nus·cule \'minəs,kyül, min'əs-\ **min·is·cule** \'minəs-\ *adj* : very small

¹min·ute \'minət\ *n* **1** : 60th part of an hour or of a degree **2** : short time **3** *pl* : official record of a meeting

²mi·nute \mī'n(y)üt, mə-\ *adj* -**nut·er; -est 1** : very small **2** : marked by close attention to details —**mi·nute·ly** *adv* —**mi·nute·ness** *n*

mir·a·cle \'mirikəl\ *n* **1** : event that cannot be explained by known laws of nature **2** : marvel —**mi·rac·u·lous** \mə'rakyələs\ *adj*—**mi·rac·u·lous·ly** *adv*

mi·rage \mə'räzh\ *n* : reflection visible at sea or in deserts of some distant object

mire \'mī(ə)r\ *n* : heavy deep mud ~ *vb* **mired; mir·ing** : stick or sink in mire —**miry** *adj*

mir·ror \'mirər\ *n* : smooth substance (as of glass) that reflects images ~ *vb* : reflect in or as if in a mirror

mirth \'mərth\ *n* : gladness and laughter —**mirth·ful** \-fəl\ *adj* —**mirth-**

ful·ly adv —**mirth·ful·ness** n —**mirth·less** adj

mis·an·thrope \'mis°n,thrōp\ n : one who hates mankind —**mis·an·throp·ic** \,mis°n'thräpik\ adj —**mis·an·thro·py** \mis'anthrəpē\ n

mis·ap·pre·hend \,mis-\ vb : misunderstand —**mis·ap·pre·hen·sion** n

mis·ap·pro·pri·ate \,mis-\ vb : take dishonestly for one's own use —**mis·ap·pro·pri·a·tion** n

mis·be·have \,mis-\ vb : behave improperly —**mis·be·hav·er** n —**mis·be·hav·ior** n

mis·cal·cu·late \mis-\ vb : calculate wrongly —**mis·cal·cu·la·tion** \,mis-\ n

mis·car·ry \mis-\ vb 1 : give birth prematurely before the fetus can survive 2 : go wrong or be unsuccessful —**mis·car·riage** n

mis·ce·ge·na·tion \mis,ejə'nāshən, ,misijə'nā-\ n : marriage between members of different races

mis·cel·la·neous \,misə'lānēəs\ adj : consisting of many things of different kinds —**mis·cel·la·neous·ly** adv —**mis·cel·la·neous·ness** n

mis·cel·la·ny \'misə,lānē\ n, pl -nies : collection of various things

mis·chance \mis-\ n : bad luck

mis·chief \'mischəf\ n : conduct esp. of a child that annoys or causes minor damage

mis·chie·vous \'mischəvəs\ adj 1 : causing annoyance or minor injury 2 : irresponsibly playful —**mis·chie·vous·ly** adv —**mis·chie·vous·ness** n

mis·con·ceive \,mis-\ vb : interpret incorrectly —**mis·con·cep·tion** n

mis·con·duct \mis-\ n 1 : mismanagement 2 : bad behavior

mis·con·strue \,mis-\ vb : misinterpret —**mis·con·struc·tion** n

mis·cre·ant \'miskrēənt\ n : one who behaves criminally or viciously —**miscreant** adj

mis·deed \mis-\ n : wrong deed

mis·de·mean·or \,misdi'mēnər\ n : crime less serious than a felony

mi·ser \'mīzər\ n : person who hoards money —**mi·ser·li·ness** \-lēnəs\ n —**mi·ser·ly** adv

mis·er·a·ble \'mizərbəl, 'miz(ə)rəbəl\ adj 1 : wretchedly deficient 2 : causing extreme discomfort —**mis·er·a·ble·ness** n —**mis·er·a·bly** \-blē\ adv

mis·ery \'miz(ə)rē\ n, pl -er·ies : suffering and want caused by distress or poverty

mis·fire \mis-\ vb 1 : fail to fire 2 : miss an intended effect —**misfire** n

mis·fit \'mis,fit, mis'fit\ n : person poorly adjusted to his environment

mis·for·tune \mis-\ n 1 : bad luck 2 : unfortunate condition or event

mis·giv·ing \mis-\ n : doubt or concern

mis·guid·ed \mis-\ adj : mistaken, uninformed, or deceived

mis·hap \'mis,hap\ n : accident

mis·in·form \,mis°n'fȯrm\ vb : give false information to —**mis·in·for·ma·tion** \,mis-\ n

mis·in·ter·pret \,mis°n'tərprət\ vb : understand or explain wrongly —**mis·in·ter·pre·ta·tion** \-,tərprə-'tāshən\ n

mis·judge \mis-\ vb : judge incorrectly or unjustly —**mis·judg·ment** n

mis·lay \mis-\ vb -laid; -lay·ing : misplace

mis·lead \mis-\ vb -led; -lead·ing : lead in a wrong direction or into error —**mis·lead·ing·ly** adv

mis·man·age \mis-\ vb : manage badly —**mis·man·age·ment** n

mis·no·mer \mis'nōmər\ n : wrong name

mi·sog·y·nist \mə'säjənəst\ n : one who hates or distrusts women —**mi·sog·y·ny** \-nē\ n

mis·place \mis-\ vb : put in an unremembered place or in the wrong place

mis·print \'mis,print, mis'-\ n : error in something printed

mis·pro·nounce \,mis-\ vb : pronounce incorrectly —**mis·pro·nun·ci·a·tion** n

mis·quote \mis-\ vb : quote incorrectly —**mis·quo·ta·tion** \,mis-\ n

mis·read \mis-\ vb -read; -read·ing : read or interpret incorrectly

mis·rep·re·sent \,mis-\ vb : represent falsely or unfairly —**mis·rep·re·sen·ta·tion** n

mis·rule \mis-\ vb : govern badly ~ n 1 : bad or corrupt government 2 : disorder

¹**miss** \'mis\ vb 1 : fail to hit, reach, or contact 2 : notice the absence of 3 : fail to obtain 4 : avoid 5 : omit —**miss** n

²**miss** n : young unmarried woman or girl —often used as a title

mis·sal \'misəl\ n : book containing what is said at mass during the year

mis·shap·en \mis(h)'shāpən\ adj : distorted

mis·sile \'misəl\ n : object (as a stone or rocket) thrown or shot

miss·ing \'misiŋ\ adj : absent or lost

mis·sion \'mishən\ n 1 : ministry sent by a church to spread its teaching 2

204

: group of diplomats sent to a foreign country **3** : task

mis·sion·ary \'misho,nerē\ *adj* : relating to religious missions ~ *n, pl* **-ar·ies** : person sent to spread religious faith

mis·sive \'misiv\ *n* : letter

mis·spell \mis-\ *vb* : spell incorrectly —**mis·spell·ing** *n*

mis·state \mis-\ *vb* : state incorrectly —**mis·state·ment** *n*

mis·step \mis-\ *n* **1** : wrong step **2** : mistake

mist \'mist\ *n* : particles of water falling as fine rain

mis·take \mə'stāk\ *n* **1** : misunderstanding or wrong belief **2** : wrong action or statement —**mistake** *vb*

mis·tak·en \-'stākən\ *adj* : having a wrong opinion or incorrect information —**mis·tak·en·ly** *adv*

mis·ter \'mistər\ *n* : sir —used without a name in addressing a man

mis·tle·toe \'misəl,tō\ *n* : parasitic green plant

mis·treat \mis'trēt\ *vb* : treat badly —**mis·treat·ment** *n*

mis·tress \'mistrəs\ *n* **1** : woman in control **2** : woman with whom a man lives unmarried

mis·tri·al \mis'trī(ə)l\ *n* : trial that has no legal effect

mis·trust \-'trəst\ *n* : lack of confidence ~ *vb* : have no confidence in —**mis·trust·ful** \-fəl\ *adj* —**mis·trust·ful·ly** *adv* —**mis·trust·ful·ness** *n*

misty \'mistē\ *adj* **mist·i·er; -est** : obscured by mist —**mist·i·ly** *adv* —**mist·i·ness** *n*

mis·un·der·stand \,mis,əndər'stand\ *vb* **1** : fail to understand **2** : interpret incorrectly

mis·un·der·stand·ing \-'standiŋ\ *n* **1** : wrong interpretation **2** : disagreement

mis·use \mish'üz, mis(h)'yüz\ *vb* **1** : use incorrectly **2** : mistreat —**misuse** \-'üz, -'yüs\ *n*

mite \'mīt\ *n* **1** : tiny spiderlike animal **2** : small amount

mi·ter, mi·tre \'mītər\ *n* **1** : bishop's headdress **2** : angular joint in wood ~ *vb* **-tered** *or* **-tred; -ter·ing** *or* **-tring** \'mītəriŋ\ : bevel the ends of for a miter joint

mit·i·gate \'mitə,gāt\ *vb* **-gat·ed; -gat·ing** : make less severe —**mit·i·ga·tion** \,mitə'gāshən\ *n* —**mit·i·ga·tive** \'mitə,gātiv\ *adj*

mi·to·sis \mī'tōsəs\ *n, pl* **-to·ses** \-,sēz\ : process of forming **2** cell nuclei from one —**mi·tot·ic** \-'tätik\ *adj*

mitt \'mit\ *n* : mittenlike baseball glove

mit·ten \'mit³n\ *n* : hand covering without finger sections

mix \'miks\ *vb* : combine or join into one mass or group ~ *n* : commercially prepared food mixture —**mix·able** *adj* —**mix·er** *n* —**mix up** *vb* : confuse

mix·ture \'miks-chər\ *n* : act or product of mixing

mix-up *n* : instance of confusion

mne·mon·ic \ni'mänik\ *adj* : assisting memory

moan \'mōn\ *n* : low prolonged sound of pain or grief —**moan** *vb*

moat \'mōt\ *n* : deep wide trench around a castle

mob \'mäb\ *n* **1** : large disorderly crowd **2** : criminal gang ~ *vb* **-bb-** : crowd around and attack or annoy

mo·bile \'mōbəl, -,bēl, -,bīl\ *adj* : capable of moving or being moved ~ \'mō,bēl\ *n* : suspended art construction with freely moving parts —**mo·bil·i·ty** \mō'bilətē\ *n*

i.io·bi·lize \'mōbə,līz\ *vb* **-lized; -liz·ing** : assemble and make ready for war duty —**mo·bi·li·za·tion** \,mōbələ'zāshən\ *n* —**mo·bi·liz·er** \'mōbə,līzər\ *n*

moc·ca·sin \'mäkəsən\ *n* **1** : heelless shoe **2** : venomous U.S. snake

mock \'mäk, 'mòk\ *vb* **1** : ridicule **2** : mimic in derision ~ *adj* **1** : simulated **2** : phony —**mock·er** *n* —**mock·ery** \-(ə)rē\ *n* —**mock·ing·ly** *adv*

mock·ing·bird \'mäkiŋ,bərd, 'mòk-\ *n* : songbird that mimics other birds

mode \'mōd\ *n* **1** : particular form or variety **2** : style —**mod·al** \-ᵊl\ *adj* —**mod·ish** \'mōdish\ *adj*

mod·el \'mäd³l\ *n* **1** : structural design **2** : miniature representation **3** : something worthy of copying **4** : one who poses for an artist or displays clothes **5** : type or design ~ *vb* **-eled** *or* **-elled; -el·ing** *or* **-el·ling 1** : shape **2** : work as a model ~ *adj* **1** : serving as a pattern **2** : being a miniature representation of

mod·er·ate \'mäd(ə)rət\ *adj* : avoiding extremes ~ \'mädə,rāt\ *vb* **-at·ed; -at·ing 1** : lessen the intensity of **2** : act as a moderator —**moderate** *n* —**mod·er·ate·ly** *adv* —**mod·er·ate·ness** *n* —**mod·er·a·tion** \,mädə'rāshən\ *n* —**mod·er·a·tor** \'mädə,rātər\ *n* : one who presides

mod·ern \'mädərn\ *adj* : relating to or characteristic of the present —**modern** *n* —**mo·der·ni·ty** \mə'dərnətē\ *n*

—**mod·ern·iza·tion** \,mädərnə-'zāshən\ *n* —**mod·ern·ize** \'mädər,nīz\ *vb* —**mod·ern·iz·er** \'mädər,nīzər\ *n* —**mod·ern·ly** *adv* —**mod·ern·ness** *n*

mod·est \'mädəst\ *adj* **1** : having a moderate estimate of oneself **2** : reserved or decent in thoughts or actions **3** : limited in size, amount, or aim —**mod·est·ly** *adv* —**mod·es·ty** \-əstē\ *n*

mod·i·cum \'mädikəm\ *n* : small amount

mod·i·fy \'mädə,fī\ *vb* **-fied; -fy·ing 1** : limit the meaning of **2** : change —**mod·i·fi·ca·tion** \,mädəfə'kāshən\ *n* —**mod·i·fi·er** \'mädə,fī(ə)r\ *n*

mod·u·lar \'mäjələr\ *adj* : built with standardized units —**mod·u·lar·ized** \-lə,rīzd\ *adj*

mod·u·late \'mäjə,lāt\ *vb* **-lat·ed; -lat·ing 1** : keep in proper measure or proportion **2** : vary a radio wave —**mod·u·la·tion** \,mäjə'lāshən\ *n* —**mod·u·la·tor** \'mäjə,lātər\ *n* —**mod·u·la·to·ry** \-lə,tōrē\ *adj*

mod·ule \'mäjül\ *n* : standardized unit

mo·gul \'mōgəl, mō'gəl\ *n* : important person

mo·hair \'mō,haər\ *n* : fabric made from the hair of the Angora goat

moist \'mȯist\ *adj* : slightly or moderately wet —**moist·en** \'mȯis³n\ *vb* —**moist·en·er** \'mȯisnər, -³nər\ *n* —**moist·ly** *adv* —**moist·ness** *n*

mois·ture \'mȯischər\ *n* : small amount of liquid that causes dampness

mo·lar \'mōlər\ *n* : grinding tooth —**molar** *adj*

mo·las·ses \mə'lasəz\ *n* : thick brown syrup from raw sugar

¹mold \'mōld\ *n* : crumbly organic soil

²mold *n* : frame or cavity for forming ~ *vb* : shape in or as if in a mold —**mold·er** *n*

³mold *n* : surface growth of fungus ~ *vb* : become moldy —**mold·i·ness** \'mōldēnəs\ *n* —**moldy** *adj*

mol·der \'mōldər\ *vb* : crumble

mold·ing \'mōldiŋ\ *n* : decorative surface, plane, or strip

¹mole \'mōl\ *n* : spot on the skin

²mole *n* : small burrowing mammal —**mole·hill** *n*

mol·e·cule \'mäli,kyül\ *n* : small particle of matter —**mol·e·cu·lar** \mə'lekyələr\ *adj*

mole·skin \-,skin\ *n* : heavy cotton fabric

mo·lest \mə'lest\ *vb* : annoy esp. by improper or rough handling —**mo-**

les·ta·tion \,mōl,es'tāshən\ *n* —**mo·lest·er** *n*

mol·li·fy \'mälə,fī\ *vb* **-fied; -fy·ing** : soothe in temper —**mol·li·fi·ca·tion** \,mäləfə'kāshən\ *n*

mol·lusk, mol·lusc \'mäləsk\ *n* : shelled aquatic invertebrate —**mol·lus·can** \mə'ləskən\ *adj*

mol·ly·cod·dle \'mälē,käd³l\ *vb* **-dled; -dling** : pamper

molt \'mōlt\ *vb* : shed hair, feathers, outer skin, or horns periodically —**molt** *n* —**molt·er** *n*

mol·ten \'mōlt³n\ *adj* : fused or liquefied by heat

mom \'mäm, 'mȯm\ *n* : mother

mo·ment \'mōmənt\ *n* **1** : tiny portion of time **2** : time of excellence **3** : importance

mo·men·tar·i·ly \,mōmən'terəlē\ *adv* **1** : for a moment **2** : at any moment

mo·men·tary \'mōmən,terē\ *adj* : continuing only a moment —**mo·men·tar·i·ness** *n*

mo·men·tous \mō'mentəs\ *adj* : very important —**mo·men·tous·ly** *adv* —**mo·men·tous·ness** *n*

mo·men·tum \-əm\ *n*, *pl* **-ta** \-ə\ *or* **-tums** : force of a moving body

mon·arch \'mänərk, -,ärk\ *n* : ruler of a kingdom or empire —**mo·nar·chi·cal** \mə'närkikəl\, **mo·nar·chic** \-'närkik\ *adj*

mon·ar·chist \'mänərkəst\ *n* : believer in monarchical government —**mon·ar·chism** \-,kizəm\ *n*

mon·ar·chy \'mänərkē\ *n*, *pl* **-chies** : realm of a monarch

mon·as·tery \'mänə,sterē\ *n*, *pl* **-ter·ies** : house for monks

mo·nas·tic \mə'nastik\ *adj* : relating to monasteries, monks, or nuns —**mo·nastic** *n* —**mo·nas·ti·cal·ly** \-ik(ə)lē\ *adv* —**mo·nas·ti·cism** \-tə,sizəm\ *n*

Mon·day \'məndē\ *n* : 2d day of the week

mon·e·tary \'mänə,terē, 'mən-\ *adj* : relating to money

mon·ey \'mənē\ *n*, *pl* **-eys** *or* **-ies** \'mənēz\ **1** : something (as coins or paper currency) used in buying **2** : wealth —**mon·eyed** \-ēd\ *adj* —**mon·ey·lend·er** *n*

mon·ger \'mȯŋgər, 'mäŋ-\ *n* : dealer

mon·gol·ism \'mäŋgə,lizəm\ *n* : congenital idiocy —**Mon·gol·oid** \-gə,lȯid\ *adj or n*

mon·goose \'mäŋ,güs, 'mäŋ-\ *n*, *pl* **-goos·es** : small agile mammal of India

mon·grel \'mäŋgrəl, 'mäŋ-\ *n* : offspring of mixed breed

mon·i·tor \'mänətər\ *n* 1 : student assistant 2 : television screen ~ *vb* : watch or observe esp. for quality

monk \'məŋk\ *n* : member of a religious order living in a monastery — **monk·ish** *adj* — **monk·ish·ly** *adv* — **monk·ish·ness** *n*

mon·key \'məŋkē\ *n, pl* -keys : small long-tailed arboreal primate ~ *vb* 1 : fool 2 : tamper

mon·key·shines \-,shīnz\ *n pl* : pranks

monks·hood \'məŋks,hùd\ *n* : poisonous herb with showy flowers

mon·o·cle \'mänikəl\ *n* : eyeglass for one eye

mo·nog·a·my \mə'nägəmē\ *n* : marriage with one person at a time — **mo·nog·a·mist** \mə'nägəmist\ *n* — **mo·nog·a·mous** \-məs\ *adj*

mono·gram \'mänə,gram\ *n* : sign of identity made of initials — **monogram** *vb*

mono·graph \-,graf\ *n* : learned treatise

mono·lin·gual \,mänə'liŋgwəl\ *adj* : using only one language

mono·lith \'mänºl,ith\ *n* 1 : single great stone 2 : single uniform massive whole — **mono·lith·ic** \,mänºl'ithik\ *adj*

mono·logue \'mänºl,óg\ *n* : long speech — **mono·logu·ist** \-,ógəst\, **mo·no·lo·gist** \mə'nälə jəst, 'mänºl,ógəst\ *n*

mono·nu·cle·o·sis \,mänō,n(y)üklē-'ōsəs\ *n* : acute infectious disease

mo·nop·o·ly \mə'näp(ə)lē\ *n, pl* -lies 1 : exclusive ownership or control of a commodity 2 : one controlling a monopoly — **mo·nop·o·list** \-ləst\ *n* — **mo·nop·o·lis·tic** \mə,näpə'listik\ *adj* — **mo·nop·o·li·za·tion** \-lə'zāshən\ *n* — **mo·nop·o·lize** \mə'näpə,līz\ *vb*

mono·rail \'mänə,rāl\ *n* : single rail for a wheeled vehicle or a vehicle or system using it

mono·syl·la·ble \-,siləbəl\ *n* : word of one syllable — **mono·syl·lab·ic** \-sə'labik\ *adj*

mono·the·ism \'mänə(,)thē,izəm\ *n* : doctrine or belief that there is only one deity — **mono·the·ist** \-,thēəst\ *n*

mono·tone \'mänə,tōn\ *n* : succession of words in one unvarying tone

mo·not·o·nous \mə'nät³nəs\ *adj* 1 : sounded in one unvarying tone 2 : tediously uniform — **mo·not·o·nous·ly** *adv* — **mo·not·o·nous·ness** *n* — **mo·not·o·ny** \-³nē\ *n*

mon·ox·ide \mə'näk,sīd\ *n* : oxide con-

taining one atom of oxygen in the molecule

mon·sieur \məs(h)(')yə(r), mə'si(ə)r\ *n, pl* **mes·sieurs** \məs(h)(')yə(r)(z), mäs-; mə'si(ə)r(z)\ : man of high rank or station —used as a title for a man esp. of French nationality

mon·si·gnor \män'sēnyər\ *n, pl* **monsignors** *or* **mon·si·gno·ri** \,män-,sēn'yōrē\ : Roman Catholic prelate —used as a title

mon·soon \män'sün\ *n* : periodic rainy season

mon·ster \'mänstər\ *n* 1 : abnormal or terrifying animal 2 : ugly, wicked, or cruel person — **mon·stros·i·ty** \män'sträsətē\ *n* — **mon·strous** \'mänstrəs\ *adj* — **mon·strous·ly** *adv*

mon·tage \män'täzh\ *n* : composite photo

month \'mənth\ *n* : 12th part of a year — **month·ly** *adv or adj or n*

mon·u·ment \'mänyəmənt\ *n* : structure erected in remembrance — **mon·u·men·tal** \,mänyə'ment³l\ *adj* — **mon·u·men·tal·ly** *adv*

moo \'mü\ *vb* : make the noise of a cow — **moo** *n*

mood \'müd\ *n* : state of mind or emotion

moody \'müdē\ *adj* **mood·i·er; -est** 1 : sad 2 : subject to changing moods and esp. to bad moods — **mood·i·ly** \'müd³lē\ *adv* — **mood·i·ness** \-ē-nəs\ *n*

moon \'mün\ *n* : earth's satellite — **moon·beam** *n* — **moon·light** *n* — **moon·lit** *adj*

moon·light \-,līt\ *vb* **-ed; -ing** : hold a 2d job — **moon·light·er** *n*

moon·shine *n* 1 : moonlight 2 : illegally distilled liquor

¹moor \'mùr\ *n* : open usu. swampy wasteland — **moor·land** \-lənd, -,land\ *n*

²moor *vb* : fasten with line or anchor

moor·ing \-iŋ\ *n* : place where boat can be moored

moose \'müs\ *n, pl* **moose** : large heavy-antlered deer

moot \'müt\ *adj* : open to question

mop \'mäp\ *n* : floor-cleaning implement ~ *vb* **-pp-** : use a mop on

mope \'mōp\ *vb* **moped; mop·ing** : be sad or listless

mo·ped \'mō,ped\ *n* : low-powered motorbike

mo·raine \mə'rān\ *n* : glacial deposit of earth and stones

mor·al \'mórəl\ *adj* 1 : relating to principles of right and wrong 2 : conforming to a standard of right behavior 3 : relating to or acting on the mind, character, or will ~ *n* 1 : point of a story 2 *pl* : moral practices or teachings —**mor·al·ist** \'mórələst\ —**mor·al·is·tic** \ˌmórə'listik\ *adj* —**mor·al·i·ty** \ma'ralətē\ *n* —**mor·al·ize** \'mórəˌlīz\ *vb* —**mor·al·ly** *adv*

mo·rale \ma'ral\ *n* : emotional attitude

mo·rass \ma'ras\ *n* : swamp

mor·a·to·ri·um \ˌmórə'tōrēəm\ *n, pl* **-ri·ums** *or* **-ria** \-ē-ə\ : suspension of activity

mo·ray \ma'rā, 'mór,ā\ *n* : savage eel

mor·bid \'mórbəd\ *adj* 1 : relating to disease 2 : gruesome —**mor·bid·i·ty** \mór'bidətē\ *n* —**mor·bid·ly** *adv* —**mor·bid·ness** *n*

mor·dant \'mórdᵊnt\ *adj* : incisive —**mor·dant·ly** *adv*

more \'mór\ *adj* 1 : greater 2 : additional ~ *adv* 1 : in addition 2 : to a greater degree ~ *n* 1 : greater quantity 2 : additional amount ~ *pron* : additional ones

mo·rel \ma'rel\ *n* : pitted edible mushroom

more·over \mór'ōvər\ *adv* : in addition

mo·res \'mór,āz, -,(ˌ)ēz\ *n, pl* : customs

morgue \'mórg\ *n* : mortuary for persons found dead

mor·i·bund \'mórə(ˌ)bənd\ *adj* : dying —**mor·i·bun·di·ty** \ˌmórə'bəndətē\ *n*

morn \'mórn\ *n* : morning

morn·ing \'mórniŋ\ *n* : time from sunrise to noon

mo·ron \'mór,än\ *n* : mentally deficient person —**mo·ron·ic** \ma'ränik\ *adj* —**mo·ron·i·cal·ly** \-ik(ə)lē\ *adv*

mo·rose \ma'rōs\ *adj* : sullen —**mo·rose·ly** *adv* —**mo·rose·ness** *n*

mor·phine \'mór,fēn\ *n* : addictive painkilling drug

mor·row \'märō\ *n* : next day

Morse code \'mórs-\ *n* : code of dots and dashes or long and short sounds used for transmitting messages

mor·sel \'mórsəl\ *n* : small piece or quantity

mor·tal \'mórtᵊl\ *adj* 1 : causing or subject to death 2 : extreme —**mortal** *n* —**mor·tal·i·ty** \mór'talətē\ *n* —**mor·tal·ly** \'mórtᵊlē\ *adv*

mor·tar \'mórtər\ *n* 1 : strong bowl 2 : short-barreled cannon 3 : masonry material that hardens —**mortar** *vb*

mort·gage \'mórgij\ *n* : transfer of property rights as security for a loan —**mortgage** *vb* —**mort·gag·ee** \ˌmórgi'jē\ *n* —**mort·ga·gor** \ˌmórgi'jór\ *n*

mor·ti·fy \'mórtəˌfī\ *vb* **-fied; -fy·ing** 1 : subdue by abstinence or self-in-

flicted pain 2 : humiliate —**mor·ti·fi·ca·tion** \ˌmórtəfə'kāshən\ *n*

mor·tu·ary \'mórchə,werē\ *n, pl* **-ar·ies** : place in which dead bodies are kept until burial

mo·sa·ic \mō'zāik\ *n* : inlaid stone decoration

Mos·lem \'mäzləm\ *var of* MUSLIM

mosque \'mäsk\ *n* : building where Muslims worship

mos·qui·to \ma'skētō\ *n, pl* **-toes** : biting insect

moss \'mós\ *n* : green seedless plant —**mossy** *adj*

most \'mōst\ *adj* 1 : majority of 2 : greatest ~ *adv* : to the greatest or a very great degree ~ *n* : greatest amount ~ *pron* : greatest number or part

-most \ˌmōst\ *adj suffix* : most : most toward

most·ly \'mōstlē\ *adv* : mainly

mote \'mōt\ *n* : small particle

mo·tel \mō'tel\ *n* : hotel with outdoor parking area

moth \'móth\ *n* : small pale insect related to the butterflies

moth·er \'mᵊthər\ *n* 1 : female parent 2 : source ~ *vb* 1 : give birth to 2 : cherish or protect —**moth·er·hood** \-,húd\ *n* —**moth·er·land** \-,land\ *n* —**moth·er·less** *adj* —**moth·er·ly** *adj*

moth·er-in-law \'mᵊth(ə)rən,ló, 'mᵊthərn,ló\ *n, pl* **mothers-in-law** : spouse's mother

mo·tif \mō'tēf\ *n* : dominant theme

mo·tion \'mōshən\ *n* 1 : proposal for action 2 : act or instance of moving ~ *vb* : direct by a motion —**mo·tion·less** *adj* —**mo·tion·less·ly** *adv* —**mo·tion·less·ness** *n*

motion picture *n* : movie

mo·ti·vate \'mōtə,vāt\ *vb* **-vat·ed; -vat·ing** : provide with a motive —**mo·ti·va·tion** \ˌmōtə'vāshən\ *n*

mo·tive \'mōtiv\ *n* : cause of a person's action ~ *adj* 1 : moving to action 2 : relating to motion —**mo·tive·less** *adj*

mot·ley \'mätlē\ *adj* : of diverse colors or elements

mo·tor \'mōtər\ *n* : unit that supplies power or motion ~ *vb* : travel by automobile —**mo·tor·ist** \-əst\ *n* —**mo·tor·ize** \'mōtə,rīz\ *vb*

mo·tor·bike *n* : lightweight motorcycle

mo·tor·boat *n* : engine-driven boat

mo·tor·car *n* : automobile

mo·tor·cy·cle *n* : 2-wheeled automotive vehicle —**mo·tor·cy·clist** *n*

mo·tor·truck *n* : automotive truck

mot·tle \\'mät^{ə}l\\ *vb* **-tled; -tling** : mark with spots of different color

mot·to \\'mäto\\ *n, pl* **-toes** : brief guiding rule

mould \\'mōld\\ *var of* MOLD

mound \\'maúnd\\ *n* : pile (as of earth)

¹mount \\'maúnt\\ *n* : mountain

²mount *vb* **1** : increase in amount **2** : get up on **3** : put in position ~ **1** : frame or support **2** : horse to ride —**mount·able** *adj* —**mount·er** *n*

moun·tain \\'maúnt^{ə}n\\ *n* : elevated land higher than a hill —**moun·tain·ous** \\'maúntənəs, -^{ə}nəs\\ *adj* —**moun·tain·top** *n*

moun·tain·eer \\,maúnt^{ə}n'iər\\ *n* : mountain resident or climber —**mountaineer** *vb*

moun·te·bank \\'maúnti,baŋk\\ *n* : impostor

mourn \\'mōrn\\ *vb* : feel or express grief —**mourn·er** *n* —**mourn·ful** \\-fal\\ *adj* —**mourn·ful·ly** *adv* —**mourn·ful·ness** *n* —**mourn·ing** *n*

mouse \\'maús\\ *n, pl* **mice** \\'mīs\\ : small rodent —**mouse·trap** *n or vb*

mous·tache \\'məs,tash, (,)məs'tash\\ *var of* MUSTACHE

mouth \\'maúth\\ *n* : opening through which an animal takes in food ~ \\'maúth\\ *vb* : speak —**mouthed** \\'maúthd, 'maúth\\ *adj* —**mouth·ful** \\-,fúl\\ *n*

mouth·piece *n* **1** : part (as of a musical instrument) held in or to the mouth **2** : spokesman

mou·ton \\'mü,tän\\ *n* : processed sheepskin

move \\'müv\\ *vb* **moved; mov·ing 1** : go or cause to go to another point **2** : change residence **3** : change or cause to change position **4** : take or cause to take action **5** : make a formal request **6** : stir the emotions ~ *n* : act or instance of moving —**mov·able, move·able** \\-əbəl\\ *adj* —**movement** *n* —**mov·er** *n*

mov·ie \\'müvē\\ *n* : projected picture in which persons and objects seem to move

¹mow \\'maú\\ *n* : part of a barn where hay or straw is stored

²mow \\'mō\\ *vb* **mowed; mowed** *or* **mown** \\'mōn\\; **mow·ing** : cut with a machine —**mow·er** *n*

Mr. \\,mistər\\ *n, pl* **Messrs.** \\,mesərz\\ —conventional title for a man

Mrs. \\,misəz, -əs, *esp South* ,mizəz, -əs, *or* (,)miz, *or before first names* (,)mis\\ *n, pl* **Mes·dames** \\mā'däm, -'dam\\ —conventional title for a married woman

Ms. \\(')miz\\ *n* —conventional title for a woman

much \\'məch\\ *adj* **more** \\'mōr\\; **most** \\'mōst\\ : great in quantity, extent, or degree ~ *adv* **more; most** : to a great degree or extent ~ *n* : great quantity, extent, or degree

mu·ci·lage \\'myüs(ə)lij\\ *n* : weak glue —**mu·ci·lag·i·nous** \\,myüsə'lajənəs\\ *adj*

muck \\'mək\\ *n* : manure, dirt, or mud —**mucky** *adj*

mu·cus \\'myükəs\\ *n* : slippery protective secretion of membranes (**mucous membranes**) lining body cavities —**mu·cous** \\-kəs\\ *adj*

mud \\'məd\\ *n* : soft wet earth —**mud·di·ly** \\'məd^{ə}lē\\ *adv* —**mud·di·ness** \\-ēnəs\\ *n* —**mud·dy** *adj or vb*

mud·dle \\'məd^{ə}l\\ *vb* **-dled; -dling 1** : make, be, or act confused **2** : make a mess of —**muddle** *n* —**mud·dle·head·ed** \\,məd^{ə}l'hedəd\\ *adj*

mu·ez·zin \\m(y)ü'ez^{ə}n\\ *n* : Muslim who calls the hour of daily prayer

¹muff \\'məf\\ *n* : tubular hand covering

²muff *vb* : bungle —**muff** *n*

muf·fin \\'məfən\\ *n* : soft biscuit baked in a cup-shaped container

muf·fle \\'məfəl\\ *vb* **-fled; -fling 1** : wrap up **2** : dull the sound of —**muf·fler** \\'məflər\\ *n*

muf·ti \\'məftē\\ *n* : civilian clothes

¹mug \\'məg\\ *n* : drinking cup ~ *vb* **-gg-** : make faces

²mug *vb* **-gg-** : assault with intent to rob —**mug·ger** *n*

mug·gy \\'məgē\\ *adj* **-gi·er; -est** : hot and humid —**mug·gi·ness** *n*

Mu·ham·mad·an \\mō'hamədən, -'häm-; mü-\\ *n* : Muslim —**Mu·ham·mad·an·ism** \\-,izəm\\ *n*

mu·lat·to \\m(y)ü'lató, -lätó, -lät-\\ *n, pl* **-toes** *or* **tos** : 1st-generation offspring of a Negro and a white

mul·ber·ry \\'məl,berē\\ *n* : tree with small edible fruit

mulch \\'məlch\\ *n* : protective ground covering —**mulch** *vb*

mulct \\'məlkt\\ *n or vb* : fine

¹mule \\'myül\\ *n* **1** : offspring of a male ass and a female horse **2** : stubborn person —**mul·ish** \\'myülish\\ *adj* —**mul·ish·ly** *adv* —**mul·ish·ness** *n*

²mule *n* : backless shoe

mull \\'məl\\ *vb* : ponder

mul·let \\'mələt\\ *n, pl* **-let** *or* **lets** : marine food fish

multi- *comb form* **1** : many or multiple **2** : many times over

multiarmed multibarreled

multibillion
multibranched
multibuilding
multicenter
multichambered
multichannel
multicolored
multicounty
multicultural
multidenominational
multidimensional
multidirectional
multidisciplinary
multidivisional
multidwelling
multifaceted
multifamily
multifilament
multifunction
multifunctional
multigrade
multiheaded
multihospital
multihued
multilane
multilevel

multimedia
multimember
multimillion
multimillionaire
multipart
multipartite
multiparty
multiplant
multipolar
multiproblem
multiproduct
multipurpose
multiracial
multiroomed
multisense
multiservice
multisided
multispeed
multistage
multistep
multistory
multisyllabic
multitalented
multitrack
multiunion
multiunit
multiuse
multiwarhead
multiyear

mul·ti·far·i·ous \,məltə'farēəs\ adj : diverse

mul·ti·lat·er·al \,məlti'latərəl, -,tī-, -'latrəl\ adj : having many sides or participants

mul·ti·lin·gual \-'lingwəl\ adj : involving several languages **—mul·ti·lin·gual·ism** \-gwə,lizəm\ n

mul·ti·ple \'məltəpəl\ adj 1 : several or many 2 : complex ~ n : product of one number by another

multiple sclerosis n : brain or spinal disease affecting muscle control

mul·ti·pli·ca·tion \,məltəplə'kāshən\ n 1 : increase 2 : short method of repeated addition

mul·ti·plic·i·ty \,məltə'plisətē\ n, pl -ties : great number or variety

mul·ti·ply \'məltə,plī\ vb -plied; -plying 1 : increase in number 2 : perform multiplication **—mul·ti·pli·er** \-,plī(ə)r\ n

mul·ti·tude \'məltə,t(y)üd\ n : great number **—mul·ti·tu·di·nous** \,məltə't(y)üdnəs, -'nəs\ adj

¹mum \'məm\ adj : silent

²mum n : chrysanthemum

mum·ble \'məmbəl\ vb -bled; -bling : speak indistinctly **—mumble** n **—mum·bler** n **—mum·bly** \-b(ə)lē\ adj

mum·mer \'məmər\ n 1 : actor esp. in

a pantomime 2 : diguised merry-maker **—mum·mery** n

mum·my \'məmē\ n, pl -mies : embalmed body **—mum·mi·fi·ca·tion** \,məmifə'kāshən\ n **—mum·mi·fy** \'məmi,fī\ vb

mumps \'məmps\ n sing or pl : virus disease with swelling esp. of the salivary glands

munch \'mənch\ vb : chew

mun·dane \,mən'dān, 'mən,-\ adj 1 : relating to the world 2 : lacking concern for the ideal or spiritual **—mun·dane·ly** adv

mu·nic·i·pal \myü'nisəpəl\ adj : of or relating to a town or city **—mu·nic·i·pal·i·ty** \myü,nisə'palətē\ n **—mu·nic·i·pal·ly** adv

mu·nif·i·cent \myü'nifəsənt\ adj : generous **—mu·nif·i·cence** \-səns\ n

mu·ni·tions \myü'nishənz\ n pl : armaments

mu·ral \'myürəl\ adj : relating to a wall ~ n : wall painting **—mu·ra·list** n

mur·der \'mərdər\ n : unlawful killing of a person ~ vb : commit a murder **—mur·der·er** n **—mur·der·ess** \-əs\ n **—mur·der·ous** \-əs\ adj **—mur·der·ous·ly** adv

murk \'mərk\ n : darkness **—murk·i·ly** \'mərkəlē\ adv **—murk·i·ness** \-kēnəs\ n **—murky** adj

mur·mur \'mərmər\ n 1 : muttered complaint 2 : low indistinct sound **—murmur** vb **—mur·mur·er** n **—mur·mur·ous** adj

mus·ca·tel \,məskə'tel\ n : sweet wine

mus·cle \'məsəl\ n 1 : body tissue capable of contracting 2 : strength ~ vb -cled; -cling : force one's way **—mus·cled** adj **—mus·cu·lar** \'məskyələr\ adj **—mus·cu·lar·i·ty** \,məskyə'larətē\ n

muscular dystrophy n : disease marked by progressive wasting of muscles

mus·cu·la·ture \'məskyələ,chūr\ n : bodily muscles

¹muse \'myüz\ vb mused; mus·ing : ponder **—mus·ing·ly** adv

²muse n : source of inspiration

mu·se·um \myü'zēəm\ n : institution displaying objects of interest

mush \'məsh\ n 1 : corn meal boiled in water or something of similar consistency 2 : sentimental nonsense **—mushy** adj

mush·room \'məsh,rüm, -,rúm\ n : caplike organ of a fungus ~ vb : grow rapidly

mu·sic \'myüzik\ n : vocal or instrumental sounds —mu·si·cal \-zikəl\ adj or n —mu·si·cal·ly adv

mu·si·cian \myü'zishən\ n : composer or performer of music —mu·si·cian·ly adj —mu·si·cian·ship n

musk \'məsk\ n : strong-smelling substance from an Asiatic deer used in perfume —musk·i·ness \'məskēnəs\ n —musky adj

mus·kel·lunge \'məskə,lənj\ n, pl -lunge : large No. American pike

mus·ket \'məskət\ n : former shoulder firearm —mus·ke·teer \,məskə'tiər\ n

musk·mel·on \'məsk,melən\ n : small edible melon

musk-ox \'məsk,äks\ n : shaggy-coated wild ox of the arctic

musk·rat \'məs,krat\ n, pl -rat or -rats : No. American water rodent

Mus·lim \'məzləm\ n : adherent of the religion founded by Muhammad

mus·lin \'məzlən\ n : cotton fabric

muss \'məs\ n : untidy state ~ vb : disarrange —muss·i·ly \'məsəlē\ adv —muss·i·ness \-ēnəs\ n —mussy adj

mus·sel \'məsəl\ n : edible mollusk

must \'(')məst\ vb —used as an auxiliary esp. to express a command, obligation, or necessity ~ \'məst\ n : something necessary

mus·tache \'məs,tash, (,)məs'-\ n : hair of the human upper lip

mus·tang \'məs,tan\ n : wild horse of Western America

mus·tard \'məstərd\ n : pungent yellow seasoning

mus·ter \'məstər\ vb 1 : assemble 2 : rouse ~ n : assembled group

musty \'məstē\ adj mus·ti·er; -est : stale —must·i·ly adv —must·i·ness n

mu·ta·ble \'myütəbəl\ adj : changeable —mu·ta·bil·i·ty \,myütə'bilətē\ n

mu·tant \'myüt³nt\ adj : relating to or produced by mutation —mutant n

mu·tate \'myü,tāt\ vb -tat·ed; -tat·ing : undergo mutation —mu·ta·tive \'myü,tātiv, myütāt-\ adj

mu·ta·tion \myü'tāshən\ n : change in a hereditary character —mu·ta·tion·al adj

mute \'myüt\ adj mut·er; mut·est 1 : unable to speak 2 : silent ~ n 1 : one who is speechless 2 : muffling device ~ vb mut·ed; mut·ing : muffle —mute·ly adv —mute·ness n

mu·ti·late \'myüt³l,āt\ vb -lat·ed; -lat·ing : damage seriously (as by cutting off or altering an essential part) —mu·ti·la·tion \,myüt³l'āshən\ n —mu·ti·la·tor \'myüt³l,ātər\ n

mu·ti·ny \'myüt(ə)nē\ n, pl -nies : rebellion —mu·ti·neer \,myüt³n'iər\ n —mu·ti·nous \'myüt³nəs\ adj —mu·ti·nous·ly adv

mutt \'mət\ n : mongrel

mut·ter \'mətər\ vb 1 : speak indistinctly or softly 2 : grumble —mutter n

mut·ton \'mət³n\ n : flesh of a mature sheep —mut·tony adj

mu·tu·al \'myücha(wə)l\ adj 1 : given or felt by one another in equal amount 2 : common —mu·tu·al·ly adv

muz·zle \'məzəl\ n 1 : nose and jaws of an animal 2 : muzzle covering to immobilize an animal's jaws 3 : discharge end of a gun ~ vb -zled; -zling : restrain with or as if with a muzzle

my \(')mī, mə\ adj 1 : relating to me or myself 2 —used interjectionally esp. to express surprise

my·na, my·nah \'mīnə\ n : Asian starling

my·o·pia \mī'ōpēə\ n : nearsightedness —my·o·pic \-'ōpik, -'äpik\ adj —my·o·pi·cal·ly \-(ə)lē\ adv

myr·i·ad \'mirēəd\ n : indefinitely large number —myriad adj

myrrh \'mər\ n : aromatic plant gum

myr·tle \'mərt³l\ n : shiny evergreen

my·self \mī'self, mə-\ pron : I, me —used reflexively or for emphasis

mys·tery \'mist(ə)rē\ n, pl -ter·ies 1 : religious truth 2 : something not understood 3 : puzzling or secret quality or state —mys·te·ri·ous \mis'tirēəs\ adj —mys·te·ri·ous·ly adv —mys·te·ri·ous·ness n

mys·tic \'mistik\ adj : mystical or mysterious ~ n : one who has mystical experiences —mys·ti·cism \-tə,sizəm\ n

mys·ti·cal \'mistikəl\ adj 1 : spiritual 2 : relating to direct communion with God —mys·ti·cal·ly \-k(ə)lē\ adv

mys·ti·fy \'mistə,fī\ vb -fied; -fy·ing : perplex —mys·ti·fi·ca·tion \,mistəfə'kāshən\ n

mys·tique \mis'tēk\ n : beliefs and attitudes associated with something

myth \'mith\ n 1 : legendary narrative explaining a belief or phenomenon 2 : imaginary person or thing —myth·i·cal \-ikəl\ adj

my·thol·o·gy \mith'äləjē\ n, pl -gies : body of myths —myth·o·log·i·cal \,mithə'läjikəl\ adj —my·thol·o·gist \mith'äləjəst\ n

N

n \'en\ *n, pl* **n's** *or* **ns** \'enz\ : 14th letter of the alphabet

nab \'nab\ *vb* **-bb-** : seize or arrest

na·dir \'nā,diər, 'nādər\ *n* : lowest point

¹nag \'nag\ *n* : old or decrepit horse

²nag *vb* **-gg-** **1** : scold or urge continually **2** : be persistently annoying ~ *n* : one who nags habitually

na·iad \'nāad, 'nī--,ad\ *n, pl* **-iads** *or* **-ia·des** \-ə,dēz\ : mythological water nymph

nail \'nāl\ *n* **1** : horny sheath at the end of each finger and toe **2** : pointed metal fastener ~ *vb* : fasten with a nail —**nail·er** *n*

na·ive, na·ïve \nä'ēv\ *adj* **-iv·er; -est 1** : innocent and unsophisticated **2** : easily deceived —**na·ive·ly** *adv* —**na·ive·ness** *n*

na·ive·té, na·ïve·té \,nä,ēv(ə)'tā, nä-'ēvə,-\ *n* : quality or state of being naive

na·ked \'nākəd, 'nekəd\ *adj* **1** : having no clothes on **2** : uncovered **3** : plain or obvious **4** : unaided —**na·ked·ly** *adv* —**na·ked·ness** *n*

nam·by-pam·by \,nambē'pambē\ *adj* : weak or indecisive

name \'nām\ *n* **1** : word by which a person or thing is known **2** : disparaging word for someone **3** : distinguished reputation ~ *vb* **named; nam·ing 1** : give a name to **2** : mention or identify by name **3** : nominate or appoint ~ *adj* **1** : relating to a name **2** : prominent —**name·able** *adj* —**name·less** *adj* —**name·less·ly** *adv*

name·ly \'nāmlē\ *adv* : that is to say

name·sake \-,sāk\ *n* : one named after another

¹nap \'nap\ *vb* **-pp- 1** : sleep briefly **2** : be off guard ~ *n* : short sleep

²nap *n* : soft downy surface —**nap·less** *adj* —**napped** \'napt\ *adj*

na·palm \'nä,pä(l)m\ *n* : gasoline in the form of a jelly

nape \'nāp, 'nap\ *n* : back of the neck

naph·tha \'nafthə, 'nap-\ *n* : flammable solvent

nap·kin \'napkən\ *n* : small cloth for use at the table

nar·cis·sism \'närsə,sizəm\ *n* : self-love —**nar·cis·sist** \-səst\ *n or adj* —**nar·cis·sis·tic** \,närsə'sistik\ *adj*

nar·cis·sus \när'sisəs\ *n, pl* **-cis·sus** *or* **-cis·sus·es** *or* **-cis·si** \-'sis,ī, -,ē\

: plant with flowers usu. borne separately

nar·cot·ic \när'kätik\ *n* : painkilling addictive drug —**narcotic** *adj*

nar·rate \'nar,āt\ *vb* **nar·rat·ed; nar·rat·ing** : tell (a story) —**nar·ra·tion** \na'rāshən\ *n* —**nar·ra·tive** \'närə-tiv\ *n or adj* —**nar·ra·tor** \'nar,ātər\ *n*

nar·row \'narō\ *adj* **1** : of less than standard width **2** : limited **3** : not liberal **4** : barely successful ~ *vb* : make narrow —**nar·row·ly** *adv* —**nar·row·ness** *n*

nar·row-mind·ed \,narō'mīndəd\ *adj* : shallow, provincial, or bigoted

nar·rows \'narōz\ *n pl* : narrow passage

nar·whal \'när,hwäl, 'närwəl\ *n* : sea mammal with a tusk

na·sal \'nāzəl\ *adj* : relating to or uttered through the nose —**na·sal·ly** *adv*

nas·tur·tium \nə'stərshəm, na-\ *n* : herb with showy flowers

nas·ty \'nastē\ *adj* **nas·ti·er; -est 1** : filthy **2** : indecent **3** : malicious or spiteful —**nas·ti·ly** \'nastəlē\ *adv* —**nas·ti·ness** \-tēnəs\ *n*

na·tal \'nāt⁹l\ *adj* : relating to birth

na·tion \'nāshən\ *n* **1** : people of similar characteristics **2** : community with its own territory and government —**na·tion·al** \'nash(ə)nəl\ *adj or n* —**na·tion·al·ly** *adv* —**na·tion·hood** *n*

na·tion·al·ism \'nash(ə)nəl,izəm\ *n* : devotion to national interests, unity, and independence —**na·tion·al·ist** \-əst\ *n or adj* —**na·tion·al·is·tic** \,nash(ə)nəl'istik\ *adj*

na·tion·al·i·ty \,nash(ə)nə'lalətē\ *n, pl* **-ties 1** : national character **2** : membership in a nation **3** : political independence **4** : ethnic group

na·tion·al·ize \'nash(ə)nəl,īz\ *vb* **-ized; -iz·ing 1** : make national **2** : place under government control —**na·tion·al·iza·tion** \,nash(ə)nələ'zāshən\ *n*

na·tive \'nātiv\ *adj* **1** : belonging to a person at or by way of birth **2** : born or produced in a particular place ~ *n* : one who belongs to a country by birth

Na·tiv·i·ty \nə'tivətē, nā-\ *n, pl* **-ties 1** : birth of Christ **2** : Christmas **3** *not cap* : birth

nat·ti·ly \'natēlē\ *adj* **-ti·er; -est** : smartly dressed **—nat·ti·ly** \'nat°lē\ *adv* **—nat·ti·ness** \-ēnəs\ *n*

nat·u·ral \'nach(ə)rəl\ *adj* **1** : relating to or determined by nature **2** : not artificial **3** : simple and sincere **4** : lifelike **—nat·u·ral·ness** *n*

nat·u·ral·ism \'nach(ə)rə,lizəm\ *n* : realism in art and literature **—nat·u·ral·is·tic** \,nach(ə)rə'listik\ *adj*

nat·u·ral·ist \-ləst\ *n* **1** : one who practices naturalism **2** : student of animals or plants

nat·u·ral·ize \-,līz\ *vb* **-ized; -iz·ing 1** : become or cause to become established **2** : confer citizenship on **—nat·u·ral·iza·tion** \,nach(ə)rələ-'zāshən\ *n*

nat·u·ral·ly \'nach(ə)rəlē, 'nachərlē\ *adv* **1** : in a natural way **2** : as might be expected

na·ture \'nāchər\ *n* **1** : basic quality of something **2** : kind **3** : disposition **4** : physical universe **5** : natural environment **—natured** *adj*

naught \'nòt, 'nät\ *n* **1** : nothing **2** : zero

naugh·ty \'nòtē, 'nät-\ *adj* **-ti·er; -est 1** : disobedient or misbehaving **2** : improper **—naught·i·ly** \'nòt°lē, 'nät-\ *adv* **—naught·i·ness** \-ēnəs\ *n*

nau·sea \'nòzēə, -shə\ *n* **1** : sickness of the stomach with a desire to vomit **2** : extreme disgust **—nau·seous** \-shəs, -zēəs\ *adj*

nau·se·ate \'nòz(h)ē,āt, -(sh)ē-\ *vb* **-at·ed; -at·ing** : affect or become affected with nausea **—nau·se·at·ing·ly** \-,ātiŋlē\ *adv*

nau·ti·cal \'nòtikəl\ *adj* : relating to ships and sailing **—nau·ti·cal·ly** \-k(ə)lē\ *adv*

nau·ti·lus \'nòt°ləs\ *n, pl* **-lus·es** *or* **-li** \-°l,ī, -,ē\ : sea mollusk

na·val \'nāvəl\ *adj* : relating to a navy

nave \'nāv\ *n* : central part of a church

na·vel \'nāvəl\ *n* : depression in the abdomen

nav·i·ga·ble \'navigəbəl\ *adj* : capable of being navigated **—nav·i·ga·bil·i·ty** \,navigə'bilətē\ *n* **—nav·i·ga·bly** \'navigəblē\ *adv*

nav·i·gate \'navə,gāt\ *vb* **-gat·ed; -gat·ing 1** : sail on or through **2** : direct the course of **—nav·i·ga·tion** \,navə'gāshən\ *n* **—nav·i·ga·tor** \'navə,gātər\ *n*

na·vy \'nāvē\ *n, pl* **-vies 1** : fleet **2** : nation's organization for sea warfare

nay \'nā\ *adv* : no—used in oral voting ~ *n* : negative vote

Na·zi \'nätsē, 'nat-\ *n* : member of a German fascist party from 1933 to 1945 **—Nazi** *adj* **—Na·zism** \'nät-,sizəm, 'nat-\, **Na·zi·ism** \-sē,izəm\ *n*

near \'niər\ *adv* : at or close to ~ *prep* : close to ~ *adj* **1** : not far away **2** : very much like ~ *vb* : approach **—near·ly** *adv* **—near·ness** *n*

near·by \niər'bī, 'niər,bī\ *adv or adj* : near

near·sight·ed \'niər'sītəd\ *adj* : seeing well at short distances only **—near·sight·ed·ly** *adv* **—near·sight·ed·ness** *n*

neat \'nēt\ *adj* **1** : not diluted **2** : tastefully simple **3** : orderly and clean **—neat** *adv* **—neat·ly** *adv* **—neat·ness** *n*

neb·u·la \'nebyələ\ *n, pl* **-lae** \-,lē, -,lī\ : large cloud of interstellar gas **—neb·u·lar** \-lər\ *adj*

neb·u·lous \-ləs\ *adj* : indistinct

nec·es·sary \'nesə,serē\ *n, pl* **-sar·ies** : indispensable item ~ *adj* **1** : inevitable **2** : compulsory **3** : positively needed **—nec·es·sar·i·ly** \,nesə-'serəlē\ *adv*

ne·ces·si·tate \ni'sesə,tāt\ *vb* **-tat·ed; -tat·ing** : make necessary

ne·ces·si·ty \ni'sesətē\ *n, pl* **-ties 1** : very great need **2** : something that is necessary **3** : poverty **4** : circumstances that force a course of action or that cannot be changed

neck \'nek\ *n* **1** : body part connecting the head and trunk **2** : part of a garment at the neck **3** : narrow part ~ *vb* : kiss and caress **—necked** \'nekt\ *adj*

neck·er·chief \'nekərchəf, -,chēf\ *n, pl* **-chiefs** \-chəfs, -,chēfs\ : cloth worn tied about the neck

neck·lace \'nekləs\ *n* : ornamental chain for the neck

neck·tie *n* : ornamental cloth tied under a collar

ne·crol·o·gy \nə'kräləjē\ *n, pl* **-gies** : obituary list

nec·ro·man·cy \'nekrə,mansē\ *n* : art of conjuring **—nec·ro·man·cer** \-sər\ *n*

ne·cro·sis \nə'krōsəs, ne-\ *n, pl* **-cro·ses** \-,sēz\ : death of body tissue **—ne·crot·ic** \-'krätik\ *adj*

nec·tar \'nektər\ *n* : sweet plant secretion

nec·tar·ine \,nektə'rēn\ *n* : smooth-skinned peach

née, nee \'nā\ *adj*—used to identify a married woman by maiden name

need \'nēd\ *n* **1** : obligation **2** : lack of something or what is lacking **3** : poverty ~ *vb* **1** : be in want **2** : have

cause for **3** : be under obligation —
need·ful \-fəl\ *adj* —**need·less** *adj*
—**need·less·ly** *adv* —**needy** *adj*

nee·dle \'nēd'l\ *n* **1** : pointed sewing
implement or something like it **2**
: movable bar in a compass **3** : hollow instrument for injecting or withdrawing material — *vb* -**dled**; -**dling**
: incite to action by repeated gibes
—**nee·dle·work** \-,wərk\ *n*

nee·dle·point \'nēd'l,pȯint\ *n* **1** : lace
work **2** : embroidery on canvas —
needlepoint *adj*

ne·far·i·ous \ni'fareəs\ *adj* : very
wicked —**ne·far·i·ous·ly** *adv*

ne·gate \ni'gāt\ *vb* -**gat·ed**; -**gat·ing 1**
: deny **2** : nullify —**ne·ga·tion**
\-'gāshən\ *n*

neg·a·tive \'negətiv\ *adj* **1** : marked by
denial or refusal **2** : showing a lack
of something suspected or desirable
3 : less than zero **4** : having more
electrons than protons **5** : having
light and shadow images reversed —
n **1** : negative word or vote **2** : negative photographic image —**neg·a·**
tive·ly *adv*

ne·glect \ni'glekt\ *vb* **1** : disregard **2**
: leave unattended to ~ *n* **1** : act of
neglecting **2** : condition of being ne-
glected —**ne·glect·ful** *adj*

neg·li·gee \,negla'zhā\ *n* : woman's
loose robe

neg·li·gent \'neglijənt\ *adj* : marked by
neglect —**neg·li·gence** \-jəns\ *n* —
neg·li·gent·ly *adv*

neg·li·gi·ble \'neglijəbəl\ *adj* : insignificant

ne·go·ti·ate \ni'gōshē,āt\ *vb* -**at·ed**; -**at·**
ing 1 : confer with another to settle
a matter **2** : obtain cash for **3** : get
through successfully —**ne·go·tia·ble**
\-sh(ē)əbəl\ *adj* —**ne·go·ti·a·tion**
\-,gōsh(ē)'āshən\ *n* —**ne·go·ti·a·tor**
\-'gōshē,ātər\ *n*

Ne·gro \'nēgrō\ *n, pl* -**groes** : member
of the black race —**Negro** *adj* —**Ne·**
groid \'nē,grȯid\ *n or adj, often not*
cap

neigh \'nā\ *n* : cry of a horse —**neigh**
vb

neigh·bor \'nābər\ *n* **1** : one living
nearby **2** : fellowman ~ *vb* : be near
or next to —**neigh·bor·hood** \-,hud\
n —**neigh·bor·li·ness** *n* —**neigh·bor·**
ly *adj*

nei·ther \'nēthər, 'nī-\ *pron or adj*
: not the one or the other ~ *conj* **1**
: not either **2** : nor

nem·e·sis \'neməsəs\ *n, pl* -**e·ses**
\-ə,sēz\ **1** : old and usu. frustrating
rival **2** : retaliation

ne·ol·o·gism \nē'älə,jizəm\ *n* : new
word

ne·on \'nē,än\ *n* : gaseous colorless
chemical element —**neon** *adj*

neo·phyte \'nēə,fīt\ *n* : beginner

neph·ew \'nefyü, *chiefly Brit* 'nev-\ *n*
: a son of one's brother, sister,
brother-in-law, or sister-in-law

nep·o·tism \'nepə,tizəm\ *n* : favoritism
shown in hiring a relative

nerve \'nərv\ *n* **1** : strand of body tissue that connects the brain with
other parts of the body **2** : self-control **3** : daring **4** *pl* : nervousness —
nerved \'nərvd\ *adj* —**nerve·less** *adj*

ner·vous \'nərvəs\ *adj* **1** : relating to
or made up of nerves **2** : easily excited **3** : fearful —**ner·vous·ly** *adv* —
ner·vous·ness *n*

nervy \'nərvē\ *adj* **nerv·i·er**; -**est** : insolent or presumptuous

-ness \nəs\ *n suffix* : condition or quality

nest \'nest\ *n* **1** : shelter prepared by
a bird for its eggs **2** : place where
eggs (as of insects or fish) are laid
and hatched **3** : snug retreat **4** : set
of objects fitting one inside or under
another ~ *vb* : build or occupy a nest

nes·tle \'nesəl\ *vb* -**tled**; -**tling** : settle
snugly (as in a nest)

¹net \'net\ *n* : fabric with spaces between strands or something made of
this ~ *vb* -**tt-** : cover with or catch
in a net

²net *adj* : remaining after deductions
~ *vb* -**tt-** : have as profit

neth·er \'nethər\ *adj* : situated below

net·tle \'net'l\ *n* : coarse herb with
stinging hairs ~ *vb* -**tled**; -**tling** : provoke or vex —**net·tle·some** *adj*

net·work *n* : system of crossing or connected elements

neu·ral \'n(y)ůrəl\ *adj* : relating to a
nerve

neu·ral·gia \n(y)ů'raljə\ *n* : pain along
a nerve —**neu·ral·gic** \-jik\ *adj*

neu·ri·tis \n(y)ů'rītəs\ *n, pl* -**ri·ti·des**
\-'rītə,dēz\ *or* -**ri·tis·es** : inflammation of a nerve —**neu·rit·ic** \-'ritik\
adj or n

neu·rol·o·gy \n(y)ů'räləjē\ *n* : study of
the nervous system —**neu·ro·log·i·**
cal \,n(y)ůrə'läjikəl\, **neu·ro·log·ic**
\-ik\ *adj* —**neu·ro·log·i·cal·ly** *adv* —
neu·rol·o·gist \n(y)ů'rälajəst\ *n*

neu·ro·sis \n(y)ů'rōsəs\ *n, pl* -**ro·ses**
\-,sēz\ : nervous disorder

neu·rot·ic \n(y)ů'rätik\ *adj* : relating to
neurosis ~ *n* : unstable person —
neu·rot·i·cal·ly \-ik(ə)lē\ *adv*

neu·ter \\'n(y)ütǝr\\ *adj* : neither masculine nor feminine

neu·tral \\'n(y)ütrǝl\\ *adj* 1 : not favoring either side 2 : being neither one thing nor the other 3 : not decided in color 4 : not electrically charged ~ *n* 1 : one that is neutral 2 : position of gears that are not engaged —**neu·tral·iza·tion** \\,n(y)ütrǝlǝ'zāshǝn\\ *n* —**neu·tral·ize** \\'n(y)ütrǝ,līz\\ *vb*

neu·tral·i·ty \\n(y)ü'tralǝtē\\ *n* : state of being neutral

neu·tron \\'n(y)ü,trän\\ *n* : uncharged atomic particle

nev·er \\'nevǝr\\ *adv* 1 : not ever 2 : not in any degree, way, or condition

nev·er·more *adv* : never again

nev·er·the·less *adv* : in spite of that

new \\'n(y)ü\\ *adj* 1 : not old or familiar 2 : different from the former 3 : recently discovered or learned 4 : not accustomed 5 : refreshed or regenerated 6 : being such for the first time ~ *adv* : newly —**new·ish** *adj* —**new·ness** *n*

new·born *adj* 1 : recently born 2 : born anew ~ *n, pl* -**born** *or* -**borns** : newborn individual

new·ly \\'n(y)ülē\\ *adv* : recently

news \\'n(y)üz\\ *n* : report of recent events —**news·let·ter** *n* —**news·mag·a·zine** *n* —**news·man** \\-mǝn, -,man\\ *n* —**news·pa·per** *n* —**news·pa·per·man** \\-,man\\ *n* —**news·stand** *n* —**news·wor·thy** *adj*

news·cast \\-,kast\\ *n* : broadcast of news —**news·cast·er** \\-,kastǝr\\ *n*

news·print *n* : cheap paper made from wood pulp

newsy \\'n(y)üzē\\ *adj* **news·i·er; -est** : filled with news

newt \\'n(y)üt\\ *n* : small salamander

New Year *n* : New Year's Day

New Year's Day *n* : January 1 observed as a legal holiday

next \\'nekst\\ *adj* : immediately preceding or following ~ *adv* 1 : in the time or place nearest 2 : at the first time yet to come ~ *prep* : nearest to

nex·us \\'neksǝs\\ *n, pl* -**us·es** \\-sǝsǝz\\ *or* -**us** \\-sǝs, -,süs\\ : connection or bond

nib \\'nib\\ *n* : pen point

nib·ble \\'nibǝl\\ *vb* -**bled; -bling** : bite gently or bit by bit ~ *n* : small bite

nice \\'nīs\\ *adj* **nic·er; nic·est** 1 : fastidious 2 : very precise or delicate 3 : pleasing 4 : respectable —**nice·ly** *adv* —**nice·ness** *n*

nice·ty \\'nīsǝtē\\ *n, pl* -**ties** 1 : dainty or elegant thing 2 : fine detail 3 : exactness

niche \\'nich\\ *n* 1 : recess in a wall 2 : fitting place, work, or use

nick \\'nik\\ *n* 1 : small broken area or chip 2 : critical moment ~ *vb* : make a nick in

nick·el \\'nikǝl\\ *n* 1 : hard silver-white metallic chemical element used in alloys 2 : U.S. 5-cent piece ~ *vb* -**eled** *or* -**elled; -el·ing** *or* -**el·ling** : plate with nickel

nick·name \\'nik,nām\\ *n* : informal substitute name —**nickname** *vb*

nic·o·tine \\'nikǝ,tēn\\ *n* : poisonous substance in tobacco

niece \\'nēs\\ *n* : a daughter of one's brother, sister, brother-in-law, or sister-in-law

nig·gard·ly \\'nigǝrdlē\\ *adj* : stingy —**nig·gard** *n* —**nig·gard·li·ness** *n*

nig·gling \\'nig(ǝ)liŋ\\ *adj* : petty and annoying

nigh \\'nī\\ *adv or adj or prep* : near

night \\'nīt\\ *n* 1 : period between dusk and dawn 2 : the coming of night —**night** *adj* —**night·ly** *adj or adv* —**night·time** *n*

night·clothes *n pl* : garments worn in bed

night·club \\-,klǝb\\ *n* : place for drinking and entertainment open at night

night crawler *n* : earthworm

night·fall *n* : the coming of night

night·gown *n* : gown worn for sleeping

night·in·gale \\'nīt·ǝn,gāl, -iŋ-\\ *n* : Old World thush that sings at night

night·mare \\'nīt,mar\\ *n* : frightening dream —**nightmare** *adj* —**night·mar·ish** \\-,marish\\ *adj*

night·shade \\'nīt,shād\\ *n* : group of plants with berries of which some forms are used as food while others are poisonous

nil \\'nil\\ *n* : nothing

nim·ble \\'nimbǝl\\ *adj* -**bler; -blest** 1 : agile 2 : clever —**nim·ble·ness** *n* —**nim·bly** \\-blē\\ *adv*

nine \\'nīn\\ *n* 1 : one more than 8 2 : 9th in a set or series —**nine** *adj or pron* —**ninth** \\'ninth\\ *adj or adv or n*

nine·pins *n* : bowling game using 9 pins

nine·teen \\nīn'tēn\\ *n* : one more than 18 —**nineteen** *adj or pron* —**nine·teenth** \\-'tēnth\\ *adj or n*

nine·ty \\'nīntē\\ *n, pl* -**ties** : 9 times 10 —**nine·ti·eth** \\-ēǝth\\ *adj or n* —**ninety** *adj or pron*

nin·ny \\'ninē\\ *n, pl* **ninnies** : fool

¹**nip** \\'nip\\ *vb* -**pp-** 1 : catch hold of and squeeze tightly 2 : pinch or bite off 3 : destroy the growth or fulfill-

ment of ~ *n* 1 : biting cold 2 : tang 3
: pinch or bite

²**nip** *n* : small quantity of liquor ~ *vb*
-pp- : take liquor in nips

nip·per \'nipər\ *n* 1 : one that nips 2 *pl*
: pincers 3 : large claw of a crustacean 4 : small boy

nip·ple \'nipəl\ *n* : tip of the breast or
something resembling it

nip·py \'nipē\ *adj* **-pi·er; -est** 1 : pungent 2 : chilly

nir·va·na \nir'vänə\ *n* : state of blissful
oblivion

nit \'nit\ *n* : parasitic insect egg

ni·ter \'nītər\ *n* : nitrate of potassium
or sodium used in gunpowder or for
fertilizer or in curing meat

ni·trate \'nī,trāt, -trət\ *n* : chemical
salt used esp. in curing meat

ni·tric \'nītrik\ *adj* : relating to nitrogen

ni·trite \-,trīt\ *n* : chemical salt used in
curing meat

ni·tro \-trō\ *n, pl* **-tros** : nitroglycerin

ni·tro·gen \-trəjən\ *n* : tasteless odorless gaseous chemical element —**ni·trog·e·nous** \nī'träjənəs\ *adj*

ni·tro·glyc·er·in, **ni·tro·glyc·er·ine**
\,nītrə'glis(ə)rən\ *n* : heavy oily explosive liquid

nit·wit \'nit,wit\ *n* : stupid person

no \(')nō\ *adv* 1 —used to express the
negative 2 : in no respect or degree
3 : not so 4 —used as an interjection
of surprise or doubt ~ *adj* 1 : not
any 2 : not a ~ *n, pl* **noes** *or* **nos**
\'nōz\ 1 : refusal 2 : negative vote

no·bil·i·ty \nō'bilətē\ *n* 1 : quality of
being noble 2 : noble rank 3 : class
of people of noble rank

no·ble \'nōbəl\ *adj* **-bler; -blest** 1 : illustrious 2 : aristocratic 3 : stately 4
: of outstanding character ~ *n* : nobleman —**no·ble·ness** *n* —**no·bly** *adv*

no·ble·man \-mən\ *n* : member of the
nobility

no·body \'nō,bädē, -bədē\ *pron* : no
person ~ *n, pl* **-bod·ies** : person of
no influence or social standing

noc·tur·nal \näk'tərnᵊl\ *adj* : relating
to, occurring at, or active at night

noc·turne \'näk,tərn\ *n* : dreamy pensive instrumental composition

nod \'näd\ *vb* **-dd-** 1 : bend the head
downward or forward (as in bowing
or going to sleep or as a sign of assent) 2 : move up and down 3 : show
by a nod of the head —**nod** *n*

node \'nōd\ *n* : stem part from which
a leaf arises —**nod·al** \-ᵊl\ *adj*

nod·ule \'näjül\ *n* : small lump or
swelling —**nod·u·lar** \'näjələr\ *adj*

no·el \nō'el\ *n* 1 : Christmas carol 2
cap : Christmas season

noes *pl of* NO

nog·gin \'nägən\ *n* 1 : small mug 2
: person's head

no·how \'nō,haů\ *adv* : in no manner

noise \'nóiz\ *n* 1 : loud or unpleasant
sound ~ *vb* **noised; nois·ing** : spread
by rumor —**noise·mak·er** *n* —**nois·i·ly** \'nóizəlē\ *adv* —**nois·i·ness**
\-zēnəs\ *n* —**noisy** \'nóizē\ *adj*

noi·some \'nóisəm\ *adj* : harmful or
offensive

no·mad \'nō,mad\ *n* : one who has no
permanent home —**nomad** *adj* —**no·mad·ic** \nō'madik\ *adj*

no·men·cla·ture \'nōmən,klāchər\ *n*
: system of names

nom·i·nal \'nämənᵊl\ *adj* 1 : being
something in name only 2 : very
small or negligible —**nom·i·nal·ly**
adv

nom·i·nate \'nämə,nāt\ *vb* **-nat·ed;
-nat·ing** : propose or choose as a candidate —**nom·i·na·tion** \,nämə'nāshən\ *n*

nom·i·na·tive \'näm(ə)nətiv\ *adj* : relating to or being a grammatical case
marking typically the subject of a
verb —**nominative** *n*

nom·i·nee \,nämə'nē\ *n* : person nominated

non- \(')nän, ,nän\ *prefix* : not, reverse
of, or absence of

nonabrasive	non-Christian
nonabsorbent	nonchurchgoer
nonacademic	noncitizen
nonaccredited	nonclassical
nonacid	nonclassified
nonaddictive	noncombat
nonadherence	noncombatant
nonadhesive	noncombustible
nonadjacent	noncommercial
nonadjustable	noncommuni-
nonaffiliated	cable
nonaggression	non-Communist
nonalcoholic	noncompliance
nonaligned	nonconclusive
nonappearance	nonconflicting
nonautomatic	nonconforming
nonbeliever	nonconsecutive
nonbinding	nonconstructive
nonbreakable	nonconsumable
noncancerous	noncontagious
noncandidate	noncontributing
noncarbonated	noncontrollable
non-Catholic	noncontroversial
nonchargeable	noncorrosive

noncriminal
noncritical
noncumulative
noncurrent
nondeductible
nondefense
nondeferrable
nondegradable
nondelivery
nondemocratic
nondenominational
nondestructive
nondiscrimination
nondiscriminatory
noneducational
nonelastic
nonelected
nonelective
nonelectric
nonelectronic
nonemotional
nonenforceable
nonenforcement
nonessential
nonexchangeable
nonexistence
nonexistent
nonexplosive
nonfat
nonfatal
nonfattening
nonfictional
nonflammable
nonflowering
nonfunctional
nongovernmental
nongraded
nonhazardous
nonhereditary
nonindustrial
nonindustrialized
noninfectious
noninflationary
nonintegrated
nonintellectual
noninterference
nonintoxicating
noninvolvement
non-Jewish
nonlegal
nonlethal
nonliterary
nonliving
nonmagnetic
nonmalignant
nonmedical
nonmember

nonmetal
nonmetallic
nonmilitary
nonmusical
nonnarcotic
nonnative
nonnegotiable
nonobjective
nonobservance
nonorthodox
nonparallel
nonparticipant
nonparticipating
nonpaying
nonpayment
nonperformance
nonperishable
nonpermanent
nonphysical
nonpoisonous
nonpolitical
nonpolluting
nonporous
nonpregnant
nonproductive
nonprofessional
nonprofit
nonracial
nonradioactive
nonrated
nonrealistic
nonrecoverable
nonrecurring
nonrefillable
nonrefundable
nonregistered
nonreligious
nonrenewable
nonrepresentative
nonresident
nonresponsive
nonrestricted
nonreversible
nonsalable
nonscientific
nonsectarian
nonsegregated
non-self-governing
nonsexist
nonsexual
nonsignificant
nonskier
nonsmoker
nonsmoking
nonspeaking
nonspecialist
nonspecific
nonstaining
nonstandard
nonstrategic

nonstriker
nonstriking
nonstudent
nonsubscriber
nonsugar
nonsurgical
nonswimmer
nontaxable
nonteaching
nontechnical
nontoxic

nontraditional
nontransferable
nontropical
nontypical
nonunion
nonuser
nonvenomous
nonverbal
nonvoter
nonwhite
nonworker

non-age \'nänij, 'nōnij\ *n* : period of youth and esp. legal minority

nonce \'näns\ *n* : present occasion ~ *adj* : occurring, used, or made only once

non-cha-lant \,nänshə'länt\ *adj* : showing indifference —**non-chalance** \-'läns\ *n* —**non-cha-lant-ly** *adv*

non-com-mis-sioned officer \,nänkə,mishənd-\ *n* : subordinate officer in the armed forces appointed from enlisted personnel

non-com-mit-tal \,nänkə'mit³l\ *adj* : indicating neither consent nor dissent

non-con-duc-tor \,nän-\ *n* : substance that is a very poor conductor

non-con-form-ist \,nän-\ *n* : one who does not conform to an established belief or mode of behavior —**noncon-for-mi-ty** *n*

non-de-script \'nändi'skript\ *adj* : not easily described

none \'nən\ *pron* : not any ~ *adv* : not at all

non-en-ti-ty \nä'nentatē\ *n* : one of no consequence

none-the-less \,nənthə'les\ *adv* : nevertheless

non-pa-reil \,nänpə'rel\ *adj* : having no equal ~ *n* 1 : one who has no equal 2 : chocolate candy disk

non-par-ti-san \'nän-\ *adj* : not influenced by political party bias

non-per-son \'nän-\ *n* : person without ordinary rights or respect

non-plus \'nän'pləs\ *vb* -**ss**- : perplex

non-pro-lif-er-a-tion \,nän-\ *adj* : aimed at ending increased use of nuclear arms

non-sched-uled \'nän-\ *adj* : licensed to carry by air without a regular schedule

non-sense \'nän,sens, -səns\ *n* : foolish or meaningless words or actions —**non-sen-si-cal** \nän'sensikəl\ *adj* —**non-sen-si-cal-ly** \-k(ə)lē\ *adv*

non-sup-port \,nän-\ *n* : failure in a

legal obligation to provide for someone's needs

non·vi·o·lence \'nän-\ n : avoidance of violence esp. in political demonstrations —**non·vi·o·lent** adj

noo·dle \'nüd³l\ n : ribbon-shaped dried food paste

nook \'núk\ n 1 : inside corner 2 : private place

noon \'nün\ n : middle of the day —**noon** adj

noon·day \-,dā\ n : noon

noon·time n : noon

noose \'nüs\ n : rope loop that slips down tight

nor \nər, (')nòr\ conj —used esp. after neither to introduce and negate the 2d member of a series

norm \'nòrm\ n : standard usu. derived from an average

nor·mal \'nòrməl\ adj : average, regular, or standard —**nor·mal·cy** \-sē\ n —**nor·mal·i·ty** \nòr'malətē\ n —**nor·mal·i·za·tion** \,nòrmələ'zāshən\ n —**nor·mal·ize** \'nòrmə,līz\ vb —**nor·mal·ly** adv

north \'nòrth\ adv : to or toward the north ~ adj : situated toward, at, or coming from the north ~ n 1 : direction to the left of one facing east 2 cap : regions to the north —**north·er·ly** \'nòrthərlē\ adv or adj —**north·ern** \-ərn\ adj —**North·ern·er** n —**north·ern·most** \-,mōst\ adj —**north·ward** \-wərd\ adv or adj —**north·wards** \-wərdz\ adv

north·east \nòrth'ēst\ n 1 : direction between north and east 2 cap : regions to the northeast —**northeast** adj or adv —**north·east·er·ly** \-'ē-,ərlē\ adv or adj —**north·east·ern** \-ərn\ adj

northern lights n pl : aurora borealis

north pole n : northernmost point of the earth

north·west \-'west\ n 1 : direction between north and west 2 cap : regions to the northwest —**northwest** adj or adv —**north·west·er·ly** \-ərlē\ adv or adj —**north·west·ern** \-ərn\ adj

nose \'nōz\ n 1 : part of the face containing the nostrils 2 : sense of smell 3 : front part ~ vb nosed; nos·ing 1 : detect by smell 2 : push aside with the nose 3 : defeat narrowly 4 : pry 5 : inch ahead —**nose·bleed** n —**nosed** \'nōzd\ adj

nose·gay \-,gā\ n : small bunch of flowers

nosh \'näsh\ vb : eat a snack —**nosh** n

nos·tal·gia \nä'staljə, nə-\ n : wistful yearning for something past —**nos·tal·gic** \-jik\ adj

nos·tril \'nästrəl\ n : opening of the nose

nos·trum \-trəm\ n : questionable medicine

nosy, nos·ey \'nōzē\ adj nos·i·er; -est : tending to pry

not \(')nät\ adv —used to make a statement negative

no·ta·ble \'nōtəbəl\ adj 1 : noteworthy 2 : distinguished ~ n : notable person —**no·ta·bil·i·ty** \nōtə'bilətē\ n —**no·ta·bly** \'nōtəblē\ adv

no·ta·rize \'nōtə,rīz\ vb -rized; -riz·ing : attest as a notary public

no·ta·ry public \'nōtərē-\ n, pl -ries public or -ry publics : public official who attests writings to make them legally authentic

no·ta·tion \nō'tāshən\ n 1 : note 2 : act, process, or method of marking things down

notch \'näch\ n : V-shaped hollow —**notch** vb

note \'nōt\ vb not·ed; not·ing 1 : notice 2 : write down ~ n 1 : musical tone 2 : written comment or record 3 : notice or heed —**note·book** n

not·ed \'nōtəd\ adj : famous

note·wor·thy \-,wərthē\ adj : worthy of special mention

noth·ing \'nəthiŋ\ pron 1 : no thing 2 : no part 3 : one of no value or importance ~ adv : not at all ~ n 1 : something that does not exist 2 : zero 3 : one of little or no importance —**noth·ing·ness** n

no·tice \'nōtəs\ n 1 : warning or announcement 2 : attention ~ vb -ticed; -tic·ing : take notice of —**no·tice·able** adj —**no·tice·ably** adv

no·ti·fy \'nōtə,fī\ vb -fied; -fy·ing : give notice of or to —**no·ti·fi·ca·tion** \,nōtəfə'kāshən\ n

no·tion \'nōshən\ n 1 : idea or opinion 2 : whim 3 pl : small sewing or personal articles

no·to·ri·ous \nō'tōrēəs\ adj : widely and unfavorably known —**no·to·ri·ety** \,nōtə'rīətē\ n —**no·to·ri·ous·ly** adv

not·with·stand·ing \,nätwith'standiŋ, -with-\ prep : in spite of ~ adv : nevertheless ~ conj : although

nou·gat \'nügət\ n : nuts or fruit pieces in a sugar paste

nought \'nòt, 'nät\ var of NAUGHT

noun \'naún\ n : word that is the name of a person, place, or thing

nour·ish \'nərish\ vb : promote the

growth of —**nour·ish·ing** *adj* —**nour·ish·ment** *n*

no·va \'nōvə\ *n, pl* **-vas** *or* **-vae** \-(,)vē, -,vī\ : star that suddenly brightens and then fades

nov·el \'nävəl\ *adj* : new or strange ~ *n* : long invented prose story —**nov·el·ist** \-(ə)ləst\ *n*

nov·el·ty \'nävəltē\ *n, pl* **-ties** 1 : something new or unusual 2 : newness 3 : small manufactured article—usu. pl.

No·vem·ber \nō'vembər\ *n* : 11th month of the year having 30 days

nov·ice \'nävəs\ *n* 1 : one preparing to take vows in a religious order 2 : one who is inexperienced or untrained

no·vi·ti·ate \nō'vishət, nə-\ *n* : period or state of being a novice

now \(')naú\ *adv* 1 : at the present time or moment 2 : forthwith 3 : under these circumstances ~ *conj* : in view of the fact ~ \'naú\ *n* : present time

now·a·days \'naú(ə),dāz\ *adv* : now

no·where \-,hwear\ *adv* : not anywhere —**no·where** *n*

nox·ious \'näkshəs\ *adj* : harmful

noz·zle \'näzəl\ *n* : device to direct or control a flow of fluid

nu·ance \'n(y)ü,äns, n(y)ü'äns\ *n* : subtle distinction or variation

nub \'nəb\ *n* 1 : knob or lump 2 : gist —**nub·by** *adj*

nu·bile \'n(y)übəl, -,bīl\ *adj* : of marriageable condition or age

nu·cle·ar \'n(y)üklēər\ *adj* : relating to the atomic nucleus or atomic energy

nu·cle·us \'n(y)üklēəs\ *n, pl* **-clei** \-klē,ī\ : central mass or part (as of a cell or an atom)

nude \'n(y)üd\ *adj* **nud·er; nud·est** : naked ~ *n* : nude human figure —**nu·di·ty** \'n(y)üdətē\ *n*

nudge \'nəj\ *vb* **nudged; nudg·ing** : touch or push gently —**nudge** *n*

nud·ism \'n(y)üd,izəm\ *n* : practice of going nude —**nud·ist** \'n(y)üdəst\ *n*

nug·get \'nəgət\ *n* : lump of gold

nui·sance \'n(y)üs⁼ns\ *n* : something annoying

null \'nəl\ *adj* : having no legal or binding force —**nul·li·ty** \'nəlotē\ *n*

nul·li·fy \'nələ,fī\ *vb* **-fied; -fy·ing** : make null or valueless —**nul·li·fi·ca·tion** \,nələfə'kāshən\ *n*

numb \'nəm\ *adj* : lacking feeling —**numb** *vb* —**numb·ly** *adv* —**numb·ness** *n*

num·ber \'nəmbər\ *n* 1 : total of individuals taken together 2 : group not specif. enumerated 3 : unit of a mathematical system 4 : numeral 5

: one in a sequence ~ *vb* 1 : count 2 : assign a number to 3 : comprise in number —**num·ber·less** *adj*

nu·mer·al \'n(y)üm(ə)rəl\ *n* : word or symbol representing a number

nu·mer·a·tor \'n(y)ümə,rātər\ *n* : part of a fraction above the line

nu·mer·i·cal \n(y)ü'merikəl\, **nu·mer·ic** \-'merik\ *adj* 1 : of or relating to numbers 2 : denoting a number or expressed in numbers —**nu·mer·i·cal·ly** \-k(ə)lē\ *adv*

nu·mer·ous \'n(y)üm(ə)rəs\ *adj* : consisting of a great number

nu·mis·mat·ics \,n(y)üməz'matiks\ *n* : study or collection of monetary objects —**nu·mis·mat·ic** \-ik\ *adj* —**nu·mis·ma·tist** \n(y)ü'mizmətəst\ *n*

nun·skull \'nən,skəl\ *n* : stupid person

nun \'nən\ *n* : woman belonging to a religious order —**nun·nery** \-(ə)rē\ *n*

nup·tial \'nəpshəl\ *adj* : relating to marriage or a wedding ~ *n* : marriage or wedding—usu. pl.

nurse \'nərs\ *n* 1 : one hired to care for children 2 : person trained to care for sick people ~ *vb* **nursed; nurs·ing** 1 : suckle 2 : care for

nurs·ery \'nərs(ə)rē\ *n, pl* **-er·ies** 1 : place where children are cared for 2 : place where young plants are grown

nursing home : private establishment where care is provided for persons who are unable to care for themselves

nur·ture \'nərchər\ *n* 1 : training or upbringing 2 : food or nourishment ~ *vb* **-tured; -tur·ing** 1 : care for or feed 2 : educate

nut \'nət\ *n* 1 : dry hard-shelled fruit or seed with a firm inner kernel 2 : metal block with a screw hole through it 3 : foolish, eccentric, or crazy person 4 : enthusiast —**nut·crack·er** *n* —**nut·shell** *n* —**nut·ty** *adj*

nut·hatch \'nət,hach\ *n* : small bird

nut·meg \'nət,meg, -,māg\ *n* : nutlike aromatic seed of a tropical tree

nu·tri·ent \'n(y)ütrēənt\ *n* : something giving nourishment —**nutrient** *adj*

nu·tri·ment \-trəmənt\ *n* : nutrient

nu·tri·tion \n(y)ü'trishən\ *n* : act or process of nourishing esp. with food —**nu·tri·tion·al** \-'trish(ə)nəl\ *adj* —**nu·tri·tious** \-'trishəs\ *adj* —**nu·tri·tive** \'n(y)ütrətiv\ *adj*

nuts \'nəts\ *adj* **1** : enthusiastic **2** : crazy

nuz·zle \'nəzəl\ *vb* **-zled; -zling 1** : touch with or as if with the nose **2** : snuggle

ny·lon \'nī,län\ *n* **1** : tough synthetic material used esp. in textiles **2** *pl* : stockings made of nylon

nymph \'nimf\ *n* **1** : lesser goddess in ancient mythology **2** : immature insect

nym·pho·ma·nia \,nimfə'mānēə, -nyə\ *n* : excessive sexual desire by a female —**nym·pho·ma·ni·ac** \-nē,ak\ *n or adj*

O

o \'ō\ *n, pl* **o's** or **os** \'ōz\ : 15th letter of the alphabet

O *var of* OH

oaf \'ōf\ *n* : stupid or awkward person —**oaf·ish** \'ōfish\ *adj*

oak \'ōk\ *n, pl* **oaks** or **oak** : tree bearing a thin-shelled nut or its wood —**oak·en** \'ōkən\ *adj*

oa·kum \'ōkəm\ *n* : loosely twisted tarred hemp or jute fiber for caulking ships

oar \'ōr\ *n* : implement used to propel a boat

oar·lock \-,läk\ *n* : device for holding an oar

oa·sis \ō'āsəs\ *n, pl* **oa·ses** \-,sēz\ : fertile area in a desert

oat \'ōt\ *n* : cereal grass or its edible seed —**oat·cake** *n* —**oat·en** \-ⁿn\ *adj* —**oat·meal** *n*

oath \'ōth\ *n, pl* **oaths** \'ōthz, 'ōths\ **1** : solemn appeal to God as a pledge of sincerity **2** : profane utterance

ob·du·rate \'äbd(y)ərət\ *adj* : stubbornly resistant —**ob·du·ra·cy** \-rəsē\ *n*

obe·di·ent \ō'bēdēənt\ *adj* : willing to obey —**obe·di·ence** \-əns\ *n* —**obe·di·ent·ly** *adv*

obei·sance \ō'bāsəns, -'bēs-\ *n* : bow of respect or submission

ob·e·lisk \'äbə,lisk\ *n* : 4-sided tapering pillar

obese \ō'bēs\ *adj* : extremely fat —**obe·si·ty** \-'bēsətē\ *n*

obey \ō'bā\ *vb* **obeyed; obey·ing 1** : follow the commands or guidance of **2** : behave in accordance with

ob·fus·cate \'äbfə,skāt\ *vb* **-cat·ed; -cat·ing** : confuse —**ob·fus·ca·tion** \,äbfəs'kāshən\ *n*

obit·u·ary \ə'bichə,werē\ *n, pl* **-ar·ies** : death notice

¹ob·ject \'äbjikt\ *n* **1** : something that may be seen or felt **2** : purpose **3** : noun or equivalent toward which the action of a verb is directed or which follows a preposition

²ob·ject \əb'jekt\ *vb* : offer opposition or disapproval —**ob·jec·tion** \-'jekshən\ *n* —**ob·jec·tion·able** \-sh(ə)nəbəl\ *adj* —**ob·jec·tor** \-'jektər\ *n*

ob·jec·tive \əb'jektiv\ *adj* **1** : relating to an object or end **2** : existing outside an individual's thoughts or feelings **3** : treating facts without distortion **4** : relating to or being a grammatical case marking objects ~ *n* : aim or end of action —**ob·jec·tive·ly** *adv* —**ob·jec·tive·ness** *n* —**ob·jec·tiv·i·ty** \,äb,jek'tivətē\ *n*

ob·li·gate \'äblə,gāt\ *vb* **-gat·ed; -gat·ing** : bind legally or morally —**ob·li·ga·tion** \,äblə'gāshən\ *n* —**oblig·a·to·ry** \ə'bligə,tōrē, 'äbligə-\ *adj*

oblige \ə'blīj\ *vb* **obliged; oblig·ing 1** : compel **2** : do a favor for —**oblig·ing·ly** *adv*

oblique \ō'blēk, -'blik\ *adj* **1** : lying at a slanting angle **2** : indirect —**oblique·ly** *adv* —**oblique·ness** *n* —**obliq·ui·ty** \-'blikwətē\ *n*

oblit·er·ate \ə'blitə,rāt\ *vb* **-at·ed; -at·ing** : completely remove or destroy —**oblit·er·a·tion** \-,blitə'rāshən\ *n*

obliv·i·on \ə'blivēən\ *n* **1** : state of having lost conscious awareness **2** : state of being unknown or forgotten

obliv·i·ous \-ēəs\ *adj* : not aware or mindful—with *to* or *of* —**obliv·i·ous·ly** *adv* —**obliv·i·ous·ness** *n*

ob·long \'äb,lόŋ\ *adj* : longer in one direction than in the other with opposite sides parallel —**oblong** *n*

ob·lo·quy \'äbləkwē\ *n, pl* **-quies 1** : strongly condemning utterance **2** : bad repute

ob·nox·ious \äb'näkshəs, əb-\ *adj* : repugnant —**ob·nox·ious·ly** *adv* —**ob·nox·ious·ness** *n*

oboe \'ōbō\ *n* : slender woodwind instrument with a reed mouthpiece —**obo·ist** \-ō,bōəst\ *n*

ob·scene \äb'sēn, əb-\ *adj* : repugnantly indecent —**ob·scene·ly** *adv* —**ob·scen·i·ty** \-'senətē\ *n*

ob·scure \äb'skyúr, əb-\ *adj* 1 : dim or hazy 2 : not well known 3 : vague ~ *vb* : make indistinct or unclear —**ob·scure·ly** *adv* —**ob·scu·ri·ty** \-'skyúrətē\ *n*

ob·se·quies \'äbsəkwēz\ *n pl* : funeral or burial rite

ob·se·qui·ous \əb'sēkwēəs\ *adj* : excessively attentive or flattering —**ob·se·qui·ous·ly** *adv*

ob·ser·va·to·ry \əb'zərvə,tōrē\ *n, pl* **-ries** : place for observing astronomical phenomena

ob·serve \əb'zərv\ *vb* **-served; -serv·ing** 1 : conform to 2 : celebrate 3 : see, watch, or notice 4 : remark —**ob·serv·able** *adj* —**ob·ser·vance** \-'zərvəns\ *n* —**ob·ser·vant** \-vənt\ *adj* —**ob·ser·va·tion** \,äbsər'vāshən, -zər-\ *n*

ob·sess \äb'ses\ *vb* : preoccupy intensely or abnormally —**ob·ses·sion** \äb'seshən, əb-\ *n* —**ob·ses·sive** \-'sesiv\ *adj* —**ob·ses·sive·ly** *adv*

ob·so·les·cent \,äbsə'les⁹nt\ *adj* : going out of use —**ob·so·les·cence** \-⁹ns\ *n*

ob·so·lete \,äbsə'lēt, 'äbsə,-\ *adj* : no longer in use

ob·sta·cle \'äbstəkəl\ *n* : something that stands in the way or opposes

ob·stet·rics \əb'stetriks\ *n sing or pl* : branch of medicine that deals with childbirth —**ob·stet·ric** \-rik\, **ob·stet·ri·cal** \-rikəl\ *adj* —**ob·ste·tri·cian** \,äbstə'trishən\ *n*

ob·sti·nate \'äbstənət\ *adj* : stubborn —**ob·sti·na·cy** \-nəsē\ *n* —**ob·sti·nate·ly** *adv*

ob·strep·er·ous \əb'strep(ə)rəs\ *adj* : uncontrollably noisy or defiant —**ob·strep·er·ous·ness** *n*

ob·struct \əb'strəkt\ *vb* : block or impede —**ob·struc·tion** \-'strəkshən\ *n* —**ob·struc·tive** \-'strəktiv\ *adj* —**ob·struc·tor** \-tər\ *n*

ob·tain \əb'tān\ *vb* 1 : gain by effort 2 : be generally recognized —**ob·tain·able** *adj*

ob·trude \əb'trüd\ *vb* **-trud·ed; -trud·ing** 1 : thrust out 2 : intrude —**ob·tru·sion** \-'trüzhən\ *n* —**ob·tru·sive** \-'trüsiv\ *adj* —**ob·tru·sive·ly** *adv*

ob·tuse \äb't(y)üs, əb-\ *adj* 1 : slow-witted 2 : exceeding 90 but less than 180 degrees —**ob·tuse·ly** *adv* —**ob·tuse·ness** *n*

ob·verse \'äb,vərs, äb'-\ *n* : principal side (as of a coin)

ob·vi·ate \'äbvē,āt\ *vb* **-at·ed; -at·ing** : make unnecessary —**ob·vi·a·tion** \,äbvē'āshən\ *n*

ob·vi·ous \'äbvēəs\ *adj* : plain or unmistakable —**ob·vi·ous·ly** *adv* —**ob·vi·ous·ness** *n*

oc·ca·sion \ə'kāzhən\ *n* 1 : favorable opportunity 2 : cause 3 : time of an event 4 : special event ~ *vb* : cause —**oc·ca·sion·al** \-'kāzh(ə)nəl\ *adj* —**oc·ca·sion·al·ly** *adv*

oc·ci·den·tal \,äksə'dent⁹l\ *adj* : western —**Occidental** *n*

oc·cult \ə'kəlt, 'äk,əlt\ *adj* : secret or mysterious

oc·cu·pan·cy \'äkyəpənsē\ *n, pl* **-cies** : an occupying

oc·cu·pant \-pənt\ *n* : one who occupies

oc·cu·pa·tion \,äkyə'pāshən\ *n* 1 : vocation 2 : action or state of occupying —**oc·cu·pa·tion·al** \-sh(ə)nəl\ *adj* —**oc·cu·pa·tion·al·ly** *adv*

oc·cu·py \'äkyə,pī\ *vb* **-pied; -py·ing** 1 : engage the attention of 2 : fill up 3 : sit or lie in 4 : reside in —**oc·cu·pi·er** \-,pī(ə)r\ *n*

oc·cur \ə'kər\ *vb* **-rr-** 1 : be found or met with 2 : take place 3 : come to mind

oc·cur·rence \ə'kərəns\ *n* : something that takes place

ocean \'ōshən\ *n* 1 : whole body of salt water 2 : large body of water —**ocean·front** *n* —**ocean·go·ing** *adj* —**ocean·ic** \,ōshē'anik\ *adj*

ocean·og·ra·phy \,ōshə'nägrəfē\ *n* : science dealing with the ocean —**ocean·og·ra·pher** \-fər\ *n* —**ocean·o·graph·ic** \-nə'grafik\ *adj*

oce·lot \'äsə,lät, 'ōsə-\ *n* : medium-sized American wildcat

ocher, ochre \'ōkər\ *n* : red or yellow pigment

o'clock \ə'kläk\ *adv* : according to the clock

oc·ta·gon \'äktə,gän\ *n* : 8-sided polygon —**oc·tag·o·nal** \äk'tagən⁹l\ *adj*

oc·tave \'äktiv\ *n* : musical interval of 8 steps or the notes within this interval

Oc·to·ber \äk'tōbər\ *n* : 10th month of the year having 31 days

oc·to·pus \'äktəpəs\ *n, pl* **-pus·es** *or* **-pi** \-,pī\ : sea mollusk with 8 arms

oc·u·lar \'äkyələr\ *adj* : relating to the eye

oc·u·list \'äkyələst\ *n* 1 : ophthalmologist 2 : optometrist

odd \'äd\ *adj* 1 : being only one of a pair or set 2 : not divisible by two without a remainder 3 : additional to what is usual or to the number mentioned 4 : queer —**odd·ly** *adv* —**odd·ness** *n*

odd·i·ty \'äd·ətē\ n, pl **-ties** : something odd

odds \'ädz\ n pl 1 : difference by which one thing is favored 2 : equalizing allowance 3 : disagreement

ode \'ōd\ n : solemn lyric poem

odi·ous \'ōdēəs\ adj : hated —**odi·ous·ly** adv —**odi·ous·ness** n

odi·um \'ōdēəm\ n 1 : merited loathing 2 : disgrace

odor \'ōdər\ n : quality that affects the sense of smell —**odor·less** adj —**odor·ous** adj

od·ys·sey \'ädəsē\ n, pl **-seys** : long wandering

o'er \'ō(ə)r\ adv or prep : OVER

of \(')əv, 'äv\ prep 1 : from 2 : distinguished by 3 : because of 4 : made with or written by 5 : made with, being, or containing 6 : belonging to or connected with 7 : about 8 : that is 9 : concerning 10 : before

off \'óf\ adv 1 : from a place 2 : unattached or removed 3 : to a state of being no longer in use 4 : away from work 5 : at a distance in time or space ~ \(')óf\ prep 1 : away from esp. the surface or top of 2 : at the expense of 3 : not engaged in or abstaining from 4 : below the usual level of ~ \(')óf\ adj 1 : not operating, up to standard, or correct 2 : remote 3 : provided for

of·fal \'ófəl\ n 1 : waste 2 : viscera and trimmings of a butchered animal

of·fend \ə'fend\ vb 1 : sin or act in violation 2 : hurt, annoy, or insult —**of·fend·er** n

of·fense, of·fence \ə'fens, 'äf,ens\ n : attack, misdeed, or insult

of·fen·sive \ə'fensiv, 'äf,en-\ adj : causing offense ~ n : attack —**of·fen·sive·ly** adv —**of·fen·sive·ness** n

of·fer \'ófər\ vb 1 : present for acceptance 2 : propose 3 : put up (an effort) ~ n 1 : proposal 2 : bid —**of·fer·ing** n

of·fer·to·ry \'ófə(r),tōrē\ n, pl **-ries** : presentation of offerings or its musical accompaniment

off·hand adv or adj : without previous thought or preparation

of·fice \'ófəs\ n 1 : position of authority (as in government) 2 : rite 3 : place where a business is transacted —**of·fice·hold·er** n

of·fi·cer \'ófəsər\ n 1 : one charged with law enforcement 2 : one who holds an office of trust or authority 3 : one who holds a commission in the armed forces

of·fi·cial \ə'fishəl\ n : one in office ~ adj : authorized or authoritative —**of·fi·cial·dom** \-dəm\ n —**of·fi·cial·ly** adv

of·fi·ci·ate \ə'fishē,āt\ vb **-at·ed; -at·ing** : perform a ceremony or function

of·fi·cious \ə'fishəs\ adj : volunteering one's services unnecessarily —**of·fi·cious·ly** adv —**of·fi·cious·ness** n

off·ing \'ófiŋ\ n : future

off·set \'óf,set\ vb **-set; -set·ting** : provide an opposite or equaling effect to

off·shoot \'óf,shüt\ n : outgrowth

off·shore adv : at a distance from the shore ~ adj : moving away from or situated off the shore

off·spring \'óf,spriŋ\ n, pl **offspring** : one coming into being through animal or plant reproduction

of·ten \'óf(t)ən\ adv : many times —**of·ten·times** adv

ogle \'ōgəl\ vb **ogled; ogling** : stare at lustily —**ogle** n —**ogler** \-(ə)lər\ n

ogre \'ōgər\ n 1 : monster 2 : dreaded person —**ogress** \'ōg(ə)rəs\ n

oh \(')ō\ interj 1—used to express an emotion 2—used in direct address

ohm \'ōm\ n : unit of electrical resistance —**ohm·ic** \-'ō-mik\ adj —**ohm·me·ter** \'ō(m),mētər\ n

oil \'óil\ n 1 : greasy liquid substance 2 : petroleum ~ vb : treat, furnish, or lubricate with oil —**oil·er** n —**oil·i·ness** \'óilēnəs\ n —**oily** \'óilē\ adj

oil·cloth n : cloth treated with oil or paint and used for coverings

oil·skin n : oiled waterproof cloth

oink \'óiŋk\ n : natural noise of a hog —**oink** vb

oint·ment \'óintmənt\ n : oily medicinal preparation

OK or **okay** \ō'kā\ adv or adj : all right ~ vb **OK'd** or **okayed**; **OK'·ing** or **okay·ing** : approve ~ n : approval

okra \'ōkrə, South also -krē\ n : leafy vegetable with edible green pods

old \'ōld\ adj 1 : of long standing 2 : of a specified age 3 : relating to a past era 4 : having existed a long time —**old·ish** \'ōldish\ adj

old·en \'ōldən\ adj : of or relating to a bygone era

old-fash·ioned \'ōl(d)'fashənd\ adj 1 : out-of-date 2 : conservative

old maid n : spinster

old-tim·er \'ōl(d)'timər\ n 1 : veteran 2 : one who is old

ole·an·der \'ōlē,andər\ n : poisonous evergreen shrub

oleo·mar·ga·rine \,ōlēō'märj(ə)rən, -'märjə,rēn\ n : margarine

ol·fac·to·ry \äl'fakt(ə)rē, ōl-\ *adj* : relating to the sense of smell

ol·i·gar·chy \'älə,gärkē, 'ōlə-\ *n, pl* **-chies 1** : government by a few people **2** : those holding power in an oligarchy **—ol·i·garch** \-,gärk\ *n* **—ol·i·gar·chic** \,älə'gärkik, ,ōlə-\, **ol·i·gar·chi·cal** -kikəl\ *adj*

ol·ive \'äliv, -əv\ *n* **1** : evergreen tree bearing small edible fruit or the fruit **2** : dull yellow to yellowish green color

om·buds·man \'äm,bủdzmən, äm'bủdz-\ *n, pl* **-men** \-mən\ : complaint investigator

om·elet, om·elette \'äm(ə)lət\ *n* : beaten eggs lightly fried and folded

omen \'ōmən\ *n* : sign or warning for the future

om·i·nous \'ämənəs\ *adj* : threatening **—om·i·nous·ly** *adv* **—om·i·nous·ness** *n*

omit \ō'mit\ *vb* **-tt- 1** : leave out **2** : fail to perform **—omis·sion** \-'mishən\ *n*

om·nip·o·tent \äm'nipətənt\ *adj* : almighty **—om·nip·o·tence** \-əns\ *n* **—om·nip·o·tent·ly** *adv*

om·ni·pres·ent \,ämni'prez³nt\ *adj* : ever-present **—om·ni·pres·ence** \-³ns\ *n*

om·ni·scient \äm'nishənt\ *adj* : all-knowing **—om·ni·science** \-əns\ *n* **—om·ni·scient·ly** *adv*

om·niv·o·rous \äm'niv(ə)rəs\ *adj* **1** : eating both meat and vegetables **2** : avid **—om·niv·o·rous·ly** *adv*

on \(')ȯn, ('ä)n\ *prep* **1** : in or to a position over and in contact with **2** : at or to **3** : about **4** : from **5** : with regard to **6** : in a state or process **7** : during the time of ~ \'ȯn, 'än\ *adv* **1** : in or into contact with **2** : forward **3** : into operation

once \'wəns\ *adv* **1** : one time only **2** : at any one time **3** : formerly ~ *n* : one time ~ *conj* : as soon as **— at once 1** : simultaneously **2** : immediately **3** : both

once-over *n* : swift examination

on·com·ing \'ȯn,kəmiŋ\ *adj* : approaching

one \'wən\ *adj* **1** : being a single thing **2** : being one in particular **3** : united ~ *pron* **1** : a single member **2** : a person in general ~ *n* **1** : 1st in a series **2** : single person or thing **—one·ness** *n*

on·er·ous \'änərəs, 'ōn-\ *adj* : oppressive

one·self \(,)wən'self\ *pron* : one's own self—usu. used reflexively or for emphasis

one-sid·ed \-'sīdəd\ *adj* **1** : unequal **2** : partial

one·time *adj* : former

one-way *adj* : made or for use in only one direction

on·go·ing *adj* : continuing

on·ion \'ənyən\ *n* : plant grown for its pungent edible bulb

on·ly \'ōnlē\ *adj* : alone in its class ~ *adv* **1** : nothing more than **2** : without respect to anyone or anything else ~ *conj* : but

on·set *n* : start

on·shore *adj* **1** : moving toward shore **2** : lying on or near the shore **—on·shore** *adv*

on·slaught \'än,slȯt, 'ȯn-\ *n* : attack

on·to \,ȯntə, ,än-; 'ȯntü, 'än-\ *prep* : to a position or point on

onus \'ōnəs\ *n* : burden (as of obligation or blame)

on·ward \'ȯnwərd, 'än-\ *adv or adj* : forward

on·yx \'äniks\ *n* : quartz used as a gem

ooze \'üz\ *n* : soft mud **—oozy** \'üzē\ *adj*

²ooze *vb* **oozed; ooz·ing** : flow or leak out slowly

opac·i·ty \ō'pasətē\ *n* : quality or state of being opaque or an opaque spot

opal \'ōpəl\ *n* : gem with delicate colors

opaque \ō'pāk\ *adj* **1** : impervious to light **2** : not easily understood **3** : dull-witted **—opaque·ly** *adv*

open \'ōpən\ *adj* **1** : not shut or shut up **2** : not secret or hidden **3** : frank or generous **4** : extended **5** : free from controls **6** : not decided ~ *vb* **1** : make or become open **2** : make or become functional **3** : start ~ *n* : outdoors **—open·er** \'ōp(ə)nər\ *n* **—open·ly** *adv* **—open·ness** *n*

open-hand·ed \-'handəd\ *adj* : generous

open·ing \'ōp(ə)niŋ\ *n* **1** : act or instance of causing to be open **2** : something that is open **3** : opportunity

op·era \'äp(ə)rə\ *n* : drama set to music **—op·er·at·ic** \,äpə'ratik\ *adj*

op·er·a·ble \'äp(ə)rəbəl\ *adj* **1** : usable or in working condition **2** : suitable for surgical treatment

op·er·ate \'äpə,rāt\ *vb* **-at·ed; -at·ing 1** : perform work **2** : perform an operation **3** : manage **—op·er·a·tor** \-,rātər\ *n*

op·er·a·tion \,äpə'rāshən\ *n* **1** : act or process of operating **2** : surgical work on a living body **3** : military action or mission —**op·er·a·tion·al** \-sh(ə)nəl\ *adj*

op·er·a·tive \'äp(ə)rətiv, 'äpə,rāt-\ *adj* : working or having an effect

op·er·et·ta \,äpə'retə\ *n* : light opera

oph·thal·mol·o·gy \,äf,thal'mäləjē, ,äp-\ *n* : branch of medicine dealing with the eye —**oph·thal·mol·o·gist** \-jəst\ *n*

opi·ate \'ōpēət, -pē,āt\ *n* : preparation or derivative of opium

opin·ion \ə'pinyən\ *n* 1 : belief 2 : judgment 3 : formal statement by an expert

opin·ion·at·ed \-yə,nātəd\ *adj* : stubborn in one's opinions

opi·um \'ōpēəm\ *n* : addictive narcotic drug that is the dried juice of a poppy

opos·sum \ə'päsəm\ *n* : common tree-dwelling mammal

op·po·nent \ə'pōnənt\ *n* : one that opposes

op·por·tune \,äpər't(y)ün\ *adj* 1 : suitable 2 : occurring at a suitable time —**op·por·tune·ly** *adv*

op·por·tun·ism \-'t(y)ü,nizəm\ *n* : a taking advantage of opportunities —**op·por·tun·ist** \-nəst\ *n* —**op·por·tu·nis·tic** \-t(y)ü'nistik\ *adj*

op·por·tu·ni·ty \-'t(y)ünətē\ *n, pl* **-ties** : favorable time

op·pose \ə'pōz\ *vb* **-posed; -pos·ing** 1 : place opposite or against something 2 : resist —**op·po·si·tion** \,äpə'zishən\ *n*

op·po·site \'äpəzət\ *n* : one that is opposed ~ *adj* 1 : set facing something that is at the other side or end 2 : opposed or contrary ~ *adv* : on opposite sides ~ *prep* : across from —**op·po·site·ly** *adv*

op·press \ə'pres\ *vb* 1 : persecute 2 : weigh down —**op·pres·sion** \ə'preshən\ *n* —**op·pres·sive** \-'presiv\ *adj* —**op·pres·sive·ly** *adv* —**op·pres·sor** \-'presər\ *n*

op·pro·bri·ous \ə'prōbrēəs\ *adj* : expressing or deserving opprobrium —**op·pro·bri·ous·ly** *adv*

op·pro·bri·um \-brēəm\ *n* 1 : something that brings disgrace 2 : infamy

opt \'äpt\ *vb* : choose

op·tic \'äptik\ *adj* : relating to vision or the eye

op·ti·cal \'äptikəl\ *adj* : relating to optics, vision, or the eye

op·ti·cian \äp'tishən\ *n* : maker of or dealer in eyeglasses

op·tics \'äptiks\ *n pl* : science of light and vision

op·ti·mal \'äptəməl\ *adj* : most favorable —**op·ti·mal·ly** *adv*

op·ti·mism \'äptə,mizəm\ *n* : tendency to hope for the best —**op·ti·mist** \-məst\ *n* —**op·ti·mis·tic** \,äptə'mistik\ *adj* —**op·ti·mis·ti·cal·ly** \-tik(ə)lē\ *adv*

op·ti·mum \'äptəməm\ *n, pl* **-ma** \-mə\ : amount or degree of something most favorable to an end

op·tion \'äpshən\ *n* 1 : ability to choose 2 : right to buy or sell a stock 3 : alternative —**op·tion·al** \-sh(ə)nəl\ *adj*

op·tom·e·try \äp'tämətrē\ *n* : profession of examining the eyes —**op·tom·e·trist** \-trəst\ *n*

op·u·lent \'äpyələnt\ *adj* : lavish —**op·u·lence** \-ləns\ *n*

opus \'ōpəs\ *n, pl* **opera** \'ōpərə, 'äpə-\ : work esp. of music

or \ər,(,)ör\ *conj* —used to indicate an alternative

-or \ər\ *n suffix* : one that performs an action

or·a·cle \'örəkəl\ *n* 1 : one held to give divinely inspired answers or revelations 2 : wise person or an utterance of such a person —**orac·u·lar** \ö'rakyələr\ *adj*

oral \'örəl, 'ōr-\ *adj* 1 : spoken 2 : relating to the mouth —**oral·ly** *adv*

or·ange \'örinj\ *n* 1 : reddish yellow citrus fruit 2 : color between red and yellow —**or·ange·ade** \,örinj'ād\ *n*

orang·utan \ə'raŋə,taŋ. -,tan\ *n* : reddish brown ape

ora·tion \ə'rāshən\ *n* : elaborate formal speech

or·a·tor \'örətər\ *n* : one who delivers an oration

or·a·to·rio \,örə'tōrē,ō\ *n, pl* **-ri·os** : major choral work

or·a·to·ry \'örə,törē\ *n* : art of public speaking —**or·a·tor·i·cal** \,örə'törikəl\ *adj*

orb \'örb\ *n* 1 : sphere 2 : celestial body

or·bit \'örbət\ *n* : path made by one body revolving around another ~ *vb* : revolve around —**or·bit·al** \-ʾl\ *adj* —**or·bit·er** *n*

or·chard \'örchərd\ *n* : place where fruit or nut trees are grown —**or·chard·ist** \-əst\ *n*

or·ches·tra \'örkəstrə\ *n* 1 : group of musicians 2 : front seats of a theater's main floor —**or·ches·tral** \ör'kestrəl\ *adj*

or·ches·trate \'örkə,strāt\ *vb* **-trat·ed; -trat·ing** : compose or arrange for an orchestra —**or·ches·tra·tion** \,örkə-'strāshən\ *n*

or·chid \'òrkəd\ n : plant with showy 3-petal flowers or its flower

or·dain \òr'dān\ vb 1 : admit to the clergy 2 : decree

or·deal \òr'dē(ə)l, 'òr,dē(ə)l\ n : severely trying experience

or·der \'òrdər\ n 1 : rank, class, or special group 2 : arrangement 3 : rule of law 4 : authoritative regulation or instruction 5 : working condition 6 : special request for a purchase or what is purchased ~ vb 1 : arrange 2 : give an order to 3 : place an order for

or·der·ly \-lē\ adj 1 : being in order or tidy 2 : well behaved ~ n, pl **-lies** 1 : officer's attendant 2 : hospital attendant —**or·der·li·ness** n

or·di·nal \'òrdnəl, -ᵊnəl\ n : number indicating order in a series

or·di·nance \-nəns, -ᵊnəns\ n : municipal law

or·di·nary \'òrdᵊn,erē\ adj : of common occurrence, quality, or ability —**or·di·nar·i·ly** \,òrdᵊn'erəlē\ adv

or·di·na·tion \,òrdᵊn'āshən\ n : act of ordaining

or·dnance \'òrdnəns\ n : military supplies

ore \'òr\ n : mineral containing a valuable constituent

or·gan \'òrgən\ n 1 : air-powered or electronic keyboard instrument 2 : animal or plant structure with special function 3 : periodical

or·gan·ic \òr'ganik\ adj 1 : relating to a bodily organ 2 : relating to living things 3 : relating to or containing carbon or its compounds —**or·gan·i·cal·ly** \-ik(ə)lē\ adv

or·gan·ism \'òrgə,nizəm\ n : living person, animal, or plant

or·gan·ist \'òrgənəst\ n : organ player

or·ga·nize \'òrgə,nīz\ vb **-nized; -niz·ing** : form parts into a functioning whole —**or·ga·ni·za·tion** \,òrg(ə)nə'zāshən\ n —**or·ga·niz·er** n

or·gasm \'òr,gazəm\ n : climax of sexual excitement

or·gy \'òrjē\ n, pl **-gies** : unrestrained indulgence

ori·ent \'òrē,ent\ vb 1 : set in a definite position 2 : acquaint with a situation —**ori·en·ta·tion** \,òrēən'tāshən\ n

ori·en·tal \,òrē'entᵊl\ adj : Eastern —**Oriental** n

or·i·fice \'òrəfəs\ n : opening

or·i·gin \'òrəjən\ n 1 : ancestry 2 : rise, beginning, or derivation from a source —**orig·i·nate** \ə'rijə,nāt\ vb —**orig·i·na·tor** n

orig·i·nal \ə'rij(ə)nəl\ n : something

from which a copy is made ~ adj 1 : first 2 : not copied from something else 3 : inventive —**orig·i·nal·i·ty** n —**orig·i·nal·ly** adv

ori·ole \'òrē,ōl\ n : American songbird

or·na·ment \'òrnəmənt\ n : something that adorns ~ vb : provide with ornament —**or·na·men·tal** \,òrnə'mentᵊl\ adj —**or·na·men·ta·tion** \-mən'tāshən\ n

or·nate \òr'nāt\ adj : elaborately decorated —**or·nate·ly** adv —**or·nate·ness** n

or·nery \'òrn(ə)rē, 'än-\ adj : irritable

or·ni·thol·o·gy \,òrnə'thäləjē\ n, pl **-gies** : study of birds —**or·ni·tho·log·i·cal** \-thə'läjikəl\ adj —**or·ni·thol·o·gist** \-'thäləjəst\ n

or·phan \'òrfən\ n : child whose parents are dead —**orphan** vb —**or·phan·age** \-(ə)nij\ n

or·tho·don·tics \,òrthə'däntiks\ n : dentistry dealing with straightening teeth —**or·tho·don·tist** \-'däntəst\ n

or·tho·dox \'òrthə,däks\ adj 1 : conforming to established doctrine 2 cap : of or relating to a Christian church originating in the Eastern Roman Empire —**or·tho·doxy** \-,däksē\ n

or·thog·ra·phy \òr'thägrəfē\ n : spelling —**or·tho·graph·ic** \,òrthə'grafik\ adj

or·tho·pe·dics \,òrthə'pēdiks\ n sing or pl : correction or prevention of skeletal deformities —**or·tho·pe·dic** \-ik\ adj —**or·tho·pe·dist** \-'pēdəst\ n

-ory \,òrē, òrē, (ə)rē\ adj suffix 1 : of, relating to, or characterized by 2 : serving for, producing, or maintaining

os·cil·late \'äsə,lāt\ vb **-lat·ed; -lat·ing** : swing back and forth —**os·cil·la·tion** \,äsə'lāshən\ n

os·mo·sis \äz'mōsəs, äs-\ n : diffusion esp. of water through a membrane —**os·mot·ic** \-'mätik\ adj

os·prey \'äsprē, -,prā\ n, pl **-preys** : large hawk

os·ten·si·ble \ä'stensəbəl\ adj : seeming —**os·ten·si·bly** \-blē\ adv

os·ten·ta·tion \,ästən'tāshən\ n : pretentious display —**os·ten·ta·tious** \-shəs\ adj —**os·ten·ta·tious·ly** adv

os·te·op·a·thy \,ästē'äpəthē\ n : system of healing that emphasizes manipulation (as of joints) —**os·te·o·path** \'ästēə,path\ n —**os·te·o·path·ic** \,ästē'pathik\ adj

os·tra·cize \'ästrə,sīz\ vb **-cize·; -ciz·ing**

: exclude by common consent —**os·tra·cism** \-,sizəm\ n

os·trich \'ästrich, 'ós-\ n : very large flightless bird

oth·er \'əthər\ adj 1 : being the one left 2 : alternate 3 : additional ~ pron 1 : remaining one 2 : different one

oth·er·wise adv 1 : in a different way 2 : in different circumstances 3 : in other respects —**otherwise** adj

ot·ter \'ätər\ n : mammal with webbed feet

ot·to·man \'ätəmən\ n : upholstered footstool

ought \'ót\ verbal auxiliary—used to express obligation, advisability, or expectation

ounce \'aúns\ n 1 : unit of weight equal to about 28.3 grams 2 : unit of capacity equal to about 29.6 milliliters

our \är, (')aü(ə)r\ adj : of or relating to us

ours \('-)aü(ə)rz, ärz\ pron : one belonging to us

our·selves \är'selvz, aü(ə)r-\ pron : we, us—used reflexively or for emphasis

-ous \əs\ adj suffix : having or having the qualities of

oust \'aúst\ vb : expel or eject

oust·er \'aústər\ n : expulsion

out \'aút\ adv 1 : away from the inside or center 2 : beyond control 3 : to extinction, exhaustion, or completion 4 : in or into the open ~ vb : become known —adj 1 : situated outside 2 : absent ~ prep 1 : out through 2 : outward on or along —**out·bound** adj —**out·build·ing** n

out·board \'aút,bórd\ adv : outside a boat or ship —**outboard** adj

out·break \'aút,brāk\ n : sudden occurrence

out·burst \-,bərst\ n : violent expression of feeling

out·cast \-,kast\ n : person cast out by society

out·come \-,kəm\ n : result

out·crop \'aút,kräp\ n : part of a rock stratum that appears above the ground —**outcrop** vb

out·cry \-,krī\ n : loud cry

out·dat·ed \aút'dātəd\ adj : out-of-date

out·dis·tance vb : go far ahead of

out·do \aút'dü\ vb -**did** \-'did\; -**done** \-'dən\; -**do·ing** \-'düiŋ\; -**does** \-'dəz\ : do better than

out·doors \aút'dórz\ adv : in or into the open air ~ n : open air —**out·door** adj

out·er \'aútər\ adj 1 : external 2 : farther out —**out·er·most** adj

out·field \'aút,fēld\ n : baseball field beyond the infield —**out·field·er** \-,fēldər\ n

out·fit \'aút,fit\ n 1 : equipment for a special purpose 2 : group ~ vb -**tt**- : equip —**out·fit·ter** n

out·go \'aút,gō\ n, pl **outgoes** : expenditure

out·go·ing \'aút,gōiŋ\ adj 1 : retiring from a position 2 : friendly

out·grow \aút'grō\ vb -**grew** \-'grü\; -**grown** \-'grōn\; -**grow·ing** 1 : grow faster than 2 : grow too large for

out·growth \'aút,grōth\ n 1 : product of growing out 2 : consequence

out·ing \'aútiŋ\ n : excursion

out·land·ish \aút'landish\ adj : very strange —**out·land·ish·ly** adv

out·last vb : last longer than

out·law \'aút,ló\ n 1 : lawless person ~ vb : make illegal

out·lay \'aút,lā\ n : expenditure

out·let \'aút,let, -lət\ n 1 : exit 2 : means of release 3 : market for goods 4 : electrical device that gives access to wiring

out·line \'aút,līn\ n 1 : line marking the outer limits 2 : summary ~ vb 1 : draw the outline of 2 : indicate the chief parts of

out·live \aút'liv\ vb : live longer than

out·look \'aút,lúk\ n 1 : viewpoint 2 : prospect for the future

out·ly·ing \'aút,līiŋ\ adj : far from a central point

out·mod·ed \aút'mōdəd\ adj : out-of-date

out·num·ber \-'nəmbər\ vb : exceed in number

out of prep 1 : out from within 2 : beyond the limits of 3 : among 4 —used to indicate absence or loss 5 : because of 6 : from or with

out-of-date adj : no longer in fashion or in use

out·pa·tient n : person treated at a hospital who does not stay

out·post n : remote military post

out·put n : amount produced ~ vb -**put·ted** or -**put**; -**put·ting** : produce

out·rage \'aút,rāj\ n 1 : violent or shameful act 2 : injury or insult ~ vb -**raged**; -**rag·ing** 1 : subject to violent injury 2 : make very angry —**out·ra·geous** \aút'rājəs\ adj —**out·ra·geous·ly** adv

out·right adv 1 : completely 2 : instantly ~ adj 1 : complete 2 : given without reservation

out·set n : beginning

out·side \aut'sīd, 'aut,-\ n 1 : place beyond a boundary 2 : exterior 3 : utmost limit ~ adj 1 : outer 2 : coming from without 3 : remote ~ adv : on or to the outside ~ prep 1 : on or to the outside of 2 : beyond the limits of

outside of prep 1 : outside 2 : besides

out·sid·er \-'sīdər\ n : one who does not belong to a group

out·skirts n pl : outlying parts (as of a city)

out·smart \aut-\ vb : outwit

out·spo·ken adj : direct and open in speech —**out·spo·ken·ness** n

out·stand·ing adj 1 : unpaid 2 : very good —**out·stand·ing·ly** adv

out·strip \aut'strip\ vb 1 : go faster than 2 : surpass

¹**out·ward** \'autwərd\ adj 1 : being toward the outside 2 : showing outwardly

²**outward, out·wards** \-wərdz\ adv : toward the outside —**out·ward·ly** adv

out·wit \aut'wit\ vb : get the better of by superior cleverness

ova pl of OVUM

oval \'ōvəl\ adj : egg-shaped —**oval** n

ova·ry \'ōv(ə)rē\ n, pl -ries 1 : egg-producing organ 2 : seed-producing part of a flower —**ovar·i·an** \ō'varēən, -'ver-\ adj

ova·tion \ō'vāshən\ n : enthusiastic applause

ov·en \'əvən\ n : chamber (as in a stove) for baking

over \'ōvər\ adv 1 : across 2 : upside down 3 : in excess or addition 4 : above 5 : at an end 6 : again ~ prep 1 : above in position or authority 2 : more than 3 : along, through, or across 4 : because of ~ adj : upper 2 : remaining 3 : ended

over- prefix 1 : so as to exceed or surpass 2 : excessive or excessively

overabundance	overassertive
overabundant	overbake
overacceptance	overbid
overachiever	overbill
overactive	overbold
overaggressive	overborrow
overambitious	overbright
overamplify	overbroad
overanalyze	overbuild
overanxiety	overburden
overanxious	overbusy
overapologetic	overbuy
overarousal	overcapacity
overarouse	overcapitalize

overcareful	overgenerous
overcautious	overglamorize
overcharge	overgraze
overcivilized	overharvest
overclean	overhasty
overcommit	overheat
overcompensate	overidealize
overcomplicate	overimaginative
overconcern	overimbibe
overconfidence	overimpressed
overconfident	overindebted
overconscien-	overindulge
tious	overindulgence
overconsume	overindulgent
overconsumption	overinflate
overcontrol	overinfluence
overcook	overinsistent
overcorrect	overintense
overcritical	overintensity
overcrowd	overinvest
overdecorate	overinvolve
overdepend	overladen
overdependent	overlarge
overdevelop	overlend
overdose	overliberal
overdramatic	overload
overdramatize	overlong
overdress	overloud
overdrink	overmedicate
overdue	overmodest
overeager	overmuch
overeat	overobvious
overeducate	overoptimistic
overelaborate	overorganize
overemotional	overpack
overemphasis	overparticular
overemphasize	overpatriotic
overenergetic	overpay
overenthusiastic	overpayment
overestimate	overpermissive
overexaggerate	overplay
overexaggeration	overpopulated
overexcite	overpossessive
overexcitement	overpraise
overexercise	overprescribe
overexert	overpressure
overexertion	overprice
overexhaust	overprivileged
overexpand	overproduce
overexpansion	overproduction
overexplain	overpromise
overexploit	overprotect
overexpose	overprotective
overextend	overpublicize
overexuberant	overqualified
overfamiliar	overrate
overfatigue	overreact
overfeed	overreaction
overfertilize	overrefine
overfill	overregulate
overfond	overregulation
	overreliance

overrepresent
overrespond
overripe
oversaturate
oversell
oversensitive
overserious
oversexed
oversimple
oversimplify
oversolicitous
overspecialize
overspend
overstaff
overstimulate
overstock
overstrain
overstress

overstretch
overstrict
oversubtle
oversupply
oversuspicious
oversweeten
overtax
overtighten
overtip
overtired
overtrain
overtreat
overuse
overutilize
overvalue
overweight
overwork
overzealous

¹over·age \,ōvər'āj\ adj : too old
²over·age \'ōv(ə)rij\ n : surplus
over·all \,ōvər'ȯl\ adj : including everything
over·alls \'ōvər,ȯlz\ n pl : work garment
over·awe vb : restrain by awe
over·bear·ing \-'ba(ə)riŋ\ adj : arrogant
over·blown \-'blōn\ adj : pretentious
over·board adv : over the side into the water
over·cast adj : clouded over ~ n : cloud covering
over·coat n : outer coat
over·come vb -came \-'kǝm\; -come; -com·ing 1 : defeat 2 : make helpless or exhausted
over·do vb -did; -done; -do·ing; -does : do too much
over·draft n : overdrawn sum
over·draw vb -drew; -drawn; -draw·ing : write checks for more than one's bank balance
over·flow \,ōvər'flō\ vb 1 : flood 2 : flow over —over·flow \'ōvər,flō\ n
over·grow vb -grew; -grown; -grow·ing : grow over
over·hand adj : made with the hand brought down from above —over·hand adv
over·hang vb -hung; -hang·ing : jut out over ~ n : something that overhangs
over·haul vb : repair 2 : overtake
over·head \,ōvər'hed\ adv : aloft ~ \'ōvər,-\ adj : situated above ~ \'ōvər,-\ n : general business expenses
over·hear vb -heard; -hear·ing : hear without the speaker's knowledge
over·joy vb : fill with joy
over·land \-,land, -lənd\ adv or adj : by, on, or across land

over·lap vb : lap over
over·lay \,ōvər'lā\ vb -laid; -lay·ing : lay over or across —over·lay \'ōvər,lā\ n
over·look \,ōvər'lùk\ vb 1 : look down on 2 : fail to see 3 : ignore 4 : pardon 5 : supervise ~ \'ōvər,-\ n : observation point
over·ly \'ōvərlē\ adv : excessively
over·night adv : through the night — overnight adj
over·pass n : bridge over a road
over·pow·er vb 1 : conquer 2 : overwhelm
over·reach \,ōvə(r)'rēch\ vb : try or seek too much
over·ride vb -rode; -rid·den; -rid·ing : neutralize action of
over·rule vb : rule against or set aside
over·run vb -ran; -run·ning 1 : swarm or flow over 2 : go beyond ~ n : an exceeding of estimated costs
over·seas adv or adj : beyond or across the sea
over·see \,ōvər'sē\ vb -saw; -seen; -see·ing : supervise —over·seer \'ōvər,sēər\ n
over·shad·ow vb : exceed in importance
over·shoe n : protective outer shoe
over·shoot vb -shot; -shoot·ing : shoot or pass beyond
over·sight n : inadvertent omission or error
over·sleep vb -slept; -sleep·ing : sleep longer than intended
over·spread vb -spread; -spread·ing : spread over or above
over·state vb : exaggerate —over·state·ment n
over·stay vb : stay too long
over·step vb : exceed
overt \ō'vərt, 'ō,vərt\ adj : not secret
over·take vb -took; -tak·en; -tak·ing : catch up with
over·throw \,ōvər'thrō\ vb -threw; -thrown; -throw·ing 1 : upset 2 : bring to defeat —over·throw \'ōvər,-\ n
over·time n : extra working time — overtime adv
over·tone n 1 : higher tone in a complex musical tone 2 : suggestion
over·ture \'ōvər,chùr, -chər\ n 1 : opening offer 2 : musical introduction
over·turn vb 1 : turn over 2 : overthrow
over·view n : brief survey
over·ween·ing \,ōvər'wēniŋ\ adj 1 : arrogant 2 : excessive
over·whelm \,ōvər'hwelm\ vb : over-

come completely —**over·whelm·ing·ly** \-'hwelmiņlē\ adv

over·wrought \,ōvə(r)'rȯt\ adj : extremely excited

ovoid \'ō,vȯid\, **ovoi·dal** \ō'vȯidᵊl\ adj : egg-shaped

ovu·late \'ävyə,lāt, 'ōv-\ vb -lat·ed; -lat·ing : produce eggs —**ovu·la·tion** \,ävyə'lāshən, ,ōv-\ n

ovum \'ōvəm\ n, pl **ova** \-və\ : female germ cell

owe \'ō\ vb **owed; ow·ing** 1 : have an obligation to pay 2 : be indebted to or for

owing to prep : because of

owl \'aúl\ n : nocturnal bird of prey —**owl·ish** adj —**owl·ish·ly** adv

own \'ōn\ adj : belonging to oneself ~ vb 1 : have as property 2 : acknowl-

edge ~ pron : one or ones belonging to oneself —**own·er** n —**own·er·ship** n

ox \'äks\ n, pl **ox·en** \'äksən\ : bovine mammal and esp. a castrated bull

ox·ide \'äk,sīd\ n : compound of oxygen

ox·i·dize \'äksə,dīz\ vb **-dized; -diz·ing** : combine with oxygen —**ox·i·da·tion** \,äksə'dāshən\ n —**ox·i·diz·able** \'äksə,dīzəbəl\ adj —**ox·i·diz·er** n

oxy·gen \'äksijən\ n : gaseous chemical element —**oxy·gen·ic** \,äksi-'jenik\ adj

oys·ter \'ȯistər\ n : bivalve mollusk —**oys·ter·ing** \'ȯist(ə)riņ\ n

ozone \'ō,zōn\ n : faintly blue form of oxygen

P

p \'pē\ n, pl **p's** or **ps** \'pēz\ : 16th letter of the alphabet

pace \'pās\ n 1 : walking step 2 : rate of progress ~ vb **paced; pac·ing** 1 : go at a pace 2 : cover with slow steps 3 : set the pace of

pace·mak·er n : electrical device to regulate heartbeat

pachy·derm \'paki,dərm\ n : elephant

pa·cif·ic \pə'sifik\ adj : calm or peaceful

pac·i·fism \'pasə,fizəm\ n : opposition to war or violence —**pac·i·fist** \-fəst\ n or adj —**pac·i·fis·tic** \,pasə'fistik\ adj

pac·i·fy \'pasə,fī\ vb **-fied; -fy·ing** : make calm —**pac·i·fi·ca·tion** \,pasəfə'kāshən\ n —**pac·i·fi·er** \'pasə,fī(ə)r\ n

pack \'pak\ n 1 : compact bundle 2 : group of animals ~ vb 1 : put into a container 2 : fill tightly or completely 3 : send without ceremony —**pack·er** n

pack·age \'pakij\ n : items bundled together ~ vb **-aged; -ag·ing** : enclose in a package

pack·et \'pakət\ n : small package

pact \'pakt\ n : agreement

pad \'pad\ n 1 : cushioning part or thing 2 : floating leaf of a water plant 3 : tablet of paper ~ vb **-dd-** 1 : furnish with a pad 2 : expand with needless matter —**pad·ding** n

pad·dle \'padᵊl\ n : implement with a flat blade ~ vb **-dled; -dling** : move, beat, or stir with a paddle

pad·dock \'padək\ n : enclosed area for racehorses

pad·dy \'padē\ n, pl **-dies** : wet land where rice is grown

pad·lock n : lock with a U-shaped catch —**padlock** vb

pa·dre \'pädrā\ n : priest

pae·an \'pēən\ n : song of praise

pa·gan \'pāgən\ n or adj : heathen —**pa·gan·ism** \-,izəm\ n

¹page \'pāj\ n : messenger ~ vb **paged; pag·ing** : summon by repeated calls

²page n : single leaf (as of a book) or one side of the leaf

pag·eant \'pajənt\ n : elaborate spectacle or procession —**pag·eant·ry** \-əntrē\ n

pa·go·da \pə'gōdə\ n : tower with roofs curving upward

paid past of PAY

pail \'pāl\ n : cylindrical container with a handle —**pail·ful** \-,fúl\ n

pain \'pān\ n 1 : punishment or penalty 2 : suffering of body or mind 3 pl : great care ~ vb : cause or experience pain —**pain·ful** \-fəl\ adj —**pain·ful·ly** adv —**pain·kill·er** n —**pain·kill·ing** adj —**pain·less** adj —**pain·less·ly** adv

pains·tak·ing \'pān,stākiņ\ adj : taking pains —**painstaking** n —**pains·tak·ing·ly** adv

paint \'pānt\ vb 1 : apply color or paint to 2 : portray in color ~ n : mixture of pigment and liquid —**paint·brush** n —**paint·er** n —**painting** n

pair \'paər\ n : a set of two ~ vb : put or go together as a pair

pa·ja·mas \pə'jäməz, -'jam-\ n pl : loose suit for sleeping

pal \'pal\ n : close friend

pal·ace \'paləs\ n 1 : residence of a sovereign 2 : mansion —**pa·la·tial** \pə'läshəl\ adj

pal·at·able \'palətəbəl\ adj : agreeable to the taste

pal·ate \'palət\ n 1 : roof of the mouth 2 : taste —**pal·a·tal** \-ət⁹l\ adj

pa·la·ver \pə'lavər, -'läv-\ n : talk —**palaver** vb

¹**pale** \'pāl\ adj **pal·er; pal·est** 1 : lacking in color or brightness 2 : light in color or shade ~ vb **paled; pal·ing** : make or become pale —**pale·ness** n

²**pale** n 1 : fence stake 2 : enclosed place

pal·ette \'palət\ n : board on which paints are laid and mixed

pal·i·sade \palə'sād\ n 1 : high fence 2 : line of cliffs

¹**pall** \'pȯl\ n 1 : cloth draped over a coffin

²**pall** vb : lose in interest or attraction

pall·bear·er n : one who attends the coffin at a funeral

pal·let \'palət\ n : makeshift bed

pal·let n : portable storage platform

pal·li·ate \'palē,āt\ vb -**at·ed; -at·ing** 1 : ease without curing 2 : cover or conceal by excusing —**pal·li·a·tion** \palē'āshən\ n —**pal·li·a·tive** \'palē,ātiv\ adj or n

pal·lid \'paləd\ adj : pale

pal·lor \'palər\ n : paleness

palm \'päm, 'pȧlm\ n 1 : tall tropical tree crowned with large leaves 2 : symbol of victory

²**palm** n : underside of the hand ~ vb 1 : conceal in the hand 2 : impose by fraud

palm·ist·ry \'päməstrē, 'pȧlmə-\ n : reading a person's character or future in his palms —**palm·ist** \'päməst, 'pȧlməst\ n

palmy \'pämē, 'pȧlmē\ adj **palm·i·er; -est** : flourishing

pal·o·mi·no \palə'mēnō\ n, pl -**nos** : light-colored horse

pal·pa·ble \'palpəbəl\ adj 1 : capable of being touched 2 : obvious —**pal·pa·bly** \-blē\ adv

pal·pi·tate \'palpə,tāt\ vb -**tat·ed; -tat·ing** : pulsate —**pal·pi·ta·tion** \palpə'tāshən\ n

pal·sy \'pȯlzē\ n, pl -**sies** 1 : paralysis 2 : condition marked by tremor —**pal·sied** \-zēd\ adj

pal·try \'pȯltrē\ adj -**tri·er; -est** : trivial

pam·pa \'pampə\ n, pl -**pas** \-pəz, -pəs\ : grassy So. American plain

pam·per \'pampər\ vb : spoil or indulge

pam·phlet \'pamflət\ n : unbound publication —**pam·phle·teer** \,pamflə-'tiər\ n

pan \'pan\ n : broad, shallow, and open container ~ vb 1 : wash gravel in a pan to search for gold 2 : criticize severely

pan·a·cea \,panə'sēə\ n : universal remedy

pan·cake n : fried flat cake

pan·creas \'paŋkrēəs, 'pan-\ n : gland that produces insulin —**pan·cre·at·ic** \,paŋkrē'atik, ,pan-\ adj

pan·da \'pandə\ n : black-and-white bearlike animal

pan·de·mo·ni·um \,pandə'mōnēəm\ n : wild uproar

pan·der \'pandər\ n 1 : pimp 2 : one who caters to others' desires or weaknesses ~ vb : act as a pander

pane \'pān\ n : sheet of glass

pan·e·gy·ric \,panə'jirik\ n : eulogistic oration —**pan·e·gy·rist** \-'jirəst\ n

pan·el \'pan⁹l\ n 1 : list of persons (as jurors) 2 : discussion group 3 : flat piece of construction material 4 : board with instruments or controls ~ vb -**eled** or -**elled; -el·ing** or -**el·ling** : decorate with panels —**pan·el·ing** n —**pan·el·ist** \-əst\ n

pang \'pan\ n : sudden sharp pain

pan·han·dle \'pan,hand⁹l\ vb -**dled; -dling** : ask for money on the street —**pan·han·dler** \-dlər, -d⁹lər\ n

pan·ic \'panik\ n : sudden overpowering fright ~ vb -**icked; -ick·ing** : affect or be affected with panic —**pan·icky** \-ikē\ adj

pan·o·ply \'panəplē\ n, pl -**plies** 1 : full suit of armor 2 : impressive array

pan·o·ra·ma \,panə'ramə, -'räm-\ n : view in every direction —**pan·oram·ic** \-'ramik\ adj

pan·sy \'panzē\ n, pl -**sies** : low-growing garden herb with showy flowers

pant \'pant\ vb 1 : breathe with great effort 2 : yearn ~ n : panting sound

pan·ta·loons \,pant⁹l'ünz\ n pl : pants

pan·ther \'panthər\ n : large wild cat

pant·ies \'pantēz\ n pl : undergarment with closed crotch and short legs

pan·to·mime \'pantə,mīm\ n 1 : play without words 2 : expression by bodily or facial movements ~ vb : represent by pantomime

pan·try \'pantrē\ n, pl -**tries** : storage room for food and dishes

pants \'pants\ *n pl* **1** : 2-legged outer garment **2** : panties

pap \'pap\ *n* : soft food

pa·pa·cy \'pāpəsē\ *n, pl* **-cies** : office of pope

pa·pal \'pāpəl\ *adj* : relating to the pope

pa·pa·ya \pə'pīə\ *n* : tropical tree with large edible fruit

pa·per \'pāpər\ *n* **1** : pliable substance used to write or print on, to wrap things in, or to cover walls **2** : printed or written document **3** : newspaper —**paper** *adj* —**pa·per·hang·er** *n* —**pa·per·weight** *n* —**pa·pery** \'pāp(ə)rē\ *adj*

pa·per·board *n* : cardboard

pa·pier-mâ·ché \,pāpərmə'shā, ,pap-,yämə-, -ma-\ *n* : molding material of waste paper

pa·poose \pa'püs, pə-\ *n* : young child of American Indian parents

pa·pri·ka \pə'prēkə, pa-\ *n* : mild red spice

pa·py·rus \pə'pīrəs\ *n, pl* **-rus·es** *or* **-ri** \-(,)rē, -,rī\ **1** : tall grasslike plant **2** : paper from papyrus

par \'pär\ *n* **1** : stated value **2** : common level **3** : accepted standard or normal condition —**par** *adj*

par·a·ble \'parəbəl\ *n* : simple story illustrating a moral truth

para·chute \'parə,shüt\ *n* : large umbrella-shaped device for making a descent from an airplane —**parachute** *vb* —**para·chut·ist** \-,shütəst\ *n*

pa·rade \pə'rād\ *n* **1** : pompous display **2** : ceremonial formation and march —*vb* **-rad·ed; -rad·ing 1** : march in a parade **2** : show off

par·a·digm \'parə,dīm, -,dim\ *n* : model

par·a·dise \'parə,dīs, -,dīz\ *n* : place of bliss

par·a·dox \'parə,däks\ *n* : statement that seems contrary to common sense yet is perhaps true —**par·a·dox·i·cal** \,parə'däksikəl\ *adj* —**par·a·dox·i·cal·ly** *adv*

par·af·fin \'parəfən\ *n* : white waxy substance used esp. for making candles and sealing foods —**paraffin** *vb* —**par·af·fin·ic** \,parə'finik\ *adj*

par·a·gon \'parə,gän, -gən\ *n* : model of perfection

para·graph \'parə,graf\ *n* : unified division of a piece of writing —*vb* : divide into paragraphs

par·a·keet \'parə,kēt\ *n* : small slender parrot

par·al·lel \'parə,lel\ *adj* **1** : lying or moving in the same direction but always the same distance apart **2** : similar —*n* **1** : parallel line, curve, or surface **2** : line of latitude **3** : similarity —*vb* **1** : compare **2** : correspond to —**par·al·lel·ism** \-,izəm\ *n*

par·al·lel·o·gram \,parə'lelə,gram\ *n* : 4-sided polygon with opposite sides equal and parallel

pa·ral·y·sis \pə'raləsəs\ *n, pl* **-y·ses** \-,sēz\ : loss of function and esp. of voluntary motion —**par·a·lyt·ic** \,parə'litik\ *adj or n*

par·a·lyze \'parə,līz\ *vb* **-lyzed; -lyz·ing** : affect with paralysis —**par·a·lyz·ing·ly** *adv*

pa·ram·e·ter \pə'ramətər\ *n* : characteristic element —**para·met·ric** \,parə'metrik\ *adj*

par·a·mount \'parə,maunt\ *adj* : superior to all others

par·amour \'parə,mur\ *n* : illicit lover

para·noia \,parə'nóiə\ *n* : mental disorder marked by irrational suspicion —**para·noid** \'parə,nóid\ *adj or n*

par·a·pet \'parəpət, -,pet\ *n* : protecting rampart in a fort

par·a·pher·na·lia \,parəfə(r)'nālyə\ *n sing or pl* : equipment

para·phrase \'parə,frāz\ *n* : restatement of a text giving the meaning in different words —**paraphrase** *vb*

para·ple·gia \,parə'plē(j)ē(ə)\ *n* : paralysis of the lower trunk and legs —**para·ple·gic** \-jik\ *adj or n*

par·a·site \'parə,sīt\ *n* : organism living on another —**par·a·sit·ic** \,parə'sitik\ *adj* —**par·a·sit·ism** \'parəsə,tizəm, -,sīt,iz-\ *n*

para·sol \'parə,sól\ *n* : umbrella used to keep off the sun

para·troops \-,trüps\ *n pl* : troops trained to parachute from an airplane —**para·troop·er** \-,trüpər\ *n*

par·boil \'pär,bóil\ *vb* : boil briefly

par·cel \'pärsəl\ *n* **1** : lot **2** : package —*vb* **-celed** *or* **-celled; -cel·ing** *or* **-cel·ling** : divide into portions

parch \'pärch\ *vb* : toast or shrivel with dry heat

parch·ment \'pärchmənt\ *n* : animal skin prepared to write on

par·don \'pärd⁸n\ *n* : excuse of an offense —*vb* : free from penalty —**par·don·able** \'pärdnəbəl, -ˀnəbal\ *adj* —**par·don·er** \-nər, -ˀnər\ *n*

pare \'paər\ *vb* **pared; par·ing 1** : trim off an outside part **2** : reduce as if by paring —**par·er** *n*

par·e·go·ric \,parə'górik\ *n* : tincture of opium and camphor

par·ent \'parənt\ *n* : one that begets

offspring —**par·ent·age** \-ij\ n —**pa-ren·tal** \pə'rent⁰l\ adj —**par·ent·hood** n

pa·ren·the·sis \pə'renthəsəs\ n, pl **-the·ses** \-ˌsēz\ 1 : word or phrase inserted in a passage 2 : one of a pair of punctuation marks ( ) —**par·en·thet·ic** \ˌparən'thetik\, **par·en·thet·i·cal** \-ikəl\ adj —**par·en·thet·i·cal·ly** \-k(ə)lē\ adv

par·fait \pär'fā\ n : layered cold dessert

pa·ri·ah \pə'rīə\ n : outcast

par·ish \'parish\ n : local church community

pa·rish·io·ner \pə'rishənər\ n : member of a parish

par·i·ty \'paratē\ n, pl **-ties** : equality

park \'pärk\ n : land reserved for recreation or beauty ~ vb : leave a vehicle standing

par·ka \'pärkə\ n : usu. hooded heavy jacket

park·way \'pärk,wā\ n : broad landscaped thoroughfare

par·lance \'pärləns\ n : manner of speaking

par·lay \'pär,lā\ n : the risking of a stake plus its winnings —**parlay** vb

par·ley \'pärlē\ n, pl **-leys** : conference about a dispute —**parley** vb

par·lia·ment \'pärləmənt\ n : legislative assembly —**par·lia·men·tar·i·an** n —**par·lia·men·ta·ry** \ˌpärlə-'ment(ə)rē\ adj

par·lor \'pärlər\ n 1 : reception room 2 : place of business

pa·ro·chi·al \pə'rōkēəl\ adj 1 : relating to a church parish 2 : provincial —**pa·ro·chi·al·ism** \-ə,lizəm\ n

par·o·dy \'parədē\ n, pl **-dies** : humorous or satirical imitation —**parody** vb

pa·role \pə'rōl\ n : conditional release of a prisoner —**parole** vb —**pa·rol·ee** \-,rō'lē, -'rō,lē\ n

par·ox·ysm \'parək,sizəm, pə'räk-\ n : spasm

par·que·try \'pärkətrē\ n, pl **-tries** : inlaid woodwork

par·ra·keet var of PARAKEET

par·rot \'parət\ n : bright-colored tropical bird

par·ry \'parē\ vb **-ried; -ry·ing** 1 : ward off a blow 2 : evade adroitly —**parry** n

parse \'pärs, 'pärz\ vb **parsed; pars·ing** : analyze grammatically

par·si·mo·ny \'pärsə,mōnē\ n : extreme frugality —**par·si·mo·ni·ous** \ˌpärsə'mōnēəs\ adj —**par·si·mo·ni·ous·ly** adv

pars·ley \'pärslē\ n : garden plant used as a seasoning

pars·nip \'pärsnəp\ n : carrotlike vegetable

par·son \'pärs⁰n\ n : minister

par·son·age \'pärsŋij, -⁰nij\ n : parson's house

part \'pärt\ n 1 : one of the units into which a larger whole is divided 2 : function or role ~ vb 1 : take leave 2 : separate 3 : go away 4 : give up

par·take \pär'tāk, pər-\ vb **-took; -tak·en; -tak·ing** : have or take a share —**par·tak·er** n

par·tial \'pärshəl\ adj 1 : favoring one over another 2 : affecting a part only —**par·tial·i·ty** \ˌpärsh(ē)'alətē\ n —**par·tial·ly** \'pärsh(ə)lē\ adv

par·tic·i·pate \pər'tisə,pāt, pär-\ vb **-pat·ed; -pat·ing** : take part in something —**par·tic·i·pant** \-pənt\ adj or n —**par·tic·i·pa·tion** \-,tisə'pāshən\ n —**par·tic·i·pa·to·ry** \-'tisəpə,tōrē\ adj

par·ti·ci·ple \'pärtə,sipəl\ n : verb form with functions of both verb and adjective —**par·ti·cip·i·al** \ˌpärtə-'sipēəl\ adj

par·ti·cle \'pärtikəl\ n : small bit

par·tic·u·lar \pə(r)'tikyələr\ adj 1 : relating to a specific person or thing 2 : individual 3 : hard to please ~ n : detail —**par·tic·u·lar·ly** adv

par·ti·san \'pärtəzən, -sən\ n 1 : adherent 2 : guerrilla —**partisan** adj —**par·ti·san·ship** n

par·tite \'pär,tīt\ adj : divided into parts

par·ti·tion \pər'tishən, pär-\ n 1 : distribution 2 : something that divides —**partition** vb

part·ly \'pärtlē\ adv : in some degree

part·ner \'pärtnər\ n 1 : associate 2 : companion 3 : business associate —**part·ner·ship** n

part of speech : class of words distinguished esp. according to function

par·tridge \'pärtrij\ n, pl **-tridge** or **-tridg·es** : stout-bodied game bird

par·tu·ri·tion \ˌpärtə'rishən, ˌpärchə-, ˌpärtyü-\ n : childbirth

par·ty \'pärtē\ n, pl **-ties** 1 : political organization 2 : participant 3 : company of persons esp. with a purpose 4 : social gathering

par·ve·nu \'pärvə,n(y)ü\ n : social upstart

pass \'pas\ vb 1 : move past, over, or through 2 : go away or die 3 : allow to elapse 4 : go unchallenged 5 : transfer or undergo transfer 6 : render a judgment 7 : occur 8

: enact 9 : undergo testing successfully 10 : be regarded 11 : decline ~ n 1 : low place in a mountain range 2 : act of passing 3 : accomplishment 4 : permission to leave, enter, or move about —**pass·able** adj —**pass·er** n —**pass·er·by** n

pas·sage \'pasij\ n 1 : process of passing 2 : means of passing 3 : voyage 4 : right to pass 5 : literary selection —**pas·sage·way** n

pass·book n : bankbook

pas·sé \pa'sā\ adj : out-of-date

pas·sen·ger \'pas³njər\ n : traveler in a conveyance

pass·ing \'pasiŋ\ n : death

pas·sion \'pashən\ n 1 : strong feeling esp. of anger, love, or desire 2 : object of affection or enthusiasm —**pas·sion·ate** \'pash(ə)nət\ adj —**pas·sion·ate·ly** adv —**pas·sion·less** adj

pas·sive \'pasiv\ adj 1 : not active but acted upon 2 : submissive —**passive** n —**pas·sive·ly** adv —**pas·siv·i·ty** \pa'sivətē\ n

Pass·over \'pas,ōvər\ n : Jewish holiday celebrated in March or April in commemoration of the Hebrews' liberation from slavery in Egypt

pass·port \'pas,pōrt\ n : government document needed for travel abroad

pass·word \'pas,wərd\ n : word or phrase spoken to pass a guard

past \'past\ adj 1 : ago 2 : just gone by 3 : having existed before the present 4 : expressing past time ~ prep or adv : beyond ~ n 1 : time gone by 2 : verb tense expressing time gone by 3 : past life

pas·ta \'pästə\ n : fresh or dried shaped dough

paste \'pāst\ n 1 : smooth ground food 2 : moist adhesive ~ vb **past·ed; past·ing** : attach with paste —**pasty** adj

paste·board n : cardboard

pas·tel \pas'tel\ n : light color —**pastel** adj

pas·teur·ize \'paschə,rīz, 'pastə-\ vb **-ized; -iz·ing** : heat (as milk) so as to kill germs —**pas·teur·iza·tion** \,paschərə'zāshən, ,pastə-\ n

pas·time \'pas,tīm\ n : amusement

pas·tor \'pastər\ n : clergyman serving a church or parish —**pas·tor·ate** \-t(ə)rət\ n

pas·to·ral \'past(ə)rəl\ adj 1 : relating to rural life 2 : of or relating to spiritual guidance or a pastor ~ n : literary work dealing with rural life

pas·try \'pāstrē\ n, pl **-ries** : sweet baked goods

pas·ture \'paschər\ n : land used for grazing ~ vb **-tured; -tur·ing** : graze

pat \'pat\ n 1 : light tap 2 : small mass ~ vb **-tt-** : tap gently ~ adj or adv 1 : apt or glib 2 : unyielding

patch \'pach\ n 1 : piece used for mending 2 : small area distinct from surrounding area ~ vb 1 : mend with a patch 2 : make of fragments 3 : repair hastily

patch·work n : something made of pieces of different materials, shapes, or colors

pate \'pāt\ n : crown of the head

pa·tel·la \pə'telə\ n, pl **-lae** \-'tel(,)ē, -,ī\ or **-las** : kneecap

¹**pa·tent** \'pat³nt, 'pāt-\ adj 1 : obvious 2 \'pat-\ : protected by a patent —**pat·ent·ly** adv

²**pat·ent** \'pat-\ n : document conferring or securing a right ~ vb : secure by patent —**pat·en·tee** \,pat³n'tē\ n

pa·ter·nal \pə'tərn³l\ adj 1 : fatherly 2 : related through or inherited from a father —**pa·ter·nal·ly** adv

pa·ter·ni·ty \pə'tərnətē\ n : fatherhood

path \'path, 'päth\ n 1 : trodden way 2 : route or course —**path·find·er** n —**path·way** n —**path·less** adj

pa·thet·ic \pə'thetik\ adj : pitiful —**pa·thet·i·cal·ly** \-ik(ə)lē\ adv

pa·thol·o·gy \pə'thäləjē\ n, pl **-gies** 1 : study of disease 2 : physical abnormality —**path·o·log·i·cal** \,pathə'läjikəl\ adj —**pa·thol·o·gist** \pə'thäləjəst\ n

pa·thos \'pā,thäs\ n : element evoking pity

pa·tience \'pāshəns\ n : habit or fact of being patient

pa·tient \'pāshənt\ adj : bearing pain or trials without complaint ~ n : person under medical care —**pa·tient·ly** adv

pa·ti·na \pə'tēnə, 'patənə\ n, pl **-nas** \-nəz\ or **-nae** \-,nē, -,nī\ : green film formed on copper and bronze

pa·tio \'patē,ō, 'pät-\ n, pl **-ti·os** : courtyard 2 : paved recreation area near a house

pa·tri·arch \'pātrē,ärk\ n 1 : man revered as father or founder 2 : venerable old man —**pa·tri·ar·chal** \,pātrē'ärkəl\ adj —**pa·tri·ar·chy** \-,ärkē\ n

pa·tri·cian \pə'trishən\ n : person of high birth —**patrician** adj

pat·ri·cide \'patrə,sīd\ n : murder of one's father

pat·ri·mo·ny \'patrə,mōnē\ n : something inherited —**pat·ri·mo·ni·al** \,patrə'mōnēəl\ adj

pa·tri·ot \'pātrēət, -,ät\ n : one who loves his country —**pa·tri·ot·ic** \'pātrē'ätik\ adj —**pa·tri·ot·i·cal·ly** \-ik(ə)lē\ adv —**pa·tri·ot·ism** \'pātrēə,tizəm\ n

pa·trol \pə'trōl\ n : a going around for observation or security 2 : group on patrol ~ vb -ll- : carry out a patrol

pa·trol·man \-mən\ n : police officer

pa·tron \'pātrən\ n 1 : special protector 2 : wealthy supporter 3 : customer

pa·tron·age \'patrənij, 'pā-\ n 1 : support or influence of a patron 2 : trade of customers 3 : control of government appointments

pa·tron·ize \'pātrə,nīz, 'pa-\ vb -ized; -iz·ing 1 : be a customer of 2 : treat with condescension

1pat·ter \'patər\ vb : talk glibly or mechanically ~ n : rapid talk

2patter vb : pat or tap rapidly ~ n : quick succession of pats or taps

pat·tern \'patərn\ n 1 : model for imitation or making things 2 : artistic design 3 : noticeable formation or set of characteristics ~ vb : form according to a pattern

pat·ty \'patē\ n, pl -ties : small flat cake

pau·ci·ty \'posətē\ n : shortage

paunch \'ponch\ n : large belly —**paunchy** adj

pau·per \'pōpər\ n : poor person —**pau·per·ism** \-pə,rizəm\ n —**pau·per·ize** \-pə,rīz\ vb

pause \'pōz\ n : temporary stop ~ vb paused; paus·ing : stop briefly

pave \'pāv\ vb paved; pav·ing : cover to smooth or firm the surface —**pave·ment** \-mənt\ n —**pav·ing** n

pa·vil·ion \pə'vilyən\ n 1 : large tent 2 : light structure used for entertainment

paw \'po\ n : foot of a 4-legged clawed animal ~ vb 1 : handle clumsily or rudely 2 : touch or strike with a paw, hoof, or foot

pawn \'pon\ n 1 : goods deposited as security for a loan 2 : state of being pledged ~ vb : deposit as a pledge —**pawn·bro·ker** n —**pawn·shop** n

pay \'pā\ vb paid \'pād\; pay·ing 1 : make due return for goods or services 2 : discharge indebtedness for 3 : requite 4 : give or make freely or as fitting 5 : be profitable ~ n 1 : status of being paid 2 : something paid —**pay·able** adj —**pay·check** n —**pay·ee** \pā'ē\ n —**pay·er** n —**pay·ment** n

pea \'pē\ n : round edible seed of a leguminous vine

peace \'pēs\ n 1 : state of calm and quiet 2 : absence of war or strife —**peace·able** \-əbəl\ adj —**peace·ably** \-blē\ adv —**peace·ful** \-fəl\ adj —**peace·ful·ly** adv —**peace·keep·er** n —**peace·keep·ing** n —**peace·mak·er** n —**peace·time** n

peach \'pēch\ n : sweet juicy fruit of a flowering tree

pea·cock \'pē,käk\ n : brilliantly colored male pheasant

peak \'pēk\ n 1 : pointed or projecting part 2 : top of a hill 3 : highest level ~ vb : reach a maximum —**peak** adj

peak·ed \'pēkəd\ adj : sickly

peal \'pēl\ n : loud sound (as of ringing bells) ~ vb : give out peals

pea·nut \'pē,nət\ n : annual herb that bears underground pods or the pod or the edible seed inside

pear \'paər\ n : fleshy fruit of a tree related to the apple

pearl \'pərl\ n : gem formed within an oyster —**pearly** \'pərlē\ adj

peas·ant \'pez³nt\ n : tiller of the soil —**peas·ant·ry** \-³ntrē\ n

peat \'pēt\ n : decayed organic deposit often dried for fuel —**peaty** adj

peb·ble \'pebəl\ n : small stone —**peb·bly** adj

pe·can \pi'kän, -'kan\ n : hickory tree bearing a smooth-shelled nut or the nut

pec·ca·dil·lo \,pekə'dilō\ n, pl -loes or -los : slight offense

1peck \'pek\ n : unit of dry measure equal to 8 quarts

2peck vb : strike or pick up with the bill ~ n : quick sharp stroke

pec·tin \'pektən\ n : water-soluble plant substance that causes fruit jellies to set —**pec·tic** \-tik\ adj

pec·to·ral \'pekt(ə)rəl\ adj : relating to the breast or chest

pe·cu·liar \pi'kyülyər\ adj 1 : characteristic of only one 2 : strange —**pe·cu·liar·i·ty** \-,kyül'yaratē, -ē'ar-\ n —**pe·cu·liar·ly** adv

pe·cu·niary \pi'kyünē,erē\ adj : relating to money

ped·a·go·gy \'pedə,gōjē, -,gäj-\ n : art or profession of teaching —**ped·a·gog·ic** \,pedə'gäjik, -'gōj-\, **ped·a·gog·i·cal** \-ikəl\ adj —**ped·a·gogue** \'pedə,gäg\ n

ped·al \'ped³l\ n : lever worked by the foot ~ adj : relating to the foot ~ vb : use a pedal

ped·ant \'ped³nt\ n : learned bore —**pe·dan·tic** \pi'dantik\ adj —**ped·ant·ry** \'ped³ntrē\ n

ped·dle \'ped³l\ vb -dled; -dling : offer

for sale **—ped·dler, ped·lar** \'pedlər\ *n*

ped·es·tal \'pedəst°l\ *n* : support or foot of something upright

pe·des·tri·an \pə'destrēən\ *adj* 1 : ordinary 2 : walking ~ *n* : person who walks

pe·di·at·rics \,pēdē'atriks\ *n* : branch of medicine dealing with children **—pe·di·at·ric** \-trik\ *adj* **—pe·di·a·tri·cian** \,pēdēə'trishən\ *n*

ped·i·gree \'pedə,grē\ *n* : line of ancestors or a record of it

ped·i·ment \'pedəmənt\ *n* : triangular gablelike decoration on a building

peek \'pēk\ *vb* 1 : look furtively 2 : glance **—peek** *n*

peel \'pēl\ *vb* 1 : strip the skin or rind from 2 : lose the outer layer ~ *n* : skin or rind **—peel·ing** *n*

¹**peep** \'pēp\ *vb or n* : cheep

²**peep** *vb* 1 : look slyly 2 : begin to emerge ~ *n* : brief view **—peep·er** *n* **—peep·hole** *n*

¹**peer** \'piər\ *n* 1 : one's equal 2 : nobleman **—peer·age** \-ij\ *n*

²**peer** *vb* : look intently or curiously

peer·less \-ləs\ *adj* : having no equal

peeve \'pēv\ *vb* : make resentful ~ *n* : complaint **—peev·ish** \-ish\ *adj* **—peev·ish·ly** *adv* **—peev·ish·ness** *n*

peg \'peg\ *n* : small pinlike piece ~ *vb* **-gg-** 1 : put a peg into 2 : fix or mark with or as if with pegs

peignoir \pān'wär, pen-\ *n* : negligee

pelf \'pelf\ *n* : money

pel·i·can \'pelikən\ *n* : large-billed seabird

pel·la·gra \pə'lagrə, -'läg-\ *n* : protein-deficiency disease

pel·let \'pelət\ *n* : little ball **—pel·let·al** \-°l\ *adj* **—pel·let·ize** \-,īz\ *vb*

pell-mell \'pel'mel\ *adv* : in confusion or haste

pel·lu·cid \pə'lüsəd\ *adj* : very clear

¹**pelt** \'pelt\ *n* : skin of a fur-bearing animal

²**pelt** *vb* : strike with blows or missiles

pel·vis \'pelvəs\ *n, pl* **-vis·es** \-vəsəz\ *or* **-ves** \-,vēz\ : cavity formed by the hip bones **—pel·vic** \-vik\ *adj*

pem·mi·can \'pemikən\ *n* : dried meat

¹**pen** \'pen\ *n* : enclosure for animals ~ *vb* **-nn-** : shut in a pen

²**pen** *n* : tool for writing with ink ~ *vb* **-nn-** : write

pe·nal \'pēn°l\ *adj* : relating to punishment

pe·nal·ize \'pēn°l,īz, 'pen-\ *vb* **-ized; -iz·ing** : put a penalty on

pen·al·ty \'pen°ltē\ *n, pl* **-ties** 1 : pun-

ishment for crime 2 : disadvantage, loss, or hardship due to an action

pen·ance \'penəns\ *n* : act performed to show repentance

pence \'pens\ *pl of* PENNY

pen·chant \'penchənt\ *n* : strong inclination

pen·cil \'pensəl\ *n* : writing or drawing tool with a solid marking substance as its core ~ *vb* **-ciled** *or* **-cilled; -cil·ing** *or* **-cil·ling** : draw or write with a pencil

pen·dant \'pendənt\ *n* : hanging ornament

pen·dent, pen·dant \'pendənt\ *adj* : hanging

pend·ing \'pendiŋ\ *prep* : while awaiting ~ *adj* : not yet decided

pen·du·lous \'penjələs, -də-\ *adj* : hanging loosely

pen·du·lum \-ləm\ *n* : weight that swings from a fixed point

pen·e·trate \'penə,trāt\ *vb* **-trat·ed; -trat·ing** 1 : enter into 2 : permeate 3 : see into **—pen·e·tra·ble** \-trəbəl\ *adj* **—pen·e·tra·tion** \,penə'trāshən\ *n* **—pen·e·tra·tive** \'penə,trātiv\ *adj*

pen·guin \'peŋgwən, 'pen-\ *n* : short-legged flightless seabird

pen·i·cil·lin \,penə'silən\ *n* : anitbiotic produced by a mold

pen·in·su·la \pə'ninsələ, -'ninchə-\ *n* : land extending out into the water **—pen·in·su·lar** \-lər\ *adj*

pe·nis \'pēnəs\ *n, pl* **-nes** \-,nēz\ *or* **-nis·es** : male organ of copulation

pen·i·tent \'penətənt\ *adj* : feeling sorrow for sins or offenses ~ *n* : penitent person **—pen·i·tence** \-təns\ *n* **—pen·i·ten·tial** \,penə'tenchəl\ *adj*

pen·i·ten·tia·ry \,penə'tench(ə)rē\ *n, pl* **-ries** : state or federal prison

pen·man·ship \'penmən,ship\ *n* : art or practice of writing

pen·nant \'penənt\ *n* : nautical or championship flag

pen·ny \'penē\ *n, pl* **-nies** \-ēz\ *or* **pence** \'pens\ 1 : monetary unit equal to 1/100 pound 2 *pl* **-nies** : cent **—pen·ni·less** \'peniləs\ *adj*

pen·sion \'penchən\ *n* : retirement income ~ *vb* : pay a pension to **—pension·er** *n*

pen·sive \'pensiv\ *adj* : thoughtful **—pen·sive·ly** *adv*

pent \'pent\ *adj* : confined

pen·ta·gon \'pentə,gän\ *n* : 5-sided polygon **—pen·tag·o·nal** \pen'tagən°l\ *adj*

pen·tam·e·ter \pen'tamətər\ *n* : line of 5 metrical feet

pent·house \'pent,haús\ *n* : rooftop apartment

pe·nu·ri·ous \pə\n(y)úrēəs\ *adj* 1 : marked by penury 2 : stingy

pen·u·ry \'penyərē\ *n* : poverty

pe·on \'pē,än, -ən\ *n, pl* **-ons** *or* **-ones** \pä'ōnēz\ : landless laborer in Spanish America —**pe·on·age** \-ənij\ *n*

pe·o·ny \'pēənē\ *n, pl* **-nies** : garden plant having large flowers

peo·ple \'pēpəl\ *n, pl* **people** 1 *pl* : human beings in general 2 *pl* : human beings in a certain group (as a family) or community 3 *pl* **peoples** : tribe, nation, or race ~ *vb* **-pled; -pling** : constitute the population of

pep \'pep\ *n* : brisk energy ~ *vb* **pepped; pep·ping** : put pep into —**pep·py** *adj*

pep·per \'pepər\ *n* 1 : pungent seasoning from the berry (**peppercorn**) of a shrub 2 : vegetable grown for its hot or sweet fruit ~ *vb* : season with pepper —**pep·pery** \-(ə)rē\ *adj*

pep·per·mint \-,mint, -mənt\ *n* : pungent aromatic mint

pep·tic \'peptik\ *adj* : relating to digestion or the effect of digestive juices

per \(')pər\ *prep* 1 : by means of 2 : for each 3 : according to

per·am·bu·late \pə'rambyə,lāt\ *vb* **-lat·ed; -lat·ing** : travel over esp. on foot —**per·am·bu·la·tion** \-,rambyə-'lāshən\ *n*

per·cale \(,)pər'kāl, 'pər,-; (,)pər'kal\ *n* : fine woven cotton cloth

per·ceive \pər'sēv\ *vb* **-ceived; -ceiving** 1 : realize 2 : become aware of through the senses —**per·ceiv·able** *adj*

per·cent \pər'sent\ *adv* : in each hundred ~ *n, pl* **-cent** *or* **-cents** 1 : one part in a hundred 2 : percentage

per·cent·age \pər'sentij\ *n* : part of a whole expressed in hundredths

per·cep·ti·ble \pər'septəbəl\ *adj* : capable of being perceived —**per·cep·ti·bly** \-blē\ *adv*

per·cep·tion \pər'sepshən\ *n* 1 : act or result of perceiving 2 : ability to perceive

per·cep·tive \pər'septiv\ *adj* : showing perception —**per·cep·tive·ly** *adv*

¹perch \'pərch\ *n* : roost for birds ~ *vb* : roost

²perch *n, pl* **perch** *or* **perch·es** : freshwater spiny-finned food fish

per·co·late \'pərkə,lāt\ *vb* **-lat·ed; -lat·ing** : trickle or cause to trickle down through a substance —**per·co·la·tor** \-,lātər\ *n*

per·cus·sion \pər'kəshən\ *n* 1 : sharp blow 2 : musical instrument sounded by striking

pe·remp·to·ry \pə'rempt(ə)rē\ *adj* 1 : imperative 2 : domineering —**pe·remp·to·ri·ly** \-t(ə)ralē\ *adv*

pe·ren·ni·al \pə'renēəl\ *adj* 1 : present at all seasons of the year 2 : continuing to live from year to year 3 : recurring regularly ~ *n* : plant that lives for a number of years —**pe·ren·ni·al·ly** *adv*

per·fect \'pərfikt\ *adj* 1 : being without fault or defect 2 : exact 3 : complete ~ *vb* : make perfect —**per·fect·i·bil·i·ty** \pər,fektə'bilətē, ,pərfik-\ *n* —**per·fect·ible** \pər'fektəbəl, 'pərfik-\ *adj* —**per·fect·ly** *adv*

per·fec·tion \pər'fekshən\ *n* 1 : quality or state of being perfect 2 : highest degree of excellence —**per·fec·tion·ist** \-sh(ə)nəst\ *n*

per·fi·dy \'pərfədē\ *n* : treachery —**per·fid·i·ous** \pər'fidēəs\ *adj* —**per·fid·i·ous·ly** *adv*

per·fo·rate \'pərfə,rāt\ *vb* **-rat·ed; -rat·ing** : make a hole in —**per·fo·ra·tion** \,pərfə'rāshən\ *n*

per·force \pər'fōrs\ *adv* : of necessity

per·form \pə(r)'fórm\ *vb* 1 : adhere to the terms of 2 : carry out 3 : give a performance —**per·form·er** *n*

per·for·mance \pər'fór,məns\ *n* 1 : act or process of performing 2 : public presentation

per·fume \pər,fyüm, pər'-\ *n* 1 : pleasant odor 2 : preparation used for scenting ~ \pər'-, 'pər,-\ *vb* **-fumed; -fum·ing** : add a pleasing smell to

per·func·to·ry \pər'fəŋkt(ə)rē\ *adj* : done merely as a duty —**per·func·to·ri·ly** \-t(ə)ralē\ *adv*

per·haps \pər'(h)aps, 'praps\ *adv* : possibly but not certainly

per·il \'perəl\ *n* : danger —**per·il·ous** *adj* —**per·il·ous·ly** *adv*

per·im·e·ter \pə'rimətər\ *n* : outer boundary of a body or figure

pe·ri·od \'pirēəd\ *n* 1 : punctuation mark . used esp. to mark the end of a declarative sentence or an abbreviation 2 : division of time 3 : stage or division in a process or development

pe·ri·od·ic \,pirē'ädik\ *adj* : occurring at regular intervals —**pe·ri·od·i·cal·ly** \-ik(ə)lē\ *adv*

pe·ri·od·i·cal \,pirē'ädikəl\ *n* : newspaper or magazine

pe·riph·ery \pə'rif(ə)rē\ *n, pl* **-er·ies**

: outer boundary —**per·iph·er·al** \-(ə)rəl\ *adj*

peri·scope \'perə,skōp\ *n* : optical instrument for viewing from a submarine

per·ish \'perish\ *vb* : die or spoil —**per·ish·able** \-əbəl\ *adj or n*

per·ju·ry \'pərj(ə)rē\ *n* : voluntary violation of an oath to tell the truth —**per·jure** \'pərjər\ *vb* —**per·jur·er** *n*

¹perk \'pərk\ *vb* 1 : thrust (as the head) up jauntily 2 : make trim or brisk 3 : gain vigor or spirit —**perky** *adj*

²perk *vb* : percolate

¹per·ma·nent \'pərmənənt\ *adj* : lasting —**per·ma·nence** \-nəns\ *n* —**per·ma·nen·cy** \-nənsē\ *n* —**per·ma·nent·ly** *adv*

²permanent *n* : long-lasting hair wave or straightening

per·me·able \'pərmēəbəl\ *adj* : permitting liquids or gases to seep through —**per·me·a·bil·i·ty** \,pərmē'bilətē\ *n*

per·me·ate \'pərmē,āt\ *vb* -**at·ed; -at·ing** 1 : seep through 2 : pervade —**per·me·ation** \,pərmē'āshən\ *n*

per·mis·si·ble \pər'misəbəl\ *adj* : that may be permitted

per·mis·sion \pər'mishən\ *n* : formal consent

per·mis·sive \pər'misiv\ *adj* : granting freedom esp. to excess —**per·mis·sive·ness** *n*

per·mit \pər'mit\ *vb* -**mit·ted; -mit·ting** 1 : give approval for 2 : make possible ~ \'pər,-, pər'-\ *n* : license

per·ni·cious \pər'nishəs\ *adj* : harmful —**per·ni·cious·ly** *adv*

per·ox·ide \pə'räk,sīd\ *n* : compound (as hydrogen peroxide) in which oxygen is joined to oxygen

per·pen·dic·u·lar \,pərpən'dikyələr\ *adj* 1 : vertical 2 : meeting another line at a right angle —**perpendicular** *n* —**per·pen·dic·u·lar·i·ty** \-,dikyə'larətē\ *n* —**per·pen·dic·u·lar·ly** *adv*

per·pe·trate \'pərpə,trāt\ *vb* -**trat·ed; -trat·ing** : be guilty of doing —**per·pe·tra·tion** \,pərpə'trāshən\ *n* —**per·pe·tra·tor** \'pərpə,trātər\ *n*

per·pet·u·al \pər'pech(ə)wəl\ *adj* 1 : continuing forever 2 : occurring continually —**per·pet·u·al·ly** *adv* —**per·pe·tu·ity** \,pərpə't(y)üətē\ *n*

per·pet·u·ate \pər'pecha,wāt\ *vb* -**at·ed; -at·ing** : make perpetual —**per·pet·u·a·tion** \-,pecha'wāshən\ *n*

per·plex \pər'pleks\ *vb* : confuse —**per·plex·i·ty** \-ətē\ *n*

per·qui·site \'pərkwəzət\ *n* : privilege or profit beyond regular pay

per·se·cute \'pərsi,kyüt\ *vb* -**cut·ed; -cut·ing** : harass in such a way as to injure or afflict —**per·se·cu·tion** \,pərsi'kyüshən\ *n* —**per·se·cu·tor** \'pərsi,kyütər\ *n*

per·se·vere \,pərsə'viər\ *vb* -**vered; -ver·ing** : persist —**per·se·ver·ance** \-'virəns\ *n*

per·sist \pər'sist, -'zist\ *vb* 1 : go on resolutely in spite of difficulties 2 : continue to exist —**per·sis·tence** \-'sistəns, -'zis-\ *n* —**per·sis·ten·cy** \-tənsē\ *n* —**per·sis·tent** \-tənt\ *adj* —**per·sis·tent·ly** *adv*

per·son \'pərsⁿn\ *n* 1 : human being 2 : human being's body or individuality 3 : reference to the speaker, one spoken to, or one spoken of

per·son·able \'pərsnəbəl, -ⁿnəbəl\ *adj* : having a pleasing personality

per·son·age \'pərsnij, -ⁿnij\ *n* : person of rank or distinction

per·son·al \'pərsnəl, -ⁿnəl\ *adj* 1 : relating to or affecting a particular person 2 : done in person 3 : affecting an individual's body 4 : indicating grammatical person —**per·son·al·ly** *adv*

per·son·al·i·ty \,pərsⁿn'alətē\ *n, pl* -**ties** 1 : offensive personal remark 2 : manner and disposition of an individual 3 : distinctive person

per·son·al·ize \'pərsna,līz, -ⁿna,līz\ *vb* -**ized; -iz·ing** : mark as belonging to a particular person

per·son·i·fy \pər'sänə,fī\ *vb* -**fied; -fy·ing** 1 : represent as a human being 2 : be the embodiment of —**per·son·i·fi·ca·tion** \-,sänəfə'kāshən\ *n*

per·son·nel \,pərsⁿn'el\ *n* : body of persons employed in an organization

per·spec·tive \pər'spektiv\ *n* 1 : apparent depth and distance in painting 2 : view of things in their true relationship or importance

per·spi·cac·i·ty \,pərspə'kasətē\ *n* : acuteness of understanding or judgment —**per·spi·ca·cious** \-'kāshəs\ *adj*

per·spire \pər'spīr\ *vb* -**spired; -spir·ing** : sweat —**per·spi·ra·tion** \,pərspə'rāshən\ *n*

per·suade \pər'swād\ *vb* -**suad·ed; -suad·ing** : cause to do or believe by argument or entreaty —**per·sua·sive** \-'swāsiv, -ziv\ *adj* —**per·sua·sive·ly** *adv* —**per·sua·sive·ness** *n*

per·sua·sion \pər'swāzhən\ *n* : act or process of persuading

pert \'pərt\ *adj* : flippant or irreverent

per·tain \pər'tān\ *vb* 1 : belong 2 : relate

per·ti·nent \'pərt⁰nənt\ *adj* : relevant
—**per·ti·nence** \-əns\ *n*

per·turb \pər'tərb\ *vb* : make uneasy
—**per·tur·ba·tion** \,pərtər'bāshən\ *n*

pe·ruse \pə'rüz\ *vb* -**rused**; -**rus·ing**
: read attentively —**pe·rus·al**
\-'rüzəl\ *n*

per·vade \pər'vād\ *vb* -**vad·ed**; -**vad·ing** : spread through every part of —
per·va·sive \-'vāsiv, -ziv\ *adj*

per·verse \pər'vərs\ *adj* 1 : corrupt 2 : unreasonably contrary —**per·verse·ly** *adv* —**per·verse·ness** *n* —**per·ver·sion** \pər'vərzhən\ *n* —**per·ver·si·ty** \-'vərsətē\ *n*

per·vert \pər'vərt\ *vb* : corrupt or distort ~ \'pər,-\ *n* : one that is perverted

pe·so \'pāsō\ *n, pl* -**sos** : monetary unit (as of Mexico)

pes·si·mism \'pesə,mizəm\ *n* : inclination to expect the worst —**pes·si·mist** \-mast\ *n* —**pes·si·mis·tic** \,pesə'mistik\ *adj*

pest \'pest\ *n* 1 : nuisance 2 : plant or animal detrimental to man —**pes·ti·cide** \'pestə,sīd\ *n*

pes·ter \'pestər\ *vb* -**tered**; -**ter·ing** : harass persistently with petty matters

pes·ti·lence \'pestələns\ *n* : plague —**pes·ti·lent** \-lənt\ *adj*

pes·tle \'pesəl, 'pest⁰l\ *n* : implement for grinding substances in a mortar

pet \'pet\ *n* 1 : domesticated animal kept for pleasure rather than utility 2 : favorite ~ *vb* -**tt**- : stroke gently or lovingly

pet·al \'pet⁰l\ *n* : modified leaf of a flower head

pe·tite \pə'tēt\ *adj* : having a small trim figure

pe·ti·tion \pə'tishən\ *n* : formal written request ~ *vb* : make a petition —**pe·ti·tion·er** *n*

pe·trel \'petrəl\ *n* : small seabird

pet·ri·fy \'petrə,fī\ *vb* -**fied**; -**fy·ing** 1 : change into stony material 2 : make rigid or inactive (as from fear) —**pet·ri·fac·tion** \,petrə'fakshən\ *n*

pe·tro·leum \pə'trōlēəm\ *n* : raw oil obtained from the ground

pet·ti·coat \'petē,kōt\ *n* : skirt worn under a dress

pet·ty \'petē\ *adj* -**ti·er**; -**est** 1 : being small or minor and of no importance 2 : narrow-minded or unsympathetic —**pet·ti·ly** \'pet⁰lē\ *adv* —**pet·ti·ness** *n*

petty officer *n* : subordinate officer in the navy or coast guard appointed from among the enlisted men

petty officer first class *n* : petty officer ranking below a chief petty officer

petty officer second class *n* : petty officer ranking below a petty officer first class

petty officer third class *n* : petty officer ranking below a petty officer second class

pet·u·lant \'pechələnt\ *adj* : irritable —**pet·u·lance** \-ləns\ *n* —**pet·u·lant·ly** *adv*

pe·tu·nia \pi't(y)ünyə\ *n* : garden plant with bright flowers

pew \'pyü\ *n* : bench with a back used in a church

pew·ter \'pyütər\ *n* : alloy of tin used for kitchen or table utensils

pH \(')pē'āch\ *n* : number expressing relative acidity and alkalinity

pha·lanx \'fā,laŋks\ *n, pl* -**lanx·es** *or* -**lan·ges** \fə'lan,jēz\ 1 : body (as of troops) in compact formation 2 *pl phalanges* : digital bone of the hand or foot

phal·lus \'faləs\ *n, pl* -**li** \'fal,ī\ *or* -**lus·es** : penis —**phal·lic** *adj*

phantasy *var of* FANTASY

phan·tom \'fantəm\ *n* : something that only appears to be real —**phantom** *adj*

pha·raoh \'fe(ə)rō, 'fārō\ *n* : ruler of ancient Egypt

phar·i·see \'farə,sē\ *n* : self-righteous or hypocritical person —**phar·i·sa·ic** \,farə'sāik\ *adj*

phar·ma·ceu·ti·cal \,färmə'sütikal\ *adj* 1 : relating to pharmacy or pharmacists 2 : medicinal —**pharmaceutical** *n*

phar·ma·col·o·gy \,färmə'käləjē\ *n* : science of drugs esp. as related to medicinal uses —**phar·ma·co·log·ic** \-kə'läjik\, **phar·ma·co·log·i·cal** \-ikal\ *adj* —**phar·ma·col·o·gist** \-'käləjəst\ *n*

phar·ma·cy \'färməsē\ *n, pl* -**cies** 1 : art or practice of preparing and dispensing drugs 2 : drugstore —**phar·ma·cist** \-səst\ *n*

phar·ynx \'fariŋks\ *n, pl* **pha·ryn·ges** \fə'rin,jēz\ : space behind the mouth into which the nostrils, esophagus, and windpipe open —**pha·ryn·ge·al** \fə'rinj(ē)əl, ,fariŋ'jēəl\ *adj*

phase \'fāz\ *n* 1 : particular appearance or stage in a recurring series of changes 2 : stage in a process

pheas·ant \'fez⁰nt\ *n, pl* -**ant** *or* -**ants**

: long-tailed brilliantly colored game bird

phe·nom·e·non \fi'nämə,nän, -nən\ *n, pl* **-na** \-nə\ *or* **-nons 1** : observable fact or event **2** *pl* **-nons** : prodigy —**phe·nom·e·nal** \-'nämən⁹l\ *adj*

phi·lan·der \fə'landər\ *vb* : make love without serious intent —**phi·lan·der·er** *n*

phi·lan·thro·py \fə'lanthrəpē\ *n, pl* **-pies** : charitable act or gift or an organization that distributes such gifts —**phil·an·throp·ic** \,filən'thrä-pik\ *adj* —**phi·lan·thro·pist** \fə'lanthrəpəst\ *n*

phi·lat·e·ly \fə'lat⁹lē\ *n* : collection and study of postage stamps —**phi·lat·e·list** \-⁹ləst\ *n*

phil·har·mon·ic \,filər'mänik, ,fil(h)är-\ *adj* : relating to a symphony orchestra

phi·lis·tine \'filə,stēn; fə'listən\ *n* : one who is smugly indifferent to ideas or art —**philistine** *adj*

philo·den·dron \,filə'dendrən\ *n, pl* **-drons** *or* **-dra** \-drə\ : plant grown for its showy leaves

phi·los·o·pher \fə'läsəfər\ *n* **1** : reflective thinker **2** : student of or specialist in philosophy

phi·los·o·phy \fə'läsəfē\ *n, pl* **-phies 1** : critical study of fundamental beliefs **2** : sciences and liberal arts exclusive of medicine, law, and theology **3** : system of ideas **4** : sum of personal convictions **5** : calmness —**phil·o·soph·ic** \,filə'säfik\, **phil·o·soph·i·cal** \-ikəl\ *adj* —**phil·o·soph·i·cal·ly** \-k(ə)lē\ *adv* —**phi·los·o·phize** \fə'läsə,fīz\ *vb*

phle·bi·tis \fli'bītəs\ *n* : inflammation of a vein

phlegm \'flem\ *n* : thick mucus in the nose and throat

phleg·mat·ic \fleg'matik\ *adj* : slow and stolid

phlox \'fläks\ *n, pl* **phlox** *or* **phlox·es** : herb grown for its flower clusters

pho·bia \'fōbēə\ *n* : irrational persistent fear

phoe·nix \'fēniks\ *n* : legendary bird held to burn itself to death and rise fresh and young from its ashes

phone \'fōn\ *n* : telephone —**phoned; phon·ing** : call on a telephone

pho·neme \'fō,nēm\ *n* : smallest distinguishable unit of speech —**pho·ne·mic** \fō'nēmik\ *adj*

pho·net·ics \fə'netiks\ *n* : study of speech sounds —**pho·net·ic** \-ik\ *adj* —**pho·ne·ti·cian** \,fōnə'tishən\ *n*

pho·no·graph \'fōnə,graf\ *n* : instrument that reproduces sounds from a grooved disc —**pho·no·graph·ic** \,fōnə'grafik\ *adj*

pho·ny, pho·ney \'fōnē\ *adj* **-ni·er; -est** : not sincere or genuine —**phony** *n*

phos·phate \'fäs,fāt\ *n* : chemical salt used in fertilizers —**phos·phat·ic** \fäs'fatik\ *adj*

phos·phor \'fäsfər\ *n* : phosphorescent substance

phos·pho·res·cence \,fäsfə'res⁹ns\ *n* : luminescence without heat —**phos·pho·res·cent** \-⁹nt\ *adj* —**phos·pho·res·cent·ly** *adv*

phos·pho·rus \'fäsf(ə)rəs\ *n* : poisonous waxy chemical element —**phos·phor·ic** \fäs'fórik, -'fär-\ *adj* —**phos·pho·rous** \'fäsf(ə)rəs; fäs'fōrəs, -'fór-\ *adj*

pho·to \'fōtō\ *n, pl* **-tos** : photograph —**photo** *vb or adj*

pho·to·elec·tric \,fōtōi'lektrik\ *adj* : relating to an electrical effect due to the interaction of light with matter

pho·to·gen·ic \,fōtə'jenik\ *adj* : suitable for being photographed

pho·to·graph \'fōtə,graf\ *n* : picture taken by photography —**photograph** *vb* —**pho·tog·ra·pher** \fə'tägrəfər\ *n*

pho·tog·ra·phy \fə'tägrəfē\ *n* : process of using light to produce images on a sensitized surface —**pho·to·graph·ic** \,fōtə'grafik\ *adj* —**pho·to·graph·i·cal·ly** \-ik(ə)lē\ *adv*

pho·to·syn·the·sis \,fōtō'sinthəsəs\ *n* : formation of carbohydrates by chlorophyll-containing plants exposed to sunlight —**pho·to·syn·the·size** \-,sīz\ *vb* —**pho·to·syn·thet·ic** \-sin'thetik\ *adj*

phrase \'frāz\ *n* **1** : brief expression **2** : group of related words that express a thought ~ *vb* **phrased; phras·ing** : express in a particular manner

phrase·ol·o·gy \,frāzē'äləjē\ *n, pl* **-gies** : manner of phrasing

phy·lum \'filəm\ *n, pl* **-la** \-lə\ : major division of the plant or animal kingdom

phys·ic \'fizik\ *n* : medicine that purges

phys·i·cal \'fizikəl\ *adj* **1** : relating to nature **2** : material as opposed to mental or spiritual **3** : relating to the body —**phys·i·cal·ly** \-k(ə)lē\ *adv*

phy·si·cian \fə'zishən\ *n* : doctor of medicine

phys·i·cist \'fizəsəst\ *n* : specialist in physics

phys·ics \'fiziks\ *n* : science that deals with matter and motion

phys·i·og·no·my \,fizē'äg)nəmē\ *n, pl* **-mies** : facial appearance esp. as a reflection of inner character

phys·i·ol·o·gy \,fizē'äləjē\ *n* **1** : science dealing with the functioning of living matter and beings **2** : functional processes in an organism —**phys·i·o·log·i·cal** \-ēə'läjikəl\, **phys·i·o·log·ic** \-ik\ *adj* —**phys·i·ol·o·gist** \-ē'äləjəst\ *n*

phy·sique \fə'zēk\ *n* : build of a person's body

pi \'pī\ *n, pl* **pis** \'pīz\ : symbol π denoting the ratio of the circumference of a circle to its diameter or the ratio itself

pi·a·nist \pē'anəst, 'pēənəst\ *n* : one who plays the piano

pi·a·no \pē'anō\ *n, pl* **-anos** : musical instrument with strings sounded by hammers operated by a keyboard

pi·az·za \pē'azə, -'atsə\ *n, pl* **-zas** *or* **-ze** \-'at(,)sä, -'ät-\ : open square in a town

pi·ca·yune \,pikē'(y)ün\ *adj* : trivial or petty

pic·co·lo \'pikə,lō\ *n, pl* **-los** : small shrill flute

¹pick \'pik\ *vb* **1** : break up with a pointed instrument **2** : remove bit by bit **3** : gather by plucking **4** : select **5** : rob **6** : provoke **7** : unlock with a wire **8** : eat sparingly ~ *n* **1** : act of choosing **2** : choicest one —**pick·er** *n* —**pick up** *vb* **1** : improve **2** : put in order

²pick *n* : pointed digging tool

pick·ax *n* : pick

pick·er·el \'pik(ə)rəl\ *n, pl* **-el** *or* **-els** : small pike

pick·et \'pikət\ *n* **1** : pointed stake (as for a fence) **2** : worker demonstrating on strike ~ *vb* : demonstrate as a picket

pick·le \'pikəl\ *n* : brine or vinegar solution for preserving foods or a food preserved in a pickle —**pickle** *vb*

pick·pock·et *n* : one who steals from pockets

pick·up \'pik,əp\ *n* **1** : revival or acceleration **2** : light truck with an open body

pic·nic \'pik,nik\ *n* : outing with food usu. eaten in the open ~ *vb* **-nicked;** **-nick·ing** : go on a picnic

pic·to·ri·al \pik'tōrēəl\ *adj* : relating to pictures

pic·ture \'pikchər\ *n* **1** : representation by painting, drawing, or photography **2** : vivid description **3** : image or copy **4** : movie ~ *vb* **-tured; -tur·ing** : form a mental image of

pic·tur·esque \,pikchə'resk\ *adj* : attractive or charming enough to be suitable for a picture —**pic·tur·esque·ness** *n*

pie \'pī\ *n* : pastry crust and a filling

pie·bald \'pī,bold\ *adj* : blotched with white and black

piece \'pēs\ *n* **1** : part of a whole **2** : one of a group or set ~ *vb* **pieced; piec·ing** : join into a whole

piece·meal \'pēs,mēl\ *adv or adj* : gradually

pied \'pīd\ *adj* : colored in blotches

pier \'piər\ *n* **1** : support for a bridge span **2** : deck or wharf built out over water **3** : pillar

pierce \'piərs\ *vb* **pierced; pierc·ing** **1** : enter or thrust into or through **2** : penetrate **3** : see through

pi·e·ty \'pīətē\ *n, pl* **-eties** : devotion to religion

pig \'pig\ *n* **1** : young swine **2** : dirty or greedy individual **3** : a casting (as of iron) run directly from a furnace into a mold —**pig·let** \-lət\ *n* —**pig·pen** *n* —**pig·sty** *n*

pi·geon \'pijən\ *n* : stout-bodied short-legged bird

pi·geon·hole *n* : small open compartment for letters or documents ~ *vb* **1** : place in a pigeonhole **2** : classify

pig·gish \'pigish\ *adj* : greedy

pig·gy·back \'pigē,bak\ *adv or adj* : up on the back and shoulders

pig·head·ed \-'hedəd\ *adj* : stubborn

pig·ment \'pigmənt\ *n* : coloring matter —**pig·men·ta·tion** *n*

pigmy *var of* PYGMY

pig·tail *n* : tight braid of hair

¹pike \'pīk\ *n, pl* **pike** *or* **pikes** : large freshwater fish

²pike *n* : former weapon consisting of a long wooden staff with a steel point —**pike·staff** *n*

³pike *n* : turnpike

pi·las·ter \'pī,lastər, pə'las-\ *n* : slightly projecting upright column

¹pile \'pīl\ *n* : supporting pillar driven into the ground

²pile *n* : quantity of things thrown on one another ~ *vb* **piled; pil·ing** : heap up or accumulate

³pile *n* : surface of fine hairs or threads —**piled** *adj*

piles \'pīlz\ *n pl* : hemorrhoids

pil·fer \'pilfər\ *vb* : steal in small quantities at a time

pil·grim \'pilgrəm\ *n* **1** : one who travels to a shrine or holy place in devotion **2** *cap* : one of the founding settlers in America in 1620

pil·grim·age \-grəmij\ *n* : pilgrim's journey

pill \'pil\ *n* : small rounded mass of medicine —**pill-box** *n*

pil·lage \'pilij\ *vb* -**laged; -lag·ing** : take booty —**pillage** *n*

pil·lar \'pilər\ *n* : upright usu. supporting column or shaft —**pil-lared** *adj*

pil·lo·ry \'pil(ə)rē\ *n, pl* -**ries** : wooden frame for public punishment with holes for the head and hands ~ *vb* -**ried; -ry·ing 1** : set in a pillory **2** : expose to public scorn

pil·low \'pilō\ *n* : soft cushion for the head —**pil-low-case** *n*

pi·lot \'pīlət\ *n* **1** : helmsman **2** : person licensed to take ships into and out of a port **3** : guide **4** : one that flies an aircraft or spacecraft ~ *vb* : act as pilot of —**pi-lot-age** \-ij\ *n* — **pi-lot-less** *adj*

pi·men·to \pə'mentō\ *n, pl* -**tos** *or* -**to 1** : pimiento **2** : allspice

pi·mien·to \pə'm(y)entō\ *n, pl* -**tos** : mild red sweet pepper fruit

pimp \'pimp\ *n* : man who solicits clients for a prostitute —**pimp** *vb*

pim·ple \'pimpəl\ *n* : small inflamed swelling on the skin —**pim-ply** \-p(ə)lē\ *adj*

pin \'pin\ *n* **1** : fastener made of a small pointed piece of wire **2** : ornament or emblem fastened to clothing with a pin **3** : wooden object used as a target in bowling ~ *vb* -**nn- 1** : fasten with a pin **2** : hold fast or immobile —**pin-hole** *n*

pin·afore \'pinə,fōr\ *n* : sleeveless dress or apron fastened at the back

pin·cer \'pinsər\ *n* **1** *pl* : gripping tool with 2 jaws **2** : pincerlike claw

pinch \'pinch\ *vb* **1** : squeeze between the finger and thumb or between the jaws of a tool **2** : compress painfully ~ *n* **1** : critical point **2** : painful effect **3** : act of pinching **4** : very small quantity

pin·cush·ion *n* : cushion for storing pins

¹**pine** \'pīn\ *n* : evergreen cone-bearing tree or its wood

²**pine** *vb* **pined; pin·ing 1** : lose health through distress **2** : yearn for intensely

pine·ap·ple *n* : tropical plant bearing an edible juicy fruit

pin·feath·er *n* : new feather just coming through the skin

¹**pinion** \'pinyən\ *vb* : restrain by binding the arms

²**pinion** *n* : small gear

pink \'pingk\ *n* **1** : plant with narrow leaves and showy flowers **2** : light red **3** : highest degree —**pink** *adj* —**pink-ish** *adj*

pink·eye *n* : contagious eye inflammation

pin·na·cle \'pinikəl\ *n* : highest point

pi·noch·le \'pē,nəkəl\ *n* : card game played with a 48-card deck

pin·point *vb* : locate, hit, or aim with great precision

pint \'pīnt\ *n* : 1/2 quart

pin·to \'pin,tō\ *n, pl* **pintos** : spotted horse

pin·worm *n* : small parasitic intestinal worm

pi·o·neer \,pīə'niər\ *n* **1** : one that originates or helps open up a new line of thought or activity **2** : early settler ~ *vb* : act as a pioneer

pi·ous \'pīəs\ *adj* **1** : conscientious in religious practices **2** : affectedly religious —**pi-ous-ly** *adv*

pipe \'pīp\ *n* **1** : tube that produces music when air is forced through **2** : bagpipe **3** : long tube for conducting a fluid **4** : smoking tool ~ *vb* **piped; pip·ing 1** : play on a pipe **2** : speak in a high voice **3** : convey by pipes —**pip-er** *n*

pipe·line *n* **1** : line of pipe **2** : channel for information

pip·ing \'pīping\ *n* **1** : music of pipes **2** : narrow fold of material used to decorate edges or seams

pi·quant \'pēkənt\ *adj* **1** : tangy **2** : provocative or charming —**pi-quan-cy** \-kənsē\ *n*

pique \'pēk\ *n* : resentment ~ *vb* **piqued; piqu·ing 1** : offend **2** : arouse

pi·qué, pi·que \pi'kā\ *n* : durable ribbed clothing fabric

pi·ra·cy \'pīrəsē\ *n, pl* -**cies 1** : robbery on the seas **2** : unauthorized use of another's production or invention

pi·ra·nha \pə'ranyə, -'rän(y)ə\ *n* : small voracious So. American fish

pi·rate \'pīrət\ *n* : one who commits piracy —**pirate** *vb* —**pi-rat-i-cal** \pə'ratikəl, pī-\ *adj*

pir·ou·ette \,pirə'wet\ *n* : full turn on the toe or ball of one foot in ballet —**pirouette** *vb*

pis *pl* of PI

pis·ta·chio \pə'stash(ē,)ō, -'stäsh-\ *n, pl* -**chios** : small tree bearing a greenish edible seed or its seed

pis·til \'pist²l\ *n* : female reproductive organ in a flower —**pis-til-late** \'pistə,lāt\ *adj*

pis·tol \'pist²l\ *n* : firearm held with one hand

pis·ton \'pistən\ *n* : sliding piece that

receives and transmits motion usu. inside a cylinder

¹**pit** \'pit\ *n* 1 : hole or shaft in the ground 2 : sunken or enclosed place for a special purpose 3 : hell 4 : hollow or indentation ~ *vb* -**tt**- 1 : form pits in 2 : become marred with pits

²**pit** *n* : stony seed of some fruits ~ *vb* -**tt**- : remove the pit from

¹**pitch** \'pich\ *n* : resin from conifers —**pitchy** *adj*

²**pitch** *vb* 1 : erect and fix firmly in place 2 : throw 3 : set at a particular level 4 : fall headlong ~ *n* 1 : action or manner of pitching 2 : degree of slope 3 : relative highness of a tone —**pitched** *adj*

pitch-blende \'pich,blend\ *n* : mineral source of uranium

¹**pitch-er** \'pichər\ *n* : container for liquids

²**pitcher** *n* : one that pitches

pitch-fork *n* : long-handled fork for pitching hay

pit-e-ous \'pitēəs\ *adj* : arousing pity —**pit-e-ous-ly** *adv*

pit-fall \'pit,fol\ *n* : hidden danger

pith \'pith\ *n* 1 : spongy plant tissue 2 : essential or meaningful part —**pithy** *adj*

piti-able \'pitēəbəl\ *adj* : pitiful

piti-ful \'pitifəl\ *adj* 1 : arousing or deserving pity 2 : contemptible —**piti-ful-ly** \-f(ə)lē\ *adv*

pit-tance \'pit³ns\ *n* : small portion or amount

pi-tu-itary \pə't(y)üə,terē\ *adj* : relating to or being a small gland attached to the brain

pity \'pitē\ *n, pl* **pi-ties** 1 : sympathetic sorrow 2 : something to be regretted ~ *vb* **pit-ied; pity-ing** : feel pity for —**piti-less** *adj* —**piti-less-ly** *adv*

piv-ot \'pivət\ *n* : fixed pin on which something turns or on which it turns or as if on a pivot —**piv-ot-al** *adj*

pix-ie, pixy \'piksē\ *n, pl* **pix-ies** : mischievous sprite

piz-za \'pētsə\ *n* : thin pie of bread dough spread with a spiced mixture (as of tomatoes, cheese, and meat)

piz-ze-ria \,pētsə'rēə\ *n* : pizza restaurant

plac-ard \'plakərd, -,ärd\ *n* : poster ~ *vb* : display placards in or on

pla-cate \'plā,kāt, 'plak,āt\ *vb* -**cat-ed; -cat-ing** : appease —**pla-ca-ble** \'plakəbəl, 'plākə-\ *adj*

place \'plās\ *n* 1 : space or room 2 : indefinite area 3 : a particular building, locality, area, or part 4 : relative position in a scale or sequence 5 : seat 6 : job ~ *vb* **placed; plac-ing** 1 : put in a place 2 : identify —**place-ment** *n*

pla-cen-ta \plə'sentə\ *n, pl* -**tas** or -**tae** \-,ē\ : structure by which a mammal is nourished before birth —**pla-cen-tal** \-'sent³l\ *adj*

plac-id \'plasəd\ *adj* : undisturbed or peaceful —**pla-cid-i-ty** \pla'sidətē\ *n* —**plac-id-ly** *adv*

pla-gia-rize \'plājə,rīz\ *vb* -**rized; -riz-ing** : use (words or ideas) of another as if your own —**pla-gia-rism** \-,rizəm\ *n* —**pla-gia-rist** \-rəst\ *n*

plague \'plāg\ *n* 1 : disastrous evil 2 : destructive contagious bacterial disease ~ *vb* **plagued; plagu-ing** 1 : afflict with disease or disaster 2 : harass

plaid \'plad\ *n* : woolen fabric with a pattern of crossing stripes or the pattern itself —**plaid** *adj*

¹**plain** \'plān\ *n* : expanse of relatively level treeless country

²**plain** *adj* 1 : lacking ornament 2 : not concealed or disguised 3 : easily understood 4 : frank 5 : not fancy or pretty —**plain-ly** *adv* —**plain-ness** \'plānnəs\ *n*

plaint \'plānt\ *n* : complaint

plain-tiff \'plāntəf\ *n* : complaining party in a lawsuit

plain-tive \'plāntiv\ *adj* : expressive of suffering or woe —**plain-tive-ly** *adv*

¹**plait** \'plāt, 'plat\ *n* 1 : pleat 2 : braid of hair or straw —**plait** *vb*

plan \'plan\ *n* 1 : drawing or diagram 2 : method for accomplishing something ~ *vb* -**nn**- 1 : form a plan of 2 : intend —**plan-less** *adj* —**plan-ner** *n*

¹**plane** \'plān\ *vb* **planed; plan-ing** : smooth or level off with a plane ~ *n* : smoothing or shaping tool —**plan-er** *n*

²**plane** *n* 1 : level surface 2 : level of existence, consciousness, or development 3 : airplane ~ *adj* 1 : flat 2 : dealing with flat surfaces or figures

plan-et \'planət\ *n* : celestial body that revolves around the sun —**plan-e-tary** \-ə,terē\ *adj*

plan-e-tar-i-um \,planə'terēəm\ *n, pl* -**iums** or -**ia** \-ē-ə\ : building or room housing a device to project images of celestial bodies

plank \'plaŋk\ *n* 1 : heavy thick board 2 : article in the platform of a political party —**plank-ing** *n*

plank-ton \'plaŋktən\ *n* : tiny aquatic animal and plant life —**plank-ton-ic** \plaŋk'tänik\ *adj*

plant \'plant\ *vb* 1 : set in the ground

to grow 2 : place firmly or forcibly ~ *n* 1 : living thing without sense organs that cannot move about 2 : land, buildings, and machinery used esp. in manufacture

¹plan·tain \'plantᵊn\ *n* : short-stemmed herb with tiny greenish flowers

²plantain *n* : banana plant with starchy greenish fruit

plan·ta·tion \plan'tāshən\ *n* : agricultural estate worked by resident laborers

plant·er \'plantər\ *n* 1 : plantation owner 2 : plant container

plaque \'plak\ *n* : commemorative tablet

plas·ma \'plazmə\ *n* : watery part of blood —**plas·mat·ic** \plaz'matik\ *adj*

plas·ter \'plastər\ *n* 1 : medicated dressing 2 : hardening paste for coating walls and ceilings ~ *vb* : cover with plaster —**plas·ter·er** *n* —**plas·tery** *adj*

plas·tic \'plastik\ *adj* : capable of being molded ~ *n* : material that can be formed into rigid objects, films, or filaments —**plas·tic·i·ty** \plas'tisətē\ *n*

plate \'plāt\ *n* 1 : flat thin piece 2 : plated metalware 3 : shallow vessel, circular dish 4 : denture or the part of it that fits to the mouth 5 : something printed from an engraving ~ *vb* **plat·ed; plat·ing** : overlay with metal —**plat·ing** *n*

pla·teau \pla'tō\ *n, pl* **-teaus** *or* **-teaux** \-'tōz\ : large level area raised above adjacent land

plat·form \'plat,förm\ *n* 1 : raised flooring or stage 2 : declaration of principles for a political party

plat·i·num \'platnəm, -ᵊnəm\ *n* : heavy silver-white metallic chemical element

plat·i·tude \'platə,t(y)üd\ *n* : trite remark —**plat·i·tu·di·nous** \,platə-'t(y)üdnəs, -ᵊnəs\ *adj*

pla·toon \plə'tün\ *n* : small military unit

platoon sergeant *n* : noncommissioned officer in the army ranking below a first sergeant

plat·ter \'platər\ *n* : large serving plate

platy·pus \'platipəs\ *n* : small aquatic egg-laying mammal

plau·dit \'plödət\ *n* : act of applause

plau·si·ble \'plözəbəl\ *adj* : reasonable or believable —**plau·si·bil·i·ty** \,plözə'bilətē\ *n* —**plau·si·bly** \-blē\ *adv*

play \'plā\ *n* 1 : action in a game 2 : recreational activity 3 : stage representation of a drama 4 : light or fitful movement 5 : free movement ~ *vb* 1 : engage in recreation 2 : move or toy with aimlessly 3 : perform music 4 : act in a drama —**play·act·ing** *n* —**play·er** *n* —**play·ful** \-fəl\ *adj* —**play·ful·ly** *adv* —**play·ful·ness** *n* —**play·pen** *n* —**play·suit** *n*

play·ground *n* : place for children to play

play·house *n* 1 : theater 2 : small house for children to play in

playing card *n* : one of a set of 24 to 78 cards marked to show its rank and suit and used to play a game of cards

play·mate *n* : companion in play

play-off *n* : contest or series of contests to determine a champion

play·thing *n* : toy

play·wright \-,rīt\ *n* : writer of plays

pla·za \'plazə, 'pläz-\ *n* : public square

plea \'plē\ *n* 1 : defendant's answer to charges 2 : urgent request

plead \'plēd\ *vb* **plead·ed** \'plēdəd\ *or* **pled** \'pled\; **plead·ing** 1 : argue for or against in court 2 : answer to a charge or indictment 3 : appeal earnestly —**plead·er** *n*

pleas·ant \'plezᵊnt\ *adj* 1 : giving pleasure 2 : marked by pleasing behavior or appearance —**pleas·ant·ly** *adv* —**pleas·ant·ness** *n*

pleas·ant·ries \-ᵊntrēz\ *n pl* : pleasant and casual conversation

please \'plēz\ *vb* **pleased; pleas·ing** 1 : give pleasure or satisfaction to 2 : desire or intend 3 : be willing to

pleas·ing \'plēziŋ\ *adj* : giving pleasure —**pleas·ing·ly** *adv*

plea·sur·able \'plezh(ə)rəbəl\ *adj* : pleasant —**plea·sur·ably** \-blē\ *adv*

plea·sure \'plezhər\ *n* 1 : desire or inclination 2 : enjoyment 3 : source of delight

pleat \'plēt\ *vb* : arrange in pleats ~ *n* : fold in cloth

ple·be·ian \pli'bēən\ *n* : one of the common people ~ *adj* : ordinary

ple·bi·scite \'plebə,sīt, -sət\ *n* : vote of the people (as of a country) on a proposal submitted to them

pledge \'plej\ *n* 1 : something given as security 2 : promise or vow ~ *vb* **pledged; pledg·ing** 1 : offer as or bind by a pledge 2 : promise

ple·na·ry \'plēnərē, 'plen-\ *adj* : full

pleni·po·ten·tia·ry \,plenəpə'tench(ə)rē, -'tenchē,erē\ *n* : diplomatic agent having full authority —**plenipotentiary** *adj*

plen·i·tude \'plenə,t(y)üd\ n 1 : completeness 2 : abundance

plen·te·ous \'plentēəs\ adj : existing in plenty

plen·ti·ful \'plentifəl\ adj : abundant —**plen·ti·ful·ly** adv

plen·ty \'plentē\ n : more than adequate number or amount

pleth·o·ra \'plethərə\ n : excess

pleu·ri·sy \'plürəsē\ n : inflammation of the chest membrane

pli·able \'plīəbəl\ adj : flexible

pli·ant \'plīənt\ adj : flexible —**pli·an·cy** \-ənsē\ n

pli·ers \'plī(ə)rz\ n pl : pinching or gripping tool

¹plight \'plīt\ vb : pledge

²plight n : bad state

plod \'pläd\ vb **-dd-** 1 : walk heavily or slowly 2 : work laboriously and monotonously —**plod·der** n —**plod·ding·ly** \-iŋlē\ adv

plot \'plät\ n 1 : small area of ground 2 : ground plan 3 : main story development (as of a book or movie) 4 : secret plan for doing something ~ vb **-tt-** 1 : make a plot or plan of 2 : plan or contrive —**plot·ter** n

plo·ver \'pləvər, 'plōvər\ n, pl **-ver** or **-vers** : shorebird related to the sandpiper

plow, plough \'plaú\ n 1 : tool used to turn soil 2 : plowlike device ~ vb 1 : break up with a plow 2 : cleave or move through like a plow —**plow·man** \-mən, -,man\ n

plow·share \-,shear\ n : plow part that cuts the earth

ploy \'plói\ n : clever plan or maneuver

pluck \'plək\ vb 1 : pull off or out 2 : tug or twitch ~ n 1 : act or instance of plucking 2 : spirit or courage

plucky \'pləkē\ adj **pluck·i·er; -est** : courageous or spirited

plug \'pləg\ n 1 : something for sealing an opening 2 : electrical connector at the end of a cord 3 : piece of favorable publicity ~ vb **-gg-** 1 : stop or make tight or secure by inserting a plug 2 : publicize

plum \'pləm\ n 1 : smooth-skinned juicy fruit 2 : fine reward

plum·age \'plümij\ n : feathers of a bird

plumb \'pləm\ n : weight on the end of a line (**plumb line**) to show vertical direction ~ adv 1 : vertically 2 : completely ~ vb : sound or test with a plumb ~ adj : vertical

plumb·er \'pləmər\ n : one who repairs usu. water pipes and fixtures

plumb·ing \'pləmiŋ\ n : system of water pipes in a building

plume \'plüm\ n : large, conspicuous, or showy feather ~ vb **plumed; plum·ing** 1 : provide or deck with feathers 2 : indulge in pride —**plumed** \'plümd\ adj

plum·met \'pləmət\ vb : drop straight down

¹plump \'pləmp\ vb : drop suddenly or heavily ~ adv 1 : suddenly and heavily 2 : directly

²plump adj : having a full rounded form —**plump·ness** n

plun·der \'pləndər\ vb : rob or take goods by force (as in war) ~ n : something taken in plundering —**plun·der·er** n

plunge \'plənj\ vb **plunged; plung·ing** 1 : thrust or drive into something 2 : begin an action suddenly 3 : dive or throw oneself forward or down ~ n : act or instance of plunging —**plung·er** n

plu·ral \'plúrəl\ adj : relating to a word form denoting more than one —**plu·ral** n

plu·ral·i·ty \plú·ralətē\ n, pl **-ties** : greatest number of votes cast when not a majority

plu·ral·ize \'plúrə,līz\ vb **-ized; -iz·ing** : make plural —**plu·ral·iza·tion** \,plúrələ'zāshən\ n

plus \'pləs\ prep : with the addition of ~ n 1 : sign + (**plus sign**) in mathematics to require addition 2 : added or positive quantity 3 : advantage ~ adj : being more or in addition

plush \'pləsh\ n : fabric with a long pile ~ adj : luxurious —**plush·ly** adv —**plushy** adj

plu·toc·ra·cy \plü'täkrəsē\ n, pl **-cies** 1 : government by the wealthy 2 : a controlling class of rich men —**plu·to·crat** \'plütə,krat\ n —**plu·to·crat·ic** \,plütə'kratik\ adj

plu·to·ni·um \plü'tōnēəm\ n : radioactive chemical element

¹ply \'plī\ n, pl **plies** : fold, thickness, or strand of which something is made

²ply vb **plied; ply·ing** 1 : use or work at 2 : keep supplying something to 3 : travel over regularly

ply·wood n : sheets of wood glued and pressed together

pneu·mat·ic \n(y)ú'matik\ adj 1 : moved by air pressure 2 : filled with compressed air —**pneu·mat·i·cal·ly** \-ik(ə)lē\ adv

pneu·mo·nia \n(y)ú'mōnyə\ n : inflammatory lung disease

¹poach \'pōch\ vb : cook in simmering liquid

²poach vb : hunt or fish illegally — **poach·er** n

pock \'päk\ n : small swelling on the skin or its scar —**pock-mark** n —**pock-marked** adj

pock-et \'päkət\ n 1 : small open bag sewn into a garment 2 : container or receptacle 3 : isolated area or group ~ vb : put in a pocket —**pock-et-ful** \-,fúl\ n

pock-et-book n 1 : purse 2 : financial resources

pock-et-knife n : knife with a folding blade for the pocket

pod \'päd\ n 1 : dry fruit that splits open when ripe 2 : detachable spacecraft compartment

po-di-a-try \pə'dīətrē, pō-\ n : branch of medicine dealing with the foot —**po-di-a-trist** \pə'dīətrəst, pō-\ n

po-di-um \'pōdēəm\ n, pl **-di-ums** or **-dia** \-ēə\ : dais

po-em \'pōəm\ n : composition in verse

po-et \'pōət\ n : writer of poetry

po-et-ry \'pōətrē\ n 1 : metrical writing 2 : poems —**po-et-ic** \pō'etik\, **po-et-i-cal** \-ikəl\ adj

po-grom \'pōgrəm, pə'gräm, 'pägrəm\ n : organized massacre

poi-gnant \'póinyənt\ adj 1 : emotionally painful 2 : deeply moving —**poi-gnan-cy** \-nyənsē\ n

poin-set-tia \póin'setēə, -'setə\ n : showy tropical American plant

point \'póint\ n 1 : individual often essential detail 2 : purpose 3 : particular place, time, or stage 4 : sharp end 5 : projecting piece of land 6 : dot or period 7 : division of the compass 8 : unit of counting ~ vb 1 : sharpen 2 : indicate direction by extending a finger 3 : direct attention to 4 : aim —**point-less** adj

point-blank adj 1 : so close to a target that a missile fired goes straight to it 2 : direct —**point-blank** adv

point-er \'póintər\ n 1 : one that points out 2 : large short-haired hunting dog 3 : hint or tip

poise \'póiz\ vb poised; pois-ing : balance ~ n : self-possessed calmness

poi-son \'póiz²n\ n : chemical that can injure or kill ~ vb 1 : injure or kill with poison 2 : apply poison to 3 : affect destructively —**poi-son-er** \-nər, -²nər\ n —**poi-son-ous** \'póiznəs, -²nəs\ adj

poke \'pōk\ vb poked; pok-ing 1 : prod 2 : dawdle ~ n : quick thrust

¹pok-er \'pōkər\ n : rod for stirring a fire

²pok-er n : card game

po-lar \'pōlər\ adj : relating to a geographical or magnetic pole

po-lar-ize \'pōla,rīz\ vb -ized; -iz-ing : cause to have magnetic poles — **po-lar-iza-tion** \,pōlərə'zāshən\ n

¹pole \'pōl\ n : long slender piece of wood or metal

²pole n 1 : either end of the earth's axis 2 : battery terminal 3 : either end of a magnet

pole-cat \'pōl,kat\ n, pl **polecats** or **polecat** 1 : European carnivorous mammal 2 : skunk

po-lem-ic \pə'lemik\ n : argument attacking another's ideas

po-lem-ics \-iks\ n sing or pl : practice of disputation —**po-lem-i-cal** \-ikəl\ adj —**po-lem-i-cist** \-əsəst\ n

po-lice \pə'lēs\ n, pl police 1 : department of government that keeps public order and enforces the laws 2 : members of the police ~ vb -liced; -lic-ing : regulate and keep in order —**po-lice-man** \-mən\ n —**po-lice-wom-an** n

¹pol-i-cy \'päləsē\ n, pl -cies : course of action selected to guide decisions

²policy n, pl -cies : insurance contract —**pol-i-cy-hold-er** n

po-lio \'pōlē,ō\ n : poliomyelitis —**po-lio** adj

po-lio-my-eli-tis \-,mīə'lītəs\ n : acute virus disease marked by fever, paralysis, and atrophy of muscles

pol-ish \'pälish\ vb 1 : make smooth and glossy 2 : develop or refine ~ n 1 : shiny surface 2 : refinement

po-lite \pə'līt\ adj -lit-er; -est : marked by correct social conduct —**po-lite-ly** adv —**po-lite-ness** n

pol-i-tic \'pälə,tik\ adj : shrewdly tactful

pol-i-tics \'pälə,tiks\ n sing or pl : practice of government and managing of public affairs —**po-lit-i-cal** \pə'litikəl\ adj —**pol-i-ti-cian** \,pälə'tishən\ n

pol-ka \'pōlkə\ n : lively couple dance —**polka** vb

poll \'pōl\ n 1 : head 2 : place where votes are cast —usu. pl. 3 : a sampling of opinion ~ vb 1 : cut off 2 : receive or record votes 3 : question in a poll —**poll-ster** \-stər\ n

pol-len \'pälən\ n : spores of a seed plant

pol-li-na-tion \,pälə'nāshən\ n : the carrying of pollen to fertilize the seed —pol·li·nate \'päle,nāt\ vb — pol·li·na·tor \-ər\ n

pol·lute \pə'lüt\ vb -lut·ed; -lut·ing : make impure esp. by contaminating with man-made waste —pol·lut·ant \-'lüt²nt\ n —pol·lut·er n —pol·lu·tion \-'lüshən\ n

pol·ly·wog, pol·li·wog \'päle,wäg\ n : tadpole

po·lo \'pōlō\ n : game played by 2 teams on horseback using long-handled mallets to drive a wooden ball

pol·troon \päl'trün\ n : coward

poly·es·ter \'päle,estər\ n : synthetic fiber

po·lyg·a·my \pə'ligəmē\ n : marriage to several spouses at the same time —po·lyg·a·mist \-məst\ n —po·lyg·a·mous \-məs\ adj

poly·gon \'päli,gän\ n : closed plane figure with straight sides

poly·syl·la·ble \'päli,siləbəl\ n : a word of more than 3 syllables —poly·syl·lab·ic \,pälisə'labik\ adj

poly·tech·nic \,päli'teknik\ adj : relating to many arts or sciences

poly·the·ism \'pälithē,izəm\ n : worship of many gods —poly·the·ist \-,thēəst\ adj or n

po·made \pō'mād, -'mäd\ n : perfumed hair ointment

pome·gran·ate \'päm(ə),granət\ n : tropical reddish fruit with many seeds

pom·mel \'pəməl, 'päm-\ n 1 : knob on the hilt of a sword 2 : knob at the front of a saddle ~ \'pəməl\ vb -meled or -melled; -mel·ing or -mel·ling : pummel

pomp \'pämp\ n 1 : brilliant display 2 : ostentation

pomp·ous \'pämpəs\ adj : pretentiously dignified —pom·pos·i·ty \päm'päsətē\ n —pomp·ous·ly adv

pon·cho \'pänchō\ n, pl -chos : blanketlike cloak

pond \'pänd\ n : small body of water

pon·der \'pändər\ vb : weigh or think in the mind

pon·der·ous \'pänd(ə)rəs\ adj 1 : very heavy 2 : clumsy 3 : oppressively dull

pon·tiff \'päntəf\ n 1 : bishop 2 : pope —pon·tif·i·cal \pän'tifikəl\ adj

pon·tif·i·cate \pän'tifə,kāt\ vb -cat·ed; -cat·ing : talk pompously

pon·toon \pän'tün\ n : flat-bottomed boat or float

po·ny \'pōnē\ n, pl -nies : small horse

poo·dle \'püd²l\ n : dog with a curly coat

¹pool \'pül\ n 1 : small body of water 2 : puddle

²pool n 1 : game of pocket billiards 2 : amount contributed by participants in a joint venture ~ vb : contribute to a common fund

poop \'püp\ n : enclosed superstructure at the stern of a ship

poor \'pür\ adj 1 : lacking material possessions 2 : less than adequate —poor·ly adv

pop \'päp\ vb -pp- 1 : move suddenly 2 : burst with or make a sharp sound 3 : protrude ~ n 1 : sharp explosive sound 2 : flavored soft drink

pop·corn \'päp,kórn\ n : corn whose kernels burst open into a white mass when heated

pope \'pōp\ n, often cap : head of the Roman Catholic Church

pop·lar \'päplər\ n : slender quick-growing tree

pop·lin \'päplən\ n : strong plain-woven fabric with crosswise ribs

pop·over \'päp,ōvər\ n : egg-rich biscuit that expands into a hollow shell as it bakes

pop·py \'päpē\ n, pl -pies : herb with showy flowers

pop·u·lace \'päpyələs\ n 1 : common people 2 : population

pop·u·lar \'päpyələr\ adj 1 : relating to the general public 2 : widely accepted 3 : commonly liked —pop·u·lar·i·ty \,päpyə'larətē\ n —pop·u·lar·ize \'päpyələ,rīz\ vb —pop·u·lar·ly \-lərlē\ adv

pop·u·late \'päpyə,lāt\ vb -lat·ed; -lat·ing : inhabit or occupy

pop·u·la·tion \,päpyə'lāshən\ n : people or number of people in a country or area

pop·u·list \'päpyələst\ n : advocate of the rights of the common people —pop·u·lism \-,lizəm\ n

pop·u·lous \'päpyələs\ adj : densely populated —pop·u·lous·ness n

por·ce·lain \'pórs(ə)lən\ n : fine-grained ceramic ware

porch \'pórch\ n : covered entrance

por·cine \'pór,sīn\ adj : relating to or suggesting swine

por·cu·pine \'pórkyə,pīn\ n : mammal with sharp quills

¹pore \'pór\ vb pored; por·ing : read attentively

²pore n : tiny hole —pored adj

pork \'pórk\ n : pig meat

por·nog·ra·phy \pór'nägrəfē\ n : depiction of erotic behavior meant chiefly to cause sexual excitement

—**por·no·graph·ic** \,pȯrnə'grafik\ adj

po·rous \'pōrəs\ adj : permeable to fluids —**po·ros·i·ty** \pə'räsətē\ n

por·poise \'pȯrpəs\ n 1 : small whale with a blunt snout 2 : dolphin

por·ridge \'pȯrij\ n : soft boiled cereal

por·rin·ger \'pȯrənjər\ n : low one-handled metal bowl or cup for children

¹port \'pȯrt\ n 1 : harbor 2 : city with a harbor

²port n 1 : inlet or outlet (as in an engine) for a fluid 2 : porthole

³port n : left side of a ship or airplane looking forward —**port** adj

⁴port n : sweet wine

por·ta·ble \'pȯrtəbəl\ adj : capable of being carried —**portable** n

por·tage \'pȯrtij, pȯr'täzh\ n : carrying of boats overland between navigable bodies of water or the route where this is done —**portage** vb

por·tal \'pȯrt⁰l\ n : entrance

por·tend \pȯr'tend\ vb : give a warning of beforehand

por·tent \'pȯr,tent\ n : something that foreshadows a coming event —**por·ten·tous** \pȯr'tentəs\ adj

por·ter \'pȯrtər\ n : baggage carrier

por·ter·house \-,haus\ n : choice cut of steak

port·fo·lio \pȯrt'fōlē,ō\ n, pl **-lios** 1 : portable case for papers 2 : investor's securities

port·hole \'pȯrt,hōl\ n : opening in the side of a ship or aircraft

por·ti·co \'pȯrti,kō\ n, pl **-coes** or **-cos** : colonnade forming a porch

por·tion \'pȯrshən\ n : part or share of a whole ~ vb : divide into or allot portions

port·ly \'pȯrtlē\ adj **-li·er; -est** : somewhat stout

por·trait \'pȯrtrət, -,trāt\ n : picture of a person —**por·trait·ist** \-əst\ n —**por·trai·ture** \'pȯrtrə,chúr\ n

por·tray \pȯr'trā\ vb 1 : make a picture of 2 : describe in words 3 : play the role of —**por·tray·al** n

pose \'pōz\ vb **posed; pos·ing** 1 : assume a posture or attitude 2 : propose 3 : pretend to take what one is not ~ n 1 : sustained posture 2 : pretense —**pos·er** n

posh \'päsh\ adj : elegant

po·si·tion \pə'zishən\ n 1 : stand taken on a question 2 : place or location 3 : status 4 : job —**position** vb

pos·i·tive \'päzətiv\ adj 1 : definite 2 : confident 3 : relating to or being an adjective or adverb form that de-

notes no increase 4 : greater than zero 5 : having a deficiency of electrons 6 : affirmative —**pos·i·tive·ly** adv —**pos·i·tive·ness** n

pos·se \'päsē\ n : emergency assistants of a sheriff

pos·sess \pə'zes\ vb 1 : have as property or as a quality 2 : control —**pos·ses·sion** \-'zeshən\ n —**pos·ses·sor** \-'zesər\ n

pos·ses·sive \pə'zesiv\ adj 1 : relating to a grammatical case denoting ownership 2 : jealous —**possessive** n —**pos·ses·sive·ness** n

pos·si·ble \'päsəbəl\ adj 1 : that can be done 2 : potential —**pos·si·bil·i·ty** \,päsə'bilətē\ n —**pos·si·bly** adv

pos·sum \'päsəm\ n : opossum

¹post \'pōst\ n : upright stake serving to support or mark ~ vb : put up or announce by a notice

²post vb 1 : mail 2 : inform

³post n 1 : sentry's station 2 : assigned task 3 : army camp ~ vb : station

post- prefix : after or subsequent to

postadolescence
postadolescent
postattack
postbaccalaureate
postbiblical
postcollege
postcolonial
postelection
postexercise
postfertilization
postflight
postgame
postgraduate
postgraduation
postharvest
posthospital
postimperial
postinaugural
postindustrial
postinoculation
postmarital
postmenopausal
postnatal
postnuptial
postproduction
postpubertal
postpuberty
postradiation
postrecession
postretirement
postrevolutionary
postseason
postsecondary
postsurgical
posttreatment
posttrial
postvaccination
postwar

post·age \'pōstij\ n : fee for mail

post·al \'pōst⁰l\ adj : relating to the mail

post·card n : card for mailing a message

post·er \'pōstər\ n : large usu. printed notice

pos·te·ri·or \pō'stirēər, pä-\ adj 1 : later 2 : situated behind ~ n : buttocks

pos·ter·i·ty \pä'sterətē\ n : succeeding generations

post·haste \'pōst'hāst\ adv : speedily

post·hu·mous \'päschəməs\ adj : occurring after one's death

post·man \'pōs(t)mən, -,man\ *n* : mailman

post·mark *n* : official mark on mail — **postmark** *vb*

post·mas·ter *n* : chief of a post office

post me·ri·di·em \'pōs(t)mə'ridēəm, -ē,em\ *adj* : being after noon

post·mor·tem \(')pōs(t)'mórtəm\ *adj* : occurring or done after death ~ *n* : medical examination of a corpse

post office *n* : agency or building for mail service

post·op·er·a·tive \(')pōst'äp(ə)rətiv, -'äpə,rāt-\ *adj* : following surgery

post·paid *adv* : with postage paid by the sender

post·par·tum \'pōs(t)'pärtəm\ *adj* : following childbirth —**postpartum** *adv*

post·pone \-'pōn\ *vb* **-poned; -pon·ing** : hold back to a later time —**post·pone·ment** *n*

post·script \'pō(s),skript\ *n* : added note

pos·tu·lant \'päschələnt\ *n* : candidate for a religious order

pos·tu·late \'päschə,lāt\ *vb* **-lat·ed; -lat·ing** : assume as true ~ *n* : assumption

pos·ture \'päschər\ *n* : bearing of the body ~ *vb* **-tured; -tur·ing** : strike a pose

po·sy \'pōzē\ *n, pl* **-sies** : flower or bunch of flowers

pot \'pät\ *n* **1** : rounded container **2** : marijuana ~ *vb* **-tt-** : place in a pot —**pot·ful** *n*

po·ta·ble \'pōtəbəl\ *adj* : drinkable

pot·ash \'pät,ash\ *n* : white chemical salt

po·tas·si·um \pə'tasēəm\ *n* : silver-white metallic chemical element

po·ta·to \pə'tātō\ *n, pl* **-toes** : edible plant tuber

pot·bel·ly *n* : paunch —**pot·bel·lied** *adj*

po·tent \'pōt²nt\ *adj* : powerful or effective —**po·ten·cy** \-²nsē\ *n*

po·ten·tate \'pōt²n,tāt\ *n* : powerful ruler

po·ten·tial \pə'tenchəl\ *adj* : capable of becoming actual ~ *n* **1** : something that can become actual **2** : degree of electrification with reference to a standard —**po·ten·ti·al·i·ty** \pə,tenchē'alətē\ *n* —**po·ten·tial·ly** *adv*

poth·er \'päthər\ *n* : fuss

po·tion \'pōshən\ *n* : liquid medicine or poison

pot·luck *n* : whatever food is available

pot·pour·ri \,pōpù'rē\ *n* : miscellaneous collection

pot·shot *n* **1** : casual or easy shot **2** : random critical remark

pot·ter \'pätər\ *n* : pottery maker

pot·tery \'pätərē\ *n, pl* **-ter·ies** : objects (as dishes) made from clay

pouch \'pauch\ *n* **1** : small bag **2** : bodily sac

poul·tice \'pōltəs\ *n* : warm medicated dressing —**poultice** *vb*

poul·try \'pōltrē\ *n* : domesticated fowl

pounce \'pauns\ *vb* **pounced; pounc·ing** : spring or swoop upon and seize

¹pound \'paund\ *n* **1** : unit of weight equal to 16 ounces **2** : monetary unit (as of the United Kingdom) —**pound·age** \-ij\ *n*

²pound *vb* **1** : crush by beating **2** : strike heavily **3** : throb

³pound *n* : shelter for stray animals

pour \'pōr\ *vb* **1** : flow or supply copiously **2** : rain hard

pout \'paut\ *vb* : look sullen —**pout** *n*

pov·er·ty \'pävərtē\ *n* **1** : lack of money or possessions **2** : poor quality

pow·der \'paudər\ *n* : dry material of fine particles ~ *vb* **1** : sprinkle or cover with powder **2** : reduce to powder —**pow·dery** *adj*

pow·er \'pau(ə)r\ *n* **1** : position of authority **2** : ability to act **3** : one that has power **4** : physical might **5** : force or energy used to do work ~ *vb* : supply with power —**pow·er·ful** \-fəl\ *adj*—**pow·er·ful·ly** *adv* —**pow·er·less** *adj*

pow·wow \'pau,wau\ *n* : conference

pox \'päks\ *n, pl* **pox** or **pox·es** : disease marked by skin rash

prac·ti·ca·ble \'praktikəbəl\ *adj* : feasible —**prac·ti·ca·bil·i·ty** \,praktikə'bilətē\ *n*

prac·ti·cal \'praktikəl\ *adj* **1** : relating to practice **2** : virtual **3** : capable of being put to use **4** : inclined to action as opposed to speculation —**prac·ti·cal·i·ty** \,prakti'kalətē\ *n* —**prac·ti·cal·ly** \'praktik(ə)lē\ *adv*

prac·tice, prac·tise \'praktəs\ *vb* **-ticed** *or* **-tised; -tic·ing** *or* **-tis·ing 1** : perform repeatedly to become proficient **2** : do or perform customarily **3** : be professionally engaged in ~ *n* **1** : actual performance **2** : habit **3** : exercise for proficiency **4** : exercise of a profession

prac·ti·tio·ner \prak'tish(ə)nər\ *n* : one who practices a profession

prag·ma·tism \'pragmə,tizəm\ *n* : practical approach to problems —**prag·mat·ic** \prag'matik\ *adj*

prai·rie \'pre(ə)rē\ *n* : broad grassy rolling tract of land

praise \'prāz\ *vb* **praised; prais·ing 1** : express approval of **2** : glorify — **praise** *n* — **praise·wor·thy** *adj*

prance \'prans\ *vb* **pranced; pranc·ing 1** : spring from the hind legs **2** : swagger — **prance** *n* — **pranc·er** *n*

prank \'praŋk\ *n* : playful or mischievous act — **prank·ster** \-stər\ *n*

prate \'prāt\ *vb* **prat·ed; prat·ing** : talk long and foolishly

prat·fall \'prat,-\ *n* : fall on the buttocks

prat·tle \'pratᵊl\ *vb* **-tled; -tling** : babble — **prattle** *n*

prawn \'prón\ *n* : shrimplike crustacean

pray \'prā\ *vb* **1** : entreat **2** : ask earnestly for something **3** : address a divinity

prayer \'praər\ *n* **1** : earnest request **2** : an addressing of a divinity **3** : words used in praying

praying mantis *n* : mantis

pre- *prefix* : before, prior to, or in advance

preadapt	precompute
preaddress	preconceive
preadmission	preconception
preadolescence	preconcerted
preadolescent	precondition
preadult	preconference
prealert	preconstruct
prealign	preconvention
preallocate	precook
preanesthetic	precool
prearraignment	precut
prearrange	predawn
prearrangement	predefine
preassemble	predelinquent
preassign	predeparture
preaudit	predesignate
preauthorize	predesignation
prebattle	predetermine
prebiblical	predischarge
prebirth	predrill
prebreakfast	predug
prebuilt	preedit
precalculate	preelection
precalculus	preelectric
precampaign	preelectronic
precancel	preemployment
precancellation	preestablish
precivilization	preexist
preclean	preexistence
preclear	preexistent
preclearance	prefight
precollege	prefilter
precolonial	preform
precombustion	pregame

preheat	prepubertal
preimmunization	prepublication
preimmunize	prepunch
preinaugural	prepurchase
preindustrial	prerecord
preinoculate	preregister
preinoculation	preregistration
preinterview	prerehearsal
prejudge	prerelease
prekindergarten	pre-Renaissance
prelaunch	preretirement
prelife	prerevolutionary
preload	prerinse
premarital	presale
premenopausal	preseason
premenstrual	preselect
premix	preset
premodern	preshrink
premodify	presoak
premoisten	presort
premold	prestamp
prenatal	presterilize
prenotification	prestrike
prenotify	presurgical
prenuptial	presweeten
preopening	pretape
preoperational	pretelevision
preordain	pretournament
prepack	pretreat
prepackage	pretreatment
prepay	pretrial
preplan	pretrip
preprocess	prewar
preproduction	prewash
preprofessional	prewrap
preprogram	

preach \'prēch\ *vb* **1** : deliver a sermon **2** : advocate earnestly — **preach·er** *n* — **preach·ment** *n*

pre·am·ble \'prē,ambəl\ *n* : introduction

pre·car·i·ous \pri'karēəs\ *adj* : dangerously insecure — **pre·car·i·ous·ly** *adv* — **pre·car·i·ous·ness** *n*

pre·cau·tion \pri'kóshən\ *n* : care taken beforehand — **pre·cau·tion·ary** \-sha,nerē\ *adj*

pre·cede \pri'sēd\ *vb* **-ced·ed; -ced·ing** : be, go, or come ahead of — **pre·ce·dence** \'presədəns, pri'sēdᵊns\ *n*

prec·e·dent \'presədənt\ *n* : something said or done earlier that serves as an example

pre·ced·ing \pri'sēdiŋ\ *adj* : that precedes

pre·cept \'prē,sept\ *n* : rule of action or conduct

pre·cep·tor \pri'septər, 'prē,sep-\ *n* : tutor

pre·cinct \'prē,siŋkt\ *n* **1** : district of a city **2** *pl* : vicinity

pre·cious \'preshəs\ *adj* **1** : of great value **2** : greatly cherished **3** : affected

prec·i·pice \'presəpəs\ *n* : steep cliff

pre·cip·i·tate \pri'sipə‚tāt\ *vb* **-tat·ed; -tat·ing 1** : cause to happen quickly or abruptly **2** : cause to separate out of a liquid ~ *n* : solid matter precipitated from a liquid ~ \-'sipətət, -ə‚tāt\ *adj* : unduly hasty —**pre·cip·i·tate·ly** *adv* —**pre·cip·i·tate·ness** *n* —**pre·cip·i·tous** \'sipətəs\ *adj* —**pre·cip·i·tous·ly** *adv*

pre·cip·i·ta·tion \pri‚sipə'tāshən\ *n* **1** : rash haste **2** : rain, snow, or hail

pré·cis \prā'sē\ *n, pl* **pré·cis** \-'sēz\ : concise summary of essential points

pre·cise \pri'sīs\ *adj* **1** : definite **2** : highly accurate —**pre·cise·ly** *adv* —**pre·cise·ness** *n*

pre·ci·sion \pri'sizhən\ *n* : quality or state of being precise

pre·clude \pri'klüd\ *vb* **-clud·ed; -clud·ing** : make impossible

pre·co·cious \pri'kōshəs\ *adj* : exceptionally advanced —**pre·co·cious·ly** *adv* —**pre·coc·i·ty** \pri'käsətē\ *n*

pre·cur·sor \pri'kərsər\ *n* : harbinger

pred·a·to·ry \'predə‚tōrē\ *adj* : preying upon others —**pred·a·tor** \'predətər\ *n*

pre·de·ces·sor \'predə‚sesər, 'prēd-\ *n* : one who has previously held a position

pre·des·tine \prē'destən\ *vb* : settle beforehand

pre·dic·a·ment \pri'dikəmənt\ *n* : difficult situation

pred·i·cate \'predikət\ *n* : part of a sentence that states something about the subject ~ \'predə‚kāt\ *vb* **-cat·ed; -cat·ing 1** : affirm **2** : establish —**pred·i·ca·tion** \‚predə'kāshən\ *n*

pre·dict \pri'dikt\ *vb* : declare in advance —**pre·dict·able** \-'diktəbəl\ *adj* —**pre·dict·ably** \-blē\ *adv* —**pre·dic·tion** \-'dikshən\ *n*

pre·di·lec·tion \‚predᵊl'ekshən, ‚prēd-\ *n* : favorable inclination

pre·dis·pose \‚prēdis'pōz\ *vb* : cause to be favorable to something beforehand —**pre·dis·po·si·tion** \‚prē‚dispə'zishən\ *n*

pre·dom·i·nate \pri'dämə‚nāt\ *vb* : be superior —**pre·dom·i·nance** \-nəns\ *n* —**pre·dom·i·nant** \-nənt\ *adj* —**pre·dom·i·nant·ly** *adv*

pre·em·i·nent \prē'emənənt\ *adj* : having highest rank —**pre·em·i·nence** \-nəns\ *n* —**pre·em·i·nent·ly** *adv*

pre·empt \prē'empt\ *vb* **1** : seize for oneself **2** : take the place of

preen \'prēn\ *vb* : dress or smooth up (as feathers)

pre·fab·ri·cat·ed \'prē'fabrə‚kātəd\ *adj* : manufactured for rapid assembly elsewhere —**pre·fab·ri·ca·tion** \‚prē‚fabri'kāshən\ *n*

pref·ace \'prefəs\ *n* : introductory comments ~ *vb* **-aced; -ac·ing** : introduce with a preface —**pref·a·to·ry** \'prefə‚tōrē\ *adj*

pre·fect \'prē‚fekt\ *n* : chief officer or judge —**pre·fec·ture** \-‚fekchər\ *n*

pre·fer \pri'fər\ *vb* **-rr- 1** : like better **2** : bring (as a charge) against a person —**pref·er·a·ble** \'pref(ə)rəbəl\ *adj* —**pref·er·a·bly** *adv* —**pref·er·ence** \-(ə)rəns\ *n* —**pref·er·en·tial** \‚prefə'renchəl\ *adj*

pre·fer·ment \pri'fərmənt\ *n* : promotion

pre·fig·ure \prē'figyər\ *vb* : foreshadow

¹pre·fix \'prē‚fiks, prē'fiks\ *vb* : place before

²pre·fix \'prē‚fiks\ *n* : affix at the beginning of a word

preg·nant \'pregnənt\ *adj* **1** : containing unborn young **2** : meaningful —**preg·nan·cy** \-nənsē\ *n*

pre·hen·sile \prē'hensəl, -‚sīl\ *adj* : adapted for grasping

pre·his·tor·ic \‚prē(h)is'tôrik\, **pre·his·tor·i·cal** \-ikəl\ *adj* : relating to the period before written history

prej·u·dice \'prejədəs\ *n* **1** : damage esp. to one's rights **2** : unreasonable attitude for or against something ~ *vb* **-diced; -dic·ing 1** : damage **2** : cause to have prejudice —**prej·u·di·cial** \‚prejə'dishəl\ *adj*

prel·ate \'prelət\ *n* : clergyman of high rank —**prel·a·cy** \-əsē\ *n*

pre·lim·i·nary \pri'limə‚nerē\ *n, pl* **-nar·ies** : something that precedes or introduces —**preliminary** *adj*

pre·lude \'prel‚(y)üd, 'prā‚lüd\ *n* : introductory performance, event, or musical piece

pre·ma·ture \‚prēmə't(y)ùər, -'chūər\ *adj* : coming before the usual or proper time —**pre·ma·ture·ly** *adv*

pre·med·i·tate \pri'medə‚tāt\ *vb* : plan beforehand —**pre·med·i·ta·tion** \-‚medə'tāshən\ *n*

pre·mier \pri'm(y)iər, 'prēmēər\ *adj* : first in rank or importance ~ *n* : prime minister —**pre·mier·ship** *n*

pre·miere \pri'myeər, -'miər\ *n* : 1st

performance ~ vb -miered; -mier-ing : give a 1st performance of

prem-ise \'premǝs\ n 1 : statement made or implied as a basis of argument 2 pl : piece of land with the structures on it

pre-mi-um \'prēmēǝm\ n 1 : bonus 2 : sum over the stated value 3 : sum paid for insurance 4 : high value

pre-mo-ni-tion \,prēmǝ'nishǝn, ,premǝ-\ n : feeling that something is about to happen —**pre-mon-i-to-ry** \pri'mänǝ,tōrē\ adj

pre-oc-cu-pied \prē'äkyǝ,pīd\ adj : lost in thought

pre-oc-cu-py \-,pī\ vb : occupy the attention of —**pre-oc-cu-pa-tion** \prē-,äkyǝ'pāshǝn\ n

pre-pare \pri'paǝr\ vb -pared; -par-ing 1 : make or get ready 2 : put together or compound —**prep-a-ra-tion** \,prepǝ'rāshǝn\ n —**pre-pa-ra-to-ry** \pri'parǝ,tōrē\ adj —**pre-pared-ness** \-'parǝdnǝs\ n

pre-pon-der-ate \pri'pändǝ,rāt\ vb -at-ed; -at-ing : exceed in weight, power, importance, or numbers —**pre-pon-der-ance** \-d(ǝ)rǝns\ n —**pre-pon-der-ant** \-d(ǝ)rǝnt\ adj —**pre-pon-der-ant-ly** adv

prep-o-si-tion \,prepǝ'zishǝn\ n : word that combines with a noun or pronoun to form a phrase —**prep-o-si-tion-al** \-'zish(ǝ)nǝl\ adj

pre-pos-sess-ing \,prēpǝ'zesiŋ\ adj : tending to create a favorable impression

pre-pos-ter-ous \pri'päst(ǝ)rǝs\ adj : absurd

pre-req-ui-site \prē'rekwǝzǝt\ n : something required beforehand —**prerequisite** n

pre-rog-a-tive \pri'rägǝtiv\ n : special right or power

pre-sage \'presij, pri'sāj\ vb -saged; -sag-ing 1 : give a warning of 2 : predict —**pre-sage** \'presij\ n

pres-by-ter \'prezbǝtǝr\ n : priest or minister

pre-science \'prēsh(ē)ǝns, 'presh-\ n : foreknowledge of events —**pre-scient** \-(ē)ǝnt\ adj

pre-scribe \pri'skrīb\ vb -scribed; -scrib-ing 1 : lay down as a guide 2 : direct the use of as a remedy

pre-scrip-tion \pri'skripshǝn\ n : written direction for the preparation and use of a medicine or the medicine prescribed

pres-ence \'prezᵊns\ n 1 : fact or condition of being present 2 : appearance or bearing

¹**pres-ent** \'prezᵊnt\ n : something given or received without compensation

²**pre-sent** \pri'zent\ vb 1 : introduce 2 : bring before the public 3 : make a gift to of 4 : bring before a court for inquiry —**pre-sent-able** adj —**pre-sen-ta-tion** \,prē,zen'tāshǝn, ,prezᵊn-\ n —**pre-sent-ment** \pri'zentmǝnt\ n

³**pres-ent** \'prezᵊnt\ adj : now existing, in progress, or attending ~ n : present time

pre-sen-ti-ment \pri'zentǝmǝnt\ n : premonition

pres-ent-ly \'prezᵊntlē\ adv 1 : soon 2 : now

present participle n : participle that typically expresses present action

pre-serve \pri'zǝrv\ vb -served; -serv-ing 1 : keep safe from danger or spoilage 2 : maintain ~ n 1 : preserved fruit —often in pl. 2 : area for protection of natural resources —**pres-er-va-tion** \,prezǝr'vāshǝn\ n —**pre-ser-va-tive** \pri'zǝrvǝtiv\ adj or n —**pre-serv-er** \-'zǝrvǝr\ n

pre-side \pri'zīd\ vb -sid-ed; -sid-ing 1 : act as chairman 2 : exercise control

pres-i-dent \'prezǝdǝnt\ n 1 : one chosen to preside 2 : chief official (as of a company or nation) —**pres-i-den-cy** \-ǝnsē\ n —**pres-i-den-tial** \,prezǝ'denchǝl\ adj

press \'pres\ n 1 : crowded condition 2 : machine or device for exerting pressure and esp. for printing 3 : pressure 4 : printing or publishing establishment 5 : news media and esp. newspapers ~ vb 1 : lie against and exert pressure on 2 : smooth with an iron or squeeze with something heavy 3 : urge 4 : crowd 5 : force one's way —**press-er** n

press-ing adj : urgent

pres-sure \'preshǝr\ n 1 : burden of distress or urgent business 2 : direct application of force —**pressure** vb —**pres-sur-iza-tion** \,presh(ǝ)rǝ-'zāshǝn\ n —**pres-sur-ize** \-,īz\ vb

pres-ti-dig-i-ta-tion \,prestǝ,dijǝ'tā-shǝn\ n : sleight of hand

pres-tige \pres'tēzh, -'tēj\ n : estimation in the eyes of people —**pres-ti-gious** \-'tijǝs\ adj

pres-to \'prestō\ adv or adj : quickly

pre-sume \pri'züm\ vb -sumed; -sum-ing 1 : assume authority without right to do so 2 : take for granted —**pre-sum-able** \-'zümǝbǝl\ adj —**pre-sum-ably** \-blē\ adv

pre-sump-tion \pri'zǝmpshǝn\ n 1

: presumptuous attitude or conduct **2** : belief supported by probability — **pre·sump·tive** \-tiv\ adj

pre·sump·tu·ous \pri'zəmpchə(wə)s\ adj : too bold or forward

pre·sup·pose \,prēsə'pōz\ vb : take for granted — **pre·sup·po·si·tion** \(,)prē-,səpə'zishən\ n

pre·tend \pri'tend\ vb **1** : act as if something is real or true when it is not **2** : act in a way that is false **3** : lay claim — **pre·tend·er** n

pre·tense, pre·tence \'prē,tens, pri-'tens\ n **1** : insincere effort **2** : deception — **pre·ten·sion** \pri'tenchən\ n

pre·ten·tious \pri'tenchəs\ adj : overly showy or self-important — **pre·ten·tious·ly** adv — **pre·ten·tious·ness** n

pre·ter·nat·u·ral \,prētər'nach(ə)rəl\ adj **1** : exceeding what is natural **2** : inexplicable by ordinary means — **pre·ter·nat·u·ral·ly** adv

pre·text \'prē,tekst\ n : falsely stated purpose

pret·ty \'pritē, 'purt-\ adj **-ti·er; -est** : pleasing by delicacy or attractiveness ~ \,pûrtē, part-, ,purt-\ adv : in some degree ~ \'pritē, 'pûrtē\ vb **-tied; -ty·ing** : make pretty — **pret·ti·ly** \'pritˀlē\ adv — **pret·ti·ness** n

pret·zel \'pretsəl\ n : twisted cracker that is glazed and salted

pre·vail \pri'vāl\ vb **1** : triumph **2** : urge successfully **3** : be frequent, widespread, or dominant

prev·a·lent \'prevələnt\ adj : widespread — **prev·a·lence** \-ləns\ n

pre·var·i·cate \pri'varə,kāt\ vb **-cat·ed; -cat·ing** : deviate from the truth — **pre·var·i·ca·tion** \-,varə'kāshən\ n — **pre·var·i·ca·tor** \-'varə,kātər\ n

pre·vent \pri'vent\ vb : keep from happening or acting — **pre·vent·able** adj — **pre·ven·tion** \-'venchən\ n — **pre·ven·tive** \-'ventiv\, **pre·ven·ta·tive** \-'ventətiv\ adj or n

pre·view \'prē,vyü\ vb : view or show beforehand — **preview** n

pre·vi·ous \'prēvēəs\ adj : having gone, happened, or existed before — **pre·vi·ous·ly** adv

prey \'prā\ n, pl **preys 1** : animal taken for food by another **2** : victim ~ vb **1** : seize and devour animals as prey **2** : have a harmful effect on

price \'prīs\ n : cost ~ vb **priced; pric·ing** : set a price on

price·less \-ləs\ adj : too precious to have a price

prick \'prik\ n **1** : tear or small wound made by a point **2** : something sharp

or pointed ~ vb : pierce slightly with a sharp point — **prick·er** n

prick·le \'prikəl\ n **1** : small sharp spine or thorn **2** : slight stinging pain ~ vb **-led; -ling** : tingle — **prick·ly** \'priklē\ adj

pride \'prīd\ n : quality or state of being proud ~ vb **prid·ed; prid·ing** : indulge in pride — **pride·ful** adj

priest \'prēst\ n : person having authority to perform the sacred rites of a religion — **priest·ess** \-əs\ n — **priest·hood** n — **priest·li·ness** \-lēnəs\ n — **priest·ly** adj

prig \'prig\ n : one who irritates by rigid or pointed observance of proprieties — **prig·gish** \-ish\ adj — **prig·gish·ly** adv

prim \'prim\ adj **-mm-** : stiffly formal and proper — **prim·ly** adv — **prim·ness** n

pri·mal \'prīmal\ adj : original or primitive

pri·ma·ry \'prī,merē, 'prīm(ə)rē\ adj : first in order of time, rank, or importance ~ n, pl **-ries** : preliminary election — **pri·mar·i·ly** \prī'merəlē\ adv

primary school n : elementary school

pri·mate n **1** \'prī,māt, -mət\ : highest-ranking bishop **2** \-,māt\ : mammal of the group that includes man and monkeys

prime \'prīm\ n : earliest or best part or period ~ adj : standing first (as in significance or quality) ~ vb **primed;**

prim·ing 1 : fill or load **2** : lay a preparatory coating on

prime minister n : chief executive of a parliamentary government

¹prim·er \'primər\ n : small introductory book

²prim·er \'prīmər\ n **1** : device for igniting an explosive **2** : material for priming a surface

pri·me·val \prī'mēvəl\ adj : relating to the earliest ages

prim·i·tive \'primətiv\ adj **1** : relating to or characteristic of an early stage of development ~ n : one that is primitive — **prim·i·tive·ly** adv — **prim·i·tive·ness** n

pri·mor·di·al \prī'mördēəl\ adj : primeval

primp \'primp\ vb : dress or groom in a finicky manner

prim·rose \'prim,rōz\ n : low herb with clusters of showy flowers

prince \'prins\ n **1** : ruler **2** : son of a king or queen — **prince·ly** adj

prin·cess \'prinsəs, -,ses\ n **1** : daughter of a king or queen 2 : wife of a prince

prin·ci·pal \'prinsəpəl\ *adj* : most important ~ *n* 1 : leading person 2 : head of a school 3 : sum lent at interest —**prin·ci·pal·ly** *adv*

prin·ci·pal·i·ty \,prinsə'palətē\ *n, pl* **-ties** : territory of a prince

prin·ci·ple \'prinsəpəl\ *n* 1 : general or fundamental law 2 : rule or code of conduct or devotion to such a code

print \'print\ *n* 1 : mark made by pressure 2 : printed state or form 3 : printed matter 4 : copy made by printing 5 : cloth with a figure stamped on it ~ *vb* 1 : produce impressions of (as from type) 2 : write in letters like those of printer's type —**print·able** *adj* —**print·er** *n*

print·ing \'printiŋ\ *n* : art or business of a printer

print·out \'print,aut\ *n* : printed record produced by a computer —**print out** \(')print'aut\ *vb*

¹**pri·or** \'prī(ə)r\ *n* : head of a religious house —**pri·or·ess** \'prīərəs\ *n* —**pri·o·ry** \'prī(ə)rē\ *n*

²**pri·or** *adj* : coming before in time, order, or importance —**pri·or·i·ty** \prī'ôrətē\ *n*

prism \'prizəm\ *n* : transparent 3-sided object that separates light into colors —**pris·mat·ic** \priz'matik\ *adj*

pris·on \'priz³n\ *n* : place where criminals are confined

pris·on·er \'priznər, -³nər\ *n* : person on trial or in prison

pris·sy \'prisē\ *adj* **-si·er; -est** : prim —**pris·si·ness** *n*

pris·tine \'pris,tēn\ *adj* : pure

pri·va·cy \'prīvəsē\ *n, pl* **-cies** : quality or state of being apart from others

pri·vate \'prīvət\ *adj* 1 : belonging to a particular individual or group 2 : carried on independently 3 : withdrawn from company or observation ~ *n* : enlisted man of the lowest rank in the marine corps or of one of the two lowest ranks in the army —**pri·vate·ly** *adv*

pri·va·teer \,prīvə'tiər\ *n* : private ship armed to attack enemy ships and commerce

private first class *n* : enlisted man ranking next below a corporal in the army and next below a lance corporal in the marine corps

pri·va·tion \prī'vāshən\ *n* : lack of what is needed for existence

priv·i·lege \'priv(ə)lij\ *n* : right granted as an advantage or favor —**privileged** *adj*

privy \'privē\ *adj* : private or secret ~ *n* : outdoor toilet —**priv·i·ly** \'privəlē\ *adv*

¹**prize** \'prīz\ *n* 1 : something offered or striven for in competition or in contests of chance 2 : something very desirable —**prize** *adj* —**prize·win·ner** *n*

²**prize** *vb* **prized** : value highly

³**prize** \'prīz\ *vb* **prized; priz·ing** : pry

prize·fight *n* : professional boxing match —**prize·fight·er** *n* —**prize·fight·ing** *n*

¹**pro** \'prō\ *n* : favorable argument or person ~ *adv* : in favor

²**pro** *n or adj* : professional

prob·a·ble \'präbəbəl\ *adj* : seeming true or real or to have a good chance of happening —**prob·a·bil·i·ty** \,präbə'bilətē\ *n* —**prob·a·bly** \'präbəblē, 'präblē\ *adv*

pro·bate \'prō,bāt\ *n* 1 : judicial determination of the validity of a will ~ *vb* **-bat·ed; -bat·ing** : establish by probate

pro·ba·tion \prō'bāshən\ *n* 1 : period of testing and trial 2 : freedom of a convict during good behavior under supervision —**pro·ba·tion·ary** \-shə,nerē\ *adj* —**pro·ba·tion·er** *n*

probe \'prōb\ *n* 1 : slender instrument for examining a cavity 2 : investigation ~ *vb* **probed; prob·ing** 1 : examine with a probe 2 : investigate

pro·bi·ty \'prōbətē\ *n* : honest behavior

prob·lem \'präbləm\ *n* 1 : question to be solved 2 : source of perplexity or vexation —**problem** *adj* —**prob·lem·at·ic** \,präblə'matik\ *adj* —**prob·lem·at·i·cal** \-ikəl\ *adj*

pro·bos·cis \prə'bäsəs\ *n, pl* **-cis·es** also **-ci·des** \-ə,dēz\ : long flexible snout

pro·ce·dure \prə'sējər\ *n* 1 : way of doing something 2 : series of steps in regular order —**pro·ce·dur·al** \-'sēj(ə)rəl\ *adj*

pro·ceed \prō'sēd\ *vb* 1 : come forth 2 : go on in an orderly way 3 : begin and carry on an action 4 : advance

pro·ceed·ing *n* 1 : procedure 2 *pl* : something said or done or its official record

pro·ceeds \'prō,sēdz\ *n pl* : total money taken in

pro·cess \'präs,es, 'prōs-\ *n, pl* **-cess·es** \-,esəz, -əsəz, -ə,sēz\ 1 : natural phenomenon marked by gradual changes 2 : series of actions or operations directed toward a result **3** : summons **4** : projecting part ~ *vb* : subject to a process —**pro·ces·sor** \-ər\ *n*

pro·ces·sion \prə'seshən\ *n* : group moving along in an orderly way

pro·ces·sion·al \-'sesh(ə)nəl\ *n* : music for a procession

pro·claim \prō'klām\ *vb* : announce publicly or with conviction —**procla·ma·tion** \,präklə'māshən\ *n*

pro·cliv·i·ty \prō'klivətē\ *n*, *pl* **-ties** : inclination

pro·cras·ti·nate \prə'krastə,nāt\ *vb* **-nat·ed; -nat·ing** : put something off until later —**pro·cras·ti·na·tion** \-,krastə'nāshən\ *n* —**pro·cras·ti·na·tor** \-'krastə,nātər\ *n*

pro·cre·ate \'prōkrē,āt\ *vb* **-at·ed; -at·ing** : produce offspring —**pro·cre·ation** \,prōkrē'āshən\ *n* —**pro·cre·ative** \'prōkrē,ātiv\ *adj* —**pro·cre·ator** \-,ātər\ *n*

proc·tor \'präktər\ *n* : supervisor of students (as at an examination) —**proctor** *vb*

pro·cure \prə'kyúr\ *vb* **-cured; -cur·ing** : get possession of —**pro·cur·able** \-'kyúrəbəl\ *adj* —**pro·cure·ment** *n* —**pro·cur·er** *n*

prod \'präd\ *vb* **-dd-** : push with or as if with a pointed instrument —**prod** *n*

prod·i·gal \'prädigəl\ *adj* : recklessly extravagant or wasteful —**prodigal** *n* —**prod·i·gal·i·ty** \,prädə'galətē\ *n*

pro·di·gious \prə'dijəs\ *adj* : extraordinary in size or degree —**pro·di·gious·ly** *adv*

prod·i·gy \'prädəjē\ *n*, *pl* **-gies** : extraordinary person or thing

pro·duce \prə'd(y)üs\ *vb* **-duced; -duc·ing 1** : present to view **2** : give birth to **3** : bring into existence ~ \'präd(,)üs, 'prōd- *also* -(,)yüs\ *n* **1** : product **2** : agricultural products for sale —**pro·duc·er** \prə'd(y)üsər\ *n*

prod·uct \'präd(,)əkt\ *n* **1** : number resulting from multiplication **2** : something produced

pro·duc·tion \prə'dəkshən\ *n* : act, process, or result of producing —**pro·duc·tive** \-'dəktiv\ *adj* —**pro·duc·tive·ness** *n* —**pro·duc·tiv·i·ty** \(,)prō,dək'tivətē, ,präd(,)ək-\ *n*

pro·fane \prō'fān\ *vb* **-faned; -fan·ing** : treat with irreverence ~ *adj* **1** : not concerned with religion **2** : serving to debase what is holy —**pro·fane·ly** *adv* —**pro·fane·ness** \-'fānnəs\ *n* —**pro·fan·i·ty** \prō'fanətē\ *n*

pro·fess \prə'fes\ *vb* **1** : declare openly **2** : confess one's faith in —**pro·fess·ed·ly** \-ədlē\ *adv*

pro·fes·sion \prə'feshən\ *n* **1** : open declaration of belief **2** : occupation requiring specialized knowledge and academic training

pro·fes·sion·al \prə'fesh(ə)nəl\ *adj* **1** : of, relating to, or engaged in a profession **2** : playing sport for pay —**professional** *n* —**pro·fes·sion·al·ism** *n* —**pro·fes·sion·al·ize** *vb* —**pro·fes·sion·al·ly** *adv*

pro·fes·sor \prə'fesər\ *n* : university or college teacher —**pro·fes·so·ri·al** \,prōfə'sōrēəl, ,präfə-\ *adj* —**pro·fes·sor·ship** *n*

prof·fer \'präfər\ *vb* **-fered; -fer·ing** : offer —**proffer** *n*

pro·fi·cient \prə'fishənt\ *adj* : very good at something —**pro·fi·cien·cy** \-ənsē\ *n* —**proficient** *n* —**pro·fi·cient·ly** *adv*

pro·file \'prō,fīl\ *n* : picture in outline —**profile** *vb*

prof·it \'präfət\ *n* **1** : valuable return **2** : excess of the selling price of goods over cost ~ *vb* : gain a profit —**prof·it·able** \'präfətəbəl, 'präftəbəl\ *adj* —**prof·it·ably** *adv* —**prof·it·less** *adj*

prof·i·teer \,präfə'tiər\ *n* : one who makes an unreasonable profit —**profiteer** *vb*

prof·li·gate \'präfligət, -lə,gāt\ *adj* **1** : shamelessly immoral **2** : wildly extravagant —**prof·li·ga·cy** \-gəsē\ *n* —**profligate** *n* —**prof·li·gate·ly** *adv*

pro·found \prə'faúnd\ *adj* **1** : marked by intellectual depth or insight **2** : deeply felt —**pro·found·ly** *adv* —**pro·fun·di·ty** \-'fəndətē\ *n*

pro·fuse \prə'fyüs\ *adj* : pouring forth liberally —**pro·fuse·ly** *adv* —**pro·fu·sion** \-'fyüzhən\ *n*

pro·gen·i·tor \prō'jenətər\ *n* : direct ancestor

prog·e·ny \'präjənē\ *n*, *pl* **-nies** : offspring

prog·no·sis \präg'nōsəs\ *n*, *pl* **-no·ses** \-,sēz\ : forecast esp. of the course of a disease

prog·nos·ti·cate \präg'nästə,kāt\ *vb* **-cat·ed; -cat·ing** : predict from signs or symptoms —**prog·nos·ti·ca·tion** \-,nästə'kāshən\ *n* —**prog·nos·ti·ca·tor** \-'nästə,kātər\ *n*

pro·gram \'prō,gram, -grəm\ *n* **1** : outline of the order to be pursued or the subjects included (as in a performance) **2** : plan of procedure **3** : coded instructions for a computer ~ *vb* **-grammed** *or* **-gramed; -gram-**

ming *or* **-gram·ing 1** : enter in a program **2** : provide a computer with a program **—pro·gram·ma·bil·i·ty** \(,)prō,gramə'bilətē\ *n* **—program·ma·ble** \'prō,gramabal\ *adj* **—pro·gram·mer** \'prō,gramər, -grəmər\ *n*

prog·ress \'prägrəs, -,res\ *n* : movement forward or to a better condition ~ \prə'gres\ *vb* **1** : move forward **2** : improve **—pro·gres·sive** \-'gresiv\ *adj* **—pro·gres·sive·ly** *adv*

pro·gres·sion \prə'greshən\ *n* **1** : act of progressing **2** : continuous connected series

pro·hib·it \prō'hibət\ *vb* : prevent by authority

pro·hi·bi·tion \,prōə'bishən\ *n* **1** : act of prohibiting **2** : legal restriction on sale or manufacture of alcoholic beverages **—pro·hi·bi·tion·ist** \-'bish(ə)nəst\ *n* **—pro·hib·i·tive** \prō'hibətiv\ *adj* **—pro·hib·i·tive·ly** *adv* **—pro·hib·i·to·ry** \-'hibə,tōrē\ *adj*

proj·ect \'präj,ekt, -ikt\ *n* : planned undertaking ~ \prə'jekt\ *vb* **1** : design or plan **2** : protrude **3** : throw forward **—pro·jec·tion** \-'jekshən\ *n*

pro·jec·tile \prə'jekt⁹l\ *n* : missile hurled by external force

pro·jec·tor \-'jektər\ *n* : device for projecting pictures on a screen

pro·le·tar·i·an \,prōlə'terēən\ *n* : member of the proletariat **—proletarian** *adj*

pro·le·tar·i·at \-ēət\ *n* : laboring class

pro·lif·er·ate \prə'lifə,rāt\ *vb* **-at·ed; -at·ing** : grow or increase in number rapidly **—pro·lif·er·a·tion** \-,lifə'rāshən\ *n*

pro·lif·ic \prə'lifik\ *adj* : producing abundantly **—pro·lif·i·cal·ly** \-ik(ə)lē\ *adv*

pro·logue \'prō,lóg, -,läg\ *n* : preface

pro·long \prə'lóŋ\ *vb* : lengthen in time or extent **—pro·lon·ga·tion** \,prō,lóŋ'gāshən\ *n*

prom \'präm\ *n* : formal school dance

prom·e·nade \,prämə'nād, -'näd\ *n* **1** : leisurely walk **2** : place for strolling **—promenade** *vb*

prom·i·nence \'präm(ə)nəns\ *n* **1** : quality, state, or fact of being readily noticeable or distinguished **2** : something that stands out **—prom·i·nent** \-nənt\ *adj* **—prom·i·nent·ly** *adv*

pro·mis·cu·ous \prə'miskyəwəs\ *adj* : not restricted to one sexual partner **—prom·is·cu·i·ty** \,prämis'kyüətē,

,prō,mis-\ *n* **—pro·mis·cu·ous·ly** *adv* **—pro·mis·cu·ous·ness** *n*

prom·ise \'präməs\ *n* **1** : statement that one will do or not do something **2** : basis for expectation **—promise** *vb* **—prom·is·so·ry** \-ə,sōrē\ *adj*

prom·is·ing \'prämasiŋ\ *adj* : likely to succeed **—prom·is·ing·ly** *adv*

prom·on·to·ry \'prämən,tōrē\ *n, pl* **-ries** : point of land jutting into the sea

pro·mote \prə'mōt\ *vb* **-mot·ed; -mot·ing 1** : advance in rank **2** : contribute to the growth, development, or prosperity of **—pro·mot·er** *n* **—pro·mo·tion** \-'mōshən\ *n* **—pro·mo·tional** \-'mōsh(ə)nəl\ *adj*

¹**prompt** \'prämpt\ *vb* **1** : incite **2** : give a cue to (an actor or singer) **—prompt·er** *n*

²**prompt** *adj* : ready and quick **—prompt·ly** *adv* **—prompt·ness** *n*

prone \'prōn\ *adj* **1** : having a tendency **2** : lying face downward **—prone·ness** \'prōnnəs\ *n*

prong \'próŋ\ *n* : sharp point of a fork **—pronged** \'próŋd\ *adj*

pro·noun \'prō,naún\ *n* : word used as a substitute for a noun

pro·nounce \prə'naúns\ *vb* **-nounced; -nounc·ing 1** : utter officially or as an opinion **2** : say or speak esp. correctly **—pro·nounce·able** *adj* **—pro·nounce·ment** *n* **—pro·nun·ci·a·tion** \-,nənsē'āshən\ *n*

pro·nounced \-'naúnst\ *adj* : strongly marked

¹**proof** \'prüf\ *n* **1** : evidence of a truth or fact **2** : trial impression or print

²**proof** *adj* : designed for or successful in resisting or repelling

proof·read *vb* : read and mark corrections in (printer's proof) **—proof·read·er** *n*

prop \'präp\ *vb* **-pp- 1** : support **2** : sustain **—prop** *n*

pro·pa·gan·da \,präpə'gandə, ,prōpə-\ *n* : the spreading of ideas or information to further or damage a cause **—pro·pa·gan·dist** \-dəst\ *n* **—pro·pa·gan·dize** \-,dīz\ *vb*

prop·a·gate \'präpə,gāt\ *vb* **-gat·ed; -gat·ing 1** : reproduce biologically **2** : cause to spread **—prop·a·ga·tion** \,präpə'gāshən\ *n*

pro·pane \'prō,pān\ *n* : heavy flammable gaseous fuel

pro·pel \prə'pel\ *vb* **-ll-** : drive forward **—pro·pel·lant, pro·pel·lent** *n or adj*

pro·pel·ler \prə'pelər\ *n* : hub with revolving blades that drives a craft

pro·pen·si·ty \prə'pensətē\ *n, pl* **-ties** : particular interest or inclination

prop·er \'präpər\ *adj* **1** : suitable or right **2** : limited to a specified thing **3** : correct **4** : strictly adhering to standards of social manners, dignity, or good taste —**prop·er·ly** *adv*

prop·er·ty \'präpərtē\ *n, pl* **-ties 1** : quality peculiar to an individual **2** : something owned **3** : piece of real estate **4** : ownership

proph·e·cy \'präfəsē\ *n, pl* **-cies** : prediction

proph·e·sy \-ˌsī\ *vb* **-sied; -sy·ing** : predict —**proph·e·si·er** \-ˌsī(ə)r\ *n*

proph·et \'präfət\ *n* : one who utters revelations or predicts events —**proph·et·ess** \-əs\ *n* —**pro·phet·ic** \prə'fetik\, **pro·phet·i·cal** \-ikəl\ *adj* —**pro·phet·i·cal·ly** \-i·k(ə)lē\ *adv*

pro·pin·qui·ty \prə'piŋkwətē\ *n* : nearness

pro·pi·ti·ate \prō'pishē,āt\ *vb* **-at·ed; -at·ing** : gain or regain the favor of —**pro·pi·ti·a·tion** \-ˌpish(ē)'āshən\ *n* —**pro·pi·ti·a·to·ry** \-'pish(ē)ə,tōrē\ *adj*

pro·pi·tious \prə'pishəs\ *adj* : favorable

pro·po·nent \prə'pōnənt\ *n* : one who argues in favor of something

pro·por·tion \prə'pōrshən\ *n* **1** : relation of one part to another or to the whole with respect to magnitude, quantity, or degree **2** : symmetry **3** : share ~ *vb* : adjust in size in relation to others —**pro·por·tion·al** \-sh(ə)nəl\ *adj* —**pro·por·tion·al·ly** *adv* —**pro·por·tion·ate** \-sh(ə)nət\ *adj* —**pro·por·tion·ate·ly** *adv*

pro·pose \prə'pōz\ *vb* **-posed; -pos·ing 1** : plan or intend **2** : make an offer of marriage **3** : present for consideration —**pro·pos·al** \-'pōzəl\ *n*

prop·o·si·tion \ˌpräpə'zishən\ *n* : something proposed ~ *vb* : suggest sexual intercourse with

pro·pound \prə'paùnd\ *vb* : set forth for consideration

pro·pri·e·tor \prə'prīətər\ *n* : owner —**pro·pri·e·tary** \-prīə,terē\ *adj* —**pro·pri·e·tor·ship** \-ər\ *n* —**pro·pri·e·tress** \-'prīətrəs\ *n*

pro·pri·e·ty \prə'prīətē\ *n, pl* **-eties** : standard of acceptability in social conduct

pro·pul·sion \prə'pəlshən\ *n* **1** : action of propelling **2** : driving power —**pro·pul·sive** \-siv\ *adj*

pro·sa·ic \prō'zāik\ *adj* : dull

pro·scribe \prō'skrīb\ *vb* **-scribed;**

-scrib·ing : prohibit —**pro·scrip·tion** \-'skripshən\ *n*

prose \'prōz\ *n* : ordinary language

pros·e·cute \'präsi,kyüt\ *vb* **-cut·ed; -cut·ing 1** : follow to the end **2** : seek legal punishment of —**pros·e·cu·tion** \ˌpräsi'kyüshən\ *n* —**pros·e·cu·tor** \'präsi,kyütər\ *n*

pros·e·lyte \'präsə,līt\ *n* : new convert —**pros·e·ly·tize** \'präs(ə)lə,tīz\ *vb*

pros·pect \'präs,pekt\ *n* **1** : extensive view **2** : something awaited **3** : potential buyer ~ *vb* : look for mineral deposits —**pro·spec·tive** \prä-'spektiv, 'präs,pek-\ *adj* —**pro·spec·tive·ly** *adv* —**pros·pec·tor** \-ˌpektər, -'pek-\ *n*

pro·spec·tus \prə'spektəs\ *n* : introductory description of an enterprise

pros·per \'präspər\ *vb* : thrive or succeed —**pros·per·ous** \-p(ə)rəs\ *adj*

pros·per·i·ty \präs'perətē\ *n* : economic well-being

pros·tate \'präs,tāt\ *n* : glandular body about the base of the male urethra —**prostate** *adj*

pros·the·sis \präs'thēsəs, 'prästhə-\ *n, pl* **-the·ses** \-ˌsēz\ : artificial replacement for a body part —**pros·thet·ic** \präs'thetik\ *adj*

pros·ti·tute \'prästə,t(y)üt\ *vb* **-tut·ed; -tut·ing** : put to corrupt or unworthy purposes ~ *n* : one who engages in sexual intercourse for pay —**pros·ti·tu·tion** \ˌprästə't(y)üshən\ *n*

pros·trate \'präs,trāt\ *adj* : stretched out with face on the ground ~ *vb* **-trat·ed; -trat·ing 1** : fall or throw (oneself) into a prostrate position **2** : reduce to helplessness —**pros·tra·tion** \präs'trāshən\ *n*

pro·tect \prə'tekt\ *vb* : shield from injury —**pro·tec·tor** \-tər\ *n*

pro·tec·tion \prə'tekshən\ *n* **1** : act of protecting **2** : one that protects —**pro·tec·tive** \-'tektiv\ *adj*

pro·tec·tor·ate \-t(ə)rət\ *n* : state dependent upon the authority of another state

pro·té·gé \'prōtə,zhā\ *n* : one under the care and protection of an influential person —**pro·té·gée** \-ˌzhā\ *n*

pro·tein \'prō,tēn\ *n* : complex combination of amino acids present in living matter

pro·test \'prō,test\ *n* **1** : organized public demonstration of disapproval **2** : strong objection ~ \prə'test\ *vb* **1** : assert positively **2** : object strongly —**pro·tes·ta·tion** \ˌprätəs-'tāshən\ *n* —**pro·test·er, pro·tes·tor** \-ər\ *n*

Prot·es·tant \'prätəstənt\ n : Christian not of a Catholic or Orthodox church —**Prot·es·tant·ism** \'prätəstənt,izəm\ n

pro·to·col \'prōtə,kȯl\ n : diplomatic etiquette

pro·ton \'prō,tän\ n : positively charged atomic particle

pro·to·plasm \'prōtə,plazəm\ n : complex colloidal living substance of plant and animal cells —**pro·to·plas·mic** \,prōtə'plazmik\ adj

pro·to·type \'prōtə,tīp\ n : original model

pro·to·zo·an \,prōtə'zōən\ n : single-celled lower invertebrate animal

pro·tract \prō'trakt\ vb : prolong

pro·trac·tor \-'traktər\ n : instrument for constructing and measuring angles

pro·trude \prō'trüd\ vb -trud·ed; -trud·ing : stick out or cause to stick out —**pro·tru·sion** \-'trüzhən\ n —**pro·tru·sive** \-'trüsiv\ adj

pro·tu·ber·ance \prō't(y)üb(ə)rəns\ n : something that protrudes —**pro·tu·ber·ant** adj

proud \'praúd\ adj 1 : having or showing excessive self-esteem 2 : highly pleased 3 : having proper self-respect 4 : glorious —**proud·ly** adv

prove \'prüv\ vb proved; proved or prov·en \'prüvən\; prov·ing 1 : test by experiment or by a standard 2 : establish the truth of by argument or evidence 3 : turn out esp. after trial or test —**prov·able** \'prüvəbəl\ adj

prov·en·der \'prävəndər\ n : dry food for domestic animals

prov·erb \'präv,ərb\ n : short meaningful popular saying —**pro·ver·bi·al** \prə'vərbēəl\ n

pro·vide \prə'vīd\ vb -vid·ed; -vid·ing 1 : take measures beforehand 2 : make a stipulation 3 : supply what is needed —**pro·vid·er** n

pro·vid·ed conj : if

prov·i·dence \'prävədəns\ n 1 often cap : divine guidance 2 cap : God 3 : quality of being provident

prov·i·dent \-ədənt\ adj 1 : making provision for the future 2 : thrifty —**prov·i·dent·ly** adv

prov·i·den·tial \,prävə'denchəl\ adj 1 : relating to Providence 2 : opportune

prov·ince \'prävəns\ n 1 : administrative district 2 pl : all of a country outside the metropolis 3 : sphere

pro·vin·cial \prə'vinchəl\ adj 1 : relating to a province 2 : not cosmopolitan —**pro·vin·cial·ism** \-,izəm\ n

pro·vi·sion \prə'vizhən\ n 1 : act of providing 2 : stock of food —usu. in pl. 3 : stipulation ~ vb : supply with provisions

pro·vi·sion·al \-'vizh(ə)nəl\ adj : provided for a temporary need

pro·vi·so \prə'vīzō\ n, pl -sos or -soes : article or clause that introduces a condition

pro·voke \prə'vōk\ vb -voked; -vok·ing 1 : incite to anger 2 : stir up on purpose —**prov·o·ca·tion** \,prävə-'kāshən\ n —**pro·voc·a·tive** \prə-'väkətiv\ adj

prow \'praú\ n : bow of a ship

prow·ess \'praúəs\ n 1 : valor 2 : extraordinary ability

prowl \'praúl\ vb : roam about stealthily —**prowl** n —**prowl·er** n

prox·i·mate \'präksəmət\ adj : very near

prox·im·i·ty \präk'simətē\ n : nearness

proxy \'präksē\ n, pl prox·ies : authority to act for another —**proxy** adj

prude \'prüd\ n : one who shows extreme modesty —**prud·ery** \'prüdərē\ n —**prud·ish** \'prüdish\ adj

pru·dent \'prüd'nt\ adj 1 : shrewd 2 : cautious 3 : thrifty —**pru·dence** \-'ns\ n —**pru·den·tial** \prü-'denchəl\ adj —**pru·dent·ly** adv

¹prune \'prün\ n : dried plum

²prune vb pruned; prun·ing : cut off unwanted parts

pru·ri·ent \'prúrēənt\ adj : lewd —**pru·ri·ence** \-ēəns\ n

¹pry \'prī\ vb pried; pry·ing : look closely or inquisitively

²pry vb pried; pry·ing : raise, move, or pull apart with a lever

psalm \'säm, 'sälm\ n : sacred song or poem —**psalm·ist** n

pseud·onym \'süd'n,im\ n : fictitious name —**pseud·on·y·mous** \sü-'dänəməs\ adj

pso·ri·a·sis \sə'rīəsəs\ n : chronic skin disease

psy·che \'sīkē\ n : soul or mind

psy·chi·a·try \sə'kīətrē, sī-\ n : branch of medicine dealing with mental disorders —**psy·chi·at·ric** \,sīkē'atrik\ adj—**psy·chi·a·trist** \sə'kīətrəst, sī-\ n

psy·chic \'sīkik\ adj 1 : relating to the psyche 2 : sensitive to supernatural forces ~ n : person sensitive to supernatural forces —**psy·chi·cal·ly** \-k(ə)lē\ adv

psy·cho·anal·y·sis \,sīkōə'naləsəs\ n

: study of the normally hidden content of the mind esp. to resolve conflicts —**psy·cho·an·a·lyst** \-'an⁹l·əst\ n —**psy·cho·an·a·lyt·ic** \-,an⁹l·'itik\ adj —**psy·cho·an·a·lyze** \-'an⁹l,īz\ vb

psy·chol·o·gy \sī'kaləjē\ n, pl -gies 1 : science of mind and behavior 2 : mental and behavioral aspect (as of an individual) —**psy·cho·log·i·cal** \,sīkə'läjikəl\ adj —**psy·cho·log·i·cal·ly** \-ik(ə)lē\ adv —**psy·chol·o·gist** \sī'käləjist\ n

psy·cho·path \'sīkə,path\ n : mentally ill or unstable person —**psy·cho·path·ic** \,sīkə'pathik\ adj

psy·cho·sis \sī'kōsəs\ n, pl -cho·ses \-,sēz\ : mental derangement (as paranoia) —**psy·chot·ic** \-'kätik\ adj or n

psy·cho·so·mat·ic \,sīkōsə'matik\ adj : caused by the interaction of mind and body

psy·cho·ther·a·py \,sīkō'therəpē\ n : treatment of mental disorder by psychological means —**psy·cho·ther·a·pist** \-pəst\ n

pto·maine \'tō,mān\ n : bacterial decay product

pu·ber·ty \'pyübərtē\ n : time of sexual maturity

pu·bic \'pyübik\ adj : relating to the lower abdominal region

pub·lic \'pəblik\ adj 1 : relating to the people as a whole 2 : civic 3 : not private 4 : open to all 5 : well-known ~ n : people as a whole —**pub·lic·ly** adv

pub·li·ca·tion \,pəblə'kāshən\ n 1 : process of publishing 2 : published work

pub·lic·i·ty \(,)pə'blisətē\ n 1 : news information given out to gain public attention 2 : public attention

pub·li·cize \'pəblə,sīz\ vb -cized; -ciz·ing : give publicity to —**pub·li·cist** \-səst\ n

pub·lish \'pəblish\ vb 1 : announce publicly 2 : reproduce for sale esp. by printing —**pub·lish·er** n

puck·er \'pəkər\ vb : pull together into folds or wrinkles ~ n : wrinkle

pud·ding \'pudiŋ\ n : creamy dessert

pud·dle \'pəd⁹l\ n : very small pool of water

pudgy \'pəjē\ adj pudg·i·er; -est : short and plump

pu·er·ile \'pyùərəl\ adj : childish

puff \'pəf\ vb 1 : blow in short gusts 2 : pant 3 : enlarge ~ n 1 : short discharge (as of air) 2 : slight swelling

3 : something light and fluffy —**puffy** adj

pug \'pəg\ n : small stocky dog

pu·gil·ism \'pyüjə,lizəm\ n : boxing —**pu·gil·ist** \-ləst\ n —**pu·gi·lis·tic** \,pyüjə'listik\ adj

pug·na·cious \,pəg'nāshəs\ adj : prone to fighting —**pug·nac·i·ty** \-'nasətē\ n

puke \'pyük\ vb puked; puk·ing : vomit —**puke** n

pul·chri·tude \'pəlkrə,t(y)üd\ n : beauty —**pul·chri·tu·di·nous** \,pəlkrə't(y)üdnəs, -'t(y)üd⁹n-əs\ adj

pull \'pùl\ vb 1 : exert force so as to draw (something) toward or out 2 : move 3 : stretch or tear ~ n 1 : act of pulling 2 : influence 3 : device for pulling something —**pull·er** n

pul·let \'pùlət\ n : young hen

pul·ley \'pùlē\ n, pl -leys : wheel with a grooved rim

Pull·man \'pùlmən\ n : railroad car with berths

pull·over \'pùl,ōvər\ adj : put on by being pulled over the head —**pull·over** \'pùl,ōvər\ n

pul·mo·nary \'pùlmə,nerē, 'pəl-\ adj : relating to the lungs

pulp \'pəlp\ n 1 : soft part of a fruit or vegetable 2 : soft moist mass (as of mashed wood) —**pulpy** adj

pul·pit \'pùl,pit\ n : raised desk used in preaching

pul·sate \'pəl,sāt\ vb -sat·ed; -sat·ing : expand and contract rhythmically —**pul·sa·tion** \,pəl'sāshən\ n

pulse \'pəls\ n : arterial throbbing caused by heart contractions —**pulse** vb

pul·ver·ize \'pəlvə,rīz\ vb -ized; -iz·ing : beat or grind into a powder

pu·ma \'p(y)ümə\ n : cougar

pum·ice \'pəməs\ n : light porous volcanic glass used in polishing

pum·mel \'pəməl\ vb -meled; -mel·ing \-(ə)liŋ\ : beat

¹**pump** \'pəmp\ n : device for moving or compressing fluids ~ vb 1 : raise (as water) with a pump 2 : fill by means of a pump —with up 3 : move like a pump —**pump·er** n

²**pump** n : woman's low shoe

pum·per·nick·el \'pəmpər,nikəl\ n : dark rye bread

pump·kin \'pəŋkən, 'pəm(p)kən\ n : large usu. orange fruit of a vine related to the gourd

pun \'pən\ n : humorous use of a word in a way that suggests two interpretations —**pun** vb

¹**punch** \'pənch\ vb 1 : strike with the

fist **2** : perforate with a punch ~ n
: quick blow with the fist —**punch·er** n

²punch n : tool for piercing or stamping

³punch n : mixed beverage often including fruit juice

punc·til·i·ous \(ˌ)pəŋkˈtiləəs\ adj
: marked by precise accordance with conventions

punc·tu·al \ˈpəŋkchə(wə)l\ adj
: prompt —**punc·tu·al·i·ty** \ˌpəŋkchəˈwalətē\ n —**punc·tu·al·ly** adv

punc·tu·ate \ˈpəŋkchəˌwāt\ vb **-at·ed;
-at·ing** : mark with punctuation

punc·tu·a·tion \ˌpəŋkchəˈwāshən\ n
: standardized marks inserted in written matter to clarify the meaning or their use

punc·ture \ˈpəŋkchər\ n : act or result of puncturing ~ vb **-tured; -tur·ing**
: make a hole in

pun·dit \ˈpəndət\ n **1** : learned person
2 : expert

pun·gent \ˈpənjənt\ adj : having a sharp or stinging odor or taste —**pun·gen·cy** \-jənsē\ n —**pun·gent·ly** adv

pun·ish \ˈpənish\ vb : impose a penalty on or for —**pun·ish·able** adj —**pun·ish·ment** n

pu·ni·tive \ˈpyünətiv\ adj : inflicting punishment

pun·kin var of PUMPKIN

¹punt \ˈpənt\ n : long narrow flat-bottomed boat ~ vb : propel (a boat) by pushing with a pole

²punt vb : kick a ball dropped from the hands ~ n : act of punting a ball

pu·ny \ˈpyünē\ adj **-ni·er; -est** : slight in power or size

pup \ˈpəp\ n : young dog

pu·pa \ˈpyüpə\ n, pl **-pae** \-(ˌ)pē, -ˌpī\ or **-pas** : insect (as a moth) when it is in a case or cocoon —**pu·pal** \-pəl\ adj

¹pu·pil \ˈpyüpəl\ n : young person in school

²pupil n : dark central opening of the iris of the eye

pup·pet \ˈpəpət\ n : small doll moved by hand or by strings —**pup·pe·teer** \ˌpəpəˈtiər\ n

pup·py \ˈpəpē\ n, pl **-pies** : young dog

pur·chase \ˈpərchəs\ vb **-chased; -chas·ing** : obtain in exchange for money ~ n **1** : act of purchasing **2** : something purchased **3** : secure grasp —**pur·chas·er** n

pure \ˈpyúr\ adj **pur·er; pur·est** : free of foreign matter, contamination, or corruption

pu·ree \pyùˈrā, -ˈrē\ n : thick liquid mass of food

pur·ga·to·ry \ˈpərgəˌtōrē\ n, pl **-ries**
: intermediate state after death for purification by expiating sins —**pur·ga·to·ri·al** \ˌpərgəˈtōrēəl\ adj

purge \ˈpərj\ vb **purged; purg·ing 1**
: purify esp. from sin **2** : have or cause free evacuation from the bowels **3** : rid (as a political party) by a purge ~ n **1** : act or result of purging **2** : something that purges —**pur·ga·tive** \ˈpərgətiv\ adj or n

pu·ri·fy \ˈpyúrəˌfī\ vb **-fied; -fy·ing**
: make or become pure —**pu·ri·fi·ca·tion** \ˌpyúrəfəˈkāshən\ n —**pu·ri·fi·er** \-ˌfī(ə)r\ n

Pu·rim \ˈpúr(ˌ)im\ n : a Jewish holiday celebrated in February or March in commemoration of the deliverance of the Jews from the massacre plotted by Haman

pu·ri·tan \ˈpyúrətʰn\ n : one who practices or preaches a very strict moral code —**pu·ri·tan·i·cal** \ˌpyúrəˈtanikəl\ adj

pu·ri·ty \ˈpyúrətē\ n : quality or state of being pure

purl \ˈpərl\ n : stitch in knitting ~ vb
: knit in purl stitch

pur·loin \(ˌ)pərˈlóin, ˈpərˌlóin\ vb
: steal

pur·ple \ˈpərpəl\ n : bluish red color —**pur·plish** \ˈpərp(ə)lish\ adj

pur·port \(ˌ)pərˈpōrt\ vb : convey outwardly as the meaning ~ \ˈpərˌpōrt\ n : meaning —**pur·port·ed·ly** \-ˌədlē\ adv

pur·pose \ˈpərpəs\ n **1** : something (as a result) aimed at **2** : resolution ~ vb **-posed; -pos·ing** : intend —**pur·pose·ful** \-fəl\ adj —**pur·pose·ful·ly** adv —**pur·pose·less** adj —**pur·pose·ly** adv

purr \ˈpər\ n : low murmur typical of a contented cat —**purr** vb

¹purse \ˈpərs\ n **1** : bag or pouch for money and small objects **2** : financial resource **3** : prize money

²purse vb **pursed; purs·ing** : pucker

pur·su·ance \pərˈsüəns\ n : act of carrying into effect

pursuant to \-ˈsüənt-\ prep : according to

pur·sue \pərˈsü\ vb **-sued; -su·ing 1**
: follow in order to overtake **2** : seek to accomplish **3** : engage in —**pur·su·er** n

pur·suit \pərˈsüt\ n **1** : act of pursuing **2** : occupation

pur·vey \(ˌ)pərˈvā\ vb **-veyed; -vey·ing**
: supply (as provisions) usu. as a business —**pur·vey·or** \-ər\ n

pus \'pəs\ *n* : thick yellowish fluid (as in a boil)

push \'pùsh\ *vb* **1** : press against to move forward **2** : urge on or provoke ~ *n* **1** : vigorous effort **2** : act of pushing **—push·cart** *n*

pushy \'pùshē\ *adj* **push·i·er; -est** : objectionably aggressive

pu·sil·lan·i·mous \,pyüsə'lanəməs\ *adj* : cowardly

pussy \'pùsē\ *n, pl* **puss·ies** : cat

pus·tule \'pəschül\ *n* : pus-filled pimple

put \'pùt\ *vb* **put; put·ting 1** : bring to a specified position or condition **2** : subject to pain, suffering, or death **3** : impose or cause to exist **4** : express **5** : cause to be used or employed **—put out** *vb* : bother or inconvenience **—put up with** : endure

pu·tre·fy \'pyütrə,fī\ *vb* **-fied; -fy·ing** : make or become putrid **—pu·tre·fac·tion** \,pyütrə'fakshən\ *n*

pu·trid \'pyütrəd\ *adj* : rotten **—pu·trid·i·ty** \pyü'tridətē\ *n*

put·ter \'pətər\ *vb* : occupy oneself with casual or unimportant work

put·ty \'pətē\ *n, pl* **-ties** : doughlike cement **—putty** *vb*

puz·zle \'pəzəl\ *vb* **-zled; -zling 1** : confuse **2** : attempt to solve **—with** *out* or *over* ~ *n* : something that confuses or tests ingenuity **—puz·zle·ment** *n* **—puz·zler** \-(ə)lər\ *n*

pyg·my \'pigmē\ *n, pl* **-mies** : dwarf **—pygmy** *adj*

py·lon \'pī,län, -lən\ *n* : tower or tall post

pyr·a·mid \'pirə,mid\ *n* : structure with a square base and 4 triangular sides meeting at a point

pyre \'pī(ə)r\ *n* : material heaped for a funeral pyre

py·ro·ma·nia \,pīrō'mānēə\ *n* : irresistible impulse to start fires **—py·ro·ma·ni·ac** \-nē,ak\ *n*

py·ro·tech·nics \,pīrə'tekniks\ *n pl* : spectacular display (as of fireworks) **—py·ro·tech·nic** \-nik\ *adj*

py·thon \'pī,thän, -thən\ *n* : very large constricting snake

Q

q \'kyü\ *n, pl* **q's** *or* **qs** \'kyüz\ : 17th letter of the alphabet

¹quack \'kwak\ *vb* : make a cry like that of a duck **—quack** *n*

²quack *n* : one who pretends to have medical or healing skill **—quack** *adj* **—quack·ery** \-ərē\ *n* **—quack·ish** *adj*

quad·ran·gle \'kwäd,rangəl\ *n* : flat geometrical figure having 4 angles and 4 sides **—quad·ran·gu·lar** \kwä-'draggyələr\ *adj*

quad·rant \'kwädrənt\ *n* : 1/4 of a circle

quad·ri·lat·er·al \,kwädrə'lat(ə)rəl\ *adj* : having 4 sides ~ *n* : 4-sided polygon

qua·drille \kwä'dril, k(w)ə-\ *n* : square dance of 5 or 6 figures in various rhythms

quad·ru·ped \'kwädrə,ped\ *n* : animal having 4 feet

qua·dru·ple \kwä'drüpəl, -'drəp-; 'kwädrəp-\ *vb* **-pled; -pling** \-(ə)liŋ\ : multiply by 4 ~ *adj* : being 4 times as great or as many

qua·dru·plet \kwä'drəplət, -'drüp-; 'kwädrəp-\ *n* : one of 4 offspring born at one birth

quaff \'kwäf, 'kwaf\ *vb* : drink deeply or repeatedly **—quaff** *n*

quag·mire \'kwag,mī(ə)r, 'kwäg-\ *n* : soft land or bog

qua·hog \'kō,hóg, 'kwó-, 'kwō-, -,häg\ *n* : thick-shelled clam

¹quail \'kwāl\ *n, pl* **quail** *or* **quails** : short-winged stout-bodied game bird

²quail *vb* : lose courage or cower in fear

quaint \'kwānt\ *adj* : pleasingly old-fashioned or odd **—quaint·ly** *adv* **—quaint·ness** *n*

quake \'kwāk\ *vb* **quaked; quak·ing** : shake or tremble ~ *n* : earthquake

qual·i·fi·ca·tion \,kwäləfə'kāshən\ *n* **1** : limitation or stipulation **2** : special skill or experience for a job

qual·i·fy \'kwälə,fī\ *vb* **-fied; -fy·ing 1** : modify or limit **2** : fit by skill or training for some purpose **3** : become eligible **—qual·i·fied** *adj* **—qual·i·fi·er** \-,fī(ə)r\ *n*

qual·i·ty \'kwälətē\ *n, pl* **-ties 1** : peculiar and essential character, nature, or feature **2** : excellence or distinction

qualm \'kwäm, 'kwälm, 'kwòm\ *n* : scruple

quan·da·ry \'kwänd(ə)rē\ *n, pl* **-ries** : state of perplexity or doubt

quan·ti·ty \'kwäntətē\ n, pl -ties 1 : something that can be measured or numbered 2 : considerable amount

quar·an·tine \'kwȯrən,tēn\ n 1 : restraint on the movements of persons or goods to prevent the spread of pests or disease 2 : place or period of quarantine —**quarantine** vb

quar·rel \'kwȯr(ə)l\ n : basis of conflict —**quarrel** vb —**quar·rel·some** \-səm\ adj

¹**quar·ry** \'kwȯrē\ n, pl quarries : prey

²**quarry** n, pl -ries : excavation for obtaining stone —**quarry** vb

quart \'kwȯrt\ n : unit of liquid measure equal to .95 liter or of dry measure equal to 1.10 liters

quar·ter \'kwȯrtər\ n 1 : 1/4 part 2 : 1/4 of a dollar 3 : city district 4 pl : place to live esp. for a time 5 : mercy ~ vb : divide into 4 equal parts

quar·ter·ly \'kwȯrtərlē\ adv or adj : at 3-month intervals ~ n, pl -lies : periodical published 4 times a year

quar·ter·mas·ter n 1 : ship's helmsman 2 : army supply officer

quar·tet \kwȯr'tet\ n 1 : music for 4 performers 2 : group of 4

quar·to \'kwȯrtō\ n, pl -tos : book printed on pages cut 4 from a sheet

quartz \'kwȯrts\ n : transparent crystalline mineral

quash \'kwäsh, 'kwȯsh\ vb 1 : set aside by judicial action 2 : suppress summarily and completely

qua·si \'kwā,zī, -sī; 'kwäzē, 'kwäs-; 'kwäzē\ adj : similar or nearly identical

qua·train \'kwä,trān\ n : unit of 4 lines of verse

qua·ver \'kwāvər\ vb : tremble or trill —**quaver** n

quay \'kē, 'kā\ n : wharf

quea·sy \'kwēzē\ adj -si·er, -est : nauseated —**quea·si·ly** \-zəlē\ adv —**quea·si·ness** \-zēnəs\ n

queen \'kwēn\ n 1 : wife or widow of a king 2 : female monarch 3 : woman of rank, power, or attractiveness 4 : fertile female of a social insect —**queen·ly** adj

queer \'kwiər\ adj : differing from the usual or normal —**queer·ly** adv —**queer·ness** n

quell \'kwel\ vb : put down

quench \'kwench\ vb 1 : put out 2 : satisfy (a thirst) —**quench·able** adj

quer·u·lous \'kwer(ə)ləs\ adj : fretful or whining —**quer·u·lous·ly** adv —**quer·u·lous·ness** n

que·ry \'kwi(ə)rē, 'kwe(ə)r-\ n, pl -ries : question —**query** vb

quest \'kwest\ n or vb : search

ques·tion \'kweschən\ n 1 : something asked 2 : subject for discussion 3 : dispute ~ vb 1 : ask questions 2 : doubt or dispute 3 : subject to analysis —**ques·tion·er** n

ques·tion·able \'kweschənəbəl\ adj 1 : not certain 2 : of doubtful truth or morality

question mark n : a punctuation mark ? used esp. at the end of a sentence to indicate a direct question

ques·tion·naire \,kweschə'na(ə)r\ n : set of questions

queue \'kyü\ n 1 : braid of hair 2 : line of persons or vehicles ~ vb queued; queu·ing or queue·ing : line up

quib·ble \'kwibəl\ n : minor objection —**quibble** vb

quick \'kwik\ adj 1 : rapid 2 : alert or perceptive ~ n : sensitive area (as under a fingernail) —**quick** adv —**quick·ly** adv —**quick·ness** n

quick·en \'kwikən\ vb 1 : come to life 2 : hurry

quick·sand n : deep mass of sand and water

quick·sil·ver n : mercury

qui·es·cent \kwī'es²nt\ adj : being at rest —**qui·es·cence** \-əns\ n

qui·et \'kwīət\ adj 1 : marked by little motion or activity 2 : gentle 3 : free from noise 4 : not showy 5 : secluded ~ vb : pacify —**quiet** adv or n —**qui·et·ly** adv —**qui·et·ness** n

qui·etude \'kwīə,t(y)üd\ n : quietness or repose

quill \'kwil\ n 1 : a large stiff feather 2 : porcupine's spine

quilt \'kwilt\ n : padded bedspread ~ vb : stitch or sew in layers with padding in between

quince \'kwins\ n : hard yellow applelike fruit

qui·nine \'kwī,nīn\ n : bitter drug used against malaria

quin·tes·sence \kwin'tes²ns\ n 1 : purest essence of something 2 : most typical example —**quint·es·sen·tial** \,kwintə'senchəl\ adj

quin·tet \kwin'tet\ n 1 : music for 5 performers 2 : group of 5

quin·tu·ple \kwin't(y)üpəl, -'təp-; 'kwintəp-\ adj 1 : having 5 units or members 2 : being 5 times as great or as many —**quintuple** n or vb

quin·tu·plet \kwin'təplət, -'t(y)üp-; 'kwintəp-\ n : one of 5 offspring at one birth

quip \'kwip\ *vb* **-pp-** : make a clever remark —**quip** *n*

quire \'kwī(ə)r\ *n* : 24 or 25 sheets of paper of the same size and quality

quirk \'kwərk\ *n* : peculiarity of action or behavior —**quirky** *adj*

quit \'kwit\ *vb* **quit; quit·ting 1** : stop **2** : leave —**quit·ter** *n*

quite \'kwīt\ *adv* **1** : completely **2** : to a considerable extent

quits \'kwits\ *adj* : even or equal with another (as by repaying a debt)

¹quiv·er \'kwivər\ *n* : case for arrows

²quiver *vb* : shake or tremble —**quiver** *n*

quix·ot·ic \kwik'sätik\ *adj* : idealistic to an impractical degree

quiz \'kwiz\ *n, pl* **quiz·zes** : short test ~ *vb* **-zz-** : question closely

quiz·zi·cal \'kwizikəl\ *adj* **1** : teasing **2** : curious

r \'är\ *n, pl* **r's** *or* **rs** \'ärz\ : 18th letter of the alphabet

rab·bet \'rabət\ *n* : groove in a board

rab·bi \'rab,ī\ *n* : Jewish religious leader —**rab·bin·ic** \rə'binik\, **rab·bin·i·cal** \-ikəl\ *adj*

rab·bin·ate \'rabənət, -,nāt\ *n* : office of a rabbi

rab·bit \'rabət\ *n, pl* **-bit** *or* **-bits** : long-eared burrowing mammal

rab·ble \'rabəl\ *n* : mob

rab·id \'rabəd\ *adj* **1** : violent **2** : fanatical **3** : affected with rabies —**rab·id·ly** *adv*

ra·bies \'rābēz\ *n, pl* **rabies** : acute deadly virus disease

rac·coon \ra'kün\ *n, pl* **-coon** *or* **-coons** : tree-dwelling mammal with a bushy ringed tail

¹race \'rās\ *n* **1** : strong current of water **2** : contest of speed **3** : election campaign ~ *vb* **raced; rac·ing 1** : run in a race **2** : rush —**race·course** *n* —**rac·er** *n* —**race·track** *n*

²race *n* **1** : family, tribe, people, or nation of the same stock **2** : division of mankind based on hereditary traits —**ra·cial** \'rāshəl\ *adj* —**ra·cial·ly** *adv*

race·horse *n* : horse used for racing

rac·ism \'rās,izəm\ *n* : discrimination based on the belief that some races are by nature superior —**rac·ist** \-əst\ *n*

rack \'rak\ *n* **1** : framework for display or storage **2** : instrument that stretches the body for torture ~ *vb* : torture with or as if with a rack

¹rack·et \'rakət\ *n* : bat with a tight netting across an open frame

²racket *n* **1** : confused noise **2** : fraudulent scheme —**rack·e·teer** \,rakə'tiər\ *n* —**rack·e·teer·ing** *n*

ra·con·teur \,rak,än'tər\ *n* : storyteller

racy \'rāsē\ *adj* **rac·i·er; -est** : risqué —**rac·i·ly** *adv* —**rac·i·ness** *n*

ra·dar \'rā,där\ *n* : radio device for determining distance and direction of distant objects

ra·di·al \'rādēəl\ *adj* : having parts arranged like rays coming from a common center —**ra·di·al·ly** *adv*

ra·di·ant \'rādēənt\ *adj* **1** : glowing **2** : beaming with happiness **3** : transmitted by radiation —**ra·di·ance** \-əns\ *n* —**ra·di·ant·ly** *adv*

ra·di·ate \'rādē,āt\ *vb* **-at·ed; -at·ing 1** : issue rays or in rays **2** : spread from a center —**ra·di·a·tion** \,rādē'āshən\ *n*

ra·di·a·tor \'rādē,ātər\ *n* : cooling or heating device

rad·i·cal \'radikəl\ *adj* **1** : fundamental **2** : extreme ~ *n* **1** : person favoring extreme changes **2** : group of atoms replaceable by one atom —**rad·i·cal·ism** \-,izəm\ *n* —**rad·i·cal·ly** *adv*

radii *pl of* RADIUS

ra·dio \'rādē,ō\ *n, pl* **-di·os 1** : transmission or reception of sound by means of electric waves **2** : radio

---

quoit \'kwāt, 'k(w)ȯit\ *n* : ring thrown at a peg in a game (quoits)

quon·dam \'kwändəm, -,dam\ *adj* : former

quo·rum \'kwōrəm\ *n* : required number of members present

quo·ta \'kwōtə\ *n* : proportional part or share

quotation mark *n* : one of a pair of punctuation marks " " or ' ' used esp. to indicate the beginning and the end of a quotation

quote \'kwōt\ *vb* **quot·ed; quot·ing 1** : speak or write another's words **2** : state (a price) —**quot·able** *adj* —**quo·ta·tion** \kwō'tāshən\ *n* —**quote** *n*

quo·tient \'kwōshənt\ *n* : number resulting from division

R

receiving set ~ *vb* : send a message to by radio —**radio** *adj*

ra·dio·ac·tiv·i·ty \ˌrādēōˌak'tivətē\ *n* : property of an element that emits energy through nuclear disintegration —**ra·dio·ac·tive** \-'aktiv\ *adj*

ra·di·ol·o·gy \ˌrādē'äləjē\ *n* : medical use of radiation —**ra·di·ol·o·gist** \-jəst\ *n*

rad·ish \'radish\ *n* : pungent fleshy root usu. eaten raw

ra·di·um \'rādēəm\ *n* : metallic radioactive chemical element

ra·di·us \'rādēəs\ *n, pl* **-dii** \-ē,ī\ 1 : line from the center of a circle or sphere to the circumference or surface 2 : area defined by a radius

raff·ish \'rafish\ *adj* : flashily vulgar —**raff·ish·ly** *adv* —**raff·ish·ness** *n*

raf·fle \'rafəl\ *n* : lottery among people who have bought tickets ~ *vb* **-fled;** **-fling** : offer in a raffle

¹**raft** \'raft\ *n* : flat floating platform ~ *vb* : travel or transport by raft

²**raft** *n* : large amount or number

raf·ter \'raftər\ *n* : usu. sloping timber of a roof

¹**rag** \'rag\ *n* : waste piece of cloth

²**rag** *n* : composition in ragtime

rag·a·muf·fin \'ragəˌməfən\ *n* : ragged dirty person

rage \'rāj\ *n* 1 : violent anger 2 : vogue ~ *vb* **raged; rag·ing** 1 : be extremely angry or violent 2 : be out of control

rag·ged \'ragəd\ *adj* : torn —**rag·ged·ly** *adv* —**rag·ged·ness** *n*

ra·gout \ra'gü\ *n* : meat stew

rag·time *n* : syncopated rhythm

rag·weed *n* : coarse weedy herb with allergenic pollen

raid \'rād\ *n* : sudden usu. surprise attack —**raid** *vb* —**raid·er** *n*

¹**rail** \'rāl\ *n* 1 : bar serving as a guard or barrier 2 : bar forming a track for wheeled vehicles 3 : railroad

²**rail** *vb* : scold someone vehemently —**rail·er** *n*

rail·ing \'rāliŋ\ *n* : rail or a barrier of rails

rail·lery \'rālərē\ *n, pl* **-ler·ies** : good-natured ridicule

rail·road \'rāl,rōd\ *n* : road for a train laid with iron rails and wooden ties ~ *vb* : force something hastily —**rail·road·er** *n* —**rail·road·ing** *n*

rail·way \-ˌwā\ *n* : railroad

rai·ment \'rāmənt\ *n* : clothing

rain \'rān\ *n* 1 : water falling in drops from the clouds 2 : shower of objects ~ *vb* : fall as or like rain —**rain·coat** *n* —**rain·drop** *n* —**rain·fall** *n* —**rain·mak·er** *n* —**rain·mak·ing** *n*

rain·storm *n* —**rain·wa·ter** *n* —**rainy** *adj*

rain·bow \-ˌbō\ *n* : arc of colors formed by the sun shining through moisture

raise \'rāz\ *vb* **raised; rais·ing** 1 : lift 2 : arouse 3 : erect 4 : collect 5 : breed, grow, or bring up 6 : increase 7 : make light ~ 1 : increase esp. in pay —**rais·er** *n*

rai·sin \'rāzᵊn\ *n* : dried grape

ra·ja, ra·jah \'räjə\ *n* : Indian prince

¹**rake** \'rāk\ *n* : tool for smoothing or sweeping ~ *vb* **raked; rak·ing** 1 : gather, loosen, or smooth with or as if with a rake 2 : sweep with gunfire

²**rake** *n* : dissolute man —**rak·ish** \'rākish\

rak·ish \'rākish\ *adj* : smart or jaunty —**rak·ish·ly** *adv* —**rak·ish·ness** *n*

ral·ly \'ralē\ *vb* **-lied; -ly·ing** 1 : bring or come together 2 : revive or recover ~ *n, pl* **-lies** 1 : act of rallying 2 : mass meeting

ram \'ram\ *n* 1 : male sheep 2 : beam used in battering down walls or doors ~ *vb* **-mm-** 1 : force or drive in or through 2 : strike against violently

ram·ble \'rambəl\ *vb* **-bled; -bling** : wander —**ramble** *n* —**ram·bler** \-blər\ *n*

ram·bunc·tious \ram'bəŋkshəs\ *adj* : unruly

ram·i·fi·ca·tion \ˌraməfə'kāshən\ *n* : consequence

ram·i·fy \'ramə,fī\ *vb* **-fied; -fy·ing** : branch out

ramp \'ramp\ *n* : sloping passage or connecting roadway

ram·page \'ram,pāj, (ˌ)ram'pāj\ *vb* **-paged; -pag·ing** : rush about wildly ~ \'ram,-\ *n* : violent or riotous action or behavior

ram·pant \'rampənt\ *adj* : widespread —**ram·pant·ly** *adv*

ram·part \'ram,pärt\ *n* : embankment of a fortification

ram·rod *n* : rod used to load or clean a gun

ram·shack·le \'ram,shakəl\ *adj* : shaky

ran *past of* RUN

ranch \'ranch\ *n* 1 : establishment for the raising of cattle, sheep, or horses 2 : specialized farm ~ *vb* : operate a ranch —**ranch·er** *n* —**ranch·land** \-,land\ *n*

ran·cid \'ransəd\ *adj* : smelling or tasting as if spoiled —**ran·cid·i·ty** \ran'sidətē\ *n* —**ran·cid·ness** *n*

ran·cor \'raŋkər\ *n* : deep hatred — **ran·cor·ous** *adj*

ran·dom \'randəm\ *adj* : occurring by chance —**ran·dom·ly** *adv* —**ran·dom·ness** *n* —**at random** : without definite aim or method

ran·dom·ize \'randə,mīz\ *vb* **-ized; -iz·ing** : distribute or treat in a random way —**ran·dom·iza·tion** \,randəmə-'zāshən\ *n*

rang *past of* RING

range \'rānj\ *n* 1 : series of things in a row 2 : open land for grazing 3 : cooking stove 4 : variation within limits 5 : place for target practice 6 : extent ~ *vb* **ranged; rang·ing** 1 : set in a row or in order 2 : roam at large, freely, or over 3 : vary within limits —**range·land** \-,land\ *n*

rang·er \'rānjər\ *n* : lawman or soldier who patrols a large area

rangy \'rānjē\ *adj* **rang·i·er; -est** : being slender with long limbs — **rang·i·ness** *n*

¹rank \'raŋk\ *adj* 1 : vigorous in growth 2 : unpleasantly strong-smelling —**rank·ly** *adv* —**rank·ness** *n*

²rank *n* 1 : line of soldiers 2 : orderly arrangement 3 : grade of official standing 4 : position within a group ~ *vb* 1 : arrange in formation or according to class 2 : take or give a relative position

rank and file *n* : general membership

ran·kle \'raŋkəl\ *vb* **-kled; -kling** : cause anger, irritation, or bitterness

ran·sack \'ran,sak\ *vb* : search through and rob

ran·som \'ransəm\ *n* : something demanded for the freedom of a captive ~ *vb* : gain the freedom of by paying a price —**ran·som·er** *n*

rant \'rant\ *vb* : talk or scold violently —**rant·er** *n* —**rant·ing·ly** *adv*

¹rap \'rap\ *n* : sharp blow or rebuke ~ *vb* **-pp-** : strike or criticize sharply

²rap *vb* **-pp-** : talk freely

ra·pa·cious \rə'pāshəs\ *adj* 1 : excessively greedy 2 : ravenous —**ra·pa·cious·ly** *adv* —**ra·pa·cious·ness** *n* —**ra·pac·i·ty** \-'pasətē\ *n*

¹rape \'rāp\ *n* : herb grown as a forage crop and for its seeds (**rape·seed**)

²rape *vb* **raped; rap·ing** : force to have sexual intercourse —**rape** *n* —**rap·er** *n* —**rap·ist** \'rāpəst\ *n*

rap·id \'rapəd\ *adj* : very fast —**ra·pid·i·ty** \rə'pidətē\ *n* —**rap·id·ly** *adv*

rap·ids \-ədz\ *n pl* : place in a stream where the current is swift

ra·pi·er \'rāpēər\ *n* : narrow 2-edged sword

rap·ine \'rapən, -,īn\ *n* : plunder

rap·port \ra'pōr\ *n* : harmonious relationship

rapt \'rapt\ *adj* : engrossed —**rapt·ly** *adv* —**rapt·ness** *n*

rap·ture \'rapchər\ *n* : spiritual or emotional ecstasy —**rap·tur·ous** \-chərəs\ *adj*

¹rare \'ra(ə)r\ *adj* **rar·er; rar·est** : having a portion relatively uncooked

²rare *adj* **rar·er; rar·est** 1 : not dense 2 : unusually fine 3 : seldom met with —**rare·ly** *adv* —**rare·ness** *n* —**rar·i·ty** \'rarətē\ *n*

rar·efy \'rarə,fī\ *vb* **-efied; -efy·ing** : make or become rare, thin, or less dense —**rar·efac·tion** \,rarə'fak-shən\ *n*

rar·ing \'ra(ə)rən, -iŋ\ *adj* : full of enthusiasm

ras·cal \'raskəl\ *n* : mean, dishonest, or mischievous person —**ras·cal·i·ty** \ras-'kal·ət·ē\ *n* —**ras·cal·ly** \'raskəlē\ *adj*

¹rash \'rash\ *adj* : too hasty in decision or action —**rash·ly** *adv* —**rash·ness** *n*

²rash *n* : a breaking out of the skin with red spots

rasp \'rasp\ *vb* 1 : rub with or as if with a rough file 2 : to speak in a grating tone ~ *n* : coarse file

rasp·ber·ry \'raz,berē, -b(ə)rē\ *n* : edible red or black berry

rat \'rat\ *n* : destructive rodent larger than the mouse

ratch·et \'rachət\ *n* : notched device for allowing motion in one direction

rate \'rāt\ *n* 1 : quantity, amount, or degree measured in relation to some other quantity : rank ~ *vb* **rat·ed; rat·ing** 1 : estimate or determine the rank or quality of 2 : deserve —**rat·er** *n*

rath·er \'rathər, 'rəth-, 'rāth-\ *adv* 1 : preferably 2 : on the other hand 3 : more properly 4 : somewhat

rat·i·fy \'ratə,fī\ *vb* **-fied; -fy·ing** : approve and accept formally —**rat·i·fi·ca·tion** \,ratəfə'kāshən\ *n*

rat·ing \'rātiŋ\ *n* : classification according to grade

ra·tio \'rāsh(ē)ō\ *n, pl* **-tios** : relation in number, quantity, or degree between things

ra·tion \'rashən, 'rāshən\ *n* : share or allotment (as of food) ~ *vb* : use or allot sparingly

ra·tio·nal \'rash(ə)nəl\ *adj* 1 : having

reason or sanity 2 : relating to reason —**ra·tio·nal·ly** adv

ra·tio·nale \,rashə'nal\ n 1 : explanation of principles of belief or practice 2 : underlying reason

ra·tio·nal·ize \-,īz\ vb **-ized; -iz·ing** : justify (as one's behavior or weaknesses) esp. to oneself —**ra·tio·nal·iza·tion** \,rash(ə)nələ'zāshən\ n

rat·tan \ra'tan, ra-\ n : palm with long stems used esp. for canes and wickerwork

rat·tle \'rat⁰l\ vb **-tled; -tling** 1 : make a series of clattering sounds 2 : say briskly 3 : confuse or upset ~ n 1 : series of clattering sounds 2 : toy that rattles

rat·tler \'ratlər\ n : rattlesnake

rat·tle·snake n : American venomous snake with a rattle at the end of the tail

rau·cous \'rókəs\ adj : harsh or boisterous —**rau·cous·ly** adv —**rau·cous·ness** n

rav·age \'ravij\ n : destructive effect ~ vb **-aged; -ag·ing** : lay waste —**rav·ag·er** n

rave \'rāv\ vb **raved; rav·ing** 1 : talk wildly in or as if in delirium 2 : talk with extreme enthusiasm ~ n 1 : act of raving 2 : enthusiastic praise

rav·el \'ravəl\ vb **-eled** or **-elled; -el·ing** or **-el·ling** 1 : unravel 2 : tangle ~ n 1 : something tangled 2 : loose thread

ra·ven \'rāvən\ n : large black bird ~ adj : black and shiny

rav·en·ous \'rav(ə)nəs\ adj : very hungry —**rav·en·ous·ly** adv —**rav·en·ous·ness** n

ra·vine \rə'vēn\ n : narrow steep-sided valley

rav·ish \'ravish\ vb 1 : seize and take away by violence 2 : overcome with joy or delight 3 : rape —**rav·ish·er** n —**rav·ish·ment** n

raw \'ró\ adj **raw·er** \'ró(ə)r\; **raw·est** \'róəst\ 1 : not cooked 2 : not processed 3 : not trained 4 : having the skin rubbed off 5 : cold and damp 6 : vulgar —**raw·ness** n

raw·hide \'ró,hīd\ n : untanned skin of cattle

ray \'rā\ n 1 : thin beam of radiant energy (as light) 2 : tiny bit

ray·on \'rā,än\ n : fabric made from cellulose fiber

raze \'rāz\ vb **razed; raz·ing** : destroy or tear down

ra·zor \'rāzər\ n : sharp cutting instrument used to shave off hair

re- \rē, ,rē, 're\ prefix 1 : again or anew 2 : back or backward

reaccelerate	rechristen
reaccept	recirculate
reacclimatize	recirculation
reaccredit	reclassification
reaccumulate	reclassify
reachieve	recolonize
reacquaint	recombine
reacquire	recompute
reactivate	reconceive
reactivation	reconnect
readapt	reconquer
readdict	reconquest
readdress	reconsider
readjust	reconsideration
readjustable	reconsolidate
readjustment	reconstruct
readmit	recontaminate
readopt	reconvene
reaffirm	reconvict
realign	recopy
realignment	re-create
reallocate	recross
reanalysis	redeal
reanalyze	redecorate
reanesthetize	rededicate
reappear	rededication
reappearance	redefine
reapply	redeposit
reappoint	redesign
reapportion	redesignate
reappraisal	redevelop
reappraise	rediscover
reapprove	rediscovery
reargue	redissolve
rearrange	redistribute
rearrest	redraft
reassemble	redraw
reassert	reemerge
reassess	reemergence
reassessment	reemphasize
reassign	reenergize
reassignment	reengage
reassociate	reenlist
reattach	reenlistment
reattain	reenroll
reawaken	reenter
rebalance	reequip
rebaptize	reestablish
rebid	reestablishment
rebind	reestimate
reborn	reevaluate
rebroadcast	reevaluation
rebuild	reexamination
rebury	reexamine
recalculate	refilm
recapture	refinance
recast	refire
recertification	refloat
recertify	reflood
rechannel	refocus
recharge	refold
recheck	reformulate

refreeze
refuel
regrow
regrowth
rehear
reheat
rehire
rehospitalization
rehospitalize
reidentify
reignite
reimplant
reimpose
reincorporate
reindict
reinfection
reinfest
reinflate
reinject
reinjection
reinoculate
reinsert
reinsertion
reinspect
reinstall
reinstitute
reintegrate
reintegration
reinter
reintroduce
reinvent
reinvestigate
reinvestigation
reinvigorate
rejudge
rekindle
reknit
relabel
relandscape
relaunch
relearn
relight
reline
reload
remarriage
remarry
remelt
remobilize
remoisten
remold
remotivate
rename
renegotiate
reoccupy
reoccur
reoccurrence
reoperate
reorchestrate
reorganization
reorganize
reorient
repack

repaint
repave
rephotograph
replan
replaster
replay
replot
repolish
repopulate
repressurize
reprice
reprint
reprocess
reprogram
repropose
reread
rerecord
reregister
reroof
reroute
resalable
resale
reschedule
reseal
resegregate
resell
resentence
reset
resettle
resew
reshoot
reshow
resod
resolidify
restage
restart
restate
restatement
restimulate
restock
restructure
restudy
restyle
resubmit
resupply
resurface
resurvey
resuspend
resynthesis
resynthesize
retarget
reteach
retell
retest
rethink
retighten
retitle
retrain
retranslate
retransmit
retransplant
retrap

retry
retune
retype
reupholster
reusable
reuse
reutilize
revaccinate

revaccination
revisit
rewash
rewax
reweave
rewind
rewire
rewrap

reach \'rēch\ *vb* **1** : stretch out **2** : touch or try to touch or grasp **3** : extend to or arrive at **4** : communicate with ~ *n* **1** : act of reaching **2** : distance or extent of reaching — **reach·able** *adj* — **reach·er** *n*

re·act \rē'akt\ *vb* **1** : act in response to some influence or stimulus **2** : undergo chemical change — **re·ac·tive** \-'aktiv\ *adj*

re·ac·tion \rē'akshən\ *n* **1** : action or emotion caused by and directly related or counter to another action **2** : chemical change

re·ac·tion·ary \-shə,nerē\ *adj* : relating to or favoring return to an earlier political order or policy ~ *n, pl* **-ar·ies** : reactionary person

re·ac·tor \rē'aktər\ *n* **1** : one that reacts **2** : apparatus for the controlled release of atomic energy

read \'rēd\ *vb* **read** \'red\; **read·ing** \'rēdiŋ\ **1** : understand written language **2** : utter aloud printed words **3** : interpret **4** : study **5** : indicate ~ *adj* \'red\ : informed by reading — **read·a·bil·i·ty** \,rēdə'bilətē\ *n* — **read·able** *adj* — **read·ably** *adv* — **read·er** *n* — **read·er·ship** *n*

read·ing \'rēdiŋ\ *n* **1** : something read or for reading **2** : particular version, interpretation, or performance **3** : indication of data made by an instrument

ready \'redē\ *adj* **readi·er; -est** : prepared or available for use or action **2** : willing to do something ~ *vb* **read·ied; ready·ing** : make ready ~ *n* : state of being ready — **read·i·ly** *adv* — **read·i·ness** *n*

real \'rē(ə)l\ *adj* **1** : actually existing **2** : genuine ~ *adv* : very — **real·ness** *n* — **for real 1** : in earnest **2** : genuine

real estate *n* : property in houses and land

re·al·ism \'rēə,lizəm\ *n* **1** : disposition to deal with facts practically **2** : faithful portrayal of reality — **re·al·ist** \-ləst\ *adj or n* — **re·al·is·tic** \,rēə'listik\ *adj* — **re·al·is·ti·cal·ly** \-tik(ə)lē\ *adv*

re·al·i·ty \rē'alətē\ *n, pl* **-ties 1** : quality

or state of being real **2** : something real

re·al·ize \'rēə,līz\ *vb* **-ized; -iz·ing 1** : make actual **2** : obtain **3** : be aware of —**re·al·iz·able** *adj* —**re·al·iza·tion** \,rēələ'zāshən\ *n*

real·ly \'rē(ə)lē\ *adv* : in truth

realm \'relm\ *n* **1** : kingdom **2** : sphere

¹ream \'rēm\ *n* : quantity of paper that is 480, 500, or 516 sheets

²ream *vb* : enlarge or clean (a hole) with a specially shaped tool (**reamer**)

reap \'rēp\ *vb* : cut or clear (as a crop) with a scythe or machine —**reap·er** *n*

¹rear \'rior\ *vb* **1** : raise upright **2** : breed or bring up **3** : rise on the hind legs

²rear *n* **1** : back **2** : position at the back of something — *adj* : being at the back —**rear·ward** \-wərd\ *adj or adv*

rear admiral *n* : commissioned officer in the navy or coast guard ranking next below a vice admiral

rea·son \'rēzᵊn\ *n* **1** : explanation or justification **2** : motive for action or belief **3** : power or process of thinking ~ *vb* **1** : use the faculty of reason **2** : try to persuade another —**rea·son·er** *n* —**rea·son·ing** \'rēz·niŋ, -ᵊnıŋ\ *n*

rea·son·able \'rēznəbəl, -ᵊnəbəl\ *adj* **1** : being within the bounds of reason **2** : inexpensive —**rea·son·able·ness** *n* —**rea·son·ably** \-blē\ *adv*

re·as·sure \,rēə'shur\ *vb* : restore one's confidence —**re·as·sur·ance** \-'shurəns\ *n* —**re·as·sur·ing·ly** *adv*

re·bate \'rē,bāt\ *n* : return of part of a payment —**rebate** *vb*

¹reb·el \'rebəl\ *n* : one that resists authority —**rebel** \'rebəl\ *adj*

²re·bel \ri'bel\ *vb* **-belled; -bel·ling 1** : resist authority **2** : feel or exhibit anger

re·bel·lion \ri'belyən\ *n* : resistance to authority and esp. to one's government

re·bel·lious \-yəs\ *adj* **1** : engaged in rebellion **2** : inclined to resist authority —**re·bel·lious·ly** *adv* —**re·bel·lious·ness** *n*

re·birth \'rē'bərth\ *n* **1** : new or second birth **2** : revival

re·bound \'rē'baund, ri-\ *vb* **1** : spring back on striking something **2** : recover from a reverse ~ \'rē,-\ *n* **1** : action of rebounding **2** : immediate reaction to a reverse

re·buff \ri'bəf\ *vb* : refuse or repulse rudely —**rebuff** *n*

re·buke \-'byük\ *vb* **-buked; -buk·ing** : reprimand sharply —**rebuke** *n*

re·bus \'rēbəs\ *n* : riddle representing syllables or words with pictures

re·but \ri'bət\ *vb* **-but·ted; -but·ting** : refute —**re·but·ter** *n*

re·but·tal \-'ᵊl\ *n* : opposing argument

re·cal·ci·trant \ri'kalsətrənt\ *adj* **1** : stubbornly resisting authority **2** : resistant to handling or treatment —**re·cal·ci·trance** \-trəns\ *n*

re·call \ri'kol\ *vb* **1** : call back **2** : remember **3** : revoke ~ \ri'-, 'rē,-\ *n* **1** : a summons to return **2** : remembrance **3** : act of revoking

re·cant \ri'kant\ *vb* : take back (something said) publicly

re·ca·pit·u·late \,rēkə'pichə,lāt\ *vb* **-lat·ed; -lat·ing** : summarize —**re·ca·pit·u·la·tion** \-,pichə'lāshən\ *n*

re·cede \ri'sēd\ *vb* **-ced·ed; -ced·ing 1** : move back or away **2** : slant backward

re·ceipt \-'sēt\ *n* **1** : act of receiving **2** : something (as payment) received —usu. in pl. **3** : writing acknowledging something received

re·ceive \ri'sēv\ *vb* **-ceived; -ceiv·ing 1** : take in or accept **2** : greet or entertain (visitors) **3** : pick up radio waves and convert into sounds or pictures —**re·ceiv·able** *adj*

re·ceiv·er \ri'sēvər\ *n* **1** : one that receives **2** : one having charge of property or money involved in a lawsuit **3** : apparatus for receiving radio waves —**re·ceiv·er·ship** *n*

re·cent \'rēsᵊnt\ *adj* **1** : lately made or used **2** : of the present time or time just past —**re·cent·ly** *adv* —**re·cent·ness** *n*

re·cep·ta·cle \ri'septikəl\ *n* : container

re·cep·tion \ri'sepshən\ *n* **1** : act of receiving **2** : social gathering at which guests are formally welcomed

re·cep·tion·ist \-sh(ə)nəst\ *n* : one who greets callers

re·cep·tive \ri'septiv\ *adj* : open and responsive to ideas, impressions, or suggestions —**re·cep·tive·ly** *adv* —**re·cep·tive·ness** *n* —**re·cep·tiv·i·ty** \,rē,sep'tivətē\ *n*

re·cess \'rē,ses, ri'ses\ *n* **1** : indentation in a line or surface **2** : suspension of a session for rest ~ *vb* **1** : make a recess or put into a recess **2** : interrupt a session for a recess

re·ces·sion \ri'seshən\ *n* **1** : departing procession **2** : period of reduced economic activity

re·ci·pe \'resə,(,)pē\ *n* : instructions for making something

re·cip·i·ent \ri'sipēənt\ *n* : one that receives

re·cip·ro·cal \ri'siprəkəl\ *adj* 1 : affecting each in the same way 2 : so related that one is equivalent to the other —**re·cip·ro·cal·ly** \-k(ə)lē\ *adv* —**re·ci·proc·i·ty** \,resə'präsətē\ *n*

re·cip·ro·cate \-,kāt\ *vb* -**cat·ed; -cat·ing** : make a return for something done or given —**re·cip·ro·ca·tion** \-,siprə'kāshən\ *n*

re·cit·al \ri'sīt²l\ *n* 1 : public reading or recitation 2 : music or dance concert or exhibition by pupils —**re·cit·al·ist** \-²ləst\ *n*

rec·i·ta·tion \,resə'tāshən\ *n* : a reciting or recital

re·cite \ri'sīt\ *vb* -**cit·ed; -cit·ing** 1 : repeat verbatim 2 : recount —**re·cit·er** *n*

reck·less \'rekləs\ *adj* : lacking caution —**reck·less·ly** *adv* —**reck·less·ness** *n*

reck·on \'rekən\ *vb* 1 : count or calculate 2 : consider

reck·on·ing *n* 1 : act or instance of reckoning 2 : settling of accounts

re·claim \ri'klām\ *vb* 1 : obtain from a waste product or by-product 2 : demand or obtain the return of —**re·claim·able** *adj* —**rec·la·ma·tion** \,reklə'māshən\ *n*

re·cline \ri'klīn\ *vb* -**clined; -clin·ing** : lean backward or lie down

re·cluse \'rek,lüs, ri'klüs\ *n* : one who lives in seclusion

rec·og·ni·tion \,rekig'nishən, -əg-\ *n* : act of recognizing or state of being recognized

re·cog·ni·zance \ri'käg(n)əzəns\ *n* : promise recorded before a court

rec·og·nize \'rekig,nīz, -əg-\ *vb* -**nized; -niz·ing** 1 : identify as previously known 2 : take notice of 3 : acknowledge esp. with appreciation —**rec·og·niz·able** \'rekəg,nīzəbəl, -ig-\ *adj* —**rec·og·niz·ably** \-blē\ *adv*

re·coil \ri'kȯil\ *vb* : draw or spring back ~ \'rē-, ri'-\ *n* : action of recoiling

rec·ol·lect \,rekə'lekt\ *vb* : remember

rec·ol·lec·tion \,rekə'lekshən\ *n* 1 : act or power of recollecting 2 : something recollected

rec·om·mend \,rekə'mend\ *vb* 1 : present as deserving of acceptance or trial 2 : advise —**rec·om·mend·able** \-'mendəbəl\ *adj*

rec·om·men·da·tion \,rekəmən'dāshən\ *n* 1 : act of recommending 2 : statement or letter recommending someone

rec·om·pense \'rekəm,pens\ *vb* -**pensed; -pens·ing** : give compensation to ~ *n* : compensation

rec·on·cile \'rekən,sīl\ *vb* -**ciled; -cil·ing** 1 : cause to be friendly again 2 : adjust or settle 3 : bring to acceptance —**rec·on·cil·able** *adj* —**rec·on·cile·ment** *n* —**rec·on·cil·er** *n* —**rec·on·cil·i·a·tion** \,rekən,silē'āshən\ *n*

rec·on·dite \'rekən,dīt\ *adj* 1 : hard to understand 2 : little known

re·con·nais·sance \ri'känəzəns, -səns\ *n* : exploratory survey of enemy territory

re·con·noi·ter, re·con·noi·tre \,rekə'nȯitər, ,rēkə-\ *vb* -**tered or -tred; -ter·ing or -tring** : make a reconnaissance of

re·cord \ri'kȯrd\ *vb* 1 : set down in writing 2 : register permanently 3 : indicate 4 : preserve (as sound or images) for later reproduction ~ \'rekərd\ *n* 1 : something recorded 2 : best performance

re·cord·er \ri'kȯrdər\ *n* 1 : one who records transactions officially 2 : wind instrument with finger holes 3 : recording device

¹**re·count** \ri'kaunt\ *vb* : relate in detail

²**re·count** \'rē-\ *vb* : count again —**re·count** \'rē-, ('rē-\ *n*

re·coup \ri'küp\ *vb* : make up for (an expense or loss)

re·course \'rē,kȯrs, ri'-\ *n* : source of aid or a turning to such a source

re·cov·er \ri'kəvər\ *vb* 1 : regain position, poise, or health 2 : recoup —**re·cov·er·able** *adj* —**re·cov·ery** \-'kəv(ə)rē\ *n*

re·cre·ation \,rekrē'āshən\ *n* : a refreshing of strength or spirits as a change from work or study —**rec·re·ation·al** \-sh(ə)nəl\ *adj*

re·crim·i·na·tion \ri,krimə'nāshən\ *n* : accusation —**re·crim·i·nate** *vb*

re·cruit \ri'krüt\ *n* : newly enlisted member ~ *vb* : enlist the membership or services of —**re·cruit·er** *n* —**re·cruit·ment** *n*

rect·an·gle \'rek,tangəl\ *n* : 4-sided figure with 4 right angles —**rect·an·gu·lar** \rek'tangyələr\ *adj*

rec·ti·fy \'rektə,fī\ *vb* -**fied; -fy·ing** : make or set right —**rec·ti·fi·ca·tion** \,rektəfə'kāshən\ *n* —**rec·ti·fi·er** \'rektə,fī(ə)r\ *n*

rec·ti·tude \'rektə,t(y)üd\ *n* : moral integrity

rec·tor \'rektər\ *n* : clergyman in charge of a parish —**rec·to·ri·al** \rek'tōrēəl\ *adj*

rec·to·ry \'rekt(ə)rē\ *n, pl* **-ries** : rector's residence

rec·tum \'rektəm\ *n, pl* **-tums** *or* **-ta** \-tə\ : last part of the intestine joining colon and anus —**rec·tal** \-t°l\ *adj*

re·cum·bent \ri'kəmbənt\ *adj* : lying down

re·cu·per·ate \ri'k(y)üpə,rāt\ *vb* **-at·ed; -at·ing** : recover (as from illness) —**re·cu·per·a·tion** \-,k(y)üpə'rāshən\ *n* —**re·cu·per·a·tive** \-'k(y)üpərātiv\ *adj*

re·cur \ri'kər\ *vb* **-rr-** 1 : return in thought or talk 2 : happen or occur again —**re·cur·rence** \-'kərəns\ *n* —**re·cur·rent** \-ənt\ *adj*

red \'red\ *n* 1 : color of blood or of the ruby 2 *cap* : communist —**red** *adj* —**red·dish** *adj* —**red·ness** *n*

red·den \'red°n\ *vb* : make or become red or reddish

re·deem \ri'dēm\ *vb* 1 : regain, free, or rescue by paying a price 2 : atone for 3 : free from sin 4 : convert into something of value —**re·deem·able** *adj* —**re·deem·er** *n*

re·demp·tion \-'dempshən\ *n* : act of redeeming —**re·demp·tive** \-tiv\ *adj* —**re·demp·to·ry** \-t(ə)rē\ *adj*

red·head \-,hed\ *n* : one having red hair —**red·head·ed** \-'hedəd\ *adj*

red·o·lent \'red°lənt\ *adj* 1 : having a fragrance 2 : suggestive —**red·o·lence** \-əns\ *n* —**red·o·lent·ly** *adv*

re·doubt \ri'daút\ *n* : small fortification

re·doubt·able \-əbəl\ *adj* : arousing dread

re·dound \ri'daúnd\ *vb* : have an effect

re·dress \ri'dres\ *vb* : set right ~ *n* 1 : relief or remedy 2 : compensation

red tape *n* : complex obstructive official routine

re·duce \ri'd(y)üs\ *vb* **-duced; -duc·ing** 1 : lessen 2 : put in a lower rank 3 : lose weight —**re·duc·er** *n* —**re·duc·ible** \-'d(y)üsəbəl\ *adj*

re·duc·tion \ri'dəkshən\ *n* 1 : act of reducing 2 : amount lost in reducing 3 : something made by reducing

re·dun·dant \ri'dəndənt\ *adj* : using more words than necessary —**re·dun·dan·cy** \-dənsē\ *n* —**re·dun·dant·ly** *adv*

red·wood *n* : tall coniferous timber tree

reed \'rēd\ *n* 1 : tall slender grass of wet areas 2 : elastic strip that vibrates to produce tones in certain wind instruments —**reedy** *adj*

reef \'rēf\ *n* : ridge of rocks or sand at or near the surface of the water

reek \'rēk\ *n* : strong or disagreeable fume or odor ~ *vb* : give off a reek

¹reel \'rēl\ *n* : revolvable device on which something flexible may be wound or quantity of something wound on it ~ *vb* 1 : wind on a reel 2 : pull in by reeling —**reel·able** *adj* —**reel·er** *n*

²reel *vb* 1 : whirl or waver as from a blow 2 : walk or move unsteadily ~ *n* : reeling motion

³reel *n* : lively dance

re·fer \ri'fər\ *vb* **-rr-** 1 : direct or send to some person or place 2 : submit for consideration or action 3 : have connection 4 : mention or allude to something —**re·fer·able** \'ref(ə)rə·bəl, ri'fər-\ *adj* —**re·fer·ral** \ri'fərəl\ *n*

ref·er·ee \,refə'rē\ *n* 1 : one to whom an issue is referred for settlement 2 : sports official ~ *vb* **-eed; -ee·ing** : act as referee

ref·er·ence \'refərns, 'ref(ə)rəns\ *n* 1 : act of referring 2 : a bearing on a matter 3 : consultation for information 4 : person who can speak for one's character or ability or a recommendation given by such a person

ref·er·en·dum \,refə'rendəm\ *n, pl* **-da** \-də\ *or* **-dums** : a seeking of voters' approval for a legislative proposal

re·fill \'rē'fil\ *vb* : fill again —**re·fill** \'rē,-\ *n* —**re·fill·able** *adj*

re·fine \ri'fīn\ *vb* **-fined; -fin·ing** 1 : free from impurities or waste matter 2 : improve or perfect 3 : free or become free of what is coarse or uncouth —**re·fine·ment** \-mənt\ *n* —**re·fin·er** *n*

re·fin·ery \ri'fīn(ə)rē\ *n, pl* **-er·ies** : place for refining (as oil or sugar)

re·flect \ri'flekt\ *vb* 1 : bend or cast back (as light or heat) 2 : bring as a result 3 : cast reproach or blame 4 : ponder —**re·flec·tion** \-'flekshən\ *n* —**re·flec·tive** \-tiv\ *adj* —**re·flec·tor** \ri'flektər\ *n*

re·flex \'rē,fleks\ *n* : automatic response to a stimulus ~ *adj* 1 : bent back 2 : relating to a reflex —**re·flex·ly** *adv*

re·flex·ive \ri'fleksiv\ *adj* : of or relating to an action directed back upon the doer or the grammatical subject —**reflexive** *n* —**re·flex·ive·ly** *adv* —**re·flex·ive·ness** *n*

re·form \ri'fórm\ *vb* : make or become better esp. by correcting bad habits —**reform** *n* —**re·form·able** *adj* —**re-**

for·ma·tive \-ˈfôrmətiv\ adj —re·form·er n

re·for·ma·to·ry \riˈfôrmə,tôrē\ n, pl -ries : penal institution for reforming young offenders

re·fract \riˈfrakt\ vb : subject to re·fraction

re·frac·tion \-ˈfrakshən\ n : the bending of a ray (as of light) when it passes from one medium into another —**re·frac·tive** \-tiv\ adj

re·frac·to·ry \riˈfrakt(ə)rē\ adj : obstinate or unmanageable

re·frain \riˈfrān\ vb : hold oneself back ~ n : verse recurring regularly in a song —**re·frain·ment** n

re·fresh \riˈfresh\ vb 1 : make or become fresh or fresher 2 : supply or take refreshment —**re·fresh·er** n —**re·fresh·ing·ly** adv

re·fresh·ment \-mənt\ n 1 : act of refreshing 2 pl : light meal

re·frig·er·ate \riˈfrijə,rāt\ vb -at·ed; -at·ing : chill or freeze (food) for preservation —**re·frig·er·ant** \-(ə)rənt\ adj or n —**re·frig·er·a·tion** \-,frijə-ˈrāshən\ n —**re·frig·er·a·tor** \-ˈrijə-,rātər\ n

ref·uge \ˈref,yüj\ n 1 : protection from danger 2 : place that provides protection

ref·u·gee \ˌrefyüˈjē\ n : one who flees for safety

re·fund \riˈfənd, ˈrē,fənd\ vb : give or put back (money) ~ \ˈrē,-\ n 1 : act of refunding 2 : sum refunded —**re·fund·able** adj

re·fur·bish \riˈfərbish\ vb : renovate

¹**re·fuse** \riˈfyüz\ vb -fused; -fus·ing : decline to accept, do, or give —**re·fus·al** \-ˈfyüzəl\ n

²**ref·use** \ˈref,yüs, -,yüz\ n : worthless matter

re·fute \riˈfyüt\ vb -fut·ed; -fut·ing : prove to be false —**ref·u·ta·tion** \ˌrefyüˈtāshən\ n —**re·fut·er** \riˈfyütər\ n

re·gain \riˈgān\ vb : get again

re·gal \ˈrēgəl\ adj 1 : befitting a king 2 : stately —**re·gal·ly** adv

re·gale \riˈgāl\ vb -galed; -gal·ing 1 : entertain richly or agreeably 2 : delight

re·ga·lia \riˈgālyə\ n pl 1 : symbols of royalty 2 : insignia of an office or order 3 : finery

re·gard \riˈgärd\ n 1 : consideration 2 : feeling of approval and liking 3 pl : friendly greetings 4 : relation ~ vb 1 : pay attention to 2 : show respect for 3 : have an opinion of 4 : look at

5 : relate to —**re·gard·ful** adj —**re·gard·less** adj

re·gard·ing prep : concerning

regardless of \riˈgärdləs-\ prep : in spite of

re·gen·er·ate \riˈjen(ə)rət\ adj 1 : formed or created again 2 : spiritually reborn ~ \-ˈjenə,rāt\ vb 1 : reform completely 2 : get new life —**re·gen·er·a·tion** \-,jenəˈrāshən\ n —**re·gen·er·a·tive** \-ˈjenə,rātiv\ adj —**re·gen·er·a·tor** \-,rātər\ n

re·gent \ˈrējənt\ n 1 : person who rules during the childhood, absence, or incapacity of the sovereign 2 : member of a governing board —**re·gen·cy** \-jənsē\ n

re·gime \rāˈzhēm, ri-\ n : government in power

reg·i·men \ˈrejəmən\ n : systematic course of treatment

reg·i·ment \ˈrejəmənt\ n : military unit ~ \-,ment\ vb : organize rigidly for control —**reg·i·men·tal** \,rejə-ˈmentᵊl\ adj —**reg·i·men·ta·tion** \-mənˈtāshən\ n

re·gion \ˈrējən\ n : indefinitely defined area —**re·gion·al** \ˈrēj(ə)nəl\ adj —**re·gion·al·ly** adv

reg·is·ter \ˈrejəstər\ n 1 : record of items or details or a book for keeping such a record 2 : device to regulate ventilation 3 : counting or recording device 4 : range of a voice or instrument ~ vb 1 : enter in a register 2 : record automatically 3 : get special care for mail by paying more postage

reg·is·trar \-,strär\ n : official keeper of records

reg·is·tra·tion \,rejəˈstrāshən\ n 1 : act of registering 2 : entry in a register

re·gress \riˈgres\ vb : go or cause to go back or to a lower level —**re·gres·sion** \-ˈgreshən\ n —**re·gres·sive** adj —**re·gres·sor** \-ˈgresər\ n

re·gret \riˈgret\ vb -tt- 1 : mourn the loss or death of 2 : be keenly sorry for ~ n 1 : sorrow or the expression of sorrow 2 pl : message declining an invitation —**re·gret·ful** \-fəl\ adj —**re·gret·ful·ly** adv —**re·gret·ta·ble** \-əbəl\ adj —**re·gret·ta·bly** \-blē\ adv —**re·gret·ter** n

reg·u·lar \ˈregyələr\ adj 1 : conforming to what is usual, normal, or average 2 : steady, uniform, or unvarying —**regular** n —**reg·u·lar·i·ty** \,regyə-ˈlaratē\ n —**reg·u·lar·ize** \ˈregyə-lə,rīz\ vb —**reg·u·lar·ly** adv

reg·u·late \ˈregyə,lāt\ vb -lat·ed; -lat·ing 1 : govern according to rule 2 : adjust to a standard —**reg·u·la·tive**

\-‚lātiv\ *adj* —**reg·u·la·tor** \-‚lātər\ *n* —**reg·u·la·to·ry** \-lə‚tōrē\ *adj*

reg·u·la·tion \‚regyə'lāshən\ *n* **1** : act of regulating **2** : rule dealing with details of procedure

re·gur·gi·tate \rē'gərjə‚tāt\ *vb* **-tat·ed; -tat·ing** : vomit —**re·gur·gi·ta·tion** \-‚gərjə'tāshən\ *n*

re·ha·bil·i·tate \‚rēh(ə)'bilə‚tāt\ *vb* **-tat·ed; -tat·ing 1** : reinstate **2** : make good or usable again —**re·ha·bil·i·ta·tion** \-‚bilə'tāshən\ *n*

re·hears·al \ri'hərsəl\ *n* : practice session or performance

re·hearse \-'hərs\ *vb* **-hearsed; -hears·ing 1** : repeat or recount **2** : engage in a rehearsal of —**re·hears·er** *n*

reign \'rān\ *n* : sovereign's authority or rule ~ *vb* : rule as a sovereign

re·im·burse \‚rēəm'bərs\ *vb* **-bursed; -burs·ing** : repay —**re·im·burs·able** *adj* —**re·im·burse·ment** *n*

rein \'rān\ *n* **1** : line of a bridle to control an animal **2** : restraining influence ~ *vb* : direct by reins

re·in·car·na·tion \‚rē‚in‚kär'nāshən\ *n* : rebirth of the soul —**re·in·car·nate** \‚rēin'kär‚nāt\ *vb*

rein·deer \'rān‚diər\ *n* : large deer of northern regions

re·in·force \‚rēən'fōrs\ *vb* : strengthen or support —**re·in·force·ment** *n* —**re·in·forc·er** *n*

re·in·state \‚rēən'stāt\ *vb* : restore to a former position —**re·in·state·ment** *n*

re·it·er·ate \rē'itə‚rāt\ *vb* : say again —**re·it·er·a·tion** \-‚itə'rāshən\ *n*

re·ject \ri'jekt\ *vb* **1** : refuse to acknowledge or grant **2** : refuse to accept or keep ~ \'rē-\ *n* : rejected person or thing —**re·jec·tion** \-'jekshən\ *n*

re·joice \ri'jóis\ *vb* **-joiced; -joic·ing** : feel joy —**re·joic·er** *n*

re·join *vb* **1** \'rē'jóin\ : join again **2** \ri'-\ : say in answer

re·join·der \ri'jóindər\ *n* : answer

re·ju·ve·nate \ri'jüvə‚nāt\ *vb* **-nat·ed; -nat·ing** : make young again —**re·ju·ve·na·tion** \-‚jüvə'nāshən\ *n*

re·lapse \ri'laps, 'rē‚laps\ *n* : recurrence of illness after a period of improvement ~ \ri-\ *vb* : suffer a relapse

re·late \ri'lāt\ *vb* **-lat·ed; -lat·ing 1** : give a report of **2** : show a connection between **3** : have a relationship —**re·lat·able** *adj* —**re·lat·er, re·la·tor** *n*

re·la·tion \-'lāshən\ *n* **1** : account **2**

: connection **3** : relationship **4** : reference **5** *pl* : dealings

re·la·tion·ship \-‚ship\ *n* : the state of being related or interrelated

rel·a·tive \'relətiv\ *n* : person connected with another by blood or marriage ~ *adj* : considered in comparison with something else —**rel·a·tive·ly** *adv* —**rel·a·tive·ness** *n*

re·lax \ri'laks\ *vb* **1** : make or become less tense or rigid **2** : make less severe **3** : seek rest or recreation —**re·lax·er** *n*

re·lax·ation \‚rē‚lak'sāshən\ *n* **1** : lessening of tension **2** : recreation

re·lay \'rē‚lā\ *n* : fresh supply (as of horses or people) arranged to relieve others ~ \'rē‚-, ri'-\ *vb* **-layed; -lay·ing** : pass along in stages

re·lease \ri'lēs\ *vb* **-leased; -leas·ing 1** : free from confinement or oppression **2** : relinquish **3** : permit publication or performance ~ *n* **1** : relief from trouble **2** : discharge from an obligation **3** : act of releasing or what is released

rel·e·gate \'relə‚gāt\ *vb* **-gat·ed; -gat·ing 1** : remove to some less prominent position **2** : assign to a particular class or sphere —**rel·e·ga·tion** \‚relə'gāshən\ *n*

re·lent \ri'lent\ *vb* : become less severe

re·lent·less \-ləs\ *adj* : mercilessly severe or persistent —**re·lent·less·ly** *adv* —**re·lent·less·ness** *n*

rel·e·vance \'reləvəns\ *n* : relation to the matter at hand —**rel·e·vant** \-vənt\ *adj* —**rel·e·vant·ly** *adv*

re·li·able \ri'līəbəl\ *adj* : fit to be trusted —**re·li·abil·i·ty** \-‚līə'bilətē\ *n* —**re·li·able·ness** *n* —**re·li·ably** \-'līəblē\ *adv*

re·li·ance \ri'līəns\ *n* : act or result of relying —**re·li·ant** \-ənt\ *adj*

rel·ic \'relik\ *n* **1** : object venerated because of its association with a saint or martyr **2** : remaining trace

re·lief \ri'lēf\ *n* **1** : lightening of something oppressive **2** : aid in the form of money or necessities

re·lieve \ri'lēv\ *vb* **-lieved; -liev·ing 1** : free from a burden or distress **2** : release from a post or duty **3** : break the monotony of —**re·liev·er** *n*

re·li·gion \ri'lijən\ *n* **1** : service and worship of God **2** : organized system of faith and worship —**re·li·gion·ist** *n*

re·li·gious \-'lijəs\ *adj* **1** : relating or devoted to the divine **2** : relating to

religious beliefs or observances —
re·li·gious·ly adv

re·lin·quish \ri-'liŋkwish, -'lin-\ vb 1
: renounce 2 : let go of —**re·lin·quish·ment** n

rel·ish \'relish\ n 1 : keen enjoyment
2 : highly seasoned sauce (as of pickles) ~ vb : enjoy —**rel·ish·able** adj

re·live \(')rē'liv\ vb : live over again
(as in the imagination)

re·lo·cate \(')rē'lō,kāt, ,rēlō'kāt\ vb
: move to a new location —**re·lo·ca·tion** \,rēlō'kāshən\ n

re·luc·tance \ri'ləktəns\ n : state of
being reluctant

re·luc·tant \-tənt\ adj : holding back
(as from acting) —**re·luc·tant·ly** adv

re·ly \ri'lī\ vb -**lied**; -**ly·ing** : place faith
or confidence—often used with on

re·main \ri'mān\ vb 1 : be left after
others have been removed 2 : be
something yet to be done 3 : stay
behind 4 : continue unchanged

re·main·der \-'māndər\ n : that which
is left over

re·mains \-'mānz\ n pl 1 : remaining
part or trace 2 : dead body

re·mark \ri'märk\ vb : express as an
observation ~ n : passing comment

re·mark·able \-'märkəbəl\ adj : extraordinary —**re·mark·able·ness** n
—**re·mark·ably** \-blē\ adv

re·me·di·al \ri'mēdēəl\ adj : intended
to remedy or improve

rem·e·dy \'remədē\ n, pl -**dies** 1 : medicine that cures 2 : something that
corrects an evil or compensates for
a loss ~ vb -**died**; -**dy·ing** : provide
or serve as a remedy for

re·mem·ber \ri'membər\ vb 1 : recall
to mind 2 : keep from forgetting 3
: convey greetings from

re·mem·brance \-brəns\ n 1 : act of
remembering 2 : something that
serves to bring to mind

re·mind \ri'mīnd\ vb : cause to remember —**re·mind·er** n

rem·i·nisce \,remə'nis\ vb -**nisced**;
-**nisc·ing** : indulge in reminiscence

rem·i·nis·cence \-'nis³ns\ n 1 : recalling of a past experience 2 : account
of a memorable experience

rem·i·nis·cent \-³nt\ adj 1 : relating to
reminiscence 2 : serving to remind
—**rem·i·nis·cent·ly** adv

re·miss \ri'mis\ adj : negligent or careless in performance of duty —**re·miss·ly** adv —**re·miss·ness** n

re·mis·sion \ri'mishən\ n 1 : act of forgiving 2 : a period of relief from or
easing of symptoms of a disease

re·mit \ri'mit\ vb -**tt**- 1 : pardon 2
: send money in payment

re·mit·tance \ri'mit³ns\ n : sum of
money remitted

rem·nant \'remnənt\ n : small part or
trace remaining

re·mod·el \'rē'mäd³l\ vb : alter the
structure of

re·mon·strance \ri'mänstrəns\ n : act
or instance of remonstrating

re·mon·strate \ri'män,strāt\ vb -**strat·ed**; -**strat·ing** : speak in protest, reproof, or opposition —**re·mon·stra·tion** \ri,män'strāshən, ,reman-\

re·morse \ri'mórs\ n : distress arising
from a sense of guilt —**re·morse·ful**
adj —**re·morse·less** adj

re·mote \ri'mōt\ adj -**mot·er**; -**est** 1
: far off in place or time 2 : hard to
reach or find 3 : slight 4 : distant in
manner —**re·mote·ly** adv —**re·mote·ness** n

re·move \ri'müv\ vb -**moved**; -**mov·ing**
1 : move by lifting or taking off or
away 2 : get rid of —**re·mov·able** adj
—**re·mov·al** \-vəl\ n —**re·mov·er** n

re·mu·ner·ate \ri'myünə,rāt\ vb -**at·ed**;
-**at·ing** : pay —**re·mu·ner·a·tion** n
—**re·mu·ner·a·tor** \-,rātər\ n

re·mu·ner·a·tive \ri'myünərətiv,
-,rāt-\ adj : gainful

re·nais·sance \,renə'säns, 'zäns\ n
: rebirth or revival

re·nal \'rēn³l\ adj : relating to the kidneys

rend \'rend\ vb rent \'rent\; **rend·ing**
: tear apart forcibly

ren·der \'rendər\ vb 1 : extract by
heating 2 : hand over or give up 3
: do (a service) for another 4 : cause
to be or become

ren·dez·vous \'rändi,vü, -dā-\ n, pl
ren·dez·vous \-,vüz\ 1 : place appointed for a meeting 2 : meeting at
an appointed place ~ vb -**voused**;
-**vous·ing** : meet at a rendezvous

ren·di·tion \ren'dishən\ n : version

ren·e·gade \'reni,gād\ n : one who deserts one faith or cause for another

re·nege \ri'nig, -'neg, -'nēg, -'nāg\ vb
-**neged**; -**neg·ing** : go back on a promise —**re·neg·er** n

re·new \ri'n(y)ü\ vb 1 : make or become new, fresh, or strong again 2
: begin again 3 : grant or obtain an
extension of —**re·new·able** adj —**re·new·al** n —**re·new·er** n

re·nounce \ri'naúns\ vb -**nounced**;
-**nounc·ing** : give up, refuse, or resign —**re·nounce·ment** n

ren·o·vate \'renə,vāt\ vb -**vat·ed**; -**vat·ing** : make like new again —**ren·o·**

va·tion \,renə'vāshən\ n —ren·o·va·tor \'renə,vātər\ n

re·nown \ri'naún\ n : state of being widely known and honored —re·nowned \-'naúnd\ adj

¹rent \'rent\ n : money paid or due for the use of another's property ~ vb : hold or give possession and use of for rent —rental n or adj —rent·er n

²rent n : a tear in cloth

re·nun·ci·a·tion \ri,nənsē'āshən\ n : act of renouncing

¹re·pair \ri'paər\ vb : go

²repair vb : restore to good condition ~ n 1 : act or instance of repairing 2 : condition —re·pair·er n —re·pair·man \-,man\ n

rep·a·ra·tion \,repə'rāshən\ n : money paid for redress—usu. pl.

rep·ar·tee \,repär'tē\ n : clever replies

re·past \ri'past, 'rē,past\ n : meal

re·pa·tri·ate \rē'pātrē,āt\ vb -at·ed; -at·ing : send back to one's own country —re·pa·tri·ate \-trēət, -trē,āt\ n —re·pa·tri·a·tion \-,pātrē'āshən\ n

re·pay \rē'pā\ vb -paid; -pay·ing : pay back —re·pay·able adj —re·pay·ment n

re·peal \ri'pēl\ vb : annul by legislative action —repeal n —re·peal·er n

re·peat \ri'pēt\ vb : say or do again ~ n 1 : act of repeating 2 : something repeated —re·peat·able adj —re·peat·ed·ly adv —re·peat·er n

re·pel \ri'pel\ vb -pelled; -pel·ling 1 : drive away 2 : disgust —re·pel·lent \-'pelənt\ adj or n

re·pent \ri'pent\ vb 1 : turn from sin 2 : regret —re·pen·tance \ri'pentⁿns\ n —re·pen·tant \-ⁿnt\ adj

re·per·cus·sion \,repər'kəshən, ,repər-\ n : effect of something done or said

rep·er·toire \'repə(r),twär\ n : pieces a company or performer can present

rep·er·to·ry \'repə(r),tōrē\ n, pl -ries 1 : repertoire 2 : theater with a resident company doing several plays

rep·e·ti·tion \,repə'tishən\ n : act or instance of repeating

rep·e·ti·tious \-'tishəs\ adj : tediously repeating —rep·e·ti·tious·ly adv —rep·e·ti·tious·ness n

re·pet·i·tive \ri'petətiv\ adj : repetitious —re·pet·i·tive·ly adv —re·pet·i·tive·ness n

re·pine \ri'pīn\ vb re·pined; re·pin·ing : feel or express discontent

re·place \ri'plās\ vb 1 : restore to a former position 2 : take the place of 3 : put something new in the place of —re·place·able adj —re·place·ment n —re·plac·er n

re·plen·ish \ri'plenish\ vb : stock or supply anew —re·plen·ish·ment n

re·plete \ri'plēt\ adj : full —re·plete·ness n —re·ple·tion \-'plēshən\ n

rep·li·ca \'replikə\ n : copy

rep·li·cate \'replə,kāt\ vb -cat·ed; -cat·ing : duplicate or repeat —rep·li·cate \-likət\ n

re·ply \ri'plī\ vb -plied; -ply·ing : say or do in answer ~ n, pl -plies : answer

re·port \ri'pōrt\ n 1 : rumor 2 : statement of information (as events or causes) 3 : explosive noise ~ vb 1 : give an account of 2 : present an account of (an event) as news 3 : present oneself 4 : make known to authorities —re·port·age \ri'pōrtij, ,repər'täzh, ,rep,ōr'-\ n —re·port·ed·ly adv —re·port·er n —re·por·to·ri·al \,repə(r)'tōrēəl\ adj

re·pose \ri'pōz\ vb -posed; -pos·ing 1 : lay or lie at rest ~ n 1 : state of resting 2 : calm or peace —re·pose·ful adj

re·pos·i·to·ry \ri'päzə,tōrē\ n, pl -ries : place where something is stored

re·pos·sess \,rēpə'zes\ vb : regain possession and legal ownership of —re·pos·ses·sion \-'zeshən\ n

rep·re·hend \,repri'hend\ vb : express disapproval of —rep·re·hen·si·ble \-'hensəbəl\ adj —rep·re·hen·si·bly adv —rep·re·hen·sion \-'henchən\ n

rep·re·sent \,repri'zent\ vb 1 : serve as a sign or symbol of 2 : act or speak for 3 : describe as having a specified quality or character —rep·re·sen·ta·tion \,repri,zen'tāshən\ n

rep·re·sen·ta·tive \,repri'zentətiv\ adj 1 : standing or acting for another 2 : carried on by elected representatives ~ n 1 : typical example 2 : one that represents another 3 : member of usu. the lower house of a legislature —rep·re·sen·ta·tive·ly adv —rep·re·sen·ta·tive·ness n

re·press \ri'pres\ vb : restrain or suppress —re·pres·sion \-'preshən\ n —re·pres·sive \-'presiv\ adj

re·prieve \ri'prēv\ vb -prieved; -priev·ing : delay the punishment or execution of —reprieve n

rep·ri·mand \'reprə,mand\ n : formal reproof —reprimand vb

re·pris·al \ri'prīzəl\ n : act in retaliation

re·prise \ri'prēz\ n : musical repetition

re·proach \ri'prōch\ n 1 : disgrace 2 : rebuke ~ vb : express disapproval to —**re·proach·ful** adj —**re·proach·ful·ly** adv —**re·proach·ful·ness** n

rep·ro·bate \'reprə‚bāt\ n : scoundrel —**reprobate** adj

rep·ro·ba·tion \‚reprə'bāshən\ n : strong disapproval

re·pro·duce \‚rēprə'd(y)üs\ vb 1 : produce again or anew 2 : bear offspring —**re·pro·duc·ible** \-'d(y)üsəbəl\ adj —**re·pro·duc·tion** \-'dəkshən\ n —**re·pro·duc·tive** \-'dəktiv\ adj

re·proof \ri'prüf\ n : blame or censure for a fault

re·prove \ri'prüv\ vb -**proved**; -**proving** : express disapproval to or of —**re·prov·er** n

rep·tile \'reptºl, -‚tīl\ n : air-breathing scaly vertebrate —**rep·til·ian** \rep'tileən\ adj or n

re·pub·lic \ri'pəblik\ n : country with representative government

re·pub·li·can \-likən\ adj 1 : relating to or resembling a republic 2 : supporting a republic —**republican** n —**re·pub·li·can·ism** n

re·pu·di·ate \ri'pyüdē‚āt\ vb -**at·ed**; -**at·ing** : refuse to have anything to do with —**re·pu·di·a·tion** \-‚pyüdē'āshən\ n

re·pug·nant \ri'pəgnənt\ adj : contrary to one's tastes or principles —**re·pug·nance** \-nəns\ n —**re·pug·nant·ly** adv

re·pulse \ri'pəls\ vb -**pulsed**; -**puls·ing** 1 : drive or beat back 2 : rebuff 3 : be repugnant to —**repulse** n —**re·pul·sion** \-'pəlshən\ n

re·pul·sive \-siv\ adj : arousing aversion or disgust —**re·pul·sive·ly** adv —**re·pul·sive·ness** n

rep·u·ta·ble \'repyətəbəl\ adj : having a good reputation —**rep·u·ta·bly** \-blē\ adv

rep·u·ta·tion \‚repyə'tāshən\ n : one's character or public esteem

re·pute \ri'pyüt\ vb -**put·ed**; -**put·ing** : think of as being ~ n : reputation —**re·put·ed·ly** adv

re·quest \ri'kwest\ n : act or instance of asking for something or a thing asked for ~ vb 1 : make a request of 2 : ask for —**re·quest·er** n

re·qui·em \'rekwēəm, 'rāk-\ n : Mass for a dead person or a musical setting for this

re·quire \ri'kwī(ə)r\ vb -**quired**; -**quir·ing** 1 : insist on 2 : call for as essential —**re·quire·ment** n

req·ui·site \'rekwəzət\ adj : necessary —**requisite** n

req·ui·si·tion \‚rekwə'zishən\ n : formal application or demand —**requisition** vb

re·quite \ri'kwīt\ vb -**quit·ed**; -**quit·ing** : make return for or to —**re·quit·al** \-'kwītºl\ n

re·scind \ri'sind\ vb : repeal or cancel —**re·scind·er** n —**re·scis·sion** \-'sizhən\ n

res·cue \'reskyü\ vb -**cued**; -**cu·ing** : set free from danger or confinement —**rescue** n —**res·cu·er** n

re·search \ri'sərch, 'rē‚sərch\ n : careful or diligent search esp. for new knowledge —**research** vb —**re·search·er** n

re·sem·ble \ri'zembəl\ vb -**sem·bled**; -**sem·bling** : be like or similar to —**re·sem·blance** \-'zembləns\ n

re·sent \ri'zent\ vb : feel or show annoyance at —**re·sent·ful** adj —**re·sent·ful·ly** adv —**re·sent·ment** n

res·er·va·tion \‚rezər'vāshən\ n 1 : act of reserving or something reserved 2 : limiting condition

re·serve \ri'zərv\ vb -**served**; -**serv·ing** 1 : store for future use 2 : set aside for special use ~ n 1 : something reserved 2 : restraint in words or bearing 3 : military forces withheld from action or not part of the regular services —**re·served** adj

res·er·voir \'rezə(r)v‚wär, -ə(r)v‚(w)ȯr, -‚ər‚vȯi\ n : place where something (as water) is kept in store

re·side \ri'zīd\ vb -**sid·ed**; -**sid·ing** 1 : make one's home 2 : be present

res·i·dence \'rezədəns\ n 1 : act or fact of residing in a place 2 : place where one lives —**res·i·dent** \-ənt\ adj or n —**res·i·den·tial** \‚rezə'denchəl\ adj

res·i·due \'rezə‚d(y)ü\ n : part remaining —**re·sid·u·al** \ri'zij(ə)wəl\ adj

re·sign \ri'zīn\ vb 1 : give up deliberately 2 : give (oneself) over without resistance —**res·ig·na·tion** \‚rezig'nāshən\ n —**re·sign·ed·ly** \-'zīnədlē\ adv

re·sil·ience \ri'zilyəns\ n : ability to recover or adjust easily

re·sil·ien·cy \-yənsē\ n : resilience

re·sil·ient \-yənt\ adj : elastic

res·in \'rezºn\ n : substance from the gum or sap of trees —**res·in·ous** adj

re·sist \ri'zist\ vb 1 : withstand the force or effect of 2 : fight against —**re·sist·ible** \-'zistəbəl\ adj —**re·sist·less** adj

re·sis·tance \ri'zistəns\ n 1 : act of resisting 2 : opposition to electric current

re·sis·tant \-tənt\ adj : giving resistance

res·o·lute \'rezə,lüt\ adj : having a fixed purpose —**res·o·lute·ly** adv —**res·o·lute·ness** n

res·o·lu·tion \,rezə'lüshən\ n 1 : process of resolving 2 : firmness of purpose 3 : statement of the opinion, will, or intent of a body

re·solve \ri'zälv\ vb **-solved; -solv·ing** 1 : find an answer to 2 : make a formal resolution ~ n 1 : something resolved 2 : steadfast purpose —**re·solv·able** adj

res·o·nant \'rezᵊnənt\ adj 1 : continuing to sound 2 : relating to intensification or prolongation of sound (as by a vibrating body) —**res·o·nance** \-əns\ n —**res·o·nant·ly** adv

re·sort \ri'zórt\ n 1 : source of help 2 : place to go for vacation ~ vb 1 : go often or habitually 2 : have recourse

re·sound \ri'zaúnd\ vb : become filled with sound

re·sound·ing \-iŋ\ adj : impressive —**re·sound·ing·ly** adv

re·source \'rē,sórs, ri'sórs\ n 1 : new or reserve source 2 pl : available funds 3 : ability to handle situations —**re·source·ful** adj —**re·source·ful·ness** n

re·spect \ri'spekt\ n 1 : relation to something 2 : high or special regard 3 : detail ~ vb : consider deserving of high regard —**re·spect·er** n —**re·spect·ful** adj —**re·spect·ful·ly** adv —**re·spect·ful·ness** n

re·spect·able \ri'spektəbəl\ adj 1 : worthy of respect 2 : fair in size, quantity, or quality —**re·spect·abil·i·ty** \-,spektə'bilətē\ n —**re·spect·ably** \-'spektəblē\ adv

re·spec·tive \-tiv\ adj : individual and specific

re·spec·tive·ly \-lē\ adv 1 : as relating to each 2 : each in the order given

res·pi·ra·tion \,respə'rāshən\ n 1 : act or process of breathing 2 : energy-yielding oxidation in living matter —**re·spi·ra·to·ry** \'resp(ə)rə,tōrē, ri'spīrə-\ adj —**re·spire** \ri'spi(ə)r\ vb

res·pi·ra·tor \'respə,rātər\ n : device for artificial respiration

re·spite \'respət\ n : temporary delay or rest

re·splen·dent \ri'splendənt\ adj : shining brilliantly —**re·splen·dence** \-dəns\ n —**re·splen·dent·ly** adv

re·spond \ri'spänd\ vb 1 : answer 2 : react —**re·spon·dent** \-'spändənt\ n or adj —**re·spond·er** n

re·sponse \ri'späns\ n 1 : act of responding 2 : answer

re·spon·si·ble \ri'spänsəbəl\ adj 1 : an-swerable for acts or decisions 2 : able to fulfill obligations 3 : having important duties —**re·spon·si·bil·i·ty** \ri,spänsə'bilətē\ n —**re·spon·si·ble·ness** n —**re·spon·si·bly** \-blē\ adv

re·spon·sive \-siv\ adj : quick to respond —**re·spon·sive·ly** adv —**re·spon·sive·ness** n

¹**rest** \'rest\ n 1 : sleep 2 : freedom from work or activity 3 : state of inactivity 4 : something used as a support ~ vb 1 : get rest 2 : cease action or motion 3 : give rest to 4 : sit or lie fixed or supported 5 : depend —**rest·ful** adj —**rest·ful·ly** adv

²**rest** n : remainder

res·tau·rant \'rest(ə)rənt, -tə,ränt\ n : public eating place

res·ti·tu·tion \,restə't(y)üshən\ n : act or fact of restoring something or repaying someone

res·tive \'restiv\ adj : uneasy or fidgety —**res·tive·ly** adv —**res·tive·ness** n

rest·less \'restləs\ adj 1 : lacking or giving no rest 2 : never resting or ceasing 3 : lacking in repose —**rest·less·ly** adv —**rest·less·ness** n

re·store \ri'stōr\ vb **-stored; -stor·ing** 1 : give back 2 : put back into use or into a former state —**re·stor·able** adj —**res·to·ra·tion** \,restə'rāshən\ n —**re·stor·ative** \ri'stōrətiv\ n or adj —**re·stor·er** n

re·strain \ri'strān\ vb : limit or keep under control —**re·strain·able** adj —**re·strained** \-'strānd\ adj —**re·strain·ed·ly** \-'strānədlē\ adv —**re·strain·er** n

re·straint \-'strānt\ n 1 : act of restraining 2 : restraining force 3 : control over feelings

re·strict \ri'strikt\ vb 1 : confine within bounds 2 : limit use of —**re·stric·tion** \-'strikshən\ n —**re·stric·tive** adj —**re·stric·tive·ly** adv

re·sult \ri'zəlt\ vb 1 : come about because of something else 2 : end ~ n 1 : thing that results 2 : something obtained by calculation or investigation —**re·sul·tant** \-'zəltᵊnt\ adj or n

re·sume \ri'züm\ vb **-sumed; -sum·ing** : return to or take up again after interruption —**re·sump·tion** \-'zəmpshən\ n

ré·su·mé \'rezə,mā, ,rezə'-\ n : summary of one's career and qualifications

re·sur·gence \ri'sərjəns\ n : a rising again —**re·sur·gent** \-jənt\ adj

res·ur·rect \,rezə'rekt\ vb 1 : raise from the dead 2 : bring to attention or use again —**res·ur·rec·tion** \-'rekshən\ *n*

re·sus·ci·tate \ri'səsə,tāt\ *vb* **-tat·ed; -tat·ing** : revive from a deathlike condition —**re·sus·ci·ta·tion** \ri,səsə'tāshən, ,rē-\ *n* —**re·sus·ci·ta·tor** \-,tātər\ *n*

re·tail \'rē,tāl\ *vb* : sell in small quantities directly to the consumer ~ *n* : business of selling to consumers — **retail** *adj or adv* —**re·tail·er** *n*

re·tain \ri'tān\ *vb* **1** : keep or hold onto **2** : engage the services of

re·tain·er *n* **1** : household servant **2** : retaining fee

re·tal·i·ate \ri'talē,āt\ *vb* **-at·ed; -at·ing** : get revenge —**re·tal·i·a·tion** \-,talē'āshən\ *n* —**re·tal·ia·to·ry** \-'talyə,tōrē\ *adj*

re·tard \ri'tärd\ *vb* : hold back —**re·tar·da·tion** \,rē,tär'däshən, ri-\ *n* —**re·tard·er** *n*

re·tard·ed \ri'tärdəd\ *adj* : slow or limited in intellectual development

retch \'rech, 'rēch\ *vb* : try to vomit

re·ten·tion \ri'tenchən\ *n* **1** : state of being retained **2** : ability to retain —**re·ten·tive** \-'tentiv\ *adj*

ret·i·cent \'retəsənt\ *adj* : inclined to be silent or secretive —**ret·i·cence** \-səns\ *n* —**ret·i·cent·ly** *adv*

ret·i·na \'ret²nə\ *n, pl* **-nas** *or* **-nae** \-²n,ē\ : sensory membrane lining the eye —**ret·i·nal** \'ret²nəl\ *adj*

ret·i·nue \'ret²n,(y)ü\ *n* : attendants or followers of a distinguished person

re·tire \ri'tī(ə)r\ *vb* **-tired; -tir·ing 1** : withdraw for privacy **2** : end a career **3** : go to bed —**re·tir·ee** \ri,tī'rē\ *n* —**re·tire·ment** *n*

re·tir·ing \ri'tī(ə)riŋ\ *adj* : shy or reserved

¹re·tort \ri'tórt\ *vb* : say in reply ~ *n* : quick, witty, or cutting answer

²re·tort \ri'tórt, 'rē,tórt\ *n* : vessel in which substances are distilled or decomposed by heat

re·trace \rē'trās\ *vb* : trace again or in reverse

re·tract \ri'trakt\ *vb* **1** : to draw back or in **2** : withdraw a charge or promise —**re·tract·able** *adj* —**re·trac·tion** \-'trakshən\ *n*

re·treat \ri'trēt\ *n* **1** : act of withdrawing **2** : place of privacy or safety or meditation and study ~ *vb* : make a retreat

re·trench \ri'trench\ *vb* : cut down (as expenses) —**re·trench·ment** *n*

re·tri·bu·tion \,retrə'byüshən\ *n* : retaliation —**re·trib·u·tive** \ri'tribyə-

tiv\ *adj* —**re·trib·u·to·ry** \-yə,tōrē\ *adj*

re·trieve \ri'trēv\ *vb* **-trieved; -triev·ing 1** : search for and bring in game **2** : recover —**re·triev·able** *adj* —**re·triev·al** \-'trēval\ *n*

re·triev·er \-'trēvər\ *n* : dog for retrieving game

ret·ro·ac·tive \,retrō'aktiv\ *adj* : made effective as of a prior date —**ret·ro·ac·tive·ly** *adv*

ret·ro·grade \'retrə,grād\ *adj* **1** : moving backward **2** : becoming worse

ret·ro·gress \,retrə'gres\ *vb* : move backward —**ret·ro·gres·sion** \-'greshən\ *n*

ret·ro·spect \'retrə,spekt\ *n* : review of past events —**ret·ro·spec·tion** \,retrə'spekshən\ *n* —**ret·ro·spec·tive** \-'spektiv\ *adj* —**ret·ro·spec·tive·ly** *adv*

re·turn \ri'tərn\ *vb* **1** : go or come back **2** : pass, give, or send back to an earlier possessor **3** : answer **4** : bring in as a profit **5** : give or do in return ~ *n* **1** : act of returning or something returned **2** *pl* : report of balloting results **3** : statement of taxable income **4** : profit —**return** *adj* —**re·turn·able** *adj or n* —**re·turn·er** *n*

re·union \rē'yünyən\ *n* **1** : act of reuniting **2** : meeting of persons who have been separated

re·vamp \(')rē'vamp\ *vb* : give a new form to old materials

re·veal \ri'vēl\ *vb* **1** : make known **2** : show plainly

rev·eil·le \'revəlē\ *n* : military signal sounded about sunrise

rev·el \'revəl\ *vb* **-eled** *or* **-elled; -el·ing** *or* **-el·ling 1** : take part in a revel **2** : take great delight ~ *n* : wild party or celebration —**rev·el·er, rev·el·ler** \-ər\ *n* —**rev·el·ry** \-rē\ *n*

rev·e·la·tion \,revə'lāshən\ *n* **1** : act of revealing **2** : something enlightening or astonishing

re·venge \ri'venj\ *vb* **-venged; -veng·ing** : inflict harm or injury in return for a wrong ~ *n* **1** : act of revenging **2** : desire to return evil —**re·venge·ful** *adj* —**re·veng·er** *n*

rev·e·nue \'revə,n(y)ü\ *n* : money collected by a government

re·ver·ber·ate \ri'vərbə,rāt\ *vb* **-at·ed; -at·ing** : resound in a series of echoes —**re·ver·ber·a·tion** \-,vərbə'rāshən\ *n*

re·vere \ri'viər\ *vb* **-vered; -ver·ing** : show honor and devotion to —**rev·er·ence** \'rev(ə)rəns\ *n* —**rev·er·ent** \-rənt\ *adj* —**rev·er·ent·ly** *adv*

rev·er·end \\'rev(ə)rənd\\ adj : worthy of reverence ~ n : clergyman

rev·er·ie \\'rev(ə)rē\\ n, pl **-er·ies** : daydream

reverse \\ri'vərs\\ adj 1 : opposite to a previous or normal condition 2 : acting in an opposite way ~ vb **-versed**; **-vers·ing** 1 : turn upside down or completely around 2 : change to the contrary or in the opposite direction ~ n 1 : something contrary 2 : change for the worse 3 : back of something —**re·ver·sal** \\-səl\\ n —**re·verse·ly** adv —**re·vers·ible** \\-'vərs-əbəl\\ adj

re·vert \\ri'vərt\\ vb : return to an original type or condition —**re·ver·sion** \\-'vərzhən\\ n

re·view \\ri'vyü\\ n 1 : formal inspection 2 : general survey 3 : critical evaluation 4 : second or repeated study or examination ~ vb 1 : examine or study again 2 : reexamine judicially 3 : view in retrospect 4 : write a critical examination of 5 : inspect —**re·view·er** n

re·vile \\ri'vīl\\ vb **-viled**; **-vil·ing** : abuse verbally —**re·vile·ment** n —**re·vil·er** n

re·vise \\ri'vīz\\ vb **-vised**; **-vis·ing** 1 : look over something written to correct or improve 2 : make a new version of —**re·vis·able** adj —**revise** n —**re·vis·er**, **re·vi·sor** \\-'vīzər\\ n —**re·vi·sion** \\-'vizhən\\ n

re·viv·al \\-'vīvəl\\ n 1 : act of reviving or state of being revived 2 : evangelistic meeting

re·vive \\-'vīv\\ vb **-vived**; **-viv·ing** 1 : return to consciousness or life 2 : bring back into use —**re·viv·er** n

rev·o·ca·tion \\,revə'kāshən\\ n : act or instance of revoking

re·voke \\ri'vōk\\ vb **-voked**; **-vok·ing** : annul by recalling —**re·vok·er** n

re·volt \\-'vōlt\\ vb 1 : throw off allegiance 2 : cause or experience disgust or shock ~ n : rebellion or revolution —**re·volt·er** n

rev·o·lu·tion \\,revə'lüshən\\ n 1 : rotation 2 : progress in an orbit 3 : sudden, radical, or complete change (as overthrow of a government) —**rev·o·lu·tion·ary** \\-shə,narē\\ adj or n

rev·o·lu·tion·ize \\-shə,nīz\\ vb **-ized**; **-iz·ing** : change radically —**rev·o·lu·tion·iz·er** n

re·volve \\ri'välv\\ vb **-volved**; **-volv·ing** 1 : ponder 2 : move in an orbit 3 : rotate —**re·volv·able** adj

re·volv·er \\ri'välvər\\ n : pistol with a revolving cylinder

re·vue \\ri'vyü\\ n : theatrical production of brief numbers

re·vul·sion \\ri'vəlshən\\ n : complete dislike or repugnance

re·ward \\ri'wörd\\ vb 1 : give a reward to or for ~ n : something offered for service or achievement

rhap·so·dy \\'rapsədē\\ n, pl **-dies** 1 : expression of extravagant praise 2 : flowing free-form musical composition —**rhap·sod·ic** \\rap'sädik\\ adj —**rhap·sod·i·cal·ly** \\-ik(ə)lē\\ adv —**rhap·so·dize** \\'rapsə,dīz\\ vb

rhet·o·ric \\'retərik\\ n : art of speaking or writing effectively —**rhe·tor·i·cal** \\ri'tòrikəl\\ adj —**rhet·o·ri·cian** \\,retə'rishən\\ n

rheu·ma·tism \\'rümə,tizəm, 'rüm-\\ n : disorder marked by inflammation or pain in muscles or joints —**rheu·mat·ic** \\rü'matik\\ adj

rhine·stone \\'rīn,stōn\\ n : a colorless imitation gem

rhi·no \\'rīnō\\ n, pl **-no** or **-nos** : rhinoceros

rhi·noc·er·os \\ri'näs(ə)rəs\\ n, pl **-noc·er·os·es** or **-noc·er·os** or **-noc·eri** \\-näsə,rī\\ : large thick-skinned mammal with 1 or 2 horns on the snout

rho·do·den·dron \\,rōdə'dendrən\\ n : flowering evergreen shrub

rhom·bus \\'rämbəs\\ n, pl **-bus·es** or **-bi** \\-,bī\\ : parallelogram with equal sides and usu. oblique angles

rhu·barb \\'rü,bärb\\ n : garden plant with edible stalks

rhyme \\'rīm\\ n 1 : correspondence in terminal sounds 2 : verse that rhymes ~ vb **rhymed**; **rhym·ing** : make or have rhymes

rhythm \\'rithəm\\ n : regular succession of sounds or motions —**rhyth·mic** \\'rithmik\\, **rhyth·mi·cal** \\-mikəl\\ adj —**rhyth·mi·cal·ly** adv

rhythm and blues n : popular music based on blues and black folk music

rib \\'rib\\ n 1 : curved bone joined to the spine 2 : riblike thing ~ vb **-bb-** 1 : furnish or mark with ribs 2 : tease —**rib·ber** n

rib·ald \\'ribəld\\ adj : coarse or vulgar —**rib·ald·ry** \\-əldrē\\ n

rib·bon \\'ribən\\ n 1 : narrow strip of fabric used esp. for decoration 2 : strip of inked cloth (as in a typewriter)

ri·bo·fla·vin \\,rībə'flāvən, 'rībə,-\\ n : growth-promoting vitamin

rice \\'rīs\\ n, pl **rice** : edible seeds of an annual cereal grass

rich \\'rich\\ adj 1 : having a lot of

money or possessions 2 : valuable 3
: containing much sugar, fat, or seasoning 4 : abundant 5 : deep and
pleasing in color or tone 6 : fertile —
rich·ly adv —**rich·ness** n

rich·es \'richəz\ n pl : wealth

rick·ets \'rikəts\ n : childhood bone
disease

rick·ety \'rikətē\ adj : shaky

rick·sha, rick·shaw \'rik,shȯ\ n : small
covered 2-wheeled vehicle pulled by
one man

ric·o·chet \'rikə,shā, Brit also -,shet\
vb -**cheted** \-,shād\ or -**chet·ted**
\-,shet-əd\; -**chet·ing** \-,shāiŋ\ or
-**chet·ting** \-,shetiŋ\ : bounce off at
an angle —**ricochet** n

rid \'rid\ vb **rid; rid·ding** : make free
of something unwanted —**rid·dance**
\'rid⁰ns\ n

rid·den \'rid⁰n\ adj : overburdened
with

¹rid·dle \'rid⁰l\ n : puzzling question
~ vb -**dled; -dling** : speak in riddles

²riddle vb -**dled; -dling** : fill full of holes

ride \'rid\ vb **rode** \'rōd\; **rid·den**
\'rid⁰n\; **rid·ing** \'ridiŋ\ 1 : be carried along 2 : sit on and cause to
move 3 : travel over a surface 4
: tease or nag ~ n 1 : trip on an
animal or in a vehicle 2 : mechanical
device ridden for amusement

rid·er n 1 : one that rides 2 : attached
clause or document —**rid·er·less** adj

ridge \'rij\ n 1 : range of hills 2 : raised
line or strip 3 : point of intersection
of 2 sloping surfaces —**ridgy** adj

rid·i·cule \'ridə,kyül\ vb -**culed; -cul-
ing** : laugh at or make fun of —**ridicule** n

ri·dic·u·lous \rə'dikyələs\ adj : arousing ridicule —**ri·dic·u·lous·ly** adv —
ri·dic·u·lous·ness n

rife \'rif\ adj : abounding —**rife** adv

riff·raff \'rif,raf\ n : mob

¹ri·fle \'rifəl\ vb -**fled; -fling** : ransack
esp. in order to steal —**ri·fler**
\-f(ə)lər\ n

²rifle n : long shoulder weapon with
spiral grooves in the bore —**ri·fle·
man** \-mən\ n —**ri·fling** n

rift \'rift\ n : separation —**rift** vb

¹rig \'rig\ vb -**gg-** 1 : fit out with rigging
2 : set up esp. as a makeshift ~ n 1
: distinctive shape, number, and arrangement of sails and masts of a
ship 2 : equipment 3 : carriage with
its horses

²rig vb -**gg-** : manipulate esp. by deceptive or dishonest means

rig·ging \'rigiŋ, -ən\ n : lines that hold

and move masts, sails, and spars of
a ship

right \'rit\ adj 1 : meeting a standard
of conduct 2 : correct 3 : genuine 4
: normal 5 : opposite of left ~ n 1
: something that is correct, just,
proper, or honorable 2 : something
to which one has a just claim 3
: something that is on the right side
~ adv 1 : according to what is right
2 : immediately 3 : completely 4 : on
the right ~ vb 1 : restore to a
proper state 2 : bring or become upright again —**right·er** n —**right·ness**
n —**right·ward** \-wərd\ adj

right angle n : angle bounded by 2 lines
perpendicular to each other —
right-an·gled \'rit'aŋgəld\ adj

righ·teous \'rīchəs\ adj : acting or
being in accordance with what is just
or moral —**right·eous·ly** adv —**righ-
teous·ness** n

right·ful \'rītfəl\ adj : lawful —**right-
ful·ly** \-ē\ adv —**right·ful·ness** n

right·ly \'rītlē\ adv 1 : justly 2 : properly 3 : correctly

rig·id \'rijəd\ adj : lacking flexibility
—**ri·gid·i·ty** \rə'jidətē\ n —**rig·id·ly**
adv

rig·ma·role \'rig(ə)mə,rōl\ n : meaningless talk or procedure

rig·or \'rigər\ n : severity —**rig·or·ous**
adj —**rig·or·ous·ly** adv

rig·or mor·tis \,rigər'mȯrtəs\ n : temporary stiffness of muscles occurring after death

rile \'rīl\ vb **riled; ril·ing** : anger

rill \'ril\ n : small brook

rim \'rim\ n : edge esp. of something
curved ~ vb -**mm-** 1 : furnish with a
rim 2 : run around the rim of

¹rime \'rīm\ n : frostlike ice formed
on exposed objects —**rimy** \'rīmē\
adj

²rime var of RHYME

rind \'rind\ n : usu. hard or tough
outer layer

¹ring \'riŋ\ n 1 : circular band used as
an ornament or for holding or fastening 2 : something circular 3
: place for contest or display 4
: group with a selfish or dishonest
aim ~ vb : surround —**ringed** adj —
ring·like adj

²ring vb **rang** \'raŋ\; **rung** \'rəŋ\; **ringing** 1 : sound resonantly when struck
2 : cause to make a metallic sound
by striking ~ n 1 : resonant sound
or tone 2 : act or instance of ringing

ring·er \'riŋər\ n 1 : one that sounds
by ringing 2 : illegal substitute

ring·lead·er \'riŋ̣ˌlēdər\ n : leader esp. of troublemakers

ring·let n : long curl

ring·worm n : a contagious fungous skin disease

rink \'riŋk\ n : enclosed place for skating

rinse \'rins\ vb **rinsed; rins·ing 1** : cleanse usu. with water only **2** : treat (hair) with a rinse ~ n : liquid used for rinsing —**rins·er** n

ri·ot \'rīət\ n **1** : violent public disorder **2** : random or disorderly profusion —**riot** vb —**ri·ot·er** n —**ri·ot·ous** adj

rip \'rip\ vb -**pp-** : cut or tear open ~ n : rent made by ripping

ripe \'rīp\ adj **rip·er; rip·est 1** : fully grown, developed, or prepared —**ripe·ly** adv —**rip·en** \'rīpən\ vb —**ripe·ness** n

rip-off n : theft —**rip off** vb

rip·ple \'ripəl\ vb -**pled; -pling 1** : become lightly ruffled on the surface **2** : sound like rippling water —**ripple** n

rise \'rīz\ vb **rose** \'rōz\; **ris·en** \'riz°n\; **ris·ing** \'rīziŋ\ **1** : get up from sitting, kneeling, or lying **2** : rebel **3** : appear above the horizon **4** : ascend **5** : gain a higher position or rank **6** : increase ~ n **1** : act of rising **2** : origin **3** : elevation **4** : increase **5** : upward slope **6** : area of high ground —**ris·er** \'rīzər\ n

risk \'risk\ n : exposure to loss or injury —**risk** vb —**risk·i·ness** n —**risky** adj

ris·qué \ris'kā\ adj : nearly indecent

rite \'rīt\ n **1** : set form for conducting a ceremony **2** : liturgy of a church **3** : ceremonial action

rit·u·al \'richəwəl\ n : rite —**ritual** adj —**rit·u·al·ism** \-ˌizəm\ n —**rit·u·al·is·tic** \ˌrich(ə)wəˈlistik\ adj —**rit·u·al·is·ti·cal·ly** \-tik(ə)lē\ adv —**rit·u·al·ly** \'rich(əw)əlē\ adv

ri·val \'rīvəl\ n **1** : competitor **2** : peer ~ vb -**valed** or -**valled; -val·ing** or -**val·ling 1** : be in competition with **2** : equal —**rival** adj —**ri·val·ry** \-rē\ n

riv·er \'rivər\ n : natural stream larger than a brook —**riv·er·bank** n —**riv·er·bed** n —**riv·er·boat** n —**riv·er·side** n

riv·et \'rivət\ n : headed metal bolt ~ vb : fasten with a rivet —**riv·et·er** n

riv·u·let \'riv(y)ələt\ n : small stream

roach \'rōch\ n : cockroach

road \'rōd\ n : open way for vehicles, persons, and animals —**road·bed** n —**road·way** n

road·block n : obstruction on a road

road·run·ner n : large fast-running bird

road·side n : strip of land along a road —**roadside** adj

roam \'rōm\ vb : wander

roan \'rōn\ adj : having a dark coat with white hairs interspersed ~ n : animal with a roan coat or its color

roar \'rōr\ vb : utter a full loud prolonged sound —**roar** n —**roar·er** n

roast \'rōst\ vb **1** : cook by dry heat **2** : criticize severely ~ n : piece of meat suitable for roasting —**roast** adj —**roast·er** n

rob \'räb\ vb -**bb- 1** : steal from **2** : commit robbery —**rob·ber** n

rob·bery \'räb(ə)rē\ n, pl -**ber·ies** : theft of something from a person by use of violence or threat

robe \'rōb\ n **1** : long flowing outer garment **2** : covering for the lower body ~ vb **robed; rob·ing** : clothe with or as if with a robe

rob·in \'räbən\ n : No. American thrush with a reddish breast

ro·bot \'rō,bät, -bət\ n **1** : machine that looks and acts like a human being **2** : efficient but insensitive person

ro·bust \rō'bəst, 'rō(ˌ)bəst\ adj : strong and vigorously healthy —**ro·bust·ly** adv —**ro·bust·ness** n

¹rock \'räk\ vb : sway or cause to sway back and forth ~ n **1** : rocking movement **2** : popular music marked by repetition and a strong beat

²rock n : mass of hard mineral material —**rock** adj —**rocky** adj

rock·er n **1** : curved piece on which a chair rocks **2** : chair that rocks

rock·et \'räkət\ n **1** : self-propelled firework or missile **2** : jet engine ~ vb : rise abruptly and rapidly —**rock·et·ry** \-ətrē\ n

rod \'räd\ n **1** : straight slender stick **2** : unit of length equal to 5½ yards

rode past of RIDE

ro·dent \'rōd°nt\ n : small gnawing mammal

ro·deo \'rōdē,ō, rə'dāō\ n, pl -**de·os** : contest of cowboy skills

roe \'rō\ n : fish eggs

rogue \'rōg\ n : dishonest or mischievous person —**ro·guery** \'rōgərē\ n —**ro·guish** \'rōgish\ adj —**ro·guish·ly** adv —**ro·guish·ness** n

roil \'roil, for 2 also 'ril\ vb **1** : make cloudy or muddy by stirring up **2** : make angry

role \'rōl\ n **1** : part to play **2** : function

roll \'rōl\ n **1** : official record or list of names **2** : something rolled up or rounded **3** : bread baked in a small rounded mass **4** : sound of rapid drum strokes **5** : heavy reverberating sound **6** : rolling movement ~ *vb* **1** : move by turning over **2** : move on wheels **3** : flow in a continuous stream **4** : swing from side to side **5** : shape or be shaped in rounded form **6** : press with a roller

roll·er *n* **1** : revolving cylinder **2** : rod on which something is rolled up

roller skate *n* : a skate with wheels instead of a runner —**roller-skate** *vb* —**roller skater** *n*

rol·lick·ing \'rälikiŋ\ *adj* : full of good spirits

Ro·man Catholic \,rōmən-\ *n* : member of a Christian church led by a pope —**Roman Catholic** *adj* —**Roman Catholicism** *n*

ro·mance \rō'mans, 'rō,mans\ *n* **1** : medieval tale of knightly adventure **2** : love story **3** : love affair ~ *vb* **-manced; -manc·ing 1** : have romantic fancies **2** : have a love affair with —**ro·manc·er** *n*

ro·man·tic \rō'mantik\ *adj* **1** : visionary or imaginative **2** : appealing to one's emotions —**ro·man·ti·cal·ly** \-ik(ə)lē\ *adv*

romp \'rämp\ *vb* : play actively and noisily —**romp** *n*

roof \'rüf, 'rüf\ *n*, *pl* **roofs** \'rüfs, 'rüfs; 'rüvz, 'rüvz\ : upper covering part of a building ~ *vb* : cover with a roof —**roofed** \'rüft, 'rüft\ *adj* —**roof·ing** *n* —**roof·less** *adj* —**roof·top** *n*

¹rook \'rük\ *n* : crowlike bird

²rook *vb* : cheat

rook·ie \'rükē\ *n* : novice

room \'rüm, 'rüm\ *n* **1** : sufficient space **2** : partitioned part of a building ~ *vb* : occupy lodgings —**room·er** *n* —**room·ful** *n* —**roomy** *adj*

room·mate *n* : one sharing the same lodgings

roost \'rüst\ *n* : support on which birds perch ~ *vb* : settle on a roost

roost·er \'rüstər, 'rüs-\ *n* : adult male domestic fowl

¹root \'rüt, 'rüt\ *n* **1** : leafless underground part of a seed plant **2** : rootlike thing or part **3** : source **4** : essential core ~ *vb* : form, fix, or become fixed by roots —**root·less** *adj* —**root·let** \-lət\ *n* —**root·like** *adj*

²root *vb* : turn up with the snout

³root \'rüt, 'rüt\ *vb* : applaud or encourage noisily —**root·er** *n*

rope \'rōp\ *n* : large strong cord of strands of fiber ~ *vb* **roped; rop·ing 1** : tie with a rope **2** : lasso

ro·sa·ry \'rōzərē\ *n*, *pl* **-ries 1** : string

of beads used in praying **2** : Roman Catholic devotion

¹rose *past of* RISE

²rose \'rōz\ *n* **1** : prickly shrub with bright flowers **2** : purplish red —**rose** *adj* —**rose·bud** *n* —**rose·bush** *n*

rose·mary \'rōz,merē\ *n*, *pl* **-mar·ies** : fragrant shrubby mint

ro·sette \rō'zet\ *n* : rose-shaped ornament

Rosh Ha·sha·nah \,rōsh(h)ə'shōnə\ *n* : Jewish New Year observed as a religious holiday in September or October

ros·in \'räz⁰n\ *n* : brittle resin

ros·ter \'rästər\ *n* : list of names

ros·trum \'rästrəm\ *n*, *pl* **-trums** *or* **-tra** \-trə\ : speaker's platform

rosy \'rōzē\ *adj* **ros·i·er; -est 1** : of the color rose **2** : hopeful —**ros·i·ly** *adv* —**ros·i·ness** *n*

rot \'rät\ *vb* **-tt-** : undergo decomposition ~ *n* **1** : decay **2** : disease in which tissue breaks down

ro·ta·ry \'rōtərē\ *adj* **1** : turning on an axis **2** : having a rotating part

ro·tate \'rō,tāt\ *vb* **-tat·ed; -tat·ing 1** : turn about an axis or a center **2** : alternate in a series —**ro·ta·tion** \rō'tāshən\ *n* —**ro·ta·tor** \'rō,tātər\ *n*

rote \'rōt\ *n* : repetition from memory

ro·tor \'rōtər\ *n* **1** : part that rotates **2** : system of rotating horizontal blades for supporting a helicopter

rot·ten \'rät⁰n\ *adj* **1** : having rotted **2** : corrupt **3** : extremely unpleasant or inferior —**rot·ten·ness** \-⁰n(n)əs\ *n*

ro·tund \rō'tənd\ *adj* : rounded —**ro·tun·di·ty** \-'təndətē\ *n*

ro·tun·da \rō'təndə\ *n* : building or room with a dome

roué \rü'ā\ *n* : man given to debauched living

rouge \'rüzh, 'rüj\ *n* : cosmetic for the cheeks —**rouge** *vb*

rough \'rəf\ *adj* **1** : not smooth **2** : not calm **3** : harsh, violent, or rugged **4** : crudely or hastily done ~ *n* : rough state or something in that state ~ *vb* **1** : roughen **2** : manhandle **3** : make roughly —**rough·ly** *adv* —**rough·ness** *n*

rough·age \'rəfij\ *n* : coarse bulky food

rough·en \'rəfən\ *vb* : make or become rough

rough·neck \'rəf,nek\ *n* : rowdy

rou·lette \rü'let\ *n* : gambling game using a whirling numbered wheel

¹round \'raund\ *adj* **1** : having every part the same distance from the center **2** : cylindrical **3** : complete **4**

: approximate 5 : blunt 6 : moving in or forming a circle ~ *n* 1 : round thing 2 : curved part 3 : series of recurring actions or events 4 : period of time or a unit of action 5 : fired shot 6 : cut of beef ~ *vb* 1 : make or become round 2 : go around 3 : finish 4 : express as an approximation —**round·ish** *adj* —**round·ly** *adv* —**round·ness** *n*

²**round** *prep or adv* : around

round·about *adj* : indirect

round·up \'raůnd,ap\ *n* 1 : gathering together of range cattle 2 : summary —**round up** *vb*

rouse \'raůz\ *vb* **roused; rous·ing** 1 : wake from sleep 2 : excite to activity

rout \'raůt\ *n* 1 : state of wild confusion 2 : disastrous defeat ~ *vb* : defeat decisively

route \'rüt, 'raůt\ *n* : line of travel ~ *vb* **rout·ed; rout·ing** : send by a selected route

rou·tine \rü'tēn\ *n* : procedure or course of action regularly followed —**routine** *adj* —**rou·tine·ly** *adv*

rove \'rōv\ *vb* **roved; rov·ing** : wander without definite direction —**rov·er** *n*

¹**row** \'rō\ *vb* 1 : propel a boat with oars 2 : travel or convey in a rowed boat ~ *n* : act of rowing —**row·boat** *n* —**row·er** \'rō(ə)r\ *n*

²**row** *n* : number of objects in a line

³**row** \'raů\ *n* : noisy quarrel —**row** *vb*

row·dy \'raůdē\ *adj* **-di·er; -est** : coarse or boisterous in behavior —**row·di·ness** *n* —**rowdy** *n* —**row·dy·ism** *n*

roy·al \'roial\ *adj* : relating to or befitting a king —**roy·al·ly** *adv*

roy·al·ty \'roialtē\ *n, pl* **-ties** 1 : state of being royal 2 : royal person 3 : payment for use of property

rub \'rəb\ *vb* **-bb-** 1 : use pressure and friction on a body 2 : scour, polish, erase, or smear by pressure and friction 3 : chafe with friction ~ *n* : difficulty

rub·ber \'rəbər\ *n* 1 : one that rubs 2 : waterproof elastic substance or something made of it —**rubber** *adj* —**rub·ber·ize** \-,īz\ *vb* —**rub·bery** *adj*

rub·bish \'rəbish\ *n* : waste or trash

rub·ble \'rəbəl\ *n* : broken stones or bricks

ru·ble \'rübəl\ *n* : monetary unit of the U.S.S.R.

ru·by \'rübē\ *n, pl* **-bies** : precious red stone

rud·der \'rədər\ *n* : steering device at the rear of a boat or aircraft

rud·dy \'rədē\ *adj* **-di·er; -est** : reddish —**rud·di·ness** *n*

rude \'rüd\ *adj* **rud·er; rud·est** 1 : roughly made 2 : impolite —**rude·ly** *adv* —**rude·ness** *n*

ru·di·ment \'rüdəmənt\ *n* 1 : something not fully developed 2 : elementary principle —**ru·di·men·ta·ry** \,rüdə'ment(ə)rē\ *adj*

rue \'rü\ *vb* **rued; ru·ing** : feel regret for ~ *n* : regret —**rue·ful** \-fəl\ *adj* —**rue·ful·ly** *adv* —**rue·ful·ness** *n*

ruf·fi·an \'rəfēən\ *n* : brutal person

ruf·fle \'rəfəl\ *vb* **-fled; -fling** 1 : draw into or provide with pleats 2 : roughen the surface of 3 : irritate ~ *n* : strip of fabric pleated on one edge

rug \'rəg\ *n* : piece of heavy fabric used as a floor covering

rug·ged \'rəgəd\ *adj* 1 : having a rough uneven surface 2 : severe 3 : strong —**rug·ged·ly** *adv* —**rug·ged·ness** *n*

ru·in \'rüən\ *n* 1 : complete collapse or destruction 2 : remains of something destroyed—usu. in pl. 3 : cause of destruction ~ *vb* 1 : destroy 2 : damage beyond repair 3 : bankrupt

ru·in·ous \'rüənəs\ *adj* : causing ruin —**ru·in·ous·ly** *adv*

rule \'rül\ *n* 1 : guide or principle for governing action 2 : usual way of doing something 3 : government 4 : straight strip (as of wood or metal) marked off in units for measuring ~ *vb* **ruled; rul·ing** 1 : govern 2 : give as a decision —**rul·er** *n*

rum \'rəm\ *n* : liquor distilled from a fermented sugarcane product

rum·ble \'rəmbəl\ *vb* **-bled; -bling** : make a low heavy rolling sound —**rumble** *n*

ru·mi·nant \'rümənənt\ *n* : hoofed mammal (as a cow or deer) that chews the cud —**ruminant** *adj*

rum·mage \'rəmij\ *vb* **-maged; -maging** : poke around looking for something —**rum·mag·er** *n*

rum·my \'rəmē\ *n* : card game

ru·mor \'rümər\ *n* 1 : common talk 2 : widespread statement not authenticated —**rumor** *vb*

rump \'rəmp\ *n* : rear part of an animal

rum·ple \'rəmpəl\ *vb* **-pled; -pling** : touse or wrinkle —**rumple** *n*

rum·pus \'rəmpəs\ *n* : disturbance

run \'rən\ *vb* **ran** \'ran\; **run; run·ning** 1 : go rapidly or hurriedly 2 : enter a race or election 3 : operate 4

: continue in force **5** : flow rapidly **6** : take a certain direction **7** : manage **8** : incur ~ *n* **1** : act of running **2** : brook **3** : continuous series **4** : usual kind **5** : freedom of movement **6** : lengthwise ravel

run·a·round *n* : evasive or delaying action

run·away \'rən·ə,wā\ *n* : fugitive ~ *adj* **1** : fugitive **2** : out of control

run-down *adj* : being in poor condition

¹rung *past part of* RING

²rung \'rəŋ\ *n* : a round of a chair or ladder

run·ner \'rənər\ *n* **1** : one that runs **2** : lengthwise supporting part of a sled, skate, or drawer

run·ner-up *n, pl* **run·ners-up** : competitor who finishes second

run·ning \'rəniŋ\ *adj* **1** : flowing **2** : continuous

runt \'rənt\ *n* : small person or animal —**runty** *adj*

run·way \'rən,wā\ *n* : strip on which aircraft land and take off

ru·pee \rü'pē, 'rü,-\ *n* : monetary unit (as of India)

rup·ture \'rəpchər\ *n* **1** : breaking or tearing apart **2** : hernia ~ *vb* **-tured; -tur·ing** : cause or undergo rupture

ru·ral \'rurəl\ *adj* : relating to the country or agriculture

ruse \'rüs, 'rüz\ *n* : trick

¹rush \'rəsh\ *n* : grasslike marsh plant

²rush *vb* **1** : move forward or act with too great haste **2** : perform in a short time ~ *n* : violent forward motion ~ *adj* : requiring speed —**rush·er** *n*

rus·set \'rəsət\ *n* **1** : reddish brown color **2** : winter apple —**russet** *adj*

rust \'rəst\ *n* **1** : reddish coating on exposed metal (as iron) **2** : reddish orange color —**rust** *vb* —**rusty** *adj*

rus·tic \'rəstik\ *adj* **1** : rural **2** : boorish ~ *n* : rustic person —**rus·ti·cal·ly** \-k(ə)lē\ *adv*

rus·tle \'rəsəl\ *vb* **-tled; -tling 1** : make or cause a rustle **2** : forage food **3** : steal cattle from the range ~ *n* : succession of small sounds —**rus·tler** \-(ə)lər\ *n*

rut \'rət\ *n* **1** : track worn by wheels or feet **2** : set routine —**rut·ted** *adj*

ruth·less \'rüthləs\ *adj* : having no pity —**ruth·less·ly** *adv* —**ruth·less·ness** *n*

-ry \rē\ *n suffix* : -ery

rye \'rī\ *n* : cereal grass grown for grain

S

s \'es\ *n, pl* **s's** *or* **ss** \'esəz\ : 19th letter of the alphabet

¹-s \s *after sounds* f, k, k̲, p, t, th; əz *after sounds* ch, j, s, sh, z, zh; z *after other sounds*\ —used to form the plural of most nouns

²-s *vb suffix* —used to form the 3d person singular present of most verbs

Sab·bath \'sabəth\ *n* **1** : Saturday observed as a day of worship by Jews and some Christians **2** : Sunday observed as a day of worship by Christians

sa·ber, sa·bre \'sābər\ *n* : cavalry sword

sa·ble \'sābəl\ *n* **1** : black **2** : dark brown mammal or its fur

sab·o·tage \'sabə,täzh\ *n* : deliberate destruction or hampering ~ *vb* **-taged; -tag·ing** : wreck through sabotage

sab·o·teur \,sabə'tər\ *n* : person who commits sabotage

sac \'sak\ *n* : baglike part

sac·cha·rin \'sak(ə)rən\ *n* : very sweet white substance

sac·cha·rine \-(ə)rən\ *adj* : nauseatingly sweet

sa·chet \sa'shā\ *n* : small bag with perfumed powder (**sachet powder**)

¹sack \'sak\ *n* : bag

²sack *vb* : plunder a captured place

sack·cloth *n* : rough garment worn as a sign of penitence

sac·ra·ment \'sakrəmənt\ *n* : formal religious act or rite —**sac·ra·men·tal** \,sakrə'ment³l\ *adj*

sa·cred \'sākrəd\ *adj* **1** : set apart for or worthy of worship **2** : worthy of reverence **3** : relating to religion —**sa·cred·ly** *adv* —**sa·cred·ness** *n*

sac·ri·fice \'sakrə,fīs\ *n* **1** : the offering of something precious to a deity or the thing offered **2** : loss or deprivation ~ *vb* **-ficed; -fic·ing** : offer or give up as a sacrifice —**sac·ri·fi·cial** \,sakrə'fishəl\ *adj*

sac·ri·lege \'sakrəlij\ *n* : violation of something sacred —**sac·ri·le·gious** \,sakrə'lijəs, -'lējəs\ *adj*

sac·ro·sanct \'sakrō,saŋkt\ *adj* : sacred

sad \'sad\ *adj* **-dd-** **1** : affected with grief or sorrow **2** : causing sorrow — **sad·den** \'sad\[?]n\ *vb* —**sad·ly** *adv* — **sad·ness** *n*

sad·dle \'sad\[?]l\ *n* : seat for riding on horseback ~ *vb* -**dled; -dling** : put a saddle on

sa·dism \'sā,dizəm, 'sad,iz-\ *n* : delight in cruelty —**sa·dist** \'sādəst, 'sad-\ *n* —**sa·dis·tic** \sə'distik\ *adj* —**sa·dis·ti·cal·ly** \-tik(ə)lē\ *adv*

sa·fa·ri \sə'färē, -'far-\ *n* : hunting expedition in Africa

safe \'sāf\ *adj* **saf·er; saf·est 1** : freed or secure from danger **2** : providing safety ~ *n* : container to keep valuables safe —**safe·keep·ing** *n* —**safe·ly** *adv*

safe·guard *n* : measure or device for preventing accidents —**safeguard** *vb*

safe·ty \'sāftē\ *n, pl* -**ties 1** : freedom from danger **2** : protective device

saf·flow·er \'saf,laü(ə)r\ *n* : herb with seeds rich in edible oil

saf·fron \'safrən\ *n* : orange powder from a crocus flower used in cooking

sag \'sag\ *vb* **-gg-** : droop, sink, or settle —**sag** *n*

sa·ga \'sägə\ *n* : story of heroic deeds

sa·ga·cious \sə'gāshəs\ *adj* : shrewd — **sa·gac·i·ty** \-'gasətē\ *n*

¹sage \'sāj\ *adj* : wise or prudent ~ *n* : wise man —**sage·ly** *adv*

²sage *n* : shrublike mint

sage·brush *n* : low shrub of the western U.S.

said *past of* SAY

sail \'sāl\ *n* **1** : fabric used to catch the wind and push a ship **2** : trip on a sailboat ~ *vb* **1** : travel on a ship **2** : glide through the air —**sail·boat** *n* —**sail·or** \'sālər\ *n*

sail·fish *n* : large fish with a very large dorsal fin

saint \'sānt, *before a name* (,)sānt *or* sənt\ *n* : holy or godly person — **saint·ed** \-əd\ *adj* —**saint·hood** \-,hüd\ *n* —**saint·li·ness** *n* —**saint·ly** *adj*

¹sake \'sāk\ *n* **1** : purpose or reason **2** : one's good or benefit

²sa·ke, sa·ki \'säkē\ *n* : Japanese rice wine

sa·la·cious \sə'lāshəs\ *adj* : sexually suggestive —**sa·la·cious·ly** *adv*

sal·ad \'saləd\ *n* : dish usu. of raw lettuce, vegetables, or fruit

sal·a·man·der \'salə,mandər\ *n* : lizardlike amphibian

sa·la·mi \sə'lämē\ *n* : highly seasoned dried sausage

sal·a·ry \'sal(ə)rē\ *n, pl* -**ries** : regular payment for services

sale \'sāl\ *n* **1** : transfer of ownership of property for money **2** : selling at bargain prices —**sal·able, sale·able** \'sāləbəl\ *adj* —**sales·man** \-mən\ *n* —**sales·per·son** *n* —**sales·wom·an** *n*

sa·lient \'sālyənt\ *adj* : standing out conspicuously

sa·line \'sā,lēn, -,līn\ *adj* : containing salt —**sa·lin·i·ty** \sā'linətē, sə-\ *n*

sa·li·va \sə'līvə\ *n* : liquid secreted into the mouth —**sal·i·vary** \'salə,verē\ *adj* —**sal·i·vate** \-,vāt\ *vb* —**sal·i·va·tion** \,salə'vāshən\ *n*

sal·low \'salō\ *adj* : of a yellowish sickly color

sal·ly \'salē\ *n, pl* -**lies 1** : rushing attack on troops **2** : witty remark —**sally** *vb*

salm·on \'samən\ *n, pl* **salmon** : soft-finned food fish

sa·lon \sə'län, 'sal,än, sa'lō[ⁿ]\ *n* : elegant room or shop

sa·loon \sə'lün\ *n* **1** : large room on a passenger ship **2** : barroom

salt \'sölt\ *n* **1** : white crystalline substance that consists of sodium and chlorine **2** : compound formed usu. from acid and metal —**salt** *vb or adj* —**salt·i·ness** *n* —**salty** *adj*

salt·wa·ter *adj* : relating to or living in salt water

sa·lu·bri·ous \sə'lübrēəs\ *adj* : good for health

sal·u·tary \'salyə,terē\ *adj* : health-giving or beneficial

sal·u·ta·tion \,salyə'tāshən\ *n* : greeting

sa·lute \sə'lüt\ *vb* -**lut·ed; -lut·ing** : honor by ceremony or formal movement —**salute** *n*

sal·vage \'salvij\ *n* : something saved from destruction ~ *vb* -**vaged; -vag·ing** : rescue or save

sal·va·tion \sal'vāshən\ *n* : saving of a person from sin or danger

salve \'sav, 'säv\ *n* : medicinal ointment ~ *vb* **salved; salv·ing** : soothe

sal·ver \'salvər\ *n* : small tray

sal·vo \'salvō\ *n, pl* -**vos** *or* -**voes** : simultaneous discharge of guns

same \'sām\ *adj* : being the one referred to ~ *pron* : the same one or ones ~ *adv* : in the same manner — **same·ness** *n*

sam·ple \'sampəl\ *n* : piece or item that shows the quality of the whole ~ *vb* -**pled; -pling** : judge by a sample

sam·pler \'samplər\ *n* : piece of needlework testing skill in embroidering

san·a·to·ri·um \,sanə'tōrēəm\ *n, pl* **-riums** *or* **-ria** \-ēə\ : hospital for the chronically ill

sanc·ti·fy \'saŋktə,fī\ *vb* **-fied; -fy·ing** : make holy —**sanc·ti·fi·ca·tion** \,saŋktəfə'kāshən\ *n*

sanc·ti·mo·nious \,saŋktə'mōnēəs\ *adj* : hypocritically pious

sanc·tion \'saŋkshən\ *n* **1** : authoritative approval **2** : coercive measure —usu. pl ~ *vb* : approve

sanc·ti·ty \'saŋktətē\ *n, pl* **-ties** : quality or state of being holy or sacred

sanc·tu·ary \'saŋkchə,werē\ *n, pl* **-ar·ies 1** : consecrated place **2** : place of refuge

sand \'sand\ *n* : loose granular particles of rock ~ *vb* : smooth with an abrasive —**sand·bank** *n* —**sand·er** *n* —**sand·storm** *n* —**sandy** *adj*

san·dal \'sand³l\ *n* : shoe consisting of a sole strapped to the foot

sand·pa·per *n* : abrasive paper —**sandpaper** *vb*

sand·pip·er \-,pīpər\ *n* : long-billed shorebird

sand·stone *n* : rock made of naturally cemented sand

sand·wich \'sand(,)wich\ *n* : 2 or more slices of bread with a filling between them ~ *vb* : squeeze or crowd in

sane \'sān\ *adj* **san·er; san·est 1** : mentally healthy **2** : sensible —**sane·ly** *adv*

sang *past of* SING

san·gui·nary \'saŋgwə,nerē\ *adj* : bloody

san·guine \'saŋgwən\ *adj* **1** : reddish **2** : cheerful

san·i·tar·i·um \,sanə'terēəm\ *n, pl* **-iums** *or* **-ia** \-ēə\ : sanatorium

san·i·tary \'sanəterē\ *adj* **1** : relating to health **2** : free from filth or infective matter

san·i·ta·tion \,sanə'tāshən\ *n* : protection of health by maintenance of sanitary conditions

san·i·ty \'sanətē\ *n* : soundness of mind

sank *past of* SINK

¹sap \'sap\ *n* **1** : vital fluid **2** : watery fluid that circulates through a vascular plant —**sap·less** *adj* —**sap·py** *adj*

²sap *vb* **-pp- 1** : undermine **2** : weaken or exhaust gradually

sa·pi·ent \'sāpēənt, 'sapē-\ *adj* : wise —**sa·pi·ence** \-əns\ *n*

sap·ling \'sapliŋ\ *n* : young tree

sap·phire \'saf,ī(ə)r\ *n* : hard transparent blue precious stone

sap·suck·er \'sap,səkər\ *n* : small American woodpecker

sar·casm \'sär,kazəm\ *n* **1** : cutting remark **2** : ironical criticism or reproach —**sar·cas·tic** \sär'kastik\ *adj* —**sar·cas·ti·cal·ly** \-tik(ə)lē\ *adv*

sar·coph·a·gus \sär'käfəgəs\ *n, pl* **-gi** \-,gī, -,jī\ : large stone coffin

sar·dine \sär'dēn\ *n* : small fish preserved esp. in oil for use as food

sar·don·ic \sär'dänik\ *adj* : bitterly disdainful —**sar·don·i·cal·ly** \-ik(ə)lē\ *adv*

sa·rong \sə'ròŋ, -'räŋ\ *n* : loose skirt worn esp. by people of the Pacific islands

sar·sa·pa·ril·la \,sas(ə)pə'rilə, särs-\ *n* : root of a tropical American plant used esp. for flavoring

sar·to·ri·al \sär'tōrēəl\ *adj* : relating to a tailor or men's clothes

¹sash \'sash\ *n* : broad band worn around the waist or over the shoulder

²sash *n, pl* **sash 1** : frame for a pane of glass in a door or window **2** : movable part of a window

sas·sa·fras \'sasə,fras\ *n* : No. American tree or its dried bark used in medicine and as flavoring

sassy \'sasē\ *adj* **sass·i·er; -est** : saucy

sat *past of* SIT

Sa·tan \'sāt³n\ *n* : devil

satch·el \'sachəl\ *n* : small bag

sate \'sāt\ *vb* **sat·ed; sat·ing** : satisfy to the full

sat·el·lite \'sat³l,īt\ *n* **1** : one that is dependent **2** : body that revolves around a larger celestial body

sa·ti·ate \'sāshē,āt\ *vb* **-at·ed; -at·ing 1** : satisfy fully **2** : surfeit —**sa·ti·ety** \sə'tīətē\ *n*

sat·in \'sat³n\ *n* : glossy fabric

sat·ire \'sa,tī(ə)r\ *n* : literary ridicule done with humor —**sa·tir·ic** \sə'tirik\, **sa·tir·i·cal** \-ikəl\ *adj* —**sa·tir·i·cal·ly** *adv* —**sat·i·rist** \'satərəst\ *n* —**sat·i·rize** \-ə,rīz\ *vb*

sat·is·fac·tion \,satəs'fakshən\ *n* : state of being satisfied —**sat·is·fac·to·ri·ly** \-'fakt(ə)rəlē\ *adv* —**sat·is·fac·to·ry** \-'fakt(ə)rē\ *adj*

sat·is·fy \'satəs,fī\ *vb* **-fied; -fy·ing 1** : make happy **2** : pay what is due to or on —**sat·is·fy·ing·ly** *adv*

sat·u·rate \'sachə,rāt\ *vb* **-rat·ed; -rat·ing** : soak or charge thoroughly —**sat·u·ra·tion** \,sachə'rāshən\ *n*

Sat·ur·day \'satərdē\ *n* : 7th day of the week

sat·ur·nine \'satər,nīn\ *adj* : sardonic or sullen

sa·tyr \'sātər, 'sat-\ *n* : partly horse-like or goatlike deity of Greek mythology

sauce \'sós\ *n* : dressing for salads or meats **—sauce·pan** *n*

sau·cer \'sósər\ *n* : small shallow dish under a cup

saucy \'sasē, 'sósē\ *adj* **sauc·i·er; -est** : insolent **—sauc·i·ly** *adv* **—sauc·i·ness** *n*

sau·er·kraut \'saú(ə)r,kraút\ *n* : finely cut and fermented cabbage

sau·na \'saúnə\ *n* : steam or dry heat bath or a room or cabinet used for such a bath

saun·ter \'sóntər, 'sánt-\ *vb* : stroll

sau·sage \'sósij\ *n* : minced and highly seasoned meat

sau·té \só'tā, sö-\ *vb* **-téed** *or* **-téd; -té·ing** : fry in a little fat **—sauté** *n*

sav·age \'savij\ *adj* : wild 2 : cruel ~ *n* : person belonging to a primitive society **—sav·age·ly** *adv* **—sav·age·ness** *n* **—sav·age·ry** *n*

¹save \'sāv\ *vb* **saved; sav·ing** 1 : rescue from danger 2 : guard from destruction 3 : redeem from sin 4 : put aside as a reserve **—sav·er** *n*

²save \(,)sāv\ *prep* : except

sav·ior, sav·iour \'sāvyər\ *n* 1 : one who saves 2 *cap* : Jesus Christ

sa·vor \'sāvər\ *n* : special flavor ~ *vb* : taste with pleasure **—sa·vory** *adj*

¹saw *past of* SEE

²saw \'só\ *n* : cutting tool with teeth ~ *vb* **sawed; sawed** *or* **sawn; saw·ing** : cut with a saw **—saw·dust** \-(,)dəst\ *n* **—saw·mill** *n* **—saw·yer** \-yər\ *n*

saw·horse *n* : support for wood being sawed

sax·o·phone \'saksə,fōn\ *n* : wind instrument with a reed mouthpiece and usu. a bent metal body

say \'sā\ *vb* **said** \'sed\; **say·ing** \'sāiŋ\; **says** \'sez\ 1 : express in words 2 : state positively ~ *n, pl* **says** \'sāz\ 1 : expression of opinion 2 : power of decision

say·ing \'sāiŋ\ *n* : commonly repeated statement

scab \'skab\ *n* 1 : protective crust over a sore or wound 2 : worker taking a striker's job ~ *vb* **-bb-** 1 : become covered with a scab 2 : work as a scab **—scab·by** *adj*

scab·bard \'skabərd\ *n* : sheath for the blade of a weapon

scaf·fold \'skafəld, -,ōld\ *n* 1 : raised platform for workmen 2 : platform on which a criminal is executed

scald \'skóld\ *vb* 1 : burn with hot liquid or steam 2 : heat to the boiling point

¹scale \'skāl\ *n* : weighing device ~ *vb* **scaled; scal·ing** : weigh

²scale *n* 1 : thin plate esp. on the body of a fish or reptile 2 : thin coating or layer ~ *vb* **scaled; scal·ing** : strip of scales **—scaled** \'skāld\ *adj* **—scale·less** *adj* **—scaly** *adj*

³scale *n* 1 : graduated series 2 : size of a sample (as a model) in proportion to the size of the actual thing 3 : standard of estimation or judgment 4 : series of musical tones ~ *vb* **scaled; scal·ing** 1 : go up by a ladder 2 : arrange in a graded series

scal·lion \'skalyən\ *n* : bulbless onion

scal·lop \'skäləp, 'skal-\ *n* 1 : marine mollusk 2 : rounded projection on a border

scalp \'skalp\ *n* : skin and flesh of the head ~ *vb* 1 : tear the scalp from 2 : sell again at a greatly increased price **—scalp·er** *n*

scal·pel \'skalpəl\ *n* : surgical knife

scamp \'skamp\ *n* : rascal

scam·per \'skampər\ *vb* : run nimbly **—scamper** *n*

scan \'skan\ *vb* **-nn-** 1 : read (verses) so as to show meter 2 : examine closely or hastily **—scan** *n* **—scan·ner** *n*

scan·dal \'skand³l\ *n* 1 : disgraceful situation 2 : malicious gossip **—scan·dal·ize** *vb* **—scan·dal·ous** *adj*

scant \'skant\ *adj* : barely sufficient ~ *vb* : stint **—scant·i·ly** *adv* **—scanty** *adj*

scape·goat \'skāp,gōt\ *n* : one that bears the blame for others

scap·u·la \'skapyələ\ *n, pl* **-lae** \-,lē\ *or* **-las** : shoulder blade

scar \'skär\ *n* : mark where a wound has healed **—scar** *vb*

scar·ab \'skarəb\ *n* : large dark beetle or an ornament representing one

scarce \'skears\ *adj* **scarc·er; scarc·est** 1 : not plentiful 2 : rare **—scar·ci·ty** \'skersətē\ *n*

scarce·ly \'skearslē\ *adv* 1 : barely 2 : almost not

scare \'skear\ *vb* **scared; scar·ing** : frighten ~ *n* : fright **—scary** *adj*

scare·crow \'skear,krō\ *n* : figure for scaring birds from crops

scarf \'skärf\ *n, pl* **scarves** \'skärvz\ *or* **scarfs** : cloth worn about the shoulders or the neck

scar·let \'skärlət\ *n* : bright red **—scarlet** *adj*

scarlet fever *n* : acute contagious disease marked by fever, sore throat, and red rash

scath·ing \\'skāthiŋ\\ *adj* : bitterly severe

scat·ter \\'skatər\\ *vb* **1** : spread about irregularly **2** : disperse

scav·en·ger \\'skavənjər\\ *n* **1** : person that collects refuse or waste **2** : animal that feeds on decayed matter — **scav·enge** \\'skavənj\\ *vb*

sce·nar·io \\sə'narē,ō\\ *n, pl* **-i·os** : plot of a movie

scene \\'sēn\\ *n* **1** : single situation in a play or movie **2** : stage setting **3** : view **4** : display of emotion — **sce·nic** \\'sēnik\\ *adj*

scen·ery \\'sēn(ə)rē\\ *n, pl* **-er·ies 1** : painted setting for a stage **2** : picturesque view

scent \\'sent\\ *vb* **1** : smell **2** : fill with odor ~ *n* **1** : odor **2** : sense of smell **3** : perfume

scep·ter \\'septər\\ *n* : staff signifying authority

scep·tic \\'skeptik\\ *var of* SKEPTIC

sched·ule \\'skejül, *esp Brit* 'shedyül\\ *n* : list showing sequence of events ~ *vb* **-uled; -ul·ing** : make a schedule of

scheme \\'skēm\\ *n* **1** : crafty plot **2** : systematic design ~ *vb* **schemed; schem·ing** : form a plot — **sche·mat·ic** \\ski'matik\\ *adj* — **schem·er** *n*

schism \\'sizəm, 'skiz-\\ *n* : split — **schis·mat·ic** \\siz'matik, skiz-\\ *n or adj*

schizo·phre·nia \\,skitsə'frēnēə\\ *n* : severe mental disorder — **schiz·oid** \\'skit,soid\\ *adj or n* — **schizo·phren·ic** \\,skitsə'frenik\\ *adj*

schol·ar \\'skälər\\ *n* : student or learned person — **schol·ar·ly** *adj*

schol·ar·ship \\-,ship\\ *n* **1** : qualities or learning of a scholar **2** : money given to a student to pay for education

scho·las·tic \\skə'lastik\\ *adj* : relating to schools, scholars, or scholarship

¹school \\'skül\\ *n* **1** : institution for learning **2** : pupils in a school **3** : group with shared beliefs ~ *vb* : teach — **school·boy** *n* — **school·girl** *n* — **school·house** *n* — **school·mate** *n* — **school·room** *n* — **school·teach·er** *n*

²school *n* : large number of fish swimming together

schoo·ner \\'skünər\\ *n* : sailing ship

sci·ence \\'sīəns\\ *n* : branch of systematic study esp. of the physical world — **sci·en·tif·ic** \\,sīən'tifik\\ *adj* — **sci·en·tif·i·cal·ly** \\-ik(ə)lē\\ *adv* — **sci·en·tist** \\'sīəntəst\\ *n*

scin·til·late \\'sint³l,āt\\ *vb* **-lat·ed; -lat-**

ing : flash — **scin·til·la·tion** \\,sint³l-'āshən\\ *n*

sci·on \\'sīən\\ *n* **1** : shoot of a plant **2** : descendant

scis·sors \\'sizərz\\ *n pl* : small shears

scle·ro·sis \\sklə'rōsəs\\ *n* : hardening of an artery — **scle·rot·ic** \\-'rätik\\ *adj*

scoff \\'skäf\\ *vb* : mock — **scoff·er** *n*

scold \\'skōld\\ *n* : person who scolds ~ *vb* : criticize severely

scoop \\'sküp\\ *n* : shovellike utensil ~ *vb* **1** : take out with a scoop **2** : dig out

scoot \\'sküt\\ *vb* : go suddenly and swiftly

scoot·er \\'skütər\\ *n* : child's foot-propelled vehicle

¹scope \\'skōp\\ *n* **1** : extent **2** : room for development

²scope *n* : viewing device (as a microscope)

scorch \\'skȯrch\\ *vb* : burn the surface of

score \\'skȯr\\ *n, pl* **scores 1** *or pl* **score** : twenty **2** : cut **3** : record of points made (as in a game) **4** : debt **5** : music of a composition ~ *vb* **scored; scor·ing 1** : record **2** : mark with lines **3** : gain in a game **4** : assign a grade to **5** : compose a score for — **score·less** *adj* — **scor·er** *n*

scorn \\'skȯrn\\ *n* : emotion involving both anger and disgust ~ *vb* : hold in contempt — **scorn·er** *n* — **scorn·ful** \\-fəl\\ *adj* — **scorn·ful·ly** *adv*

scor·pi·on \\'skȯrpēən\\ *n* : poisonous spider-like animal

scoun·drel \\'skaundrəl\\ *n* : mean worthless person

¹scour \\'skau̇(ə)r\\ *vb* : examine thoroughly

²scour *vb* : rub in order to clean

scourge \\'skərj\\ *n* **1** : whip **2** : punishment ~ *vb* **scourged; scourg·ing 1** : lash **2** : punish severely

scout \\'skau̇t\\ *vb* : inspect or observe to get information ~ *n* : person sent out to get information

scow \\'skau̇\\ *n* : large flat-bottomed boat with square ends

scowl \\'skau̇l\\ *vb* : make a face in expression of displeasure — **scowl** *n*

scrag·gly \\'skraglē\\ *adj* : irregular or unkempt

scram \\'skram\\ *vb* **-mm-** : go away at once

scram·ble \\'skrambəl\\ *vb* **-bled; -bling 1** : clamber clumsily around **2** : struggle for possession of something **3** : mix together **4** : stir during frying — **scramble** *n*

¹scrap \\'skrap\\ *n* **1** : fragment **2** : discarded material ~ *vb* **-pp-** : get rid of as useless

²**scrap** *vb* **-pp-** : fight —**scrap·per** *n*

scrap·book *n* : blank book in which mementos are kept

scrape \'skrāp\ *vb* **scraped; scrap·ing** 1 : remove by drawing a knife over 2 : clean or smooth by rubbing 3 : get (money) together 4 : get along with difficulty ~ *n* 1 : act of scraping 2 : predicament —**scrap·er** *n*

scratch \'skrach\ *vb* 1 : scrape or dig with or as if with claws or nails 2 : cause to move gratingly ~ *n* : mark or sound made in scratching —**scratchy** *adj*

scrawl \'skról\ *vb* : write hastily and carelessly —**scrawl** *n*

scraw·ny \'skrónē\ *adj* **-ni·er; -est** : very thin

scream \'skrēm\ *vb* : cry out loudly and shrilly ~ *n* : loud shrill cry

screech \'skrēch\ *vb or n* : shriek

screen \'skrēn\ *n* 1 : device or partition used to protect or decorate 2 : surface on which pictures appear (as in movies) ~ *vb* : shield or separate with or as if with a screen

screw \'skrü\ *n* 1 : grooved fastening device 2 : propeller ~ *vb* 1 : fasten by means of a screw 2 : move spirally

screw·driv·er \'skrü,drīvər\ *n* : tool for turning screws

scrib·ble \'skribəl\ *vb* **-bled; -bling** : write hastily or carelessly —**scribble** *n* —**scrib·bler** \-(ə)lər\ *n*

scribe \'skrīb\ *n* : one who writes or copies writing

scrimp \'skrimp\ *vb* : economize greatly

scrip \'skrip\ *n* 1 : paper money for less than a dollar 2 : certificate entitling one to something (as stock)

script \'skript\ *n* : text (as of a play)

scrip·ture \'skripchər\ *n* : sacred writings of a religion —**scrip·tur·al** \'skripchərəl\ *adj*

scroll \'skrōl\ *n* 1 : roll of paper for writing a document 2 : spiral or coiled design

scro·tum \'skrōtəm\ *n, pl* **-ta** \-ə\ *or* **-tums** : pouch containing the testes

scrounge \'skrau̇nj\ *vb* **scrounged; scroung·ing** : collect by or as if by foraging

¹**scrub** \'skrəb\ *n* : stunted tree or shrub or a growth of these —**scrub** *adj* —**scrub·by** *adj*

²**scrub** *vb* **-bb-** 1 : rub in washing 2 : wash by rubbing —**scrub** *n*

scruff \'skrəf\ *n* : loose skin of the back of the neck

scru·ple \'skrüpəl\ *n* : reluctance due to ethical considerations —**scruple** *vb* —**scru·pu·lous** \-pyələs\ *adj* —**scru·pu·lous·ly** *adv*

scru·ti·ny \'skrüt²nē\ *n, pl* **-nies** : careful inspection —**scru·ti·nize** \-²n,īz\ *vb*

scud \'skəd\ *vb* **-dd-** : move speedily

scuff \'skəf\ *vb* : scratch, scrape, or wear away —**scuff** *n*

scuf·fle \'skəfəl\ *vb* **-fled; -fling** 1 : struggle at close quarters 2 : shuffle one's feet —**scuffle** *n*

scull \'skəl\ *n* 1 : oar for sculling 2 : racing shell propelled with sculls ~ *vb* : propel a boat by an oar over the stern

scul·lery \'skələ(ə)rē\ *n, pl* **-ler·ies** : small room near the kitchen for cleaning

sculp·ture \'skəlpchər\ *n* : work of art carved or molded ~ *vb* **-tured; -tur·ing** : form as sculpture —**sculp·tor** \-tər\ *n* —**sculp·tur·al** \-chərəl\ *adj*

scum \'skəm\ *n* : filthy film on a liquid

scurf \'skərf\ *n* : thin dry scales of skin

scur·ri·lous \'skərələs\ *adj* : coarsely jesting

scur·ry \'skərē\ *vb* **-ried; -ry·ing** : scamper

scur·vy \'skərvē\ *n* : vitamin-deficiency disease

¹**scut·tle** \'skət²l\ *n* : pail for coal

²**scuttle** *vb* **-tled; -tling** : cut a hole in a ship to sink it

³**scuttle** *vb* **-tled; -tling** : scamper

scythe \'sīth\ *n* : mowing tool —**scythe** *vb*

sea \'sē\ *n* 1 : large body of salt water 2 : ocean 3 : rough water —**sea** *adj* —**sea·coast** *n* —**sea·food** *n* —**sea level** *n* —**sea·port** *n* —**sea·shore** *n* —**sea·wa·ter** *n*

sea·bird *n* : bird frequenting the open ocean

sea·board *n* : country's seacoast

sea·far·er \-,farər\ *n* : seaman —**sea·far·ing** \-,fariŋ\ *adj or n*

sea horse *n* : small fish with a horselike head

¹**seal** \'sēl\ *n* : large sea mammal of cold regions —**seal·skin** *n*

²**seal** *n* 1 : device for stamping a design 2 : something that closes ~ *vb* 1 : affix a seal to 2 : close up securely 3 : determine finally —**seal·ant** \-ənt\ *n* —**seal·er** *n*

sea lion *n* : large Pacific seal with external ears

seam \'sēm\ *n* : line of junction of 2

edges 2 : layer of a mineral ~ *vb* : join by sewing —**seam·less** *adj*

sea·man \'sēmən\ *n* 1 : one who helps to handle a ship 2 : enlisted man in the navy ranking next below a petty officer third class —**sea·man·ship** *n*

seaman apprentice *n* : enlisted man in the navy ranking next below a seaman

seaman recruit *n* : enlisted man of the lowest rank in the navy

seam·stress \'sēmstrəs\ *n* : woman who sews

seamy \'sēmē\ *adj* **seam·i·er; -est** : unpleasant or sordid

sé·ance \'sā,äns\ *n* : meeting for communicating with spirits

sea·plane *n* : airplane that can take off from and land on the water

sear \'siər\ *vb* : scorch

search \'sərch\ *vb* 1 : look through 2 : seek —**search** *n* —**search·er** *n* —**search·light** *n*

sea·sick *adj* : nauseated by the motion of a ship —**sea·sick·ness** *n*

¹sea·son \'sēzᵊn\ *n* 1 : division of the year 2 : customary time for something —**sea·son·al** \'sēznəl, -ᵊnəl\ *adj* —**sea·son·al·ly** *adv*

²season *vb* 1 : add spice to (food) 2 : make strong or fit for use —**sea·son·ing** \-nig, -ᵊnij\ *n*

sea·son·able \'sēznəbəl\ *adj* : occurring at a suitable time —**sea·son·ably** \-blē\ *adv*

seat \'sēt\ *n* 1 : place to sit 2 : chair, bench, or stool for sitting on 3 : place that serves as a capital or center ~ *vb* 1 : place in or on a seat 2 : provide seats for

sea·weed *n* : marine alga

sea·wor·thy *adj* : strong enough to hold up to a sea voyage

se·cede \si'sēd\ *vb* **-ced·ed; -ced·ing** : withdraw from a body (as a nation)

se·clude \si'klüd\ *vb* **-clud·ed; -clud·ing** : shut off alone —**se·clu·sion** \-'klüzhən\ *n*

¹sec·ond \'sekənd\ *adj* : next after the 1st ~ *n* 1 : one that is second 2 : one who assists (as in a duel) —**second, sec·ond·ly** *adv*

²second *n* 1 : 60th part of a minute 2 : moment

sec·ond·ary \'sekən,derē\ *adj* 1 : second in rank or importance 2 : coming after the primary or elementary

sec·ond·hand *adj* 1 : not original 2 : used before

second lieutenant *n* : commissioned officer ranking next below a first lieutenant

se·cret \'sēkrət\ *adj* 1 : hidden 2 : kept from general knowledge —**se·cre·cy** \-krəsē\ *n* —**secret** *n* —**se·cre·tive** \'sēkrətiv, si'krēt-\ *adj* —**se·cret·ly** *adv*

sec·re·tar·i·at \,sekrə'terēət\ *n* 1 : body of secretaries in an office 2 : administrative department

sec·re·tary \'sekrə,terē\ *n, pl* **-tar·ies** 1 : one hired to handle correspondence and other tasks for a superior 2 : official in charge of correspondence or records 3 : head of a government department —**sec·re·tar·i·al** \,sekrə'terēəl\ *adj*

¹se·crete \si'krēt\ *vb* **-cret·ed; -cret·ing** : produce as a secretion

²se·crete \si'krēt, 'sēkrət\ *vb* **-cret·ed; -cret·ing** : hide

se·cre·tion \si'krēshən\ *n* 1 : act or process of secreting 2 : product of glandular activity

sect \'sekt\ *n* : religious group

sec·tar·i·an \sek'terēən\ *adj* 1 : relating to a sect 2 : limited in character or scope ~ *n* : member of a sect

sec·tion \'sekshən\ *n* : distinct part —**sec·tion·al** \-sh(ə)nəl\ *adj*

sec·tor \'sektər\ *n* 1 : part of a circle between 2 radii 2 : distinctive part

sec·u·lar \'sekyələr\ *adj* 1 : not sacred 2 : not monastic

se·cure \si'kyür\ *adj* **-cur·er; -est** : free from danger or loss ~ *vb* 1 : fasten safely 2 : get —**se·cure·ly** *adv*

se·cu·ri·ty \si'kyürətē\ *n, pl* **-ties** 1 : safety 2 : something given to guarantee payment 3 *pl* : bond or stock certificates

se·dan \si'dan\ *n* 1 : chair carried by 2 men 2 : enclosed automobile

se·date \si'dāt\ *adj* : quiet and dignified —**se·date·ly** *adv*

sed·a·tive \'sedətiv\ *adj* : serving to relieve tension ~ *n* : sedative drug —**se·da·tion** \si'dāshən\ *n*

sed·en·tary \'sedᵊn,terē\ *adj* : characterized by much sitting

sedge \'sej\ *n* : grasslike marsh plant

sed·i·ment \'sedəmənt\ *n* : material that settles to the bottom of a liquid or is deposited by water or a glacier —**sed·i·men·ta·ry** \,sedə'ment(ə)rē\ *adj* —**sed·i·men·ta·tion** \-,mən-'tāshən. -,men-\ *n*

se·di·tion \si'dishən\ *n* : revolution against a government —**se·di·tious** \-əs\ *adj*

se·duce \si'd(y)üs\ *vb* **-duced; -duc·ing** 1 : lead astray 2 : entice to unlawful sexual intercourse —**se·duc·er** *n* —

se·duc·tion \-'dəkshən\ n —se·duc·tive \-'tiv\ adj

sed·u·lous \'sejələs\ adj : diligent

by which a plant is propagated **2**
see·ing **1** : perceive by the eye **2**
: notice or heed **3** : understand **4**
: make sure **5** : meet with or escort

²see n : jurisdiction of a bishop

seed \'sēd\ n, pl seed or seeds **1** : part
by which a plant is propagated **2**
: source ~ vb **1** : sow **2** : remove
seeds from —seed·less adj

seed·ling \-liŋ\ n : plant grown from
seed

seedy \-ē\ adj seed·i·er; -est **1** : full of
seeds **2** : inferior
: proper
1 : search for **2** : try to reach or
obtain —seek·er n

seem \'sēm\ vb : give the impression
of being —seem·ing·ly adv

seem·ly \-lē\ adj seem·li·er; -est
: proper

seep \'sēp\ vb : leak through fine pores
or cracks —seep·age \'sēpij\ n

seer \'siər\ n : one who foresees or
predicts events

seer·suck·er \'siər,səkər\ n : light
puckered fabric

see·saw \'sē,sȯ\ n : board balanced in
the middle —seesaw vb

seethe \'sēth\ vb seethed; seeth·ing
: become violently agitated

seg·ment \'segmənt\ n : division of a
thing —seg·ment·ed \-,mentəd\ adj

seg·re·gate \'segri,gāt\ vb -gat·ed; -gat·ing : cut off from others —seg·re·ga·tion \,segri'gāshən\ n

seine \'sān\ n : large weighted fishing
net ~ vb : fish with a seine

seis·mic \'sīzmik, 'sīs-\ adj : relating
to an earthquake

seis·mo·graph \-mə,graf\ n : apparatus
for detecting earthquakes

seize \'sēz\ vb seized; seiz·ing : take by
force —sei·zure \'sēzhər\ n

sel·dom \'seldəm\ adv : not often

se·lect \sə'lekt\ adj **1** : favored **2** : discriminating ~ vb : take by prefer-
ence —se·lec·tive \-'lektiv\ adj

se·lec·tion \sə'lekshən\ n : act of se-
lecting or thing selected

se·lect·man \si'lek(t),man, -mən\ n
: New England town official

self \'self\ n, pl selves \'selvz\ : essential person distinct from others

self- comb form **1** : oneself or itself **2**
: of oneself or itself **3** : by oneself or
automatic **4** : to, for, or toward oneself

self-addressed
self-administered
self-analysis
self-appointed
self-assertive
self-assurance
self-assured
self-awareness
self-cleaning
self-closing
self-complacent
self-conceit
self-confessed
self-confidence
self-confident
self-contained
self-contempt
self-contradic-
tion
self-contradic-
tory
self-control
self-created
self-criticism
self-defeating
self-defense
self-denial
self-denying
self-destruction
self-destructive
self-determina-
tion
self-determined
self-discipline
self-doubt
self-educated
self-employed
self-employment
self-esteem
self-evident
self-explanatory
self-expression
self-fulfilling

self-fulfillment
self-governing
self-government
self-help
self-image
self-importance
self-important
self-imposed
self-improve-
ment
self-indulgence
self-indulgent
self-inflicted
self-interest
self-love
self-operating
self-pity
self-portrait
self-possessed
self-possession
self-preservation
self-proclaimed
self-propelled
self-propelling
self-protection
self-reliance
self-reliant
self-respect
self-respecting
self-restraint
self-sacrifice
self-satisfaction
self-satisfied
self-service
self-serving
self-starting
self-styled
self-sufficiency
self-sufficient
self-supporting
self-taught
self-winding

self-cen·tered adj : concerned only
with one's own self

self-con·scious adj : ill at ease —self-
con·scious·ly adv —self-con·scious-
ness n

self·ish \'selfish\ adj : taking care of
oneself without regard for others —
self·ish·ly adv —self·ish·ness n

self·less \'selfləs\ adj : having no concern for self —self·less·ness n

self-made adj : rising by one's own
efforts

self-righ·teous adj : strongly convinced
of one's own righteousness

self·same \'self,sām\ adj : precisely
the same

sell \'sel\ vb sold \'sōld\; sell·ing **1**
: transfer (property) esp. for money

2 : deal in as a business **3** : be sold —**sell·er** n

selves pl of SELF

se·man·tic \si'mantik\ adj : relating to meaning —**se·man·tics** \-iks\ n sing or pl

sema·phore \'sema,fōr\ n 1 : visual signaling apparatus **2** : signaling by flags

sem·blance \'semblans\ n : appearance

se·men \'sēmən\ n : male reproductive fluid

se·mes·ter \sə'mestər\ n : half a school year

semi- \, semi, 'sem-. -,ī\ prefix **1** : half **2** : partial

semi·co·lon \'semi,kōlən\ n : punctuation mark ;

semi·con·duc·tor \, semi-, -,ī-\ n : substance between a conductor and a nonconductor in ability to conduct electricity —**semi·con·duct·ing** adj

semi·fi·nal \, semi-\ adj : being next to the final —**semifinal** \'semi-\ n

semi·for·mal \, semi-\ adj : being or suitable for an occasion of moderate formality

sem·i·nal \'semən²l\ adj **1** : relating to seed or semen **2** : causing or influencing later development

sem·i·nar \'sema,när\ n : conference or conferencelike study

sem·i·nary \'sema,nerē\ n, pl -nar·ies : school and esp. a theological school —**sem·i·nar·i·an** \, sema·'nerēan\ n

sen·ate \'senat\ n : upper branch of a legislature —**sen·a·tor** \-ər\ n —**sen·a·to·rial** \, sena'tōrēal\ adj

send \'send\ vb sent \'sent\, send·ing **1** : cause to go **2** : propel —**send·er** n

se·nile \'sēn,īl, 'sen-\ adj : mentally deficient through old age —**se·nil·i·ty** \si'nilətē\ n

se·nior \'sēnyər\ n : older or higher ranking —**senior** adj —**se·nior·i·ty** \, sēn'yórətē\ n

senior chief petty officer n : petty officer in the navy ranking next below a master chief petty officer

senior master sergeant n : noncommissioned officer in the air force ranking next below a chief master sergeant

sen·sa·tion \sen'sāshan\ n **1** : bodily feeling **2** : condition of excitement or the cause of it —**sen·sa·tion·al** \-sh(ə)nəl\ adj

sense \'sens\ n **1** : meaning **2** : faculty of perceiving something physical **3** : sound mental capacity ~ vb **sensed**;

sens·ing : perceive by the senses —**sense·less** adj —**sense·less·ly** adv

sen·si·bil·i·ty \, sensə'bilətē\ n, pl -ties : delicacy of feeling

sen·si·ble \'sensəbəl\ adj **1** : capable of sensing or being sensed **2** : aware or conscious **3** : intelligent —**sen·si·bly** \-blē\ adv

sen·si·tive \'sensətiv\ adj **1** : subject to excitation by or responsive to stimuli **2** : having power of feeling **3** : easily affected —**sen·si·tive·ness** n —**sen·si·tiv·i·ty** \, sensə'tivətē\ n

sen·si·tize \'sensə,tīz\ vb -tized; -tiz·ing : make or become sensitive

sen·sor \'sen,sór. -sər\ n : device that responds to a physical stimulus

sen·so·ry \'sens(ə)rē\ adj : relating to sensation or the senses

sen·su·al \'sench(ə)wəl, 'senshəl\ adj **1** : pleasing the senses **2** : devoted to the pleasures of the senses —**sen·su·al·ist** n —**sen·su·al·i·ty** \, senchə'walətē\ n —**sen·su·al·ly** adv

sen·su·ous \'sench(ə)wəs\ adj : having strong appeal to the senses

sent past of SEND

sen·tence \'sent²ns. -²nz\ n **1** : judgment of a court **2** : grammatically self-contained speech unit ~ vb -tenced; -tenc·ing : impose a sentence on

sen·ten·tious \sen'tenchəs\ adj : using pompous language

sen·tient \'sench(ē)ənt\ adj : capable of feeling

sen·ti·ment \'sentəmənt\ n **1** : belief **2** : feeling

sen·ti·men·tal \, sentə'ment²l\ adj : influenced by tender feelings —**sen·ti·men·tal·ism** n —**sen·ti·men·tal·ist** n —**sen·ti·men·tal·i·ty** \-, ment²l'ətalitē, -mən-\ n —**sen·ti·men·tal·ize** \-'ment²l,īz\ vb —**sen·ti·men·tal·ly** adv

sen·ti·nel \'sentinəl, -²nəl\ n : sentry

sen·try \'sentrē\ n, pl -tries : one who stands guard

se·pal \'sēpəl, 'sep-\ n : one of the modified leaves comprising a flower calyx

sep·a·rate \'sepə,rāt\ vb -rat·ed; -rat·ing **1** : set or keep apart **2** : become divided or detached ~ \'sep(ə)rat\ adj **1** : not connected or shared **2** : distinct from each other —**sep·a·ra·ble** \'sep(ə)rabəl\ adj —**sep·a·rate·ly** adv —**sep·a·ra·tion** \, sepə'rāshən\ n —**sep·a·ra·tor** \'sepə,rātər\ n

se·pia \'sēpēə\ n : brownish gray

Sep·tem·ber \sep'tembar\ n : 9th month of the year having 30 days

sep·tic \'septik\ *adj* : relating to or using the action of bacteria

sep·ul·cher, sep·ul·chre \'sepəlkər\ *n* 1 : burial vault —**se·pul·chral** \sə'pəlkrəl\ *adj*

se·quel \'sēkwəl\ *n* 1 : consequence or result 2 : continuation of a story

se·quence \'sēkwəns\ *n* : continuous or connected series —**se·quen·tial** \si'kwenchəl\ *adj*

se·ques·ter \si'kwestər\ *vb* : segregate

se·quin \'sēkwən\ *n* : spangle

se·quoia \si'kwȯiə\ *n* : huge California coniferous tree

sera *pl of* SERUM

ser·aph \'serəf\ *n, pl* **-a·phim** \-ə,fim\ *or* **-aphs** : angel —**se·raph·ic** \sə'rafik\ *adj*

sere \'siər\ *adj* : dried up or withered

ser·e·nade \,serə'nād\ *n* : music sung esp. to a lady —**serenade** *vb*

ser·en·dip·i·ty \,serən'dipətē\ *n* : good luck in finding things not sought for —**ser·en·dip·i·tous** \-əs\ *adj*

se·rene \sə'rēn\ *adj* : tranquil —**se·rene·ly** *adv* —**se·ren·i·ty** \sə'renətē\ *n*

serf \'sərf\ *n* : peasant obligated to work the land —**serf·dom** \-dəm\ *n*

serge \'sərj\ *n* : twilled woolen cloth

ser·geant \'särjənt\ *n* : noncommissioned officer (as in the army) ranking next below a staff sergeant

sergeant first class *n* : noncommissioned officer in the army ranking next below a master sergeant

sergeant major *n, pl* **sergeants major** *or* **sergeant majors** 1 : noncommissioned officer serving as chief administrative assistant in a headquarters 2 : noncommissioned officer in the marine corps ranking above a first sergeant

se·ri·al \'sirēəl\ *n* : story told a little bit at a time —**serial** *adj* —**se·ri·al·ly** *adv*

se·ries \'si(ə)rēz\ *n, pl* **series** : number of things in order

se·ri·ous \'sirēəs\ *adj* 1 : subdued in appearance or manner 2 : sincere 3 : of great importance —**se·ri·ous·ly** *adv* —**se·ri·ous·ness** *n*

ser·mon \'sərmən\ *n* : lecture on religion or behavior

ser·pent \'sərpənt\ *n* : snake —**ser·pen·tine** \-pən,tēn, -,tīn\ *adj*

ser·rat·ed \'ser,ātəd\ *adj* : saw-toothed

se·rum \'sirəm\ *n, pl* **-rums** *or* **-ra** \-ə\ : watery part of blood —**se·rous** \-əs\ *adj*

ser·vant \'sərvənt\ *n* : person employed for domestic work

serve \'sərv\ *vb* **served; serv·ing** 1 : work through or perform a term of service 2 : be of use 3 : prove adequate 4 : hand out (food or drink) 5 : be of service to —**serv·er** *n*

ser·vice \'sərvəs\ *n* 1 : act or means of serving 2 : required duty 3 : meeting for worship 4 : branch of public employment or the persons in it 5 : set of dishes or silverware 6 : benefit — *vb* **-viced; -vic·ing** : do repair work on —**ser·vice·able** *adj* —**ser·vice·man** \-,man, -mən\ *n* —**ser·vice·wom·an** *n*

ser·vile \'sərvəl, -,vīl\ *adj* : behaving like a slave —**ser·vil·i·ty** \sər-'vilətē\ *n*

serv·ing \'sərviŋ\ *n* : helping

ser·vi·tude \'sərvə,t(y)üd\ *n* : slavery

ses·a·me \'sesəmē\ *n* : East Indian annual herb or its seeds

ses·sion \'seshən\ *n* : meeting

set \'set\ *vb* **set; set·ting** 1 : cause to sit 2 : place 3 : settle, arrange, or adjust 4 : cause to be or do 5 : become fixed or solid 6 : sit on eggs to hatch them 7 : sink below the horizon — *adj* : settled — *n* 1 : group classed together 2 : setting for the scene of a play or film 3 : electronic apparatus 4 : collection of mathematical elements —**set forth** : begin a trip —**set off** *vb* : set forth —**set out** *vb* : begin a trip or undertaking —**set up** *vb* 1 : assemble or erect 2 : cause

set·back *n* : reverse

set·tee \se'tē\ *n* : bench or sofa

set·ter \'setər\ *n* : large long-coated hunting dog

set·ting \'setiŋ\ *n* : background or surroundings

set·tle \'setᵊl\ *vb* **-tled; -tling** 1 : come to rest 2 : sink gradually 3 : become established in a place or a home 4 : adjust or arrange 5 : calm 6 : dispose of (as by paying) 7 : decide or agree on —**set·tle·ment** \-mənt\ *n* —**set·tler** \'setlər, -ᵊlər\ *n*

sev·en \'sevən\ *n* : one more than 6 —**seven** *adj or pron* —**sev·enth** \-ənth\ *adj or adv or n*

sev·en·teen \,sevən'tēn\ *n* : one more than 16 —**seventeen** *adj or pron* —**sev·en·teenth** \-'tēnth\ *adj or n*

sev·en·ty \'sevəntē\ *n, pl* **-ties** : 7 times 10 —**sev·en·ti·eth** \-tēəth\ *adj or n* —**seventy** *adj or pron*

sev·er \'sevər\ *vb* **-ered; -er·ing** : cut off or apart —**sev·er·ance** \-(ə)rəns\ *n*

sev·er·al \'sev(ə)rəl\ *adj* 1 : distinct 2

: consisting of an indefinite but not large number —**sev·er·al·ly** \-ē\ adv

se·vere \sə'viər\ adj **-ver·er; -est** 1 : allowing no evasion or compromise 2 : restrained or unadorned 3 : painful or distressing 4 : hard to endure —**se·vere·ly** adv —**se·ver·i·ty** \-'verətē\ n

sew \'sō\ vb **sewed; sewn** \'sōn\ or **sewed; sew·ing** : fasten by stitches made with thread and needle —**sew·ing** n

sew·age \'süij\ n : liquid household waste

¹**sew·er** \'sō(ə)r\ n : one that sews

²**sew·er** \'süər\ n : pipe or channel to carry off waste matter

sex \'seks\ n 1 : either of 2 divisions of organisms distinguished respectively as male and female or the qualities which differentiate them 2 : copulation —**sexed** \'sekst\ adj —**sex·less** adj —**sex·u·al** \'seksh(əw)əl\ adj —**sex·u·al·i·ty** \,sekshə'walətē\ n —**sex·u·al·ly** adv —**sexy** adj

sex·ism \'sek,sizəm\ n : discrimination based on sex and esp. against women —**sex·ist** \'seksəst\ adj or n

sex·tant \'sekstənt\ n : instrument for navigation

sex·tet \sek'stet\ n 1 : music for 6 performers 2 : group of 6

sex·ton \'sekstən\ n : church caretaker

shab·by \'shabē\ adj **-bi·er; -est** 1 : worn and faded 2 : dressed in worn clothes 3 : not generous or fair —**shab·bi·ly** adv —**shab·bi·ness** n

shack \'shak\ n : hut

shack·le \'shakəl\ n : metal device to bind legs or arms ~ vb **-led; -ling** : fasten with shackles

shad \'shad\ n : Atlantic food fish

shade \'shād\ n 1 : space sheltered from the light esp. of the sun 2 : gradation of color 3 : small difference 4 : something that shades ~ vb **shad·ed; shad·ing** : shelter from light and heat —**shady** adj

shad·ow \'shadō\ n 1 : shade cast upon a surface by something blocking light 2 : trace 3 : gloomy influence ~ vb 1 : cast a shadow 2 : follow closely —**shad·owy** adj

shaft \'shaft\ n 1 : long slender cylindrical part 2 : deep vertical opening (as of a mine)

shag \'shag\ n : shaggy tangled mat

shag·gy \'shagē\ adj **-gi·er; -est** 1 : covered with long hair or wool 2 : not neat and combed

shah \'shä, 'sho\ n : monarch in Iran

shake \'shāk\ vb **shook** \'shuk\ **shaken** \'shākən\; **shak·ing** 1 : move or cause to move quickly back and forth 2 : distress 3 : clasp (hands) as friendly gesture —**shake** n —**shak·er** \-ər\ n

shake-up n : reorganization

shaky \'shākē\ adj **shak·i·er; -est** : not sound, stable, or reliable —**shak·i·ly** adv —**shak·i·ness** n

shale \'shāl\ n : stratified rock

shall \shəl, (')shal\ vb, past **should** \shəd, (')shùd\; pres sing & pl **shall** —used as an auxiliary to express a command, futurity, or determination

shal·low \'shalō\ adj 1 : not deep 2 : not intellectually profound

shal·lows \-ōz\ n pl : area of shallow water

sham \'sham\ adj or n or vb : fake

sham·ble \'shambəl\ vb **-bled; -bling** : shuffle along —**sham·ble** n

sham·bles \'shambəlz\ n : state of disorder

shame \'shām\ n 1 : distress over guilt or disgrace 2 : cause of shame or regret ~ vb **shamed; sham·ing** 1 : make ashamed 2 : disgrace —**shame·ful** \-fəl\ adj —**shame·ful·ly** \-ē\ adv —**shame·less** adj —**shame·less·ly** adv

shame·faced \'shām'fāst\ adj : ashamed

sham·poo \sham'pü\ vb : wash one's hair ~ n, pl **-poos** : act of or preparation used in shampooing

sham·rock \'sham,räk\ n : plant with 3-lobed leaves

shank \'shank\ n : part of the leg between the knee and ankle

shan·ty \'shantē\ n, pl **-ties** : hut

shape \'shāp\ vb **shaped; shap·ing** : form esp. in a particular structure or appearance ~ n 1 : distinctive appearance or arrangement of parts 2 : condition —**shape·less** \-ləs\ adj —**shape·li·ness** n —**shape·ly** adj

shard \'shärd\ n : broken piece

share \'sheər\ n 1 : portion belonging to one 2 : interest in a company's stock ~ vb **shared; shar·ing** : divide or use with others —**share·hold·er** n —**shar·er** n

share·crop·per \-,kräpər\ n : farmer who works another's land in return for a share of the crop —**share·crop** vb

shark \'shärk\ n : voracious sea fish

sharp \'shärp\ adj 1 : having a good point or cutting edge 2 : alert, clever, or sarcastic 3 : vigorous or fierce 4

: having prominent angles or a sudden change in direction **5** : distinct **6** : higher than the true pitch — *adv* : exactly ~ *n* : sharp note —**sharp·ly** *adv* —**sharp·ness** *n*

sharp·en \\'shärpən\\ *vb* : make sharp —**sharp·en·er** \\'shärp(ə)nər\\ *n*

sharp·shoot·er *n* : expert marksman —**sharp·shoot·ing** *n*

shat·ter \\'shatər\\ *vb* : smash or burst into fragments

shave \\'shāv\\ *vb* **shaved; shaved** or **shav·en** \\'shāvən\\; **shav·ing 1** : cut off with a razor **2** : make bare by cutting the hair from **3** : slice very thin ~ *n* : act or instance of shaving —**shav·er** *n*

shawl \\'shól\\ *n* : loose covering for the head or shoulders

she \\(')shē\\ *pron* : that female one

sheaf \\'shēf\\ *n, pl* **sheaves** \\'shēvz\\ : bundle esp. of grain stalks

shear \\'shir\\ *vb* **sheared; sheared** or **shorn** \\'shórn\\; **shear·ing 1** : trim wool from **2** : cut off with scissorlike action

shears \\'shirz\\ *n pl* : cutting tool with 2 blades fastened so that the edges slide by each other

sheath \\'shēth\\ *n, pl* **sheaths** \\'shēthz, 'shēths\\ : covering (as for a blade)

sheathe \\'shēth\\ *vb* **sheathed; sheath·ing** : put into a sheath

shed \\'shed\\ *vb* **shed; shed·ding 1** : give off (as tears or hair) **2** : cause to flow or diffuse ~ *n* : small storage building

sheen \\'shēn\\ *n* : subdued luster

sheep \\'shēp\\ *n, pl* **sheep** : domesticated mammal covered with wool —**sheep·skin** *n*

sheep·ish \\'shēpish\\ *adj* : embarrassed by awareness of a fault

sheer \\'shir\\ *adj* **1** : pure **2** : very steep **3** : very thin or transparent —**sheer** *adv*

sheet \\'shēt\\ *n* : broad flat piece (as of cloth or paper)

sheikh, sheik \\'shēk, 'shāk\\ *n* : Arab chief —**sheikh·dom, sheik·dom** \\-dəm\\ *n*

shelf \\'shelf\\ *n, pl* **shelves** \\'shelvz\\ **1** : flat narrow structure used for storage or display **2** : sandbank or rock ledge

shell \\'shel\\ *n* **1** : hard or tough outer covering **2** : case holding explosive powder and projectile for a weapon **3** : light racing boat with oars ~ *vb* **1** : remove the shell of **2** : bombard —**shelled** \\'sheld\\ *adj* —**shell·er** *n*

shel·lac \\shə'lak\\ *n* : varnish ~ *vb* -lacked; -lack·ing 1 : coat with shellac 2 : defeat —**shel·lack·ing** *n*

shell·fish *n* : water animal with a shell

shel·ter \\'sheltər\\ *n* : something that gives protection ~ *vb* : give refuge to

shelve \\'shelv\\ *vb* **shelved; shelv·ing 1** : place or store on shelves **2** : dismiss or put aside

she·nan·i·gans \\shə'nanigənz\\ *n pl* : mischievous or deceitful conduct

shep·herd \\'shepərd\\ *n* : one that tends sheep ~ *vb* : act as a shepherd or guardian —**shep·herd·ess** \\-əs\\ *n*

sher·bet \\'shərbət\\, **sher·bert** \\-bərt\\ *n* : fruit-flavored frozen dessert

sher·iff \\'sherəf\\ *n* : county law officer

sher·ry \\'sherē\\ *n, pl* -ries : type of wine

shield \\'shēld\\ *n* **1** : broad piece of armor carried on the arm **2** : something that protects —**shield** *vb*

shier *comparative of* SHY

shiest *superlative of* SHY

shift \\'shift\\ *vb* **1** : change place, position, or direction **2** : get by ~ *n* **1** : transfer **2** : scheduled work period **3** : loose-fitting dress

shift·less \\'shift(l)əs\\ *adj* : lazy

shifty \\'shiftē\\ *adj* **shift·i·er; -est** : tricky or untrustworthy

shil·le·lagh \\shə'lālē\\ *n* : club or stick

shil·ling \\'shilin\\ *n* : former British coin

shil·ly-shally \\'shilē,shalē\\ *vb* -shal-lied; -shally·ing 1 : hesitate 2 : dawdle

shim·mer \\'shimər\\ *vb or n* : glimmer

shin \\'shin\\ *n* : front part of the leg below the knee ~ *vb* **-nn-** : climb by sliding the body close along

shine \\'shin\\ *vb* **shone** \\-shōn\\ or **shined; shin·ing 1** : give off or cause to give off light **2** : be outstanding **3** : polish ~ *n* : brilliance

shin·gle \\'shingəl\\ *n* **1** : small thin piece used in covering roofs or exterior walls ~ *vb* **-gled; -gling** : cover with shingles

shin·gles \\'shingəlz\\ *n pl* : acute inflammation of spinal nerves

shin·ny \\'shinē\\ *vb* -nied; -ny·ing : shin

shiny \\'shinē\\ *adj* **shin·i·er; -est** : bright or polished

ship \\'ship\\ *n* **1** : large oceangoing vessel **2** : aircraft or spacecraft ~ *vb* -pp- **1** : put on a ship **2** : transport by carrier —**ship·board** *n* —**ship·build·er** *n* —**ship·per** *n* —**ship·yard** *n*

-ship \\,ship\\ *n suffix* **1** : state, condition, or quality **2** : rank or profession **3** : skill **4** : something showing a state or quality

ship·ment \-mənt\ *n* : goods shipped

ship·ping \'shipiŋ\ *n* 1 : ships 2 : transportation of goods

ship·shape *adj* : tidy

ship·wreck *n* : destruction or loss of a ship —**shipwreck** *vb*

shire \'shī(ə)r, *in place-name compounds* ,shiər, shər\ *n* : British county

shirk \'shərk\ *vb* : evade —**shirk·er** *n*

shirr \'shər\ *vb* 1 : gather (cloth) by drawing up parallel lines of stitches 2 : bake (eggs) in a dish

shirt \'shərt\ *n* : garment for covering the torso —**shirt·less** *adj*

shiv·er \'shivər\ *vb* : tremble —**shiver** *n* —**shiv·ery** *adj*

shoal \'shōl\ *n* : shallow place (as in a river)

¹shock \'shäk\ *n* : pile of sheaves set up in the field

²shock *n* 1 : forceful impact 2 : violent mental or emotional disturbance 3 : effect of a charge of electricity 4 : depression of the vital bodily processes ~ *vb* 1 : strike with surprise, horror, or disgust 2 : subject to an electrical shock —**shock·proof** *adj*

³shock *n* : bushy mass (as of hair)

shod·dy \'shädē\ *adj* **-di·er; -est** : cheaply or poorly made or done —**shod·di·ly** \'shäd²lē\ *adv* —**shod·di·ness** *n*

shoe \'shü\ *n* 1 : covering for the human foot 2 : horseshoe ~ *vb* **shod** \'shäd\; **shoe·ing** : put horseshoes on —**shoe·lace** *n* —**shoe·mak·er** *n*

shone *past of* SHINE

shook *past of* SHAKE

shoot \'shüt\ *vb* **shot** \'shät\; **shoot·ing** 1 : propel (as an arrow or bullet) 2 : wound or kill with a missile 3 : discharge (a weapon) 4 : drive (as a ball) at a goal 5 : photograph ~ *n* : new plant growth —**shoot·er** *n*

shop \'shäp\ *n* : place where things are made or sold ~ *vb* **-pp-** : visit stores —**shop·keep·er** *n* —**shop·per** *n*

shop·lift *vb* : steal goods from a store —**shop·lift·er** \-,liftər\ *n*

¹shore \'shōr\ *n* : land along the edge of water —**shore·less** *adj*

²shore *vb* **shored; shor·ing** : prop up ~ *n* : something that props

shore·bird *n* : bird of the seashore

shorn *past part of* SHEAR

short \'shört\ *adj* 1 : not long or tall or extending far 2 : brief in time 3 : curt 4 : not having or being enough ~ *adv* : curtly ~ *n* 1 *pl* : short drawers or trousers 2 : short circuit —

short·en \-³n\ *vb* —**short·ly** *adv* —**short·ness** *n*

short·age \'shörtij\ *n* : deficiency

short·cake *n* : dessert of biscuit with sweetened fruit

short·change *vb* : cheat esp. by giving too little change

short circuit : abnormal electric connection —**short-circuit** *vb*

short·com·ing *n* : failing

short·cut \-,kət\ *n* 1 : more direct route than that usu. taken 2 : quicker way of doing something

short·hand *n* : method of speed writing

short-lived \'shört'livd, -,livd\ *adj* : of short life or duration

short·sight·ed *adj* : lacking foresight

shot \'shät\ *n* 1 : act of shooting 2 : attempt (as at making a goal) 3 : small pellets forming a charge 4 : range or reach 5 : photograph 6 : injection of medicine 7 : portion (as of liquor) taken at one time —**shot·gun** *n*

should \shəd, (')shùd\ *past of* SHALL —used as an auxiliary to express condition, obligation, or probability

shoul·der \'shōldər\ *n* 1 : part of the body where the arm joins the trunk 2 : part that projects or lies to the side ~ *vb* : push with or take upon the shoulder

shoulder blade *n* : the flat triangular bone at the back of the shoulder

shout \'shaut\ *vb* : give voice loudly —**shout** *n*

shove \'shəv\ *vb* **shoved; shov·ing** : push along or away —**shove** *n*

shov·el \'shəvəl\ *n* : broad tool for digging or lifting ~ *vb* **-eled** *or* **-elled; -el·ing** *or* **-el·ling** : take up or dig with a shovel

show \'shō\ *vb* **showed** \'shōd\; **shown** \'shōn\ *or* **showed; show·ing** 1 : present to view 2 : reveal or demonstrate 3 : indicate 4 : conduct or escort 5 : act in (a specified manner) 6 : appear or be noticeable ~ *n* 1 : demonstrative display 2 : spectacle 3 : theatrical, radio, or television program —**show·case** *n* —**show off** *vb* 1 : display proudly 2 : act so as to attract attention — **show up** *vb* : arrive

show·down *n* : final settlement of a contested issue

show·er \'shaù(ə)r\ *n* 1 : brief fall of rain 2 : bath in which water sprinkles down on the person 3 : party at which someone gets gifts ~ *vb* 1 : fall in a shower 2 : bathe in a shower —**show·ery** *adj*

showy \'shōē\ *adj* **show·i·er; -est** : very noticeable or overly elaborate — **show·i·ly** *adv* — **show·i·ness** *n*

shrap·nel \'shrapᵊl\ *n, pl* **shrapnel** : metal fragments of a bomb

shred \'shred\ *n* : narrow strip cut or torn off ~ *vb* **-dd-** : cut or tear into shreds

shrew \'shrü\ *n* **1** : scolding woman **2** : mouselike mammal — **shrew·ish** \-ish\ *adj*

shrewd \'shrüd\ *adj* : showing cleverness or good judgment — **shrewd·ly** *adv* — **shrewd·ness** *n*

shriek \'shrēk\ *n* : shrill cry — **shriek** *vb*

shrill \'shril\ *adj* : piercing and high-pitched — **shril·ly** *adv*

shrimp \'shrimp\ *n* : small sea crustacean

shrine \'shrīn\ *n* **1** : tomb of a saint **2** : hallowed place

shrink \'shriŋk\ *vb* **shrank** \'shraŋk\; **shrunk** \'shrəŋk\ *or* **shrunk·en** \'shrəŋkən\ **1** : draw back or away **2** : become smaller — **shrink·able** *adj*

shrink·age \'shriŋkij\ *n* : amount something shrinks

shriv·el \'shrivəl\ *vb* **-eled** *or* **-elled; -el·ing** *or* **-el·ling** : shrink or wither into wrinkles

shroud \'shraud\ *n* **1** : cloth put over a corpse **2** : cover or screen ~ *vb* : veil or screen from view

shrub \'shrəb\ *n* : low woody plant — **shrub·by** *adj*

shrub·bery \'shrəb(ə)rē\ *n, pl* **-ber·ies** : growth of shrubs

shrug \'shrəg\ *vb* **-gg-** : hunch the shoulders up in doubt, indifference, or dislike — **shrug** *n*

shuck \'shək\ *vb* : strip of a shell or husk — **shuck** *n*

shud·der \'shədər\ *vb* : tremble — **shudder** *n*

shuf·fle \'shəfəl\ *vb* **-fled; -fling 1** : mix together **2** : walk with a sliding movement — **shuffle** *n*

shuf·fle·board \'shəfəl,bōrd\ *n* : game of sliding disks into a scoring area

shun \'shən\ *vb* **-nn-** : keep away from

shunt \'shənt\ *vb* : turn off to one side

shut \'shət\ *vb* **shut; shut·ting 1** : bar passage into or through (as by moving a lid or door) **2** : suspend activity — **shut out** : exclude — **shut up** *vb* : stop or cause to stop talking

shut-in *n* : invalid

shut·ter \'shətər\ *n* **1** : movable cover for a window **2** : camera part that exposes film

shut·tle \'shətᵊl\ *n* **1** : part of a weaving

machine that carries thread back and forth **2** : vehicle traveling back and forth over a short route ~ *vb* **-tled; -tling** : move back and forth frequently

shut·tle·cock \'shətᵊl,käk\ *n* : feathered object in badminton

shy \'shī\ *adj* **shi·er** *or* **shy·er** \'shī(ə)r\; **shi·est** *or* **shy·est** \'shīəst\ **1** : sensitive and hesitant in dealing with others **2** : wary **3** : lacking ~ *vb* **shied; shy·ing** : move back from fright — **shy·ly** *adv* — **shy·ness** *n*

sib·i·lant \'sibələnt\ *adj* : having the sound of the *s* or the *sh* in *sash* — **sibilant** *n*

sib·ling \'sibliŋ\ *n* : brother or sister

sick \'sik\ *adj* **1** : not in good health **2** : nauseated **3** : relating to or meant for the sick — **sick·bed** *n* — **sick·en** \-ən\ *vb* — **sick·ly** *adj* — **sick·ness** *n*

sick·le \'sikəl\ *n* : curved short-handled blade

side \'sīd\ *n* **1** : part to left or right of an object or the torso **2** : edge or surface away from the center or at an angle to top and bottom or ends **3** : contrasting or opposing position or group — **sid·ed** *adj*

side·board *n* : piece of dining-room furniture for table service

side·burns \-,bərnz\ *n pl* : whiskers in front of the ears

side·long \-,sīd,lȯŋ\ *adv or adj* : to or along the side

si·de·re·al \sī'dirēəl, sə-\ *adj* : measured by the apparent motion of fixed stars

side·show *n* : minor show at a circus

side·step *vb* **1** : step aside **2** : avoid

side·swipe \-,swīp\ *vb* : strike with a glancing blow — **sideswipe** *n*

side·track *vb* : lead aside or astray

side·walk *n* : paved walk at the side of a road

side·ways \-,wāz\ *adv or adj* **1** : to or from the side **2** : with one side to the front

sid·ing \'sīdiŋ\ *n* **1** : short railroad track **2** : material for covering the outside of a building

si·dle \'sīdᵊl\ *vb* **-dled; -dling** : move sideways or unobtrusively

siege \'sēj\ *n* : persistent attack (as on a fortified place)

si·es·ta \sē'estə\ *n* : midday nap

sieve \'siv\ *n* : utensil with holes to separate particles

sift \'sift\ *vb* **1** : pass through a sieve **2** : examine carefully — **sift·er** *n*

sigh \'sī\ *n* : audible release of the

breath (as to express weariness) —
sigh *vb*

sight \\'sīt\\ *n* **1** : something seen or
worth seeing **2** : process, power, or
range of seeing **3** : device used in
aiming **4** : view or glimpse ~ *vb* : get
sight of —**sight·ed** *adj* —**sight·less**
—**sight-see·ing** *adj* —**sight·seer**
\\-,sēər\\ *n*

sign \\'sīn\\ *n* **1** : symbol **2** : gesture
expressing a command or thought **3**
: public notice to advertise or warn
4 : trace ~ *vb* **1** : mark with or make
a sign **2** : write one's name on —**sign·**
er *n*

sig·nal \\'signᵊl\\ *n* **1** : sign of command
or warning **2** : electronic transmission ~ *vb* **-naled** *or* **-nalled; -nal·ing**
or **-nal·ling** : communicate or notify
by signals

sig·na·to·ry \\'signə,tōrē\\ *n, pl* **-ries**
: person or government that signs
jointly with others

sig·na·ture \\'signə,chùr\\ *n* : one's
name written by oneself

sig·net \\'signət\\ *n* : small seal

sig·nif·i·cance \\signifikəns\\ *n* **1**
: meaning **2** : importance —**sig·nif·i·**
cant \\-kənt\\ *adj* —**sig·nif·i·cant·ly**
adv

sig·ni·fy \\'signə,fī\\ *vb* **-fied; -fy·ing 1**
: show by a sign **2** : mean —**sig·ni·fi·**
ca·tion \\,signəfə'kāshən\\ *n*

si·lence \\'sīləns\\ *n* : state of being without sound ~ *vb* **-lenced; -lenc·**
ing : keep from making noise or
sound —**si·lenc·er** *n*

si·lent \\'sīlənt\\ *adj* : having or producing no sound —**si·lent·ly** *adv*

sil·hou·ette \\,silə'wet\\ *n* : outline filled
in usu. with black —**etted; -ett·ing**
: represent by a silhouette

sil·i·ca \\'silikə\\ *n* : mineral found as
quartz and opal

sil·i·con \\'silikən, 'silə,kän\\ *n* : nonmetallic chemical element

silk \\'silk\\ *n* **1** : fine strong lustrous
protein fiber from moth larvae (**silk-**
worms \\-,wərmz\\) **2** : thread or cloth
made from silk —**silk·en** \\'silkən\\
adj —**silky** *adj*

sill \\'sil\\ *n* : bottom part of a window
frame or a doorway

sil·ly \\'silē\\ *adj* **sil·li·er; -est** : foolish
or stupid —**sil·li·ness** *n*

si·lo \\'sīlō\\ *n, pl* **-los** : building for stor-
ing animal feed

silt \\'silt\\ *n* : fine earth carried by rivers ~ *vb* : obstruct or cover with silt

sil·ver \\'silvər\\ *n* **1** : white ductile metallic chemical element **2** : silver-

ware ~ *adj* : having the color of silver —**sil·very** *adj*

sil·ver·ware \\-,waər\\ *n* : eating and
serving utensils

sim·i·lar \\'simələr\\ *adj* : resembling
each other in some ways —**sim·i·lar·**
i·ty \\,simə'larətē\\ *n* —**sim·i·lar·ly**
\\'simələrlē\\ *adv*

sim·i·le \\'simə,)lē\\ *n* : comparison of
unlike things using *like* or *as*

sim·mer \\'simər\\ *vb* : stew gently

sim·per \\'simpər\\ *vb* : give a silly smile
—**simper** *n*

sim·ple \\'simpəl\\ *adj* **-pler; -plest 1**
: not combined **2** : not other than **3**
: not complex or fancy **4** : naive —
sim·ple·ness *n* —**sim·ply** \\-plē\\ *adv*

sim·ple·ton \\'simpəltən\\ *n* : fool

sim·plic·i·ty \\sim'plisətē\\ *n* : state or
fact of being simple

sim·pli·fy \\'simplə,fī\\ *vb* **-fied; -fy·ing**
: make easier —**sim·pli·fi·ca·tion**
\\,simpləfə'kāshən\\ *n*

sim·u·late \\'simyə,lāt\\ *vb* **-lat·ed; -lat·**
ing : create the effect or appearance
of —**sim·u·la·tion** \\,simyə'lāshən\\ *n*

si·mul·ta·ne·ous \\,sīməl'tānēəs\\ *adj*
: occurring or operating at the same
time —**si·mul·ta·ne·ous·ly** *adv* —**si·**
mul·ta·ne·ous·ness *n*

sin \\'sin\\ *n* : offense against God — *vb*
-nn- : commit a sin —**sin·ful** \\-fəl\\
adj —**sin·less** *adj* —**sin·ner** *n*

since \\(')sins\\ *adv* **1** : from a past time
until now **2** : backward in time ~
prep **1** : in the period after **2** : con-
tinuously from ~ *conj* **1** : from the
time when **2** : because

sin·cere \\sin'siər\\ *adj* **-cer·er; -cer·est**
: genuine or honest —**sin·cere·ly** *adv*
—**sin·cer·i·ty** \\-'serətē\\ *n*

si·ne·cure \\'sīni,kyùər, 'sini-\\ *n*
: well-paid job that requires little
work

sin·ew \\'sinyü\\ *n* **1** : tendon **2** : physical
strength —**sin·ewy** *adj*

sing \\'siŋ\\ *vb* **sang** \\'saŋ\\ *or* **sung**
\\'səŋ\\; **sung; sing·ing** : produce
musical tones with the voice —**sing·**
er *n*

singe \\'sinj\\ *vb* **singed; singe·ing**
: scorch lightly

sin·gle \\'siŋgəl\\ *adj* **1** : one only **2**
: unmarried *n* : separate one —**sin·**
gle·ness *n* —**sin·gly** \\-glē\\ *adv* —**sin·**
gle out *vb* : select or set aside

sin·gu·lar \\'siŋgyələr\\ *adj* **1** : relating
to a word form denoting one **2** : outstanding or superior **3** : queer —**sin·**
gular *n* —**sin·gu·lar·i·ty** \\,siŋgyə-
'larətē\\ *n* —**sin·gu·lar·ly** \\'siŋgyə-
lərlē\\ *adv*

sin·is·ter \'sinəstər\ *adj* : threatening evil

sink \'siŋk\ *vb* **sank** \'saŋk\ *or* **sunk** \'səŋk\; **sunk; sink·ing 1** : submerge or descend **2** : grow worse **3** : make by digging or boring **4** : invest ~ *n* : basin with a drain

sink·er \'siŋkər\ *n* : weight to sink a fishing line

sin·u·ous \'sinyəwəs\ *adj* : winding in and out —**sin·u·os·i·ty** \,sinyə-'wäsətē\ *n* —**sin·u·ous·ly** *adv*

si·nus \'sīnəs\ *n* : skull cavity connecting with the nostrils

sip \'sip\ *vb* **-pp-** : drink in small quantities —**sip** *n*

si·phon \'sīfən\ *n* : tube that draws liquid by suction —**siphon** *vb*

sir \(')sər\ *n* **1** —used before the first name of a knight or baronet **2** —used in addressing a man without using his name

sire \'sī(ə)r\ *n* : father ~ *vb* **sired; sir·ing** : beget

si·ren \'sīrən\ *n* **1** : seductive woman **2** : wailing warning whistle —**siren** *adj*

sir·loin \'sər,loin\ *n* : cut of beef

sirup *var of* SYRUP

si·sal \'sīsəl, -zəl\ *n* : strong rope fiber

sis·sy \'sisē\ *n, pl* **-sies** : timid or effeminate boy

sis·ter \'sistər\ *n* : female sharing one or both parents with another person —**sis·ter·hood** \-,hůd\ *n* —**sis·ter·ly** *adj*

sis·ter-in-law \'sistə(r)ən,lȯ\ *n, pl* **sis·ters-in-law** \'sistə(r)z-...\ —**tərzən-**\ : sister of one's husband or wife or wife of one's brother

sit \'sit\ *vb* **sat** \'sat\; **sit·ting 1** : rest on the buttocks or haunches **2** : roost **3** : hold a session **4** : pose for a portrait **5** : have a location **6** : rest or fix in place —**sit·ter** *n*

site \'sīt\ *n* : place

sit·u·at·ed \'sicha,wātəd\ *adj* : located

sit·u·a·tion \,sicha'wäshən\ *n* **1** : location **2** : condition **3** : job

six \'siks\ *n* : one more than 5 —**six** *adj or pron* —**sixth** \'siksth\ *adj or adv or n*

six·teen \siks'tēn\ *n* : one more than 15 —**sixteen** *adj or pron* —**six·teenth** \-'tēnth\ *adj or n*

six·ty \'sikstē\ *n, pl* **sixties** : 6 times 10 —**six·ti·eth** \-ēəth\ *adj or n* —**sixty** *adj or pron*

siz·able, size·able \'sīzəbəl\ *adj* : quite large —**siz·ably** \-blē\ *adv*

size \'sīz\ *n* : measurement of the amount of space something takes up ~ *vb* : grade according to size

siz·zle \'sizəl\ *vb* **-zled; -zling** : fry with a hissing sound —**sizzle** *n*

skate \'skāt\ *n* **1** : metal runner on a shoe for gliding over ice **2** : roller skate —**skate** *vb* —**skat·er** *n*

skein \'skān\ *n* : loosely twisted quantity (as of yarn)

skel·e·ton \'skelət⁀n\ *n* : bony framework —**skel·e·tal** \-ət⁀l\ *adj*

skep·tic \'skeptik\ *n* : one who is critical or doubting —**skep·ti·cal** \-tikəl\ *adj* —**skep·ti·cism** \-tə,sizəm\ *n*

sketch \'skech\ *n* **1** : rough drawing **2** : small story or essay —**sketch** *vb* —**sketchy** *adj*

skew·er \'skyüər\ *n* : pin for holding roasting meat —**skewer** *vb*

ski \'skē\ *n, pl* **skis** : long strip bound to the shoe for gliding over snow or water —**ski** *vb* —**ski·er** *n*

skid \'skid\ *n* **1** : plank for supporting something or on which it slides **2** : act of skidding ~ *vb* **-dd-** : slide sideways

skiff \'skif\ *n* : small open boat

skill \'skil\ *n* : developed or learned ability —**skilled** \'skild\ *adj* —**skill·ful** \-fəl\ *adj* —**skill·ful·ly** *adv*

skil·let \'skilət\ *n* : pan for frying

skim \'skim\ *vb* **-mm- 1** : take off from the top of a liquid **2** : read or move over swiftly **3** : having the cream removed —**skim·mer** *n*

skimp \'skimp\ *vb* : give too little of something —**skimpy** *adj*

skin \'skin\ *n* **1** : outer layer of an animal body **2** : rind ~ *vb* **-nn-** : take the skin from —**skin·less** *adj* —**skinned** *adj* —**skin·tight** *adj*

skin·flint \'skin,flint\ *n* : stingy person

skin·ny \'skinē\ *adj* **-ni·er; -est** : very thin

skip \'skip\ *vb* **-pp- 1** : move with leaps **2** : read past or ignore —**skip** *n*

skip·per \'skipər\ *n* : ship's master —**skipper** *vb*

skir·mish \'skərmish\ *n* : minor combat —**skirmish** *vb*

skirt \'skərt\ *n* : garment or part of a garment that hangs below the waist ~ *vb* : pass around the edge of

skit \'skit\ *n* : brief usu. humorous story

skit·tish \'skitish\ *adj* : easily frightened

skulk \'skəlk\ *vb* : move furtively

skull \'skəl\ *n* : bony case that protects the brain

skunk \'skəŋk\ *n* : mammal that can forcibly eject an ill-smelling fluid

sky \'skī\ *n, pl* **skies** 1 : upper air 2 : heaven —**sky•ey** \'skīē\ *adj* —**sky•line** *n* —**sky•ward** \-wərd\ *adv or adj*

sky•lark \'skī,lärk\ *n* : European lark noted for its song

sky•light *n* : window in a roof or ceiling

sky•rock•et *n* : shooting firework ~ *vb* : rise suddenly

sky•scrap•er \-,skrāpər\ *n* : very tall building

slab \'slab\ *n* : thick slice

slack \'slak\ *adj* 1 : careless 2 : not taut 3 : not busy ~ *n* 1 : part hanging loose 2 *pl* : casual trousers —**slack•en** *vb* —**slack•ly** *adv* —**slack•ness** *n*

slag \'slag\ *n* : waste from melting of ores

slain *past part of* SLAY

slake \'slāk\ *vb* **slaked; slak•ing** : quench

slam \'slam\ *n* : heavy jarring impact ~ *vb* **-mm-** : shut, strike, or throw violently and loudly

slan•der \'slandər\ *n* : malicious gossip ~ *vb* : hurt (someone) with slander —**slan•der•er** *n* —**slan•der•ous** *adj*

slang \'slaŋ\ *n* : informal nonstandard vocabulary —**slang** *adj*

slant \'slant\ *vb* 1 : slope 2 : present with a special viewpoint ~ *n* : sloping direction, line, or plane

slap \'slap\ *vb* **-pp-** : strike sharply with the open hand —**slap** *n*

slash \'slash\ *vb* 1 : cut with sweeping strokes 2 : reduce sharply ~ *n* : gash

slat \'slat\ *n* : thin narrow flat strip

slate \'slāt\ *n* 1 : dense fine-grained layered rock 2 : roofing tile or writing tablet of slate 3 : list of candidates ~ *vb* **slat•ed; slat•ing** : designate

slat•tern \'slatərn\ *n* : untidy woman —**slat•tern•ly** *adj*

slaugh•ter \'slótər\ *n* 1 : butchering of livestock for market 2 : great and cruel destruction of lives ~ *vb* : commit slaughter upon —**slaugh•ter•house** *n*

slave \'slāv\ *n* : one owned and forced into service by another ~ *vb* **slaved; slav•ing** : work as or like a slave —**slave** \'slāv\ *adj* —**slav•ery** \'slāv(ə)rē\ *n*

sla•ver \'slavər, 'slāv-\ *vb or n* : slobber

slav•ish \'slāvish\ *adj* : of or like a slave —**slav•ish•ly** *adv*

slay \'slā\ *vb* **slew** \'slü\; **slain** \'slān\; **slay•ing** : kill —**slay•er** *n*

slea•zy \'slēzē, 'slā-\ *adj* **-zi•er; -est** : shabby or flimsy

sled \'sled\ *n* : vehicle on runners —**sled** *vb*

¹**sledge** \'slej\ *n* : sledgehammer

²**sledge** *n* : heavy sled

sledge•ham•mer *n* : heavy long-handled hammer —**sledgehammer** *adj or vb*

sleek \'slēk\ *adj* : smooth or glossy —**sleek** *vb*

sleep \'slēp\ *n* : natural suspension of consciousness ~ *vb* **slept** \'slept\; **sleep•ing** : rest in a state of sleep —**sleep•er** *n* —**sleep•less** *adj*

sleep•walk•er *n* : one who walks during sleep

sleepy \'slēpē\ *adj* **sleep•i•er; -est** 1 : ready for sleep 2 : quietly inactive —**sleep•i•ly** \'slēpəlē\ *adv* —**sleep•i•ness** \-pēnəs\ *n*

sleet \'slēt\ *n* : frozen rain —**sleet** *vb* —**sleety** *adj*

sleeve \'slēv\ *n* : part of a garment for the arm —**sleeve•less** *adj*

sleigh \'slā\ *n* : horse-drawn sled with seats ~ *vb* : drive or ride in a sleigh

sleight of hand \'slīt-\ : skillful manual manipulation or a trick requiring it

slen•der \'slendər\ *adj* 1 : thin esp. in physique 2 : scanty

sleuth \'slüth\ *n* : detective

slew \'slü\ *past of* SLAY

slice \'slīs\ *n* : thin flat piece ~ *vb* **sliced; slic•ing** : cut a slice from

slick \'slik\ *adj* 1 : very smooth 2 : clever —**slick** *vb*

slick•er \'slikər\ *n* : waterproof raincoat

slide \'slīd\ *vb* **slid** \'slid\; **slid•ing** \'slīdiŋ\ : move smoothly along a surface ~ *n* 1 : act of sliding 2 : surface on which something slides 3 : transparent picture for projection

slier *comparative of* SLY

sliest *superlative of* SLY

slight \'slīt\ *adj* 1 : slender 2 : frail 3 : small in degree ~ *vb* 1 : ignore or treat as unimportant —**slight** *n* —**slight•ly** *adv*

slim \'slim\ *adj* **-mm-** 1 : slender 2 : scanty ~ *vb* **-mm-** : make or become slender

slime \'slīm\ *n* : dirty slippery film (as on water) —**slimy** *adj*

sling \'sliŋ\ *vb* **slung** \'sləŋ\; **sling•ing** : hurl with or as if with a sling ~ *n* 1 : strap for swinging and hurling stones 2 : looped strap or bandage to lift or support

sling•shot *n* : forked stick with elastic bands for shooting small stones or shot

slink \'sliŋk\ *vb* **slunk** \'sləŋk\; **slink•ing** : move stealthily or sinuously —**slinky** *adj*

¹**slip** \'slip\ *vb* **-pp-** 1 : escape quietly

or secretly **2** : slide along smoothly **3** : make a mistake **4** : to pass without being noticed or done **5** : fall off from a standard ~ *n* **1** : ship's berth **2** : sudden mishap **3** : mistake **4** : woman's undergarment

²slip *n* **1** : plant shoot **2** : small strip (as of paper)

slip·per \'slipər\ *n* : shoe that slips on easily

slip·pery \'slip(ə)rē\ *adj* **-peri·er**; **-est 1** : slick enough to slide on **2** : tricky —**slip·peri·ness** *n*

slip·shod \'slip'shäd\ *adj* : careless

slit \'slit\ *vb* **slit**; **slit·ting** : make a slit in ~ *n* : long narrow cut

slith·er \'slithər\ *vb* : glide along like a snake —**slith·ery** *adj*

sliv·er \'slivər\ *n* : splinter

slob \'släb\ *n* : untidy person

slob·ber \'släbər\ *vb* : dribble saliva —**slobber** *n*

slo·gan \'slōgən\ *n* : word or phrase expressing the aim of a cause

sloop \'slüp\ *n* : one-masted sailboat

slop \'släp\ *n* : food waste for animal feed ~ *vb* **-pp-** : spill

slope \'slōp\ *vb* **sloped**; **slop·ing** : deviate from the vertical or horizontal ~ *n* : upward or downward slant

slop·py \'släpē\ *adj* **-pi·er**; **-est 1** : muddy **2** : untidy

slot \'slät\ *n* : narrow opening

sloth \'slōth, 'slòth\ *n*, *pl* **sloths** \with ths *or* thz\ **1** : laziness **2** : slow-moving mammal —**sloth·ful** *adj*

slouch \'slauch\ *n* **1** : drooping posture **2** : lazy or incompetent person ~ *vb* : walk or stand with a slouch

¹slough \'slü\ *n* : swamp or muddy place

²slough \'sləf\, **sluff** *vb* : cast off (a skin)

slov·en·ly \'sləvənlē\ *adj* : untidy

slow \'slō\ *adj* **1** : sluggish or stupid **2** : moving, working, or happening at less than the usual speed ~ *vb* **1** : make slow **2** : go slower —**slow** *adv* —**slow·ly** *adv* —**slow·ness** *n*

sludge \'sləj\ *n* : slushy mass (as of treated sewage)

slug \'sləg\ *n* **1** : mollusk related to the snails **2** : bullet **3** : metal disk ~ *vb* **-gg-** : strike forcibly —**slug·ger** *n*

slug·gish \'sləgish\ *adj* : slow in movement or flow —**slug·gish·ly** *adv* —**slug·gish·ness** *n*

sluice \'slüs\ *n* : channel for water ~ *vb* **sluiced**; **sluic·ing** : wash in running water

slum \'sləm\ *n* : thickly populated area marked by poverty

slum·ber \'sləmbər\ *vb or n* : sleep

slump \'sləmp\ *vb* **1** : sink suddenly **2** : slouch —**slump** *n*

slung *past of* SLING

slunk *past of* SLINK

¹slur \'slər\ *vb* **-rr-** : run (words or notes) together —**slur** *n*

²slur *n* : malicious or insulting remark —**slur** *vb*

slurp \'slərp\ *vb* : eat or drink noisily —**slurp** *n*

slush \'sləsh\ *n* : partly melted snow —**slushy** *adj*

slut \'slət\ *n* **1** : untidy woman **2** : prostitute —**slut·tish** \'slətish\ *adj*

sly \'slī\ *adj* **sli·er** \'slī(ə)r\; **sli·est** \'slīəst\ : given to or showing secrecy and deception —**sly·ly** *adv* —**sly·ness** *n*

¹smack \'smak\ *n* : characteristic flavor ~ *vb* : have a taste or hint

²smack *vb* **1** : move (the lips) so as to make a sharp noise **2** : kiss or slap with a loud noise ~ *n* **1** : sharp noise made by the lips **2** : noisy slap

³smack *adv* : squarely and sharply

⁴smack *n* : fishing ship

small \'smòl\ *adj* **1** : little in size or amount **2** : few in number **3** : trivial —**small·ish** *adj* —**small·ness** *n*

small·pox \'smòl,päks\ *n* : contagious virus disease marked by fever and eruption

smart \'smärt\ *vb* **1** : cause or feel stinging pain **2** : endure distress ~ *adj* **1** : intelligent or resourceful **2** : stylish —**smart** *n* —**smart·ly** *adv* —**smart·ness** *n*

smash \'smash\ *vb* : break or be broken into pieces ~ *n* **1** : smashing blow **2** : act or sound of smashing

smat·ter·ing \'smatəriŋ\ *n* **1** : superficial knowledge **2** : small scattered number or amount

smear \'smir\ *n* : greasy stain ~ *vb* **1** : spread (something sticky) **2** : smudge **3** : slander

smell \'smel\ *vb* **smelled** \'smeld\ *or* **smelt** \'smelt\; **smell·ing 1** : perceive the odor of **2** : have or give off an odor ~ *n* **1** : sense by which one perceives odor **2** : odor —**smelly** *adj*

¹smelt \'smelt\ *n*, *pl* **smelts** *or* **smelt** : small food fish

²smelt *vb* : melt or fuse (ore) in order to separate the metal —**smelt·er** *n*

smile \'smīl\ *n* : facial expression with the mouth turned up usu. to show pleasure —**smile** *vb*

smirk \'smərk\ *vb* : wear a conceited smile —**smirk** *n*

smite \'smīt\ *vb* **smote** \'smōt\; **smit-**

ten \'smit⁹n\ *or* smote; smit·ing \'smītiŋ\ 1 : strike heavily or kill 2 : affect strongly

smith \'smith\ *n* : worker in metals and esp. a blacksmith

smithy \'smithē\ *n, pl* smith·ies : a smith's workshop

smock \'smäk\ *n* : loose dress or protective coat

smog \'smäg, 'smòg\ *n* : fog and smoke —smog·gy *adj*

smoke \'smōk\ *n* : sooty gas from burning ~ *vb* smoked; smok·ing 1 : give off smoke 2 : inhale the fumes of burning tobacco 3 : cure (as meat) with smoke —smoke·less *adj* —smok·er *n* —smoky *adj*

smoke·stack *n* : chimney through which smoke is discharged

smol·der, smoul·der \'smōldər\ *vb* 1 : burn and smoke without flame 2 : be suppressed but active —smolder *n*

smooth \'smüth\ *adj* 1 : having a surface without irregularities 2 : not jarring or jolting ~ *vb* : make smooth —smooth·ly *adv* —smooth·ness *n*

smor·gas·bord \'smòrgəs,bòrd\ *n* : buffet consisting of many foods

smoth·er \'sməthər\ *vb* 1 : kill by depriving of air 2 : cover thickly

smudge \'sməj\ *vb* smudged; smudg·ing : soil or blur by rubbing ~ *n* 1 : thick smoke 2 : dirty spot

smug \'sməg\ *adj* -gg- : content in one's own virtue or accomplishment —smug·ly *adv* —smug·ness *n*

smug·gle \'sməgəl\ *vb* -gled; -gling : import or export secretly or illegally —smug·gler \'sməglər\ *n*

smut \'smət\ *n* 1 : something that smudges 2 : indecent language or matter 3 : fungous disease of plants —smut·ty *adj*

snack \'snak\ *n* : light meal

snag \'snag\ *n* : unexpected difficulty ~ *vb* -gg- : become caught on something that sticks out

snail \'snāl\ *n* : small mollusk with a spiral shell

snake \'snāk\ *n* : long-bodied limbless crawling reptile —snake·bite *n*

snap \'snap\ *vb* -pp- 1 : bite at something 2 : utter angry words 3 : break suddenly with a sharp sound ~ *n* 1 : act or sound of snapping 2 : fastening that closes with a click 3 : something easy to do —snap·per *n* —snap·pish *adj* —snap·py *adj*

snap·drag·on *n* : garden plant with spikes of showy flowers

snap·shot \'snap,shät\ *n* : casual photograph

snare \'snaər\ *n* : trap for catching game ~ *vb* : capture or hold with or as if with a snare

¹snarl \'snärl\ *n* : tangle ~ *vb* : cause to become knotted

²snarl *vb or n* : growl

snatch \'snach\ *vb* 1 : try to grab something suddenly 2 : seize or take away suddenly ~ *n* 1 : act of snatching 2 : something brief or fragmentary

sneak \'snēk\ *vb* : move or take in a furtive manner ~ *n* : one who acts in a furtive manner —sneak·ing·ly *adv* —sneaky *adj*

sneak·er \'snēkər\ *n* : sports shoe

sneer \'sniər\ *vb* : smile scornfully —sneer *n*

sneeze \'snēz\ *vb* sneezed; sneez·ing : force the breath out with sudden and involuntary violence —sneeze *n*

snick·er \'snikər\ *n* : partly suppressed laugh —snicker *vb*

snide \'snīd\ *adj* : subtly ridiculing

sniff \'snif\ *vb* 1 : draw air audibly up the nose 2 : detect by smelling —sniff *n*

¹snipe \'snīp\ *n, pl* snipes *or* snipe : bird of marshy areas

²snipe *vb* sniped; snip·ing : shoot at an enemy from a concealed position —snip·er *n*

snips \'snips\ *n pl* : scissorslike tool

sniv·el \'sniv-al\ *vb* -eled *or* -elled; -eling *or* -el·ling 1 : have a running nose 2 : whine —snivel *n*

snob \'snäb\ *n* : one who acts superior to others —snob·bery \-(ə)rē\ *n* —snob·bish \-bish\ *adj* —snob·bish·ly *adv* —snob·bish·ness *n*

snoop \'snüp\ *vb* : pry in a furtive way ~ *n* : prying person

snooze \'snüz\ *vb* snoozed; snooz·ing : take a nap —snooze *n*

snore \'snòr\ *vb* snored; snor·ing : breathe with a hoarse noise while sleeping —snore *n*

snort \'snòrt\ *vb* : force air noisily through the nose —snort *n*

snout \'snaút\ *n* : long projecting muzzle (as of a swine)

snow \'snō\ *n* : crystals formed from water vapor ~ *vb* : fall as snow —snow·ball *n* —snow·bank *n* —snow·drift *n* —snow·fall *n* —snow·plow *n* —snow·storm *n* —snowy *adj*

snow·shoe *n* : frame of wood strung with thongs for walking on snow

snub \'snəb\ *vb* **-bb-** : ignore or avoid through disdain —**snub** *n*

¹snuff \'snəf\ *vb* : put out (a candle) —**snuff·er** *n*

²snuff *vb* : draw forcibly into the nose ~ *n* : pulverized tobacco

snug \'snəg\ *adj* **-gg-** 1 : warm, secure, and comfortable 2 : fitting closely —**snug·ly** *adv* —**snug·ness** *n*

snug·gle \'snəgəl\ *vb* **-gled; -gling** : curl up comfortably

so \('\)sō\ *adv* 1 : in the manner or to the extent indicated 2 : in the same way 3 : therefore 4 : finally 5 : thus ~ *conj* : for that reason

soak \'sōk\ *vb* 1 : lie in a liquid 2 : absorb ~ *n* : act of soaking

soap \'sōp\ *n* : cleaning substance —**soap** *vb* —**soapy** *adj*

soar \'sōr\ *vb* : fly upward on or as if on wings

sob \'säb\ *vb* **-bb-** : weep with convulsive heavings of the chest —**sob** *n*

so·ber \'sōbər\ *adj* 1 : not drunk 2 : serious or solemn —**so·ber·ly** *adv*

so·bri·ety \sə'brīətē, sō-\ *n* : quality or state of being sober

soc·cer \'säkər\ *n* : game played by kicking a ball

so·cia·ble \'sōshəbəl\ *adj* : friendly —**so·cia·bil·i·ty** \,sōshə'bilətē\ *n* —**so·cia·bly** \'sōshəblē\ *adv*

so·cial \'sōshəl\ *adj* 1 : relating to pleasant companionship 2 : naturally living or growing in groups 3 : relating to human society ~ *n* : social gathering —**so·cial·ly** *adv*

so·cial·ism \'sōshə,lizəm\ *n* : social organization based on government control of the production and distribution of goods —**so·cial·ist** \'sōsh(ə)ləst\ *n or adj* —**so·cial·is·tic** \,sōshə'listik\ *adj*

so·cial·ize \'sōshə,līz\ *vb* **-ized; -iz·ing** 1 : regulate by socialism 2 : adapt to social needs 3 : participate in a social gathering —**so·cial·iza·tion** \,sōsh(ə)lə'zāshən\ *n*

social work *n* : services concerned with aiding the poor and socially maladjusted —**social worker** *n*

so·ci·ety \sə'sīətē\ *n, pl* **-eties** 1 : companionship 2 : community life 3 : rich or fashionable class 4 : voluntary group

so·ci·ol·o·gy \,sōs(h)ē'äläjē\ *n* : study of social relationships —**so·cio·log·i·cal** \-ē'ä'läjikəl\ *adj* —**so·ci·ol·o·gist** \-'äləjəst\ *n*

¹sock \'säk\ *n, pl* **socks** *or* **sox** : short stocking

²sock *vb or n* : punch

sock·et \'säkət\ *n* : hollow part that holds something

sod \'säd\ *n* : turf ~ *vb* **-dd-** : cover with sod

so·da \'sōdə\ *n* 1 : carbonated water or a soft drink 2 : ice cream drink made with soda

sod·den \'säd³n\ *adj* 1 : lacking spirit 2 : soaked or soggy

so·di·um \'sōdēəm\ *n* : soft waxy silver white metallic chemical element

so·fa \'sōfə\ *n* : wide padded chair

soft \'sȯft\ *adj* 1 : not hard, rough, or harsh 2 : nonalcoholic —**soft·ly** *adv* —**soft·ness** \'sȯf(t)nəs\ *n*

soft·ball *n* : game like baseball

soft·en \'sȯfən\ *vb* : make or become soft —**soft·en·er** \-(ə)nər\ *n*

sog·gy \'sägē\ *adj* **-gier; -est** : heavy with moisture —**sog·gi·ness** \-ēnəs\ *n*

¹soil \'sȯil\ *vb* : make or become dirty ~ *n* : embedded dirt

²soil *n* : loose surface material of the earth

so·journ \'sō,jərn, sō'jərn\ *vb* : reside temporarily —**so·journ** *n*

so·lace \'säləs\ *n or vb* : comfort

so·lar \'sōlər\ *adj* 1 : relating to the sun or the energy in sunlight

sold *past of* SELL

sol·der \'sädər, 'sȯd-\ *n* : metallic alloy melted to join metallic surfaces ~ *vb* : cement with solder

sol·dier \'sōljər\ *n* : person in military service ~ *vb* : serve as a soldier —**sol·dier·ly** *adj or adv*

¹sole \'sōl\ *n* : bottom of the foot or a shoe —**soled** *adj*

²sole *n* : flatfish caught for food

³sole *adj* : single or only —**sole·ly** \'sō(l)lē\ *adv*

sol·emn \'säləm\ *adj* 1 : dignified and ceremonial 2 : highly serious 3 : of great importance or responsibility —**so·lem·ni·ty** \sə'lemnətē\ *n* —**sol·emn·ly** *adv* —**sol·emn·ness** *n*

so·lic·it \sə'lisət\ *vb* : ask for —**so·lic·i·ta·tion** \-,lisə'tāshən\ *n*

so·lic·i·tor \sə'lisətər\ *n* 1 : one that solicits 2 : lawyer

so·lic·i·tous \sə'lisətəs\ *adj* : showing or expressing concern —**so·lic·i·tous·ly** *adv* —**so·lic·i·tude** \sə'lisə,t(y)üd\ *n*

sol·id \'säləd\ *adj* 1 : not hollow 2 : having 3 dimensions 3 : hard 4 : of good quality 5 : of one character ~ *n* 1 : 3-dimensional figure 2 : substance in solid form —**solid** *adv* —**so·lid·i·ty** \sə'lidətē\ *n* —**sol·id·ly** *adv* —**sol·id·ness** *n*

sol•i•dar•i•ty \ˌsälə'darətē\ *n* : unity of purpose

so•lid•i•fy \sə'lidə,fī\ *vb* **-fied; -fy•ing** : make or become solid —**so•lid•i•fi•ca•tion** \-ˌlidəfə'kāshən\ *n*

so•lil•o•quy \sə'liləkwē\ *n, pl* **-quies** : dramatic monologue —**so•lil•o•quize** \-ˌkwīz\ *vb*

sol•i•taire \ˈsälə,taar\ *n* **1** : solitary gem **2** : card game for one person

sol•i•tary \ˌterē\ *adj* **1** : alone **2** : secluded **3** : single

sol•i•tude \ˌt(y)üd\ *n* : state of being alone

so•lo \ˈsōlō\ *n, pl* **-los** : performance by only one person — *adv* : alone — **solo** *adj or vb* —**so•lo•ist** *n*

sol•stice \ˈsälstəs\ *n* : time of the year when the sun is farthest north or south of the equator

sol•u•ble \ˈsälyəbəl\ *adj* : capable of being dissolved **2** : capable of being solved —**sol•u•bil•i•ty** \ˌsälyə'bilətē\ *n*

so•lu•tion \sə'lüshən\ *n* **1** : answer to a problem **2** : homogeneous liquid mixture

solve \ˈsälv\ *vb* **solved; solv•ing** : find a solution —**solv•able** *adj*

sol•vent \ˈsälvənt\ *adj* **1** : able to pay all debts **2** : dissolving or able to dissolve ~ *n* : substance that dissolves or disperses another substance —**sol•ven•cy** \-vənsē\ *n*

som•ber, som•bre \ˈsämbər\ *adj* **1** : dark **2** : grave —**som•ber•ly** *adv*

som•bre•ro \səm'bre(ə)rō\ *n, pl* **-ros** : broad-brimmed hat

some \(ˈ)səm\ *adj* **1** : one unspecified **2** : unspecified or indefinite number of **3** : at least a few or a little ~ \ˈsəm\ *pron* : a certain number or amount

-some \səm\ *adj suffix* : characterized by a thing, quality, state, or action

some•body \ˈsəm,bädē, -bəd-\ *pron* : some person

some•day \ˈsəm,dā\ *adv* : at some future time

some•how \ˌhaů\ *adv* : by some means

some•one \-(ˌ)wən\ *pron* : some person

som•er•sault \ˈsəmər,sôlt\ *n* : body flip —**somersault** *vb*

some•thing \ˈsəmthiŋ\ *pron* : some undetermined or unspecified thing

some•time \ˈsəm,tīm\ *adv* : at a future, unknown, or unnamed time

some•times \ˌtīmz\ *adv* : occasionally

some•what \ˌhwät, -ˌhwət\ *adv* : in some degree

some•where \-ˌhwear\ *adv* : in, at, or to an unknown or unnamed place

som•no•lent \ˈsämnələnt\ *adj* : sleepy —**som•no•lence** \-ləns\ *n*

son \ˈsən\ *n* : male offspring

so•nar \ˈsō,när\ *n* : apparatus that locates underwater objects by reflected vibrations

so•na•ta \sə'nätə\ *n* : instrumental composition

song \ˈsóŋ\ *n* : music and words to be sung

song•bird *n* : bird with musical tones

son•ic \ˈsänik\ *adj* : relating to sound waves or the speed of sound

son–in–law *n, pl* **sons–in–law** : husband of one's daughter

son•net \ˈsänət\ *n* : poem of 14 lines

so•no•rous \sə'nōrəs, 'sänərəs\ *adj* **1** : loud, deep, or rich in sound **2** : impressive —**so•nor•i•ty** \sə'nórətē\ *n*

soon \ˈsün\ *adv* **1** : before long **2** : promptly **3** : early

soot \ˈsüt, 'sət, 'süt\ *n* : fine black substance formed by combustion — **sooty** *adj*

soothe \ˈsüth\ *vb* **soothed; sooth•ing** : calm or comfort —**sooth•er** *n*

sooth•say•er \ˈsüth,sāər\ *n* : prophet —**sooth•say•ing** \-iŋ\ *n*

sop \ˈsäp\ *n* : conciliatory bribe, gift, or concession ~ *vb* **-pp- 1** : dip in a liquid **2** : soak **3** : mop up

so•phis•ti•cat•ed \sə'fistə,kātəd, sə-\ *adj* **1** : complex **2** : wise, cultured, or shrewd in human affairs —**so•phis•ti•ca•tion** \-ˌfistə'kāshən\ *n*

soph•ist•ry \ˈsäfəstrē\ *n* : subtly fallacious reasoning or argument —**soph•ist** \ˈsäfəst\ *n* —**so•phis•tic** \sə'fistik, sə-\, **so•phis•ti•cal** \-tikəl\ *adj*

soph•o•more \ˈsäf,mōr, 'säf,mōr\ *n* : 2d-year student

so•po•rif•ic \ˌsäpə'rifik, ˌsōp-\ *adj* : causing sleep or drowsiness

so•pra•no \sə'pranō\ *n, pl* **-nos** : highest singing voice

sor•cery \ˈsórs(ə)rē\ *n* : witchcraft —**sor•cer•er** \-rər\ *n* —**sor•cer•ess** \-rəs\ *n*

sor•did \ˈsórdəd\ *adj* : vulgar, degrading, or corrupt —**sor•did•ly** *adv* —**sor•did•ness** *n*

sore \ˈsór\ *adj* **sor•er; sor•est 1** : causing pain or distress **2** : severe or intense **3** : angry ~ *n* : sore usu. infected spot on the body —**sore•ly** *adv* —**sore•ness** *n*

sor•ghum \ˈsórgəm\ *n* : forage grass

so•ror•i•ty \sə'rórətē\ *n, pl* **-ties** : club usu. for college women

sor•rel \ˈsórəl\ *n* : herb with sour juice

sor•row \ˈsärō\ *n* : deep distress and

regret or a cause of this **—sor·row·ful** \-fəl\ *adj* **—sor·row·ful·ly** \-f(ə)lē\ *adv*

sor·ry \'särē\ *adj* **-ri·er; -ri·est** 1 : feeling sorrow, regret, or penitence 2 : dismal

sort \'sort\ *n* 1 : kind 2 : nature ~ *vb* : classify **—out of sorts** : grouchy

sor·tie \'sortē, sor'tē\ *n* : military attack esp. against besiegers

SOS \,es,(,)ō'es\ *n* : call for help

so–so \'sō'sō\ *adv or adj* : barely acceptable

sot \'sät\ *n* : drunkard **—sot·tish** *adj*

souf·flé \sü'flā\ *n* : baked dish made light with beaten egg whites

sought *past of* SEEK

soul \'sōl\ *n* 1 : immaterial essence of an individual life 2 : essential nature 3 : person

soul·ful \'sōlfəl\ *adj* : full of or expressing deep feeling **—soul·ful·ly** *adv*

¹**sound** \'saund\ *adj* 1 : free from fault, error, or illness 2 : firm or hard 3 : showing good judgment **—sound·ly** *adv* **—sound·ness** *n*

²**sound** *n* 1 : sensation experienced by hearing 2 : noise ~ *vb* 1 : make or cause to make a noise 2 : seem **—sound·proof** *adj or vb*

³**sound** *n* 1 : wide strait ~ *vb* 1 : measure the depth of (water) 2 : investigate

soup \'süp\ *n* : broth usu. containing pieces of solid food **—soupy** *adj*

sour \'saü(ə)r\ *adj* 1 : having an acid or tart taste 2 : disagreeable ~ *vb* : become or make sour **—sour·ish** *adj* **—sour·ly** *adv* **—sour·ness** *n*

source \'sōrs\ *n* 1 : point of origin 2 : one that provides something needed

souse \'saüs\ *vb* **soused; sous·ing** 1 : pickle 2 : plunge into a liquid 3 : intoxicate ~ *n* 1 : something pickled 2 : drunkard

south \'saüth\ *adv* : to or toward the south ~ *adj* : situated toward, at, or coming from the south ~ *n* 1 : direction to the right of sunrise 2 *cap* : regions to the south **—south·er·ly** \'səthərlē\ *adv or adj* **—south·ern** \'səthərn\ *adj* **—South·ern·er** *n* **—south·ern·most** \-,mōst\ *adj* **—south·ward** \'saüthwərd\ *adv or adj* **—south·wards** \-wərdz\ *adv*

south·east \saüth'ēst, *naut* saü'ēst\ *n* 1 : direction between south and east 2 *cap* : regions to the southeast **—southeast** *adj or adv* **—south·east·er·ly** *adv or adj* **—south·east·ern** \-ərn\ *adj*

south pole *n* : the southernmost point of the earth

south·west \saüth'west, *naut* saü'west\ *n* 1 : direction between south and west 2 *cap* : regions to the southwest **—southwest** *adj or adv* **—south·west·er·ly** *adv or adj* **—south·west·ern** \-ərn\ *adj*

sou·ve·nir \'süvə,niər\ *n* : something that is a reminder of a place or event

sov·er·eign \'säv(ə)rən\ *n* 1 : supreme ruler 2 : gold coin of the United Kingdom ~ *adj* 1 : supreme 2 : independent **—sov·er·eign·ty** \-tē\ *n*

¹**sow** \'saú\ *n* : female swine

²**sow** \'sō\ *vb* **sowed; sown** \'sōn\ *or* **sowed, sow·ing** 1 : plant or strew with seed 2 : scatter abroad **—sow·er** \'sō(ə)r\ *n*

sox *pl of* SOCK

soy·bean \'soi,bēn, -,bēn\ *n* : legume with edible beans

spa \'spä\ *n* : resort at a mineral spring

space \'spās\ *n* 1 : period of time 2 : area in, around, or between 3 : region beyond earth's atmosphere 4 : accommodations ~ *vb* **spaced; spac·ing** : separate **—space·craft** *n* **—space·flight** *n* **—space·ship** *n*

spa·cious \'spāshəs\ *adj* : large or roomy **—spa·cious·ly** *adv* **—spa·cious·ness** *n*

¹**spade** \'spād\ *n* : shovel with a flat blade ~ *vb* **spad·ed; spad·ing** : dig with a spade **—spade·ful** *n*

²**spade** *n* : playing card marked with a black figure like an inverted heart

spa·ghet·ti \spə'getē\ *n* : pasta strings

span \'span\ *n* 1 : amount of time 2 : distance between supports ~ *vb* **-nn-** : extend across

span·gle \'spaŋgəl\ *n* : small disk of shining metal **—spangle** *vb*

span·iel \'spanyəl\ *n* : small dog with drooping ears

spank \'spaŋk\ *vb* : strike the buttocks of with the open hand

¹**spar** \'spär\ *n* : pole or boom

²**spar** *vb* **-rr-** : practice boxing

spare \'spaər\ *adj* 1 : held in reserve 2 : thin or scanty ~ *vb* **spared; spar·ing** 1 : reserve or avoid using 2 : avoid punishing or killing **—spare** *n*

spar·ing \'spa(ə)riŋ\ *adj* : thrifty **—spar·ing·ly** *adv*

spark \'spärk\ *n* 1 : tiny hot and glowing particle 2 : smallest beginning or germ 3 : visible electrical discharge ~ *vb* 1 : emit or produce sparks 2 : stir to activity

spar·kle \'spärkəl\ *vb* **-kled; -kling** 1

: flash **2** : effervesce ~ *n* : gleam —
spark·ler \-k(ə)lər\ *n*

spar·row \sparō\ *n* : small singing bird

sparse \spärs\ *adj* **spars·er; spars·est**
: thinly scattered **—sparse·ly** *adv*

spasm \spazəm\ *n* **1** : involuntary
muscular contraction **2** : sudden,
violent, and temporary effort or feeling **—spas·mod·ic** \spaz'mädik\ *adj*

spas·tic \spastik\ *adj* : relating to or
marked by muscular spasm **—spas-
tic** *n*

¹spat \spat\ *past of* SPIT

²spat *n* : petty dispute

spa·tial \spāshəl\ *adj* : relating to
space **—spa·tial·ly** \-ē\ *adv*

spat·ter \spatər\ *vb* : splash with
drops of liquid **—spatter** *n*

spat·u·la \spachələ\ *n* : flexible knife-
like utensil

spawn \spón\ *vb* **1** : produce eggs or
offspring **2** : bring forth ~ *n* : egg
cluster

spay \spā\ *vb* : remove the ovaries
from (an animal)

speak \spēk\ *vb* **spoke** \spōk\; **spoken** \spōkən\; **speak·ing 1** : utter
words **2** : express orally **3** : address
an audience **4** : use (a language) in
speaking **—speak·er** *n*

spear \spiər\ *n* : long pointed weapon
~ *vb* : strike or pierce with a spear

spear·head *n* : leading force, element,
or influence **—spearhead** *vb*

spear·mint *n* : aromatic garden mint

spe·cial \speshəl\ *adj* **1** : unusual or
unique **2** : particularly favored **3**
: set aside for a particular use **—
special** *n* **—spe·cial·ly** *adv*

spe·cial·ist \spesh(ə)ləst\ *n* **1** : one devoted to a branch of learning or activity **2** : any of four enlisted ranks
in the army corresponding to the
grades of corporal through sergeant
first class

spe·cial·ize \speshə,līz\ *vb* **-ized; -iz-
ing** : concentrate one's efforts **—
spe·cial·iza·tion** \,speshələ'zāshən\ *n*

spe·cial·ty \speshəltē\ *n, pl* **-ties** : area
or field in which one specializes

spe·cie \spēshē, -sē\ *n* : money in coin

spe·cies \spēshēz, -sēz\ *n, pl* **species**
: biological grouping of closely related organisms

spe·cif·ic \spi'sifik\ *adj* : definite or exact **—spe·cif·i·cal·ly** \-ik(ə)lē\ *adv*

spec·i·fi·ca·tion \,spesəfə'kāshən\ *n* **1**
: item specified **2** : detailed description of work to be done —usu. pl.

spec·i·fy \spesə,fī\ *vb* **-fied; -fy·ing**
: mention precisely or by name

spec·i·men \-əmən\ *n* : typical example

spe·cious \spēshəs\ *adj* : apparently
but not really genuine or correct

speck \spek\ *n* : tiny particle or blemish **—speck** *vb*

speck·led \spekəld\ *adj* : marked with
spots

spec·ta·cle \spektikəl\ *n* **1** : impressive
public display **2** *pl* : eyeglasses

spec·tac·u·lar \spek'takyələr\ *adj*
: sensational or showy

spec·ta·tor \spek,tātər\ *n* : one who
looks on

spec·ter, spec·tre \spektər\ *n* **1** : ghost
2 : haunting vision

spec·tral \spektrəl\ *adj* : relating to or
resembling a specter or spectrum

spec·trum \spektrəm\ *n, pl* **-tra** \-trə\
or **-trums** : series of colors formed
when white light is dispersed into its
components

spec·u·late \spekyə,lāt\ *vb* **-lat·ed;
-lat·ing 1** : think about things yet unknown **2** : risk money in a business
deal in hope of high profit **—spec·u-
la·tion** \,spekyə'lāshən\ *n* **—spec·u-
la·tive** \spekyə,lātiv\ *adj* **—spec·u-
la·tor** \-,lātər\ *n*

speech \spēch\ *n* **1** : power, act, or
manner of speaking **2** : talk given to
an audience **—speech·less** *adj*

speed \spēd\ *n* **1** : quality of being fast
2 : rate of motion or performance ~
vb **sped** \sped\ *or* **speed·ed; speed·
ing** : go at a great or excessive rate
of speed **—speed·boat** *n* **—speed·er** *n*
—speed·i·ly \spēd°lē\ *adv* **—speed·
up** \-,əp\ *n* **—speedy** *adj*

speed·om·e·ter \spi'dämətər\ *n* : instrument for indicating speed

¹spell \spel\ *n* : influence of or like
magic

²spell *vb* **1** : name, write, or print the
letters of **2** : mean **—spell·er** *n*

³spell *vb* : substitute for or relieve
(someone) ~ *n* **1** : turn at work **2**
: period of time

spell·bound *adj* : held by a spell

spend \spend\ *vb* **spent** \spent\;
spend·ing 1 : pay out **2** : occupy oneself during (a period of time) **—
spend·er** *n*

spend·thrift \spen(d),thrift\ *n*
: wasteful person

sperm \spərm\ *n, pl* **sperm** *or* **sperms**
: semen or a germ cell in it

spew \spyü\ *vb* : gush out in a stream

sphere \sfiər\ *n* **1** : figure with every
point on its surface at an equal distance from the center **2** : round body
3 : range of action or influence **—
spher·i·cal** \sfirikəl, 'sfer-\ *adj*

spher·oid \'sfi(ə)r,ȯid, 'sfe(ə)r-\ n : spherelike figure

spice \'spīs\ n 1 : aromatic plant product for seasoning food 2 : interesting quality —**spice** vb —**spicy** adj

spi·der \'spīdər\ n : small insectlike animal with 8 legs —**spi·dery** adj

spig·ot \'spigət, 'spikət\ n : faucet

spike \'spīk\ n : very large nail ~ vb **spiked; spik·ing** : fasten or pierce with a spike —**spiked** \'spīkt\ adj

spill \'spil\ vb : cause or allow unintentionally to fall, flow, or run out ~ n 1 : act of spilling 2 : something spilled —**spill·able** adj

spill·way n : passage for surplus water

spin \'spin\ vb **spun** \'spən\; **spin·ning** 1 : draw out fiber and twist into thread 2 : form thread from a sticky body fluid 3 : revolve or cause to revolve extremely fast ~ n : rapid rotating motion —**spin·ner** n

spin·ach \'spinich\ n : garden herb with edible leaves

spi·nal \'spīnᵊl\ adj : relating to the backbone —**spi·nal·ly** adv

spinal cord n : thick strand of nervous tissue that extends from the brain along the back within the backbone

spin·dle \'spindᵊl\ n 1 : stick used for spinning thread 2 : shaft around which something turns

spin·dly \'spindlē\ adj : tall and slender

spine \'spīn\ n : backbone 2 : stiff sharp projection on a plant or animal —**spine·less** adj —**spiny** adj

spin·et \'spinət\ n : small piano

spin·ster \'spinstər\ n : woman who has never married

spi·ral \'spīrəl\ adj : circling or winding around a single point or line —**spiral** n or vb —**spi·ral·ly** adv

spire \'spī(ə)r\ n : steeple —**spiry** adj

spir·it \'spirət\ n : life-giving force 2 cap : presence of God 3 : ghost 4 : mood 5 : vivacity or enthusiasm 6 pl : alcoholic liquor ~ vb : carry off secretly —**spir·it·ed** adj —**spir·it·less** adj

spir·i·tu·al \'spirich(əw)əl\ adj 1 : relating to the spirit or sacred matters 2 : deeply religious ~ n : religious folk song —**spir·i·tu·al·i·ty** \,spirichə'walətē\ n —**spir·i·tu·al·ly** adv

spir·i·tu·al·ism \'spirich(əw)ə,lizəm\ n : belief that spirits communicate with the living —**spir·i·tu·al·ist** \-list\ n —**spir·i·tu·al·is·tic** \,spirich(əw)ə'listik\ adj

¹spit \'spit\ n 1 : rod for holding and turning meat over a fire 2 : point of land that runs into the water

²spit vb **spit** or **spat** \'spat\; **spit·ting** : eject saliva from the mouth ~ n 1 : saliva 2 : perfect likeness

spite \'spīt\ n : grudge with a wish to injure ~ vb **spit·ed; spit·ing** : treat insultingly —**spite·ful** \-fəl\ adj —**spite·ful·ly** adv —**in spite of** : in defiance or contempt of

spit·tle \'spitᵊl\ n : saliva

spit·toon \spi'tün\ n : receptacle for spit

splash \'splash\ vb : scatter a liquid on —**splash** n

splat·ter \'splatər\ vb : spatter —**splat·ter** n

splay \'splā\ vb 1 : spread out 2 : slope or slant outward —**splay** n or adj

spleen \'splēn\ n 1 : organ for maintenance of the blood 2 : spite or anger

splen·did \'splendəd\ adj 1 : impressive in beauty or brilliance 2 : outstanding —**splen·did·ly** adv

splen·dor \'splendər\ n 1 : brilliance 2 : magnificence

splice \'splīs\ vb **spliced; splic·ing** : join (2 things) end to end —**splice** n

splint \'splint\ n 1 : thin strip of wood 2 : something that keeps an injured body part in place

splin·ter \'splintər\ n : thin needlelike piece ~ vb : break into splinters

split \'split\ vb **split; split·ting** : divide lengthwise or along a grain —**split** n

splotch \'spläch\ n : blotch

splurge \'splərj\ vb **splurged; splurg·ing** : indulge oneself —**splurge** n

splut·ter \'splətər\ n : sputter —**splut·ter** vb

spoil \'spȯil\ n : plunder ~ vb **spoiled** \'spȯild, 'spȯilt\ or **spoilt** \'spȯilt\; **spoil·ing** 1 : pillage 2 : ruin 3 : rot —**spoil·age** \'spȯilij\ n —**spoil·er** n

¹spoke \'spōk\ past of SPEAK

²spoke n : rod from the hub to the rim of a wheel

spo·ken past part of SPEAK

spokes·man \'spōksmən\ n : one who speaks for others —**spokes·wom·an** \-,wŭmən\ n

sponge \'spənj\ n 1 : porous mass that forms the skeleton of some marine animals 2 : spongelike material used for wiping ~ vb **sponged; spong·ing** 1 : wipe with a sponge 2 : live at another's expense —**spongy** adj

spon·sor \'spänsər\ n : one who assumes responsibility for another or

who provides financial support —
sponsor *vb* —**spon·sor·ship** *n*

spon·ta·ne·ous \spän'tānēəs\ *adj*
: done, produced, or occurring naturally or without planning —**spon·ta-
ne·i·ty** \,späntən'ēətē\ *n* —**spon·ta-
ne·ous·ly** \spän'tānēəslē\ *adv*

spoof \'spüf\ *vb* : make good-natured
fun of —**spoof** *n*

spook \'spük\ *n* : ghost ~ *vb* : frighten
—**spooky** *adj*

spool \'spül\ *n* : cylinder on which
something is wound

spoon \'spün\ *n* : utensil consisting of
a shallow bowl with a handle —
spoon *vb* —**spoon·ful** \-,ful\ *n*

spoor \'spur, 'spōr\ *n* : track or trail
esp. of a wild animal

spo·rad·ic \spə'radik\ *adj* : occasional
—**spo·rad·i·cal·ly** \-ik(ə)lē\ *adv*

spore \'spōr\ *n* : primitive usu. one-
celled reproductive body

sport \'spōrt\ *vb* **1** : frolic **2** : wear or
display ostentatiously ~ *n* **1** : physical activity engaged in for pleasure
2 : jest **3** : likable person —**sport·ive**
\-iv\ *adj* —**sporty** *adj*

sports·cast \'spōrts,kast\ *n* : broadcast
of a sports event —**sports·cast-
er** \-,kastər\ *n*

sports·man \-mən\ *n* : one who enjoys
hunting and fishing

sports·man·ship \-mən,ship\ *n* : ability
to be gracious in winning or losing

spot \'spät\ *n* **1** : blemish **2** : distinctive
small part **3** : location ~ *vb* **-tt-** **1**
: mark with spots **2** : see or recognize
~ *adj* : made at random or in limited
numbers —**spot·less** *adj* —**spot·less-
ly** *adv*

spot·light *n* **1** : intense beam of light **2**
: center of public interest —**spotlight**
vb

spot·ty \'spätē\ *adj* **-ti·er; -est** : uneven
in quality

spouse \'spaus\ *n* : one's husband or
wife

spout \'spaut\ *vb* **1** : shoot forth in a
stream **2** : say pompously ~ *n* **1**
: opening through which liquid
spouts **2** : jet of liquid

sprain \'sprān\ *n* : twisting injury to a
joint ~ *vb* : injure with a sprain

sprat \'sprat\ *n* : small or young herring

sprawl \'sprol\ *vb* : lie or sit with limbs
spread out —**sprawl** *n*

¹spray \'sprā\ *n* : branch or arrangement of flowers

²spray *n* **1** : mist **2** : device that dis-
charges liquid as a mist —**spray** *vb*
—**spray·er** *n*

spread \'spred\ *vb* **spread; spread·ing**
1 : open up or unfold **2** : scatter or
smear over a surface **3** : cause to be
known or to exist over a wide area
~ *n* **1** : extent to which something is
spread **2** : cloth cover **3** : something
intended to be spread —**spread·er** *n*

spree \'sprē\ *n* : burst of indulging in
something

sprig \'sprig\ *n* : small shoot or twig

spright·ly \'sprītlē\ *adj* **-li·er; -est**
: lively —**spright·li·ness** *n*

spring \'sprin\ *vb* **sprang** \'spran\ *or*
sprung \'sprən\; **sprung; spring·ing**
1 : move or shoot up quickly or by
elastic force **2** : make known suddenly ~ *n* **1** : source **2** : flow of water
from underground **3** : season between winter and summer **4** : elastic
body or device (as a coil of wire) **5**
: leap **6** : elastic power —**springy** *adj*

sprin·kle \'sprinkəl\ *vb* **-kled; -kling**
: scatter in small drops or particles
~ *n* : light rainfall —**sprin·kler**
\-k(ə)lər\ *n*

sprint \'sprint\ *n* : short run at top
speed —**sprint** *vb* —**sprint·er** *n*

sprite \'sprīt\ *n* : elf or elfish person

sprock·et \'spräkət\ *n* : tooth on a
wheel (**sprocket wheel**) shaped so as
to interlock with a chain

sprout \'spraut\ *vb* : send out new
growth ~ *n* : plant shoot

¹spruce \'sprüs\ *n* : conical evergreen
tree

²spruce *adj* **spruc·er; spruc·est** : neat
and stylish in appearance ~ *vb*
spruced; spruc·ing : make or become
neat

spry \'sprī\ *adj* **spri·er** *or* **spry·er**
\'sprī(ə)r\; **spri·est** *or* **spry·est**
\'sprīəst\ : agile and active

spume \'spyüm\ *n* : froth

spun *past of* SPIN

spunk \'spənk\ *n* : courage —**spunky**
adj

spur \'spər\ *n* **1** : pointed device used
to urge on a horse **2** : something that
urges to action **3** : projecting part ~
vb **-rr-** : urge on —**spurred** *adj*

spu·ri·ous \'spyūrēəs\ *adj* : not genuine

spurn \'spərn\ *vb* : reject

¹spurt \'spərt\ *n* : burst of effort,
speed, or activity ~ *vb* : make a
spurt

²spurt *vb* : gush out ~ *n* : sudden gush

sput·ter \'spətər\ *vb* **1** : talk hastily and
indistinctly in excitement **2**
: make popping sounds —**sputter** *n*

spu·tum \'spyütəm\ *n*, *pl* **-ta** \-ə\ : ex-
pectorated saliva and mucus

spy \'spī\ *vb* **spied; spy·ing** : watch or try to gather information about someone secretly —**spy** *n*

squab \'skwäb\ *n, pl* **squabs** *or* **squab** : young pigeon

squab·ble \'skwäbəl\ *n or vb* : dispute

squad \'skwäd\ *n* : small group

squad·ron \'skwädrən\ *n* : small military unit

squal·id \'skwäləd\ *adj* : filthy or wretched

squall \'skwól\ *n* : sudden violent brief storm —**squally** *adj*

squa·lor \'skwälər\ *n* : quality or state of being squalid

squan·der \'skwändər\ *vb* : waste

square \'skwaər\ *n* **1** : instrument for measuring right angles **2** : flat figure that has 4 equal sides and 4 right angles **3** : open area in a city **4** : product of number multiplied by itself ~ *adj* **squar·er; squar·est** **1** : being a square in form **2** : having sides meet at right angles **3** : multiplied by itself **4** : being a square unit of area **5** : honest **6** : even or tied ~ *vb* **squared; squar·ing** **1** : form into a square **2** : multiply a number by itself **3** : conform **4** : settle —**square·ly** *adv*

¹**squash** \'skwäsh, 'skwósh\ *vb* **1** : press flat **2** : suppress

²**squash** *n, pl* **squash·es** *or* **squash** : garden vegetable

squat \'skwät\ *vb* **-tt- 1** : stoop or sit on one's heels **2** : settle on land one does not own ~ *n* : act or posture of squatting ~ *adj* **squat·ter; squat·test** : short and thick —**squat·ter** *n*

squaw \'skwó\ *n* : Indian woman

squawk \'skwók\ *n* : harsh loud cry —**squawk** *vb*

squeak \'skwēk\ *vb* : make a thin high-pitched sound —**squeak** *n* —**squeaky** *adj*

squeal \'skwēl\ *vb* **1** : make a shrill sound or cry **2** : protest —**squeal** *n*

squea·mish \'skwēmish\ *adj* : easily nauseated or disgusted

squeeze \'skwēz\ *vb* **squeezed; squeez·ing 1** : apply pressure to **2** : extract by pressure —**squeeze** *n* —**squeez·er** *n*

squelch \'skwelch\ *vb* : suppress (as with a retort) —**squelch** *n*

squid \'skwid\ *n, pl* **squid** *or* **squids** : 10-armed long-bodied sea mollusk

squint \'skwint\ *vb* : look with the eyes partly closed —**squint** *n or adj*

squire \'skwī(ə)r\ *n* **1** : knight's aide **2** : country landholder **3** : lady's de-voted escort ~ *vb* **squired; squir·ing** : escort

squirm \'skwərm\ *vb* : wriggle

squir·rel \'skwər(ə)l\ *n* : rodent with a long bushy tail

squirt \'skwərt\ *vb* : eject liquid in a spurt —**squirt** *n*

stab \'stab\ *n* **1** : wound given by a pointed weapon **2** : quick thrust **3** : attempt ~ *vb* **-bb-** : pierce or wound with or as if with a pointed weapon

¹**sta·ble** \'stābəl\ *n* : building for livestock ~ *vb* **-bled; -bling** : keep in a stable

²**stable** *adj* **sta·bler; sta·blest 1** : firmly established **2** : mentally well-balanced **3** : steady —**sta·bil·i·ty** \stə'bilətē\ *n* —**sta·bil·i·za·tion** \,stābələ'zāshən\ *n* —**sta·bi·lize** \'stābə,līz\ *vb* —**sta·bi·liz·er** *n*

stac·ca·to \stə'kätō\ *adj* : disconnected

stack \'stak\ *n* : large pile ~ *vb* : pile up

sta·di·um \'stādēəm\ *n* : outdoor sports arena

staff \'staf\ *n, pl* **staffs** \'stafs, stavz\ *or* **staves** \'stavz, 'stāvz\ **1** : rod or supporting cane **2** : people assisting a leader **3** : 5 horizontal lines on which music is written ~ *vb* : supply with workers —**staff·er** *n*

staff sergeant *n* : noncommissioned officer ranking in the army next below a sergeant first class, in the air force next below a technical sergeant, and in the marine corps next below a gunnery sergeant

stag \'stag\ *n, pl* **stags** *or* **stag** : male deer ~ *adj* : for men ~ *adv* : without a date

stage \'stāj\ *n* **1** : raised platform for a speaker or performers **2** : theater **3** : step in a process ~ *vb* **staged; stag·ing** : produce (a play) —**stagy** \'stājē\ *adj*

stage·coach *n* : passenger coach

stag·ger \'stagər\ *vb* **1** : reel or cause to reel from side to side **2** : overlap or alternate —**stagger** *n* —**stag·ger·ing·ly** *adv*

stag·nant \'stagnənt\ *adj* : not moving or active —**stag·nate** \-,nāt\ *vb* —**stag·na·tion** \stag'nāshən\ *n*

¹**staid** \'stād\ *adj* : sedate

²**staid** *past of* STAY

stain \'stān\ *vb* **1** : discolor **2** : dye (as wood) **3** : disgrace ~ *n* **1** : discolored area **2** : dishonor **3** : coloring preparation —**stain·less** *adj*

stair \'staər\ *n* **1** : step in a series for

going from one level to another 2 *pl* : flight of steps —**stair·way** *n*

stair·case \'stā(ə)r, kās\ *n* : series of steps with their framework

stake \'stāk\ *n* 1 : small post driven into the ground 2 : bet 3 : prize in a contest ~ *vb* staked; stak·ing 1 : mark or secure with a stake 2 : place as a bet

sta·lac·tite \stə'lak, tīt\ *n* : icicle-shaped deposit hanging in a cavern

sta·lag·mite \stə'lag, mīt\ *n* : icicle-shaped deposit on a cavern floor

stale \'stāl\ *adj* **stal·er; stal·est** : not fresh —**stale** *vb*

stale·mate \'stāl, māt\ *n* : deadlock —**stalemate** *vb*

¹**stalk** \'stok\ *vb* 1 : walk stiffly or proudly 2 : pursue stealthily

²**stalk** *n* : plant stem —**stalked** \'stokt\ *adj*

¹**stall** \'stol\ *n* 1 : compartment in a stable 2 : booth where articles are sold

²**stall** *vb* : bring or come to a standstill unintentionally

³**stall** *vb* : delay, evade, or keep a situation going to gain advantage or time

stal·lion \'stalyən\ *n* : male horse

stal·wart \'stolwərt\ *adj* : strong or brave

sta·men \'stāmən\ *n* : flower organ that produces pollen

stam·i·na \'stamənə\ *n* : endurance

stam·mer \'stamər\ *vb* : hesitate in speaking —**stammer** *n*

stamp \'stamp *also* 'stämp *or* 'stomp\ *vb* 1 : pound with the sole of the foot or a heavy implement 2 : impress with a mark 3 : cut out with a die 4 : attach a postage stamp to ~ *n* 1 : device for stamping 2 : act of stamping 3 : government seal showing a tax or fee has been paid

stam·pede \stam'pēd\ *n* : headlong rush of frightened animals ~ *vb* **-ped·ed; -ped·ing** : flee in panic

stance \'stans\ *n* : way of standing

¹**stanch** \'stonch, 'stänch\ *vb* : stop the flow of (as blood)

²**stanch** *var of* STAUNCH

stan·chion \'stanchən\ *n* : upright support

stand \'stand\ *vb* **stood** \'stüd\; **stand·ing** 1 : be at rest in or assume an upright position 2 : remain unchanged 3 : be steadfast 4 : maintain a relative position or rank 5 : set upright 6 : undergo or endure ~ *n* 1 : act or place of standing, staying, or resisting 2 : sales booth 3 : structure for holding something upright 4

: group of plants growing together 5 *pl* : tiered seats —**stand** *n*

stan·dard \'standərd\ *n* 1 : symbolic figure or flag 2 : model, rule, or guide 3 : upright support —**standard** *adj* —**stan·dard·iza·tion** \,standərdə'zāshən\ *n* —**stan·dard·ize** \'standərd,īz\ *vb*

standard time *n* : time established over a region or country

stand·ing \'standiŋ\ *n* 1 : relative position or rank 2 : duration

stand·still *n* : state of rest

stank *past of* STINK

stan·za \'stanzə\ *n* : division of a poem

¹**sta·ple** \'stāpəl\ *n* : U-shaped wire fastener —**staple** *vb* —**sta·pler** \-p(ə)lər\ *n*

²**staple** *n* : chief commodity or item —**staple** *adj*

star \'stär\ *n* 1 : celestial body visible as a point of light 2 : 5- or 6-pointed figure representing a star 3 : leading performer ~ *vb* **-rr-** 1 : mark with a star 2 : play the leading role —**star·dom** \'stärdəm\ *n* —**star·less** *adj* —**star·light** *n* —**star·ry** *adj*

star·board \'stärbərd\ *n* : right side of a ship or airplane looking forward —**starboard** *adj*

starch \'stärch\ *n* : nourishing carbohydrate from plants also used in adhesives and laundering ~ *vb* : stiffen with starch —**starchy** *adj*

stare \'staər\ *vb* **stared; star·ing** : look intently with wide-open eyes —**stare** *n* —**star·er** *n*

stark \'stärk\ *adj* 1 : absolute 2 : severe or bleak —**stark** *adv* —**stark·ly** *adv*

star·ling \'stärliŋ\ *n* : bird related to the crows

start \'stärt\ *vb* 1 : twitch or jerk (as from surprise) 2 : perform or show performance of the first part of an action or process ~ *n* 1 : sudden involuntary motion 2 : beginning —**start·er** *n*

star·tle \'stärt²l\ *vb* **-tled; -tling** : frighten or surprise suddenly

starve \'stärv\ *vb* **starved; starv·ing** 1 : suffer or die from hunger 2 : kill with hunger —**star·va·tion** \stär-'vāshən\ *n*

state \'stāt\ *n* 1 : condition of being 2 : condition of mind 3 : nation or a political unit within it ~ *vb* **stat·ed; stat·ing** 1 : express in words 2 : establish —**state·hood** \-,hùd\ *n*

state·ly \'stātlē\ *adj* **-li·er; -est** : having impressive dignity —**state·li·ness** *n*

state·ment \ˈstātmənt\ n 1 : something stated 2 : financial summary

state·room n : private room on a ship

states·man \ˈstātsmən\ n : one skilled in government or diplomacy — **states·man·like** adj — **states·man·ship** n

stat·ic \ˈstatik\ adj 1 : relating to bodies or forces at rest 2 : not moving 3 : relating to stationary charges of electricity ~ n : noise on radio or television from electrical disturbances

sta·tion \ˈstāshən\ n 1 : place of duty 2 : regular stop on a bus or train route 3 : social standing 4 : place where radio or television programs originate ~ vb : assign to a station

sta·tion·ary \ˈstāshə,nerē\ adj 1 : not moving or not movable 2 : not changing

sta·tio·nery \ˈstāshə,nerē\ n : letter paper with envelopes

sta·tis·tic \stəˈtistik\ n : single item of statistics

sta·tis·tics \-tiks\ n pl : numerical facts collected for study — **sta·tis·ti·cal** \-tikəl\ adj — **sta·tis·ti·cal·ly** adv — **stat·is·ti·cian** \,statəˈstishən\ n

stat·u·ary \ˈstachə,werē\ n, pl -ar·ies : collection of statues

stat·ue \ˈstachü\ n : sculptured likeness of a being — **stat·u·ette** \,stachəˈwet\ n

stat·u·esque \,stachəˈwesk\ adj : well-proportioned or of dignified bearing

stat·ure \ˈstachər\ n 1 : height 2 : status gained by achievement

sta·tus \ˈstātəs, ˈstat-\ n : relative situation or condition

sta·tus quo \-ˈkwō\ n : existing state of affairs

stat·ute \ˈstachüt\ n : law — **stat·u·to·ry** \ˈstachə,tōrē\ adj

staunch \ˈstȯnch\ adj : steadfast — **staunch·ly** adv

stave \ˈstāv\ n : narrow strip of wood ~ vb **staved** or **stove** \ˈstōv\; **stav·ing** 1 : break a hole in 2 : drive away

staves pl of STAFF

¹**stay** \ˈstā\ n : support ~ vb **stayed**; **stay·ing** 1 : prop up 2 : satisfy for a time

²**stay** vb **stayed** or **staid** \ˈstād\; **stay·ing** 1 : pause 2 : lodge 3 : remain 4 : stop or postpone ~ n : a staying

stead \ˈsted\ n : one's place, job, or function — **in good stead** : to advantage

stead·fast \-,fast\ adj : faithful or determined — **stead·fast·ly** adv

steady \ˈstedē\ adj **stead·i·er; -est** 1

: firm in position or sure in movement 2 : calm or reliable 3 : constant 4 : regular ~ vb **stead·ied; steady·ing** : make or become steady — **steadi·ly** \ˈsted³lē\ adv — **steadi·ness** n — **steady** adv

steak \ˈstāk\ n : thick slice of meat

steal \ˈstēl\ vb **stole** \ˈstōl\; **sto·len** \ˈstōlən\; **steal·ing** 1 : take and carry away wrongfully and with intent to keep 2 : move secretly or slowly

stealth \ˈstelth\ n : secret or underhand procedure — **stealth·i·ly** \-thəlē\ adv — **stealthy** adj

steam \ˈstēm\ n : vapor of boiling water ~ vb : give off steam — **steam·boat** n — **steam·ship** n — **steamy** adj

steed \ˈstēd\ n : horse

steel \ˈstēl\ n : tough carbon-containing iron ~ vb : make able to resist — **steel** adj — **steely** adj

¹**steep** \ˈstēp\ adj : having a very sharp slope or great elevation — **steep·ly** adv — **steep·ness** n

²**steep** vb : soak in a liquid

stee·ple \ˈstēpəl\ n : usu. tapering church tower

stee·ple·chase n : race over hurdles

¹**steer** \ˈstiər\ n : castrated ox

²**steer** vb 1 : direct the course of (as a ship or car) 2 : guide

steer·age \ˈsti(ə)rij\ n : section in a ship for people paying the lowest fares

stein \ˈstīn\ n : mug

stel·lar \ˈstelər\ adj : relating to stars or resembling a star

¹**stem** \ˈstem\ n : main upright part of a plant ~ vb -mm- 1 : derive 2 : make progress against — **stem·less** adj — **stemmed** adj

²**stem** vb -mm- : stop the flow of

stench \ˈstench\ n : stink

sten·cil \ˈstensəl\ n : printing sheet cut with letters to let ink pass through — **stencil** vb

ste·nog·ra·phy \stəˈnägrəfē\ n : art or process of writing in shorthand — **ste·nog·ra·pher** \-fər\ n — **steno·graph·ic** \,stenəˈgrafik\ adj

sten·to·ri·an \sten·tōrēən\ adj : extremely loud

step \ˈstep\ n 1 : single action of a leg in walking or running 2 : rest for the foot in going up or down 3 : degree, rank, or stage 4 : way of walking ~ vb -pp- 1 : move by steps 2 : press with the foot

step- \ˈstep-\ comb form : related by a remarriage and not by blood

step·lad·der n : light portable set of steps in a hinged frame

steppe \\'step\\ *n* : dry grassy land esp. of Asia

-ster \\stər\\ *n suffix* 1 : one that does, makes, or uses 2 : one that is associated with or takes part in 3 : one that is

ste·reo \\'sterē,ō, 'stir-\\ *n, pl* **-reos** : stereophonic sound system — **stereo** *adj*

ste·reo·phon·ic \\,sterēə'fänik, ,stir-\\ *adj* : relating to a 3-dimensional effect of reproduced sound

ste·reo·typed \\'sterēə,tīpt, 'stir-\\ *adj* : represented as lacking originality or individuality

ster·ile \\'sterəl\\ *adj* 1 : unable to bear fruit, crops, or offspring 2 : free from disease germs —**ster·il·i·ty** \\stə'rilətē\\ *n* —**ster·il·iza·tion** \\,sterələ'zāshən\\ *n* —**ster·il·ize** \\-ə,līz\\ *vb* —**ster·il·iz·er** *n*

ster·ling \\'stərliŋ\\ *adj* 1 : having a fixed standard of purity represented by an alloy of 925 parts of silver with 75 parts of copper 2 : made of sterling silver 3 : excellent

¹stern \\'stərn\\ *adj* : severe —**stern·ly** *adv* —**stern·ness** *n*

²stern *n* : back end of a boat

ster·num \\'stərnəm\\ *n, pl* **-nums** *or* **-na** \\-nə\\ : long flat chest bone joining the 2 sets of ribs

stetho·scope \\'stethə,skōp\\ *n* : instrument used for listening to sounds in the chest

ste·ve·dore \\'stēvə,dōr\\ *n* : worker who loads and unloads ships

stew \\'st(y)ü\\ *n* : dish of boiled meat and vegetables —**stew** *vb*

stew·ard \\'st(y)üərd\\ *n* 1 : manager of an estate or an organization 2 : person on a ship or airliner who looks after passenger comfort —**stew·ard·ess** \\-əs\\ *n* —**stew·ard·ship** *n*

¹stick \\'stik\\ *n* 1 : cut or broken branch 2 : long thin piece of wood or something resembling it

²stick *vb* **stuck** \\'stək\\; **stick·ing** 1 : stab 2 : thrust or project 3 : hold fast to something 4 : attach 5 : become jammed or fixed

stick·er \\'stikər\\ *n* : gummed label

stick·ler \\'stik(ə)lər\\ *n* : one who insists on exactness or completeness

sticky \\'stikē\\ *adj* **stick·i·er; -est** 1 : adhesive 2 : gluey

stiff \\'stif\\ *adj* 1 : not bending easily 2 : tense 3 : formal 4 : strong 5 : severe —**stiff·ly** *adv* —**stiff·ness** *n*

stiff·en \\'stifən\\ *vb* : make or become stiff —**stiff·en·er** \\-(ə)nər\\ *n*

sti·fle \\'stīfəl\\ *vb* **-fled; -fling** 1 : smother or suffocate 2 : suppress

stig·ma \\'stigmə\\ *n, pl* **-ma·ta** \\stig-'mätə, 'stigmətə\\ *or* **-mas** : mark of disgrace —**stig·ma·tize** \\'stigmə,tīz\\ *vb*

stile \\'stīl\\ *n* : steps for crossing a fence

sti·let·to \\stə'letō\\ *n, pl* **-tos** *or* **-toes** : slender dagger

¹still \\'stil\\ *adj* 1 : motionless 2 : silent ~ *vb* : make or become still ~ *adv* 1 : without motion 2 : up to and during this time 3 : in spite of that ~ *n* : silence —**still·ness** *n*

²still *n* : apparatus used in distillation

still-born *adj* : born dead —**still-birth** *n*

stilt \\'stilt\\ *n* : one of a pair of poles for walking

stilt·ed \\'stiltəd\\ *adj* : pompous

stim·u·lant \\'stimyələnt\\ *n* : substance that temporarily increases the activity of an organism —**stimulant** *adj*

stim·u·late \\-,lāt\\ *vb* **-lat·ed; -lat·ing** : make active —**stim·u·la·tion** \\,stimyə'lāshən\\ *n*

stim·u·lus \\'stimyələs\\ *n, pl* **-li** \\-,lī\\ : something that stimulates

sting \\'stiŋ\\ *vb* **stung** \\'stəŋ\\; **sting·ing** 1 : prick painfully 2 : hurt with an intense burning pain ~ *n* : act of stinging —**sting·er** *n*

stin·gy \\'stinjē\\ *adj* **stin·gi·er; -est** : not generous —**stin·gi·ness** *n*

stink \\'stiŋk\\ *vb* **stank** \\'staŋk\\ *or* **stunk** \\'stəŋk\\; **stunk; stink·ing** : have a strong offensive odor —**stink** *n* —**stink·er** *n*

stint \\'stint\\ *vb* : be sparing or stingy ~ *n* : restraint 2 : quantity or period of work

sti·pend \\'stī,pend, -pənd\\ *n* : money paid periodically

stip·ple \\'stipəl\\ *vb* **-pled; -pling** : engrave, paint, or draw with dots instead of lines —**stipple** *n*

stip·u·late \\'stipyə,lāt\\ *vb* **-lat·ed; -lat·ing** : demand as a condition —**stip·u·la·tion** \\,stipyə'lāshən\\ *n*

stir \\'stər\\ *vb* **-rr-** 1 : move slightly 2 : prod or push into activity 3 : mix by continued circular movement ~ *n* : act or result of stirring

stir·rup \\'stərəp\\ *n* : saddle loop for the foot

stitch \\'stich\\ *n* 1 : loop formed by a needle in sewing 2 : sudden sharp pain ~ *vb* 1 : fasten or decorate with stitches 2 : sew

stock \\'stäk\\ *n* 1 : block or part of wood 2 : original from which others derive 3 : farm animals 4 : supply of goods kept by a merchant 5 : money

invested in a large business **6** *pl*
: instrument of punishment like a pillory with holes for the feet or feet
and hands ~ *vb* : provide with stock

stock-ade \stä′kād\ *n* : defensive or
confining enclosure

stock-ing \′stäkiŋ\ *n* : close-fitting covering for the foot and leg

stock-pile *n* : reserve supply —**stockpile**
vb

stock-yard *n* : yard for livestock to be
slaughtered or shipped

stocky \′stäkē\ *adj* **stock-i-er; -est**
: short and relatively thick

stodgy \′stäjē\ *adj* **stodg-i-er; -est** : dull

sto-ic \′stōik\, **sto-i-cal** -ikəl\ *adj*
: showing indifference to pain —
stoic *n* —**sto-i-cal-ly** \-ik(ə)lē\ *adv* —
sto-i-cism \′stōə,sizəm\ *n*

stoke \′stōk\ *vb* **stoked; stok-ing** : stir
up a fire or supply fuel to a furnace
—**stok-er** *n*

¹**stole** \′stōl\ *past of* STEAL

²**stole** *n* : long wide scarf

stolen *past part of* STEAL

stol-id \′stäləd\ *adj* : having or showing little or no emotion —**sto-lid-i-ty**
\stä′lidətē\ *n* —**stol-id-ly** \′stäləd-lē\
adv

stom-ach \′stəmək, -ik\ *n* **1** : saclike
digestive organ **2** : abdomen **3** : appetite or desire —**stom-ach-ache** *n*

stood *past of* STAND

stool \′stül\ *n* **1** : seat usu. without
back or arms **2** : footstool **3** : discharge of feces

¹**stoop** \′stüp\ *vb* **1** : bend over **2**
: lower oneself ~ *n* **1** : act of bending
over **2** : bent position of shoulders

²**stoop** *n* : small porch at a house door

stop \′stäp\ *vb* **-pp- 1** : block an opening **2** : end or cause to end **3** : pause
for rest or a visit in a journey ~ *n* **1**
: plug **2** : act or place of stopping **3**
: delay in a journey —**stop-light** *n* —
stop-page \-ij\ *n* —**stop-per** *n*

stop-gap *n* : temporary measure or
thing

stor-age \′stōrij\ *n* : safekeeping of
goods (as in a warehouse)

store \′stōr\ *vb* **stored; stor-ing** : put
aside for future use ~ *n* **1** : something stored **2** : retail business establishment —**store-house** *n* —**store-
keep-er** *n* —**store-room** *n*

stork \′stōrk\ *n* : large wading bird

storm \′stȯrm\ *n* **1** : heavy fall of rain
or snow **2** : violent outbreak ~ *vb* **1**
: rain or snow heavily **2** : rage **3**
: make an attack against —**stormy**
adj

¹**sto-ry** \′stōrē\ *n*, *pl* **-ries 1** : narrative
2 : report —**sto-ry-tell-er** *n*

²**story** *n*, *pl* **-ries** : floor of a building

stout \′staút\ *adj* **1** : firm or strong **2**
: thick or bulky —**stout-ly** *adv* —
stout-ness *n*

stove \′stōv\ *n* : apparatus for providing heat (as for cooking or heating)

²**stove** *past of* STAVE

stow \′stō\ *vb* **1** : pack in a compact
mass **2** : put or hide away

strad-dle \′strad²l\ *vb* **-dled; -dling**
: stand over or sit on with legs on
opposite sides —**straddle** *n*

strafe \′strāf\ *vb* **strafed; straf-ing** : fire
upon with machine guns from a low-
flying airplane

strag-gle \′stragəl\ *vb* **-gled; -gling**
: wander or become separated from
others —**strag-gler** \-(ə)lər\ *n*

straight \′strāt\ *adj* **1** : having no
bends, turns, or twists **2** : just,
proper, or honest **3** : neat and orderly ~ *adv* : in a straight manner

straight-en \′strāt²n\ *vb* : make or become straight

straight-for-ward \strāt′fȯrwərd\ *adj*
: frank or honest

straight-way *adv* : immediately

¹**strain** \′strān\ *n* **1** : lineage **2** : trace

²**strain** *vb* **1** : exert to the utmost **2**
: filter or remove by filtering **3** : injure by improper use ~ *n* **1** : excessive tension or exertion **2** : bodily
injury from excessive effort —
strain-er *n*

strait \′strāt\ *n* **1** : narrow channel connecting **2** bodies of water **2** *pl*
: distress

strait-en \′strāt²n\ *vb* **1** : hem in **2**
: make distressing or difficult

¹**strand** \′strand\ *vb* **1** : drive or cast
upon the shore **2** : leave helpless

²**strand** *n* **1** : twisted fiber of a rope **2**
: length of something ropelike

strange \′strānj\ *adj* **strang-er; strang-
est 1** : unusual or queer **2** : new —
strange-ly *adv* —**strange-ness** *n*

strang-er \′strānjər\ *n* : person with
whom one is not acquainted

stran-gle \′straŋgəl\ *vb* **-gled; -gling**
: choke to death —**stran-gler**
\-g(ə)lər\ *n*

stran-gu-la-tion \,straŋgyə′lāshən\ *n*
: act or process of strangling

strap \′strap\ *n* : narrow strip of flexible material used esp. for fastening

~ vb 1 : secure with a strap 2 : beat with a strap —**strap·less** n

strap·ping \'strapiŋ\ adj : large

strat·a·gem \'stratəjəm, -jem\ n : deceptive scheme or maneuver

strat·e·gy \'stratəjē\ n, pl -gies : carefully worked out plan of action —**stra·te·gic** \strə'tējik\ adj —**strat·e·gist** \'stratəjist\ n

strat·i·fy \'stratə,fī\ vb -fied; -fy·ing : form or arrange in layers —**strat·i·fi·ca·tion** \,stratəfə'kāshən\ n

strato·sphere \'stratə,sfiər\ n : earth's atmosphere from about 7 to 37 miles above the earth's surface —**strato·spher·ic** \,stratə'sfi(ə)rik, -'sfer-\ adj

stra·tum \'strātəm, 'strat-\ n, pl -ta \'strātə, 'strat-\ : layer

straw \'strȯ\ n 1 : grass stems after grain is removed 2 : tube for drinking ~ adj : made of straw

straw·ber·ry \'strȯ,berē, -b(ə)rē\ n : red pulpy fruit

stray \'strā\ vb : wander from a course or herd ~ n : person or animal that strays ~ adj : separated from or not related to anything close by

streak \'strēk\ n 1 : mark of a different color 2 : narrow band of light 3 : trace 4 : run (as of luck) or series ~ vb 1 : form streaks in or on 2 : move fast

stream \'strēm\ n 1 : flow of water on land 2 : steady flow (as of water or air) ~ vb 1 : flow in a stream 2 : pour out streams

stream·er \'strēmər\ n : long ribbon or ribbonlike flag

stream·lined \-,līnd, -'līnd\ adj 1 : made with contours to reduce air or water resistance 2 : simplified 3 : modernized —**streamline** vb

street \'strēt\ n : thoroughfare esp. in a city or town

street·car \'strēt-\ n : passenger vehicle running on rails in the streets

strength \'streŋth\ n 1 : quality of being strong 2 : toughness 3 : intensity

strength·en \'streŋthən\ vb : make, grow, or become stronger —**strength·en·er** \'streŋth(ə)nər\ n

stren·u·ous \'strenyəwəs\ adj : requiring or showing energetic effort —**stren·u·ous·ly** adv

stress \'stres\ n 1 : pressure or strain that tends to distort a body 2 : relative prominence given to one thing among others 3 : state of physical or mental tension or something inducing it ~ vb : put stress on

stretch \'strech\ vb 1 : spread or reach out 2 : draw out in length or breadth 3 : make taut 4 : exaggerate 5 : become extended without breaking ~ n : act of extending beyond normal limits

stretch·er \'strechər\ n : cot with handles for carrying a disabled person

strew \'strü\ vb strewed; strewed or strewn \'strün\; strew·ing 1 : scatter 2 : cover by scattering something over

strick·en \'strikən\ adj : afflicted with disease

strict \'strikt\ adj 1 : severe and unyielding 2 : precise —**strict·ly** adv —**strict·ness** n

stric·ture \'strikchər\ n : hostile criticism

stride \'strīd\ vb strode \'strōd\; strid·den \'stridᵊn\; strid·ing \'strīdiŋ\ : walk or run with long steps ~ n 1 : long step 2 : manner of striding

stri·dent \'strīdᵊnt\ adj : loud and harsh

strife \'strīf\ n : conflict

strike \'strīk\ vb struck \'strək\; struck; strik·ing \'strikiŋ\ 1 : hit sharply 2 : delete 3 : produce by impressing 4 : cause to sound 5 : afflict 6 : occur to or impress 7 : cause (a match) to ignite by rubbing 8 : refrain from working 9 : find 10 : take on (as a pose) ~ n 1 : act or instance of striking 2 : work stoppage 3 : military attack —**strik·er** n —**strike out** vb : start out vigorously —**strike up** n : start

strik·ing \'strīkiŋ\ adj : very noticeable —**strik·ing·ly** adv

string \'striŋ\ n 1 : line usu. of twisted threads 2 : series 3 pl : stringed instruments ~ vb strung \'strəŋ\; string·ing 1 : thread on or with a string 2 : hang or fasten by a string

stringed \'striŋd\ adj : having strings

strin·gent \'strinjənt\ adj : severe

stringy \'striŋē\ adj string·i·er, -est : tough or fibrous

¹**strip** \'strip\ vb -pp- 1 : take the covering or clothing from 2 : undress —**strip·per** n

²**strip** n : long narrow flat piece

stripe \'strīp\ n : distinctive line or long narrow section ~ vb striped \'strīpt\; strip·ing : make stripes on

striped \'strīpt, 'strīpəd\ adj : having stripes or streaks

strive \'strīv\ vb strove \'strōv\; striv·en \'strivən\ or strived; striv·ing \'striviŋ\ 1 : struggle 2 : try hard

strode past of STRIDE

stroke \'strōk\ *vb* **stroked; strok·ing** : rub gently ~ *n* **1** : act of swinging or striking **2** : sudden action

stroll \'strōl\ *vb* : walk leisurely —**stroll** *n* —**stroll·er** *n*

strong \'stroŋ\ *adj* **1** : capable of exerting great force or of withstanding stress or violence **2** : healthy **3** : zealous —**strong·ly** *adv*

strong·hold *n* : fortified place

stron·tium \'stränch(ē)əm, 'stränt-ēəm\ *n* : soft malleable metallic chemical element

struck *past of* STRIKE

struc·ture \'strəkchər\ *n* **1** : building **2** : arrangement of elements ~ *vb* **-tured; -tur·ing** : make into a structure —**struc·tur·al** \-chərəl, -shrəl\ *adj*

strug·gle \'strəgəl\ *vb* **-gled; -gling 1** : make strenuous efforts to overcome an adversary **2** : proceed with great effort ~ *n* **1** : strenuous effort **2** : intense competition for superiority

strum \'strəm\ *vb* **-mm-** : play (a musical instrument) by brushing the strings with the fingers

strum·pet \'strəmpət\ *n* : prostitute

strung *past of* STRING

strut \'strət\ *vb* **-tt-** : walk in a proud or showy manner ~ *n* **1** : proud walk **2** : supporting bar or rod

strych·nine \'strik,nīn, -nən, -,nēn\ *n* : bitter poisonous alkaloid

stub \'stəb\ *n* : short end or section ~ *vb* **-bb-** : strike against something

stub·ble \'stəbəl\ *n* : short growth left after cutting —**stub·bly** *adj*

stub·born \'stəbərn\ *adj* **1** : determined not to yield **2** : hard to control —**stub·born·ly** *adv* —**stub·born·ness** *n*

stub·by \'stəbē\ *adj* : short, blunt, and thick

stuc·co \'stəkō\ *n, pl* **-cos** *or* **-coes** : plaster for coating outside walls ~ *vb* : coat with stucco

stuck *past of* STICK

stuck-up \'stək'əp\ *adj* : conceited

¹stud \'stəd\ *n* : male horse kept for breeding

²stud *n* **1** : upright wall support **2** : projecting nail, pin, or rod ~ *vb* **-dd-** : supply or dot with studs

stu·dent \'st(y)üd²nt\ *n* : one who studies

stud·ied \'stədēd\ *adj* : premeditated

stu·dio \'st(y)üdē,ō\ *n, pl* **-dios 1** : artist's workroom **2** : place where movies are made or television or radio shows are broadcast

stu·di·ous \'st(y)üdēəs\ *adj* : devoted to study —**stu·di·ous·ly** *adv*

study \'stədē\ *n, pl* **stud·ies 1** : act or process of learning about something **2** : branch of learning **3** : careful examination **4** : room for reading or studying ~ *vb* **stud·ied; study·ing** : apply the attention and mind to a subject

stuff \'stəf\ *n* **1** : personal property **2** : raw or fundamental material **3** : unspecified often worthless material or things ~ *vb* : fill esp. by packing tightly —**stuff·ing** *n*

stuffy \'stəfē\ *adj* **stuff·i·er; -est 1** : lacking fresh air **2** : unimaginative or pompous

stul·ti·fy \'stəltə,fī\ *vb* **-fied; -fy·ing** : cause to appear foolish —**stul·ti·fi·ca·tion** \,stəltəfə'kāshən\ *n*

stum·ble \'stəmbəl\ *vb* **-bled; -bling 1** : lose one's balance or fall in walking or running **2** : speak or act clumsily **3** : come by chance —**stumble** *n*

stump \'stəmp\ *n* : part left when something is cut off ~ *vb* : confuse —**stumpy** *adj*

stun \'stən\ *vb* **-nn- 1** : make senseless or dizzy by or as if by a blow **2** : bewilder

stung *past of* STING

stunk *past of* STINK

stun·ning \'stəniŋ\ *adj* : strikingly beautiful —**stun·ning·ly** *adv*

¹stunt \'stənt\ *vb* : hinder the normal growth of

²stunt *n* : spectacular feat

stu·pe·fy \'st(y)üpə,fī\ *vb* **-fied; -fy·ing 1** : make insensible by or as if by drugs **2** : amaze —**stu·pe·fac·tion** \,st(y)üpə'fakshən\ *n*

stu·pen·dous \st(y)ü'pendəs\ *adj* : very big or impressive —**stu·pen·dous·ly** *adv*

stu·pid \'st(y)üpəd\ *adj* : not sensible or intelligent —**stu·pid·i·ty** \st(y)ü'pidətē\ *n* —**stu·pid·ly** *adv*

stu·por \'st(y)üpər\ *n* : state of being conscious but not aware or sensible —**stu·por·ous** *adj*

stur·dy \'stərdē\ *adj* **-di·er; -est** : strong —**stur·di·ly** \'stərd³lē\ *adv* —**stur·di·ness** *n*

stur·geon \'stərjən\ *n* : fish whose roe is caviar

stut·ter \'stətər\ *vb or n* : stammer

¹sty \'stī\ *n, pl* **sties** : pig pen

²sty, stye \'stī\ *n, pl* **sties** *or* **styes** : inflamed swelling on the edge of an eyelid

style \'stīl\ *n* **1** : distinctive way of speaking, writing, or acting **2** : elegant or fashionable way of living ~ *vb* **styled; styl·ing 1** : name **2** : give a particular design or style to —**styl·ish** \'stīlish\ *adj* —**styl·ish·ly** *adv* —**styl·ish·ness** *n* —**styl·ist** \-əst\ *n* —**styl·ize** \'stī(ə)l,īz\ *vb*

sty·lus \'stīləs\ *n, pl* **-li** \'stī(ə)l,ī\ **1** : pointed writing tool **2** : phonograph needle

sty·mie \'stīmē\ *vb* **-mied; -mie·ing** : block or frustrate

suave \'swäv\ *adj* : well-mannered and gracious —**suave·ly** *adv*

¹sub \'səb\ *n or adj* : substitute

²sub *n* : submarine

sub- \,səb, 'səb\ *prefix* **1** : under or beneath **2** : subordinate or secondary **3** : subordinate portion of **4** : with repetition of a process so as to form, stress, or deal with subordinate parts or relations **5** : somewhat **6** : nearly

subacute	subindustry
subagency	sublease
subagent	sublethal
subarctic	sublevel
subarea	subliterate
subatmospheric	subnetwork
subaverage	suboceanic
subbase	suborder
subbasement	subpar
subbranch	subpart
subcabinet	subplot
subcategory	subpolar
subclass	subprincipal
subclassification	subprocess
subclassify	subprogram
subcommission	subproject
subcommunity	subregion
subcomponent	subsea
subconcept	subsection
subcontract	subsense
subcontractor	subspecialty
subculture	subspecies
subdean	substage
subdepartment	subsurface
subdistrict	subsystem
subentry	subtemperate
subequatorial	subtheme
subfamily	subtopic
subfreezing	subtotal
subgroup	subtreasury
subhead	subtype
subheading	subunit
subhuman	subvariety
subindex	

sub·con·scious \,səb'känchəs, 'səb-\ *adj* : existing without conscious awareness ~ *n* : part of the mind concerned with subconscious activities —**sub·con·scious·ly** *adv*

sub·di·vide \,səbdə'vīd, 'səbdə,vīd\ *vb* **1** : divide into several parts **2** : divide (land) into building lots —**sub·di·vi·sion** \-'vizhən, -,vizh-\ *n*

sub·due \səb'd(y)ü\ *vb* **-dued; -du·ing 1** : bring under control **2** : reduce the intensity of

sub·ject \'səbjikt\ *n* **1** : person under the authority of another **2** : something being discussed or studied **3** : word or word group about which something is said in a sentence ~ *adj* **1** : being under one's authority **2** : prone **3** : dependent on some condition or act ~ \səb'jekt\ *vb* **1** : bring under control **2** : cause to undergo —**sub·jec·tion** \-'jekshən\ *n*

sub·jec·tive \(,)səb'jektiv\ *adj* : deriving from an individual viewpoint or bias —**sub·jec·tive·ly** *adv* —**sub·jec·tiv·i·ty** \-,jek'tivətē\ *n*

sub·ju·gate \'səbji,gāt\ *vb* **-gat·ed; -gat·ing** : bring under one's control —**sub·ju·ga·tion** \,səbji'gāshən\ *n*

sub·junc·tive \səb'jəŋktiv\ *adj* : relating to a verb form which expresses possibility or contingency —**subjunctive** *n*

sub·let \'səb'let\ *vb* **-let; -let·ting** : rent (a property) from a lessee

sub·lime \sə'blīm\ *adj* : splendid —**sub·lim·i·ty** \-'blimətē\ *n*

sub·ma·rine \'səbmə,rēn, ,səbmə'-\ *adj* : existing, acting, or growing under the sea ~ *n* : underwater boat

sub·merge \səb'mərj\ *vb* **-merged; -merg·ing** : put or plunge under the surface of water —**sub·mer·gence** \-'mərjəns\ *n* —**sub·mers·ible** \səb'mərsəbəl\ *adj* —**sub·mer·sion** \-'mərzhən\ *n*

sub·mit \səb'mit\ *vb* **-tt- 1** : yield **2** : give or offer —**sub·mis·sion** \-'mishən\ *n* —**sub·mis·sive** \-'misiv\ *adj*

sub·nor·mal \,səb'nórməl\ *adj* : falling below what is normal

sub·or·di·nate \sə'bórdnət, -ᵊnət\ *adj* : lower in rank ~ *n* : one that is subordinate ~ \sə'bórdᵊn,āt\ *vb* **-nat·ed; -nat·ing** : place in a lower rank or class —**sub·or·di·na·tion** \-,bórdᵊn'āshən\ *n*

sub·poe·na \sə'pēnə\ *n* : summons to appear in court ~ *vb* **-naed; -na·ing** : summon with a subpoena

sub·scribe \səb'skrīb\ *vb* **-scribed; -scrib·ing 1** : give consent or approval **2** : agree to support or to receive and pay for —**sub·scrib·er** *n*

sub·scrip·tion \səb'skripshən\ *n* : order for regular receipt of a publication

sub·se·quent \'səbsikwənt, -sə,kwent\ *adj* : following after —**sub·se·quent·ly** \-,kwentlē, -kwənt-\ *adv*

sub·ser·vi·ence \səb'sərvēəns\ *n* : obsequious submission —**sub·ser·vi·en·cy** \-ənsē\ *n* —**sub·ser·vi·ent** \-ənt\ *adj*

sub·side \səb'sīd\ *vb* -**sid·ed**; -**sid·ing** : die down in intensity

sub·sid·iary \səb'sidē,erē\ *adj* 1 : furnishing support 2 : controlled by a main company —**subsidiary** *n*

sub·si·dize \'səbsə,dīz\ *vb* -**dized**; -**diz·ing** : aid with a subsidy

sub·si·dy \'səbsədē\ *n, pl* -**dies** : gift of supporting funds

sub·sist \səb'sist\ *vb* : acquire the necessities of life —**sub·sis·tence** \-'sistəns\ *n*

sub·stance \'səbstəns\ *n* 1 : essence or essential part 2 : physical material 3 : wealth

sub·stan·dard \,səb'standərd, 'səb-\ *adj* : falling short of a standard or norm

sub·stan·tial \səb'stanchəl\ *adj* 1 : plentiful 2 : considerable —**sub·stan·tial·ly** *adv*

sub·stan·ti·ate \səb'stanchē,āt\ *vb* -**at·ed**; -**at·ing** : verify —**sub·stan·ti·a·tion** \-,stanchē'āshən\ *n*

sub·sti·tute \'səbstə,t(y)üt\ *n* : replacement ~ *vb* -**tut·ed**; -**tut·ing** : put or serve in place of another —**substitute** *adj* —**sub·sti·tu·tion** \,səbstə-'t(y)üshən\ *n*

sub·ter·fuge \'səbtər,fyüj\ *n* : deceptive trick

sub·ter·ra·nean \,səbtə'rānēən\ *adj* : lying or being underground

sub·ti·tle \'səb,tīt⁰l\ *n* : movie caption

sub·tle \'sət⁰l\ *adj* -**tler** \'sətlər, -⁰lər\; -**tlest** \-ləst, -⁰ləst\ 1 : hardly noticeable 2 : clever —**sub·tle·ty** \-tē\ *n* —**sub·tly** \-lē, -⁰lē\ *adv*

sub·tract \səb'trakt\ *vb* : take away (as one number from another) —**sub·trac·tion** \-'trakshən\ *n*

sub·urb \'səb,ərb\ *n* : residential area adjacent to a city —**sub·ur·ban** \sə'bərbən\ *adj or n* —**sub·ur·ban·ite** \-bə,nīt\ *n*

sub·vert \səb'vərt\ *vb* : overthrow or ruin —**sub·ver·sion** \-'vərzhən\ *n* —**sub·ver·sive** \-'vərsiv\ *adj*

sub·way \'səb,wā\ *n* : underground electric railway

suc·ceed \sək'sēd\ *vb* 1 : follow (someone) in a job, role, or title 2 : attain a desired object or end

suc·cess \-'ses\ *n* 1 : satisfactory completion of something 2 : gaining of wealth and fame 3 : one that succeeds —**suc·cess·ful** \-fəl\ *adj* —**suc·cess·ful·ly** *adv*

suc·ces·sion \sək'seshən\ *n* 1 : order, act, or right of succeeding 2 : series

suc·ces·sive \-'sesiv\ *adj* : following in order —**suc·ces·sive·ly** *adv*

suc·ces·sor \-'sesər\ *n* : one that succeeds another

suc·cinct \(,)sək'siŋkt, sə'siŋkt\ *adj* : brief —**suc·cinct·ly** *adv* —**suc·cinct·ness** *n*

suc·cor \'səkər\ *n or vb* : help

suc·co·tash \'səkə,tash\ *n* : beans and corn cooked together

suc·cu·lent \'səkyələnt\ *adj* : juicy —**suc·cu·lence** \-ləns\ *n* —**succulent** *n*

suc·cumb \sə'kəm\ *vb* 1 : give up 2 : die

such \('),səch, (,)sich\ *adj* 1 : of this or that kind 2 : having a specified quality —**such** *pron or adv*

suck \'sək\ *vb* 1 : draw in liquid with the mouth 2 : draw liquid from by or as if by mouth —**suck** *n*

suck·er \'səkər\ *n* 1 : one that sucks or clings 2 : shoot from the roots or lower part of a plant 3 : easily deceived person

suck·le \'səkəl\ *vb* -**led**; -**ling** : give or draw milk from the breast or udder

suck·ling \'səkliŋ\ *n* : young unweaned mammal

su·crose \'sü,krōs, -,krōz\ *n* : cane or beet sugar

suc·tion \'səkshən\ *n* 1 : act of sucking 2 : act or process of drawing in by partially exhausting the air

sud·den \'səd⁰n\ *adj* 1 : happening quickly or unexpectedly 2 : steep 3 : hasty —**sud·den·ly** *adv* —**sud·den·ness** *n*

suds \'sədz\ *n pl* : soapy water esp. when frothy —**sudsy** \'sədzē\ *adj*

sue \'sü\ *vb* **sued**; **su·ing** 1 : petition 2 : bring legal action against

suede, suède \'swād\ *n* : leather with a napped surface

su·et \'süət\ *n* : hard beef fat

suf·fer \'səfər\ *vb* 1 : experience pain, loss, or hardship 2 : permit —**suf·fer·er** *n*

suf·fer·ing \-(ə)riŋ\ *n* : pain or hardship

suf·fice \sə'fīs\ *vb* -**ficed**; -**fic·ing** : be sufficient

suf·fi·cient \sə'fishənt\ *adj* : adequate —**suf·fi·cien·cy** \-ənsē\ *n* —**suf·fi·cient·ly** *adv*

suf·fix \'səf,iks\ *n* : letters added at the end of a word —**suffix** \'səfiks,

(,)sə'fiks\ vb —suf·fix·a·tion \,səf,ik'sāshən\

suf·fo·cate \'səfə,kāt\ vb -cat·ed; -cat·ing : suffer or die or cause to die from lack of air —**suf·fo·cat·ing·ly** adv —**suf·fo·ca·tion** \,səfə'kāshən\ n

suf·frage \'səfrij\ n : right to vote

suf·fuse \sə'fyüz\ vb -fused; -fus·ing : spread over or through

sug·ar \'shủgər\ n : sweet substance ~ vb : mix, cover, or sprinkle with sugar —**sug·ar·cane** n —**sug·ary** adj

sug·gest \sə(g)'jest\ vb 1 : put into someone's mind 2 : remind one by association of ideas —**sug·gest·ible** \-'jestəbəl\ adj —**sug·ges·tion** \-'jeschən\ n

sug·ges·tive \-'jestiv\ adj : suggesting something improper —**sug·ges·tive·ly** adv —**sug·ges·tive·ness** n

sui·cide \'süə,sīd\ n 1 : act of killing oneself purposely 2 : one who commits suicide —**sui·cid·al** \,süə'sīd⁰l\ adj

suit \'süt\ n 1 : action in court to recover a right or claim 2 : number of things used or worn together 3 : one of the 4 sets of playing cards ~ vb 1 : be appropriate or becoming to 2 : meet the needs of —**suit·abil·i·ty** \,sütə'bilətē\ n —**suit·able** \'sütəbəl\ adj —**suit·ably** adv

suit·case n : flat rectangular traveling bag

suite \'swēt, for 2 also 'süt\ n 1 : group of rooms 2 : set of matched furniture

suit·or \'sütər\ n : one who seeks to marry a woman

sul·fur, sul·phur \'səlfər\ n : nonmetallic yellow chemical element —**sul·fu·ric** \,səl'fyůrik\ adj —**sul·fu·rous** \-'fyůrəs, 'səlf(y)ərəs\ adj

sulk \'səlk\ vb : be moodily silent —**sulk** n

sulky \'səlkē\ adj : inclined to sulk ~ n : light 2-wheeled cart —**sulk·i·ly** \'səlkəlē\ adv —**sulk·i·ness** \-kēnəs\ n

sul·len \'sələn\ adj 1 : gloomily silent 2 : dismal —**sul·len·ly** adv —**sul·len·ness** n

sul·ly \'səlē\ vb -lied; -ly·ing : cast doubt or disgrace on

sul·tan \'səlt⁰n\ n : sovereign of a Muslim state —**sul·tan·ate** \-,āt\ n

sul·try \'səltrē\ adj -tri·er; -est : very hot and moist

sum \'səm\ n 1 : amount 2 : gist : result of addition ~ vb -mm- : find the sum of

su·mac \'s(h)ü,mak\ n : shrub with spikes of berries

sum·ma·ry \'səmərē\ adj 1 : concise 2 : done without delay or formality ~ n, pl -ries : concise statement —**sum·mar·i·ly** \(,)sə'merəlē, 'səmərəlē\ adv —**sum·ma·rize** \'səmə,rīz\ vb

sum·ma·tion \(,)sə'māshən\ n : a summing up esp. in court

sum·mer \'səmər\ n : season in which the sun shines most directly —**sum·mery** adj

sum·mit \'səmət\ n : highest point

sum·mon \'səmən\ vb 1 : send for or call together 2 : order to appear in court —**sum·mon·er** n

sum·mons \'səmənz\ n, pl **summons·es** : an order to answer charges in court

sump·tu·ous \'səmpchə(wə)s\ adj : lavish

sun \'sən\ n 1 : shining celestial body around which the planets revolve 2 : light of the sun ~ vb -nn- : expose to the sun —**sun·beam** n —**sun·burn** n —**sun·glass·es** n pl —**sun·light** n —**sun·ny** adj —**sun·rise** n —**sun·set** n —**sun·shine** n —**sun·tan** n

sun·dae \'sənde\ n : ice cream with topping

Sun·day \'sənde\ n : 1st day of the week

sun·di·al \-,dī(ə)l\ n : device for showing time by the sun's shadow

sun·dries \'səndrēz\ n, pl : various small articles

sun·dry \-drē\ adj : several

sun·fish n : perchlike freshwater fish

sun·flow·er n : tall plant grown for its oil-rich seeds

sung past of SING

sunk past of SINK

sunk·en \'səŋkən\ adj 1 : submerged 2 : fallen in

sun·spot n : dark spot on the sun

sun·stroke n : heatstroke from the sun

sup \'səp\ vb -pp- : eat the evening meal

super \'süpər\ adj : very fine

super- \,süpər, 'sü-\ prefix 1 : higher in quantity, quality, or degree than 2 : in addition 3 : exceeding a norm 4 : in excessive degree or intensity 5 : surpassing others of its kind 6 : situated above, on, or at the top of 7 : more inclusive than 8 : superior in status or position

superabundance	superathlete
superabundant	superbomb
superambitious	superclean

supercold
superpowerful
supercolossal
superrefined
superconvenient
superrich
supercop
supersalesman
superdense
superscout
supereffective
supersecrecy
superefficiency
supersecret
superefficient
supersensitive
superenthusiasm
supership
superenthu-
supersize
siastic
supersized
superfast
superslick
supergood
supersmooth
supergovern-
supersoft
ment
superspecial
supergroup
superspecialist
superhard
superspy
superhero
superstar
superheroine
superstate
superhuman
superstrength
superintellectual
superstrong
superintelligence
supersuccessful
superintelligent
supersystem
superman
supertanker
supermodern
superthick
superpatriot
superthin
superpatriotic
supertight
superpatriotism
supertough
superplane
superweak
superpolite
superweapon
superport
superwoman

su·perb \su̇ˈpərb\ *adj* : outstanding —**su·perb·ly** *adv*

su·per·cil·ious \ˌsüpərˈsiləs\ *adj* : haughtily contemptuous

su·per·fi·cial \ˌsüpərˈfishəl\ *adj* : relating to what is only apparent —**su·per·fi·ci·al·i·ty** \-ˌfishēˈalət·ē\ *n* —**su·per·fi·cial·ly** *adv*

su·per·flu·ous \su̇ˈpərfləwəs\ *adj* : more than necessary —**su·per·flu·i·ty** \ˌsüpərˈflüətē\ *n*

su·per·im·pose \ˌsüpərimˈpōz\ *vb* : lay over and above something

su·per·in·tend \ˌsüp(ə)rinˈtend\ *vb* : have charge and oversight of —**su·per·in·ten·dence** \-ˈtendəns\ *n* —**su·per·in·ten·den·cy** \-dənsē\ *n* —**su·per·in·ten·dent** \-dənt\ *n*

su·pe·ri·or \su̇ˈpirēər\ *adj* 1 : higher, better, or more important 2 : haughty —**superior** *n* —**su·pe·ri·or·i·ty** \-ˌpirēˈorət·ē\ *n*

su·per·la·tive \su̇ˈpərlət·iv\ *adj* 1 : relating to or being an adjective or adverb form that denotes an extreme level 2 : surpassing others —**superlative** *n* —**su·per·la·tive·ly** *adv*

su·per·mar·ket \ˈsüpərˌmärkət\ *n* : self-service grocery store

su·per·nat·u·ral \ˌsüpərˈnach(ə)rəl\ *adj* : beyond the observable physical world —**su·per·nat·u·ral·ly** *adv*

su·per·sede \ˌsüpərˈsēd\ *vb* -**sed·ed;** -**sed·ing** : take the place of

su·per·son·ic \-ˈsänik\ *adj* : relating to speeds 1 to 5 times the speed of sound

su·per·sti·tion \ˌsüpərˈstishən\ *n* : beliefs based on ignorance, fear of the unknown, or trust in magic —**su·per·sti·tious** \-əs\ *adj*

su·per·struc·ture \ˈsüpərˌstrəkchər\ *n* : something built on a base or as a vertical extension

su·per·vise \ˈsüpərˌvīz\ *vb* -**vised;** -**vis·ing** : have charge of —**su·per·vi·sion** \ˌsüpərˈvizhən\ *n* —**su·per·vi·sor** \ˈsüpərˌvīzər\ *n* —**su·per·vi·so·ry** \ˌsüpərˈvīz(ə)rē\ *adj*

su·pine \su̇ˈpīn\ *adj* 1 : lying on the back 2 : indifferent or abject

sup·per \ˈsəpər\ *n* : evening meal

sup·plant \səˈplant\ *vb* : take the place of

sup·ple \ˈsəpəl\ *adj* -**pler;** -**plest** : able to bend easily

sup·ple·ment \ˈsəpləmənt\ *n* : something that adds to or makes up for a lack —**supplement** *vb* —**sup·ple·men·tal** \ˌsəpləˈmentᵊl\ *adj* —**sup·ple·men·ta·ry** \-ˈment(ə)rē\ *adj*

sup·pli·ant \ˈsəplēənt\ *n* : one who supplicates

sup·pli·cate \ˈsəpləˌkāt\ *vb* -**cat·ed;** -**cat·ing** 1 : pray to God 2 : ask earnestly and humbly —**sup·pli·cant** \-likənt\ *n* —**sup·pli·ca·tion** \ˌsəpləˈkāshən\ *n*

sup·ply \səˈplī\ *vb* -**plied;** -**ply·ing** : furnish ~ *n, pl* -**plies** 1 : amount needed or available 2 *pl* : provisions —**sup·pli·er** \-ˈplī(ə)r\ *n*

sup·port \səˈpōrt\ *vb* 1 : take sides with 2 : provide with food, clothing, and shelter 3 : hold up or serve as a foundation for —**support** *n* —**sup·port·able** *adj* —**sup·port·er** *n*

sup·pose \səˈpōz\ *vb* -**posed;** -**pos·ing** 1 : assume to be true 2 : expect 3 : think probable —**sup·po·si·tion** \ˌsəpəˈzishən\ *n*

sup·pos·i·to·ry \səˈpäzəˌtōrē\ *n, pl* -**ries** : medicated material for insertion (as into the rectum)

sup·press \səˈpres\ *vb* 1 : put an end to by authority 2 : keep from being known —**sup·pres·sion** \-ˈpreshən\ *n*

sup·pu·rate \ˈsəpyəˌrāt\ *vb* -**rat·ed;** -**rat·ing** : form or give off pus —**sup·pu·ra·tion** \ˌsəpyəˈrāshən\ *n*

su·prem·a·cy \sù'preməsē\ n, pl -cies : supreme power or authority

su·preme \sù'prēm\ adj 1 : highest in rank or authority 2 : greatest possible —**su·preme·ly** adv

Supreme Being n : God

sur·charge \'sər,chärj\ n 1 : excessive load or burden 2 : extra fee or cost

sure \'shùr\ adj **sur·er; sur·est** 1 : confident 2 : reliable 3 : not to be disputed 4 : bound to happen ~ adv : surely —**sure·ly** adv —**sure·ness** n

sure·ty \'shùrətē\ n, pl -ties 1 : guarantee 2 : one who gives a guarantee for another person

surf \'sərf\ n : waves that break on the shore ~ vb : ride the surf —**surf·board** n —**surf·er** n —**surf·ing** n

sur·face \'sərfəs\ n 1 : the outside of an object 2 : outward aspect ~ vb -**faced; -fac·ing** : rise to the surface

sur·feit \'sərfət\ n 1 : excess 2 : excessive indulgence (as in food or drink) 3 : disgust caused by excess ~ vb : feed, supply, or indulge to the point of surfeit

surge \'sərj\ vb **surged; surg·ing** : rise and fall in or as if in waves ~ n : sudden increase

sur·geon \'sərjən\ n : physician who specializes in surgery

sur·gery \'sərj(ə)rē\ n, pl -ger·ies : medical treatment involving cutting open the body

sur·gi·cal \'sərjikəl\ adj : relating to surgeons or surgery —**sur·gi·cal·ly** adv

sur·ly \'sərlē\ adj -li·er; -est : cross —**sur·li·ness** n

sur·mise \sər'mīz\ vb -mised; -mis·ing : guess —**surmise** n

sur·mount \-'maùnt\ vb 1 : defeat 2 : get to or be the top of

sur·name \'sər,nām\ n : family name

sur·pass \sər'pas\ vb : go beyond or exceed —**sur·pass·ing·ly** adv

sur·plice \'sərpləs\ n : loose white outer ecclesiastical vestment

sur·plus \'sər(,)pləs\ n : quantity left over

sur·prise \sə(r)'prīz\ vb -prised; -pris·ing 1 : come upon or affect unexpectedly 2 : amaze —**surprise** n —**sur·pris·ing** adj —**sur·pris·ing·ly** adv

sur·ren·der \sə'rendər\ vb : give up oneself or a possession to another ~ n : act of surrendering

sur·rep·ti·tious \,sərəp'tishəs\ adj : done, made, or acquired by stealth —**sur·rep·ti·tious·ly** adv

sur·rey \'sərē\ n, pl -reys : horse-drawn carriage

sur·ro·gate \'sərəgāt, -gət\ n : substitute

sur·round \sə'raùnd\ vb : enclose on all sides

sur·round·ings \sə'raùndiŋz\ n pl : objects, conditions, or area around something

sur·veil·lance \sər'vāləns, -'vālyəns, -'vāəns\ n : careful watch

sur·vey \sər'vā\ vb -veyed; -vey·ing 1 : look over and examine closely 2 : make a survey of (as a tract of land) ~ \'sər,-\ n, pl -veys 1 : inspection 2 : process of measuring (as land) —**sur·vey·or** \-'vāər\ n

sur·vive \sər'vīv\ vb -vived; -viv·ing 1 : remain alive or in existence 2 : outlive or outlast —**sur·viv·al** n —**sur·vi·vor** \-'vīvər\ n

sus·cep·ti·ble \sə'septəbəl\ adj : likely to allow or be affected by something —**sus·cep·ti·bil·i·ty** \-,septə'bilətē\ n

sus·pect \'səs,pekt, sə'spekt\ adj : regarded with suspicion ~ \'səs,pekt\ n : one who is suspected (as of a crime) ~ \sə'spekt\ vb 1 : have doubts of 2 : believe guilty without proof 3 : guess

sus·pend \sə'spend\ vb 1 : temporarily stop or keep from a function or job 2 : withhold (judgment) temporarily 3 : hang

sus·pend·er \sə'spendər\ n : one of 2 supporting straps for trousers which pass over the shoulders

sus·pense \sə'spens\ n : excitement and uncertainty as to outcome —**sus·pense·ful** adj

sus·pen·sion \sə'spenchən\ n : act of suspending or the state or period of being suspended

sus·pi·cion \sə'spishən\ n : act of suspecting something 2 : trace

sus·pi·cious \-əs\ adj 1 : arousing suspicion 2 : inclined to suspect —**sus·pi·cious·ly** adv

sus·tain \sə'stān\ vb 1 : provide with nourishment 2 : keep going 3 : hold up 4 : suffer 5 : support or prove

sus·te·nance \'səstənəns\ n 1 : nourishment 2 : something that sustains or supports

swab \'swäb\ n 1 : mop 2 : wad of absorbent material for applying medicine ~ vb -**bb-** : use a swab on

swad·dle \'swäd²l\ vb -dled; -dling \'swädliŋ, -²liŋ\ : bind (an infant) in bands of cloth

swag·ger \'swagər\ vb -gered; -ger·ing 1 : walk with a conceited swing 2 : boast —**swagger** n

¹**swal·low** \'swälō\ n : small migratory bird

²**swallow** vb **1** : take into the stomach through the throat **2** : envelop or take in **3** : accept too easily **4** : endure **5** : retract or repress —**swallow** n

swam past of SWIM

swamp \'swämp\ n : wet spongy land ~ vb : deluge (as with water) —**swampy** adj

swan \'swän\ n : white long-necked swimming bird

swap \'swäp\ vb **-pp-** : trade —**swap** n

swarm \'swórm\ n **1** : mass of honeybees leaving a hive to start a new colony **2** : large crowd moving together ~ vb : gather in a swarm

swar·thy \'swórthē, -thē\ adj **-thi·er;** **-est** : dark in complexion

swash·buck·ler \'swäsh,bəklər\ n : boasting blustering soldier or daredevil —**swash·buck·ling** \-,bək(ə)liŋ\ adj

swat \'swät\ vb **-tt-** : hit sharply —**swat** n —**swat·ter** n

swatch \'swäch\ n : sample piece (as of fabric)

swath \'swäth, 'swóth\, **swathe** \'swäth, 'swóth, 'swāth\ n : row or path cut (as through grass)

swathe \'swäth, 'swóth, 'swāth\ vb **swathed; swath·ing** : wrap with or as if with a bandage

sway \'swā\ vb **1** : swing gently from side to side **2** : influence ~ n **1** : gentle swinging from side to side **2** : controlling power or influence

swear \'swaər\ vb **swore** \'swōr\; **sworn** \'swórn\; **swear·ing 1** : make or cause to make a solemn statement under oath **2** : use profane language —**swear·er** n —**swear·ing** n

sweat \'swet\ vb **sweat** or **sweat·ed;** **sweat·ing 1** : excrete salty moisture from glands of the skin **2** : form drops of moisture on the surface **3** : work or cause to work hard ~ n **1** : liquid exuded through pores from glands (**sweat glands**) of the skin **2** : moisture gathering on a surface in drops —**sweaty** adj

sweat·er \'swetər\ n : knitted jacket or pullover

sweep \'swēp\ vb **swept** \'swept\; **sweep·ing 1** : remove or clean by a brush or a single forceful wipe (as of the hand) **2** : move over with speed and force (as of the hand) **3** : move or extend in a wide curve ~ n **1** : a clearing off or away **2** : single forceful wipe or swinging movement **3** : scope —**sweep·er** n —**sweep·ing** adj

sweep·stakes \'swēp,stāks\ n, pl **sweep·stakes** : contest in which the entire prize may go to the winner

sweet \'swēt\ adj **1** : being or causing the pleasing taste typical of sugar **2** : not stale or spoiled **3** : not salted **4** : pleasant **5** : regarded with love or fondness ~ n : something sweet —**sweet·ly** adv —**sweet·ness** n

sweet·en \'swēt²n\ vb : make sweet —**sweet·en·er** \-²nər\ n

sweet·heart n : person one loves

sweet potato n : sweet yellow edible root of a tropical vine

swell \'swel\ vb **swelled; swelled** or **swol·len** \'swōlən\; **swell·ing 1** : enlarge **2** : bulge **3** : fill or be filled with emotion ~ n **1** : increase **2** : long crestless wave —**swell·ing** n

swel·ter \'sweltər\ vb : be uncomfortable from excessive heat

swept past of SWEEP

swerve \'swərv\ vb **swerved; swerv·ing** : move abruptly aside from a course —**swerve** n

¹**swift** \'swift\ adj **1** : moving with great speed **2** : occurring suddenly —**swift·ly** adv —**swift·ness** n

²**swift** n : small insect-eating bird

swig \'swig\ vb **-gg-** : drink in gulps —**swig** n

swill \'swil\ vb : swallow greedily ~ n **1** : animal food of refuse and liquid **2** : garbage

swim \'swim\ vb **swam** \'swam\; **swum** \'swəm\; **swim·ming 1** : propel oneself in water **2** : float in or be surrounded with a liquid **3** : have a sensation of dizziness ~ n : act or period of swimming —**swim·mer** n

swin·dle \'swind²l\ vb **-dled; -dling** \-(d)liŋ, -d²liŋ\ : cheat (someone) of money or property —**swindle** n —**swin·dler** \-(d)lər, -d²lər\ n

swine \'swīn\ n, pl **swine** : short-legged hoofed mammal with a snout —**swin·ish** \'swīnish\ adj

swing \'swiŋ\ vb **swung** \'swəŋ\; **swing·ing 1** : move rapidly in an arc **2** : sway or cause to sway back and forth **3** : hang so as to sway or sag **4** : turn on a hinge or pivot **5** : accomplish through effort or influence ~ n **1** : act or instance of swinging **2** : swinging movement (as in trying to hit something) **3** : suspended seat for swinging —**swing** adj —**swing·er** n

swipe \'swīp\ n : strong sweeping blow ~ vb **swiped; swip·ing 1** : strike or wipe with a sweeping motion **2** : steal esp. with a quick movement

swirl \'swərl\ *vb* : eddy —**swirl** *n*

swish \'swish\ *n* : hissing, sweeping, or brushing sound —**swish** *vb*

switch \'swich\ *n* **1** : slender flexible whip or twig **2** : blow with a switch **3** : shift, change, or reversal of **4** : device that opens or closes an electrical circuit ~ *vb* **1** : punish or urge on with a switch **2** : change or reverse roles, positions, or subjects **3** : operate a switch of

switch·board *n* : panel of switches to control electrical circuits

swiv·el \'swivəl\ *vb* **-eled** *or* **-elled**; **-el·ing** *or* **-el·ling** : swing or turn on a pivot —**swivel** *n*

swollen *past part of* SWELL

swoon \'swün\ *n* : faint —**swoon** *vb*

swoop \'swüp\ *vb* : make a swift diving attack —**swoop** *n*

sword \'sòrd\ *n* : sharp cutting weapon with a long blade

sword·fish *n* : large ocean fish with a long swordlike projection

swore *past of* SWEAR

sworn *past part of* SWEAR

swum *past part of* SWIM

swung *past of* SWING

syc·a·more \'sikə₁mòr\ *n* : shade tree

sy·co·phant \'sikəfənt\ *n* : servile flatterer —**syc·o·phan·tic** \₁sikə'fantik\ *adj*

syl·la·ble \'siləbəl\ *n* : unit of a spoken word —**syl·lab·ic** \sə'labik\ *adj*

syl·la·bus \'siləbəs\ *n, pl* **-bi** \-₁bī\ *or* **-bus·es** : summary of main topics (as of a course of study)

syl·van \'silvən\ *adj* **1** : living or located in a wooded area **2** : abounding in woods

sym·bol \'simbəl\ *n* : something that represents or suggests another thing —**sym·bol·ic** \sim'bälik\ *adj* —**sym·bol·i·cal·ly** *adv*

sym·bol·ism \'simbə₁lizəm\ *n* : representation of meanings with symbols

sym·bol·ize \'simbə₁līz\ *vb* **-ized**; **-iz·ing** : serve as a symbol of —**sym·bol·iza·tion** \₁simbələ'zāshən\ *n*

sym·me·try \'simətrē\ *n, pl* **-tries** : regularity and balance in the arrangement of parts —**sym·met·ri·cal** \sə'metrikəl\ *adj* —**sym·met·ri·cal·ly** \-k(ə)lē\ *adv*

sym·pa·thize \'simpə₁thīz\ *vb* **-thized**; **-thiz·ing** : feel or show sympathy —**sym·pa·thiz·er** *n*

sym·pa·thy \'simpəthē\ *n, pl* **-thies 1** : ability to understand or share the

feelings of another **2** : expression of sorrow for another's misfortune —**sym·pa·thet·ic** \₁simpə'thetik\ *adj* —**sym·pa·thet·i·cal·ly** \-ik(ə)lē\ *adv*

sym·pho·ny \'simfənē\ *n, pl* **-nies** : composition for an orchestra or the orchestra itself —**sym·phon·ic** \sim'fänik\ *adj*

sym·po·sium \sim'pōzēəm\ *n, pl* **-sia** \-zēə\ *or* **-siums** : conference at which a topic is discussed

symp·tom \'simptəm\ *n* : unusual feeling or reaction that is a sign of disease —**symp·tom·at·ic** \₁simptə'matik\ *adj*

syn·a·gogue, syn·a·gog \'sinə₁gäg\ *n* : Jewish house of worship

syn·chro·nize \'siŋkrə₁nīz, 'sin-\ *vb* **-nized**; **-niz·ing 1** : occur or cause to occur at the same instant **2** : cause to agree in time —**syn·chro·ni·za·tion** \₁siŋkrənə'zāshən, ₁sin-\ *n*

syn·co·pa·tion \₁siŋkə'pāshən, ₁sin-\ *n* : shifting of the regular musical accent to the weak beat —**syn·co·pate** \'siŋkə₁pāt, 'sin-\ *vb*

syn·di·cate \'sindikət\ *n* : business association ~ \-də₁kāt\ *vb* **-cat·ed**; **-cat·ing 1** : form a syndicate **2** : publish through a syndicate

syn·drome \'sin₁drōm\ *n* : particular group of symptoms

syn·onym \'sinə₁nim\ *n* : word with the same meaning as another —**syn·on·y·mous** \sə'nänəməs\ *adj* —**syn·on·y·my** \-mē\ *n*

syn·op·sis \sə'näpsəs\ *n, pl* **-op·ses** \-₁sēz\ : condensed statement or outline

syn·tax \'sin₁taks\ *n* : way in which words are put together —**syn·tac·tic** \sin'taktik\ *adj* —**syn·tac·ti·cal** \-tikəl\ *adv*

syn·the·sis \'sinthəsəs\ *n, pl* **-the·ses** \-₁sēz\ : combination of parts or elements into a whole —**syn·the·size** \-₁sīz\ *vb*

syn·thet·ic \sin'thetik\ *adj* : artificially made —**synthetic** *n* —**syn·thet·i·cal·ly** \-ik(ə)lē\ *adv*

syph·i·lis \'sif(ə)ləs\ *n* : venereal disease —**syph·i·lit·ic** \₁sifə'litik\ *adj or n*

sy·ringe \sə'rinj, 'sirinj\ *n* : plunger device for injecting or withdrawing liquids

syr·up \'sərəp, 'sirəp\ *n* : thick sticky sweet liquid —**syr·upy** *adj*

sys·tem \'sistəm\ *n* **1** : arrangement of units that function together **2** : regular order —**sys·tem·at·ic** \₁sistə-

'matik\ *adj* —**sys·tem·at·i·cal·ly** *adv*
—**sys·tem·atize** \'sistəmə,tīz\ *vb*

sys·tem·ic \sis'temik\ *adj* : relating to the whole body

T

t \'tē\ *n*, *pl* **t's** or **ts** \'tēz\ : 20th letter of the alphabet

tab \'tab\ *n* 1 : short projecting flap 2 *pl* : careful watch

tab·by \'tabē\ *n*, *pl* **-bies** : domestic cat

tab·er·na·cle \'tabər,nakəl\ *n* : house of worship

ta·ble \'tābəl\ *n* 1 : piece of furniture having a smooth slab fixed on legs 2 : supply of food 3 : condensed list —**ta·ble·cloth** *n* —**ta·ble·top** *n* —**ta·ble·ware** *n* —**tab·u·lar** \'tabyələr\ *adj*

tab·leau \'tab,lō\ *n*, *pl* **-leaux** \-,lōz\ 1 : graphic description 2 : depiction of a scene by people in costume

ta·ble·spoon *n* 1 : large serving spoon 2 : measuring spoon holding ½ fluidounce —**ta·ble·spoon·ful** \-,ful\ *n*

tab·let \'tablət\ *n* 1 : flat slab suited for an inscription 2 : collection of sheets of paper glued together at one edge 3 : disk-shaped pill

tab·loid \'tab,lòid\ *n* : newspaper of small page size

ta·boo \tə'bü, ta-\ *adj* : banned esp. as immoral or dangerous —**taboo** *n* or *vb*

tab·u·late \'tabyə,lāt\ *vb* **-lat·ed; -lat·ing** : put in the form of a table —**tab·u·la·tion** \,tabyə'lāshən\ *n* —**tab·u·la·tor** \'tabyə,lātər\ *n*

tac·it \'tasət\ *adj* : implied but not expressed —**tac·it·ly** *adv* —**tac·it·ness** *n*

tac·i·turn \'tasə,tərn\ *adj* : not inclined to talk —**tac·i·tur·ni·ty** \,tasə'tərnətē\ *n*

tack \'tak\ *n* 1 : small sharp nail 2 : course of action ~ *vb* 1 : fasten with tacks 2 : add

tack·le \'takəl, *naut often* 'tāk-\ *n* 1 : equipment 2 : arrangement of ropes and pulleys 3 : act of tackling ~ *vb* **-led; -ling** 1 : seize or throw down 2 : start dealing with

¹**tacky** \'takē\ *adj* **tack·i·er; -est** : sticky to the touch

²**tacky** *adj* **tack·i·er; -est** : cheap or gaudy

tact \'takt\ *n* : sense of the proper thing to say or do —**tact·ful** \-fəl\ *adj* —**tact·ful·ly** *adv* —**tact·less** *adj* —**tact·less·ly** *adv*

tac·tic \'taktik\ *n* : action as part of a plan

tac·tics \'taktiks\ *n sing or pl* 1 : science of maneuvering forces in combat 2 : skill of using available means to reach an end —**tac·ti·cal** \-tikəl\ *adj* —**tac·ti·cian** \tak'tishən\ *n*

tac·tile \'takt⁹l, -,tīl\ *adj* : relating to or perceptible through the sense of touch

tad·pole \'tad,pōl\ *n* : larval frog or toad with tail and gills

taf·fe·ta \'tafətə\ *n* : crisp lustrous fabric (as of silk)

taf·fy \'tafē\ *n*, *pl* **-fies** : candy stretched until porous

¹**tag** \'tag\ *n* : piece of hanging or attached material ~ *vb* **-gg-** 1 : provide or mark with a tag 2 : follow closely

²**tag** *n* : children's game of trying to catch one another ~ *vb* : touch a person in tag

tail \'tāl\ *n* 1 : rear end or a growth extending from the rear end of an animal 2 : back or last part 3 : the reverse of a coin ~ *vb* : follow —**tailed** \'tāld\ *adj* —**tail·less** *adj*

tail·light *n* : red warning light at the back of a vehicle

tai·lor \'tālər\ *n* : one who makes or alters garments ~ *vb* 1 : fashion or alter (clothes) 2 : make or adapt for a special purpose

tail·spin *n* : spiral dive by an airplane

taint \'tānt\ *vb* : affect or become affected with something bad and esp. decay ~ *n* : trace of decay or corruption

take \'tāk\ *vb* **took** \'tùk\; **tak·en** \'tākən\; **tak·ing** 1 : get into one's possession 2 : become affected by 3 : receive into one's body (as by eating) 4 : pick out or remove 5 : use for transportation 6 : need or make use of 7 : lead, carry, or cause to go to another place 8 : undertake and do, make, or perform ~ *n* : amount taken —**take·over** *n* —**tak·er** *n* —**take advantage of** : profit by —**take exception** : object —**take off** *vb* 1 : remove 2 : go away 3 : mimic 4 : begin flight —**take over** *vb* : assume control or possession of or responsibility for

take·off *n* : act or instance of taking off

talc \'talk\ *n* : soft mineral used in making toilet powder (**tal·cum pow·der** \'talkəm-\)

tale \\tāl\\ n 1 : story or anecdote 2 : falsehood

tal·ent \\talənt\\ n : natural mental or creative ability —**tal·ent·ed** adj

tal·is·man \\taləsmən, -əz-\\ n, pl -mans : object thought to act as a charm

talk \\tȯk\\ vb 1 : express one's thoughts in speech 2 : discuss 3 : influence to a position or course of action by talking ~ n 1 : act of talking 2 : formal discussion 3 : rumor 4 : informal lecture —**talk·ative** \\-ətiv\\ adj —**talk·er** n

tall \\tȯl\\ adj : extending to a great or specified height —**tall·ness** n

tal·low \\talō\\ n : hard white animal fat used esp. in soap and lubricants

tal·ly \\talē\\ n, pl -lies : recorded amount ~ vb -lied; -ly·ing 1 : add or count up 2 : match

tal·on \\talən\\ n : bird's claw

tam \\tam\\ n : tam-o'-shanter

tam·bou·rine \\,tambə'rēn\\ n : small drum with loose disks at the sides

tame \\tām\\ adj **tam·er; tam·est** 1 : changed from being wild to being controllable by man 2 : docile 3 : dull ~ vb **tamed; tam·ing** : make or become tame —**tam·able, tame·able** adj —**tame·ly** adv —**tam·er** n

tam-o'-shan·ter \\'tamə,shantər\\ n : Scottish woolen cap with a wide flat circular crown

tamp \\tamp\\ vb : drive down or in by a series of light blows

tam·per \\tampər\\ vb : interfere so as to change for the worse

tan \\tan\\ vb -nn- 1 : change (hide) into leather esp. by soaking in a liquid containing tannin 2 : make or become brown (as by exposure to the sun) ~ n 1 : brown skin color induced by the sun 2 : light yellowish brown —**tan·ner** n —**tan·nery** \\'tan(ə)rē\\ n

tan·dem \\tandəm\\ adv : one behind another

tang \\taŋ\\ n : sharp distinctive flavor —**tangy** adj

tan·gent \\tanjənt\\ adj : touching a curve or surface ~ n 1 : tangent line, curve, or surface 2 : abrupt change of course —**tan·gen·tial** \\tan'jenchəl\\ adj

tan·ger·ine \\'tanjə,rēn, ,tanjə'-\\ n : deep orange citrus fruit

tan·gi·ble \\tanjəbəl\\ adj 1 : able to be touched 2 : substantially real —**tan·gi·bil·i·ty** \\,tanjə'bilətē\\ n —**tan·gi·bly** adv

tan·gle \\taŋgəl\\ vb -gled; -gling : unite in intricate confusion ~ n : tangled twisted mass

tan·go \\taŋgō\\ n, pl -gos : dance of Spanish-American origin —**tango** vb

tank \\taŋk\\ n 1 : large artificial receptacle for liquids 2 : armored military vehicle —**tank·ful** n

tan·kard \\taŋkərd\\ n : tall one-handled drinking vessel

tank·er \\taŋkər\\ n : vehicle or vessel with tanks for transporting a liquid

tan·nin \\tanən\\ n : substance of plant origin used in tanning and dyeing

tan·ta·lize \\'tant³l,īz\\ vb -lized; -liz·ing : tease or torment by keeping something desirable just out of reach —**tan·ta·liz·er** n —**tan·ta·liz·ing·ly** adv

tan·ta·mount \\'tantə,maunt\\ adj : equivalent in value or meaning

tan·trum \\tantrəm\\ n : fit of bad temper

¹**tap** \\tap\\ n 1 : faucet 2 : act of tapping ~ vb -pp- 1 : pierce so as to draw off fluid 2 : connect into —**tap·per** n

²**tap** vb -pp- : rap lightly ~ n : light stroke or its sound

tape \\tāp\\ n 1 : narrow flexible strip (as of cloth, plastic, or metal) 2 : tape measure ~ vb **taped; tap·ing** 1 : fasten with tape 2 : record on tape

tape measure n : strip of tape marked in units for use in measuring

ta·per \\tāpər\\ n 1 : slender wax candle 2 : gradual lessening of width in a long object ~ vb 1 : make or become smaller toward one end 2 : diminish gradually

tap·es·try \\tapəstrē\\ n, pl -tries : heavy handwoven ruglike wall hanging

tape·worm n : long flat intestinal worm

tap·i·o·ca \\,tapē'ōkə\\ n : a granular starch used esp. in puddings

tar \\tär\\ n : thick dark sticky liquid distilled (as from coal) ~ vb -rr- : treat or smear with tar

ta·ran·tu·la \\tə'ranch(ə)lə, -'rant³l]ə\\ n : large hairy usu. harmless spider

tar·dy \\tärdē\\ adj -di·er; -est : late —**tar·di·ly** \\'tärd³lē\\ adv —**tar·di·ness** n

tar·get \\tärgət\\ n 1 : mark to shoot at 2 : goal to be achieved ~ vb 1 : make a target of 2 : establish as a goal

tar·iff \\'tarəf\\ n 1 : duty or rate of duty imposed on imported goods 2 : schedule of tariffs, rates, or charges

tar·nish \\tärnish\\ vb : make or become dull or discolored —**tarnish** n

tar·pau·lin \ tär′pōlən, ′tärpə-\ n
: waterproof protective covering

tar·ry \ ′tarē\ vb -ried; -ry·ing : be slow
in leaving

¹tart \ ′tärt\ adj 1 : pleasantly sharp to
the taste 2 : caustic —**tart·ly** adv —
tart·ness n

²tart n : small pie

tar·tan \ ′tärt⁰n\ n : woolen fabric with
a plaid design

tar·tar \ ′tärtər\ n : hard crust on the
teeth

task \ ′task\ n : assigned work

task·mas·ter n : one that burdens another with labor

tas·sel \ ′tasəl, ′täs-\ n : hanging ornament made of a bunch of cords fastened at one end

taste \ ′tāst\ vb tast·ed; tast·ing 1 : try
or determine the flavor of 2 : eat or
drink in small quantities 3 : have a
specific flavor ~ n 1 : small amount
tasted 2 : bit 3 : special sense that
identifies sweet, sour, bitter, or salty
qualities 4 : individual preference 5
: critical appreciation of quality —
taste·ful \ -fəl\ adj —**taste·ful·ly** adv
—**taste·less** adj —**taste·less·ly** adv —
tast·er n —**tasty** adj

tat·ter \ ′tatər\ n 1 : part torn and left
hanging 2 pl : tattered clothing ~ vb
: make or become ragged

tat·tle \ ′tat⁰l\ vb -tled; -tling : inform
on someone —**tat·tler** \ ′tatlər, -⁰lər\
n

tat·tle·tale n : one that tattles

tat·too \ ta′tü\ vb : mark the skin with
indelible designs or figures —**tattoo**
n

taught past of TEACH

taunt \ ′tȯnt\ n : sarcastic challenge or
insult —**taunt** vb —**taunt·er** n

taut \ ′tȯt\ adj : tightly drawn —**taut·**
ly adv —**taut·ness** n

tav·ern \ ′tavərn\ n : establishment
where liquors are sold to be drunk
on the premises

taw·dry \ ′tȯdrē\ adj -dri·er; -est
: cheap and gaudy

taw·ny \ ′tȯnē\ adj -ni·er; -est : brownish orange

tax \ ′taks\ vb 1 : impose a tax on 2
: charge 3 : put under stress ~ n 1
: charge by authority for public purposes 2 : strain —**tax·able** adj —**tax·**
a·tion \ tak′sāshən\ n —**tax·pay·er** n
—**tax·pay·ing** adj

taxi \ ′taksē\ n, pl tax·is \ -sēz\ : automobile transporting passengers for a
fare ~ vb tax·ied; taxi·ing or taxy·
ing; tax·is or tax·ies 1 : transport or

go by taxi 2 : move along the ground
before takeoff or after landing

taxi·cab \ ′taksē,kab\ n : taxi

taxi·der·my \ ′taksə,dərmē\ n : art of
stuffing and mounting animal skins
—**taxi·der·mist** \ -məst\ n

tea \ ′tē\ n : cured leaves of an oriental
shrub or a drink made from these —
tea·cup n —**tea·pot** n

teach \ ′tēch\ vb taught \ ′tȯt\; teach·
ing 1 : tell or show the fundamentals
or skills of something 2 : cause to
know the consequences 3 : impart
knowledge of —**teach·able** adj —
teach·er n —**teach·ing** n

teak \ ′tēk\ n : East Indian timber tree
or its wood

tea·ket·tle \ ′tē,ket⁰l, -,kit-\ n : covered
kettle with a handle and spout for
boiling water

teal \ ′tēl\ n, pl teal or teals : small
short-necked wild duck

team \ ′tēm\ n 1 : draft animals har-
nessed together 2 : number of people
organized for a game or work ~ vb
: form or work together as a team —
team adj —**team·mate** n —**team·**
work n

team·ster \ ′tēmstər\ n : one that drives
a team or truck

¹tear \ ′tiər\ n : drop of salty liquid that
moistens the eye —**tear·ful** \ -fəl\ adj
—**tear·ful·ly** adv

²tear \ ′taər\ vb tore \ ′tōr\; torn
\ ′tōrn\; tear·ing 1 : separate or pull
apart by force 2 : move or act with
violence or haste ~ n : act or result
of tearing

tease \ ′tēz\ vb teased; teas·ing : annoy
by goading, coaxing, or tantalizing
~ n 1 : act of teasing or state of being
teased 2 : one that teases

tea·spoon \ ′tē,spün\ n 1 : small spoon
for stirring or sipping 2 : measuring
spoon holding ⅙ fluidounce —**tea·**
spoon·ful \ -,ful\ n

teat \ ′tit, ′tēt\ n : protuberance
through which milk is drawn from
an udder or breast

tech·ni·cal \ ′teknikal\ adj : having or
relating to special mechanical or scientific knowledge 2 : by strict interpretation of rules —**tech·ni·cal·ly**
\ -k(ə)lē\ adv

tech·ni·cal·i·ty \ ,teknə′kalətē\ n, pl
-ties : detail meaningful only to a specialist

technical sergeant n : noncommissioned officer in the air force ranking
next below a master sergeant

tech·ni·cian \ tek′nishən\ n : person

with the technique of a specialized skill

tech·nique \tek'nēk\ n : manner of accomplishing something

tech·nol·o·gy \tek'näləjē\ n, pl -gies : applied science —**tech·no·log·i·cal** \,teknə'läjikəl\ adj

te·dious \'tēdēəs, 'tējəs\ adj : wearisome from length or dullness —**te·dious·ly** adv —**te·dious·ness** n

te·di·um \'tēdēəm\ n : tedious state or quality

tee \'tē\ n : mound or peg on which a golf ball is placed before beginning play —**tee** vb

teem \'tēm\ vb : become filled to overflowing

teen·age \'tēn,āj\, **teen·aged** \-,ājd\ adj : relating to people in their teens —**teen·ag·er** \-,ājər\ n

teens \'tēnz\ n pl : years 13 to 19 in a person's life

tee·pee var of TEPEE

tee·ter \'tētər\ vb 1 : move unsteadily 2 : seesaw —**teeter** n

teeth pl of TOOTH

teethe \'tēth\ vb teethed; teeth·ing : grow teeth

tele·cast \'teli,kast\ vb -cast; -cast·ing : broadcast by television —**telecast** n —**tele·cast·er** n

tele·gram \'telə,gram\ n : message sent by telegraph

tele·graph \-,graf\ n : system for communication by electrical transmission of coded signals ~ vb : send by telegraph —**tele·gra·pher** \tə'legrəfər\ n —**tele·graph·ic** \,telə'grafik\ adj

te·leph·a·thy \tə'lepəthē\ n : apparent communication without known sensory means —**tele·path·ic** \,telə'pathik\ adj —**tele·path·i·cal·ly** \-ik(ə)lē\ adv

tele·phone \'telə,fōn\ n : instrument or system for electrical transmission of spoken words ~ vb -phoned; -phon·ing : communicate with by telephone —**tele·phon·er** n

tele·scope \-,skōp\ n : tube-shaped optical instrument for viewing distant objects ~ vb -scoped; -scop·ing : slide or cause to slide inside another similar section —**tele·scop·ic** \,telə'skäpik\ adj

tele·vise \'telə,vīz\ vb -vised; -vis·ing : broadcast by television

tele·vi·sion \-,vizhən\ n : transmission and reproduction of images by radio waves

tell \'tel\ vb told \'tōld\; tell·ing 1 : count 2 : relate in detail 3 : reveal 4 : give information or an order to 5 : determine

tell·er \'telər\ n 1 : one that relates or counts 2 : bank employee handling money

te·mer·i·ty \tə'merətē\ n, pl -ties : boldness

tem·per \'tempər\ vb 1 : dilute or soften 2 : toughen ~ n 1 : characteristic attitude or feeling 2 : toughness 3 : disposition or control over one's emotions

tem·per·a·ment \'temp(ə)rəmənt\ n : characteristic frame of mind —**tem·per·a·men·tal** \,temp(ə)rə'ment[ə]l\ adj

tem·per·ance \'temp(ə)rəns\ n : moderation in or abstinence from indulgence and esp. the use of intoxicating drink

tem·per·ate \'temp(ə)rət\ adj : moderate

tem·per·a·ture \'tempər,chúr, -p(ə)rə,chúr, -chər\ n 1 : degree of hotness or coldness 2 : fever

tem·pest \'tempəst\ n : violent storm —**tem·pes·tu·ous** \tem'peschəwəs\ adj

¹**tem·ple** \'tempəl\ n : place of worship

²**temple** n : flattened space on each side of the forehead

tem·po \'tempō\ n, pl -pi \-,pē\ or -pos : rate of speed

tem·po·ral \'temp(ə)rəl\ adj : relating to time or to secular concerns

tem·po·rary \'tempə,rerē\ adj : lasting for a short time only —**tem·po·rar·i·ly** \,tempə'rerəlē\ adv

tempt \'tem(p)t\ vb 1 : coax or persuade to do wrong 2 : attract or provoke —**tempt·er** n —**tempt·ing·ly** adv —**tempt·ress** \'temptrəs\ n

temp·ta·tion \temp'tāshən\ n 1 : act of tempting 2 : something that tempts

ten \'ten\ n 1 : one more than 9 2 : 10th in a set or series 3 : thing having 10 units —**ten** adj or pron —**tenth** \'tenth\ adj or adv or n

ten·a·ble \'tenəbəl\ adj : capable of being held or defended —**ten·a·bil·i·ty** \,tenə'bilətē\ n

te·na·cious \tə'nāshəs\ adj 1 : holding fast 2 : retentive —**te·na·cious·ly** adv —**te·nac·i·ty** \tə'nasətē\ n

ten·ant \'tenənt\ n : one who occupies a rented dwelling —**ten·an·cy** \-ənsē\ n

¹**tend** \'tend\ vb : take care of or supervise something

²**tend** vb 1 : move in a particular direction 2 : show a tendency

ten·den·cy \'tendənsē\ n, pl -cies : likelihood to move, think, or act in a particular way

1tender \'tendər\ *adj* 1 : soft or delicate 2 : expressing or responsive to love or sympathy 3 : sensitive (as to touch) —**ten·der·ly** *adv* —**ten·der·ness** *n*

2tender \'tendər\ *n* 1 : one that tends 2 : vehicle attached to a steam locomotive 3 : transport to a larger ship

3tender *n* 1 : offer of a bid for a contract 2 : something that may be offered in payment —**tender** *vb*

ten·der·ize \'tendə,rīz\ *vb* **-ized; -iz·ing** : make (meat) tender —**ten·der·iz·er** \'tendə,rīzər\ *n*

ten·der·loin \'tendər,loin\ *n* : tender beef or pork strip from near the backbone

ten·don \'tendən\ *n* : cord of tissue attaching muscle to bone —**ten·di·nous** \-dənəs\ *adj*

ten·dril \'tendrəl\ *n* : slender coiling growth of some climbing plants

ten·e·ment \'tenəmənt\ *n* 1 : house divided into apartments 2 : shabby dwelling

te·net \'tenət\ *n* : principle of belief

ten·nis \'tenəs\ *n* : racket-and-ball game played across a net

ten·or \'tenər\ *n* 1 : general drift or meaning 2 : highest natural adult male voice

ten·pin \'ten,pin\ *n* : bottle-shaped pin bowled at in a game (**tenpins**)

1tense \'tens\ *n* : distinct verb form that indicates time

2tense *adj* **tens·er; tens·est** 1 : stretched tight 2 : marked by nervous tension —**tense** *vb* —**tense·ly** *adv* —**tense·ness** *n* —**ten·si·ty** \'tensətē\ *n*

ten·sile \'tensəl, -,sīl\ *adj* : relating to tension

ten·sion \'tenchən\ *n* 1 : tense condition 2 : state of mental unrest or of potential hostility or opposition

tent \'tent\ *n* : collapsible shelter

ten·ta·cle \'tentikəl\ *n* : long flexible projection of an insect or mollusk —**ten·ta·cled** \-kəld\ *adj* —**ten·tac·u·lar** \ten'takyələr\ *adj*

ten·ta·tive \'tentətiv\ *adj* : subject to change or discussion —**ten·ta·tive·ly** *adv*

ten·u·ous \'tenyəwəs\ *adj* 1 : not dense or thick 2 : flimsy or weak —**te·nu·i·ty** \te'n(y)üətē, tə-\ *n*

ten·ure \'tenyər\ *n* : act, right, manner, or period of holding something —**ten·ured** \-yərd\ *adj*

te·pee \'tē(,)pē\ *n* : conical tent

tep·id \'tepəd\ *adj* : moderately warm

term \'tərm\ *n* 1 : period of time 2 : mathematical expression 3 : special word or phrase 4 *pl* : conditions 5 *pl* : relations ~ *vb* : name

ter·mi·nal \'tərmən°l\ *n* 1 : end 2 : device for making an electrical connection 3 : station at end of a transportation line —**terminal** *adj*

ter·mi·nate \'tərmə,nāt\ *vb* **-nat·ed; -nat·ing** : bring or come to an end —**ter·mi·na·ble** \-nəbəl\ *adj* —**ter·mi·na·tion** \,tərmə'nāshən\ *n*

ter·mi·nol·o·gy \,tərmə'näləjē\ *n* : terms used in a particular subject

ter·mi·nus \'tərmənəs\ *n, pl* **-ni** \-,nī\ *or* **-nus·es** 1 : end 2 : end point of a transportation line

ter·mite \'tər,mīt\ *n* : wood-eating insect

tern \'tərn\ *n* : small sea bird

ter·race \'terəs\ *n* 1 : balcony or patio 2 : bank with a flat top ~ *vb* **-raced; -rac·ing** : landscape in a series of banks

ter·ra-cot·ta \,terə'kätə\ *n* : reddish brown earthenware

ter·rain \tə'rān\ *n* : features of the land

ter·ra·pin \'terəpən\ *n* : No. American turtle

ter·rar·i·um \tə'rareəm\ *n, pl* **-ia** \-ēə\ *or* **-i·ums** : container for keeping plants or animals

ter·res·tri·al \tə'rest(r)ēəl\ *adj* 1 : relating to the earth or its inhabitants 2 : living or growing on land

ter·ri·ble \'terəbəl\ *adj* 1 : exciting terror 2 : distressing 3 : intense 4 : of very poor quality —**ter·ri·bly** \-blē\ *adv*

ter·ri·er \'terēər\ *n* : small dog

ter·rif·ic \tə'rifik\ *adj* 1 : exciting terror 2 : extraordinary

ter·ri·fy \'terə,fī\ *vb* **-fied; -fy·ing** : fill with terror —**ter·ri·fy·ing·ly** *adv*

ter·ri·to·ry \'terə,tōrē\ *n, pl* **-ries** : particular geographical region —**ter·ri·to·ri·al** \,terə'tōrēəl\ *adj*

ter·ror \'terər\ *n* : intense fear and panic or a cause of it

ter·ror·ism \-,izəm\ *n* : systematic covert warfare to produce terror for political coercion —**ter·ror·ist** \-əst\ *adj or n*

ter·ror·ize \-,īz\ *vb* **-ized; -iz·ing** 1 : fill with terror 2 : coerce by threat or violence

ter·ry \'terē\ *n, pl* **-ries** : absorbent fabric with a loose pile

terse \'tərs\ *adj* **ters·er; ters·est** : concise —**terse·ly** *adv* —**terse·ness** *n*

ter·tia·ry \'tərshē,erē\ *adj* : of 3d rank, importance, or value

test \'test\ *n* : examination or evaluation ~ *vb* : examine by a test —**tester** *n*

tes-ta-ment \'testəmənt\ *n* **1** *cap* : division of the Bible **2** : will —**tes-ta-men-ta-ry** \,testə'ment(ə)rē\ *adj*

tes-ti-cle \'testikəl\ *n* : testis

tes-ti-fy \'testə,fī\ *vb* **-fied; -fy-ing 1** : give testimony **2** : serve as evidence

tes-ti-mo-ni-al \,testə'mōnēəl\ *n* **1** : favorable recommendation **2** : tribute —**testimonial** *adj*

tes-ti-mo-ny \'testə,mōnē\ *n, pl* **-nies** : statement given as evidence in court

tes-tis \'testəs\ *n, pl* **-tes** \-,tēz\ : male reproductive gland

tes-ty \'testē\ *adj* **-ti-er; -est** : easily annoyed

tet-a-nus \'tet³nəs\ *n* : bacterial disease producing violent spasms

tête-à-tête \,tātə'tāt\ *adv* : privately ~ *n* : private conversation ~ *adj* : private

teth-er \'tethər\ *n* : leash ~ *vb* : restrain with a leash

text \tekst\ *n* **1** : author's words **2** : main body of printed or written matter on a page **3** : textbook **4** : scriptural passage used as the theme of a sermon **5** : topic —**tex-tu-al** \'tekschə(wə)l\ *adj*

text-book \'teks(t),bůk\ *n* : book on a school subject

tex-tile \'tek,stīl, 'tekst³l\ *n* : fabric

tex-ture \'tekschər\ *n* **1** : feel and appearance of something **2** : structure

than \thən, (')than\ *conj or prep* — used in comparisons

thank \'thaŋk\ *vb* : express gratitude to

thank-ful \-fəl\ *adj* : giving thanks —**thank-ful-ly** *adv* —**thank-ful-ness** *n*

thank-less *adj* : not appreciated

thanks \'thaŋks\ *n pl* : expression of gratitude

Thanks-giv-ing \thaŋks'giviŋ\ *n* : 4th Thursday in November observed as a legal holiday for giving thanks for divine goodness

that \(,)that\ *pron, pl* those \(')thōz\ **1** : something indicated or understood **2** : the one farther away ~ *adj, pl* those : being the one mentioned or understood or farther away ~ \that, (,)that\ *conj or pron* —used to introduce a clause ~ \'that\ *adv* : to such an extent

thatch \'thach\ *vb* : cover with thatch ~ *n* : covering of matted straw

thaw \'thò\ *vb* : melt or cause to melt —**thaw** *n*

the \thə, *before vowel sounds usu* thē\ *definite article* : that particular one ~ *adv* —used before a comparative or superlative

the-ater, the-atre \'thēətər\ *n* **1** : building or room for viewing a play or movie **2** : dramatic arts

the-at-ri-cal \thē'atrikəl\ *adj* **1** : relating to the theater **2** : involving exaggerated emotion

thee \(')thē\ *pron, objective case of* THOU

theft \'theft\ *n* : act of stealing

their \thər, (,)theər\ *adj* : relating to them

theirs \'theərz\ *pron* : their one or ones

the-ism \'thē,izəm\ *n* : belief in the existence of a god or gods —**the-ist** \-əst\ *n or adj* —**the-is-tic** \thē'istik\ *adj*

them \(th)əm, (')them\ *pron, objective case of* THEY

theme \'thēm\ *n* **1** : subject matter **2** : essay **3** : melody developed in a piece of music —**the-mat-ic** \thi'matik\ *adj*

them-selves \thəm'selvz, them-\ *pron pl* : they, them —used reflexively or for emphasis

then \(')then\ *adv* **1** : at that time **2** : soon after that **3** : in addition **4** : in that case **5** : consequently ~ \'then\ *n* : that time ~ *adj* : existing at that time

thence \'thens, 'thens\ *adv* : from that place or fact

the-oc-ra-cy \thē'äkrəsē\ *n, pl* **-cies** : government by officials regarded as divinely inspired —**the-o-crat-ic** \,thēə'kratik\ *adj*

the-ol-o-gy \thē'äləjē\ *n, pl* **-gies** : study of religion —**the-o-lo-gian** \,thēə'lōjən\ *n* —**the-o-log-i-cal** \-'läjikəl\ *adj*

the-o-rem \'thēərəm, 'thirəm\ *n* : provable statement of truth

the-o-ret-i-cal \,thēə'retikəl\ *adj* : relating to or being theory —**the-o-ret-i-cal-ly** *adv*

the-o-rize \'thēə,rīz\ *vb* **-rized; -riz-ing** : put forth theories —**the-o-rist** *n*

the-o-ry \'thēərē, 'thirē\ *n, pl* **-ries 1** : general principles of a subject **2** : plausible or scientifically acceptable explanation **3** : judgment, guess, or opinion

ther-a-peu-tic \,therə'pyütik\ *adj* : offering or relating to remedy —**ther-a-peu-ti-cal-ly** \-ik(ə)lē\ *adv*

ther·a·py \'therəpē\ *n, pl* **-pies** : treatment for mental or physical disorder —**ther·a·pist** \-pəst\ *n*

there \'thaͅər, 'theͅar\ *adv* 1 : in, at, or to that place 2 : in that respect ~ \(ͅ)thaͅ(ͅə)r, (ͅ)theͅ(ͅə)r, thar\ *pron* — used to introduce a sentence or clause ~ \'thaͅər, 'theͅar\ *n* : that place or point

there·abouts, there·about \ͅtharə-'baut(s), 'tharə-,-, ͅthera-, 'thera, \ *adv* : near that place, time, number, or quantity

there·af·ter \thar'aftər, ther-\ *adv* : after that

there·by \thar'bī, ther-, 'tha(ͅə)r,bī, 'the(ͅə)r,bī\ *adv* 1 : by that 2 : connected with or with reference to that

there·fore \'tha(ͅə)r,fōr, 'the(ͅə)r-\ *adv* : for that reason

there·in \thar'in, ther-\ *adv* 1 : in or into that place, time, or thing 2 : in that respect

there·of \-'əv, -'äv\ *adv* 1 : of that or it 2 : from that

there·upon \'tharə,pón, 'ther-, -,pän; ͅtharə'pón, -'pän, ͅther-\ *adv* 1 : on that matter 2 : therefore 3 : immediately after that

there·with \thar'with, ther-, -'with\ *adv* : with that

ther·mal \'thərməl\ *adj* : relating to, caused by, or conserving heat — **ther·mal·ly** *adv*

ther·mo·dy·nam·ics \ͅthərmōdī'nam-iks\ *n* : physics of heat

ther·mom·e·ter \thə(r)'mämətər\ *n* : instrument for measuring temperature —**ther·mo·met·ric** \ͅthərmə'metrik\ *adj* —**ther·mo·met·ri·cal·ly** \-rik(ə)lē\ *adv*

ther·mos \'thərməs\ *n* : double-walled bottle used to keep liquids hot or cold

ther·mo·stat \'thərmə,stat\ *n* : automatic temperature control —**ther·mo·stat·ic** \ͅthərmə'statik\ *adj* —**ther·mo·stat·i·cal·ly** \-ik(ə)lē\ *adv*

the·sau·rus \thi'sóras\ *n, pl* **-sau·ri** \-'sór,ī\ *or* **-sau·rus·es** \-'sórasaz\ : book of words and esp. synonyms

these *pl of* THIS

the·sis \'thēsəs\ *n, pl* **the·ses** \'thē,sēz\ 1 : proposition to be argued for 2 : essay embodying results of original research

thes·pi·an \'thespēan\ *adj* : dramatic ~ *n* : actor

they \(')thā\ *pron* 1 : those ones 2 : people in general

thi·a·mine \'thīəmən, -,mēn\ *n* : essential vitamin

thick \'thik\ *adj* 1 : having relatively great mass from front to back or top to bottom 2 : viscous ~ *n* : most crowded or thickest part —**thick·ly** *adv* —**thick·ness** *n*

thick·en \'thikən\ *vb* : make or become thick —**thick·en·er** \-(ə)nər\ *n*

thick·et \'thikət\ *n* : dense growth of bushes or small trees

thick-skinned \-'skind\ *adj* : insensitive to criticism

thief \'thēf\ *n, pl* **thieves** \'thēvz\ : one that steals

thieve \'thēv\ *vb* **thieved; thiev·ing** : steal —**thiev·ery** *n*

thigh \'thī\ *n* : upper part of the leg

thigh·bone \'thī'bōn, -,bōn\ *n* : femur

thim·ble \'thimbəl\ *n* : protective cap for the finger in sewing —**thim·ble·ful** *n*

thin \'thin\ *adj* **-nn-** 1 : having relatively little mass from front to back or top to bottom 2 : not closely set or placed 3 : relatively free flowing 4 : lacking substance, fullness, or strength ~ *vb* **-nn-** : make or become thin —**thin·ly** *adv* —**thin·ness** *n*

thing \'thiŋ\ *n* 1 : matter of concern 2 : event or act 3 : object 4 *pl* : possessions

think \'thiŋk\ *vb* **thought** \'thót; **think·ing** 1 : form or have in the mind 2 : have as an opinion 3 : ponder 4 : devise by thinking 5 : imagine —**think·er** *n*

thin-skinned *adj* : extremely sensitive to criticism

third \'thərd\ *adj* : being number 3 in a countable series ~ *n* 1 : one that is third 2 : one of 3 equal parts —**third, third·ly** *adv*

third dimension *n* : thickness or depth —**third-dimensional** *adj*

thirst \'thərst\ *n* 1 : dryness in mouth and throat 2 : intense desire ~ *vb* : feel thirst —**thirsty** *adj*

thir·teen \ͅthər'tēn, 'thər-\ *n* : one more than 12 —**thirteen** *adj or pron* —**thir·teenth** \-'tēnth\ *adj or n*

thir·ty \'thərtē\ *n, pl* **thirties** : 3 times 10 —**thir·ti·eth** \-ēəth\ *adj or n* —**thirty** *adj or pron*

this \(')this\ *pron, pl* **these** \(')thēz\ : something close or under immediate discussion ~ *adj, pl* **these** : being the one near, present, just mentioned, or more immediately under observation ~ \'this\ *adv* : to such an extent or degree

this·tle \'thisəl\ *n* : tall prickly herb

thith·er \'thithər\ *adv* : to that place

thong \'thȯŋ\ n : strip of leather or hide

tho·rax \'thȯr,aks\ n, pl **-rax·es** or **-ra·ces** \'thȯrə,sēz\ 1 : part of the body between neck and abdomen 2 : middle of 3 divisions of an insect body —**tho·rac·ic** \thə'rasik\ adj

thorn \'thȯrn\ n : sharp spike on a plant or a plant bearing these —**thorny** adj

thor·ough \'thərō\ adj : omitting or overlooking nothing —**thor·ough·ly** adv —**thor·ough·ness** n

thor·ough·bred \'thərə,bred\ n 1 cap : light speedy racing horse 2 : one of excellent quality —**thoroughbred** adj

thor·ough·fare \'thərə,faar\ n : public road

those pl of THAT

thou \(')thau̇\ pron, archaic : you

though \'thō\ adv : however ~ \(,)thō\ conj 1 : despite the fact that 2 : granting that

thought \'thȯt\ past of THINK ~ n 1 : process of thinking 2 : serious consideration 3 : idea

thought·ful \-fəl\ adj 1 : absorbed in or showing thought 2 : considerate of others —**thought·ful·ly** adv —**thought·ful·ness** n

thought·less \-ləs\ adj 1 : careless or reckless 2 : lacking concern for others —**thought·less·ly** adv

thou·sand \'thau̇zənd\ n, pl **-sands** or **-sand** : 10 times 100 —**thousand** adj —**thou·sandth** \-ᵗnth\ adj or n

thrash \'thrash\ vb 1 : thresh 2 : beat 3 : move about violently —**thrash·er** n

thread \'thred\ n 1 : fine line of fibers 2 : train of thought 3 : ridge around a screw ~ vb 1 : pass thread through 2 : put together on a thread 3 : make one's way through or between

thread·bare adj 1 : worn so that the thread shows 2 : trite

threat \'thret\ n 1 : expression of intention to harm 2 : thing that threatens

threat·en \'thretᵊn\ vb 1 : utter threats 2 : show signs of being near or impending —**threat·en·ing·ly** adv

three \'thrē\ n 1 : one more than 2 2 : 3d in a set or series —**three** adj or pron

three·fold \'thrē,fōld, -'fōld\ adj : triple —**three·fold** \-'fōld\ adv

three·score adj : being 3 times 20

thresh \'thrash, 'thresh\ vb : beat to separate grain —**thresh·er** n

thresh·old \'thresh,ōld\ n 1 : sill of a door 2 : beginning stage

threw past of THROW

thrice \'thrīs\ adv : 3 times

thrift \'thrift\ n : careful management or saving of money —**thrift·i·ly** \'thriftəlē\ adv —**thrift·less** adj —**thrifty** adj

thrill \'thril\ vb 1 : have or cause to have a sudden sharp feeling of excitement 2 : tremble —**thrill** n —**thrill·er** n —**thrill·ing·ly** adv

thrive \'thrīv\ vb **throve** \'thrōv\ or **thrived**; **thriv·en** \'thrivən\ 1 : grow vigorously 2 : prosper

throat \'thrōt\ n 1 : front part of the neck 2 : passage to the stomach —**throat·ed** adj —**throaty** adj

throb \'thräb\ vb **-bb-** : pulsate —**throb** n

throe \'thrō\ n 1 : pang or spasm 2 pl : hard or painful struggle

throne \'thrōn\ n : chair representing power or sovereignty

throng \'thrȯŋ\ n or vb : crowd

throt·tle \'thrätᵊl\ vb **-tled; -tling** : choke ~ n : valve regulating volume of fuel and air delivered to engine cylinders

through \(')thrü\ prep 1 : into at one side and out at the other side of 2 : by way of 3 : among, between, or all around 4 : because of 5 : throughout the time of ~ \'thrü\ adv 1 : from one end or side to the other 2 : from beginning to end 3 : to the core 4 : into the open ~ \'thrü\ adj 1 : going directly from origin to destination 2 : finished

through·out \thrü'au̇t\ adv 1 : everywhere 2 : from beginning to end ~ prep 1 : in or to every part of 2 : during the whole of

throve past of THRIVE

throw \'thrō\ vb **threw** \'thrü\; **thrown** \'thrōn\; **throw·ing** 1 : propel through the air 2 : cause to fall or fall off 3 : put suddenly in a certain position or condition 4 : move quickly as if throwing 5 : put on or off hastily —**throw** n —**throw·er** \'thrō(ə)r\ n —**throw up** : vomit

thrush \'thrəsh\ n : songbird

thrust \'thrəst\ vb **thrust**; **thrust·ing** 1 : shove forward 2 : stab or pierce —**thrust** n

thud \'thəd\ n : dull sound of something falling —**thud** vb

thug \'thəg\ n : ruffian or gangster

thumb \'thəm\ n 1 : short thick division of the hand opposing the fingers 2 : glove part for the thumb ~ vb

: leaf through with the thumb — **thumb·nail** n

thump \'thəmp\ vb : strike with something thick or heavy causing a dull heavy sound —**thump** n

thun·der \'thəndər\ n : sound following lightning —**thunder** vb —**thun·der·clap** n —**thun·der·ous** \'thən-d(ə)rəs\ adj —**thun·der·ous·ly** adv

thun·der·bolt \-,bōlt\ n : discharge of lightning with thunder

thun·der·show·er \'thəndər,shaù(ə)r\ n : shower with thunder and lightning

thun·der·storm n : storm with thunder and lightning

Thurs·day \'thərzdē\ n : 5th day of the week

thus \'thəs\ adv 1 : in this or that way 2 : to this degree or extent 3 : because of this or that

thwart \'thwórt\ vb : block or defeat

thy \(,)thī\ adj, archaic : your

thyme \'tīm, 'thīm\ n : cooking herb

thy·roid \'thī,róid\ adj : relating to a large endocrine gland (**thyroid gland**)

thy·self \thī'self\ pron, archaic : yourself

ti·ara \tē'arə, -'er-, -'är-\ n : decorative formal headband

tib·ia \'tibēə\ n, pl -**i·ae** \-ē,ē\ : bone between the knee and ankle

tic \'tik\ n : twitching of facial muscles

¹**tick** \'tik\ n : small 8-legged blood-sucking animal

²**tick** n 1 : light rhythmic tap or beat 2 : check mark ~ vb 1 : make ticks 2 : mark with a tick 3 : operate

tick·er \'tikər\ n 1 : something (as a watch) that ticks 2 : telegraph instrument that prints on paper tape

tick·et \'tikət\ n 1 : tag showing price, payment of a fee or fare, or a traffic offense 2 : list of candidates ~ vb : put a ticket on

tick·ing \'tikiŋ\ n : fabric covering of a mattress

tick·le \'tikəl\ vb -**led, -ling** 1 : please or amuse 2 : touch lightly causing uneasiness, laughter, or spasmodic movements —**tickle** n

tick·lish \'tik(ə)lish\ adj 1 : sensitive to tickling 2 : requiring delicate handling —**tick·lish·ly** adv —**tick·lish·ness** n

tid·al wave \'tīd³l-\ n : high sea wave following an earthquake

tid·bit \'tid,bit\ n : choice morsel

tide \'tīd\ n : alternate rising and falling of the sea ~ vb **tid·ed; tid·ing** : be enough to allow (one) to get by

for a time —**tid·al** \'tīd³l\ adj —**tide·wa·ter** n

tid·ings \'tīdiŋz\ n pl : news or message

ti·dy \'tīdē\ adj -**di·er; -est** 1 : well ordered and cared for 2 : large or substantial —**ti·di·ness** n —**tidy** vb

tie \'tī\ n 1 : line or ribbon for fastening, uniting, or closing 2 : cross support to which railroad rails are fastened 3 : uniting force 4 : equality in score or tally or a deadlocked contest 5 : necktie ~ vb **tied; ty·ing** or **tie·ing** 1 : fasten or close by wrapping and knotting a tie 2 : form a knot in 3 : gain the same score or tally as an opponent

tier \'tiər\ n : one of a stepike series of rows

tiff \'tif\ n : petty quarrel —**tiff** vb

ti·ger \'tīgər\ n : large black-striped flesh-eating mammal —**ti·ger·ish** \-g(ə)rish\ adj —**ti·gress** \-grəs\ n

tight \'tīt\ adj 1 : fitting close together esp. so as not to allow air or water in 2 : held very firmly 3 : taut 4 : fitting too snugly 5 : difficult 6 : stingy 7 : evenly contested 8 : low in supply —**tight** adv —**tight·en** \-³n\ vb —**tight·ly** adv —**tight·ness** n

tights \'tīts\ n pl : skintight garments

tight·wad \'tīt,wäd\ n : stingy person

tile \'tīl\ n : thin piece of stone or fired clay used on roofs, floors, or walls ~ vb : cover with tiles

¹**till** \(,)til\ prep or conj : until

²**till** \'til\ vb : cultivate (soil) —**till·able** adj

³**till** \'til\ n : money drawer

till·er \'tilər\ n : lever for turning a boat's rudder

tilt \'tilt\ vb : cause to incline ~ n : slant

tim·ber \'timbər\ n 1 : cut wood for building 2 : large squared piece of wood 3 : wooded land or trees for timber ~ vb : cover, frame, or support with timbers —**tim·bered** adj —**tim·ber·land** \-,land\ n

tim·bre \'tambər, 'tim-\ n : sound quality

time \'tīm\ n 1 : period during which something exists or continues or can be accomplished 2 : point at which something happens 3 : customary hour 4 : age 5 : tempo 6 : moment, hour, day, or year as indicated by a clock or calendar 7 : one's experience during a particular period ~ vb **timed; tim·ing** 1 : arrange or set the time of 2 : determine or record the time, duration, or rate of **—time-keep·er** n **—time·less** adj **—time·less·ness** n **—time·li·ness** n **—time·ly** adv **—tim·er** n

time·piece n : device to show time

times \ˈtīmz\ prep : multiplied by

time·ta·ble \ˈtīm‚tābəl\ n : table of departure and arrival times

tim·id \ˈtiməd\ adj : lacking in courage or self-confidence **—ti·mid·i·ty** \təˈmidətē\ n **—tim·id·ly** adv

tim·o·rous \ˈtim(ə)rəs\ adj : fearful **—tim·o·rous·ly** adv **—tim·o·rous·ness** n

tim·pa·ni \ˈtimpənē\ n pl : set of kettledrums **—tim·pa·nist** \-nəst\ n

tin \ˈtin\ n 1 : soft white metallic chemical element 2 : metal food can

tinc·ture \ˈtiŋkchər\ n : alcoholic solution of a medicine

tin·der \ˈtindər\ n : substance used to kindle a fire

tine \ˈtīn\ n : one of the points of a fork

tin·foil \ˈtin‚fȯil\ n : thin metal sheeting

tinge \ˈtinj\ vb **tinged; tinge·ing** or **ting·ing** \ˈtinjiŋ\ 1 : color slightly 2 : affect with a slight odor ~ n : slight coloring or flavor

tin·gle \ˈtiŋgəl\ vb **-gled; -gling** : feel a ringing, stinging, or thrilling sensation **—tingle** n

tin·ker \ˈtiŋkər\ vb : experiment in repairing something **—tin·ker·er** n

tin·kle \ˈtiŋkəl\ vb **-kled; -kling** : make or cause to make a high ringing sound **—tinkle** n

tin·sel \ˈtinsəl\ n : decorative thread or strip of glittering metal or paper

tint \ˈtint\ n 1 : slight or pale coloration 2 : color shade ~ vb : give a tint to

ti·ny \ˈtīnē\ adj **-ni·er; -est** : very small

¹tip \ˈtip\ vb **-pp-** 1 : overturn 2 : lean ~ n : act or state of tipping

²tip n : pointed end of something ~ vb **-pp-** 1 : furnish with a tip 2 : cover the tip of

³tip n : small sum given for a service performed ~ vb : give a tip to

⁴tip n : piece of confidential information ~ vb **-pp-** : give confidential information to

tip-off \ˈtip‚ȯf\ n : indication

tip·ple \ˈtipəl\ vb **-pled; -pling** : drink intoxicating liquor esp. habitually or excessively **—tip·pler** \-(ə)lər\ n

tip·sy \ˈtipsē\ adj **-si·er; -est** : unsteady or foolish from alcohol

tip·toe \ˈtip‚tō\ n : the toes of the feet ~ adv or adj : supported on tiptoe ~ vb **-toed; -toe·ing** : walk quietly or on tiptoe

tip-top n : highest point ~ adj : excellent

ti·rade \ˈtī‚rād, ˈtī‚-\ n : prolonged speech of abuse

¹tire \ˈtī(ə)r\ vb **tired; tir·ing** 1 : make or become weary 2 : wear out the patience of **—tire·less** adj **—tire·less·ly** adv **—tire·less·ness** n **—tire·some** \-səm\ adj **—tire·some·ly** adv **—tire·some·ness** n

²tire n : rubber cushion encircling a car wheel

tired \ˈtī(ə)rd\ adj : weary

tis·sue \ˈtishü\ n 1 : soft absorbent paper 2 : layer of cells forming a basic structural element of an animal or plant body

ti·tan·ic \tīˈtanik, tə-\ adj : gigantic

ti·ta·ni·um \tīˈtānēəm, tə-\ n : gray light strong metallic chemical element

tithe \ˈtīth\ n : tenth part paid or given esp. for the support of a church **—tithe** vb **—tith·er** n

tit·il·late \ˈtitᵊl‚āt\ vb **-lat·ed; -lat·ing** : excite pleasurably **—tit·il·la·tion** \‚titᵊlˈāshən\ n

ti·tle \ˈtītᵊl\ n 1 : legal ownership 2 : distinguishing name 3 : designation of honor, rank, or office 4 : championship **—ti·tled** adj

tit·ter \ˈtitər\ n : nervous or affected laugh **—titter** vb

tit·u·lar \ˈtich(ə)lər\ adj 1 : existing in title only 2 : relating to or bearing a title

TNT \‚tē‚en·ˈtē\ n : high explosive

to \tə, (ˈ)tü\ prep 1 : in the direction of 2 : at, on, or near 3 : resulting in 4 : before or until 5 —used to show a relationship or object of a verb 6 —used with an infinitive ~ \ˈtü\ adv 1 : forward 2 : to a state of consciousness

toad \ˈtōd\ n : tailless leaping amphibian

toad·stool \-‚stül\ n : mushroom esp. when inedible or poisonous

toady \ˈtōdē\ n, pl **toad·ies** : one who flatters to gain favors **—toady** vb

toast \ˈtōst\ vb 1 : make (as a slice of bread) crisp and brown 2 : drink in honor of someone or something 3 : warm ~ n 1 : toasted sliced bread 2 : act of drinking in honor of someone **—toast·er** n

to·bac·co \təˈbakō\ n, pl **-cos** : broad-leaved herb or its leaves prepared for smoking or chewing

to·bog·gan \təˈbägən\ n : long flat-bottomed light sled ~ vb : coast on a toboggan

to·day \tə'dā\ *adv* **1** : on or for this day **2** : at the present time ~ *n* : present day or time

tod·dle \'täd^əl\ *vb* **-dled; -dling** : walk with tottering steps like a young child —**toddle** *n* —**tod·dler** \'tädlər, -^ələr\ *n*

to-do \tə'dü\ *n, pl* **to-dos** \-'düz\ : disturbance or fuss

toe \'tō\ *n* : one of the 5 end divisions of the foot —**toe·nail** *n*

to·ga \'tōgə\ *n* : loose outer garment of ancient Rome

to·geth·er \tə'gethər\ *adv* **1** : in or into one place or group **2** : in or into contact or association **3** : at one time **4** : as a group —**to·geth·er·ness** *n*

toil \'tȯil\ *vb* : work hard and long — **toil** *n* —**toil·er** *n* —**toil·some** *adj*

toi·let \'tȯilət\ *n* **1** : dressing and grooming oneself **2** : bathroom **3** : water basin to urinate and defecate in

toils \'tȯilz\ *n pl* : net or trap

to·ken \'tōkən\ *n* **1** : outward sign or expression of something **2** : small part representing the whole **3** : piece resembling a coin

told *past of* TELL

tol·er·a·ble \'tälərəbəl\ *adj* **1** : capable of being endured **2** : moderately good —**tol·er·a·bly** \-blē\ *adv*

tol·er·ance \'tälərəns\ *n* **1** : lack of opposition to beliefs or practices differing from one's own **2** : capacity for enduring **3** : allowable deviation —**tol·er·ant** *adj* —**tol·er·ant·ly** *adv*

tol·er·ate \'tälə,rāt\ *vb* **-at·ed; -at·ing 1** : allow to be or to be done without opposition **2** : endure or resist the action of —**tol·er·a·tion** \,tälə'rāshən\ *n*

¹toll \'tōl\ *n* **1** : fee paid for a privilege or service **2** : cost of achievement in loss or suffering —**toll·booth** *n* —**toll·gate** *n*

²toll *vb* **1** : cause the sounding of a (bell) **2** : sound with slow measured strokes ~ *n* : sound of a tolling bell

tom·a·hawk \'tämə,hȯk\ *n* : light ax used as a weapon by Indians

to·ma·to \tə'mātō, -'mät-\ *n, pl* **-toes** : tropical American herb or its fruit

tomb \'tüm\ *n* : house, vault, or grave for burial

tom·boy \'täm,bȯi\ *n* : girl with boyish behavior

tomb·stone *n* : stone marking a grave

tom·cat \'täm,kat\ *n* : male cat

tome \'tōm\ *n* : large or weighty book

to·mor·row \tə'märō\ *adv* : on or for the day after today —**tomorrow** *n*

tom–tom \'täm,täm\ *n* : small-headed drum beaten with the hands

ton \'tən\ *n* : unit of weight equal to 2000 pounds

tone \'tōn\ *n* **1** : vocal or musical sound **2** : sound of definite pitch **3** : manner of speaking that expresses an emotion or attitude **4** : color quality **5** : healthy condition **6** : general character or quality ~ *vb* : soften or muffle —often used with *down* —**ton·al** \-^əl\ *adj* —**to·nal·i·ty** \tō'nalətē\ *n*

tongs \'täŋz, 'tȯŋz\ *n pl* : grasping device of 2 joined or hinged pieces

tongue \'təŋ\ *n* **1** : fleshy movable organ of the mouth **2** : language **3** : something long and flat and fastened at one end —**tongued** \'təŋd\ *adj* —**tongue·less** *adj*

ton·ic \'tänik\ *n* : something (as a drug) that invigorates or restores health —**tonic** *adj*

to·night \tə'nīt\ *adv* : on this night ~ *n* : present or coming night

ton·sil \'tänsəl\ *n* : either of a pair of oval masses in the throat —**ton·sil·lec·to·my** \,tänsə'lektəmē\ *n* —**ton·sil·li·tis** \-'lītəs\ *n*

too \'tü\ *adv* **1** : in addition **2** : excessively

took *past of* TAKE

tool \'tül\ *n* : device worked by hand ~ *vb* : shape or finish with a tool

toot \'tüt\ *vb* : sound or cause to sound esp. in short blasts —**toot** *n*

tooth \'tüth\ *n, pl* **teeth** \'tēth\ **1** : one of the hard structures in the jaws for chewing **2** : one of the projections on the edge of a gear wheel —**tooth·ache** *n* —**tooth·brush** *n* —**toothed** \'tütht\ *adj* —**tooth·less** *adj* —**tooth·paste** *n* —**tooth·pick** *n*

tooth·some \'tüthsəm\ *adj* **1** : delicious **2** : attractive

¹top \'täp\ *n* **1** : highest part or level of something **2** : lid or covering ~ *vb* **-pp- 1** : cover with a top **2** : surpass **3** : go over the top of ~ *adj* : being at the top —**topped** *adj*

²top *n* : spinning toy

to·paz \'tō,paz\ *n* : hard gem

top·coat *n* : lightweight overcoat

top·ic \'täpik\ *n* : subject for discussion or study

top·i·cal \-ikəl\ *adj* **1** : relating to or arranged by topics **2** : relating to current or local events —**top·i·cal·ly** \-k(ə)lē\ *adv*

top·most \'täp,mōst\ *adj* : highest of all

top–notch \-'näch\ *adj* : of the highest quality

to·pog·ra·phy \tə'pägrəfē\ *n* **1** : art of mapping the physical features of a place **2** : outline of the form of a place —**to·pog·ra·pher** \-fər\ *n* —**top·o·graph·ic** \,täpə'grafik, top·o·graph·i·cal \ -ikəl\ *adj*

top·ple \'täpəl\ *vb* -**pled**; -**pling** : fall or cause to fall

top·sy–tur·vy \,täpsē'tərvē\ *adv or adj* **1** : upside down **2** : in utter confusion

torch \'torch\ *n* : flaming light —**torch·bear·er** *n* —**torch·light** *n*

tore *past of* TEAR

tor·ment \'tor,ment\ *n* : extreme pain or anguish or a source of this ~ *vb* **1** : cause severe anguish to **2** : harass —**tor·men·tor** \-ər\ *n*

torn *past part of* TEAR

tor·na·do \tor'nādō\ *n, pl* -**does** *or* -**dos** : violent destructive whirling wind

tor·pe·do \tor'pēdō\ *n, pl* -**does** : self-propelled explosive submarine missile ~ *vb* : hit with a torpedo

tor·pid \'torpəd\ *adj* **1** : having lost motion or the power of exertion **2** : lacking vigor —**tor·pid·i·ty** \tor'pidətē\ *n*

tor·por \'torpər\ *n* : extreme sluggishness or lethargy

torque \'tork\ *n* : turning force

tor·rent \'torənt\ *n* **1** : rushing stream **2** : tumultuous outburst —**tor·ren·tial** \to'renchəl, tə-\ *adj*

tor·rid \'torəd\ *adj* **1** : parched with heat **2** : impassioned

tor·sion \'torshən\ *n* : a twisting or being twisted —**tor·sion·al** \'torsh(ə)nəl\ *adj* —**tor·sion·al·ly** *adv*

tor·so \'torsō\ *n, pl* -**sos** *or* -**si** \-,sē\ : trunk of the human body

tor·til·la \tor'tē(y)ə\ *n* : round flat cornmeal bread

tor·toise \'tortəs\ *n* : sea turtle

tor·tu·ous \'torch(ə)wəs\ *adj* **1** : winding **2** : tricky

tor·ture \'torchər\ *n* **1** : use of pain to punish or force **2** : agony ~ *vb* -**tured**; -**tur·ing** : inflict torture on —**tor·tur·er** *n*

toss \'tos, 'tas\ *vb* **1** : move to and fro or up and down violently **2** : throw with a quick light motion **3** : move restlessly —**toss** *n*

toss–up *n* **1** : a deciding by flipping a coin **2** : even chance

tot \'tät\ *n* : small child

to·tal \'tōt'l\ *n* : entire amount ~ *vb* -**taled** *or* -**talled**; -**tal·ing** *or* -**tal·ling** **1**

: add up **2** : amount to —**total** *adj* —**to·tal·ly** *adv*

to·tal·i·tar·i·an \tō,talə'terēən\ *adj* : relating to a political system in which the government has complete control over the people —**totalitarian** *n* —**to·tal·i·tar·i·an·ism** \-ēə,nizəm\ *n*

to·tal·i·ty \tō'talətē\ *n, pl* -**ties** : whole amount or entirety

tote \'tōt\ *vb* -**ed**; **tot·ing** : carry

to·tem \'tōtəm\ *n* : often carved figure used as a family or tribe emblem

tot·ter \'tätər\ *vb* **1** : sway as if about to fall **2** : stagger

touch \'təch\ *vb* **1** : make contact with so as to feel **2** : be or cause to be in contact **3** : take into the hands or mouth **4** : treat or mention a subject **5** : relate or concern **6** : move to sympathetic feeling ~ *n* **1** : light stroke **2** : act or fact of touching or being touched **3** : sense of feeling **4** : trace **5** : state of being in contact

touch·down \'təch,daůn\ *n* : scoring of 6 points in football

touch·stone *n* : test or criterion of genuineness or quality

touchy \'təchē\ *adj* **touch·i·er**; -**est** **1** : easily offended **2** : requiring tact

tough \'təf\ *adj* **1** : strong but elastic **2** : not easily chewed **3** : severe or disciplined **4** : difficult to influence or overcome ~ *n* : rowdy or belligerent person —**tough·ly** *adv* —**tough·ness** *n*

tough·en \'təfən\ *vb* : make or become tough

tou·pee \tü'pā\ *n* : small wig for a bald spot

tour \'tůr, *1 is also* 'taů(ə)r\ *n* **1** : period of time spent at work or on an assignment **2** : journey with a return to the starting point ~ *vb* : travel over to see the sights —**tour·ist** \'tůrəst\ *n*

tour·na·ment \'tůrnəmənt, 'tər-\ *n* **1** : medieval jousting competition **2** : championship series of games

tour·ney \-nē\ *n, pl* -**neys** : tournament

tour·ni·quet \'tůrnikət, 'tər-\ *n* : twisted bandage for stopping blood flow

tou·sle \'taůzəl\ *vb* -**sled**; -**sling** : dishevel (as someone's hair)

tout \'taůt, 'tüt\ *vb* : praise or publicize loudly

tow \'tō\ *vb* : pull along behind —**tow** *n*

to·ward, to·wards \(')tō(ə)rd(z), tə'word(z)\ *prep* **1** : in the direction of 2 : with respect to 3 : in part payment on

tow·el \'taủ(ə)l\ *n* : absorbent cloth or paper for wiping or drying

tow·er \'taủ(ə)r\ *n* : tall structure ~ *vb* : rise to a great height —**tow·ered** \'taủ(ə)rd\ *adj* —**tow·er·ing** *adj*

tow·head \'tō,hed\ *n* : person having white or light blond hair —**tow·head·ed** \-,hedəd\ *adj*

town \'taủn\ *n* 1 : small residential area 2 : city —**towns·peo·ple** \'taủnz-,pēpəl\ *n pl*

town·ship \'taủn,ship\ *n* 1 : unit of local government 2 : 36 square miles of U.S. public land

tox·ic \'täksik\ *adj* : poisonous —**tox·ic·i·ty** \täk'sisətē\ *n*

tox·in \'täksən\ *n* : poison produced by an organism

toy \'tòi\ *n* : something for a child to play with ~ *vb* : amuse oneself or play with something ~ *adj* 1 : designed as a toy 2 : very small

¹**trace** \'trās\ *vb* **traced**; **trac·ing** 1 : mark over the lines of (a drawing) 2 : follow the trail or the development of ~ *n* 1 : track 2 : tiny amount or residue —**trace·able** *adj* —**trac·er** *n*

²**trace** *n* : line of a harness

tra·chea \'trākēə\ *n*, *pl* **-che·ae** \-kē,ē\ : windpipe —**tra·che·al** \-kēəl\ *adj*

track \'trak\ *n* 1 : trail left by wheels or footprints 2 : racing course 3 : train rails 4 : awareness of a progression 5 : looped belts propelling a vehicle ~ *vb* 1 : follow the tracks of 2 : make tracks on —**track·er** *n*

track–and–field *adj* : relating to athletic contests of running, jumping, and throwing events

¹**tract** \'trakt\ *n* : pamphlet of propaganda

²**tract** *n* 1 : stretch of land 2 : system of body organs

trac·ta·ble \'traktəbəl\ *adj* : easily controlled

trac·tion \'trakshən\ *n* : gripping power to permit movement —**trac·tion·al** \-sh(ə)nəl\ *adj* —**trac·tive** \'traktiv\ *adj*

trac·tor \'traktər\ *n* 1 : farm vehicle used esp. for pulling 2 : truck for hauling a trailer

trade \'trād\ *n* 1 : one's regular business 2 : occupation requiring skill 3 : the buying and selling of goods 4 : act of trading ~ *vb* **trad·ed**; **trad·ing** 1 : give in exchange for something 2 : buy and sell goods 3 : be a

regular customer —**trades·peo·ple** \'trādz,pēpəl\ *n pl*

trade·mark \'trād,märk\ *n* : word or mark identifying a manufacturer —**trademark** *vb*

trades·man \'trādzmən\ *n* : shopkeeper

tra·di·tion \trə'dishən\ *n* : belief or custom passed from generation to generation —**tra·di·tion·al** \-'dish(ə)nəl\ *adj* —**tra·di·tion·al·ly** *adv*

tra·duce \trə'd(y)üs\ *vb* **-duced**; **-duc·ing** : lower the reputation of —**tra·duc·er** *n*

traf·fic \'trafik\ *n* 1 : business dealings 2 : movement along a route ~ *vb* : do business —**traf·fick·er** *n* —**traffic light** *n*

trag·e·dy \'trajədē\ *n*, *pl* **-dies** 1 : serious drama describing a conflict and having a sad end 2 : disastrous event

trag·ic \'trajik\ *adj* : being a tragedy —**trag·i·cal·ly** \-ik(ə)lē\ *adv*

trail \'trāl\ *vb* 1 : hang down and drag along the ground 2 : draw along behind 3 : follow the track of 4 : dwindle ~ *n* 1 : something that trails 2 : path or evidence left by something

trail·er \'trālər\ *n* : vehicle intended to be hauled

train \'trān\ *n* 1 : trailing part of a gown 2 : retinue or procession 3 : connected series 4 : group of linked railroad cars ~ *vb* 1 : cause to grow as desired 2 : make or become prepared or skilled 3 : point —**train·ee** *n* —**train·er** *n* —**train·load** *n* —**train·man** \-mən\ *n*

trait \'trāt\ *n* : distinguishing quality

trai·tor \'trātər\ *n* : one who betrays a trust or commits treason —**trai·tor·ous** *adj*

tra·jec·to·ry \trə'jekt(ə)rē\ *n*, *pl* **-ries** : path of something moving through air or space

tram·mel \'traməl\ *vb* **-meled** *or* **-melled**; **-mel·ing** *or* **-mel·ling** \-(ə)liŋ\ : impede —**trammel** *n*

tramp \'tramp, 2 *is also* 'trämp, 'trȯmp\ *vb* 1 : walk or hike 2 : tread on ~ *n* : beggar or vagrant

tram·ple \'trampəl\ *vb* **-pled**; **-pling** : walk or step on so as to bruise or crush —**trample** *n* —**tram·pler** \-p(ə)lər\ *n*

tram·po·line \,trampə'lēn, 'trampə,-\ *n* : resilient canvas-and-springs surface used for bouncing —**tram·po·lin·er** *n* —**tram·po·lin·ist** \-əst\ *n*

trance \'trans\ *n* 1 : sleeplike condition 2 : state of mystical absorption

tran·quil \'traŋkwəl, 'tran-\ *adj* : quiet

and undisturbed —**tran·quil·ize**
\-kwə‚līz\ *vb* —**tran·quil·iz·er** *n*
—**tran·quil·i·ty, tran·quil·i·ty** \tran-
'kwilətē, traŋ-\ *n* —**tran·quil·ly** *adv*

trans·act \trans'akt, tranz-\ *vb* : conduct (business)

trans·ac·tion \-'akshən\ *n* 1 : business
deal 2 *pl* : records of proceedings

tran·scend \tran'send\ *vb* : rise above
or surpass —**tran·scen·dent**
\-'endənt\ *adj* —**tran·scen·den·tal**
\‚trans‚en'dentᵊl, -ən-\ *adj*

tran·scribe \trans'krīb\ *vb* -scribed;
-scrib·ing : make a copy, arrangement, or recording of —**tran·scrip·
tion** \trans'kripshən\ *n*

tran·script \'trans‚kript\ *n* : official
copy

tran·sept \'trans‚ept\ *n* : part of a
church that crosses the nave at right
angles

trans·fer \trans'fər, 'trans‚fər\ *vb* -rr-
1 : move from one person, place, or
situation to another 2 : convey ownership of 3 : print or copy by contact
4 : change to another vehicle or
transportation line ~ \'trans‚fər\ *n*
1 : act or process of transferring 2
: one that transfers or is transferred
3 : ticket permitting one to transfer
—**trans·fer·able** \trans'fərəbəl\ *adj*
—**trans·fer·al** \-əl\ *n* —**trans·fer·
ence** \-əns\ *n*

trans·fig·ure \trans'figyər\ *vb* -ured;
-ur·ing 1 : change the form or appearance of 2 : glorify —**trans·fig·u·
ra·tion** \‚trans‚fig(y)ə'rāshən\ *n*

trans·fix \trans'fiks\ *vb* 1 : pierce
through 2 : hold motionless

trans·form \-'form\ *vb* 1 : change in
structure, appearance, or character
2 : change (an electric current) in
potential or type —**trans·for·ma·tion**
\‚transfər'māshən\ *n* —**trans·form·
er** \trans'förmər\ *n*

trans·fuse \trans'fyüz\ *vb* -fused; -fus·
ing 1 : diffuse into or through 2
: transfer (as blood) into a vein —
trans·fu·sion \-'fyüzhən\ *n*

trans·gress \trans'gres, tranz-\ *vb* : sin
—**trans·gres·sion** \-'greshən\ *n* —
trans·gres·sor \-'gresər\ *n*

tran·sient \'tranchənt\ *adj* : not lasting
or staying long —**transient** *n* —**tran·
sient·ly** *adv*

tran·sis·tor \tranz'istər, trans-\ *n*
: small electronic device used to
regulate flow of electricity —**tran·
sis·tor·ize** \-tə‚rīz\ *vb*

tran·sit \'transət, 'tranz-\ *n* 1 : movement over, across, or through 2

: local and esp. public transportation
3 : surveyor's instrument

tran·si·tion \trans'ishən, tranz-\ *n*
: passage from one state, stage, or
subject to another —**tran·si·tion·al**
\-'ish(ə)nəl\ *adj*

tran·si·to·ry \'transə‚tōrē, 'tranz-\ *adj*
: of brief duration

trans·late \trans'lāt, tranz-\ *vb* -lat·ed;
-lat·ing : change into another language —**trans·lat·able** *adj* —**trans·la·
tion** \-'lāshən\ *n* —**trans·la·tor**
\-'lātər\ *n*

trans·lu·cent \trans'lüsᵊnt, tranz-\ *adj*
: diffusing light so that objects beyond cannot be distinguished —
trans·lu·cence \-ᵊns\ *n* —**trans·lu·
cen·cy** \-ᵊnsē\ *n* —**trans·lu·cent·ly**
adv

trans·mis·sion \-'mishən\ *n* 1 : act or
process of transmitting 2 : system of
gears between a car engine and drive
wheels

trans·mit \-'mit\ *vb* -tt- 1 : transfer
from one person or place to another
2 : pass on by inheritance 3 : broadcast —**trans·mis·si·ble** \-'misəbəl\
adj —**trans·mit·ta·ble** \-'mitəbəl\
adj —**trans·mit·tal** \-'mitᵊl\ *n* —
trans·mit·ter *n*

tran·som \'transəm\ *n* : window above
a door

trans·par·ent \trans'parənt\ *adj* 1
: clear enough to see through 2
: obvious —**trans·par·en·cy** \-ənsē\
n —**trans·par·ent·ly** *adv*

tran·spire \trans'pī(ə)r\ *vb* -spired;
-spir·ing : take place —**tran·spi·ra·
tion** \‚transpə'rāshən\ *n*

trans·plant \trans'plant\ *vb* 1 : dig up
and move to another place 2 : transfer from one body part or person to
another —**transplant** \'trans‚-\ *n* —
trans·plan·ta·tion \‚trans‚plan-
'tāshən\ *n*

trans·port \trans'pōrt\ *vb* 1 : carry or
deliver to another place 2 : carry
away by emotion ~ \'trans‚-\ *n* 1
: act of transporting 2 : rapture 3
: ship or plane for carrying troops or
supplies —**trans·por·ta·tion** \‚trans‚-
pər'tāshən\ *n* —**trans·port·er** *n*

trans·pose \trans'pōz\ *vb* -posed; -pos·
ing : change the position, sequence,
or key —**trans·po·si·tion** \‚transpə'zishən\ *n*

tran·ship \tran(ch)'ship, trans-\ *vb*
: transfer from one mode of transportation to another —**tran·ship·ment**
n

trans·verse \trans'vərs, tranz-\ *adj*

: lying across —**trans·verse** \'trans-, ,vers, 'tranz-\ n —**trans·verse·ly** adv

trap \'trap\ n 1 : device for catching animals 2 : something by which one is caught unawares 3 : device to allow one thing to pass through while keeping other things out ~ vb -**pp**- : catch in a trap —**trap·per** n

trap·door n : door in a floor or roof

tra·peze \tra'pēz\ n : suspended bar used by acrobats

trap·e·zoid \'trapə,zoid\ n : plane 4-sided figure with 2 parallel sides —**trap·e·zoi·dal** \,trapə'zoid³l\ adj

trap·pings \'trapiŋz\ n pl 1 : ornamental covering 2 : outward decoration or dress

trash \'trash\ n : something that is no good —**trashy** adj

trau·ma \'traůma, 'trȯ-\ n, pl -ma·ta \-mətə\ or -mas : bodily or mental injury —**trau·mat·ic** \trə'matik, trȯ-, traů-\ adj

tra·vail \trə'vāl, 'trav,āl\ n : painful work or exertion ~ vb : labor hard

trav·el \'travəl\ vb -eled or -elled; -el·ing or -el·ling 1 : take a trip or tour 2 : move or be carried from point to point ~ n : journey —often pl. —**trav·el·er, trav·el·ler** n

tra·verse \trə'vərs, tra'vərs, 'travərs\ vb -versed; -vers·ing : go or extend across —**tra·verse** \'travərs\ n

trav·es·ty \'travəstē\ n, pl -ties : terrible distortion or imitation of something —**travesty** vb

trawl \'trȯl\ vb : fish or catch with a trawl ~ n : large cone-shaped net —**trawl·er** n

tray \'trā\ n : shallow flat-bottomed receptacle for holding or carrying something

treach·er·ous \'trechərəs\ adj : disloyal or dangerous —**treach·er·ous·ly** adv

treach·ery \'trechərē\ n, pl -er·ies : betrayal of a trust

tread \'tred\ vb trod \'träd\; trod·den \'träd³n\ or tred; tread·ing 1 : step on or over 2 : walk 3 : press or crush with the feet ~ n 1 : way of walking 2 : sound made in walking 3 : part on which a thing runs

trea·dle \'tred³l\ n : foot pedal operating a machine

tread·mill n 1 : mill worked by walking persons or animals 2 : wearisome routine

trea·son \'trēz³n\ n : attempt to overthrow the government —**trea·son·able** \'trēznəbəl, -³nəbəl\ adj —**trea·son·ous** \-nəs, -³nəs\ adj

trea·sure \'trezhər, 'trāzh-\ n : wealth stored up 2 : something of great value ~ vb -sured; -sur·ing : keep as precious

trea·sur·er \'trezhərər, 'trāzhərər, 'trāzh-\ n : officer who handles funds

trea·sury \'trezh(ə)rē, 'trāzh-\ n, pl -sur·ies : place or office for keeping and distributing funds

treat \'trēt\ vb 1 : have as a topic 2 : pay for the food or entertainment of 3 : act toward or regard in a certain way 4 : give medical care for ~ n 1 : food or entertainment paid for by another 2 : something special and enjoyable —**treat·ment** \-mənt\ n

trea·tise \'trētəs\ n : systematic written exposition or argument

trea·ty \'trētē\ n, pl -ties : agreement between governments

tre·ble \'trebəl\ n 1 : highest part in music 2 : upper half of the musical range ~ adj : triple in number or amount ~ vb -bled; -bling : make triple —**tre·bly** adv

tree \'trē\ n : tall woody plant ~ vb treed; tree·ing : force up a tree —**tree·less** adj

trek \'trek\ n : difficult trip ~ vb -kk- : make a trek

trel·lis \'treləs\ n : structure of crossed strips

trem·ble \'trembəl\ vb -bled; -bling 1 : shake from fear or cold 2 : move or sound as if shaken

tre·men·dous \tri'mendəs\ adj : amazingly large, powerful, or excellent —**tre·men·dous·ly** adv

trem·or \'tremər\ n : a trembling

trem·u·lous \'tremyələs\ adj : trembling or quaking

trench \'trench\ n : long narrow cut in land

tren·chant \'trenchənt\ adj : sharply perceptive

trend \'trend\ n : prevailing tendency, direction, or style

trep·i·da·tion \,trepə'dāshən\ n : nervous apprehension

tres·pass \'trespəs, -,pas\ n 1 : sin 2 : unauthorized entry onto someone's property ~ vb 1 : sin 2 : enter illegally —**tres·pass·er** n

tress \'tres\ n : long lock of hair

tres·tle \'tresəl\ n 1 : support with a horizontal piece and spreading legs 2 : framework bridge

tri·ad \'trī,ad, -əd\ n : union of 3

tri·al \'trī(ə)l\ n 1 : hearing and judgment of a matter in court 2 : source of great annoyance **3** : test use or experimental effort —**trial** *adj*

tri·an·gle \'trī,aṇgəl\ *n* : plane figure with 3 sides and 3 angles —**tri·an·gu·lar** \trī'aṇgyələr\ *adj*

tribe \'trīb\ *n* : social group of numerous families —**trib·al** \'trībəl\ *adj* —**tribes·man** \'trībzmən\ *n*

trib·u·la·tion \,tribyə'lāshən\ *n* : suffering from oppression

tri·bu·nal \trī'byün°l, trib'yün-\ *n* **1** : court **2** : something that decides

trib·u·tary \'tribyə,terē\ *n, pl* **-tar·ies** : stream that flows into a river or lake

trib·ute \'trib(,)yüt, -yət\ *n* **1** : payment to acknowledge submission **2** : tax **3** : gift or act showing respect

trick \'trik\ *n* **1** : scheme to deceive **2** : prank **3** : deceptive or ingenious feat **4** : mannerism **5** : knack **6** : tour of duty ~ *vb* : deceive by cunning —**trick·ery** \-(ə)rē\ *n* —**trick·ster** \-stər\ *n*

trick·le \'trikəl\ *vb* **-led; -ling** : run in drops or a thin stream —**trickle** *n*

tricky \'trikē\ *adj* **trick·i·er; -est** **1** : inclined to trickery **2** : requiring skill or caution

tri·cy·cle \'trī,sikəl\ *n* : 3-wheeled bicycle

tri·dent \'trīd°nt\ *n* : 3-pronged spear

tri·en·ni·al \trī'enēəl\ *adj* : lasting, occurring, or done every 3 years —**triennial** *n*

tri·fle \'trīfəl\ *n* : something of little value or importance ~ *vb* **-fled; -fling** **1** : speak or act in a playful or flirting way **2** : toy —**tri·fler** *n*

tri·fling \'trīfliṇ\ *adj* : trivial

trig·ger \'trigər\ *n* : finger-piece of a firearm lock that releases the hammer ~ *vb* : set into motion —**trigger** *adj* —**trig·gered** \-ərd\ *adj*

trig·o·nom·e·try \,trigə'nämətrē\ *n* : mathematics dealing with triangular measurement —**trig·o·no·met·ric** \-nə'metrik\ *adj*

trill \'tril\ *n* **1** : rapid alternation between 2 adjacent tones **2** : rapid vibration in speaking ~ *vb* : utter in or with a trill

tril·lion \'trilyən\ *n* : 1000 billions —**trillion** *adj* —**tril·lionth** \-yənth\ *adj or n*

tril·o·gy \'triləjē\ *n, pl* **-gies** : 3-part literary or musical composition

trim \'trim\ *vb* **-mm- 1** : decorate **2** : make neat or reduce by cutting ~ *adj* **-mm-** : neat and compact ~ *n* **1** : state or condition **2** : ornaments —**trim·ly** *adv* —**trim·mer** *n*

trim·ming \'trimiṇ\ *n* **1** : something that ornaments or completes **2** *pl* : scraps left after cutting

Trin·i·ty \'trinətē\ *n* : divine unity of Father, Son, and Holy Spirit

trin·ket \'triṇkət\ *n* : small ornament

trio \'trēō\ *n, pl* **tri·os** **1** : music for 3 performers **2** : group of 3

trip \'trip\ *vb* **-pp- 1** : step lightly **2** : stumble or cause to stumble **3** : make or cause to make a mistake **4** : release (as a spring or switch) ~ *n* **1** : journey **2** : stumble **3** : drug-induced experience

tri·par·tite \trī'pär,tīt\ *adj* : having 3 parts or parties

tripe \'trīp\ *n* **1** : animal's stomach used as food **2** : trash

tri·ple \'tripəl\ *vb* **-pled; -pling** : make 3 times as great ~ *n* : group of 3 ~ *adj* **1** : having 3 units **2** : being 3 times as great as any number

trip·let \'triplət\ *n* **1** : group of 3 **2** : one of 3 offspring born together

trip·li·cate \'triplikət\ *adj* : made in 3 identical copies ~ *n* : one of 3 copies

tri·pod \'trī,päd\ *n* : a stand with 3 legs —**tripod**, **tri·po·dal** \'tripəd°l, 'trī,päd-\ *adj*

tri·sect \'trī,sekt, trī'-\ *vb* : divide into 3 usu. equal parts —**tri·sec·tion** \'trī,sekshən\ *n*

trite \'trīt\ *adj* **trit·er; trit·est** : too much used

tri·umph \'trīəmf\ *n, pl* **-umphs** \-əmfs, -əm(p)s\ : victory or great success ~ *vb* : obtain or celebrate victory —**tri·um·phal** \trī'əmfəl\ *adj* —**tri·um·phant** \-fənt\ *adj* —**tri·um·phant·ly** *adv*

tri·um·vi·rate \trī'əmvərət\ *n* : ruling body of 3 persons

triv·et \'trivət\ *n* **1** : 3-legged stand **2** : stand to hold a hot dish

triv·ia \'trivēə\ *n sing or pl* : unimportant details

triv·i·al \'trivēəl\ *adj* : of little importance —**triv·i·al·i·ty** \,trivē'alətē\ *n*

trod *past of* TREAD

trod·den *past part of* TREAD

troll \'trōl\ *n* : dwarf or giant of folklore inhabiting caves or hills

trol·ley \'trälē\ *n, pl* **-leys** : streetcar run by overhead electric wires

trol·lop \'träləp\ *n* : untidy or immoral woman

trom·bone \träm'bōn, 'träm,-\ *n* : musical instrument with a long sliding tube —**trom·bon·ist** \-'bōnəst, -,bō-\ *n*

troop \'trüp\ *n* **1** : cavalry unit **2** *pl* : soldiers **3** : collection of people or things ~ *vb* : move or gather in crowds

troop·er \'trüpər\ *n* 1 : cavalry soldier 2 : policeman on horseback or state policeman

tro·phy \'trōfē\ *n, pl* **-phies** : prize gained by a victory

trop·ic \'träpik\ *n* 1 : either of the 2 parallels of latitude one 23½ degrees north of the equator (**tropic of Cancer** \-'kansər\) and one 23½ degrees south of the equator (**tropic of Capri·corn** \-'kaprə,kȯrn\) 2 *pl* : region lying between the tropics —**tropic, trop·i·cal** \-ikəl\ *adj*

trot \'trät\ *n* : moderately fast gait esp. of a horse with diagonally paired legs moving together ~ *vb* -tt- : go at a trot —**trot·ter** *n*

troth \'träth, 'trȯth, 'trōth\ *n* 1 : pledged faithfulness 2 : betrothal

trou·ba·dour \'trübə,dȯr\ *n* : medieval lyric poet

trou·ble \'trəbəl\ *vb* **-bled; -bling** 1 : disturb 2 : afflict 3 : make an effort ~ *n* 1 : cause of mental or physical distress 2 : effort —**trou·ble·mak·er** *n* —**trou·ble·some** *adj* —**trou·ble·some·ly** *adv*

trough \'trȯf, 'trȯth\ *n, pl* **troughs** \'trȯfs, 'trȯvz; 'trȯths, 'trō(th)z\ 1 : narrow container for animal feed or water 2 : long channel or depression (as between waves)

trounce \'traúns\ *vb* **trounced; trounc·ing** : thrash, punish, or defeat severely

troupe \'trüp\ *n* : group of stage performers —**troup·er** *n*

trou·sers \'traúzərz\ *n pl* : long pants for men or boys —**trouser** *adj*

trous·seau \'trüsō, trü'sō\ *n, pl* **-seaux** \-sōz, -'sōz\ *or* **-seaus** : bride's collection of clothing and personal items

trout \'traút\ *n, pl* **trout** : freshwater food and game fish

trow·el \'traúəl\ *n* 1 : tool for spreading or smoothing 2 : garden scoop —**trowel** *vb*

troy \'trȯi\ *n* : system of weights based on a pound of 12 ounces

tru·ant \'trüənt\ *n* 1 : one who shirks duty 2 : one absent from school without permission —**tru·an·cy** \-ənsē\ *n* —**truant** *adj*

truce \'trüs\ *n* : agreement to halt fighting

truck \'trək\ *n* 1 : wheeled frame for moving heavy objects 2 : automotive vehicle for transporting heavy loads

~ *vb* : transport on a truck —**truck·er** *n* —**truck·load** *n*

truck·le \'trəkəl\ *vb* **-led; -ling** : yield slavishly to another

tru·cu·lent \'trəkyələnt\ *adj* : aggressively self-assertive —**tru·cu·lence** \-ləns\ *n* —**tru·cu·len·cy** \-lənsē\ *n* —**tru·cu·lent·ly** *adv*

trudge \'trəj\ *vb* **trudged; trudg·ing** : walk or march steadily and with difficulty

true \'trü\ *adj* **tru·er; tru·est** 1 : loyal 2 : in agreement with fact or reality 3 : genuine ~ *adv* 1 : truthfully 2 : accurately —**tru·ly** *adv*

true-blue *adj* : loyal

truf·fle \'trəfəl, 'trüf-\ *n* : edible fruit of an underground fungus

tru·ism \'trü,izəm\ *n* : obvious truth

trump \'trəmp\ *n* : card of a designated suit any of whose cards will win over other cards ~ *vb* : take with a trump

trumped-up \'trəm(p)t'əp\ *adj* : made-up

trum·pet \'trəmpət\ *n* : tubular brass wind instrument with a flaring end ~ *vb* 1 : blow a trumpet 2 : proclaim loudly —**trum·pet·er** *n*

trun·cate \'trəŋ,kāt, 'trən-\ *vb* **-cat·ed; -cat·ing** : cut short —**trun·ca·tion** \,trəŋ'kāshən\ *n*

trun·dle \'trənd⁸l\ *vb* **-dled; -dling** : roll along

trunk \'trəŋk\ *n* 1 : main part (as of a body or tree) 2 : long muscular nose of an elephant 3 : storage chest 4 : storage space in a car 5 *pl* : shorts

truss \'trəs\ *vb* : bind tightly ~ *n* 1 : set of structural parts forming a framework 2 : appliance worn to hold a hernia in place

trust \'trəst\ *n* 1 : reliance on another 2 : assured hope 3 : credit 4 : property held or managed in behalf of another 5 : combination of firms that reduces competition 6 : something entrusted to another's care 7 : custody ~ *vb* 1 : depend 2 : hope 3 : entrust 4 : have faith in —**trust·ful** \-fəl\ *adj* —**trust·ful·ly** *adv* —**trust·ful·ness** *n* —**trust·worth·i·ness** *n* —**trust·wor·thy** *adj*

trust·ee \,trəs'tē\ *n* : person holding property in trust —**trust·ee·ship** *n*

trusty \'trəstē\ *adj* **trust·i·er; -est** : dependable

truth \'trüth\ *n, pl* **truths** \'trüthz, 'trüths\ 1 : real state of things 2 : true or accepted statement 3 : agreement with fact or reality —

truth·ful \-fəl\ *adj* —**truth·ful·ly** *adv* —**truth·ful·ness** *n*

try \'trī\ *vb* **tried; try·ing** 1 : conduct the trial of 2 : put to a test 3 : strain 4 : make an effort at ~ *n, pl* **tries** : act of trying

try·out *n* : competitive test of performance esp. for athletes or actors —**try out** *vb*

tryst \'trist, 'trist\ *n* : secret rendezvous of lovers

tsar \'zär, 'tsär\ *var of* CZAR

T-shirt \'tē,shərt\ *n* : collarless pullover shirt with short sleeves

tub \'təb\ *n* 1 : wide bucketlike vessel 2 : bathtub

tu·ba \'t(y)übə\ *n* : large low-pitched brass wind instument

tube \'t(y)üb\ *n* 1 : hollow cylinder 2 : round container from which a substance can be squeezed 3 : airtight circular tube of rubber inside a tire 4 : electronic device consisting of a sealed usu. glass container with electrodes inside —**tubed** \'t(y)übd\ *adj* —**tube·less** *adj*

tu·ber \'t(y)übər\ *n* : fleshy underground growth (as of a potato) —**tuber·ous** \-rəs\ *adj*

tu·ber·cu·lo·sis \t(y)ů,bərkyə'lōsəs\ *n, pl* **-lo·ses** \-,sēz\ : bacterial disease esp. of the lungs —**tu·ber·cu·lar** \-'bərkyələr\ *adj* —**tu·ber·cu·lous** \-ləs\ *adj*

tub·ing \'t(y)übiŋ\ *n* : series or arrangement of tubes

tu·bu·lar \'t(y)übyələr\ *adj* : of or like a tube

tuck \'tək\ *vb* 1 : pull up into a fold 2 : put into a snug often concealing place 3 : make snug in bed —with *in* ~ *n* 1 : fold in a cloth

tuck·er \'təkər\ *vb* : fatigue

Tues·day \'t(y)üzdē\ *n* : 3d day of the week

tuft \'təft\ *n* : clump (as of hair or feathers) —**tuft·ed** \'təftəd\ *adj*

tug \'təg\ *vb* **-gg-** 1 : pull hard 2 : move by pulling ~ *n* 1 : act of tugging 2 : tugboat

tug·boat *n* : boat for towing or pushing ships through a harbor

tug-of-war \,təgə(v)'wȯr\ *n, pl* **tugs-of-war** : pulling contest between 2 teams

tu·ition \t(y)ů'ishən\ *n* : cost of instruction

tu·lip \'t(y)üləp\ *n* : herb with cup-shaped flowers

tum·ble \'təmbəl\ *vb* **-bled; -bling** 1 : perform gymnastic feats of rolling and turning 2 : fall or cause to fall

suddenly 3 : toss ~ *n* : act of tumbling

tum·bler \'təmblər\ *n* 1 : acrobat 2 : drinking glass 3 : obstruction in a lock that can be moved (as by a key)

tu·mid \'t(y)üməd\ *adj* : turgid

tum·my \'təmē\ *n, pl* **-mies** : belly

tu·mor \'t(y)ümər\ *n* : abnormal and useless growth of tissue —**tu·mor·ous** *adj*

tu·mult \'t(y)ü,məlt\ *n* 1 : confusion of loud noise and movement 2 : violent agitation of mind or feelings —**tu·mul·tu·ous** \t(y)ù'məlch(ə)wəs, -'məlchəs\ *adj*

tun \'tən\ *n* : large cask

tu·na \'t(y)ünə\ *n, pl* **-na** *or* **-nas** : large sea food fish

tun·dra \'təndrə\ *n* : treeless arctic plain

tune \'t(y)ün\ *n* 1 : melody 2 : correct musical pitch 3 : harmonious relationship ~ *vb* **tuned; tun·ing** 1 : bring or come into harmony 2 : adjust in musical pitch 3 : adjust a receiver so as to receive a broadcast 4 : put in first-class working order —**tune·ful** \-fəl\ *adj* —**tun·er** *n*

tung·sten \'təŋstən\ *n* : metallic element used for electrical purposes and in hardening alloys (as steel)

tu·nic \'t(y)ünik\ *n* 1 : ancient knee-length garment 2 : hip-length blouse or jacket

tun·nel \'tən²l\ *n* : underground passageway ~ *vb* **-neled** *or* **-nelled; -neling** *or* **-nel·ling** : make a tunnel through or under something

tur·ban \'tərbən\ *n* : wound headdress worn esp. by Muslims

tur·bid \'tərbəd\ *adj* 1 : dark with stirred-up sediment 2 : confused —**tur·bid·i·ty** \,tər'bidətē\ *n*

tur·bine \'tərbən, -,bīn\ *n* : engine turned by the force of gas or water on fan blades

tur·bo·jet \'tərbō,jet\ *n* : airplane powered by a jet engine having a turbine-driven air compressor or the engine itself

tur·bo·prop \'tərbō,präp\ *n* : airplane powered by a propeller turned by a jet engine-driven turbine

tur·bu·lent \'tərbyələnt\ *adj* 1 : causing violence or disturbance 2 : marked by agitation or tumult —**tur·bu·lence** \-ləns\ *n* —**tur·bu·lent·ly** *adv*

tu·reen \tə'rēn, tyù-\ *n* : deep bowl for serving soup

turf \'tərf\ *n* : upper layer of soil bound by grass and roots

tur·gid \'tərjəd\ *adj* 1 : swollen 2 : too highly embellished in style —**tur·gid·i·ty** \,tər'jidətē\ *n*

tur·key \'tərkē\ *n, pl* **-keys** : large American bird raised for food

tur·moil \'tər,mȯil\ *n* : extremely agitated condition

turn \'tərn\ *vb* 1 : move or cause to move around an axis 2 : twist (a mechanical part) to operate 3 : wrench 4 : cause to face or move in a different direction 5 : reverse the sides or surfaces of 6 : upset 7 : go around 8 : become or cause to become 9 : seek aid from a source ~ *n* 1 : act or instance of turning 2 : change 3 : place at which something turns 4 : place, time, or opportunity to do something in order —**turn down** *vb* : decline to accept —**turn in** *vb* 1 : deliver or report to authorities 2 : go to bed —**turn off** *vb* : stop the functioning of —**turn out** *vb* 1 : expel 2 : produce 3 : come together 4 : prove to be in the end —**turn up** *vb* 1 : discover or appear 2 : happen unexpectedly

turn·coat *n* : traitor

tur·nip \'tərnəp\ *n* : edible root of an herb

turn·out \'tərn,au̇t\ *n* 1 : gathering of people for a special purpose 2 : size of a gathering

turn·over *n* 1 : upset or reversal 2 : filled pastry 3 : volume of business 4 : movement (as of goods or people) into, through, and out of a place

turn·pike \'tərn,pīk\ *n* : expressway on which tolls are charged

turn·stile \-,stīl\ *n* : post with arms pivoted on the top that allows people to pass one by one

turn·ta·ble *n* : platform that turns a phonograph record

tur·pen·tine \'tərpən,tīn\ *n* : oil distilled from pine-tree resin and used as a solvent

tur·pi·tude \'tərpə,t(y)üd\ *n* : inherent baseness

tur·quoise \'tər,k(w)ȯiz\ *n* : blue or greenish gray gemstone

tur·ret \'tərət\ *n* 1 : little tower on a building 2 : revolving tool holder or gun housing

tur·tle \'tərt'l\ *n* : reptile with the trunk enclosed in a bony shell

tur·tle·dove *n* : wild pigeon

tur·tle·neck *n* : high close-fitting collar that can be turned over on a sweater with this collar

tusk \'təsk\ *n* : long protruding tooth (as of an elephant) —**tusked** \'təskt\ *adj*

tus·sle \'təsəl\ *n or vb* : struggle

tu·te·lage \'t(y)üt'lij\ *n* 1 : act of protecting 2 : instruction esp. of an individual

tu·tor \'t(y)ütər\ *n* : private teacher ~ *vb* : teach usu. individually

tux·e·do \,tək'sēdō\ *n, pl* **-dos** *or* **-does** : semiformal evening clothes for a man

TV \'tē'vē\ *n* : television

twain \'twān\ *n* : two

twang \'twaŋ\ *n* 1 : harsh sound like that of a plucked bowstring 2 : nasal speech or resonance ~ *vb* : sound or speak with a twang

tweak \'twēk\ *vb* : pinch and pull playfully —**tweak** *n*

tweed \'twēd\ *n* 1 : rough woolen fabric 2 *pl* : tweed clothing

tweet \'twēt\ *n* : chirping note —**tweet** *vb*

twee·zers \'twēzərz\ *n pl* : small pincerlike tool

twelve \'twelv\ *n* 1 : one more than 11 2 : 12th in a set or series 3 : something having 12 units —**twelfth** \'twelfth\ *adj or n* —**twelve** *adj or pron*

twen·ty \'twentē\ *n, pl* **-ties** : 2 times 10 —**twen·ti·eth** \-ēəth\ *adj or n* —**twenty** *adj or pron*

twice \'twīs\ *adv* 1 : on 2 occasions 2 : 2 times

twig \'twig\ *n* : small branch —**twig·gy** *adj*

twi·light \'twī,līt\ *n* : light from the sky at dusk or dawn —**twilight** *adj*

twill \'twil\ *n* : fabric with a weave that gives an appearance of diagonal lines in the fabric

twilled \'twild\ *adj* : made with a twill weave

twin \'twin\ *adj* 1 : born with one another or as a pair at one birth 2 : made up of 2 similar parts ~ *n* : either of 2 offspring born together

twine \'twīn\ *n* : strong twisted thread ~ *vb* **twined; twin·ing** 1 : twist together 2 : coil about a support —**twin·er** *n* —**twiny** *adj*

twinge \'twinj\ *vb* **twinged; twing·ing** *or* **twinge·ing** : affect with or feel a sudden sharp pain ~ *n* : sudden sharp stab (as of pain)

twin·kle \'twiŋkəl\ *vb* **-kled; -kling** : shine with a flickering light ~ *n* 1 : wink 2 : intermittent shining —**twin·kler** \-k(ə)lər\ *n*

twirl \'twərl\ *vb* : whirl round ~ *n* 1 : act of twirling 2 : coil —**twirl·er** *n*

twist \'twist\ *vb* 1 : unite by winding (threads) together 2 : wrench 3 : move in or have a spiral shape 4 : follow a winding course ~ *n* 1 : act or result of twisting 2 : unexpected development

twist·er \'twistər\ *n* : tornado

twit \'twit\ *vb* **-tt-** : taunt

twitch \'twich\ *vb* : move or pull with a sudden motion ~ *n* : act of twitching

twit·ter \'twitər\ *vb* : make chirping noises ~ *n* : small intermittent noise

two \'tü\ *n, pl* **twos** 1 : one more than one 2 : the 2d in a set or series 3 : something having 2 units —**two** *adj or pron*

two·fold \'tü,föld, -'föld\ *adj* : double —**two·fold** \-'föld\ *adv*

two·some \'tüsəm\ *n* : couple

-ty *n suffix* : quality, condition, or degree

ty·coon \tī'kün\ *n* : powerful and successful businessman

tying *pres part of* TIE

tyke \'tīk\ *n* : small child

tym·pa·num \'timpənəm\ *n, pl* **-na** \-nə\ : eardrum or the cavity which it closes externally —**tym·pan·ic** \tim'panik\ *adj*

type \'tīp\ *n* 1 : class, kind, or group set apart by common characteristics 2 : special design of printed letters ~ *vb* **typed; typ·ing** 1 : produce on a typewriter 2 : identify or classify as a particular type

type·writ·er *n* : keyboard machine that produces printed material by striking with raised letters through an inked ribbon —**type·write** *vb*

ty·phoid \'tī,föid, tī'-\ *adj* : relating to or being a communicable bacterial disease (**typhoid fever**)

ty·phoon \tī'fün\ *n* : hurricane of the western Pacific ocean

ty·phus \'tīfəs\ *n* : severe disease with fever, delirium, and rash

typ·i·cal \'tipikəl\ *adj* : having the essential characteristics of a group —**typ·i·cal·i·ty** \,tipə'kalətē\ *n* —**typ·i·cal·ly** *adv* —**typ·i·cal·ness** *n*

typ·i·fy \'tipə,fī\ *vb* **-fied; -fy·ing** : be typical of

typ·ist \'tīpəst\ *n* : one who operates a typewriter

ty·pog·ra·phy \tī'pägrəfē\ *n* 1 : art of printing with type 2 : style, arrangement, or appearance of matter printed from type —**ty·po·graph·ic** \,tīpə'grafik\, **ty·po·graph·i·cal** \-ikəl\ *adj* —**ty·po·graph·i·cal·ly** *adv*

ty·ran·ni·cal \tə'ranikəl, tī-\ *adj* : relating to a tyrant —**ty·ran·ni·cal·ly** *adv*

tyr·an·nize \'tirə,nīz\ *vb* **-nized; -niz·ing** : rule or deal with in the manner of a tyrant —**tyr·an·niz·er** *n*

tyr·an·ny \'tiranē\ *n, pl* **-nies** : unjust use of absolute governmental power

tyr·ant \'tīrənt\ *n* : harsh ruler having absolute power

ty·ro \'tīrō\ *n, pl* **-ros** : beginner

tzar \'zär, '(t)sär\ *var of* CZAR

U

u \'yü\ *n, pl* **u's** *or* **us** \'yüz\ : 21st letter of the alphabet

ubiq·ui·tous \yü'bikwətəs\ *adj* : ever-present —**ubiq·ui·tous·ly** *adv* —**ubiq·ui·ty** \-wətē\ *n*

ud·der \'ədər\ *n* : animal sac containing milk glands and nipples

ug·ly \'əglē\ *adj* **ugli·er; -est** 1 : offensive to look at 2 : mean or quarrelsome —**ug·li·ness** *n*

uku·le·le \,yükə'lālē\ *n* : small 4-string guitar

ul·cer \'əlsər\ *n* : eroded sore —**ul·cer·ous** *adj*

ul·cer·ate \'əlsə,rāt\ *vb* **-at·ed; -at·ing** : cause or become affected with an ulcer —**ul·cer·a·tion** \,əlsə'rāshən\ *n* —**ul·cer·a·tive** \'əlsə,rātiv\ *adj*

ul·na \'əlnə\ *n* : bone of the forearm opposite the thumb

ul·te·ri·or \,əl'tirēər\ *adj* : not revealed

ul·ti·mate \'əltəmət\ *adj* : final, maximum, or extreme —**ultimate** *n* —**ul·ti·mate·ly** *adv*

ul·ti·ma·tum \,əltə'mātəm, -'mät-\ *n, pl* **-tums** *or* **-ta** \-ə\ : final proposition or demand carrying or implying a threat

ul·tra·vi·o·let \,əltrə'vīələt\ *adj* : having a wavelength shorter than visible light

um·bil·i·cus \,əmbə'līkəs, ,əm'bili-\ *n, pl* **-li·ci** \-bə'lī,kī, -,sī; -'bilə,kī, -,kē\ *or* **-li·cus·es** : small depression on the abdominal wall marking the site of the cord (**umbilical cord**) that joins the unborn fetus to its mother —**um·bil·i·cal** \,əm'bilikəl\ *adj*

um·brage \'əmbrij\ *n* : resentment

um·brel·la \,əm'brelə\ *n* : collapsible

fabric device to protect from sun or rain

um·pire \\'əm,pī(ə)r\\ *n* **1** : arbitrator **2** : sport official —**umpire** *vb*

ump·teen \\'əmp'tēn\\ *adj* : very numerous —**umpteenth** \\-'tēnth\\ *adj*

un- \\,ən, 'ən\\ *prefix* **1** : not **2** : opposite of

unable	uncontrolled
unabridged	unconventional
unacceptable	unconventionally
unaccompanied	unconverted
unaccounted	uncooked
unacquainted	uncooperative
unaddressed	uncoordinated
unadorned	uncovered
unadulterated	uncultivated
unafraid	undamaged
unaided	undated
unalike	undeclared
unambiguous	undefeated
unambitious	undemocratic
unannounced	undependable
unanswered	undeserving
unanticipated	undesirable
unappetizing	undetected
unappreciated	undetermined
unapproved	undeveloped
unassisted	undeviating
unattended	undignified
unattractive	undisturbed
unauthorized	undivided
unavailable	undomesticated
unavoidable	undrinkable
unbearable	unearned
unbelievable	uneducated
unbelievably	unemotional
unbiased	unending
unbranded	unendurable
unbreakable	unenforceable
uncensored	unenlightened
unchallenged	unethical
unchangeable	unexcitable
unchanged	unexciting
unchanging	unexplainable
uncharacteristic	unexplored
uncharged	unfair
unchaste	unfairly
uncivilized	unfairness
unclaimed	unfavorable
unclear	unfavorably
uncleared	unfeigned
unclothed	unfilled
uncluttered	unfinished
uncombed	unflattering
uncomfortable	unforeseeable
uncomfortably	unforeseen
uncomplimentary	unforgivable
unconfirmed	unforgiving
uncontested	unfulfilled
	unfurnished

ungenerous	unobtainable
ungentlemanly	unobtrusive
ungraceful	unobtrusively
ungrammatical	unofficial
unharmed	unopened
unhealthful	unopposed
unhurt	unorganized
unidentified	unoriginal
unimaginable	unorthodox
unimaginative	unpaid
unimportant	unpardonable
unimpressed	unpatriotic
uninformed	unpaved
uninhabited	unpleasant
uninjured	unpleasantly
uninsured	unpleasantness
unintelligent	unpopular
unintelligible	unpopularity
unintelligibly	unposed
unintended	unpredictable
unintentional	unpredictably
unintentionally	unprejudiced
uninterested	unprepared
uninteresting	unpretentious
uninterrupted	unproductive
uninvited	unprofitable
unjust	unproved
unjustifiable	unproven
unjustified	unprovoked
unjustly	unpunished
unknowing	unqualified
unknowingly	unquenchable
unknown	unquestioning
unleavened	unreachable
unlicensed	unreadable
unlikable	unready
unlike	unrealistic
unlikelihood	unreasonable
unlikely	unreasonably
unlikeness	unrefined
unlimited	unrelated
unlovable	unreliable
unmanageable	unremembered
unmarked	unrepentant
unmarried	unrequited
unmerciful	unresolved
unmercifully	unresponsive
unmerited	unrestrained
unmolested	unrestricted
unmotivated	unrewarding
unmoving	unripe
unnamed	unsafe
unnavigable	unsalted
unnecessarily	unsanitary
unnecessary	unsatisfactory
unneeded	unsatisfied
unneighborly	unsatisfying
unnoticeable	unscented
unnoticed	unscheduled
unobjectionable	unseasoned
unobservable	unseen
unobservant	

unselfish   untanned
unselfishly   unthankful
unselfishness   untidy
unshaped   untouched
unshaved   untrained
unshaven   untreated
unskillful   untrue
unskillfully   untrustworthy
unsolicited   untruthful
unsolved   unusable
unsophisticated   unusual
unsound   unvarying
unsoundly   unverified
unsoundness   unwanted
unspecified   unwarranted
unspoiled   unwary
unsteadily   unwavering
unsteadiness   unweaned
unsteady   unwed
unstructured   unwelcome
unsubstantiated   unwholesome
unsuccessful   unwilling
unsuitable   unwillingly
unsuitably   unwillingness
unsuited   unwise
unsupervised   unwisely
unsupported   unworkable
unsure   unworthily
unsuspecting   unworthiness
unsweetened   unworthy
unsympathetic   unyielding
untamed

un·ac·cus·tomed \,ən-\ *adj* 1 : not customary 2 : not accustomed

un·af·fect·ed \,ən-\ *adj* 1 : not influenced or changed by something 2 : natural and sincere —**un·af·fect·ed·ly** *adv*

unan·i·mous \yü'nanəməs\ *adj* 1 : showing no disagreement 2 : formed with the agreement of all —**una·nim·i·ty** \,yünə'nimətē\ *n* —**unan·i·mous·ly** *adv*

un·armed \,ən-\ *adj* : not armed or armored

un·as·sum·ing \,ən-\ *adj* : not bold or arrogant

un·at·tached \,ən-\ *adj* 1 : not attached 2 : not married or engaged

un·aware \,ən-\ *adv* : unawares ~ *adj* : not aware

un·awares \,ənə'waərz\ *adv* 1 : without warning 2 : unintentionally

un·bal·anced \,ən-\ *adj* 1 : not balanced 2 : mentally unstable

un·beat·en \,ən-\ *adj* : not beaten

un·be·com·ing \,ən-\ *adj* : not proper or suitable —**un·be·com·ing·ly** *adv*

un·bend \,ən-\ *vb* -**bent**; -**bend·ing** : make or become more relaxed and friendly

un·bend·ing \,ən-\ *adj* : formal and inflexible

un·bind \,ən-, 'ən-\ *vb* -**bound**; -**bind·ing** 1 : remove bindings from 2 : release

un·bolt \,ən-, 'ən-\ *vb* : open or unfasten by withdrawing a bolt

un·born \,ən-, 'ən-\ *adj* : not yet born

un·bo·som \,ən-, 'ən-\ *vb* : disclose thoughts or feelings

un·bowed \,ən'baúd, 'ən-\ *adj* : not defeated or subdued

un·bri·dled \,ən'brid³ld, 'ən-\ *adj* : unrestrained

un·bro·ken \,ən-, 'ən-\ *adj* 1 : not damaged 2 : not interrupted

un·buck·le \,ən-, 'ən-\ *vb* : unfasten the buckle of

un·bur·den \,ən-, 'ən-\ *vb* : relieve (oneself) of anxieties

un·but·ton \,ən-, 'ən-\ *vb* : unfasten the buttons of

un·called-for \,ən-\ *adj* : too harsh or rude for the occasion

un·can·ny \ən'kanē\ *adj* 1 : weird 2 : suggesting superhuman powers —**un·can·ni·ly** \-'kan²lē\ *adv*

un·ceas·ing \,ən-\ *adj* : never ceasing —**un·ceas·ing·ly** *adv*

un·cer·e·mo·ni·ous \,ən-\ *adj* : acting without ordinary courtesy —**un·cer·e·mo·ni·ous·ly** *adv*

un·cer·tain \,ən-, 'ən-\ *adj* 1 : not determined, sure, or definitely known 2 : subject to chance or change —**un·cer·tain·ly** *adv* —**un·cer·tain·ty** *n*

un·chris·tian \,ən-, 'ən-\ *adj* : not consistent with Christian teachings

un·cle \'ənkəl\ *n* 1 : brother of one's father or mother 2 : husband of one's aunt

un·clean \,ən-, 'ən-\ *adj* : not clean or pure —**un·clean·ness** *n*

un·clog \,ən-, 'ən-\ *vb* : remove an obstruction from

un·coil \,ən-, 'ən-\ *vb* : release or become released from a coiled state

un·com·mit·ted \,ən-\ *adj* : not pledged to a particular allegiance or course of action

un·com·mon \,ən-, 'ən-\ *adj* 1 : rare 2 : superior —**un·com·mon·ly** *adv*

un·com·pro·mis·ing \'ən-\ *adj* : not making or accepting a compromise

un·con·cerned \,ən-\ *adj* 1 : disinterested 2 : not anxious —**un·con·cern·ed·ly** *adv*

un·con·di·tion·al \,ən-\ *adj* : not limited in any way —**un·con·di·tion·al·ly** *adv*

un·con·scio·na·ble \,ən-, 'ən-\ *adj*

: shockingly unjust or unscrupulous
—un·con·scio·na·bly adv

un·con·scious \,ən-, 'ən-\ adj 1 : not awake or aware of one's surroundings 2 : not consciously done ~ n : part of one's mental life that one is not aware of —un·con·scious·ly adv —un·con·scious·ness n

un·con·sti·tu·tion·al \,ən-, 'ən-\ adj : not according to or consistent with a constitution

un·con·trol·la·ble \,ən-\ adj : incapable of being controlled —un·con·trol·la·bly adv

un·count·ed \,ən-\ adj : countless

un·couth \,ən'küth, 'ən-\ adj : rude and vulgar

un·cov·er \,ən-, 'ən-\ vb 1 : reveal 2 : expose by removing a covering

unc·tion \'əŋkshən\ n 1 : rite of anointing 2 : exaggerated or insincere earnestness

unc·tu·ous \'əŋkchə(wə)s\ adj 1 : oily 2 : excessively or insincerely ingratiating —unc·tu·ous·ly adv

un·cut \,ən-, 'ən-\ adj 1 : not cut down, into, off, or apart 2 : not shaped by cutting 3 : not abridged

un·daunt·ed \,ən-, 'ən-\ adj : not discouraged —un·daunt·ed·ly adv

un·de·cid·ed \,ən-\ adj 1 : not settled 2 : not having made up one's mind

un·de·ni·able \,ən-\ adj : plainly true —un·de·ni·ably adv

un·der \'əndər\ adv : below or beneath something ~ \,əndər, 'ən-\ prep 1 : lower than and sheltered by 2 : below the surface of 3 : covered or concealed by 4 : subject to the authority of 5 : less than ~ \'əndər\ adj 1 : lying below or beneath 2 : subordinate 3 : less than usual, proper, or desired

un·der·brush \'əndər,brəsh\ n : shrubs and small trees growing beneath large trees

un·der·clothes \'əndər,klō(th)z\ n pl : underwear

un·der·cloth·ing \-,klōthiŋ\ n : underwear

un·der·cov·er \'əndər-\ adj : employed or engaged in secret investigation

un·der·cur·rent \'əndər-\ n : hidden tendency or opinion

un·der·cut \,əndər-\ vb -cut; -cut·ting : offer to sell or to work at a lower rate than

un·der·de·vel·oped \,əndər-\ adj : not normally or adequately developed esp. economically

un·der·dog \'əndər-\ n : contestant given least chance of winning

un·der·done \,əndər-\ adj : not thoroughly done or cooked

un·der·es·ti·mate \,əndər-\ vb : estimate too low

un·der·ex·pose \,əndər-\ vb : give less than normal exposure to —un·der·ex·po·sure n

un·der·feed \,əndər-\ vb -fed; -feed·ing : feed inadequately

un·der·foot \,əndər-\ adv 1 : under the feet 2 : in the way of another

un·der·gar·ment \'əndər-\ n : garment to be worn under another

un·der·go \,əndər-\ vb -went \-'went\; -gone; -go·ing 1 : endure 2 : pass through (as an experience)

un·der·grad·u·ate \,əndər-\ n : university or college student

un·der·ground \,əndər-\ adv 1 : beneath the surface of the earth 2 : in secret ~ \'əndər-\ adj 1 : being or growing under the surface of the ground 2 : secret ~ \'əndər-\ n : secret political movement or group

un·der·growth \'əndər-\ n : low growth on the floor of a forest

un·der·hand \'əndər-\ adv or adj 1 : with secrecy and deception 2 : with the hand kept below the waist

un·der·hand·ed \'əndər-\ adj or adv : underhand —un·der·hand·ed·ly adv —un·der·hand·ed·ness n

un·der·line \'əndər-\ vb 1 : draw a line under 2 : stress —underline n

un·der·ling \'əndərliŋ\ n : inferior

un·der·ly·ing \,əndər,liiŋ\ adj : basic

un·der·mine \,əndər-\ vb 1 : excavate beneath 2 : weaken or wear away secretly or gradually

un·der·neath \,əndər'nēth\ prep : directly under ~ adv 1 : below a surface or object 2 : on the lower side

un·der·nour·ished \,əndər-\ adj : insufficiently nourished —un·der·nour·ish·ment n

un·der·pants \'əndər,pants\ n pl : pants worn as underwear

un·der·pass \-,pas\ n : passage underneath

un·der·pin·ning \'əndər,piniŋ\ n : support

un·der·priv·i·leged \,əndər-\ adj : poor

un·der·rate \,əndə(r)'rāt\ vb : rate or value too low

un·der·score \'əndər-\ vb or n : underline

un·der·sea \'əndər,sē\ adj : being, carried on, or used beneath the surface of the sea ~ \,əndər'sē\, un·der·seas \-'sēz\ adv : beneath the surface of the sea

un·der sec·re·tary \,əndər-\ *n* : deputy secretary

un·der·sell \,əndər-\ *vb* **-sold; -sell·ing** : sell articles cheaper than

un·der·shirt \'əndər,shərt\ *n* : shirt worn as underwear

un·der·shorts \'əndər,shórts\ *n pl* : short underpants

un·der·side \'əndər,sīd, ,əndər'sīd\ *n* : side or surface lying underneath

un·der·sized \,əndər'sīzd\ *adj* : unusually small

un·der·stand \,əndər'stand\ *vb* **-stood** \-'stúd\; **-stand·ing 1** : be aware of the meaning of **2** : deduce **3** : have a sympathetic attitude **—un·der·stand·able** \-'standəbəl\ *adj* **—un·der·stand·ably** \-blē\ *adv*

un·der·stand·ing \,əndər'standiŋ\ *n* **1** : intelligence **2** : ability to comprehend and judge **3** : mutual agreement ~ *adj* : sympathetic

un·der·state \,əndər-\ *vb* **1** : represent as less than is the case **2** : state with restraint **—un·der·state·ment** *n*

un·der·stood \,əndər'stúd\ *adj* **1** : agreed upon **2** : implicit

un·der·study \'əndər,, ,əndər-\ *vb* : study another actor's part in order to substitute **—understudy** \'əndər-\ *n*

un·der·take \,əndər-\ *vb* **-took; -tak·en; -tak·ing 1** : attempt (a task) or assume (a responsibility) **2** : guarantee

un·der·tak·er \'əndər,tākər\ *n* : one in the funeral business

un·der·tak·ing \'əndər-, ,əndər-\ *n* **1** : something (as work) that is undertaken **2** : promise

under–the–counter *adj* : illicit

un·der·tone \'əndər-\ *n* : low or subdued tone or utterance

un·der·tow \-,tō\ *n* : current beneath the waves that flows seaward

un·der·val·ue \,əndər-\ *vb* : value too low

un·der·wa·ter \,əndər-\ *adj* : being or used below the surface of the water **—underwater** *adv*

under way *adv* : in motion or in progress

un·der·wear \'əndər-\ *n* : clothing worn next to the skin and under ordinary clothes

un·der·world \'əndər-\ *n* **1** : place of departed souls **2** : world of organized crime

un·der·write \'əndə(r)-, ,əndə(r)-\ *vb* **-wrote; -writ·ten; -writ·ing** \-,rītiŋ, -'rīt-\ **1** : provide insurance for **2** : guarantee financial support of **—un·der·writ·er** *n*

un·dies \'əndēz\ *n pl* : underwear

un·do \,ən-, 'ən-\ *vb* **-did; -done; -do·ing 1** : unfasten **2** : reverse **3** : ruin **—un·do·ing** *n*

un·doubt·ed \,ən-, 'ən-\ *adj* : certain **—un·doubt·ed·ly** *adv*

un·dress \,ən-, 'ən-\ *vb* : remove one's clothes

un·due \,ən-, 'ən-\ *adj* : excessive **—un·du·ly** *adv*

un·du·late \'ənjə,lāt\ *vb* **-lat·ed; -lat·ing** : rise and fall regularly

un·dy·ing \,ən-, 'ən-\ *adj* : immortal or perpetual

un·earth \,ən-, 'ən-\ *vb* : dig up or discover

un·earth·ly \,ən-, 'ən-\ *adj* : supernatural

un·easy \,ən-\ *adj* **1** : awkward or embarrassing **2** : disturbed or worried **—un·eas·i·ly** *adv* **—un·eas·i·ness** *n*

un·em·ployed \,ən-, 'ən-\ *adj* : not having a job **—un·em·ploy·ment** *n*

un·equal \,ən-, 'ən-\ *adj* : not equal or uniform **—un·equal·ly** *adv*

un·equaled, un·equalled \,ən-, 'ən-\ *adj* : having no equal

un·equiv·o·cal \,ən-\ *adj* : leaving no doubt **—un·equiv·o·cal·ly** *adv*

un·err·ing \,ən-, 'ən-\ *adj* : infallible **—un·err·ing·ly** *adv*

un·even \,ən-, 'ən-\ *adj* **1** : not smooth **2** : not regular or consistent **—un·even·ly** *adv* **—un·even·ness** *n*

un·event·ful \,ən-\ *adj* : lacking interesting or noteworthy incidents

un·ex·pect·ed \,ənik'spektəd\ *adj* : not expected **—un·ex·pect·ed·ly** *adv*

un·fail·ing \,ən-, 'ən-\ *adj* : steadfast **—un·fail·ing·ly** *adv*

un·faith·ful \,ən-, 'ən-\ *adj* : not loyal **—un·faith·ful·ly** *adv* **—un·faith·ful·ness** *n*

un·fa·mil·iar \,ən-\ *adj* **1** : not well known **2** : not acquainted **—un·fa·mil·iar·i·ty** *n*

un·fas·ten \,ən-, 'ən-\ *vb* : release a catch or lock

un·feel·ing \,ən-\ *adj* : lacking feeling or compassion **—un·feel·ing·ly** *adv*

un·fit \,ən-\ *adj* : not suitable **—un·fit·ness** *n*

un·flap·pa·ble \,ən'flapəbəl, ,ən-\ *adj* : not easily upset or panicked **—un·flap·pa·bly** *adv*

un·fold \,ən-, 'ən-\ *vb* **1** : open the folds of **2** : reveal **3** : develop

un·for·get·ta·ble \,ən-\ *adj* : memorable **—un·for·get·ta·bly** *adv*

un·for·tu·nate \,ən-\ *adj* **1** : not lucky

or successful 2 : deplorable —**unfor-tunate** *n* —**un·for·tu·nate·ly** *adv*

un·found·ed \,ən-, 'ən-\ *adj* : lacking a sound basis

un·freeze \,ən-\ *vb* —**froze; fro-zen; -freez·ing** : thaw

un·friend·ly \,ən-, 'ən-\ *adj* : not friendly or kind —**un·friend·li·ness** *n*

un·furl \,ən-, 'ən-\ *vb* : unfold or unroll

un·gain·ly \,ən-, 'ən-\ *adj* : clumsy —**un·gain·li·ness** *n*

un·god·ly \,ən'gädlē, -'göd-, 'ən-\ *adj* : wicked —**un·god·li·ness** *n*

un·grate·ful \,ən-, 'ən-\ *adj* : not thankful for favors —**un·grate·ful·ly** \-lē\ *adv* —**un·grate·ful·ness** *n*

un·guent \'əngwənt, 'ən-\ *n* : ointment

un·hand \,ən-, 'ən-\ *vb* : let go

un·hap·py \,ən-, 'ən-\ *adj* 1 : unfortunate 2 : sad —**un·hap·pi·ly** *adv* —**un·hap·pi·ness** *n*

un·healthy \,ən-, 'ən-\ *adj* 1 : not wholesome 2 : not well

un·heard-of \,ən'hərdəv, 'ən-, -,əv\ *adj* : unprecedented

un·hinge \,ən'hinj, 'ən-\ *vb* 1 : take from the hinges 2 : make unstable (as one's mind)

un·hitch \,ən-, 'ən-\ *vb* : unfasten (something hitched)

un·ho·ly \,ən-, 'ən-\ *adj* : sinister or shocking —**un·ho·li·ness** *n*

un·hook \,ən-, 'ən-\ *vb* : release from a hook

uni·cel·lu·lar \,yüni'selyələr\ *adj* : of or having a single cell

uni·corn \'yünə,körn\ *n* : legendary animal with one horn in the middle of the forehead

uni·cy·cle \'yüni,sīkəl\ *n* : pedal-powered vehicle with only a single wheel

uni·di·rec·tion·al \,yünidə'reksh(ə)nəl, -dī-\ *adj* : working in only a single direction

uni·form \'yünə,förm\ *adj* : not changing or showing any variation ~ *n* : distinctive dress worn by members of a particular group —**uni·for·mi·ty** \,yünə'förmətē\ *n* —**uni·form·ly** *adv*

uni·fy \'yünə,fī\ *vb* —**fied; -fy·ing** : make into a coherent whole —**uni·fi·ca·tion** \,yünəfə'kāshən\ *n*

uni·lat·er·al \,yünə'lat(ə)rəl\ *adj* : having, affecting, or done by one side only —**uni·lat·er·al·ly** *adv*

un·im·peach·able \,ən-\ *adj* 1 : blameless 2 : not to be doubted

un·in·hib·it·ed \,ən-\ *adj* : free of restraint —**un·in·hib·it·ed·ly** *adv*

union \'yünyən\ *n* 1 : act or instance

of joining 2 or more things into one or the state of being so joined 2 : confederation of nations or states 3 : organization of workers (**labor union, trade union**)

union·ize \'yünyə,nīz\ *vb* —**ized; -iz·ing** : form into a labor union —**union·iza·tion** \,yünyənə'zāshən\ *n*

unique \yü'nēk\ *adj* 1 : being the only one of its kind 2 : very unusual —**unique·ly** *adv* —**unique·ness** *n*

uni·son \'yünəsən, -nəzən\ *n* 1 : sameness in pitch 2 : exact agreement

unit \'yünət\ *n* 1 : smallest whole number 2 : definite amount or quantity used as a standard of measurement 3 : single part of a whole —**unit** *adj*

unite \yü'nīt\ *vb* **unit·ed; unit·ing** : put or join together

uni·ty \'yünətē\ *n, pl* **-ties** 1 : quality or state of being united or a unit 2 : harmony

uni·ver·sal \,yünə'vərsəl\ *adj* 1 : relating to or affecting everyone or everything 2 : present or occurring everywhere —**uni·ver·sal·ly** *adv*

uni·verse \'yünə,vərs\ *n* : the complete system of all things that exist

uni·ver·si·ty \,yünə'vərs(ə)tē\ *n, pl* **-ties** : institution of higher learning

un·kempt \,ən-, 'ən-\ *adj* : not neat or combed

un·kind \,ən-, 'ən-\ *adj* : mean or severe —**un·kind·li·ness** *n* —**un·kind·ly** *adv* —**un·kind·ness** *n*

un·law·ful \,ən-, 'ən-\ *adj* : illegal —**un·law·ful·ly** *adv*

un·leash \,ən-, 'ən-\ *vb* : free from control or restraint

un·less \ən,les, ,ən-\ *conj* : except on condition that

un·load \,ən-, 'ən-\ *vb* 1 : take (cargo) from a vehicle, vessel, or plane 2 : take a load from 3 : discard

un·lock \,ən-, 'ən-\ *vb* 1 : unfasten through release of a lock 2 : release or reveal

un·lucky \,ən-, 'ən-\ *adj* 1 : experiencing bad luck 2 : likely to bring misfortune —**un·luck·i·ly** *adv*

un·mis·tak·able \,ən-\ *adj* : not capable of being mistaken or misunderstood —**un·mis·tak·ably** *adv*

un·moved \,ən-\ *adj* 1 : not emotionally affected 2 : remaining in the same place or position

un·nat·u·ral \,ən-, 'ən-\ *adj* 1 : not natural or spontaneous 2 : abnormal —**un·nat·u·ral·ly** *adv* —**un·nat·u·ral·ness** *n*

un·nerve \,ən-, 'ən-\ *vb* : deprive of courage

un·oc·cu·pied \‚ən-, ‚ən-\ *adj* 1 : not busy 2 : not occupied

un·pack \‚ən-, ‚ən-\ *vb* 1 : remove (things packed) from a container 2 : remove the contents of (a package)

un·par·al·leled \‚ən-, ‚ən-\ *adj* : having no equal

un·plug \‚ən-, ‚ən-\ *vb* 1 : unclog by removing a plug 2 : disconnect from an electric circuit by removing a plug

un·prec·e·dent·ed \‚ən-, ‚ən-\ *adj* : unlike or superior to anything known before

un·prin·ci·pled \‚ən-, ‚ən-\ *adj* : unscrupulous

un·ques·tion·able \‚ən-, ‚ən-\ *adj* : acknowledged as beyond doubt —**un·ques·tion·ably** *adv*

un·rav·el \‚ən-, ‚ən-\ *vb* 1 : separate the threads of 2 : solve

un·re·al \‚ən-, ‚ən-\ *adj* : not real or genuine —**un·re·al·i·ty** \‚ən-\ *n*

un·rea·son·ing \‚ən-, ‚ən-\ *adj* : not using or being guided by reason

un·re·lent·ing \‚ən-\ *adj* : not yielding or easing —**un·re·lent·ing·ly** *adv*

un·rest \‚ən-, ‚ən-\ *n* : turmoil

un·ri·valed \‚ən-, ‚ən-\ *adj* : having no rival

un·roll \‚ən-, ‚ən-\ *vb* 1 : unwind a roll of 2 : become unrolled

un·ruf·fled \‚ən-, ‚ən-\ *adj* : not agitated or upset

un·ru·ly \‚ən'rülē, ‚ən-\ *adj* : not readily controlled or disciplined —**un·ru·li·ness** *n*

un·scathed \‚ən'skāthd, ‚ən-\ *adj* : unharmed

un·sci·en·tif·ic \‚ən-, ‚ən-\ *adj* : not in accord with the principles and methods of science

un·screw \‚ən-, ‚ən-\ *vb* : loosen or remove by withdrawing screws or by turning

un·scru·pu·lous \‚ən-, ‚ən-\ *adj* : being or acting in total disregard of conscience, ethical principles, or rights of others —**un·scru·pu·lous·ly** *adv* —**un·scru·pu·lous·ness** *n*

un·seal \‚ən-, ‚ən-\ *vb* : break or remove the seal of

un·sea·son·able \‚ən-, ‚ən-\ *adj* : not appropriate or usual for the season —**un·sea·son·ably** *adv*

un·seem·ly \‚ən'sēmlē, ‚ən-\ *adj* : not polite or in good taste —**un·seem·li·ness** *n*

un·set·tle \‚ən-, ‚ən-\ *vb* : disturb —**un·set·tled** *adj*

un·skilled \‚ən-, ‚ən-\ *adj* : not having or requiring a particular skill

un·snap \‚ən-, ‚ən-\ *vb* : loosen by undoing a snap

un·speak·able \‚ən'spēkəbəl, ‚ən-\ *adj* : extremely bad —**un·speak·ably** \-blē\ *adv*

un·sta·ble \‚ən-, ‚ən-\ *adj* 1 : not mentally or physically balanced 2 : tending to change

un·stop \‚ən-, ‚ən-\ *vb* 1 : unclog 2 : remove a stopper from

un·strung \‚ən'strəŋ, ‚ən-\ *adj* : nervously tired or anxious

un·sung \‚ən'səŋ, ‚ən-\ *adj* : not celebrated in song or verse

un·tan·gle \‚ən-, ‚ən-\ *vb* 1 : free from a state of being tangled 2 : find a solution to

un·think·able \‚ən'thiŋkəbəl, ‚ən-\ *adj* : not to be thought of or considered possible

un·think·ing \‚ən-, ‚ən-\ *adj* : careless —**un·think·ing·ly** *adv*

un·tie \‚ən-, ‚ən-\ *vb* -tied; -ty·ing or -tie·ing : open by releasing ties

un·til \(‚)ən,til\ *prep* : up to the time of ~ *conj* : to the time that

un·time·ly \‚ən-, ‚ən-\ *adj* 1 : premature 2 : coming at an unfortunate time

un·to \‚əntə, ‚ən(‚)tü\ *prep* : to

un·told \‚ən-, ‚ən-\ *adj* 1 : not told 2 : too numerous to count

un·to·ward \‚ən'tō(ə)rd\ *adj* 1 : difficult to manage 2 : inconvenient

un·truth \‚ən-, ‚ən-\ *n* 1 : lack of truthfulness 2 : lie

un·used \‚ən'yüst, ‚ən-, -'yüzd\ *adj* 1 \-'yüzd\ : not accustomed 2 \-'yüzd\ : not used

un·well \‚ən-, ‚ən-\ *adj* : sick

un·wieldy \‚ən'wēldē, ‚ən-\ *adj* : too big or awkward to manage easily

un·wind \‚ən-, ‚ən-\ *vb* -wound; -wind·ing 1 : undo something that is wound 2 : become unwound 3 : relax

un·wit·ting \‚ən-, ‚ən-\ *adj* 1 : not intended 2 : not knowing —**un·wit·ting·ly** *adv*

un·wont·ed \‚ən-, ‚ən-\ *adj* 1 : unusual 2 : not accustomed by experience

un·wrap \‚ən-, ‚ən-\ *vb* : remove the wrappings from

un·writ·ten \‚ən-, ‚ən-\ *adj* : made or passed on only in speech or through tradition

un·zip \‚ən-, ‚ən-\ *vb* : zip open

up \'əp\ *adv* 1 : in or to a higher position or level 2 : from beneath a surface or level 3 : in or into an upright position 4 : out of bed 5 : to or with greater intensity 6 : into existence, evidence, or knowledge 7

: away **8**—used to indicate a degree of success, completion, or finality **9** : in or into parts ~ *adj* **1** : in the state of having risen **2** : raised to or at a higher level **3** : moving, inclining, or directed upward **4** : in a state of greater intensity **5** : at an end ~ *vb* **upped** *or in 1 up* **1 up** **1** : act abruptly **2** : move or cause to move upward ~ *prep* **1** : to, toward, or at a higher point of **2** : along or toward the beginning of

up·braid \əp'brād\ *vb* : criticize or scold

up·bring·ing \'əp-\ *n* : process of bringing up and training

up·com·ing \'əp,kəmiŋ\ *adj* : approaching

up·date \əp'dāt\ *vb* : bring up to date —**update** \'əp,dāt\ *n*

up·end \əp-\ *vb* : stand or rise on end

up·grade \'əp,grād\ *n* **1** : upward slope **2** : increase \'əp,-, ,'əp'-\ ~ *vb* : raise to a higher position

up·heav·al \əp'hēvəl\ *n* **1** : a heaving up (as of part of the earth's crust) **2** : violent change

up·hill \'əp'hil\ *adv* : upward on a hill or incline ~ \'əp-\ *adj* **1** : going up **2** : difficult

up·hold \əp'hōld\ *vb* **-held; -hold·ing** : support or defend —**up·hold·er** *n*

up·hol·ster \əp'hōlstər\ *vb* : cover (furniture) with padding and fabric (**up·hol·stery** \-st(ə)rē\) —**up·hol·ster·er** *n*

up·keep \'əp,kēp\ *n* : act or cost of keeping up or maintaining

up·land \'əplənd, -,land\ *n* : high land —**upland** *adj*

up·lift \,əp'lift\ *vb* **1** : lift up **2** : improve the condition or spirits of —**up·lift** \'əp,-\ *n*

up·on \ə'pȯn, -'pän\ *prep* : on

up·per \'əpər\ *adj* : higher in position, rank, or order ~ *n* : top part of a shoe

up·per·most \'əpər,mōst\ *adv* : in or into the highest or most prominent position —**uppermost** *adj*

up·right \'əp,rīt\ *adj* **1** : vertical **2** : erect in posture **3** : morally correct ~ *n* : something that stands upright —**upright** *adv* —**up·right·ly** *adv* —**up·right·ness** *n*

up·ris·ing \'əp,rīziŋ\ *n* : revolt

up·roar \'əp,rōr\ *n* : state of commotion or violent disturbance

up·roar·i·ous \,əp'rōrēəs\ *adj* **1** : marked by uproar **2** : extremely funny —**up·roar·i·ous·ly** *adv*

up·root \,əp-\ *vb* : remove by or as if by pulling up by the roots

up·set \,əp'set\ *vb* **-set; -set·ting** **1** : force or be forced out of the usual position **2** : disturb emotionally or physically ~ \'əp,-\ *n* **1** : act of throwing into disorder **2** : minor physical disorder

up·shot \'əp,shät\ *n* : final result

up·side down \,əp,sīd'daᵫn\ *adv* **1** : turned so that the upper and lower parts are reversed **2** : in or into confusion or disorder —**upside-down** *adj*

up·stairs \'əp-\ *adv* : up the stairs or to the next floor ~ *adj* : situated on the floor above ~ *n sing or pl* : part of a building above the ground floor

up·stand·ing \,əp'standiŋ, 'əp,-\ *adj* : honest

up·start \'əp,stärt\ *n* : one who claims more personal importance than is warranted —**upstart** \,əp-\ *adj*

up·swing \'əp,swiŋ\ *n* : marked increase (as in activity)

up·tight \'əp'tīt\ *adj* **1** : tense **2** : angry **3** : rigidly conventional

up-to-date *adj* : current —**up-to-date·ness** *n*

up·town \'əp-\ *n* : upper part of a town or city —**uptown** *adj or adv*

up·ward \'əpwərd\, **up·wards** \-wərdz\ *adv* **1** : in a direction from lower to higher **2** : toward a higher or greater state or number ~ *adj* : directed toward or situated in a higher place

up·wind \'əp'wind\ *adv or adj* : in the direction from which the wind is blowing

ura·ni·um \yᵫ'rānēəm\ *n* : metallic radioactive chemical element

ur·ban \'ərbən\ *adj* : characteristic of a city

ur·bane \,ər'bān\ *adj* : polished in manner —**ur·ban·i·ty** \,ər'banətē\ *n*

ur·chin \'ərchən\ *n* : mischievous youngster

-ure *n suffix* : act or process

ure·thra \yᵫ'rēthrə\ *n, pl* **-thras** *or* **-thrae** \-(,)thrē\ : canal that carries off urine from the bladder —**ure·thral** \-thrəl\ *adj*

urge \'ərj\ *vb* **urged; urging** **1** : earnestly plead for or insist on (an action) **2** : try to persuade **3** : impel to a course of activity ~ *n* : force or impulse that moves one to action

ur·gent \'ərjənt\ *adj* **1** : calling for immediate attention **2** : urging insistently —**ur·gen·cy** \-jənsē\ *n* —**ur·gent·ly** *adv*

uri·nal \\'yúrən⁹l\\ *n* : receptacle to urinate in

uri·nate \\'yúrə,nāt\\ *vb* -nat·ed; -nat·ing : discharge urine —**uri·na·tion** \\,yúrə'nāshən\\ *n*

urine \\'yúrən\\ *n* : liquid waste material from the kidneys —**uri·nary** \\-ə,nerē\\ *adj*

urn \\'ərn\\ *n* 1 : vaselike or cuplike vessel on a pedestal 2 : large coffee pot

us \\(')əs\\ *pron, objective case of* WE

us·able \\'yüzəbəl\\ *adj* : suitable or fit for use —**us·abil·i·ty** \\,yüzə'bilətē\\ *n*

us·age \\'yüsij, -zij\\ *n* 1 : customary practice 2 : way of doing or of using something

use \\'yüs\\ *n* 1 : act or practice of putting something into action 2 : state of being used 3 : way of using 4 : privilege, ability, or power to use something 5 : utility or function 6 : occasion or need to use ~ \\'yüz\\ *vb* **used** \\'yüzd; "used to" usu 'yüstə\\; **us·ing** \\'yüziŋ\\ 1 : accustom 2 : put into action or service 3 : consume 4 : behave toward 5 — used in the past tense with *to* to indicate a former practice —**use·ful** \\'yüsfəl\\ *adj* —**use·ful·ly** *adv* —**use·ful·ness** *n* —**use·less** \\-ləs\\ *adj* —**use·less·ly** *adv* —**use·less·ness** *n* —**us·er** *n*

used \\'yüzd\\ *adj* : not new

ush·er \\'əshər\\ *n* 1 : one who escorts people to their seats ~ *vb* : conduct to a place —**ush·er·ette** \\,əshə'ret\\ *n*

usu·al \\'yüzhə(wə)l\\ *adj* : being what is expected according to custom or habit —**usu·al·ly** \\'yüzh(ə)wəlē, 'yüzh(ə)lē\\ *adv*

usurp \\yủ'sərp, -'zərp\\ *vb* : seize and hold by force or without right —**usur·pa·tion** \\,yüsər'pāshən, -zər-\\ *n* —**usurp·er** *n*

usu·ry \\'yüzh(ə)rē\\ *n, pl* -ries 1 : lending of money at excessive interest or the rate or amount of such interest —**usu·rer** \\-zhərər\\ *n* —**usu·ri·ous** \\yủ'zhúrēəs\\ *adj*

uten·sil \\yủ'tensəl\\ *n* 1 : eating or cooking tool 2 : useful article

uter·us \\'yütərəs\\ *n, pl* **uteri** \\-,rī\\ : organ for containing and nourishing an unborn offspring —**uter·ine** \\-,rīn, -rən\\ *adj*

util·i·tar·i·an \\yü,tilə'terēən\\ *adj* : being or meant to be useful rather than beautiful

util·i·ty \\yü'tilətē\\ *n, pl* -ties 1 : usefulness 2 : regulated business providing a public service (as electricity)

uti·lize \\'yüt⁹l,īz\\ *vb* -lized; -liz·ing : make use of —**uti·li·za·tion** \\,yüt⁹lə'zāshən\\ *n*

ut·most \\'ət,mōst\\ *adj* 1 : most distant 2 : of the greatest or highest degree or amount —**utmost** *n*

uto·pia \\yủ'tōpēə\\ *n* : place of ideal perfection —**uto·pi·an** \\-pēən\\ *adj or n*

ut·ter \\'ətər\\ *adj* : absolute ~ *vb* : express with the voice —**ut·ter·ly** *adv*

ut·ter·ance \\'ətərəns, 'ətrəns\\ *n* : what one says

V

v \\'vē\\ *n, pl* **v's** *or* **vs** \\'vēz\\ : 22d letter of the alphabet

va·can·cy \\'vākənsē\\ *n, pl* -cies 1 : state of being vacant 2 : unused or unoccupied place or office

va·cant \\-kənt\\ *adj* 1 : not occupied, filled, or in use 2 : foolish or without expression —**va·cant·ly** *adv*

va·cate \\-,kāt\\ *vb* -cat·ed; -cat·ing 1 : annul 2 : leave unfilled or unoccupied

va·ca·tion \\vā'kāshən, və-\\ *n* : extended period of rest from routine —**vacation** *vb* —**va·ca·tion·er** *n*

vac·ci·nate \\'vaksə,nāt\\ *vb* -nat·ed; -nat·ing : inoculate

vac·ci·na·tion \\,vaksə'nāshən\\ *n* : act of or the scar left by vaccinating

vac·cine \\vak'sēn, 'vak,-\\ *n* : substance to induce immunity to a disease

vac·il·late \\'vasə,lāt\\ *vb* -lat·ed; -lat·ing : waver between courses or opinions —**vac·il·la·tion** \\,vasə'lāshən\\ *n*

vac·u·ous \\'vakyəwəs\\ *adj* 1 : empty 2 : dull or inane —**va·cu·ity** \\va-'kyüətē, va-\\ *n* —**vac·u·ous·ly** *adv* —**vac·u·ous·ness** *n*

vac·u·um \\'vakyùəm, -(,)yüm, -yəm\\ *n, pl* **vac·u·ums** *or* **vac·ua** \\-yəwə\\ : empty space with no air ~ *vb* : clean with a vacuum cleaner

vacuum cleaner *n* : appliance that cleans by suction

vag·a·bond \\'vagə,bänd\\ *n* : wanderer with no home —**vagabond** *adj*

va·ga·ry \ˈvāgərē, vəˈge(ə)rē\ n, pl **-ries** : whim

va·gi·na \vəˈjīnə\ n, pl **-nae** -(,)nē or **-nas** : canal that leads out from the uterus —**vag·i·nal** \ˈvajənᵊl\ adj

va·grant \ˈvāgrənt\ n : person with no home and no job —**va·gran·cy** \-grənsē\ n —**vagrant** adj

vague \ˈvāg\ adj **vagu·er; vagu·est** : not clear, definite, or distinct —**vague·ly** adv —**vague·ness** n

vain \ˈvān\ adj **1** : of no value **2** : unsuccessful **3** : conceited —**vain·ly** adv —**in vain** : without result or success

va·lance \ˈvaləns, ˈval-\ n : border drapery

vale \ˈvāl\ n : valley

vale·dic·to·ri·an \,valə,dikˈtōrēən\ n : student giving the farewell address at commencement

vale·dic·to·ry \-ˈdikt(ə)rē\ adj : bidding farewell —**valedictory** n

va·lence \ˈvāləns\ n : degree of combining power of a chemical element

val·en·tine \ˈvalən,tīn\ n : sweetheart or a card sent to a sweetheart or friend on St. Valentine's Day

va·let \ˈvalət, ˈval(,)ā, vaˈlā\ n : male personal servant

val·iant \ˈvalyənt\ adj : brave or heroic —**val·iant·ly** adv

val·id \ˈvaləd\ adj **1** : proper and legally binding **2** : founded on truth or fact —**va·lid·i·ty** \vəˈlidətē, va-\ n —**val·id·ly** adv

val·i·date \ˈvalə,dāt\ vb **-dat·ed; -dat·ing** : establish as valid —**val·i·da·tion** \,valəˈdāshən\ n

va·lise \vəˈlēs\ n : bag for a traveler's clothing and personal articles

val·ley \ˈvalē\ n, pl **-leys** : long depression between ranges of hills

val·or \ˈvalər\ n : bravery or heroism —**val·or·ous** \ˈvalərəs\ adj

valu·able \ˈvalyə(wə)bəl\ adj **1** : worth a lot of money **2** : being of great importance or use —**valuable** n

val·u·a·tion \,valyəˈwāshən\ n **1** : act or process of valuing **2** : market value of a thing

val·ue \ˈvalyü\ n **1** : fair return or equivalent for something exchanged **2** : how much something is worth **3** : distinctive quality (as of a color or sound) **4** : guiding principle or ideal—usu. pl. ~ vb **val·ued; valu·ing 1** : estimate the worth of **2** : appreciate the importance of —**valued** adj —**val·ue·less** adj —**val·u·er** n

valve \ˈvalv\ n : structure or device to control flow of a liquid or gas —**valved** \ˈvalvd\ adj —**valve·less** adj

vam·pire \ˈvam,pī(ə)r\ n **1** : legendary night-wandering dead body that sucks human blood **2** : bat that feeds on the blood of animals

¹van \ˈvan\ n : vanguard

²van n : enclosed truck

va·na·di·um \vəˈnādēəm\ n : soft ductile metallic chemical element

van·dal \ˈvandᵊl\ n : one who willfully defaces or destroys property —**van·dal·ism** \-,izəm\ n —**van·dal·ize** \-,īz\ vb

vane \ˈvān\ n : bladelike device designed to be moved by force of air or water

van·guard \ˈvan,gärd\ n **1** : troops moving at the front of an army **2** : forefront of an action or movement

va·nil·la \vəˈnilə\ n : tropical orchid with pods yielding a flavoring substance

van·ish \ˈvanish\ vb : disappear suddenly

van·i·ty \ˈvanətē\ n, pl **-ties 1** : futility or something that is futile **2** : undue pride in oneself **3** : makeup table

van·quish \ˈvaŋkwish, ˈvan-\ vb **1** : overcome in battle or in a contest **2** : gain mastery over

van·tage \ˈvantij\ n : position of advantage or perspective

va·pid \ˈvapəd, ˈvāpəd\ adj : lacking spirit, liveliness, or zest —**va·pid·i·ty** \vaˈpidətē\ n —**vap·id·ly** \ˈvapədlē\ adv —**vap·id·ness** n

va·por \ˈvāpər\ n **1** : fine separated particles floating in and clouding the air **2** : gaseous form of an ordinarily liquid substance ~ vb : give off vapor —**va·por·ish** \-p(ə)rish\ adj —**va·por·ous** \-p(ə)rəs\ adj

va·por·ize \ˈvāpə,rīz\ vb **-ized; -iz·ing** : convert into vapor —**va·por·iza·tion** \,vāpərəˈzāshən\ n —**va·por·iz·er** n

vari·able \ˈverēəbəl\ adj : apt to vary —**vari·abil·i·ty** \,verēəˈbilətē\ n —**variable** n —**vari·able·ness** n —**vari·ably** adv

vari·ance \ˈverēəns\ n **1** : instance or degree of variation **2** : legal permission to build contrary to a zoning law

vari·ant \-ənt\ n : something that differs from others of its kind —**variant** adj

vari·a·tion \,verēˈāshən\ n : instance or extent of varying

var·i·cose \ˈvarə,kōs\ adj : abnormally swollen

var·ied \'verēd\ *adj* : showing variety
—**var·ied·ly** *adv*

var·ie·gate \'verēə,gāt, 'veri,gāt\ *vb*
-gat·ed; -gat·ing : diversify in appearance esp. with different colors
—**var·ie·gat·ed** *adj* —**var·ie·ga·tion** \,verēə'gāshən, ,veri'gā-\ *n*

va·ri·ety \və'rīətē\ *n, pl* **-et·ies** 1 : state of being different 2 : collection of different things 3 : something that differs from others of its kind

var·i·ous \'verēəs\ *adj* : being many and unlike —**var·i·ous·ly** *adv*

var·nish \'värnish\ *n* : liquid that dries to a hard glossy protective coating ~ *vb* : cover with varnish

var·si·ty \'värsətē, -stē\ *n, pl* **-ties** : principal team representing a school

vary \'verē\ *vb* **var·ied; vary·ing** 1 : alter 2 : make or be different kinds

vas·cu·lar \'vaskyələr\ *adj* : relating to a channel for the conveyance of a body fluid (as blood or sap)

vase \'vās, 'vāz\ *n* : tall usu. ornamental container to hold flowers and water

vas·sal \'vasəl\ *n* 1 : one acknowledging another as feudal lord 2 : one in a dependent position —**vas·sal·age** \-əlij\ *n*

vast \'vast\ *adj* : very great in size, extent, or amount —**vast·ly** *adv* —**vast·ness** *n*

vat \'vat\ *n* : large tub- or barrel-shaped container

vaude·ville \'vód(ə)vəl, 'väd-, 'vód-, -(ə),vil\ *n* : stage entertainment of unrelated acts

¹vault \'vólt\ *n* 1 : masonry arch 2 : usu. underground storage or burial room ~ *vb* : form or cover with a vault —**vault·ed** *adj* —**vaulty** *adj*

²vault *vb* : spring over esp. with the help of the hands or a pole ~ *n* : act of vaulting —**vault·er** *n* —**vault·ing** *adj*

vaunt \'vónt\ *vb* : boast —**vaunt** *n*

veal \'vēl\ *n* : flesh of a young calf

veer \'viər\ *vb* : change course esp. gradually —**veer** *n*

veg·e·ta·ble \'vej(ə)təbəl\ *adj* 1 : relating to or obtained from plants 2 : like that of a plant ~ *n* 1 : plant 2 : plant grown for food

veg·e·tar·i·an \,vejə'terēən\ *n* : person who eats no meat —**vegetarian** *adj* —**veg·e·tar·i·an·ism** \-ē·ə,nizəm\ *n*

veg·e·tate \'vejə,tāt\ *vb* **-tat·ed; -tat·ing** : lead a dull inert life

veg·e·ta·tion \,vejə'tāshən\ *n* : plant life —**veg·e·ta·tion·al** \-sh(ə)nəl\ *adj*

ve·he·ment \'vēəmənt\ *adj* : showing strong esp. violent feeling —**ve·he·mence** \-məns\ *n* —**ve·he·ment·ly** *adv*

ve·hi·cle \'vē,(h)ikəl, 'vēəkəl\ *n* 1 : medium through which something is expressed, applied, or administered 2 : structure for transporting something esp. on wheels —**ve·hic·u·lar** \vē'hikyələr\ *adj*

veil \'vāl\ *n* 1 : sheer material to hide something or to cover the face and head 2 : something that hides ~ *vb* : cover with a veil

vein \'vān\ *n* 1 : rock fissure filled with deposited mineral matter 2 : vessel that carries blood toward the heart 3 : sap-carrying tube in a leaf 4 : distinctive nature or mode of expression —**veined** \'vānd\ *adj*

ve·loc·i·ty \və'läs(ə)tē\ *n, pl* **-ties** : speed

ve·lour, ve·lours \və'lúr\ *n, pl* **velours** \-'lúrz\ : fabric with a velvetlike pile

vel·vet \'velvət\ *n* : fabric with a short soft pile —**velvet** *adj* —**vel·vety** *adj*

ve·nal \'vēn°l\ *adj* : capable of being corrupted esp. by money —**ve·nal·i·ty** \vi'nalətē\ *n* —**ve·nal·ly** *adv*

vend \'vend\ *vb* : sell —**vend·ible** *adj* —**ven·dor** \'vendər\ *n*

ven·det·ta \ven'detə\ *n* : feud between clans

ve·neer \və'niər\ *n* 1 : thin layer of fine wood glued over a cheaper wood 2 : superficial display ~ *vb* : overlay with a veneer

ven·er·a·ble \'venər(ə)bəl, 'venrəbəl\ *adj* : deserving of respect

ven·er·ate \'venə,rāt\ *vb* **-at·ed; -at·ing** : respect esp. with reverence —**ven·er·a·tion** \,venə'rāshən\ *n*

venereal disease \və,nirēəl-\ *n* : contagious disease spread through copulation

ven·geance \'venjəns\ *n* : punishment in retaliation for an injury or offense

venge·ful \'venjfəl\ *adj* : filled with a desire for revenge —**venge·ful·ly** *adv*

ve·nial \'vēnēəl, -nyəl\ *adj* : capable of being forgiven

ven·i·son \'venəsən, -əzən\ *n* : deer meat

ven·om \'venəm\ *n* 1 : poison secreted by certain animals 2 : ill will —**ven·om·ous** \-əməs\ *adj*

vent \'vent\ *vb* 1 : provide with or let out at a vent 2 : give expression to ~ *n* : opening for passage or for relieving pressure

ven·ti·late \'vent³l,āt\ *vb* -**lat·ed**; -**lat·ing** : allow fresh air to circulate through —**ven·ti·la·tion** \,vent³l'āshən\ *n* —**ven·ti·la·tor** \'vent³l,ātər\ *n*

ven·tri·cle \'ventrikəl\ *n* : heart chamber that pumps blood into the arteries of the brain

ven·tril·o·quist \ven'trilə,kwəst\ *n* : one who can make the voice appear to come from another source —**ven·tril·o·quism** \-,kwizəm\ *n* —**ven·tril·o·quy** \-kwē\ *n*

ven·ture \'venchər\ *vb* -**tured**; -**tur·ing** 1 : risk or take a chance on 2 : put forward (an opinion) ~ *n* : speculative business enterprise

ven·ture·some \-səm\ *adj* : brave or daring —**ven·ture·some·ly** *adv* —**ven·ture·some·ness** *n*

ven·ue \'venyü\ *n* : scene of an action or event

ve·rac·i·ty \və'rasətē\ *n, pl* -**ties** : truthfulness or accuracy —**ve·ra·cious** \və'rāshəs\ *adj*

ve·ran·da, ve·ran·dah \və'randə\ *n* : large open porch

verb \'vərb\ *n* : word that expresses action or existence

ver·bal \'vərbəl\ *adj* 1 : having to do with or expressed in words 2 : oral 3 : relating to or formed from a verb —**ver·bal·iza·tion** \,vərbələ'zāshən\ *n* —**ver·bal·ize** \'vərbə,līz\ *vb* —**ver·bal·ly** \-ē\ *adv*

verbal auxiliary *n* : auxiliary verb

ver·ba·tim \(,)vər'bātəm\ *adv or adj* : using the same words

ver·biage \'vərbēij\ *n* : excess of words

ver·bose \(,)vər'bōs\ *adj* : using more words than are needed —**ver·bos·i·ty** \-'bäsətē\ *n*

ver·dant \'vərd³nt\ *adj* : green with growing plants —**ver·dant·ly** *adv*

ver·dict \'vər,dikt\ *n* : decision of a jury

ver·dure \'vərjər\ *n* : green growing vegetation or its color

verge \'vərj\ *vb* **verged**; **verg·ing** : be almost on the point of happening or doing something ~ *n* : edge 2 : threshold

ver·i·fy \'verə,fī\ *vb* -**fied**; -**fy·ing** : establish the truth, accuracy, or reality of —**ver·i·fi·able** *adj* —**ver·i·fi·ca·tion** \,verəfə'kāshən\ *n*

ver·i·ly \'verəlē\ *adv* : truly or confidently

ver·i·ta·ble \'verətəbəl\ *adj* : actual —often used to suggest the aptness of a metaphor —**ver·i·ta·bly** *adv*

ver·i·ty \'veratē\ *n, pl* -**ties** : truth

ver·mi·cel·li \,vərmə'chelē, -'sel-\ *n* : thin spaghetti

ver·min \'vərmən\ *n, pl* **vermin** : small animal pest

ver·nac·u·lar \və(r)'nakyələr\ *adj* : relating to a native language or dialect and esp. its normal spoken form ~ *n* : vernacular language

ver·nal \'vərn³l\ *adj* : relating to spring

ver·sa·tile \'vərsət³l\ *adj* : having many abilities or uses —**ver·sa·til·i·ty** \,vərsə'tilətē\ *n*

verse \'vərs\ *n* 1 : line or stanza of poetry 2 : poetry 3 : short division of a chapter in the Bible

versed \'vərst\ *adj* : familiar from experience, study, or practice

ver·sion \'vərzhən\ *n* 1 : translation of the Bible 2 : account or description from a particular point of view

ver·sus \'vərsəs\ *prep* : opposed to or against

ver·te·bra \'vərtəbrə\ *n, pl* -**brae** \-,brā, -(,)brē\ *or* -**bras** : segment of the backbone —**ver·te·bral** \(,)vər'tēbrəl, 'vərtə-\ *adj*

ver·te·brate \'vərtəbrət, -,brāt\ *n* : animal with a backbone —**vertebrate** *adj*

ver·tex \'vər,teks\ *n, pl* **ver·ti·ces** \'vərtə,sēz\ 1 : point of intersection of lines or surfaces 2 : highest point

ver·ti·cal \'vərtikəl\ *adj* : rising straight up from a level surface —**vertical** *n* —**ver·ti·cal·i·ty** \,vərtə'kalətē\ *n* —**ver·ti·cal·ly** *adv*

ver·ti·go \'vərti,gō\ *n, pl* -**goes** *or* -**gos** : dizziness

verve \'vərv\ *n* : liveliness or vividness

very \'verē\ *adj* -**er; -est** 1 : exact 2 : exactly suitable 3 : precisely the same ~ *adv* : to a high degree

ves·i·cle \'vesikəl\ *n* : membranous cavity —**ve·sic·u·lar** \və'sikyələr\ *adj*

ves·pers \'vespərz\ *n pl* : late afternoon or evening worship service

ves·sel \'vesəl\ *n* 1 : a container (as a barrel, bottle, pan, or cup) for a liquid 2 : craft for navigation esp. on water 3 : tube in which a body fluid is circulated

¹**vest** \'vest\ *vb* 1 : give a particular authority, right, or property to 2 : clothe with or as if with a garment

²**vest** *n* : sleeveless garment worn under a suit coat

ves·ti·bule \'vestə,byül\ *n* : enclosed

entrance —ves·tib·u·lar \ve-
'stibyələr\ adj

ves·tige \'vestij\ n : visible trace or
remains —ves·ti·gial \ve'stijēəl\ adj
—ves·ti·gial·ly adv

vest·ment \'ves(t)mənt\ n : clergyman's garment

ves·try \'vestrē\ n, pl -tries : church
storage room for garments and articles

vet·er·an \'vet(ə)rən\ n 1 : former
member of the armed forces 2 : person with long experience —veteran
adj

Veterans Day n : 4th Monday in October or formerly November 11 observed as a legal holiday in commemoration of the end of war in 1918
and 1945

vet·er·i·nar·i·an \,vet(ə)rən'erēən,
,vetᵊn-\ n : doctor of animals —vet·
er·i·nary \'vet(ə)rən,erē, 'vetᵊn-\
adj

ve·to \'vētō\ n, pl -toes 1 : power to
forbid and esp. the power of a chief
executive to prevent a bill from becoming law 2 : exercise of the veto
~ vb 1 : forbid 2 : reject a legislative
bill

vex \'veks\ vb vexed; vex·ing : trouble,
distress, or annoy —vex·a·tion \vek-
'sāshən\ n —vex·a·tious \-shəs\ adj

via \'vīə, 'vēə\ prep : by way of

vi·a·ble \'vīəbəl\ adj : capable of sur-
viving or growing 2 : practical or
workable —vi·a·bil·i·ty \,vīə'bilətē\
n —vi·a·bly \'vīəblē\ adv

via·duct \'vīə,dəkt\ n : high road or
railway bridge

vi·al \'vī(ə)l\ n : small bottle

vi·brant \'vībrənt\ adj 1 : vibrating 2
: pulsing with vigor or activity 3
: sounding from vibration —vi·bran-
cy \-brənsē\ n

vi·brate \'vī,brāt\ vb -brat·ed; -brat-
ing 1 : move or cause to move
quickly back and forth or side to side
2 : respond sympathetically —vi·
bra·tion \vī'brāshən\ n —vi·bra·tor
\'vī,brātər\ n —vi·bra·tory \'vībrə,
tōrē\ adj

vic·ar \'vikər\ n : parish clergyman
—vi·car·i·ate \-ēət\ n

vi·car·i·ous \vī'kerēəs, -'kar-\ adj : experienced imaginatively or sympathetically —vi·car·i·ous·ly adv —vi·
car·i·ous·ness n

vice \'vīs\ n 1 : immoral habit 2 : de-
pravity

vice- \'(,)vīs, ,vīs\ prefix : one that
takes the place of

vice-chairman   vice-mayor
vice-chairman-   vice-premier
 ship   vice-presidency
vice-chancellor vice-president
vice-chancellor- vice-presidential
 ship   vice-principal
vice-consul   vice-regent

vice admiral n : commissioned officer
in the navy or coast guard ranking
above a rear admiral

vice·roy \'vīs,rói\ n : provincial governor who represents the sovereign

vice ver·sa \,vīsi'vərsə, (')vīs'vər-\
adv : with the order reversed

vi·cin·i·ty \və'sinətē\ n, pl -ties : surrounding area

vi·cious \'vishəs\ adj 1 : wicked 2
: savage 3 : malicious —vi·cious·ly
adv —vi·cious·ness n

vi·cis·si·tude \və'sisə,t(y)üd, vī-\ n : irregular, unexpected, or surprising
change —usu. used in pl.

vic·tim \'viktəm\ n : person killed,
hurt, or abused

vic·tim·ize \'viktə,mīz\ vb -ized; -iz·ing
: make a victim of —vic·tim·iza·tion
\,viktəmə'zāshən\ n —vic·tim·iz·er
\'viktə,mīzər\ n

vic·tor \'viktər\ n : winner

Vic·to·ri·an \vik'tōrēən\ adj : relating
to the reign of Queen Victoria of
England or the art, taste, or
standards of her time ~ n : one of
the Victorian period

vic·to·ri·ous \vik'tōrēəs\ adj : having
won a victory —vic·to·ri·ous·ly adv

vic·to·ry \'vikt(ə)rē\ n, pl -ries : success in defeating an enemy or opponent or in overcoming difficulties

vict·uals \'vitᵊlz\ n pl : food

vid·eo \'vidē,ō\ adj : relating to the
television image

vid·eo·tape \'vidēō,tāp\ vb : make a
recording of (a television production) on special tape —videotape n

vie \'vī\ vb vied; vy·ing : contend —vi·
er \'vī(ə)r\ n

view \'vyü\ n 1 : process of seeing or
examining 2 : opinion 3 : area of
landscape that can be seen 4 : range
of vision 5 : purpose or object ~ vb
1 : look at 2 : think about or consider
—view·er n

view·point n : position from which
something is considered

vig·il \'vijəl\ n 1 : day of devotion before a religious feast 2 : act or time
of keeping awake 3 : long period of
keeping watch (as over a sick or
dying person)

vig·i·lant \'vijələnt\ adj : alert esp. to

avoid danger —**vig·i·lance** \-ləns\ *n*
—**vig·i·lant·ly** *adv*

vig·i·lan·te \ˌvijəˈlantē\ *n* : one of a group independent of the law working to suppress crime

vi·gnette \vinˈyet\ *n* : short descriptive literary piece

vig·or \ˈvigər\ *n* **1** : energy or strength **2** : intensity or force —**vig·or·ous** \ˈvig(ə)rəs\ *adj* —**vig·or·ous·ly** *adv* —**vig·or·ous·ness** *n*

vile \ˈvīl\ *adj* **vil·er**; **vil·est** : thoroughly bad or contemptible —**vile·ly** *adv* —**vile·ness** *n*

vil·i·fy \ˈviləˌfī\ *vb* **-fied**; **-fy·ing** : speak evil of —**vil·i·fi·ca·tion** \ˌviləfəˈkāshən\ *n* —**vil·i·fi·er** \ˈviləˌfī(ə)r\ *n*

vil·la \ˈvilə\ *n* : country estate

vil·lage \ˈvilij\ *n* : small country town —**vil·lag·er** *n*

vil·lain \ˈvilən\ *n* : bad person —**vil·lain·ess** \-ənəs\ *n* —**vil·lainy** *n*

vil·lain·ous \-ənəs\ *adj* : evil or corrupt —**vil·lain·ous·ly** *adv* —**vil·lain·ous·ness** *n*

vim \ˈvim\ *n* : energy

vin·di·cate \ˈvindəˌkāt\ *vb* **-cat·ed**; **-cat·ing 1** : avenge **2** : exonerate **3** : justify —**vin·di·ca·tion** \ˌvindəˈkāshən\ *n* —**vin·di·ca·tor** \ˈvindəˌkātər\ *n*

vin·dic·tive \vinˈdiktiv\ *adj* : seeking or meant for revenge —**vin·dic·tive·ly** *adv* —**vin·dic·tive·ness** *n*

vine \ˈvīn\ *n* : climbing or trailing plant

vin·e·gar \ˈvinigər\ *n* : acidic liquid obtained by fermentation —**vin·e·gary** \-g(ə)rē\ *adj*

vine·yard \ˈvinyərd\ *n* : plantation of grapevines

vin·tage \ˈvintij\ *n* **1** : season's yield of grapes or wine **2** : period of origin ~ *adj* : of enduring interest

vi·nyl \ˈvīnᵊl\ *n* : strong plastic

vi·o·la \vēˈōlə\ *n* : instrument of the violin family tuned lower than the violin —**vi·o·list** \-ləst\ *n*

vi·o·late \ˈvīəˌlāt\ *vb* **-lat·ed**; **-lat·ing 1** : act with disrespect or disregard of **2** : rape **3** : desecrate —**vi·o·la·tion** \ˌvīəˈlāshən\ *n* —**vi·o·la·tor** \ˈvīəˌlātər\ *n*

vi·o·lence \ˈvīələns\ *n* : intense physical force that causes or is intended to cause injury or destruction —**vi·o·lent** \-lənt\ *adj* —**vi·o·lent·ly** *adv*

vi·o·let \ˈvīələt\ *n* **1** : small flowering plant **2** : reddish blue

vi·o·lin \ˌvīəˈlin\ *n* : bowed stringed instrument —**vi·o·lin·ist** \-əst\ *n*

VIP \ˌvēˌīˈpē\ *n*, *pl* **VIPs** \-ˈpēz\ : very important person

vi·per \ˈvīpər\ *n* **1** : venomous snake **2** : treacherous or malignant person

vi·ra·go \vəˈrägō, -ˈrä-; ˈvirəˌgō\ *n*, *pl* **-goes** *or* **-gos** : shrew

vi·ral \ˈvīrəl\ *adj* : relating to or caused by a virus

vir·gin \ˈvərjən\ *n* : unmarried or chaste woman ~ *adj* **1** : chaste **2** : natural and unspoiled —**vir·gin·al** \-əl\ *adj* —**vir·gin·al·ly** *adv* —**vir·gin·i·ty** \vərˈjinətē\ *n*

vir·gule \ˈvərgyül\ *n* : mark / used esp. to denote "or" or "per"

vir·ile \ˈvirəl\ *adj* : masculine —**vi·ril·i·ty** \vəˈrilətē\ *n*

vir·tu·al \ˈvərchə(wə)l\ *adj* : being almost the same —**vir·tu·al·ly** *adv*

vir·tue \ˈvərchü\ *n* **1** : moral excellence **2** : effective or commendable quality **3** : chastity

vir·tu·os·i·ty \ˌvərchəˈwäsətē\ *n*, *pl* **-ties** : great skill (as in music)

vir·tu·o·so \ˌvərchəˈwōsō, -zō\ *n*, *pl* **-sos** *or* **-si** \-sē, -zē\ : highly skilled performer esp. of music —**virtuoso** *adj*

vir·tu·ous \ˈvərch(ə)wəs\ *adj* **1** : morally good **2** : chaste —**vir·tu·ous·ly** *adv*

vir·u·lent \ˈvir(y)ələnt\ *adj* **1** : bitterly hostile **2** : extremely severe or infectious —**vir·u·lence** \-ləns\ *n* —**vir·u·lent·ly** *adv*

vi·rus \ˈvīrəs\ *n* : tiny disease-causing agent

vi·sa \ˈvēzə, -sə\ *n* : authorization to enter a foreign country

vis·age \ˈvizij\ *n* : face

vis·cera \ˈvisərə\ *n pl* : internal bodily organs esp. of the trunk

vis·cer·al \ˈvisərəl\ *adj* **1** : bodily **2** : instinctive **3** : deeply or crudely emotional —**vis·cer·al·ly** *adv*

vis·cid \ˈvisəd\ *adj* : viscous —**vis·cid·i·ty** \visˈidətē\ *n*

vis·count \ˈvīˌkaunt\ *n* : British nobleman ranking below an earl and above a baron —**vis·count·ess** \-əs\ *n*

vis·cous \ˈviskəs\ *adj* : having a thick or sticky consistency —**vis·cos·i·ty** \visˈkäsətē\ *n*

vise \ˈvīs\ *n* : device for clamping something being worked on

vis·i·bil·i·ty \ˌvizəˈbilətē\ *n*, *pl* **-ties** : degree or range to which something can be seen

vis·i·ble \ˈvizəbəl\ *adj* **1** : capable of being seen **2** : manifest —**vis·i·bly** *adv*

vi·sion \'vizhən\ *n* 1 : vivid picture seen in a dream or trance or in the imagination 2 : foresight 3 : power of seeing ~ *vb* : imagine

vi·sion·ary \'vizhə,nerē\ *adj* 1 : given to dreaming or imagining 2 : illusory 3 : not practical ~ *n* : one with great dreams or projects

vis·it \'vizət\ *vb* 1 : go or come to see 2 : stay with for a time as a guest 3 : cause or be a reward, affliction, or punishment ~ *n* : short stay as a guest —**vis·it·able** *adj* —**vis·i·tor** \-ər\ *n*

vis·i·ta·tion \,vizə'tāshən\ *n* 1 : official visit 2 : divine punishment or favor 3 : severe trial

vi·sor \'vīzər\ *n* 1 : front piece of a helmet 2 : part (as on a cap or car windshield) that shades the eyes

vis·ta \'vistə\ *n* : distant view

vi·su·al \'vizh(əw)əl\ *adj* 1 : relating to sight 2 : visible —**vi·su·al·ly** *adv*

vi·su·al·ize \'vizh(ə)wə,līz\ *vb* -**ized**; -**iz·ing** : form a mental image of —**vi·su·al·iza·tion** \,vizhə(wə)lə'zāshən\ *n* —**vi·su·al·iz·er** \'vizh(wə),līzər\ *n*

vi·tal \'vīt²l\ *adj* 1 : relating to or characteristic of life 2 : full of life and vigor 3 : basic 4 : very important —**vi·tal·ly** *adv*

vi·tal·i·ty \vī'talətē\ *n, pl* -**ties** 1 : life force 2 : energy

vi·ta·min \'vītəmən\ *n* : natural or organic substance essential to health

vi·ti·ate \'vishē,āt\ *vb* -**at·ed**; -**at·ing** 1 : spoil or impair 2 : invalidate —**vi·ti·a·tion** \,vishē'āshən\ *n* —**vi·ti·a·tor** \'vishē,ātər\ *n*

vit·re·ous \'vitrēəs\ *adj* : relating to or resembling glass

vit·ri·ol \'vitrēəl\ *n* : something caustic, corrosive, or biting —**vit·ri·ol·ic** \,vitrē'älik\ *adj*

vi·tu·per·ate \vī't(y)üpə,rāt, və-\ *vb* -**at·ed**; -**at·ing** : abuse in words —**vi·tu·per·a·tion** \-,t(y)üpə'rāshən\ *n* —**vi·tu·per·a·tive** \-'t(y)üp(ə)rativ, -pə,rāt-\ *adj* —**vi·tu·per·a·tive·ly** *adv*

vi·va·cious \və·vāshəs, vī-\ *adj* : lively —**vi·va·cious·ly** *adv* —**vi·va·cious·ness** *n* —**vi·vac·i·ty** \-'vasətē\ *n*

viv·id \'vivəd\ *adj* 1 : lively 2 : brilliant 3 : intense or sharp —**viv·id·ly** *adv* —**viv·id·ness** *n*

viv·i·fy \'vivə,fī\ *vb* -**fied**; -**fy·ing** : give life or vividness to

vivi·sec·tion \,vivə'sekshən, 'vivə,-\ *n* : experimental operation on a living animal

vix·en \'viksən\ *n* 1 : female fox 2 : scolding woman

vo·cab·u·lary \vō'kabyə,lerē\ *n, pl* -**lar·ies** 1 : list or collection of words 2 : terminology of a person or subject

vo·cal \'vōkəl\ *adj* 1 : relating to or produced by or for the voice 2 : speaking out freely and usu. emphatically

vocal cords *n pl* : membranous folds in the larynx that are important in making vocal sounds

vo·cal·ist \'vōkəlist\ *n* : singer

vo·cal·ize \-,līz\ *vb* -**ized**; -**iz·ing** : give vocal expression to

vo·ca·tion \vō'kāshən\ *n* : regular employment —**vo·ca·tion·al** \-sh(ə)nəl\ *adj*

vo·cif·er·ous \vō'sif(ə)rəs\ *adj* : noisy and insistent —**vo·cif·er·ous·ly** *adv*

vod·ka \'vädkə\ *n* : colorless distilled grain liquor

vogue \'vōg\ *n* : brief but intense popularity

voice \'vòis\ *n* 1 : sound produced through the mouth by humans and many animals 2 : power of speaking 3 : right of choice or opinion ~ *vb* : express in words —**voiced** \'vòist\ *adj*

void \'vòid\ *adj* 1 : containing nothing 2 : lacking —with *of* 3 : not legally binding ~ *n* 1 : empty space 2 : feeling of hollowness ~ *vb* 1 : discharge (as body waste) 2 : make (as a contract) void —**void·able** *adj* —**void·er** *n*

vol·a·tile \'välət²l\ *adj* 1 : readily vaporizing at a relatively low temperature 2 : explosive or easily stirred to violence 3 : changeable —**vol·a·til·i·ty** \,välə'tilətē\ *n* —**vol·a·til·ize** \'välət²l,īz\ *vb*

vol·ca·no \väl'kānō\ *n, pl* -**noes** *or* -**nos** : opening in the earth's crust from which molten rock and steam come out —**vol·ca·nic** \-'kanik\ *adj*

vo·li·tion \vō'lishən\ *n* : free will —**vo·li·tion·al** \-'lish(ə)nəl\ *adj*

vol·ley \'välē\ *n, pl* -**leys** 1 : flight of missiles (as arrows or bullets) 2 : simultaneous shooting of many weapons

vol·ley·ball *n* : game of batting a large ball over a net

volt \'vōlt\ *n* : unit for measuring the force that moves an electric current

volt·age \'vōltij\ *n* : quantity of volts

vol·u·ble \'välyəbəl\ *adj* : fluent and smooth in speech —**vol·u·bil·i·ty**

\,vālyə'bilətē\ *n* —**vol·u·bly** \'väl-yəblē\ *adv*

vol·ume \'välyəm\ *n* **1** : book **2** : space occupied as measured by cubic units **3** : amount **4** : intensity of a sound

vo·lu·mi·nous \və'lümənəs\ *adj* : large or bulky

vol·un·tary \'välən,terē\ *adj* **1** : done, made, or given freely and without expecting compensation **2** : relating to or controlled by the will —**vol·un·tari·ly** *adv*

vol·un·teer \,välən'tiər\ *n* : person who offers to help or work without expecting payment or reward ~ *vb* **1** : offer or give voluntarily **2** : offer oneself as a volunteer

vo·lup·tuous \və'ləpchə(wə)s\ *adj* **1** : luxurious **2** : having a full and sexually attractive figure —**vo·lup·tuous·ly** *adv* —**vo·lup·tuous·ness** *n*

vom·it \'vämət\ *vb* : throw up the contents of the stomach —**vomit** *n*

voo·doo \'vüdü\ *n, pl* **voodoos 1** : religion derived from African ancestor worship and involving sorcery **2** : one who practices voodoo **3** : charm or fetish used in voodoo —**voodoo** *adj* —**voo·doo·ism** \,izəm\ *n*

vo·ra·cious \vȯ'rāshəs, və-\ *adj* : greedy or exceedingly hungry —**vo·ra·cious·ly** *adv* —**vo·ra·cious·ness** *n* —**vo·rac·i·ty** \-'rasətē\ *n*

vor·tex \'vȯr,teks\ *n, pl* **vor·ti·ces** \'vȯrtə,sēz\ : whirling liquid

vo·ta·ry \'vōtərē\ *n, pl* **-ries 1** : devoted participant, adherent, admirer, or worshiper

vote \'vōt\ *n* **1** : individual expression of preference in choosing or reaching a decision **2** : right to indicate one's preference or the preference expressed ~ *vb* **vot·ed; vot·ing 1** : cast a vote **2** : choose or defeat by vote —**vote·less** *adj* —**vot·er** *n*

vo·tive \'vōtiv\ *adj* : offered or performed in fulfillment of a vow or in petition, gratitude, or devotion

vouch \'vaůch\ *vb* : give a guarantee or personal assurance

vouch·er \'vaůchər\ *n* : written record or receipt that serves as proof of a transaction

vouch·safe \vaůch'sāf\ *vb* **-safed; -saf·ing** : grant

vow \'vaů\ *n* : solemn promise to do something or to live or act a certain way —**vow** *vb*

vow·el \'vaů(ə)l\ *n* **1** : speech sound produced without obstruction or friction in the mouth **2** : letter representing such a sound

voy·age \'vȯiij\ *n* : long journey esp. by water or through space ~ *vb* **-aged; -ag·ing** : make a voyage —**voy·ag·er** *n*

vul·ca·nize \'vəlkə,nīz\ *vb* **-nized; -niz·ing** : treat (as rubber) to make more elastic or stronger —**vul·ca·ni·za·tion** \,vəlkənə'zāshən\ *n*

vul·gar \'vəlgər\ *adj* **1** : relating to the common people **2** : lacking refinement **3** : offensive in manner or language —**vul·gar·ism** \-,rizəm\ *n* —**vul·gar·ize** \-,rīz\ *vb* —**vul·gar·ly** *adv*

vul·gar·i·ty \,vəl'garətē\ *n, pl* **-ties 1** : state of being vulgar **2** : vulgar language or act

vul·ner·a·ble \'vəln(ə)rəbəl\ *adj* : susceptible to attack or damage —**vul·ner·a·bil·i·ty** \,vəln(ə)rə'bilətē\ *n* —**vul·ner·a·bly** *adv*

vul·ture \'vəlchər\ *n* : large flesh-eating bird

vul·va \'vəlvə\ *n, pl* **-vae** \-,vē, -,vī\ : external genital parts of the female

vying *pres part of* VIE

W

w \'dəbəl(,)yü\ *n, pl* **w's** *or* **ws** \-(,)yüz\ : 23d letter of the alphabet

wad \'wäd\ *n* **1** : little mass **2** : soft mass of fibrous material **3** : pliable plug to retain a powder charge ~ *vb* **1** : form into a wad **2** : stuff with a wad

wad·dle \'wäd²l\ *vb* **-dled; -dling** : walk with short steps swaying from side to side —**waddle** *n*

wade \'wād\ *vb* **wad·ed; wad·ing 1** : step in or through (as water) **2** : move with difficulty —**wade** *n* —**wad·er** *n*

wa·fer \'wāfər\ *n* **1** : thin crisp cake or cracker **2** : waferlike thing

waf·fle \'wäfəl\ *n* : crisped cake of batter cooked in a hinged utensil (**waffle iron**)

waft \'wäft, 'waft\ *vb* : cause to move lightly by wind or waves —**waft** *n*

1wag \'wag\ *vb* **-gg-** : sway or swing from side to side or to and fro —**wag** *n*

²**wag** n : wit —**wag-gish** adj

wage \'wāj\ vb **waged; wag-ing** : engage in ~ n 1 : payment for labor or services 2 : compensation

wa-ger \'wājər\ n or vb : bet

wag-gle \'wagəl\ vb **-gled; -gling** : wag —**waggle** n

wag-on \'wagən\ n 1 : 4-wheeled vehicle drawn by animals 2 : child's 4-wheeled cart

waif \'wāf\ n : homeless child

wail \'wāl\ vb 1 : mourn 2 : make a sound like a mournful cry —**wail** n

wain-scot \'wānskət, -,skōt, -,skät\ n : usu. paneled wooden lining of an interior wall —**wainscot** vb

waist \'wāst\ n 1 : narrowed part of the body between chest and hips 2 : waistlike part —**waist-line** n

wait \'wāt\ vb 1 : remain in readiness or expectation 2 : delay 3 : attend as a waiter ~ n 1 : concealment 2 : act or period of waiting

wait-er \'wātər\ n : man who waits on tables

wait-ress \'wātrəs\ n : woman who waits on tables

waive \'wāv\ vb **waived; waiv-ing** : give up claim to

waiv-er \'wāvər\ n : act of waiving right, claim, or privilege

¹**wake** \'wāk\ vb **woke** \'wōk\ **wo-ken** \'wōkən\ **wak-ing 1** : keep watch 2 : bring or come back to consciousness after sleep ~ n 1 : state of being awake 2 : watch held over a dead body

²**wake** n : track left by a ship

wake-ful \'wākfəl\ adj : not sleeping or able to sleep —**wake-ful-ness** n

wak-en \'wākən\ vb : wake

wale \'wāl\ n : ridge on cloth

walk \'wók\ vb 1 : move or cause to move on foot 2 : pass over, through, or along by walking ~ n 1 : a going on foot 2 : place or path for walking 3 : distance to be walked 4 : way of living 5 : way of walking 6 : slow 4-beat gait of a horse —**walk-er** n

wall \'wól\ n 1 : structure for defense or for enclosing something 2 : upright enclosing part of a building or room 3 : something like a wall ~ vb : provide, separate, surround, or close with a wall —**walled** \'wóld\ adj

wal-la-by \'wäləbē\ n, pl **-bies** : small or medium-sized kangaroo

wal-let \'wälət\ n : pocketbook with compartments

wall-flow-er n 1 : mustardlike plant with showy fragrant flowers 2 : one who remains on the sidelines of social activity

wal-lop \'wäləp\ n 1 : powerful blow 2 : ability to hit hard ~ vb 1 : defeat soundly 2 : hit hard

wal-low \'wälō\ vb 1 : roll about in deep mud 2 : live with excessive pleasure ~ n : place for wallowing

wall-pa-per n : decorative paper for walls —**wallpaper** vb

wal-nut \'wól,(ʌ)nət\ n 1 : edible nut with a furrowed shell and adherent husk 2 : tree on which this nut grows or its brown wood 3 : hickory nut or tree

wal-rus \'wólrəs, 'wäl-\ n, pl **-rus** or **-rus-es** : large sealike mammal of northern seas

waltz \'wólts\ n : gliding dance to music having 3 beats to the measure or the music —**waltz** vb

wam-pum \'wämpəm\ n : strung shell beads used by No. American Indians as money

wan \'wän\ adj **-nn-** : sickly or pale —**wan-ly** adv —**wan-ness** n

wand \'wänd\ n : slender staff

wan-der \'wändər\ vb 1 : move about aimlessly 2 : stray 3 : become delirious —**wan-der-er** n

wan-der-lust \'wändər,ləst\ n : strong urge to wander

wane \'wän\ vb **waned; wan-ing 1** : grow smaller or less 2 : lose power, prosperity, or influence —**wane** n

wan-gle \'wangəl\ vb **-gled; -gling** : obtain by sly or indirect means

want \'wónt\ vb 1 : lack 2 : need 3 : desire earnestly ~ n 1 : deficiency 2 : dire need 3 : something wanted

want-ing \-iŋ\ adj 1 : not present or in evidence 2 : falling below standards 3 : lacking in ability ~ prep 1 : lacking 2 : diminished by

wan-ton \'wónt²n\ adj 1 : lewd 2 : having no regard for justice or for others' feelings, rights, or safety ~ n : lewd or immoral person ~ vb : be wanton —**wan-ton-ly** adv —**wan-ton-ness** n

wa-pi-ti \'wäpətē\ n, pl **-ti** or **-tis** : elk

war \'wór\ n 1 : armed fighting between nations 2 : state of hostility or conflict 3 : struggle between opposing forces or for a particular end ~ vb **-rr-** : engage in warfare —**war-less** \-ləs\ adj —**war-time** n

war-ble \'wórbəl\ n 1 : melodious succession of low pleasing sounds 2 : musical trill ~ vb **-bled; -bling** : sing or utter in a trilling way

war-bler \'wórblər\ n 1 : small thrushlike singing bird 2 : small bright-colored insect-eating bird

ward \'wȯrd\ n 1 : a guarding or being under guard or guardianship 2 : division of a prison or hospital 3 : electoral or administrative division of a city 4 : person under protection of a guardian or a law court ~ vb : turn aside —ward·ship n

1.ward \wȯrd\ adj suffix 1 : that moves, tends, faces, or is directed toward 2 : that occurs or is situated in the direction of

2.ward, -wards adv suffix 1 : in a (specified) direction 2 : toward a (specified) point, position, or area

war·den \'wȯrdᵊn\ n 1 : guardian 2 : official charged with supervisory duties or enforcement of laws 3 : official in charge of a prison

ward·er \'wȯrdər\ n : watchman or warden

ward·robe \'wȯrd,rōb\ n 1 : clothes closet 2 : collection of wearing apparel

ware \'waar\ n 1 : articles for sale — often pl. 2 : items of fired clay

ware·house \-,haús\ n : place for storage of merchandise —warehouse vb —ware·house·man \-,man\ n —ware·hous·er \-,haúzər, -,sər\ n

war·fare \'wȯr,faar\ n 1 : military operations between enemies 2 : struggle

war·head \-,hed\ n : part of a missile (as a bomb) holding the charge

war·like adj : fond of or threatening war

warm \'wȯrm\ adj 1 : having or giving out moderate or adequate heat 2 : serving to retain heat 3 : showing strong feeling 4 : giving a pleasant impression of warmth, cheerfulness, or friendliness ~ vb : make or become warm 2 : give warmth or energy to 3 : become increasingly ardent, interested, or competent —warm·er n —warm·ly adv

war·mon·ger \'wȯr,məggər, -,mäŋ-\ n : one who attempts to stir up war

warmth \'wȯrmth\ n 1 : quality or state of being warm 2 : enthusiasm

warn \'wȯrn\ vb 1 : put on guard 2 : notify in advance —warn·ing \-iŋ\ n or adj

warp \'wȯrp\ n 1 : lengthwise threads in a woven fabric 2 : twist ~ vb 1 : twist out of shape 2 : lead astray 3 : distort

war·rant \'wȯrənt, 'wär-\ n 1 : authorization 2 : legal writ authorizing action ~ vb 1 : declare or maintain

positively 2 : guarantee 3 : approve 4 : justify

warrant officer n 1 : officer in the armed forces ranking next below a commissioned officer 2 : commissioned officer in the navy or coast guard ranking below an ensign

war·ran·ty \'wȯrəntē, 'wär-\ n, pl -ties : guarantee of the integrity of a product

war·ren \'wȯrən, 'wär-\ n : area for the keeping of small game as rabbits

war·rior \'wȯryər, 'wȯrēər; 'wärē-, 'wäryər\ n : man engaged or experienced in warfare

war·ship \'wȯr,ship\ n : armed military ship

wart \'wȯrt\ n 1 : small projection on the skin caused by a virus 2 : wartlike protuberance

wary \'wa(ə)rē\ adj wari·er; -est : careful in guarding against danger or deception

was past 1st & 3d sing of BE

wash \'wȯsh, 'wäsh\ vb 1 : cleanse with or as if with a liquid (as water) 2 : wet thoroughly with liquid 3 : flow along the border of 4 : flow in a stream 5 : move or remove by or as if by the action of water 6 : cover or daub lightly with a liquid 7 : undergo laundering ~ n 1 : act of washing or being washed 2 : articles to be washed 3 : surging action of water or disturbed air

wash·able \-əbəl\ adj : capable of being washed without damage

wash·board n : grooved board to scrub clothes on

wash·bowl n : large bowl for water for washing hands and face

wash·cloth n : cloth used for washing one's face and body

wash·er \'wȯshər, 'wäsh-\ n 1 : machine for washing 2 : ring used around a bolt or screw to ensure tightness or relieve friction

wash·ing \'wȯshiŋ, 'wäsh-\ n : articles to be washed

Washington's Birthday n : the 3d Monday in February or formerly February 22 observed as a legal holiday

wash·out n 1 : washing out or away of earth 2 : place where earth is washed away 3 : failure

wash·room n : room with washing and toilet facilities

wasp \'wäsp, 'wȯsp\ n : slender-bodied winged insect related to the bees and having a formidable sting

wasp·ish \'wäspish, 'wȯs-\ *adj* : irritable

was·sail \'wäsəl, wä'säl\ *n* **1** : toast to someone's health **2** : liquor drunk on festive occasions **3** : riotous drinking —**wassail** *vb*

waste \'wāst\ *n* **1** : sparsely settled or barren region **2** : act or an instance of wasting **3** : refuse (as garbage or rubbish) **4** : material (as feces) produced but not used by a living body ~ *vb* **wast·ed; wast·ing 1** : ruin **2** : spend or use carelessly **3** : lose substance or energy ~ *adj* **1** : wild and uninhabited **2** : being of no further use —**wast·er** *n* —**waste·ful** \-fəl\ *adj* —**waste·ful·ly** *adv* —**waste·ful·ness** *n*

waste·bas·ket \'wās(t),baskət\ *n* : receptacle for refuse

waste·land \'wäst,land, -lənd\ *n* : barren uncultivated land

wast·rel \'wāstrəl, 'wästrəl\ *n* : one who wastes

watch \'wäch, 'wȯch\ *vb* **1** : be or stay awake intentionally **2** : be on the lookout for danger **3** : observe **4** : keep oneself informed about ~ *n* **1** : act of keeping awake to guard **2** : close observation **3** : one that watches **4** : period of duty on a ship or those on duty during this period **5** : timepiece carried on the person —**watch·er** *n*

watch·dog *n* **1** : dog kept to guard property **2** : one that protects

watch·ful \-fəl\ *adj* : steadily attentive —**watch·ful·ly** *adv* —**watch·ful·ness** *n*

watch·man \-mən\ *n* : person assigned to watch

watch·word *n* **1** : secret word used as a signal **2** : slogan

wa·ter \'wȯtər, 'wät-\ *n* **1** : liquid that descends as rain and forms rivers, lakes, and seas **2** : liquid containing or resembling water ~ *vb* **1** : supply with or get water **2** : dilute with or as if with water **3** : form or secrete watery matter

water buffalo *n* : common oxlike often domesticated Asian buffalo

wa·ter·col·or *n* **1** : paint whose liquid part is water **2** : picture made with watercolors

wa·ter·course *n* : stream of water

wa·ter·cress \-,kres\ *n* : perennial salad plant found chiefly in clear running water

wa·ter·fall *n* : steep descent of the water of a stream

wa·ter·fowl *n* **1** : bird that frequents the water **2** **waterfowl** *pl* : swimming game birds

wa·ter·front *n* : land fronting a body of water

water lily *n* : aquatic plant with floating leaves and showy flowers

wa·ter·logged \-,lȯgd, -,lägd\ *adj* : filled or soaked with water

wa·ter·mark *n* **1** : mark showing how high water has risen **2** : a marking in paper visible under light ~ *vb* : mark (paper) with a watermark

wa·ter·mel·on *n* : large fruit with sweet juicy usu. red pulp

water moccasin *n* : venomous snake of the southern U.S.

wa·ter·pow·er *n* : power of moving water used to run machinery

wa·ter·proof *adj* : not letting water through ~ *vb* : make waterproof —**wa·ter·proof·ing** *n*

wa·ter·shed \-,shed\ *n* : dividing ridge between two drainage areas or one of these areas

water ski *n* : ski used on water when the wearer is towed —**wa·ter·ski** *vb* —**wa·ter·ski·er** *n*

wa·ter·spout *n* **1** : pipe from which water is spouted **2** : tornado over a body of water

wa·ter·tight *adj* **1** : so tight as not to let water in **2** : so worded that its meaning cannot be misunderstood or its purpose defeated

wa·ter·way *n* : navigable body of water

wa·ter·works *n pl* : system by which water is supplied (as to a city)

wa·tery \'wȯtərē, 'wät-\ *adj* **1** : containing, full of, or giving out water **2** : being like water **3** : soft and soggy

watt \'wät\ *n* : unit of electric power —**watt·age** \'wätij\ *n*

wat·tle \'wät[ə]l\ *n* **1** : framework of flexible branches used for fencing **2** : fleshy process hanging usu. about the head or neck (as of a bird) —**wat·tled** \-[ə]ld\ *adj*

wave \'wāv\ *vb* **waved; wav·ing 1** : flutter **2** : signal with the hands **3** : wave to and fro with the hand **4** : curve up and down like a wave ~ *n* **1** : moving swell on the surface of water **2** : wavelike shape **3** : waving motion **4** : surge **5** : disturbance that transfers energy from point to point —**wave·let** \-lət\ *n* —**wave·like** *adj* —**wavy** *adj*

wave·length \'wāv,leṅth\ *n* : distance from crest to crest in the line of advance of a wave

wa·ver \'wāvər\ *vb* **1** : fluctuate in opinion, allegiance, or direction **2**

: flicker **3** : falter —**wa·ver** n —**wa·**
ver·er n —**wa·ver·ing·ly** adv
¹**wax** \'waks\ n **1** : yellowish plastic
substance secreted by bees **2** : substance resembling beeswax ~ vb
: treat or rub with wax esp. for polishing
²**wax** vb **1** : grow larger **2** : become
wax·en \'waksən\ adj : made of or resembling wax
waxy \'waksē\ adj **wax·i·er;**
: made of, full of, or resembling wax
way \'wā\ n **1** : thoroughfare for travel
or passage **2** : route **3** : course of
action **4** : method **5** : detail **6** : usual
or characteristic state of affairs **7**
: condition **8** : distance **9** : progress
along a course —**by way of 1** : for the
purpose of **2** : by the route through
—**out of the way** : remote —**under**
way : in motion or progress
way·bill n : paper that accompanies a
shipment and gives details of goods,
route, and charges
way·far·er \'wā,farər\ n : traveler esp.
on foot —**way·far·ing** \-,farin\ adj
way·lay \'wā,lā\ vb **-laid** \-,lād\; **-lay-**
ing : lie in wait for
way·side n : side of a road
way·ward \'wāwərd\ adj **1** : disobedient **2** : unpredictable **3** : opposite to
what is desired
we \(')wē\ pron —used of a group that
includes the speaker or writer
weak \'wēk\ adj **1** : lacking strength
or vigor **2** : deficient in vigor of mind
or character **3** : deficient in the usual
ingredients **4** : not having or exerting
authority —**weak·en** \'wēkən\ vb —
weak·ly adv
weak·ling \-lin\ n : person who is physically, mentally, or morally weak
weak·ly \'wēklē\ adj : feeble
weak·ness \-nəs\ n **1** : quality or state
of being weak **2** : fault **3** : object of
special liking
wealth \'welth\ n **1** : abundant possessions or resources **2** : profusion
wealthy \'welthē\ adj **wealth·i·er;** -est
: having wealth
wean \'wēn\ vb **1** : accustom (a young
mammal) to take food otherwise
than by nursing **2** : free from de-
pendence
weap·on \'wepən\ n **1** : something (as
a gun) that may be used to fight with
2 : means by which one contends
against another
wear \'waər\ vb **wore** \'wōr\; **worn**
\'wōrn\; **wear·ing 1** : use as an article of clothing or adornment **2**
: carry on the person **3** : show an

appearance of **4** : decay by use or by
scraping **5** : lessen the strength of **6**
: endure use ~ n **1** : act of wearing
2 : clothing **3** : lasting quality **4**
: result of use —**wear·able** \'war-
əbəl\ adj —**wear·er** n —**wear out**
~ vb **1** : make or become useless by
wear **2** : tire
wea·ri·some \'wirēsəm\ adj : causing
weariness —**wea·ri·some·ly** adv —
wea·ri·some·ness n
wea·ry \'wi(ə)rē\ adj -**ri·er;** -est **1**
: worn out in strength, freshness, or
patience **2** : expressing or characteristic of weariness ~ vb -**ried; -ry·ing**
: make or become weary —**wea·ri·ly**
adv —**wea·ri·ness** n
wea·sel \'wēzəl\ n **1** : small slender
flesh-eating mammals
weath·er \'wethər\ n : condition of the
atmosphere ~ vb **1** : expose to or
endure the action of weather **2** : endure
weath·er-beat·en adj : altered by exposure to the weather
weath·er·man \-,man\ n : one who
forecasts and reports the weather
weath·er·proof adj : able to withstand
exposure to weather —**weatherproof**
vb
weather vane n : movable device that
shows the way the wind blows
weave \'wēv\ vb **wove** \'wōv\ or
weaved; wo·ven \'wōvən\ or
weaved; weav·ing 1 : form by interlacing strands of material **2** : contrive **3** : make a coherent whole **4**
: follow a winding course ~ n : pattern or method of weaving —**weav-**
er n
web \'web\ n **1** : cobweb **2** : animal or
plant membrane **3** : network ~ vb
-bb- : cover or provide with a web
webbed \'webd\ adj : having or being
toes or fingers united by a web
web·bing \'webin\ n : strong closely
woven tape
wed \'wed\ vb **-dd- 1** : marry **2** : unite
wed·ding \'wedin\ n : marriage ceremony and celebration
wedge \'wej\ n : V-shaped object used
for splitting, raising, forcing open,
or tightening ~ vb **wedged; wedg·ing**
1 : tighten or split with a wedge **2**
: force into a narrow space
wed·lock \'wed,läk\ n : marriage
Wednes·day \'wenzdē\ n : 4th day of
the week
wee \'wē\ adj : very small
weed \'wēd\ n **1** : unwanted plant ~ vb
: remove weeds or other unwanted
items —**weed·er** n —**weedy** adj

weeds *n pl* : mourning clothes

week \'wēk\ *n* 1 : 7 successive days 2 : calendar period of 7 days beginning with Sunday and ending with Saturday 3 : the working or school days of the calendar week

week·day \'wēk,dā\ *n* : any day except Sunday and often Saturday

week·end \-,end\ *n* : Saturday and Sunday ~ *vb* : spend the weekend

week·ly \'wēklē\ *adj* : occurring, done, produced, or issued every week ~ *adv* : once a week ~ *n, pl* **-lies** : weekly publication —**weekly** *adv*

weep \'wēp\ *vb* **wept** \'wept\; **weep·ing** : shed tears —**weep·er** *n* —**weepy** *adj*

wee·vil \'wēvəl\ *n* : small injurious beetle with a long head usu. curved into a snout —**wee·vily, wee·vil·ly** \'wēv(ə)lē\ *adj*

weft \'weft\ *n* : woof

weigh \'wā\ *vb* 1 : determine the heaviness of 2 : have a specified weight 3 : consider carefully 4 : heave up (an anchor) 5 : press down or burden

weight \'wāt\ *n* 1 : amount that something weighs 2 : relative heaviness 3 : heavy object 4 : burden or pressure 5 : importance ~ *vb* 1 : load with a weight 2 : oppress —**weight·less** \-ləs\ *adj* —**weight·less·ness** *n* —**weighty** \'wātē\ *adj*

weird \'wiərd\ *adj* 1 : unearthly or mysterious 2 : strange —**weird·ly** *adv* —**weird·ness** *n*

wel·come \'welkəm\ *vb* **-comed; -com·ing** : accept or greet cordially ~ *adj* : received or permitted gladly ~ *n* : cordial greeting or reception

weld \'weld\ *vb* : unite by heating, hammering, or pressing ~ *n* : union by welding —**weld·er** *n*

wel·fare \'wel,faər\ *n* 1 : prosperity 2 : relief

¹well \'wel\ *n* 1 : spring 2 : hole sunk in the earth to obtain a natural deposit (as of oil) 3 : source of supply 4 : open space extending vertically through floors ~ *vb* : flow forth

²well *adv* **bet·ter** \'betər\; **best** \'best\ 1 : in a good or proper manner 2 : satisfactorily 3 : fully 4 : considerably ~ *adj* 1 : satisfactory 2 : prosperous 3 : desirable 4 : healthy

well-ad·vised \,weləd'vīzd\ *adj* : prudent

well-be·ing \'wel'bēiŋ\ *n* : state of being happy, healthy, or prosperous

well-bred \-'bred\ *adj* : having good manners

well-done *adj* 1 : properly performed 2 : cooked thoroughly

well-heeled \-'hēld\ *adj* : financially well-off

well-mean·ing *adj* : having good intentions

well-nigh *adv* : nearly

well-off *adj* : being in good condition esp. financially

well-read \-'red\ *adj* : well informed through reading

well-round·ed \-'raúndəd\ *adj* : broadly developed

well·spring *n* : source

well-to-do \,welta'dü\ *adj* : prosperous

well-worn \-'wórn\ *adj* 1 : worn by much use 2 : trite

welsh \'welsh, 'welch\ *vb* : default dishonorably

Welsh rabbit *n* : melted often seasoned cheese poured over toast or crackers

Welsh rare·bit \-'raərbət\ *n* : Welsh rabbit

welt \'welt\ *n* 1 : narrow strip of leather between a shoe upper and sole 2 : ridge raised on the skin usu. by a blow ~ *vb* : hit hard

wel·ter \'weltər\ *vb* 1 : toss about 2 : wallow ~ *n* : confused jumble

wen \'wen\ *n* : cyst formed by blockage of a skin gland

wench \'wench\ *n* : young woman

wend \'wend\ *vb* : direct one's course

went *past of* GO

wept *past of* WEEP

were *2d sing, past pl, or past subjunctive of* BE

were·wolf \'wer,wúlf, 'wir-\ *n, pl* **-wolves** \-,wúlvz\ : person held to be able to change into a wolf

west \'west\ *adv* : to or toward the west ~ *adj* : situated toward or at or coming from the west ~ *n* 1 : direction of sunset 2 *cap* : regions to the west —**west·er·ly** \'westərlē\ *adv or adj* —**west·ward** \-wərd\ *adv or adj* —**west·wards** \-wərdz\ *adv*

west·ern \'westərn\ *adj* 1 *cap* : of a region designated West 2 : lying toward or coming from the west — **West·ern·er** *n*

wet \'wet\ *adj* **-tt-** 1 : consisting of or covered or soaked with liquid 2 : not dry ~ *n* : moisture ~ *vb* **-tt-** : make or become moist —**wet·ly** *adv* —**wet·ness** *n*

whack \'hwak\ *vb* : strike sharply ~ *n* 1 : sharp blow 2 : proper working order 3 : chance 4 : try

¹whale \'hwāl\ *n, pl* **whales** *or* **whale**

360

: large marine mammal ~ *vb* **whaled**; **whal·ing** : hunt for whales —**whale·boat** *n* —**whal·er** *n*

²**whale** *vb* **whaled**; **whal·ing** : strike or hit vigorously

whale·bone *n* : horny substance attached to the upper jaw of some large whales (**whalebone whales**)

wharf \'hwȯrf\ *n, pl* **wharves** \'hwȯrvz\ : structure alongside which boats lie to load or unload

what \(')hwät\ *pron* 1 —used to inquire the identity or nature of something 2 : that which 3 : whatever ~ *adv* : to what degree or in what respect ~ *adj* 1 —used to inquire about the identity or nature of something 2 : how remarkable or surprising 3 : whatever

what·ev·er \hwät'evǝr\ *pron* 1 : anything or everything that 2 : no matter what ~ *adj* : of any kind at all

what·not \'hwät,nät\ *pron* : any of various other things that might be mentioned

what·so·ev·er \,hwätsǝ'wevǝr\ *pron or adj* : whatever

wheal \'hwēl\ *n* : a welt on the skin

wheat \'hwēt\ *n* : cereal grain that yields flour —**wheat·en** *adj*

whee·dle \'hwēd°l\ *vb* **-dled**; **-dling** : coax or tempt by flattery

wheel \'hwēl\ *n* 1 : disk or circular frame capable of turning on a central axis 2 : device of which the main part is a wheel ~ *vb* 1 : convey or move on wheels or a wheeled vehicle 2 : rotate 3 : turn so as to change direction —**wheeled** *adj* —**wheel·er** *n* —**wheel·less** *adj*

wheel·bar·row \-,barō\ *n* : one-wheeled vehicle for carrying small loads

wheel·base *n* : distance in inches between the front and rear axles of an automotive vehicle

wheel·chair *n* : chair mounted on wheels esp. for the use of invalids

wheeze \'hwēz\ *vb* **wheezed**; **wheez·ing** : breathe with difficulty and with a whistling sound —**wheeze** *n* —**wheezy** *adj*

whelk \'hwelk\ *n* : large sea snail

whelp \'hwelp\ *n* : one of the young of various carnivorous mammals (as a dog) ~ *vb* : bring forth whelps

when \(')hwen, hwǝn\ *adv* —used to inquire about or designate a particular time ~ *conj* 1 : at or during the time that 2 : every time that 3 : if 4 : although ~ \,hwen\ *pron* : what time

whence \(')hwens\ *adv* 1 : from what place, source, or cause 2 : from or out of which

when·ev·er \hwen'evǝr, hwǝn-\ *conj* or *adv* : at whatever time

where \(')hwear\ *adv* 1 : at, in, or to what place 2 : at, in, or to what situation, position, direction, circumstances, or respect ~ *conj* 1 : at, in, or to what place, position, or circumstance 2 : at, in, or to which place ~ \'hwear\ *n* 1 : place 2 : what place

where·abouts \-ǝ,baúts\ *adv* : about where ~ *n sing or pl* : place where a person or thing is

where·as \hwer'az\ *conj* 1 : because 2 : while on the contrary

where·by *conj* : by, through, or in accordance with which

where·fore \'hwear,fōr\ *adv* 1 : why 2 : therefore ~ *n* : cause

where·in \hwer'in\ *adv* : in what respect

where·of \-'ǝv, -äv\ *conj* : of what, which, or whom

where·up·on \'hwera,pón, -,pän\ *conj* —used to introduce a result or consequence

wher·ev·er \hwer'evǝr\ *adv* : where ~ *conj* : at, in, or to whatever place or circumstance

where·with·al \'hwerwith,ȯl, -with-\ *n* : resources and esp. money

whet \'hwet\ *vb* **-tt-** 1 : sharpen by rubbing (as with a stone) 2 : stimulate —**whet·stone** *n*

whether \'hwethǝr\ *conj* 1 : if it is or was true that 2 : if it is or was better 3 : whichever is the case

whey \'hwā\ *n* : watery part of sour milk

which \(')hwich\ *adj* 1 : being what one or ones out of a group 2 : whichever ~ *pron* 1 : which one or ones 2 : whichever

which·ev·er \hwich'evǝr\ *pron or adj* : no matter what one

whiff \'hwif\ *n* 1 : slight gust 2 : inhalation of odor, gas, or smoke 3 : slight trace ~ *vb* : inhale an odor

while \'hwīl\ *n* 1 : period of time 2 : time and effort used ~ \(,)hwīl\ *conj* 1 : during the time that 2 : as long as 3 : although ~ \'hwīl\ *vb* **whiled**; **whil·ing** : cause to pass esp. pleasantly

whim \'hwim\ *n* : sudden or brief idea or wish

whim·per \'hwimpǝr\ *vb* : cry softly —**whimper** *n*

whim·si·cal \'hwimzikǝl\ *adj* 1 : full of

whims 2 : erratic —whim·si·cal·i·ty \ˌhwimzə'kalətē\ n —whim·si·cal·ly adv

whim·sy, whim·sey \'hwimzē\ n, pl -sies or -seys 1 : whim 2 : fanciful creation

whine \'hwīn\ vb whined; whin·ing 1 : utter a usu. high-pitched plaintive or distressed cry 2 : complain — whine n

whin·ny \'hwinē\ vb -nied; -ny·ing : neigh —whinny n

whip \'hwip\ vb -pp- 1 : move quickly 2 : strike with something slender and flexible 3 : defeat 4 : incite 5 : beat into a froth ~ n 1 : flexible device used for whipping 2 : party leader responsible for discipline 3 : thrashing motion —whip·per n

whip·cord n 1 : thin tough cord 2 : cloth made of hard-twisted yarns

whip·lash n : injury from a sudden sharp movement of the neck and head

whip·per·snap·per \'hwipər,snapər\ n : small, insignificant, or presumptuous person

whip·pet \'hwipət\ n : small swift dog often used for racing

whip·poor·will \'hwipər,wil\ n : American nocturnal bird

whir \'hwər\ vb -rr- : move, fly, or revolve with a whizzing sound ~ n : continuous fluttering or vibratory sound

whirl \'hwərl\ vb 1 : move or drive in a circle 2 : spin 3 : move or turn quickly 4 : reel ~ n 1 : rapid circular movement 2 : state of commotion or confusion

whirl·pool n : whirling mass of water having a depression in the center

whirl·wind n : whirling wind storm

whisk \'hwisk\ n 1 : quick light sweeping or brushing motion 2 : usu. wire kitchen implement for beating ~ vb 1 : move or convey briskly 2 : beat 3 : brush lightly

whisk broom n : small broom

whis·ker \'hwiskər\ n 1 pl : beard 2 : long bristle or hair near an animal's mouth —whis·kered \-kərd\ adj

whis·key, whis·ky \'hwiskē\ n, pl -keys or -kies : liquor distilled from a fermented mash of grain

whis·per \'hwispər\ vb 1 : speak softly 2 : tell by whispering ~ n 1 : soft low sound 2 : rumor

whist \'hwist\ n : card game

whis·tle \'hwisəl\ n 1 : device by which a shrill sound is produced 2 : shrill clear sound made by a whistle

or through the lips ~ vb -tled; -tling 1 : make or utter a whistle 2 : signal or call by a whistle 3 : produce by whistling —whis·tler n

whis·tle-stop n 1 : small community 2 : brief political appearance

whit \'hwit\ n : bit

white \'hwīt\ adj whit·er; -est 1 : free from color 2 : of the color of new snow or milk 3 : having light skin ~ n 1 : color of maximum lightness 2 : white part or thing 3 : person who is light-skinned —white·ness n

white·bait \'hwīt,bāt\ n : young of a herring

white blood cell n : blood cell that does not contain hemoglobin

white·cap \'hwīt,kap\ n : wave crest breaking into foam

white-col·lar adj : relating to salaried employees with duties not requiring protective or work clothing

white elephant n : unwanted often useless item

white·fish \'hwīt,fish\ n : freshwater food fish

whit·en \'hwīt⁰n\ vb : make or become white —whit·en·er \'hwītnər, -⁰nər\ n

white slave n : woman or girl held unwillingly for purposes of prostitution —white slavery n

white·tail \'hwīt,tāl\ n : No. American deer

white·wash vb 1 : whiten with a composition (as of lime and water) 2 : gloss over or cover up faults or wrongdoing —whitewash n

whith·er \'hwithər\ adv 1 : to what place 2 : to what situation, position, degree, or end

¹whit·ing \'hwītiŋ\ n : usu. light or silvery food fish

²whit·ing n : pulverized chalk or limestone

whit·ish \'hwītish\ adj : somewhat white

whit·tle \'hwit⁰l\ vb -tled; -tling 1 : pare 2 : shape by paring 3 : reduce gradually

whiz, whizz \'hwiz\ vb -zz- : make a sound like a speeding object —whiz, whizz n

who \(')hü\ pron 1 —used to inquire the identity of an indicated person or group 2 : person or persons that 3 \(,)hü, ü\ —used to introduce a relative clause

who·dun·it \hü'dənət\ n : detective or mystery story

who·ev·er \hü'evər\ pron : no matter who

whole \'hōl\ *adj* **1** : being in healthy or sound condition **2** : having all its parts or elements **3** : constituting the total sum of ~ *n* **1** : complete amount or sum **2** : coherent complex system **—on the whole 1** : considering all circumstances **2** : in general **—whole-ness** *n*

whole-heart-ed \'hōl'härtəd\ *adj* : sincere

whole number *n* : integer

whole-sale *n* : sale of goods in quantity usu. for resale by a retail merchant ~ *adj* **1** : of or relating to wholesaling **2** : performed on a large scale ~ *vb* **-saled; -sal-ing** : sell at wholesale **—wholesale** *adv* **—whole-sal-er** *n*

whole-some \-səm\ *adj* **1** : promoting mental, spiritual, or bodily health **2** : healthy **—whole-some-ness** *n*

whole wheat *adj* : made of ground entire wheat kernels

whol-ly \'hōl(l)ē\ *adv* **1** : totally **2** : solely

whom \(')hüm\ *pron, objective case of* WHO

whom-ev-er \hüm'evər\ *pron, objective case of* WHOEVER

whoop \'h(w)üp, 'h(w)u̇p\ *vb* : shout loudly ~ *n* : shout

whooping cough *n* : infectious disease marked by convulsive coughing fits

whop-per \'hwäpər\ *n* **1** : something unusually large or extreme of its kind **2** : monstrous lie

whop-ping \'hwäpiŋ\ *adj* : extremely large

whore \'hōr\ *n* : prostitute

whorl \'hwȯrl, 'hwərl\ *n* : spiral **—whorled** *adj*

whose \(')hüz\ *adj* : of or relating to whom or which ~ *pron* : whose one or ones

who-so-ev-er \,hüsə'wevər\ *pron* : whoever

why \(')hwī\ *adv* : for what reason, cause, or purpose ~ *conj* **1** : reason for which **2** : for which ~ \'hwī, *pl* **whys** : reason ~ *interj* \(,)wī, (,)hwī\ —used esp. to express surprise

wick \'wik\ *n* : cord that draws up oil, tallow, or wax to be burned

wick-ed \'wikəd\ *adj* **1** : morally bad **2** : harmful or troublesome **3** : very unpleasant **4** : mischievous **—wick-ed-ly** *adv* **—wick-ed-ness** *n*

wick-er \'wikər\ *n* **1** : small pliant branch **2** : wickerwork **—wicker** *adj*

wick-er-work *n* : work made of wickers

wick-et \'wikət\ *n* **1** : small gate, door,

or window **2** : frame in cricket or arch in croquet

wide \'wīd\ *adj* **wid-er; wid-est 1** : covering a vast area **2** : measured at right angles to the length **3** : having extension from side to side **4** : opened fully **5** : far from the goal ~ *adv* **wid-er; wid-est 1** : over a great distance **2** : so as to leave considerable space between **3** : fully **—wide-ly** *adv* **—wid-en** \'wīd°n\ *vb*

wide-awake *adj* : alert

wide-eyed *adj* **1** : having the eyes wide open **2** : amazed **3** : naive

wide-spread *adj* : widely extended

wid-ow \'widō\ *n* : woman who has lost her husband by death and has not married again ~ *vb* : cause to become a widow **—wid-ow-hood** *n*

wid-ow-er \'widəwər\ *n* : man who has lost his wife by death and has not married again

width \'width\ *n* **1** : distance from side to side **2** : largeness of extent **3** : measured and cut piece of material

wield \'wēld\ *vb* **1** : use or handle esp. effectively **2** : exert **—wield-er** *n*

wie-ner \'wēnər\ *n* : frankfurter

wife \'wīf\ *n, pl* **wives** \'wīvz\ : married woman **—wife-hood** *n* **—wife-less** *adj* **—wife-ly** *adj*

wig \'wig\ *n* : manufactured covering of hair for the head

wig-gle \'wigəl\ *vb* **-gled; -gling 1** : move with quick jerky or shaking movements **2** : wriggle **—wiggle** *n* **—wig-gler** *n*

wig-gly \-(ə)lē\ *adj* **1** : tending to wiggle **2** : wavy

wig-wag \'wig,wag\ *vb* : signal by a flag or light waved according to a code or by the hand or arm

wig-wam \'wig,wäm\ *n* : American Indian hut consisting of a framework of poles overlaid with bark, rush mats, or hides

wild \'wīld\ *adj* **1** : living or being in a state of nature and not domesticated or cultivated **2** : unrestrained **3** : turbulent **4** : crazy **5** : uncivilized **6** : erratic ~ *n* **1** : wilderness **2** : undomesticated state ~ *adv* : without control **—wild-ly** *adv* **—wild-ness** *n*

wild-cat \'wīl(d),kat\ *n* **1** : any of various undomesticated cats (as a lynx) **2** : oil or gas well drilled in an area not known to be productive ~ *adj* **1** : not sound or safe **2** : unauthorized ~ *vb* **-tt-** : drill a wildcat oil or gas well

wil-der-ness \'wildərnəs\ *n* : uncultivated and uninhabited region

wild-fire \'wīl(d),fī(ə)r\ n : sweeping and destructive fire

wild-fowl n : game waterfowl

wild-life \'wīl(d),līf\ n : undomesticated animals

wile \'wīl\ n : trick to snare or deceive ~ vb **wiled**; **wil-ing** : lure

will \wəl, (ə)l, (')wil\ vb, past **would** \wəd, (ə)d, (')wủd\; pres sing & pl **will** 1 : wish 2 —used as an auxiliary verb to express (1) desire or willingness (2) customary action (3) simple future time (4) capability (5) determination (6) probability (7) inevitability or (8) a command 3 \'wil\ : dispose of by a will ~ \'wil\ n 1 : often determined wish 2 : act, process, or experience of willing 3 : power of controlling one's actions or emotions 4 : legal document disposing of property after death

will-ful, wil-ful \'wilfəl\ adj 1 : governed by will without regard to reason 2 : intentional —**will-ful-ly** adv

will-ing \'wiliŋ\ adj 1 : inclined or favorably disposed in mind 2 : prompt to act 3 : done, borne, or accepted voluntarily or without reluctance —**will-ing-ly** adv —**will-ing-ness** n

will-o'-the-wisp \,wilə(thə)'wisp\ n 1 : light that appears at night over marshy grounds 2 : misleading or elusive goal or hope

wil-low \'wilō\ n : quick-growing shrub or tree with flexible shoots

wil-lowy \'wiləwē\ adj : gracefully tall and slender

will-pow-er \'wil,pau̇(ə)r\ n : energetic determination

wil-ly–nil-ly \,wilē'nilē\ adv or adj : without regard for one's choice

wilt \'wilt\ vb 1 : lose or cause to lose freshness and become limp 2 : grow weak

wily \'wīlē\ adj **wil-i-er**; **-est** : full of craftiness —**wil-i-ness** n

win \'win\ vb **won** \'wən\; **win-ning** 1 : gain victory in a contest 2 : get possession of esp. by effort 3 : gain in battle or contest 4 : make friendly or favorable ~ n : victory

wince \'wins\ vb **winced**; **winc-ing** : shrink back involuntarily —**wince** n

winch \'winch\ n : machine for hoisting or pulling with a drum around which rope is wound —**winch** vb

¹wind \'wind\ n 1 : movement of the air 2 : breath 3 : gas in the stomach or intestines 4 : air carrying a scent 5 : intimation ~ vb 1 : get a scent of 2 : cause to be out of breath

²wind \'wīnd\ vb **wound** \'waủnd\; **wind-ing** 1 : have or follow a curving course 2 : move or lie to encircle 3 : encircle or cover with something pliable 4 : tighten the spring of ~ n : turn or coil —**wind-er** n

wind-break n : trees and shrubs to break the force of the wind

wind-fall \'win(d),fȯl\ n 1 : thing blown down by wind 2 : unexpected benefit

wind instrument n : musical instrument (as a flute or horn) sounded by wind and esp. by the breath

wind-lass \'windləs\ n : winch esp. for hoisting anchor

wind-mill \'win(d),mil\ n : machine worked by the wind turning vanes

win-dow \'windō\ n 1 : opening in the wall of a building to let in light and air 2 : pane in a window —**win-dow-less** adj

win-dow-shop vb : look at the displays in store windows —**win-dow-shop-per** n

wind-pipe \'win(d),pīp\ n : passage for the breath from the larynx to the lungs

wind-shield \'win(d),shēld\ n : transparent screen in front of the occupants of a vehicle

wind-up \'wīn,dəp\ n : end —**wind up** \(')wīn'dəp\ vb

wind-ward \'win(d)wərd\ adj : moving toward or situated on the side toward the direction from which the wind is blowing ~ n : direction from which the wind is blowing

windy \'windē\ adj **wind-i-er**; **-est** 1 : having wind 2 : indulging in useless talk

wine \'wīn\ n 1 : fermented grape juice 2 : usu. fermented juice of a plant product (as fruit) used as a beverage ~ vb : treat to or drink wine

wing \'wiŋ\ n 1 : movable paired appendage for flying 2 : winglike thing 3 pl : area at the side of the stage out of sight 4 : faction ~ vb 1 : fly 2 : let fly —**winged** adj —**wing-less** adj —**on the wing** : in flight —**under one's wing** : in one's charge or care

wink \'wiŋk\ vb 1 : close and open the eyes quickly 2 : avoid seeing or noticing something 3 : twinkle 4 : close and open one eye quickly as a signal or hint ~ n 1 : brief sleep 2 : act of winking 3 : instant —**wink-er** n

win-ner \'winər\ n : one that wins

win-ning \'-iŋ\ n 1 : victory 2 : money won at gambling ~ adj 1 : victorious 2 : charming

win·now \'winō\ *vb* **1** : remove (as chaff from grain) by a current of air **2** : get rid of something unwanted or separate something

win·some \'winsəm\ *adj* **1** : causing joy **2** : cheerful or gay —**win·some·ly** *adv* —**win·some·ness** *n*

win·ter \'wintər\ *n* : season between autumn and spring ~ *adj* : sown in autumn in time for harvest the next spring or summer ~ *vb* : pass the winter —**win·ter·time** *n*

win·ter·green \'wintər,grēn\ *n* : low heathlike evergreen plant with red berries

win·try \'wintrē\, **win·tery** \'wint-(ə)rē\ *adj* **win·tri·er**; **-est 1** : characteristic of winter **2** : cold in feeling

wipe \'wīp\ *vb* **wiped**; **wip·ing 1** : clean or dry by rubbing **2** : remove by rubbing or cleaning **3** : erase completely **4** : destroy **5** : pass (as a cloth) over a surface ~ *n* : act or instance of wiping —**wip·er** *n*

wire \'wī(ə)r\ *n* **1** : thread of metal **2** : work made of wire **3** : telegram or cablegram ~ *vb* **1** : provide with wire **2** : bind or mount with wire **3** : telegraph —**wire·less** *adj*

wire·less \-ləs\, *chiefly Brit* : radio

wire·tap *vb* : connect into a telephone or telegraph wire to get information —**wiretap** *n* —**wire·tap·per** *n*

wir·ing \'wī(ə)riŋ\ *n* : system of wire esp. for distributing electricity through a building

wiry \'wī(ə)rē\ *adj* **wir·i·er** \'wīrēər\; **-est 1** : resembling wire **2** : slender yet strong and sinewy —**wir·i·ness** *n*

wis·dom \'wizdəm\ *n* **1** : accumulated learning **2** : good sense

wisdom tooth *n* : last tooth on each half of each jaw in man

¹wise \'wīz\ *n* : manner

²wise *adj* **wis·er**; **wis·est 1** : having or showing wisdom, good sense, or good judgment **2** : aware of what is going on —**wise·ly** *adv*

wise·crack *n* : clever, smart, or flippant remark ~ *vb* : make a wisecrack

wish \'wish\ *vb* **1** : have a desire **2** : express a wish concerning **3** : request ~ *n* **1** : a wishing or desire **2** : expressed will or desire

wish·bone *n* : forked bone in front of the breastbone in most birds

wish·ful \-fəl\ *adj* **1** : expressive of a wish **2** : according with wishes rather than fact

wishy-washy \'wishē,wȯshē, -,wäsh-\ *adj* : weak or insipid

wisp \'wisp\ *n* **1** : small bunch of hay

or straw **2** : thin strand, strip, fragment, or streak **3** : something frail, slight, or fleeting —**wispy** *adj*

wis·te·ria \wis'tirēə\ *n* : pealike woody vine with long clusters of flowers

wist·ful \'wistfəl\ *adj* : full of longing —**wist·ful·ly** *adv* —**wist·ful·ness** *n*

wit \'wit\ *n* **1** : reasoning power **2** : mental soundness —usu. pl. **3** : quickness and cleverness in handling words and ideas **4** : talent for clever remarks or one noted for witty remarks —**wit·less** *adj* —**wit·less·ly** *adv* —**wit·less·ness** *n* —**wit·ted** *adj*

witch \'wich\ *n* **1** : person believed to have magic power **2** : ugly old woman ~ *vb* : bewitch —**witch·craft** *n*

witch·ery \'wich(ə)rē\ *n*, *pl* **-er·ies 1** : witchcraft **2** : charm

witch ha·zel \'wich,hāzəl\ *n* **1** : shrub having small yellow flowers in fall **2** : alcoholic solution of material from witch hazel bark used as a lotion

witch-hunt *n* **1** : searching out and persecution of supposed witches **2** : harassment of those with unpopular views

with \'wich, '(,)with\ *prep* **1** : against, to, or toward **2** : in support of **3** : because of **4** : in the company of **5** : having **6** : despite **7** : containing **8** : by means of

with·draw \with'drȯ, with-\ *vb* **-drew** \-'drü\; **-drawn** \-'drȯn\; **-draw·ing** \-'drȯiŋ\ **1** : take back or away **2** : call back or retract **3** : go away **4** : terminate one's participation in or use of —**with·draw·al** \-'drȯ(ə)l\ *n*

with·drawn \with'drȯn\ *adj* : socially detached and unresponsive

with·er \'withər\ *vb* **1** : shrivel **2** : lose or cause to lose energy, force, or freshness

with·ers \'withərz\ *n pl* : ridge between the shoulder bones of a horse

with·hold \with'hōld, with-\ *vb* **-held** \-'held\; **-hold·ing 1** : hold back **2** : refrain from giving

with·in \with'in, with-\ *adv* **1** : in or into the interior **2** : inside oneself ~ *prep* **1** : in or to the inner part of **2** : in the limits or compass of ~ *n* : inner place or area

with·out \with'aut, with-\ *prep* **1** : outside **2** : lacking **3** : unaccompanied or unmarked by —**without** *adv*

with·stand \with'stand, with-\ *vb* **-stood** \-'stud\; **-stand·ing** : oppose successfully

wit·ness \'witnəs\ *n* **1** : testimony **2**

: one who testifies **3** : one present at a transaction to testify that it has taken place **4** : one who has personal knowledge or experience **5** : something serving as proof ~ *vb* **1** : bear witness **2** : act as legal witness of **3** : furnish proof of **4** : be a witness of **5** : be the scene of

wit·ti·cism \'witə,sizəm\ *n* : witty saying or phrase

wit·ting \'witiŋ\ *adj* : intentional —**wit·ting·ly** *adv*

wit·ty \'witē\ *adj* -ti•er; -est : marked by or full of wit —**wit·ti·ly** \'witᵊlē\ *adv* —**wit·ti·ness** *n*

wives *pl of* WIFE

wiz·ard \'wizərd\ *n* **1** : magician **2** : very clever person —**wiz·ard·ry** \-ə(r)drē\ *n*

wiz·ened \'wizᵊnd\ *adj* : dried up

wob·ble \'wäbəl\ *vb* -bled; -bling **1** : move or cause to move with an irregular rocking motion **2** : tremble **3** : waver —**wobble** *n* —**wob·bly** \'wäb(ə)lē\ *adj*

woe \'wō\ *n* **1** : deep suffering **2** : misfortune

woe·be·gone \'wōbi,gòn\ *adj* : exhibiting woe, sorrow, or misery

woe·ful \'wōfəl\ *adj* **1** : full of woe **2** : bringing woe —**woe·ful·ly** *adv*

woke *past of* WAKE

woken *past part of* WAKE

wolf \'wulf\ *n*, *pl* **wolves** \'wulvz\ : large doglike predatory mammal — *vb* : eat greedily —**wolf·ish** *adj*

wol·fram \'wulfrəm\ *n* : tungsten

wol·ver·ine \,wulvə'rēn\ *n*, *pl* -ines : flesh-eating mammal related to the sables

wom·an \'wumən\ *n*, *pl* **wom·en** \'wimən\ **1** : adult female person **2** : womankind **3** : feminine nature —**wom·an·hood** \-,hud\ *n* —**wom·an·ish** *adj*

wom·an·kind \-,kind\ *n* : females of the human race

wom·an·ly \-lē\ *adj* : having qualities characteristic of a woman —**wom·an·li·ness** \-lēnəs\ *n*

womb \'wum\ *n* : uterus

won *past of* WIN

won·der \'wəndər\ *n* **1** : cause of astonishment or surprise **2** : feeling (as of astonishment) aroused by something extraordinary — *vb* **1** : feel surprise **2** : feel curiosity or doubt

won·der·ful \'wəndərfəl\ *adj* **1** : exciting wonder **2** : unusually good —**won·der·ful·ly** \-f(ə)lē\ *adv* —**won·der·ful·ness** *n*

won·der·land \-,land, -lənd\ *n* **1** : fairy-like imaginary realm **2** : place that excites admiration or wonder

won·der·ment \-mənt\ *n* : wonder

won·drous \'wəndrəs\ *adj* : wonderful —**won·drous·ly** *adv* —**won·drous·ness** *n*

wont \'wònt, 'wōnt\ *adj* : accustomed ~ *n* : habit —**wont·ed** *adj*

woo \'wu\ *vb* : try to gain the love or favor of —**woo·er** *n*

wood \'wud\ *n* **1** : dense growth of trees usu. smaller than a forest — often pl. **2** : hard fibrous substance of trees and shrubs beneath the bark **3** : wood prepared for some use (as burning) — *adj* **1** : wooden **2** : suitable for working with wood **3** : of woods \'wudz\ : living or growing in woods —**wood·chop·per** *n* —**wood·pile** *n* —**wood·shed** *n*

wood·bine \'wud,bīn\ *n* : climbing vine

wood·chuck \-,chək\ *n* : thick-bodied grizzled animal of No. America

wood·craft *n* **1** : skill and practice in matters relating to the woods **2** : skill in making articles from wood

wood·cut \-,kət\ *n* **1** : relief printing surface engraved on wood **2** : print from a woodcut

wood·ed \'wudəd\ *adj* : covered with woods

wood·en \'wudᵊn\ *adj* **1** : made of wood **2** : lacking resilience **3** : lacking ease, liveliness or interest —**wood·en·ly** *adv* —**wood·en·ness** *n*

wood·land \-lənd, -,land\ *n* : land covered with trees

wood·peck·er \'wud,pekər\ *n* : brightly marked bird with a hard bill for drilling into trees

woods·man \'wudzmən\ *n* : one who works in the woods

wood·wind \'wud,wind\ *n* : one of a group of wind instruments (as a flute or oboe)

wood·work *n* : work (as interior house fittings) made of wood

woody \'wudē\ *adj* **wood·i·er**; -est **1** : abounding with woods **2** : of, containing, or like wood fibers —**wood·i·ness** *n*

woof \'wuf\ *n* : threads in a woven fabric that cross the warp

wool \'wul\ *n* **1** : soft hair of some mammals and esp. the sheep **2** : something (as a textile) made of wool —**wooled** \'wuld\ *adj*

wool·en, wool·len \'wulən\ *adj* **1** : made of wool **2** : relating to the manufacture of woolen products — *n* **1** : woolen fabric **2** : woolen garments —usu. pl.

wool·gath·er·ing *n* : act of indulging in idle daydreaming

wool·ly \'wu̇lē\ *adj* **-li·er; -est** 1 : of, relating to, or bearing wool 2 : consisting of or resembling wool 3 : confused or turbulent

woo·zy \'wüzē\ *adj* **-zi·er; -est** 1 : confused 2 : somewhat dizzy, nauseated, or weak —**woo·zi·ness** *n*

word \'wərd\ *n* 1 : brief remark or 2 : speech sound or series of speech sounds that communicates a meaning 3 : written representation of a word 4 : order 5 : news 6 : promise 7 *pl* : dispute ~ *vb* : express in words —**word·less** *adj*

word·ing \'wərdiŋ\ *n* : verbal expression

wordy \'wərdē\ *adj* **word·i·er; -est** : using many words —**word·i·ness** *n*

wore *past of* WEAR

work \'wərk\ *n* 1 : labor 2 : employment 3 : task 4 : something (as an artistic production) produced by mental effort or physical labor 5 *pl* : buildings, grounds, and machinery of a factory 6 *pl* : moving parts of a mechanism 7 : workmanship ~ *adj* 1 : suitable for wear while working 2 : used for work ~ *vb* **worked** \'wərkt\ *or* **wrought** \'ròt\, **work·ing** 1 : bring to pass 2 : create by expending labor upon 3 : bring or get into a form or condition 4 : set or keep in operation 5 : solve 6 : cause to labor 7 : arrange 8 : excite 9 : labor 10 : perform work regularly for wages 11 : function according to plan or design 12 : produce a desired effect —**work·bag** *n* —**work·bas·ket** *n* —**work·bench** *n* —**work·man** \-mən\ *n* —**work·room** *n* —**in the works** : in preparation

work·able \'wərkəbəl\ *adj* 1 : capable of being worked 2 : feasible —**work·able·ness** *n*

work·a·day \'wərkə,dā\ *adj* 1 : relating to or suited for working days 2 : ordinary

work·er \'wərkər\ *n* : person who works esp. for wages

work·horse *n* 1 : horse used chiefly for labor 2 : person who undertakes difficult labor

work·house *n* : place of confinement for persons who have committed minor offenses

work·ing \'wərkiŋ\ *adj* 1 : adequate to allow work to be done 2 : adopted or assumed to help further work or activity ~ *n* : operation

work·ing·man \'wərkiŋ,man\ *n* : one who works for wages usu. at manual labor

work·man·like \-,līk\ *adj* : worthy of a good workman

work·man·ship \-,ship\ *n* 1 : art or skill of a workman 2 : quality imparted to a piece of work

work·out \'wərk,au̇t\ *n* : exercise to improve one's fitness

work·shop *n* 1 : small establishment for manufacturing or handicrafts 2 : seminar emphasizing exchange of ideas and practical methods

world \'wərld\ *n* 1 : universe 2 : earth with its inhabitants and all things upon it 3 : people in general 4 : great number or quantity 5 : class of persons or their sphere of interest

world·ly \'wərldlē\ *adj* 1 : devoted to this world and its pursuits rather than to religion 2 : sophisticated —**world·li·ness** *n*

world·ly-wise *adj* : possessing understanding of human affairs

world·wide *adj* : extended throughout the entire world

worm \'wərm\ *n* 1 : earthworm or a similar animal 2 *pl* : disorder caused by parasitic worms ~ *vb* 1 : move or cause to move in a slow and indirect way 2 : free from worms —**wormy** *adj*

worm·wood \'wərm,wu̇d\ *n* 1 : aromatic woody herb related to the daisies 2 : something bitter or grievous

worn *past part of* WEAR

worn-out \'wòrn'au̇t\ *adj* : exhausted or used up by or as if by wear

wor·ri·some \'wərēsəm\ *adj* 1 : causing worry 2 : inclined to worry

wor·ry \'wərē\ *vb* **-ried; -ry·ing** 1 : shake and mangle with the teeth 2 : disturb 3 : feel or express anxiety ~ *n, pl* **-ries** 1 : anxiety 2 : cause of anxiety —**wor·ri·er** *n*

worse \'wərs\ *adj, comparative of* BAD *or of* ILL 1 : bad or evil in a greater degree 2 : more unwell ~ *n* 1 : one that is worse 2 : greater degree of badness ~ *adv, comparative of* BAD *or of* ILL : in a worse manner

wors·en \'wərs°n\ *vb* : make or become worse

wor·ship \'wərshəp\ *n* 1 : reverence toward a divine being or supernatural power 2 : expression of reverence 3 : extravagant respect or devotion ~ *vb* **-shiped** *or* **-shipped; -ship·ing** *or* **-ship·ping** 1 : honor or reverence 2 : perform or take part in worship \—wor·ship·er, wor·ship·per n

worst \'wərst\ adj, superlative of BAD or of ILL **1** : most bad, evil, ill, or corrupt **2** : most unfavorable, unpleasant, or painful ~ n **1** : one that is worst **2** : greatest degree of badness ~ adv, superlative of ILL or of BAD or BADLY : to the extreme degree of badness ~ vb : defeat

wor·sted \'wústəd, 'wərstəd\ n : smooth compact wool yarn or fabric made from such yarn

worth \'wərth\ prep **1** : equal in value to **2** : deserving of ~ n **1** : monetary value **2** : value of something measured by its qualities or by the esteem in which it is held **3** : moral merit

worth·less \-ləs\ adj **1** : lacking worth **2** : useless —**worth·less·ness** n

worth·while \-'hwil\ adj : being worth the time or effort spent

wor·thy \'wərthē\ adj **-thi·er; -est 1** : having worth or value **2** : having sufficient worth ~ n, pl **-thies** : worthy person —**wor·thi·ly** adv —**wor·thi·ness** n

would \wəd, əd, d, (')wúd\ past of WILL —used to express (1) preference (2) intent (3) habitual action (4) contingency (5) probability or (6) a request

would-be \,wúd,bē\ adj : desiring or professing to be

¹wound \'wünd\ n **1** : injury in which the skin is broken **2** : mental hurt ~ vb : inflict a wound to or in

²wound \'waúnd\ past of WIND

wove past of WEAVE

woven past part of WEAVE

wrack \'rak\ n : ruin

wraith \'rāth\ n, pl **wraiths** \'rāths, 'rāthz\ **1** : ghost **2** : insubstantial appearance

wran·gle \'raŋgəl\ vb or n : quarrel —**wran·gler** n

wrap \'rap\ vb **-pp- 1** : cover esp. by winding or folding **2** : envelop and secure for transportation or storage **3** : enclose, surround, or conceal wholly **4** : coil, fold, draw, or twine about something ~ n **1** : wrapper or wrapping **2** : outer garment (as a shawl)

wrap·per \'rapər\ n **1** : that in which something is wrapped **2** : one that wraps

wrap·ping n : something used to wrap an object

wrath \'rath\ n : violent anger —**wrath·ful** \-fəl\ adj

wreak \'rēk\ vb **1** : inflict **2** : bring about

wreath \'rēth\ n, pl **wreaths** \'rēthz, 'rēths\ : something (as boughs) intertwined into a circular shape

wreathe \'rēth\ vb **wreathed; wreath·ing 1** : shape into or take on the shape of a wreath **2** : surround

wreck \'rek\ n **1** : broken remains (as of a ship or vehicle) after much damage **2** : something disabled or in a state of ruin **3** : an individual who has become weak or infirm **4** : action of breaking up or destroying something ~ vb : ruin or damage by breaking up

wreck·age \'rekij\ n **1** : act of wrecking **2** : remains of a wreck

wreck·er \-ər\ n **1** : one that wrecks or tears down and removes buildings **2** : automotive vehicle for removing disabled cars

wren \'ren\ n : small mostly brown singing bird

wrench \'rench\ vb **1** : pull with violent twisting or force **2** : injure or disable by a violent twisting or straining ~ n **1** : forcible twisting **2** : tool for exerting a twisting force

wrest \'rest\ vb **1** : pull or move by a forcible twisting movement **2** : gain with difficulty ~ n **1** : forcible twist

wres·tle \'resəl, 'ras-\ vb **-tled; -tling 1** : scuffle with an opponent in attempt to throw him down **2** : contend against in wrestling **3** : struggle (as with a problem) ~ n : action or an instance of wrestling —**wres·tler** \'reslər, 'ras-\ n

wres·tling \'resliŋ\ n : sport in which 2 opponents try to throw and pin each other

wretch \'rech\ n **1** : miserable unhappy person **2** : vile person

wretch·ed \'rechəd\ adj **1** : deeply afflicted, dejected, or distressed **2** : grievous **3** : inferior —**wretch·ed·ness** n

wrig·gle \'rigəl\ vb **-gled; -gling 1** : twist and turn restlessly **2** : move or advance by twisting and turning —**wriggle** n —**wrig·gler** \'rig(ə)lər\ n

wring \'riŋ\ vb **wrung** \'rəŋ\; **wring·ing 1** : squeeze or twist out moisture **2** : get by or as if by forcible exertion **3** : twist together in anguish **4** : pain —**wring·er** n

wrin·kle \'riŋkəl\ n : crease or small fold on a surface (as in the skin or in cloth) ~ vb **-kled; -kling** : develop or cause to develop wrinkles —**wrin-kly** \-kəlē\ *adj*

wrist \'rist\ *n* : joint or region between the hand and the arm

writ \'rit\ *n* 1 : something written 2 : legal order in writing

write \'rīt\ *vb* **wrote** \'rōt\; **writ-ten** \'rit²n\; **writ-ing** \'rītiŋ\ 1 : form letters or words on a surface 2 : form the letters or the words of (as on paper) 3 : make up and set down for others to read 4 : write a letter to — **write off** *vb* : cancel

writ-er \'rītər\ *n* : one that writes esp. as a business or occupation

writhe \'rīth\ *vb* **writhed**; **with-ing** : move or proceed with twists and turns

writ-ing \'rītiŋ\ *n* 1 : act of one that writes 2 : handwriting 3 : something written or printed

wrong \'roŋ\ *n* 1 : unfair or unjust act 2 : something that is contrary to justice 3 : state of being or doing wrong ~ *adj* **wrong-er** \'roŋər\; **wrong-est**

\'roŋəst\ 1 : sinful 2 : not right according to a standard 3 : unsuitable 4 : incorrect ~ *adv* 1 : in a wrong direction or manner 2 : incorrectly ~ *vb* **wronged**; **wrong-ing** 1 : do wrong to 2 : treat unjustly —**wrong-ly** *adv*

wrong-do-er \-'düər\ *n* : one who does wrong —**wrong-do-ing** \-'düiŋ\ *n*

wrong-ful \-fəl\ *adj* 1 : wrong 2 : illegal —**wrong-ful-ly** *adv* —**wrong-ful-ness** *n*

wrong-head-ed \'roŋ'hedəd\ *adj* : obstinately wrong —**wrong-head-ed-ly** *adv* —**wrong-head-ed-ness** *n*

wrote *past of* WRITE

wrought \'rot\ *adj* 1 : formed 2 : hammered into shape 3 : deeply stirred

wrung *past of* WRING

wry \'rī\ *adj* **wri-er** \'rī(ə)r\; **wri-est** \'rīəst\ 1 : turned abnormally to one side 2 : twisted 3 : cleverly and often ironically humorous —**wry-ly** *adv* —**wry-ness** *n*

X

x \'eks\ *n, pl* **x's** *or* **xs** \'eksəz\ 1 : 24th letter of the alphabet 2 : unknown quantity ~ *vb* **x-ed**; **x-ing** *or* **x'ing** : cancel with a series of x's—usu. with *out*

xe-non \'zē,nän,'zen,än\ *n* : heavy gaseous chemical element

xe-no-pho-bia \,zenə'fōbēə, ,zēn-\ *n* : fear and hatred of foreign people and things —**xe-no-phobe** \'zenə ,fōb. 'zēn-\ *n*

Xmas \'krisməs *also* 'eksməs\ *n* : Christmas

x-ra-di-a-tion *n* 1 : exposure to X rays 2 : radiation consisting of X rays

x-ray \'eks,rā\ *vb* : examine, treat, or photograph with X rays

X ray *n* 1 : radiation of short wavelength that is able to penetrate solids 2 : photograph taken with X rays

xy-lo-phone \'zīlə,fōn\ *n* : musical instrument with wooden bars that are struck —**xy-lo-phon-ist** \-,fōnəst\ *n*

Y

y \'wī\ *n, pl* **y's** *or* **ys** \'wīz\ : 25th letter of the alphabet

¹-y \ē\ *adj suffix* 1 : composed of full of 2 : like 3 : performing or apt to perform an action 4 : somewhat

²-y \ē\ *n suffix, pl* **-ies** 1 : state, condition, or quality 2 : activity, place of business, or goods dealt with 3 : whole group

yacht \'yät\ *n* : luxurious pleasure boat ~ *vb* : race or cruise in a yacht

ya-hoo \'yähü, 'yä-\ *n, pl* **-hoos** : uncouth or rowdy person

yak \'yak\ *n* : big hairy Asian ox

yam \'yam\ *n* 1 : edible root of a trop-

ical vine 2 : deep orange sweet potato

yam-mer \'yamər\ *vb* 1 : whimper 2 : chatter —**yammer** *n*

yank \'yaŋk\ *n* : strong sudden pull — **yank** *vb*

Yank \'yaŋk\ *n* : Yankee

Yan-kee \'yaŋkē\ *n* : native or inhabitant of New England, the northern U.S., or the U.S.

yap \'yap\ *vb* **-pp-** 1 : yelp 2 : chatter —**yap** *n*

¹yard \'yärd\ *n* 1 : 3 feet 2 : long spar for supporting and extending a sail —**yard-age** \-ij\ *n*

²**yard** *n* 1 : enclosed roofless area 2 : grounds of a building 3 : work area

yard·arm \'yärd‚ärm\ *n* : end of the yard of a square-rigged ship

yard·stick *n* 1 : measuring stick 3 feet long 2 : standard for judging

yarn \'yärn\ *n* 1 : spun fiber for weaving or knitting 2 : tale

yaw \'yò\ *vb* : deviate erratically from a course —**yaw** *n*

yawl \'yòl\ *n* : sailboat with 2 masts and one or more jibs

yawn \'yòn\ *vb* : open the mouth wide ~ *n* : deep breath through a wide-open mouth —**yawn·er** *n*

ye \(')yē\ *pron* : you

yea \'yā\ *adv* 1 : yes 2 : truly ~ *n* : affirmative vote

year \'yiər\ *n* 1 : period of about 365 days 2 *pl* : age

year·book *n* : annual report of the year's events

year·ling \'yiərliŋ, 'yərlən\ *n* : one that is or is rated as a year old

year·ly \'yiərlē\ *adj* : annual —**yearly** *adv*

yearn \'yərn\ *vb* 1 : feel desire esp. for what one cannot have 2 : feel tenderness or compassion

yearn·ing \-iŋ\ *n* : tender or urgent desire

yeast \'yēst\ *n* : froth or sediment in sugary liquids containing a tiny fungus and used in making alcoholic liquors and as a leaven in baking —**yeasty** *adj*

yell \'yel\ *vb* : utter a loud cry —**yell** *n*

yel·low \'yelō\ *adj* 1 : of the color yellow 2 : sensational 3 : cowardly ~ *vb* : make or turn yellow ~ *n* 1 : color of lemons 2 : yolk of an egg —**yel·low·ish** \'yelōwish\ *adj*

yellow fever *n* : virus disease marked by prostration, jaundice, fever, and often hemorrhage

yellow jacket *n* : wasp with yellow stripes

yelp \'yelp\ *vb* : utter a sharp quick shrill cry —**yelp** *n*

yen \'yen\ *n* : strong desire

yeo·man \'yōmən\ *n* 1 : attendant or officer in a royal or noble household 2 : small farmer 3 : naval petty officer with clerical duties —**yeo·man·ry** \-rē\ *n*

-yer —see ER

yes \'yes\ *adv* —used to express consent or agreement ~ *n* : affirmative reply

yes-man \'yes‚man\ *n* : toady

yes·ter·day \'yestərdē\ *adv* 1 : on the day preceding today 2 : only a short time ago ~ *n* 1 : day last past 2 : time not long past

yet \('\)yet\ *adv* 1 : in addition 2 : up to now 3 : so soon as now 4 : nevertheless ~ *conj* : but

yew \'yü\ *n* : evergreen tree or shrubs with dark stiff poisonous needles

yield \'yēld\ *vb* 1 : surrender 2 : grant 3 : bear as a crop 4 : produce 5 : cease opposition or resistance ~ *n* : quantity produced or returned

yo·del \'yōd²l\ *vb* **-deled** *or* **-delled; -del·ing** *or* **-del·ling** : sing by abruptly alternating between chest voice and falsetto —**yodel** *n* —**yo·del·er** \'yōdlər, -²lər\ *n*

yo·ga \'yōgə\ *n* : system of exercises for attaining bodily or mental control and well-being

yo·gi \'yōgē\ *n* : person who practices yoga

yo·gurt, yo·ghurt \'yōgərt\ *n* : fermented slightly acid soft nearly fluid food made from milk

yoke \'yōk\ *n* 1 : neck frame for coupling draft animals or for carrying loads 2 : clamp 3 : slavery 4 : tie or link 5 : piece of a garment esp. at the shoulder ~ *vb* **yoked; yok·ing** 1 : couple with a yoke 2 : join

yo·kel \'yōkəl\ *n* : bumpkin

yolk \'yō(l)k\ *n* : yellow part of an egg —**yolked** \'yō(l)kt\ *adj*

Yom Kip·pur \‚yòmki'pùr, ‚yäm-‚kipər\ *n* : Jewish holiday observed in September or October with fasting and prayer as a day of atonement

yon \'yän\ *adj or adv* : YONDER

yon·der \'yändər\ *adv* : at or to that place ~ *adj* : distant

yore \'yōr\ *n* : time long past

you \('\)yü, yə\ *pron* 1 : person or persons addressed 2 : person in general

young \'yəŋ\ *adj* **younger** \'yəŋgər\; **youn·gest** \'yəŋgəst\ 1 : being in the first or an early stage of life, growth, or development 2 : recently come into being 3 : having the qualities (as vigor) of youth ~ *n, pl* **young** : persons or lower animals that are young —**young·ish** \-ish\ *adj*

young·ster \-stər\ *n* 1 : young person 2 : child

your \yər, ('\)yúr, ('\)yōr\ *adj* : relating to you or yourself

yours \'yúrz, 'yōrz\ *pron* : the ones belonging to you

your·self \yər'self\ *pron, pl* **yourselves** \-'selvz\ : you —used reflexively or for emphasis

youth \'yüth\ *n, pl* **youths** \'yüthz,

'yuths\ **1** : period between childhood and maturity **2** : young man **3** : young persons **4** : state or quality of being young, fresh, or vigorous

youth·ful \'yüthfəl\ *adj* **1** : relating to or appropriate to youth **2** : young **3** : vigorous —**youth·ful·ly** *adv* —**youth·ful·ness** *n*

yowl \'yau̇l\ *vb* : utter a loud long mournful cry —**yowl** *n*

yo–yo \'yō(,)yō\ *n, pl* **-yos** : toy that falls from or rises to the hand as it unwinds and rewinds on a string

yuc·ca \'yəkə\ *n* : any of several plants related to the lilies that grow in dry regions

yule \'yül\ *n* : Christmas —**yule·tide** \-,tīd\ *n*

yum·my \'yəmē\ *adj* **-mi·er; -est** : highly attractive or pleasing

Z

z \'zē\ *n, pl* **z's** *or* **zs** : 26th letter of the alphabet

za·ny \'zānē\ *n, pl* **-nies 1** : clown **2** : silly person ~ *adj* **-ni·er; -est** : crazy or foolish —**za·ni·ly** *adv* —**za·ni·ness** *n*

zeal \'zēl\ *n* : enthusiasm

zeal·ot \'zelət\ *n* : fanatical partisan

zeal·ous \'zeləs\ *adj* : filled with zeal —**zeal·ous·ly** *adv* —**zeal·ous·ness** *n*

ze·bra \'zēbrə\ *n* : horselike African mammal marked with light and dark stripes

zeit·geist \'tsīt,gīst, 'zīt-\ *n* : general spirit of an era

ze·nith \'zēnəth\ *n* : highest point

zeph·yr \'zefər\ *n* : gentle breeze

zep·pe·lin \'zep(ə)lən\ *n* : cylindrical rigid airship

ze·ro \'zērō\ *n, pl* **-ros 1** : number represented by the symbol 0 or the symbol itself **2** : starting point **3** : lowest point ~ *adj* : having no size or quantity

zest \'zest\ *n* **1** : quality of enhancing enjoyment **2** : keen enjoyment —**zest·ful** \-fəl\ *adj* —**zest·ful·ly** *adv* —**zest·ful·ness** *n*

zig·zag \'zig,zag\ *n* : one of a series of short sharp turns or angles ~ *adj* : having zigzags ~ *adv* : in or by a zigzag path ~ *vb* **-gg-** : proceed along a zigzag path

zil·lion \'zilyən\ *n* : large indeterminate number

zinc \'zink\ *n* : bluish white crystalline metallic chemical element

zing \'zin\ *n* **1** : shrill humming noise **2** : energy —**zing** *vb*

zin·nia \'zinēə, 'zēnyə\ *n* : American herb widely grown for its showy flowers

¹zip \'zip\ *vb* **-pp-** : move or act with speed ~ *n* : energy

²zip *vb* **-pp-** : close or open with a zipper

zip code *n* : 5-digit number that identifies a U.S. postal delivery area

zip·per \'zipər\ *n* : fastener consisting of 2 rows of interlocking teeth

zip·py \'zipē\ *adj* **-pi·er; -est** : brisk

zir·con \'zər,kän\ *n* : zirconium-containing mineral sometimes used in jewelry

zir·co·ni·um \,zər'kōnēəm\ *n* : heat-resistant and corrosion-resistant metallic element

zith·er \'zithər, 'zith-\ *n* : stringed musical instrument played by plucking

zo·di·ac \'zōdē,ak\ *n* : imaginary belt in the heavens encompassing the paths of the planets and divided into 12 signs used in astrology —**zo·di·a·cal** \zō'dīəkəl\ *adj*

zom·bie \'zämbē\ *n* : supernatural power held to enter a dead body and bring it back to life

zon·al \'zōn°l\ *adj* : of, relating to, or having the form of a zone —**zon·al·ly** *adv*

zone \'zōn\ *n* **1** : division of the earth's surface based on latitude and climate **2** : distinctive area ~ *vb* **zoned; zon·ing 1** : mark off into zones **2** : reserve for special purposes —**zo·na·tion** \zō'nāshən\ *n*

zoo \'zü\ *n, pl* **zoos** : collection of living animals usu. for public display

zo·ol·o·gy \zō'äləjē\ *n* : science of animals —**zo·o·log·i·cal** \,zōə'läjikəl\ *adj* —**zo·ol·o·gist** \zō'äləjəst\ *n*

zoom \'züm\ *vb* **1** : move with a loud hum or buzz **2** : move or increase with great speed —**zoom** *n*

zuc·chi·ni \zü'kēnē\ *n, pl* **-ni** *or* **-nis** : summer squash with smooth cylindrical dark green fruits

zwie·back \'swēbak, 'swī-, 'zwē-, 'zwī-\ *n* : biscuit of baked, sliced, and toasted bread

zy·gote \'zī,gōt\ *n* : cell formed by the union of 2 sexual cells —**zy·got·ic** \zī'gätik\ *adj*

Abbreviations

Most of these abbreviations have been given in one form. Variation in use of periods, in type, and in capitalization is frequent and widespread (as *mph*, *MPH*, *m.p.h.*, *Mph*).

abbr	abbreviation	**bet**	between
AC	alternating current	**biog**	biographer, biographical, biography
acad	academic, academy	**biol**	biologic, biological, biologist, biology
AD	in the year of our Lord	**bldg**	building
adj	adjective	**blvd**	boulevard
adv	adverb, advertisement	**Brit**	Britain, British
AF	air force, audio frequency	**bro**	brother, brothers
agric	agricultural, agriculture	**bu**	bureau, bushel
AK	Alaska	**c**	carat, cent, centimeter, century, chapter, circa, cup
aka	also known as	**C**	Celsius, centigrade
AL, Ala	Alabama	**ca**	circa
alg	algebra	**CA, Cal, Calif**	California
Alta	Alberta	**Can, Canad**	Canada, Canadian
a.m., AM	before noon	**cap**	capacity, capital, capitalize, capitalized
Am, Amer	America, American	**Capt**	captain
amp	ampere	**CB**	citizens band
amt	amount	**CDT**	central daylight time
anc	ancient	**cen**	central
anon	anonymous	**cert**	certificate, certification, certified, certify
ans	answer	**cf**	compare
ant	antonym	**chap**	chapter
APO	army post office	**chem**	chemistry
approx	approximate, approximately	**cir**	circle, circuit, circular, circumference
Apr	April	**civ**	civil, civilian
apt	apartment, aptitude	**cm**	centimeter
AR	Arkansas	**co**	company, county
arith	arithmetic	**CO**	Colorado
Ariz	Arizona	**c/o**	care of
Ark	Arkansas	**COD**	cash on delivery, collect on delivery
art	article, artificial	**col**	colonial, colony, color, colored, column, counsel
assn	association	**Col**	colonel, Colorado
asst	assistant	**Colo**	Colorado
att	attached, attention, attorney	**comp**	comparative, compensation, compiled, compiler, composition, compound
attn	attention	**cong**	congress, congressional
atty	attorney	**conj**	conjunction
Aug	August	**Conn**	Connecticut
auth	authentic, author, authorized	**cont**	continued
aux, auxil	auxiliary		
av	avoirdupois		
AV	audiovisual		
ave	avenue		
avg	average		
AZ	Arizona		
bal	balance		
bar	barrel		
bbl	barrel, barrels		
BC	before Christ, British Columbia		

contr contract, contraction
corp corporal, corporation
corr corrected, correction
cp compare, coupon
cr credit, creditor
CSA Confederate States of America
CST central standard time
ct carat, cent, count, court
CT central time, certified teacher, Connecticut
cu cubic
cur currency, current
CZ Canal Zone
d penny
DA district attorney
dag dekagram
dal dekaliter
dam dekameter
dbl double
DC direct current, District of Columbia
DDS doctor of dental science, doctor of dental surgery
DE Delaware
dec deceased, decrease
Dec December
deg degree
Del Delaware
Dem Democrat, Democratic
dept department
det detached, detachment, detail, determine
dg decigram
dia, diam diameter
diag diagonal, diagram
dict dictionary
dif, diff difference
dim dimension, diminished
dir director
disc discount
dist distance, district
div divided, dividend, division, divorced
dkg dekagram
dkl dekaliter
dkm dekameter
dl deciliter
dm decimeter
DMD doctor of dental medicine
DOB date of birth
doz dozen
DP data processing
dr dram, drive, drum
Dr doctor
DST daylight saving time
dz dozen
E east, eastern, excellent
ea each
ecol ecological, ecology
econ economics, economist, economy
EDT eastern daylight time

e.g. for example
elec electric, electrical, electricity
elem elementary
eng engine, engineer, engineering
Eng England, English
esp especially
EST eastern standard time
ET eastern time
et al and others
etc et cetera
exec executive
f false, female, feminine
F, Fah, Fahr Fahrenheit
Feb February
fed federal, federation
fem female, feminine
FL, Fla Florida
FPO fleet post office
fr father, friar, from
Fri Friday
ft feet, foot, fort
fut future
g gram
G good
Ga, GA Georgia
gal gallery, gallon
gen general
geog geographic, geographical, geography
geol geologic, geological, geology
geom geometric, geometrical, geometry
gm gram
GMT Greenwich mean time
GOP Grand Old Party (Republican)
gov government, governor
GP general practice, general practitioner
gr grade, grain, gram
gram grammar, grammatical
gt great
GU Guam
hd head
hf half
hgt height
HI Hawaii
hist historian, historical, history
hon honor, honorable, honorary
hr here, hour
HS high school
ht height
HT Hawaii time
hwy highway
i intransitive, island, isle
Ia, IA Iowa
ID Idaho, identification
i.e. that is
IL, Il Illinois
imp imperative, imperfect
in inch
IN Indiana
inc incomplete, incorporated

ind independent
Ind Indian, Indiana
inf infinitive
int interest
interj interjection
ital italic, italicized
Jan January
JD juvenile delinquent
jour journal, journeyman
JP justice of the peace
jr, jun junior
JV junior varsity
Kan, Kans Kansas
kg kilogram
km kilometer
KS Kansas
kw kilowatt
Ky, KY Kentucky
l late, left, liter
L large, long
La, LA Louisiana
lb pound
lg large, long
lib liberal, librarian, library
m male, masculine, meter, mile
M medium
MA Massachusetts
Man Manitoba
Mar March
masc masculine
Mass Massachusetts
math mathematical, mathematician
max maximum
Md Maryland
MD doctor of medicine, Maryland
MDT mountain daylight time
Me, ME Maine
med medium
mg milligram
mgr manager
MI, Mich Michigan
mid middle
min minimum, minor, minute
Minn Minnesota
misc miscellaneous
Miss Mississippi
ml milliliter
mm millimeter
MN Minnesota
mo month
Mo, MO Missouri
Mon Monday
Mont Montana
mpg miles per gallon
mph miles per hour
MS Mississippi
MST mountain standard time
mt mount, mountain
MT Montana, mountain time
n neuter, noun
N north, northern
NA North America, not applicable

nat national, native, natural
naut nautical
NB New Brunswick
NC North Carolina
ND, N Dak North Dakota
NE, Neb, Nebr Nebraska
neg negative
neut neuter
Nev Nevada
Nfld Newfoundland
NH New Hampshire
NJ New Jersey
NM, N Mex New Mexico
no north, number
Nov November
NS Nova Scotia
NV Nevada
NWT Northwest Territories
NY New York
NYC New York City
O Ohio
obj object, objective
occas occasionally
Oct October
off office, officer, official
OH Ohio
OK, Okla Oklahoma
ON, Ont Ontario
opp opposite
OR, Ore, Oreg Oregon
orig original, originally
oz ounce, ounces
p page
Pa Pennsylvania
PA Pennsylvania, public address
par paragraph, parallel
part participle, particular
pass passenger, passive
pat patent
PC percent, postcard
pd paid
PD police department
PDT Pacific daylight time
PEI Prince Edward Island
Penn, Penna Pennsylvania
pg page
pk park, peak, peck
pkg package
pl place, plural
p.m., PM afternoon
PO post office
pop popular, population
pos position, positive
poss possessive
pp pages
PQ Province of Quebec
pr pair, price, printed
PR public relations, Puerto Rico
prep preposition
pres present, president
prob probable, probably, problem
prof professor

pron pronoun
prov province
PS postscript, public school
PST Pacific standard time
psych psychology
pt part, payment, pint, point
PT Pacific time
pvt private
qr quarter
qt quantity, quart
Que Quebec
quot quotation
r right, river
rd road, rod, round
recd received
reg region, register, registered, regular, regulation
rel relating, relative, religion
rep report, reporter, representative, republic
Rep Republican
res residence
rev reverse, review, revised, revision, revolution
Rev reverend
RFD rural free delivery
RI Rhode Island
rm room
RPM revolutions per minute
RR railroad, rural route
RSVP please reply
rt right
rte route
S small, south, southern
SA South America
Sask Saskatchewan
Sat Saturday
SC South Carolina
sci science, scientific
SD, S Dak South Dakota
secy secretary
sen senator, senior
Sept, Sep September
sing singular
sm small
so south, southern
soph sophomore
sp spelling
spec special, specifically
sq square
sr senior
Sr sister
SSR Soviet Socialist Republic
st street

St saint
std standard
subj subject
Sun Sunday
supt superintendent
syn synonym
t teaspoon, temperature, ton, transitive, troy, true
T tablespoon
tbs, tbsp tablespoon
TD touchdown
tech technical, technician, technology
Tenn Tennessee
terr territory
Tex Texas
Th, Thu, Thurs Thursday
TN Tennessee
trans translated, translation, translator
tsp teaspoon
Tu, Tue, Tues Tuesday
TX Texas
UN United Nations
univ universal, university
US United States
USA United States of America
USSR Union of Soviet Socialist Republics
usu usual, usually
UT Utah
v verb, versus
Va, VA Virginia
var variant, variety
vb verb
VG very good
VI Virgin Islands
vol volcano, volume, volunteer
VP vice president
vs versus
Vt, VT Vermont
W west, western
WA, Wash Washington
Wed Wednesday
WI, Wis, Wisc Wisconsin
wk week, work
wt weight
WV, W Va West Virginia
WY, Wyo Wyoming
XL extra large, extra long
yd yard
yr year, younger, your
YT Yukon Territory

Handbook of Style

Punctuation

The English writing system uses punctuation marks to separate groups of words for meaning and emphasis; to convey an idea of the variations of pitch, volume, pauses, and intonations of speech; and to help avoid ambiguity. English punctuation marks, together with general rules and bracketed examples of their use, follow.

APOSTROPHE '

1. indicates the possessive case of nouns and indefinite pronouns ⟨the boy's mother⟩ ⟨the boys' mothers⟩ ⟨It is anyone's guess.⟩
2. marks omissions in contracted words ⟨didn't⟩ ⟨o'clock⟩
3. often forms plurals of letters, figures, and words referred to as words ⟨You should dot your *i*'s and cross your *t*'s.⟩ ⟨several 8's⟩ ⟨She has trouble pronouncing her *the*'s.⟩

BRACKETS [ ]

1. set off extraneous data such as editorial additions esp. within quoted material ⟨wrote that the author was "trying to dazzle his readers with phrases like *jeu de mots* [play on words]"⟩
2. function as parentheses within parentheses ⟨Bowman Act (22 Stat., ch. 4, § [or sec.] 4, p. 50⟩

COLON :

1. introduces word, clause, or phrase that explains, illustrates, amplifies, or restates what has gone before ⟨The sentence was poorly constructed: it lacked both unity and coherence.⟩
2. introduces a series ⟨Three countries were represented: England, France, and Belgium⟩
3. introduces lengthy quoted material set off from the rest of a text by indentation but not by quotation marks ⟨I quote from the text of Chapter One:⟩
4. separates data in time-telling and data in bibliographic and biblical references ⟨8:30 a.m.⟩ ⟨New York: Smith Publishing Co.⟩ ⟨John 4:10⟩
5. separates titles and subtitles (as of books) ⟨*The Tragic Dynasty: A History of the Romanovs*⟩
6. follows the salutation in formal correspondence ⟨Dear Sir:⟩ ⟨Gentlemen:⟩

COMMA ,

1. separates main clauses joined by a coordinating conjunction (as *and, but, or, nor,* or *for*) and very short clauses not so joined ⟨She knew very little about him, and he volunteered nothing.⟩ ⟨I came, I saw, I conquered.⟩
2. sets off an adverbial clause (or a long phrase) that precedes the main clause ⟨When she found that her friends had deserted her, she sat down and cried.⟩
3. sets off from the rest of the sentence transitional words and expressions (as *on the contrary, on the other hand*), conjunctive adverbs (as *consequently, furthermore, however*), and expressions that introduce an illustration or example (as *namely, for example*) ⟨Your second question, on the other hand, remains open.⟩ ⟨The mystery, however, remains

unsolved.⟩ ⟨She expects to travel through two countries, namely, France and England.⟩
4. **separates words, phrases, or clauses in series and coordinate adjectives modifying a noun** ⟨Men, women, and children crowded into the square.⟩ ⟨The harsh, cold wind was strong.⟩
5. **sets off from the rest of the sentence parenthetic elements (as nonrestrictive modifiers)** ⟨Our guide, who wore a blue beret, was an experienced traveler.⟩ ⟨We visited Gettysburg, the site of a famous battle.⟩
6. **introduces a direct quotation, terminates a direct quotation that is neither a question nor an exclamation, and encloses split quotations** ⟨John said, "I am leaving."⟩ ⟨"I am leaving," John said.⟩ ⟨"I am leaving," John said with determination, "even if you want me to stay."⟩
7. **sets off words in direct address, absolute phrases, and mild interjections** ⟨You may go, Mary, if you wish.⟩ ⟨I fear the encounter, his temper being what it is.⟩ ⟨Ah, that's my idea of an excellent dinner.⟩
8. **separates a question from the rest of the sentence which it ends** ⟨It's a fine day, isn't it?⟩
9. **indicates the omission of a word or words, and esp. a word or words used earlier in the sentence** ⟨Common stocks are preferred by some investors; bonds, by others.⟩
10. **is used to avoid ambiguity** ⟨To Mary, Jane was someone special.⟩
11. **is used to group numbers into units of three in separating thousands, millions, etc.; however, it is generally not used in numbers of four figures, in page numbers, in dates, or in street numbers** ⟨Smithville, pop. 100,000⟩ *but* ⟨3600 rpm⟩ ⟨the year 1973⟩ ⟨page 1411⟩ ⟨4507 Smith Street⟩
12. **punctuates an inverted name** ⟨Smith, John W., Jr.⟩
13. **separates a proper name from a following academic, honorary, governmental, or military title** ⟨John Smith, M.D.⟩
14. **sets off geographical names (as state or country from city), items in dates, and addresses from the rest of a text** ⟨Shreveport, Louisiana, is the site of a large air base.⟩ ⟨On Sunday, June 23, 1940, he was wounded.⟩ ⟨Number 10 Downing Street, London, is a famous address.⟩
15. **follows the salutation in informal correspondence and follows the closing line of a formal or informal letter** ⟨Dear Mary,⟩ ⟨Affectionately,⟩ ⟨Very truly yours,⟩

DASH —

1. **usu. marks an abrupt change or break in the continuity of a sentence** ⟨When in 1960 the stockpile was sold off—indeed, dumped as surplus—natural-rubber sales were hard hit.—Barry Commoner⟩
2. **introduces a summary statement after a series** ⟨Oil, steel, and wheat—these are the sinews of industrialization.⟩
3. **often precedes the attribution of a quotation** ⟨My foot is on my native heath . . . . —Sir Walter Scott⟩

ELLIPSIS . . . .

1. **indicates the omission of one or more words within a quoted passage** ⟨The head is not more native to the heart . . . than is the throne of Denmark to thy father.—Shakespeare⟩
2. **indicates halting speech or an unfinished sentence in dialogue** ⟨"I'd like to . . . that is . . . if you don't mind . . . ." He faltered and then stopped speaking.⟩
3. **indicates the omission of one or more sentences within a quoted passage or the omission of words at the end of a sentence by using four spaced dots the last of which represents the period** ⟨That recovering

the manuscripts would be worth almost any effort is without question. . . . The monetary value of a body of Shakespeare's manuscripts would be almost incalculable—Charlton Ogburn⟩

4. usu. indicates omission of one or more lines of poetry when ellipsis is extended the length of the line

⟨Thus driven
By the bright shadow of that lovely dream,
. . . .
He fled.
—P. B. Shelley⟩

EXCLAMATION POINT !

1. **terminates an emphatic phrase or sentence** ⟨Get out of here!⟩
2. **terminates an emphatic interjection** ⟨Encore!⟩

HYPHEN -

1. **marks separation or division of a word at the end of a line** ⟨mill-[end of line]stone⟩ ⟨pas-[end of line]sion⟩
2. **is used between some prefix and word combinations, as prefix + proper name; ⟨pre-Renaissance⟩ prefix ending with a vowel + word beginning often with the same vowel ⟨co-opted⟩ ⟨re-ink⟩; stressed prefix + word, esp. when this combination is similar to a different one ⟨re=cover a sofa⟩ *but* ⟨recover from an illness⟩**
3. **is used in some compounds, esp. those containing prepositions ⟨pres-ident-elect⟩ ⟨sister-in-law⟩**
4. **is often used between elements of a unit modifier in attributive position in order to avoid ambiguity ⟨He is a small-business man.⟩ ⟨She has gray-green eyes.⟩**
5. **suspends the first part of a hyphened compound when used with another hyphened compound ⟨a six- or eight-cylinder engine⟩**
6. **is used in writing out compound numbers between 21 and 99 ⟨thirty=four⟩ ⟨one hundred twenty-eight⟩**
7. **is used between the numerator and the denominator in writing out fractions esp. when they are used as modifiers ⟨a two-thirds majority of the vote⟩**
8. **serves instead of the phrase "(up) to and including" between numbers and dates ⟨pages 40-98⟩ ⟨the decade 1960-69⟩**

HYPHEN, DOUBLE =

is used in the end-of-line division of a hyphened compound to indicate that the compound is hyphened and not closed ⟨self-[end of line]seeker⟩ *but* ⟨self-[end of line]same⟩

PARENTHESES ( )

1. **set off supplementary, parenthetic, or explanatory material when the interruption is more marked than that usu. indicated by commas ⟨Three old destroyers (all now out of commission) will be scrapped.⟩ ⟨He is hoping (as we all are) that this time he will succeed.⟩**
2. **enclose numerals which confirm a written number in a text ⟨Delivery will be made in thirty (30) days.⟩**
3. **enclose numbers or letters in a series ⟨We must set forth (1) our long-term goals, (2) our immediate objectives, and (3) the means at our disposal.⟩**

PERIOD

1. **terminates sentences or sentence fragments that are neither interrogatory nor exclamatory** ⟨Obey the law.⟩ ⟨He obeyed the law.⟩
2. **follows some abbreviations and contractions** ⟨Dr.⟩ ⟨Jr.⟩ ⟨etc.⟩ ⟨cont.⟩

QUESTION MARK   ?

1. **terminates a direct question** ⟨Who threw the bomb?⟩ ⟨"Who threw the bomb?" he asked.⟩ ⟨To ask the question Who threw the bomb? is unnecessary.⟩
2. **indicates the writer's ignorance or uncertainty** ⟨Omar Khayyám, Persian poet (?–?1123)⟩

QUOTATION MARKS, DOUBLE   " "

1. **enclose direct quotations in conventional usage** ⟨He said, "I am leaving."⟩
2. **enclose words or phrases borrowed from others, words used in a special way, and often slang when it is introduced into formal writing** ⟨He called himself "emperor," but he was really just a dictator.⟩ ⟨He was arrested for smuggling "smack."⟩
3. **enclose titles of short poems, short stories, articles, lectures, chapters of books, songs, short musical compositions, and radio and TV programs** ⟨Robert Frost's "Dust of Snow"⟩ ⟨Pushkin's "Queen of Spades"⟩ ⟨The third chapter of *Treasure Island* is entitled "The Black Spot."⟩ ⟨"America the Beautiful"⟩ ⟨Ravel's "Bolero"⟩ ⟨NBC's "Today Show"⟩
4. **are used with other punctuation marks in the following ways: the period and the comma fall *within* the quotation marks** ⟨"I am leaving," he said.⟩ ⟨His camera was described as "waterproof," but "moisture-resistant" would have been a better description.⟩ **the semicolon falls *outside* the quotation marks** ⟨He spoke of his "little cottage in the country"; he might have called it a mansion.⟩ **the dash, the question mark, and the exclamation point fall *within* the quotation marks when they refer to the quoted matter only; they fall *outside* when they refer to the whole sentence** ⟨He asked, "When did you leave?"⟩ ⟨What is the meaning of "the open door"?⟩ ⟨The sergeant shouted, "Halt!"⟩ ⟨Save us from his "mercy"!⟩

QUOTATION MARKS, SINGLE   ' '

enclose a quotation within a quotation in conventional usage ⟨The witness said, "I distinctly heard him say, 'Don't be late,' and then I heard the door close."⟩

SEMICOLON   ;

1. **links main clauses not joined by coordinating conjunctions** ⟨Some people have the ability to write well; others do not.⟩
2. **links main clauses joined by conjunctive adverbs (as *consequently, furthermore, however*)** ⟨Speeding is illegal; furthermore, it is very dangerous.⟩
3. **links clauses which themselves contain commas even when such clauses are joined by coordinating conjunctions** ⟨Mr. King, whom you met yesterday, will be our representative on the committee; but you should follow the proceedings carefully yourself, because they are vitally important to us.⟩

VIRGULE /

1. **separates alternatives** ⟨. . . designs intended for high-heat and/or high-speed applications—F. S. Badger, Jr.⟩
2. **separates successive divisions (as months or years) of an extended period of time** ⟨the fiscal year 1972/73⟩
3. **serves as a dividing line between run-in lines of poetry** ⟨Say, sages, what's the charm on earth/Can turn death's dart aside?—Robert Burns⟩
4. **often represents *per* in abbreviations** ⟨9 ft/sec⟩ ⟨20 km/hr⟩

Italicization

The following are usually italicized in print and underlined in manuscript:

1. **titles of books, magazines, newspapers, plays, movies, works of art, and longer musical compositions** ⟨Eliot's *The Waste Land*⟩ ⟨*Saturday Review*⟩ ⟨*Christian Science Monitor*⟩ ⟨Shakespeare's *Othello*⟩ ⟨the movie *Gone With the Wind*⟩ ⟨Gainsborough's *Blue Boy*⟩ ⟨Mozart's *Don Giovanni*⟩
2. **names of ships and aircraft, and often spacecraft** ⟨M.V. *West Star*⟩ ⟨Lindbergh's *Spirit of St. Louis*⟩ ⟨*Apollo 13*⟩
3. **words, letters, and figures when referred to as words, letters, and figures** ⟨The word *receive* is often misspelled.⟩ ⟨The *g* in *align* is silent.⟩ ⟨The first *2* and the last *0* in the address are barely legible.⟩
4. **foreign words and phrases that have not been naturalized in English** ⟨*che sarà, sarà*⟩ ⟨*ich dien*⟩
5. **New Latin scientific names of genera, species, subspecies, and varieties (but not groups of higher rank) in botanical and zoological names** ⟨a thick-shelled American clam (*Mercenaria mercenaria*)⟩

Capitalization

Capitals are used for two broad purposes in English: they mark a beginning (as of a sentence) and they signal a proper noun or adjective.

1. **The first word of a sentence or sentence fragment is capitalized.** ⟨The play lasted nearly three hours.⟩ ⟨How are you feeling?⟩ ⟨Bravo!⟩
2. **The first word of a direct quotation is capitalized.** ⟨And God said, Let there be light.—Gen 1:3⟩ ⟨He replied, "We can stay only a few minutes."⟩
3. **The first word of a direct question within a sentence is capitalized.** ⟨That question is this: Is man an ape or an angel?—Benjamin Disraeli⟩
4. **The first word of a line of poetry is conventionally capitalized.** ⟨The best lack all conviction, while the worst
Are full of passionate intensity.—W. B. Yeats⟩
5. **Words in titles are capitalized with the exception of internal conjunctions, prepositions, and articles.** ⟨*The Way of the World*⟩ ⟨*Of Mice and Men*⟩
6. **The first word of the salutation of a letter and the first word of the closing line are capitalized.** ⟨Dear Mary⟩ ⟨My dear Mrs. Smith⟩ ⟨Sincerely yours⟩
7. **The names of persons and places, of organizations and their members, of congresses and councils, and of historical periods and events are capitalized.** ⟨Noah Webster⟩ ⟨Rome⟩ ⟨Texas⟩ ⟨England⟩ ⟨Rotary International⟩ ⟨Baptists⟩ ⟨the Atomic Energy Commission⟩ ⟨the Yalta Conference⟩ ⟨the Middle Ages⟩ ⟨World War II⟩

8. **The names of ships, aircraft, and spacecraft are capitalized.** ⟨Lindbergh's *Spirit of St. Louis*⟩
9. **Words designating peoples and languages are capitalized.** ⟨Canadians⟩ ⟨Iroquois⟩ ⟨Latin⟩
10. **Derivatives of proper nouns are capitalized when used in their primary sense.** ⟨Roman customs⟩ ⟨Shakespearean comedies⟩ ⟨the Edwardian era⟩
11. **Words of family relationship preceding the name of a person are capitalized.** ⟨Uncle George⟩
12. **Titles preceding the name of a person and epithets used instead of a name are capitalized.** ⟨President Roosevelt⟩ ⟨Professor Harris⟩ ⟨Pope Paul⟩ ⟨Old Hickory⟩ ⟨the Iron Chancellor⟩
13. **The pronoun *I* is capitalized.** ⟨only I know the real story⟩
14. **Words designating the Deity (and pronouns referring thereto) are often capitalized.** ⟨God⟩ ⟨Jehovah⟩ ⟨Allah⟩ ⟨the Supreme Being in His great wisdom⟩
15. **Personifications are capitalized.** ⟨She dwells with Beauty—John Keats⟩
16. **The days of the week, the months of the year, and holidays and holy days are capitalized.** ⟨Tuesday⟩ ⟨June⟩ ⟨Thanksgiving⟩ ⟨Yom Kippur⟩
17. **Names of specific courts of law are capitalized.** ⟨the United States Court of Appeals for the Second Circuit⟩
18. **Names of treaties are capitalized.** ⟨Treaty of Versailles⟩ ⟨Kellogg-Briand Pact⟩
19. **Registered trademarks and other registered marks are capitalized.** ⟨Orlon⟩ ⟨Air Express⟩
20. **Geological eras, periods, epochs, strata, and names of prehistoric divisions are capitalized.** ⟨Silurian period⟩ ⟨Age of Reptiles⟩ ⟨Neolithic age⟩
21. **Planets, constellations, asteroids, stars, and groups of stars are capitalized; however, sun, earth, and moon are not capitalized unless they are listed with other capitalized astronomical names.** ⟨Venus⟩ ⟨Big Dipper⟩ ⟨Sirius⟩
22. **Genera in scientific names in zoology and botany are capitalized; names of species are not.** ⟨a cabbage butterfly (*Pieris rapae*)⟩

Plurals

The plurals of English words are regularly formed by the addition of the suffix -*s* or -*es* to the singular, as
⟨dog → dogs⟩ ⟨race → races⟩ ⟨guy → guys⟩ ⟨monarch → monarchs⟩ ⟨grass → grasses⟩ ⟨dish → dishes⟩ ⟨buzz → buzzes⟩ ⟨branch → branches⟩

The plurals of words that follow other patterns, as
⟨army → armies⟩ ⟨duo → duos⟩ ⟨ox → oxen⟩ ⟨foot → feet⟩ ⟨p. → pp.⟩ ⟨sheep → sheep⟩ ⟨phenomenon → phenomena *or* phenomenons⟩ ⟨libretto → librettos *or* libretti⟩ ⟨curriculum → curricula⟩ ⟨alga → algae⟩ ⟨corpus → corpora⟩ ⟨sergeant major → sergeants major *or* sergeant majors⟩ are given at the appropriate entries in the main body of the dictionary.